Lecture Notes in Computer Science   13681

More information about this series at https://link.springer.com/bookseries/558

Shai Avidan · Gabriel Brostow ·
Moustapha Cissé · Giovanni Maria Farinella ·
Tal Hassner (Eds.)

Computer Vision – ECCV 2022

17th European Conference
Tel Aviv, Israel, October 23–27, 2022
Proceedings, Part XXI

Springer

Editors
Shai Avidan
Tel Aviv University
Tel Aviv, Israel

Gabriel Brostow ⓘ
University College London
London, UK

Moustapha Cissé
Google AI
Accra, Ghana

Giovanni Maria Farinella ⓘ
University of Catania
Catania, Italy

Tal Hassner ⓘ
Facebook (United States)
Menlo Park, CA, USA

ISSN 0302-9743   ISSN 1611-3349 (electronic)
Lecture Notes in Computer Science
ISBN 978-3-031-19802-1   ISBN 978-3-031-19803-8 (eBook)
https://doi.org/10.1007/978-3-031-19803-8

This Springer imprint is published by the registered company Springer Nature Switzerland AG
The registered company address is: Gewerbestrasse 11, 6330 Cham, Switzerland

Foreword

Organizing the European Conference on Computer Vision (ECCV 2022) in Tel-Aviv during a global pandemic was no easy feat. The uncertainty level was extremely high, and decisions had to be postponed to the last minute. Still, we managed to plan things just in time for ECCV 2022 to be held in person. Participation in physical events is crucial to stimulating collaborations and nurturing the culture of the Computer Vision community.

There were many people who worked hard to ensure attendees enjoyed the best science at the 16th edition of ECCV. We are grateful to the Program Chairs Gabriel Brostow and Tal Hassner, who went above and beyond to ensure the ECCV reviewing process ran smoothly. The scientific program includes dozens of workshops and tutorials in addition to the main conference and we would like to thank Leonid Karlinsky and Tomer Michaeli for their hard work. Finally, special thanks to the web chairs Lorenzo Baraldi and Kosta Derpanis, who put in extra hours to transfer information fast and efficiently to the ECCV community.

We would like to express gratitude to our generous sponsors and the Industry Chairs, Dimosthenis Karatzas and Chen Sagiv, who oversaw industry relations and proposed new ways for academia-industry collaboration and technology transfer. It's great to see so much industrial interest in what we're doing!

Authors' draft versions of the papers appeared online with open access on both the Computer Vision Foundation (CVF) and the European Computer Vision Association (ECVA) websites as with previous ECCVs. Springer, the publisher of the proceedings, has arranged for archival publication. The final version of the papers is hosted by SpringerLink, with active references and supplementary materials. It benefits all potential readers that we offer both a free and citeable version for all researchers, as well as an authoritative, citeable version for SpringerLink readers. Our thanks go to Ronan Nugent from Springer, who helped us negotiate this agreement. Last but not least, we wish to thank Eric Mortensen, our publication chair, whose expertise made the process smooth.

October 2022

Rita Cucchiara
Jiří Matas
Amnon Shashua
Lihi Zelnik-Manor

Preface

Welcome to the proceedings of the European Conference on Computer Vision (ECCV 2022). This was a hybrid edition of ECCV as we made our way out of the COVID-19 pandemic. The conference received 5804 valid paper submissions, compared to 5150 submissions to ECCV 2020 (a 12.7% increase) and 2439 in ECCV 2018. 1645 submissions were accepted for publication (28%) and, of those, 157 (2.7% overall) as orals.

846 of the submissions were desk-rejected for various reasons. Many of them because they revealed author identity, thus violating the double-blind policy. This violation came in many forms: some had author names with the title, others added acknowledgments to specific grants, yet others had links to their github account where their name was visible. Tampering with the LaTeX template was another reason for automatic desk rejection.

ECCV 2022 used the traditional CMT system to manage the entire double-blind reviewing process. Authors did not know the names of the reviewers and vice versa. Each paper received at least 3 reviews (except 6 papers that received only 2 reviews), totalling more than 15,000 reviews.

Handling the review process at this scale was a significant challenge. To ensure that each submission received as fair and high-quality reviews as possible, we recruited more than 4719 reviewers (in the end, 4719 reviewers did at least one review). Similarly we recruited more than 276 area chairs (eventually, only 276 area chairs handled a batch of papers). The area chairs were selected based on their technical expertise and reputation, largely among people who served as area chairs in previous top computer vision and machine learning conferences (ECCV, ICCV, CVPR, NeurIPS, etc.).

Reviewers were similarly invited from previous conferences, and also from the pool of authors. We also encouraged experienced area chairs to suggest additional chairs and reviewers in the initial phase of recruiting. The median reviewer load was five papers per reviewer, while the average load was about four papers, because of the emergency reviewers. The area chair load was 35 papers, on average.

Conflicts of interest between authors, area chairs, and reviewers were handled largely automatically by the CMT platform, with some manual help from the Program Chairs. Reviewers were allowed to describe themselves as senior reviewer (load of 8 papers to review) or junior reviewers (load of 4 papers). Papers were matched to area chairs based on a subject-area affinity score computed in CMT and an affinity score computed by the Toronto Paper Matching System (TPMS). TPMS is based on the paper's full text. An area chair handling each submission would bid for preferred expert reviewers, and we balanced load and prevented conflicts.

The assignment of submissions to area chairs was relatively smooth, as was the assignment of submissions to reviewers. A small percentage of reviewers were not happy with their assignments in terms of subjects and self-reported expertise. This is an area for improvement, although it's interesting that many of these cases were reviewers hand-picked by AC's. We made a later round of reviewer recruiting, targeted at the list of authors of papers submitted to the conference, and had an excellent response which helped provide enough emergency reviewers. In the end, all but six papers received at least 3 reviews.

The challenges of the reviewing process are in line with past experiences at ECCV 2020. As the community grows, and the number of submissions increases, it becomes ever more challenging to recruit enough reviewers and ensure a high enough quality of reviews. Enlisting authors by default as reviewers might be one step to address this challenge.

Authors were given a week to rebut the initial reviews, and address reviewers' concerns. Each rebuttal was limited to a single pdf page with a fixed template.

The Area Chairs then led discussions with the reviewers on the merits of each submission. The goal was to reach consensus, but, ultimately, it was up to the Area Chair to make a decision. The decision was then discussed with a buddy Area Chair to make sure decisions were fair and informative. The entire process was conducted virtually with no in-person meetings taking place.

The Program Chairs were informed in cases where the Area Chairs overturned a decisive consensus reached by the reviewers, and pushed for the meta-reviews to contain details that explained the reasoning for such decisions. Obviously these were the most contentious cases, where reviewer inexperience was the most common reported factor.

Once the list of accepted papers was finalized and released, we went through the laborious process of plagiarism (including self-plagiarism) detection. A total of 4 accepted papers were rejected because of that.

Finally, we would like to thank our Technical Program Chair, Pavel Lifshits, who did tremendous work behind the scenes, and we thank the tireless CMT team.

October 2022

Gabriel Brostow
Giovanni Maria Farinella
Moustapha Cissé
Shai Avidan
Tal Hassner

Organization

General Chairs

Rita Cucchiara   University of Modena and Reggio Emilia, Italy
Jiří Matas   Czech Technical University in Prague, Czech
                              Republic
Amnon Shashua   Hebrew University of Jerusalem, Israel
Lihi Zelnik-Manor   Technion – Israel Institute of Technology, Israel

Program Chairs

Shai Avidan   Tel-Aviv University, Israel
Gabriel Brostow   University College London, UK
Moustapha Cissé   Google AI, Ghana
Giovanni Maria Farinella   University of Catania, Italy
Tal Hassner   Facebook AI, USA

Program Technical Chair

Pavel Lifshits   Technion – Israel Institute of Technology, Israel

Workshops Chairs

Leonid Karlinsky   IBM Research, Israel
Tomer Michaeli   Technion – Israel Institute of Technology, Israel
Ko Nishino   Kyoto University, Japan

Tutorial Chairs

Thomas Pock   Graz University of Technology, Austria
Natalia Neverova   Facebook AI Research, UK

Demo Chair

Bohyung Han   Seoul National University, Korea

Social and Student Activities Chairs

Tatiana Tommasi   Italian Institute of Technology, Italy
Sagie Benaim   University of Copenhagen, Denmark

Diversity and Inclusion Chairs

Xi Yin   Facebook AI Research, USA
Bryan Russell   Adobe, USA

Communications Chairs

Lorenzo Baraldi   University of Modena and Reggio Emilia, Italy
Kosta Derpanis   York University & Samsung AI Centre Toronto,
                                   Canada

Industrial Liaison Chairs

Dimosthenis Karatzas   Universitat Autònoma de Barcelona, Spain
Chen Sagiv   SagivTech, Israel

Finance Chair

Gerard Medioni   University of Southern California & Amazon,
                                   USA

Publication Chair

Eric Mortensen   MiCROTEC, USA

Area Chairs

Lourdes Agapito   University College London, UK
Zeynep Akata   University of Tübingen, Germany
Naveed Akhtar   University of Western Australia, Australia
Karteek Alahari   Inria Grenoble Rhône-Alpes, France
Alexandre Alahi   École polytechnique fédérale de Lausanne,
                                   Switzerland
Pablo Arbelaez   Universidad de Los Andes, Columbia
Antonis A. Argyros   University of Crete & Foundation for Research
                                   and Technology-Hellas, Crete
Yuki M. Asano   University of Amsterdam, The Netherlands
Kalle Åström   Lund University, Sweden
Hadar Averbuch-Elor   Cornell University, USA

Matthijs Douze	Facebook AI Research, USA
Mohamed Elhoseiny	King Abdullah University of Science and Technology, Saudi Arabia
Sergio Escalera	University of Barcelona, Spain
Yi Fang	New York University, USA
Ryan Farrell	Brigham Young University, USA
Alireza Fathi	Google, USA
Christoph Feichtenhofer	Facebook AI Research, USA
Basura Fernando	Agency for Science, Technology and Research (A*STAR), Singapore
Vittorio Ferrari	Google Research, Switzerland
Andrew W. Fitzgibbon	Graphcore, UK
David J. Fleet	University of Toronto, Canada
David Forsyth	University of Illinois at Urbana-Champaign, USA
David Fouhey	University of Michigan, USA
Katerina Fragkiadaki	Carnegie Mellon University, USA
Friedrich Fraundorfer	Graz University of Technology, Austria
Oren Freifeld	Ben-Gurion University, Israel
Thomas Funkhouser	Google Research & Princeton University, USA
Yasutaka Furukawa	Simon Fraser University, Canada
Fabio Galasso	Sapienza University of Rome, Italy
Jürgen Gall	University of Bonn, Germany
Chuang Gan	Massachusetts Institute of Technology, USA
Zhe Gan	Microsoft, USA
Animesh Garg	University of Toronto, Vector Institute, Nvidia, Canada
Efstratios Gavves	University of Amsterdam, The Netherlands
Peter Gehler	Amazon, Germany
Theo Gevers	University of Amsterdam, The Netherlands
Bernard Ghanem	King Abdullah University of Science and Technology, Saudi Arabia
Ross B. Girshick	Facebook AI Research, USA
Georgia Gkioxari	Facebook AI Research, USA
Albert Gordo	Facebook, USA
Stephen Gould	Australian National University, Australia
Venu Madhav Govindu	Indian Institute of Science, India
Kristen Grauman	Facebook AI Research & UT Austin, USA
Abhinav Gupta	Carnegie Mellon University & Facebook AI Research, USA
Mohit Gupta	University of Wisconsin-Madison, USA
Hu Han	Institute of Computing Technology, Chinese Academy of Sciences, China

Bohyung Han	Seoul National University, Korea
Tian Han	Stevens Institute of Technology, USA
Emily Hand	University of Nevada, Reno, USA
Bharath Hariharan	Cornell University, USA
Ran He	Institute of Automation, Chinese Academy of Sciences, China
Otmar Hilliges	ETH Zurich, Switzerland
Adrian Hilton	University of Surrey, UK
Minh Hoai	Stony Brook University, USA
Yedid Hoshen	Hebrew University of Jerusalem, Israel
Timothy Hospedales	University of Edinburgh, UK
Gang Hua	Wormpex AI Research, USA
Di Huang	Beihang University, China
Jing Huang	Facebook, USA
Jia-Bin Huang	Facebook, USA
Nathan Jacobs	Washington University in St. Louis, USA
C.V. Jawahar	International Institute of Information Technology, Hyderabad, India
Herve Jegou	Facebook AI Research, France
Neel Joshi	Microsoft Research, USA
Armand Joulin	Facebook AI Research, France
Frederic Jurie	University of Caen Normandie, France
Fredrik Kahl	Chalmers University of Technology, Sweden
Yannis Kalantidis	NAVER LABS Europe, France
Evangelos Kalogerakis	University of Massachusetts, Amherst, USA
Sing Bing Kang	Zillow Group, USA
Yosi Keller	Bar Ilan University, Israel
Margret Keuper	University of Mannheim, Germany
Tae-Kyun Kim	Imperial College London, UK
Benjamin Kimia	Brown University, USA
Alexander Kirillov	Facebook AI Research, USA
Kris Kitani	Carnegie Mellon University, USA
Iasonas Kokkinos	Snap Inc. & University College London, UK
Vladlen Koltun	Apple, USA
Nikos Komodakis	University of Crete, Crete
Piotr Koniusz	Australian National University, Australia
Philipp Kraehenbuehl	University of Texas at Austin, USA
Dilip Krishnan	Google, USA
Ajay Kumar	Hong Kong Polytechnic University, Hong Kong, China
Junseok Kwon	Chung-Ang University, Korea
Jean-Francois Lalonde	Université Laval, Canada

Vittorio Murino   Istituto Italiano di Tecnologia, Italy
P. J. Narayanan   International Institute of Information Technology,
                                Hyderabad, India
Ram Nevatia   University of Southern California, USA
Natalia Neverova   Facebook AI Research, UK
Richard Newcombe   Facebook, USA
Cuong V. Nguyen   Florida International University, USA
Bingbing Ni   Shanghai Jiao Tong University, China
Juan Carlos Niebles   Salesforce & Stanford University, USA
Ko Nishino   Kyoto University, Japan
Jean-Marc Odobez   Idiap Research Institute, École polytechnique
                                fédérale de Lausanne, Switzerland
Francesca Odone   University of Genova, Italy
Takayuki Okatani   Tohoku University & RIKEN Center for
                                Advanced Intelligence Project, Japan
Manohar Paluri   Facebook, USA
Guan Pang   Facebook, USA
Maja Pantic   Imperial College London, UK
Sylvain Paris   Adobe Research, USA
Jaesik Park   Pohang University of Science and Technology,
                                Korea
Hyun Soo Park   The University of Minnesota, USA
Omkar M. Parkhi   Facebook, USA
Deepak Pathak   Carnegie Mellon University, USA
Georgios Pavlakos   University of California, Berkeley, USA
Marcello Pelillo   University of Venice, Italy
Marc Pollefeys   ETH Zurich & Microsoft, Switzerland
Jean Ponce   Inria, France
Gerard Pons-Moll   University of Tübingen, Germany
Fatih Porikli   Qualcomm, USA
Victor Adrian Prisacariu   University of Oxford, UK
Petia Radeva   University of Barcelona, Spain
Ravi Ramamoorthi   University of California, San Diego, USA
Deva Ramanan   Carnegie Mellon University, USA
Vignesh Ramanathan   Facebook, USA
Nalini Ratha   State University of New York at Buffalo, USA
Tammy Riklin Raviv   Ben-Gurion University, Israel
Tobias Ritschel   University College London, UK
Emanuele Rodola   Sapienza University of Rome, Italy
Amit K. Roy-Chowdhury   University of California, Riverside, USA
Michael Rubinstein   Google, USA
Olga Russakovsky   Princeton University, USA

Mathieu Salzmann   École polytechnique fédérale de Lausanne,
                              Switzerland
Dimitris Samaras   Stony Brook University, USA
Aswin Sankaranarayanan   Carnegie Mellon University, USA
Imari Sato   National Institute of Informatics, Japan
Yoichi Sato   University of Tokyo, Japan
Shin'ichi Satoh   National Institute of Informatics, Japan
Walter Scheirer   University of Notre Dame, USA
Bernt Schiele   Max Planck Institute for Informatics, Germany
Konrad Schindler   ETH Zurich, Switzerland
Cordelia Schmid   Inria & Google, France
Alexander Schwing   University of Illinois at Urbana-Champaign, USA
Nicu Sebe   University of Trento, Italy
Greg Shakhnarovich   Toyota Technological Institute at Chicago, USA
Eli Shechtman   Adobe Research, USA
Humphrey Shi   University of Oregon & University of Illinois at
                              Urbana-Champaign & Picsart AI Research,
                              USA
Jianbo Shi   University of Pennsylvania, USA
Roy Shilkrot   Massachusetts Institute of Technology, USA
Mike Zheng Shou   National University of Singapore, Singapore
Kaleem Siddiqi   McGill University, Canada
Richa Singh   Indian Institute of Technology Jodhpur, India
Greg Slabaugh   Queen Mary University of London, UK
Cees Snoek   University of Amsterdam, The Netherlands
Yale Song   Facebook AI Research, USA
Yi-Zhe Song   University of Surrey, UK
Bjorn Stenger   Rakuten Institute of Technology
Abby Stylianou   Saint Louis University, USA
Akihiro Sugimoto   National Institute of Informatics, Japan
Chen Sun   Brown University, USA
Deqing Sun   Google, USA
Kalyan Sunkavalli   Adobe Research, USA
Ying Tai   Tencent YouTu Lab, China
Ayellet Tal   Technion – Israel Institute of Technology, Israel
Ping Tan   Simon Fraser University, Canada
Siyu Tang   ETH Zurich, Switzerland
Chi-Keung Tang   Hong Kong University of Science and
                              Technology, Hong Kong, China
Radu Timofte   University of Würzburg, Germany & ETH Zurich,
                              Switzerland
Federico Tombari   Google, Switzerland & Technical University of
                              Munich, Germany

James Tompkin   Brown University, USA
Lorenzo Torresani   Dartmouth College, USA
Alexander Toshev   Apple, USA
Du Tran   Facebook AI Research, USA
Anh T. Tran   VinAI, Vietnam
Zhuowen Tu   University of California, San Diego, USA
Georgios Tzimiropoulos   Queen Mary University of London, UK
Jasper Uijlings   Google Research, Switzerland
Jan C. van Gemert   Delft University of Technology, The Netherlands
Gul Varol   Ecole des Ponts ParisTech, France
Nuno Vasconcelos   University of California, San Diego, USA
Mayank Vatsa   Indian Institute of Technology Jodhpur, India
Ashok Veeraraghavan   Rice University, USA
Jakob Verbeek   Facebook AI Research, France
Carl Vondrick   Columbia University, USA
Ruiping Wang   Institute of Computing Technology, Chinese
                                     Academy of Sciences, China
Xinchao Wang   National University of Singapore, Singapore
Liwei Wang   The Chinese University of Hong Kong,
                                     Hong Kong, China
Chaohui Wang   Université Paris-Est, France
Xiaolong Wang   University of California, San Diego, USA
Christian Wolf   NAVER LABS Europe, France
Tao Xiang   University of Surrey, UK
Saining Xie   Facebook AI Research, USA
Cihang Xie   University of California, Santa Cruz, USA
Zeki Yalniz   Facebook, USA
Ming-Hsuan Yang   University of California, Merced, USA
Angela Yao   National University of Singapore, Singapore
Shaodi You   University of Amsterdam, The Netherlands
Stella X. Yu   University of California, Berkeley, USA
Junsong Yuan   State University of New York at Buffalo, USA
Stefanos Zafeiriou   Imperial College London, UK
Amir Zamir   École polytechnique fédérale de Lausanne,
                                     Switzerland
Lei Zhang   Alibaba & Hong Kong Polytechnic University,
                                     Hong Kong, China
Lei Zhang   International Digital Economy Academy (IDEA),
                                     China
Pengchuan Zhang   Meta AI, USA
Bolei Zhou   University of California, Los Angeles, USA
Yuke Zhu   University of Texas at Austin, USA

Todd Zickler   Harvard University, USA
Wangmeng Zuo   Harbin Institute of Technology, China

Technical Program Committee

Davide Abati
Soroush Abbasi
   Koohpayegani
Amos L. Abbott
Rameen Abdal
Rabab Abdelfattah
Sahar Abdelnabi
Hassan Abu Alhaija
Abulikemu Abuduweili
Ron Abutbul
Hanno Ackermann
Aikaterini Adam
Kamil Adamczewski
Ehsan Adeli
Vida Adeli
Donald Adjeroh
Arman Afrasiyabi
Akshay Agarwal
Sameer Agarwal
Abhinav Agarwalla
Vaibhav Aggarwal
Sara Aghajanzadeh
Susmit Agrawal
Antonio Agudo
Touqeer Ahmad
Sk Miraj Ahmed
Chaitanya Ahuja
Nilesh A. Ahuja
Abhishek Aich
Shubhra Aich
Noam Aigerman
Arash Akbarinia
Peri Akiva
Derya Akkaynak
Emre Aksan
Arjun R. Akula
Yuval Alaluf
Stephan Alaniz
Paul Albert
Cenek Albl

Filippo Aleotti
Konstantinos P.
   Alexandridis
Motasem Alfarra
Mohsen Ali
Thiemo Alldieck
Hadi Alzayer
Liang An
Shan An
Yi An
Zhulin An
Dongsheng An
Jie An
Xiang An
Saket Anand
Cosmin Ancuti
Juan Andrade-Cetto
Alexander Andreopoulos
Bjoern Andres
Jerone T. A. Andrews
Shivangi Aneja
Anelia Angelova
Dragomir Anguelov
Rushil Anirudh
Oron Anschel
Rao Muhammad Anwer
Djamila Aouada
Evlampios Apostolidis
Srikar Appalaraju
Nikita Araslanov
Andre Araujo
Eric Arazo
Dawit Mureja Argaw
Anurag Arnab
Aditya Arora
Chetan Arora
Sunpreet S. Arora
Alexey Artemov
Muhammad Asad
Kumar Ashutosh

Sinem Aslan
Vishal Asnani
Mahmoud Assran
Amir Atapour-Abarghouei
Nikos Athanasiou
Ali Athar
ShahRukh Athar
Sara Atito
Souhaib Attaiki
Matan Atzmon
Mathieu Aubry
Nicolas Audebert
Tristan T.
   Aumentado-Armstrong
Melinos Averkiou
Yannis Avrithis
Stephane Ayache
Mehmet Aygün
Seyed Mehdi
   Ayyoubzadeh
Hossein Azizpour
George Azzopardi
Mallikarjun B. R.
Yunhao Ba
Abhishek Badki
Seung-Hwan Bae
Seung-Hwan Baek
Seungryul Baek
Piyush Nitin Bagad
Shai Bagon
Gaetan Bahl
Shikhar Bahl
Sherwin Bahmani
Haoran Bai
Lei Bai
Jiawang Bai
Haoyue Bai
Jinbin Bai
Xiang Bai
Xuyang Bai

Yang Bai
Yuanchao Bai
Ziqian Bai
Sungyong Baik
Kevin Bailly
Max Bain
Federico Baldassarre
Wele Gedara Chaminda
  Bandara
Biplab Banerjee
Pratyay Banerjee
Sandipan Banerjee
Jihwan Bang
Antyanta Bangunharcana
Aayush Bansal
Ankan Bansal
Siddhant Bansal
Wentao Bao
Zhipeng Bao
Amir Bar
Manel Baradad Jurjo
Lorenzo Baraldi
Danny Barash
Daniel Barath
Connelly Barnes
Ioan Andrei Bârsan
Steven Basart
Dina Bashkirova
Chaim Baskin
Peyman Bateni
Anil Batra
Sebastiano Battiato
Ardhendu Behera
Harkirat Behl
Jens Behley
Vasileios Belagiannis
Boulbaba Ben Amor
Emanuel Ben Baruch
Abdessamad Ben Hamza
Gil Ben-Artzi
Assia Benbihi
Fabian Benitez-Quiroz
Guy Ben-Yosef
Philipp Benz
Alexander W. Bergman

Urs Bergmann
Jesus Bermudez-Cameo
Stefano Berretti
Gedas Bertasius
Zachary Bessinger
Petra Bevandić
Matthew Beveridge
Lucas Beyer
Yash Bhalgat
Suvaansh Bhambri
Samarth Bharadwaj
Gaurav Bharaj
Aparna Bharati
Bharat Lal Bhatnagar
Uttaran Bhattacharya
Apratim Bhattacharyya
Brojeshwar Bhowmick
Ankan Kumar Bhunia
Ayan Kumar Bhunia
Qi Bi
Sai Bi
Michael Bi Mi
Gui-Bin Bian
Jia-Wang Bian
Shaojun Bian
Pia Bideau
Mario Bijelic
Hakan Bilen
Guillaume-Alexandre
  Bilodeau
Alexander Binder
Tolga Birdal
Vighnesh N. Birodkar
Sandika Biswas
Andreas Blattmann
Janusz Bobulski
Giuseppe Boccignone
Vishnu Boddeti
Navaneeth Bodla
Moritz Böhle
Aleksei Bokhovkin
Sam Bond-Taylor
Vivek Boominathan
Shubhankar Borse
Mark Boss

Andrea Bottino
Adnane Boukhayma
Fadi Boutros
Nicolas C. Boutry
Richard S. Bowen
Ivaylo Boyadzhiev
Aidan Boyd
Yuri Boykov
Aljaz Bozic
Behzad Bozorgtabar
Eric Brachmann
Samarth Brahmbhatt
Gustav Bredell
Francois Bremond
Joel Brogan
Andrew Brown
Thomas Brox
Marcus A. Brubaker
Robert-Jan Bruintjes
Yuqi Bu
Anders G. Buch
Himanshu Buckchash
Mateusz Buda
Ignas Budvytis
José M. Buenaposada
Marcel C. Bühler
Tu Bui
Adrian Bulat
Hannah Bull
Evgeny Burnaev
Andrei Bursuc
Benjamin Busam
Sergey N. Buzykanov
Wonmin Byeon
Fabian Caba
Martin Cadik
Guanyu Cai
Minjie Cai
Qing Cai
Zhongang Cai
Qi Cai
Yancheng Cai
Shen Cai
Han Cai
Jiarui Cai

Bowen Cai
Mu Cai
Qin Cai
Ruojin Cai
Weidong Cai
Weiwei Cai
Yi Cai
Yujun Cai
Zhiping Cai
Akin Caliskan
Lilian Calvet
Baris Can Cam
Necati Cihan Camgoz
Tommaso Campari
Dylan Campbell
Ziang Cao
Ang Cao
Xu Cao
Zhiwen Cao
Shengcao Cao
Song Cao
Weipeng Cao
Xiangyong Cao
Xiaochun Cao
Yue Cao
Yunhao Cao
Zhangjie Cao
Jiale Cao
Yang Cao
Jiajiong Cao
Jie Cao
Jinkun Cao
Lele Cao
Yulong Cao
Zhiguo Cao
Chen Cao
Razvan Caramalau
Marlène Careil
Gustavo Carneiro
Joao Carreira
Dan Casas
Paola Cascante-Bonilla
Angela Castillo
Francisco M. Castro
Pedro Castro

Luca Cavalli
George J. Cazenavette
Oya Celiktutan
Hakan Cevikalp
Sri Harsha C. H.
Sungmin Cha
Geonho Cha
Menglei Chai
Lucy Chai
Yuning Chai
Zenghao Chai
Anirban Chakraborty
Deep Chakraborty
Rudrasis Chakraborty
Souradeep Chakraborty
Kelvin C. K. Chan
Chee Seng Chan
Paramanand Chandramouli
Arjun Chandrasekaran
Kenneth Chaney
Dongliang Chang
Huiwen Chang
Peng Chang
Xiaojun Chang
Jia-Ren Chang
Hyung Jin Chang
Hyun Sung Chang
Ju Yong Chang
Li-Jen Chang
Qi Chang
Wei-Yi Chang
Yi Chang
Nadine Chang
Hanqing Chao
Pradyumna Chari
Dibyadip Chatterjee
Chiranjoy Chattopadhyay
Siddhartha Chaudhuri
Zhengping Che
Gal Chechik
Lianggangxu Chen
Qi Alfred Chen
Brian Chen
Bor-Chun Chen
Bo-Hao Chen

Bohong Chen
Bin Chen
Ziliang Chen
Cheng Chen
Chen Chen
Chaofeng Chen
Xi Chen
Haoyu Chen
Xuanhong Chen
Wei Chen
Qiang Chen
Shi Chen
Xianyu Chen
Chang Chen
Changhuai Chen
Hao Chen
Jie Chen
Jianbo Chen
Jingjing Chen
Jun Chen
Kejiang Chen
Mingcai Chen
Nenglun Chen
Qifeng Chen
Ruoyu Chen
Shu-Yu Chen
Weidong Chen
Weijie Chen
Weikai Chen
Xiang Chen
Xiuyi Chen
Xingyu Chen
Yaofo Chen
Yueting Chen
Yu Chen
Yunjin Chen
Yuntao Chen
Yun Chen
Zhenfang Chen
Zhuangzhuang Chen
Chu-Song Chen
Xiangyu Chen
Zhuo Chen
Chaoqi Chen
Shizhe Chen

Xiaotong Chen
Xiaozhi Chen
Dian Chen
Defang Chen
Dingfan Chen
Ding-Jie Chen
Ee Heng Chen
Tao Chen
Yixin Chen
Wei-Ting Chen
Lin Chen
Guang Chen
Guangyi Chen
Guanying Chen
Guangyao Chen
Hwann-Tzong Chen
Junwen Chen
Jiacheng Chen
Jianxu Chen
Hui Chen
Kai Chen
Kan Chen
Kevin Chen
Kuan-Wen Chen
Weihua Chen
Zhang Chen
Liang-Chieh Chen
Lele Chen
Liang Chen
Fanglin Chen
Zehui Chen
Minghui Chen
Minghao Chen
Xiaokang Chen
Qian Chen
Jun-Cheng Chen
Qi Chen
Qingcai Chen
Richard J. Chen
Runnan Chen
Rui Chen
Shuo Chen
Sentao Chen
Shaoyu Chen
Shixing Chen

Shuai Chen
Shuya Chen
Sizhe Chen
Simin Chen
Shaoxiang Chen
Zitian Chen
Tianlong Chen
Tianshui Chen
Min-Hung Chen
Xiangning Chen
Xin Chen
Xinghao Chen
Xuejin Chen
Xu Chen
Xuxi Chen
Yunlu Chen
Yanbei Chen
Yuxiao Chen
Yun-Chun Chen
Yi-Ting Chen
Yi-Wen Chen
Yinbo Chen
Yiran Chen
Yuanhong Chen
Yubei Chen
Yuefeng Chen
Yuhua Chen
Yukang Chen
Zerui Chen
Zhaoyu Chen
Zhen Chen
Zhenyu Chen
Zhi Chen
Zhiwei Chen
Zhixiang Chen
Long Chen
Bowen Cheng
Jun Cheng
Yi Cheng
Jingchun Cheng
Lechao Cheng
Xi Cheng
Yuan Cheng
Ho Kei Cheng
Kevin Ho Man Cheng

Jiacheng Cheng
Kelvin B. Cheng
Li Cheng
Mengjun Cheng
Zhen Cheng
Qingrong Cheng
Tianheng Cheng
Harry Cheng
Yihua Cheng
Yu Cheng
Ziheng Cheng
Soon Yau Cheong
Anoop Cherian
Manuela Chessa
Zhixiang Chi
Naoki Chiba
Julian Chibane
Kashyap Chitta
Tai-Yin Chiu
Hsu-kuang Chiu
Wei-Chen Chiu
Sungmin Cho
Donghyeon Cho
Hyeon Cho
Yooshin Cho
Gyusang Cho
Jang Hyun Cho
Seungju Cho
Nam Ik Cho
Sunghyun Cho
Hanbyel Cho
Jaesung Choe
Jooyoung Choi
Chiho Choi
Changwoon Choi
Jongwon Choi
Myungsub Choi
Dooseop Choi
Jonghyun Choi
Jinwoo Choi
Jun Won Choi
Min-Kook Choi
Hongsuk Choi
Janghoon Choi
Yoon-Ho Choi

Yukyung Choi
Jaegul Choo
Ayush Chopra
Siddharth Choudhary
Subhabrata Choudhury
Vasileios Choutas
Ka-Ho Chow
Pinaki Nath Chowdhury
Sammy Christen
Anders Christensen
Grigorios Chrysos
Hang Chu
Wen-Hsuan Chu
Peng Chu
Qi Chu
Ruihang Chu
Wei-Ta Chu
Yung-Yu Chuang
Sanghyuk Chun
Se Young Chun
Antonio Cinà
Ramazan Gokberk Cinbis
Javier Civera
Albert Clapés
Ronald Clark
Brian S. Clipp
Felipe Codevilla
Daniel Coelho de Castro
Niv Cohen
Forrester Cole
Maxwell D. Collins
Robert T. Collins
Marc Comino Trinidad
Runmin Cong
Wenyan Cong
Maxime Cordy
Marcella Cornia
Enric Corona
Huseyin Coskun
Luca Cosmo
Dragos Costea
Davide Cozzolino
Arun C. S. Kumar
Aiyu Cui
Qiongjie Cui

Quan Cui
Shuhao Cui
Yiming Cui
Ying Cui
Zijun Cui
Jiali Cui
Jiequan Cui
Yawen Cui
Zhen Cui
Zhaopeng Cui
Jack Culpepper
Xiaodong Cun
Ross Cutler
Adam Czajka
Ali Dabouei
Konstantinos M. Dafnis
Manuel Dahnert
Tao Dai
Yuchao Dai
Bo Dai
Mengyu Dai
Hang Dai
Haixing Dai
Peng Dai
Pingyang Dai
Qi Dai
Qiyu Dai
Yutong Dai
Naser Damer
Zhiyuan Dang
Mohamed Daoudi
Ayan Das
Abir Das
Debasmit Das
Deepayan Das
Partha Das
Sagnik Das
Soumi Das
Srijan Das
Swagatam Das
Avijit Dasgupta
Jim Davis
Adrian K. Davison
Homa Davoudi
Laura Daza

Matthias De Lange
Shalini De Mello
Marco De Nadai
Christophe De
    Vleeschouwer
Alp Dener
Boyang Deng
Congyue Deng
Bailin Deng
Yong Deng
Ye Deng
Zhuo Deng
Zhijie Deng
Xiaoming Deng
Jiankang Deng
Jinhong Deng
Jingjing Deng
Liang-Jian Deng
Siqi Deng
Xiang Deng
Xueqing Deng
Zhongying Deng
Karan Desai
Jean-Emmanuel Deschaud
Aniket Anand Deshmukh
Neel Dey
Helisa Dhamo
Prithviraj Dhar
Amaya Dharmasiri
Yan Di
Xing Di
Ousmane A. Dia
Haiwen Diao
Xiaolei Diao
Gonçalo José Dias Pais
Abdallah Dib
Anastasios Dimou
Changxing Ding
Henghui Ding
Guodong Ding
Yaqing Ding
Shuangrui Ding
Yuhang Ding
Yikang Ding
Shouhong Ding

Haisong Ding
Hui Ding
Jiahao Ding
Jian Ding
Jian-Jiun Ding
Shuxiao Ding
Tianyu Ding
Wenhao Ding
Yuqi Ding
Yi Ding
Yuzhen Ding
Zhengming Ding
Tan Minh Dinh
Vu Dinh
Christos Diou
Mandar Dixit
Bao Gia Doan
Khoa D. Doan
Dzung Anh Doan
Debi Prosad Dogra
Nehal Doiphode
Chengdong Dong
Bowen Dong
Zhenxing Dong
Hang Dong
Xiaoyi Dong
Haoye Dong
Jiangxin Dong
Shichao Dong
Xuan Dong
Zhen Dong
Shuting Dong
Jing Dong
Li Dong
Ming Dong
Nanqing Dong
Qiulei Dong
Runpei Dong
Siyan Dong
Tian Dong
Wei Dong
Xiaomeng Dong
Xin Dong
Xingbo Dong
Yuan Dong

Samuel Dooley
Gianfranco Doretto
Michael Dorkenwald
Keval Doshi
Zhaopeng Dou
Xiaotian Dou
Hazel Doughty
Ahmad Droby
Iddo Drori
Jie Du
Yong Du
Dawei Du
Dong Du
Ruoyi Du
Yuntao Du
Xuefeng Du
Yilun Du
Yuming Du
Radhika Dua
Haodong Duan
Jiafei Duan
Kaiwen Duan
Peiqi Duan
Ye Duan
Haoran Duan
Jiali Duan
Amanda Duarte
Abhimanyu Dubey
Shiv Ram Dubey
Florian Dubost
Lukasz Dudziak
Shivam Duggal
Justin M. Dulay
Matteo Dunnhofer
Chi Nhan Duong
Thibaut Durand
Mihai Dusmanu
Ujjal Kr Dutta
Debidatta Dwibedi
Isht Dwivedi
Sai Kumar Dwivedi
Takeharu Eda
Mark Edmonds
Alexei A. Efros
Thibaud Ehret

Max Ehrlich
Mahsa Ehsanpour
Iván Eichhardt
Farshad Einabadi
Marvin Eisenberger
Hazim Kemal Ekenel
Mohamed El Banani
Ismail Elezi
Moshe Eliasof
Alaa El-Nouby
Ian Endres
Francis Engelmann
Deniz Engin
Chanho Eom
Dave Epstein
Maria C. Escobar
Victor A. Escorcia
Carlos Esteves
Sungmin Eum
Bernard J. E. Evans
Ivan Evtimov
Fevziye Irem Eyiokur
    Yaman
Matteo Fabbri
Sébastien Fabbro
Gabriele Facciolo
Masud Fahim
Bin Fan
Hehe Fan
Deng-Ping Fan
Aoxiang Fan
Chen-Chen Fan
Qi Fan
Zhaoxin Fan
Haoqi Fan
Heng Fan
Hongyi Fan
Linxi Fan
Baojie Fan
Jiayuan Fan
Lei Fan
Quanfu Fan
Yonghui Fan
Yingruo Fan
Zhiwen Fan

Zicong Fan
Sean Fanello
Jiansheng Fang
Chaowei Fang
Yuming Fang
Jianwu Fang
Jin Fang
Qi Fang
Shancheng Fang
Tian Fang
Xianyong Fang
Gongfan Fang
Zhen Fang
Hui Fang
Jiemin Fang
Le Fang
Pengfei Fang
Xiaolin Fang
Yuxin Fang
Zhaoyuan Fang
Ammarah Farooq
Azade Farshad
Zhengcong Fei
Michael Felsberg
Wei Feng
Chen Feng
Fan Feng
Andrew Feng
Xin Feng
Zheyun Feng
Ruicheng Feng
Mingtao Feng
Qianyu Feng
Shangbin Feng
Chun-Mei Feng
Zunlei Feng
Zhiyong Feng
Martin Fergie
Mustansar Fiaz
Marco Fiorucci
Michael Firman
Hamed Firooz
Volker Fischer
Corneliu O. Florea
Georgios Floros

Wolfgang Foerstner
Gianni Franchi
Jean-Sebastien Franco
Simone Frintrop
Anna Fruehstueck
Changhong Fu
Chaoyou Fu
Cheng-Yang Fu
Chi-Wing Fu
Deqing Fu
Huan Fu
Jun Fu
Kexue Fu
Ying Fu
Jianlong Fu
Jingjing Fu
Qichen Fu
Tsu-Jui Fu
Xueyang Fu
Yang Fu
Yanwei Fu
Yonggan Fu
Wolfgang Fuhl
Yasuhisa Fujii
Kent Fujiwara
Marco Fumero
Takuya Funatomi
Isabel Funke
Dario Fuoli
Antonino Furnari
Matheus A. Gadelha
Akshay Gadi Patil
Adrian Galdran
Guillermo Gallego
Silvano Galliani
Orazio Gallo
Leonardo Galteri
Matteo Gamba
Yiming Gan
Sujoy Ganguly
Harald Ganster
Boyan Gao
Changxin Gao
Daiheng Gao
Difei Gao

Chen Gao
Fei Gao
Lin Gao
Wei Gao
Yiming Gao
Junyu Gao
Guangyu Ryan Gao
Haichang Gao
Hongchang Gao
Jialin Gao
Jin Gao
Jun Gao
Katelyn Gao
Mingchen Gao
Mingfei Gao
Pan Gao
Shangqian Gao
Shanghua Gao
Xitong Gao
Yunhe Gao
Zhanning Gao
Elena Garces
Nuno Cruz Garcia
Noa Garcia
Guillermo
    Garcia-Hernando
Isha Garg
Rahul Garg
Sourav Garg
Quentin Garrido
Stefano Gasperini
Kent Gauen
Chandan Gautam
Shivam Gautam
Paul Gay
Chunjiang Ge
Shiming Ge
Wenhang Ge
Yanhao Ge
Zheng Ge
Songwei Ge
Weifeng Ge
Yixiao Ge
Yuying Ge
Shijie Geng

Zhengyang Geng
Kyle A. Genova
Georgios Georgakis
Markos Georgopoulos
Marcel Geppert
Shabnam Ghadar
Mina Ghadimi Atigh
Deepti Ghadiyaram
Maani Ghaffari Jadidi
Sedigh Ghamari
Zahra Gharaee
Michaël Gharbi
Golnaz Ghiasi
Reza Ghoddoosian
Soumya Suvra Ghosal
Adhiraj Ghosh
Arthita Ghosh
Pallabi Ghosh
Soumyadeep Ghosh
Andrew Gilbert
Igor Gilitschenski
Jhony H. Giraldo
Andreu Girbau Xalabarder
Rohit Girdhar
Sharath Girish
Xavier Giro-i-Nieto
Raja Giryes
Thomas Gittings
Nikolaos Gkanatsios
Ioannis Gkioulekas
Abhiram
    Gnanasambandam
Aurele T. Gnanha
Clement L. J. C. Godard
Arushi Goel
Vidit Goel
Shubham Goel
Zan Gojcic
Aaron K. Gokaslan
Tejas Gokhale
S. Alireza Golestaneh
Thiago L. Gomes
Nuno Goncalves
Boqing Gong
Chen Gong

Yuanhao Gong
Guoqiang Gong
Jingyu Gong
Rui Gong
Yu Gong
Mingming Gong
Neil Zhenqiang Gong
Xun Gong
Yunye Gong
Yihong Gong
Cristina I. González
Nithin Gopalakrishnan
    Nair
Gaurav Goswami
Jianping Gou
Shreyank N. Gowda
Ankit Goyal
Helmut Grabner
Patrick L. Grady
Ben Graham
Eric Granger
Douglas R. Gray
Matej Grcić
David Griffiths
Jinjin Gu
Yun Gu
Shuyang Gu
Jianyang Gu
Fuqiang Gu
Jiatao Gu
Jindong Gu
Jiaqi Gu
Jinwei Gu
Jiaxin Gu
Geonmo Gu
Xiao Gu
Xinqian Gu
Xiuye Gu
Yuming Gu
Zhangxuan Gu
Dayan Guan
Junfeng Guan
Qingji Guan
Tianrui Guan
Shanyan Guan

Denis A. Gudovskiy
Ricardo Guerrero
Pierre-Louis Guhur
Jie Gui
Liangyan Gui
Liangke Gui
Benoit Guillard
Erhan Gundogdu
Manuel Günther
Jingcai Guo
Yuanfang Guo
Junfeng Guo
Chenqi Guo
Dan Guo
Hongji Guo
Jia Guo
Jie Guo
Minghao Guo
Shi Guo
Yanhui Guo
Yangyang Guo
Yuan-Chen Guo
Yilu Guo
Yiluan Guo
Yong Guo
Guangyu Guo
Haiyun Guo
Jinyang Guo
Jianyuan Guo
Pengsheng Guo
Pengfei Guo
Shuxuan Guo
Song Guo
Tianyu Guo
Qing Guo
Qiushan Guo
Wen Guo
Xiefan Guo
Xiaohu Guo
Xiaoqing Guo
Yufei Guo
Yuhui Guo
Yuliang Guo
Yunhui Guo
Yanwen Guo

Akshita Gupta
Ankush Gupta
Kamal Gupta
Kartik Gupta
Ritwik Gupta
Rohit Gupta
Siddharth Gururani
Fredrik K. Gustafsson
Abner Guzman Rivera
Vladimir Guzov
Matthew A. Gwilliam
Jung-Woo Ha
Marc Habermann
Isma Hadji
Christian Haene
Martin Hahner
Levente Hajder
Alexandros Haliassos
Emanuela Haller
Bumsub Ham
Abdullah J. Hamdi
Shreyas Hampali
Dongyoon Han
Chunrui Han
Dong-Jun Han
Dong-Sig Han
Guangxing Han
Zhizhong Han
Ruize Han
Jiaming Han
Jin Han
Ligong Han
Xian-Hua Han
Xiaoguang Han
Yizeng Han
Zhi Han
Zhenjun Han
Zhongyi Han
Jungong Han
Junlin Han
Kai Han
Kun Han
Sungwon Han
Songfang Han
Wei Han

Xiao Han
Xintong Han
Xinzhe Han
Yahong Han
Yan Han
Zongbo Han
Nicolai Hani
Rana Hanocka
Niklas Hanselmann
Nicklas A. Hansen
Hong Hanyu
Fusheng Hao
Yanbin Hao
Shijie Hao
Udith Haputhanthri
Mehrtash Harandi
Josh Harguess
Adam Harley
David M. Hart
Atsushi Hashimoto
Ali Hassani
Mohammed Hassanin
Yana Hasson
Joakim Bruslund Haurum
Bo He
Kun He
Chen He
Xin He
Fazhi He
Gaoqi He
Hao He
Haoyu He
Jiangpeng He
Hongliang He
Qian He
Xiangteng He
Xuming He
Yannan He
Yuhang He
Yang He
Xiangyu He
Nanjun He
Pan He
Sen He
Shengfeng He

Songtao He
Tao He
Tong He
Wei He
Xuehai He
Xiaoxiao He
Ying He
Yisheng He
Ziwen He
Peter Hedman
Felix Heide
Yacov Hel-Or
Paul Henderson
Philipp Henzler
Byeongho Heo
Jae-Pil Heo
Miran Heo
Sachini A. Herath
Stephane Herbin
Pedro Hermosilla Casajus
Monica Hernandez
Charles Herrmann
Roei Herzig
Mauricio Hess-Flores
Carlos Hinojosa
Tobias Hinz
Tsubasa Hirakawa
Chih-Hui Ho
Lam Si Tung Ho
Jennifer Hobbs
Derek Hoiem
Yannick Hold-Geoffroy
Aleksander Holynski
Cheeun Hong
Fa-Ting Hong
Hanbin Hong
Guan Zhe Hong
Danfeng Hong
Lanqing Hong
Xiaopeng Hong
Xin Hong
Jie Hong
Seungbum Hong
Cheng-Yao Hong
Seunghoon Hong

Yi Hong
Yuan Hong
Yuchen Hong
Anthony Hoogs
Maxwell C. Horton
Kazuhiro Hotta
Qibin Hou
Tingbo Hou
Junhui Hou
Ji Hou
Qiqi Hou
Rui Hou
Ruibing Hou
Zhi Hou
Henry Howard-Jenkins
Lukas Hoyer
Wei-Lin Hsiao
Chiou-Ting Hsu
Anthony Hu
Brian Hu
Yusong Hu
Hexiang Hu
Haoji Hu
Di Hu
Hengtong Hu
Haigen Hu
Lianyu Hu
Hanzhe Hu
Jie Hu
Junlin Hu
Shizhe Hu
Jian Hu
Zhiming Hu
Juhua Hu
Peng Hu
Ping Hu
Ronghang Hu
MengShun Hu
Tao Hu
Vincent Tao Hu
Xiaoling Hu
Xinting Hu
Xiaolin Hu
Xuefeng Hu
Xiaowei Hu

Yang Hu
Yueyu Hu
Zeyu Hu
Zhongyun Hu
Binh-Son Hua
Guoliang Hua
Yi Hua
Linzhi Huang
Qiusheng Huang
Bo Huang
Chen Huang
Hsin-Ping Huang
Ye Huang
Shuangping Huang
Zeng Huang
Buzhen Huang
Cong Huang
Heng Huang
Hao Huang
Qidong Huang
Huaibo Huang
Chaoqin Huang
Feihu Huang
Jiahui Huang
Jingjia Huang
Kun Huang
Lei Huang
Sheng Huang
Shuaiyi Huang
Siyu Huang
Xiaoshui Huang
Xiaoyang Huang
Yan Huang
Yihao Huang
Ying Huang
Ziling Huang
Xiaoke Huang
Yifei Huang
Haiyang Huang
Zhewei Huang
Jin Huang
Haibin Huang
Jiaxing Huang
Junjie Huang
Keli Huang

Lang Huang
Lin Huang
Luojie Huang
Mingzhen Huang
Shijia Huang
Shengyu Huang
Siyuan Huang
He Huang
Xiuyu Huang
Lianghua Huang
Yue Huang
Yaping Huang
Yuge Huang
Zehao Huang
Zeyi Huang
Zhiqi Huang
Zhongzhan Huang
Zilong Huang
Ziyuan Huang
Tianrui Hui
Zhuo Hui
Le Hui
Jing Huo
Junhwa Hur
Shehzeen S. Hussain
Chuong Minh Huynh
Seunghyun Hwang
Jaehui Hwang
Jyh-Jing Hwang
Sukjun Hwang
Soonmin Hwang
Wonjun Hwang
Rakib Hyder
Sangeek Hyun
Sarah Ibrahimi
Tomoki Ichikawa
Yerlan Idelbayev
A. S. M. Iftekhar
Masaaki Iiyama
Satoshi Ikehata
Sunghoon Im
Atul N. Ingle
Eldar Insafutdinov
Yani A. Ioannou
Radu Tudor Ionescu

Umar Iqbal
Go Irie
Muhammad Zubair Irshad
Ahmet Iscen
Berivan Isik
Ashraful Islam
Md Amirul Islam
Syed Islam
Mariko Isogawa
Vamsi Krishna K. Ithapu
Boris Ivanovic
Darshan Iyer
Sarah Jabbour
Ayush Jain
Nishant Jain
Samyak Jain
Vidit Jain
Vineet Jain
Priyank Jaini
Tomas Jakab
Mohammad A. A. K.
   Jalwana
Muhammad Abdullah
   Jamal
Hadi Jamali-Rad
Stuart James
Varun Jampani
Young Kyun Jang
YeongJun Jang
Yunseok Jang
Ronnachai Jaroensri
Bhavan Jasani
Krishna Murthy
   Jatavallabhula
Mojan Javaheripi
Syed A. Javed
Guillaume Jeanneret
Pranav Jeevan
Herve Jegou
Rohit Jena
Tomas Jenicek
Porter Jenkins
Simon Jenni
Hae-Gon Jeon
Sangryul Jeon

Boseung Jeong
Yoonwoo Jeong
Seong-Gyun Jeong
Jisoo Jeong
Allan D. Jepson
Ankit Jha
Sumit K. Jha
I-Hong Jhuo
Ge-Peng Ji
Chaonan Ji
Deyi Ji
Jingwei Ji
Wei Ji
Zhong Ji
Jiayi Ji
Pengliang Ji
Hui Ji
Mingi Ji
Xiaopeng Ji
Yuzhu Ji
Baoxiong Jia
Songhao Jia
Dan Jia
Shan Jia
Xiaojun Jia
Xiuyi Jia
Xu Jia
Menglin Jia
Wenqi Jia
Boyuan Jiang
Wenhao Jiang
Huaizu Jiang
Hanwen Jiang
Haiyong Jiang
Hao Jiang
Huajie Jiang
Huiqin Jiang
Haojun Jiang
Haobo Jiang
Junjun Jiang
Xingyu Jiang
Yangbangyan Jiang
Yu Jiang
Jianmin Jiang
Jiaxi Jiang

Jing Jiang
Kui Jiang
Li Jiang
Liming Jiang
Chiyu Jiang
Meirui Jiang
Chen Jiang
Peng Jiang
Tai-Xiang Jiang
Wen Jiang
Xinyang Jiang
Yifan Jiang
Yuming Jiang
Yingying Jiang
Zeren Jiang
ZhengKai Jiang
Zhenyu Jiang
Shuming Jiao
Jianbo Jiao
Licheng Jiao
Dongkwon Jin
Yeying Jin
Cheng Jin
Linyi Jin
Qing Jin
Taisong Jin
Xiao Jin
Xin Jin
Sheng Jin
Kyong Hwan Jin
Ruibing Jin
SouYoung Jin
Yueming Jin
Chenchen Jing
Longlong Jing
Taotao Jing
Yongcheng Jing
Younghyun Jo
Joakim Johnander
Jeff Johnson
Michael J. Jones
R. Kenny Jones
Rico Jonschkowski
Ameya Joshi
Sunghun Joung

Felix Juefei-Xu
Claudio R. Jung
Steffen Jung
Hari Chandana K.
Rahul Vigneswaran K.
Prajwal K. R.
Abhishek Kadian
Jhony Kaesemodel Pontes
Kumara Kahatapitiya
Anmol Kalia
Sinan Kalkan
Tarun Kalluri
Jaewon Kam
Sandesh Kamath
Meina Kan
Menelaos Kanakis
Takuhiro Kaneko
Di Kang
Guoliang Kang
Hao Kang
Jaeyeon Kang
Kyoungkook Kang
Li-Wei Kang
MinGuk Kang
Suk-Ju Kang
Zhao Kang
Yash Mukund Kant
Yueying Kao
Aupendu Kar
Konstantinos Karantzalos
Sezer Karaoglu
Navid Kardan
Sanjay Kariyappa
Leonid Karlinsky
Animesh Karnewar
Shyamgopal Karthik
Hirak J. Kashyap
Marc A. Kastner
Hirokatsu Kataoka
Angelos Katharopoulos
Hiroharu Kato
Kai Katsumata
Manuel Kaufmann
Chaitanya Kaul
Prakhar Kaushik

Yuki Kawana
Lei Ke
Lipeng Ke
Tsung-Wei Ke
Wei Ke
Petr Kellnhofer
Aniruddha Kembhavi
John Kender
Corentin Kervadec
Leonid Keselman
Daniel Keysers
Nima Khademi Kalantari
Taras Khakhulin
Samir Khaki
Muhammad Haris Khan
Qadeer Khan
Salman Khan
Subash Khanal
Vaishnavi M. Khindkar
Rawal Khirodkar
Saeed Khorram
Pirazh Khorramshahi
Kourosh Khoshelham
Ansh Khurana
Benjamin Kiefer
Jae Myung Kim
Junho Kim
Boah Kim
Hyeonseong Kim
Dong-Jin Kim
Dongwan Kim
Donghyun Kim
Doyeon Kim
Yonghyun Kim
Hyung-Il Kim
Hyunwoo Kim
Hyeongwoo Kim
Hyo Jin Kim
Hyunwoo J. Kim
Taehoon Kim
Jaeha Kim
Jiwon Kim
Jung Uk Kim
Kangyeol Kim
Eunji Kim

Daeha Kim
Dongwon Kim
Kunhee Kim
Kyungmin Kim
Junsik Kim
Min H. Kim
Namil Kim
Kookhoi Kim
Sanghyun Kim
Seongyeop Kim
Seungryong Kim
Saehoon Kim
Euyoung Kim
Guisik Kim
Sungyeon Kim
Sunnie S. Y. Kim
Taehun Kim
Tae Oh Kim
Won Hwa Kim
Seungwook Kim
YoungBin Kim
Youngeun Kim
Akisato Kimura
Furkan Osman Kınlı
Zsolt Kira
Hedvig Kjellström
Florian Kleber
Jan P. Klopp
Florian Kluger
Laurent Kneip
Byungsoo Ko
Muhammed Kocabas
A. Sophia Koepke
Kevin Koeser
Nick Kolkin
Nikos Kolotouros
Wai-Kin Adams Kong
Deying Kong
Caihua Kong
Youyong Kong
Shuyu Kong
Shu Kong
Tao Kong
Yajing Kong
Yu Kong

Zishang Kong
Theodora Kontogianni
Anton S. Konushin
Julian F. P. Kooij
Bruno Korbar
Giorgos Kordopatis-Zilos
Jari Korhonen
Adam Kortylewski
Denis Korzhenkov
Divya Kothandaraman
Suraj Kothawade
Iuliia Kotseruba
Satwik Kottur
Shashank Kotyan
Alexandros Kouris
Petros Koutras
Anna Kreshuk
Ranjay Krishna
Dilip Krishnan
Andrey Kuehlkamp
Hilde Kuehne
Jason Kuen
David Kügler
Arjan Kuijper
Anna Kukleva
Sumith Kulal
Viveka Kulharia
Akshay R. Kulkarni
Nilesh Kulkarni
Dominik Kulon
Abhinav Kumar
Akash Kumar
Suryansh Kumar
B. V. K. Vijaya Kumar
Pulkit Kumar
Ratnesh Kumar
Sateesh Kumar
Satish Kumar
Vijay Kumar B. G.
Nupur Kumari
Sudhakar Kumawat
Jogendra Nath Kundu
Hsien-Kai Kuo
Meng-Yu Jennifer Kuo
Vinod Kumar Kurmi

Yusuke Kurose
Keerthy Kusumam
Alina Kuznetsova
Henry Kvinge
Ho Man Kwan
Hyeokjun Kweon
Heeseung Kwon
Gihyun Kwon
Myung-Joon Kwon
Taesung Kwon
YoungJoong Kwon
Christos Kyrkou
Jorma Laaksonen
Yann Labbe
Zorah Laehner
Florent Lafarge
Hamid Laga
Manuel Lagunas
Shenqi Lai
Jian-Huang Lai
Zihang Lai
Mohamed I. Lakhal
Mohit Lamba
Meng Lan
Loic Landrieu
Zhiqiang Lang
Natalie Lang
Dong Lao
Yizhen Lao
Yingjie Lao
Issam Hadj Laradji
Gustav Larsson
Viktor Larsson
Zakaria Laskar
Stéphane Lathuilière
Chun Pong Lau
Rynson W. H. Lau
Hei Law
Justin Lazarow
Verica Lazova
Eric-Tuan Le
Hieu Le
Trung-Nghia Le
Mathias Lechner
Byeong-Uk Lee

Chen-Yu Lee
Che-Rung Lee
Chul Lee
Hong Joo Lee
Dongsoo Lee
Jiyoung Lee
Eugene Eu Tzuan Lee
Daeun Lee
Saehyung Lee
Jewook Lee
Hyungtae Lee
Hyunmin Lee
Jungbeom Lee
Joon-Young Lee
Jong-Seok Lee
Joonseok Lee
Junha Lee
Kibok Lee
Byung-Kwan Lee
Jangwon Lee
Jinho Lee
Jongmin Lee
Seunghyun Lee
Sohyun Lee
Minsik Lee
Dogyoon Lee
Seungmin Lee
Min Jun Lee
Sangho Lee
Sangmin Lee
Seungeun Lee
Seon-Ho Lee
Sungmin Lee
Sungho Lee
Sangyoun Lee
Vincent C. S. S. Lee
Jaeseong Lee
Yong Jae Lee
Chenyang Lei
Chenyi Lei
Jiahui Lei
Xinyu Lei
Yinjie Lei
Jiaxu Leng
Luziwei Leng

Jan E. Lenssen
Vincent Lepetit
Thomas Leung
María Leyva-Vallina
Xin Li
Yikang Li
Baoxin Li
Bin Li
Bing Li
Bowen Li
Changlin Li
Chao Li
Chongyi Li
Guanyue Li
Shuai Li
Jin Li
Dingquan Li
Dongxu Li
Yiting Li
Gang Li
Dian Li
Guohao Li
Haoang Li
Haoliang Li
Haoran Li
Hengduo Li
Huafeng Li
Xiaoming Li
Hanao Li
Hongwei Li
Ziqiang Li
Jisheng Li
Jiacheng Li
Jia Li
Jiachen Li
Jiahao Li
Jianwei Li
Jiazhi Li
Jie Li
Jing Li
Jingjing Li
Jingtao Li
Jun Li
Junxuan Li
Kai Li

Kailin Li
Kenneth Li
Kun Li
Kunpeng Li
Aoxue Li
Chenglong Li
Chenglin Li
Changsheng Li
Zhichao Li
Qiang Li
Yanyu Li
Zuoyue Li
Xiang Li
Xuelong Li
Fangda Li
Ailin Li
Liang Li
Chun-Guang Li
Daiqing Li
Dong Li
Guanbin Li
Guorong Li
Haifeng Li
Jianan Li
Jianing Li
Jiaxin Li
Ke Li
Lei Li
Lincheng Li
Liulei Li
Lujun Li
Linjie Li
Lin Li
Pengyu Li
Ping Li
Qiufu Li
Qingyong Li
Rui Li
Siyuan Li
Wei Li
Wenbin Li
Xiangyang Li
Xinyu Li
Xiujun Li
Xiu Li

Xu Li
Ya-Li Li
Yao Li
Yongjie Li
Yijun Li
Yiming Li
Yuezun Li
Yu Li
Yunheng Li
Yuqi Li
Zhe Li
Zeming Li
Zhen Li
Zhengqin Li
Zhimin Li
Jiefeng Li
Jinpeng Li
Chengze Li
Jianwu Li
Lerenhan Li
Shan Li
Suichan Li
Xiangtai Li
Yanjie Li
Yandong Li
Zhuoling Li
Zhenqiang Li
Manyi Li
Maosen Li
Ji Li
Minjun Li
Mingrui Li
Mengtian Li
Junyi Li
Nianyi Li
Bo Li
Xiao Li
Peihua Li
Peike Li
Peizhao Li
Peiliang Li
Qi Li
Ren Li
Runze Li
Shile Li

Sheng Li
Shigang Li
Shiyu Li
Shuang Li
Shasha Li
Shichao Li
Tianye Li
Yuexiang Li
Wei-Hong Li
Wanhua Li
Weihao Li
Weiming Li
Weixin Li
Wenbo Li
Wenshuo Li
Weijian Li
Yunan Li
Xirong Li
Xianhang Li
Xiaoyu Li
Xueqian Li
Xuanlin Li
Xianzhi Li
Yunqiang Li
Yanjing Li
Yansheng Li
Yawei Li
Yi Li
Yong Li
Yong-Lu Li
Yuhang Li
Yu-Jhe Li
Yuxi Li
Yunsheng Li
Yanwei Li
Zechao Li
Zejian Li
Zeju Li
Zekun Li
Zhaowen Li
Zheng Li
Zhenyu Li
Zhiheng Li
Zhi Li
Zhong Li

Zhuowei Li
Zhuowan Li
Zhuohang Li
Zizhang Li
Chen Li
Yuan-Fang Li
Dongze Lian
Xiaochen Lian
Zhouhui Lian
Long Lian
Qing Lian
Jin Lianbao
Jinxiu S. Liang
Dingkang Liang
Jiahao Liang
Jianming Liang
Jingyun Liang
Kevin J. Liang
Kaizhao Liang
Chen Liang
Jie Liang
Senwei Liang
Ding Liang
Jiajun Liang
Jian Liang
Kongming Liang
Siyuan Liang
Yuanzhi Liang
Zhengfa Liang
Mingfu Liang
Xiaodan Liang
Xuefeng Liang
Yuxuan Liang
Kang Liao
Liang Liao
Hong-Yuan Mark Liao
Wentong Liao
Haofu Liao
Yue Liao
Minghui Liao
Shengcai Liao
Ting-Hsuan Liao
Xin Liao
Yinghong Liao
Teck Yian Lim

Che-Tsung Lin
Chung-Ching Lin
Chen-Hsuan Lin
Cheng Lin
Chuming Lin
Chunyu Lin
Dahua Lin
Wei Lin
Zheng Lin
Huaijia Lin
Jason Lin
Jierui Lin
Jiaying Lin
Jie Lin
Kai-En Lin
Kevin Lin
Guangfeng Lin
Jiehong Lin
Feng Lin
Hang Lin
Kwan-Yee Lin
Ke Lin
Luojun Lin
Qinghong Lin
Xiangbo Lin
Yi Lin
Zudi Lin
Shijie Lin
Yiqun Lin
Tzu-Heng Lin
Ming Lin
Shaohui Lin
SongNan Lin
Ji Lin
Tsung-Yu Lin
Xudong Lin
Yancong Lin
Yen-Chen Lin
Yiming Lin
Yuewei Lin
Zhiqiu Lin
Zinan Lin
Zhe Lin
David B. Lindell
Zhixin Ling

Zhan Ling
Alexander Liniger
Venice Erin B. Liong
Joey Litalien
Or Litany
Roee Litman
Ron Litman
Jim Little
Dor Litvak
Shaoteng Liu
Shuaicheng Liu
Andrew Liu
Xian Liu
Shaohui Liu
Bei Liu
Bo Liu
Yong Liu
Ming Liu
Yanbin Liu
Chenxi Liu
Daqi Liu
Di Liu
Difan Liu
Dong Liu
Dongfang Liu
Daizong Liu
Xiao Liu
Fangyi Liu
Fengbei Liu
Fenglin Liu
Bin Liu
Yuang Liu
Ao Liu
Hong Liu
Hongfu Liu
Huidong Liu
Ziyi Liu
Feng Liu
Hao Liu
Jie Liu
Jialun Liu
Jiang Liu
Jing Liu
Jingya Liu
Jiaming Liu

Jun Liu
Juncheng Liu
Jiawei Liu
Hongyu Liu
Chuanbin Liu
Haotian Liu
Lingqiao Liu
Chang Liu
Han Liu
Liu Liu
Min Liu
Yingqi Liu
Aishan Liu
Bingyu Liu
Benlin Liu
Boxiao Liu
Chenchen Liu
Chuanjian Liu
Daqing Liu
Huan Liu
Haozhe Liu
Jiaheng Liu
Wei Liu
Jingzhou Liu
Jiyuan Liu
Lingbo Liu
Nian Liu
Peiye Liu
Qiankun Liu
Shenglan Liu
Shilong Liu
Wen Liu
Wenyu Liu
Weifeng Liu
Wu Liu
Xiaolong Liu
Yang Liu
Yanwei Liu
Yingcheng Liu
Yongfei Liu
Yihao Liu
Yu Liu
Yunze Liu
Ze Liu
Zhenhua Liu

Zhenguang Liu
Lin Liu
Lihao Liu
Pengju Liu
Xinhai Liu
Yunfei Liu
Meng Liu
Minghua Liu
Mingyuan Liu
Miao Liu
Peirong Liu
Ping Liu
Qingjie Liu
Ruoshi Liu
Risheng Liu
Songtao Liu
Xing Liu
Shikun Liu
Shuming Liu
Sheng Liu
Songhua Liu
Tongliang Liu
Weibo Liu
Weide Liu
Weizhe Liu
Wenxi Liu
Weiyang Liu
Xin Liu
Xiaobin Liu
Xudong Liu
Xiaoyi Liu
Xihui Liu
Xinchen Liu
Xingtong Liu
Xinpeng Liu
Xinyu Liu
Xianpeng Liu
Xu Liu
Xingyu Liu
Yongtuo Liu
Yahui Liu
Yangxin Liu
Yaoyao Liu
Yaojie Liu
Yuliang Liu

Yongcheng Liu
Yuan Liu
Yufan Liu
Yu-Lun Liu
Yun Liu
Yunfan Liu
Yuanzhong Liu
Zhuoran Liu
Zhen Liu
Zheng Liu
Zhijian Liu
Zhisong Liu
Ziquan Liu
Ziyu Liu
Zhihua Liu
Zechun Liu
Zhaoyang Liu
Zhengzhe Liu
Stephan Liwicki
Shao-Yuan Lo
Sylvain Lobry
Suhas Lohit
Vishnu Suresh Lokhande
Vincenzo Lomonaco
Chengjiang Long
Guodong Long
Fuchen Long
Shangbang Long
Yang Long
Zijun Long
Vasco Lopes
Antonio M. Lopez
Roberto Javier
    Lopez-Sastre
Tobias Lorenz
Javier Lorenzo-Navarro
Yujing Lou
Qian Lou
Xiankai Lu
Changsheng Lu
Huimin Lu
Yongxi Lu
Hao Lu
Hong Lu
Jiasen Lu

Juwei Lu
Fan Lu
Guangming Lu
Jiwen Lu
Shun Lu
Tao Lu
Xiaonan Lu
Yang Lu
Yao Lu
Yongchun Lu
Zhiwu Lu
Cheng Lu
Liying Lu
Guo Lu
Xuequan Lu
Yanye Lu
Yantao Lu
Yuhang Lu
Fujun Luan
Jonathon Luiten
Jovita Lukasik
Alan Lukezic
Jonathan Samuel Lumentut
Mayank Lunayach
Ao Luo
Canjie Luo
Chong Luo
Xu Luo
Grace Luo
Jun Luo
Katie Z. Luo
Tao Luo
Cheng Luo
Fangzhou Luo
Gen Luo
Lei Luo
Sihui Luo
Weixin Luo
Yan Luo
Xiaoyan Luo
Yong Luo
Yadan Luo
Hao Luo
Ruotian Luo
Mi Luo

Tiange Luo
Wenjie Luo
Wenhan Luo
Xiao Luo
Zhiming Luo
Zhipeng Luo
Zhengyi Luo
Diogo C. Luvizon
Zhaoyang Lv
Gengyu Lyu
Lingjuan Lyu
Jun Lyu
Yuanyuan Lyu
Youwei Lyu
Yueming Lyu
Bingpeng Ma
Chao Ma
Chongyang Ma
Congbo Ma
Chih-Yao Ma
Fan Ma
Lin Ma
Haoyu Ma
Hengbo Ma
Jianqi Ma
Jiawei Ma
Jiayi Ma
Kede Ma
Kai Ma
Lingni Ma
Lei Ma
Xu Ma
Ning Ma
Benteng Ma
Cheng Ma
Andy J. Ma
Long Ma
Zhanyu Ma
Zhiheng Ma
Qianli Ma
Shiqiang Ma
Sizhuo Ma
Shiqing Ma
Xiaolong Ma
Xinzhu Ma

Gautam B. Machiraju
Spandan Madan
Mathew Magimai-Doss
Luca Magri
Behrooz Mahasseni
Upal Mahbub
Siddharth Mahendran
Paridhi Maheshwari
Rishabh Maheshwary
Mohammed Mahmoud
Shishira R. R. Maiya
Sylwia Majchrowska
Arjun Majumdar
Puspita Majumdar
Orchid Majumder
Sagnik Majumder
Ilya Makarov
Farkhod F.
   Makhmudkhujaev
Yasushi Makihara
Ankur Mali
Mateusz Malinowski
Utkarsh Mall
Srikanth Malla
Clement Mallet
Dimitrios Mallis
Yunze Man
Dipu Manandhar
Massimiliano Mancini
Murari Mandal
Raunak Manekar
Karttikeya Mangalam
Puneet Mangla
Fabian Manhardt
Sivabalan Manivasagam
Fahim Mannan
Chengzhi Mao
Hanzi Mao
Jiayuan Mao
Junhua Mao
Zhiyuan Mao
Jiageng Mao
Yunyao Mao
Zhendong Mao
Alberto Marchisio

Diego Marcos
Riccardo Marin
Aram Markosyan
Renaud Marlet
Ricardo Marques
Miquel Martí i Rabadán
Diego Martin Arroyo
Niki Martinel
Brais Martinez
Julieta Martinez
Marc Masana
Tomohiro Mashita
Timothée Masquelier
Minesh Mathew
Tetsu Matsukawa
Marwan Mattar
Bruce A. Maxwell
Christoph Mayer
Mantas Mazeika
Pratik Mazumder
Scott McCloskey
Steven McDonagh
Ishit Mehta
Jie Mei
Kangfu Mei
Jieru Mei
Xiaoguang Mei
Givi Meishvili
Luke Melas-Kyriazi
Iaroslav Melekhov
Andres Mendez-Vazquez
Heydi Mendez-Vazquez
Matias Mendieta
Ricardo A. Mendoza-León
Chenlin Meng
Depu Meng
Rang Meng
Zibo Meng
Qingjie Meng
Qier Meng
Yanda Meng
Zihang Meng
Thomas Mensink
Fabian Mentzer
Christopher Metzler

Gregory P. Meyer
Vasileios Mezaris
Liang Mi
Lu Mi
Bo Miao
Changtao Miao
Zichen Miao
Qiguang Miao
Xin Miao
Zhongqi Miao
Frank Michel
Simone Milani
Ben Mildenhall
Roy V. Miles
Juhong Min
Kyle Min
Hyun-Seok Min
Weiqing Min
Yuecong Min
Zhixiang Min
Qi Ming
David Minnen
Aymen Mir
Deepak Mishra
Anand Mishra
Shlok K. Mishra
Niluthpol Mithun
Gaurav Mittal
Trisha Mittal
Daisuke Miyazaki
Kaichun Mo
Hong Mo
Zhipeng Mo
Davide Modolo
Abduallah A. Mohamed
Mohamed Afham
   Mohamed Aflal
Ron Mokady
Pavlo Molchanov
Davide Moltisanti
Liliane Momeni
Gianluca Monaci
Pascal Monasse
Ajoy Mondal
Tom Monnier

Aron Monszpart
Gyeongsik Moon
Suhong Moon
Taesup Moon
Sean Moran
Daniel Moreira
Pietro Morerio
Alexandre Morgand
Lia Morra
Ali Mosleh
Inbar Mosseri
Sayed Mohammad
    Mostafavi Isfahani
Saman Motamed
Ramy A. Mounir
Fangzhou Mu
Jiteng Mu
Norman Mu
Yasuhiro Mukaigawa
Ryan Mukherjee
Tanmoy Mukherjee
Yusuke Mukuta
Ravi Teja Mullapudi
Lea Müller
Matthias Müller
Martin Mundt
Nils Murrugarra-Llerena
Damien Muselet
Armin Mustafa
Muhammad Ferjad Naeem
Sauradip Nag
Hajime Nagahara
Pravin Nagar
Rajendra Nagar
Naveen Shankar Nagaraja
Varun Nagaraja
Tushar Nagarajan
Seungjun Nah
Gaku Nakano
Yuta Nakashima
Giljoo Nam
Seonghyeon Nam
Liangliang Nan
Yuesong Nan
Yeshwanth Napolean

Dinesh Reddy
    Narapureddy
Medhini Narasimhan
Supreeth
    Narasimhaswamy
Sriram Narayanan
Erickson R. Nascimento
Varun Nasery
K. L. Navaneet
Pablo Navarrete Michelini
Shant Navasardyan
Shah Nawaz
Nihal Nayak
Farhood Negin
Lukáš Neumann
Alejandro Newell
Evonne Ng
Kam Woh Ng
Tony Ng
Anh Nguyen
Tuan Anh Nguyen
Cuong Cao Nguyen
Ngoc Cuong Nguyen
Thanh Nguyen
Khoi Nguyen
Phi Le Nguyen
Phong Ha Nguyen
Tam Nguyen
Truong Nguyen
Anh Tuan Nguyen
Rang Nguyen
Thao Thi Phuong Nguyen
Van Nguyen Nguyen
Zhen-Liang Ni
Yao Ni
Shijie Nie
Xuecheng Nie
Yongwei Nie
Weizhi Nie
Ying Nie
Yinyu Nie
Kshitij N. Nikhal
Simon Niklaus
Xuefei Ning
Jifeng Ning

Yotam Nitzan
Di Niu
Shuaicheng Niu
Li Niu
Wei Niu
Yulei Niu
Zhenxing Niu
Albert No
Shohei Nobuhara
Nicoletta Noceti
Junhyug Noh
Sotiris Nousias
Slawomir Nowaczyk
Ewa M. Nowara
Valsamis Ntouskos
Gilberto Ochoa-Ruiz
Ferda Ofli
Jihyong Oh
Sangyun Oh
Youngtaek Oh
Hiroki Ohashi
Takahiro Okabe
Kemal Oksuz
Fumio Okura
Daniel Olmeda Reino
Matthew Olson
Carl Olsson
Roy Or-El
Alessandro Ortis
Guillermo Ortiz-Jimenez
Magnus Oskarsson
Ahmed A. A. Osman
Martin R. Oswald
Mayu Otani
Naima Otberdout
Cheng Ouyang
Jiahong Ouyang
Wanli Ouyang
Andrew Owens
Poojan B. Oza
Mete Ozay
A. Cengiz Oztireli
Gautam Pai
Tomas Pajdla
Umapada Pal

Simone Palazzo
Luca Palmieri
Bowen Pan
Hao Pan
Lili Pan
Tai-Yu Pan
Liang Pan
Chengwei Pan
Yingwei Pan
Xuran Pan
Jinshan Pan
Xinyu Pan
Liyuan Pan
Xingang Pan
Xingjia Pan
Zhihong Pan
Zizheng Pan
Priyadarshini Panda
Rameswar Panda
Rohit Pandey
Kaiyue Pang
Bo Pang
Guansong Pang
Jiangmiao Pang
Meng Pang
Tianyu Pang
Ziqi Pang
Omiros Pantazis
Andreas Panteli
Maja Pantic
Marina Paolanti
Joao P. Papa
Samuele Papa
Mike Papadakis
Dim P. Papadopoulos
George Papandreou
Constantin Pape
Toufiq Parag
Chethan Parameshwara
Shaifali Parashar
Alejandro Pardo
Rishubh Parihar
Sarah Parisot
JaeYoo Park
Gyeong-Moon Park

Hyojin Park
Hyoungseob Park
Jongchan Park
Jae Sung Park
Kiru Park
Chunghyun Park
Kwanyong Park
Sunghyun Park
Sungrae Park
Seongsik Park
Sanghyun Park
Sungjune Park
Taesung Park
Gaurav Parmar
Paritosh Parmar
Alvaro Parra
Despoina Paschalidou
Or Patashnik
Shivansh Patel
Pushpak Pati
Prashant W. Patil
Vaishakh Patil
Suvam Patra
Jay Patravali
Badri Narayana Patro
Angshuman Paul
Sudipta Paul
Rémi Pautrat
Nick E. Pears
Adithya Pediredla
Wenjie Pei
Shmuel Peleg
Latha Pemula
Bo Peng
Houwen Peng
Yue Peng
Liangzu Peng
Baoyun Peng
Jun Peng
Pai Peng
Sida Peng
Xi Peng
Yuxin Peng
Songyou Peng
Wei Peng

Weiqi Peng
Wen-Hsiao Peng
Pramuditha Perera
Juan C. Perez
Eduardo Pérez Pellitero
Juan-Manuel Perez-Rua
Federico Pernici
Marco Pesavento
Stavros Petridis
Ilya A. Petrov
Vladan Petrovic
Mathis Petrovich
Suzanne Petryk
Hieu Pham
Quang Pham
Khoi Pham
Tung Pham
Huy Phan
Stephen Phillips
Cheng Perng Phoo
David Picard
Marco Piccirilli
Georg Pichler
A. J. Piergiovanni
Vipin Pillai
Silvia L. Pintea
Giovanni Pintore
Robinson Piramuthu
Fiora Pirri
Theodoros Pissas
Fabio Pizzati
Benjamin Planche
Bryan Plummer
Matteo Poggi
Ashwini Pokle
Georgy E. Ponimatkin
Adrian Popescu
Stefan Popov
Nikola Popović
Ronald Poppe
Angelo Porrello
Michael Potter
Charalambos Poullis
Hadi Pouransari
Omid Poursaeed

Shraman Pramanick
Mantini Pranav
Dilip K. Prasad
Meghshyam Prasad
B. H. Pawan Prasad
Shitala Prasad
Prateek Prasanna
Ekta Prashnani
Derek S. Prijatelj
Luke Y. Prince
Véronique Prinet
Victor Adrian Prisacariu
James Pritts
Thomas Probst
Sergey Prokudin
Rita Pucci
Chi-Man Pun
Matthew Purri
Haozhi Qi
Lu Qi
Lei Qi
Xianbiao Qi
Yonggang Qi
Yuankai Qi
Siyuan Qi
Guocheng Qian
Hangwei Qian
Qi Qian
Deheng Qian
Shengsheng Qian
Wen Qian
Rui Qian
Yiming Qian
Shengju Qian
Shengyi Qian
Xuelin Qian
Zhenxing Qian
Nan Qiao
Xiaotian Qiao
Jing Qin
Can Qin
Siyang Qin
Hongwei Qin
Jie Qin
Minghai Qin

Yipeng Qin
Yongqiang Qin
Wenda Qin
Xuebin Qin
Yuzhe Qin
Yao Qin
Zhenyue Qin
Zhiwu Qing
Heqian Qiu
Jiayan Qiu
Jielin Qiu
Yue Qiu
Jiaxiong Qiu
Zhongxi Qiu
Shi Qiu
Zhaofan Qiu
Zhongnan Qu
Yanyun Qu
Kha Gia Quach
Yuhui Quan
Ruijie Quan
Mike Rabbat
Rahul Shekhar Rade
Filip Radenovic
Gorjan Radevski
Bogdan Raducanu
Francesco Ragusa
Shafin Rahman
Md Mahfuzur Rahman
    Siddiquee
Hossein Rahmani
Kiran Raja
Sivaramakrishnan
    Rajaraman
Jathushan Rajasegaran
Adnan Siraj Rakin
Michaël Ramamonjisoa
Chirag A. Raman
Shanmuganathan Raman
Vignesh Ramanathan
Vasili Ramanishka
Vikram V. Ramaswamy
Merey Ramazanova
Jason Rambach
Sai Saketh Rambhatla

Clément Rambour
Ashwin Ramesh Babu
Adín Ramírez Rivera
Arianna Rampini
Haoxi Ran
Aakanksha Rana
Aayush Jung Bahadur
    Rana
Kanchana N. Ranasinghe
Aneesh Rangnekar
Samrudhdhi B. Rangrej
Harsh Rangwani
Viresh Ranjan
Anyi Rao
Yongming Rao
Carolina Raposo
Michalis Raptis
Amir Rasouli
Vivek Rathod
Adepu Ravi Sankar
Avinash Ravichandran
Bharadwaj Ravichandran
Dripta S. Raychaudhuri
Adria Recasens
Simon Reiß
Davis Rempe
Daxuan Ren
Jiawei Ren
Jimmy Ren
Sucheng Ren
Dayong Ren
Zhile Ren
Dongwei Ren
Qibing Ren
Pengfei Ren
Zhenwen Ren
Xuqian Ren
Yixuan Ren
Zhongzheng Ren
Ambareesh Revanur
Hamed Rezazadegan
    Tavakoli
Rafael S. Rezende
Wonjong Rhee
Alexander Richard

Christian Richardt
Stephan R. Richter
Benjamin Riggan
Dominik Rivoir
Mamshad Nayeem Rizve
Joshua D. Robinson
Joseph Robinson
Chris Rockwell
Ranga Rodrigo
Andres C. Rodriguez
Carlos Rodriguez-Pardo
Marcus Rohrbach
Gemma Roig
Yu Rong
David A. Ross
Mohammad Rostami
Edward Rosten
Karsten Roth
Anirban Roy
Debaditya Roy
Shuvendu Roy
Ahana Roy Choudhury
Aruni Roy Chowdhury
Denys Rozumnyi
Shulan Ruan
Wenjie Ruan
Patrick Ruhkamp
Danila Rukhovich
Anian Ruoss
Chris Russell
Dan Ruta
Dawid Damian Rymarczyk
DongHun Ryu
Hyeonggon Ryu
Kwonyoung Ryu
Balasubramanian S.
Alexandre Sablayrolles
Mohammad Sabokrou
Arka Sadhu
Aniruddha Saha
Oindrila Saha
Pritish Sahu
Aneeshan Sain
Nirat Saini
Saurabh Saini

Takeshi Saitoh
Christos Sakaridis
Fumihiko Sakaue
Dimitrios Sakkos
Ken Sakurada
Parikshit V. Sakurikar
Rohit Saluja
Nermin Samet
Leo Sampaio Ferraz
    Ribeiro
Jorge Sanchez
Enrique Sanchez
Shengtian Sang
Anush Sankaran
Soubhik Sanyal
Nikolaos Sarafianos
Vishwanath Saragadam
István Sárándi
Saquib Sarfraz
Mert Bulent Sariyildiz
Anindya Sarkar
Pritam Sarkar
Paul-Edouard Sarlin
Hiroshi Sasaki
Takami Sato
Torsten Sattler
Ravi Kumar Satzoda
Axel Sauer
Stefano Savian
Artem Savkin
Manolis Savva
Gerald Schaefer
Simone Schaub-Meyer
Yoni Schirris
Samuel Schulter
Katja Schwarz
Jesse Scott
Sinisa Segvic
Constantin Marc Seibold
Lorenzo Seidenari
Matan Sela
Fadime Sener
Paul Hongsuck Seo
Kwanggyoon Seo
Hongje Seong

Dario Serez
Francesco Setti
Bryan Seybold
Mohamad Shahbazi
Shima Shahfar
Xinxin Shan
Caifeng Shan
Dandan Shan
Shawn Shan
Wei Shang
Jinghuan Shang
Jiaxiang Shang
Lei Shang
Sukrit Shankar
Ken Shao
Rui Shao
Jie Shao
Mingwen Shao
Aashish Sharma
Gaurav Sharma
Vivek Sharma
Abhishek Sharma
Yoli Shavit
Shashank Shekhar
Sumit Shekhar
Zhijie Shen
Fengyi Shen
Furao Shen
Jialie Shen
Jingjing Shen
Ziyi Shen
Linlin Shen
Guangyu Shen
Biluo Shen
Falong Shen
Jiajun Shen
Qiu Shen
Qiuhong Shen
Shuai Shen
Wang Shen
Yiqing Shen
Yunhang Shen
Siqi Shen
Bin Shen
Tianwei Shen

Xi Shen
Yilin Shen
Yuming Shen
Yucong Shen
Zhiqiang Shen
Lu Sheng
Yichen Sheng
Shivanand Venkanna
    Sheshappanavar
Shelly Sheynin
Baifeng Shi
Ruoxi Shi
Botian Shi
Hailin Shi
Jia Shi
Jing Shi
Shaoshuai Shi
Baoguang Shi
Boxin Shi
Hengcan Shi
Tianyang Shi
Xiaodan Shi
Yongjie Shi
Zhensheng Shi
Yinghuan Shi
Weiqi Shi
Wu Shi
Xuepeng Shi
Xiaoshuang Shi
Yujiao Shi
Zenglin Shi
Zhenmei Shi
Takashi Shibata
Meng-Li Shih
Yichang Shih
Hyunjung Shim
Dongseok Shim
Soshi Shimada
Inkyu Shin
Jinwoo Shin
Seungjoo Shin
Seungjae Shin
Koichi Shinoda
Suprosanna Shit

Palaiahnakote
    Shivakumara
Eli Shlizerman
Gaurav Shrivastava
Xiao Shu
Xiangbo Shu
Xiujun Shu
Yang Shu
Tianmin Shu
Jun Shu
Zhixin Shu
Bing Shuai
Maria Shugrina
Ivan Shugurov
Satya Narayan Shukla
Pranjay Shyam
Jianlou Si
Yawar Siddiqui
Alberto Signoroni
Pedro Silva
Jae-Young Sim
Oriane Siméoni
Martin Simon
Andrea Simonelli
Abhishek Singh
Ashish Singh
Dinesh Singh
Gurkirt Singh
Krishna Kumar Singh
Mannat Singh
Pravendra Singh
Rajat Vikram Singh
Utkarsh Singhal
Dipika Singhania
Vasu Singla
Harsh Sinha
Sudipta Sinha
Josef Sivic
Elena Sizikova
Geri Skenderi
Ivan Skorokhodov
Dmitriy Smirnov
Cameron Y. Smith
James S. Smith
Patrick Snape

Mattia Soldan
Hyeongseok Son
Sanghyun Son
Chuanbiao Song
Chen Song
Chunfeng Song
Dan Song
Dongjin Song
Hwanjun Song
Guoxian Song
Jiaming Song
Jie Song
Liangchen Song
Ran Song
Luchuan Song
Xibin Song
Li Song
Fenglong Song
Guoli Song
Guanglu Song
Zhenbo Song
Lin Song
Xinhang Song
Yang Song
Yibing Song
Rajiv Soundararajan
Hossein Souri
Cristovao Sousa
Riccardo Spezialetti
Leonidas Spinoulas
Michael W. Spratling
Deepak Sridhar
Srinath Sridhar
Gaurang Sriramanan
Vinkle Kumar Srivastav
Themos Stafylakis
Serban Stan
Anastasis Stathopoulos
Markus Steinberger
Jan Steinbrener
Sinisa Stekovic
Alexandros Stergiou
Gleb Sterkin
Rainer Stiefelhagen
Pierre Stock

Ombretta Strafforello
Julian Straub
Yannick Strümpler
Joerg Stueckler
Hang Su
Weijie Su
Jong-Chyi Su
Bing Su
Haisheng Su
Jinming Su
Yiyang Su
Yukun Su
Yuxin Su
Zhuo Su
Zhaoqi Su
Xiu Su
Yu-Chuan Su
Zhixun Su
Arulkumar Subramaniam
Akshayvarun Subramanya
A. Subramanyam
Swathikiran Sudhakaran
Yusuke Sugano
Masanori Suganuma
Yumin Suh
Yang Sui
Baochen Sun
Cheng Sun
Long Sun
Guolei Sun
Haoliang Sun
Haomiao Sun
He Sun
Hanqing Sun
Hao Sun
Lichao Sun
Jiachen Sun
Jiaming Sun
Jian Sun
Jin Sun
Jennifer J. Sun
Tiancheng Sun
Libo Sun
Peize Sun
Qianru Sun

Shanlin Sun
Yu Sun
Zhun Sun
Che Sun
Lin Sun
Tao Sun
Yiyou Sun
Chunyi Sun
Chong Sun
Weiwei Sun
Weixuan Sun
Xiuyu Sun
Yanan Sun
Zeren Sun
Zhaodong Sun
Zhiqing Sun
Minhyuk Sung
Jinli Suo
Simon Suo
Abhijit Suprem
Anshuman Suri
Saksham Suri
Joshua M. Susskind
Roman Suvorov
Gurumurthy Swaminathan
Robin Swanson
Paul Swoboda
Tabish A. Syed
Richard Szeliski
Fariborz Taherkhani
Yu-Wing Tai
Keita Takahashi
Walter Talbott
Gary Tam
Masato Tamura
Feitong Tan
Fuwen Tan
Shuhan Tan
Andong Tan
Bin Tan
Cheng Tan
Jianchao Tan
Lei Tan
Mingxing Tan
Xin Tan

Zichang Tan
Zhentao Tan
Kenichiro Tanaka
Masayuki Tanaka
Yushun Tang
Hao Tang
Jingqun Tang
Jinhui Tang
Kaihua Tang
Luming Tang
Lv Tang
Sheyang Tang
Shitao Tang
Siliang Tang
Shixiang Tang
Yansong Tang
Keke Tang
Chang Tang
Chenwei Tang
Jie Tang
Junshu Tang
Ming Tang
Peng Tang
Xu Tang
Yao Tang
Chen Tang
Fan Tang
Haoran Tang
Shengeng Tang
Yehui Tang
Zhipeng Tang
Ugo Tanielian
Chaofan Tao
Jiale Tao
Junli Tao
Renshuai Tao
An Tao
Guanhong Tao
Zhiqiang Tao
Makarand Tapaswi
Jean-Philippe G. Tarel
Juan J. Tarrio
Enzo Tartaglione
Keisuke Tateno
Zachary Teed

Ajinkya B. Tejankar
Bugra Tekin
Purva Tendulkar
Damien Teney
Minggui Teng
Chris Tensmeyer
Andrew Beng Jin Teoh
Philipp Terhörst
Kartik Thakral
Nupur Thakur
Kevin Thandiackal
Spyridon Thermos
Diego Thomas
William Thong
Yuesong Tian
Guanzhong Tian
Lin Tian
Shiqi Tian
Kai Tian
Meng Tian
Tai-Peng Tian
Zhuotao Tian
Shangxuan Tian
Tian Tian
Yapeng Tian
Yu Tian
Yuxin Tian
Leslie Ching Ow Tiong
Praveen Tirupattur
Garvita Tiwari
George Toderici
Antoine Toisoul
Aysim Toker
Tatiana Tommasi
Zhan Tong
Alessio Tonioni
Alessandro Torcinovich
Fabio Tosi
Matteo Toso
Hugo Touvron
Quan Hung Tran
Son Tran
Hung Tran
Ngoc-Trung Tran
Vinh Tran

Phong Tran
Giovanni Trappolini
Edith Tretschk
Subarna Tripathi
Shubhendu Trivedi
Eduard Trulls
Prune Truong
Thanh-Dat Truong
Tomasz Trzcinski
Sam Tsai
Yi-Hsuan Tsai
Ethan Tseng
Yu-Chee Tseng
Shahar Tsiper
Stavros Tsogkas
Shikui Tu
Zhigang Tu
Zhengzhong Tu
Richard Tucker
Sergey Tulyakov
Cigdem Turan
Daniyar Turmukhambetov
Victor G. Turrisi da Costa
Bartlomiej Twardowski
Christopher D. Twigg
Radim Tylecek
Mostofa Rafid Uddin
Md. Zasim Uddin
Kohei Uehara
Nicolas Ugrinovic
Youngjung Uh
Norimichi Ukita
Anwaar Ulhaq
Devesh Upadhyay
Paul Upchurch
Yoshitaka Ushiku
Yuzuko Utsumi
Mikaela Angelina Uy
Mohit Vaishnav
Pratik Vaishnavi
Jeya Maria Jose Valanarasu
Matias A. Valdenegro Toro
Diego Valsesia
Wouter Van Gansbeke
Nanne van Noord

Simon Vandenhende
Farshid Varno
Cristina Vasconcelos
Francisco Vasconcelos
Alex Vasilescu
Subeesh Vasu
Arun Balajee Vasudevan
Kanav Vats
Vaibhav S. Vavilala
Sagar Vaze
Javier Vazquez-Corral
Andrea Vedaldi
Olga Veksler
Andreas Velten
Sai H. Vemprala
Raviteja Vemulapalli
Shashanka
    Venkataramanan
Dor Verbin
Luisa Verdoliva
Manisha Verma
Yashaswi Verma
Constantin Vertan
Eli Verwimp
Deepak Vijaykeerthy
Pablo Villanueva
Ruben Villegas
Markus Vincze
Vibhav Vineet
Minh P. Vo
Huy V. Vo
Duc Minh Vo
Tomas Vojir
Igor Vozniak
Nicholas Vretos
Vibashan VS
Tuan-Anh Vu
Thang Vu
Mårten Wadenbäck
Neal Wadhwa
Aaron T. Walsman
Steven Walton
Jin Wan
Alvin Wan
Jia Wan

Jun Wan
Xiaoyue Wan
Fang Wan
Guowei Wan
Renjie Wan
Zhiqiang Wan
Ziyu Wan
Bastian Wandt
Dongdong Wang
Limin Wang
Haiyang Wang
Xiaobing Wang
Angtian Wang
Angelina Wang
Bing Wang
Bo Wang
Boyu Wang
Binghui Wang
Chen Wang
Chien-Yi Wang
Congli Wang
Qi Wang
Chengrui Wang
Rui Wang
Yiqun Wang
Cong Wang
Wenjing Wang
Dongkai Wang
Di Wang
Xiaogang Wang
Kai Wang
Zhizhong Wang
Fangjinhua Wang
Feng Wang
Hang Wang
Gaoang Wang
Guoqing Wang
Guangcong Wang
Guangzhi Wang
Hanqing Wang
Hao Wang
Haohan Wang
Haoran Wang
Hong Wang
Haotao Wang

Hu Wang
Huan Wang
Hua Wang
Hui-Po Wang
Hengli Wang
Hanyu Wang
Hongxing Wang
Jingwen Wang
Jialiang Wang
Jian Wang
Jianyi Wang
Jiashun Wang
Jiahao Wang
Tsun-Hsuan Wang
Xiaoqian Wang
Jinqiao Wang
Jun Wang
Jianzong Wang
Kaihong Wang
Ke Wang
Lei Wang
Lingjing Wang
Linnan Wang
Lin Wang
Liansheng Wang
Mengjiao Wang
Manning Wang
Nannan Wang
Peihao Wang
Jiayun Wang
Pu Wang
Qiang Wang
Qiufeng Wang
Qilong Wang
Qiangchang Wang
Qin Wang
Qing Wang
Ruocheng Wang
Ruibin Wang
Ruisheng Wang
Ruizhe Wang
Runqi Wang
Runzhong Wang
Wenxuan Wang
Sen Wang

Shangfei Wang
Shaofei Wang
Shijie Wang
Shiqi Wang
Zhibo Wang
Song Wang
Xinjiang Wang
Tai Wang
Tao Wang
Teng Wang
Xiang Wang
Tianren Wang
Tiantian Wang
Tianyi Wang
Fengjiao Wang
Wei Wang
Miaohui Wang
Suchen Wang
Siyue Wang
Yaoming Wang
Xiao Wang
Ze Wang
Biao Wang
Chaofei Wang
Dong Wang
Gu Wang
Guangrun Wang
Guangming Wang
Guo-Hua Wang
Haoqing Wang
Hesheng Wang
Huafeng Wang
Jinghua Wang
Jingdong Wang
Jingjing Wang
Jingya Wang
Jingkang Wang
Jiakai Wang
Junke Wang
Kuo Wang
Lichen Wang
Lizhi Wang
Longguang Wang
Mang Wang
Mei Wang

Min Wang
Peng-Shuai Wang
Run Wang
Shaoru Wang
Shuhui Wang
Tan Wang
Tiancai Wang
Tianqi Wang
Wenhai Wang
Wenzhe Wang
Xiaobo Wang
Xiudong Wang
Xu Wang
Yajie Wang
Yan Wang
Yuan-Gen Wang
Yingqian Wang
Yizhi Wang
Yulin Wang
Yu Wang
Yujie Wang
Yunhe Wang
Yuxi Wang
Yaowei Wang
Yiwei Wang
Zezheng Wang
Hongzhi Wang
Zhiqiang Wang
Ziteng Wang
Ziwei Wang
Zheng Wang
Zhenyu Wang
Binglu Wang
Zhongdao Wang
Ce Wang
Weining Wang
Weiyao Wang
Wenbin Wang
Wenguan Wang
Guangting Wang
Haolin Wang
Haiyan Wang
Huiyu Wang
Naiyan Wang
Jingbo Wang

Jinpeng Wang
Jiaqi Wang
Liyuan Wang
Lizhen Wang
Ning Wang
Wenqian Wang
Sheng-Yu Wang
Weimin Wang
Xiaohan Wang
Yifan Wang
Yi Wang
Yongtao Wang
Yizhou Wang
Zhuo Wang
Zhe Wang
Xudong Wang
Xiaofang Wang
Xinggang Wang
Xiaosen Wang
Xiaosong Wang
Xiaoyang Wang
Lijun Wang
Xinlong Wang
Xuan Wang
Xue Wang
Yangang Wang
Yaohui Wang
Yu-Chiang Frank Wang
Yida Wang
Yilin Wang
Yi Ru Wang
Yali Wang
Yinglong Wang
Yufu Wang
Yujiang Wang
Yuwang Wang
Yuting Wang
Yang Wang
Yu-Xiong Wang
Yixu Wang
Ziqi Wang
Zhicheng Wang
Zeyu Wang
Zhaowen Wang
Zhenyi Wang

Zhenzhi Wang
Zhijie Wang
Zhiyong Wang
Zhongling Wang
Zhuowei Wang
Zian Wang
Zifu Wang
Zihao Wang
Zirui Wang
Ziyan Wang
Wenxiao Wang
Zhen Wang
Zhepeng Wang
Zi Wang
Zihao W. Wang
Steven L. Waslander
Olivia Watkins
Daniel Watson
Silvan Weder
Dongyoon Wee
Dongming Wei
Tianyi Wei
Jia Wei
Dong Wei
Fangyun Wei
Longhui Wei
Mingqiang Wei
Xinyue Wei
Chen Wei
Donglai Wei
Pengxu Wei
Xing Wei
Xiu-Shen Wei
Wenqi Wei
Guoqiang Wei
Wei Wei
XingKui Wei
Xian Wei
Xingxing Wei
Yake Wei
Yuxiang Wei
Yi Wei
Luca Weihs
Michael Weinmann
Martin Weinmann

Congcong Wen
Chuan Wen
Jie Wen
Sijia Wen
Song Wen
Chao Wen
Xiang Wen
Zeyi Wen
Xin Wen
Yilin Wen
Yijia Weng
Shuchen Weng
Junwu Weng
Wenming Weng
Renliang Weng
Zhenyu Weng
Xinshuo Weng
Nicholas J. Westlake
Gordon Wetzstein
Lena M. Widin Klasén
Rick Wildes
Bryan M. Williams
Williem Williem
Ole Winther
Scott Wisdom
Alex Wong
Chau-Wai Wong
Kwan-Yee K. Wong
Yongkang Wong
Scott Workman
Marcel Worring
Michael Wray
Safwan Wshah
Xiang Wu
Aming Wu
Chongruo Wu
Cho-Ying Wu
Chunpeng Wu
Chenyan Wu
Ziyi Wu
Fuxiang Wu
Gang Wu
Haiping Wu
Huisi Wu
Jane Wu

Jialian Wu
Jing Wu
Jinjian Wu
Jianlong Wu
Xian Wu
Lifang Wu
Lifan Wu
Minye Wu
Qianyi Wu
Rongliang Wu
Rui Wu
Shiqian Wu
Shuzhe Wu
Shangzhe Wu
Tsung-Han Wu
Tz-Ying Wu
Ting-Wei Wu
Jiannan Wu
Zhiliang Wu
Yu Wu
Chenyun Wu
Dayan Wu
Dongxian Wu
Fei Wu
Hefeng Wu
Jianxin Wu
Weibin Wu
Wenxuan Wu
Wenhao Wu
Xiao Wu
Yicheng Wu
Yuanwei Wu
Yu-Huan Wu
Zhenxin Wu
Zhenyu Wu
Wei Wu
Peng Wu
Xiaohe Wu
Xindi Wu
Xinxing Wu
Xinyi Wu
Xingjiao Wu
Xiongwei Wu
Yangzheng Wu
Yanzhao Wu

Yawen Wu
Yong Wu
Yi Wu
Ying Nian Wu
Zhenyao Wu
Zhonghua Wu
Zongze Wu
Zuxuan Wu
Stefanie Wuhrer
Teng Xi
Jianing Xi
Fei Xia
Haifeng Xia
Menghan Xia
Yuanqing Xia
Zhihua Xia
Xiaobo Xia
Weihao Xia
Shihong Xia
Yan Xia
Yong Xia
Zhaoyang Xia
Zhihao Xia
Chuhua Xian
Yongqin Xian
Wangmeng Xiang
Fanbo Xiang
Tiange Xiang
Tao Xiang
Liuyu Xiang
Xiaoyu Xiang
Zhiyu Xiang
Aoran Xiao
Chunxia Xiao
Fanyi Xiao
Jimin Xiao
Jun Xiao
Taihong Xiao
Anqi Xiao
Junfei Xiao
Jing Xiao
Liang Xiao
Yang Xiao
Yuting Xiao
Yijun Xiao

Yao Xiao

Zeyu Xiao

Zhisheng Xiao

Zihao Xiao

Binhui Xie

Christopher Xie

Haozhe Xie

Jin Xie

Guo-Sen Xie

Hongtao Xie

Ming-Kun Xie

Tingting Xie

Chaohao Xie

Weicheng Xie

Xudong Xie

Jiyang Xie

Xiaohua Xie

Yuan Xie

Zhenyu Xie

Ning Xie

Xianghui Xie

Xiufeng Xie

You Xie

Yutong Xie

Fuyong Xing

Yifan Xing

Zhen Xing

Yuanjun Xiong

Jinhui Xiong

Weihua Xiong

Hongkai Xiong

Zhitong Xiong

Yuanhao Xiong

Yunyang Xiong

Yuwen Xiong

Zhiwei Xiong

Yuliang Xiu

An Xu

Chang Xu

Chenliang Xu

Chengming Xu

Chenshu Xu

Xiang Xu

Huijuan Xu

Zhe Xu

Jie Xu

Jingyi Xu

Jiarui Xu

Yinghao Xu

Kele Xu

Ke Xu

Li Xu

Linchuan Xu

Linning Xu

Mengde Xu

Mengmeng Frost Xu

Min Xu

Mingye Xu

Jun Xu

Ning Xu

Peng Xu

Runsheng Xu

Sheng Xu

Wenqiang Xu

Xiaogang Xu

Renzhe Xu

Kaidi Xu

Yi Xu

Chi Xu

Qiuling Xu

Baobei Xu

Feng Xu

Haohang Xu

Haofei Xu

Lan Xu

Mingze Xu

Songcen Xu

Weipeng Xu

Wenjia Xu

Wenju Xu

Xiangyu Xu

Xin Xu

Yinshuang Xu

Yixing Xu

Yuting Xu

Yanyu Xu

Zhenbo Xu

Zhiliang Xu

Zhiyuan Xu

Xiaohao Xu

Yanwu Xu

Yan Xu

Yiran Xu

Yifan Xu

Yufei Xu

Yong Xu

Zichuan Xu

Zenglin Xu

Zexiang Xu

Zhan Xu

Zheng Xu

Zhiwei Xu

Ziyue Xu

Shiyu Xuan

Hanyu Xuan

Fei Xue

Jianru Xue

Mingfu Xue

Qinghan Xue

Tianfan Xue

Chao Xue

Chuhui Xue

Nan Xue

Zhou Xue

Xiangyang Xue

Yuan Xue

Abhay Yadav

Ravindra Yadav

Kota Yamaguchi

Toshihiko Yamasaki

Kohei Yamashita

Chaochao Yan

Feng Yan

Kun Yan

Qingsen Yan

Qixin Yan

Rui Yan

Siming Yan

Xinchen Yan

Yaping Yan

Bin Yan

Qingan Yan

Shen Yan

Shipeng Yan

Xu Yan

Yan Yan
Yichao Yan
Zhaoyi Yan
Zike Yan
Zhiqiang Yan
Hongliang Yan
Zizheng Yan
Jiewen Yang
Anqi Joyce Yang
Shan Yang
Anqi Yang
Antoine Yang
Bo Yang
Baoyao Yang
Chenhongyi Yang
Dingkang Yang
De-Nian Yang
Dong Yang
David Yang
Fan Yang
Fengyu Yang
Fengting Yang
Fei Yang
Gengshan Yang
Heng Yang
Han Yang
Huan Yang
Yibo Yang
Jiancheng Yang
Jihan Yang
Jiawei Yang
Jiayu Yang
Jie Yang
Jinfa Yang
Jingkang Yang
Jinyu Yang
Cheng-Fu Yang
Ji Yang
Jianyu Yang
Kailun Yang
Tian Yang
Luyu Yang
Liang Yang
Li Yang
Michael Ying Yang

Yang Yang
Muli Yang
Le Yang
Qiushi Yang
Ren Yang
Ruihan Yang
Shuang Yang
Siyuan Yang
Su Yang
Shiqi Yang
Taojiannan Yang
Tianyu Yang
Lei Yang
Wanzhao Yang
Shuai Yang
William Yang
Wei Yang
Xiaofeng Yang
Xiaoshan Yang
Xin Yang
Xuan Yang
Xu Yang
Xingyi Yang
Xitong Yang
Jing Yang
Yanchao Yang
Wenming Yang
Yujiu Yang
Herb Yang
Jianfei Yang
Jinhui Yang
Chuanguang Yang
Guanglei Yang
Haitao Yang
Kewei Yang
Linlin Yang
Lijin Yang
Longrong Yang
Meng Yang
MingKun Yang
Sibei Yang
Shicai Yang
Tong Yang
Wen Yang
Xi Yang

Xiaolong Yang
Xue Yang
Yubin Yang
Ze Yang
Ziyi Yang
Yi Yang
Linjie Yang
Yuzhe Yang
Yiding Yang
Zhenpei Yang
Zhaohui Yang
Zhengyuan Yang
Zhibo Yang
Zongxin Yang
Hantao Yao
Mingde Yao
Rui Yao
Taiping Yao
Ting Yao
Cong Yao
Qingsong Yao
Quanming Yao
Xu Yao
Yuan Yao
Yao Yao
Yazhou Yao
Jiawen Yao
Shunyu Yao
Pew-Thian Yap
Sudhir Yarram
Rajeev Yasarla
Peng Ye
Botao Ye
Mao Ye
Fei Ye
Hanrong Ye
Jingwen Ye
Jinwei Ye
Jiarong Ye
Mang Ye
Meng Ye
Qi Ye
Qian Ye
Qixiang Ye
Junjie Ye

Sheng Ye
Nanyang Ye
Yufei Ye
Xiaoqing Ye
Ruolin Ye
Yousef Yeganeh
Chun-Hsiao Yeh
Raymond A. Yeh
Yu-Ying Yeh
Kai Yi
Chang Yi
Renjiao Yi
Xinping Yi
Peng Yi
Alper Yilmaz
Junho Yim
Hui Yin
Bangjie Yin
Jia-Li Yin
Miao Yin
Wenzhe Yin
Xuwang Yin
Ming Yin
Yu Yin
Aoxiong Yin
Kangxue Yin
Tianwei Yin
Wei Yin
Xianghua Ying
Rio Yokota
Tatsuya Yokota
Naoto Yokoya
Ryo Yonetani
Ki Yoon Yoo
Jinsu Yoo
Sunjae Yoon
Jae Shin Yoon
Jihun Yoon
Sung-Hoon Yoon
Ryota Yoshihashi
Yusuke Yoshiyasu
Chenyu You
Haoran You
Haoxuan You
Yang You

Quanzeng You
Tackgeun You
Kaichao You
Shan You
Xinge You
Yurong You
Baosheng Yu
Bei Yu
Haichao Yu
Hao Yu
Chaohui Yu
Fisher Yu
Jin-Gang Yu
Jiyang Yu
Jason J. Yu
Jiashuo Yu
Hong-Xing Yu
Lei Yu
Mulin Yu
Ning Yu
Peilin Yu
Qi Yu
Qian Yu
Rui Yu
Shuzhi Yu
Gang Yu
Tan Yu
Weijiang Yu
Xin Yu
Bingyao Yu
Ye Yu
Hanchao Yu
Yingchen Yu
Tao Yu
Xiaotian Yu
Qing Yu
Houjian Yu
Changqian Yu
Jing Yu
Jun Yu
Shujian Yu
Xiang Yu
Zhaofei Yu
Zhenbo Yu
Yinfeng Yu

Zhuoran Yu
Zitong Yu
Bo Yuan
Jiangbo Yuan
Liangzhe Yuan
Weihao Yuan
Jianbo Yuan
Xiaoyun Yuan
Ye Yuan
Li Yuan
Geng Yuan
Jialin Yuan
Maoxun Yuan
Peng Yuan
Xin Yuan
Yuan Yuan
Yuhui Yuan
Yixuan Yuan
Zheng Yuan
Mehmet Kerim Yücel
Kaiyu Yue
Haixiao Yue
Heeseung Yun
Sangdoo Yun
Tian Yun
Mahmut Yurt
Ekim Yurtsever
Ahmet Yüzügüler
Edouard Yvinec
Eloi Zablocki
Christopher Zach
Muhammad Zaigham
   Zaheer
Pierluigi Zama Ramirez
Yuhang Zang
Pietro Zanuttigh
Alexey Zaytsev
Bernhard Zeisl
Haitian Zeng
Pengpeng Zeng
Jiabei Zeng
Runhao Zeng
Wei Zeng
Yawen Zeng
Yi Zeng

Yiming Zeng

Tieyong Zeng

Huanqiang Zeng

Dan Zeng

Yu Zeng

Wei Zhai

Yuanhao Zhai

Fangneng Zhan

Kun Zhan

Xiong Zhang

Jingdong Zhang

Jiangning Zhang

Zhilu Zhang

Gengwei Zhang

Dongsu Zhang

Hui Zhang

Binjie Zhang

Bo Zhang

Tianhao Zhang

Cecilia Zhang

Jing Zhang

Chaoning Zhang

Chenxu Zhang

Chi Zhang

Chris Zhang

Yabin Zhang

Zhao Zhang

Rufeng Zhang

Chaoyi Zhang

Zheng Zhang

Da Zhang

Yi Zhang

Edward Zhang

Xin Zhang

Feifei Zhang

Feilong Zhang

Yuqi Zhang

GuiXuan Zhang

Hanlin Zhang

Hanwang Zhang

Hanzhen Zhang

Haotian Zhang

He Zhang

Haokui Zhang

Hongyuan Zhang

Hengrui Zhang

Hongming Zhang

Mingfang Zhang

Jianpeng Zhang

Jiaming Zhang

Jichao Zhang

Jie Zhang

Jingfeng Zhang

Jingyi Zhang

Jinnian Zhang

David Junhao Zhang

Junjie Zhang

Junzhe Zhang

Jiawan Zhang

Jingyang Zhang

Kai Zhang

Lei Zhang

Lihua Zhang

Lu Zhang

Miao Zhang

Minjia Zhang

Mingjin Zhang

Qi Zhang

Qian Zhang

Qilong Zhang

Qiming Zhang

Qiang Zhang

Richard Zhang

Ruimao Zhang

Ruisi Zhang

Ruixin Zhang

Runze Zhang

Qilin Zhang

Shan Zhang

Shanshan Zhang

Xi Sheryl Zhang

Song-Hai Zhang

Chongyang Zhang

Kaihao Zhang

Songyang Zhang

Shu Zhang

Siwei Zhang

Shujian Zhang

Tianyun Zhang

Tong Zhang

Tao Zhang

Wenwei Zhang

Wenqiang Zhang

Wen Zhang

Xiaolin Zhang

Xingchen Zhang

Xingxuan Zhang

Xiuming Zhang

Xiaoshuai Zhang

Xuanmeng Zhang

Xuanyang Zhang

Xucong Zhang

Xingxing Zhang

Xikun Zhang

Xiaohan Zhang

Yahui Zhang

Yunhua Zhang

Yan Zhang

Yanghao Zhang

Yifei Zhang

Yifan Zhang

Yi-Fan Zhang

Yihao Zhang

Yingliang Zhang

Youshan Zhang

Yulun Zhang

Yushu Zhang

Yixiao Zhang

Yide Zhang

Zhongwen Zhang

Bowen Zhang

Chen-Lin Zhang

Zehua Zhang

Zekun Zhang

Zeyu Zhang

Xiaowei Zhang

Yifeng Zhang

Cheng Zhang

Hongguang Zhang

Yuexi Zhang

Fa Zhang

Guofeng Zhang

Hao Zhang

Haofeng Zhang

Hongwen Zhang

Hua Zhang
Jiaxin Zhang
Zhenyu Zhang
Jian Zhang
Jianfeng Zhang
Jiao Zhang
Jiakai Zhang
Lefei Zhang
Le Zhang
Mi Zhang
Min Zhang
Ning Zhang
Pan Zhang
Pu Zhang
Qing Zhang
Renrui Zhang
Shifeng Zhang
Shuo Zhang
Shaoxiong Zhang
Weizhong Zhang
Xi Zhang
Xiaomei Zhang
Xinyu Zhang
Yin Zhang
Zicheng Zhang
Zihao Zhang
Ziqi Zhang
Zhaoxiang Zhang
Zhen Zhang
Zhipeng Zhang
Zhixing Zhang
Zhizheng Zhang
Jiawei Zhang
Zhong Zhang
Pingping Zhang
Yixin Zhang
Kui Zhang
Lingzhi Zhang
Huaiwen Zhang
Quanshi Zhang
Zhoutong Zhang
Yuhang Zhang
Yuting Zhang
Zhang Zhang
Ziming Zhang

Zhizhong Zhang
Qilong Zhangli
Bingyin Zhao
Bin Zhao
Chenglong Zhao
Lei Zhao
Feng Zhao
Gangming Zhao
Haiyan Zhao
Hao Zhao
Handong Zhao
Hengshuang Zhao
Yinan Zhao
Jiaojiao Zhao
Jiaqi Zhao
Jing Zhao
Kaili Zhao
Haojie Zhao
Yucheng Zhao
Longjiao Zhao
Long Zhao
Qingsong Zhao
Qingyu Zhao
Rui Zhao
Rui-Wei Zhao
Sicheng Zhao
Shuang Zhao
Siyan Zhao
Zelin Zhao
Shiyu Zhao
Wang Zhao
Tiesong Zhao
Qian Zhao
Wangbo Zhao
Xi-Le Zhao
Xu Zhao
Yajie Zhao
Yang Zhao
Ying Zhao
Yin Zhao
Yizhou Zhao
Yunhan Zhao
Yuyang Zhao
Yue Zhao
Yuzhi Zhao

Bowen Zhao
Pu Zhao
Bingchen Zhao
Borui Zhao
Fuqiang Zhao
Hanbin Zhao
Jian Zhao
Mingyang Zhao
Na Zhao
Rongchang Zhao
Ruiqi Zhao
Shuai Zhao
Wenda Zhao
Wenliang Zhao
Xiangyun Zhao
Yifan Zhao
Yaping Zhao
Zhou Zhao
He Zhao
Jie Zhao
Xibin Zhao
Xiaoqi Zhao
Zhengyu Zhao
Jin Zhe
Chuanxia Zheng
Huan Zheng
Hao Zheng
Jia Zheng
Jian-Qing Zheng
Shuai Zheng
Meng Zheng
Mingkai Zheng
Qian Zheng
Qi Zheng
Wu Zheng
Yinqiang Zheng
Yufeng Zheng
Yutong Zheng
Yalin Zheng
Yu Zheng
Feng Zheng
Zhaoheng Zheng
Haitian Zheng
Kang Zheng
Bolun Zheng

Haiyong Zheng
Mingwu Zheng
Sipeng Zheng
Tu Zheng
Wenzhao Zheng
Xiawu Zheng
Yinglin Zheng
Zhuo Zheng
Zilong Zheng
Kecheng Zheng
Zerong Zheng
Shuaifeng Zhi
Tiancheng Zhi
Jia-Xing Zhong
Yiwu Zhong
Fangwei Zhong
Zhihang Zhong
Yaoyao Zhong
Yiran Zhong
Zhun Zhong
Zichun Zhong
Bo Zhou
Boyao Zhou
Brady Zhou
Mo Zhou
Chunluan Zhou
Dingfu Zhou
Fan Zhou
Jingkai Zhou
Honglu Zhou
Jiaming Zhou
Jiahuan Zhou
Jun Zhou
Kaiyang Zhou
Keyang Zhou
Kuangqi Zhou
Lei Zhou
Lihua Zhou
Man Zhou
Mingyi Zhou
Mingyuan Zhou
Ning Zhou
Peng Zhou
Penghao Zhou
Qianyi Zhou

Shuigeng Zhou
Shangchen Zhou
Huayi Zhou
Zhize Zhou
Sanping Zhou
Qin Zhou
Tao Zhou
Wenbo Zhou
Xiangdong Zhou
Xiao-Yun Zhou
Xiao Zhou
Yang Zhou
Yipin Zhou
Zhenyu Zhou
Hao Zhou
Chu Zhou
Daquan Zhou
Da-Wei Zhou
Hang Zhou
Kang Zhou
Qianyu Zhou
Sheng Zhou
Wenhui Zhou
Xingyi Zhou
Yan-Jie Zhou
Yiyi Zhou
Yu Zhou
Yuan Zhou
Yuqian Zhou
Yuxuan Zhou
Zixiang Zhou
Wengang Zhou
Shuchang Zhou
Tianfei Zhou
Yichao Zhou
Alex Zhu
Chenchen Zhu
Deyao Zhu
Xiatian Zhu
Guibo Zhu
Haidong Zhu
Hao Zhu
Hongzi Zhu
Rui Zhu
Jing Zhu

Jianke Zhu
Junchen Zhu
Lei Zhu
Lingyu Zhu
Luyang Zhu
Menglong Zhu
Peihao Zhu
Hui Zhu
Xiaofeng Zhu
Tyler (Lixuan) Zhu
Wentao Zhu
Xiangyu Zhu
Xinqi Zhu
Xinxin Zhu
Xinliang Zhu
Yangguang Zhu
Yichen Zhu
Yixin Zhu
Yanjun Zhu
Yousong Zhu
Yuhao Zhu
Ye Zhu
Feng Zhu
Zhen Zhu
Fangrui Zhu
Jinjing Zhu
Linchao Zhu
Pengfei Zhu
Sijie Zhu
Xiaobin Zhu
Xiaoguang Zhu
Zezhou Zhu
Zhenyao Zhu
Kai Zhu
Pengkai Zhu
Bingbing Zhuang
Chengyuan Zhuang
Liansheng Zhuang
Peiye Zhuang
Yixin Zhuang
Yihong Zhuang
Junbao Zhuo
Andrea Ziani
Bartosz Zieliński
Primo Zingaretti

Nikolaos Zioulis
Andrew Zisserman
Yael Ziv
Liu Ziyin
Xingxing Zou
Danping Zou
Qi Zou

Shihao Zou
Xueyan Zou
Yang Zou
Yuliang Zou
Zihang Zou
Chuhang Zou
Dongqing Zou

Xu Zou
Zhiming Zou
Maria A. Zuluaga
Xinxin Zuo
Zhiwen Zuo
Reyer Zwiggelaar

Contents – Part XXI

Active Label Correction Using Robust Parameter Update and Entropy Propagation

Kwang In Kim$^{(\boxtimes)}$ (iD)

UNIST, Ulsan, Korea
`kimki@unist.ac.kr`

Abstract. Label noise is prevalent in real-world visual learning applications and correcting all label mistakes can be prohibitively costly. Training neural network classifiers on such noisy datasets may lead to significant performance degeneration. Active label correction (ALC) attempts to minimize the re-labeling costs by identifying examples for which providing correct labels will yield maximal performance improvements. Existing ALC approaches typically select the examples that the classifier is least confident about (e.g. with the largest entropies). However, such confidence estimates can be unreliable as the classifier itself is initially trained on noisy data. Also, naïvely selecting a batch of low confidence examples can result in redundant labeling of spatially adjacent examples. We present a new ALC algorithm that addresses these challenges. Our algorithm robustly estimates label confidence values by regulating the contributions of individual examples in the parameter update of the network. Further, our algorithm avoids redundant labeling by promoting diversity in batch selection through propagating the confidence of each newly labeled example to the entire dataset. Experiments involving four benchmark datasets and two types of label noise demonstrate that our algorithm offers a significant improvement in re-labeling efficiency over state-of-the-art ALC approaches.

Keywords: Active label correction · Uncertainty sampling · Diffusion

1 Introduction

Deep neural networks can provide state-of-the-art performance on a variety of inference problems. This success often relies on the availability of large amounts of annotated data, but building large-scale annotations is a costly and erroneous process. For example, reliable annotations for medical imaging or astronomical imaging require expensive domain experts, and hence less costly (but less reliable) crowdsourcing might be employed [22,36,44]. Noisy labels can also be

Supplementary Information The online version contains supplementary material available at https://doi.org/10.1007/978-3-031-19803-8_1.

found in automatically annotated data [26], data collected by noisy sensors [18], and label corruptions caused by adversarial attacks [1,42].

As such, *noisy annotations* are invariably used in training. Naïvely training deep neural networks on noisy data can severely limit their generalization capability as they tend to memorize data [41]. One approach to reduce labeling costs (or label correction or proofreading costs) is *active label correction* (ALC). ALC approaches attempt to identify examples for which correct labeling will provide the most significant performance improvement.

A common approach to ALC is to incrementally determine important examples. Initially, a deep network h is trained on the noisy training set D where only a small portion is provided with *clean* labels. By analyzing the predictions $h|_D$ of h on D, an ALC algorithm suggests examples to query. Once an oracle provided correct labels to these examples, h is retrained yielding improved predictions $h|_D$. This process is repeated until the labeling budget is exhausted.

Inspired by the success of active learning (AL), most existing ALC algorithms select examples with the largest entropy (or loss) values of the class-conditional probability distributions of $h|_D$ [2,19,25]. Using entropy is an intuitive and reliable approach to AL as the highest entropy examples are the most ambiguous to classify by h, and hence labeling them could significantly reduce the uncertainties that h has on D. However, its application to ALC is limited in that the estimated entropy values can be unreliable as h itself is trained on the initially noisy dataset: It is possible that a small portion of *clean* examples exhibit relatively high entropy values, even though re-labeling them would not help improve network performance. Also, selecting a large *batch* of high entropy points is redundant: If an example x_* has a high entropy value then its spatial neighbors tend to show similar high entropies (Fig. 1), but labeling them along with x_* would be unnecessary as re-training h on x_* can resolve the uncertainties of its neighbors. On the other hand, employing small batches of high entropy points would require frequent retraining of h, leading to increased computational costs.

Our algorithm addresses these difficulties by robustly estimating the entropy values of $h|_D$. During the update of h-parameters, the loss gradients of individual examples are weighted by the respective contribution parameters. These parameters are continuously adjusted based on the progressions of loss estimates, gradually suppressing the influence of outlier examples. Further, we explicitly diversify batch selection by iteratively regulating the entropy estimates of h: Once a point x_* is labeled, its updated entropy value (of zero) is propagated along D such that the entropies of neighboring points are suppressed. Instantiating these contributions into a learning framework lets our algorithm robustly train deep networks with efficient acquisition of labels.

We conducted experiments on four benchmark datasets with two different types of label noise. The results demonstrate that our robust parameter update strategy and entropy propagation approach contribute individually and collectively to improving ACL performance, outperforming existing approaches by a large margin.

2   Related Work

Active Label Correction. Typically, active label correction algorithms select examples to query by assessing the *confidences* of predictions made by the classifier on given training sets. For example Nallapati et al.'s *CorrActive learning* prioritizes misclassified examples (those exhibiting high training losses) [21] while Rebbapragada et al.'s *Active Label Correction* algorithm queries examples with the highest entropy values [25]. For support vector machine classifiers, predictive confidences can be evaluated based on their margins, leading to margin-based sample strategies [31]. Similarly, Henter et al.proposed to label examples showing the smallest difference between the class probabilities of the best and second-best hypotheses [13] and Bernhardt et al.'s *Active Label Cleaning* algorithm selects examples with the highest predictive losses and predictive entropy [2]. These algorithms demonstrated significant performance gains over random selection, but they do not explicitly model the underlying noise generation processes.

Kremer et al.'s robust ACL algorithm employs explicit noise modeling to measure the expected change of the classifier when examples are newly labeled: Such changes are measured based on the difference between the total losses obtained with and without labeling candidate examples. For logistic regression, with the aid of its noise model, this quantity can be evaluated without having to actually label the candidates. However, its extension to deep neural networks is not straightforward. Similarly to [2,25], Li et al.'s *Dual Active Label Correction* algorithm queries high-entropy examples [19]. Further, this algorithm achieved noise robustness by incorporating a noise model into classifier training: It estimates the probabilities of class transitions caused by noise and uses them to rectify the classifier outputs in the loss evaluation achieving significant improvements over existing ALC algorithms. In the experiments, we show that our method outperforms these existing methods [2,19,21,25].

Inspired by the intuition that examples that lie in label-homogeneous regions are likely to be clean, Urner et al.presented a theoretical sample complexity analysis [34]. Instantiating this theoretical analysis into practical algorithms remains an open problem.

Related Problems. Active learning (AL) with noisy annotators is a closely related problem. Zhang and Chaudhuri presented a theoretical AL framework where weak and strong oracles respectively provide clean and noisy labels [40]. This problem differs from ALC in that the identities of clean labels (provided by strong oracles) are known a priori [40]. Similarly, Yan et al.presented an AL scenario where oracles occasionally provide noisy labels [38]. Younesian et al.considered a learning problem where multiple annotators have varying levels of experience, presenting labels of diverse quality [39]. Their algorithm actively selects not only the examples to query but also the oracles who will annotate the queried examples. Under the presence of multiple noisy annotators (e.g.from crowdsourcing) Parde and Nielsen proposed to assign varying weights to the labels of each example via estimating the reliability of individual annotators [22].

Sheng et al.'s algorithm queries an example for additional labels when existing labels are discrepant [30].

Explicit detection of noisy examples is another closely related domain. Shen and Sanghavi used the loss values to determine noisy examples. Their algorithm alternates between filtering out examples with the highest losses and retraining the classifier on the remaining training set [29]. Zhu et al. proposed to construct *soft labels* based on local feature aggregations and used them to define a score function [43]. This enables to detect noisy examples without having to train a task-specific model. Huang et al.proposed to avoid memorization of noisy data by cyclically transferring the status of the learner from overfitting to underfitting via controlling its learning rate [14]. This strategy achieved improved performance over traditional noise-robust learning approaches. However, it relies on known numbers of noisy examples. We show that our algorithm offers improved labeling efficiency even without requiring the number of noisy examples (Sect. 3.1). Park et al.'s algorithm assesses how labeling individual examples influences the change of the classifier parameters and their evaluations on validation data [23]. Its application to ALC is not straightforward as clean validation sets are seldom available in ALC problems.

3 Robust Active Label Acquisition

Problem Setting and Algorithm Overview. We consider classification problems where one learns a neural network as a function h from the input space $\mathcal{X}$ to the output class-encoding space $\mathcal{Y}$. We employ one-hot class encoding such that $\mathcal{Y}$ forms a probability simplex of dimension M where M is the number of classes, and h generates class-conditional probabilities as outputs. When h does not generate probabilistic outputs, one could apply softmax activations to construct pseudo probabilities.

For a given *clean* training set $\widehat{D} = \{(x_j, y_j)\}_{j=1}^{N}$ sampled from an underlying distribution p of $\mathcal{X} \times \mathcal{Y}$, h can be constructed by minimizing the sum of losses:

$$L(h) = \sum_{j=1}^{N} l(h(x_j), y_j) \tag{1}$$

for a loss function $l : \mathcal{Y} \times \mathcal{Y} \rightarrow \mathbb{R}^+$. We use the cross-entropy loss $l(z, y) = -\sum_{k=1}^{M} z^k \log(y^k)$ where z^k is the k-th component of z, while our method is applicable to other losses as well. In active label correction (ALC) problems, a subset $D^N \subset \widehat{D}$ of data is contaminated with label noise forming a (partially) noisy dataset D, e.g.the labels in $D^N \subset D$ are randomly flipped or altered with underlying class transition probabilities [16,20,35], and the number and identities of such noisy examples are not known. ALC algorithms are then provided with a labeling budget G such that they can select and query the true labels of G examples to an oracle. Typically, these algorithms identify iteratively such examples: Initially, a network h^0 is trained on $D^0 = D$. At iteration t, the outputs

$h^{t-1}|_{D^{t-1}}$ of h^{t-1} trained on D^{t-1} are analyzed to determine a batch $B^t \subset D$ of examples to query. Once $B^t \subset D$ is labeled, D^t is accordingly updated.

In active learning (AL), B^t is often selected as the most *ambiguous* examples, i.ethose with the highest entropy values of the corresponding class-conditional probabilities $h(x)$. However, naïvely applying this strategy to ALC can be suboptimal as it can select already clean examples (in $D^C = D \setminus D^N$): As D^N is not known a priori, h^t trains on the entire dataset D^t, possibly memorizing noisy data $D^N \subset D^t$, and hence it can generate relatively high entropy values even on the examples in D^C.

Similarly to existing AL and ALC approaches, we employ entropy as the main batch selection criterion but we enhance its labeling efficiency by 1) robustifying the training of h^t via suppressing the contributions of label noise in its parameter update (Sect. 3.1). This helps improve the estimation of entropy values as well as classification accuracy. Also, 2) we iteratively regulate the estimated entropy values during batch selection (Sect. 3.2). Each time a single example is labeled, its updated entropy value is instantly propagated to D^t suppressing the entropies of the other points. This helps avoid selecting accumulations of adjacent examples and diversify label selection without having to retrain h per stage.

3.1 Robust Update of Classifier Parameters

In the standard stochastic gradient descent-based learning, the parameter vector W of h is iteratively updated using a mini-batch subset D_i of D, minimizing L:

$$W(i+1) = W(i) - \eta(i) \sum_{(x_k, y_k) \in D_i} \overline{\alpha}_k(i) \nabla_W l(h(x_k), y_k), \qquad (2)$$

where i is the pass index of an iteration, $\eta(i)$ is the learning rate, and the contribution parameters $\{\overline{\alpha}_k\}$ are kept at a constant value of $\frac{1}{N}$. In this case, clean and noisy examples contribute equally to the update of W potentially distracting the training process.

Our algorithm dynamically adjusts $\{\overline{\alpha}_k(i)\}$ according to the learning progress of h. At each epoch, the global weights $\{\alpha_j\}_{j=1}^N$ are determined as convex combination coefficients of the entire dataset D ($\alpha_j \geq 0$, $\sum_{j=1}^N \alpha_j = 1$) and $\{\overline{\alpha}_k(i)\}$ is selected from $\{\alpha_j\}_{j=1}^N$ according to its mini-batch index[1]. In the first epoch, $\boldsymbol{\alpha}(1) = [\alpha_1(1), \dots, \alpha_N(1)]^\top$ is uniformly initialized and W is updated according to Eq. 2. Thereafter, at epoch q, $\boldsymbol{\alpha}(q)$ is updated based on the following rule:

$$\boldsymbol{\alpha}(q+1) = (1 - \delta^\alpha)\boldsymbol{\alpha}(q) + \delta^\alpha \frac{\mathbf{g}(q)}{\|\mathbf{g}(q)\|_1}, \qquad (3)$$

where $\mathbf{g}(q) = [g(l(h^q(x_1), y_1)), \dots, g(l(h^q(x_N), y_N))]^\top$ and

$$g(z) = \exp\left(-\frac{z^2}{\sigma^\alpha}\right) \qquad (4)$$

---

[1] We denote a single update step of W for a given mini-batch (Eq. 2) by 'pass' while an 'epoch' involves multiple mini-batch passes including all the training examples.

for the step hyperparameter $0 \leq \delta^\alpha \leq 1$ and scale hyperparameter $\sigma^\alpha \geq 0$. Once $\boldsymbol{\alpha}(q+1)$ is obtained, it is normalized such that $\|\boldsymbol{\alpha}(q+1)\|_1 = 1$. As $g(l(h(x_j), y_j))$ is inversely proportional to the loss l incurred at (x_j, y_j), the iterative update process of Eq. 2 tends to ignore examples that *consistently* (during the iteration) exhibit large errors. The parameter δ^α controls the speed of α evolution: At large (close to one) δ^α, $\{\alpha_j\}$ evolves rapidly, emphasizing the latest observed loss values while small δ^α places more emphasis on the previous loss trajectory of each example. σ^α determines how aggressively losses are penalized: For small δ^α values, even small losses are heavily penalized and only a small number of examples contribute to the parameter update, while as $\delta^\alpha \rightarrow \infty$, $g \rightarrow 1$ independently of individual loss values, producing an even $\{\alpha_j\}$ distribution.

Discussion. Using the training loss as a noise indicator is a common practice in ACL. For example, Bernhardt et al.'s active cleaning strategy queries points with large loss values [2]. Empirically evaluating this approach in preliminary experiments, we observed that determining the optimal timing to measure losses is challenging: At early training epochs, the classifier h might not have gained sufficient information on the problem to faithfully estimate the target outputs of clean data. On the other hand, at later epochs, h can overfit to D, generating low loss values even on D^N. Our approach bypasses this step by accumulating the contribution parameters over time and *gradually* suppressing the outliers. When our algorithm suggested candidates for labeling, on average (across a varying number of labels) 97.9% of these examples were noisy while using [2] achieved only around 91.1% accuracy: As (re-)labeling already clean examples is redundant, ALC algorithms need to select noisy examples for querying (Table 1).

Our framework (Eq. 3) can be considered as an instance of example re-weighting for robust learning: As the gradient is a linear operator, weighting the loss gradient per example is equivalent to weighting individual examples. However, adapting these approaches to ALC is non-trivial. For example, Ren et al.'s meta-learning approach requires clean validation labels [27]. While this might be reasonable for general robust learning, in ALC, such labels are seldom available.

An alternative to our strategy is to explicitly pre-select clean examples $D^C \subset D$: One could first apply data cleaning algorithms e.g. [14, 23, 43] to identify clean examples and subsequently apply active learning. Once D^C can be successfully estimated, in principle, this choice would lead to improved performance. However, Fig. 4 demonstrates that precisely identifying D^C is challenging even when the number of noisy examples is assumed known as in [14].

3.2   Entropy Propagation for Iterative Label Selection

Querying the most *uncertain* examples (e.g. with the highest entropy values) for labeling has been commonly exercised in AL and ALC. An ideal setting in this case would be *fine-grained* incremental learning: At stage t, the single most uncertain example $x_* \in D^{t-1}$ is queried for labeling and D^t is accordingly updated. Then, a new classifier h^t is trained on D^t yielding the uncertainty estimates for the next stage. However, in deep learning, this strategy is not

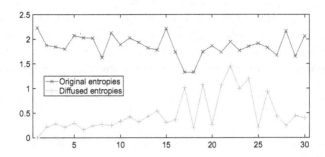

Fig. 1. An example of entropy diffusion on *CIFAR-10* dataset. A point x_* is newly labeled and the corresponding entropy is updated to zero. The entropies of the remaining examples in D are accordingly adjusted. The x-axis shows the indices of data points ordered inversely according to the distance to x_*. The first entry is x_*. When x_* has originally a high entropy value, its spatial neighbors also exhibit high entropy values (the average entropy on D was less than 0.7). Applying diffusion on D suppressed the entropies of points near x_*. Note that the degrees of suppression are proportional to the similarity to x_*.

directly applicable as it requires frequently retraining the classifier, incurring prohibitively high computational costs. Instead, a batch B^t of examples are selected at once as examples with the highest entropies in D^{t-1}.

This naïve batch selection strategy often generates redundant labelings: When h^t assigns a high entropy value $e(x_*)$ to an example x_*, it is likely that other examples in its neighborhood $\mathcal{N}(x_*)$ also have high entropies (Fig. 1) and therefore, included in B^t along with x_* (Fig. 1). However, when h^t is trained with the ground-truth label of x_*, it may acquire sufficient information to resolve uncertainty in $\mathcal{N}(x_*)$. In this case, it would be more efficient to select examples outside $\mathcal{N}(x_*)$. Our approach is to *diversify* batch selection by simulating a diffusion process on the manifold of data points $\mathcal{X}$.

Entropy Diffusion on Data Manifolds. On a Riemannian manifold $\mathcal{X}$ equipped with a data-generating distribution $p(x)$, a diffusion of a smooth function $g \in C^\infty(\mathcal{X})$ is described as a time evolution equation:

$$\frac{\partial g}{\partial t} = \Delta_p g, \tag{5}$$

where Δ_p is the (p-normalized) Laplacian on $\mathcal{X}$. This process gradually *propagates* the *mass* $g(x)$ at location x to the entire manifold weighted by p [28] and it has been used in denoising smooth functions and data points [12], semi-supervised learning [3], and simulating information spread on social networks [24]. We consider the entropy values e as a smooth function to be diffused along $\mathcal{X}$. Suppose that at stage t, h^t is trained and the corresponding entropy estimation on $\mathcal{X}$ is made. Then, the example x_* with the maximum entropy is queried for labeling, and the corresponding entropy value $e(x_*)$ is set to zero. This *new information* is spread over $\mathcal{X}$ suppressing the entropies of the related points.

Entropy Propagation Algorithm. In practice, the manifold $\mathcal{X}$ is not directly observed and instead a point cloud $X = \{x_j\}_{j=1}^N$ sampled from p is presented as an embedding of $\mathcal{X}$ onto a Euclidean space (i.e. $X \subset \mathbb{R}^d$ with d being the data dimensionality). In this case, the analytic diffusion process can be spatially discretized as

$$\frac{\partial \mathbf{e}}{\partial t} = -L\mathbf{e}, \tag{6}$$

where $\mathbf{e} = [e(x_1), \ldots, e(x_N)]^\top$, L is the probability-normalized graph Laplacian constructed based on X:

$$L = I - D^{-1}A, \tag{7}$$

$$A^{jk} = \begin{cases} \exp\left(-\frac{\|x_j - x_k\|^2}{\sigma^L}\right), & \text{if } x_j = \mathcal{N}(x_k) \text{ or } x_k = \mathcal{N}(x_j) \\ 0, & \text{otherwise,} \end{cases}$$

$$D^{jk} = \begin{cases} \sum_m^N A^{jm}, & \text{if } j = k \\ 0, & \text{otherwise,} \end{cases}$$

$\mathcal{N}(x)$ is the nearest neighbors of x, and $\sigma^L > 0$ is a scaling hyperparameter. When the sample size N grows to infinity, X becomes a precise representation of $\mathcal{M}$ and in this case, $-L$ converges to the true Laplacian Δ_p [11].

Our entropy propagation algorithm is obtained by time-discretizing the continuous evolution of Eq. 6 using the explicit Euler scheme [4]:

$$\mathbf{e}(i+1) = \mathbf{e}(i) - \delta^L L \mathbf{e}(i) \tag{8}$$

with a time-discretization step size $\delta^L > 0$. This helps simulate fine-grained incremental learning without the need to actually retrain h for each newly added label. Figure 1 shows that high entropy values are indeed spatially correlated, and our diffusion process can effectively suppress the entropies of nearby points.

Discussion. The diffusion process in Eq. 6 jointly updates the entropy values $\mathbf{e}$ of the entire training set D. This offers the capability of not only suppressing the entropies of neighbors $\mathcal{N}(x_*)$ of a newly labeled example x_* but also regularizing potentially noisy entropies (as h trains on noisy data D). The latter can be seen by noting that for a manifold $\mathcal{X}$ with a compactly supported data distribution p, the time-discretization of the diffusion process in Eq. 5 corresponds to a single gradient-descent step for minimizing the following energy:

$$E(g; g^{t-1}) = \|g - g^{t-1}\|^2 + \delta\langle \nabla g, \nabla g \rangle \tag{9}$$

where ∇g is the gradient of g. This is a direct consequence of Stokes' theorem [10]: Our diffusion promotes *first-order smoothness* of the solution $\mathbf{e}$ along $\mathcal{X}$.

3.3 Active Label Correction Algorithm

Our final algorithm is obtained by incorporating the robust classifier training steps (Sect. 3.1) into the incremental label selection process (Sect. 3.2): At iteration t, the classifier parameter W and contribution parameters $\{\alpha_j\}_{j=1}^N$ are

---

Algorithm 1. Robust active label correction algorithm

1: **Input:** Noisy data $D = \{(x_i, y_i)\}_{i=1}^N$, and labeling batch size Q and budget G.
2: **Initialization:** $D^0 = \emptyset$, $B^0 = \emptyset$, $S^0 = \emptyset$, and $t = 1$.
3: **repeat**
4:    $\alpha_j = \frac{1}{N}$ for $j = 1 \ldots, N$.
5:    **if** mod $(t, Q) = 0$ **then**
6:       $S^t = S^{t-1} \cup B^{t-1}$.
7:       **repeat**
8:          Update the classifier h parameter W according to Eq 2.
9:          Update the contribution coefficients $\{\alpha_j\}_{j=1}^N$ using Eq 3.
10:       **until** maximum epoch reached.
11:       Train h with $\{\alpha_j\}_{j=1}^N$.
12:       Evaluate the entropy values **e** using h on D.
13:       $B^t = \emptyset$.
14:    **end if**
15:    Sample the candidate set C from $D \setminus S^t$ using p^S.
16:    Select an example $x_* \in C$ with the largest entropy e.
17:    **repeat**
18:       Assign zero to $e(x_*)$.
19:       Update **e** using Eq. 8.
20:    **until** maximum diffusion steps reached.
21:    $B^t = B^t \cup \{x_*\}$.
22:    $t = t + 1$.
23: **until** labeling budget reached.
24: **Output:** Trained classifier h^t and (partially) cleaned label set S^t.

---

estimated using Eqs. 2 and 3, and the entropy estimates $\{e(x_j)\}_{j=1}^N$ are obtained by evaluating h^t on D^t. Then, a batch B^t of data are constructed by iterating through 1) sampling a set C of candidate examples from the probability distribution p^S on $\{1, \ldots, N\}$ formed by $p_j^S = \frac{1-\alpha_j}{\sum_{k=1}^N 1 - \alpha_k}$: For experiments, we sampled candidates from p^S by ranking p^S); 2) adding the example x_* with the highest entropy value in C to B^t; and 3) iteratively updating the entropy estimates $\{e(x_j)\}_{j=1}^N$ using Eq 8. Algorithm 1 summarizes the training process.

Hyperparameters and Complexity. Our algorithm requires determining several hyperparameters. This is a difficult problem in the ALC setting: Often, the hyperparameters of learning algorithms are tuned based on separate validation sets. However, in ALC, labels are inherently limited and such validation sets might not be available. For our experiments (Sect. 4), we determined these parameters based on heuristics commonly employed in related problem domains and fixed them across the entire datasets. The Laplacian scaling parameter σ^L (Eq. 7) was determined as the squared mean of pairwise data distances in D following [32]. The scale parameter $\sigma^\alpha > 0$ (Eq. 4) was determined similarly. The number of entropy diffusion steps (Eq. 8) was fixed at 10. The size of the neighborhood $\mathcal{N}(x)$ in building L was fixed at 10 as commonly exercised in semi-supervised learning [12]. The explicit Euler discretization (Eq. 8) of the continuous diffusion process (Eq. 6) is numerically stable only for small step sizes $\delta^L > 0$ [15] and we fixed it at 0.1. The update parameter $\delta^\alpha > 0$ is fixed at the same value.

The time complexity of our algorithm is linear in the number N of total examples and the number M of classes: The main computational bottleneck is in the assessment of the loss and entropy values on D, and the diffusion step of the entropies (Eq. 8). As the graph Laplacian L is sparse, the multiplication Le takes linear time $\mathcal{O}(|\mathcal{N}| \times N)$. On *CIFAR-100* dataset, selecting a single label took 0.003 s on average.

4   Experiments

Datasets. We evaluated our method on four benchmark datasets: *CIFAR-10* [17], *CIFAR-100* [17], Fashion MNIST (*F-MNIST*) [37], and *Caltech-256* [7]. These datasets are widely used in active label correction (ALC) and learning with noisy labels [2,5,8,14,19]. For all datasets, initially 80% of the ground-truth labels were corrupted using noise models and the remaining clean labels were augmented by performing ALC with a labeling budget G and a batch size Q of 15,000 and 1,000, respectively: The classifier h was trained at every 1,000-th stages, and during the intermediate stages, ALC algorithms queried 1,000 examples to label. The numbers and identities of the original clean labels were not known to ALC algorithms. We considered two label noise models. The *uniform noise* model replaces the ground-truth labels with labels randomly selected from uniform class distributions [2,25]. In the *class-symmetry flipping* model, a class transition probability matrix $T \in \mathbb{R}^{M \times M}$ is first constructed such that T^{ij} is the probability of transition from class i to class j. For each point with class i, a noise label is sampled from the distribution corresponding to the i-th row of T. The entries of T are randomly sampled from the uniform distribution in $[0, 1]$ and each row was probabilistically normalized.

Baselines. We compared with random sampling of labels (*Random*), Nallapati et al.'s CorrActive learning (*CorrActive*) [21], Rebbapragada et al.'s ACL approach [25] which selects a batch of examples with the highest entropies (*Entropy*; the ALC disagreement criterion in [25]), a method that combines the loss and entropy values, inspired by Bernhardt et al.'s active label cleaning approach [2] (*LossEnt*)[2], and Li et al.'s dual active label correction (*DALC*) [19]. Similarly to *Entropy*, *DALC* selects high-entropy examples, and additionally, it estimates the class transition matrix T (as a noise model) to adjust the estimated outputs of h during training: For *uncertain* examples identified during training, a modified loss l' was applied:

$$l'(h(x), y) = l(T^\top h(x), y). \tag{10}$$

---

[2] This algorithm cannot be directly applied to our setting as it requires multiple annotations for each newly labeled example. Our approach selects the points with the largest sums of the loss and entropy values.

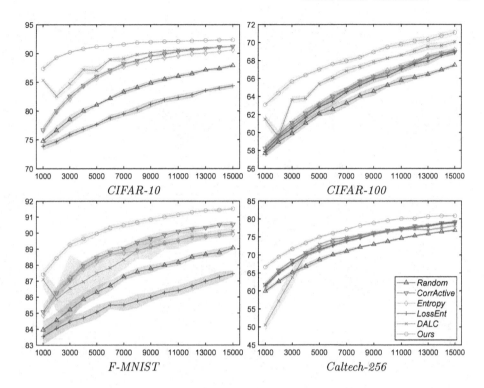

Fig. 2. Mean accuracy (%) with standard deviation (shaded) of different active label correction algorithms under uniform noise. The x-axis corresponds to the number of queried labels. All ALC algorithms outperformed *Random* except for *LossEnt* on *CIFAR-10* and *F-MNIST*. *DALC* demonstrated competitive performance in *CIFAR-10*, *CIFAR-100*, and later learning stages of *Caltech-256*. Our algorithm achieved further significant and consistent improvements.

For all datasets and ALC methods, we conducted experiments 10 times and averaged the results. All experiments were performed on a machine with NVIDIA RTX 3090 GPU, Intel Core i7-11700KF CPU, and 32 GB of RAM. We used the classifier that consists of fixed ResNet-101 [9] pretrained on ImageNet and four fully-connected layers. This configuration constantly outperformed fully trained ResNet-50 and VGG-16 on *CIFAR-10*. We used stochastic gradient descent with an initial learning rate of 0.01, a momentum value of 0.9, and a weight decay factor of 10^{-4}. The learning rate was scaled by 0.1 every 10 epochs.

Results. Figures 2 and 3 summarize the results. All algorithms showed increasing accuracy as more labels were corrected, and they showed similar accuracy progressions for both uniform noise and class-symmetry flipping noise. *Entropy* and *CorrActive* achieved noticeable improvements from *Random* while *LossEnt* was worse than *Random* when the number of classes are limited (*CIFAR-10* and *F-MNIST*). *DALC* demonstrated further significant performance gains by

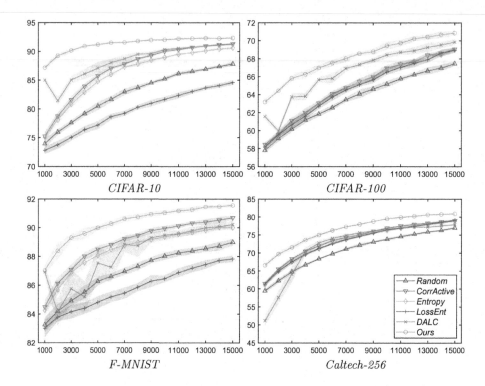

Fig. 3. Mean accuracy (%) with standard deviation (shaded) of different active label correction algorithms under class-symmetry flipping noise.

learning the class transition matrices[3]. Interestingly, it achieved high accuracy even when uniform noise was used: *DALC*'s noise model does not directly match this type of noise. However, simultaneously selecting a batch of examples with the highest entropy values can produce redundant labeling (Fig. 1 shows that high entropy values are indeed spatially correlated). By robustifying classifier training and entropy estimation through the contribution-weighted parameter update (Eq. 2), and promoting diversity in batch selection using entropy diffusion (Eq. 8), our algorithm achieved even more pronounced performance improvements. On *CIFAR-10*, our algorithm reached 90% accuracy at only 3,000 labels, while *DALC* and *CorrActive* required, 9,000 and 11,000 labels, respectively, offering 3- and 3.6-times higher labeling efficiency. Importantly, our algorithm was never significantly worse than other algorithms. Our results on *Caltech-256* (with 256 classes) indicate that it gracefully scales with the number of classes.

---

[3] DACL's accuracy often decreased in the second iteration as it switches from the entire dataset D to the labeled dataset S^t in estimating the class transition matrix T. At early ALC stages, these data points are limited and the corresponding T estimation is unreliable, leading to degraded performances.

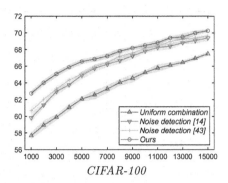

CIFAR-100

Fig. 4. Performance of our robust parameter update approach (Eq. 2), the standard uniform gradient combination, and the explicit noise detection methods of [14,43]. x- and y-axes show the number of acquired labels and the corresponding classification accuracy (%), respectively. Our *soft* gradient combination approach provides considerably higher labeling efficiency than *hard* noise detection and uniform gradient averaging.

Selection Accuracy of Noisy Examples, and Contributions of Robust Parameter Update and Entropy Propagation. As the number and identities of clean examples D^C are not known and (re-)labeling such examples is redundant, ALC algorithms must select examples for querying from $D \setminus D^C$. Table 1 shows that the superior overall performance of our algorithm can be (partially) explained by its ability to select examples from $D \setminus D^C$.

Figures 4 and 5 demonstrate the effectiveness of our robust parameter update and entropy propagation components.

Table 1. Average noisy example selection accuracy (%) of different ALC algorithms defined as the ratio between the number of queried points in $D \setminus D^C$ and the total number of queries; *CIFAR-100*. Our algorithm consistently achieved the highest selection accuracy.

# labels	1,000	3,000	5,000	7,000	9,000	11,000	13,000	15,000
Random	81.20	80.50	81.50	82.00	80.50	80.00	81.00	82.10
Entropy	90.30	91.30	90.00	91.50	92.60	90.70	90.80	91.40
LossEnt	93.70	93.98	93.02	93.41	93.70	93.79	94.27	93.22
CorrActive	87.60	89.70	87.50	87.60	89.20	89.10	89.70	90.20
DALC	89.10	92.10	91.70	91.10	91.10	90.20	88.30	88.80
Ours	97.90	98.00	97.30	97.80	97.80	97.80	98.10	97.60

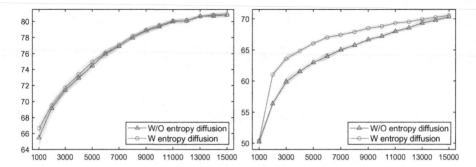

Fig. 5. (Left) Performance of our algorithm with and without entropy diffusion (*Caltech-256*). (Right) Pure label acquisition efficiency of the conventional batch entropy-based selection method and our entropy diffusion method: 15,000 labels were acquired from initial 1,000 known labels (*CIFAR-100*). Entropy diffusion contributes to consistent and statistically significant performance improvements.

5   Conclusions

Existing active label correction (ALC) approaches rely on uncertainty predictions made by unreliable classifiers (trained on noisy samples). Further, simultaneously selecting a batch of ambiguous examples can lead to redundant labeling. Our method addresses these limitations by regulating the contributions of individual parameter gradients via monitoring the progression of losses, and diffusing the entropy value of each newly labeled point avoiding the selection of spatial accumulations. Combining these contributions into a learning framework, our algorithm offers robustness in training under label noise and efficiency in label acquisition without having to know the identity or number of noisy examples. Evaluated on four benchmark datasets, our algorithm demonstrated a significant and consistent performance gain over state-of-the-art methods.

Limitations and Future Work. Our method assumes a uniform cost per label while in practice, the labeling cost can vary across examples: Labeling the most ambiguous examples can rapidly improve classifier performance, but it could also involve considerable annotation time and effort. In such cases, one should carefully trade between the gain of the information and the associated annotation cost. Adjusting our original entropy-based label selection criterion by incorporating a label cost estimation module (e.g., [6,33]) might be possible, but this would involve modifying the entire label acquisition process. Our method is agnostic to the noise generation process and therefore, complementary to noise model-based approaches including DALC. Future work should investigate the possibility of combing the strengths of model-based approaches and ours.

Acknowledgments. We thank James Tompkin for fruitful discussions and the anonymous reviewers for their insightful comments. This work was supported by the National Research Foundation of Korea (NRF) grant (No. 2021R1A2C2012195, Data efficient machine learning for estimating skeletal pose across multiple domains, 1/2) and Institute of Information & Communications Technology Planning & Evaluation (IITP) grant (No. 2021-0-00537, Visual common sense through self-supervised learning for restoration of invisible parts in images, 1/2) both funded by the Korea government (MSIT).

References

1. Arachie, C., Huang, B.: A general framework for adversarial label learning. JMLR **22**, 1–33 (2021)
2. Bernhardt, M., et al.: Active label cleaning: improving dataset quality under resource constraints. In: arXiv:2109.00574 (2021)
3. Budninskiy, M., Abdelaziz, A., Tong, Y., Desbrun, M.: Laplacian-optimized diffusion for semi-supervised learning. Comput. Aided Geom. Des. **79** (2020)
4. Shampine, L.F.: Tolerance proportionality in ODE codes. In: Bellen, A., Gear, C.W., Russo, E. (eds.) Numerical Methods for Ordinary Differential Equations. LNM, vol. 1386, pp. 118–136. Springer, Heidelberg (1989). https://doi.org/10.1007/BFb0089235
5. Fang, T., Lu, N., Niu, G., Sugiyama, M.: Rethinking importance weighting for deep learning under distribution shift. In: NeurIPS (2020)
6. Gao, R., Saar-Tsechansky, M.: Cost-accuracy aware adaptive labeling for active learning. In: AAAI, pp. 2569–2576 (2020)
7. Griffin, G., Holub, A., Perona, P.: Caltech-256 object category dataset. Technical report. California Institute of Technology (2007)
8. Han, B., et al.: Co-teaching: robust training of deep neural networks with extremely noisy labels. In: NIPS (2018)
9. He, K., Zhang, X., Ren, S., Sun, J.: Deep residual learning for image recognition. In: CVPR, pp. 770–778 (2016)
10. Hein, M.: Geometrical Aspects of Statistical Learning Theory. Ph.D. thesis. Technical University of Darmstadt, Germany (2005)
11. Hein, M., Audibert, J.-Y., von Luxburg, U.: From graphs to manifolds – weak and strong pointwise consistency of graph laplacians. In: Auer, P., Meir, R. (eds.) COLT 2005. LNCS (LNAI), vol. 3559, pp. 470–485. Springer, Heidelberg (2005). https://doi.org/10.1007/11503415_32
12. Hein, M., Maier, M.: Manifold denoising. In: NIPS, pp. 561–568 (2007)
13. Henter, D., Stahlt, A., Ebbecke, M., Gillmann, M.: Classifier self-assessment: active learning and active noise correction for document classification. In: ICDAR, pp. 276–280 (2015)
14. Huang, J., Qu, L., Jia, R., Zhao, B.: O2U-Net: a simple noisy label detection approach for deep neural networks. In: ICCV, pp. 3326–3334 (2019)
15. Iserles, A.: A First Course in the Numerical Analysis of Differential Equations. Cambridge University Press, 2nd edn. (2012)
16. Kremer, J., Sha, F., Igel, C.: Robust active label correction. In: AISTATS, pp. 308–316 (2018)
17. Krizhevsky, A.: Learning Multiple Layers of Features from Tiny Images. Technical report. University of Toronto (2009)
18. Krüger, M., Novo, A.S., Nattermann, T., Mohamed, M., Bertram, T.: Reducing noise in label annotation: a lane change prediction case study. In: IFAC Symposium on Intelligent Autonomous Vehicles, pp. 221–226 (2019)
19. Li, S.-Y., Shi, Y., Huang, S.-J., Chen, S.: Improving deep label noise learning with dual active label correction. Mach. Learn. **111**, 1–22 (2021). https://doi.org/10.1007/s10994-021-06081-9

20. Liu, T., Tao, D.: Classification with noisy labels by importance reweighting. IEEE TPAMI **38**(3), 447–461 (2016)
21. Nallapati, R., Surdeanu, M., Manning, C.: CorrActive learning: learning from noisy data through human interaction. In: IJCAI Workshop on Intelligence and Interaction (2009)
22. Parde, N., Nielsen, R.D.: Finding patterns in noisy crowds: regression-based annotation aggregation for crowdsourced data. In: EMNLP, pp. 1907–1912 (2017)
23. Park, S., Jo, D.U., Choi, J.Y.: Over-fit: noisy-label detection based on the overfitted model property. In: arXiv:2106.07217 (2021)
24. Pierri, F., Piccardi, C., Ceri, S.: Topology comparison of twitter diffusion networks effectively reveals misleading information. Sci. Rep. **10**(1372), 1–19 (2020)
25. Rebbapragada, U., Brodley, C.E., Sulla-Menashe, D., Friedl, M.A.: Active label correction. In: ICDM, pp. 1080–1085 (2012)
26. Rehbein, I., Ruppenhofer, J.: Detecting annotation noise in automatically labelled data. In: ACL, pp. 1160–1170 (2018)
27. Ren, M., Zeng, W., Yang, B., Urtasun, R.: Learning to reweight examples for robust deep learning. In: ICML (2018)
28. Rosenberg, S.: The Laplacian on a Riemannian Manifold. Cambridge University Press (2009)
29. Shen, Y., Sanghavi, S.: Learning with bad training data via iterative trimmed loss minimization. In: ICML (2019)
30. Sheng, V.S., Provost, F., Ipeirotis, P.G.: Get another label? improving data quality and data mining using multiple, noisy labelers. In: KDD, pp. 614–622 (2009)
31. Stokes, J.W., Kapoor, A., Ray, D.: Asking for a second opinion: re-querying of noisy multi-class labels. In: ICASSP, pp. 2329–2333 (2016)
32. Szlam, A.D., Maggioni, M., Coifman, R.R.: Regularization on graphs with function-adapted diffusion processes. JMLR **9**, 1711–1739 (2008)
33. Tajbakhsh, N., Jeyaseelan, L., Li, Q., Chiang, J.N., Wu, Z., Ding, X.: Embracing imperfect datasets: a review of deep learning solutions for medical image segmentation. Med. Image Anal. **63** (2020)
34. Urner, R., David, S.B., Shamir, O.: Learning from weak teachers. In: AISTATS, pp. 1252–1260 (2012)
35. van Rooyen, B., Menon, A.K., Williamson, R.C.: Learning with symmetric label noise: the importance of being unhinged. In: NIPS (2015)
36. Wang, S., et al.: Annotation-efficient deep learning for automatic medical image segmentation. Nat. Commun. **12**(1), 1–13 (2021)
37. Xiao, H., Rasul, K., Vollgraf, R.: FashionMNIST: a novel image dataset for benchmarking machine learning algorithms. arXiv:1708.07747 (2017)
38. Yan, S., Chaudhuri, K., Javidi, T.: Active learning from imperfect labelers. In: NIPS (2016)
39. Younesian, T., Epema, D., Chen, L.Y.: Active learning for noisy data streams using weak and strong labelers. arXiv:2010.14149v1 (2020)
40. Zhang, C., Chaudhuri, K.: Active learning from weak and strong labelers. In: NIPS (2015)
41. Zhang, C., Bengio, S., Hardt, M., Recht, B., Vinyals, O.: Understanding deep learning requires rethinking generalization. In: ICLR (2017)
42. Zhang, M., Hu, L., Shi, C., Wang, X.: Adversarial label-flipping attack and defense for graph neural networks. In: ICDM (2020)
43. Zhu, Z., Dong, Z., Liu, Y.: Detecting corrupted labels without training a model to predict. In: ICML (2022)
44. Ørting, S.N., et al.: A survey of crowdsourcing in medical image analysis. Hum. Comput. **7**, 1–26 (2020)

Unpaired Image Translation via Vector Symbolic Architectures

Justin Theiss[1,2]($\boxtimes$), Jay Leverett[1], Daeil Kim[1], and Aayush Prakash[1]

[1] Meta Reality Labs, Burlingame, USA
{theiss,jayleverett,daeilkim,aayushp}@fb.com
[2] University of California, Berkeley, CA 94720, USA

Abstract. Image-to-image translation has played an important role in enabling synthetic data for computer vision. However, if the source and target domains have a large semantic mismatch, existing techniques often suffer from source content corruption aka semantic flipping. To address this problem, we propose a new paradigm for image-to-image translation using Vector Symbolic Architectures (VSA), a theoretical framework which defines algebraic operations in a high-dimensional vector (hypervector) space. We introduce VSA-based constraints on adversarial learning for source-to-target translations by learning a hypervector mapping that inverts the translation to ensure consistency with source content. We show both qualitatively and quantitatively that our method improves over other state-of-the-art techniques.

Keywords: Image-to-image translation · Adversarial learning · Vector symbolic architectures · Semantic flipping

1 Introduction

Image-to-image translation techniques [8,12,14,23,25,30,33,39] have been instrumental in improving synthetic data for computer vision. They have been used to bridge the domain gap for synthetic data [12,30,39] and for photorealistic enhancement in virtual reality and gaming applications [33]. Some researchers [7,16,31] argue that the domain gap can be further factorized into a content (shift in semantic statistics) and appearance gap. In this work, we are interested in the unpaired image-to-image translation method in the challenging scenario where the content gap between the source and target domains is large.

There are several techniques for unpaired image-to-image translation [12,30, 39]. Some approaches assume that content and style can be separated in order to translate style without corrupting content (e.g., [12]). Others have used a bijective mapping to reconstruct the source image from the translated image (i.e., a "cyclic loss" [39]). However, these methods do not work well if there is a *large*

Supplementary Information The online version contains supplementary material available at https://doi.org/10.1007/978-3-031-19803-8_2.

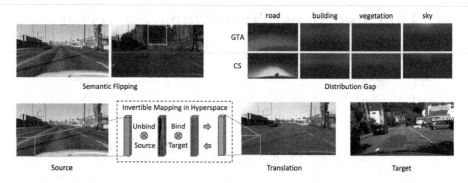

Fig. 1. We propose Vector Symbolic Architecture based image-to-image translation technique (VSAIT) which addresses semantic flipping (source content corruption) that happens when the distribution gap (shift in semantic statistics) between source and target domains is large. Our method learns a mapping in high-dimensional vector space (hyperspace), which encourages translated images to be consistent with the source domain. Conceptually, our approach aims to "unbind" source-related information (e.g., texture and color) and "bind" target-related information as well as vice versa to recover source content. (Color figure online)

shift in distribution between source and target domains leading to the problem of *semantic flipping*. Semantic flipping is characterized by image artifacts, object or feature hallucinations that are a result of adversarial training for datasets with a large content gap. Specifically, this is observed as a change in content between source and translated images (e.g., sky to trees in Fig. 1). Semantic flipping is a critical issue for improving photorealism in computer graphics applications [33] as well as training downstream tasks using translated images, as we want to preserve the source semantic labels of translations.

Relatively few works have directly focused on the semantic flipping problem; however, they can be broadly categorized into three approaches: image-level consistency, domain-invariant encoding, and task-level consistency. Methods using an image-level consistency loss attempt to ensure that pixel-level information is highly correlated between source and translated images [3,8]. Such methods may fail to account for feature-level differences that do not correlate well with pixel-level differences. Approaches that focus on domain-invariant encoding train the generator to encode domain-invariant content either using a shared latent space [23] or contrastive learning [14]. These methods will fail to reduce semantic flipping if content and style cannot be sufficiently disentangled. Finally, others have used pre-trained task networks to generate pseudo-labels for each domain to ensure a consistent translation with respect to source labels (i.e., semantic masks) [11,33]. However, these methods fail if the task network cannot generate pseudo-labels for both domains. We instead focus on a method that provides feature-level consistency between source and translated images without explicit assumptions of domain-invariant encoding or quality of pseudo-labels. This addresses gaps in previous methods which make them vulnerable to semantic flipping.

In the current paper, we propose a novel usage of a theoretical framework known as vector symbolic architectures (VSA [9,15]; also referred to as hyperdimensional computing) as a new paradigm for unpaired image-to-image translation. Although much of the VSA research has been conducted in theoretical neuroscience (see [20,21]), it has more recently been applied to computer vision problems using extracted features from deep neural networks [27,28]. VSA defines a high-dimensional vector (hypervector) space and operators used for symbolic computation, which allows for mathematical formulations of conceptual queries such as, "what color is the car?". In the case of unpaired image translation, such formulations are useful because they enable us to recover attributes from the source image and ensure consistent relationships among features when translating images from one domain to another. VSA is well suited for this approach as it can represent arbitrary symbols and formulations generally without supervision or training [32]. The important difference from previous methods addressing semantic flipping is that VSA ensures that hypervector representations of different semantic content are almost orthogonal to each other (e.g., sky and trees) [15]. The cosine distance between translated and source hypervectors therefore is greatest when semantic flipping occurs.

Using this framework, we propose a method for learning a hypervector mapping between source and target domains that is robust to semantic flipping (Fig. 1). By inverting this mapping, we are able to minimize the distance between features extracted from source and translated images without requiring that content and style be fully disentangled. We demonstrate qualitatively and quantitatively that this approach significantly reduces the image artifacts and hallucinations observed for unpaired image translation between domains with a large content gap. We hope that our work provides inspiration for incorporating VSA into new areas of computer vision research. Our contributions include:

- Our method addresses important artifacts and feature hallucinations (semantic flipping) that often occur with other unsupervised image translation methods as a result of content gap between source and target domains.
- To the best of our knowledge, we are the first to show that Vector Symbolic Architectures (VSA) can be used for a challenging task of image translations in the wild. We hope this opens up an exciting area of research around VSA.
- We demonstrate qualitative and quantitative improvement over state-of-the-art methods that directly address semantic flipping across multiple experiments with unmatched semantic statistics.

2 Related Work

Unpaired Image-to-Image Translation. Unpaired image-to-image translation is a widely studied problem with many existing techniques [2,3,8,12–14, 18,23,25,30,33,38,39]. One popular approach is to impose the cycle-consistency constraint [18,38,39], which states that a source-to-target generator and a target-to-source generator are bijections. Building on cycle-consistency, UNIT [25]

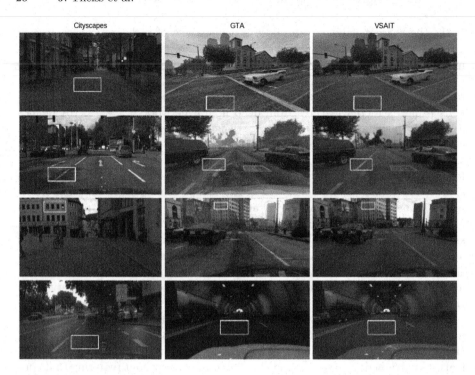

Fig. 2. Example GTA translations from our method (VSAIT) alongside representative examples from Cityscapes. We can see that VSAIT successfully translates GTA images to Cityscapes' style and that, in particular, our method is able to learn specific textures and attributes (e.g. gray cobblestone, white lane lines rather than yellow) that are commonly found in Cityscapes images. Moreover, VSAIT is able to handle unseen scenarios (e.g. tunnel) that do not occur in Cityscapes without semantic flipping. (Color figure online)

mapped the source and target domains to a shared latent space, while DRIT [23] and other methods [2,12] factorized the latent space into a shared content space and a domain-specific style space. DistanceGAN [3] showed that source to target translations can be learnt unidirectionally. CUT [30] subsequently proposed a unidirectional method based on contrastive learning. Whereas some of these methods require separate networks per domain or assume that content and style can be disentangled, our method uses a single generator without assumption of disentanglement.

Semantic Flipping. The body of research on semantic flipping is relatively small. Methods based on cycle-consistency combat semantic flipping through pixel-level reconstruction, but they are unable to prevent semantic flipping in the face of large distributional shifts. GcGAN [8] enforces geometry-consistent constraints on image translations by ensuring robustness for transformations such as flipping or rotation. This does not necessarily address semantic flipping for small, local features that could still be geometry-consistent. EPE [33] addresses semantic flipping by conditioning on G-buffers (e.g. albedo, glossiness, depth, normals) as well as incorporating semantic segmentation pseudo-labels into the discriminator. Although their method addresses semantic flipping, it does not generalize to many tasks or datasets since it assumes access to the synthetic image rendering process and a downstream task network that can generate pseudo-labels for both source and target domains. Alternatively, SRUNIT [14] proposed to address semantic flipping by using contrastive learning (following CUT [30]) to encode domain-invariant semantic representations that are robust to small feature-space perturbations. Although their approach does not require access to any labels or rendering process like EPE, it does not sufficiently address semantic flipping. Unlike these approaches, we reduce semantic flipping by inverting the translation in hyperspace using VSA in order to ensure recovery of source information.

Computer Vision Applications of VSA. Although much of the research associated with VSA has been conducted in theoretical neuroscience, Neubert et al. [28] provided examples of how VSA can be used for computer vision tasks such as object and place recognition, which demonstrated how image features extracted from pre-trained neural networks can be used within the VSA framework. Other works have used VSA for visual question answering [26] and scene transformation [17], albeit with simple shapes or MNIST digits. More recently, Osipov et al. [29] used VSA to learn to unbind category representations among unlabelled data vectors bound to a shared representational space. This is most similar to the challenge that we are addressing in the current paper, as we can consider the source and target features to be bound to a similar content space; however, unlike their study we do not have access to the underlying shared representational space.

3   Method

3.1   Preliminary: VSA

Vector Symbolic Architectures (VSA) [9,15] provide a framework for encoding and manipulating information in a hypervector space (hyperspace) with high capacity and robustness to noise [15]. In VSA framework, hypervectors are randomly sampled from a vector space $\mathbb{V} = [-1,1]^n$ (where $n >> 1000$) in order to represent symbols that can be typically manipulated using two operators – binding/unbinding (element-wise multiplication) and bundling (element-wise addition). The binding operator can be used to assign an attribute to a symbol (e.g., "gray car"), whereas bundling can be used to group symbols together (e.g., "gray car and red bike"). These operators define the Multiplication-Addition-Permutation (MAP) architecture. Other operators and architectures (see [35]) are beyond the scope of our work.

The benefit of using VSA framework for image translation is its versatility in representing arbitrary symbols without supervision. This allows us to infer underlying representational spaces (e.g., content distribution) without explicitly defining them. Since the challenge of semantic flipping in unpaired image translation is typically to constrain the generator, we do not need to learn how to generate images from hypervectors but instead learn a mapping that ensures we recover the same source information for a given translated hypervector.

In order to assign random hypervectors to image features, Neubert et al. [28] used locality sensitive hashing (LSH) to project image features extracted using a pre-trained neural network (AlexNet [22]) to a relatively lower-dimensional space (from $13 \times 13 \times 384$ to 8192). In this case, the entire image was encoded into a single hypervector; however, image patches can also be encoded as separate hypervectors [27]. As an example, imagine an image patch from the source domain that contains a car and pedestrian. We can assume without loss of generality that the image patch is represented as a hypervector:

$$v_{src} = c \otimes c_{src} + p \otimes p_{src}, \tag{1}$$

where c and p are hypervectors representing the car and pedestrian bound with source-specific hypervectors c_{src} and p_{src}, respectively.

Since we do not have access to the underlying symbols associated with source and target domains, instead we must learn a mapping that unbinds source-specific information and binds target-specific information (and vice versa). Specifically, we would like to learn a hypervector mapping that can unbind these source-specific attributes and bind target-specific attributes in order to obtain a target representation v_{tgt} as shown in Eq. 2.

$$v_{src} \otimes u_{src \leftrightarrow tgt} \approx v_{tgt}, \\ \text{where } u_{src \leftrightarrow tgt} = (c_{src} \otimes c_{tgt} + p_{src} \otimes p_{tgt}) \tag{2}$$

Since the binding/unbinding operation is invertible, c_{src} and p_{src} are unbound while c_{tgt} and p_{tgt} are correspondingly bound. Importantly, since these random hypervectors are very likely to be almost orthogonal, binding/unbinding the incorrect attributes (i.e., $c \otimes p_{src}$) simply adds noise to the resulting vector as demonstrated in Eq. 3.

$$\begin{aligned} v_{src} \otimes u_{src \leftrightarrow tgt} &= c \otimes c_{src} \otimes (c_{src} \otimes c_{tgt} + p_{src} \otimes p_{tgt}) \\ &\quad + p \otimes p_{src} \otimes (c_{src} \otimes c_{tgt} + p_{src} \otimes p_{tgt}) \\ &= (c \otimes c_{tgt} + noise) + (noise + p \otimes p_{tgt}) \\ &= c \otimes c_{tgt} + p \otimes p_{tgt} + noise \approx v_{tgt} \end{aligned} \tag{3}$$

It is also worth noting that $u_{src \leftrightarrow tgt}$ is equivalent to $u_{tgt \leftrightarrow src}$, which means a single vector can be used to map between the domains. Hence, $v_{tgt} \otimes u_{src \leftrightarrow tgt} \approx v_{src}$. Note that hypervectors in the VSA framework are distributed representations that are very robust to noise [1] and further that cosine similarity will still be high relative to similarity with random vectors. The above example demonstrates the unique properties of the VSA framework, which allow for algebraic formulations of symbolic representations.

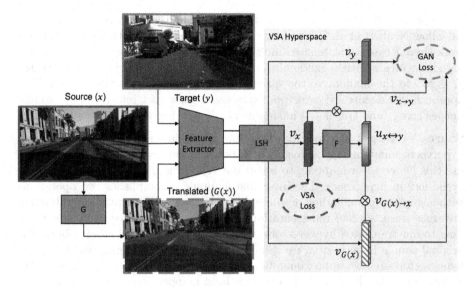

Fig. 3. Our method addresses semantic flipping by learning an invertible mapping in a high-dimensional vector space (VSA hyperspace) in order to ensure consistency between source and translated images. We extract features and use locality sensitive hashing (LSH) to encode source (x, blue), target (y, green), and translated ($G(x)$, striped green) images into this random VSA hyperspace. We use a GAN loss to train G to generate images with hypervectors similar to those in the target domain. Finally, the hypervector mapping ($u_{x\leftrightarrow y}$, green-and-blue vertical bar) is used to invert our translation (Eq. 4) to recover the source hypervectors (VSA Loss). See Sect. 3.3 for more details. (Color figure online)

3.2 VSA-Based Image Translation (VSAIT)

Overview. Our goal is to translate images from a source to target domain, while minimizing semantic flipping caused by differences in the content distribution between the two domains. As shown in Fig. 3, our method uses a hypervector adversarial loss (GAN Loss in Fig. 3) that operates on VSA-based hypervector representations of image patches. In order to address semantic flipping we constrain the generator to preserve the content of the source domain via a VSA-based cyclic loss (VSA Loss in Fig. 3). We do so by leveraging VSA to invert our translation in hypervector space to ensure consistency with the source content. We will cover these two loss functions later in this section. Our method has three major network components– Generator G, Discriminator D_Y and Mapper F that we will discuss next. We present training details in Sect. 3.3.

Generator. Our approach uses a generator $G : X \rightarrow Y$ (shown in Fig. 3) and feature-level discriminator D_Y in order to learn an unpaired image translation between X (source) and Y (target) domains, where D_Y is trained to discriminate between hypervectors extracted from target and translated images.

As previously introduced in Sect. 3.1, to assign hypervectors to image patches, we follow Neubert et al. [28] and extract features using a pre-trained neural network (in our case, concatenated multiple layers of VGG19 [36]). These concatenated features are then randomly projected from the extracted feature vector $f_i \in \mathbb{R}^m$ to the random vector space $\mathbb{V} = [-1, 1]^n$ where $m >> n$. Using this approach, we denote hypervectors extracted from target images as v_Y, source images as v_X, and translated images as $v_{G(X)}$ (see Fig. 3).

Source $\leftrightarrow$ Target Mapper. Furthermore, we train a network F to generate a hypervector mapping $u_{X \leftrightarrow Y}$ (e.g., Eq. 3) between source and target domains. We use this hypervector mapping to invert our translation, providing a VSA-based cyclic loss in hyperspace. The invertible mapping accomplishes two operations with a single step: unbinding of source (resp. target) representations and binding of target (resp. source) representations. This means that if we apply this mapping to our translated hypervectors $v_{G(X)}$, we should approximately obtain the original source hypervectors v_X. Similarly, if we apply this mapping to source hypervectors v_X, we approximately obtain translated hypervectors $v_{G(X)}$. We denote translated hypervectors that have been mapped to the source domain as $v_{G(X) \to X}$ and those mapped from source to target domain as $v_{X \to Y}$ as shown in Eq. 4 as well as Fig. 3.

$$v_{G(X)} \otimes u_{X \leftrightarrow Y} = v_{G(X) \to X} \approx v_X$$
$$v_X \otimes u_{X \leftrightarrow Y} = v_{X \to Y} \approx v_{G(X)}$$
(4)

Hypervector Adversarial Loss. In order to train G, D_Y and F to translate images that match the target distribution, we use an adversarial loss [10]. Specifically, we want the hypervectors of our translated image $v_{G(X)}$ to be similar to those from the target domain v_Y. Furthermore, by binding the hypervector mapping $u_{X \leftrightarrow Y}$ to source vectors v_X, we should obtain a hypervector of the source features mapped to the target domain (Eq. 4). Therefore, we train F along with G and D_Y using the following adversarial loss:

$$\mathcal{L}_{GAN}(G, D_Y, F, X, Y) = \mathbb{E}_{y \sim p_Y(y)}[\log D_Y(v_y)]$$
$$+ \mathbb{E}_{x \sim p_X(x)}[\log(1 - D_Y(v_{G(x)}))]$$
$$+ \mathbb{E}_{x \sim p_X(x)}[\log(1 - D_Y(v_x \otimes F(v_x)))],$$
(5)

where G and F networks are trained to fool the discriminator D_Y, thereby minimizing the objective while D_Y attempts to maximize it.

VSA-Based Cyclic Loss. Although adversarial training provides a method to generate images that match the target distribution, the differences in content between domains will result in semantic flipping. We therefore need a loss that constrains the generator to preserve source content and reduce semantic flipping. To do so, we incorporate our VSA-based cyclic loss, which ensures that the same hypervectors are obtained when mapping translated vectors back from target to source domain ($v_{G(X) \to X}$):

$$\mathcal{L}_{VSA}(G, X) = \mathbb{E}_{x \sim p_X(x)} \left[\frac{1}{n} \sum_{i=1}^{n} dist \left(v_x^i, v_{G(x) \to x}^i \right) \right], \qquad (6)$$

where $dist(\cdot, \cdot)$ is the cosine distance averaged across the n hypervectors (representing image patches indexed by i) for the image x. By minimizing the cosine distance ($1 -$ cosine similarity) between $v_{G(X) \to X}$ and v_X, we ensure that the same features are recovered after inverting our translation (i.e., representations of "car" and "pedestrian" are maintained in the example from Eq. 1).

Our overall objective combines our adversarial and VSA-based cyclic losses, training G to generate images matching the target domain and F to invert the translation to ensure consistency with the source domain:

$$\mathcal{L}(G, D_Y, F, X, Y) = \mathcal{L}_{GAN}(G, D_Y, F, X, Y) + \lambda \mathcal{L}_{VSA}(G, X), \qquad (7)$$

where λ controls the relative importance of our VSA-based cyclic loss.

3.3 VSAIT Training

We train our method with a GAN-based training framework using the objective described in Eq. 7. We begin by randomly sampling an image from each domain and translating the source image into the target domain via the generator G. In order to use the VSA framework, we must first encode data into the hypervector space. Therefore, we extract features from each image (source, target, and translated) at multiple layers of a pre-trained neural network (Feature Extractor in Fig. 3) as the first step in encoding image patches into the VSA hyperspace. We consider each image patch to be represented by the extracted features sharing its receptive field. We flatten and concatenate these features across layers, resulting in a set of feature vectors (one per image patch) with a dimensionality of m.

We then use LSH (Fig. 3) to reduce the dimensionality of the extracted feature vectors into our random hyperspace $\mathbb{V}$, which reduces the dimensionality to $n << m$. Specifically, we normalize and project the extracted feature vectors using a random matrix where each row is sampled from a standard normal distribution and normalized to unit length. The resulting vectors are therefore in the range $[-1, 1]$, which is necessary to implement the VSA binding operation as described in Sect. 3.1. These hypervectors represent the image patches for the source, target, and translated images as shown in Fig. 3. Note that this process does not require training nor is it necessarily dependent on a specific feature extractor, although different feature extractors may encode different information.

Finally, we use F to generate a hypervector mapping for each source hypervector. We use these hypervector mappings ($u_{x \leftrightarrow y}$ in Fig. 3) to unbind source (resp. target) information and correspondingly bind target (resp. source) information (Eq. 4). By applying this mapping to the source hypervectors, we should obtain a hypervector representation of the source image translated into the target domain ($v_{x \to y}$ in Fig. 3), which is used in our adversarial loss (Eq. 5) to train F. The ultimate goal of this step, however, is to use the mapping to invert our translation $v_{G(x)}$ and ensure that we recover the same source information v_x (Eq. 6). Doing so will reduce semantic flipping by constraining G to generate images that have hypervectors that are consistent with the source domain.

4 Experiments

We evaluate our method using experiments across multiple datasets. First, we compare against baseline techniques for GTA [34] to Cityscapes [6], where the two domains have inherent semantic differences. We then perform experiments using datasets sub-sampled to create differences in semantic statistics. Specifically, we follow the method in [14] to sub-sample the Google Maps [13] dataset, which is typically designed for paired image translation tasks. We show that VSAIT works as intended to reduce semantic flipping while still generating diverse image translations. Our qualitative results in Fig. 2 demonstrate that the hyperspace mapping constrains the generator to translate features that are consistent between source and target domains. Furthermore, we show that other methods still have significant artifacts and hallucinations related to semantic flipping (Fig. 4). Our quantitative results show improvements against the other baselines, particularly for the GTA to Cityscapes task. Finally, we perform an ablation study to evaluate the contributions of different components in VSAIT.

4.1 Implementation Details

We follow CUT [30] in our choice of the generator network architecture. For the discriminator network, we use a three-layer fully-convolutional network with 1×1 convolutional filters. For the mapping network F, we use a two-layer fully-convolutional network. We train VSAIT using the Adam optimizer [19] ($\beta_1 = 0$, $\beta_2 = 0.9$) with a batch size of 1 and learning rate of 0.0001 for the generator (and mapping network F) and 0.0004 for the discriminator. To improve adversarial training, we use the "hinge loss" [24] rather than the negative log-likelihood objective in $\mathcal{L}_{GAN}$ (Eq. 5). For GTA to Cityscapes, we use $\lambda = 10$ in Eq. 7 and $\lambda = 5$ for other experiments. See Supplemental for more details.

4.2 Datasets

We perform our experiments using three datasets: GTA [34], Cityscapes [6], and Google Maps [13]. GTA [34] is a synthetic dataset of 24966 images generated from the video game Grand Theft Auto V. Cityscapes [6] is a real dataset of driving scenarios accompanied with finely-annotated semantic segmentation labels, which includes 2975 training and 500 validation images. The Google Maps dataset [13] is a collection of 2194 paired maps and aerial photos (1096 training and 1098 validation images).

4.3   Baselines

We compare our method against several baselines that are relevant to the semantic flipping problem: GcGAN, DRIT, CUT, SRUNIT, and EPE. We choose these methods for comparison as they reflect the recent approaches focused on reducing semantic flipping. Specifically, they represent methods that use image-level consistency (GcGAN [8]), domain-invariant encoding (DRIT [23], CUT [30], SRUNIT [14]), and task-level consistency (EPE [33]). It is worth reiterating that EPE only works for synthetic datasets with access to G-buffers (e.g., albedo, glossiness, depth, normals), which are not publicly available for GTA and do not exist for real datasets (e.g., Google Maps). Therefore we compare qualitatively to EPE and rely on quantitative values reported in their work.

4.4   GTA → Cityscapes

We first demonstrate our method using GTA to Cityscapes, which are unpaired datasets that naturally differ in their semantic statistics. For training, we use 20000 of GTA images for our source dataset and all 2975 training images for our target dataset. Following [33], we evaluate our image translation performance using the Kernel Inception Distance (KID) [4] which measures the distance of extracted features from translated and target images using the pre-trained InceptionV3 network [37]. As seen in the Table 2, our method outperforms the baseline methods in the KID metric. As shown in Fig. 4, only EPE has similar quality of image translations for GTA to Cityscapes. However, whereas other methods hallucinate trees and Mercedes hood ornaments, EPE has a tendency to remove palm trees and add unnatural lighting to cars even in dark scenes.

We additionally evaluate translation quality via semantic segmentation metrics computed using DeepLab V3 [5] pretrained on Cityscapes. In line with [14], we report three metrics related to semantic segmentation performance (Table 1): pixel accuracy, class accuracy, and mean intersection over union (mIoU). As shown in Table 1, we outperform the other baselines by a wide margin. Whereas KID computes the distance between translated and target images in feature space, semantic segmentation metrics better reflect semantic flipping directly. As seen in Fig. 4, other methods often generate trees and other features in the sky, which will lower semantic segmentation performance in those regions.

4.5   Google Map → Aerial Photo

We then demonstrate performance on the Google Maps [13] dataset. Here we sub-sample the 1096 training images using K-means clustering of the histograms from grayscale map images to obtain two datasets with different semantic statistics (as in [14]). We evaluate translation performance on all 1098 validation images and report three pixel-level metrics (Table 1). The first metric is the L2 distance between translated and target images. We also report pixel accuracy defined as the percentage of pixels with a maximum absolute difference less than a given threshold (i.e., $max(|r_i - r_i'|, |g_i - g_i'|, |b_i - b_i'|) < \delta$). For the map

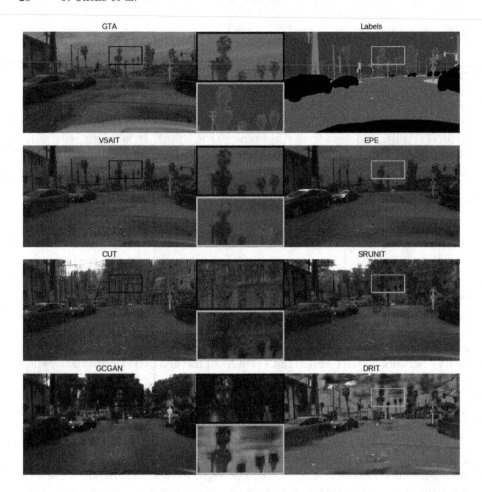

Fig. 4. We compare our VSAIT translation to those of baseline methods on an example GTA image. Typical methods often suffer from semantic flipping in open sky regions of GTA, as such regions are observed less often in Cityscapes (i.e., content gap). Here we see that SRUNIT [14], CUT [30], GcGAN [8] and DRIT [23] each suffer from sky hallucinations, while EPE [33] removes palm trees (features that are absent from Cityscapes) in the distance. Meanwhile, our method is able to translate to Cityscapes style while preserving semantics from the original GTA image.

to aerial photo task, we use thresholds of $\delta = 30, 50$ [14]. Similar to GTA to Cityscapes, our approach substantially outperforms the baseline methods. Particularly interesting is the improvement we see in the pixel accuracy for both thresholds ($\delta = 30, 50$), whereas the other methods perform very similarly.

Table 1. Quantitative evaluation across datasets with unmatched semantics. The metrics included are average pixel prediction accuracy (pxAcc), average class prediction accuracy (clsAcc), mean IoU (mIoU), average L2 distance (Dist), and pixel accuracy with task-specific thresholds (Acc).

Method	GTA → Cityscapes			Map → Photo			Photo → Map		
	pxAcc	clsAcc	mIoU	Dist	Acc (δ_1)	Acc (δ_2)	Dist	Acc (δ_1)	Acc (δ_2)
GcGAN [8]	65.62	32.38	22.64	71.47	28.87	43.48	23.62	15.00	30.65
DRIT [23]	64.28	32.17	20.99	70.87	28.97	43.56	24.19	13.94	29.01
CUT [30]	64.59	32.19	20.35	70.28	28.86	44.07	23.44	16.25	31.34
SRUNIT [14]	67.21	32.97	22.69	68.55	30.41	45.91	23.00	**17.67**	**32.78**
VSAIT (ours)	**76.48**	**45.33**	**30.89**	**64.98**	**45.3**	**69.28**	**22.86**	15.2	32.13

4.6   Aerial Photo → Google Map

We additionally demonstrate performance for the task of photo to map using the same sub-sampled datasets obtained from the Google Maps training dataset as described above. For this experiment, we evaluate the same metrics as with map to photo but with pixel accuracy threshold of $\delta = 3, 5$ [14] (Table 1). Although we outperform the baseline methods on the L2 distance metric (Dist in Table 1), we did not observe improvements in the pixel accuracy metrics. We do believe that our approach using VSA is capable of improving these metrics with a more suitable encoding method (as opposed to VGG) for images that have regions without contours or complex features (as is the case for some regions in Google Map images representing landscape or water). However, we leave study of encoding methods for VSA in computer vision applications to future research.

4.7   Ablation Study

We demonstrate the effect of VSAIT by evaluating the contribution of the VSA-based cyclic loss (Eq. 6), the learned hypervector mapping $u_{X \leftrightarrow Y}$, and the hypervector dimensionality. We use the GTA to Cityscapes task to evaluate these ablations on semantic segmentation performance metrics (Table 2). We first demonstrate that by removing the VSA-based cyclic loss, the generator learns to translate images without preserving content, demonstrating the serious problem of semantic flipping (Fig. 5B). Next, we show the importance of the invertible mapping $u_{X \leftrightarrow Y}$ by generating a random hypervector mapping instead of learning the mapping adversarially (Eq. 5). When using a random hypervector instead of the learned mapping generated by F, the generator maintains global structure but since the invertible mapping does not recover the source hypervector (Eq. 4) the local content is often changed (semantic flipping shown in Fig. 5C). Finally, we demonstrate the importance of using the VSA hypervector space by reducing the dimensionality of $\mathbb{V}$ from 4096 to 128. Reducing the dimensionality of the hyperspace from 4096 to 128 results in noisy image translations that seem to only reflect global changes in style. However, even using a low-dimensional hypervector VSAIT still outperforms most methods compared in Table 1.

Table 2. Evaluations on GTA to Cityscapes. Left: quantitative comparison for KID metric. *Mean values reported in [33]. Right: ablation study task demonstrating the contributions for each component of VSAIT method.

Method	KID	Ablation	pxAcc	clsAcc	mIoU
CUT	21.18*				
SRUNIT	16.27	w/o VSA Loss	52.17	16.14	10.21
DRIT	14.69	Random Hypervector Mapping	65.75	29.32	17.53
GcGAN	12.32	Reduced Hypervector Dim	66.42	40.34	25.04
EPE	10.95*	VSAIT (ours)	**76.48**	**45.33**	**30.89**
VSAIT (ours)	**8.74**				

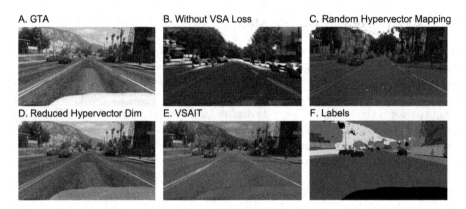

Fig. 5. Ablation study for GTA to Cityscapes. (A) and (F) show the ground truth image and semantic labels for the GTA source image, respectively. (B) demonstrates the challenge of semantic flipping when using GAN-based methods without constraining the generator. (C) shows the importance of learning the hypervector mapping. (D) demonstrates the importance of high-dimensional space for this method. (E) shows the effect on image translation when incorporating all components of our approach.

5   Conclusion

In this paper, we address the semantic flipping problem in unpaired image translation using a novel approach based on VSA framework [9,15]. We show important qualitative and quantitative improvements over previous methods that have attempted to address this problem, demonstrating that VSA can be used to invert image translations and ensure consistency with the source domain. Given its inherent versatility, we hope this work inspires future research using VSA in more computer vision applications.

Acknowledgments. We thank Mihir Jain, Shingo Takagi, Patrick Rodriguez, Sarah Watson, Zijian He, Peizhao Zhang, and Tao Xu for their helpful feedback.

References

1. Ahmad, S., Hawkins, J.: Properties of sparse distributed representations and their application to hierarchical temporal memory. arXiv preprint arXiv:1503.07469 (2015)
2. Almahairi, A., Rajeshwar, S., Sordoni, A., Bachman, P., Courville, A.: Augmented cyclegan: Learning many-to-many mappings from unpaired data. In: International Conference on Machine Learning, pp. 195–204. PMLR (2018)
3. Benaim, S., Wolf, L.: One-sided unsupervised domain mapping. In: Advances in neural Information Processing Systems 30 (2017)
4. Bińkowski, M., Sutherland, D.J., Arbel, M., Gretton, A.: Demystifying mmd gans. arXiv preprint arXiv:1801.01401 (2018)
5. Chen, L.C., Papandreou, G., Schroff, F., Adam, H.: Rethinking atrous convolution for semantic image segmentation. arXiv preprint arXiv:1706.05587 (2017)
6. Cordts, M., et al.: The cityscapes dataset for semantic urban scene understanding. In: CVPR (2016)
7. Devaranjan, J., Kar, A., Fidler, S.: Meta-sim2: unsupervised learning of scene structure for synthetic data generation. In: European Conference on Computer Vision, pp. 715–733. Springer (2020). https://doi.org/10.1007/978-3-030-58520-4_42
8. Fu, H., Gong, M., Wang, C., Batmanghelich, K., Zhang, K., Tao, D.: Geometry-consistent generative adversarial networks for one-sided unsupervised domain mapping. In: Proceedings of the IEEE/CVF Conference on Computer Vision and Pattern Recognition, pp. 2427–2436 (2019)
9. Gayler, R.W.: Vector symbolic architectures answer jackendoff's challenges for cognitive neuroscience. arXiv preprint cs/0412059 (2004)
10. Goodfellow, I., et al.: Generative adversarial nets. In: Advances in Neural Information Processing Systems 27 (2014)
11. Hoffman, J., et al.: Cycada: cycle-consistent adversarial domain adaptation. In: International Conference on Machine Learning, pp. 1989–1998. PMLR (2018)
12. Huang, X., Liu, M.Y., Belongie, S., Kautz, J.: Multimodal unsupervised image-to-image translation. In: Proceedings of the European Conference on Computer Vision (ECCV), pp. 172–189 (2018)
13. Isola, P., Zhu, J.Y., Zhou, T., Efros, A.A.: Image-to-image translation with conditional adversarial networks. In: Proceedings of the IEEE Conference on Computer Vision and Pattern Recognition, pp. 1125–1134 (2017)
14. Jia, Z., et al.: Semantically robust unpaired image translation for data with unmatched semantics statistics. In: Proceedings of the IEEE/CVF International Conference on Computer Vision, pp. 14273–14283 (2021)
15. Kanerva, P.: Hyperdimensional computing: an introduction to computing in distributed representation with high-dimensional random vectors. Cogn. Comput. $1(2)$, 139–159 (2009). https://doi.org/10.1007/s12559-009-9009-8
16. Kar, A., et al: Meta-sim: learning to generate synthetic datasets. In: Proceedings of the IEEE/CVF International Conference on Computer Vision, pp. 4551–4560 (2019)
17. Kent, S., Olshausen, B.: A vector symbolic approach to scene transformation. Cognitive computational neuroscience (ccn 2017) (extended abstract) [link] (2017)
18. Kim, T., Cha, M., Kim, H., Lee, J.K., Kim, J.: Learning to discover cross-domain relations with generative adversarial networks. In: International Conference on Machine Learning, pp. 1857–1865. PMLR (2017)

19. Kingma, D.P., Ba, J.: Adam: a method for stochastic optimization. In: ICLR (2015)
20. Kleyko, D., Rachkovskij, D.A., Osipov, E., Rahim, A.: A survey on hyperdimensional computing aka vector symbolic architectures, part ii: applications, cognitive models, and challenges. arXiv preprint arXiv:2112.15424 (2021)
21. Kleyko, D., Rachkovskij, D.A., Osipov, E., Rahimi, A.: A survey on hyperdimensional computing aka vector symbolic architectures, part i: models and data transformations. arXiv preprint arXiv:2111.06077 (2021)
22. Krizhevsky, A., Sutskever, I., Hinton, G.E.: Imagenet classification with deep convolutional neural networks. In: Advances in Neural Information Processing Systems 25 (2012)
23. Lee, H.Y., Tseng, H.Y., Huang, J.B., Singh, M., Yang, M.H.: Diverse image-to-image translation via disentangled representations. In: Proceedings of the European Conference on Computer Vision (ECCV), pp. 35–51 (2018)
24. Lim, J.H., Ye, J.C.: Geometric gan. arXiv preprint arXiv:1705.02894 (2017)
25. Liu, M.Y., Breuel, T., Kautz, J.: Unsupervised image-to-image translation networks. In: Advances in Neural Information Processing Systems 30 (2017)
26. Montone, G., O'Regan, J.K., Terekhov, A.V.: Hyper-dimensional computing for a visual question-answering system that is trainable end-to-end. arXiv preprint arXiv:1711.10185 (2017)
27. Neubert, P., Schubert, S.: Hyperdimensional computing as a framework for systematic aggregation of image descriptors. In: Proceedings of the IEEE/CVF Conference on Computer Vision and Pattern Recognition, pp. 16938–16947 (2021)
28. Neubert, P., Schubert, S., Protzel, P.: An introduction to hyperdimensional computing for robotics. KI-Künstliche Intelligenz 33(4), 319–330 (2019). https://doi.org/10.1007/s13218-019-00623-z
29. Osipov, E., et al.: Hyperseed: unsupervised learning with vector symbolic architectures. arXiv preprint arXiv:2110.08343 (2021)
30. Park, T., Efros, A.A., Zhang, R., Zhu, J.Y.: Contrastive learning for unpaired image-to-image translation. In: European Conference on Computer Vision, pp. 319–345. Springer (2020). https://doi.org/10.1007/978-3-030-58545-7_19
31. Prakash, A., Debnath, S., Lafleche, J.F., Cameracci, E., Birchfield, S., Law, M.T., et al.: Self-supervised real-to-sim scene generation. In: Proceedings of the IEEE/CVF International Conference on Computer Vision, pp. 16044–16054 (2021)
32. Purdy, S.: Encoding data for htm systems. arXiv preprint arXiv:1602.05925 (2016)
33. Richter, S.R., AlHaija, H.A., Koltun, V.: Enhancing photorealism enhancement. arXiv preprint arXiv:2105.04619 (2021)
34. Richter, S.R., Vineet, V., Roth, S., Koltun, V.: Playing for data: Ground truth from computer games. In: European Conference on Computer Vision, pp. 102–118. Springer (2016). https://doi.org/10.1007/978-3-319-46475-6_7
35. Schlegel, K., Neubert, P., Protzel, P.: A comparison of vector symbolic architectures. Artif. Intell. Rev. 1–33 (2021). https://doi.org/10.1007/s10462-021-10110-3
36. Simonyan, K., Zisserman, A.: Very deep convolutional networks for large-scale image recognition. arXiv preprint arXiv:1409.1556 (2014)
37. Szegedy, C., Vanhoucke, V., Ioffe, S., Shlens, J., Wojna, Z.: Rethinking the inception architecture for computer vision. In: Proceedings of the IEEE Conference on Computer Vision and Pattern Recognition, pp. 2818–2826 (2016)
38. Yi, Z., Zhang, H., Tan, P., Gong, M.: Dualgan: unsupervised dual learning for image-to-image translation. In: Proceedings of the IEEE International Conference on Computer Vision, pp. 2849–2857 (2017)
39. Zhu, J.Y., Park, T., Isola, P., Efros, A.A.: Unpaired image-to-image translation using cycle-consistent adversarial networks. In: Proceedings of the IEEE International Conference on Computer Vision, pp. 2223–2232 (2017)

UniNet: Unified Architecture Search with Convolution, Transformer, and MLP

Jihao Liu[1,2], Xin Huang[1], Guanglu Song[2], Hongsheng Li[1(✉)], and Yu Liu[2]

[1] CUHK, MMLab, Hong Kong, China
hsli@ee.cuhk.edu.hk
[2] SenseTime Research, Hong Kong, China

Abstract. Recently, transformer and multi-layer perceptron (MLP) architectures have achieved impressive results on various vision tasks. However, how to effectively combine those operators to form high-performance hybrid visual architectures still remains a challenge. In this work, we study the learnable combination of convolution, transformer, and MLP by proposing a novel unified architecture search approach. Our approach contains two key designs to achieve the search for high-performance networks. First, we model the very different searchable operators in a unified form, and thus enable the operators to be characterized with the same set of configuration parameters. In this way, the overall search space size is significantly reduced, and the total search cost becomes affordable. Second, we propose context-aware downsampling modules (DSMs) to mitigate the gap between the different types of operators. Our proposed DSMs are able to better adapt features from different types of operators, which is important for identifying high-performance hybrid architectures. Finally, we integrate configurable operators and DSMs into a unified search space and search with a Reinforcement Learning-based search algorithm to fully explore the optimal combination of the operators. To this end, we search a baseline network and scale it up to obtain a family of models, named UniNets, which achieve much better accuracy and efficiency than previous ConvNets and Transformers. In particular, our UniNet-B5 achieves 84.9% top-1 accuracy on ImageNet, outperforming EfficientNet-B7 and BoTNet-T7 with 44% and 55% fewer FLOPs respectively. By pretraining on the ImageNet-21K, our UniNet-B6 achieves 87.4%, outperforming Swin-L with 51% fewer FLOPs and 41% fewer parameters. Code is available at https://github.com/Sense-X/UniNet.

Keywords: Deep learning architectures · Neural architecture search

1 Introduction

Convolutional Neural Networks (CNNs) dominate the learning of visual representations and show effectiveness on various visual tasks, including image classification, object detection, semantic segmentation, etc. Recently, convolution-free backbones show impressive performances on image classification [7]. Vision

© The Author(s), under exclusive license to Springer Nature Switzerland AG 2022
S. Avidan et al. (Eds.): ECCV 2022, LNCS 13681, pp. 33–49, 2022.
https://doi.org/10.1007/978-3-031-19803-8_3

Transformer (ViT) [8] demonstrates that pure transformer architecture that is mainly built on multi-head self-attentions (MSAs) can attain state-of-the-art performance when trained on large-scale datasets (e.g., ImageNet-21K, JFT-300M). MLP-Mixer [32] introduced a pure multi-layer perceptron (MLP) architecture that can almost match ViT's performance without using the time-consuming attention mechanism. The main operators in those networks perform differently in terms of efficiency and data utilization. On the one hand, convolutions in CNNs are locally connected and their weights are input-independent, which makes it effective at extracting low-level representations and efficient under the low-data regime. On the other hand, MSAs in the transformer capture long-range dependency, and the attention weights are dynamically dependent on the input representations. Hence, it is more data and computation demanding. The token-mixing in MLP-Mixer performs like a depthwise convolution of a full receptive field with parameter sharing, which is also data demanding. It is an important topic to study how to combine them effectively to form high-performance hybrid visual architectures, which, however, remains a challenge.

There were recent papers on attempting to manually combine the different types of operators to form hybrid visual networks. In ViT [8], a hybrid architecture using ResNet and transformer is also studied and improves upon pure transformers for smaller model sizes. Besides, many other works [5,6,9,11,13,42,43] also explored the combination of convolution and transformer to form hybrid architectures to improve data or computation efficiency. Furthermore, the combination of convolution and MLP is studied in [18], and the combination of gated MLP and MSA is studied in [19]. Those approaches focus on combining two distinct operators and can achieve satisfactory performances to some extent. However, a unified view and a systematical study are missed in prior arts.

We identify two key challenges when building high-performance hybrid architectures: (1) The operators can be implemented with various styles, and it is infeasible to manually explore all possible implementations and combinations. Although we can automate the exploration with Neural Architecture Search (NAS) techniques, the search space should be properly designed so that the search cost is affordable. (2) Each operator has its own characteristics, and simply combining them together does not lead to optimal results. We conduct a simple pilot study on directly stacking different operators to form hybrid networks. As shown in Table 1, however, the straightforward stacking of different operators achieves even worse performance than the vanilla ViT.

Table 1. ImageNet top-1 accuracy of different operator combinations. T and M refer to transformer block and MLP-Mixer block respectively. Different block numbers are chosen so that their computations are comparable.

Model	Configuration	#Params (M)	#FLOPs (G)	Top-1 Acc.
ViT	12 T	22	4.6	**78.0**
MLP-Mixer	18 M	23	4.7	76.8
ViT-MLP	7 T + 7 M	22	4.5	76.5
MLP-ViT	7 M + 7 T	22	4.5	77.8

In this paper, we study the learnable combination of convolution, transformer, and MLP by proposing a novel unified architecture search approach. Our

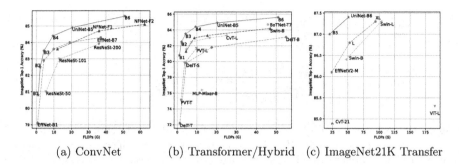

(a) ConvNet   (b) Transformer/Hybrid   (c) ImageNet21K Transfer

Fig. 1. ImageNet top-1 accuracy vs. FLOPs. Our UniNet-B5 achieve 84.9% with ImageNet-1K dataset, outperforming EfficientNet-B7 and BoTNet-T7 with 44% and 55% fewer FLOPs, respectively. Our UniNet-B6 achieve 87.4% on ImageNet-1K with ImageNet-21K pre-training, outperforming EfficientNetV2-XL with 46% fewer FLOPs.

approach has two key designs to address the challenges mentioned above. First, we model distinct operators in a unified form, and use the same set of searchable configuration parameters (i.e., *OP type, expansion, channels*, etc.) to characterize each of the different operators. The unified design enables us to greatly reduce the overall search space, and as a result, the total search cost becomes affordable. Besides, we propose context-aware downsampling modules (DSMs) to harmonize the combination of different operators. The proposed DSMs can be instantiated into three types, i.e., Local-DSM (L-DSM), Local-Global-DSM (LG-DSM), and Global-DSM (G-DSM), aiming to better adapt the representations from one operator to another. Based on these designs, we build a unified search space consisting of a large family of different general operators (GOPs), DSMs, and network size, and jointly optimize model accuracy and FLOPs for identifying high-performance hybrid networks. We illustrate the search space and the backbone in Fig. 2.

The discovered network, named UniNet, exhibits strong performance and efficiency improvements over common ConvNets, Transformers, or hybrid architectures on various visual benchmarks. Our experiments show that UniNet has the following characteristics: (1) placing convolutions in the shallow layers and transformers in the deep layers, (2) allocating a similar amount of FLOPs for both convolutions and transformers, and (3) inserting L-DSM to downsample for convolutions and LG-DSM for transformers. Our analysis shows that the conclusion is consistent among the top-5 models.

To go even further, we build a family of high-performance UniNet models by scaling up the searched baseline network, which achieves better accuracy and efficiency in both small and large model sizes. In particular, our UniNet-B5 achieves comparable accuracy (+0.1%) to EfficientNet-B7 while requires much less computation cost (−44%) (Fig. 1 (a)). By pretraining on large-scale ImageNet-21K, our UniNet-B6 achieves 87.4% accuracy, outperforming Swin-L with fewer FLOPs (−51%) and parameters (−41%) (Fig. 1(c)).

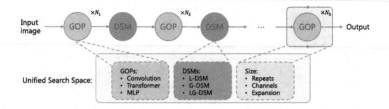

Fig. 2. Unified Architecture Search. We jointly search different types of operators as well as downsampling modules (DSM) and network size in a unified search space. We construct UniNet architecture in a multi-stage fashion. Between two successive stages, one of the DSMs is inserted to change the spatial dimension or channels.

2   Related Works

Convolution, Transformer, and MLP. A host of ConvNets have been proposed to push forward the state-of-the-art computer vision approaches such as [14,28,30]. Despite the numerous CNN models, their basic operators, convolution, are the same. Recently, [8] proposed a pure transformer-based image classification model ViT, which achieves impressive performance on the ImageNet benchmark. DeiT [34] shows that well-trained ViT can obtain a better performance-speed trade-off than ConvNets. PVT [41] and Swin [21] propose multi-stage vision transformers, which can be easily transferred to other downstream tasks. On the other hand, recent papers are attempting to use only MLP as the building block. MLP-Mixer [32], ResMLP [33], and ViP [15] show that pure MLP architectures can also achieve near state-of-the-art performance.

Combination of Different Operators. Another line of work tries to combine different operators to form new networks. CvT [42] propose to incorporate self-attention and convolution by generating Q, K, and V in self-attention with convolution. ConViT [6] tries to unify convolution and self-attention with gated positional self-attention and is more sample-efficient than self-attention. Many other works [5,9,11,13] also explored the combination of convolution and transformer to form hybrid architectures to improve the data or computation efficiency. Besides, ConvMLP [18] studied the combination of convolution and MLP, and gMLP [19] studied the combination of gated MLP and multi-head self-attentions (MSA). Instead of requiring manual exploration of the hybrid architectures, we propose a unified architecture search approach to automatically search for high-performance hybrid architecture.

3   Method

3.1   Unified Architecture Search

As discussed in previous works [6], an appropriate combination of convolution and transformer operators can lead to performance improvements. However, the previous approaches [42,43] only adopt convolution in self-attention or feed-forward network (FFN) sub-layers and stack them repeatedly. Their approaches did not fully explore the combinations to take advantage of their different characteristics.

Prior arts [40,44] show that the downsampling module plays an important role in visual tasks. Most previous approaches adopt hand-crafted downsampling operations, i.e., strided convolution, max-pooling, or avg-pooling, to downsample the feature map based on only the local context. However, these operations are specifically designed for ConvNets, and might not be suitable to the transformer or MLP based architectures, which capture representation globally.

In this paper, we investigate the learnable combination of convolution, transformer, and MLP[1], trying to assemble them to create high-performance hybrid visual network architectures. For better transmitting features across different operator blocks, we proposed context-aware downsampling modules. We jointly search the operators, downsampling modules, and network size in a unified search space. In contrast, previous Neural Architecture Search (NAS) works achieved state-of-the-art performances mainly via searching the network sizes. We show that the searched hybrid architecture by our unified architecture search approach can achieve very promising performance.

In the remaining parts of the section, we firstly present how to properly define different operators into a unified search space and search them jointly. We then present the challenge of incorporating downsampling modules with different operators and present our proposed context-aware downsampling module. Finally, we will introduce our UniNet architectures and NAS pipeline.

3.2 Modeling Convolution, Transformer, MLP with a Unified Searchable Form

Recently, transformer and MLP based architectures are able to achieve comparable performance to convolution networks on different visual tasks. To achieve better performance, it is intuitive to assemble all the types of operators to build high-performance hybrid networks. Actually, a few works [6,42,43] have been studied to empirically combine convolution and self-attention. However, manually searching network architectures is quite time-consuming and cannot ensure optimal performances with different computational budgets.

We introduce a unified search space that contains General Operators (GOPs, including convolution, transformer, and MLP), and then search for the optimal combination of those operators jointly. Compared with prior arts, we propose a unified form to characterize different operators. Specifically, we use the inverted residual [24] to model a general block, which first expands the input channel c to a larger size ec, and then projects the ec channels back to c for residual connection. The e is defined as the expansion ratio, which is usually a small integer number, e.g., 4. The general operation block is therefore modeled as

---

[1] Here, MLP refers to a MLP-style sub-layer that captures spatial representations [15,32,33], instead of pure 1×1 convolution.

$$y = x + \text{Operation}(x), \tag{1}$$

where Operation can be convolution, MLP, or transformer, and x, y represent input and output features, respectively. For convolution, we place the convolution operation inside the bottleneck [24], which can be expressed as

$$\text{Operation}(x) = \text{Proj}_{ec \to c}(\text{Conv}(\text{Proj}_{c \to ec}(x))). \tag{2}$$

The Conv operation can be either regular convolution or depth-wise convolution (DWConv) [3], and the Proj represents a linear projection. For self-attention in transformer and token-mixing in MLP, the computation cost on the large bottleneck feature map is quite huge. Following previous works [8,32], we separate them from the bottleneck for computation efficiency, and the Proj is implemented inside the FFN [37] sub-layer. Each transformer block has a query-key-value self-attention sub-layer and an FFN sub-layer, and the token-mixing in the MLP block is implemented by transpose-FFN-transpose as that in [32],

$$y = y' + \text{FFN}(y'), \tag{3}$$
$$y' = x + \text{SA}(x) \text{ or } x + \text{MLP}(x), \tag{4}$$
$$\text{FFN}(y') = \text{Proj}_{ec \to c}(\text{Proj}_{c \to ec}(y')), \tag{5}$$

where SA can be either vanilla self-attention or local self-attention LSA, and MLP refers to the token-mixing operation.

There are two main advantages of representing the different types of operators in a unified search space: (1) We can characterize each operator with the same set of configuration parameters (i.e., *OP type, expansion, channels*, etc). As a result, the overall search space is greatly reduced, and the total search cost becomes affordable. (2) With the unified form, the comparison between operators is fairer, which is important for NAS [29] to identify the optimal hybrid architecture.

3.3   Context-Aware Downsampling Modules

As discussed in Sect. 3.1, the downsampling module (DSM) plays an important role in visual tasks. In addition to hand-crafted DSM (i.e., max-pooling or avg-pooling), a few works [10,23,40] tried to preserve more information via downsampling with the learnable or dynamic kernel. Most of the approaches utilized downsampling based on local context, which suits conventional ConvNets well. However, in our unified search space, operators with different receptive fields can be assembled unrestrictedly to form a hybrid architecture, where the local context might be destroyed and therefore the previous downsampling operations might not be suitable.

In this paper, we propose context-aware DSM, which is instanced with Local-DSM (L-DSM), Local-Global-DSM (LG-DSM), and Global-DSM (G-DSM). The main difference between those DSMs is the considered context when performing

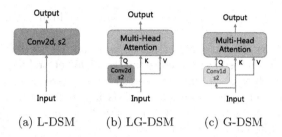

(a) L-DSM   (b) LG-DSM   (c) G-DSM

Fig. 3. Structures of the context-aware downsampling modules. The three DSMs are described in Sect. 3.3. Shortcuts are omitted for better visualization.

downsampling. For L-DSM, only local context is involved, which fits ConvNets well as shown in previous works [21,41]. For G-DSM, only global context is used for downsampling, which may fit other operators, e.g., transformers. The LG-DSM combines the characteristics of L-DSM and G-DSM. It uses both local and global context for downsampling. Our intuition is that one of the largest dissimilarities of different operators is the receptive field. Transformer and MLP naturally have global receptive filed, while convolution has local receptive field, e.g., 3×3. When combining those operators, there is no single optimal DSM that satisfies all scenarios.

The proposed DSMs are visualized in Fig. 3. To downsample based on global cues, we utilize the self-attention mechanism to capture global context, which is missed by the prior art. For G-DSM, we use `Conv1D` with stride 2 to downsample the query and use the downsampled query features to aggregate key features with downsampled output resolution. Note that, there is no local context preserved after downsampling of G-DSM. For LG-DSM, we first reshape the flattened token sequences back to the spatial grid and apply `Conv2D` with stride 2 to downsample the query, and then flatten the query back to calculate the attention weights.

Compared with previous works, which mainly try to improve ConvNets, our proposed DSMs are not designed for a specific architecture. Our motivation is that different DSMs might be suitable for different operators. For example, the optimal DSM might be L-DSM for ConvNets, but G-DSM for transformers. As thousands of operator combinations would be trained in our NAS process, it is unfeasible to decide which DSM to use by hand. To obtain the optimal architecture, we jointly search DSMs with other operators. In our searched optimal architecture, L-DSM is indeed used between operators with the local receptive field while LG-DSM is favored by operators with a global receptive field. The results validate the effectiveness of our proposed context-aware DSMs.

3.4   UniNet Architecture

As shown in recent studies, combining different operators [42,43] can bring performance improvements. Most previous approaches only repeatedly stack the same operator in the whole architecture and search only different channels in different stages. These approaches do not allow large architecture diversity in each block, which we show is crucial for achieving high accuracy for hybrid architectures.

On the contrary, in our UniNet, the operators are not fixed but searched from the unified search space. We construct our UniNet architecture in a multi-stage fashion, which can be easily transferred to downstream tasks. Between two successive stages, one of our proposed DSMs is inserted to reduce the spatial dimension. We jointly search the GOP and DSM for all stages. The GOP could be different for different stages but repeated multiple times in one stage, which can greatly reduce the search space size as pointed out before [29]. The overall architecture and unified search space are illustrated in Fig. 2.

Thanks to our unified form of GOPs, the network size of each stage can be configured with the repeat number r, channel size c, and expansion ratio e. To obtain better computation-accuracy trade-off, we jointly search the network size with the GOP and DSM. For GOP, we search for convolution, transformer, MLP, and their promising variants, i.e., {SA, LSA, Conv, DWConv, MLP}, as defined in Sect. 3.2; for e, we search from {2, 3, 4, 5, 6}. The kernel size for convolution operation is fixed to 3 × 3. The head dimension in self-attention is fixed to 32. We start the architecture search with an initial architecture, whose network size is determined based on a reference architecture, e.g., EfficientNetV2 [31]. The initial channels and repeats are set according to the reference architecture. For c and r, we search from the sets {0.5, 0.75, 1.0, 1.25, 1.5} and {−2, −1, 0, 1, 2}, respectively. Channels are set to be divisible by 32 for self-attention. Suppose we partition the network into K stages, and each stage has a sub-search space of size S. Then the total search space is S^K. In our implementation, K is set to 5 and S equals 1,875. As a result, our search space size is about 2×10^{16} and covers a large set of operators with quite different characteristics.

3.5 Search Algorithm

We use Reinforcement Learning (RL)-based search algorithm to search for high-performance hybrid architecture in our unified search space by jointly optimizing the model accuracy and FLOPs. Concretely, we follow previous work [20,29] and map an architecture in the unified search space to a list of tokens, which are determined by a sequence of actions generated by a Recurrent Neural Network (RNN). The RNN is optimized with the PPO algorithm [25] by maximizing the expected reward. In our implementation, we simultaneously optimize accuracy and the theoretical computation cost (FLOPs). To handle the multi-objective optimization problem, we use a weighted product customized as [29] to approximate Pareto optimal. For a sampled architecture m, the reward is formulated as $r(m) = a(m) \times (\frac{t}{f(m)})^\alpha$, where function $a(m)$ and $f(m)$ return the accuracy and the FLOPs of m, t is the target FLOPs, and α is a weight factor that balances the accuracy and computation cost. We include more details of the RL algorithm in the supplementary materials.

During the search process, thousands of combinations of GOPs and DSMs are trained on a proxy task with the same setting, which gives us a fair comparison between those combinations. When the search is over, the top-5 architectures with the highest reward are trained with full epochs, and the top-performing one is kept for model scaling and transferring to other downstream tasks.

4   Experimental Setup and Implementation

To find the optimal architecture in our search space, we directly search on the large-scale dataset, ImageNet-1K. We reserve 50 k images from the training set as a validation set. We employ a proxy task setting in the search phase. For each sampled architecture, we train it for 5 epochs and calculate the reward of the architecture with its FLOPs and the accuracy on the validation set. We set the target FLOPs t and weight factor α in the reward function to 550 M and 0.07 respectively [30]. During the search process, totally 2 K models are trained on the proxy task. After that, we fully train the top-5 architectures on ImageNet-1K and preserve the top-performing one for model scaling and transferring to other downstream tasks.

For full training on the ImageNet-1K dataset, we follow the popular training recipe in DeiT [34]. We employ AdamW optimizer [17] with an initial learning rate of 0.001 and weight decay of 0.05 to train UniNet. The total batch size is set to 1024. We totally train for 300 epochs with a cosine learning rate decay and 5 epochs of linear warm-up. We follow the augmentation strategy in DeiT [34] and apply small augmentation for small models and heavy augmentation for large models as introduced in [27,35]. For training efficiency, UniNet-B5 and UniNet-B6 are trained with 224×224 input size and then finetuned on the large resolution. We also pre-train UniNet on a larger ImageNet-21K dataset, which contains 14.2 million images and 21 K classes, to further test UniNet. We pretrain for 90 epochs with AdamW optimizer. We then finetune on ImageNet-1K for 30 epochs and compare the top-1 accuracy on ImageNet-1K with other approaches. We list the details of training and finetuning hyper-parameters in the supplementary materials.

Besides, we also transfer UniNet to downstream tasks, e.g., object detection and instance segmentation on COCO and semantic segmentation on ADE20K. For COCO training, we use the various detection frameworks and train UniNet with the widely-used 1x (12 epochs) and 3x (36 epochs) schedules. For ADE20K training, we use the UperNet framework and train with the same setting as [21]. The training details are listed in the supplementary materials.

5   Main Results

In this section, we firstly present our searched UniNet architecture. We then show the performance of the scaled UniNets on classification, object detection, and semantic segmentation.

Table 2. UniNet-B0 architecture. GOP and DSM represent General Operators and downsampling module respectively. DWConv and SA are described in Sect. 3.2.

Stage	Operator		Network size			FLOPs(M)
	GOP	DSM	e	c	r	
0	DWConv	L-DSM	4	48	2	68
1	DWConv	L-DSM	6	80	4	135
2	DWConv	L-DSM	3	128	4	42
3	SA	LG-DSM	2	128	4	63
4	SA	LG-DSM	5	256	8	187

Table 3. Performance of Top-5 models after fully training. D and A are short for DWConv and SA respectively.

Rank	Configuration	Top-1 Acc.
0	**DDDAA**	**79.1**
1	DDDAA	78.7
2	DDDAD	77.9
3	DDDAA	78.6
4	DDDAA	78.4

5.1 UniNet Model Family

Table 2 shows our searched UniNet-B0 architecture. Our searched architecture has the following characteristics: (1) Placing convolution in the shallow layers and transformers with SA in the deep layers. While the previous work [8] shows that the early-stage transformer blocks learn to gather local representations, our searched architecture directly applies convolution at early stages, which is more efficient. We further compare the top-5 searched models in Table 3, and find the conclusion is close to consistent. The exception is the 3rd model, which uses DWConv at the last stage, but with inferior performance. (2) Allocating a similar amount of computations for both convolutions and transformers. Shown in Table 2, the DWConv stages consume 245 M FLOPs, and SA stages consume 250 M FLOPs. While the operator combination has been studied in prior arts, the computation allocating for different operators is neglected. Our work shed some light on this question by jointly searching the network size in our unified search space. (3) Inserting L-DSM to downsample for convolutions and LG-DSM for transformers. Our search results show that the widely-used downsampling module is sub-optimal for hybrid architectures. We also notice that the MLP operator has not been chosen in the searched UniNet. We empirically find that the MLP-style operation breaks the spatial structure which is important for visual tasks [16], leading to inferior performance when combined with other operators. We add the visualization in the supplementary materials.

To go even further, we build a family of high-performance UniNet models by scaling up the searched UniNet-B0. We utilize the compound scaling [30] to scale depth, width, and resolution simultaneously. Note that the resolution is scaled with a smaller coefficient compared to EfficientNet [30] for training and memory efficiency. We list the details of UniNet-B1 to UniNet-B6 in the supplementary materials. While most previous transformer-based architectures outperform convolution-based architectures in large model sizes but underperform in small model sizes, UniNet achieves consistently better accuracy and efficiency across B0 to B6.

Table 4. UniNet performance on ImageNet. All UniNet models are trained on the ImageNet-1K dataset with 1.28 M images. C, T, and H denote convolution, transformer, and hybrid architecture respectively.

Model	Family	Input Size	#FLOPs (G)	#Params (M)	Top-1 Acc.
EffNet-B0 [30]	C	224	0.39	5.3	77.1
EffNetV2-B0 [31]	C	240	0.7	7.4	78.7
DeiT-Tiny [34]	T	224	1.3	5.7	72.2
PVT-Tiny [41]	T	224	1.9	13.2	75.1
ConViT-Ti+ [6]	H	224	2	10	76.7
UniNet-B0	H	160	0.56	11.5	79.1
EffNet-B2 [30]	C	260	1	9.2	80.1
EffNetV2-B1 [31]	C	260	1.2	8.1	79.8
RegNetY-4G [22]	C	224	4	20.6	81.9
DeiT-Small [34]	T	224	4.3	22	79.8
PVT-Small [41]	T	224	3.8	24.5	79.8
UniNet-B1	H	224	1.1	11.5	80.8
EffNet-B3 [30]	C	300	1.8	12	81.6
EffNetV2-B3 [31]	C	300	3	14	82.1
Swin-T [21]	T	224	4.5	29	81.3
CoAtNet-0 [5]	H	224	4.2	25	81.6
UniNet-B2	H	256	2.2	16.2	82.5
EffNet-B4 [30]	C	380	4.2	19	82.9
NFNet-F0 [1]	C	256	12.4	71.5	83.6
Swin-B [21]	T	224	15.4	88	83.5
ConViT-B+ [6]	H	224	30	152	82.5
CoAtNet-1 [5]	H	224	8.4	42	83.3
CvT-21 [42]	H	384	24.9	32	83.3
UniNet-B3	H	288	4.3	24	83.5
EffNet-B7 [30]	C	600	37	66	84.3
EffNetV2-M [31]	C	480	24	54	85.1
NFNet-F2 [1]	C	352	62.6	193.8	85.1
BoTNet-T7 [26]	T	384	45.8	75.1	84.7
CoAtNet-1 [5]	H	384	27.4	42	85.1
UniNet-B4	H	320	9.4	43.8	84.4
UniNet-B5	H	384	20.4	72.9	84.9
UniNet-B6	H	448	51	117	85.6

Table 5. Performance on ImageNet with ImageNet-21K pre-train. All models are pre-trained on ImageNet-21K and fine-tuned on ImageNet-1K.

Model	Family	Input Size	#FLOPs (G)	#Params (M)	Top-1 Acc.
EffNetV2-M [31]	C	480	24	55	86.1
ViT-L/16 [8]	T	384	190.7	304	85.3
HaloNet-H4 [36]	T	384	–	85	85.6
Swin-B [21]	T	384	47.1	88	86.4
CvT-21 [42]	H	384	25	32	84.9
UniNet-B5	H	384	20.4	72.9	87
EffNetV2-L [31]	C	480	53	121	86.8
EffNetV2-XL [31]	C	512	94	208	87.3
Swin-L [21]	T	384	103.9	197	87.3
CoAtNet-2 [5]	H	384	49.8	75	87.1
CoAtNet-2 [5]	H	512	96.7	75	87.3
UniNet-B6	H	448	51	117	87.4

Table 6. Comparison with previous efficient architectures. UniNet is trained with knowledge distillation for a more fair comparison.

Model	Family	#FLOPs (M)	Top-1 Acc.
AttentiveNAS [39]	C	491	80.1
AlphaNet [38]	C	491	80.3
FBNetv3 [4]	C	557	80.5
OFA [2]	C	595	80.0
LeViT [12]	H	658	80.0
UniNet-B0	H	555	80.8

5.2   ImageNet Classification Performance

ImageNet-1K. Table 4 presents the performance comparison of our searched UniNet with previous proposed architectures. Our searched UniNet has better accuracy and computation efficiency than previous ConvNets, Transformers, or hybrid architectures.

As shown in Table 4, under mobile setting, our UniNet-B0 achieves 79.1% top-1 accuracy with 555 M FLOPs, outperforming EfficientNetV2-B0 [31] with less FLOPs. In the middle FLOPs setting, our UniNet-B3 achieves 83.5% top-1 accuracy with 4.3 G FLOPs, which outperforms the pure convolution-based EfficientNet-B4, pure transformer-based Swin-B, and hybrid architecture CvT-21. For larger models, our UniNet-B5 achieves 84.9% with 20 G FLOPs, outperforming EfficientNet-B7 and BoTNet-T7 with 44% and 55% fewer FLOPs, respectively. Figure 1(a, b) further visualizes the comparison of UniNet with other architectures in terms of accuracy and FLOPs.

Table 7. Object detection, instance segmentation, and semantic segmentation performance on the COCO val2017 and ADE20K val set. All UniNet models are pre-trained on the ImageNet-1K dataset.

Backbone	#Params (M) Det/Seg	#FLOPs (G) Det/Seg	Mask R-CNN 1x		Mask R-CNN 3x		UperNet mIoU (%)
			AP@box	AP@mask	AP@box	AP@mask	
ResNet18 [14]	31/ −	207/885	34.0	31.2	36.9	33.6	−
ResNet50 [14]	44/ −	260/951	38.0	34.4	41.0	37.1	−
PVT-Tiny [41]	33/ −	208/945	36.7	35.1	39.8	37.4	−
UniNet-B1	28/38	211/877	40.5	37.5	44.4	40.1	42.7
ResNet101 [14]	63/86	336/1029	40.4	36.4	42.8	38.5	44.9
PVT-Small [41]	44/ −	245/1039	40.4	37.8	43.0	39.9	−
Swin-T [21]	48/60	267/945	43.7	39.8	46.0	41.6	44.5
UniNet-B3	42/51	270/940	45.2	41.1	47.9	42.9	48.5

Table 8. Performance on the COCO val2017 with various detection frameworks. The AP@box is reported.

Framework	Cascade-Mask-R-CNN	ATSS	Sparse-R-CNN	Mask-R-CNN
ResNet50 [14]	46.3	43.5	44.5	41.0
Swin-T [21]	50.5	47.2	47.9	46.0
UniNet-B3	51.3	49.8	48.9	47.9

We further compare UniNet-B0 to previous searched efficient architectures in Table 6. Note that for a more fair comparison, we train UniNet-B0 with knowledge distillation. The details of distillation are listed in the supplementary materials. Shown in Table 6, UniNet-B0 achieves 80.8% accuracy with 555 M FLOPs, outperforming other efficient convolution-based or hybrid architectures.

ImageNet-21K. Table 5 presents the performance comparison of UniNet and other architectures with ImageNet-21K pretrain. Notably, UniNet-B5 obtains 87% top-1 accuracy, which outperforms Swin-L with 4× less computation. UniNet-B6 achieves 87.4% top-1 accuracy, which outperforms CoAtNet-2 [5] with 47% less computation. We further visualize the comparison in Fig. 1(c).

5.3   Object Detection and Semantic Segmentation Performance

For object detection and semantic segmentation, we pick UniNet-B1 and UniNet-B3 and use them as the backbone networks for detection and segmentation frameworks. We compare our UniNet with other convolution or transformer-based architectures. For COCO object detection, we use various detection frameworks and compare the performance under 1× and 3× schedules. For ADE20K semantic segmentation we use the UperNet framework and report mIoU (%) for different architectures under the same training setting.

As shown in Table 7, our searched UniNet consistently outperforms convolution-based ResNet [14] and transformer-based PVT [41] or Swin-Transformer [21]. UniNet-B1 achieves 40.5 AP@box, which is 3.8% better than PVT-Tiny but with 15% fewer parameters. UniNet-B3 achieves 45.2 AP@box with 1× schedule and 47.9 AP@box with 3× schedule, which is 1.5% and 1.9% better than Swin-T, respectively. We further test various detection framework and show the results in Table 8, and find that UniNet achieves consistently better performance among others. For ADE20K semantic segmentation, we achieve 48.5% mIoU with 51 M parameters. Compared with transformer-based Swin-T, our UniNet outperforms 4.0% mIoU with a similar parameter size. Besides, compared with convolution-based ResNet101, we achieve 3.6% higher mIoU with 41% fewer parameters. All the results show the effectiveness of our searched UniNet.

6 Ablative Studies and Analysis

In this section, we study the impact of joint search of General Operators and discuss the importance of context-aware downsampling modules (DSMs).

6.1 Single Operator vs. General Operators

Previous works [29,30] mostly focus on the network size search, which uses a single operator, convolution, as the main feature extractor. In comparison, we jointly search the combination of different General Operators (GOPs), i.e., convolution, transformer, MLP, and their promising variants. To verify the importance of GOPs, we keep only one type of operator in the search space and re-run the search experiments under the same settings. After the search, we fully train the top-5 architectures with the highest reward on ImageNet-1K and report the best performance.

Table 9. Performance on ImageNet with different search settings. One type of operator is kept for comparison with the hybrid UniNet.

Model	#FLOPs (G)	#Params (M)	Top-1 Acc.
UniNet-B0	0.56	11.5	**79.1**
Convolution-Only	0.59	11.0	77.7
Transformer-Only	1.2	11.2	78.2
MLP-Only	0.95	11.4	76.8

As shown in Table 9, our searched hybrid architecture consistently achieves better accuracy compared to single-operator-based architectures. The result verifies the effectiveness of our unified architecture search of GOPs, which can take advantage of the characteristics of different operators.

6.2 Fixed vs. Context-Aware Downsampling

When combining different operators into a unified network, the traditional downsampling module, such as strided-conv or pooling, could be sub-optimal. To verify the effectiveness of our proposed context-aware DSMs, we replace the DSMs of our search UniNet with one fixed DSM and compare their performance under the same training setting.

As shown in Table 10, our searched UniNet consistently outperforms its variants that use a single-fixed DSM in all stages. Although we see that using G-DSM or LG-DSM in all stages brings more computation and parameters, the performance does not become better. The result emphasizes the importance of our joint search of GOPs and DSMs.

Table 10. Performance on ImageNet of UniNet with different DSMs. Note that the traditional strided-conv downsampling module is shown in row 2.

Model	#FLOPs (G)	#Params (M)	Top-1 Acc
UniNet	0.56	11.5	**79.1**
w/L-DSM	0.54	11.3	78.5
w/G-DSM	0.77	12.7	76.8
w/LG-DSM	0.72	14.1	78.9

Table 11. Performance comparison on ImageNet of different backbones when equipped with our proposed DSMs.

Model	#FLOPs (G)	#Params (M)	Top-1 Acc.
PVT-Tiny [41]	1.9	13.2	75.1
w/LG-DSM	3.1	17.3	78.6
w/L→LG-DSM	2.0	14.3	77.5
Swin-T [21]	4.5	29.0	81.2
w/LG-DSM	6.4	33.4	81.9
w/L→LG-DSM	4.7	30.0	81.6

Besides, we transfer our proposed DSMs to other popular transformer-based architectures, Swin-Transformer [21] and PVT [41]. Both Swin and PVT have 4 stages. We compare 2 settings: 1) using LG-DSM for 4 stages, as both PVT and Swin are pure transformer architectures 2) using L-DSM for the first two stages while LG-DSM for the latter two stages, which requires less computation. As shown in Table 11, our proposed LG-DSM improves PVT-Tiny and Swin-T for 3.5% and 0.7%, respectively. Using L-DSM in the first two stages has a similar computation compared with the baseline, which improves PVT-Tiny and Swin-T for 2.4% and 0.4%, respectively. To note that, PVT uses a strided-conv for downsampling. As discussed in Sect. 3.3, it is harmful to the main operator in PVT, which has a global receptive field. On the contrary, our proposed DSMs are able to downsample based on both local and global context, and can greatly improve the performance.

7 Conclusion

In this paper, we propose a novel unified architecture search approach to jointly search the combination of convolution, transformer, and MLP. We empirically identify that the widely-used downsampling modules become the performance bottlenecks when the operators are combined. To further improve the performance, we propose context-aware downsampling modules and jointly search them with all operators. We scale the search baseline network up and obtain a family of models, named UniNet, which achieve much better accuracy and efficiency than previous ConvNets and Transformers.

Acknowledgememt. Hongsheng Li is also a Principal Investigator of Centre for Perceptual and Interactive Intelligence Limited (CPII). This work is supported in part by CPII, in part by the General Research Fund through the Research Grants Council of Hong Kong under Grants (Nos. 14204021, 14207319), in part by CUHK Strategic Fund.

References

1. Brock, A., De, S., Smith, S.L., Simonyan, K.: High-performance large-scale image recognition without normalization. arXiv preprint arXiv:2102.06171 (2021)
2. Cai, H., Gan, C., Wang, T., Zhang, Z., Han, S.: Once-for-all: Train one network and specialize it for efficient deployment. arXiv preprint arXiv:1908.09791 (2019)
3. Chollet, F.: Xception: deep learning with depthwise separable convolutions. In: Proceedings of the IEEE Conference on Computer Vision and Pattern Recognition, pp. 1251–1258 (2017)
4. Dai, X., et al.: Fbnetv3: joint architecture-recipe search using neural acquisition function (2020)
5. Dai, Z., Liu, H., Le, Q.V., Tan, M.: Coatnet: marrying convolution and attention for all data sizes. arXiv preprint arXiv:2106.04803 (2021)
6. d'Ascoli, S., Touvron, H., Leavitt, M., Morcos, A., Biroli, G., Sagun, L.: Convit: improving vision transformers with soft convolutional inductive biases. arXiv preprint arXiv:2103.10697 (2021)
7. Deng, J., Dong, W., Socher, R., Li, L.J., Li, K., Fei-Fei, L.: Imagenet: a large-scale hierarchical image database. In: 2009 IEEE Conference on Computer Vision and Pattern Recognition, pp. 248–255. IEEE (2009)
8. Dosovitskiy, A., et al.: An image is worth 16×16 words: transformers for image recognition at scale. arXiv preprint arXiv:2010.11929 (2020)
9. Gao, P., Lu, J., Li, H., Mottaghi, R., Kembhavi, A.: Container: context aggregation network. arXiv preprint arXiv:2106.01401 (2021)
10. Gao, Z., Wang, L., Wu, G.: Lip: Local importance-based pooling. In: Proceedings of the IEEE/CVF International Conference on Computer Vision, pp. 3355–3364 (2019)
11. Gong, C., et al.: Nasvit: neural architecture search for efficient vision transformers with gradient conflict aware supernet training. In: International Conference on Learning Representations (2021)
12. Graham, B., et al.: Levit: a vision transformer in convnet's clothing for faster inference. In: Proceedings of the IEEE/CVF International Conference on Computer Vision, pp. 12259–12269 (2021)
13. Guo, J., et al.: Cmt: convolutional neural networks meet vision transformers. arXiv preprint arXiv:2107.06263 (2021)
14. He, K., Zhang, X., Ren, S., Sun, J.: Deep residual learning for image recognition. In: Proceedings of the IEEE Conference on Computer Vision and Pattern Recognition, pp. 770–778 (2016)
15. Hou, Q., Jiang, Z., Yuan, L., Cheng, M.M., Yan, S., Feng, J.: Vision permutator: a permutable mlp-like architecture for visual recognition. arXiv preprint arXiv:2106.12368 (2021)
16. Islam, M.A., Jia, S., Bruce, N.D.: How much position information do convolutional neural networks encode? arXiv preprint arXiv:2001.08248 (2020)
17. Kingma, D.P., Ba, J.: Adam: a method for stochastic optimization. arXiv preprint arXiv:1412.6980 (2014)
18. Li, J., Hassani, A., Walton, S., Shi, H.: Convmlp: hierarchical convolutional mlps for vision. arXiv preprint arXiv:2109.04454 (2021)
19. Liu, H., Dai, Z., So, D., Le, Q.: Pay attention to mlps. In: Advances in Neural Information Processing Systems 34 (2021)
20. Liu, J., et al.: Fnas: uncertainty-aware fast neural architecture search. arXiv preprint arXiv:2105.11694 (2021)

21. Liu, Z., et al.: Swin transformer: hierarchical vision transformer using shifted windows. arXiv preprint arXiv:2103.14030 (2021)
22. Radosavovic, I., Kosaraju, R.P., Girshick, R., He, K., Dollár, P.: Designing network design spaces. In: Proceedings of the IEEE/CVF Conference on Computer Vision and Pattern Recognition, pp. 10428–10436 (2020)
23. Saeedan, F., Weber, N., Goesele, M., Roth, S.: Detail-preserving pooling in deep networks. In: Proceedings of the IEEE Conference on Computer Vision and Pattern Recognition, pp. 9108–9116 (2018)
24. Sandler, M., Howard, A., Zhu, M., Zhmoginov, A., Chen, L.C.: Mobilenetv 2: inverted residuals and linear bottlenecks. In: Proceedings of the IEEE Conference on Computer Vision and Pattern Recognition, pp. 4510–4520 (2018)
25. Schulman, J., Wolski, F., Dhariwal, P., Radford, A., Klimov, O.: Proximal policy optimization algorithms. arXiv preprint arXiv:1707.06347 (2017)
26. Srinivas, A., Lin, T.Y., Parmar, N., Shlens, J., Abbeel, P., Vaswani, A.: Bottleneck transformers for visual recognition. In: Proceedings of the IEEE/CVF Conference on Computer Vision and Pattern Recognition, pp. 16519–16529 (2021)
27. Steiner, A., Kolesnikov, A., Zhai, X., Wightman, R., Uszkoreit, J., Beyer, L.: How to train your vit? data, augmentation, and regularization in vision transformers. arXiv preprint arXiv:2106.10270 (2021)
28. Szegedy, C., et al.: Going deeper with convolutions. In: Proceedings of the IEEE Conference on Computer Vision and Pattern Recognition, pp. 1–9 (2015)
29. Tan, M., et al.: Mnasnet: platform-aware neural architecture search for mobile. In: Proceedings of the IEEE/CVF Conference on Computer Vision and Pattern Recognition, pp. 2820–2828 (2019)
30. Tan, M., Le, Q.: Efficientnet: rethinking model scaling for convolutional neural networks. In: International Conference on Machine Learning, pp. 6105–6114. PMLR (2019)
31. Tan, M., Le, Q.V.: Efficientnetv2: smaller models and faster training. arXiv preprint arXiv:2104.00298 (2021)
32. Tolstikhin, I., et al.: Mlp-mixer: an all-mlp architecture for vision. arXiv preprint arXiv:2105.01601 (2021)
33. Touvron, H., et al.: Resmlp: feedforward networks for image classification with data-efficient training. arXiv preprint arXiv:2105.03404 (2021)
34. Touvron, H., Cord, M., Douze, M., Massa, F., Sablayrolles, A., Jégou, H.: Training data-efficient image transformers & distillation through attention. In: International Conference on Machine Learning, pp. 10347–10357. PMLR (2021)
35. Touvron, H., Cord, M., Sablayrolles, A., Synnaeve, G., Jégou, H.: Going deeper with image transformers. arXiv preprint arXiv:2103.17239 (2021)
36. Vaswani, A., Ramachandran, P., Srinivas, A., Parmar, N., Hechtman, B., Shlens, J.: Scaling local self-attention for parameter efficient visual backbones. In: Proceedings of the IEEE/CVF Conference on Computer Vision and Pattern Recognition, pp. 12894–12904 (2021)
37. Vaswani, A., et al.: Attention is all you need. In: Advances in Neural Information Processing Systems, pp. 5998–6008 (2017)
38. Wang, D., Gong, C., Li, M., Liu, Q., Chandra, V.: Alphanet: Improved training of supernets with alpha-divergence. In: International Conference on Machine Learning, pp. 10760–10771. PMLR (2021)
39. Wang, D., Li, M., Gong, C., Chandra, V.: Attentivenas: improving neural architecture search via attentive sampling. In: Proceedings of the IEEE/CVF Conference on Computer Vision and Pattern Recognition, pp. 6418–6427 (2021)

40. Wang, J., Chen, K., Xu, R., Liu, Z., Loy, C.C., Lin, D.: Carafe++: unified content-aware reassembly of features. In: IEEE Transactions on Pattern Analysis and Machine Intelligence (2021)
41. Wang, W., et al.: Pyramid vision transformer: a versatile backbone for dense prediction without convolutions. arXiv preprint arXiv:2102.12122 (2021)
42. Wu, H., et al.: Cvt: introducing convolutions to vision transformers. arXiv preprint arXiv:2103.15808 (2021)
43. Yuan, K., Guo, S., Liu, Z., Zhou, A., Yu, F., Wu, W.: Incorporating convolution designs into visual transformers. arXiv preprint arXiv:2103.11816 (2021)
44. Zhang, R.: Making convolutional networks shift-invariant again. In: ICML (2019)

AMixer: Adaptive Weight Mixing for Self-attention Free Vision Transformers

Yongming Rao[1,2], Wenliang Zhao[1,2], Jie Zhou[1,2], and Jiwen Lu[1,2(✉)]

[1] Department of Automation, Tsinghua University, Beijing, China
zhaowl20@mails.tsinghua.edu
[2] Beijing National Research Center for Information Science and Technology, Beijing, China
{jzhou,lujiwen}@tsinghua.edu.cn

Abstract. Vision Transformers have shown state-of-the-art results for various visual recognition tasks. The dot-product self-attention mechanism that replaces convolution to mix spatial information is commonly recognized as the indispensable ingredient behind the success of vision Transformers. In this paper, we thoroughly investigate the key differences between vision Transformers and recent all-MLP models. Our empirical results show the superiority of vision Transformers mainly comes from the data-dependent token mixing strategy and the multi-head scheme instead of query-key interactions. Inspired by this observation, we propose a computationally and parametrically efficient operation named adaptive weight mixing to generate attention weights without token-token interactions. Based on this operation, we develop a new architecture named as AMixer to capture both long-term and short-term spatial dependencies without self-attention. Extensive experiments demonstrate that our adaptive weight mixing is more efficient and effective than previous weight generation methods and our AMixer can achieve a better trade-off between accuracy and complexity than vision Transformers and MLP models on both ImageNet and downstream tasks. Code is available at https://github.com/raoyongming/AMixer.

Keywords: Vision transformers · Adaptive weight mixing

1 Introduction

Recent advances on vision Transformers have pushed the state-of-the-art of various visual recognition tasks, including image classification [12,28,35,54], semantic segmentation [8,28,55], object detection [4,28] and action recognition [1,2]. As a step towards less inductive bias in architecture designs, Vision Transformers

Supplementary Information The online version contains supplementary material available at https://doi.org/10.1007/978-3-031-19803-8_4.

(ViT) [12] and its variants utilize the self-attention mechanism [45] to capture the interactions between different spatial locations by directly learning from the raw data, different from conventional CNNs that are largely relied on human prior knowledge and hand-made choices. More recently, the pure multi-layer perceptrons (MLP) models [41,42] are proposed to further simplify the designs of vision Transformers. By replacing the self-attention layers with spatial MLPs, all-MLP models exhibit a simple and more efficient approach to mix spatial information for visual recognition tasks. However, empirical results suggest all-MLP models without self-attention usually perform inferiorly compared to vision Transformers [28,42].

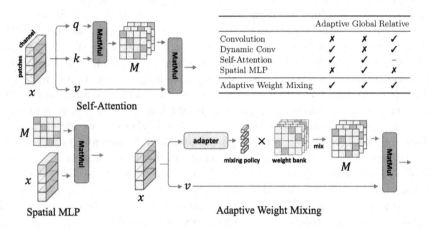

Fig. 1. The main idea of *AMixer*. By analyzing the differences between self-attention and spatial MLP, we propose a new operation named *adaptive weight mixing* to efficiently generate data-dependent spatial mixing weights without token-token interaction. We compare the proposed adaptive weight mixing with prevalent operations by considering three key factors: the input-dependent weight (*adaptive*), global interactions among spatial locations (*global*) and weights based on the relative positions (*relative*) "indicates that only a weak regularization of position-relative weight based on positional embeddings is imposed to self-attention". Our method combines the advantages of previous operations.

The self-attention mechanism is commonly recognized as the key ingredient behind the success of vision Transformers. Self-attention fully considers the relationships among all spatial locations by generating the spatial mixing weights (*i.e.*, attention weights) using the dot product of two projected versions of the input (*i.e.*, queries and keys) and applying the weights to another projected input (*i.e.*, values). Benefiting from the communications among all tokens, vision Transformers can better model long-range dependencies with fewer blocks compared to convolutions [12,51]. Since spatial MLP models also consider all possible interactions between any two spatial locations with learnable mixing weights, it is natural to ask: *which specific designs make self-attention more effective? Is there a more efficient way to learn the spatial mixing weights?*

In this paper, we thoroughly investigate the key differences between vision Transformers and recent all-MLP models. Starting from a simple and neat all-MLP architecture [42], we gradually add the designs in vision Transformers to verify their effects. Our empirical results show the superiority of vision Transformers mainly comes from the data-dependent spatial mixing strategy and the multi-head scheme instead of the query-key interactions in self-attention. Based on this observation, we propose a computationally and parametrically efficient operation called *Adaptive Weight Mixing* to generate attention weights without token-token interactions. Our operation is inspired by the spatial MLP in all-MLP models, where the spatial mixing weights are memory-like model parameters and are learned through standard back-propagation. Different from previous methods that generate the weights with dot-product (*e.g.*, self-attention) or another MLP (*e.g.*, dynamic convolution [15]), our solution makes the static memory *adaptive* to the input by predicting a small weight mixing matrix that linearly blends a set of static weights from a weight bank. By doing so, we avoid the heavy computation of dot-product ($\mathcal{O}(N^2D)$ for N tokens with D-dim features) and a large number of parameters for weight generation ($\mathcal{O}(N^2D)$ for generating $N \times N$ weights from a D-dim feature). Moreover, inspired by the relative positional embeddings [28,37,38], we propose to add the symmetric regularization to the weight bank, where the weight of two positions is only related to their relative position instead of their absolute positions. This strategy can largely reduce the number of parameters in the weight bank since only $\mathcal{O}(N)$ parameters need to be stored. The relative weight also adds the structural priors to the model and makes the input resolution of our model more flexible. Our key idea is illustrated in Fig. 1. We also summarize the differences between our method and other prevalent operations in deep vision models.

Our new adaptive weight mixing operation can serve as a plug-and-play module to replace the self-attention in vision Transformers or spatial MLP in all-MLP models. We propose a new architecture *AMixer* by replacing the self-attention in various vision Transformers with the new operation, which is able to adaptively capture both long-term and short-term spatial dependencies like vision Transformers while having a more efficient weight generation strategy. Equipped with our adaptive weight mixing operation, the enhanced all-MLP models ResMLP [42] and Swin-Mixer [28] can surpass their vision Transformers counterparts DeiT [43] and Swin Transformers [28]. We also scale up AMixer to obtain a series of hierarchical models with different complexities. Extensive experiments show that our adaptive weight mixing is more efficient and effective than previous weight generation methods. AMixer can attain a better trade-off between accuracy and complexity than vision Transformers and MLP models on both ImageNet [36] and downstream tasks.

2   Related Work

Vision Transformers. The Transformer architecture that is originally designed for the NLP tasks [45] has shown promising results on various vision problems since Dosovitskiy *et al.* [12] introduce it to the image classification problem with a patch-based design. A large number of works aim to design more suitable architectures for vision tasks. Some methods are also proposed to improve the training strategy and inference efficiency. Although quite a few kinds of powerful models are designed, most of them are still based on the dot-product self-attention mechanism. In this work, we show that the query-key interaction in vision Transformer may not be necessary, which may provide a new view to design more efficient vision Transformers.

MLP-Like Models. Recently, there are several works that question the importance of self-attention in the vision Transformers and propose to use spatial MLP to replace the self-attention layer in the Transformers [27,41,42]. Although these models are more efficient than the counterpart vision Transformers by removing the dot-product self-attention, this simple modification may bring two drawbacks: (1) the memory-like static spatial MLP usually exhibit weaker expressive power compared to Transformers [28,42]; (2) unlike Transformers, MLP-based models are hard to scale up to a new resolution since the weights of the spatial MLPs have fixed sizes. Our work aims to resolve the above issues in MLP-like models by introducing a new weight generation scheme. Since we store the relative weights instead of the absolute weights in the weight bank, our model can adapt to different input resolutions by interpolating the weight bank.

Dynamic Weights. The self-attention mechanism [45] can be viewed as one of the most popular methods to generate dynamic weights. Learning dynamic weights that are conditioned on the input is also a widely studied problem for CNN models. Previous efforts based on convolutional networks usually focus on predicting adaptive convolution kernels that are shared for the different locations [7,14,21]. Some works also propose to generate region or position-specific weights to better exploit the location information in CNNs [20,26]. However, their methods are designed for generating relatively small kernels (*e.g.*, 3 × 3), which are widely used in CNN-based models. We argue that their generation methods are computational and parametrically expensive to generate large kernels, which makes them hard to scale up to the global interactions considered in this paper. The most related work is Synthesizer [40] which proposes to predict the attention weights using an MLP for NLP tasks. Different from them, we propose a new framework to generate weights by linearly blending weights in a bank, avoiding the large computation and storage cost.

3 Approach

3.1 Vision Transformers and MLP Models: An Unified View

Since vision Transformers [12,28] start to dominate vision tasks, many Transformer-style architectures that pursue the same goal of reducing inductive bias emerged [33,41,42]. Among those, MLP models [27,41,42] replace the self-attention by MLPs that are applied across spatial locations, which are very efficient on modern accelerators. However, the performances of current all-MLP models lag far behind their Transformer counterparts, *e.g.*, 76.6% (ResMLP-12 [42]) *vs* 79.8% (Deit-S [43]) on ImageNet. To examine where the performance drop comes from, we aim to provide an in-depth analysis of the two families of models from a unified perspective. Both vision Transformers and MLP models are built with the following basic block ($\mathbf{X} \in \mathbb{R}^{N \times D}$ is the input, $N = N_H N_W$):

$$\mathbf{X} \leftarrow \mathbf{X} + \mathrm{Mixer}(\mathbf{X}), \tag{1}$$

$$\mathbf{X} \leftarrow \mathbf{X} + \mathrm{MLP}(\mathbf{X}), \tag{2}$$

where the Mixer and the MLP perform spatial mixing and channel mixing, respectively. Generally, the Mixer function can be written in the following form:

$$\mathrm{Mixer}(\mathbf{X}) = \underset{1 \leq h \leq H}{\mathrm{Concat}}(\mathbf{M}_h(\mathbf{X})\mathbf{V}_h(\mathbf{X}))\mathbf{C},$$
$$\mathbf{M}_h \in \mathbb{R}^{N \times N}, \mathbf{V}_h \in \mathbb{R}^{N \times D_h}, \mathbf{C} \in \mathbb{R}^{D \times D}. \tag{3}$$

We consider the multi-head occasion in the above formula. For the h-th head, the $\mathbf{M}_h$ matrix characterizes the interactions among the tokens, and the $\mathbf{V}_h$ projects input to $D_h = D/H$ dimension as the *value*. The $\{\mathbf{V}_h\}_{h=1}^H$ weighted by the $\{\mathbf{M}_h\}_{h=1}^H$ are then concatenated and projected by another matrix $\mathbf{C}$. For vision Transformers [12,28,43], the widely used multi-head self-attention (MHSA) can be derived from Eq. (3) by setting $\mathbf{V}_h(\mathbf{X}) = \mathbf{X}\mathbf{W}_h^V, \mathbf{C} = \mathbf{W}^O$, and

$$\mathbf{M}_h(\mathbf{X}) = \mathrm{Softmax}\left(\frac{\mathbf{Q}_h(\mathbf{X})\mathbf{K}_h(\mathbf{X})^\top}{\sqrt{D_h}}\right),$$
$$\mathbf{Q}_h(\mathbf{X}) = \mathbf{X}\mathbf{W}_h^Q, \mathbf{K}_h(\mathbf{X}) = \mathbf{X}\mathbf{W}_h^K, \tag{4}$$

where the $\mathbf{W}_h^Q, \mathbf{W}_h^K, \mathbf{W}_h^V \in \mathbb{R}^{D \times D_h}$ and $\mathbf{W}^O \in \mathbb{R}^{D \times D}$ are the learnable parameters. For all-MLP models [41,42], the spatial mixing operation is simply performed by a linear layer without the multi-head operation, *i.e.*,

$$H = 1, \mathbf{V}_1(\mathbf{X}) = \mathbf{X}, \mathbf{M}_1(\mathbf{X}) = \mathbf{W}, \mathbf{C} = \mathbf{I}. \tag{5}$$

3.2   Rethinking Self-attention in ViTs

From the analysis in Sect. 3.1, we can identify the differences between the vision Transformers and the all-MLP models. Specifically, vision Transformers contain four components that the all-MLP models do not have: (1) the multi-head scheme; (2) the softmax operation; (3) the V-projection ($\mathbf{V}_h$) and the C-projection ($\mathbf{C}$); (4) the dot-product between the query and the key. In this section, we will investigate whether these factors can bring improvements to the vanilla MLP models. The step-by-step results of our analysis are summarized in Table 1.

Multi-head Scheme. The multi-head self-attention [45] is originally proposed to help the model to attend to multiple positions. One nice property of the multi-head scheme is that it does not induce extra FLOPs. However, it is interesting

Table 1. Starting from ResMLP [42] and surpassing DeiT [43]. We gradually add key ingredients to an all-MLP model ResMLP [42] and show the final model (AMixer) outperform the Transformer DeiT [43] with fewer FLOPs and parameters.

Model	Params.	FLOPs	Acc. (%)
ResMLP-12 [42]	15 M	3.0 G	76.6
+ Multi-head scheme	19 M	3.0 G	$77.4_{(+0.8)}$
+ Extra projections	22 M	3.7 G	$78.0_{(+1.4)}$
+ Softmax	22 M	3.7 G	$78.2_{(+1.6)}$
+ Adaptive weight mixing	26 M	3.9 G	$79.9_{(+3.3)}$
+ Relative attention weight	19 M	3.9 G	$\mathbf{80.3}_{(+3.7)}$
DeiT-S [43]	22 M	4.6 G	79.8

to see that there are rare previous efforts that apply the multi-head scheme to MLPs except [28]. In our experiments, we implement a multi-head MLP model based on ResMLP [42] and find the accuracy on ImageNet can be improved from 76.6% to 77.4%.

Extra Projections. The V-projection and the C-projection are also important, especially when the multi-head scheme is used. Without these projections, interactions across different heads are cut off. We then add the extra projections and find they can further boost the performance by 0.6%.

Softmax. Another difference between self-attention and MLP is the softmax operation. Softmax makes the weighted sum of the row of $\mathbf{V}_h(\mathbf{X})$ bounded and we find it can improve the accuracy to 78.2%.

By far, the performance of the modified MLP is still lower than DeiT [43] and the only difference now is how $\mathbf{M}_h$ is generated. In vision Transformers, the $\mathbf{M}_h(\mathbf{X})$ matrix is *adaptive* because the dot-product between $\mathbf{Q}_h$ and $\mathbf{K}_h$ is conditioned on the input $\mathbf{X}$ while $\mathbf{M}_h$ is simply a memory-like weight in MLPs. Then we ask: can we find another implementation of the adaptive $\mathbf{M}_h(\mathbf{X})$, which is better than the standard dot-product self-attention? To make an attempt towards this interesting question, we propose adaptive weight mixing, a better alternative to self-attention.

3.3   Adaptive Weight Mixing

To obtain the adaptive weights $\{\mathbf{M}_h\}_{h=1}^{H}$, self-attention requires $2ND^2$ FLOPs to compute the query and key and N^2D to perform the dot-product, such that the total FLOPs is

$$\text{FLOPs(SA)} = \underbrace{N^2D}_{\text{dot-product}} + \underbrace{2ND^2}_{\text{compute query and key}} . \tag{6}$$

In this paper, we propose a more efficient method named *adaptive weight mixing* to achieve a similar function to self-attention. Briefly speaking, our adaptive weight mixing learns a weight bank of size B and predicts a mixing policy for each token to generate the $\mathbf{M}_h$ adaptively. Formally, let the weight bank be $\mathcal{W} \in \mathbb{R}^{B \times N \times N}$, which is learnable during training. We then use an adapter to predict the mixing policy based on the input $\mathbf{X}$:

$$\mathbf{\Pi}(\mathbf{X}) = \text{Adapter}(\mathbf{X}) \in \mathbb{R}^{N \times H \times B}. \tag{7}$$

The mixing policy $\mathbf{\Pi}(\mathbf{X})$ is sample-specific and head-specific, which largely increases the diversity. To reduce extra costs induced by predicting the policy, our adapter is designed to be very lightweight as a two-layer MLP.

$$\mathbf{Y} = \text{GELU}\left(\mathbf{X}\mathbf{W}_1^{D \times D'}\right)\mathbf{W}_2^{D' \times HB}, \text{Adapter}(\mathbf{X}) = \text{Reshape}(\mathbf{Y}), \tag{8}$$

where $D' = D/r$ is the hidden dimension with reduction ratio r to reduce computational costs following [21]. With the mixing policy, we can construct the $\mathbf{M}_h$ by

$$\mathbf{M}_{h,i} = \text{Softmax}\left(\sum_{b=1}^{B} \mathbf{\Pi}_{i,h,b}\mathcal{W}_{b,i}\right), \tag{9}$$

where $\mathbf{M}_{h,i}$ denotes the weighting coefficient for the h-th head and the i-th token. The above equation also suggests that our $\mathbf{M}_{h,i}$ is taken from a B-dimension linear space spanned by $\mathcal{W}_{:,i}$. Distinct from self-attention, our method only requires

$$\text{FLOPs}(\text{Ada}) = \underbrace{\frac{ND^2}{r} + \frac{NDHB}{r}}_{\text{adapter}} + \underbrace{N^2BH}_{\text{mixing}} \tag{10}$$

to generate $\mathbf{M}_h$. In our experiments, the typical values of the hyper-parameters are: $B = 16, H = 8, r = 4$. It is easy to show our adaptive weight mixing is more efficient than self-attention since D is usually much larger than BH (*e.g.*, $D = 384$ in DeiT-S [43]). With adaptive weight mixing, we can achieve 79.9% top-1 accuracy on ImageNet, surpassing DeiT-S [43].

Relative Attention Weight. The vanilla design of the weight bank contains too many parameters ($\mathcal{O}(BN^2)$). To make the weight bank more memory-friendly, we propose another variant that considers 2D relative position following the practice in [28]. Consider two points i, j with coordinates (i_h, i_w) and (j_h, j_w), we assume the relation between i, j is only related to their relative position $(i_h - j_h, i_w - j_w)$ and irrelevant to their absolute positions. Therefore, there are only $(2N_H - 1) \times (2N_W - 1)$ possible relative positions and we only need to store a weight bank $\mathcal{W}^{\text{rel}} \in \mathbb{R}^{B \times (2N_H - 1) \times (2N_W - 1)}$ instead of the vanilla version $\mathcal{W} \in \mathbb{R}^{B \times N_H N_W \times N_H N_W}$. As is shown in Table 1, the relative attention weight can further bring an improvement of 0.4% on accuracy and significantly reduce the number of parameters of our model.

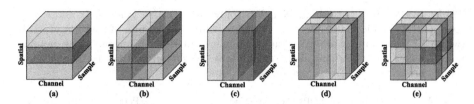

Fig. 2. Comparisons of different weight generation methods. We categorize the methods by whether the weights are data-dependent, spatial-aware, or channel-specific. Some typical operations in each category are: (a) Spatial MLP [42]; (b) Multihead MLP (Sect. 3.2); (c) Convolution; (d) Dynamic Convolution [7,14]; (e) Self-attention [45], Synthesizer [40], and Adaptive Weight Mixing (Sect. 3.3).

Discussions. In Fig. 2, we illustrate various weight generation methods in terms of whether they are data-dependent, spatial-aware, or channel-specific. Among those, Dynamic Convolution [7] aggregates the whole convolutional weights through predicted attention coefficients. Our adaptive weight mixing, however, allows more diverse weights since our mixing policies are different across the heads. Besides, convolution-based methods (Dynamic Convolution [7] and Dynamic Depth-wise Convolution [14]) generate spatial-shared weights while our method can produce unique weights for different spatial locations. Our method is also much more efficient than methods that directly predict the parameters using an MLP including Synthesizer [40] and Dynamic Depth-wise Convolution [14]. Our empirical results also show our method is more effective and efficient than existing dynamic weight generation models (see Sect. 4.3).

3.4 Architecture Variants

The adaptive weight mixing can be easily applied to various network architectures based on self-attention and spatial MLP. Apart from the ViT-like architectures, as is already shown in Table 1, our method is conceptually compatible with hierarchical architectures like Swin Transformers and Swin Mixer [28]. We directly apply our adaptive weight mixing to Swin Transformers to build our hierarchical models, including three variants named AMixer-T, AMixer-S, and AMixer-B. We follow the hierarchical design in Swin [28], where a 4-stage architecture is adopted with $[2, 2, n, 2]$ blocks in each stage. We adjust the number of blocks in the third stage, number of heads, and the MLP ratio to scale our model to have similar FLOPs with the Swin [28] series. Different from Swin, we find setting the MLP ratio to 3 can lead to a better trade-off between accuracy and complexity for our models. We also enlarge the window size to 14 for the third stage benefiting from the proposed highly efficient weight generation method without query-key interactions. We also further scale the ViT-like architecture to 17 layers to match the complexity of the original DeiT-S model. We fix the ratio of the bank size B to the number of heads H as 1.5 for our models due to the decent trade-off between complexity and performance. Note that our models enjoy more diversity with more heads but the performance of standard vision

Table 2. Main results on ImageNet. We apply our adaptive weight mixing to ViT-style and hierarchical architectures. We also include the results of multi-head MLP (MH-MLP) for comparison. We find the multi-head mechanism can bring notable improvements to MLPs and show our adaptive weight mixing can further enhance the performance of MLPs, surpassing self-attention.

Model	Params	FLOPs	Acc(%)	Model	Params	FLOPs	Acc(%)
DeiT-S [43]	22 M	4.6 G	79.8	Swin-T [28]	29 M	4.5 G	81.3
ResMLP-12 [42]	15 M	3.0 G	76.6	Swin-Mixer-T/D6 [28]	23 M	4.0 G	79.7
ResMLP-24 [42]	30 M	6.0 G	79.4	Swin-Mixer-B/D24 [28]	61 M	10.4 G	81.3
MH-MLP-DeiT-S	22M	4.5 G	79.2	MH-MLP-T	27 M	4.5 G	80.7
AMixer-DeiT-S	21M	4.5 G	**80.8**	AMixer-T	28 M	4.5 G	**82.0**

Transformers saturates with the number of heads increasing as shown in [44]. We follow the settings of Swin and do not add any extra convolutional layers except the patch embedding [12] and merging layers [28], while many previous works obtain significant improvement by adding more convolutional layers to capture local patterns [10,22,47,49]. Moreover, we develop a series of pure MLP models that have identical architecture and designs (including all techniques discussed in Sect. 3.2 and relative attention weight) to AMixer series except the adaptive weight mixing strategy as the static counterpart of our models. We refer to them as "MH-MLP" (multi-head MLP) models. More details can be found in Supplementary Material.

4   Experiments

We conduct extensive experiments to verify the effectiveness of our AMixer models and the new adaptive weight mixing operation. We present the main results on ImageNet [36] and compare them with various state-of-the-art vision Transformers and MLP-like architectures. We also test our models on the downstream transfer learning task on relatively small datasets [24,25,31] and semantic segmentation task on the challenging ADE20K [56] dataset. Lastly, we investigate the effectiveness and efficiency of our new designs, and provide the visualization for a better intuitive understanding of our method.

4.1   ImageNet Classification

Setups. We conduct our main experiments on ImageNet [36], a large-scale benchmark dataset for image classification. We follow the standard protocol to train our model on the training set that contains 1.2 M images and evaluate the model on the 50,000 validation images reporting the single-crop top-1 classification accuracy over the 1,000 categories. To fairly compare with previous works on vision Transformers and MLP-like models, we follow the training strategy proposed in DeiT [43], where the model is trained for 300 epochs with the

Table 3. Comparisons with state-of-the-art vision Transformers and MLP-like models on ImageNet. We report the top-1 accuracy on ImageNet as well as the number of parameters and the theoretical complexity in FLOPs. We divide models into three groups based on their complexities. AMixer series exhibit very competitive performances with previous state-of-the-art methods.

Model	Params	FLOPs	Acc(%)	Model	Params	FLOPs	Acc(%)	Model	Params	FLOPs	Acc(%)
gMLP-S [27]	20 M	4.5 G	79.4	ResMLP-36 [42]	45 M	8.9 G	79.7	MLP-Mixer-B [41]	46 M	–	76.4
DeiT-S [43]	22 M	4.6 G	79.8	PVT-Large [47]	61 M	9.8 G	81.7	ViT-B [12]	86 M	17.5 G	79.7
PVT-M [47]	44 M	6.7 G	81.2	T2T-ViT$_t$-19 [53]	39 M	9.8 G	82.2	gMLP-S [27]	73 M	15.8 G	81.6
Swin-T [28]	29 M	4.5 G	81.3	CrossViT-18 [5]	43 M	9.0 G	82.5	DeiT-B [43]	86 M	17.5 G	81.8
CPVT-S [11]	23 M	4.6 G	81.5	GFNet-H-B [33]	54 M	8.6 G	82.9	CPVT-B [11]	88 M	17.6 G	82.3
GFNet-H-S [33]	32 M	4.6 G	81.5	Swin-S [28]	50M	8.7 G	83.0	T2T-ViT$_t$-24 [53]	64 M	15.0 G	82.6
T2T-ViT-14 [53]	22 M	5.2 G	81.5	CycleMLP-B4 [6]	52 M	10.1 G	83.0	Swin-B [28]	88 M	15.4 G	83.3
CycleMLP-B2 [6]	27 M	3.9 G	81.6	Twins-SVT-B [10]	56 M	8.3 G	83.2	Twins-SVT-L [10]	99 M	14.8 G	83.7
AMixer-T	26 M	4.5 G	**82.0**	AMixer-S	46 M	9.0 G	**83.5**	AMixer-B	83 M	16.0G	**84.0**

AdamW optimizer [29] and cosine learning rate scheduler. For ViT-style models, we directly adopt the data augmentation and training strategy of DeiT [43]. For hierarchical models, we follow the training techniques of Swin Transformers [28], where EMA model [32] and repeated augmentation [19] are not used during training. Note that we do not use any extra training tricks [22] to directly compare with baseline methods.

Comparisons with Baseline Models. We apply our new adaptive weight mixing operation to two types of widely used architectures: the original ViT [43] model enhanced with DeiT training strategy [43], and high-performance hierarchical models based on Swin Transformers [28]. We also include the results of our multi-head MLP (MH-MLP) for comparison. The results are presented in Table 2. With similar network architecture and identical training configurations, we see our AMixer achieves +1% performance improvement over DeiT model. By applying our operations to a Swin-Mixer-T/D6 and scaling the model to match the complexity, we also observe that our method outperforms the original Swin-T model by 0.7%. Besides, we find that the multi-head mechanism can bring notable improvements to MLPs, where our modified MLP models can largely improve the ResMLP-12 [42] and Swin-Mixer-T/D6 models by 2.6% and 1.0%. The performance gap between AMixer and MH-MLP (+1.6% and 1.3% for ViT and Swin style model respectively) also clearly shows the neat improvement brought by the adaptive weight mixing. These results strongly demonstrate that our adaptive weight mixing is a more efficient and effective method to generate attention weights than self-attention.

Comparisons with State-of-the-Art Models. By further scaling up AMixer models, we build a series of models based on Swin Transformers to compare with state-of-the-art vision Transformers and MLP-like models as shown in Table 3. We see our method achieves very competitive results compared to previous state-of-the-art networks with a relatively simple design. The building block of AMixer

Table 4. Results on transfer learning datasets. We report the top-1 accuracy on the four datasets and the FLOPs of the models.

Model	FLOPs	CIFAR10	CIFAR100	Flowers	Cars
ResNet50 [16]	4.1 G	–	–	96.2	90.0
EfficientNet-B7 [39]	37 G	98.9	**91.7**	98.8	**94.7**
ViT-L/16 [12]	190.7 G	97.9	86.4	89.7	–
DeiT-B/16 [43]	17.5 G	**99.1**	90.8	98.4	92.1
ResMLP-24 [42]	6.0 G	98.7	89.5	97.9	89.5
Swin-T [28]	4.5 G	98.7	88.7	99.6	91.6
AMixer-T	4.5 G	98.9	89.9	99.6	92.9
AMixer-B	16.0 G	**99.1**	91.0	**99.8**	92.9

consists of only MLPs and our adaptive weight mixing operations, while many previous works add convolutions [10, 47] to better capture local information or use a more sophisticated architecture [5] instead of the standard four-stage network. Since the mainstream research of developing more powerful vision Transformers still uses self-attention as an indispensable ingredient, we believe our method has the potential of applying to most vision Transformers variants and improving their efficiency.

4.2   Downstream Tasks

Transfer Learning. To evaluate the transferability of our AMixer architecture and the learned representation, we follow the commonly used experimental settings [12, 39, 43] to evaluate AMixer on a set of transfer learning benchmark datasets that contain a relatively small number of samples while having substantial domain gaps from the upstream ImageNet dataset. Specifically, we test our lightweight AMixer-T model and a more powerful model AMixer-B on CIFAR-10 [25], CIFAR-100 [25], Stanford Cars [24] and Flowers-102 [31]. Following the setting of previous works, we initialize the models with the ImageNet pre-trained weights and fine-tune them on the new datasets. The results are presented in Table 4. Our models generally have strong transferability on various downstream datasets. Our models also show competitive performance compared to state-of-the-art CNNs and large-scale vision Transformers with relatively low complexity.

Semantic Segmentation. Semantic segmentation is a widely used downstream task to verify the generality of vision Transformers on dense prediction tasks with high input resolution. We evaluate our AMixer model on the challenging ADE20K [56] dataset following previous works [28, 47], where we train two AMixer models that have similar computational complexities with the basic ResNet-50 and ResNet-101 models [16]. We see in Table 5 that our model outperforms the strong Swin models with a similar level of complexity, which suggests our method generalizes well to dense prediction tasks.

4.3 Analysis and Visualization

Robustness & Generalization Ability. We further perform experiments to show our AMixer also has better robustness and generalization ability. For robustness, we consider ImageNet-A, ImageNet-C, FGSM and PGD. ImageNet-A [18] (IN-A) is a challenging dataset that contains natural adversarial examples. ImageNet-C [17] (IN-C) is used to validate the robustness of the model under various types of corruption. We use the mean corruption error (mCE, lower is better) on ImageNet-C as the evaluation metric. FGSM [13] and PGD [30]

Table 5. Semantic segmentation on ADE20K. We report the mIoU on the validation set as well as the number of parameters and theoretical complexity in FLOPs. The models are equipped with the prevalent semantic segmentation method Semantic FPN [23] and UperNet [50]. The FLOPs are measured with 1024 × 1024 input. We divide the models into two groups that have the similar complexities of widely used ResNet-50 and ResNet-101 models [16] respectively.

Backbone	Semantic FPN [23] 80 k			UperNet [50] 160 k		
	FLOPs	Params	mIoU (%)	FLOPs	Params	mIoU (%)
ResNet50 [16]	183 G	29 M	36.7	952 G	67 M	42.1
Swin-T [28]	182 G	32 M	41.5	940 G	60 M	44.5
AMixer-T	169 G	31 M	**43.7**	927 G	58 M	**46.0**
ResNet101 [16]	260 G	48 M	38.8	1029 G	86 M	43.8
Swin-S [28]	274 G	53 M	45.2	1033 G	81 M	47.6
AMixer-S	249 G	51 M	**45.9**	1021 G	78 M	**47.7**

Table 6. Evaluation of robustness and generalization ability. We measure the robustness from different aspects, including the adversarial robustness by adopting adversarial attack algorithms including FGSM and PGD and the performance on corrupted/out-of-distribution datasets including ImageNet-A [18] (top-1 accuracy) and ImageNet-C [17] (mCE, lower is better). The generalization ability is evaluated on ImageNet-V2 [34] and ImageNet-Real [3].

Model	FLOPs	Params	ImageNet		Generalization		Robustness			
			Top-1↑	Top5↑	IN-V2↑	IN-Real↑	FGSM↑	PGD↑	IN-C↓	IN-A↑
DeiT-S	4.6 G	22 M	79.8	95.0	68.4	85.6	40.7	**16.7**	54.6	18.9
Swin-T	4.5 G	28 M	81.2	95.5	69.6	86.6	33.7	7.3	62.0	21.6
AMixer-T	4.5 G	26 M	**82.0**	**96.0**	**71.2**	**87.3**	40.8	13.3	54.0	**25.4**
DeiT-B	17.6 G	87 M	82.0	95.6	70.9	86.7	46.4	21.3	48.5	27.4
Swin-B	15.4 G	88 M	83.4	96.5	72.5	87.8	49.2	21.3	54.4	35.8
AMixer-B	16.0 G	83 M	**84.0**	**96.7**	**73.5**	**88.0**	**51.1**	**26.8**	48.6	**36.5**

are two widely used algorithms that are targeted to evaluate the adversarial robustness of the model by single-step attack and multi-step attack, respectively. For generalization ability, we adopt two variants of ImageNet validation set: ImageNet-V2 [34] (IN-V2) and ImageNet-Real [3] (IN-Real). ImageNet-V2 is a re-collected version of ImageNet validation set following the same data collection procedure of ImageNet, while ImageNet-Real contains the same images as ImageNet validation set but has reassessed labels. We compare two of our models AMixer-T and AMixer-B to both the DeiT [43] and Swin [28] counterparts and find the AMixer models enjoy better generalization ability and robustness (Table 6).

Comparisons with Existing Weight Generation Methods. We first analyze the effectiveness of our new weight generation method compared to previous ones as shown in Table 7. We compare our method with self-attention (DeiT [43]), Synthesizer [40], location-shared weight generation with MLP (DyConv-G [14]) and weight selection (DyConv-S [7]). Under a carefully controlled setting (identical training method following DeiT [43] and same network configurations), we show that our method achieves the best performance among competitive baseline methods with high efficiency, where suggests our method is more suitable and efficient in the scenarios of vision Transformers.

Comparisons with Other Efficient Self-attentions. We compare our adaptive weight mixing with other methods to efficiently approximate self-attention, including Linformer [46], Performer [9], Nystroformer [52] and the linear attention in PVTv2 [48]. For fair comparisons, we use DeiT-S [43] as the basic archi-

Table 7. Comparisons with other weight generation and efficient attention methods. We fix the training strategy and the number of layers or FLOPs to test the effectiveness of different methods.

Model	Params	FLOPs	Acc (%)	Model	FLOPs	Acc (%)
DeiT-S [43]	22 M	4.6 G	79.8	Linformer [46]	4.5 G	77.8
Synthesizer [40]	19 M	3.9 G	78.4	Performer [9]	4.6 G	72.1
DyConv-G [14]	287 M	4.0 G	79.2	Nystroformer [52]	4.6 G	77.1
DyConv-S [7]	30 M	3.7 G	78.6	PVTv2 [48]	4.5 G	79.1
AMixer	19 M	3.9 G	**80.3**	AMixer	4.5 G	**80.8**

Table 8. Data efficiency & convergence speed. We compare the performance of our model and the baseline vision Transformer when trained with fewer data or fewer epochs on ImageNet.

Model	Data ratio			Training epoch		
	10%	50%	100%	50	100	300
DeiT-S [43]	34.0	72.9	79.8	65.7	74.4	79.8
AMixer-DeiT-S	**48.7**	**76.3**	**80.8**	**69.2**	**76.9**	**80.8**

tecture and directly replace the standard self-attention with different efficient self-attentions. We also ensure the FLOPs of all the models to be ~4.6G by stacking enough layers. The results are summarized in Table 7b. We find those efficient self-attentions all fail to bring improvement over the DeiT-S, while our AMixer-Deit-S can outperform the baseline by a significant margin.

Data Efficiency and Convergence Speed. We compare the performance of our model and the baseline vision Transformer when trained with fewer data or fewer epochs on ImageNet. The results are shown in Table 8. We see the advantage of our model becomes more significant when the model is trained with fewer data or epochs. The results indicate that our adaptive weight mixing operation performs better when data and computation resources are limited.

Adaptive Weights Visualization. To investigate how our **M** matrices vary with the input images, we visualize our adaptive weights **M** in Fig. 3. For each image, we first find the token (indicated by the red box) that has the highest classification score on the ground truth category, and visualize the weights corresponded to that token. We include the weights of the 1, 3, 5, 7, 10 and 12-th layer and weights of different heads are averaged. Firstly, we find the weights exhibit notable diversity across different images. Secondly, we show our model tends to attend to the most discriminative part of the images (*e.g.*, in the first row, the weights have higher values near the head of the dog). These visualizations show that our adaptive weights generated without token-token interactions have the similar behavior to the weights obtained by self-attention [12].

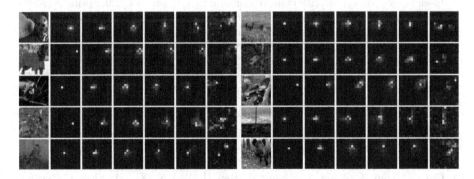

Fig. 3. Our method can generate data-dependent attention weights without token-token interactions. The attention weights in shallow layers usually focus on local regions while the weights of deeper layers adaptively attends to the shape of the whole object.

5 Conclusion

In this paper, we have thoroughly studied the key differences between vision Transformers and recent all-MLP models. Inspired by our empirical results, we

have proposed a new operation named adaptive weight mixing to generate attention weights without token-token interactions. Based on this operation, we have
developed a new architecture AMixer that is computationally and parametrically
more efficient than vision Transformers. Extensive experiments have shown that
our adaptive weight mixing is more efficient and effective than previous weight
generation methods. Our models achieve a better trade-off between accuracy
and complexity than vision Transformers and MLP models on both ImageNet
and downstream tasks.

Acknowledgment. This work was supported in part by the National Key Research
and Development Program of China under Grant 2017YFA0700802, in part by the
National Natural Science Foundation of China under Grant 62125603 and Grant
U1813218, in part by a grant from the Beijing Academy of Artificial Intelligence
(BAAI).

References

1. Arnab, A., Dehghani, M., Heigold, G., Sun, C., Lučić, M., Schmid, C.: Vivit: A
   video vision transformer. arXiv preprint arXiv:2103.15691 (2021)
2. Bertasius, G., Wang, H., Torresani, L.: Is space-time attention all you need for
   video understanding? arXiv preprint arXiv:2102.05095 (2021)
3. Beyer, L., Hénaff, O.J., Kolesnikov, A., Zhai, X., Oord, A.v.d.: Are we done with
   imagenet? arXiv preprint arXiv:2006.07159 (2020)
4. Carion, N., Massa, F., Synnaeve, G., Usunier, N., Kirillov, A., Zagoruyko, S.: End-
   to-end object detection with transformers. In: ECCV. pp. 213–229. Springer (2020)
5. Chen, C.F., Fan, Q., Panda, R.: Crossvit: Cross-attention multi-scale vision transformer for image classification. arXiv preprint arXiv:2103.14899 (2021)
6. Chen, S., Xie, E., Ge, C., Liang, D., Luo, P.: Cyclemlp: A mlp-like architecture for
   dense prediction. arXiv preprint arXiv:2107.10224 (2021)
7. Chen, Y., Dai, X., Liu, M., Chen, D., Yuan, L., Liu, Z.: Dynamic convolution:
   Attention over convolution kernels. In: CVPR. pp. 11030–11039 (2020)
8. Cheng, B., Schwing, A.G., Kirillov, A.: Per-pixel classification is not all you need
   for semantic segmentation. NeurIPS (2021)
9. Choromanski, K., Likhosherstov, V., Dohan, D., Song, X., Gane, A., Sarlos, T.,
   Hawkins, P., Davis, J., Mohiuddin, A., Kaiser, L., et al.: Rethinking attention with
   performers. ICLR (2021)
10. Chu, X., Tian, Z., Wang, Y., Zhang, B., Ren, H., Wei, X., Xia, H., Shen, C.: Twins:
    Revisiting the design of spatial attention in vision transformers. In: NeurIPS 2021
    (2021)
11. Chu, X., Tian, Z., Zhang, B., Wang, X., Wei, X., Xia, H., Shen, C.: Conditional
    positional encodings for vision transformers. arXiv preprint arXiv:2102.10882
    (2021)
12. Dosovitskiy, A., Beyer, L., Kolesnikov, A., Weissenborn, D., Zhai, X., Unterthiner,
    T., Dehghani, M., Minderer, M., Heigold, G., Gelly, S., Uszkoreit, J., Houlsby, N.:
    An image is worth 16x16 words: Transformers for image recognition at scale. arXiv
    preprint arXiv:2010.11929 (2020)
13. Goodfellow, I.J., Shlens, J., Szegedy, C.: Explaining and harnessing adversarial
    examples. arXiv preprint arXiv:1412.6572 (2014)

14. Han, Q., Fan, Z., Dai, Q., Sun, L., Cheng, M.M., Liu, J., Wang, J.: Demystifying local vision transformer: Sparse connectivity, weight sharing, and dynamic weight. arXiv preprint arXiv:2106.04263 (2021)
15. Han, Y., Huang, G., Song, S., Yang, L., Wang, H., Wang, Y.: Dynamic neural networks: A survey. arXiv preprint arXiv:2102.04906 (2021)
16. He, K., Zhang, X., Ren, S., Sun, J.: Deep residual learning for image recognition. In: CVPR. pp. 770–778 (2016)
17. Hendrycks, D., Dietterich, T.: Benchmarking neural network robustness to common corruptions and perturbations. arXiv preprint arXiv:1903.12261 (2019)
18. Hendrycks, D., Zhao, K., Basart, S., Steinhardt, J., Song, D.: Natural adversarial examples. In: CVPR. pp. 15262–15271 (2021)
19. Hoffer, E., Ben-Nun, T., Hubara, I., Giladi, N., Hoefler, T., Soudry, D.: Augment your batch: Improving generalization through instance repetition. In: CVPR. pp. 8129–8138 (2020)
20. Hu, J., Shen, L., Albanie, S., Sun, G., Vedaldi, A.: Gather-excite: Exploiting feature context in convolutional neural networks. arXiv preprint arXiv:1810.12348 (2018)
21. Hu, J., Shen, L., Sun, G.: Squeeze-and-excitation networks. In: CVPR. pp. 7132–7141 (2018)
22. Jiang, Z., Hou, Q., Yuan, L., Zhou, D., Jin, X., Wang, A., Feng, J.: Token labeling: Training a 85.5% top-1 accuracy vision transformer with 56m parameters on imagenet. arXiv preprint arXiv:2104.10858 (2021)
23. Kirillov, A., Girshick, R., He, K., Dollár, P.: Panoptic feature pyramid networks. In: CVPR. pp. 6399–6408 (2019)
24. Krause, J., Stark, M., Deng, J., Fei-Fei, L.: 3d object representations for fine-grained categorization. In: ICCVW. pp. 554–561 (2013)
25. Krizhevsky, A., Hinton, G., et al.: Learning multiple layers of features from tiny images (2009)
26. Li, D., Hu, J., Wang, C., Li, X., She, Q., Zhu, L., Zhang, T., Chen, Q.: Involution: Inverting the inherence of convolution for visual recognition. In: CVPR. pp. 12321–12330 (2021)
27. Liu, H., Dai, Z., So, D.R., Le, Q.V.: Pay attention to mlps. arXiv preprint arXiv:2105.08050 (2021)
28. Liu, Z., Lin, Y., Cao, Y., Hu, H., Wei, Y., Zhang, Z., Lin, S., Guo, B.: Swin transformer: Hierarchical vision transformer using shifted windows. arXiv preprint arXiv:2103.14030 (2021)
29. Loshchilov, I., Hutter, F.: Decoupled weight decay regularization. arXiv preprint arXiv:1711.05101 (2017)
30. Madry, A., Makelov, A., Schmidt, L., Tsipras, D., Vladu, A.: Towards deep learning models resistant to adversarial attacks. arXiv preprint arXiv:1706.06083 (2017)
31. Nilsback, M.E., Zisserman, A.: Automated flower classification over a large number of classes. In: ICVGIP. pp. 722–729 (2008)
32. Polyak, B.T., Juditsky, A.B.: Acceleration of stochastic approximation by averaging. SIAM journal on control and optimization $30(4)$, 838–855 (1992)
33. Rao, Y., Zhao, W., Zhu, Z., Lu, J., Zhou, J.: Global filter networks for image classification. In: NeurIPS (2021)
34. Recht, B., Roelofs, R., Schmidt, L., Shankar, V.: Do imagenet classifiers generalize to imagenet? In: ICML. pp. 5389–5400. PMLR (2019)
35. Riquelme, C., Puigcerver, J., Mustafa, B., Neumann, M., Jenatton, R., Pinto, A.S., Keysers, D., Houlsby, N.: Scaling vision with sparse mixture of experts. arXiv preprint arXiv:2106.05974 (2021)

36. Russakovsky, O., Deng, J., Su, H., Krause, J., Satheesh, S., Ma, S., Huang, Z., Karpathy, A., Khosla, A., Bernstein, M., et al.: Imagenet large scale visual recognition challenge. IJCV **115**(3), 211–252 (2015)
37. Shaw, P., Uszkoreit, J., Vaswani, A.: Self-attention with relative position representations. arXiv preprint arXiv:1803.02155 (2018)
38. Srinivas, A., Lin, T.Y., Parmar, N., Shlens, J., Abbeel, P., Vaswani, A.: Bottleneck transformers for visual recognition. In: Proceedings of the IEEE/CVF Conference on Computer Vision and Pattern Recognition. pp. 16519–16529 (2021)
39. Tan, M., Le, Q.: Efficientnet: Rethinking model scaling for convolutional neural networks. In: ICML. pp. 6105–6114. PMLR (2019)
40. Tay, Y., Bahri, D., Metzler, D., Juan, D.C., Zhao, Z., Zheng, C.: Synthesizer: Rethinking self-attention for transformer models. In: ICML. pp. 10183–10192. PMLR (2021)
41. Tolstikhin, I., Houlsby, N., Kolesnikov, A., Beyer, L., Zhai, X., Unterthiner, T., Yung, J., Keysers, D., Uszkoreit, J., Lucic, M., et al.: Mlp-mixer: An all-mlp architecture for vision. arXiv preprint arXiv:2105.01601 (2021)
42. Touvron, H., Bojanowski, P., Caron, M., Cord, M., El-Nouby, A., Grave, E., Joulin, A., Synnaeve, G., Verbeek, J., Jégou, H.: Resmlp: Feedforward networks for image classification with data-efficient training. arXiv preprint arXiv:2105.03404 (2021)
43. Touvron, H., Cord, M., Douze, M., Massa, F., Sablayrolles, A., Jégou, H.: Training data-efficient image transformers & distillation through attention. arXiv preprint arXiv:2012.12877 (2020)
44. Touvron, H., Cord, M., Sablayrolles, A., Synnaeve, G., Jégou, H.: Going deeper with image transformers. arXiv preprint arXiv:2103.17239 (2021)
45. Vaswani, A., Shazeer, N., Parmar, N., Uszkoreit, J., Jones, L., Gomez, A.N., Kaiser, Ł., Polosukhin, I.: Attention is all you need. In: NeurIPS. pp. 5998–6008 (2017)
46. Wang, S., Li, B.Z., Khabsa, M., Fang, H., Ma, H.: Linformer: Self-attention with linear complexity. arXiv preprint arXiv:2006.04768 (2020)
47. Wang, W., Xie, E., Li, X., Fan, D.P., Song, K., Liang, D., Lu, T., Luo, P., Shao, L.: Pyramid vision transformer: A versatile backbone for dense prediction without convolutions (2021)
48. Wang, W., Xie, E., Li, X., Fan, D.P., Song, K., Liang, D., Lu, T., Luo, P., Shao, L.: Pvtv 2: Improved baselines with pyramid vision transformer. Computational Visual Media **8**(3), 1–10 (2022)
49. Wu, H., Xiao, B., Codella, N., Liu, M., Dai, X., Yuan, L., Zhang, L.: Cvt: Introducing convolutions to vision transformers. arXiv preprint arXiv:2103.15808 (2021)
50. Xiao, T., Liu, Y., Zhou, B., Jiang, Y., Sun, J.: Unified perceptual parsing for scene understanding. In: ECCV. pp. 418–434 (2018)
51. Xie, E., Wang, W., Yu, Z., Anandkumar, A., Alvarez, J.M., Luo, P.: Segformer: Simple and efficient design for semantic segmentation with transformers. arXiv preprint arXiv:2105.15203 (2021)
52. Xiong, Y., Zeng, Z., Chakraborty, R., Tan, M., Fung, G., Li, Y., Singh, V.: Nyströmformer: A nyström-based algorithm for approximating self-attention (2021)
53. Yuan, L., Chen, Y., Wang, T., Yu, W., Shi, Y., Jiang, Z., Tay, F.E., Feng, J., Yan, S.: Tokens-to-token vit: Training vision transformers from scratch on imagenet. ICCV (2021)
54. Zhai, X., Kolesnikov, A., Houlsby, N., Beyer, L.: Scaling vision transformers. arXiv preprint arXiv:2106.04560 (2021)

55. Zheng, S., Lu, J., Zhao, H., Zhu, X., Luo, Z., Wang, Y., Fu, Y., Feng, J., Xiang, T., Torr, P.H., et al.: Rethinking semantic segmentation from a sequence-to-sequence perspective with transformers. arXiv preprint arXiv:2012.15840 (2020)
56. Zhou, B., Zhao, H., Puig, X., Fidler, S., Barriuso, A., Torralba, A.: Scene parsing through ade20k dataset. In: CVPR. pp. 633–641 (2017)

TinyViT: Fast Pretraining Distillation for Small Vision Transformers

Kan Wu[1,3], Jinnian Zhang[2,4], Houwen Peng[3]([✉]), Mengchen Liu[4], Bin Xiao[4],
Jianlong Fu[3], and Lu Yuan[4]

[1] Sun Yat-sen University, Guangzhou, China
[2] University of Wisconsin-Madison, Madison, USA
[3] Microsoft Research Asia, Beijing, China
houwen.peng@microsoft.com
[4] Microsoft Cloud+AI, Redmond, USA

Abstract. Vision transformer (ViT) recently has drawn great attention in computer vision due to its remarkable model capability. However, most prevailing ViT models suffer from huge number of parameters, restricting their applicability on devices with limited resources. To alleviate this issue, we propose TinyViT, a new family of tiny and efficient small vision transformers pretrained on large-scale datasets with our proposed fast distillation framework. The central idea is to transfer knowledge from large pretrained models to small ones, while enabling small models to get the dividends of massive pretraining data. More specifically, we apply distillation during pretraining for knowledge transfer. The logits of large teacher models are sparsified and stored in disk in advance to save the memory cost and computation overheads. The tiny student transformers are automatically scaled down from a large pretrained model with computation and parameter constraints. Comprehensive experiments demonstrate the efficacy of TinyViT. It achieves a top-1 accuracy of 84.8% on ImageNet-1k with only 21M parameters, being comparable to Swin-B pretrained on ImageNet-21k while using 4.2 times fewer parameters. Moreover, increasing image resolutions, TinyViT can reach 86.5% accuracy, being slightly better than Swin-L while using only 11% parameters. Last but not the least, we demonstrate a good transfer ability of TinyViT on various downstream tasks. Code and models are available at https://github.com/microsoft/Cream/tree/main/TinyViT.

Keywords: Pretraining · Knowledge distillation · Small transformer

K. Wu, J. Zhang and H. Peng—Equal contribution. Work done when Kan and Jinnian were interns of Microsoft.

Supplementary Information The online version contains supplementary material available at https://doi.org/10.1007/978-3-031-19803-8_5.

1   Introduction

Transformer [62] has taken computer vision domain by storm and are becoming increasingly popular in both research and practice [8,20,75]. One of the recent trends for vision transforms (ViT) is to continue to grow in model size while yielding improved performance on standard benchmarks [41,54,75]. For example, V-MoE [54] uses 305 million images to train an extremely large model with 14.7 billion parameters, achieving state-of-the-art performance on image classification. Meanwhile, the Swin transformer uses 3 billion parameters with 70 million pretraining images, to attain promising results on downstream detection and segmentation tasks [41,42]. Such large model sizes and the accompanying heavy pretraining costs make these models unsuitable for applications involving limited computational budgets, such as mobile and IoT edge devices [77].

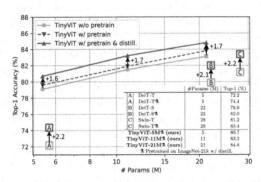

Fig. 1. Comparison of our TinyViT with other small vision transformer models [42,61] on ImageNet-1k in terms of w/ and w/o ImageNet-21k pretraining and distillation. Pretraining with distillation can effectively improve the performance of all these small transformer models, further unveiling their capacities. Best viewed in color. (Color figure online)

In contrast to scaling up models to large scales, this work turns attention to downsizing vision transformers, aiming to generate a new family of tiny models and elevate their transfer capacities in downstream tasks. In particular, we explore the following key issue: *how to effectively transfer the knowledge of existing large-scale transformers to small ones, as well as unleash the power of large-scale data to elevate the representability of small models?* In computer vision, it has long been recognized that large models pretrained on large datasets often achieve better results, while small models easily become saturated (or underfitting) as the growth of data [41,75]. Is there any possible way for small models to absorb knowledge from massive data and further unveil their capacities?

To answer this question, we introduce a fast knowledge distillation method to pretrain small models, and show that small models can also get the dividends of massive pretraining data with the guidance of large models. More specifically, we observe that direct pretraining of small models suffers from performance saturation, especially when the data scale increases. But if we impose distillation during pretraining, using a powerful model as the teacher, the potentials of large-scale pretraining data can be unlocked for small models, as demonstrated in Fig. 1. Meanwhile, the distilled small models can be transferred well to downstream tasks, since they have learned a great deal of knowledge about how to generalize from the large model as well as the large-scale pretraining data. We give a detailed discussion in Sect. 4 exploring the underlying reasons why pretraining distillation is able to further unveil the capacities of small models.

Pretraining models with distillation is inefficient and costly, because a considerable proportion of computing resources is consumed on passing training data through the large teacher model in each iteration, rather than training the target small student. Also, a giant teacher may occupy the most GPU memory, significantly slowing down the training speed of the students (due to limited batch size). To address this issue, we propose a fast and scalable distillation strategy. More concretely, we propose to generate a sparse probability vector as the soft label of each input image in advance, and store it into label files together with the corresponding data augmentation information like random cropping, RandAugment [17], CutMix [73], *etc.* During training, we reuse the stored sparse soft labels and augmentations to precisely replicate the distillation procedure, successfully omitting the forward computation and storage of large teacher models. Such strategy has two advantages: 1) Fast. It largely saves the memory cost and computation overheads of generating teachers' soft labels during training. Thus, the distillation of small models can be largely speed up because it is able to use much larger batch size. Besides, since the teacher logits per epoch are independent, they can be saved in parallel, instead of epoch-by-epoch in conventional methods. 2) Scalable. It can mimic any kind of data augmentation and generate the corresponding soft labels. We just need to forward the large teacher model for only once, and reuse the soft labels for arbitrary student models.

We verify the efficacy of our fast pretraining distillation framework not only on existing small vision transformers, such as DeiT-T [61] and Swin-T [42], but also over our new designed tiny architectures. Specifically, following [21], we adopt a progressive model contraction approach to scale down a large model and generate a family of tiny vision transformers (TinyViT). With our fast pretraining distillation on ImageNet-21k [18], TinyViT with 21M parameters achieves 84.8% top-1 accuracy on ImageNet-1k, being 4.2 times smaller than the pretrained Swin-B (85.2% accuracy with 88M parameters). With higher resolution, our model can reach 86.5% top-1 accuracy, establishing new state-of-the-art performance on ImageNet-1k under aligned settings. Moreover, TinyViT models demonstrate good transfer capacities on downstream tasks. For instance, TinyViT-21M gets an AP of 50.2 on COCO object detection benchmark, being 2.1 points superior to Swin-T using 28M parameters.

In summary, the main contributions of this work are twofold.

- We propose a fast pretraining distillation framework to unleash the capacity of small models by fully leveraging the large-scale pretraining data. To our best knowledge, this is the first work exploring small model pretraining.

– We release a new family of tiny vision transformer models, which strike a good trade-off between computation and accuracy. With pretraining distillation, such models demonstrate good transfer ability on downstream tasks.

2   Related Work

In this section, we review the related work on large-scale pretraining, small vision transformers, and knowledge distillation. It is notable that our work is orthogonal to existing literature on model compression techniques such as quantization [26, 35,43,43] and pruning [38,69,70,81]. These techniques can be used as a post-processing for our TinyViT to further improve model efficiency.

Large-Scale Pretraining. Bommasani *et al.* [6] first coined the concept of foundation models that are pretrained from large-scale data and have outstanding performance in various downstream tasks. For example, BERT [19] and GPT-3 [51] have been demonstrated to be effective foundation models in natural language processing. Recently, there are some research efforts in developing foundation models in computer vision, including CLIP [50], Align [36] and Florence [72]. They have shown impressive transfer and zero-shot capabilities. However, these large models are unsuitable for downstream applications with limited computational budgets. By contrast, our work investigates the pretraining method for small models and improves their transferability to various downstream tasks.

Small Vision Transformers. Lightweight CNNs have powered many mobile vision tasks [33,59]. Recently, there are several attempts developing light vision transformers (ViTs). Mehta *et al.* [44] combined standard convolutions and transformers to develop MobileViT, which outperforms the prevailing MobileNets [33] and ShuffleNet [79]. Gong *et al.* [22] employed NAS and identified a family of efficient ViTs with MACs ranging from 200M to 800M, surpassing the state-of-the-art. Graham *et al.* [24] optimized the inference time of small and medium-sized ViTs and generated a family of throughput-efficient ViTs. Different from these manually designed or automatically searched small models, our work explores model contraction to generate small models by progressively slimming a large seed model, which can be considered as a complementary work to existing literature on scaling-up large vision transformers [12,41,54,75].

Knowledge Distillation. Distillation in a teacher-student framework [31] is widely used to leverage knowledge from large teacher models. It has been extensively studied in convolutional networks [23]. Recently, there are several research works in developing distillation techniques for ViTs [70,80]. For example, Touvron et al. [61] introduced a distillation token to allow the transformer to learn from a ConvNet teacher, while Jia et al. [37] proposed to excavate knowledge from the teacher transformer via the connection between images and patches. Distillation for ViTs is still under-explored, especially for pretraining distillation.

In knowledge distillation, the mostly related work to ours is the recent FKD [56]. Both methods share a similar spirit on saving teacher logits to promote training efficiency, but our framework has two advantages. 1) More efficient. Instead of saving the explicit information of each transformation in data augmentation using hundreds of bytes, such as crop coordinates and rotation degree, our framework only needs 4 bytes to store a random seed. The seed will be used as the initial state of the random number generator to reproduce the number sequence that controls the transformations in data augmentation to generate crop coordinates and rotation degree, *etc.* 2) More general. Our framework supports all existing types of data augmentation including the complex Mixup [76] and Cutmix [73], which are not explored in FKD. Moreover, the studied problem in [56] is different to ours. We focus on pretraining-stage distillation for transformers, while FKD explores finetune-stage distillation for CNN models.

3   TinyViT

This section proposes TinyViT, a new family of tiny and efficient models with fast pretraining distillation on large-scale data. We first introduce the fast knowledge distillation framework for small model pretraining in Sect. 3.1. Then we design a new tiny model family with good computation/accuracy trade-off by progressivley scaling down a large seed model in Sect. 3.2.

3.1   Fast Pretraining Distillation

We observe that direct pretraining of small models on massive data does not bring much gains, especially when transferring them to downstream tasks, as

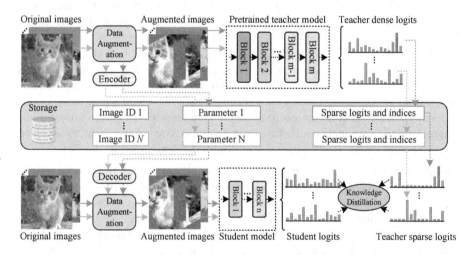

Fig. 2. Our fast pretraining distillation framework. **Top:** the branch for saving teacher logits. Encoded data augmentation and sparsified teacher logits are saved. **Middle:** the disk for storing information. **Bottom:** the branch for training the student. The decoder reconstructs the data augmentation, and distillation is conducted between the teacher logits and student outputs. Note that the two branches are independent and asynchronous.

presented in Fig. 1. To address this issue, we resort to knowledge distillation to further unveil the power of pretraining for small models. Different from prior work that pays most attention to finetune-stage distillation [61], we focus on pretraining distillation, which not only allows small models to learn from large-scale model, but also elevates their transfer capacities for downstream tasks.

Pretraining with distillation is inefficient and costly, because a considerable proportion of computing resources is consumed on passing training data through the large teacher model in each iteration, rather than training the target small student. Also, a giant teacher may occupy the most GPU memory, slowing down the training speed of the target students (due to limited batch size). To solve this problem, we propose a fast pretraining distillation framework. As depicted in Fig. 2, we store the information of data augmentation and teacher predictions in advance. During training, we reuse the stored information to precisely replicate the distillation procedure, successfully omitting the forward computation and memory occupation of the large teacher model.

Mathematically, for an input image x with strong data augmentation $\mathcal{A}$, such as RandAugment [17] and CutMix [73], we store both $\mathcal{A}$ and teacher prediction $\hat{y} = T(\mathcal{A}(x))$, where $T(\cdot)$ and $\mathcal{A}(x)$ are the teacher model and the augmented image. It is notable that passing the same image through the same data augmentation pipeline multiple times will generate different augmented images due to the inherent randomness in data augmentation. Therefore, the pair $(\mathcal{A}, \hat{y})$ needs to be saved for each image in each iteration, as illustrated in Fig. 2.

In the training process, we only need to recover the pairs $(\mathcal{A}, \hat{y})$ from stored files, and optimize the following objective function for student model distillation:

$$\mathcal{L} = CE\left(\hat{\mathbf{y}}, S(\mathcal{A}(x))\right), \tag{1}$$

where $S(\cdot)$ and $CE(\cdot)$ are the student model and cross entropy loss, respectively. Note that our framework is label-free, *i.e.*, with no need for ground-truth labels, because we only use the soft labels generated by teacher models for training. Therefore, it can utilize numerous off-the-shelf web data without labels for large-scale pretraining. Such a label-free strategy is workable in practice because the soft labels are accurate enough while carrying a lot of discriminative information for classification such as category relations. We also observe that distillation with ground-truth would cause slight performance drops. The reason may be that not all the labels in ImageNet-21k [18] are mutually exclusive [53], including correlative pairs like "chair" and "furniture", "horse" and "animal". Therefore, the one-hot ground-truth label could not describe an object precisely, and in some cases it suppresses either child classes or parent classes during training. Moreover, our distillation framework is as fast as training models without distillation since the cumbersome teacher $T(\cdot)$ is removed during training in Eq. (1).

Besides, our distillation framework is fast due to two key components: sparse soft labels and data augmentation encoding. They can largely reduce the storage consumption while improving memory efficiency during training.

Sparse Soft Labels. Let's consider the teacher model outputs C logits for the prediction. It often consumes much storage space to save the whole dense logits of all augmented images if C is large, $e.g.$, $C = 21,841$ for ImageNet-21k. Therefore, we just save the most important part of the logits, $i.e.$, sparse soft labels. Formally, we select the top-K values in $\hat{\mathbf{y}}$, $i.e.$, $\{\hat{y}_{\mathcal{I}(k)}\}_{k=1}^{K} \in \hat{\mathbf{y}}$, and store them along with their indices $\{\mathcal{I}(k)\}_{k=1}^{K}$ into our label files. During training, we only reuse the stored sparse labels for distillation with label smoothing [55,58], which is defined as

$$\hat{y}_c = \begin{cases} \hat{y}_{\mathcal{I}(k)} & \text{if } c = \mathcal{I}(k), \\ \frac{1 - \sum_{k=1}^{K} \hat{y}_{\mathcal{I}(k)}}{C - K} & \text{otherwise,} \end{cases} \tag{2}$$

where $\hat{y}_c$ is the recovered teacher logits for student model distillation, $i.e.$, $\hat{\mathbf{y}} = [\hat{y}_1, \ldots, \hat{y}_c, \ldots, \hat{y}_C]$. When the sparsity factor K is small, $i.e.$ $K \ll C$, it can reduce logits' storage by orders of magnitude. Moreover, we empirically show that such sparse labels can achieve comparable performance to the dense labels for knowledge distillation, as presented in Sect. 5.2.

Data Augmentation Encoding. Data augmentation involves a set of parameters $\mathbf{d}$, such as the rotation degree and crop coordinates, to transform the input image. Since $\mathbf{d}$ is different for each image in each iteration, saving it directly becomes memory-inefficient. To solve this problem, we encode $\mathbf{d}$ by a single parameter $d_0 = \mathcal{E}(\mathbf{d})$, where $\mathcal{E}(\cdot)$ is the encoder in Fig. 2. Then in the training process, we recover $\mathbf{d} = \mathcal{E}^{-1}(d_0)$ after loading d_0 in the storage files, where $\mathcal{E}^{-1}(\cdot)$ is viewed as the decoder. Therefore, the data augmentation can be accurately reconstructed. In practice, a common choice for the decoder is the pseudo-random number generator (i.e. PCG [47]). It takes a single parameter as the input and generates a sequence of parameters. As for the encoder, we simply implement it by a generator for d_0 and reusing the decoder $\mathcal{E}^{-1}(\cdot)$. It outputs $\mathbf{d} = \mathcal{E}^{-1}(d_0)$ for the teacher model. d_0 is saved for the decoder to reproduce $\mathbf{d}$ when training the student. Thus, the implementation becomes more efficient.

3.2   Model Architectures

In this subsection, we present a new family of tiny vision transformers by scaling down a large model seed with a progressive model contraction approach [21]. Specifically, we start with a large model and define a basic set of contraction factors. Then in each step, smaller candidate models are generated around the current model by adjusting the contraction factors. We select models that satisfy both constraints on the number of parameters and throughput. The model with the best validation accuracy will be utilized for further reduction in the next step until the target is achieved. This is a form of *constrained local search* [32] in the model space spanned by the contraction factors.

We adopt a hierarchical vision transformer as the basic architecture, for the convenience of dense prediction downstream tasks like detection that require multi-scale features. More concretely, our base model consists of four stages with a gradual reduction in resolution similar to Swin [42] and LeViT [24]. The patch embedding block consists of two convolutions with kernel size 3, stride 2 and padding 1. We apply lightweight and efficient MBConvs [33] in Stage 1 and down sampling blocks, since convolutions at earlier layers are capable of learning low-level representation efficiently due to their strong inductive biases [24,67]. The last three stages are constructed by transformer blocks, with window attention to reduce computational cost. The attention biases [24] and a 3×3 depthwise convolution between attention and MLP are introduced to capture local information [15,66]. Residual connection [28] is applied on each block in Stage 1, as well as attention blocks and MLP blocks. All activation functions are GELU [30]. The normalization layers of convolution and linear are BatchNorm [34] and LayerNorm [3], respectively.

Contraction Factors. We consider the following factors to form a model:

- $\gamma_{D_{1-4}}$: embeded dimension of four stages respectively. Decreasing them results in a thinner network with fewer heads in multi-head self-attention.
- $\gamma_{N_{1-4}}$: the number of blocks in four stages respectively. The depth of the model is decreased by reducing these values.
- $\gamma_{W_{2-4}}$: window size in the last three stages respectively. As these values become smaller, the model has fewer parameters and higher throughput.
- γ_R: channel expansion ratio of the MBConv block. We can obtain a smaller model size by reducing this factor.
- γ_M: expansion ratio of MLP for all transformer blocks. The hidden dimension of MLP will be smaller if scaling down this value.
- γ_E: the dimension of each head in multi-head attention. The number of heads will be increased when scaling it down, bringing lower computation cost.

We scale down the above factors with a progressive model contraction approach [21] and generate a new family of tiny vision transformers: All models share the same factors: $\{\gamma_{N_1}, \gamma_{N_2}, \gamma_{N_3}, \gamma_{N_4}\} = \{2, 2, 6, 2\}$, $\{\gamma_{W_2}, \gamma_{W_3}, \gamma_{W_4}\} = \{7, 14, 7\}$ and $\{\gamma_R, \gamma_M, \gamma_E\} = \{4, 4, 32\}$. For the embeded dimensions $\{\gamma_{D_1}, \gamma_{D_2}, \gamma_{D_3}, \gamma_{D_4}\}$, TinyViT-21M: $\{96, 192, 384, 576\}$, TinyViT-11M: $\{64, 128, 256, 448\}$ and TinyViT-5M: $\{64, 128, 160, 320\}$.

4   Analysis and Discussions

In this section, we provide analysis and discussions on two key questions: 1) What are the underlying factors limiting small models to fit large data? 2) Why distillation can unlock the power of large data for small models? To answer the above questions, we conduct experiments on the widely used large-scale benchmark ImageNet-21k [18], which contains 14M images with 21,841 categories.

What are the Underlying Factors Limiting Small Models to Fit Large Data? We observe that there are many hard samples existing in IN-21k, *e.g.*, images with wrong labels and similar images with different labels due to the existence of multiple equally prominent objects in the images. This is also recognized by existing literature [5,53,74] and approximately 10% images in ImageNet are considered as hard samples. Small models struggle to fit these hard samples, leading to low

Table 1. Impact of hard samples. Models are pretrained on IN-21k and then finetuned on IN-1k.

#	Model	Pretraining Dataset	IN-1k Top-1(%)	IN-Real [5] Top-1(%)	IN-V2 [52] Top-1(%)
0	Swin-T [42]	Train from scratch on IN-1k	81.2	86.7	69.7
1		Original IN-21k	81.9(+0.7)	87.0(+0.3)	70.6(+0.9)
2		Cleaned IN-21k	82.2(+1.0)	87.3(+0.6)	71.1(+1.4)
3		Original IN-21k w/ distillation	83.4(+2.2)	88.0(+1.3)	72.6(+2.9)
4	TinyViT-21M (**ours**)	Train from scratch on IN-1k	83.1	88.1	73.1
5		Original IN-21k	83.8(+0.7)	88.4(+0.3)	73.8(+0.7)
6		Cleaned IN-21k	84.2(+1.1)	88.5(+0.4)	73.8(+0.7)
7		Original IN-21k w/ distillation	84.8(+1.7)	88.9(+0.8)	75.1(+2.0)

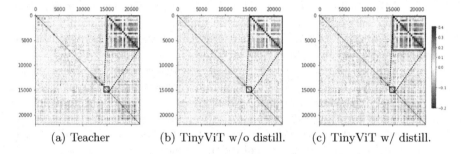

(a) Teacher   (b) TinyViT w/o distill.   (c) TinyViT w/ distill.

Fig. 3. Pearson correlations of output predictions on ImageNet-21k. (Color figure online)

training accuracy compared to large models (TinyViT-21M: 53.2% *vs.* Swin-L-197M [42]: 57.1%) and limited transferability on ImageNet-1k (TinyViT-21M w/ pretraining: 83.8% *vs.* w/o pretraining: 83.1%).

To verify the impact of hard samples, we resort to two techniques. 1) Inspired by [5], we exploit the powerful pretrained model Florence [72] finetuned on ImageNet-21k to identify the images whose labels lie outside the top-5 predictions of Florence. Through this procedure, we remove 2M images from ImageNet-21k, approximately 14%, and then pretrain TinyViT-21M and Swin-T on the cleaned dataset. 2) We perform distillation to pretrain TinyViT-21M/Swin-T using Florence as the teacher model, which generates soft labels to replace the polluted groundtruth labels in ImageNet-21k. The results of the pretrained models with finetuning on ImageNet-1k are reported in Table 1.

We obtain several insights from the results. 1) Pretraining small models on the original ImageNet-21k dataset brings limited performance gains on ImageNet-1k (0.7% for both Swin-T and TinyViT-21M). 2) After removing parts of the hard samples in ImageNet-21k, both models can better leverage the large data and achieve higher performance gains (1.0%/1.1% for Swin-T/TinyViT-21M). 3) Distillation is able to avoid the defects of hard samples, because it does

Table 2. Ablation study on different pretraining strategies for Swin [42] and DeiT [61]. The performance on IN-1k is reported.

Model	#Params (M)	Train on IN-1k	Pretrain on IN-21k	
			w/o distill.	w/ distill.
DeiT-Ti [61]	5	72.2	73.0(+0.8)	74.4(+2.2)
DeiT-S [61]	22	79.9	80.5(+0.6)	82.0(+2.1)
Swin-T [42]	28	81.2	81.9(+0.7)	83.4(+2.2)

not use the groundtruth labels that are the main cause of hard samples. Thus, it gets higher improvements (2.2%/1.7% for Swin-T and TinyViT-21M).

Why can Distillation Improve the Performance of Small Models on Large Datasets? The answer is that the student models can directly learn domain knowledge from teachers. Namely, the teacher injects class relationship prior when training the student, while filtering noisy labels (hard samples) for small student models.

To analyze the class relationships of teacher predictions, we select 8 images per class from IN-21k with totally 21,841 classes. These images are then fed into Florence [72] to extract prediction logits. Following [60], we can generate the heatmap of Pearson correlation coefficients between classes on the prediction logits. In Fig. 3(a), simialr or related classes clearly have a high correlations with each other (red), illustrated by the block diagonal structure. In addition, the teacher model can also capture uncorrelated classes (shown in blue). This observation verifies that teacher predictions indeed reveal class relationships.

We compare the Pearson correlations on the predictions of TinyViT-21M w/o and w/ distillation, as shown in Fig. 3(b) and Fig. 3(c) respectively. The block diagonal structure is less obvious without distillation, indicating that the small model is difficult to capture more class relations. However, distillation can guide the student model to imitate the teacher behaviors, leading to better excavating knowledge from large datasets. As shown in Fig. 3(c), the Pearson correlations of TinyViT with distillation are closer to the teacher.

5 Experiments

In this section, we first provide ablation studies on our proposed fast pretraining distillation framework. Next, we compare our TinyViT with other state-of-the-art models. At last, we demonstrate the transferability on downstream tasks.

5.1 Implementation Details

Pretraining on ImageNet. For the pretraining on IN-21k [18], we pretrain TinyViT for 90 epochs, then finetune the pretrained models for 30 epochs on IN-1k. For the training from scratch on IN-1k, we train our models for 300 epochs. More details are shown in *Supplementary Materials* (Sec. B).

Knowledge Distillation. We pre-store the top-100 logits of teacher models for IN-21k, including Swin-L [42], BEiT-L [4], CLIP-ViT-L/14 [20,50] and Florence [72] for all 90 epochs. Note that CLIP-ViT-L/14 and Florence are finetuned on IN-21k for 30 epochs to serve as teachers. Then, we distill the student models using the stored teacher logits with the same hyper-parameters as the distillation involving the teacher model. The distillation temperature is set to 1.0. We disable Mixup [76] and Cutmix [73] for pretraining distillation on TinyViT. All models are implemented using PyTorch [49] with timm library [65].

5.2   Ablation Study

Impact of Pretraining Distillation on Existing Small ViTs. We study the effectiveness of our proposed fast pretraining distillation framework on two popular vision transformers: DeiT [61] and Swin [42]. As shown in Table 2, comparing to training from scratch on IN-1k, pretraining without distillation on IN-21k can only bring limited gains, *i.e.* 0.8%/0.6%/0.7% for DeiT-Ti/DeiT-S/Swin-T, respectively. However, our proposed fast pretraining distillation framework increases the accuracy by 2.2%/2.1%/2.2% respectively. It indicates that pretraining distillation allows small models to benefit more from large-scale datasets.

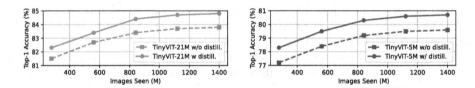

Fig. 4. Comparison on pretrained TinyViT-21M/5M over training data size.

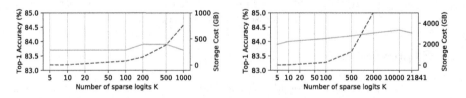

Fig. 5. The accuracy on IN-1k and storage cost of TinyViT-21M along different saved logits K. **Left:** distill TinyViT-21M on IN-1k **Right:** distill TinyViT-21M on IN-21k then finetune it on IN-1k.

Impact of Pretraining Data Scale. We investigate the representation quality of TinyViT-5M/21M with respect to the total number of images "seen" (batch size times number of steps) during pretraining on IN-21k, following the strategies in [75]. We use CLIP-ViT-L/14 [20,50] as the teacher. The results on IN-1k after finetuning are shown in Fig. 4. We have the following observations. 1) For both models, pretraining distillation can consistently brings performance gains over different data size. 2) All models tends to saturate as the number of epochs increase, which may be bottlenecked by the model capacities.

Impact of the Number of Saved Logits. The effects of sparse logits on distilling TinyViT-21M by using Swin-L [42] as the teacher model are shown in Fig. 5. On both IN-1k and IN-21k, we observe that the accuracy increases as the number of sparse logits K grows until saturation, meanwhile the storage cost grows linearly.

This observation is aligned with existing work on knowledge distillation [56, 60], where teacher logtis capture class relationships but also contain noise. This makes it possible to sparsify teacher logits such that the class relationships are reserved while reducing noise. Moreover, memory consumption also impose constraints on the choice of K. To obtain comparable accuracy under limited storage space, we select the slightly larger K, where $K=10$ (1.0% logits) on IN-1k for 300 epochs and $K=100$ (0.46% logits) on IN-21k for 90 epochs using 16 GB/481 GB storage cost, respectively.

Impact of Teacher Models. We evaluate the impact of teacher models for pretraining distillation. As shown in Table 3, a better teacher can yield better student models (#1 *vs.* #2 *vs.* #3 and #4). TinyViT-21M distilled by Florence on IN-21k is 1.0%/0.6%/1.0% higher in top-1 accuracy on three benchmark datasets than trained from scratch on IN-21k (#0 *vs.* #4). However, better teacher models are often large in model size, resulting in high GPU memory consumption and long training time, e.g., Florence (#4) with 682M parameters occupies 11GB GPU memory and leads to 2.4 times longer training time.

Table 3. Ablation study on different teacher models for pretraining distillation. Teacher performance are listed in the brackets: (the number of parameters, linear probe performance on IN-1k). We report the training time cost and memory consumption of teacher models on NVIDIA V100 GPUs without using our proposed fast pretraining distillation.

#	IN-21k Pretrained Teacher	IN-1k Top-1(%)	IN-Real Top-1(%)	IN-V2 Top-1(%)	Training Time (GPU Hours)	Memory (GB)
0	w/o distill.	83.8	88.4	73.8	3,360	0
1	BEiT-L (326M, 84.1) [4]	84.1	88.4	73.8	6,415 (1.9×)	3.9
2	Swin-L (229M, 84.4) [42]	84.2	88.6	73.9	5,804 (1.7×)	6.8
3	CLIP-ViT-L/14 (321M, 85.2) [50]	84.8	88.9	75.1	7,087 (2.1×)	2.7
4	Florence (682M, 86.2) [72]	84.8	89.0	74.8	7,942 (2.4×)	10.7

Note that our fast pretraining distillation framework simply loads the teacher logits from a hard disk during training. Therefore, it does not require additional GPU memory and has the same training time as #0. Moreover, the framework is compatible with all types of teacher models. Therefore, the performance of TinyViT can be further improved by introducing more powerful teachers Table 4.

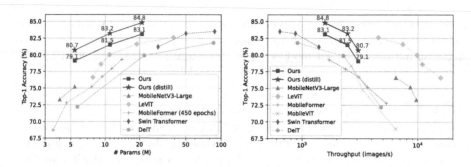

Fig. 6. Comparison with state-of-the-art methods on IN-1k.

5.3   Results on ImageNet

In this section, we compare our scaled TinyViT models with state-of-the-art methods on IN-1k [18]. The performance is reported in Fig. 6. The models with 🐟: indicates pretraining on IN-21k with the proposed fast distillation framework using CLIP-ViT-L/14 [20,50] as the teacher. It shows that, without distillation, our TinyViT models achieve comparable performance to current prevailing methods, such as Swin transformer [42] and LeViT [24], with similar param-

Table 4. TinyViT performance on IN-1k [18] with comparisons to state-of-the-art models. MACs (multiply-accumulate operations) and Throughput are measured using the GitHub repository of [1,24] and a V100 GPU. 🐟: pretrain on IN-21k with the proposed fast distillation; ↑: finetune with higher resolution.

	Model	Top-1 (%)	Top-5 (%)	#Params (M)	MACs (G)	Throughput (images/s)	Input	Arch.
5–10M #Params	MoblieViT-S [44]	78.4	-	6	1.8	2,661	256	Hybrid
	ViTAS-DeiT-A [57]	75.5	92.4	6	1.3	3,504	224	Trans
	GLiT-Tiny [9]	76.3	-	7	1.5	3,262	224	Trans
	Mobile-Former-214M [14]	76.7	-	9	0.2	3,105	224	Hybrid
	CrossViT-9 [10]	77.1	-	9	2.0	2,659	224	Trans
	TinyViT-5M (ours)	**79.1**	94.8	5.4	1.3	3,060	224	Hybrid
	TinyViT-5M🐟 (ours)	80.7	95.6	5.4	1.3	3,060	224	Hybrid
11–20M	ResNet-18 [28]	70.3	86.7	12	1.8	8,714	224	CNN
	PVT-Tiny [63]	75.1	-	13	1.9	2,791	224	Trans
	ResT-Small [78]	79.6	94.9	14	2.1	2,037	224	Trans
	LeViT-256 [24]	81.6	-	19	1.1	7,386	224	Hybrid
	CoaT-Lite Small [68]	81.9	95.6	20	4.0	1,138	224	Trans
	TinyViT-11M (ours)	**81.5**	95.8	11	2.0	2,468	224	Hybrid
	TinyViT-11M🐟 (ours)	83.2	96.5	11	2.0	2,468	224	Hybrid
>20M	DeiT-S [61]	79.9	95.0	22	4.6	2,276	224	Trans
	T2T-ViT-14 [71]	81.5	95.7	21	4.8	1,557	224	Trans
	AutoFormer-S [11]	81.7	95.7	23	5.1	1,341	224	Trans
	Swin-T [42]	81.2	95.5	28	4.5	1,393	224	Trans
	CrossViT-15 [10]	82.3	-	28	6.1	1,306	224	Trans
	EffNet-B5 [59]	83.6	96.7	30	9.9	330	456	CNN
	TinyViT-21M (ours)	**83.1**	96.5	21	4.3	1,571	224	Hybrid
	TinyViT-21M🐟 (ours)	84.8	97.3	21	4.3	1,571	224	Hybrid
	TinyViT-21M🐟 ↑384 (ours)	86.2	97.8	21	13.8	394	384	Hybrid
	TinyViT-21M🐟 ↑512 (ours)	86.5	97.9	21	27.0	167	512	Hybrid

eters. This indicates the effectiveness of the proposed new architectures and the model scaling techniques. Moreover, with the fast pretraining distillation, the performance of TinyViT can be largely improved, outperforming the state-of-the-art CNN, transformer and hybrid models. In particular, using only 21M parameters, TinyViT trained from scratch on IN-1k gets 1.9%/3.2% higher top-1 accuracy than Swin-T [42] and DeiT-S [61] respectively, while after pretraining with distillation on IN-21k, the improvements arise to 3.6% and 4.9%. With higher resolution, TinyViT-21M reaches a top-1 accuracy of 86.5%, establishing new state-of-the-art performance on IN-1k for small models. Besides, TinyViT surpasses automatically searched models, such as AutoFormer [11] and GLiT [9].

5.4   Transfer Learning Results

Linear Probe. For linear probe, we follow the same setting as in MOCO v3 [13], *i.e.*, replacing the head of TinyViT models with a linear layer, while only finetuning the linear layer on downstream datasets and frozing other weights. We consider five classification benchmarks: CIFAR-10 [39], CIFAR-100 [39], Flowers [46], Cars [2] and Pets [48]. The results are reported in Table 5.

We compare the performance of TinyViT-21M with 4 different training settings. It is clear that distillation can improve the linear probe performance of TinyViT (#0 *vs.* #1, #2 *vs.* #3). Besides, when trained on larger datasets (*i.e.*, IN-21k), TinyViT gets more than 10% gains over CIFAR-100, Flowers and Cars (#0,#1 *vs.* #2, #3), indicating better representability. Thus, pretraining with distillation on large-scale datasets achieves the best representability (#3).

Few-Shot Learning. We also evaluate the transferability of TinyViT with different training settings on few-shot learning benchmark [25]. The benchmark datasets include: CropDisease [45], EuroSAT [29], ISIC 2018 [16] and ChestX [64]. The average accuracy over 600 episodes is reported in Table 5. We obtain same observations as the linear probe results, except of ChestX, where gray-scale medical images are the least similar to natural images, as well as few in the training dataset for the teacher models and the student models. In combination of these results, we can conclude that pretraining distillation is significant in improving the representability of small models, and thus our proposed fast pretraining distillation framework is effective.

Object Detection. We also investigate the transfer ability of our TinyViT on object detection task [40]. We use Cascade R-CNN [7] with Swin-T [42] as our baseline. We follow the same training settings used in Swin transformer [42]. The results on COCO 2017 validation set are reported in Table 6. Under the same training recipe, our TinyViT architecture achieves better performance than Swin-T, getting 1.5% AP improvements. Furthermore, after applying pretraining distillation, TinyViT gets another 0.6% AP improvements, being 2.1% higher than Swin-T. This clearly demonstrates our fast pretraining distillation framework is effective and capable of improving the transfer ability of small models.

Table 5. Performance of TinyViT-21M w/ and w/o pretraining for linear probe and few-shot image classification.

#	Training dataset	Linear probe					5-shot				20-shot				50-shot			
		CIFAR-10	CIFAR-100	Flowers	Cars	Pets	ISIC	EuroSAT	CropD	ChestX	ISIC	EuroSAT	CropD	ChestX	ISIC	EuroSAT	CropD	ChestX
0	IN-1k	91.7	75.2	80.9	56.3	86.5	42.9	82.4	92.2	24.8	56.7	91.0	97.4	29.0	63.7	94.2	98.6	31.8
1	IN-1k🔥	91.7	74.5	82.4	61.7	85.5	43.0	83.0	94.2	24.4	58.5	91.8	97.9	28.6	66.2	94.3	98.9	31.8
2	IN-21k	96.3	84.7	99.7	67.7	92.6	52.5	87.4	97.4	24.6	66.5	93.7	99.1	29.4	73.4	95.5	99.5	33.4
3	IN-21k🔥	96.9	86.6	99.7	75.1	93.8	53.5	88.1	98.0	24.7	67.3	93.9	99.3	29.5	74.2	96.0	99.5	33.2

Table 6. Comparison on COCO [40] object detection using Cascade Mask R-CNN [7, 27] for 12 epochs. We report the number of parameters of the backbone.

#	Backbone	#Params	IN-1k	AP	AP_{50}	AP_{75}	AP_S	AP_M	AP_L
0	Swin-T [42]	28M	81.2	48.1	67.1	52.1	31.1	51.2	63.5
1	TinyViT-21M	21M	83.1	49.6 (+1.5)	68.5	54.2	32.3	53.2	64.8
2	TinyViT-21M🔥	21M	84.8	50.2 (+2.1)	69.4	54.4	32.9	53.9	65.2

6 Conclusions

We have proposed a new family of tiny and efficient vision transformers pretrained on large-scale datasets with our proposed fast distillation framework, named TinyViT. Extensive experiments demonstrate the efficacy of TinyViT on ImageNet-1k, and its superior transferability on various downstream benchmarks. In future work, we will consider using more data to further unlock the representability of small models with the assistance of more powerful teacher models. Designing a more effective scaling down method to generate small models with better computation/accuracy is another interesting research direction.

References

1. fvcore library. https://github.com/facebookresearch/fvcore/
2. 3d object representations for fine-grained categorization. In: 3dRR (2013)
3. Ba, J.L., Kiros, J.R., Hinton, G.E.: Layer normalization. arXiv (2016)
4. Bao, H., Dong, L., Wei, F.: BEiT: BERT pre-training of image transformers. In: ICLR (2022)
5. Beyer, L., Hénaff, O.J., Kolesnikov, A., Zhai, X., Oord, A.V.D.: Are we done with imagenet? arXiv (2020)
6. Bommasani, R., et al.: On the opportunities and risks of foundation models (2021)
7. Cai, Z., Vasconcelos, N.: Cascade R-CNN: delving into high quality object detection. In: CVPR (2018)
8. Carion, N., Massa, F., Synnaeve, G., Usunier, N., Kirillov, A., Zagoruyko, S.: End-to-End object detection with transformers. In: Vedaldi, A., Bischof, H., Brox, T., Frahm, J.-M. (eds.) ECCV 2020. LNCS, vol. 12346, pp. 213–229. Springer, Cham (2020). https://doi.org/10.1007/978-3-030-58452-8_13

9. Chen, B., et al.: Glit: neural architecture search for global and local image transformer. In: ICCV (2021)
10. Chen, C.F., Fan, Q., Panda, R.: CrossViT: cross-attention multi-scale vision transformer for image classification. ICCV (2021)
11. Chen, M., Peng, H., Fu, J., Ling, H.: AutoFormer: searching transformers for visual recognition. In: ICCV (2021)
12. Chen, W., Huang, W., Du, X., Song, X., Wang, Z., Zhou, D.: Auto-scaling vision transformers without training. In: ICLR (2021)
13. Chen, X., Xie, S., He, K.: An empirical study of training self-supervised vision transformers. In: ICCV (2021)
14. Chen, Y., et al.: Mobile-former: bridging mobileNet and transformer. In: CVPR (2022)
15. Chu, X., et al.: Conditional positional encodings for vision transformers. arXiv (2021)
16. Codella, et al.: Skin lesion analysis toward melanoma detection 2018: a challenge hosted by the international skin imaging collaboration (isic). arXiv (2019)
17. Cubuk, E.D., Zoph, B., Shlens, J., Le, Q.V.: Randaugment: practical automated data augmentation with a reduced search space. In: CVPR (2020)
18. Deng, J., Dong, W., Socher, R., Li, L.J., Li, K., Fei-Fei, L.: ImageNet: a large-scale hierarchical image database. In: CVPR (2009)
19. Devlin, J., Chang, M.W., Lee, K., Toutanova, K.: BERT: pre-training of deep bidirectional transformers for language understanding. In: NAACL-HLT (1) (2019)
20. Dosovitskiy, A., et al.: An image is worth 16x16 words: transformers for image recognition at scale. ICLR (2021)
21. Feichtenhofer, C.: X3d: expanding architectures for efficient video recognition. In: CVPR (2020)
22. Gong, C., et al.: NASVit: neural architecture search for efficient vision transformers with gradient conflict aware supernet training. In: ICLR (2022)
23. Gou, J., Yu, B., Maybank, S.J., Tao, D.: Knowledge distillation: a survey. IJCV (2021)
24. Graham, B., et al.: LeViT: a vision transformer in convnet's clothing for faster inference. In: ICCV (2021)
25. Guo, Y., et al.: A broader study of cross-domain few-shot learning. In: ECCV (2020)
26. Han, S., Mao, H., Dally, W.J.: Deep compression: compressing deep neural networks with pruning, trained quantization and Huffman coding. arXiv (2015)
27. He, K., Gkioxari, G., Dollár, P., Girshick, R.: Mask R-CNN. In: ICCV (2017)
28. He, K., Zhang, X., Ren, S., Sun, J.: Deep residual learning for image recognition. In: CVPR (2016)
29. Helber, P., Bischke, B., Dengel, A., Borth, D.: EuroSAT: a novel dataset and deep learning benchmark for land use and land cover classification. IEEE J. Sel. Top. Appl. Earth Obs. Remote Sens. $12(7)$, 2217–2226 (2019)
30. Hendrycks, D., Gimpel, K.: Gaussian error linear units (gelus). arXiv (2016)
31. Hinton, G., Vinyals, O., Dean, J.: Distilling the knowledge in a neural network. arXiv (2015)
32. Hoos, H.H., Stützle, T.: Stochastic local search: foundations and applications. Elsevier (2004)
33. Howard, A., Sandler, M., Chu, G., Chen, L.C., Chen, B., Tan, M., Wang, W., Zhu, Y., Pang, R., Vasudevan, V., et al.: Searching for mobilenetv3. In: ICCV (2019)
34. Ioffe, S., Szegedy, C.: Batch normalization: accelerating deep network training by reducing internal covariate shift. In: ICML (2015)

35. Jacob, B., et al.: Quantization and training of neural networks for efficient integer-arithmetic-only inference. In: CVPR (2018)

36. Jia, C., et al.: Scaling up visual and vision-language representation learning with noisy text supervision. In: ICML (2021)

37. Jia, D., et al.: Efficient vision transformers via fine-grained manifold distillation. arXiv (2021)

38. Kong, Z., et al.: SPVit: enabling faster vision transformers via soft token pruning. arXiv (2021)

39. Krizhevsky, A., Hinton, G., et al.: Learning multiple layers of features from tiny images (2009)

40. Lin, T.-Y., et al.: Microsoft COCO: common objects in context. In: Fleet, D., Pajdla, T., Schiele, B., Tuytelaars, T. (eds.) ECCV 2014. LNCS, vol. 8693, pp. 740–755. Springer, Cham (2014). https://doi.org/10.1007/978-3-319-10602-1_48

41. Liu, Z., et al.: Swin transformer v2: scaling up capacity and resolution. In: CVPR (2022)

42. Liu, Z., et al.: Swin transformer: hierarchical vision transformer using shifted windows. In: ICCV (2021)

43. Liu, Z., Wang, Y., Han, K., Zhang, W., Ma, S., Gao, W.: Post-training quantization for vision transformer. NeurIPS **34**(2021), 28092–28103 (2021)

44. Mehta, S., Rastegari, M.: MobileViT: light-weight, general-purpose, and mobile-friendly vision transformer. In: ICLR (2021)

45. Mohanty, S.P., Hughes, D.P., Salathé, M.: Using deep learning for image-based plant disease detection. Front. Plant Sci. **7**, 1419 (2016)

46. Nilsback, M.E., Zisserman, A.: A visual vocabulary for flower classification. In: CVPR (2006)

47. O'Neill, M.E.: PCG: a family of simple fast space-efficient statistically good algorithms for random number generation. TOMS (2014)

48. Parkhi, O.M., Vedaldi, A., Zisserman, A., Jawahar, C.: Cats and dogs. In: CVPR (2012)

49. Paszke, A., et al.: Pytorch: an imperative style, high-performance deep learning library. NeurIPS (2019)

50. Radford, A., et al.: Learning transferable visual models from natural language supervision. In: ICML (2021)

51. Radford, A., Narasimhan, K., Salimans, T., Sutskever, I., et al.: Improving language understanding by generative pre-training (2018)

52. Recht, B., Roelofs, R., Schmidt, L., Shankar, V.: Do imagenet classifiers generalize to imagenet? In: ICML (2019)

53. Ridnik, T., Ben-Baruch, E., Noy, A., Zelnik-Manor, L.: ImageNet-21k pretraining for the masses. In: NeurIPS (2021)

54. Riquelme, C., et al.: Scaling vision with sparse mixture of experts. In: NeurIPS (2021)

55. Shen, Z., Liu, Z., Xu, D., Chen, Z., Cheng, K.T., Savvides, M.: Is label smoothing truly incompatible with knowledge distillation: an empirical study. In: ICLR (2020)

56. Shen, Z., Xing, E.: A fast knowledge distillation framework for visual recognition. arXiv (2021)

57. Su, X., et al.: Vitas: vision transformer architecture search. arXiv (2021)

58. Szegedy, C., Vanhoucke, V., Ioffe, S., Shlens, J., Wojna, Z.: Rethinking the inception architecture for computer vision. In: CVPR (2016)

59. Tan, M., Le, Q.: Efficientnet: rethinking model scaling for convolutional neural networks. In: ICML (2019)

60. Tang, J., et al.: Understanding and improving knowledge distillation (2020)
61. Touvron, H., Cord, M., Douze, M., Massa, F., Sablayrolles, A., Jégou, H.: Training data-efficient image transformers & distillation through attention. In: ICML. PMLR (2021)
62. Vaswani, A., et al.: Attention is all you need. In: NeurIPS (2017)
63. Wang, W., et al.: Pyramid vision transformer: a versatile backbone for dense prediction without convolutions. In: ICCV (2021)
64. Wang, X., Peng, Y., Lu, L., Lu, Z., Bagheri, M., Summers, R.M.: ChestX-ray8: hospital-scale chest x-ray database and benchmarks on weakly-supervised classification and localization of common thorax diseases. In: CVPR (2017)
65. Wightman, R.: Pytorch image models (2019)
66. Wu, K., Peng, H., Chen, M., Fu, J., Chao, H.: Rethinking and improving relative position encoding for vision transformer. In: ICCV (2021)
67. Xiao, T., Dollar, P., Singh, M., Mintun, E., Darrell, T., Girshick, R.: Early convolutions help transformers see better. NeurIPS **34**, 30392–30400 (2021)
68. Xu, W., Xu, Y., Chang, T., Tu, Z.: Co-scale conv-attentional image transformers. In: ICCV (2021)
69. Yang, H., Yin, H., Molchanov, P., Li, H., Kautz, J.: NViT: vision transformer compression and parameter redistribution. arXiv (2021)
70. Yu, S., et al.: Unified visual transformer compression. In: ICLR (2022)
71. Yuan, L., et al.: Tokens-to-token ViT: training vision transformers from scratch on ImageNet. In: ICCV (2021)
72. Yuan, L., et al.: Florence: a new foundation model for computer vision. ArXiv (2021)
73. Yun, S., Han, D., Oh, S.J., Chun, S., Choe, J., Yoo, Y.: CutMix: regularization strategy to train strong classifiers with localizable features. In: ICCV (2019)
74. Yun, S., Oh, S.J., Heo, B., Han, D., Choe, J., Chun, S.: Re-labeling ImageNet: from single to multi-labels, from global to localized labels. In: CVPR (2021)
75. Zhai, X., Kolesnikov, A., Houlsby, N., Beyer, L.: Scaling vision transformers. In: CVPR (2022)
76. Zhang, H., Cisse, M., Dauphin, Y.N., Lopez-Paz, D.: mixup: beyond empirical risk minimization. In: ICLR (2018)
77. Zhang, J., et al.: MiniViT: compressing vision transformers with weight multiplexing. In: CVPR (2022)
78. Zhang, Q., bin Yang, Y.: Rest: an efficient transformer for visual recognition. In: NeurIPS (2021)
79. Zhang, X., Zhou, X., Lin, M., Sun, J.: ShuffleNet: an extremely efficient convolutional neural network for mobile devices. In: CVPR (2018)
80. Zhou, W., Xu, C., McAuley, J.: Meta learning for knowledge distillation (2022)
81. Zhu, M., Tang, Y., Han, K.: Vision transformer pruning. In: KDD Workshop on Model Mining (2021)

Equivariant Hypergraph Neural Networks

Jinwoo Kim[1], Saeyoon Oh[1], Sungjun Cho[2], and Seunghoon Hong[1,2](✉)

[1] KAIST, Daejeon, South Korea
seunghoon.hong@kaist.ac.kr
[2] LG AI Research, Seoul, South Korea

Abstract. Many problems in computer vision and machine learning can be cast as learning on hypergraphs that represent higher-order relations. Recent approaches for hypergraph learning extend graph neural networks based on message passing, which is simple yet fundamentally limited in modeling long-range dependencies and expressive power. On the other hand, tensor-based equivariant neural networks enjoy maximal expressiveness, but their application has been limited in hypergraphs due to heavy computation and strict assumptions on fixed-order hyperedges. We resolve these problems and present Equivariant Hypergraph Neural Network (EHNN), the first attempt to realize maximally expressive equivariant layers for general hypergraph learning. We also present two practical realizations of our framework based on hypernetworks (EHNN-MLP) and self-attention (EHNN-Transformer), which are easy to implement and theoretically more expressive than most message passing approaches. We demonstrate their capability in a range of hypergraph learning problems, including synthetic k-edge identification, semi-supervised classification, and visual keypoint matching, and report improved performances over strong message passing baselines. Our implementation is available at https://github.com/jw9730/ehnn.

Keywords: Hypergraph neural network · Graph neural network · Permutation equivariance · Semi-supervised classification · Keypoint matching

1   Introduction

Reasoning about a system that involves a set of entities and their relationships requires relational data structures. Graph represents relational data with nodes and edges, where a node corresponds to an entity and an edge represents a relationship between a pair of nodes. However, pairwise edges are often insufficient to represent more complex relationships. For instance, many geometric configurations of entities such as angles and areas can only be captured by considering higher-order relationships between three or more nodes. Hypergraph is a general

---

Supplementary Information The online version contains supplementary material available at https://doi.org/10.1007/978-3-031-19803-8_6.

S. Avidan et al. (Eds.): ECCV 2022, LNCS 13681, pp. 86–103, 2022.
https://doi.org/10.1007/978-3-031-19803-8_6

data structure that represents such higher-order relationships with hyperedges, *i.e.*, edges associating more than two nodes at a time [6]. Thus, it is widely used to represent various visual data such as scenes [19,30], feature correspondence [4,41,49,55], and polygonal mesh [8,46,58], as well as general relational data such as social networks [10,37,52], biological networks [22,33], linguistic structures [15], and combinatorial optimization problems [28].

To learn deep representation of hypergraphs, recent works developed specialized hypergraph neural networks by generalizing the message passing operator of graph neural networks (GNNs) [2,3,13,16,18,26]. In these networks, node and (hyper)edge features are updated recurrently by aggregating features of neighboring nodes and edges according to the connectivity of input (hyper)graph. Despite such simplicity, message passing networks have fundamental limitations. Notably, the local and recurrent operations of message passing prevents them from handling dependencies between any pair of nodes with distance longer than the number of propagation steps [21,32]. It is also known that this locality is related to oversmoothing that hinders the use of deep networks [11,26,39,47].

A more general and potentially powerful approach for hypergraph learning is to find *all* possible permutation equivariant linear operations on the input (hyper)graph and use them as bases of linear layers that constitute *equivariant GNNs* [43,54]. While message passing is one specific, locally restricted case of equivariant operation, the maximal set of equivariant operations extends further, involving various global interactions over possibly disconnected nodes and (hyper)edges [32]. The formulation naturally extends to higher-order layers that can handle hypergraphs in principle and even mixed-order layers where input and output are of different orders (e.g., graph in, hypergraph out). Despite the advantages, the actual usage of equivariant GNNs has been mainly limited to sets and graphs [32,43,51,59], and they have not been realized for general hypergraph learning. This is mainly due to the prohibitive parameter dimensionality of higher-order layers and a bound in the input and output hyperedge orders that comes from fixed-order tensor representation.

We propose *Equivariant Hypergraph Neural Network (EHNN)* as the first attempt to realize equivariant GNNs for general hypergraph learning. We begin by establishing a simple connection between sparse, arbitrarily structured hypergraphs and dense, fixed-order tensors, from which we derive the maximally expressive equivariant linear layer for undirected hypergraphs. Then, we impose an intrinsic parameter sharing within the layer via hypernetworks [23], which (1) retains maximal expressiveness, (2) practically bounds the number of parameters, and (3) allows processing hyperedges with arbitrary and possibly unseen orders. Notably, the resulting layer (EHNN-MLP) turns out to be a simple augmentation of an MLP-based message passing with hyperedge order embedding and global pooling. This leads to efficient implementation and also allows incorporation of any advances in the message passing literature. We further extend into a Transformer counterpart (EHNN-Transformer) by introducing self-attention to achieve a higher expressive power with the same asymptotic cost. In a challenging synthetic k-edge identification task where message passing networks fail, we show that the high expressiveness of EHNN allows fine-grained global reasoning to perfectly solve the task, and demonstrate their generalizability towards unseen hyperedge orders. We also demonstrate their state-of-the-art performance in several transductive and inductive hypergraph learning benchmarks, including semi-supervised classification and visual correspondence matching.

2   Preliminary and Related Work

Let us introduce preliminary concepts from permutation equivariant learning [32, 43,51]. We first describe higher-order tensors, then describe maximally expressive permutation equivariant linear layers that compose equivariant GNNs [43].

We begin with some notations. We denote a set as $\{a, ..., b\}$, a tuple as $(a, ..., b)$, and $[n] = \{1, ..., n\}$. We denote the space of order-k tensors as $\mathbb{R}^{n^k \times d}$ with feature dimension d. For an order-k tensor $\mathbf{A} \in \mathbb{R}^{n^k \times d}$, we use a multi-index $\mathbf{i} = (i_1, ..., i_k) \in [n]^k$ to index an element $\mathbf{A}_{\mathbf{i}} = \mathbf{A}_{i_1,...,i_k} \in \mathbb{R}^d$. Let S_n denote all permutations of $[n]$. A node permutation $\pi \in S_n$ acts on a multi-index $\mathbf{i}$ by $\pi(\mathbf{i}) = (\pi(i_1), ..., \pi(i_k))$, and acts on a tensor $\mathbf{A}$ by $(\pi \cdot \mathbf{A})_{\mathbf{i}} = \mathbf{A}_{\pi^{-1}(\mathbf{i})}$.

Higher-Order Tensors. Prior work on equivariant learning regard a hypergraph data as $G = (V, \mathbf{A})$ where V is a set of n nodes and $\mathbf{A} \in \mathbb{R}^{n^k \times d}$ is a tensor that encodes hyperedge features [32,43,51]. The order k of the tensor $\mathbf{A}$ indicates the type of hypergraph. First-order tensor encodes a set of features (*e.g.*, point cloud) where $\mathbf{A}_i$ is feature of node i. Second-order tensor encodes pairwise edge features (*e.g.*, adjacency) where $\mathbf{A}_{i_1,i_2}$ is feature of edge (i_1, i_2). Generally, an order-k tensor encodes *hyperedge* features (*e.g.*, mesh normal) where $\mathbf{A}_{i_1,...,i_k}$ is feature of hyperedge $(i_1, ..., i_k)$. We begin our discussion from tensors, but will arrive at the familiar notion of hypergraphs with any-order undirected hyperedges [18].

Permutation Invariance and Equivariance. In (hyper)graph learning, we are interested in building a function f that takes a (higher-order) tensor $\mathbf{A}$ as input and outputs some value T. Since the tensor representation of the graph changes dramatically with the permutation of node indices, the function f should be invariant or equivariant under node permutations. Formally, if the output T is a single vector, f is required to be *permutation invariant*, always satisfying $f(\pi \cdot \mathbf{A}) = f(\mathbf{A})$; if we want T to be a tensor $T = \mathbf{T}$, f is required to be *permutation equivariant*, always satisfying $f(\pi \cdot \mathbf{A}) = \pi \cdot f(\mathbf{A})$. As a neural network f is often built as a stack of linear layers and non-linearities, its construction reduces to finding invariant and equivariant *linear* layers.

Invariant and Equivariant Linear Layers. Many (hyper)graph neural networks rely on message passing [18,20], which is a restricted equivariant operator. Alternatively, tensor-based *maximally expressive* linear layers have been characterized by Maron el. al. (2019) [43]. Specifically, invariant linear layers $L_{k\to 0} : \mathbb{R}^{n^k \times d} \to \mathbb{R}^{d'}$ and equivariant linear layers $L_{k\to l} : \mathbb{R}^{n^k \times d} \to \mathbb{R}^{n^l \times d'}$ were identified (note that invariance is a special case of equivariance with $l = 0$). Given an order-k input $\mathbf{A} \in \mathbb{R}^{n^k \times d}$, the order-$l$ output of an equivariant linear layer $L_{k\to l}$ is written as follows, with indicator $\mathbb{1}$ and multi-indices $\mathbf{i} \in [n]^k, \mathbf{j} \in [n]^l$:

$$L_{k\to l}(\mathbf{A})_{\mathbf{j}} = \sum_{\mu}\sum_{\mathbf{i}} \mathbb{1}_{(\mathbf{i},\mathbf{j})\in\mu}\mathbf{A}_{\mathbf{i}}w_{\mu} + \sum_{\lambda} \mathbb{1}_{\mathbf{j}\in\lambda}b_{\lambda}, \qquad (1)$$

where $w_{\mu} \in \mathbb{R}^{d\times d'}$, $b_{\lambda} \in \mathbb{R}^{d'}$ are weight and bias parameters, and μ and λ are *equivalence classes* of order-$(k+l)$ and order-l multi-indices, respectively.

The equivalence classes can be interpreted as a partitioning of a multi-index space. The equivalence classes μ for the weight specifies a partitioning of the space of order-$(k+l)$ multi-indices $[n]^{k+l}$, and λ for the bias specifies a partitioning of the space of order-l multi-indices $[n]^l$. The total number of the equivalence classes (the size of partitioning) depends only on orders k and l. With b(k) the k-th Bell number, there exist b$(k+l)$ equivalence classes μ for the weight and b(l) equivalence classes λ for the bias. For first-order layer $L_{1\to 1}$, there exist b$(2) = 2$ equivalence classes μ_1, μ_2 for the weight, specifying the partitioning of $[n]^2$ as $\{\mu_1,\mu_2\}$ where $\mu_1 = \{(i,j)|i = j\}$ and $\mu_2 = \{(i,j)|i \neq j\}$. For further details, we guide the readers to Maron et al. (2019) [43] and Kim et al. (2021) [32].

Equivariant GNNs. Based on the maximally expressive equivariant linear layers (Eq. (1)), a bouquet of permutation invariant or equivariant neural networks were formulated. A representative example is *equivariant GNN* [43] (also called k-IGN [12,42]) built by stacking the equivariant linear layers and non-linearity. Their theoretical expressive power has been extensively studied [12,29,42,44,59], leading to successful variants in set and graph learning [31,32,45,51]. In particular, practical variants such as Higher-order Transformer [32] and TokenGT [31] unified equivariant GNNs and Transformer architecture [36,53], surpassing the graph learning performance of message passing GNNs by a large margin.

Challenges in Hypergraph Learning. Despite the theoretical and practical advantages, to our knowledge, equivariant GNN and its variants were rarely considered for general hypergraph learning with higher-order data [1], and never implemented except for highly restricted k-uniform hyperedge prediction [32,51]. We identify two main challenges. First, although the asymptotic cost can be reduced to a practical level with recent tricks [32], the number of parameters still grows rapidly to Bell number of input order [5]. This makes any layer $L_{k\to l}$ with $k + l > 4$ challenging to use, as $k + l = 5$ already leads to 52 weight matrices. Second, in inductive learning [24,60] where a model is tested on unseen nodes or hypergraphs, the model can be required to process unseen-order hyperedges that possibly surpass the max order in the training data. This is not straightforward for equivariant GNNs, because fixed-order tensors that underlie $L_{k\to l}$ require to pre-specify the max hyperedge order (k,l) that the model can process.

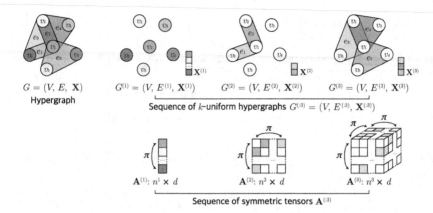

Fig. 1. Example of a hypergraph represented as a sequence of k-uniform hypergraphs (Definition 1), or equivalently a sequence of symmetric higher-order tensors (Definition 3). Note that nodes are handled as first-order hyperedges.

3   Equivariant Hypergraph Neural Network

We now proceed to our framework on practical equivariant GNNs for general hypergraph data. All proofs can be found in Appendix A.1. In practical setups that assume undirected hypergraphs [2,3,13,16,18,57], a hypergraph $G = (V, E, \mathbf{X})$ is defined by a set of n nodes V, a set of m hyperedges E, and features $\mathbf{X} \in \mathbb{R}^{m \times d}$ of the hyperedges. Each hyperedge $e \in E$ is a subset of node set V, and its order $|e|$ indicates its type. For example, a first-order edge $\{i\}$ represents an i-th node; a second-order edge $\{i, j\}$ represents a pairwise link of i-th and j-th nodes; in general, an order-k edge $\{i_1, ..., i_k\}$ represents a hyperedge that links k nodes. By $\mathbf{X}_e \in \mathbb{R}^d$ we denote the feature attached to a hyperedge e. We assume that node and hyperedge features are both d-dimensional [12,32,42,43]; to handle different dimensionalities, we simply let $d = (d_v + d_e)$ and place node features at first d_v channels and hyperedge features at last d_e channels.

Note that above notion of hypergraphs $(V, E, \mathbf{X})$ does not directly align to higher-order tensors $\mathbf{A} \in \mathbb{R}^{n^k \times d}$ (Sect. 2) – unlike them, hypergraphs of our interest are sparse, undirected, and each hyperedge contains unique node indices. As equivariant GNNs (Sect. 2) build upon higher-order tensors, it is necessary to establish a connection between hypergraphs and the higher-order tensors.

3.1   Hypergraph as a Sequence of Higher-Order Tensors

To describe hypergraphs $(V, E, \mathbf{X})$ using higher-order tensors $\mathbf{A} \in \mathbb{R}^{n^k \times d}$, it is convenient to introduce k-*uniform hypergraphs*. A hypergraph is k-uniform if all of its hyperedges are exactly of order-k. For example, a graph without self-loops is

2-uniform, and a triangle mesh is 3-uniform. From that, we can define equivalent representation of a hypergraph as a *sequence* of k-uniform hypergraphs:

Definition 1. *The sequence representation of a hypergraph* $(V, E, \mathbf{X})$ *with max hyperedge order K is a sequence of k-uniform hypergraphs with $k \leq K$, written as* $(V, E^{(k)}, \mathbf{X}^{(k)})_{k \leq K} = (V, E^{(:K)}, \mathbf{X}^{(:K)})$ *where $E^{(k)}$ as the set of all order-k hyperedges in E and $\mathbf{X}^{(k)}$ as a row stack of features $\{\mathbf{X}_e | e \in E^{(k)}\}$.*

As the collection $(E^{(k)})_{k \leq K}$ forms a partition of E, we can retrieve the original hypergraph $(V, E, \mathbf{X})$ from its sequence representation $(V, E^{(k)}, \mathbf{X}^{(k)})_{k \leq K}$ by using the union of $(E^{(k)})_{k \leq K}$ for E and the concatenation of $(\mathbf{X}^{(k)})_{k \leq K}$ for $\mathbf{X}$.

The concept of uniform hypergraph is convenient because we can draw an equivalent representation as a *symmetric* higher-order tensor [13,35]. An order-k tensor $\mathbf{A}$ is symmetric if its entries are invariant under reordering of indices, *e.g.*, $\mathbf{A}_{ij} = \mathbf{A}_{ji}$, $\mathbf{A}_{ijk} = \mathbf{A}_{kij} = ...$, and so on. From that, we can define the equivalent representation of a k-uniform hypergraph as an order-k symmetric tensor[1]:

Definition 2. *The tensor representation of k-uniform hypergraph* $(V, E^{(k)}, \mathbf{X}^{(k)})$ *is an order-k symmetric tensor* $\mathbf{A}^{(k)} \in \mathbb{R}^{n^k \times d}$ *defined as follows:*

$$\mathbf{A}^{(k)}_{(i_1,...,i_k)} = \begin{cases} \mathbf{X}^{(k)}_e & \text{if } e = \{i_1, ..., i_k\} \in E^{(k)} \\ 0 & \text{otherwise} \end{cases}. \tag{2}$$

From $\mathbf{A}^{(k)}$, we can retrieve the original k-uniform hypergraph $(V, E^{(k)}, \mathbf{X}^{(k)})$ by first identifying the indices of all nonzero entries of $\mathbf{A}^{(k)}$ to construct $E^{(k)}$, and then using $E^{(k)}$ to index $\mathbf{A}^{(k)}$ to construct $\mathbf{X}^{(k)}$.

Now, directly combining Definition 1 and 2, we can define the equivalent representation of a hypergraph as a sequence of higher-order tensors:

Definition 3. *The tensor sequence representation of a hypergraph* $(V, E, \mathbf{X})$ *with maximum hyperedge order K is a sequence of symmetric higher-order tensors* $(\mathbf{A}^{(k)})_{k \leq K} = \mathbf{A}^{(:K)}$, *where each $\mathbf{A}^{(k)}$ is the tensor representation (Definition 2) of each k-uniform hypergraph* $(V, E^{(k)}, \mathbf{X}^{(k)})$ *that comes from the sequence representation of the hypergraph* $(V, E^{(k)}, \mathbf{X}^{(k)})_{k \leq K} = (V, E^{(:K)}, \mathbf{X}^{(:K)})$ *(Definition 1).*

An illustration is in Fig. 1. Note that we can include node features as $\mathbf{A}^{(1)}$. Now, our problem of interest reduces to identifying a function f that operates on sequences of tensors $\mathbf{A}^{(:K)}$ that represent hypergraphs. The concept of permutation invariance and equivariance (Sect. 2) applies similarly here. A node permutation $\pi \in S_n$ acts on a tensor sequence $\mathbf{A}^{(:K)}$ by jointly acting on each tensor, $\pi \cdot \mathbf{A}^{(:K)} = (\pi \cdot \mathbf{A}^{(k)})_{k \leq K}$. An invariant f always satisfies $f(\pi \cdot \mathbf{A}^{(:K)}) = f(\mathbf{A}^{(:K)})$, and an equivariant f always satisfies $f(\pi \cdot \mathbf{A}^{(:K)}) = \pi \cdot f(\mathbf{A}^{(:K)})$.

---

[1] Higher-order tensors can in principle represent directed hypergraphs as well; we constrain them to be symmetric to specifically represent undirected hypergraphs.

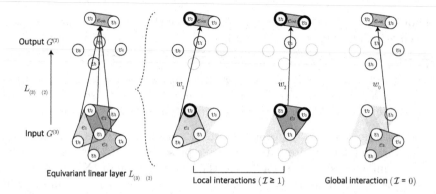

Fig. 2. Conceptual illustration of an equivariant linear layer $L_{(3)\to(2)}$ as in Eq. (3). The layer uses different weights $w_{\mathcal{I}}$ for different overlaps $\mathcal{I}$ between input and output hyperedges. This gives rise to local interactions similar to message-passing ($\mathcal{I} \geq 1$) and global interactions ($\mathcal{I} = 0$) implemented as global sum-pooling.

3.2   Equivariant Linear Layers for Hypergraphs

In Definition 3, we represented a hypergraph as a sequence of symmetric higher-order tensors $(\mathbf{A}^{(k)})_{k \leq K}$, each $\mathbf{A}^{(k)}$ representing a k-uniform hypergraph. We now utilize equivariant linear layers $L_{k \to l} : \mathbb{R}^{n^k \times d} \to \mathbb{R}^{n^l \times d'}$ (Eq. (1)) in Sect. 2 to formalize equivariant linear layers that input and output hypergraphs. The idea is to find and combine all pairwise linear maps between tensors (*i.e.*, k-uniform hypergraphs) of input and output sequences. Although seemingly simple, this gives the *maximally expressive* equivariant linear layer for hypergraphs.

Equivariant Linear Layers for k-Uniform Hypergraphs. In Sect. 2, we argued that the equivariant linear layer $L_{k \to l}$ cannot be practically used due to the prohibitive number of b($k + l$) weights and b(l) biases. Yet, when the input and output tensors are restricted to k- and l-uniform hypergraphs respectively, we can show that the layer reduces to $\mathcal{O}(k + l)$ weights and a single bias:

Proposition 1. *Assume that the input and output of equivariant linear layer $L_{k \to l}$ (Eq. (1)) are constrained to symmetric tensors that represent k- and l-uniform hypergraphs respectively (Eq. (2)). Then it reduces to $L_{(k)\to(l)}$ below:*

$$L_{(k)\to(l)}(\mathbf{A}^{(k)})_{\mathbf{j}} = \mathbb{1}_{|\mathbf{j}|=l}\left(\sum_{\mathcal{I}=1}^{\min(k,l)}\sum_{\mathbf{i}}\mathbb{1}_{|\mathbf{i}\cap\mathbf{j}|=\mathcal{I}}\mathbf{A}_{\mathbf{i}}^{(k)}w_{\mathcal{I}} + \sum_{\mathbf{i}}\mathbf{A}_{\mathbf{i}}^{(k)}w_0 + b_l\right), \quad (3)$$

where $w_o, w_{\mathcal{I}} \in \mathbb{R}^{d \times d'}$, $b_l \in \mathbb{R}^{d'}$ are weight and bias, $|\mathbf{i}|$ is number of distinct elements in $\mathbf{i}$, and $|\mathbf{i} \cap \mathbf{j}|$ is number of distinct intersecting elements in $\mathbf{i}$ and $\mathbf{j}$.

The idea for the proof is that, if input and output are constrained to tensors from Eq. (2), a large number of parameters in the original layer are tied to adhere to the symmetry. This leads to much less parameters compared to the original Bell number version ($L_{k \to l}$). Still, note that $L_{(k) \to (l)}$ (Eq. (3)) is still a maximally expressive linear layer as it produces the identical outputs with $L_{k \to l}$.

Notably, Eq. (3) reveals that maximal expressiveness is composed of sophisticated local message passing augmented with global interaction. In the first term of Eq. (3), the constraint $\mathbb{1}_{|i \cap j| > 0}$ specifies local dependency between *incident* input and output hyperedges having at least one overlapping nodes. Yet, this local interaction is more *fine-grained* than conventional message passing, as it uses separate weights $w_{\mathcal{I}}$ for different numbers of overlapping nodes $\mathcal{I}$ (Fig. 2). This is reminiscent of recent work in subgraph message passing [7] that improve expressive power of GNNs. In addition, the layer contains intrinsic global interaction via pooling in second term of Eq. (3), which reminds of virtual node or global attention [27, 34, 38, 40, 48, 56] that also improve expressive power [48].

Equivariant Linear Layers for Hypergraphs. We now construct maximally expressive equivariant linear layers for undirected hypergraphs. We begin by representing a hypergraph as a sequence of tensors $(\mathbf{A}^{(k)})_{k \leq K} = \mathbf{A}^{(:K)}$ (Definition 3). The goal is to construct the linear layer $L_{(:K) \to (:L)}$ to input and output those tensor sequences while being equivariant $L_{(:K) \to (:L)}(\pi \cdot \mathbf{A}^{(:K)}) = \pi \cdot L_{(:K) \to (:L)}(\mathbf{A}^{(:K)})$. For this, we use all pairwise linear layers $L_{(k) \to (l)}$ (Eq. (3)) between tensors of input and output sequences:

$$L_{(:K) \to (:L)}(\mathbf{A}^{(:K)}) = \left(\sum_{k \leq K} L_{(k) \to (l)}(\mathbf{A}^{(k)}) \right)_{l \leq L}. \tag{4}$$

For better interpretation, we plug Eq. (3) into Eq. (4) and rewrite it with respect to **j**-th entry of l-th (order-l) output tensor:

$$L_{(:K) \to (:L)}(\mathbf{A}^{(:K)})_{l,\mathbf{j}} = \mathbb{1}_{|\mathbf{j}|=l} \sum_{k \leq K} \sum_{\mathcal{I}=1}^{\min(k,l)} \sum_{\mathbf{i}} \mathbb{1}_{|\mathbf{i} \cap \mathbf{j}|=\mathcal{I}} \mathbf{A}_{\mathbf{i}}^{(k)} w_{k,l,\mathcal{I}}$$

$$+ \mathbb{1}_{|\mathbf{j}|=l} \sum_{k \leq K} \sum_{\mathbf{i}} \mathbf{A}_{\mathbf{i}}^{(k)} w_{k,l,0} + \mathbb{1}_{|\mathbf{j}|=l} b_l. \tag{5}$$

Note that we added subscripts (k, l) to w_0, $w_{\mathcal{I}}$ to differentiate between weights from each sublayer $L_{(k) \to (l)}$ as they are involved in different computations. On the other hand, the biases from sublayers $(L_{(k) \to (l)})_{k \leq K}$ carry out exactly the same computation, and can be merged to a single bias b_l. As a result, $L_{(:K) \to (:L)}$ contains $\sum_{l \leq L, k \leq K}(1 + \min(k, l))$ weights and L biases, achieving a better scalability than the original $L_{K \to L}$ that has exponentially many weights and biases.

Similar to sublayers $L_{(k) \to (l)}$ (Eq. (3)), we see that the combined layer for general hypergraphs $L_{(:K) \to (:L)}$ (Eq. (5)) is a mixture of fine-grained local message passing and global interaction. In this case, the local interactions utilize different weights $w_{k,l,\mathcal{I}}$ for each triplet $(k, l, \mathcal{I})$ that specifies dependency between order-k input and order-l output hyperedges with $\mathcal{I}$ overlapping nodes. Similarly, global interactions (pooling) utilize different weights $w_{k,l,0}$ for each pair (k, l), specifying global dependency between all order-k input and order-l output hyperedges. Finally, different biases b_l are assigned for each output hyperedge order l.

Importantly, we can show the following:

Theorem 1. $L_{(:K) \to (:L)}$ *(Eq. (4)) is the maximally expressive equivariant linear layer for undirected hypergraphs represented as tensor sequences.*

Similar as in Proposition 1, the idea for the proof is to appropriately constraint the input and output of the maximally expressive equivariant linear layer $L_{K \to L}$, and observe that most of its parameters are tied and reduced, leading to $L_{(:K) \to (:L)}$. Still, the layer retains maximal expressiveness of the original layer $(L_{K \to L})$ as it produces the identical output.

3.3   Equivariant Hypergraph Neural Networks (EHNN)

In Sect. 3.2, we introduced equivariant linear layers for general undirected hypergraphs $L_{(:K) \to (:L)}$ by composing order-specific sublayers $L_{(k) \to (l)}$ for $k \leq K$, $l \leq L$ and proved their maximal expressiveness. Yet, these layers are still unsuitable to be used in practice because they cannot input or output hypergraphs with orders exceeding (K, L), and the number of weights and biases grows at least linearly to (K, L) that can reach several hundreds in practice. To resolve the problems jointly, we propose the concept of *Equivariant Hypergraph Neural Network* (EHNN) that introduces intrinsic trainable parameter sharing via *hypernetworks* [23]. More specifically, we impose parameter sharing within $L_{(:K) \to (:L)}$ and across all sublayers $L_{(k) \to (l)}$ via two hypernetworks, each for weights and biases[2]. As a result, an EHNN layer is defined as follows, with hypernetworks $\mathcal{W} : \mathbb{N}^3 \to \mathbb{R}^{d \times d'}$ and $\mathcal{B} : \mathbb{N} \to \mathbb{R}^{d'}$ inferring all weights $w_{k,l,\mathcal{I}}$ and biases b_l (Eq. (5)) from the subscripts $(k, l, \mathcal{I})$ and (l) respectively:

$$\text{EHNN}(\mathbf{A}^{(:K)})_{l,\mathbf{j}} = \mathbb{1}_{|\mathbf{j}|=l} \sum_{k \leq K} \sum_{\mathcal{I}=1}^{\min(k,l)} \sum_{\mathbf{i}} \mathbb{1}_{|\mathbf{i} \cap \mathbf{j}| = \mathcal{I}} \mathbf{A}_{\mathbf{i}}^{(k)} \mathcal{W}(k, l, \mathcal{I})$$

$$+ \mathbb{1}_{|\mathbf{j}|=l} \sum_{k \leq K} \sum_{\mathbf{i}} \mathbf{A}_{\mathbf{i}}^{(k)} \mathcal{W}(k, l, 0) + \mathbb{1}_{|\mathbf{j}|=l} \mathcal{B}(l). \tag{6}$$

In principle, this preserves maximal expressiveness of $L_{(:K) \to (:L)}$ when $\mathcal{W}$ and $\mathcal{B}$ are parameterized as MLPs, as by universal approximation they can learn any lookup table that maps subscripts to weights and biases [25]. Furthermore, as hypernetworks $\mathcal{W}$ and $\mathcal{B}$ can produce weights for arbitrary hyperedge orders $(k, l, \mathcal{I})$, we can remove the bound in hyperedge orders from the specification of the layer and use a single EHNN layer with bounded parameters to any hypergraphs with unbounded or unseen hyperedge orders. Conclusively, EHNN layer is by far the first attempt that is maximally expressive while being able to process arbitrary-order hypergraphs by construction.

---

[2] Note that we do not share the hypernetworks across different levels of layers.

3.4   Practical Realization of EHNN

The EHNN layer in Eq. (6) is conceptually elegant, but in practice it can be costly as we need to explicitly hold all output matrices of the hypernetwork $\mathcal{W}(k, l, \mathcal{I}) \in \mathbb{R}^{d \times d'}$ in memory. This motivates us to seek for simpler realizations of EHNN that can be implemented efficiently while retaining the maximal expressiveness (*i.e.*, being able to model $L_{(:K) \rightarrow (:L)}$ (Theorem 1) thus exhausting the full space of equivariant linear layers on undirected hypergraphs). To this end, we propose EHNN-MLP that utilizes three consecutive MLPs to approximate the role of the weight hypernetwork, and also propose its extension EHNN-Transformer with attention mechanism. Then, we finish the section by providing a comparative analysis of EHNN-MLP and EHNN-Transformer with respect to the existing message passing hypergraph neural networks.

Realization with MLP. We first introduce *EHNN-MLP*, a simple realization of EHNN with three elementwise MLPs $\phi_{1:3}$ where each $\phi_p : \mathbb{N} \times \mathbb{R}^{d_p} \rightarrow \mathbb{R}^{d'_p}$ takes a positive integer as an auxiliary input. The intuition here is to *decompose* the weight application with hypernetwork $\mathcal{W}(k, l, \mathcal{I})$ into three consecutive MLPs $\phi_1(k, \cdot)$, $\phi_2(\mathcal{I}, \cdot)$, and $\phi_3(l, \cdot)$, eliminating the need to explicitly store the inferred weights for each triplet $\mathcal{W}(k, l, \mathcal{I})$. We characterize EHNN-MLP as follows:

$$\text{EHNN-MLP}(\mathbf{A}^{(:K)})_{l,\mathbf{j}} = \phi_3 \left(l, \sum_{\mathcal{I} \geq 0} \phi_2 \left(\mathcal{I}, \sum_{k \leq K} \sum_{\mathbf{i}} \mathbf{B}_{\mathbf{i},\mathbf{j}}^{\mathcal{I}} \phi_1(k, \mathbf{A}_{\mathbf{i}}^{(k)}) \right) \right) + \mathcal{B}(l),$$

$$(7)$$

$$\text{where } \mathbf{B}_{\mathbf{i},\mathbf{j}}^{\mathcal{I}} = \begin{cases} \mathbb{1}_{|\mathbf{i} \cap \mathbf{j}| = \mathcal{I}} & \text{if } \mathcal{I} \geq 1 \\ 1 & \text{if } \mathcal{I} = 0 \end{cases}, \qquad (8)$$

where we omit the output constraint $\mathbb{1}_{|\mathbf{j}| = l}$ for brevity, and introduce a binary scalar $\mathbf{B}_{\mathbf{i},\mathbf{j}}^{\mathcal{I}}$ to write local ($\mathcal{I} \geq 1$) and global ($\mathcal{I} = 0$) interactions together.

Now we show that an EHNN-MLP layer can realize any EHNN layer:

Theorem 2. *An EHNN-MLP layer (Eq. (7)) can approximate any EHNN layer (Eq. (6)) to an arbitrary precision.*

The proof is done by leveraging the universal approximation property [25] to model appropriate functions with MLPs $\phi_{1:3}$, so that the output of EHNN-MLP (Eq. (7)) accurately approximates the output of EHNN (Eq. (6)). As a result, with EHNN-MLP, we now have a practical model that can approximate the maximally expressive linear layer for general undirected hypergraphs.

In our implementation of the MLPs $\phi_{1:3}$, we first transform the input order (k, l or $\mathcal{I}$) into a continuous vector called *order embedding*, and combine it with the input feature through concatenation. This way, the order embeddings are served similarly as the positional encoding used in Transformer [53] with a subtle difference that it indicates the order of the input or output hyperedges. We employ sinusoidal encoding [53] to obtain order embedding due to its efficiency and, more importantly, to aid extrapolation to unseen hyperedge orders in testing.

Realization as a Transformer. While EHNN-MLP (Eq. (7)) theoretically inherits the high expressive power of EHNN, in practice, its static sum-pooling can be limited in accounting for relative importance of input hyperedges. A solution for this is to introduce more sophisticated pooling. In particular, the attention mechanism of Transformers [53] was shown to offer a large performance gain in set and (hyper)graph modeling [13,31,32,36] via dynamic weighting of input elements. Thus, we extend EHNN-MLP with multihead attention coefficients $\alpha_{i,j}^{h,\mathcal{I}}$ and introduce *EHNN-Transformer*, an advanced realization of EHNN:

$$\text{Attn}(\mathbf{A}^{(:K)})_{l,\mathbf{j}} = \phi_3 \left(l, \sum_{\mathcal{I} \geq 0} \phi_2 \left(\mathcal{I}, \sum_{h=1}^{H} \sum_{k \leq K} \sum_{\mathbf{i}} \alpha_{i,j}^{h,\mathcal{I}} \phi_1(k, \mathbf{A}_{\mathbf{i}}^{(k)}) w_h^V \right) \right), \quad (9)$$

$$\text{EHNN-Transformer}(\mathbf{A}^{(:K)}) = \text{Attn}(\mathbf{A}^{(:K)}) + \text{MLP}(\text{Attn}(\mathbf{A}^{(:K)})), \quad (10)$$

where we omit the output constraint $\mathbb{1}_{|\mathbf{j}|=l}$ and bias $\mathcal{B}(l)$ for brevity. H denotes the number of heads and $w_h^V \in \mathbb{R}^{d \times d_v}$ denotes the value weight matrix. To compute attention coefficients $\alpha_{i,j}^{h,\mathcal{I}}$ from the input, we introduce additional query and key (hyper)networks $\mathcal{Q} : \mathbb{N} \to \mathbb{R}^{H \times d_H}$ and $\mathcal{K} : \mathbb{N} \times \mathbb{R}^d \to \mathbb{R}^{H \times d_H}$ and characterize scaled dot-product attention [53] as follows:

$$\alpha_{i,j}^{h,\mathcal{I}} = \begin{cases} \sigma \left(\mathcal{Q}(\mathcal{I})_h \mathcal{K} \left(\mathcal{I}, \phi_1(k, \mathbf{A}_{\mathbf{i}}^{(k)}) \right)_h^\top / \sqrt{d_H} \cdot \mathbb{1}_{|\mathbf{i} \cap \mathbf{j}| = \mathcal{I}} \right) & \text{if } \mathcal{I} \geq 1 \\ \sigma \left(\mathcal{Q}(0)_h \mathcal{K} \left(\mathcal{I}, \phi_1(k, \mathbf{A}_{\mathbf{i}}^{(k)}) \right)_h^\top / \sqrt{d_H} \right) & \text{if } \mathcal{I} = 0 \end{cases}, \quad (11)$$

where $\sigma(\cdot)$ denotes activation, often chosen as softmax normalization. Note that the query $\mathcal{Q}(\mathcal{I})$ is agnostic to output index $\mathbf{j}$, following prior works on set and (hyper)graph attention [13,36]. Although this choice of attention mechanism has a drawback that assigning importance to input (**i**) depending on output (**j**) is not straightforward, we choose it in favor of scalability.

Comparison to Message Passing Networks. We finish the section by providing a comparative analysis of EHNNs with respect to the existing message passing networks for hypergraphs. We specifically compare against *AllSet* [13], as it represents a highly general framework that subsumes most existing hypergraph neural networks. Their MLP-based characterization *AllDeepSets* can be written with two MLPs ϕ_1 and ϕ_2 as follows:

$$\text{AllDeepSets}(\mathbf{A}^{(:K)})_{l,\mathbf{j}} = \mathbb{1}_{|\mathbf{j}|=l} \phi_2 \left(\sum_{k \leq K} \sum_{\mathbf{i}} \mathbb{1}_{|\mathbf{i} \cap \mathbf{j}| \geq 1} \phi_1(\mathbf{A}_{\mathbf{i}}^{(k)}) \right). \quad (12)$$

We show the below by reducing EHNN-MLP to AllDeepSets through ablation:

Theorem 3. *An AllDeepSets layer (Eq. (12)) is a special case of EHNN-MLP layer (Eq. (7)), while the opposite is not true.*

Finally, Theorem 3 leads to the following corollary:

Corollary 1. *An EHNN-MLP layer is more expressive than an AllDeepSets layer and also all hypergraph neural networks that AllDeepSets subsumes.*

We provide an in-depth discussion including the comparison between EHNN-Transformer and AllSetTransformer [13] in Appendix A.2.

4 Experiments

We test EHNN on a range of hypergraph learning problems including synthetic node classification problem, real-world semi-supervised classification, and visual keypoint matching. For the real-world tasks, we use 10 semi-supervised classification datasets used in Chien et al. [13] and two visual keypoint matching datasets used in Wang et al. [55]. Details including the datasets and hyperparameters are in Appendix A.3. Additional experiments including comparative and ablation studies, and runtime and memory cost analysis are in Appendix A.4.

4.1 Synthetic k-edge Identification

We devise a simple but challenging synthetic node classification task termed k-edge identification to demonstrate how the expressive power of EHNN can help learn complex hypergraph functions. In input hypergraph, we pick a random hyperedge and mark its nodes with a binary label. The task is to identify all other nodes whose hyperedge order is the same with the marked one. The model is required to propagate the information of marked hyperedge globally, while also reasoning about fine-grained structure of individual hyperedges for comparison. We use 100 train and 20 test hypergraphs, each with 100 nodes and randomly wired 10 hyperedges of orders $\in \{2, ..., 10\}$. To further test generalization to unseen orders, we add two training sets where hyperedges are sampled *without* order-$\{5, 6, 7\}$ hyperedges (interpolation) or order-$\{8, 9, 10\}$ hyperedges (extrapolation). We evaluate the performance of EHNN-MLP/-Transformer with AllDeepSets and AllSetTransformer [13] as message passing baselines.

The test performances are in Table 1. EHNN achieves significant improvement over message passing nets, producing almost perfect prediction. The result

Table 1. Results for synthetic order-k hyperedge identification. We show averaged best test accuracy (%) over 5 runs with standard deviation.

	Test involves only seen k	Test involves unseen k	
		Interpolation	Extrapolation
AllDeepSets	76.99 ± 0.98	79.6 ± 0.86	79.01 ± 2.82
AllSetTransformer	77.61 ± 2.27	78.61 ± 2.367	77.35 ± 1.89
EHNN-MLP	98.02 ± 0.73	90.70 ± 2.90	85.65 ± 2.89
EHNN-Transformer	**99.69 ± 0.31**	**92.31 ± 1.47**	**90.19 ± 5.51**

Table 2. Results for semi-supervised node classification. Average accuracy (%) over 20 runs are shown, and standard deviation can be found in Appendix A.3. Gray shade indicate the best result, and blue shade indicate results within one standard deviation of the best. Baseline scores are taken from Chien et al. [13].

	Zoo	20Newsgroups	mushroom	NTU2012	ModelNet40	Yelp	House(1)	Walmart(1)	House(0.6)	Walmart(0.6)	avg. rank (↓)
MLP	87.18	81.42	100.00	85.52	96.14	31.96	67.93	45.51	81.53	63.28	6.4
CEGCN	51.54	OOM	95.27	81.52	89.92	OOM	62.80	54.44	64.36	59.78	11.5
CEGAT	47.88	OOM	96.60	82.21	92.52	OOM	69.09	51.14	77.25	59.47	10.5
HNHN	93.59	81.35	100.00	89.11	97.84	31.65	67.80	47.18	78.78	65.80	5.9
HGNN	92.50	80.33	98.73	87.72	95.44	33.04	61.39	62.00	66.16	77.72	7.8
HCHA	93.65	80.33	98.70	87.48	94.48	30.99	61.36	62.45	67.91	77.12	8.1
HyperGCN	N/A	81.05	47.90	56.36	75.89	29.42	48.31	44.74	78.22	55.31	12.4
UniGCNII	93.65	81.12	99.96	89.30	98.07	31.70	67.25	54.45	80.65	72.08	5.8
HAN (full batch)	85.19	OOM	90.86	83.58	94.04	OOM	71.05	OOM	83.27	OOM	9.9
HAN (minibatch)	75.77	79.72	93.45	80.77	91.52	26.05	62.00	48.57	82.04	63.1	10.6
AllDeepSets	95.39	81.06	99.99	88.09	96.98	30.36	67.82	64.55	80.70	78.46	5.4
AllSetTransformer	97.50	81.38	100.00	88.69	98.20	36.89	69.33	65.46	83.14	78.46	2.4
EHNN-MLP	91.15	81.31	99.99	87.35	97.74	35.80	67.41	65.65	82.29	78.80	5.0
EHNN-Transformer	93.27	81.42	100.00	89.60	98.28	36.48	71.53	68.73	85.09	80.05	1.6

Table 3. Hypergraph matching accuracy (%) on Willow test set.

	Car	Duck	Face	Motor	Wine	Avg.
GMN	38.85	38.75	78.85	28.08	45.00	45.90
NGM	77.50	85.87	99.81	77.50	89.71	86.08
NHGM	69.13	83.08	99.81	73.37	88.65	82.81
NMGM	74.95	81.33	99.83	78.26	92.06	85.29
IPCA-GM	79.58	80.20	99.70	73.37	83.75	83.32
CIE-H	9.37	8.87	9.88	11.84	9.84	9.96
BBGM	96.15	90.96	**100.00**	96.54	**99.23**	96.58
GANN-MGM	92.11	90.11	**100.00**	96.21	98.26	95.34
NGM-v2	94.81	89.04	**100.00**	96.54	95.87	95.25
NHGM-v2	89.33	83.17	**100.00**	92.60	95.96	92.21
EHNN-MLP	94.71	91.92	**100.00**	97.21	97.79	96.33
EHNN-Transformer	**97.02**	**92.69**	**100.00**	**97.60**	98.08	**97.08**

advocates that even for simple tasks there are cases where high expressive power of a network is essential. Furthermore, we observe evidences that the model can interpolate or even extrapolate to unseen hyperedge orders. This supports the use of hypernetworks to infer parameters for potentially unseen orders.

4.2 Semi-supervised Classification

To test EHNN in real-world hypergraph learning, we use 10 transductive semi-supervised node classification datasets [13]. The data is randomly split into 50% training, 25% validation, and 25% test. We run the experiment 20 times with random splits and initialization, and report aggregated classification accuracy.

Table 4. Hypergraph matching accuracy (%) on PASCAL-VOC test set.

	Aero	Bike	Bird	Boat	Botl	Bus	Car	Cat	Chair	Cow	Desk
GMN	40.67	57.62	58.19	51.38	77.55	72.48	66.90	65.04	40.43	61.56	65.17
PCA-GM	51.46	62.43	64.70	58.56	81.94	75.18	69.56	71.05	44.53	65.81	39.00
NGM	12.09	10.01	17.44	21.73	12.03	21.40	20.16	14.26	15.10	12.07	14.50
NHGM	12.09	10.01	17.44	21.73	12.03	21.40	20.16	14.26	15.10	12.07	14.50
IPCA-GM	50.78	62.29	63.87	58.94	79.46	74.18	72.60	71.52	41.42	64.12	36.67
CIE-H	52.26	66.79	69.09	59.76	83.38	74.61	69.93	71.04	43.36	69.20	76.00
BBGM	**60.06**	71.32	78.21	78.97	88.63	**95.57**	**89.52**	80.53	**59.34**	**77.80**	76.00
GANN-MGM	14.75	32.20	21.31	24.43	67.23	36.35	21.09	17.20	25.73	21.00	37.50
NGM-v2	42.88	61.70	63.63	75.62	84.66	90.58	75.34	72.26	44.42	66.67	74.50
NHGM-v2	57.04	71.88	76.06	**79.96**	**89.79**	93.70	86.16	80.76	56.36	76.70	74.33
EHNN-MLP	57.34	**73.89**	76.41	78.41	89.40	94.51	85.58	79.83	56.39	76.56	**91.00**
EHNN-Transformer	60.04	72.36	**78.25**	78.59	87.61	93.77	87.99	**80.78**	58.76	76.29	81.17
	Dog	Horse	Mbk	Prsn	Plant	Sheep	Sofa	Train	Tv	Avg.	
GMN	61.56	62.18	58.96	37.80	78.39	66.89	39.74	79.84	90.94	61.66	
PCA-GM	67.82	65.18	65.71	46.21	83.81	70.51	49.88	80.87	93.07	65.36	
NGM	12.83	12.05	15.69	09.76	21.00	17.10	15.12	31.11	24.88	16.52	
NHGM	12.83	12.05	15.67	09.76	21.00	17.10	14.66	31.11	24.83	16.49	
IPCA-GM	69.11	66.05	65.88	46.97	83.09	68.97	51.83	79.17	92.27	64.96	
CIE-H	69.68	71.18	66.14	46.76	87.22	71.08	59.16	82.84	92.60	69.10	
BBGM	**80.39**	77.80	76.48	**65.99**	98.52	**78.07**	76.65	97.61	94.36	**80.09**	
GANN-MGM	16.16	20.16	25.92	19.20	53.76	18.34	26.16	46.30	72.32	30.85	
NGM-v2	67.83	68.92	68.86	47.40	96.69	70.57	70.01	95.13	92.49	71.51	
NHGM-v2	76.75	77.45	**76.81**	58.56	98.21	75.34	76.42	98.10	94.80	78.76	
EHNN-MLP	76.57	**78.65**	75.54	58.92	98.31	76.53	**81.14**	98.08	**95.01**	79.90	
EHNN-Transformer	78.30	76.91	75.79	63.78	97.60	76.47	78.04	**98.53**	93.83	79.74	

The test performances are in Table 2. Our methods often achieve favorable scores over strong baselines *e.g.*, AllDeepSets and AllSetTransformer – our models improve the state-of-the art by 3.27% in Walmart (1), 1.82% in House (0.6), and 1.54% in Walmart (0.6). Notably, EHNN-Transformer gives state-of-the-art performance in most cases. This supports the notion that attention strengthens equivariant networks [32, 36], and also implies that high expressiveness of EHNN makes it strong on general hypergraph learning setups involving not only social networks but also vision and graphics (NTU2012 and ModelNet40).

4.3 Visual Keypoint Matching

To test EHNN in computer vision problems represented as hypergraph learning, we tackle visual keypoint matching. The task is considered challenging due to discrepancy between the two images in terms of viewpoint, scale, and lighting. Following previous work [55], we view the problem as *hypergraph matching* where keypoints of each image form an hypergraph. This is considered helpful as the hyperedge features can capture rotation- and scale-invariant geometric features such as angles. We then cast hypergraph matching to binary node classification on a single association hypergraph as in previous work [55].

We use two standard datasets [55]: Willow ObjectClass [14] and PASCAL-VOC [9,17]. The Willow dataset consists of 256 images with 5 object categories. The PASCAL-VOC dataset contains 11,530 images with 20 object categories, and is considered challenging due to large variance in illumination and pose. We follow the training setup of NHGM-v2 [55] and only replace the hypergraph neural network module to EHNN-MLP/-Transformer. The key difference between NHGM-v2 and our models is that NHGM-v2 utilizes two *separate* message passing networks, one on 2-edges and another on 3-edges, and aggregates node features as a weighted sum. In contrast, EHNN *mixes* the information from 2-edges and 3-edges extensively via shared MLP hypernetworks and global interactions.

The results are in Tables 3 and 4. On Willow, EHNN-Transformer gives the best performance, improving over NHGM-v2 by 4.87%. On PASCAL-VOC, EHNNs improve over NHGM-v2 by $\sim 1\%$, and are competitive to the best model (BBGM; 0.19% gap) that relies on sophisticated combinatorial solver [50]. We conjecture that intrinsic and global mix of 2-edge (distance) and 3-edge (angle) feature improves hypergraph learning and consequently also keypoint matching.

5   Conclusion

We proposed a family of hypergraph neural networks coined Equivariant Hypergraph Neural Network (EHNN). EHNN extends theoretical foundations of equivariant GNNs to general undirected hypergraphs by representing a hypergraph as a sequence of tensors and combining equivariant linear layers on them. We further proposed EHNN-MLP/-Transformer, practical realizations of EHNN based on MLP hypernetworks. We show that EHNN is theoretically more expressive than most message passing networks and provide empirical evidences.

Acknowledgement. This work was supported by Institute of Information & communications Technology Planning & Evaluation (IITP) (No. 2021-0-00537, 2019-0-00075 and 2021-0-02068), the National Research Foundation of Korea (NRF) (No. 2021R1C1C1012540 and 2021R1A4A3032834), and Korea Meteorological Administration Research and Development Program "Development of AI techniques for Weather Forecasting" under Grant (KMA2021-00121).

References

1. Albooyeh, M., Bertolini, D., Ravanbakhsh, S.: Incidence networks for geometric deep learning. arXiv (2019)
2. Arya, D., Gupta, D.K., Rudinac, S., Worring, M.: Hypersage: generalizing inductive representation learning on hypergraphs. arXiv (2020)
3. Bai, S., Zhang, F., Torr, P.H.S.: Hypergraph convolution and hypergraph attention. Pattern Recognit. (2021)
4. Belongie, S.J., Malik, J., Puzicha, J.: Shape matching and object recognition using shape contexts. IEEE Trans. Pattern Anal. Mach. Intell. (2002)

5. Berend, D., Tassa, T.: Improved bounds on bell numbers and on moments of sums of random variables. Probability and Mathematical Statistics. (2010)
6. Berge, C., Minieka., E.: Graphs and Hypergraphs. North-Holland Publishing Company (1981)
7. Bevilacqua, B., et al.: Equivariant subgraph aggregation networks. In: ICLR (2022)
8. Botsch, M., Pauly, M., Kobbelt, L., Alliez, P., Lévy, B.: Geometric modeling based on polygonal meshes. In: Eurographics Tutorials (2008)
9. Bourdev, L., Malik, J.: Poselets: body part detectors trained using 3d human pose annotations. In: ICCV (2009)
10. Bu, J., et al.: Music recommendation by unified hypergraph: combining social media information and music content. In: Proceedings of the 18th International Conference on Multimedia 2010, Firenze, Italy, 25–29 October, 2010 (2010)
11. Cai, C., Wang, Y.: A note on over-smoothing for graph neural networks. arXiv (2020)
12. Chen, Z., Chen, L., Villar, S., Bruna, J.: Can graph neural networks count substructures? In: NeurIPS (2020)
13. Chien, E., Pan, C., Peng, J., Milenkovic, O.: You are allset: a multiset function framework for hypergraph neural networks. In: ICLR (2022)
14. Cho, M., Alahari, K., Ponce, J.: Learning graphs to match. In: ICCV (2013)
15. Ding, K., Wang, J., Li, J., Li, D., Liu, H.: Be more with less: hypergraph attention networks for inductive text classification. In: Proceedings of the 2020 Conference on Empirical Methods in Natural Language Processing, EMNLP 2020, Online, 16–20 November, 2020 (2020)
16. Dong, Y., Sawin, W., Bengio, Y.: HNHN: hypergraph networks with hyperedge neurons. arXiv (2020)
17. Everingham, M., Van Gool, L., Williams, C.K., Winn, J., Zisserman, A.: The pascal visual object classes (voc) challenge. Int. J. Comput. Vis. (2010)
18. Feng, Y., You, H., Zhang, Z., Ji, R., Gao, Y.: Hypergraph neural networks. In: AAAI (2019)
19. Gao, Y., Wang, M., Tao, D., Ji, R., Dai, Q.: 3-d object retrieval and recognition with hypergraph analysis. IEEE Trans. Image Process. (2012)
20. Gilmer, J., Schoenholz, S.S., Riley, P.F., Vinyals, O., Dahl, G.E.: Neural message passing for quantum chemistry. In: ICML (2017)
21. Gu, F., Chang, H., Zhu, W., Sojoudi, S., Ghaoui, L.E.: Implicit graph neural networks. In: NeurIPS (2020)
22. Gu, S., Yang, M., Medaglia, J.D., Gur, R.C., Gur, R.E., Satterthwaite, T.D., Bassett, D.S.: Functional hypergraph uncovers novel covariant structures over neurodevelopment. Human Brain Mapp. (2017)
23. Ha, D., Dai, A.M., Le, Q.V.: Hypernetworks. In: ICLR (2017)
24. Hamilton, W.L., Ying, Z., Leskovec, J.: Inductive representation learning on large graphs. In: NeurIPS (2017)
25. Hornik, K., Stinchcombe, M.B., White, H.: Multilayer feedforward networks are universal approximators. Neural Networks (1989)
26. Huang, J., Yang, J.: Unignn: a unified framework for graph and hypergraph neural networks. In: IJCAI (2021)
27. Ishiguro, K., ichi Maeda, S., Koyama, M.: Graph warp module: an auxiliary module for boosting the power of graph neural networks in molecular graph analysis. arXiv (2019)
28. Kalai, G.: Linear programming, the simplex algorithm and simple polytopes. Math. Program. (1997)

29. Keriven, N., Peyré, G.: Universal invariant and equivariant graph neural networks. In: NeurIPS (2019)
30. Kim, E., Kang, W., On, K., Heo, Y., Zhang, B.: Hypergraph attention networks for multimodal learning. In: CVPR (2020)
31. Kim, J., et al.: Pure transformers are powerful graph learners. arXiv (2022)
32. Kim, J., Oh, S., Hong, S.: Transformers generalize deepsets and can be extended to graphs and hypergraphs. In: NeurIPS (2021)
33. Klimm, F., Deane, C.M., Reinert, G., Estrada, E.: Hypergraphs for predicting essential genes using multiprotein complex data. J. Complex Networks **9**, cnaa028 (2021)
34. Knyazev, B., Taylor, G.W., Amer, M.R.: Understanding attention and generalization in graph neural networks. In: NeurIPS (2019)
35. Kofidis, E., Regalia, P.A.: On the best rank-1 approximation of higher-order super-symmetric tensors. Siam J. Matrix Anal. Appl. **23**, 863–884 (2002)
36. Lee, J., et al.: Set transformer: a framework for attention-based permutation-invariant neural networks. In: ICML (2019)
37. Li, D., Xu, Z., Li, S., Sun, X.: Link prediction in social networks based on hyper-graph. In: 22nd International World Wide Web Conference, WWW '13, Rio de Janeiro, Brazil, 13–17 May 2013, Companion Volume (2013)
38. Li, J., Cai, D., He, X.: Learning graph-level representation for drug discovery. arXiv (2017)
39. Li, Q., Han, Z., Wu, X.: Deeper insights into graph convolutional networks for semi-supervised learning. In: AAAI (2018)
40. Louis, S.M., et al.: Global attention based graph convolutional neural networks for improved materials property prediction. arXiv (2020)
41. Lowe, D.G.: Object recognition from local scale-invariant features. In: ICCV (1999)
42. Maron, H., Ben-Hamu, H., Serviansky, H., Lipman, Y.: Provably powerful graph networks. In: NeurIPS (2019)
43. Maron, H., Ben-Hamu, H., Shamir, N., Lipman, Y.: Invariant and equivariant graph networks. In: ICLR (2019)
44. Maron, H., Fetaya, E., Segol, N., Lipman, Y.: On the universality of invariant networks. In: ICML (2019)
45. Maron, H., Litany, O., Chechik, G., Fetaya, E.: On learning sets of symmetric elements. In: ICML (2020)
46. Milano, F., Loquercio, A., Rosinol, A., Scaramuzza, D., Carlone, L.: Primal-dual mesh convolutional neural networks. In: NeurIPS (2020)
47. Oono, K., Suzuki, T.: Graph neural networks exponentially lose expressive power for node classification. In: ICLR (2020)
48. Puny, O., Ben-Hamu, H., Lipman, Y.: From graph low-rank global attention to 2-fwl approximation. In: ICML (2020)
49. Ray, L.A.: 2-d and 3-d image registration for medical, remote sensing, and indus-trial applications. J. Electronic Imaging (2005)
50. Rolínek, M., Swoboda, P., Zietlow, D., Paulus, A., Musil, V., Martius, G.: Deep graph matching via Blackbox differentiation of combinatorial solvers. In: Vedaldi, A., Bischof, H., Brox, T., Frahm, J.-M. (eds.) ECCV 2020. LNCS, vol. 12373, pp. 407–424. Springer, Cham (2020). https://doi.org/10.1007/978-3-030-58604-1_25
51. Serviansky, H., et al.: Set2graph: learning graphs from sets. In: NeurIPS (2020)
52. Tan, S., Bu, J., Chen, C., He, X.: Using rich social media information for music recommendation via hypergraph model. In: Hoi, S., Luo, J., Boll, S., Xu, D., Jin, R., King, I. (eds.) Social Media Modeling and Computing. Springer, London (2011). https://doi.org/10.1007/978-0-85729-436-4_10

53. Vaswani, A., et al.: Attention is all you need. In: NeurIPS (2017)
54. Velikovic, P.: Message passing all the way up. arXiv (2022)
55. Wang, R., Yan, J., Yang, X.: Neural graph matching network: Learning lawler's quadratic assignment problem with extension to hypergraph and multiple-graph matching. IEEE Trans. Pattern Anal. Mach. Intell. (2021)
56. Wu, Z., Jain, P., Wright, M.A., Mirhoseini, A., Gonzalez, J.E., Stoica, I.: Representing long-range context for graph neural networks with global attention. arXiv (2021)
57. Yadati, N., Nimishakavi, M., Yadav, P., Nitin, V., Louis, A., Talukdar, P.P.: Hypergcn: A new method for training graph convolutional networks on hypergraphs. In: NeurIPS (2019)
58. Yavartanoo, M., Hung, S., Neshatavar, R., Zhang, Y., Lee, K.M.: Polynet: Polynomial neural network for 3d shape recognition with polyshape representation. In: 3DV (2021)
59. Zaheer, M., Kottur, S., Ravanbakhsh, S., Póczos, B., Salakhutdinov, R., Smola, A.J.: Deep sets. In: NeurIPS (2017)
60. Zhang, M., Cui, Z., Neumann, M., Chen, Y.: An end-to-end deep learning architecture for graph classification. In: AAAI (2018)

ScaleNet: Searching for the Model to Scale

Jiyang Xie[1], Xiu Su[2], Shan You[3], Zhanyu Ma[1(✉)], Fei Wang[4],
and Chen Qian[3]

[1] Pattern Recognition and Intelligent Systems Laboratory,
Beijing University of Posts and Telecommunications, Beijing, China
{xiejiyang2013,mazhanyu}@bupt.edu.cn
[2] The University of Sydney, Camperdown, Australia
xisu5992@uni.sydney.edu.au
[3] SenseTime Research Centre, Beijing, China
{youshan,qianchen}@sensetime.com
[4] University of Science and Technology of China, Hefei, China
wangfei91@mail.ustc.edu.cn

Abstract. Recently, community has paid increasing attention on model scaling and contributed to developing a model family with a wide spectrum of scales. Current methods either simply resort to a one-shot NAS manner to construct a non-structural and non-scalable model family or rely on a manual yet fixed scaling strategy to scale an unnecessarily best base model. In this paper, we bridge both two components and propose ScaleNet to jointly search base model and scaling strategy so that the scaled large model can have more promising performance. Concretely, we design a super-supernet to embody models with different spectrum of sizes (*e.g.*, FLOPs). Then, the scaling strategy can be learned interactively with the base model via a Markov chain-based evolution algorithm and generalized to develop even larger models. To obtain a decent super-supernet, we design a hierarchical sampling strategy to enhance its training sufficiency and alleviate the disturbance. Experimental results show our scaled networks enjoy significant performance superiority on various FLOPs, but with at least 2.53× reduction on search cost. Codes are available at https://github.com/luminolx/ScaleNet.

Keywords: Neural architecture search (NAS) · Model scaling · Hierarchical sampling strategy · Markov chain-based evolution algorithm

This work was supported in part by Beijing Natural Science Foundation Project No. Z200002 and in part by National Natural Science Foundation of China (NSFC) No. 61922015, U19B2036, 62225601.

Supplementary Information The online version contains supplementary material available at https://doi.org/10.1007/978-3-031-19803-8_7.

1   Introduction

Convolutional neural networks (CNNs) have achieved great performance in computer vision with various model architectures [4,5,8,11,12,21,34–37,40,42] proposed for better feature extraction abilities. Previous work [22–25,39] usually focused on how to automatically design a model architecture under a certain resource budget (*e.g.*, floating-point operations per second, FLOPs) with neural architecture search (NAS) algorithms and gained significant improvements. However, due to different levels of budgets which may occur in various applications, multi-scale architectures should be considered in practice and can be independently generated by the NAS. Nevertheless, typical NAS methods [22–25,39] have to search one a time for each scale, and the searching cost will be approximated linearly scaled as well [29] (see baseline in Fig. 1).

In contrast, recent work [3,6,7,10,15–17,28,31,33,41,43] get down to paying attention on model scale and designing a model family in a more straightforward way. Two frameworks have been proposed as shown in Fig. 1, including one-shot NAS-based pipeline (*e.g.*, BigNAS [41] and Once-for-All (OFA) [3]) and two-step pipeline (*e.g.*, EfficientNet [28] and EfficientNet-X [15]). The former directly designed an overcomplete one-shot supernet to embody multiple (finite) scales and searched models by NAS. However, they are difficult to extend the searched models to a larger one, since finding a specific scaling strategy that adapts all the non-structurally searched architectures is infeasible. The latter decomposed the large model generation with two steps, *i.e.*, first acquiring an optimal base model, then scaling it on three dimensions, including depth, width, and resolution, using some pre-defined strategies, *e.g.*, compound scaling [28] and fast compound scaling [7]. However, the best base model is unnecessarily optimal for scaling. How to combine the advantages of both, *i.e.*, *automatically and jointly searching the base model and scaling strategy by NAS and freely extending the scaling strategy into infinite scales*, should be carefully considered.

Different with manually designed rule-based scaling strategies [7,28,38], we propose to *directly discover* the optimal scaling strategies within base model search. One-shot NAS can search model architectures based on a trained supernet that contains all the possible architectures (so-called paths). For improving search efficiency, we apply an even-larger supernet dubbed super-supernet to embody multi-scale networks. However, a common one-shot space usually has a uni-modal distribution of FLOPs of paths under uniform sampling [9,41]. In this way, the super-supernet tends to favor the intermediate-FLOPs and cannot accommodate all FLOPs budgets well, which will in turn hampers the optimality of searched scaling strategies. Inspired by ancestral sampling [1], we propose a hierarchical sampling strategy (HSS) that splits the search space into partitions and the sampling is implemented respectively. The search space and the sampling distribution of the super-supernet for FLOPs are carefully designed according to the budgets of various scaling stages and undertake a multi-modal form distribution.

Secondly, considering that our goal is to find a base model architecture with the strongest scaling capability (instead of the best performance) and its corre-

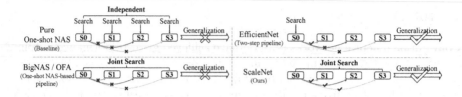

Fig. 1. Comparisons of different methods to generate a model family S0–S3. Red, blue, and green arrows are the scaling strategy searching for scaling stage 1, 2, and 3, respectively. The pure one-shot NAS (baseline) independently searched various models without either scaling strategy modeling between scaling stages or larger-scale architecture generalization. BigNAS [41] jointly searched the model family from an entire supernet, although it obtained non-structural then non-scalable architectures. Then in EfficientNet [28], the base model (*i.e.*, S0) and the scaling strategy to S1 were only searched independently for architecture generalizing. In our ScaleNet, we combine the two components and jointly search base model and all scaling strategies to scale the model into infinite ones. (Color figure online)

sponding optimal scaling strategies, we propose a joint search for them, dubbed Markov chain-based evolution algorithm (MCEA), by iteratively and interactively optimizing both of them. After obtaining the searched scaling strategies, we model the trends of depth, width, and resolution, respectively, and generalize them to develop even larger models. We theoretically derive a group of generalization functions in the three dimensions for larger-scale architectures, with which moderate performance can be actually achieved.

The contributions of this paper are four-fold:

- We propose ScaleNet to jointly search the base model and a group of the scaling strategies based on one-shot NAS framework. The scaling strategies of larger scales are generalized by the searched ones with our theoretically derived generalization functions.
- We carefully design the search space and a multi-modal distribution for FLOPs budgets for hierarchical sampling strategy (HSS) in the one-shot NAS-based scaling search algorithm to enhance the training sufficiency of paths in super-supernet.
- We propose a joint search algorithm for both the base model and the scaling strategies, namely Markov chain-based evolution algorithm (MCEA), by iteratively and interactively optimizing both of them.
- Experimental results show that the searched architectures by the proposed ScaleNet with various FLOPs budgets can outperform the referred methods on various datasets including ImageNet-1k. Meanwhile, search time can be significantly reduced at least $2.53\times$.

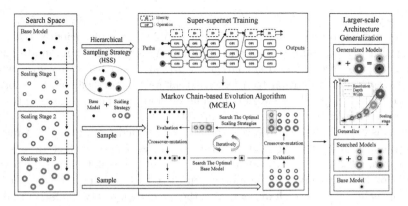

Fig. 2. Framework of the proposed ScaleNet. Based on the carefully designed search space with multiple scaling stage (the left box), we apply the proposed hierarchical sampling strategy (HSS) for sampling paths (one path is generated by a base model and a scaling strategy) in one-shot super-supernet training (the upper box). Then, we utilize the proposed Markov chain-based evolution algorithm (MCEA) to iteratively and interactively search the optimal base model and scaling strategies (the lower box). In each iteration, an evolution procedure with crossover-mutation and evaluation is undertaken for searching the optimal base model or scaling strategies based on the search space. Finally, after obtaining the optimal ones, we generalize them to larger-scale architectures by the estimations of the trends of depth, width, and resolution, respectively (the right box). All the obtained architectures will be applied for retraining and inference.

2   Related Work

2.1   One-Shot NAS-Based Model Family Searching

FBNets [6,31,33] optimized CNN architectures for mobile devices and generated a family of models in order to avoid training individual architectures separately and reduce resource consuming. Cai *et al.* [3] proposed to train a once-for-all (OFA) model that supports diverse architectural settings by decoupling training and search, in order to reduce the cost. BigNAS [41] challenged the conventional pipeline that post-processing of model weights is necessary to achieve good performance and constructed big single-stage models without extra retraining or post-processing. However, the main drawback of these methods is that they only searched for a model family by training a joint or even a group of independent supernet(s), but did not analyze the structural relationship and explicit scaling strategies between the architectures with different budgets in the model family. It is difficult and even infeasible to extend the scaling strategies to larger scales.

2.2   Model Scaling

Tan and Le [28] systematically studied model scaling and found that carefully balancing depth, width, and resolution of a model can lead to better performance. They proposed to empirically obtain the optimal compound scaling that effectively scales a specific base model up to gain a model family, *i.e.*, Efficient-Net. Its variant versions, such as EfficientNetV2 [29] and EfficientNet-X [15], improved it in trade-off on speed and accuracy. A simple fast compound scaling strategy [7] was proposed to encourage to primarily scale model width, while scaling depth and resolution to a lesser extent for memory efficiency. Another work [16] built an greedy network enlarging method based on the reallocation of computations in order to enlarge the capacity of CNNs by improving the three dimensions on stage level. However, the aforementioned work always estimated the optimal scaling strategy for theoretical double-FLOPs budget by a small grid search, which is computationally expensive and does not match the actual FLOPs budgets. Meanwhile, they only considered to find the strategy for the smallest scaling stage, which did not learn the dependency between larger scaling stages. Furthermore, the relation between a base model and scaling strategies did not be investigated, which means the base is not the optimal for scaling.

3   ScaleNet

Due to the drawbacks of the one-shot NAS-based model family searching and compound scaling-based model scaling, we propose to combine their advantages together and fill the gap between them. Here, ScaleNet jointly searches a base model with the strongest scaling capability and the optimal scaling strategies based on one-shot NAS framework by training a super-supernet as shown in Fig. 2. The super-supernet training and joint searching procedures are carefully designed for the goal. Then, when obtaining the searched scaling strategies, we model the trends of depth, width, and resolution, respectively, and generalize to develop even larger architectures. All the searched and generalized scaling strategies will be applied for the final model family construction and training.

3.1   One-Shot Joint Search Space for Model Scaling

The FLOPs budget of the base model is selected according to the mean FLOPs of the search space as shown in Fig. 3 (Detailed information of the search space are shown in supplementary material). Then for various scaling stages, their FLOPs budgets are exponentially expanded by that of the base model α. As scaling strategies $\{\boldsymbol{S}_j = [d_j, w_j, r_j]\}_{j=0}^{M}$ with maximum scaling stage as M, including the change ratios of depth d_j, width w_j, and resolution r_j (real numbers that are not smaller than one), have their corresponding FLOPs budgets, respectively, we assign a scaling strategy to

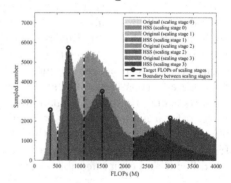

Fig. 3. Sampling distribution based on the proposed HSS, compared with that of the original uniform sampling in [41]. We took 750,000 paths for each to simulate actual super-supernet training.

each base model architecture to compute the mean FLOPs and find the center point of the search space of scaling stage j according to its FLOPs budget. The detailed settings of the whole search space are elaborated in the supplementary material.

3.2   Hierarchical Sampling Strategy for Super-Supernet Training

Applying the original one-shot NAS framework [9,41] by utilizing uniform sampling to train the super-supernet means each operation has equal probability to be selected. It has two disadvantages: 1) the original bell-shape sampling distribution towards one specific FLOPs budget for the whole search space is not suitable for the multiple scaling stages with various budgets, where paths cannot be fairly trained in each scaling stage (see the red histogram in Fig. 3); 2) the search space is almost $300\times$ larger and the size of super-supernet is $8\times$ larger (statistics with base model and three scaling stages trained) than before, which increase the difficulty of super-supernet training. As we need to search architectures in different scaling stages, the paths with the less selected FLOPs budgets in super-supernet training are not sufficiently trained and those in one scaling stage are not fairly trained. Here, we propose a hierarchical sampling strategy (HSS) by implementing a multi-modal sampling distribution to address the above issues (see the blue histogram in Fig. 3).

As we assigned d_j, w_j, and r_j into scaling stages in the search space, we treat the target multi-modal sampling distribution $p(\boldsymbol{\alpha}, \boldsymbol{S})$ as a mixture model, $i.e.$,

$$p(\boldsymbol{\alpha}, \boldsymbol{S}) = p(\boldsymbol{\alpha}) \cdot p(\boldsymbol{S}) = p(\boldsymbol{\alpha}) \cdot \left(\sum_{j=0}^{M} \eta_j p_j(\boldsymbol{S}) \right), \qquad (1)$$

where $p(\boldsymbol{\alpha})$ and $p_j(\boldsymbol{S})$ are the sampling distributions of base model $\boldsymbol{\alpha}$ and scaling stage j, respectively, and η_j is normalized component weight, $\sum_{j=0}^{M} \eta_j = 1$ and $\eta_j \geq 0$. Here, we can empirically set equal component weights, $i.e.$, $\eta_j = \frac{1}{M+1}$, or normalized combination ratios of scaling strategies in the search space.

In sampling, we apply the ancestral sampling of a probabilistic graphic model [1] that is a two-step hierarchical strategy for the scaling strategies. We firstly select a scaling stage m given the conditional distribution $p(m|\eta_1, \cdots, \eta_M)$, which is a categorical distribution as

$$p(m = j|\eta_1, \cdots, \eta_M) = \eta_j. \qquad (2)$$

Then, we uniformly sample a scaling strategy $\boldsymbol{S}$ in scaling stage m. Meanwhile, a base model $\boldsymbol{\alpha}$ is sampled as well based on the original uniform sampling.

The one-shot super-supernet training process based on the proposed HSS is

$$\boldsymbol{W}^* = \underset{\boldsymbol{W}}{\operatorname{argmin}} \, loss_{\boldsymbol{\alpha}, \boldsymbol{S} \sim p(\boldsymbol{\alpha}, \boldsymbol{S})} \left(\boldsymbol{W}(\boldsymbol{\alpha}, \boldsymbol{S}); \boldsymbol{D}_{train} \right), \qquad (3)$$

where $\boldsymbol{W}$ is a set of super-supernet parameters, $\boldsymbol{W}^*$ is a set of the optimal parameters, $loss$ is training loss function (commonly cross-entropy loss), $\boldsymbol{W}(\boldsymbol{\alpha}, \boldsymbol{S})$ means a path that is constructed by $\boldsymbol{\alpha}$ and $\boldsymbol{S}$, and $\boldsymbol{D}_{train}$ is training set.

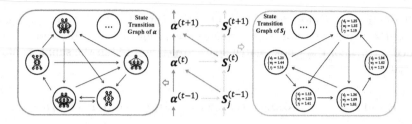

Fig. 4. The interactive search in the proposed Markov chain-based evolution algorithm (MCEA) with a coupled Markov chain. The coupled Markov chain combines both the left ((5)–(6)) and the right ((7)–(8)) ones for the interaction.

3.3   Interactive Search for Base Model and Multiple Scaling Strategy

After completing the super-supernet training, we usually search both base model and a group of scaling strategies by an evolution algorithm (EA). The original objective of the optimization is globally maximizing the weighted sum of the validation accuracies ACC of the M scaling stages [32] as

$$\max_{\boldsymbol{\alpha},\{\boldsymbol{S}_j\}} \left[\sum_{j=1}^{M} \pi_j ACC\left(\boldsymbol{W}^*(\boldsymbol{\alpha}, \boldsymbol{S}_j); \boldsymbol{D}_{val}\right) \right], \tag{4}$$
$$\text{s.t. } \boldsymbol{\alpha} \in \boldsymbol{\Omega}_\alpha, \boldsymbol{S}_j \in \boldsymbol{\Omega}_j, \text{FLOPs}(\boldsymbol{W}^*(\boldsymbol{\alpha}, \boldsymbol{S}_j)) = f_j,$$

where π_j is the normalized weight of scaling stage j (constrained by $\sum_{j=1}^{M} \pi_j = 1$), ACC is the validation accuracy of a path, $\boldsymbol{D}_{val}$ is validation set, $\boldsymbol{\Omega}_\alpha$ and $\boldsymbol{\Omega}_j$ are the search space of base model and scaling stage j, respectively, and f_j is the FLOPs budget of scaling stage j.

However, both the too large search space and constrained computational resource restrict the search. Meanwhile, searching the globally optimal group of architectures from the search space is difficult and expensive, since redundant information and noises may affect the search.

Here, inspired by Markov process, we propose a so-called Markov chain-based evolution algorithm (MCEA) with a coupled Markov chain, which iteratively and interactively optimizes $\boldsymbol{\alpha}$ and $\{\boldsymbol{S}_j\}$, to overcome the global search issue. As shown in Fig. 4, with maximum iteration number T and iteration index $t = 1, \cdots, T$, we transfer the optimization problem in (4) to iteratively and interactively solving the limiting distributions $\gamma(\boldsymbol{\alpha})$ and $\gamma(\{\boldsymbol{S}_j\})$ to obtain the optimal $\boldsymbol{\alpha}^*$ and $\boldsymbol{S}_j^*$, respectively, as

$$\boldsymbol{\alpha}^* = \underset{\boldsymbol{\alpha}}{\operatorname{argmax}}\, \gamma(\boldsymbol{\alpha}) = \operatorname{argmax}_{\boldsymbol{\alpha}} \left[\lim_{t \to \infty} p(\boldsymbol{\alpha}^{(t)}) \right], \tag{5}$$

$$p(\boldsymbol{\alpha}^{(t)}) = \sum_{\boldsymbol{\alpha}^{(t-1)}} p(\boldsymbol{\alpha}^{(t)} | \boldsymbol{\alpha}^{(t-1)}, \{\boldsymbol{S}_j\}_{j=1}^{M} = \{\boldsymbol{S}_j^{(t-1)}\}_{j=1}^{M}) p(\boldsymbol{\alpha}^{(t-1)}), \tag{6}$$

$$\boldsymbol{S}_j^* = \underset{\boldsymbol{S}_j}{\operatorname{argmax}}\, \gamma(\boldsymbol{S}_j) = \operatorname{argmax}_{\boldsymbol{S}_j} \left[\lim_{t \to \infty} p(\boldsymbol{S}_j^{(t)}) \right], \tag{7}$$

$$p(\boldsymbol{S}_j^{(t)}) = \sum_{\boldsymbol{S}_j^{(t-1)}} p(\boldsymbol{S}_j^{(t)} | \boldsymbol{S}_j^{(t-1)}, \boldsymbol{\alpha} = \boldsymbol{\alpha}^{(t)}) p(\boldsymbol{S}_j^{(t-1)}), \tag{8}$$

where $p(\boldsymbol{\alpha}^{(t-1)})$ and $p(\boldsymbol{S}_j^{(t-1)})$ are the state probabilities of the discrete variable $\boldsymbol{\alpha}^{(t-1)}$ and $\boldsymbol{S}_j^{(t-1)}$, respectively, with the enumerable search space as state space.

$$p(\boldsymbol{\alpha}^{(t)}|\boldsymbol{\alpha}^{(t-1)}, \{\boldsymbol{S}_j\}_{j=1}^M = \{\boldsymbol{S}_j^{(t-1)}\}_{j=1}^M) \propto \sum_{j=1}^M \pi_j ACC\left(\boldsymbol{W}^*(\boldsymbol{\alpha}, \boldsymbol{S}_j^{(t-1)}); \boldsymbol{D}_{val}\right)$$

and $p(\boldsymbol{S}_j^{(t)}|\boldsymbol{S}_j^{(t)}, \boldsymbol{\alpha} = \boldsymbol{\alpha}^{(t-1)}) \propto ACC\left(\boldsymbol{W}^*(\boldsymbol{\alpha}^{(t)}, \boldsymbol{S}_j); \boldsymbol{D}_{val}\right)$ are transition matrices and are approximated implemented by the crossover-mutation process under FLOPs budgets given the obtained scaling strategies or base model, respectively. $\boldsymbol{S}_j^{(0)}$ is the initial scaling strategy of the jth scaling stage, where probability $p(\boldsymbol{S}_j^{(0)}) \propto \frac{1}{K}\sum_{k=1}^K ACC\left(\boldsymbol{W}^*(\boldsymbol{\alpha}_k^{(0)}, \boldsymbol{S}_j); \boldsymbol{D}_{val}\right)$ is obtained by a group of randomly selected base models $\{\boldsymbol{\alpha}_k^{(0)}\}_{k=1}^K$ under the FLOPs budget of base model.

3.4 Larger-Scale Architecture Generalization with Searched Scaling Strategies

The scaling strategies of larger scales are generalized by the searched ones. We define the optimal scales of $M + 1$ scaling stages as $\{\hat{\boldsymbol{S}}_j\}_{j=0}^M$. We should note that we pre-define $\hat{\boldsymbol{S}}_0$ as $\hat{d}_0 = \hat{w}_0 = \hat{r}_0 = 1$ for the base model.

We argue that depth, width, and resolution should have distinct growth rates, respectively, since they perform different roles in the model scaling. Meanwhile, j is exponentially proportional to FLOPs budgets in our setting, but $\hat{\boldsymbol{S}}_j, j = 1, \cdots, M$ are under almost linear- or quadratic-level. Therefore, inspired by [28], we propose to utilize the independent regression functions for depth, width, and resolution for the larger-scale generalization with

$$\begin{cases} \hat{d}_j = a_0^{(d)} \cdot \left(\left(a_1^{(d)}\right)^j - 1\right) + 1 \\ \hat{w}_j = a_0^{(w)} \cdot \left(\left(a_1^{(w)}\right)^j - 1\right) + 1 \\ \hat{r}_j = a_0^{(r)} \cdot \left(\left(a_1^{(r)}\right)^j - 1\right) + 1 \end{cases} \tag{9}$$

to guarantee the values in $\hat{\boldsymbol{S}}_0$, where a_0 and a_1 are parameters which can be directly optimized by stochastic gradient descent (SGD) or other optimization algorithms. As we can learn different values of the parameters, respectively, the three dimensions can obtain distinct growth rates.

Derivation of Larger-scale Architecture Generalization Functions. We define FLOPs budget as f here. We can obtain the relation between f and scaling stage j as $f \propto 2^{\theta \times j}$ where $\propto$ means "proportional to", $\theta > 0$ is a parameter. As the depth $\hat{d}$, width $\hat{w}$, resolution $\hat{r}$ are positively correlated with f, we have $\theta^{(d)}$, $\theta^{(w)}$, and $\theta^{(r)}$ with $\theta = \theta^{(d)} + \theta^{(w)} + \theta^{(r)}$ for the three, and obtain

$$2^{(\theta^{(d)}+\theta^{(w)}+\theta^{(r)})\times j} \stackrel{.}{\propto} \hat{d} \times \hat{w}^2 \times \hat{r}^2, \tag{10}$$

where $\stackrel{.}{\propto}$ means "positively correlated with", but not "proportional to". We formulate the relation between j and $\hat{d}$ as $2^{\theta^{(d)} \times j} \stackrel{.}{\propto} \hat{d}$ and introduce a linear

Table 1. Comparisons with other state-of-the-art methods on ImageNet-1k dataset. Top-1 and Top-5 accuracies (%), FLOPs (G), and numbers of parameters (#Param., M) are reported. The best results are highlighted in **bold**.

Model	Top-1	Top-5	FLOPs	#Param.
FBNetV2-L1 [31]	77.2	N/A	0.33	N/A
OFA-80 [3]	76.8	93.3	0.35	6.1
GreedyNAS-A [39]	77.1	93.3	0.37	6.5
EfficientNet-B0 [28]	76.3	93.2	0.39	5.3
ScaleNet-S0 (ours)	**77.5**	**93.7**	**0.35**	**4.4**
EfficientNet-B1 [28]	78.8	94.4	0.70	7.8
OFA-200 [3]	79.0	94.5	0.78	11.0
RegNetY-800MF [19]	76.3	N/A	0.80	6.3
EfficientNet-X-B0 [15]	77.3	N/A	0.91	7.6
ScaleNet-S1 (ours)	**79.9**	**94.8**	**0.80**	**7.4**
EfficientNet-B2 [28]	79.8	94.9	1.00	9.2
BigNASModel-XL [41]	80.9	N/A	1.04	9.5
EfficientNet-X-B1 [15]	79.4	N/A	1.58	9.6
RegNetY-1.6GF [19]	78.0	N/A	1.60	11.2
ScaleNet-S2 (ours)	**81.3**	**95.6**	**1.45**	**10.2**
EfficientNet-B3 [28]	81.1	95.5	1.80	12.0
EfficientNet-X-B2 [15]	80.0	N/A	2.30	10.0
RegNetY-3.2GF [19]	79.0	N/A	3.20	19.4
RegNetY-4GF [19]	79.4	N/A	4.00	20.6
ScaleNet-S3 (ours)	**82.2**	**95.9**	**2.76**	**13.2**
RegNetY-500M→4GF [7]	81.7	N/A	4.10	36.2
EfficientNet-B4 [28]	82.6	96.3	4.20	19.0
EfficientNet-X-B3 [15]	81.4	N/A	4.30	13.3
RegNetY-8GF [19]	81.7	N/A	8.00	39.2
ScaleNet-S4 (ours)	**83.2**	**96.6**	**5.97**	**16.1**
EfficientNet-B5 [28]	83.3	96.7	9.90	30.0
EfficientNet-X-B4 [15]	83.0	N/A	10.40	21.6
RegNetY-500M→16GF [7]	83.1	N/A	16.20	134.8
EfficientNet-B0 →16GF [7]	83.2	N/A	16.20	122.8
ScaleNet-S5 (ours)	**83.7**	**97.1**	**10.22**	**20.9**

approximation as $2^{\theta^{(d)} \times j} \approx \beta \hat{d} + \delta \Rightarrow \hat{d} \approx \frac{1}{\beta} \cdot 2^{\theta^{(d)} \times j} - \frac{\delta}{\beta}$, where β and δ are parameters. Here, we define $a_0^{(d)} = \frac{1}{\beta}$, $a_1^{(d)} = 2^{\theta^{(d)}}$, $a_2^{(d)} = -\frac{\delta}{\beta}$ and obtain

$$\hat{d} = a_0^{(d)} \cdot \left(a_1^{(d)} \right)^j + a_2^{(d)}. \qquad (11)$$

Note that as $a_0^{(d)}$, $a_1^{(d)}$, and $a_2^{(d)}$ are parameters, "$\approx$" can be transferred to "$=$".

Table 2. Performance in five fine-tuning tasks. Top-1 accuracies (%), FLOPs (G), parameter numbers (#Param., M) are reported. The best results are in **bold**.

Dataset	Model	Top-1	FLOPs	#Param.
FGVC Aircraft [18]	Inception-v4 [26]	90.9	13.00	41
	EfficientNet-B3 [28]	90.7	1.80	10
	ScaleNet-S3 (ours)	**91.4**	**2.76**	11
Stanford Cars [13]	Inception-v4 [26]	93.4	13.00	41
	EfficientNet-B3 [28]	93.6	1.80	10
	ScaleNet-S3 (ours)	**94.4**	**2.76**	11
Food-101 [2]	Inception-v4 [26]	90.8	13.00	41
	EfficientNet-B4 [28]	91.5	4.20	17
	ScaleNet-S4 (ours)	**92.0**	**5.97**	14
CIFAR-10 [14]	NASNet-A [44]	98.0	42.00	85
	EfficientNet-B0 [28]	98.1	0.39	4
	ScaleNet-S0 (ours)	**98.3**	**0.35**	3
CIFAR-100 [14]	NASNet-A [44]	87.5	42.00	85
	EfficientNet-B0 [28]	88.1	0.39	4
	ScaleNet-S0 (ours)	**88.4**	**0.35**	3

Then, due to $\hat{d} = 1$ for the base model (*i.e.*, scaling stage 0), we should guarantee the relation. Thus, we put $\hat{d} = 1, j = 0$ into (11) and obtain $a_2^{(d)} = 1 - a_0^{(d)}$. We re-put it into (11) and obtain the depth function in (9) as

$$\hat{d} = a_0^{(d)} \cdot \left(a_1^{(d)}\right)^j + \left(1 - a_0^{(d)}\right) = a_0^{(d)} \cdot \left(\left(a_1^{(d)}\right)^j - 1\right) + 1. \tag{12}$$

Similarly, we can achieve the relation between i and $\hat{w}$, $\hat{r}$, respectively, as

$$\hat{w} \approx \sqrt{\frac{1}{\beta'} \cdot 2^{\theta^{(w)} \times i} - \frac{\delta'}{\beta'}} \approx \frac{1}{\sqrt{\beta'}} \sqrt{2}^{\theta^{(w)} \times i} - \sqrt{\frac{\delta'}{\beta'}}, \tag{13}$$

$$\hat{r} \approx \sqrt{\frac{1}{\beta''} \cdot 2^{\theta^{(r)} \times i} - \frac{\delta''}{\beta''}} \approx \frac{1}{\sqrt{\beta''}} \sqrt{2}^{\theta^{(r)} \times i} - \sqrt{\frac{\delta''}{\beta''}}, \tag{14}$$

where β', δ', β'', and δ'' are parameters.

4   Experimental Results and Discussions

4.1   Performance of ScaleNet on ImageNet-1k

We conducted experiments on ImageNet-1k dataset [20] for the proposed ScaleNet with recently proposed methods. Note that we divided a mini validation set (50 images per class) from the training set for evaluation in the MCEA. The search models are named by Sj, where S0 is the base model, S1, S2, and S3 are searched by the MCEA, and S4 and S5 are the generalized ones. The FLOPs budgets are selected according to Fig. 3. Detailed settings are in the supplementary material. In Table 1 with different FLOPs budgets, the searched models of our ScaleNet can achieve the best performance among those with similar FLOPs.

Table 3. Ablation studies. Top-1 accuracies (%) of s0-s4 models on ImageNet-100 dataset are reported. In column "Sampl.", "U" and "H" are the original uniform sampling and the proposed HSS, respectively. M and T are the maximum scaling stage and the iteration of the proposed MCEA. "Val" (for T only) means the validation accuracy (%) in the MCEA. The best results are shown in **bold**.

Sampl.	M	T	Val	s0	s1	s2	s3	s4
U	3	4	N/A	84.16	86.96	87.72	89.26	90.02
H	1	4	N/A	84.06	86.30	87.93	88.86	90.30
H	2	4	N/A	84.42	86.24	88.02	89.12	90.14
H	3	1	63.58	84.18	86.34	**88.12**	88.90	89.76
H	3	2	63.38	84.20	85.86	88.00	89.44	90.18
H	3	4	**63.61**	**84.76**	**87.18**	88.10	**89.90**	90.46
H	3	6	63.59	84.44	86.42	87.80	89.54	**90.48**
H	3	8	63.53	84.50	86.48	87.64	89.30	90.36

4.2 Transferability to Fine-tuning Tasks

In addition to the experiments on ImageNet-1k, we also transferred the searched architectures to fine-tuning tasks by fine-tuning our ImageNet-pretrained models. Experimental settings can be found in the supplementary material. Table 2 shows the transfer learning results. Ours can outperform different referred models, respectively. When applying larger models, we can gain further improvement.

4.3 Ablation Studies

We discuss the effect of the proposed components for the ScaleNet on ImageNet-100 dataset [20,30]. We divided a mini validation set (50 images per class) from the training set. All the following validation accuracies were calculated by the mini one. Searched models are named by sj, where s0 (120M FLOPs) is the base model, s1 (240M FLOPs), s2 (480M FLOPs), and s3 (960M FLOPs) are searched by the MCEA, and s4 (1920M FLOPs) is the generalized one. The experimental results are shown in Table 3. Detailed experimental settings and visualization of search space are in supplementary material.

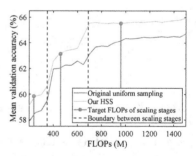

Fig. 5. Mean validation accuracies in the 4th iteration of the MCEA by using original uniform sampling in [41] and our HSS, respectively. The accuracies are grouped based on FLOPs. Each non-overlapping group contains recent 50M FLOPs paths. We merely show the performance of the three scaling stages, as we only evaluate them in the MCEA, except those of the base model.

Table 4. Performance comparison of three coefficients (%), including Pearson, Spearman, and Kendall coefficients, for validation accuracies by using original uniform sampling ("Original") in [41] and our HSS, respectively, to evaluate the sampling strategies in super-supernet training. We sampled 6,000 paths.

Method	Pearson	Spearman	Kendall
Original	35.3	80.1	64.1
Our HSS	**73.6**	**83.9**	**66.2**

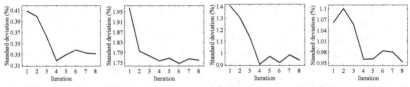

(a) Base model.   (b) Scaling stage 1. (c) Scaling stage 2. (d) Scaling stage 3.

Fig. 6. Standard deviations (Stds) of validation accuracies in each iteration of the MCEA. In different scaling stages, the Stds decrease significantly in the first four iterations, while they then tend to be steady and convergent.

Effect of HSS: We compare the proposed HSS with the original uniform sampling in [41]. Our HSS improves the searched results with better retrained accuracies of s0–s4.

Furthermore, we illustrate the validation accuracies of paths by using both of them to evaluate the sufficiency of the super-supernet training. In Fig. 5, the accuracies of our HSS are generally larger than those of the original one in addition to the FLOPs interval of [360, 440], as the interval is the mode of the original uniform sampling distribution. This means the proposed HSS can improve the sufficiency of the super-supernet training.

We further analyze the Pearson, Spearman, and Kendall coefficients for validation accuracies of the two ones, respectively. All of them are the larger the better. Detailed settings are in the supplementary material. Table 4 shows the values of our HSS significantly outperform the corresponding ones of the original. Specifically, our Pearson one is more than double of the original's.

Effect of Maximum Scaling Stage in Searching: We set the maximum scaling stage M to be one, two, or three in the MCEA for searching. ScaleNet can gain better performance with larger M, which means a more suitable base model for scaling can be found. More scaling stages can achieve better performance by obtaining better base model architecture for scaling, which is a common sense. This means we do not have to validate with much larger M.

Effect of Iteration in Searching: We set the iteration T as one, two, four, six, or eight in the MCEA for searching. When increasing T from one to four, better base models and scaling strategies can be obtained with top-1 accuracies improved in most of the scaling stages. This means that larger T can improve

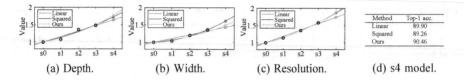

(a) Depth.   (b) Width.   (c) Resolution.   (d) s4 model.

Fig. 7. Comparison of larger-scale architecture generalization functions. The definitions of the compared ones are in the supplementary material. We generalized the three ones of s4 and retrained the scaled models on ImageNet-100 in (d).

Table 5. Comparisons of search cost (GPU/TPU days). Those of supernet (super-supernet) training and searching are compared, respectively. "Ratio-to-ScaleNet" is the ratio between total cost of a model to that of the proposed ScaleNet, the smaller the better. "†" means we estimated the lower-bound time. "N/A" means the work does not have the step. "*" means the work has the step but did not specifically mentioned in the paper. The best result is in **bold**.

Model	Device	Training	Searching	Total	Ratio-to-ScaleNet
MnasNet [27][†]	TPUv2	N/A	211,571	211,571	436.23×
EfficientNet-X [15][†]	TPUv3	N/A	>1,765	>1,765	>3.64×
EfficientNet [28][†]	TPUv3	N/A	>1,714	>1,714	>3.53×
FBNetV2 [31][†]	V100	*	*	>1,633	>3.37×
OFA [3][†]	V100	*	*	>1,486	>3.06×
BigNAS [41][†]	TPUv3	>960	> 268	>1,228	> 2.53×
ScaleNet (ours)	**V100**	**379**	**106**	**485**	**1×**

the searched results. However, when increasing T from four to eight, similar performance can be found. This means about four iterations is enough for the search. Meanwhile, we can find that the retraining accuracies of s0-4 is relative to the validation accuracy in the MCEA, which shows the effectiveness of it.

In addition, we show the standard deviations (Stds) of validation accuracies in each iteration of the MCEA in Fig. 6 to analyze their convergence. In different scaling stages, the Stds decrease significantly in the first four iterations, while they then tend to be steady and convergent. This shows that our ScaleNet can effectively search the optimal ones and gradually minimize the Stds.

Effect of Larger-Scale Architecture Generalization: We experimentally compare the proposed exponential one with commonly used polynomial functions, such as linear and squared ones. As shown in Fig. 7(a)–(c), three cases can precisely fit the trends of the depth, width, and resolution, respectively. Ours function can perform with different trends in the three dimensions. For depth and resolution, ours obtains rapid increase similar to the squared one, while it achieves gradual changes for width as the linear one. The total trends of ours are various, which is similar to the conclusion in [28], but the other two always perform the uppermost or the lowest, which are unreasonable.

We also trained all the scaled s4 models with three generalized scaling strategies, respectively, shown in Fig. 7(d). The proposed one can achieve the best top-1 performance as 90.46%, superior to the other two functions. This shows the effectiveness of our larger-scale architecture generalization.

4.4   Discussion of Search Cost

We discuss the efficiency of our ScaleNet, compared with a few recent strategies, including both one-shot NAS-based and two-step pipelines. We estimated the search cost for the referred ones under our FLOPs budgets, as they applied with various FLOPs budgets. The estimations are all shown in the supplementary material. As shown in Table 5, the proposed ScaleNet can remarkably reduce the total search cost, which contains the cost of (super-)supernet training and searching. It can decrease at least 2.53× and even 436.23×. Meanwhile, the proposed ScaleNet in the two parts of cost can still significantly improve the efficiency, respectively. Note that we used V100 for our experiments, while some others utilized TPUv3, which are much better than ours. This means we can achieve a larger decrease on the total search time under same resource conditions.

4.5   Discussion of the Trend of Scaling Strategies

We discuss the trend of learned scaling strategies for different scaling stages (Fig. 8) in order to promote further scaling strategy design.

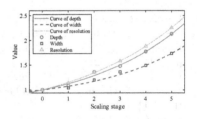

Fig. 8. Trends of depth, width, and resolution on ImageNet-1k.

- Depth, width, and resolution change in an exponential order. They have different values of their change rates among scaling stages. Depth and resolution change similarly, while that of width is slightly smaller, which is similar to EfficientNet [28].
- Their values are not completely restricted by the theoretical constraint in [28], but merely focus on the actual FLOPs budgets in each scaling stage. This means the searching process of ours is more fair.
- After obtaining the searched ones that are good enough under the corresponding FLOPs budgets, the extended ones can be precisely constructed in FLOPs of generalized architectures as well under our estimation and work well in experiments.

5   Conclusion

In this paper, we proposed ScaleNet to jointly search the base model and a group of the scaling strategies based on one-shot NAS framework. We improved the super-supernet training by the proposed HSS. Then, we jointly searched the base model and the scaling strategies by the proposed MCEA. The scaling strategies of larger scales were decently generalized by the searched ones. Experimental results show that the searched architectures by the proposed ScaleNet with various FLOPs budgets can outperform the referred methods on various datasets, including ImageNet-1k and fine-tuning tasks. Meanwhile, the searching time can be significantly reduced, compared with those one-shot NAS-based and manually designed two-step pipelines.

References

1. Bishop, C.M.: Pattern Recognition and Machine Learning. Springer Science+Business Media LLC, Berlin (2006)
2. Bossard, L., Guillaumin, M., Van Gool, L.: Food-101 – mining discriminative components with random forests. In: Fleet, D., Pajdla, T., Schiele, B., Tuytelaars, T. (eds.) ECCV 2014. LNCS, vol. 8694, pp. 446–461. Springer, Cham (2014). https://doi.org/10.1007/978-3-319-10599-4_29
3. Cai, H., Gan, C., Wang, T., Zhang, Z., Han, S.: Once-for-All: train one network and specialize it for efficient deployment. In: ICLR (2020)
4. Chang, D., Pang, K., Zheng, Y., Ma, Z., Song, Y.Z., Guo, J.: Your "flamingo" is my "bird": fine-grained, or not. In: CVPR, pp. 11476–11485 (2021)
5. Cheng, Z., Su, X., Wang, X., You, S., Xu, C.: Sufficient vision transformer. In: KDD (2022)
6. Dai, X., et al.: FBNetV3: joint architecture-recipe search using predictor pretraining. In: CVPR, pp. 16276–16285 (2021)
7. Dollar, P., Singh, M., Girshick, R.: Fast and accurate model scaling. In: CVPR, pp. 924–932 (2021)
8. Du, R., Xie, J., Ma, Z., Chang, D., Song, Y.Z., Guo, J.: Progressive learning of category-consistent multi-granularity features for fine-grained visual classification. IEEE TPAMI (2021)
9. Guo, Z.: Single path one-shot neural architecture search with uniform sampling. In: Vedaldi, A., Bischof, H., Brox, T., Frahm, J.-M. (eds.) ECCV 2020. LNCS, vol. 12361, pp. 544–560. Springer, Cham (2020). https://doi.org/10.1007/978-3-030-58517-4_32
10. Han, K., Wang, Y., Zhang, Q., Zhang, W., Xu, C., Zhang, T.: Model Rubik's cube: twisting resolution, depth and width for TinyNets. In: NeurIPS (2020)
11. He, K., Zhang, X., Ren, S., Sun, J.: Deep residual learning for image recognition. In: CVPR (2016)
12. Howard, A., et al.: Searching for mobilenetV3. In: ICCV (2019)
13. Krause, J., Stark, M., Deng, J., Fei-Fei, L.: 3D object representations for fine-grained categorization. In: CVPRW, pp. 554–561 (2013)
14. Krizhevsky, A.: Learning multiple layers of features from tiny images. Technical Report, CIFAR (2009)
15. Li, S., et al.: Searching for fast model families on datacenter accelerators. In: CVPR, pp. 8085–8095 (2021)
16. Liu, C., et al.: Greedy network enlarging. ArXiv preprint, arXiv:2108.00177 (2021)
17. Lou, W., Xun, L., Sabet, A., Bi, J., Hare, J., Merrett, G.V.: Dynamic-OFA: Runtime DNN architecture switching for performance scaling on heterogeneous embedded platforms. In: CVPRW, pp. 3110–3118 (2021)

18. Maji, S., Rahtu, E., Kannala, J., Blaschko, M., Vedaldi, A.: Fine-grained visual classification of aircraft. ArXiv preprint, arXiv:1306.5151 (2013)
19. Radosavovic, I., Kosaraju, R.P., Girshick, R., He, K., Dollar, P.: Designing network design spaces. In: CVPR (2020)
20. Russakovsky, O., et al.: ImageNet large scale visual recognition challenge. IJCV **115**(3), 211–252 (2015)
21. Sandler, M., Howard, A., Zhu, M., Zhmoginov, A., Chen, L.C.: MobileNetV2: Inverted residuals and linear bottlenecks. In: CVPR (2018)
22. Su, X., et al.: Prioritized architecture sampling with Monto-Carlo tree search. In: CVPR, pp. 10968–10977 (2021)
23. Su, X., et al.: Locally free weight sharing for network width search. ArXiv preprint, arXiv:2102.05258 (2021)
24. Su, X., You, S., Wang, F., Qian, C., Zhang, C., Xu, C.: BCNet: searching for network width with bilaterally coupled network. In: CVPR, pp. 2175–2184 (2021)
25. Su, X., et al.: ViTAS: vision transformer architecture search. ArXiv preprint, arXiv:2106.13700 (2021)
26. Szegedy, C., Ioffe, S., Vanhoucke, V., Alemi, A.A.: Inception-v4, Inception-ResNet and the impact of residual connections on learning. In: AAAI (2017)
27. Tan, M., et al.: MnasNet: Platform-aware neural architecture search for mobile. In: CVPR (2019)
28. Tan, M., Le, Q.: EfficientNet: Rethinking model scaling for convolutional neural networks. In: ICML, pp. 6105–6114 (2019)
29. Tan, M., Le, Q.V.: EfficientNetV2: smaller models and faster training. ArXiv preprint, arXiv:2104.00298 (2021)
30. Tian, Y., Krishnan, D., Isola, P.: Contrastive multiview coding. In: Vedaldi, A., Bischof, H., Brox, T., Frahm, J.-M. (eds.) ECCV 2020. LNCS, vol. 12356, pp. 776–794. Springer, Cham (2020). https://doi.org/10.1007/978-3-030-58621-8_45
31. Wan, A., et al.: FBNetV2: differentiable neural architecture search for spatial and channel dimensions. In: CVPR (2020)
32. Wang, C., Xu, C., Yao, X., Tao, D.: Evolutionary generative adversarial networks. IEEE Trans. Evol. Comput. **23**(6), 921–934 (2019)
33. Wu, B., et al.: FBNet: hardware-aware efficient ConvNet design via differentiable neural architecture search. In: CVPR (2019)
34. Xie, J., Ma, Z., Chang, D., Zhang, G., Guo, J.: GPCA: a probabilistic framework for Gaussian process embedded channel attention. IEEE TPAMI (2021)
35. Xie, J., et al.: Advanced dropout: a model-free methodology for Bayesian dropout optimization. IEEE TPAMI (2021)
36. Xie, J., et al.: DS-UI: dual-supervised mixture of gaussian mixture models for uncertainty inference in image recognition. IEEE TIP **30**, 9208–9219 (2021)
37. Xu, H., Su, X., Wang, Y., Cai, H., Cui, K., Chen, X.: Automatic bridge crack detection using a convolutional neural network. Appl. Sci. **9**(14), 2867 (2019)
38. Yang, Z., Liu, D., Wang, C., Yang, J., Tao, D.: Modeling image composition for complex scene generation. ArXiv preprint, arXiv:2206.00923 (2022)
39. You, S., Huang, T., Yang, M., Wang, F., Qian, C., Zhang, C.: GreedyNAS: towards fast one-shot NAS with greedy supernet. In: CVPR (2020)
40. You, S., Xu, C., Xu, C., Tao, D.: Learning from multiple teacher networks. In: KDD, pp. 1285–1294 (2017)
41. Yu, J., et al.: BigNAS: scaling up neural architecture search with big single-stage models. In: Vedaldi, A., Bischof, H., Brox, T., Frahm, J.-M. (eds.) ECCV 2020. LNCS, vol. 12352, pp. 702–717. Springer, Cham (2020). https://doi.org/10.1007/978-3-030-58571-6_41

42. Zagoruyko, S., Komodakis, N.: Wide residual networks. ArXiv preprint, arXiv:1605.07146 (2016)
43. Zhai, X., Kolesnikov, A., Houlsby, N., Beyer, L.: Scaling vision transformers. ArXiv preprint, arXiv:2106.04560 (2021)
44. Zoph, B., Vasudevan, V., Shlens, J., Le, Q.V.: Learning transferable architectures for scalable image recognition. In: CVPR (2018)

Complementing Brightness Constancy with Deep Networks for Optical Flow Prediction

Vincent Le Guen[1,2,3(✉)], Clément Rambour[2], and Nicolas Thome[2,4]

[1] EDF R&D, Chatou, France
vincent.le-guen@edf.fr
[2] Conservatoire National des Arts et Métiers, CEDRIC, Paris, France
[3] SINCLAIR AI Lab, Palaiseau, France
[4] Sorbonne Université, CNRS, ISIR, 75005 Paris, France

Abstract. State-of-the-art methods for optical flow estimation rely on deep learning, which require complex sequential training schemes to reach optimal performances on real-world data. In this work, we introduce the COMBO deep network that explicitly exploits the brightness constancy (BC) model used in traditional methods. Since BC is an approximate physical model violated in several situations, we propose to train a physically-constrained network complemented with a data-driven network. We introduce a unique and meaningful flow decomposition between the physical prior and the data-driven complement, including an uncertainty quantification of the BC model. We derive a joint training scheme for learning the different components of the decomposition ensuring an optimal cooperation, in a supervised but also in a semi-supervised context. Experiments show that COMBO can improve performances over state-of-the-art supervised networks, *e.g.* RAFT, reaching state-of-the-art results on several benchmarks. We highlight how COMBO can leverage the BC model and adapt to its limitations. Finally, we show that our semi-supervised method can significantly simplify the training procedure.

1 Introduction

Optical flow estimation is a classical problem in computer vision, consisting in computing the per-pixel motion between video frames. This is a core visual task useful in many applications, such as video compression [1], medical imaging [4] or object tracking [11]. Yet, this remains a particularly challenging task for real-world scenes, especially in presence of fast-moving objects, occlusions, changes of illumination or textureless surfaces.

Traditional model-based estimation methods [17,35] assume that the intensity of pixels is conserved during motion $\mathbf{w}$: $I_{t-1}(\mathbf{x}) = I_t(\mathbf{x} + \mathbf{w})$, which is

---

Supplementary Information The online version contains supplementary material available at https://doi.org/10.1007/978-3-031-19803-8_8.

known as the *brightness constancy* (BC) model. Linearizing this constraint for small motion leads to the famous optical flow partial differential equation (PDE) solved by variational methods since the seminal work of Horn and Schunk [17]:

$$\frac{\partial I}{\partial t}(t, \mathbf{x}) + \mathbf{w}(t, \mathbf{x}) \cdot \nabla I(t, \mathbf{x}) = 0 \tag{1}$$

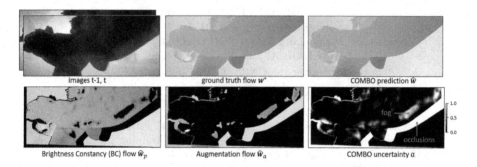

Fig. 1. Proposed COMBO model for flow estimation between two images I_1 and I_2. We explicitly leverage the brightness constancy (BC) assumption in Eq. (1) for estimating the physical flow prediction $\hat{\mathbf{w}}_p$. Since BC is an approximate model violated in several usual situations, COMBO learns an uncertainty map $\hat{\alpha}$ specifying areas where $\hat{\mathbf{w}}_p$ is relevant, and an augmentation data-driven flow $\hat{\mathbf{w}}_a$ to compensate for the BC violations (in this example, related to fog and occlusions). The final COMBO prediction combining $(\hat{\mathbf{w}}_a, \hat{\mathbf{w}}_p, \hat{\alpha})$ is both physically-regularized and accurate.

However this physical model for optical flow is only a rather coarse approximation of the reality. The BC assumption is violated in many situations: in presence of occlusions, global or local illumination changes, specular reflexions, or complex natural situations such as fog. The correspondence problem is also ambiguous for textureless surfaces. To solve this ill-posed inverse problem, this is necessary to inject prior knowledge about the flow, such as spatial smoothness, sparsity or small total variation.

In contrast to these traditional model-based approaches, deep neural networks have become state-of-the-art for learning optical flow in a pure data-driven fashion [13,18,20,44,51,53,61]. However, since flow labelling on real images is expensive, supervised deep learning methods mostly use complex curriculum training schemes on synthetic datasets to progressively adapt to the complexity of real-world scenes.

More recently, unsupervised deep learning approaches are closer in spirit to traditional approaches [22,24,30,39,45,49]. Without ground-truth labels, they rely on a photometric reconstruction loss based on the BC assumption, and additional regularization losses like spatial smoothness. They also use of specific modules, *e.g.* occlusion detection, to identify images areas where the BC in Eq. (1) is violated.

In this work, we introduce a hybrid model-based machine learning (MB/ML) model dedicated to optical flow estimation, which COMplements Brightness constancy with deep networks for accurate Optical flow prediction (COMBO). As illustrated in Fig. 1, COMBO decomposes the estimation process into a physical flow based on the simplified Brightness Constancy (BC) hypothesis and a data-driven augmentation for compensating for the limitations of the physical model. COMBO also simultaneously learns an uncertainty model of the brightness constancy, useful for fusing the two flow branches into an accurate flow estimation. Importantly, the two branches are learned jointly and a principled optimization ensures an optimal cooperation between them.

Our contributions are the following:

- We propose a principled way to regularize supervised flow models with an explicit exploitation of the BC assumption. We introduce with COMBO a meaningful and unique flow decomposition into a physical part optimizing the BC and an augmentation part compensating for its limitations.
- We propose to jointly learn the physical, augmented flows and a uncertainty measure of the BC validity, generalizing occlusion detection approaches or robust photometric losses. It also enables to exploit the model in semi-supervised contexts for non-annotated pixels where we know that the BC assumption is satisfied.
- To learn the COMBO model, we define and compute a fine-grained supervision by decomposing the ground-truth flow into a BC flow, a residual flow and an uncertainty map.
- Experiments (Sect. 4) show that when included into a state-of-the-art supervised network, i.e. RAFT, COMBO can improve performances consistently over datasets and training curriculum steps. COMBO also reaches state-of-the-art performances on several benchmarks, and we show that the semi-supervised scheme can be leveraged to grandly simplify the training curriculum. We also provide detailed ablations and qualitative analyses attesting the benefits of our principled decomposition framework.

2   Related Work

Traditional Optical Flow. Since the seminal works of Lucas-Kanade [35] and Horn-Schunck [17], optical flow estimation is traditionally casted as an optimization problem over the space of motion fields between a pair of images [8,40,58]. As mentionned in introduction, the cost function is usually based on the conservation assumption of an image descriptor during motion, i.e. the *brightness constancy* (BC). Since the number of optical flow variables is twice the number of observations, the search problem is underconstrained. Existing methods typically add spatial smoothness constraints on the flow to regularize the problem, enabling to propagate information from non-ambiguous to ambiguous pixels, *e.g.* occluded. Since, progress has been made for handling the limitations of the brightness constancy with more robust matching loss, such as the gradient constancy [7], the structural similarity (SSIM), the Charbonnier loss [9], the census loss [39] or involving descriptors learned by deep neural networks [3,59]. However, these traditional methods are limited for handling large motion and often suffer from a high computational cost.

Deep Supervised Methods. Deep neural networks have proven effective for directly learning the optical flow end-to-end from a labelled dataset [13,18,20, 23,44,51,53]. Although some methods borrow ideas from traditional methods such as cost volume processing [61] and pyramidal coarse-to-fine warping [44], they do not rely anymore on the conservation of an image descriptor. One of the current state-of-the-art architectures is the Recurrent All-Pairs Field Transforms (RAFT) [53]. This model exploits the correlation volume between all pairs of pixels and iteratively refines the flow with a recurrent neural network. Since obtaining ground-truth flow annotations is very expensive, supervised methods mostly train on synthetic datasets. This leads to a non-negligible generalization gap when transferring to real-world datasets. Consequently, complex curriculum learning schemes are needed to progressively adapt the learned optical flow from synthetic data to real scenarios [50,53].

Deep Unsupervised Methods. More recently, unsupervised approaches proved to outperform traditional methods even without flow labels [22,24,30,39,45,49]. They revisit the brightness constancy assumption by warping the target image with the estimated flow and optimizing a photometric loss. However they still lag behind supervised methods and require additional mechanisms for overcoming the limitations of the BC assumption, *e.g.* occlusion reasoning [39,57] or self-supervision [24,31,32]. Occlusions were traditionally treated as outliers in a robust estimation setting [7], or estimated with a forward-backward consistency check [2,39]. More recent approaches jointly learn occlusion maps with convolutional neural networks in a supervised way (i.e. with ground-truth occlusions) [19,20,37] or unsupervised way [15,21,63]. Nonetheless, most of these methods focus on specific cases of deviations from the brightness constancy assumption, *e.g.* occlusions or illumination changes. Our approach is more general and learns to compensate for any failure case of this simplified assumption. Besides, we learn from supervised flow data a confidence model of the BC assumption, which enables to learn our model in a semi-supervised setting [26,60].

Hybrid MB/ML. Combining model-based (MB) and machine learning (ML) models is a long-standing subject [42,46,54] that yet remains widely open nowadays. Leveraging physical knowledge enables to design machine learning models that learn from less data, and offer better generalization while conserving physical plausibility. Many ideas were explored, such as imposing soft physical constraints [28,34,43,48,56] in the training loss function or hard constraints in the network architectures [6,12,16,27,36,41]. However, most existing approaches assume a fully-known prior physical model. Very few works have investigated how to exploit incomplete physical models with deep neural networks [29,33,38,47,62]. Besides, exploiting incomplete physical knowledge in a deep hybrid model has never been explored for optical flow to the best of our knowledge.

3   COMBO Model for Optical Flow

Given a pair of frames I_{t-1} and $I_t \in \mathbb{R}^{W \times H \times 3}$, the optical flow task consists in estimating the dense motion field $\mathbf{w} = (u, v) \in \mathbb{R}^{W \times H \times 2}$ that maps each pixel from the source image I_{t-1} to its corresponding relative location in the target image I_t.

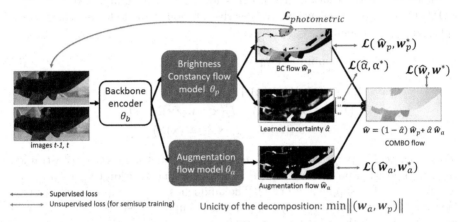

Fig. 2. Our proposed COMBO model for optical flow estimation. Given a pair of input frames (I_{t-1}, I_t), COMBO first extract convolutional features. The model is composed of three branches that compute an estimate for the physical flow $\hat{\mathbf{w}}_p$, the augmentation flow $\hat{\mathbf{w}}_a$ and the uncertainty map $\hat{\alpha}$.

We introduce COMBO, a deep learning model that explicitly exploits the brightness constancy (BC) assumption and learns the complementary information to compensate for the BC modeling errors.

The COMBO model is depicted in Fig. 2. The model takes a pair of input frames (I_{t-1}, I_t) and first encodes them into a feature space. From this common representation space, the rationale of COMBO is to decompose the dense flow $\hat{\mathbf{w}}$ using 3 main quantities: a physical term $\hat{\mathbf{w}}_p \in \mathbb{R}^{W \times H \times 2}$ fulfilling the BC assumption, an augmentation term $\hat{\mathbf{w}}_a \in \mathbb{R}^{W \times H \times 2}$ dedicated to capture the remaining information for accurate flow prediction. For each pixel, our decomposition also involves an uncertainty map $\hat{\alpha} \in [0, 1]^{W \times H}$ representing the violation of the BC assumption at each pixel.

In Sect. 3.1, we present our proposed BC augmentation framework, ensuring a unique and meaningful decomposition of $\hat{\mathbf{w}}$ between the physical $\hat{\mathbf{w}}_p$, augmented $\hat{\mathbf{w}}_a$ and uncertainty $\hat{\alpha}$ terms. From this formulation, we derive in Sect. 3.2 a training scheme to learn the model parameters, including a supervised but also a semi-supervised variant leveraging the learned BC confidence $\hat{\alpha}$.

3.1   BC-Augmented Flow Decomposition

We consider the flow $\mathbf{w}(\mathbf{x})$ representing the displacement of pixel $\mathbf{x} = (x, y)$ from $I_{t-1}(\mathbf{x})$ to $I_t(\mathbf{x})$. Let us define the brightness constancy divergence as

$\mathcal{L}_{BC}(\mathbf{x}, \mathbf{w}) := \ell(I_{t-1}(\mathbf{x}) - I_t(\mathbf{x} + \mathbf{w}))$ measured with the photometric loss ℓ (*e.g.* the L1 loss). In COMBO, we propose to decompose the ground truth flow $\mathbf{w}^*$ between a physical flow $\mathbf{w}_p^*$, an augmentation flow $\mathbf{w}_a^*$ and an uncertainty map α^*:

$$\mathbf{w}^*(\mathbf{x}) = (1 - \alpha^*(\mathbf{x})) \, \mathbf{w}_p^*(\mathbf{x}) + \alpha^*(\mathbf{x}) \, \mathbf{w}_a^*(\mathbf{x}). \tag{2}$$

Since the decomposition in Eq. (2) is not necessarily unique, we define the COMBO decomposition $(\mathbf{w}_p^*, \mathbf{w}_a^*, \alpha^*)$ as the solution of the following constrained optimization problem:

$$\min_{\mathbf{w}_p, \mathbf{w}_a} \quad \|(\mathbf{w}_a, \mathbf{w}_p)\| \qquad \text{subject to:} \tag{3}$$

$$\begin{cases} (1 - \alpha^*(\mathbf{x})) \, \mathbf{w}_p(\mathbf{x}) + \alpha(\mathbf{x}) \, \mathbf{w}_a(\mathbf{x}) = \mathbf{w}^*(\mathbf{x}) \\ (1 - \alpha^*(\mathbf{x})) \, |I_1(\mathbf{x}) - I_2(\mathbf{x} + \mathbf{w}_p(\mathbf{x}))| = 0 \\ \alpha^*(\mathbf{x}) = \sigma\left(|I_1(\mathbf{x}) - I_2(\mathbf{x} + \mathbf{w}^*(\mathbf{x}))|\right). \end{cases}$$

Theoretical Properties of the Decomposition: Under these constraints, the decomposition problem in Eq. (3) admits a unique solution $(\mathbf{w}_p^*, \mathbf{w}_a^*, \alpha^*)$ (we detail the proof in supplementary 1). The uniqueness in decomposition of a given flow into the three $(\mathbf{w}_p^*, \mathbf{w}_a^*, \alpha^*)$ components is important since it ensures a well posed problem for learning the different terms.

Beyond its sound mathematical formulation, the decomposition in Eq. (3) is also meaningful. It ensures to properly and explicitly exploit the BC model and to overcome its limitations to represent real data in diverse and complex situations. We detail now each component of this decomposition problem:

Brightness Constancy Flow $\hat{\mathbf{w}}_p(\mathbf{x})$: We define the brightness constancy flow $\hat{\mathbf{w}}_p$ as a minimizer of the BC condition, similarly to traditional and unsupervised methods. The BC is a very useful constraint not fully exploited in deep supervised methods. However, as mentioned in introduction, this BC assumption is often violated in real data, *e.g.* in case of occlusions, illumination changes, textureless surfaces, *etc.*. When directly minimizing $\mathcal{L}_{BC}(\mathbf{x}, \mathbf{w}) = \ell(I_{t-1}(\mathbf{x}) - I_t(\mathbf{x} + \mathbf{w}))$, for a given pixel $\mathbf{x}$ in the source image, there may exist multiple possible matches in the target image satisfying the BC constraint. Therefore, the BC constraint is only applied to $\mathbf{w}_p$ in Eq. (3), not to the final flow vector $\mathbf{w}^*$, and is weighted by the BC confidence measure $(1 - \alpha^*(\mathbf{x}))$. This is done on purpose, since the BC constraint is not always verified when training a model from ground truth supervision, making this term possibly conflicting with the supervised objective. We verify experimentally that a naive incorporation of the BC loss during training is not effective. In contrast, COMBO exploits an augmented flow to jointly incorporate the BC knowledge with an adaptive compensation for its violation.

BC Augmented Flow $\hat{\mathbf{w}}_a(\mathbf{x})$: In contrast to traditional and unsupervised methods, we do not leverage prior knowledge on the flow but instead rely on a data-driven augmentation $\hat{\mathbf{w}}_a$ to learn how to optimally compensate for the simplified model, as investigated by several recent augmented physical models [29,33,38,47,55,62]. To ensure a unique decomposition in Eq. (3), we minimize the norm of the concatenated vector $(\hat{\mathbf{w}}_a, \hat{\mathbf{w}}_p)$. The rationale is to compensate with the minimal correction $\|\hat{\mathbf{w}}_a\|$ from the brightness constancy assumption. This least-action augmentation also prevents $\hat{\mathbf{w}}_p(\mathbf{x})$ from being too large: the BC flow is enforced to be as close as possible to the ground-truth flow $\mathbf{w}^*$. Minimizing the norm of $\hat{\mathbf{w}}_p$ also prevents degenerate cases with possibly several admissible $\hat{\mathbf{w}}_p$ equidistant to $\mathbf{w}^*$ (see supplementary 1 for a discussion).

BC Uncertainty $\alpha^*(\mathbf{x})$: We weight the decomposition between $\hat{\mathbf{w}}_p$ and $\hat{\mathbf{w}}_a$ in Eq. (3) with the uncertainty map $\alpha^*(\mathbf{x}) = \sigma(\mathcal{L}_{BC}(\mathbf{x}, \mathbf{w}^*))$ quantifying the per-pixel validity of the BC assumption, where σ is a nonlinear function[1] ensuring that the uncertainty values spread over $[0; 1]$. When $\alpha^*(\mathbf{x}) = 0$, the BC assumption is verified; in that case, our decomposition reduces to the physical flow $\hat{\mathbf{w}}(\mathbf{x}) = \hat{\mathbf{w}}_p(\mathbf{x})$ as in traditional methods. On the contrary, when the BC is violated $(\alpha^*(\mathbf{x}) > 0)$, the errors of the brightness constancy modelling are compensated by the data-driven model $\hat{\mathbf{w}}_a$. This leads to a meaningful decomposition between $\hat{\mathbf{w}}_p$ and $\hat{\mathbf{w}}_a$.

3.2 Training

In this section, we propose to jointly learn the three quantities $\mathbf{w}_p^*$, $\mathbf{w}_a^*$ and α^* of the flow decomposition Eq. (2) with a deep neural architecture named COMBO. We introduce a practical learning framework to solve the decomposition problem in Eq. (3) in the supervised and semi-supervised settings. Given a dataset of labelled image pairs $\mathcal{D}_{sup} = \{(I_{t-1}, I_t, \mathbf{w}^*)_i\}_{i=1}^{N_{sup}}$ and unlabelled image pairs $\mathcal{D}_{unsup} = \{(I_{t-1}, I_t)_i\}_{i=1}^{N_{unsup}}$, the goal is to learn the parameters $\theta = \{\theta_b, \theta_p, \theta_a\}$ of the COMBO model depicted in Fig. 2, where θ_b are the backbone encoder parameters, θ_p the parameters of the BC flow model, θ_a are the parameters of the augmented flow model.

The general loss for learning the COMBO model is the following:

$$\mathcal{L}(\mathcal{D}, \theta) = \lambda_p \|\hat{\mathbf{w}}_p - \mathbf{w}_p^*\|_2^2 + \lambda_a \|\hat{\mathbf{w}}_a - \mathbf{w}_a^*\|_2^2 + \lambda_{total} \|\hat{\mathbf{w}} - \mathbf{w}^*\|_2^2$$
$$+ \lambda_{photo} \mathcal{L}_{photo}(\mathcal{D}, \theta) + \lambda_w \|(\hat{\mathbf{w}}_a, \hat{\mathbf{w}}_p)\|^2 + \lambda_\alpha \mathcal{L}_\alpha(\mathcal{D}, \theta), \quad (4)$$

where $\hat{\mathbf{w}}(\mathbf{x}) = (1 - \hat{\alpha}(\mathbf{x})) \hat{\mathbf{w}}_p(\mathbf{x}) + \hat{\alpha}(\mathbf{x}) \hat{\mathbf{w}}_a(\mathbf{x})$ is the flow predicted by COMBO.

The total loss in Eq. (4) is composed of supervised losses on the final flow $\hat{\mathbf{w}}$, the BC flow $\hat{\mathbf{w}}_p$ and the augmentation flow $\hat{\mathbf{w}}_a$. In addition to the supervised loss on $\hat{\mathbf{w}}_p$, we also use a photometric loss similarly to traditional and unsupervised methods. We use the L1 loss weighted by the certainty measure $(1 - \alpha^*(\mathbf{x}))$:

$$\mathcal{L}_{photo}(\mathcal{D}, \theta) = \sum_{I_1, I_2 \in \mathcal{D}} \sum_{\mathbf{x}} (1 - \alpha^*(\mathbf{x})) |I_1(\mathbf{x}) - I_2(\mathbf{x} + \hat{\mathbf{w}}_p)|_1. \quad (5)$$

---

[1] We choose in this work the sigmoid function centered at 0.5 for image pixels in the range $[0; 1]$.

With the L1 loss, the physical branch of COMBO directly models the brightness conservation at the pixel level and the learned uncertainty captures the limitations of this hypothesis. Other photometric losses more robust to the brightness constancy limitations could have been chosen, *e.g.* the Charbonnier [9], SSIM [24] or census loss [39], that would produce a different physical flow. Our augmentation framework can seamlessly adapt to the level of approximation of the BC model at each pixel. Note that the photometric loss is complementary with the supervised loss $\|\hat{\mathbf{w}}_p - \mathbf{w}_p^*\|_2^2$: a small error on the predicted flow $\hat{\mathbf{w}}_p$ results in a small endpoint error (EPE) but can have a large photometric error if $\hat{\mathbf{w}}_p$ leads to a large photometric change in the target image.

Finally, we define the uncertainty loss as:

$$\mathcal{L}_\alpha(\mathcal{D}_{sup}, \theta) = \sum_{I_1, I_2 \in \mathcal{D}_{sup}} \sum_{\mathbf{x}} \|\hat{\alpha}(\mathbf{x}) - \sigma(\mathcal{L}_{BC}(\mathbf{x}, \mathbf{w}^*))\|_2^2. \tag{6}$$

Curriculum Learning for the BC Uncertainty: In the COMBO decomposition $\hat{\mathbf{w}}(\mathbf{x}) = (1 - \hat{\alpha}(\mathbf{x})) \, \hat{\mathbf{w}}_p(\mathbf{x}) + \hat{\alpha}(\mathbf{x}) \, \hat{\mathbf{w}}_a(\mathbf{x})$, a bad estimate of the uncertainty α could be harmful for learning $\hat{\mathbf{w}}_p$ and $\hat{\mathbf{w}}_a$. Therefore, similarly to the *teacher forcing* strategy in sequential models, we choose a scheduled sampling strategy [5] where we use the ground truth α^* with high probability at the beginning of learning, and decrease progressively this probability towards 0 to rely more and more on the prediction $\hat{\alpha}$ (see Algorithm 1).

Supervised Learning: In the supervised learning setting, we only exploit the supervised set $\mathcal{D}_{sup}$. We minimize the total loss in Eq. (4) by using the fine-grained supervision on $(\mathbf{w}_p^*, \mathbf{w}_a^*, \alpha^*)$ that we have created (see supplementary 3.1 for examples of tuples $(\mathbf{w}_p^*, \mathbf{w}_a^*, \alpha^*)$ for each dataset).

Semi-supervised Learning: COMBO can be also favorably used in a semi-supervised training setting, which consists in exploiting the information of non-annotated images in $\mathcal{D}_{unsup}$ in addition to the annotated frames in $\mathcal{D}_{sup}$. This is an important context in practice since labelling flow images is expensive at scale (in general $N_{unsup} \gg N_{sup}$). Leveraging unlabelled data directly on the target dataset is an appealing way for unsupervised domain adaptation.

When learning in semi-supervised mode (see Algorithm 1), we mix in a mini-batch labelled image pairs from $\mathcal{D}_{sup}$ and unlabelled image pairs from $\mathcal{D}_{unsup}$. For labelled images, we again minimize the supervised loss $\mathcal{L}$ defined in Eq. (4). For unlabelled frames, we refine the estimation of $\hat{\mathbf{w}}_p$ by exploiting the photometric loss on pixels that are likely to satisfy the BC constraint (measured by the uncertainty map α learned with ground-truth data). We only minimize in that case the photometric loss $\mathcal{L}_{photo}(\mathcal{D}_{unsup}, \theta)$, which corresponds to the particular case of Eq. (4) by setting $\lambda_{photo} = 1$ and $\lambda_p = \lambda_a = \lambda_{total} = \lambda_w = \lambda_\alpha = 0$. Importantly, for unlabelled images, we block the gradient flow in the uncertainty branch α since α can only be estimated in supervised mode.

Algorithm 1: COMBO optimization:

Parameters: $\lambda_p, \lambda_a, \lambda_{total}, \lambda_{photo}, \lambda_w, \lambda_\alpha \geq 0, \tau > 0$;

for $epoch = 1 : N_{epochs}$ **do**

    for $each\ batch\ b = (b_{sup}, b_{unsup})$ **do**

        If $Rand(0,1) < 1 - epoch/50$ **Then:**   # scheduled sampling

        $\hat{\mathbf{w}}(\mathbf{x}) = (1 - \alpha^*(\mathbf{x}))\ \hat{\mathbf{w}}_p(\mathbf{x}) + \alpha^*(\mathbf{x})\ \hat{\mathbf{w}}_a(\mathbf{x})$

        Else:

        $\hat{\mathbf{w}}(\mathbf{x}) = (1 - \hat{\alpha}(\mathbf{x}))\ \hat{\mathbf{w}}_p(\mathbf{x}) + \hat{\alpha}(\mathbf{x})\ \hat{\mathbf{w}}_a(\mathbf{x})$

        Compute $\mathcal{L}_{sup} = \mathcal{L}(b_{sup}, \theta, \lambda_{sup}, \lambda_{photo}, \lambda_w, \lambda_\alpha)$ with Eq. (4)

        Compute $\mathcal{L}_{unsup} = \mathcal{L}_{photo}(b_{unsup}, \theta)$

        $\theta_{j+1} = \theta_j - \tau\ \nabla(\mathcal{L}_{sup} + \mathcal{L}_{unsup})$

---

4 Experiments

We evaluate and compare COMBO to recent state-of-the-art models on the optical flow datasets FlyingChairs [13], MPI Sintel [10] and KITTI-2015 [14], in the supervised and semi-supervised contexts. For model analysis, we perform a train/test resplit of the Sintel and KITTI training datasets, as done by [30]. Our code is available at https://github.com/vincent-leguen/COMBO.

4.1 Experimental Setup

We adopt for the backbone encoder and flow network the RAFT architecture [53], which is one of the current state-of-the-art methods for supervised optical flow. The encoder is composed of convolutional layers that extract features from images I_{t-1} and I_t at resolution 1/8. Then visual similarity is modelled by constructing a 4D correlation volume that computes matching costs for all possible displacements. The optical flow branch is a gated recurrent unit (GRU) that progressively refines the flow from an initial estimate, with lookups on the correlation volume. The final flow is the sum of residual refinements from the GRU, upsampled at full resolution.

Table 1. Performances of COMBO compared to the RAFT model (run with online code). COMBO consistently outperforms RAFT on the three training stages, illustrating the relevance of leveraging the BC physical model and complementing its failure cases.

Stage	Method	Chairs	Sintel-test-resplit		KITTI-test-resplit	
			Clean	Final	Fl-epe	Fl-all
C	RAFT	0.82	1.11	1.76	10.7	39.7
C	COMBO	**0.74**	**1.04**	**1.58**	**10.2**	**39.3**
C+T	RAFT	1.15	0.82	1.17	5.67	17.9
C+T	COMBO	**1.09**	**0.77**	**0.96**	**5.46**	**17.3**
C+T+	RAFT	1.23	0.57	0.76	1.79	7.12
S+H+K	COMBO	**1.16**	**0.56**	**0.71**	**1.75**	**6.58**

Table 2. State-of-the-art performance comparison on FlyingChairs, Sintel-train and KITTI-train, when learning on FlyingChairs (C) and FlyingChairs+FlyingThings (C+T). Scores are reported from corresponding papers.

Stage	Method	Chairs	Sintel (train)		KITTI-15 (train)	
			Clean	Final	Fl-epe	Fl-all
C	RAFT [53]	0.82	2.26	4.52	10.67	39.72
C	GMA [23]	0.79	2.32	**4.10**	10.32	**36.91**
C	COMBO	**0.74**	**2.19**	4.37	**10.19**	39.02
C+T	LiteFlowNet [20]	-	2.48	4.04	10.39	28.5
C+T	PWC-Net [51]	-	2.55	3.93	10.35	33.7
C+T	VCN [61]	-	2.21	3.68	8.36	25.1
C+T	MaskFlowNet [63]	-	2.25	3.61	-	23.1
C+T	RAFT [53]	1.15	1.43	2.71	5.01	17.5
C+T	GMA [23]	1.19	**1.31**	2.73	**4.69**	17.1
C+T	COMBO	**1.09**	**1.31**	**2.58**	4.69	**16.5**

In the COMBO model, the encoder and correlation volume are shared, and each branch has its own GRU initialized from zero. The uncertainty branch is simply adapted to provide a unique output channel. We give details on the network architectures and hyperparameters in supplementary 2. The code of COMBO will be released if accepted. Note that our method is agnostic to the optical flow backbone. Any other deep architecture than RAFT could be used for computing the physical, augmentation flow and the uncertainty map.

4.2   Supervised State-of-the-Art Comparison

Following the supervised learning curriculum of prior works [23,52,53,63], we pretrain our models successively on the synthetic datasets FlyingChairs [13] and FlyingThings3D [37]. We then finetune on Sintel [10] by combining data from Sintel, KITTI-2015 and HD1K [25]. We finally finetune on KITTI-2015 with only data from KITTI.

In Table 1, we compare the endpoint error (EPE) of COMBO with RAFT [53], by running the code from the authors. Since we rely on a RAFT architecture, the results in Table 1 directly evaluate the impact of the proposed augmented model and learning scheme. We see that COMBO consistently outperforms RAFT on FlyingChairs, Sintel-test-resplit and KITTI-test-resplit from all stages of the curriculum. This confirms the relevance of leveraging the BC constraint for regularizing supervised models, and the use of the augmentation for compensating its violations.

In Table 2, we compare COMBO to competitive supervised optical flow baselines, from the stages FlyingChairs (C) and FlyingChairs+FlyingThings (C+T). When generalizing to Sintel-train and KITTI-train, COMBO outperforms RAFT [53] in all cases, and is superior or equivalent to the recent GMA model [23] in 6/8 cases. Note also that COMBO outperforms all other methods on FlyingChairs.

Table 3. Comparison with RAFT on KITTI-test-resplit from the FlyingChairs (C) and Sintel (S) checkpoints, with supervised and semisup training on KITTI. We see that COMBO in semisup from Chairs is almost equivalent to COMBO from Sintel, showing that the training curriculum can be drastically reduced.

Model	Mode	Checkpoint	KITTI (test-resplit)	
			F1-epe	F1-all
RAFT [53]	sup	C	2.28	7.60
COMBO	sup	C	2.19	7.30
COMBO	semisup	C	**1.75**	**6.88**
RAFT [53]	sup	S	1.79	7.12
COMBO	sup	S	1.75	**6.58**
COMBO	semisup	S	**1.74**	**6.58**

4.3 Semi-supervised Results

We analyze the performances of COMBO in a semi-supervised learning setting in Table 3. We evaluate the different models on KITTI test-resplit, using for training the annotated images of KITTI train-resplit (sup) and the additional unlabelled images of KITTI (semisup). When training on KITTI from the earliest stage of the curriculum (FlyingChairs), we can see that COMBO-semisup (F1-epe=1.75) largely improves over RAFT-sup (2.28) and COMBO-sup (2.19). It confirms that leveraging the vast amount of unlabelled frames is crucial for adapting the model to a target dataset from an early checkpoint. Interestingly, the semisup training from Chairs is almost equivalent to the COMBO model trained from the Sintel checkpoint (1.74). It shows that COMBO trained in a semisup context enables to greatly simplify the training curriculum to reach similar performances. This feature of COMBO is of crucial interest in many domains for transferring models to target datasets from a single synthetic training stage.

To further analyze the semi-supervised learning ability of COMBO, we progressively reduce the number of training images on KITTI-resplit and compare the performances of RAFT and COMBO-semisup trained from the FlyingChairs checkpoint. In Fig. 3, we observe that RAFT degrades much more sharply than COMBO with fewer training images, and the difference in EPE becomes very large with 10% of training images (EPE=11.6 for RAFT v.s. 4.4 for COMBO). It highlights the crucial ability of COMBO to leverage the BC assumption on unlabelled frames.

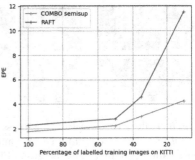

Fig. 3. Performances on KITTI-resplit trained from the Chairs, w.r.t. the number of labelled frames.

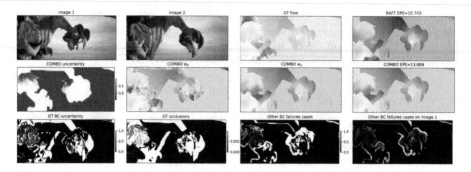

Fig. 4. Qualitative prediction results on MPI Sintel. We observe that in zones of high uncertainty of the BC, the physical flow $\hat{\mathbf{w}}_p$ is ill-defined; the augmentation flow $\hat{\mathbf{w}}_a$ successfully complements it for accurate flow estimation. We also show that the uncertainty learned by COMBO is consistent with the GT BC uncertainty, and that it detects other cases of violation of the BC different from occlusions.

Fig. 5. Qualitative prediction results on KITTI 2015. We see that at the bottom of the image where the road becomes occluded, the physical flow $\hat{\mathbf{w}}_p$ is ill-defined and is complements by $\hat{\mathbf{w}}_a$ for accurate prediction.

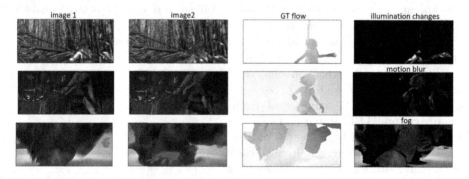

Fig. 6. Failure cases of the brightness constancy detected by COMBO different from occlusions. The last column corresponds to image 1 masked by the map of thresholded uncertainty $\hat{\alpha}$ deprived of the ground-truth occlusions. From top to bottom, COMBO captures: illumination change, motion blur and fog.

4.4   Ablation Study

We perform in Table 4 an ablation study on FlyingChairs to analyze the behaviour of the COMBO model. We first show that two RAFT branches trained with different seeds and mixed 50:50 improve over RAFT but is largely inferior to COMBO, show that the performances of COMBO do not simply come from an augmentation of the parameters or an ensembling effect. Then, we see that a single RAFT branch with the photometric loss $\mathcal{L}_{photo}$ in Eq. (5) (epe = 0.794) is far inferior to COMBO (0.743). This is because the BC regularization helps in improving generalization in regions where the BC assumption is fulfilled, but is detrimental in regions where the BC assumption does not hold. In contrast, COMBO can leverage the BC assumption and complement it in an adaptive manner when it is violated, overcoming the conflict issues between the two terms.

Moreover, the linear decomposition $\hat{\mathbf{w}} = \hat{\mathbf{w}}_p + \hat{\mathbf{w}}_a$ without the uncertainty branch, i.e. we set $\alpha(\mathbf{x}) = 1/2$ everywhere, is clearly inferior to COMBO. It shows the crucial necessity to account for the uncertainty of the BC. Finally, when we remove the minimization of $\|(\hat{\mathbf{w}}_a, \hat{\mathbf{w}}_p)\|$ from COMBO (then the decomposition is not unique anymore), the performances also decrease, highlighting the superiority of the well-posed and unique decomposition of COMBO.

We then report in Table 5 the performances of the individual $\hat{\mathbf{w}}_p$ (resp. $\hat{\mathbf{w}}_a$) branches weighted by the certainty of the BC (resp. uncertainty). For example, we compute $EPE_{weighted}(\hat{\mathbf{w}}_p, \mathbf{w}^*) = \sum_{\mathbf{x}}(1 - \alpha^*(\mathbf{x}))\|\hat{\mathbf{w}}_p(\mathbf{x}) - \mathbf{w}^*(\mathbf{x})\|_2$. We see that both $\hat{\mathbf{w}}_p$ and $\hat{\mathbf{w}}_a$ are superior to RAFT on areas where they apply. In particular the performance gap compared to RAFT widens on areas with high BC uncertainty (EPE= 2.20 $v.s.$ 0.52), showing the benefits of the COMBO decomposition to greatly improve the estimation on challenging zones.

Table 4. Ablation study on FlyingChairs, showing the benefits of the meaningful and principled decomposition of COMBO, compared to the backbone RAFT.

Method	EPE (FlyingChairs)
RAFT [53]	0.818
2 RAFT branches mixed equally	0.800
RAFT + BC photometric loss	0.794
COMBO $\hat{\mathbf{w}}_p + \hat{\mathbf{w}}_a$ (no weighting by uncertainty)	0.769
COMBO without min $\|(\hat{\mathbf{w}}_a, \hat{\mathbf{w}}_p)\|$	0.752
COMBO	**0.743**

4.5 COMBO Analysis

We provide qualitative flow predictions of the COMBO model for Sintel-test-resplit in Fig. 4 and KITTI-test-resplit in Fig. 5. In uncertain zones ($\hat{\alpha} \approx 1$, for example in the occluded region of the bird in Fig. 4 or at the bottom of Fig. 5), we can see that $\hat{\mathbf{w}}_p$ gives incoherent results, as expected. In that case, the flow is efficiently complemented by $\hat{\mathbf{w}}_a$ to produce the COMBO flow.

Occlusion Detection: To analyze the ability of COMBO to detect occlusions, we represent in supplementary 3.2 the precision-recall curve of the COMBO

Table 5. Performances of the individual BC $\hat{\mathbf{w}}_p$ and residual $\hat{\mathbf{w}}_a$ flow branches on areas with high BC confidence (resp. high BC uncertainty).

Method	EPE weighted (FlyingChairs)
RAFT on BC certain zones	0.48
COMBO $\hat{\mathbf{w}}_p$ on certain zones	**0.30**
RAFT on BC uncertain zones	2.29
COMBO $\hat{\mathbf{w}}_a$ on uncertain zones	**0.52**

uncertainty detector with respect to the ground-truth occlusion masks (which are known for Sintel). COMBO obtains an Average Precision (AP) of 59%, which is a lower bound of the true AP of COMBO for occlusions (since COMBO also captures other failure cases than occlusions). This means that COMBO is able to efficiently detect occlusions without any ground-truth occlusion supervision, compared to the random classifier which reaches 7% (ratio of occluded pixels).

Detection of Other Failure Cases of the BC: In the third line of Fig. 4, we show the ground-truth (GT) BC uncertainty mask (defined as $\mathcal{L}_{BC} > \epsilon$, $\epsilon = 0.01$ in Fig. 4) and the ground-truth occlusions of Sintel. We observe that the COMBO uncertainty globally aligns with the GT BC uncertainty, and covers a larger area than the GT occlusions. To investigate this, we display the thresholded uncertainty mask α deprived of the GT occlusions: it shows that COMBO can capture other failure cases of the BC different than occlusions. Applying this mask on image 1 (bottom right of Fig. 4) shows that this corresponds to illumination changes for this example.

We further analyze the other failure cases of the BC in Fig. 6. We can see that COMBO can detect other cases of violation of the BC, without any supervision masks on these cases. The top row of Fig. 6 shows that the uncertainty α detects the illumination change on the arm of the woman. On the middle row, the uncertainty concentrates on the woman running, which causes motion blur. The bottom row shows a BC uncertainty on a large part of the image, caused by the presence of fog. We provide additional visualizations in supplementary 3.4.

5   Conclusion

We have introduced COMBO, a new physically-constrained architecture for optical flow estimation that explicitly exploits the simplified brightness constancy constraint. COMBO learns the uncertainty of the BC and how to complement it with a data-driven network. COMBO reaches state-of-the-art results on several benchmarks, and is able to greatly simplify the training curriculum with a semi-supervised learning scheme. An appealing perspective would be to investigate the application of augmented physical models to multi-frame optical flow estimation.

References

1. Agustsson, E., Minnen, D., Johnston, N., Balle, J., Hwang, S.J., Toderici, G.: Scale-space flow for end-to-end optimized video compression. In: Proceedings of the IEEE/CVF Conference on Computer Vision and Pattern Recognition, pp. 8503–8512 (2020)
2. Alvarez, L., Deriche, R., Papadopoulo, T., Sánchez, J.: Symmetrical dense optical flow estimation with occlusions detection. Int. J. Comput. Vision **75**(3), 371–385 (2007)
3. Bailer, C., Varanasi, K., Stricker, D.: Cnn-based patch matching for optical flow with thresholded hinge embedding loss. In: Proceedings of the IEEE Conference on Computer Vision and Pattern Recognition, pp. 3250–3259 (2017)
4. Balakrishnan, G., Zhao, A., Sabuncu, M.R., Guttag, J., Dalca, A.V.: An unsupervised learning model for deformable medical image registration. In: Proceedings of the IEEE Conference on Computer Vision and Pattern Recognition, pp. 9252–9260 (2018)
5. Bengio, S., Vinyals, O., Jaitly, N., Shazeer, N.: Scheduled sampling for sequence prediction with recurrent neural networks. In: Advances in Neural Information Processing Systems 28 (2015)
6. de Bezenac, E., Pajot, A., Gallinari, P.: Deep learning for physical processes: incorporating prior scientific knowledge. In: ICLR (2018)
7. Brox, T., Bruhn, A., Papenberg, N., Weickert, J.: High accuracy optical flow estimation based on a theory for warping. In: Pajdla, T., Matas, J. (eds.) ECCV 2004. LNCS, vol. 3024, pp. 25–36. Springer, Heidelberg (2004). https://doi.org/10.1007/978-3-540-24673-2_3
8. Brox, T., Malik, J.: Large displacement optical flow: descriptor matching in variational motion estimation. IEEE Trans. Pattern Anal. Mach. Intell. **33**(3), 500–513 (2010)
9. Bruhn, A., Weickert, J., Schnörr, C.: Lucas/kanade meets horn/schunck: combining local and global optic flow methods. Int. J. Comput. Vision **61**(3), 211–231 (2005)
10. Butler, D.J., Wulff, J., Stanley, G.B., Black, M.J.: A naturalistic open source movie for optical flow evaluation. In: Fitzgibbon, A., Lazebnik, S., Perona, P., Sato, Y., Schmid, C. (eds.) ECCV 2012. LNCS, vol. 7577, pp. 611–625. Springer, Heidelberg (2012). https://doi.org/10.1007/978-3-642-33783-3_44
11. Corpetti, T., Mémin, É., Pérez, P.: Dense estimation of fluid flows. IEEE Trans. Pattern Anal. Mach. Intell. **24**(3), 365–380 (2002)
12. Daw, A., Thomas, R.Q., Carey, C.C., Read, J.S., Appling, A.P., Karpatne, A.: Physics-guided architecture (pga) of neural networks for quantifying uncertainty in lake temperature modeling. In: Proceedings of the 2020 SIAM International Conference on Data Mining, pp. 532–540. SIAM (2020)
13. Dosovitskiy, A., et al.: Flownet: learning optical flow with convolutional networks. In: Proceedings of the IEEE International Conference on Computer Vision (ICCV), pp. 2758–2766 (2015)
14. Geiger, A., Lenz, P., Stiller, C., Urtasun, R.: Vision meets robotics: the kitti dataset. Int. J. Robot. Res. **32**(11), 1231–1237 (2013)
15. Godet, P., Boulch, A., Plyer, A., Le Besnerais, G.: Starflow: a spatiotemporal recurrent cell for lightweight multi-frame optical flow estimation. In: 2020 25th International Conference on Pattern Recognition (ICPR), pp. 2462–2469. IEEE (2021)

16. Greydanus, S., Dzamba, M., Yosinski, J.: Hamiltonian neural networks. In: Advances in Neural Information Processing Systems (NeurIPS), pp. 15353–15363 (2019)
17. Horn, B.K., Schunck, B.G.: Determining optical flow. Artif. intell. **17**(1–3), 185–203 (1981)
18. Hui, T.W., Tang, X., Loy, C.C.: Liteflownet: a lightweight convolutional neural network for optical flow estimation. In: Proceedings of the IEEE Conference on Computer Vision and Pattern Recognition (CVPR), pp. 8981–8989 (2018)
19. Hur, J., Roth, S.: Iterative residual refinement for joint optical flow and occlusion estimation. In: Proceedings of the IEEE/CVF Conference on Computer Vision and Pattern Recognition, pp. 5754–5763 (2019)
20. Ilg, E., Mayer, N., Saikia, T., Keuper, M., Dosovitskiy, A., Brox, T.: Flownet 2.0: evolution of optical flow estimation with deep networks. In: Proceedings of the IEEE Conference on Computer Vision and Pattern Recognition, pp. 2462–2470 (2017)
21. Janai, J., Güney, F., Ranjan, A., Black, M., Geiger, A.: Unsupervised learning of multi-frame optical flow with occlusions. In: Ferrari, V., Hebert, M., Sminchisescu, C., Weiss, Y. (eds.) ECCV 2018. LNCS, vol. 11220, pp. 713–731. Springer, Cham (2018). https://doi.org/10.1007/978-3-030-01270-0_42
22. Yu, J.J., Harley, A.W., Derpanis, K.G.: Back to basics: unsupervised learning of optical flow via brightness constancy and motion smoothness. In: Hua, G., Jégou, H. (eds.) ECCV 2016. LNCS, vol. 9915, pp. 3–10. Springer, Cham (2016). https://doi.org/10.1007/978-3-319-49409-8_1
23. Jiang, S., Campbell, D., Lu, Y., Li, H., Hartley, R.: Learning to estimate hidden motions with global motion aggregation. In: CVPR (2021)
24. Jonschkowski, R., Stone, A., Barron, J.T., Gordon, A., Konolige, K., Angelova, A.: What matters in unsupervised optical flow. In: Vedaldi, A., Bischof, H., Brox, T., Frahm, J.-M. (eds.) ECCV 2020. LNCS, vol. 12347, pp. 557–572. Springer, Cham (2020). https://doi.org/10.1007/978-3-030-58536-5_33
25. Kondermann, D., et al.: The hci benchmark suite: stereo and flow ground truth with uncertainties for urban autonomous driving. In: Proceedings of the IEEE Conference on Computer Vision and Pattern Recognition Workshops, pp. 19–28 (2016)
26. Lai, W.S., Huang, J.B., Yang, M.H.: Semi-supervised learning for optical flow with generative adversarial networks. In: Proceedings of the 31st International Conference on Neural Information Processing Systems, pp. 353–363 (2017)
27. Le Guen, V., Thome, N.: Disentangling physical dynamics from unknown factors for unsupervised video prediction. In: CVPR (2020)
28. Li, Z., Kovachki, N., Azizzadenesheli, K., Liu, B., Bhattacharya, K., Stuart, A., Anandkumar, A.: Fourier neural operator for parametric partial differential equations. arXiv preprint arXiv:2010.08895 (2020)
29. Linial, O., Eytan, D., Shalit, U.: Generative ODE modeling with known unknowns. In: ICLR 2020 Deep Differential Equations Workshop (2020)
30. Liu, L., et al.: Learning by analogy: reliable supervision from transformations for unsupervised optical flow estimation. In: Proceedings of the IEEE/CVF Conference on Computer Vision and Pattern Recognition, pp. 6489–6498 (2020)
31. Liu, P., King, I., Lyu, M.R., Xu, J.: Ddflow: learning optical flow with unlabeled data distillation. In: Proceedings of the AAAI Conference on Artificial Intelligence, vol. 33, pp. 8770–8777 (2019)

32. Liu, P., Lyu, M., King, I., Xu, J.: Selflow: self-supervised learning of optical flow. In: Proceedings of the IEEE/CVF Conference on Computer Vision and Pattern Recognition, pp. 4571–4580 (2019)
33. Long, Y., She, X., Mukhopadhyay, S.: Hybridnet: integrating model-based and data-driven learning to predict evolution of dynamical systems. In: Conference on Robot Learning (CoRL) (2018)
34. Lu, L., Jin, P., Karniadakis, G.E.: Deeponet: learning nonlinear operators for identifying differential equations based on the universal approximation theorem of operators. arXiv preprint arXiv:1910.03193 (2019)
35. Lucas, B.D., Kanade, T., et al.: An iterative image registration technique with an application to stereo vision. Vancouver, British Columbia (1981)
36. Lutter, M., Ritter, C., Peters, J.: Deep lagrangian networks: using physics as model prior for deep learning. arXiv preprint arXiv:1907.04490 (2019)
37. Mayer, N., et al.: A large dataset to train convolutional networks for disparity, optical flow, and scene flow estimation. In: Proceedings of the IEEE Conference on Computer Vision and Pattern Recognition, pp. 4040–4048 (2016)
38. Mehta, V., Char, I., Neiswanger, W., Chung, Y., Schneider, J.: Neural dynamical systems. In: ICLR 2020 Deep Differential Equations Workshop (2020)
39. Meister, S., Hur, J., Roth, S.: Unflow: unsupervised learning of optical flow with a bidirectional census loss. In: Thirty-Second AAAI Conference on Artificial Intelligence (2018)
40. Mémin, E., Pérez, P.: Dense estimation and object-based segmentation of the optical flow with robust techniques. IEEE Trans. Image Process. **7**(5), 703–719 (1998)
41. Mohan, A.T., Lubbers, N., Livescu, D., Chertkov, M.: Embedding hard physical constraints in neural network coarse-graining of 3d turbulence. arXiv preprint arXiv:2002.00021 (2020)
42. Psichogios, D.C., Ungar, L.H.: A hybrid neural network-first principles approach to process modeling. AIChE J. **38**(10), 1499–1511 (1992)
43. Raissi, M.: Deep hidden physics models: deep learning of nonlinear partial differential equations. J. Mach. Learn. Res. **19**(1), 932–955 (2018)
44. Ranjan, A., Black, M.J.: Optical flow estimation using a spatial pyramid network. In: Proceedings of the IEEE Conference on Computer Vision and Pattern Recognition (CVPR), pp. 4161–4170 (2017)
45. Ren, Z., Yan, J., Ni, B., Liu, B., Yang, X., Zha, H.: Unsupervised deep learning for optical flow estimation. In: Thirty-First AAAI Conference on Artificial Intelligence (2017)
46. Rico-Martinez, R., Anderson, J., Kevrekidis, I.: Continuous-time nonlinear signal processing: a neural network based approach for gray box identification. In: Proceedings of IEEE Workshop on Neural Networks for Signal Processing, pp. 596–605. IEEE (1994)
47. Saha, P., Dash, S., Mukhopadhyay, S.: PhICNet: physics-incorporated convolutional recurrent neural networks for modeling dynamical systems. arXiv preprint arXiv:2004.06243 (2020)
48. Sirignano, J., Spiliopoulos, K.: Dgm: a deep learning algorithm for solving partial differential equations. J. Comput. Phys. **375**, 1339–1364 (2018)
49. Stone, A., Maurer, D., Ayvaci, A., Angelova, A., Jonschkowski, R.: Smurf: self-teaching multi-frame unsupervised raft with full-image warping. In: Proceedings of the IEEE/CVF Conference on Computer Vision and Pattern Recognition, pp. 3887–3896 (2021)

50. Sun, D., et al.: Autoflow: learning a better training set for optical flow. In: Proceedings of the IEEE/CVF Conference on Computer Vision and Pattern Recognition, pp. 10093–10102 (2021)

51. Sun, D., Yang, X., Liu, M.Y., Kautz, J.: Pwc-net: Cnns for optical flow using pyramid, warping, and cost volume. In: Proceedings of the IEEE Conference on Computer Vision and Pattern Recognition (CVPR), pp. 8934–8943 (2018)

52. Sun, D., Yang, X., Liu, M.Y., Kautz, J.: Models matter, so does training: An empirical study of CNNs for optical flow estimation. IEEE Trans. Pattern Anal. Mach. Intell. **42**(6), 1408–1423 (2019)

53. Teed, Z., Deng, J.: RAFT: recurrent all-pairs field transforms for optical flow. In: Vedaldi, A., Bischof, H., Brox, T., Frahm, J.-M. (eds.) ECCV 2020. LNCS, vol. 12347, pp. 402–419. Springer, Cham (2020). https://doi.org/10.1007/978-3-030-58536-5_24

54. Thompson, M.L., Kramer, M.A.: Modeling chemical processes using prior knowledge and neural networks. AIChE J. **40**(8), 1328–1340 (1994)

55. Wang, Q., Li, F., Tang, Y., Xu, Y.: Integrating model-driven and data-driven methods for power system frequency stability assessment and control. IEEE Trans. Power Syst. **34**(6), 4557–4568 (2019)

56. Wang, S., Wang, H., Perdikaris, P.: Learning the solution operator of parametric partial differential equations with physics-informed deeponets. arXiv preprint arXiv:2103.10974 (2021)

57. Wang, Y., Yang, Y., Yang, Z., Zhao, L., Wang, P., Xu, W.: Occlusion aware unsupervised learning of optical flow. In: Proceedings of the IEEE Conference on Computer Vision and Pattern Recognition, pp. 4884–4893 (2018)

58. Wedel, A., Cremers, D., Pock, T., Bischof, H.: Structure-and motion-adaptive regularization for high accuracy optic flow. In: 2009 IEEE 12th International Conference on Computer Vision, pp. 1663–1668. IEEE (2009)

59. Xu, J., Ranftl, R., Koltun, V.: Accurate optical flow via direct cost volume processing. In: Proceedings of the IEEE Conference on Computer Vision and Pattern Recognition, pp. 1289–1297 (2017)

60. Yan, W., Sharma, A., Tan, R.T.: Optical flow in dense foggy scenes using semi-supervised learning. In: Proceedings of the IEEE/CVF Conference on Computer Vision and Pattern Recognition, pp. 13259–13268 (2020)

61. Yang, G., Ramanan, D.: Volumetric correspondence networks for optical flow. Adv. Neural. Inf. Process. Syst. **32**, 794–805 (2019)

62. Yin, Y., et al.: Augmenting physical models with deep networks for complex dynamics forecasting. In: Ninth International Conference on Learning Representations ICLR 2021 (2021)

63. Zhao, S., Sheng, Y., Dong, Y., Chang, E.I., Xu, Y., et al.: Maskflownet: asymmetric feature matching with learnable occlusion mask. In: Proceedings of the IEEE/CVF Conference on Computer Vision and Pattern Recognition, pp. 6278–6287 (2020)

ViTAS: Vision Transformer Architecture Search

Xiu Su[1], Shan You[2,3]([✉]), Jiyang Xie[4], Mingkai Zheng[1], Fei Wang[5],
Chen Qian[2], Changshui Zhang[3], Xiaogang Wang[2,6], and Chang Xu[1]

[1] School of Computer Science, Faculty of Engineering, The University of Sydney,
Camperdown, Australia
xisu5992@uni.sydney.edu.au, c.xu@sydney.edu.au
[2] SenseTime Research, Beijing, China
{youshan,qianchen}@sensetime.com
[3] Department of Automation, THUAI, BNRist, Tsinghua University, Beijing, China
zcs@mail.tsinghua.edu.cn
[4] Beijing University of Posts and Telecommunications, Beijing, China
xiejiyang2013@bupt.edu.cn
[5] University of Science and Technology of China, Hefei, China
wangfei91@mail.ustc.edu.cn
[6] The Chinese University of Hong Kong, Hong Kong, China
xgwang@ee.cuhk.edu.hk

Abstract. Vision transformers (ViTs) inherited the success of NLP but
their structures have not been sufficiently investigated and optimized for
visual tasks. One of the simplest solutions is to directly search the optimal
one via the widely used neural architecture search (NAS) in CNNs. However, we empirically find this straightforward adaptation would encounter
catastrophic failures and be frustratingly unstable for the training of
superformer. In this paper, we argue that since ViTs mainly operate
on token embeddings with little inductive bias, imbalance of channels
for different architectures would worsen the weight-sharing assumption
and cause the training instability as a result. Therefore, we develop a
new cyclic weight-sharing mechanism for token embeddings of the ViTs,
which enables each channel could more evenly contribute to all candidate
architectures. Besides, we also propose identity shifting to alleviate the
many-to-one issue in superformer and leverage weak augmentation and
regularization techniques for more steady training empirically. Based on
these, our proposed method, ViTAS, has achieved significant superiority in both DeiT- and Twins-based ViTs. For example, with only 1.4G
FLOPs budget, our searched architecture achieves 3.3% higher accuracy than the baseline DeiT on ImageNet-1k dataset. With 3.0G FLOPs,
our results achieve 82.0% accuracy on ImageNet-1k, and 45.9% mAP on
COCO2017, which is 2.4% superior than other ViTs.

Supplementary Information The online version contains supplementary material
available at https://doi.org/10.1007/978-3-031-19803-8_9.

Keywords: Vision transformer (ViT) · nerual architecture search (NAS) · Cyclic weight sharing mechanism · Identity shifting · Weak augmentation

1   Introduction

Transformer, as a self-attention characterized neural network, has been widely leveraged for natural language processing (NLP) tasks [1,9,31,32]. Amazingly, recent breakthrough of vision transformers (ViTs) [11,40] further revealed the huge potential of transformers in computer vision (CV) tasks [37,46–48,51,61,63,64]. With no use of inductive biases, self-attention layers in the transformer introduce a global receptive field, which conveys refresh solutions to process vision data. Following ViTs, there have been quite a few works on vision transformers for a variety of tasks, such as image recognition [7,12,20,53,58,62], object detection [25,67], and semantic segmentation [25].

Despite the remarkable achievements of ViTs, the design of their architectures is still rarely investigated. Current ViTs simply split an image into a sequence of patches (*i.e.*, tokens) and stack transformer blocks as NLP tasks. Nevertheless, this vanilla protocol does not necessarily ensure the optimality for vision tasks. Stacking manner and intrinsic structure of the blocks need to be further analyzed and determined, such as patch size of input, head number in multihead self-attention (MHSA), output dimensions of parametric layers, operation type, and depth of the whole model. Therefore, we raise questions that *What makes a better vision transformer? How can we obtain it?* Inspired by the success of one-shot neural architecture search (NAS) in ConvNets (CNNs), our intuition is also to directly search for an optimal architecture for ViTs, which in turn gives us insight about designing more promising ViTs.

Unlike the sliding convolutions of CNNs, ViTs project the patches into a sequence of token embeddings, and the features are extracted sequentially. In this way, how to specify an appropriate configuration (dimension) for token embeddings of all layers play an important role for the architecture of ViTs [50]. To search [42] for the optimal token embedding dimension, recent work [4,21] simply borrow the ordinal weight sharing [14,59] in CNNs for the superformer (a.k.a. supernet in CNNs) to accommodate different token dimension. However, this ordinal mechanism would inevitably introduce imbalance among channels during training, causing the superformer cannot evaluate each token dimension well and induces sub-optimal architectures consequently. Though recent bilateral mechanism [36] was proposed to handle this issue, the training cost has to be doubled yet the imbalance of channels still exist to some extent.

In this paper, we propose a novel *cyclic* weight sharing mechanism for superformer to embody various token embedding dimensions of all layers. Concretely, we encourage balanced *training fairness* and *influence uniformity* for each channel in the superformer. With these two conditions, the cyclic rule could be learned as an index mapping to indicate each dimension of token embeddings (see Fig. 1), so that each could be more evenly evaluated. Besides, since the cyclic rule is a single-pass mapping, computation cost of training the superformer is similar to that of a ordinal [4,59] one.

Based on the customized cyclic manner, we propose a corresponding NAS method for ViTs dubbed vision transformer architecture search (ViTAS). However, we empirically observe that the training of superformer tends to be frustratingly instable. We argue that the space size of ViTs are way too huger (even 1.1×10^{54}), and propose to calibrate the space with an identity shifting technique. Besides, we find that strong augmentation and regularization are critic to further stabilize the superformer training. Extensive experimental results have shown the superiority of our ViTAS.

2   Related Work

Vision Transformer. ViT was first proposed by Dosovitskiy et al. [11] to extend the applications of transformers into computer vision fields by cascading manually designed multilayer perceptrons (MLPs) and MHSA modules. Touvron et al. [40] introduced a teacher-student strategy and a distillation token into the ViT, namely data-efficient image transformers (DeiT). Recently, other variants of ViT were proposed and all introduced inductive bias and prior knowledge to extract local information for better feature extraction. Tokens-to-Token (T2T) ViT [60] added a layer-wise T2T transformation and a deep-narrow backbone to overcome limitations of local structure modeling. Then, Han et al. [15]

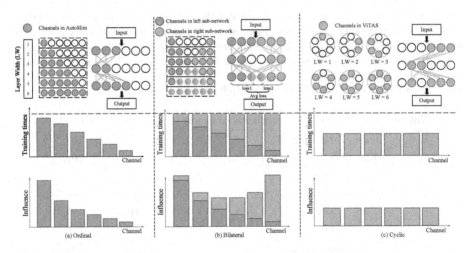

Fig. 1. Comparison between (a) ordinal [4,59], (b) bilateral [36] and (c) our cyclic forms with a toy example of six groups of channels. In (a), channels cannot be fairly trained in terms of training times and influence. Channels in (b) need double training cost compared to the others and also unevenly distributed influence. Then in (c), the proposed cyclic pattern overcomes the defects of (a) and (b) and achieves fairly training of channels w.r.t. training times and influence while maintaining half training cost than the bilateral form.

proposed to model both patch- and pixel-level representations by transformer-in-transformer (TNT). Swin Transformer [25] generated various patch scales by shifted windows for better representing highly changeable visual elements. Wu et al. [44] reintroduced convolutions into the ViT, namely convolutional vision transformer (CvT). Pyramid vision transformer (PVT) [43] trained on dense partitions of the image to achieve high output resolution and used a progressive shrinking pyramid to reduce computations of large feature maps. Another Twins ViT framework [5] was proposed, which introduced spatially separable self-attention (SSSA) to replace the less efficient global sub-sampled attention in PVT. All the aforementioned transformer structures were manually designed according to expert experience.

One-Shot NAS Method. Differentiable architecture search (DARTS) [19, 24,55,56] first formulated the NAS task in a differentiable manner based on the continuous relaxation. In contrast, single path one-shot (SPOS) framework [35,52,57] adopted an explicit path sampler to construct a simplified supernet, such as uniform sampler [14,37], greedy sampler [18,52,57] and Monte-Carlo tree sampler [34]. Some work also attempted to investigate the channel dimension by direct searching [35,36] or pruning from pretrained models [26,38]. As for ViTs, AutoFormer [4] first adopted the one-shot NAS framework for the ViT based architecture search. BossNAS [21] implemented the search with an self-supervised training scheme and leveraged a hybrid CNN-transformer search space for boosting the performance.

Table 1. Macro transformer space for the ViTAS of Twins-based architecture. "TBS" indicates that layer type is searched from parametric operation and identity operation for depth search. "Embedding" represents the patch embedding layer. "Max$_a$" and "Max$_m$" indicates the max dimension of attention layer ("Max$_a$" also used for patch embedding layer) and mlp layer, respectively. "Ratio" means the reduction ratio from the "Max Output Dim". A larger "Ratio" indicates a larger dimension.

Number	OP	Type	Patch size/#Heads	Max$_a$	Max$_m$	Ratio
1	False	Embeding	4	128	–	$\{i/10\}_{i=1}^{10}$
4	TBS	Local	$\{2,4,8,16\}$	480	512	$\{i/10\}_{i=1}^{10}$
		Global				
1	False	Embeding	2	256	–	$\{i/10\}_{i=1}^{10}$
4	TBS	Local	$\{2,4,8,16\}$	960	1024	$\{i/10\}_{i=1}^{10}$
		Global				
1	False	Embeding	2	512	–	$\{i/10\}_{i=1}^{10}$
12	TBS	Local	$\{2,4,8,16\}$	1920	2048	$\{i/10\}_{i=1}^{10}$
		Global				
1	False	Embeding	2	1024	–	$\{i/10\}_{i=1}^{10}$
6	TBS	Local	$\{2,4,8,16\}$	3840	4096	$\{i/10\}_{i=1}^{10}$
		Global				

3   Revisiting One-Shot NAS Towards Transformer Space

One-Shot NAS & Dimension Search. Towards the search of a decent architecture $\alpha \in \mathcal{A}$ from a huge transformer space $\mathcal{A}$ (*i.e.*, transformer space), a weight sharing strategy is commonly leveraged to avoid exhausted path training from scratch. For a superformer $\mathcal{N}$ with weights $\mathcal{W}$, each path α inherits its weights from $\mathcal{W}$. The one-shot NAS is thus formulated as a two-stage optimization problem, *i.e.*, superformer training and then architecture searching. Base on the above settings, many researchers leveraged dimension search algorithms, *e.g.*, AutoSlim [4,59] and BCNet [36], to perform the search of the dimensions for fine grained architectures. We define $\mathcal{C}$ as the set of candidate dimensions for a certain operation, where $c \in \mathcal{C}$ indicates the dimensions within α. Thus, the optimization function is as

$$W_{\mathcal{A},\mathcal{C}}^* = \underset{W_{\mathcal{A},\mathcal{C}}}{\operatorname{argmin}}\, loss_{\text{train}}\left(\mathcal{N}(\mathcal{A},\mathcal{C},W_{\mathcal{A},\mathcal{C}})\right), \tag{1}$$

$$\alpha^*, c^* = \underset{(\alpha,c)\in(\mathcal{A},\mathcal{C})}{\operatorname{argmax}}\, Acc_{\text{val}}\left(\mathcal{N}(\alpha,c,W_{\alpha,c}^*)\right), \tag{2}$$

$$\text{s.t. FLOPs}(\mathcal{N}(\alpha,c,W_{\alpha,c}^*)) \le f,$$

where $loss_{\text{train}}$ is training loss, Acc_{val} is validation accuracy, $W_{\mathcal{A},\mathcal{C}}^*$ is a set of trained weights, α^* is the searched optimal architecture, and f is resource budget. Following the one-shot framework, the superformer is trained by uniformly sampling different (α, c) from $(\mathcal{A}, \mathcal{C})$, and then we search the optimal architecture (α^*, c^*) according to W^*. After these, the selected α^* will be retrained for evaluation.

Table 2. Macro transformer space for the ViTAS of DeiT-based architecture. "TBS" indicates that layer type is searched from vanilla ViT block or identity operation for depth search. "Ratio" means the reduction ratio from the "Max Dim". A larger "Ratio" means a larger dimension.

Number	OP	Type	Patch size/#Heads	Max Dim	Ratio
1	False	Linear	$\{14,16,32\}$	384	$\{i/10\}_{i=1}^{10}$
16	TBS	MHSA	$\{3,6,12,16\}$	1440	$\{i/10\}_{i=1}^{10}$
		MLP	–	1440	$\{i/10\}_{i=1}^{10}$

Towards Transformer Space. To explore the possibility of the optimal ViT architecture in the arch-level, we incorporate all the essential elements in our transformer space, including *head number, patch size, operation type, output dimension of each layer,* and *depth of the architectures,* as shown in Table 1[1]

---

[1] In the superformer, Max_a indicates the output of the first fully connected (FC) layer, which should be able to be divided by all "ratios" and "Heads", *i.e.*, $\text{Max}_a | (Ratio \times Heads), \forall Ratio, Heads$. Therefore, we select least common multiple of "ratios" and "Heads" for Max_a.

and Table 2^2. More details of transformer space is elaborated in the Section A.2 of Appendix. With the Twins-small based transformer space in Table 1 as an example, the size of transformer space amounts to 1.1×10^{54} and the FLOPs (parameters) ranges from 0.02G (0.16M) to 11.2G (86.1M). Similarly in Table 2, with the DeiT-small transformer space, the size of space amounts to 5.4×10^{34} and the FLOPs (parameters) ranges from 0.1G (0.5M) to 20.0G (97.5M).

4   Cyclic Channels for Token Embeddings

Previous work [4,59] proposed the ordinal weight sharing paradigm, which is widely leveraged in many CNN and Transformer NAS papers [4,41,54]. Concretely, as illustrated in Fig. 1(a), to search for a dimension i at a layer with maximum of l channels, the ordinal pattern assigns the left i channels in the superformer to indicate the corresponding architecture as

$$\boldsymbol{a}_A(i) = [1:i], \ i \le l, \tag{3}$$

where $\boldsymbol{a}_A(i)$ means the selected i channels from the left (smaller-index) side.

However, this channel configuration imposes a strong constraint on the channels and leads to imbalanced training for each channel in the superformer. As in Fig. 1(a), with the ordinal pattern, channels that are close to the left side are used in both large and small dimension. Since different dimensions are uniformly sampled during searching, the training times $\mathcal{C}_A(i)$ of the i-th channel used in all dimensions with the ordinal pattern can be represented as

$$\mathcal{C}_A(i) = l - i + 1. \tag{4}$$

Therefore, channels closer to the left side will gain more times of training, which induces evaluation bias among different channels and leads to sub-optimal searching results.

To remove the evaluation bias among channels of the superformer, we introduce a condition for constructing a mapping for channels:

Theorem 1 (training fairness). *Each channel should obtain same training times for fairer training of superformer.*

With the aims of **Theorem** 1 and keep the same computation cost as AutoSlim [4,59] (*i.e.*, ordinal pattern), we introduce indicator matrix β with $\beta_{i,j} \in \{0,1\}$ (one means using the channel) to represent whether channel i being used in dimension j. Two conditions need to be satisfied: (1) for each row β_i, which is the training times of the channel i in each dimension, the sum of it should be equal with that of all the other channels, and (2) for each column β_j, which demonstrates the training times of channels in dimension j, the sum of it

---

[2] In the superformer, "Max Dim" indicates the output dimensions of both attention and MLP blocks.

should be the dimension of itself. Finally, the constraints of β can be represented as follows

$$\sum_j \beta_{i,j} = (1+l)/2, \ \forall i, \tag{5}$$

$$\sum_i \beta_{i,j} = j, \ \forall j. \tag{6}$$

Infinite solutions can be solved under aforementioned constraints only. Here, the bilateral pattern in BCNet [36] is a special case of the aforementioned settings with double training times as $l+1$.

Although forcing the channels to be trained for same training times can boost the fairness, constructing a path only constrained by condition 1 cannot emerge the actual performance of the path due to the difference of training saturation between one-shot-based sampling and training from scratch [27].

This means that in order to more precisely rank various paths, we need to mimic the process of the latter and balance the influence of each channels.

Theorem 2 (influence uniformity). *Each channel needs to have the same sum of influence among all its related dimensions for training.*

Concretely, we should carefully design the weight sharing mechanism based on **Theorem 2**. Here, we define $\psi_{i,j}$ to indicate the influence of channel i in dimension j. For each channel pair, we have

$$\begin{cases} \psi_{i_1,j} = \psi_{i_2,j}, \ \forall i_1, i_2 \\ \psi_{i,j_1} \geq \psi_{i,j_2}, \ \forall j_1 \leq j_2 \end{cases} . \tag{7}$$

Considering that transformer architectures are mainly consist of full-connected (FC) layers. Specifically, for an FC layer with j input channels $x_i, i = 1, \cdots, j$ and a certain output channel $y = \sum_{i=1}^{j} y_i, y_i = w_i x_i$ with parameters $w_i, i = 1, \cdots, j$, we can obtain the gradient of w_i as

$$\nabla w_i = \frac{\partial loss_{\text{train}}}{\partial y} \cdot \frac{\partial y}{\partial y_i} \cdot \frac{\partial y_i}{\partial x_i}. \tag{8}$$

Meanwhile, for a dimension sampled from the FC layer with one random input channel x_i, the gradient of w_i here can be represented as

$$(\nabla w_i)' = \frac{\partial loss_{\text{train}}}{\partial y'} \cdot \frac{\partial y'}{\partial y_i} \cdot \frac{\partial y_i}{\partial x_i}, \tag{9}$$

where $y' = y_i$. Therefore, in the former case, the influence $\psi_{i,j}$ of the i-th channel can be defined as the contribution of the channel to its gradient as

$$\psi_{i,j} = \frac{(\nabla w_i)'}{\nabla w_i} = \frac{\frac{\partial y'}{\partial y_i}}{\frac{\partial y}{\partial y_i}}, \tag{10}$$

assuming $\frac{\partial loss_{\text{train}}}{\partial y} = \frac{\partial loss_{\text{train}}}{\partial y'}$. We can also assume $y_i \approx y_{i'}, i \neq i'$, as the distributions of w_i or x_i can be similar to each i, respectively, when randomly sampling the dimensions in each batch. In this case, we can obtain $y \approx j \times y_i$, and $\psi_{i,j} = \frac{1}{j}$ for Eqs. (7) and (10).

Note that channel i may be shared w.r.t.different dimensions. To keep all the channels being treated equally, any two channels i_1 and i_2 should have the same influence among all the dimensions, *i.e.*,

$$\sum_j \beta_{i_1,j}\psi_{i_1,j} = \sum_j \beta_{i_2,j}\psi_{i_2,j}, \ \forall i_1, i_2. \tag{11}$$

Optimization of Cyclic Mapping. Combining Eq. (5)–Eq. (11), we can obtain the specialized weight sharing paradigm for the cyclic superformer. In practice, since $\frac{1+l}{2}$ may not be an integer, Eq. (5) may not be completely satisfied. Thus, for any two channels i_1 and i_2, we can relax the constraint in Eq. (5) by

$$\left| \sum_j \beta_{i_1,j} - \sum_j \beta_{i_2,j} \right| \le 1, \ \forall i_1, i_2. \tag{12}$$

To facilitate the search of the optimal weight sharing paradigm, we should make sure all the channels being fairly trained with almost the same influence among all the dimensions. Therefore, we can update Eq. (11) to an objective as

$$\min_\beta \sum_{i_1,i_2} \left(\beta_{i_1,j}\psi_{i_1,j} - \beta_{i_2,j}\psi_{i_2,j}\right)^2, \tag{13}$$

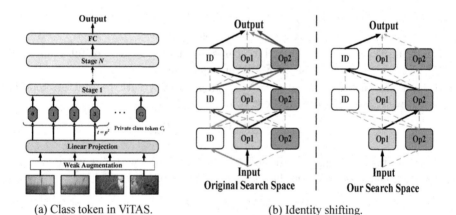

(a) Class token in ViTAS.   (b) Identity shifting.

Fig. 2. Private class token and identity shifting search space in ViTAS. (a) For transformer architectures with class token settings, with different patch sizes p, we assign one independent class tokens for each and obtain $p \times p$ patches and a private class token under one patch size setting. (b) Comparison between currently mainstream ID search strategy (left) and ours ID oriented method (right). From left, a group of paths in the superformer, *i.e.*, red, **blue** and **black** paths, corresponds to one same architecture, which may performs differently. This can hinder the search for decent architectures. While for our method, each architecture corresponds to only one path in the superformer, which reduces the redundancy in it and boosts the search performance. (Color figure online)

The overall problem is thus a QCQP (quadratically constrained quadratic program), which can be efficiently solved by many off-the-shelf solvers [10,29]. We have presented detailed experimental settings and simulations of β and $\psi_{i,j}$ in Section A.15 of Appendix.

5   Further Stabilizing the Training of Superformer

Training the superformer is for fair estimation of each architecture's performance, which is essential for the next optimal architecture searching stage. Here, we argue that superformer requires an efficient and simple transformer space and training recipe for boosting the search. For the transformer space of ViTAS, we propose the identity shifting strategy to solve the many-to-one issue as in Fig. 2b. Besides, for architectures with class tokens, $i.e.$DeiT [40], we introduce private class token w.r.t. each patch size to cater for different paths. For the training recipe of ViTAS, we underline that weak augmentation & regularization rather than complex and tricky ones [5,40] can prevent the search from unsteady.

Identity Shifting. Given a pre-defined NAS transformer space, as in Fig. 2b, identity (ID) operation serves as the significant part and has a large effect on the searched results for three reasons: 1) it defines the depth of the searched architecture, 2) compared to other operations, the non-parametric ID is much more different with other parametric operations, which will involve in a higher variance on paths, and 3) stacking manner and intrinsic structure of a transformer architecture within each stage lead to complicatedly many-to-one correspondence between architectures in the superformer and transformer space. These introduce a huge ambiguous for NAS. Here, we propose to search the operations with identity shifting strategy, as depicted in the right side of Fig. 2b. In each stage, we remove the ambiguous between transformer space and superformer by sampling the number of ID and arrange them at the deeper layers of the stage in order to remove the redundancy in superformer. Typically, with three operations (including ID) and twelve searched layers, the transformer space of operations can be reduced from 3^{12} to $2^{13} - 1$.

Private Class Token. Notably, pure vision transformer architectures, $e.g.$, DeiT [40], usually introduce a trainable vector named class token for the output classification. The class token is appended to the patch tokens before the first layer and then go through the transformer blocks for the prediction task. These class tokens often take a small size, which changes with the pre-defined patch size P ($i.e.$, $\frac{H \times W}{P \times P}$), and performs significant in performance. Towards these attributes, we propose to privatize the class token for each P. As shown in Fig. 2a, for different patch sizes, we assign private ones for each. In this way, the affect between class tokens can be avoided with only negligible computation cost or memory cost introduced. Ablations of the private class token are presented in Section A.6 of Appendix.

Weak Augmentation & Regularization. We explore the superformer training strategy of the ViTAS, including data augmentation and regularization. We conducted the evaluations with Twins-based architecture and 1.4G FLOPs budget on ImageNet-1k dataset. Compared with one single ViT, the superformer

Table 3. Searched Twins-based ViT architectures w.r.t. different FLOPs and GPU throughput on ImageNet-1k. We abbreviate the name of tiny, short, base, and large for T, S, B, and L, respectively. ⋆ indicates that the re-implementation results of important baseline methods with our recipe. Our results are highlighted in bold.

Method	FLOPs (G)	Throughput (image/s)	Params (M)	Top-1 (%)	Top-5 (%)
ResNet-18 [17]	1.8	4458.4	12	69.8	89.1
DeiT-T⋆ [40]	1.3	2728.5	5	72.3	91.4
Twins-T⋆ [5]	1.4	1580.7	11.5	77.8	94.1
AutoFormer-T⋆ [4]	1.3	3055.4	5.7	74.7	91.9
ViTAS-Twins-T	1.4	1686.3	13.8	**79.4**	**94.8**
DeiT-S⋆ [40]	4.6	437.0	22.1	79.9	95.0
PVT-S [43]	3.8	820	24.5	79.8	–
Twins-SVT-S⋆ [5]	2.9	1059	24	81.6	95.9
AutoFormer-S⋆ [4]	5.1	1231.7	22.9	79.8	95.0
BossNet-T0 [21]	5.7	–	–	81.6	–
Twins-PCPVT-S⋆ [5]	3.8	815	24.1	81.2	95.6
Swin-T⋆ [25]	4.5	766	29	81.2	95.5
ViTAS-Twins-S	3.0	958.6	30.5	**82.0**	**95.7**
T2T-ViT$_t$-19 [60]	8.9	–	39.2	81.4	–
BoTNet-S1-59 [33]	7.3	–	33.5	81.7	–
BossNet-T1 [21]	7.9	–	–	82.2	–
Twins-PCPVT-B [5]	6.7	525	43.8	82.7	–
Swin-S⋆ [25]	8.7	444	50	83.0	96.2
Twins-SVT-B⋆ [5]	8.6	469	56	83.2	96.3
ViTAS-Twins-B	8.8	362.7	66.0	**83.5**	**96.5**
DeiT-B⋆ [40]	17.6	292	86.6	81.8	95.7
TNT-B [15]	14.1	–	66	82.8	–
CrossViT-B [2]	21.2	–	104.7	82.2	–
ViTAS-Twins-L	16.1	260.7	124.8	**84.0**	**96.9**

training is much more difficult to converge, which needs a simply yet effective training strategy.

From Table 4, as group 0, the superformer performs badly with the default training strategy [5,40]. To facility the search, we first removed the stochastic depth, since our identity search performs the similar effect in the superformer training. Then, we gradually dropped other data augmentation and/or regularization and find that a weak augmentation can largely promote retraining accuracy with searching a better architecture. Table 5 presents the ViTAS training recipe for our experiments. We provide a detailed analysis of weak augmentation in Section A.14 of Appendix.

Table 4. Ablation studies of training recipe of superformer of the ViTAS. "✓"/"✗" indicates that we used/not used the corresponding method. We implemented the search on the ImageNet-1k with 1.4G budget of Twins. We report the top-1 accuracy of the best architectures in both ViTAS (*i.e.*, searching) and retraining. "RD": Rand-Augment. "MP": Mixup. "CM": CutMix. "CJ": Color Jitter. "Era": Erasing. "SD": Stoch Depth. "RA": Repeated Augmentation. "WD": Weight Decay. Best results are in bold.

	Data augmentation				Regularization				ViTAS	Retraining
#	RD	MP	CM	CJ	Era	SD	RA	WD	Acc(%)	Acc(%)
0	✓	✓	✓	✓	✓	✓	✓	✓	59.4%	77.9%
1	✓	✓	✓	✓	✓	✗	✓	✓	61.2%	78.0%
2	✓	✓	✓	✓	✓	✗	✗	✓	61.5%	78.2%
3	✓	✗	✗	✓	✓	✗	✗	✓	62.3%	78.6%
4	✗	✗	✗	✓	✓	✗	✗	✓	64.9%	78.8%
7	✗	✗	✗	✗	✓	✗	✗	✓	65.6%	78.9%
8	✗	✗	✗	✗	✗	✗	✗	✓	66.1%	79.1%
9	✗	✗	✗	✗	✗	✗	✗	✗	**67.7%**	**79.4%**

Table 5. Training recipe of the ViTAS with parameter settings. BS: batch size, LR: learning rate, WD: weight decay. We will conduct the ViTAS according to the following recipe in experiments.

Epochs	BS	Optimizer	LR	LR decay	Warmup
300	1024	AdamW	0.001	cosine	5

6 Experimental Results

We perform the ViTAS on the challenging ImageNet-1k dataset [8] for image classification, and COCO2017 [13] and ADE20k [66] for object detection, instance segmentation, and semantic segmentation. To promote the search, we randomly sample 50K images from the training set as the local validation set and the rest images are leveraged for training. All experiments are implemented with PyTorch [30] and trained on V100 GPUs. Please find detailed experimental settings in Section A.1 and A.3 of Appendix.

6.1 Efficient Search of ViTAS on ImageNet-1k

In Table 3, we compare our results with recent precedent ViT architectures. To evaluate our methods with other existing algorithms, we based on the Twins transformer space[3] and present the search results with both FLOPs and GPU

---

[3] We constructed the ViTAS-Twins-T transformer space from Twins-S similar to Table 1, and the Twins-T was uniformly scaled from Twins-S.

Table 6. Searched ViT architectures that do not involve inductive bias w.r.t. different FLOPs and GPU throughput on ImageNet-1k. ⋆ indicates that the re-implementation results of important baseline methods with our recipe. Our results are in bold.

Method	FLOPs (G)	Throughput (image/s)	Params (M)	Top-1 (%)	Top-5 (%)
ResNet-18 [17]	1.8	4458.4	12	69.8	89.1
DeiT-T⋆ [40]	1.3	2728.5	5	72.3	91.4
AutoFormer-T⋆ [4]	1.3	2955.4	5.7	74.7	91.9
ViTAS-DeiT-A	1.4	2831.1	6.6	**75.6**	**92.5**
ResNet-50 [17]	4.1	1226.1	25	76.2	91.4
DeiT-S⋆ [40]	4.6	940.4	22	79.9	95.0
AutoFormer-S⋆ [4]	5.1	1231.7	22.9	79.8	95.0
ViTAS-DeiT-B	4.9	1189.4	2.3	**80.2**	**95.1**

throughput. With different FLOPs budgets, The search ones (ViTAS-Twins-T/S/B/L) can outperform the referred transformers. For example, ViTAS-Twins-T can improve Top-1 accuracy by 1.6%, compared with Twins-T. For larger architectures, the search ones can moderately surpass all the corresponding referred ones as well, respectively.

In addition, we also searched the optimal architectures based on pure ViT and DeiT space, shown in Table 6. With only 1.4G FLOPs and similar GPU throughput, our searched ViTAS-DeiT-A model achieves 75.6% on Top-1 accuracy and is 3.4% superior than DeiT-T, which indicates the effectiveness of our proposed ViTAS method. Furthermore, with 4.9G FLOPs budget, our ViTAS-DeiT-B model also achieves superior performance of 80.2% on Top-1 accuracy with 0.3% surpassing the DeiT-S.

6.2   Transferability of ViTAS with Semantic Segmentation on ADE20K

In addition to search the optimal ViT architectures on the ImageNet-1k, we evaluated the generalization ability of the ViTAS by transferring the searched architectures to other tasks. With the same recipe as Twins [5], we fintuned on ADE20k [66] by using our ImageNet-pretrained models as backbones for semantic segmentation, shown in Table 8. Under different FLOPs budgets, our models can obtain significant performance improvement as 2% ∼ 4% on mIoU, compared with corresponding referred methods. For example, with semantic FPN [5] method as baseline, ViTAS-Twins-B surpasses the second best one, Twins-SVT-B, by more than 4% on mIoU.

6.3   Transferability to Object Detection and Instance Segmentation

With the same recipe as Twins [5], we undertook both object detection and instance segmentation on COCO2017 [23] by using our ImageNet-pretrained models as backbones, respectively. In Table 7, with mask R-CNN and RetinaNet

Table 7. Object detection and instance segmentation performance with searched backbones on the COCO2017 dataset with Mask R-CNN framework and RatinaNet framework. We followed the same training and evaluation setting as [5]. "FLOPs" and "Param" are in giga and million, respectively. ⋆ indicates the re-implementation results of important baseline methods with our recipe. Our results are highlighted in bold.

Backbone	Mask R-CNN 1× [16]								RetinaNet 1× [22]							
	FLOPs	Param	AP^b	AP^b_{50}	AP^b_{75}	AP^m	AP^m_{50}	AP^m_{75}	FLOPs	Param	AP^b	AP^b_{50}	AP^b_{75}	AP_S	AP_M	AP_L
ResNet50 [17]	174	44.2	38.0	58.6	41.4	34.4	55.1	35.7	111	37.7	36.3	55.3	38.6	19.3	40.0	48.8
PVT-Small [43]	178	44.1	40.4	62.9	43.8	37.8	60.1	40.3	118	34.2	40.4	61.3	43.0	25.0	42.9	55.7
Twins-PCPVT-S [5]	178	44.3	42.9	65.8	47.1	40.0	62.7	42.9	118	34.4	43.0	64.1	46.0	27.5	46.3	57.3
Swin-T [25]	177	47.8	42.2	64.6	46.2	39.1	61.6	42.0	118	38.5	41.5	62.1	44.2	25.1	44.9	55.5
Twins-SVT-S⋆ [5]	164	44.0	43.5	66.0	47.8	40.1	62.9	43.1	104	34.3	42.2	63.3	44.9	26.4	45.6	57.0
ViTAS-Twins-S	168	44.2	**45.9**	**67.8**	**50.3**	**41.5**	**64.7**	**45.0**	108	41.3	**44.4**	**65.3**	**47.6**	**27.5**	**48.3**	**60.0**
ResNet101 [17]	210	63.2	40.4	61.1	44.2	36.4	57.7	38.8	149	56.7	38.5	57.8	41.2	21.4	42.6	51.1
ResNeXt101 [49]	212	62.8	41.9	62.5	45.9	37.5	59.4	40.2	151	56.4	39.9	59.6	42.7	22.3	44.2	52.5
PVT-Medium [5]	211	63.9	42.0	64.4	45.6	39.0	61.6	42.1	151	53.9	41.9	63.1	44.3	25.0	44.9	57.6
Twins-PCPVT-B [5]	211	64.0	44.6	66.7	48.9	40.9	63.8	44.2	151	54.1	44.3	65.6	47.3	27.9	47.9	59.6
Swin-S [25]	222	69.1	44.8	66.6	48.9	40.9	63.4	44.2	162	59.8	44.5	65.7	47.5	27.4	48.0	59.9
Twins-SVT-B⋆ [5]	224	76.3	45.5	67.4	50.0	41.4	64.5	44.5	163	67.0	44.4	65.6	47.4	28.5	47.9	59.5
ViTAS-Twins-B	227	85.4	**47.6**	**69.2**	**52.2**	**42.9**	**66.3**	**46.5**	167	76.2	**46.0**	**66.7**	**49.6**	**29.1**	**50.2**	**62.0**
Twins-SVT-L⋆ [5]	292	119.7	45.9	67.9	49.9	41.6	65.0	45.0	232	110.9	45.2	66.6	48.4	29.0	48.6	60.9
ViTAS-Twins-L	301	144.1	**48.2**	**69.9**	**52.9**	**43.3**	**66.9**	**46.7**	246	135.5	**47.0**	**67.8**	**50.3**	**29.6**	**50.9**	**62.4**

as baseline, we achieve state-of-the-art performance with remarkably improvement on each AP metrics. The aforementioned experimental results in both of the tasks can demonstrate the effectiveness of ViTAS.

6.4 Ablation Studies

Effect of ViTAS as a Superformer. To validate the effectiveness of our proposed ViTAS, as in Table 9, we implemented the search with 1.4G FLOPs budget and Twins transformer space on ImageNet-1k dataset. Our baseline superformers are AutoFormer [4,59] and BCNet [36] that adopt ordinal or bilateral weight sharing mechanism, respectively, to evaluate a sampled architecture. With all settings in our paper, our cyclic pattern (79.4%) can enjoy a gain of 0.9% or 1.3% on Top-1 accuracy compare to bilateral (78.5%) or ordinal (78.1%) pattern, respectively. In addition, when only searching with the cyclic weight pattern and without additional strategies, our method (77.9%) can still attain 0.3% or 0.7% performance gain compare to baseline methods of bilateral (77.6%) and

Table 8. Performance comparison with searched backbones on ADE20K validation dataset. Architectures were implemented with the same training recipe as [5]. All backbones were pretrained on ImageNet-1k, except for SETR, which was pretrained on ImageNet-21k dataset. ⋆ indicates the re-implementation results of important baseline methods with our recipe. Our results are highlighted in bold.

Backbone	Semantic FPN 80k [5]			Upernet 160k [25]		
	FLOPs (G)	Param (M)	mIoU (%)	FLOPs (G)	Param (M)	mIoU (%)
ResNet50 [17]	45	28.5	36.7	–	–	–
Twins-PCPVT-S [5]	40	28.4	44.3	234	54.6	46.2
Swin-T [25]	46	31.9	41.5	237	59.9	44.5
Twins-SVT-S⋆ [5]	37	28.3	43.6	228	54.4	45.9
ViTAS-Twins-S	38	35.1	**46.6**	229	61.7	**47.9**
ResNet101 [17]	66	47.5	38.8	–	–	–
Twins-PCPVT-B [5]	55	48.1	44.9	250	74.3	47.1
Swin-S [25]	70	53.2	45.2	261	81.3	47.6
Twin-SVT-B⋆ [5]	67	60.4	45.5	261	88.5	47.7
ViTAS-Twins-B	67	69.6	**49.5**	261	97.7	**50.2**
ResNetXt101 [49]	-	86.4	40.2	–	–	–
PVT-Large [5]	71	65.1	42.1	–	–	–
Twins-PCPVT-L [5]	71	65.3	46.4	269	91.5	48.6
Swin-B [25]	107	91.2	46.0	299	121	48.1
Twins-SVT-L⋆ [5]	102	103.7	46.9	297	133	48.8
ViTAS-Twins-L	108	128.2	**50.4**	303	158.7	**51.3**
Backnone	PUP (SETR [65])			MLA (SETR [65])		
T-Large (SETR) [65]	–	310	50.1	–	308	48.6

Table 9. Ablation studies of the proposed ViTAS. We implemented the search on the ImageNet-1k set with 1.4G FLOPs budget. Weak_aug (WA), private token (PT), and Identity shifting (IF) in Twins space on ImageNet.

	None	PT	WA	IF	PT+WA	PT+IF	WA+IF	PT+WA+IF
Ordinal [4,59]	77.2	77.3	77.5	77.4	77.8	77.6	77.9	78.1
Bilateral [36]	77.6	77.7	78.0	77.8	78.1	77.9	78.2	78.5
Cyclic	77.9	78.2	78.7	78.6	78.8	78.4	79.0	79.4

ordinal (77.2%) weight sharing mechanism. We also conduct the ablations of ViTAS w.r.t. DeiT seach space in section A.7 of Appendix.

Comparison of AutoFormer [4,59], BCNet [36], and ViTAS w.r.t weight sharing paradigm of superformer training. AutoFormer, BCNet, and ViTAS adopt the ordinal, bilaterally, and cyclic weight sharing paradigm, respectively. As in Fig. 3a, we depict the average of training loss in each epoch w.r.t. three weight sharing mechanisms. In general, two obvious phenomena can be concluded as follows:

- In the first few epochs (*e.g.*, ≤ 20), the ordinal superformer has the fastest convergence, then is the bilateral pattern, the last is our cyclic one.
- After a few epochs (*e.g.*, ≥ 100), the superformer with the cyclic pattern can be best trained with the lowest loss value, while the bilateral pattern has the second convergence speed, and ordinal pattern performs the worst for training superformer.

It is because the ordinal pattern has the largest bias in training channels. As shown in Fig. 3a, a part of the channels converges the fastest in the first few epochs. The bilateral pattern performs similar due to no influence uniformity considered. However, after training more epochs, many channels do not obtain well treated in the superformer of the ordinal and bilateral patterns, thus they present larger average loss values than the cyclic one.

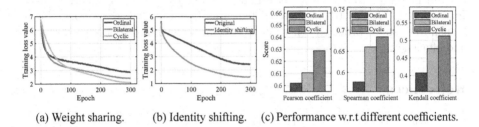

(a) Weight sharing.   (b) Identity shifting.   (c) Performance w.r.t different coefficients.

Fig. 3. Comparisons of superformer training loss values and performance comparison of coefficients. (a) Superformer training loss w.r.t. ordinal, bilateral, and cyclic weight sharing mechanisms on ImageNet-1k dataset. (b) Superformer training loss w.r.t. identity shifting and original setting on ImageNet-100. (c) Performance comparison of coefficients w.r.t. ordinal, bilateral, and cyclic mechanisms with 2000 sampled paths.

Effect of Identity Shifting Strategy. As in Fig. 3b, we present the training losses of the ViTAS using identity shifting strategy and original setting, respectively, with ImageNet-100 dataset [8,39]. With the redundancy paths removed, our method can converge to a much smaller loss than the original one, which indicates the proposed identity shifting strategy can promote the training of the superformer. Concretely, the training loss of original and identity shifting decrease to 2.4 and 1.5 at the final, respectively, which indicates that our method promote to better convergence for superformer. Moreover, the results trained from scratch of the searched architectures with identity shifting or original setting is 90.4% and 88.3%, respectively.

Performance comparison of AutoFormer [4,59], BCNet [36], and ViTAS w.r.t. Weight Sharing Paradigm with 2,000 Sampled Paths. To perform the search, we uniformly assign 8 budget range from 1G to 8G FLOPs, with 250 paths in each weight sharing mechanism. Generally, we assume the performance of architectures are positively correlated with FLOPs. Thus, we can obtain the scores of the three patterns w.r.t. Pearson, Spearman, and Kendall coefficients on different FLOPs groups. As shown in Fig. 3c, our method achieves remarkable improvements comparing to the others, which indicates that our superformer can provide more precisely ranking for architectures. Details of coefficients are elaborated in Section A.5 of Appendix.

7   Conclusion

In this paper, we presented a vision transformer architecture search (*i.e.*, ViTAS) framework with the formulated cyclic weight sharing paradigm for the fair ranking of dimensions and also search efficiency. Besides, we propose the identity shifting strategy to arrange the ID operation at the deeper layers for removing the redundant paths in the superformer. Moreover, we also investigated the training strategy of the superformer and proposed the weak augmentation strategy during search to boost the performance of ViTAS. Extensive experiments on ImageNet-1k, COCO2017, and ADE20k datasets w.r.t. Twins- and DeiT-based transformer space prove the effectiveness of our ViTAS in terms of performance and efficiency.

References

1. Brown, T.B., et al.: Language models are few-shot learners. arXiv preprint arXiv:2005.14165 (2020)
2. Chen, C.F., Fan, Q., Panda, R.: Crossvit: cross-attention multi-scale vision transformer for image classification. arXiv preprint arXiv:2103.14899 (2021)
3. Chen, K., et al.: Mmdetection: ppen mmlab detection toolbox and benchmark. arXiv preprint arXiv:1906.07155 (2019)
4. Chen, M., Peng, H., Fu, J., Ling, H.: AutoFormer: searching transformers for visual recognition. In: Proceedings of the IEEE/CVF International Conference on Computer Vision (ICCV), pp. 12270–12280, October 2021
5. Chu, X., et al.: Twins: revisiting the design of spatial attention in vision transformers. arXiv preprint arXiv:2104.13840 (2021)
6. Deb, K., Pratap, A., Agarwal, S., Meyarivan, T.: A fast and elitist multiobjective genetic algorithm: Nsga-ii. IEEE Trans. Evol. Comput. **6**(2), 182–197 (2002)
7. Deng, C., Yang, E., Liu, T., Tao, D.: Two-stream deep hashing with class-specific centers for supervised image search. IEEE Trans. Neural Networks Learn. Syst. **31**(6), 2189–2201 (2019)
8. Deng, J., Dong, W., Socher, R., Li, L.J., Li, K., Fei-Fei, L.: Imagenet: a large-scale hierarchical image database. In: 2009 IEEE Conference on Computer Vision and Pattern Recognition, pp. 248–255. IEEE (2009)
9. Devlin, J., Chang, M.W., Lee, K., Toutanova, K.: Bert: pre-training of deep bidirectional transformers for language understanding. arXiv preprint arXiv:1810.04805 (2018)
10. Diamond, S., Boyd, S.: Cvxpy: a python-embedded modeling language for convex optimization. J. Mach. Learn. Res. **17**(1), 2909–2913 (2016)
11. Dosovitskiy, A., et al.: An image is worth 16×16 words: transformers for image recognition at scale. arXiv preprint arXiv:2010.11929 (2020)

12. Du, R., Xie, J., Ma, Z., Chang, D., Song, Y.Z., Guo, J.: Progressive learning of category-consistent multi-granularity features for fine-grained visual classification (2021)
13. Everingham, M., Van Gool, L., Williams, C.K.I., Winn, J., Zisserman, A.: The pascal visual object classes (voc) challenge. Int. J. Comput. Vision **88**(2), 303–338 (2010)
14. Guo, Z., Zhang, X., Mu, H., Heng, W., Liu, Z., Wei, Y., Sun, J.: Single path one-shot neural architecture search with uniform sampling. In: Vedaldi, A., Bischof, H., Brox, T., Frahm, J.-M. (eds.) ECCV 2020. LNCS, vol. 12361, pp. 544–560. Springer, Cham (2020). https://doi.org/10.1007/978-3-030-58517-4_32
15. Han, K., Xiao, A., Wu, E., Guo, J., Xu, C., Wang, Y.: Transformer in transformer. arXiv preprint arXiv:2103.00112 (2021)
16. He, K., Gkioxari, G., Dollár, P., Girshick, R.: Mask r-cnn. In: Proceedings of the IEEE International Conference on Computer Vision, pp. 2961–2969 (2017)
17. He, K., Zhang, X., Ren, S., Sun, J.: Deep residual learning for image recognition. In: Proceedings of the IEEE Conference on Computer Vision and Pattern Recognition, pp. 770–778 (2016)
18. Huang, T., et al.: Greedynasv2: Greedier search with a greedy path filter. arXiv preprint arXiv:2111.12609 (2021)
19. Huang, T., et al.: Explicitly learning topology for differentiable neural architecture search. arXiv preprint arXiv:2011.09300 (2020)
20. Huang, T., et al.: Dyrep: bootstrapping training with dynamic re-parameterization. In: Proceedings of the IEEE/CVF Conference on Computer Vision and Pattern Recognition, pp. 588–597 (2022)
21. Li, C., et al.: BossNAS: exploring hybrid CNN-transformers with block-wisely self-supervised neural architecture search (2021)
22. Lin, T.Y., Goyal, P., Girshick, R., He, K., Dollár, P.: Focal loss for dense object detection. In: Proceedings of the IEEE International Conference on Computer Vision, pp. 2980–2988 (2017)
23. Lin, T.-Y., Maire, M., Belongie, S., Hays, J., Perona, P., Ramanan, D., Dollár, P., Zitnick, C.L.: Microsoft COCO: common objects in context. In: Fleet, D., Pajdla, T., Schiele, B., Tuytelaars, T. (eds.) ECCV 2014. LNCS, vol. 8693, pp. 740–755. Springer, Cham (2014). https://doi.org/10.1007/978-3-319-10602-1_48
24. Liu, H., Simonyan, K., Yang, Y.: DARTS: differentiable architecture search. In: 7th International Conference on Learning Representations, ICLR 2019, New Orleans, LA, USA, May 6–9 (2019)
25. Liu, Z., et al.: Swin transformer: Hierarchical vision transformer using shifted windows. arXiv preprint arXiv:2103.14030 (2021)
26. Liu, Z., Li, J., Shen, Z., Huang, G., Yan, S., Zhang, C.: Learning efficient convolutional networks through network slimming. In: Proceedings of the IEEE International Conference on Computer Vision, pp. 2736–2744 (2017)
27. Liu, Z., Sun, M., Zhou, T., Huang, G., Darrell, T.: Rethinking the value of network pruning. arXiv preprint arXiv:1810.05270 (2018)
28. Loshchilov, I., Hutter, F.: Decoupled weight decay regularization. arXiv preprint arXiv:1711.05101 (2017)
29. Park, J., Boyd, S.: General heuristics for nonconvex quadratically constrained quadratic programming. arXiv preprint arXiv:1703.07870 (2017)
30. Paszke, A., Gross, S., Chintala, S., Chanan, G.: Pytorch: Tensors and dynamic neural networks in python with strong gpu acceleration. PyTorch: tensors and dynamic neural networks in Python with strong GPU acceleration 6 (2017)

31. Radford, A., Narasimhan, K., Salimans, T., Sutskever, I.: Improving language understanding with unsupervised learning. Tech. rep, OpenAI (2018)
32. Radford, A., Wu, J., Child, R., Luan, D., Amodei, D., Sutskever, I.: Language models are unsupervised multitask learners. OpenAI blog **1**(8), 9 (2019)
33. Srinivas, A., Lin, T.Y., Parmar, N., Shlens, J., Abbeel, P., Vaswani, A.: Bottleneck transformers for visual recognition. In: Proceedings of the IEEE/CVF Conference on Computer Vision and Pattern Recognition, pp. 16519–16529 (2021)
34. Su, X., et al.: Prioritized architecture sampling with monto-carlo tree search. In: Proceedings of the IEEE/CVF Conference on Computer Vision and Pattern Recognition, pp. 10968–10977 (2021)
35. Su, X., et al.: Locally free weight sharing for network width search. arXiv preprint arXiv:2102.05258 (2021)
36. Su, X., You, S., Wang, F., Qian, C., Zhang, C., Xu, C.: Bcnet: searching for network width with bilaterally coupled network. In: Proceedings of the IEEE/CVF Conference on Computer Vision and Pattern Recognition, pp. 2175–2184 (2021)
37. Su, X., et al.: K-shot nas: Learnable weight-sharing for nas with k-shot supernets. arXiv preprint arXiv:2106.06442 (2021)
38. Tang, Y., You, S., Xu, C., Han, J., Qian, C., Shi, B., Xu, C., Zhang, C.: Reborn filters: pruning convolutional neural networks with limited data. In: Proceedings of the AAAI Conference on Artificial Intelligence, pp. 5972–5980 (2020)
39. Tian, Y., Krishnan, D., Isola, P.: Contrastive multiview coding. In: Vedaldi, A., Bischof, H., Brox, T., Frahm, J.-M. (eds.) Contrastive multiview coding. LNCS, vol. 12356, pp. 776–794. Springer, Cham (2020). https://doi.org/10.1007/978-3-030-58621-8_45
40. Touvron, H., Cord, M., Douze, M., Massa, F., Sablayrolles, A., Jégou, H.: Training data-efficient image transformers & distillation through attention. arXiv preprint arXiv:2012.12877 (2020)
41. Wan, A., et al.: Fbnetv2: differentiable neural architecture search for spatial and channel dimensions. In: Proceedings of the IEEE/CVF Conference on Computer Vision and Pattern Recognition, pp. 12965–12974 (2020)
42. Wang, C., Xu, C., Yao, X., Tao, D.: Evolutionary generative adversarial networks. IEEE Trans. Evol. Comput. **23**(6), 921–934 (2019). https://doi.org/10.1109/TEVC.2019.2895748
43. Wang, W., et al.: Pyramid vision transformer: a versatile backbone for dense prediction without convolutions. arXiv preprint arXiv:2102.12122 (2021)
44. Wu, H., et al.: Cvt: introducing convolutions to vision transformers. arXiv preprint arXiv:2103.15808 (2021)
45. Xiao, T., Liu, Y., Zhou, B., Jiang, Y., Sun, J.: Unified perceptual parsing for scene understanding. In: Ferrari, V., Hebert, M., Sminchisescu, C., Weiss, Y. (eds.) Unified perceptual parsing for scene understanding. LNCS, vol. 11209, pp. 432–448. Springer, Cham (2018). https://doi.org/10.1007/978-3-030-01228-1_26
46. Xie, J., Ma, Z., Chang, D., Zhang, G., Guo, J.: GPCA: a probabilistic framework for Gaussian process embedded channel attention (2021)
47. Xie, J., et al.: Advanced dropout: a model-free methodology for Bayesian dropout optimization (2021)
48. Xie, J., et al.: DS-UI: Dual-supervised mixture of Gaussian mixture models for uncertainty inference in image recognition 30, 9208–9219 (2021)
49. Xie, S., Girshick, R., Dollár, P., Tu, Z., He, K.: Aggregated residual transformations for deep neural networks. In: Proceedings of the IEEE Conference on Computer Vision and Pattern Recognition, pp. 1492–1500 (2017)

50. Xu, H., Su, X., Wang, D.: Cnn-based local vision transformer for covid-19 diagnosis. arXiv preprint arXiv:2207.02027 (2022)
51. Xu, H., Su, X., Wang, Y., Cai, H., Cui, K., Chen, X.: Automatic bridge crack detection using a convolutional neural network. Appl. Sci. **9**(14), 2867 (2019)
52. Xu, H., et al.: Data agnostic filter gating for efficient deep networks. In: ICASSP 2022–2022 IEEE International Conference on Acoustics, Speech and Signal Processing (ICASSP), pp. 3503–3507. IEEE (2022)
53. Xu, H., Wang, D., Sowmya, A.: Multi-scale alignment and spatial roi module for covid-19 diagnosis. arXiv preprint arXiv:2207.01345 (2022)
54. Yan, Z., Dai, X., Zhang, P., Tian, Y., Wu, B., Feiszli, M.: Fp-nas: fast probabilistic neural architecture search. In: Proceedings of the IEEE/CVF Conference on Computer Vision and Pattern Recognition, pp. 15139–15148 (2021)
55. Yang, Y., Li, H., You, S., Wang, F., Qian, C., Lin, Z.: Ista-nas: Efficient and consistent neural architecture search by sparse coding. Advances in Neural Information Processing Systems 33 (2020)
56. Yang, Y., You, S., Li, H., Wang, F., Qian, C., Lin, Z.: Towards improving the consistency, efficiency, and flexibility of differentiable neural architecture search. In: Proceedings of the IEEE/CVF Conference on Computer Vision and Pattern Recognition, pp. 6667–6676 (2021)
57. You, S., Huang, T., Yang, M., Wang, F., Qian, C., Zhang, C.: Greedynas: towards fast one-shot nas with greedy supernet. In: Proceedings of the IEEE/CVF Conference on Computer Vision and Pattern Recognition, pp. 1999–2008 (2020)
58. You, S., Xu, C., Xu, C., Tao, D.: Learning from multiple teacher networks. In: Proceedings of the 23rd ACM SIGKDD International Conference on Knowledge Discovery and Data Mining, pp. 1285–1294 (2017)
59. Yu, J., Huang, T.: Autoslim: Towards one-shot architecture search for channel numbers. arXiv preprint arXiv:1903.11728 8 (2019)
60. Yuan, L., et al.: Tokens-to-token vit: Training vision transformers from scratch on imagenet. arXiv preprint arXiv:2101.11986 (2021)
61. Zheng, M., et al.: Weakly supervised contrastive learning. In: Proceedings of the IEEE/CVF International Conference on Computer Vision, pp. 10042–10051 (2021)
62. Zheng, M., You, S., Huang, L., Wang, F., Qian, C., Xu, C.: Simmatch: semi-supervised learning with similarity matching. In: Proceedings of the IEEE/CVF Conference on Computer Vision and Pattern Recognition, pp. 14471–14481 (2022)
63. Zheng, M., You, S., Wang, F., Qian, C., Zhang, C., Wang, X., Xu, C.: Ressl: relational self-supervised learning with weak augmentation. Adv. Neural. Inf. Process. Syst. **34**, 2543–2555 (2021)
64. Zheng, M., et al.: Relational self-supervised learning. arXiv preprint arXiv:2203.08717 (2022)
65. Zheng, S., et al.: Rethinking semantic segmentation from a sequence-to-sequence perspective with transformers. In: Proceedings of the IEEE/CVF Conference on Computer Vision and Pattern Recognition, pp. 6881–6890 (2021)
66. Zhou, B., Zhao, H., Puig, X., Fidler, S., Barriuso, A., Torralba, A.: Scene parsing through ade20k dataset. In: Proceedings of the IEEE Conference on Computer Vision and Pattern Recognition, pp. 633–641 (2017)
67. Zhu, X., Su, W., Lu, L., Li, B., Wang, X., Dai, J.: Deformable detr: deformable transformers for end-to-end object detection. arXiv preprint arXiv:2010.04159 (2020)

LidarNAS: Unifying and Searching Neural Architectures for 3D Point Clouds

Chenxi Liu[(✉)], Zhaoqi Leng, Pei Sun, Shuyang Cheng, Charles R. Qi, Yin Zhou, Mingxing Tan, and Dragomir Anguelov

Waymo LLC, Mountain View, USA
{cxliu,lengzhaoqi,peis,shuyangcheng,rqi,yinzhou,
tanmingxing,dragomir}@waymo.com

Abstract. Developing neural models that accurately understand objects in 3D point clouds is essential for the success of robotics and autonomous driving. However, arguably due to the higher-dimensional nature of the data (as compared to images), existing neural architectures exhibit a large variety in their designs, including but not limited to the views considered, the format of the neural features, and the neural operations used. Lack of a unified framework and interpretation makes it hard to put these designs in perspective, as well as systematically explore new ones. In this paper, we begin by proposing a unified framework of such, with the key idea being factorizing the neural networks into a series of view transforms and neural layers. We demonstrate that this modular framework can reproduce a variety of existing works while allowing a fair comparison of backbone designs. Then, we show how this framework can easily materialize into a concrete neural architecture search (NAS) space, allowing a principled NAS-for-3D exploration. In performing evolutionary NAS on the 3D object detection task on the Waymo Open Dataset, not only do we outperform the state-of-the-art models, but also report the interesting finding that NAS tends to discover the same macro-level architecture concept for both the vehicle and pedestrian classes.

1 Introduction

Being able to recognize, segment, or detect objects in 3D is one of the fundamental goals of computer vision. In this paper we consider the point cloud input representation for the wide usage of RGBD cameras in robotics applications, as well as LiDAR sensors in autonomous driving. There has been a lot of research in this area, including various deep learning based approaches.

But which neural architecture should you choose? PointNet [32]? VoxelNet [55]? PointPillars [18]? Range Sparse Net [43]? It is easy to get overwhelmed by the diverse set of concepts present in these names as well as the variety in the architectures themselves.

Supplementary Information The online version contains supplementary material available at https://doi.org/10.1007/978-3-031-19803-8_10.

© The Author(s), under exclusive license to Springer Nature Switzerland AG 2022
S. Avidan et al. (Eds.): ECCV 2022, LNCS 13681, pp. 158–175, 2022.
https://doi.org/10.1007/978-3-031-19803-8_10

This level of variety at the macro-level is not observed in other areas, e.g., neural architectures developed for 2D images. The root cause is the higher-dimensional nature of the data. There are three major reasons in particular:

- *Views*: 2D images are captured by an egocentric photographer. A similar view exists for 3D, that is the perspective view, or range images. But when the scan is not egocentric, we have an unordered point set that can no longer be indexed by pixel coordinates. In addition, gravity makes the z axis special, and often times a natural choice is to view an object from top-down. Each view has its unique properties and (dis)advantages.
- *Sparsity*: Images are dense in the sense that each pixel has an RGB value between 0 and 255. But in 3D, range images may have pixels that correspond to infinite depth. Also, objects typically occupy a small percentage of the space, meaning that when a scene is voxelized, the number of non-empty voxels is typically small compared with the total number of voxels.
- *Neural operations*: Due to views and sparsity, 2D convolution does not always apply, resulting in more diverse neural operations.

Our first contribution in this paper is a *unified framework* that can interpret and organize the variety of neural architecture designs, while adhering to the principles listed above. This framework allows us to put existing designs in perspective and enables us to explore new designs. The key idea is to factorize the entire neural network into a series of *transforms* and *layers*. The framework supports four views (point, voxel, pillar, perspective) and two formats (dense, sparse), as well as the *transforms* between them. It is also possible to merge features from different views, building parallelism into the sequential stages. But once a view-format combination is set, it restricts the types of *layers* that can be applied. When visualized, this framework is a trellis, and any neural architecture corresponds to a connected subset of this trellis. We provide several examples of how popular architectures can be refactored and reproduced under this framework, proving its generality.

A direct benefit of this framework is that it can easily materialize into a search space, which immediately unlocks and enables NAS. NAS stands for neural architecture search [57], which tries to replace human labor and manual designs with machine computation and automatic discoveries. Despite its success on 2D architectures [44], its usage on 3D has been limited. In this paper we conduct a principled NAS-for-3D explorations, by not only considering the micro-level (such as the number of channels), but also embracing the macro-level (such as transforms between various views and formats).

We conduct our LidarNAS experiments on the 3D object detection task on the Waymo Open Dataset [42]. Using regularized evolution [35], our search finds LidarNASNet, which outperforms the state-of-the-art RSN model [43] on both the vehicle and the pedestrian classes. In addition to the superior accuracy and the competitive latency, there are also interesting observations about the Lidar-NASNet architecture itself. First of all, though the search/evolution was conducted separately on vehicle and pedestrian, the found architectures have essentially the same high-level design concept. Second, the modifications discovered by NAS coincidentally reflects ideas from human designs. We also analyze the hundreds of architectures sampled in the process and draw useful lessons that should inform future designs.

To summarize, the main contributions of this paper are:

- A unified framework general enough to include a wide range of backbones for 3D data processing
- A search space and an algorithm challenging enough to cover both the micro-level and the macro-level
- A successful NAS experiment which leads to state-of-the-art performance on the Waymo Open Dataset

2 Related Work

2.1 Neural Architectures for 3D

We partition neural architectures for 3D into four categories, according to the primary view(s) used. Since this paper studies *backbone* design for 3D object detection, we will mostly cover detection but will also talk about segmentation and classification.

The first category is **top-down primary**, which includes voxel and pillar. The main idea is to divide 3D points into 3D voxels [8,9,11,49,50,55] or 2D pillars [18], which then become regular. The advantage is that voxelization enables locality, which in turn enables convolution operations. But the main limitation is memory consumption, which grows cubically (or quadratically). This either limits the maximum detection range or sacrifices the voxelization granularity. Even if sparse operations may be used, for egocentric scans, the point densities at long-range and short-range are different, posing challenges in learning.

The second category is **point primary**, which treats the point cloud as unorganized sets. Originally developed for classification and segmentation [32,33], the idea can also be used on detection [29,31]. The advantage is that it is more memory-friendly than voxelization based approaches. However, its limitation is that the neural layers do not perform as well, possibly due to irregular coordinates. In addition, to achieve locality, nearest neighbor search is typically needed for the input, which can be expensive.

The third category is **perspective primary**, operating directly on the range image [5,6,12,28]. This is also very memory-friendly and can utilize powerful 2D convolution layers which have been extensively researched. However, as the depth can change drastically for adjacent pixels, these methods exhibit more difficulty in localizing the objects accurately, as well as handling occlusions.

The fourth and final category is **fusion** methods, which use two or more of the representations discussed above. The fusion may be either sequential and parallel. For example, RSN [43] sequentially performs foreground segmentation on the perspective view and delivers detection output on the top-down view. PVCNN [25] and SPVCNN [45] fuses information from the point view and the voxel view in a parallel fashion. MVF [54] fuses feature from perspective view, point view, and pillar view, also in a parallel fashion. The hope is that fusion methods can combine the best of multiple worlds, which is why it is important to keep all options when doing architecture exploration.

2.2 Neural Architecture Search

Early works on neural architecture search primarily focused on the **search algorithm**. A variety of methods were introduced, including reinforcement learning [3,57], evolution [35,36], performance prediction [23], weight-sharing [24,30]. Essentially, different methods make different approximations about the search process.

These search algorithm explorations started on image classification. The following phase consists of extending to other **tasks**, such as semantic segmentation [7,22] and object detection [14,48]. For 3D tasks, NAS research has been done on medical imaging [2,17,47,52,56]. However, the *volumetric* CT scans are different from *point* clouds, and as a result the search space is greatly simplified. There are also works on 3D shape classification [19,26], but their overall frameworks do not exceed that set by [24]. [20,45] is closer to our work, in the sense that it uses NAS to optimize for segmentation and detection on 3D scenes (KITTI [13]). But generalizing the terminology used in [22], we believe there is also a two-level hierarchy in 3D neural architecture designs, with the outer macro-level controlling the views of the data/features, and the inner micro-level being the specifics of the neural layers. Under this terminology, [20,45] keeps the macro-level fixed, while our search covers both.

3   Unifying Neural Architectures for 3D

3.1   Philosophy

In order to offer a unified interpretation of the growing variety of neural networks for 3D, we need to pinpoint their high-level design principles. Fortunately, we find these underlying principles to be surprisingly congruent, and we characterize them as: finding *some neighborhood* of the 3D points and then *aggregating information* within. The "aggregation" part is typically done through some form of convolution and/or pooling. The "neighborhood" part has different choices:

- PointNet [32]: the neighborhood alternates between the point itself (MLP) and all points (max-pooling)
- PointNet++ [33]: the neighborhood is an Euclidean ball with a certain radius
- VoxelNet [55]: 3D neighborhood measured by Manhattan distance of Cartesian coordinates (x, y, z)
- PointPillars [18]: 2D neighborhood measured by Manhattan distance of (part of) Cartesian coordinates (x, y)
- LaserNet [28]: 2D neighborhood measured by Manhattan distance of pixel coordinates (i, j)

These common "neighborhood" choices have been typically expressed through the views of the data/features: point, voxel, pillar, perspective. We point out that there have been and will be more views being proposed, which is why we feel the "neighborhood" interpretation is more generic. Notably, different data views can *transform* between each other back and forth. However, once the data view is determined, it *restricts* the type of *layers* that can be applied. This factorization of "transforms" and "layers" as well as their relationship will be reflected in our framework described next.

3.2   A Unified Framework

In this subsection, we build upon the aforementioned high-level ideas and describe the main framework we use to think about neural architectures throughout this work. We describe its different levels of detail from fine to coarse.

Views and Formats. We consider a total of four views (point, pillar, voxel, perspective) and up to two data formats (dense and sparse):

- **Point**: The features for all N 3D points are stored in a matrix of size $[N, C]$, where C is the number of channels. The Cartesian coordinates (x, y, z) for each point are stored in a separate matrix of size $[N, 3]$, where the indices of the points are aligned between the two matrices.
- **Pillar**: In this view, we store a fixed-length feature for each pillar when viewing the scene from top-down. We allow the pillar view to be either dense or sparse. If dense, the features are stored in a tensor of size $[B, X, Y, C]$, where B is the batch size, X and Y are the number of pillars along the corresponding dimension. If sparse, the features are stored in a matrix of size $[N, C]$, where N is the number of *non-empty* pillars and a separate matrix of size $[N, 3]$ is used to store the indices (both batch and spatial) of these non-empty pillars. In both data formats, unlike the point view, the Cartesian coordinates of each pillar('s center) can be easily calculated from its spatial index (`origin + index * pillar size`).
- **Voxel**: Different from the pillar view, the voxel view partitions the scene along all three spatial dimensions. The additional partition along the z axis makes fitting a tensor of size $[B, X, Y, Z, C]$ into memory very challenging. Therefore, in this work we only consider the sparse format for the voxel view. Features are stored in a matrix of size $[N, C]$, where N is the number of *non-empty* voxels. A separate matrix of size $[N, 4]$ is used to store their indices (both batch and spatial).
- **Perspective**: For egocentric 3D scans or RGBD images, simply using the original perspective view is a natural choice. We consider both the dense and sparse formats for this view. If dense, features are stored in a tensor of size $[B, H, W, C]$, where H and W consist of the size of the range image. A separate tensor of size $[B, H, W, 3]$ is used to store the Cartesian coordinates of each pixel on the range image. If sparse, features are stored in a matrix of

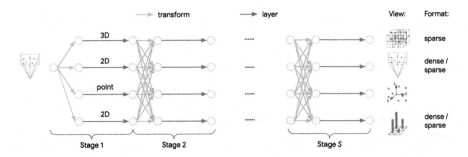

Fig. 1. The LidarNAS framework for interpreting neural architectures on 3D point clouds. The entire backbone consists of S stages. Each stage consists of view & format transforms followed by corresponding neural layers. Within this framework, a backbone architecture corresponds to a *connected subset* of the S-stage trellis.

size $[N, C]$ and Cartesian coordinates a separate matrix of size $[N, 3]$, similar to the point view.

Transforms. Now that the views and formats are established, the framework shall be general enough to include possible transforms from one to the other. The transforms are intended to be lightweight: powerful neural feature update is a non-goal. Since there are totally six possible representations (four views, with pillar and perspective having two formats), we have up to $6^2 = 36$ different transforms. Though this number may seem daunting, some of these transforms have more familiar and friendly names. For example, the transform to itself is identity. The one from a sparse format to its dense counterpart is densification (by padding zero vectors). The point to voxel transform is voxelization. The reverse transform is devoxelization. The point to perspective transform is projection.

Layers. Once a view-format combination is set, we can apply neural layers to update the features. Generally, we do not put constraint on the number or form of the layers: it can be as simple as a one-layer convolution, or as complicated as an entire U-Net [37]. But the one constraint is that it conforms to the view-format combination for both its input and output. This is because, for instance, 2D convolution cannot be applied on 3D inputs; sparse convolution does not work on dense features. Notably, 2D layer implementations can interchangeably work for both the pillar view and the perspective view.

Stages. Putting these concepts together, we define a stage to be the sequential pair of possible transforms and their associated layers. Figure 1 visualizes the concatenation of S stages. Within this framework, the backbone of a neural network for 3D corresponds to a *connected subset of this S-stage trellis*. A head can then be added to the end to perform 3D classification/detection/segmentation.

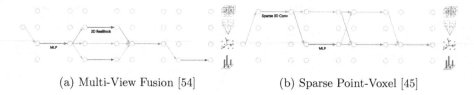

(a) Multi-View Fusion [54]   (b) Sparse Point-Voxel [45]

Fig. 2. Examples of how existing designs may be interpreted within the LidarNAS framework.

We emphasize that the word choice is "subset" but not "path", meaning that a stage can have more than one view present. This makes our framework more general, as it supports not only sequential designs but also parallel ones. Consequently, we may have multiple different views in stage $s-1$ transforming to the same view in stage s. In these cases, after applying individual transforms, we merge these transformed features through either concatenation (default in this work) or summation.

3.3 Inclusion of Existing Designs

In Fig. 2 and Fig. 3, we visualize several examples of how existing designs may be interpreted within the framework described above. Our framework is flexible enough to cover both entirely sequential designs such as Range Sparse Net [43] and more parallel designs such as Multi-View Fusion [54]. In addition to these networks developed for 3D detection, it can also explain those beyond, such as SPV [45]. More architecture designs fit in, including but not limited to [18,29, 46,49,55], but we skip visualization due to space limitations.

4 Searching Neural Architectures for 3D

The framework described in the previous section brings many benefits, one of which is the potential to search novel and better architectures. This section focuses on how the framework materializes into a search space (Sect. 4.1), as well as our choice of search algorithm (Sect. 4.2).

4.1 From Framework to Search Space

Figure 2 demonstrated how, at a high level, various architectures fall within the LidarNAS framework. But delving into the details, specific implementations of the modules are going to differ across works. While this is very much expected and understandable, the variety and freedom in "layers" alone would make constructing a meaningful search space infeasible. We now discuss how we materialize the framework into a search space by making specific choices.

Transforms. Among the 36 possible transforms, we did not implement the transforms from pillar to voxel, as nothing more can be done other than copying the same features along the z axis. From the voxel view, our implementation only supported transforms to the pillar view. Supporting 31/36 transforms is still high coverage.

Layers. We need at least one type of neural layer for each of the following: point, 2D dense, 2D sparse, 3D sparse. Our search space picked one representative for each:

- **Point:** Multiple layers of dense-normalization-ReLU. The normalization can either be batch normalization [16] or layer normalization [1]. The number of units F in the dense layers is a hyperparameter that can be searched.
- **2D dense:** A U-Net [37] with residual blocks [15]. We use up to five downsampling and upsampling scales. The number of channels for each scale are $[F, 4F, 8F, 8F, 16F]$ with F being the hyperparameter that can be searched. The number of blocks per scale is 2 except for the highest resolution scale which is 1.
- **2D sparse:** Also a U-Net with residual blocks, except that each convolution is a sparse convolution (kernel size 3×3). We use up to 3 downsampling and upsampling scales, and the number of blocks are [1, 2, 3] and [0, 2, 2]. We use the same number of channels F for all downsampling and upsampling blocks.
- **3D sparse:** Also a U-Net with residual blocks, except that 3D sparse convolution is used. The kernel size can either be $3 \times 3 \times 3$ or $3 \times 3 \times 1$, and the corresponding stride for each scale is $2 \times 2 \times 2$ or $2 \times 2 \times 1$. The other details follow the 2D sparse case above.

These choices of layer specifics, especially those for 2D and 3D, try to exactly follow RSN [43].

Stages Our search space considers $S = 3$ stages. For simplicity, we also have the constraint that the last stage can only have one view. Inspired by RSN, we add the option to perform foreground segmentation immediately after the first perspective branch that appears.

4.2   Regularized Evolution

We choose regularized evolution to be our search algorithm, which follows [35]. Compared against other major classes of NAS methods, evolution arguably makes the least amount of approximations, which is desirable especially since we are exploring a less explored task and a complicated search space. We do not use weight-sharing NAS for GPU memory considerations. 3D tasks are understandably more memory intensive than 2D tasks, and the batch size on each GPU was already small (<10). However, even the best weight-sharing NAS (a recent example is [4]) implementations require $2 - 3\times$ extra GPU memory.

Our mutation algorithm works by first randomly selecting a stage s and then randomly applying one of the following six mutation choices to this stage:

- *Add a view:* if the stage does not have all four views, then randomly add a view not yet present in this stage. A random view present in the previous stage is selected as its predecessor. A random view present in the next stage is selected as its successor. A default layer of the corresponding type is used for this addition. The number of channels for all layers in this stage are halved.
- *Remove a view:* if the stage has more than one view, then randomly remove an existing view. Usage of the removed view in the next stage is also removed. The number of channels for all layers in this stage are doubled.
- *Switch the view:* if the stage has exactly one view, then switch the view to another. All usage of the old view in the next stage is changed to the new view.
- *Adjust the pillar/voxel size:* a key parameter in many of the transforms is the pillar/voxel size. Multiply the pillar/voxel size by either 0.8 or 1.2 for all views.
- *Adjust the number of channels:* multiply the number of channels for all layers in the stage by either 0.8 or 1.2.
- *Adjust the layer progression:*
  - Point: Either increase or decrease the number of dense-normalization-ReLU by 1.
  - 2D dense: Either increase or decrease the number of scales by 1.
  - 2D/3D sparse: Increase or decrease the number of downsampling/upsampling scales by 1.

If a mutation fails (e.g., if the precondition does not hold, such as trying to remove a view when the stage only has one view), the algorithm mutates again until it succeeds.

The first four mutation choices focus on the "transform" aspect of a stage, while the last two mutation choices focus on the "layer" aspect. This level of coverage and variety makes the search comprehensive yet challenging.

5   Experimental Results

5.1   Experimental Setting

We perform 3D object detection experiments on the challenging Waymo Open Dataset [42]. It provides LiDAR scans in the range image form, which makes experiments on the perspective view much more natural and convenient. It contains 1150 LiDAR sequences with 798 train, 202 validation, and 150 test ones. Each sequence is 20 s at 10 frames per second. Experiments are conducted on both the vehicle and the pedestrian classes, using the official evaluation metrics of 3D/BEV AP.

5.2   Existing Architectures Under LidarNAS

In this subsection, we use the LidarNAS framework (Sect. 3) to reimplement several existing neural architectures for 3D. The goal here is to prove the generality and correctness of the LidarNAS framework interpretation, as well as validate our implementation of individual modules.

We selected four existing architectures: RSN [43], PointPillars [18], Laser-Net [28], and MVF++ [34]. These are selected to cover a variety of views as well as topology. Note that the LidarNAS framework focuses on *backbone* design. In our reimplementation, we use an anchor-free detection *head* that is the same as RSN if the backbone output is sparse voxels but also works for pillar and perspective views (details are described in the supplementary material). This means that our RSN reimplementation is exact but the others are not, and we add the suffix "-like" to indicate this difference.

Table 1. A diverse set of existing 3D detection architectures under the LidarNAS framework. The second number in the batch size multiplication is the number of GPUs/TPU shards. The metric (last two columns) is L1 3D AP.

model	class	frame	device	batch	steps	lr	voxelization (m)	LidarNAS AP	previous AP
RSN-exact	Veh	3	GPU	2×16	120k	0.006	$0.2 \times 0.2 \times 0.2$	77.2	77.2 [43]
	Ped	3	GPU	3×16	120k	0.006	$0.1 \times 0.1 \times 20.0$	79.1	79.1 [43]
PointPillars-like	Veh	1	GPU	2×16	120k	0.006	0.32×0.32	69.3	63.3 [43] / 60.3 [34]
	Ped	1	GPU	3×16	120k	0.006	0.32×0.32	66.1	68.9 [43] / 60.1 [34]
LaserNet-like	Veh	1	GPU	1×16	360k	0.001	-	47.1	52.1 [43] / 56.1 [6]
	Ped	1	GPU	1×16	240k	0.003	-	59.0	63.4 [43] / 62.9 [6]
MVF++-like	Veh	1	TPU	2×128	43k	0.003	0.32×0.32	73.6	74.6 [34]
	Ped	1	TPU	2×128	43k	0.003	0.32×0.32	70.4	78.0 [34]

Table 1 summarizes the results, using L1 3D AP. Key hyperparameter values are also provided. We use no color if our reimplementation is within 1% absolute of the previously reported number; green if higher than > 5%; yellow if lower than ≤ 5%; and red if lower than > 5%. Considering the diversity of these architectures, overall we consider our reimplementation to be acceptable and successful, validating our implementation of (some of the) transforms and layers modules. Notice that our implementation can support multi-frame, as well as both GPU and TPU.

Looking into individual neural architectures, our reproduction of RSN is exact. Interestingly, PointPillars-like significantly outperforms previous reports on the vehicle class. This is an important reminder that revisiting previous architectures may be necessary and beneficial, as they may still be competitive when coupled with latest developments in other areas (e.g., anchor-free detection head). However, the performance on the pedestrian class is slightly worse. This is also observed on MVF++-like, where the vehicle class is within 1% but the pedestrian class is significantly worse. Our hypothesis is that comparatively speaking, our detection head is better suited on larger objects but struggles more on smaller objects. Finally, our LaserNet-like performs noticeably worse than any network that detects on the top-down view (meaning pillar or voxel), despite training for $2 - 3\times$ longer steps. This proves that detection from the perspective view needs more specialized operations, such as those described in the original paper, or some recent developments [6, 12].

5.3 Searching for New Architectures

In this subsection, we perform and analyze neural architecture search experiments, using the search space and algorithm described in Sect. 4.

Table 2. 3D object detection results for the vehicle and pedestrian classes on the Waymo Open Dataset validation set. The AP is difficulty L1. The unit of latency is ms. Multi-frame models are grayed. §: Slightly different from PointPillars-like in Table 1, because here we have to swap the original layers with the U-Net explained in Sect. 4.1. †: our measurement using identical setting: average on 10 scenes, each has more than 100 vehicles/pedestrians.

model	year	frame	Vehicle			Pedestrian		
			3D AP	BEV AP	latency	3D AP	BEV AP	latency
LaserNet [28]	CVPR 19		52.1	71.2	64.3	63.4	70.0	64.3
PointPillars [18]	CVPR 19		63.3	82.5	49.0	68.9	76.0	49.0
PV-RCNN [38]	CVPR 20		70.3	83.0	-	-	-	-
Pillar-based [46]	ECCV 20	1	69.8	87.1	66.7	72.5	78.5	66.7
PV-RCNN [39]	WOD 20	2	77.5	-	300	78.9	-	300
RCD [5]	CoRL 20	1	69.0	82.1	-	-	-	-
MVF++ [34]	CVPR 21	1	74.6	87.6	-	78.0	83.3	-
CenterPoint [51]	CVPR 21	2	76.7	-	-	79.0	-	-
PPC [6]	CVPR 21		65.2	80.8	-	75.5	82.2	-
RangeDet [12]	ICCV 21	1	72.9	-	-	75.9	-	-
PointPillars-like§		1	67.6	85.3	-	-	-	-
LidarNASNet-P (ours)		1	**73.2**	**88.2**	-	-	-	-
RSN [43]	CVPR 21	1	75.2	87.7	46.5†	77.1	81.7	21.0†
LidarNASNet-R (ours)		1	**75.6**	**88.6**	49.3†	**77.4**	**82.0**	22.6†

Evolving Past the State-of-the-Art. Based on the analysis above, picking a random architecture as the starting point would take much longer time for the performance to ramp up, so we use *warm starting* [40, 41] to speed up and save up. Each search lasts 100 architectures, each trained using batch size 2×8 GPUs for 12k steps (10% of the standard number of steps) using cosine learning rate. All architectures operate on single-frame. The population size and tournament size for the regularized evolution algorithm are 20 and 5 respectively. We also measure the V100 latency of the network on a (random) training batch immediately after 11k training steps. The measurement is taken close to the end of the training because for architectures that perform foreground segmentation, the latency may change throughout training. We comment that this search phase latency measurement is noisy, not only because the data batch is random, but also because the scheduler may allocate a GPU shared with other jobs. Regardless, we use 100 * L1 3D AP - 0.5 * latency in ms[1] as the objective to guide the evolution. Once an architecture is identified, we increase the per-GPU batch size from 2 to 5, and train for 120k steps as the final evaluation.

We conduct a separate search/evolution from three different starting points: PointPillars-like vehicle, RSN CarXL, and RSN PedL[2]. We name our found architecture LidarNASNet-P/R depending on whether the starting point was PointPillars-like or RSN, and compare them against other models in Table 2.

We first compare LidarNASNet-P against PointPillars-like, the evolution baseline. The L1 3D AP improves from 67.6 to 73.2, with a significant gap of +5.6. The gain on BEV AP is also significant at +2.9. The large improvement and competitive end result clearly showcase the effectiveness of our search. When running the same evolution from RSN, LidarNASNet-R outperforms by 0.4 and 0.3 3D AP on vehicle and pedestrian respectively, and the gains on BEV AP are even larger. As we will see soon, LidarNASNet-R has an additional branch, so the latency is higher, but only slightly. To put this in perspective, we did an ablation study[3] where we increase the number of channels in the sparse U-Net of RSN for vehicle (from 64 to 91) to reach AP parity with LidarNASNet-R. The latency of this architecture is 60.8 ms, which is significantly higher.

Comparing against other architectures, LidarNASNet-R also performs very competitively. Not only is this reflected in the superior AP especially among single-frame models, but also in the small latency. We reiterate that our total search cost is about 80 GPU days, which is only 10 times the cost of training a single RSN (8 GPU days).

Visualizing and Analyzing LidarNASNet. We visualize the macro-level architecture of LidarNASNet in Fig. 3. We start by discussing LidarNASNet-P. At the macro-level, the evolution decided to add a 2D U-Net that enhances the features for each range image pixel before voxelization to the pillar view. This change alone improves the 3D AP from 67.6 to 72.3. The evolution also learned to increase the voxelization granularity from 0.32×0.32 to 0.25×0.25, which is a micro-level change that is not reflected in Fig. 3. This change further improves the 3D AP to the 73.2 reported in Table 2.

For LidarNASNet-R, notice that though the search was conducted separately for the vehicle and pedestrian class, *the same macro-level architecture design was found*, which is a positive signal regarding the generality of the found design. Specifically, LidarNASNet-R adds a pillar view in the first stage, as well as the associated sparse 2D U-Net. The idea of adding a pillar view resembles MVF [34,54] (though the sparse format is used here while MVF did not consider sparse operations), making LidarNASNet-R a hybrid between RSN and MVF,

---

[1] We empirically picked these multipliers; did not tune them heavily.

[2] We skipped PointPillars-like pedestrian, because the corresponding number in Table 1 is yellow not green.

[3] In fact this architecture was sampled/discovered during our evolution.

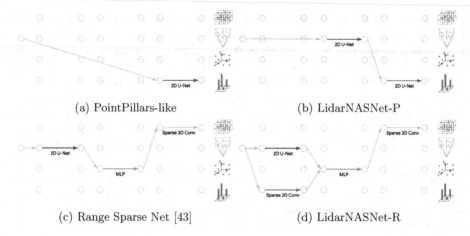

(a) PointPillars-like   (b) LidarNASNet-P

(c) Range Sparse Net [43]   (d) LidarNASNet-R

Fig. 3. The *macro-level* architecture of the found LidarNASNet-P/R. Note that the illustration in (d) applies for *both* vehicle and pedestrian. It adds a sparse convolution on the pillar view in the first stage, utilizing all four views and two formats considered in this work.

two very successful human designs. The voxelization granularity of this sparse 2D U-Net is 0.32×0.32, and the number of channels F is 16. In the vehicle variant, the number of channels for the original perspective view is halved (from 16 to 8). In the pedestrian variant, this is reduced even more aggressively (from 16 to 3).

The Search Space is Challenging. A common critique on some of the NAS literature is that the search space can be "easy" in the sense that even random sampling of architectures (and taking the argmax) can find high-quality architectures indistinguishable from those found by NAS [21]. We prove our search space is not trivial, by training 100 architectures randomly generated by the procedure detailed in the supplementary material. Figure 4 shows the side-by-side comparison of these random architectures against our LidarNAS evolution. It is clear that randomly sampled architectures have much worse qualities, in terms of both detection AP and latency. Not only does this illustrate that

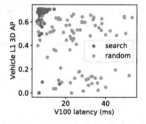

Fig. 4. Randomly sampled architectures (orange) in the LidarNAS search space have worse average and higher variance, calling for warm starting (blue). (Color figure online)

the search space we consider is challenging and nontrivial, but also justifies our use of warm starting.

Lessons from the Sampled Architectures. In addition to fixating on the top-performing architecture, there are also lessons to be learned in the hundreds of architectures sampled. We now choose a few angles to analyze these data.

Using the LidarNAS evolution data points, we investigate architectures that only mutated the "layer" aspect (i.e. the last two mutation choices in Sect. 4.2) versus the rest. The AP standard deviation of the two subsets are 0.04 and 0.14 respectively, which confirms that on average, mutating "transforms" results in more aggressive changes than mutating "layers" only.

Using the random architectures data points, we study which views and stages have the most direct effect on detection quality. Specifically, we run a linear regression from the 12-dimensional binary feature indicating whether the corresponding branch exists in the architecture to the L1 3D AP. The coefficients are visualized in Fig. 5. By comparing the columns, it is clear that later stages have a much more direct influence on the detection AP than earlier stages. By comparing the rows of the last column, top-down views (voxel and pillar) positively influence the detection AP, while the perspective view impacts it negatively. This again resonates with the belief that detection from the perspective view tends to be more challenging and requires more specialized treatment.

Using the random architectures data points, we also study the effect of dense vs sparse on latency. Recall that in our LidarNAS framework, the perspective view and the pillar view are the two that allow both dense and sparse formats. For each view, we run a linear regression to latency from a 3-dimensional feature, indicating the total number of empty/dense/sparse branches. For the perspective view, the coefficients are $[-5.24, -1.65, 6.90]$. For the pillar view, the coefficients are $[-3.03, 3.06, -0.03]$. The first coefficient is the most negative for both, which is expected, because the more empty

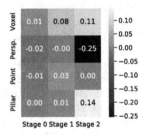

Fig. 5. Linear regression from the presence of individual views and stages to detection AP.

branches you have, the smaller the latency is. Interestingly, the coefficients reveal that on the perspective view, using more sparse branches results in larger latency, whereas on the pillar view, using more sparse branches results in smaller latency. This shows that sparse operations can offer speedup but not always: it depends on whether the view inherently has high sparsity.

6 Conclusion

This paper aims to achieve two goals for neural architecture research for 3D: first, a unified framework that summarizes and organizes existing designs, and second, an architecture search exploration enabled by this framework. We demonstrate the generality of our LidarNAS framework, not only through pictorial illustration, but also through empirical experiments. Then, we successfully and automatically discovered LidarNASNet, which achieves state-of-the-art results on the Waymo Open Dataset 3D object detection. The searched architecture is interesting: not only is it identical when searching on two different classes, but also embodies and reaffirms shades from existing designs.

There are still many limitations in this work, and we look forward to addressing them in future research. First, while the *transforms* coverage is fairly complete, the *layers* currently implemented do not capture much diversity, and we shall add more powerful layer choices into the search space, such as Transformers [10,27,53]. Second, all search experiments are single-frame; in extending to multi-frame, challenges include more memory pressure and the additional complication over which stage to perform temporal fusion.

References

1. Ba, J.L., Kiros, J.R., Hinton, G.E.: Layer normalization. arXiv preprint arXiv:1607.06450 (2016)
2. Bae, W., Lee, S., Lee, Y., Park, B., Chung, M., Jung, K.-H.: Resource optimized neural architecture search for 3D medical image segmentation. In: Shen, D., et al. (eds.) MICCAI 2019. LNCS, vol. 11765, pp. 228–236. Springer, Cham (2019). https://doi.org/10.1007/978-3-030-32245-8_26
3. Baker, B., Gupta, O., Naik, N., Raskar, R.: Designing neural network architectures using reinforcement learning. arXiv preprint arXiv:1611.02167 (2016)
4. Bender, G., et al.: Can weight sharing outperform random architecture search? an investigation with tunas. In: Proceedings of the IEEE/CVF Conference on Computer Vision and Pattern Recognition, pp. 14323–14332 (2020)
5. Bewley, A., Sun, P., Mensink, T., Anguelov, D., Sminchisescu, C.: Range conditioned dilated convolutions for scale invariant 3d object detection. arXiv preprint arXiv:2005.09927 (2020)
6. Chai, Y., et al.: To the point: efficient 3d object detection in the range image with graph convolution kernels. In: Proceedings of the IEEE/CVF Conference on Computer Vision and Pattern Recognition, pp. 16000–16009 (2021)
7. Chen, L.C., et al.: Searching for efficient multi-scale architectures for dense image prediction. arXiv preprint arXiv:1809.04184 (2018)
8. Chen, X., Ma, H., Wan, J., Li, B., Xia, T.: Multi-view 3d object detection network for autonomous driving. In: Proceedings of the IEEE conference on Computer Vision and Pattern Recognition, pp. 1907–1915 (2017)
9. Deng, J., Shi, S., Li, P., Zhou, W., Zhang, Y., Li, H.: Voxel R-CNN: towards high performance voxel-based 3d object detection. arXiv preprint arXiv:2012.15712 (2020)
10. Engel, N., Belagiannis, V., Dietmayer, K.: Point transformer. IEEE Access **9**, 134826–134840 (2021)
11. Engelcke, M., Rao, D., Wang, D.Z., Tong, C.H., Posner, I.: Vote3deep: Fast object detection in 3d point clouds using efficient convolutional neural networks. In: 2017 IEEE International Conference on Robotics and Automation (ICRA), pp. 1355–1361. IEEE (2017)
12. Fan, L., Xiong, X., Wang, F., Wang, N., Zhang, Z.: Rangedet: in defense of range view for lidar-based 3d object detection. arXiv preprint arXiv:2103.10039 (2021)
13. Geiger, A., Lenz, P., Urtasun, R.: Are we ready for autonomous driving? the KITTI vision benchmark suite. In: 2012 IEEE Conference on Computer Vision and Pattern Recognition, pp. 3354–3361. IEEE (2012)

14. Ghiasi, G., Lin, T.Y., Le, Q.V.: Nas-fpn: Learning scalable feature pyramid architecture for object detection. In: Proceedings of the IEEE/CVF Conference on Computer Vision and Pattern Recognition, pp. 7036–7045 (2019)
15. He, K., Zhang, X., Ren, S., Sun, J.: Deep residual learning for image recognition. In: Proceedings of the IEEE Conference on Computer Vision and Pattern Recognition, pp. 770–778 (2016)
16. Ioffe, S., Szegedy, C.: Batch normalization: accelerating deep network training by reducing internal covariate shift. In: International Conference on Machine Learning, pp. 448–456. PMLR (2015)
17. Kim, S., et al.: Scalable neural architecture search for 3D medical image segmentation. In: Shen, D., et al. (eds.) MICCAI 2019. LNCS, vol. 11766, pp. 220–228. Springer, Cham (2019). https://doi.org/10.1007/978-3-030-32248-9_25
18. Lang, A.H., Vora, S., Caesar, H., Zhou, L., Yang, J., Beijbom, O.: Pointpillars: fast encoders for object detection from point clouds. In: Proceedings of the IEEE/CVF Conference on Computer Vision and Pattern Recognition, pp. 12697–12705 (2019)
19. Li, G., Qian, G., Delgadillo, I.C., Muller, M., Thabet, A., Ghanem, B.: SGAS: sequential greedy architecture search. In: Proceedings of the IEEE/CVF Conference on Computer Vision and Pattern Recognition, pp. 1620–1630 (2020)
20. Li, G., Xu, M., Giancola, S., Thabet, A., Ghanem, B.: LC-NAS: latency constrained neural architecture search for point cloud networks. arXiv preprint arXiv:2008.10309 (2020)
21. Li, L., Talwalkar, A.: Random search and reproducibility for neural architecture search. In: Uncertainty in Artificial Intelligence, pp. 367–377. PMLR (2020)
22. Liu, C., et al.: Auto-Deeplab: hierarchical neural architecture search for semantic image segmentation. In: Proceedings of the IEEE/CVF Conference on Computer Vision and Pattern Recognition, pp. 82–92 (2019)
23. Liu, C., et al.: Progressive neural architecture search. In: Proceedings of the European Conference on Computer Vision (ECCV), pp. 19–34 (2018)
24. Liu, H., Simonyan, K., Yang, Y.: Darts: differentiable architecture search. arXiv preprint arXiv:1806.09055 (2018)
25. Liu, Z., Tang, H., Lin, Y., Han, S.: Point-voxel CNN for efficient 3d deep learning. arXiv preprint arXiv:1907.03739 (2019)
26. Ma, Z., Zhou, Z., Liu, Y., Lei, Y., Yan, H.: Auto-orvnet: orientation-boosted volumetric neural architecture search for 3d shape classification. IEEE Access 8, 12942–12954 (2019)
27. Mao, J., et al.: Voxel transformer for 3d object detection. In: Proceedings of the IEEE/CVF International Conference on Computer Vision, pp. 3164–3173 (2021)
28. Meyer, G.P., Laddha, A., Kee, E., Vallespi-Gonzalez, C., Wellington, C.K.: Lasernet: an efficient probabilistic 3d object detector for autonomous driving. In: Proceedings of the IEEE/CVF Conference on Computer Vision and Pattern Recognition, pp. 12677–12686 (2019)
29. Ngiam, J., et al.: Starnet: targeted computation for object detection in point clouds. arXiv preprint arXiv:1908.11069 (2019)
30. Pham, H., Guan, M., Zoph, B., Le, Q., Dean, J.: Efficient neural architecture search via parameters sharing. In: International Conference on Machine Learning, pp. 4095–4104. PMLR (2018)
31. Qi, C.R., Litany, O., He, K., Guibas, L.J.: Deep Hough voting for 3D object detection in point clouds. In: Proceedings of the IEEE/CVF International Conference on Computer Vision, pp. 9277–9286 (2019)

32. Qi, C.R., Su, H., Mo, K., Guibas, L.J.: PointNet: deep learning on point sets for 3D classification and segmentation. In: Proceedings of the IEEE Conference on Computer Vision and Pattern Recognition, pp. 652–660 (2017)

33. Qi, C.R., Yi, L., Su, H., Guibas, L.J.: Pointnet++: Deep hierarchical feature learning on point sets in a metric space. arXiv preprint arXiv:1706.02413 (2017)

34. Qi, C.R., et al.: Offboard 3D object detection from point cloud sequences. In: Proceedings of the IEEE/CVF Conference on Computer Vision and Pattern Recognition, pp. 6134–6144 (2021)

35. Real, E., Aggarwal, A., Huang, Y., Le, Q.V.: Regularized evolution for image classifier architecture search. In: Proceedings of the AAAI Conference on Artificial Intelligence, vol. 33, pp. 4780–4789 (2019)

36. Real, E., et al.: Large-scale evolution of image classifiers. In: International Conference on Machine Learning, pp. 2902–2911. PMLR (2017)

37. Ronneberger, O., Fischer, P., Brox, T.: U-Net: convolutional networks for biomedical image segmentation. In: Navab, N., Hornegger, J., Wells, W.M., Frangi, A.F. (eds.) MICCAI 2015. LNCS, vol. 9351, pp. 234–241. Springer, Cham (2015). https://doi.org/10.1007/978-3-319-24574-4_28

38. Shi, S., et al.: PV-RCNN: point-voxel feature set abstraction for 3D object detection. In: Proceedings of the IEEE/CVF Conference on Computer Vision and Pattern Recognition, pp. 10529–10538 (2020)

39. Shi, S., Guo, C., Yang, J., Li, H.: PV-RCNN: the top-performing lidar-only solutions for 3D detection/3d tracking/domain adaptation of waymo open dataset challenges. arXiv preprint arXiv:2008.12599 (2020)

40. So, D., Le, Q., Liang, C.: The evolved transformer. In: International Conference on Machine Learning, pp. 5877–5886. PMLR (2019)

41. So, D.R., Mańke, W., Liu, H., Dai, Z., Shazeer, N., Le, Q.V.: Primer: searching for efficient transformers for language modeling. arXiv preprint arXiv:2109.08668 (2021)

42. Sun, P., et al.: Scalability in perception for autonomous driving: Waymo open dataset. In: Proceedings of the IEEE/CVF Conference on Computer Vision and Pattern Recognition, pp. 2446–2454 (2020)

43. Sun, P., et al.: RSN: range sparse net for efficient, accurate lidar 3D object detection. In: Proceedings of the IEEE/CVF Conference on Computer Vision and Pattern Recognition, pp. 5725–5734 (2021)

44. Tan, M., Le, Q.: EfficientNet: rethinking model scaling for convolutional neural networks. In: International Conference on Machine Learning, pp. 6105–6114. PMLR (2019)

45. Tang, H., et al.: Searching efficient 3D architectures with sparse point-voxel convolution. In: Vedaldi, A., Bischof, H., Brox, T., Frahm, J.-M. (eds.) ECCV 2020. LNCS, vol. 12373, pp. 685–702. Springer, Cham (2020). https://doi.org/10.1007/978-3-030-58604-1_41

46. Wang, Y., et al.: Pillar-based object detection for autonomous driving. In: Vedaldi, A., Bischof, H., Brox, T., Frahm, J.-M. (eds.) ECCV 2020. LNCS, vol. 12367, pp. 18–34. Springer, Cham (2020). https://doi.org/10.1007/978-3-030-58542-6_2

47. Wong, K.C.L., Moradi, M.: SegNAS3D: network architecture search with derivative-free global optimization for 3D image segmentation. In: Shen, D., et al. (eds.) MICCAI 2019. LNCS, vol. 11766, pp. 393–401. Springer, Cham (2019). https://doi.org/10.1007/978-3-030-32248-9_44

48. Xu, H., Yao, L., Zhang, W., Liang, X., Li, Z.: Auto-FPN: automatic network architecture adaptation for object detection beyond classification. In: Proceedings of the IEEE/CVF International Conference on Computer Vision, pp. 6649–6658 (2019)

49. Yan, Y., Mao, Y., Li, B.: Second: sparsely embedded convolutional detection. Sensors **18**(10), 3337 (2018)

50. Yang, B., Luo, W., Urtasun, R.: Pixor: Real-time 3d object detection from point clouds. In: Proceedings of the IEEE conference on Computer Vision and Pattern Recognition, pp. 7652–7660 (2018)

51. Yin, T., Zhou, X., Krahenbuhl, P.: Center-based 3D object detection and tracking. In: Proceedings of the IEEE/CVF Conference on Computer Vision and Pattern Recognition, pp. 11784–11793 (2021)

52. Yu, Q., et al.: C2FNAS: coarse-to-fine neural architecture search for 3D medical image segmentation. In: Proceedings of the IEEE/CVF Conference on Computer Vision and Pattern Recognition, pp. 4126–4135 (2020)

53. Zhao, H., Jiang, L., Jia, J., Torr, P.H., Koltun, V.: Point transformer. In: Proceedings of the IEEE/CVF International Conference on Computer Vision, pp. 16259–16268 (2021)

54. Zhou, Y., et al.: End-to-end multi-view fusion for 3D object detection in lidar point clouds. In: Conference on Robot Learning, pp. 923–932. PMLR (2020)

55. Zhou, Y., Tuzel, O.: VoxelNet: end-to-end learning for point cloud based 3D object detection. In: Proceedings of the IEEE Conference on Computer Vision and Pattern Recognition, pp. 4490–4499 (2018)

56. Zhu, Z., Liu, C., Yang, D., Yuille, A., Xu, D.: V-NAS: neural architecture search for volumetric medical image segmentation. In: 2019 International Conference on 3D Vision (3DV), pp. 240–248. IEEE (2019)

57. Zoph, B., Le, Q.V.: Neural architecture search with reinforcement learning. arXiv preprint arXiv:1611.01578 (2016)

Uncertainty-DTW for Time Series and Sequences

Lei Wang[1,2] and Piotr Koniusz[1,2(✉)]

[1] Australian National University, Canberra, Australia
{lei.wang,piotr.koniusz}@data61.csiro.au
[2] Data61/CSIRO, Canberra, Australia

Abstract. Dynamic Time Warping (DTW) is used for matching pairs of sequences and celebrated in applications such as forecasting the evolution of time series, clustering time series or even matching sequence pairs in few-shot action recognition. The transportation plan of DTW contains a set of paths; each path matches frames between two sequences under a varying degree of time warping, to account for varying temporal intra-class dynamics of actions. However, as DTW is the smallest distance among all paths, it may be affected by the feature uncertainty which varies across time steps/frames. Thus, in this paper, we propose to model the so-called aleatoric uncertainty of a differentiable (soft) version of DTW. To this end, we model the heteroscedastic aleatoric uncertainty of each path by the product of likelihoods from Normal distributions, each capturing variance of pair of frames. (The path distance is the sum of base distances between features of pairs of frames of the path.) The Maximum Likelihood Estimation (MLE) applied to a path yields two terms: (i) a sum of Euclidean distances weighted by the variance inverse, and (ii) a sum of log-variance regularization terms. Thus, our uncertainty-DTW is the smallest weighted path distance among all paths, and the regularization term (penalty for the high uncertainty) is the aggregate of log-variances along the path. The distance and the regularization term can be used in various objectives. We showcase forecasting the evolution of time series, estimating the Fréchet mean of time series, and supervised/unsupervised few-shot action recognition of the articulated human 3D body joints.

Keywords: Time series · Aleatoric uncertainty · Few-shot · Actions

L. Wang and P. Koniusz—Equal contribution. Code: https://github.com/LeiWangR/uDTW.

Supplementary Information The online version contains supplementary material available at https://doi.org/10.1007/978-3-031-19803-8_11.

S. Avidan et al. (Eds.): ECCV 2022, LNCS 13681, pp. 176–195, 2022.
https://doi.org/10.1007/978-3-031-19803-8_11

1   Introduction

Dynamic Time Warping (DTW) [6] is a method popular in forecasting the evolution of time series, estimating the Fréchet mean of time series, or classifying generally understood actions. The key property of DTW is its sequence matching transportation plan that allows any two sequences that are being matched to progress at different 'speeds' not only in the global sense but locally in the temporal sense. As DTW is non-differentiable, a differentiable 'soft' variant of DTW, soft-DTW [7], uses a soft-minimum function which enables backpropagation.

The role of soft-DTW is to evaluate the (relaxed) DTW distance between a pair of sequences $\boldsymbol{\Psi} \equiv [\boldsymbol{\psi}_1, ..., \boldsymbol{\psi}_\tau] \in \mathbb{R}^{d' \times \tau}$, $\boldsymbol{\Psi}' \equiv [\boldsymbol{\psi}'_1, ..., \boldsymbol{\psi}'_{\tau'}] \in \mathbb{R}^{d' \times \tau'}$ of lengths τ and τ', respectively. Under its transportation plan $\mathcal{A}_{\tau, \tau'}$, each path $\boldsymbol{\Pi} \in \mathcal{A}_{\tau, \tau'}$ is evaluated to ascertain the path distance, and the smallest distance is 'selected' by the soft minimum:

$$d_{\text{DTW}}^2(\boldsymbol{\Psi}, \boldsymbol{\Psi}') = \text{SoftMin}_\gamma \left([\langle \boldsymbol{\Pi}, \boldsymbol{D}(\boldsymbol{\Psi}, \boldsymbol{\Psi}') \rangle]_{\boldsymbol{\Pi} \in \mathcal{A}_{\tau, \tau'}} \right), \tag{1}$$

where $\text{SoftMin}_\gamma(\boldsymbol{\alpha}) = -\gamma \log \sum_i \exp(-\alpha_i / \gamma)$ is the soft minimum, $\gamma \geq 0$ controls its relaxation (hard vs. soft path selection), and $\boldsymbol{D} \in \mathbb{R}_+^{\tau \times \tau'} \equiv [d_{\text{base}}^2(\boldsymbol{\psi}_m, \boldsymbol{\psi}'_n)]_{(m,n) \in \mathcal{I}_\tau \times \mathcal{I}_{\tau'}}$ contains pair-wise distances between all possible pairings of frame-wise feature representations of sequences $\boldsymbol{\Psi}$ and $\boldsymbol{\Psi}'$, and $d_{\text{base}}^2(\cdot, \cdot)$ may be the squared Euclidean distance.

However, the path distance $\langle \boldsymbol{\Pi}, \boldsymbol{D}(\boldsymbol{\Psi}, \boldsymbol{\Psi}') \rangle$ of path $\boldsymbol{\Pi}$ ignores the observation uncertainty of frame-wise feature representations by simply relying on the Euclidean distances stored in $\boldsymbol{D}$. Thus, we resort to the notion of the so-called aleatoric uncertainty known from a non-exhaustive list of works about uncertainty [14,15,17,18,28].

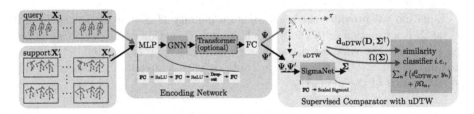

Fig. 1. Supervised few-shot action recognition of the articulated human 3D body joints with the uncertainty-DTW (uDTW). Frames from a query and support sequences are split into short-term temporal blocks $\mathbf{X}_1, ..., \mathbf{X}_\tau$ and $\mathbf{X}'_1, ..., \mathbf{X}'_{\tau'}$ of length M given stride S. We pass all skeleton coordinates via Encoding Network to obtain feature tensors $\boldsymbol{\Psi}$ and $\boldsymbol{\Psi}'$, which are directed to the Supervised Comparator with uDTW. For each query-support pair $(\boldsymbol{\Psi}_n, \boldsymbol{\Psi}'_n)$, uDTW computes the base-distance matrix $\mathbf{D}_n$ reweighted by uncertainty $\boldsymbol{\Sigma}_n^\dagger$ to compare $\tau \times \tau'$ blocks, and SigmaNet generates underlying block-wise uncertainty parameters $\boldsymbol{\Sigma}_n$. uDTW finds the warping path with the smallest distance, and returns its Ω_n penalty (uncertainty aggregated along the path).

Specifically, to capture the aleatoric uncertainty of the Euclidean distance (or regression, *etc.*), one should tune the observation noise parameter of sequences. Instead of the homoscedastic model (constant observation noise), we opt for the so-called heteroscedastic aleatoric uncertainty model (the observation noise may vary with each frame/sequence). To this end, we model each path distance by the product of likelihoods of Normal distributions (we also investigate other distributions in Appendix Sec. F).

Our (soft) uncertainty-DTW takes the following generalized form:

$$
\begin{cases}
d^2_{\mathrm{uDTW}}(\boldsymbol{D}, \boldsymbol{\Sigma}^\dagger) = \mathrm{SoftMin}_\gamma \Big(\underbrace{\big[\big\langle \boldsymbol{\Pi}, \boldsymbol{D} \odot \boldsymbol{\Sigma}^\dagger \big\rangle\big]_{\boldsymbol{\Pi} \in \mathcal{A}_{\tau,\tau'}}}_{\boldsymbol{w}} \Big) & (2) \\[2ex]
\Omega(\boldsymbol{\Sigma}) = \mathrm{SoftMinSel}_\gamma \Big(\boldsymbol{w}, \big[\langle \boldsymbol{\Pi}, \log \boldsymbol{\Sigma} \rangle\big]_{\boldsymbol{\Pi} \in \mathcal{A}_{\tau,\tau'}} \Big), & (3)
\end{cases}
$$

where $\boldsymbol{D} \equiv \boldsymbol{D}(\boldsymbol{\Psi}, \boldsymbol{\Psi}')$, $\boldsymbol{\Sigma} \equiv \boldsymbol{\Sigma}(\boldsymbol{\Psi}, \boldsymbol{\Psi}')$ and $\boldsymbol{\Sigma}^\dagger = \mathrm{inv}(\boldsymbol{\Sigma})$,

where $\odot$ is the Hadamard product, $\boldsymbol{\Sigma}^\dagger(\boldsymbol{\Psi}, \boldsymbol{\Psi}')$ is the element-wise inverse of matrix $\boldsymbol{\Sigma} \in \mathbb{R}_+^{\tau \times \tau'} \equiv [\sigma^2(\boldsymbol{\psi}_m, \boldsymbol{\psi}'_n)]_{(m,n) \in \mathcal{I}_\tau \times \mathcal{I}_{\tau'}}$ which contains pair-wise variances between all possible pairings of frame-wise feature representations from sequences $\boldsymbol{\Psi}$ and $\boldsymbol{\Psi}'$. $\mathrm{SoftMin}_\gamma(\boldsymbol{\alpha}) = \sum_i \alpha_i \frac{\exp(-(\alpha_i - \mu_\alpha)/\gamma)}{\sum_j \exp(-(\alpha_j - \mu_\alpha)/\gamma)}$ with μ_α (the mean over coefficients of $\boldsymbol{\alpha}$) subtracted from each coefficient α_i to attain stability of the softmax (into which we feed $(\alpha_i - \mu_\alpha)$). Moreover, $\mathrm{SoftMinSel}_\gamma(\boldsymbol{\alpha}, \boldsymbol{\beta}) = \sum_i \beta_i \frac{\exp(-(\alpha_i - \mu_\alpha)/\gamma)}{\sum_j \exp(-(\alpha_j - \mu_\alpha)/\gamma)}$ is a soft-selector returning $(\beta_{i^*} : i^* = \arg\min_i \alpha_i)$ if γ approaches zero.

Equation (2) yields the uncertainty-weighted time warping distance $d^2_{\mathrm{uDTW}}(\boldsymbol{D}, \boldsymbol{\Sigma}^\dagger)$ between sequences $\boldsymbol{\Psi}$ and $\boldsymbol{\Psi}'$ because $\boldsymbol{D}$ and $\boldsymbol{\Sigma}^\dagger$ are both functions of $(\boldsymbol{\Psi}, \boldsymbol{\Psi}')$.

Equation (3) provides the regularization penalty $\Omega(\boldsymbol{\Sigma})$ for sequences $\boldsymbol{\Psi}$ and $\boldsymbol{\Psi}'$ (as $\boldsymbol{\Sigma}$ is a function of $(\boldsymbol{\Psi}, \boldsymbol{\Psi}')$) which is the aggregation of log-variances along the path with the smallest distance, *i.e.*, path matrix $((\boldsymbol{\Pi}_{i^*} \in \{0,1\}^{\tau \times \tau'}) : i^* = \arg\min_k w_k)$ if $\gamma = 0$, and vector $\boldsymbol{w}$ contains path-aggregated distances for all possible paths of the plan $\mathcal{A}_{\tau,\tau'}$.

Contributions. The celebrated DTW warps the matching path between a pair of sequences to recover the best matching distance under varying temporal within-class dynamics of each sequence. The recovered path, and the distance corresponding to that path, may be suboptimal if frame-wise (or block-wise) features contain noise (frames that are outliers, contain occlusions or large within-class object variations, *etc.*)

To this end, we propose several contributions:

i. We introduce the uncertainty-DTW, dubbed as uDTW, whose role is to take into account the uncertainty of in frame-wise (or block-wise) features

(a) sDTW$_{\gamma=0.01}$ (b) sDTW$_{\gamma=0.1}$ (c) uDTW$_{\gamma=0.01}$ (d) uDTW$_{\gamma=0.1}$ (e) uDTW uncert.

Fig. 2. Plots (a)–(d) show paths of sDTW and uDTW (in white) for a pair of sequences. We power-normalized pixels of plots (by the power of 0.1) to see also darker paths better. With higher γ that controls softness, in (b) & (d) more paths become 'active' (fuzzy effect). In (c), uDTW has two possible routes *vs.* sDTW (a) due to uncertainty modeling. In (e), we visualise uncertainty Σ. We binarize plot (c) and multiply it by the Σ to display uncertainty values on the path (white pixels = high uncertainty). The middle of the main path is deemed uncertain, which explains why an additional path merges in that region with the main path. See also the histogram of values of Σ.

by selecting the path which maximizes the Maximum Likelihood Estimation (MLE). The parameters (such as variance) of a distribution (*i.e.*, the Normal distribution) are thus used within MLE (and uDTW) to model the uncertainty.

ii. As pairs of sequences are often of different lengths, optimizing the free-form variable of variance is impossible. To that end, we equip each of our pipelines with SigmaNet, whose role is to take frames (or blocks) of sequences, and generate the variance end-to-end (the variance is parametrized by SigmaNet).

iii. We provide several pipelines that utilize uDTW for (1) forecasting the evolution of time series, (2) estimating the Fréchet mean of time series, (3) supervised few-shot action recognition, and (4) unsupervised few-shot action recognition.

Notations. $\mathcal{I}_\tau$ is the index set $\{1, 2, ..., \tau\}$. Concatenation of α_i into a vector $\boldsymbol{\alpha}$ is denoted by $[\alpha_i]_{i \in \mathcal{I}_I}$. Concatenation of α_{ij} into matrix $\mathbf{A}$ is denoted by $[\alpha_{ij}]_{(i,j) \in \mathcal{I}_I \times \mathcal{I}_J}$. Dot-product between two matrices equals the dot-product of vectorized $\boldsymbol{\Pi}$ and $\boldsymbol{D}$, that is $\langle \boldsymbol{\Pi}, \boldsymbol{D} \rangle \equiv \langle \text{vec}(\boldsymbol{\Pi}), \text{vec}(\boldsymbol{D}) \rangle$. Mathcal symbols are sets, *e.g.*, $\mathcal{A}$ is a transportation plan, capitalized bold symbols are matrices, *e.g.*, $\boldsymbol{D}$ is the distance matrix, lowercase bold symbols are vectors, *e.g.*, $\boldsymbol{w}$ contains weighted distances. Regular fonts are scalars.

1.1 Similarity Learning with uDTW

In further chapters, based on the distance in Eq. (2) and the regularization term in Eq. (3), we define specific loss functions for several problems such as forecasting the evolution of time series, clustering time series or even matching sequence pairs in few-shot action recognition. Below is an example of a generic similarity learning loss:

$$\arg\min_{\mathcal{P}} \sum_n \ell\left(d_{\text{uDTW}}^2(\boldsymbol{D}(\boldsymbol{\Psi}_n, \boldsymbol{\Psi}_n'), \boldsymbol{\Sigma}^\dagger(\boldsymbol{\Psi}_n, \boldsymbol{\Psi}_n')), \delta_n\right) + \beta\Omega(\boldsymbol{\Sigma}(\boldsymbol{\Psi}_n, \boldsymbol{\Psi}_n')), \quad (4)$$

or

$$\arg\min_{\mathcal{P}, \boldsymbol{\Sigma} > 0} \sum_n \ell\left(d_{\text{uDTW}}^2(\boldsymbol{D}(\boldsymbol{\Psi}_n, \boldsymbol{\Psi}_n'), \boldsymbol{\Sigma}^\dagger), \delta_n\right) + \beta\Omega(\boldsymbol{\Sigma}), \quad (5)$$

where $\boldsymbol{\Psi}_n = f(\mathbf{X}_n; \mathcal{P})$ and $\boldsymbol{\Psi}_n' = f(\mathbf{X}_n'; \mathcal{P})$ are obtained from some backbone encoder $f(\cdot; \mathcal{P})$ with parameters $\mathcal{P}$ and $(\mathbf{X}_n, \mathbf{X}_n') \in \mathcal{X}$ is a sequence pair to compare with the similarity label $\delta_n \in \{0, 1\}$ (where $\delta_n = 0$ if $y_n = y_n'$ and $\delta_n = 1$ otherwise), (y_n, y_n') is a pair of class labels for $(\boldsymbol{\Psi}_n, \boldsymbol{\Psi}_n')$, and $\beta \geq 0$ controls the penalty for high matching uncertainty. Figure 2 illustrates the impact of uncertainty on uDTW.

Note that minimizing Eq. (5) w.r.t. $(\mathcal{P}, \boldsymbol{\Sigma})$ assumes that $\boldsymbol{\Sigma} \in \mathbb{R}_+^{\tau \times \tau'}$ is a free variable to minimize over (derivation in Section 1.2). However, as sequence pairs vary in length, $i.e.$, $\tau \neq \tau'$, optimizing one global $\boldsymbol{\Sigma}$ is impossible (its size changes). Thus, for problems we tackle, we minimize loss functions with the distance/penalty in Eq. (4) and (5) where $\boldsymbol{\Sigma}$ is parametrized by $(\boldsymbol{\Psi}_n, \boldsymbol{\Psi}_n')$:

$$d_{\text{uDTW}\bullet}^2(\boldsymbol{\Psi}, \boldsymbol{\Psi}') \equiv d_{\text{uDTW}}^2(\boldsymbol{D}(\boldsymbol{\Psi}, \boldsymbol{\Psi}'), \boldsymbol{\Sigma}^\dagger(\boldsymbol{\Psi}, \boldsymbol{\Psi}')), \quad (6)$$
$$\Omega_\bullet(\boldsymbol{\Psi}, \boldsymbol{\Psi}') \equiv \Omega(\boldsymbol{\Sigma}(\boldsymbol{\Psi}, \boldsymbol{\Psi}')). \quad (7)$$

To that end, we devise a small MLP unit $\sigma(\cdot; \mathcal{P}_\sigma)$ or $\sigma(\cdot, \cdot; \mathcal{P}_\sigma)$ and obtain:

$$\boldsymbol{\Sigma} = 0.5 \cdot [(\sigma^2(\boldsymbol{\psi}_m; \mathcal{P}_\sigma) + \sigma^2(\boldsymbol{\psi}_n'; \mathcal{P}_\sigma))]_{(m,n) \in \mathcal{I}_\tau \times \mathcal{I}_{\tau'}} \quad (8)$$
or
$$\boldsymbol{\Sigma}' = [\sigma^2(\boldsymbol{\psi}_m, \boldsymbol{\psi}_n'; \mathcal{P}_\sigma)]_{(m,n) \in \mathcal{I}_\tau \times \mathcal{I}_{\tau'}}, \quad (9)$$

where Eq. (8) uses additive variance terms generated for individual frames $\boldsymbol{\psi}_m$ and $\boldsymbol{\psi}_n'$, whereas (9) is a jointly generated variance for $(\boldsymbol{\psi}_m, \boldsymbol{\psi}_n')$.

1.2   Derivation of uDTW

We proceed by modeling an arbitrary path $\boldsymbol{\Pi}_i$ from the transportation plan of $\mathcal{A}_{\tau, \tau'}$ as the following Maximum Likelihood Estimation (MLE) problem:

$$\arg\max_{\{\sigma_{mn}\}_{(m,n) \in \boldsymbol{\Pi}_i}} \prod_{(m,n) \in \boldsymbol{\Pi}_i} p(\|\boldsymbol{\psi}_m - \boldsymbol{\psi}_n'\|, \sigma_{mn}^2), \quad (10)$$

where p may be some arbitrary distribution, σ are distribution parameters, and $\| \cdot \|$ is an arbitrary norm. For the Normal distribution $\mathcal{N}$ which relies on the squared Euclidean distance $\| \cdot \|_2^2$, we have:

$$\underset{\{\sigma_{mn}\}_{(m,n)\in\Pi_i}}{\arg\max} \prod_{(m,n)\in\Pi_i} \mathcal{N}(\boldsymbol{\psi}_m; \boldsymbol{\psi}_n', \sigma_{mn}^2) \tag{11}$$

$$= \underset{\{\sigma_{mn}\}_{(m,n)\in\Pi_i}}{\arg\max} \log \prod_{(m,n)\in\Pi_i} \frac{1}{(2\pi)^{\frac{d'}{2}}\sigma^{d'}} \exp\left(-\frac{\|\boldsymbol{\psi}_m - \boldsymbol{\psi}_n'\|_2^2}{\sigma_{mn}^2}\right) \tag{12}$$

$$= \underset{\{\sigma_{mn}\}_{(m,n)\in\Pi_i}}{\arg\max} \sum_{(m,n)\in\Pi_i} -\frac{d'}{2}\log(2\pi) - d'\log(\sigma) - \frac{\|\boldsymbol{\psi}_m - \boldsymbol{\psi}_n'\|_2^2}{\sigma_{mn}^2} \tag{13}$$

$$= \underset{\{\sigma_{mn}\}_{(m,n)\in\Pi_i}}{\arg\min} \sum_{(m,n)\in\Pi_i} d'\log(\sigma) + \frac{\|\boldsymbol{\psi}_m - \boldsymbol{\psi}_n'\|_2^2}{\sigma_{mn}^2}, \tag{14}$$

where d' is the length of feature vectors $\boldsymbol{\psi}$. Having recovered uncertainty parameters $\{\sigma_{mn}\}_{(m,n)\in\Pi_i}$, we obtain a combination of penalty terms and reweighted squared Euclidean distances:

$$\beta\Omega_{\Pi_i} + d_{\Pi_i}^2 = \sum_{(m,n)\in\Pi_i} \beta\log(\sigma_{mn}) + \frac{\|\boldsymbol{\psi}_m - \boldsymbol{\psi}_n'\|_2^2}{\sigma_{mn}^2}, \tag{15}$$

where $\beta \geq 0$ (generally $\beta \neq d'$) adjusts the penalty for large uncertainty. Separating the uncertainty penalty $\log(\sigma_{mn})$ from the uncertainty-weighted distance (both aggregated along path Π_i) yields:

$$\begin{cases} d_{\Pi_i}^2 = \left\langle \boldsymbol{\Pi}_i, \boldsymbol{D}(\boldsymbol{\Psi}, \boldsymbol{\Psi}') \odot \boldsymbol{\Sigma}^\dagger \right\rangle \\ \Omega_{\Pi_i} = \left\langle \boldsymbol{\Pi}_i, \log\boldsymbol{\Sigma} \right\rangle, \end{cases} \tag{16}$$

where $\boldsymbol{D} \in \mathbb{R}_+^{\tau\times\tau'} \equiv \left[\frac{d_2^2(\boldsymbol{\psi}_m, \boldsymbol{\psi}_n')}{\sigma_{mn}^2}\right]_{(m,n)\in\mathcal{I}_\tau\times\mathcal{I}_{\tau'}}$ and $\boldsymbol{\Sigma} \in \mathbb{R}_+^{\tau\times\tau'} \equiv [\sigma_{mn}^2]_{(m,n)\in\mathcal{I}_\tau\times\mathcal{I}_{\tau'}}$. Derivations for other distributions, *i.e.*, Laplace or Cauchy, follow the same reasoning.

2   Related Work

Different Flavors of Dynamic Time Warping. DTW [6], which seeks a minimum cost alignment between time series is computed by dynamic programming in quadratic time, is not differentiable and is known to get trapped in bad local minima. In contrast, soft-DTW (sDTW) [7] addresses the above issues by replacing the minimum over alignments with a soft minimum, which has the effect of inducing a 'likelihood' field over all possible alignments. However, sDTW has been successfully applied in many computer vision tasks including audio/music score alignment [31], action recognition [4,39], and end-to-end differentiable text-to-speech synthesis [10]. Despite its successes, sDTW has some limitations: (i) it can be negative when used as a loss (ii) it may still get trapped in bad local minima. Thus, soft-DTW divergences (sDTW div.) [3], inspired by sDTW, attempts to overcome such issues.

Other approaches inspired by DTW have been used to improve the inference or adapt to modified or additional constraints, *i.e.*, OPT [38] and OWDA [40] treat the alignment as the optimal transport problem with temporal regularization. TAP [39] directly predicts the alignment through a lightweight CNN, thus is does not follow a principled transportation plan, and is not guaranteed to find a minimum cost path.

Our uDTW differs from these methods in that the transportation plan is executed under the uncertainty estimation, thus various feature-level noises and outliers are less likely to lead to the selection of a sub-optimal cost path.

Alignment-Based Time Series Problems. Distance between sequences plays an important role in time series retrieval [40], forecasting [3,7], classification [3, 7,9,49], clustering [12,35], *etc.* Various temporal nuisance noises such as initial states, different sampling rates, local distortions, and execution speeds make the measurement of distance between sequences difficult. To tackle these issues, typical feature-based methods use RNNs to encode sequences and measure the distance between corresponding features [34]. Other existing methods [20,43, 45] either encode each sequence into features that are invariant to temporal variations [1,26] or adopt alignment for temporal correspondence calibration [38]. However, none of these methods is modeling the aleatoric uncertainty. As we model it along the time warping path, the observation noise may vary with each frame or block.

Few-Shot Action Recognition. Most existing few-shot action recognition methods [44,46,47] follow the metric learning paradigm. Signal Level Deep Metric Learning [30] and Skeleton-DML [29] one-shot FSL approaches encode signals into images, extract features using a deep residual CNN and apply multi-similarity miner losses. TAEN [2] and FAN [41] encode actions into representations and apply vector-wise metrics.

Most methods identify the importance of temporal alignment for handling the non-linear temporal variations, and various alignment-based models are proposed to compare the sequence pairs, *e.g.*, permutation-invariant spatial-temporal attention reweighted distance in ARN [50], a variant of DTW used in OTAM [4], temporal attentive relation network [32], a two-stage temporal alignment network (TA2N) [22], a temporal CrossTransformer [33], a learnable sequence matching distance called TAP [39].

In all cases, temporal alignment is a well-recognized tool, however lacking the uncertainty modeling, which impacts the quality of alignment. Such a gap in the literature inspires our work on uncertainty-DTW.

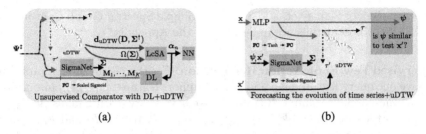

(a)   (b)

Fig. 3. In (a) is the unsupervised comparator for unsupervised few-shot action recognition. The unsupervised head is wired with the Encoding Network from Fig. 1, and trained from scratch without labels. In (b) is the pipeline for forecasting the evolution of time series (a.k.a. multistep-ahead prediction).

3   Pipeline Formulations

Below we provide our several pipeline formulations for which uDTW is used as an indispensable component embedded with the goal of measuring the distance for warped paths under uncertainty.

3.1   Few-Shot Action Recognition

For both supervised and unsupervised few-shot pipelines, we employ the Encoder Network (EN) and the Supervised Comparator (similarity learning) as in Fig. 1, or Unupervised Comparator (based on dictionary learning) as in Fig. 3a.

Encoding Network (EN). Our EN contains a simple 3-layer MLP unit (FC, ReLU, FC, ReLU, Dropout, FC), GNN, with transformer [11] and FC. The MLP unit takes M neighboring frames, each with J skeleton body joints given by Cartesian coordinates (x, y, z), forming one temporal block[1]. In total, depending on stride S, we obtain some τ temporal blocks (each block captures the short temporal dependency), whereas the long temporal dependency will be modeled by uDTW. Each temporal block is encoded by the MLP into a $d \times J$ dimensional feature map. Subsequently, query feature maps of size τ and support feature maps of size τ' are forwarded to a simple linear GNN model, and transformer, and an FC layer, which returns $\boldsymbol{\Psi} \in \mathbb{R}^{d' \times \tau}$ query feature maps and $\boldsymbol{\Psi}' \in \mathbb{R}^{d' \times \tau'}$ support feature maps. Such encoded feature maps are passed to the Supervised Comparator with uDTW.

Specifically, let support maps $\boldsymbol{\Psi}' \equiv [f(\boldsymbol{X}'_1; \mathcal{P}), ..., f(\boldsymbol{X}'_{\tau'}; \mathcal{P})]$ and query maps $\boldsymbol{\Psi} \equiv [f(\boldsymbol{X}_1; \mathcal{P}), ..., f(\boldsymbol{X}_{\tau}; \mathcal{P})]$ (where $\boldsymbol{\Psi} \in \mathbb{R}^{d' \times \tau}, \boldsymbol{\Psi}' \in \mathbb{R}^{d' \times \tau'}$), for query and support frames per block $\mathbf{X}, \mathbf{X}' \in \mathbb{R}^{3 \times J \times M}$. We define $f(\mathbf{X}; \mathcal{P}) = \text{FC}(\text{Transf}(\text{S}^2\text{GC}(\text{MLP}(\mathbf{X}; \mathcal{P}_{MLP}); \mathcal{P}_{S^2GC}); \mathcal{P}_{Transf}); \mathcal{P}_{FC})$, where $\mathcal{P} \equiv [\mathcal{P}_{MLP}, \mathcal{P}_{S^2GC}, \mathcal{P}_{Transf}, \mathcal{P}_{FC}, \mathcal{P}_{SN}]$ is the set of parameters of EN, where $\mathcal{P}_{SN}$

---

[1] We use temporal blocks as they were shown more robust than frame-wise FSAR [50] models.

are parameters of SigmaNet, and S^2GC is a Simple Spectral Graph Convolution (S^2GC) [51] whose details are in Sec. H.3 of the Appendix.

Supervised Few-Shot Action Recognition. For the N-way Z-shot problem, we have one query feature map and $N \times Z$ support feature maps per episode. We form a mini-batch containing B episodes. We have query feature maps $\{\boldsymbol{\Psi}_b\}_{b \in \mathcal{I}_B}$ and support feature maps $\{\boldsymbol{\Psi}'_{b,n,z}\}_{b \in \mathcal{I}_B, n \in \mathcal{I}_N, z \in \mathcal{I}_Z}$. Moreover, $\boldsymbol{\Psi}_b$ and $\boldsymbol{\Psi}'_{b,1,:}$ share the same class (drawn from N classes per episode), forming the subset $C^{\ddagger} \equiv \{c_1, ..., c_N\} \subset \mathcal{I}_C \equiv \mathcal{C}$. To be precise, labels $y(\boldsymbol{\Psi}_b) = y(\boldsymbol{\Psi}'_{b,1,z}), \forall b \in \mathcal{I}_B, z \in \mathcal{I}_Z$ while $y(\boldsymbol{\Psi}_b) \neq y(\boldsymbol{\Psi}'_{b,n,z}), \forall b \in \mathcal{I}_B, n \in \mathcal{I}_N \setminus \{1\}, z \in \mathcal{I}_Z$. Thus the similarity label $\delta_1 = 0$, whereas $\delta_{n \neq 1} = 1$. Note that the selection of $C^{\ddagger}$ per episode is random. For the N-way Z-shot protocol, the Supervised Comparator is minimized w.r.t. $\mathcal{P}$ ($\boldsymbol{\Psi}_b$ and $\boldsymbol{\Psi}'$ depend on $\mathcal{P}$) as:

$$\arg\min_{\mathcal{P}} \sum_{b \in \mathcal{I}_B} \sum_{n \in \mathcal{I}_N} \sum_{z \in \mathcal{I}_Z} \left(d^2_{\mathrm{uDTW}\bullet}(\boldsymbol{\Psi}_b, \boldsymbol{\Psi}'_{b,n,z}) - \delta_n \right)^2 + \beta \Omega_{\bullet}(\boldsymbol{\Psi}_b, \boldsymbol{\Psi}'_{b,n,z}). \quad (17)$$

Unsupervised Few-Shot Action Recognition. Below we propose a very simple unsupervised variant with so-called Unsupervised Comparator. The key idea is that with uDTW, invariant to local temporal speed changes can be used to learn a dictionary which, with some dictionary coding method should outperform at reconstructing the sequences. This means we can learn an unsupervised comparator by projecting sequences onto the dictionary space. To this end, let the protocol remain as for the supervised few-shot learning with the exception that class labels are not used during training, and only support images in testing are labeled for sake of evaluation the accuracy by deciding which support representation each query is the closest to in the nearest neighbor sense.

Firstly, in each training episode, we combine the query sequences $\boldsymbol{\Psi}_b$ with the support sequences $\boldsymbol{\Psi}'_{b,n,z}$ into episode sequences denoted as $\boldsymbol{\Psi}^{\ddagger}_{b,n}$ where $b \in \mathcal{I}_B$ enumerates over B episodes, and $n \in \mathcal{I}_{(N \cdot Z + 1)}$. For the feature coding, we use Locality-constrained Soft Assignment (LCSA) [19, 21, 25] and a simple dictionary update based on the least squares computation.

For each episode $b \in \mathcal{I}_B$, we iterate over the following three steps:

i. The LCSA coding step which expresses each $\boldsymbol{\Psi}^{\ddagger}_{b,n}$ as $\boldsymbol{\alpha}_{b,n} \in \mathbb{R}^K_+$ that assign $\boldsymbol{\Psi}^{\ddagger}_{b,n}$ into a dictionary with K sequences $\boldsymbol{M}_1, ..., \boldsymbol{M}_K \in \mathbb{R}^{d' \times \tau'}$ (dictionary anchors):

$$\forall_{k,n}, \ \alpha_{k,b,n} = \begin{cases} \dfrac{\exp\left(-\frac{1}{\gamma'} d^2_{\mathrm{uDTW}\bullet}\left(\boldsymbol{\Psi}^{\ddagger}_{b,n}, M_k\right)\right)}{\displaystyle\sum_{l \in \mathcal{M}(\boldsymbol{\Psi}^{\ddagger}_{b,n}; K')} \exp\left(-\frac{1}{\gamma'} d^2_{\mathrm{uDTW}\bullet}\left(\boldsymbol{\Psi}^{\ddagger}_{b,n}, M_l\right)\right)} & \text{if } M_k \in \mathcal{M}\left(\boldsymbol{\Psi}^{\ddagger}_{b,n}; K'\right), \\[4mm] 0 & \text{otherwise,} \end{cases} \quad (18)$$

where $0 < K' \leq K$ is a subset size for K' nearest anchors of $\boldsymbol{\Psi}^{\ddagger}_{b,n}$ retrieved by operation $\mathcal{M}(\boldsymbol{\Psi}^{\ddagger}_{b,n}; K')$ (based on uDTW) from $\boldsymbol{M}_1, ..., \boldsymbol{M}_K$, τ' is set to the mean of τ (over training set), and $\gamma' = 0.7$ is a so-called smoothing factor;

ii. The dictionary update step updates $M_1, ..., M_K$ given $\alpha_{b,n}$ from Eq. (18):
for i=1,...,dict_iter:

$$\forall_k, \; M_k := M_k - \lambda_{\mathrm{DL}} \sum_{n=1}^{N \cdot Z + 1} \nabla_{M_k} d^2_{\mathrm{uDTW} \bullet} \left(\Psi^{\ddagger}_{b,n}, \sum_{l=1}^{K} \alpha_{l,b,n} M_l \right), \quad (19)$$

where dict_iter is set to 10 and $\lambda_{\mathrm{DL}} = 0.001$;

iii. The main loss for the Feature Encoder update step is given as ($\lambda_{\mathrm{EN}} = 0.001$):

$$\mathcal{P} := \mathcal{P} - \lambda_{\mathrm{EN}} \sum_{n=1}^{N \cdot Z + 1} \nabla_{\mathcal{P}} d^2_{\mathrm{uDTW} \bullet} \left(\Psi^{\ddagger}_{b,n}, M' \right) + \beta \Omega_{\bullet} \left(\Psi^{\ddagger}_{b,n}, M' \right), \quad (20)$$

where $M' = \sum_{l=1}^{K} \alpha_{l,b,n} M_l$.

During testing, we use the learnt dictionary, pass new support and query sequences via Eq. (18) and obtain α codes. Subsequently, we compare the LCSA code of the query sequence with LCSA codes of support sequences via the histogram intersection kernel. The closest match in the support set determines the test label of the query sequence.

3.2   Time Series Forecasting and Classification

One of key applications of DTW and sDTW is learning with time series, including forecasting the evolution of time series as in Fig. 3b and time series classification.

Forecasting the Evolution of Time Series. Let $\mathbf{x} \in \mathbb{R}^t$ and $\mathbf{x}' \in \mathbb{R}^{\tau - t}$ be the training and testing parts of one time series corresponding to timesteps $1, ..., t$ and $t + 1, ..., \tau$, respectively. The goal is to learn encoder $f(\mathbf{x}; \mathcal{P}) \in \mathbb{R}^{\tau - t}$ which will be able to take $\mathbf{x}$ as input, learn to translate it to $\mathbf{x}'$. Figure 3b show the full pipeline. We took the Encoding Network from the original soft-DTW pipeline [7]. Our training objective is:

$$\arg \min_{\mathcal{P}} \sum_{n \in \mathcal{I}_N} d^2_{\mathrm{uDTW} \bullet} (\psi_n, \mathbf{x}'_n) + \beta \Omega_{\bullet} (\psi_n, \mathbf{x}'_n), \quad (21)$$

where $\psi = f(\mathbf{x}; \mathcal{P})$ and N is the number of training time series, $\mathcal{P} \equiv [\mathcal{P}_{MLP}, \mathcal{P}_{SN}]$ is the set of parameters of EN and SigmaNet. In order to obtain Σ, vectors ψ and $\mathbf{x}'$ are passed via SigmaNet. After training, at the test time, for a previously unseen testing sample $\mathbf{x}$, $f(\cdot)$ has to predict the remaining part of the time series given by $\mathbf{x}'$.

Time Series Classification. Below we follow the setting for this classical task according to the original soft-DTW paper [7], and define the **nearest centroid** classifier. We estimate the Fréchet mean of training time series of each class separately. We do not use any Encoding Network but the raw features. Let $\mathbf{x} \in \mathbb{R}^\tau$ be training samples and $\boldsymbol{\mu} \in \mathbb{R}^{\tau'}$ be class prototypes (τ' is set to average of τ across all classes). We have:

$$\forall_c, \; \underset{\mathcal{P}}{\arg\min} \sum_{n \in \mathcal{I}_{N_c}} d^2_{\text{uDTW}\bullet}(\mathbf{x}_n, \boldsymbol{\mu}_c) + \beta\Omega_\bullet(\mathbf{x}_n, \boldsymbol{\mu}_c), \tag{22}$$

where N_c is the number of samples for class $c \in \mathcal{I}_C$ and $\mathcal{P} \equiv [\mathcal{P}_{SN}, \boldsymbol{\mu}_c]$. During testing, we apply $\arg\min_{c \in \mathcal{I}_C} d^2_{\text{uDTW}\bullet}(\mathbf{x}, \boldsymbol{\mu}_c) + \beta\Omega_\bullet(\mathbf{x}, \boldsymbol{\mu}_c)$ for $\mathbf{x}$ to find its nearest neighbor and label it. The variances of $\mathbf{x}$ are recovered through SigmaNet while variances of $\boldsymbol{\mu}_c$ were obtained during training (adding both yields $\boldsymbol{\Sigma}$ of testing sample). As in soft-DTW paper [7], we use uDTW to directly find the **nearest neighbor** of $\mathbf{x}$ across training samples to label $\mathbf{x}$ (for uncertainty, we use SigmaNet from the nearest centroid task).

4 Experiments

Below we apply uDTW in several scenarios such as (i) forecasting the evolution of time series, (ii) clustering/classifying time series, (iii) supervised few-shot action recognition, and (iv) unsupervised few-shot action recognition.

Datasets. The following datasets are used in our experiments:

i. *UCR* archive [8] is a dataset for time series classification archive. This dataset contains a wide variety of fields (astronomy, geology, medical imaging) and lengths, and can be used for time series classification/clustering and forecasting tasks.

ii. *NTU RGB+D (NTU-60)* [36] contains 56,880 video sequences and over 4 million frames. NTU-60 has variable sequence lengths and high intra-class variations.

iii. *NTU RGB+D 120 (NTU-120)* [24], an extension of NTU-60, contains 120 action classes (daily/health-related), and 114,480 RGB+D video samples captured with 106 distinct human subjects from 155 different camera viewpoints.

iv. *Kinetics* [16] is a large-scale collection of 650,000 video clips that cover 400/600/700 human action classes. It includes human-object interactions such as *playing instruments*, as well as human-human interactions such as *shaking hands* and *hugging*. We follow approach [48] and use the estimated joint locations in the pixel coordinate system as the input to our pipeline. As OpenPose produces the 2D body joint coordinates and Kinetics-400 does not offer multiview or depth data, we use a network of Martinez et al. [27] pre-trained on Human3.6M [5], combined with the 2D OpenPose output to estimate 3D coordinates from 2D coordinates. The 2D OpenPose and the latter network give us (x, y) and z coordinates, respectively.

4.1 Fréchet Mean of Time Series

Below, we visually inspect the Fréchet mean for the Euclidean, sDTW and our uDTW distance, respectively.

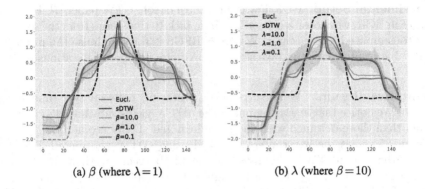

(a) β (where $\lambda = 1$)   (b) λ (where $\beta = 10$)

Fig. 4. Interpolation between two time series (grey and black dashed lines) on the Gun Point dataset. We compute the barycenter by solving $\arg\min\limits_{\mu, \sigma_\mu} \sum_{n=1}^2 d^2_{\mathrm{uDTW}}(D, \Sigma^\dagger) + \beta\Omega(\Sigma) + \lambda\Omega'(\Sigma)$ where $D = (\mathbf{x}_n \mathbf{1}^\top - \mathbf{1}\mu^\top)^2$ and $\Sigma = \mathbf{1}\mathbf{1}^\top + \mathbf{1}\sigma_\mu^\top$ where $\mathbf{x}_n$ is the given n-th time series. $\beta \geq 0$ controls the penalty for high matching uncertainty, Ω' is defined as in Eq. (3) but element-wise $\log \Sigma$ is replaced by element-wise $(\Sigma - 1)^2$ so that $\lambda \geq 0$ favours uncertainty to remain close to one. β and λ control the uncertainty estimation and yield different barycenters than the Euclidean (green color) and sDTW (blue color) distances. As Ω and Ω' act similar, we only use Ω in our experiments. (Color figure online)

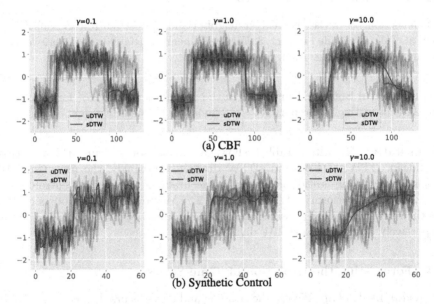

Fig. 5. Comparison of barycenter based on sDTW or uDTW on CBF and Synthetic Control. We visualize uncertainty around the barycenters in red color for uDTW. Our uDTW generates reasonable barycenters even when higher γ values are used, *e.g.*, $\gamma = 10.0$. Higher γ value leads to smooth barycenter but introducing higher uncertainty. (Color figure online)

Experimental Setup. We follow the protocol of soft-DTW paper [7]. For each dataset in UCR, we choose a class at random, pick 10 time series from the selected class to compute its barycenter. We use L-BFGS [23] to minimise the proposed uDTW barycenter objective. We set the maximum number of iterations to 100.

Qualitative Results. We first perform averaging between two time series (Fig. 4). We notice that averaging under the uDTW yields substantially different results than those obtained with the Euclidean and sDTW geometry.

Figure 5 shows the barycenters obtained using sDTW and our uDTW. We observe that our uDTW yields more reasonable barycenters than sDTW even when large γ are used, $e.g.$, for $\gamma = 10$ (right column of plots in Fig. 5), the change points of red curve look sharper. We also notice that both uDTW and sDTW with low smoothing parameter $\gamma = 0.1$ can get stuck in some bad local minima, but our uDTW has fewer sharp peaks compared with sDTW (barycenters of uDTW are improved by the uncertainty measure). Moreover, higher γ values smooth the barycenter but introducing higher uncertainty (see uncertainty visualization around the barycenters by comparing, $e.g.$, $\gamma = 0.1$ $vs.$ $\gamma = 10.0$). With $\gamma = 1$, the barycenters of sDTW and uDTW match well with the time series. More visualizations can be found in Appendix Sec. D.

4.2   Classification of Time Series

In this section, we devise the nearest neighbor and nearest centroid classifiers [13] with uDTW, as detailed in Sect. 3. For the K-nearest neighbor classifier, we used softmax for the final decision. See Appendix Sec. H.4 for details.

Experimental Setup. We use 50% of the data for training, 25% for validation and 25% for testing. We report $K = 1$, 2 and 3 for the nearest neighbor classifier.

Quantitative Results. Table 1 shows a comparison of our uDTW versus Euclidean, DTW, sDTW, and sDTW div. Unsurprisingly, the use of uDTW for barycenter computation improves the accuracy of the nearest centroid classifier, and it outperforms sDTW div. by $\sim 2\%$. Moreover, uDTW boosts results for the nearest neighbor classifier given $K=1$, 2 and 3 by 1.4%, 1.7% and 3.2%, respectively, compared to sDTW div.

4.3   Forecasting the Evolution of Time Series

Experimental setup. We use the training and test sets pre-defined in the UCR archive. For both training and test, we use the first 60% of timesteps of series as input and the remaining 40% as output, ignoring the class information.

Table 1. Classification accuracy (mean±std) on UCR archive by the nearest neighbor and the nearest centroid classifiers. In the column we indicate which distance was used for computing the class prototypes. K is the number of nearest neighbors in this context.

	Nearest neighbor			Nearest centroid
	$K = 1$	$K = 3$	$K = 5$	
Euclidean	71.2±17.5	72.3±18.1	73.0±16.7	61.3±20.1
DTW [6]	74.2±16.6	75.0±17.0	75.4±15.8	65.9±18.8
sDTW [7]	76.2±16.6	77.2±15.9	78.0±16.5	70.5±17.6
sDTW div. [3]	78.6±16.2	79.5±16.7	80.1±16.5	70.9±17.8
uDTW	80.0±15.0	81.2±17.8	83.3±16.2	72.2±16.0

Qualitative Results. The visualization of the predictions are given in Fig. 6. Although the predictions under the sDTW and uDTW losses sometimes agree with each other, they can be visibly different. Predictions under uDTW can confidently predict the abrupt and sharp changes. More visualizations can be found in Appendix Sec. E.

Quantitative Results. We also provide quantitive results to validate the effectiveness of uDTW. We use ECG5000 dataset from the UCR archive which is composed of 5000 electrocardiograms (ECG) (500 for training and 4500 for testing) of length 140. To better evaluate the predictions, we use 2 different metrics (i) MSE for the predicted errors of each time step (ii) DTW, sDTW div. and uDTW for comparing the 'shape' of time series. We use such shape metrics for evaluation as the length of time series generally varies, and the MSE metric may lead to biased results which ignore the shape trend of time series. We then use the Student's t-test (with significance level 0.05) to highlight the best performance in each experiment (averaged over 100 runs). Table 2 shows that our uDTW achieves almost the best performance on both MSE and shape evaluation metrics (lower score is better).

4.4 Few-Shot Action Recognition

Below, we use uDTW as a distance in our objectives for few-shot action recognition (AR) tasks. We implement supervised and unsupervised pipelines (which is also novel).

Experimental Setup. For NTU-120, we follow the standard one-shot protocols [24]. Base on this protocol, we create a similar one-shot protocol for NTU-60, with 50/10 action classes used for training/testing respectively (see Appendix Sec. C for details). We also evaluate the model on both 2D and 3D Kinetics-skeleton. We split the whole Kinetics-skeleton into 200 actions for training (the

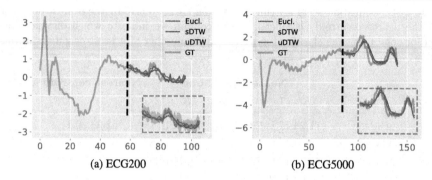

Fig. 6. Given the first part of a time series, we train 3 multi-layer perception (MLP) to predict the remaining part, we use the Euclidean, sDTW or uDTW distance per MLP. We use ECG200 and ECG5000 in UCR archive, and display the prediction obtained for the given test sample with either of these 3 distances and the ground truth (GT). Oftentimes, we observe that uDTW helps predict the sudden changes well.

Table 2. Time series forecasting results evaluated with MSE, DTW, sDTW div. and uDTW metrics on ECG5000, averaged over 100 runs (mean±std). Best method(s) are highlighted in bold using Student's t-test. Column-wise distances indicate the distance used during training. Row-wise distances indicate the distance used to compare prediction with the groundtruth at the test time (lower values are better).

	MSE	DTW	sDTW div.	uDTW
Euclidean	**32.1±1.62**	20.0±0.18	15.3±0.16	14.4±0.18
sDTW [7]	38.6±6.30	**17.2±0.80**	22.6±3.59	32.1±2.25
sDTW div. [3]	24.6±1.37	38.9±5.33	**20.0±2.44**	15.4±1.62
uDTW	23.0±1.22	**16.7±0.08**	16.8±1.62	**8.27±0.79**

rest is used for testing). We choose Matching Nets (MatchNets) and Prototypical Net (ProtoNet) as baselines as these two models are very popular baselines, and we adapt these methods to skeleton-based action recognition. We reshape and resize each video block into 224×224 color image, and pass this image into MatchNets and ProtoNet to learn the feature representation per video block. We compare uDTW *vs.* Euclidean, sDTW, sDTW div. and recent TAP.

Quantitative Results. Table 3, 4 and 5 show that our uDTW performs better than sDTW and sDTW div. on both supervised and unsupervised few-shot action recognition. On Kinetics-skeleton dataset, we gain 2.4% and 4.4% improvements on 3D skeletons for supervised and unsupervised settings. On supervised setting, we outperform TAP by ∼ 4% and 2% on NTU-60 and NTU-120 respectively. Moreover, we outperform sDTW by ∼ 2% and 3% on NTU-60 and NTU-120 for the unsupervised setting. More evaluations on few-shot action recognition are in Appendix Sec. F.

Table 3. Evaluations on NTU-60.

#classes	10	20	30	40	50
			Supervised		
MatchNets [42]	46.1	48.6	53.3	56.3	58.8
ProtoNet [37]	47.2	51.1	54.3	58.9	63.0
TAP [39]	54.2	57.3	61.7	64.7	68.3
Euclidean	38.5	42.2	45.1	48.3	50.9
sDTW [7]	53.7	56.2	60.0	63.9	67.8
sDTW div. [3]	54.0	57.3	62.1	65.7	69.0
uDTW	56.9	61.2	64.8	68.3	72.4
			Unsupervised		
Euclidean	20.9	23.7	26.3	30.0	33.1
sDTW [7]	35.6	45.2	53.3	56.7	61.7
sDTW div. [3]	36.0	46.1	54.0	57.2	62.0
uDTW	37.0	48.3	55.3	58.0	63.3

Table 4. Evaluations on NTU-120.

#classes	20	40	60	80	100
			Supervised		
MatchNets [42]	20.5	23.4	25.1	28.7	30.0
ProtoNet [37]	21.7	24.0	25.9	29.2	32.1
TAP [39]	31.2	37.7	40.9	44.5	47.3
Euclidean	18.7	21.3	24.9	27.5	30.0
sDTW [7]	30.3	37.2	39.7	44.0	46.8
sDTW div. [3]	30.8	38.1	40.0	44.7	47.3
uDTW	32.2	39.0	41.2	45.3	49.0
			Unsupervised		
Euclidean	13.5	16.3	20.0	24.9	26.2
sDTW [7]	20.1	25.3	32.0	36.9	40.9
sDTW div. [3]	20.8	26.0	33.2	37.5	42.3
uDTW	22.7	28.3	35.9	39.4	44.0

Table 5. Evaluations on 2D and 3D Kinetics-skeleton.

	Supervised		Unsupervised	
	2D	3D	2D	3D
Euclidean	21.2	23.1	12.7	13.3
TAP [39]	32.9	36.0	-	-
sDTW [7]	34.7	39.6	23.3	28.3
sDTW div. [3]	35.0	40.1	24.0	28.9
uDTW	35.5	42.0	25.9	32.7

5 Conclusions

We have introduced the uncertainty-DTW which handles the uncertainty estimation of frame- and/or block-wise features to improve the path warping of the celebrated soft-DTW. Our uDTW produces the uncertainty-weighted distance along the path and returns the regularization penalty aggregated along the path, which follows sound principles of classifier regularization. We have provided several pipelines for time series forecasting, and supervised and unsupervised action recognition, which use uDTW as a distance. Our simple uDTW achieves better sequence alignment in several benchmarks.

References

1. Abid, A., Zou, J.: AutoWarp: learning a warping distance from unlabeled time series using sequence autoencoders. In: NIPS 2018. Curran Associates Inc., Red Hook (2018)

2. Ben-Ari, R., Shpigel Nacson, M., Azulai, O., Barzelay, U., Rotman, D.: TAEN: temporal aware embedding network for few-shot action recognition. In: 2021 IEEE/CVF Conference on Computer Vision and Pattern Recognition Workshops (CVPRW), pp. 2780–2788 (2021)

3. Blondel, M., Mensch, A., Vert, J.P.: Differentiable divergences between time series. In: Banerjee, A., Fukumizu, K. (eds.) Proceedings of the 24th International Conference on Artificial Intelligence and Statistics. Proceedings of Machine Learning Research, vol. 130, pp. 3853–3861. PMLR (2021)

4. Cao, K., Ji, J., Cao, Z., Chang, C.Y., Niebles, J.C.: Few-shot video classification via temporal alignment. In: CVPR (2020)

5. Ionescu, C., Papava, D., Olaru, V., Sminchisescu, C.: Human3.6m: large scale datasets and predictive methods for 3D human sensing in natural environments. IEEE Trans. Pattern Anal. Mach. Intell. **36**, 1325–1339 (2014)

6. Cuturi, M.: Fast global alignment kernels. In: International Conference on Machine Learning (ICML) (2011)

7. Cuturi, M., Blondel, M.: Soft-DTW: a differentiable loss function for time-series. In: International Conference on Machine Learning (ICML) (2017)

8. Dau, H.A., et al.: The UCR Time Series Classification Archive (2018). https://www.cs.ucr.edu/~eamonn/time_series_data_2018/

9. Dempster, A., Schmidt, D.F., Webb, G.I.: MINIROCKET: a very fast (almost) deterministic transform for time series classification. In: Proceedings of the 27th ACM SIGKDD Conference on Knowledge Discovery & Data Mining, KDD 2021, pp. 248–257. Association for Computing Machinery, New York (2021). https://doi.org/10.1145/3447548.3467231

10. Donahue, J., Dieleman, S., Binkowski, M., Elsen, E., Simonyan, K.: End-to-end adversarial text-to-speech. In: International Conference on Learning Representations (2021)

11. Dosovitskiy, A., et al.: An image is worth 16×16 words: transformers for image recognition at scale. In: International Conference on Learning Representations (2020)

12. García-García, D., Parrado Hernández, E., Díaz-de María, F.: A new distance measure for model-based sequence clustering. IEEE Trans. Pattern Anal. Mach. Intell. **31**(7), 1325–1331 (2009). https://doi.org/10.1109/TPAMI.2008.268

13. Hastie, T., Tibshirani, R., Friedman, J.: The Elements of Statistical Learning. Springer Series in Statistics, Springer, New York (2001)

14. Hüllermeier, E., Waegeman, W.: Aleatoric and epistemic uncertainty in machine learning: an introduction to concepts and methods. Mach. Learn. **110**(3), 457–506 (2021). https://doi.org/10.1007/s10994-021-05946-3

15. Indrayan, A.: Medical Biostatistics, 2nd edn. Chapman & Hall/CRC, Boca Raton (2008). https://www.loc.gov/catdir/toc/ecip0723/2007030353.html

16. Kay, W., et al.: The kinetics human action video dataset (2017)

17. Kendall, A., Gal, Y.: What uncertainties do we need in Bayesian deep learning for computer vision? In: Guyon, I., et al. (eds.) Advances in Neural Information Processing Systems, vol. 30. Curran Associates, Inc. (2017)

18. Kiureghian, A.D., Ditlevsen, O.: Aleatory or epistemic? Does it matter? Struct. Saf. **31**(2), 105–112 (2009). https://doi.org/10.1016/j.strusafe.2008.06.020. Risk Acceptance and Risk Communication
19. Koniusz, P., Mikolajczyk, K.: Soft assignment of visual words as linear coordinate coding and optimisation of its reconstruction error. In: 2011 18th IEEE International Conference on Image Processing, pp. 2413–2416 (2011). https://doi.org/10.1109/ICIP.2011.6116129
20. Koniusz, P., Wang, L., Cherian, A.: Tensor representations for action recognition. TPAMI **44**, 648–665 (2020)
21. Koniusz, P., Yan, F., Mikolajczyk, K.: Comparison of mid-level feature coding approaches and pooling strategies in visual concept detection. Comput. Vis. Image Underst. **117**(5), 479–492 (2013). https://doi.org/10.1016/j.cviu.2012.10.010
22. Li, S., et al.: TTAN: two-stage temporal alignment network for few-shot action recognition. CoRR (2021)
23. Liu, D.C., Nocedal, J.: On the limited memory BFGS method for large scale optimization. Math. Program. **45**, 503–528 (1989)
24. Liu, J., Shahroudy, A., Perez, M., Wang, G., Duan, L.Y., Kot, A.C.: NTU RGB+D 120: a large-scale benchmark for 3D human activity understanding. IEEE Trans. Pattern Anal. Mach. Intell. (2019). https://doi.org/10.1109/TPAMI.2019.2916873
25. Liu, L., Wang, L., Liu, X.: In defense of soft-assignment coding. In: 2011 International Conference on Computer Vision, pp. 2486–2493 (2011). https://doi.org/10.1109/ICCV.2011.6126534
26. Lohit, S., Wang, Q., Turaga, P.: Temporal transformer networks: joint learning of invariant and discriminative time warping. In: Proceedings of the IEEE/CVF Conference on Computer Vision and Pattern Recognition (CVPR) (2019)
27. Martinez, J., Hossain, R., Romero, J., Little, J.J.: A simple yet effective baseline for 3D human pose estimation. In: 2017 IEEE International Conference on Computer Vision (ICCV), pp. 2659–2668 (2017). https://doi.org/10.1109/ICCV.2017.288
28. Matthies, H.G.: Quantifying uncertainty: modern computational representation of probability and applications. In: Ibrahimbegovic, A., Kozar, I. (eds.) Extreme Man-Made and Natural Hazards in Dynamics of Structures, pp. 105–135. Springer, Netherlands, Dordrecht (2007). https://doi.org/10.1007/978-1-4020-5656-7_4
29. Memmesheimer, R., Häring, S., Theisen, N., Paulus, D.: Skeleton-DML: deep metric learning for skeleton-based one-shot action recognition (2021)
30. Memmesheimer, R., Theisen, N., Paulus, D.: Signal level deep metric learning for multimodal one-shot action recognition (2020)
31. Mensch, A., Blondel, M.: Differentiable dynamic programming for structured prediction and attention. In: Dy, J., Krause, A. (eds.) Proceedings of the 35th International Conference on Machine Learning. Proceedings of Machine Learning Research, vol. 80, pp. 3462–3471. PMLR (2018)
32. Mina, B., Zoumpourlis, G., Patras, I.: Tarn: temporal attentive relation network for few-shot and zero-shot action recognition. In: Sidorov, K., Hicks, Y. (eds.) Proceedings of the British Machine Vision Conference (BMVC), pp. 130.1–130.14. BMVA Press (2019). https://doi.org/10.5244/C.33.130
33. Perrett, T., Masullo, A., Burghardt, T., Mirmehdi, M., Damen, D.: Temporal-relational crosstransformers for few-shot action recognition. In: Proceedings of the IEEE/CVF Conference on Computer Vision and Pattern Recognition (CVPR), pp. 475–484 (2021)
34. Ramachandran, P., Liu, P.J., Le, Q.V.: Unsupervised pretraining for sequence to sequence learning (2018)

35. Sakoe, H., Chiba, S.: Dynamic programming algorithm optimization for spoken word recognition. IEEE Trans. Acoust. Speech Signal Process. **26**(1), 43–49 (1978). https://doi.org/10.1109/TASSP.1978.1163055

36. Shahroudy, A., Liu, J., Ng, T.T., Wang, G.: NTU RGB+D: a large scale dataset for 3D human activity analysis. In: IEEE Conference on Computer Vision and Pattern Recognition (2016)

37. Snell, J., Swersky, K., Zemel, R.S.: Prototypical networks for few-shot learning. In: Guyon, I., et al. (eds.) Advances in Neural Information Processing Systems 30: Annual Conference on Neural Information Processing Systems, Long Beach, CA, USA, 4–9 December 2017, pp. 4077–4087 (2017)

38. Su, B., Hua, G.: Order-preserving optimal transport for distances between sequences. IEEE Trans. Pattern Anal. Mach. Intell. **41**(12), 2961–2974 (2019). https://doi.org/10.1109/TPAMI.2018.2870154

39. Su, B., Wen, J.R.: Temporal alignment prediction for supervised representation learning and few-shot sequence classification. In: International Conference on Learning Representations (2022)

40. Su, B., Zhou, J., Wu, Y.: Order-preserving Wasserstein discriminant analysis. In: 2019 IEEE/CVF International Conference on Computer Vision (ICCV), pp. 9884–9893 (2019). https://doi.org/10.1109/ICCV.2019.00998

41. Tan, S., Yang, R.: Learning similarity: feature-aligning network for few-shot action recognition. In: International Joint Conference on Neural Networks (IJCNN), pp. 1–7 (2019)

42. Vinyals, O., Blundell, C., Lillicrap, T., Kavukcuoglu, K., Wierstra, D.: Matching networks for one shot learning. In: Lee, D.D., Sugiyama, M., von Luxburg, U., Guyon, I., Garnett, R. (eds.) Advances in Neural Information Processing Systems 29: Annual Conference on Neural Information Processing Systems, Barcelona, Spain, 5–10 December 2016, pp. 3630–3638 (2016)

43. Wang, L.: Analysis and evaluation of Kinect-based action recognition algorithms. Master's thesis, School of the Computer Science and Software Engineering, The University of Western Australia (2017)

44. Wang, L., Huynh, D.Q., Koniusz, P.: A comparative review of recent Kinect-based action recognition algorithms. IEEE Trans. Image Process. **29**, 15–28 (2020)

45. Wang, L., Huynh, D.Q., Mansour, M.R.: Loss switching fusion with similarity search for video classification. In: ICIP (2019)

46. Wang, L., Koniusz, P.: Self-supervising action recognition by statistical moment and subspace descriptors, pp. 4324–4333. Association for Computing Machinery, New York (2021). https://doi.org/10.1145/3474085.3475572

47. Wang, L., Koniusz, P., Huynh, D.Q.: Hallucinating IDT descriptors and I3D optical flow features for action recognition with CNNs. In: The IEEE International Conference on Computer Vision (ICCV) (2019)

48. Yan, S., Xiong, Y., Lin, D.: Spatial temporal graph convolutional networks for skeleton-based action recognition. In: AAAI (2018)

49. Yang, C.H.H., Tsai, Y.Y., Chen, P.Y.: Voice2series: reprogramming acoustic models for time series classification. In: Meila, M., Zhang, T. (eds.) Proceedings of the 38th International Conference on Machine Learning. Proceedings of Machine Learning Research, vol. 139, pp. 11808–11819. PMLR (2021)
50. Zhang, H., Zhang, L., Qi, X., Li, H., Torr, P.H.S., Koniusz, P.: Few-shot action recognition with permutation-invariant attention. In: Vedaldi, A., Bischof, H., Brox, T., Frahm, J.-M. (eds.) ECCV 2020. LNCS, vol. 12350, pp. 525–542. Springer, Cham (2020). https://doi.org/10.1007/978-3-030-58558-7_31
51. Zhu, H., Koniusz, P.: Simple spectral graph convolution. In: International Conference on Learning Representations (ICLR) (2021)

Black-Box Few-Shot Knowledge Distillation

Dang Nguyen$^{(\boxtimes)}$, Sunil Gupta, Kien Do, and Svetha Venkatesh

Applied Artificial Intelligence Institute (A^{2}I^2), Deakin University, Geelong, Australia
{d.nguyen,sunil.gupta,k.do,svetha.venkatesh}@deakin.edu.au

Abstract. Knowledge distillation (KD) is an efficient approach to transfer the knowledge from a large "teacher" network to a smaller "student" network. Traditional KD methods require lots of *labeled* training samples and a *white-box* teacher (parameters are accessible) to train a good student. However, these resources are not always available in real-world applications. The distillation process often happens at an external party side where we do not have access to much data, and the teacher does not disclose its parameters due to security and privacy concerns. To overcome these challenges, we propose a black-box few-shot KD method to train the student with *few unlabeled* training samples and a *black-box* teacher. Our main idea is to expand the training set by generating a diverse set of out-of-distribution synthetic images using MixUp and a conditional variational auto-encoder. These synthetic images along with their labels obtained from the teacher are used to train the student. We conduct extensive experiments to show that our method significantly outperforms recent SOTA few/zero-shot KD methods on image classification tasks. The code and models are available at: https://github.com/nphdang/FS-BBT.

1 Introduction

Despite achieving many great successes in real-world applications [11,34,43], deep neural networks often have millions of weights to train, thus require heavy computation and storage [31]. To make deep neural networks smaller and applicable to real-time devices, especially for edge devices with limited resources, knowledge distillation (KD) methods have been proposed [2,10,17].

The main goal of KD is to transfer the knowledge from a large pre-trained network (called *teacher*) to a smaller network (called *student*) so that the student can perform as well as the teacher [17,36]. Most of existing KD methods follow the idea introduced by Hinton et al. [17], which suggests to use both the ground-truth labels and the teacher's predictions as training signals for the student. The intuition behind this approach is that if the student network not only learns from its training data but also is guided by a powerful teacher network pre-trained on a large-scale data, then the student will improve its classification accuracy.

The success of existing KD methods relies on two strong assumptions. First, the student's training set must be *very large and labeled* (it is usually the same as the teacher's training set) [2,17,19,36]. Second, the teacher is a *white-box* model so that the student has access to the teacher's internal details (e.g. gradient, parameters, feature maps, logits) [1,3,8,40]. However, these assumptions rarely hold in real-world applications. Typically, the distillation happens at an external party side where we can only access to few unlabeled samples. For example, DeepFace [35] developed by Facebook was trained on 4 million non-public facial images. For distilling a student network from DeepFace, an external party may not have access to the face database used by Facebook due to various reasons including privacy. Instead, its training set would typically comprise of a few thousands images that are accessible at the external party side. In some cases, the pre-trained teacher models are *black-box* i.e. they are released without disclosing their parameters, which is often the case with cloud-deployed machine learning web-services. For example, IBM Watson Speech-to-Text [32] only provides its APIs to end-users to convert audio and voice to written text.

To mitigate the demand of large training data, several few-shot KD methods were proposed for KD with few samples [3,20], but they still require a white-box teacher. To the best of our knowledge, there is only one method named BBKD [37] to train the student with few samples and a black-box teacher. BBKD uses MixUp to synthesize training images and active learning to select the most uncertain mixup images to query the teacher model. Although BBKD shows significant improvements over current SOTA few/zero-shot KD methods, it exhibits two notable limitations. First, it has to synthesize *a huge pool of candidate images*. For example, given $N = 1000$ original images, it constructs $C = 10^6$ candidate images, and selects $M = 20000$ synthetic images from C to train the student. Since the number of candidate images C is very large, it requires expensive computation and consumes large memory resource. Second, it has to train the student multiple times until a stopping criteria. Although the student network is smaller than the teacher network, it is still a deep neural network. Training the student multiple times must be avoided since it costs both resources and training time. *Therefore, few-shot KD with a black-box teacher in a resource- and time-efficient manner is an open problem.*

Our Method. To solve the above problem, we propose a novel *unsupervised black-box few-shot* KD method i.e. training the student with only *few unlabeled* images and a *black-box* teacher. Our method offers a resource- and time-efficient KD process, which addresses the bottlenecks of BBKD. First, it does not need to create any pool of candidate images; instead it directly generates M synthetic images from N original images to train the student. Second, it only trains the student network in one-pass; no active learning is required and no multiple student models are repeatedly created.

Our method has three main steps. First, we generate synthetic images from a given *small* set of original images. Second, the synthetic images are sent to the teacher model to query their *soft-labels* (i.e. class probabilities). Finally, the original and synthetic images along with their soft-labels are used to train the student network. Our method is illustrated in Fig. 1.

The key component in our method is the image generator, where we propose two approaches to generate synthetic images. First, we use the MixUp method

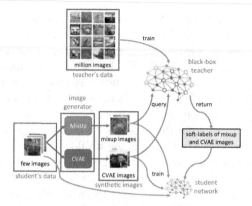

Fig. 1. Knowledge distillation with few samples and black-box teacher. Given a black-box teacher and a small set of original images, we propose to employ MixUp method and CVAE generative model to generate synthetic images to train the student network.

[4,12,18] to synthesize a virtual image by a weighted combination of two original images. Mixup images help us to cover the manifold of natural images. Second, we use Conditional Variational Autoencoder (CVAE) [33] – a generative model to generate additional synthetic images. While MixUp is useful to some extent, mixup images too close to original images do not add much value to the training data. Such disqualified mixup images are replaced by images generated from CVAE. Using CVAE, we can generate interpolated images i.e. the output image semantically mixes characteristics from the original images. As a result, we can enrich the training set and improve the diversity of training images, which is very useful when training the student network.

Our Contribution. To summarize, we make the following contributions.

1. We propose **FS-BBT** (*knowledge distillation with $\underline{F}ew$ $\underline{S}amples$ and $\underline{B}lack$-$\underline{B}ox$ $\underline{T}eacher$), a novel method offers a successful KD process even with few unlabeled training samples and a black-box teacher model.
2. We develop an efficient approach to train the student network in resource- and time-efficient manner, where we do not need to create a large pool of candidate images and only train the student network one time.
3. We empirically validate our proposed method on several image classification tasks, comparing it with both standard and SOTA few/zero-shot KD methods. The experimental results show that our method significantly outperforms competing baselines.

2   Related Works

Knowledge Distillation. Knowledge distillation (KD) has become popular since Hinton et al. introduced its concept in their teacher-student framework [17]. The main goal of KD is to train a compact student network by mimicking the softmax output of a high-capacity teacher network. Many KD methods have been proposed, and they can be categorized into three groups: *relation-based*, *feature-based*, and *response-based* methods. Relation-based methods not only use the teacher's output but also explore the relationships between different layers of teacher when training the student network. Examples include [23,30,40]. Feature-based methods leverage both the teacher's output at the last layer and the intermediate layers when training student network [1,19,30]. Response-based methods directly mimic the final prediction of the teacher network [7,17,26,29].

Knowledge Distillation with Limited Data. To successfully train the student network, most KD methods assume that both the student's training data and the teacher's training data are identical. For example, [6,17] pointed out that the student only achieved its best accuracy when it had accessed to the teacher's training data. Similarly, [27] mentioned the typical setting in KD methods was the student network trained on the teacher's training data. Recent SOTA methods [2,19,36] also trained both teacher and student networks on the same dataset. In practice, the teacher's training data could be unavailable due to transmission limitation or privacy while we could only collect few samples for the student's training data. Several few/zero-shot KD methods were developed to deal with this situation [3,8,20,28,41]. However, all of these methods require a *white-box* teacher to access to its internal details (e.g. gradient information, weights, feature maps, logits...) to generate synthetic training samples. As far as we know, only BBKD [37] requires few training samples and zero knowledge of the teacher (i.e. *black-box* teacher). However, it is computation and resource intensive as it requires a large pool of candidate images and extensive iterative training.

3 Framework

3.1 Problem Definition

Given a small set of *unlabeled* images $\mathcal{X} = \{x_i\}_{i=1}^N$ and a black-box teacher T, our goal is to train a student S on $\mathcal{X}$ s.t. S's performance is comparable to T's.

A direct solution for the above problem is to apply the standard KD method [17]. We first query the teacher to obtain the *hard-label* (i.e. one-hot encoding) y_i for each sample $x_i \in \mathcal{X}$, and then create a labeled training set $\mathcal{D} = \{x_i, y_i\}_{i=1}^N$. Finally, we train the student network with the standard KD loss function:

$$\mathcal{L} = \sum_{(x_i, y_i) \in \mathcal{D}} (1 - \omega)\mathcal{L}_{CE}(y_{x_i}^S, y_i) + \omega \mathcal{L}_{KL}(y_{x_i}^S, y_{x_i}^T), \qquad (1)$$

where $y_{x_i}^S$, $y_{x_i}^T$, y_i are the student's softmax output, the teacher's softmax output, and the hard-label of a sample x_i, $\mathcal{L}_{CE}$ is the cross-entropy loss, $\mathcal{L}_{KL}$ is the Kullback–Leibler divergence loss, and ω is a trade-off factor to balance the two loss terms. Equation (1) does not use the *temperature* factor as in Hinton's KD method [17] since this requires access to the pre-softmax activations (logits) of teacher, which violates our assumption of "black-box" teacher.

Although training the student network via Eq. (1) is a possible way, it is not a good solution as $\mathcal{X}$ only contains very few samples while standard KD methods typically require lots of training samples [2,17,19,36].

3.2 Proposed Method FS-BBT

We propose a novel method to solve the above problem, which has three main steps: (1) we generate mixup images from original images contained in $\mathcal{X}$, (2) we replace disqualified mixup images by images generated from CVAE, and (3) we train the student with a combination of original, mixup, and CVAE images.

Generating Mixup Images. Our idea is to use MixUp [18] – one of recently proposed data augmentation techniques to expand the training set $\mathcal{X}$.

Inspired by BBKD [37], we generate M mixup images from N original images (typically, $N \ll M$). Given two original images $x_i, x_j \in \mathcal{X}$, we use MixUp to generate a synthetic image by a weighted combination between x_i and x_j:

$$x_{mu}(\lambda) = \lambda x_i + (1 - \lambda)x_j, \tag{2}$$

where the coefficient $\lambda \in [0, 1]$ is sampled from a Beta distribution.

Let $X = [x_1, x_2, ..., x_N]$ be the vector of original images. We first sample two M-length vectors $X^1 = [x_1^1, x_2^1, ..., x_M^1]$ and $X^2 = [x_1^2, x_2^2, ..., x_M^2]$, where $x_i^1, x_i^2 \sim X$. We then sample a vector $\lambda = [\lambda_1, \lambda_2, ..., \lambda_M]$ from a Beta distribution, and mixup each pair of two images in X^1 and X^2 using Eq. (2):

$$X_{mu} = \begin{bmatrix} \lambda_1 x_1^1 + (1 - \lambda_1)x_1^2 \\ \lambda_2 x_2^1 + (1 - \lambda_2)x_2^2 \\ ... \\ \lambda_M x_M^1 + (1 - \lambda_M)x_M^2 \end{bmatrix} \tag{3}$$

The goal of mixing up original images is to expand the initial set of training images $\mathcal{X}$ as much as possible to cover the manifold of natural images.

However, when mixing up two original images, there is a case that the mixup image is very similar to one of two original images, making it useless. This problem happens when $\lambda_i \approx 0$ or $\lambda_i \approx 1$. Figure 2 shows two examples of desirable vs. disqualified mixup images.

To remove disqualified mixup images, we set a threshold $\alpha \in [0, 0.5]$, and discard mixup images generated with coefficient $\lambda_i \leq \alpha$ or $\lambda_i \geq (1 - \alpha)$.

Let M_1 be the number of remaining mixup images after we filter out the disqualified ones. Our

$\lambda = 0.58$ $\lambda = 0.98$

Fig. 2. Desirable vs. disqualified mixup images. At $\lambda = 0.58$, the mixup image shows a good combination between two original images "horse" and "ship" but at $\lambda = 0.98$, it looks almost the same as "horse".

next step is to generate $M_2 = M - M_1$ synthetic images from CVAE (we call them CVAE images).

Generating CVAE Images. We first query the teacher model to obtain the hard-label y_i for each sample $x_i \in \mathcal{X}$ to create a labeled training set $\mathcal{D} =$

$\{x_i, y_i\}_{i=1}^N$. We then train a Conditional Variational Autoencoder (CVAE) model [33] using $\mathcal{D}$ to learn the distribution of the latent variable $z \in \mathbb{R}^d$, where d is the dimension of z. CVAE is a generative model consisting of an encoder and a decoder. We use the encoder network to map an image along with its label $(x, y) \in \mathcal{D}$ to a latent vector z that follows $P(z \mid y)$. From the latent vector z conditioned on the label y, we use the decoder network to reconstruct the input image x. Following [33], we train CVAE by maximizing the variational lower bound objective:

$$\log P(x \mid y) \geq \mathbb{E}(\log P(x \mid z, y)) - \mathrm{KL}(Q(z \mid x, y), P(z \mid y)), \qquad (4)$$

where $Q(z \mid x, y)$ is parameterized by the encoder network that maps input image x and its label y to the latent vector z, $P(x \mid z, y)$ is parameterized by the decoder network that reconstructs input image x from the latent vector z and label y, $\mathbb{E}(\log P(x \mid z, y))$ is the expected likelihood, which is implemented by a cross-entropy loss between the input image and the reconstructed image, and $P(z \mid y) \equiv \mathcal{N}(0, I)$ is the prior distribution of z conditioned on y.

After the CVAE model is trained, we can generate images via $G(z, y)$, where $z \sim \mathcal{N}(0, I)$, y is a label, and G is the trained decoder network.

Covering Both In-Distribution and Out-of-Distribution Samples. To generate M_2 CVAE images, we sample $(\frac{M_2}{2})$-length vector $z^{\mathcal{N}}$ from the normal distribution $\mathcal{N}(0, I)$ and $(\frac{M_2}{2})$-length vector $z^{\mathcal{U}}$ from the uniform distribution $\mathcal{U}([-3, 3]^d)$ (we choose the range $[-3, 3]$ following [13, 16]). We create vector $z = z^{\mathcal{N}} \oplus z^{\mathcal{U}}$, where $\oplus$ is the concatenation operator. We manually define a M_2-length vector y_{cvae}, which contains the classes of generated images such that the number of generated images for each class is equivalent. Finally, we generate CVAE images $x_{cvae} = G(z, y_{cave})$.

The intuition behind our generation process is that: (1) Generating images from $z^{\mathcal{N}} \sim \mathcal{N}(0, I)$ will provide *synthetic images within the distribution* of $\mathcal{X}$. These images are interpolated versions of original images. (2) Generating images from $z^{\mathcal{U}} \sim \mathcal{U}([-3, 3]^d)$ will provide *synthetic images out-of the distribution* of $\mathcal{X}$. These images are far way from the original ones, but they are expected to better cover *unseen images,* which improves the student's generalization.

Discussion. One can sample $\lambda_i \in [\alpha, 1 - \alpha]$ to generate M_1 qualified mixup images, then generate M_2 CVAE images. This way requires two hyper-parameters M_1 and M_2. While this is definitely possible, for simplicity we choose to aggregate these two hyper-parameters into a single hyper-parameter M that controls the total number of synthetic images. In experiments, we set the same values for M as those in other few-shot KD methods [3,37] while M_1 and M_2 are automatically computed based on M and α.

Training the Student Network. After the above steps, we obtain two types of synthetic images – mixup and CVAE images. We send them to the teacher model to obtain their softmax outputs (i.e. their class probabilities) as the *soft-labels* for the images. We train the student network with the original and synthetic images along with their soft-labels using the following loss:

$$\mathcal{L} = \sum_{x_i \in \mathcal{X} \cup \mathcal{X}_{mu} \cup \mathcal{X}_{cvae}} \mathcal{L}_{CE}(y^S_{x_i}, y^T_{x_i}), \tag{5}$$

where $y^S_{x_i}$, $y^T_{x_i}$ are the student's and the teacher's softmax output, $\mathcal{X}$, $\mathcal{X}_{mu}$, $\mathcal{X}_{cvae}$ are the set of original, mixup, and CVAE images, and $\mathcal{L}_{CE}$ is the cross-entropy loss. Although we train the student by matching the teacher's softmax outputs, our loss function is still applicable in case the teacher only returns top-1 labels [39]. Algorithm 1 summarizes our proposed method **FS-BBT**.

Algorithm 1: The proposed **FS-BBT** algorithm.

Input: T: pre-trained *black-box* teacher network
Input: $\mathcal{X} = \{x_i\}_{i=1}^N$: *unlabeled* training set
Input: M: number of synthetic images
Input: α: threshold to select mixup images
Output: S: student network

1 **begin**
2   query teacher T to obtain hard-label y_i for each $x_i \in \mathcal{X}$;
3   train CVAE model using $\mathcal{D} = \{x_i, y_i\}_{i=1}^N$;
4   sample $\lambda = [\lambda_1, ..., \lambda_M]$ from a Beta distribution;
5   select M_1 instances of λ_i s.t. $\alpha < \lambda_i < 1 - \alpha$;
6   generate M_1 mixup images $\mathcal{X}_{mu}$ using Eq. (3);
7   compute $M_2 = M - M_1$;
8   sample $(\frac{M_2}{2})$-length vector $z^{\mathcal{N}} \sim \mathcal{N}(0, I)$;
9   sample $(\frac{M_2}{2})$-length vector $z^{\mathcal{U}} \sim \mathcal{U}([-3, 3]^d)$;
10   create vector $z = z^{\mathcal{N}} \oplus z^{\mathcal{U}}$;
11   design M_2-length vector y_{cvae} with class balance;
12   generate M_2 CVAE images $\mathcal{X}_{cvae} = G(z, y_{cvae})$;
13   query teacher T to obtain soft-labels for $\mathcal{X}, \mathcal{X}_{mu}, \mathcal{X}_{cvae}$;
14   train student S with $\mathcal{X}, \mathcal{X}_{mu}, \mathcal{X}_{cvae}$ and their soft-labels using Eq. (5);

---

4 Experiments and Discussions

We conduct extensive experiments on five benchmark image datasets to evaluate the classification performance of our method, comparing it with SOTA baselines. Our main goal is to show that with the same number of original and synthetic images, our method is much better than existing few/zero-shot KD methods.

4.1 Datasets

We use five image datasets, namely MNIST, Fashion-MNIST, CIFAR-10, CIFAR-100, and Tiny-ImageNet. These datasets were often used to evaluate the classification performance of KD methods [3,8,17,28,37].

4.2   Baselines

We compare our method **FS-BBT** with the following baselines:

- *Student-Alone*: the student network is trained on the student's training data $\mathcal{D}$ from scratch.
- *Standard-KD*: the student network is trained with the standard KD loss in Eq. (1). We choose the trade-off factor $\omega = 0.9$, which is a common value used in KD methods [17, 25, 36, 42].
- *FSKD* [3]: this is a few-shot KD method, which generates synthetic training images using adversarial technique. It requires a *white-box* teacher model to generate adversarial samples to train the student network.
- *WaGe* [20]: this few-shot KD method integrates a Wasserstein-based loss with the standard KD loss to improve the student's generalization.
- *BBKD* [37]: this method uses few original images and a *black-box* teacher model to train the student model. Its main idea is to use MixUp and active learning to generate synthetic images. Since this is the closest work to ours, we consider BBKD as our main competitor.

To have a fair comparison, we use the same teacher-student network architecture, the same number of original and synthetic images N and M as in FSKD and BBKD. We also set the same hyper-parameters (e.g. batch size and the number of epochs) for Student-Alone, Standard-KD, and our **FS-BBT**. We use threshold $\alpha = 0.05$ to select qualified mixup images across all experiments. In an ablation study in Sect. 4.7, we will investigate how different values for α affect our method's performance. We repeat each experiment five times with random seeds, and report the averaged accuracy. For the baselines FSKD, WaGe, and BBKD, we obtain their accuracy from the papers [20, 37][1]. We also compare with several well-known zero-shot KD methods in Sect. 4.6.

4.3   Results on MNIST and Fashion-MNIST

Experiment Settings Following [3, 28], we use the LeNet5 architecture [22] for the teacher and LeNet5-Half (a modified version with half number of channels per layer) for the student. We train the teacher network with a batch size of 64 and 20 epochs. As shown in Table 1, our teacher model achieves comparable accuracy with that reported by BBKD in [37] (99.18% vs. 99.29% for MNIST and 90.15% vs. 90.80% for Fashion-MNIST). We train the student network with a batch size of 64 and 50 epochs. We train the CVAE with feed-forward neural networks for both encoder and decoder, using a latent dimension of 2, a batch size of 256, and 100 (200) epochs for MNIST (Fashion-MNIST). Following FSKD [3] and BBKD [37], we set $N = 2000$ and $M = 24000$ for MNIST and $N = 2000$ and $M = 48000$ for Fashion-MNIST.

The MNIST and Fashion-MNIST datasets have 60K training images and 10K testing images from 10 classes ($[0, 1, ..., 9]$).

---

[1] This is possible because we use benchmark datasets, and the training and test splits are fixed.

Table 1. Classification results on MNIST and Fashion-MNIST. "Teacher" indicates the accuracy of the teacher network on the test set. "Model" indicates whether the teacher network is a *black-box* model. "*N*" shows the number of original images used by each method. "Accuracy" is the accuracy of the student network on the test set. The results of FSKD, WaGe, and BBKD* are obtained from [20,37]. "*⋆*" means the BBKD* and **FS-BBT*** methods use the same architecture (LeNet5) for both teacher and student networks.

Dataset	Method	Teacher	Model	N	Accuracy
MNIST	Student-Alone	-	-	2,000	95.97%
	Standard-KD	99.18%	Black	2,000	95.99%
	FSKD [3]	99.29%	White	2,000	80.43%
	BBKD* [37]	99.29%	Black	2,000	98.74%
	FS-BBT (Ours)	99.18%	Black	2,000	98.42%
	FS-BBT* (Ours)	99.18%	Black	2,000	**98.91%**
Fashion-MNIST	Student-Alone	-	-	2,000	81.37%
	Standard-KD	90.15%	Black	2,000	83.87%
	FSKD [3]	90.80%	White	2,000	68.64%
	WaGe [20]	92.00%	White	1,000	85.18%
	BBKD* [37]	90.80%	Black	2,000	80.90%
	FS-BBT (Ours)	90.15%	Black	2,000	84.73%
	FS-BBT* (Ours)	90.15%	Black	2,000	**86.53%**

Quantitative Results. From Table 1, we can see that our method **FS-BBT** outperforms Student-Alone and Standard-KD on both MNIST and Fashion-MNIST. **FS-BBT** achieves 98.42% (MNIST) and 84.73% (Fashion-MNIST), which is much better than Student-Alone achieving 95.97% and 81.37%. With a support from the teacher model, Standard-KD is always better than Student-Alone, for example, 83.87% vs. 81.37% on Fashion-MNIST.

Compared with FSKD and WaGe, **FS-BBT** significantly outperforms FSKD on both MNIST and Fashion-MNIST while **FS-BBT** is similar with WaGe on Fashion-MNIST.

Compared with BBKD, **FS-BBT** achieves a comparable accuracy with BBKD on MNIST while **FS-BBT** outperforms BBKD by a large margin on Fashion-MNIST, where our accuracy improvement is around 4%. Since BBKD uses the same architecture LeNet5 for both teacher and student networks, we also report the accuracy of our method with this setting, indicated by **FS-BBT***. With LeNet5 for the student network, we further achieve 2% gain (i.e. an improvement of 6% over BBKD) on Fashion-MNIST.

4.4 Results on CIFAR-10 and CIFAR-100

Experiment Settings. Following [3,28], we use AlexNet [21] and AlexNet-Half (50% filters are removed) for teacher and student networks on CIFAR-10. We train the teacher network with a batch size of 512 and 50 epochs. Our teacher model achieves a comparable accuracy with that reported by BBKD in [37] (84.07% vs. 83.07%). We train the student network with a batch size of 128 and 100 epochs. We use ResNet-32 [15] for the teacher and ResNet-20 for the student on CIFAR-100. We train student and teacher networks with a batch size of 16/32 and 200 epochs. For both CIFAR-10 and CIFAR-100, we train the CVAE model with convolutional neural networks for both encoder and decoder, using a latent dimension of 2, a batch size of 64, and 600 epochs. Like BBKD [37] and WaGe [20], we set $N = 2000$ for CIFAR-10, $N = 5000$ for CIFAR-100, and $M = 40000$ for both datasets.

CIFAR-10 is set of RGB images with 10 classes, 50K training images, and 10K testing images while CIFAR-100 is with 100 classes, and each class contains 500 training images and 100 testing images. Since neither the accuracy reference nor the source code is available for BBKD on CIFAR-100, we implement BBKD by ourselves, and use the same teacher as in our method for a fair comparison.

Table 2. Classification results on CIFAR-10 and CIFAR-100. "N" shows the number of original images used by each method. The results of FSKD, WaGe, and BBKD* are obtained from [20,37]. "*" means the BBKD* and **FS-BBT*** methods use the same architecture (AlexNet) for both teacher and student networks. "†" means the result is based on our own implementation.

Dataset	Method	Teacher	Model	N	Accuracy
CIFAR-10	Student-Alone	-	-	2,000	54.59%
	Standard-KD	84.07%	Black	2,000	58.96%
	FSKD [3]	83.07%	White	2,000	40.58%
	WaGe [20]	89.00%	White	5,000	73.08%
	BBKD* [37]	83.07%	Black	2,000	74.60%
	FS-BBT (Ours)	84.07%	Black	2,000	74.10%
	FS-BBT* (Ours)	84.07%	Black	2,000	**76.17%**
CIFAR-100	Student-Alone	-	-	5,000	32.85%
	Standard-KD	69.08%	Black	5,000	36.79%
	WaGe [20]	47.00%	White	5,000	20.32%
	BBKD† [37]	69.08%	Black	5,000	53.41%
	FS-BBT (Ours)	69.08%	Black	5,000	**56.28%**

Quantitative Results. From Table 2 we observe the similar results as in MNIST and Fashion-MNIST. Student-Alone does not have a good accuracy. Standard-KD improves 4% of accuracy over Student-Alone with the knowledge transferred from the teacher.

On CIFAR-10, WaGe and BBKD greatly outperform FSKD, and our **FS-BBT** is comparable with WaGe and BBKD. When we use the same architecture

Table 3. Classification results on Tiny-ImageNet. "N" shows the number of original images used by each method. "†" means the result is based on our own implementation.

Dataset	Method	Teacher	Model	N	Accuracy
Tiny-ImageNet	Student-Alone (full)	-	-	100,000	48.81%
	Student-Alone	-	-	10,000	23.19%
	Standard-KD	52.02%	Black	10,000	35.81%
	BBKD† [37]	52.02%	Black	10,000	40.01%
	FS-BBT (Ours)	52.02%	Black	10,000	**43.29%**

AlexNet for both teacher and student as in BBKD, our variant **FS-BBT**⋆ is the best method, where it outperforms BBKD (the second best method) by around 2%. **FS-BBT**⋆ outperforms WaGe by around 3% even though WaGe uses much more original training samples than ours (5K vs. 2K), and more powerful teacher (89% vs. 84%).

On CIFAR-100, Student-Alone achieves low accuracy at around 32%. Standard-KD is better than Student-Alone around 4% thanks to the knowledge transferred from the teacher. Interestingly, WaGe works very poorly (only 20.32% of accuracy), becoming the worst method. Its unsatisfactory performance can be a consequence of distilling from a low-accuracy teacher. BBKD is significantly better than other methods with an improvement around 20–30%. Using the same number of original and synthetic images, our method **FS-BBT** achieves 3% gains over BBKD thanks to the CVAE images generated in Sect. 3.2.

The above results suggest that replacing disqualified mixup images by synthetic images generated from CVAE is an effective solution to improve the robustness and generalization of the student network on the unseen testing samples, as we discussed in Sect. 3.2.

4.5   Results on Tiny-ImageNet

Experiment Settings. We use ResNet-32 and ResNet-20 for the teacher and student. We train teacher and student networks with a batch size of 32 and 100 epochs. Our teacher model achieves a similar accuracy with literature [5] (52.02% vs. 48.26%). We train CVAE in the same way as in CIFAR-100. We set $N = 10000$ and $M = 50000$. Tiny-ImageNet has 100K training images, 10K testing images, and 200 classes.

Quantitative Results Table 3 shows that Student-Alone reaches a very low accuracy due to a large number of classes presented in this dataset. Standard-KD is significantly better than Student-Alone with an improvement more than 12%. Our method **FS-BBT** achieves 3% gains over BBKD (the second-best baseline).

We also train Student-Alone with full 100K original images and their soft-labels provided by the teacher. This can be considered as an upper bound of all few-shot KD methods as it uses the full set of training images. **FS-BBT** drops only 5% accuracy from Student-Alone with full training data although it requires only 10% of training data. This proves the efficacy of our proposed framework.

4.6 Comparison with Zero-Shot (or Data-Free) KD Methods

We also compare with several popular zero-shot KD methods, including *Meta-KD* [24], *ZSKD* [28], *DAFL* [8], *DFKD* [38], and *ZSDB3KD* [39].

Table 4 reports the classification accuracy on MNIST, Fashion-MNIST, and CIFAR-10. Our method is much better than other methods on Fashion-MNIST and CIFAR-10 while it is comparable on MNIST.

Table 4. Classification comparison with zero-shot KD methods. The results of baselines are obtained from [39].

Method	Model	MNIST	Fashion-MNIST	CIFAR-10
Meta-KD [24]	White	92.47%	-	-
ZSKD [28]	White	98.77%	79.62%	69.56%
DAFL [8]	White	98.20%	-	66.38%
DFKD [38]	White	**99.08%**	-	73.91%
ZSDB3KD [39]	Black	96.54%	72.31%	59.46%
FS-BBT (Ours)	Black	98.91%	**86.53%**	**76.17%**

4.7 Ablation Study

As there are several components and a hyper-parameter α in our method, we further conduct some ablation experiments to analyze how each of them affects to our overall classification accuracy. We select CIFAR-10 for this analysis.

Different Types of Synthetic Images. As described in Sect. 3.2, we generate three types of synthetic images to train the student network. First, we generate *mixup images*. Second, we sample $z^{\mathcal{N}} \sim \mathcal{N}(0, I)$ to generate CVAE images within the distribution of the original images (we call them *CVAE-WD images*). Finally, we sample $z^{\mathcal{U}} \sim \mathcal{U}([-3, 3]^d)$ to generate CVAE images out-of the distribution of the original images (we call them *CVAE-OOD images*).

Figure 3 shows original images and three types of synthetic images for four true classes "car", "deer", "ship", and "dog". Our synthetic images have good quality, where the objects are clearly recognized and visualized. These synthetic images provide a comprehensive coverage of real images in the test set, resulting in the great improvement of the student network trained on them.

Table 5 reports the accuracy of various types of our synthetic images. The standard KD method achieves only 58.96% of accuracy. By utilizing mixup

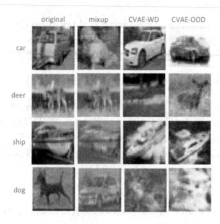

Fig. 3. Original images (1st column) and three types of synthetic images: mixup images (2nd column), CVAE-WD images (3rd column), and CVAE-OOD images (4th column). The text on the left indicates the true labels of original images.

images, our method achieves up to 71.67% of accuracy. However, using solely mixup images has disadvantages as we discussed in Sect. 3.2. By combining mixup images with CVAE-WD images or CVAE-OOD images, our method further improves its accuracy up to 72.60% and 73.25% of accuracy respectively. Finally, when combining all three types of synthetic images, our method achieves the best performance at 74.10% of accuracy.

Table 5. Effectiveness of different types of synthetic images on our method **FS-BBT**.

	KD	FS-BBT (Ours)						
Mixup images		✓				✓	✓		✓
CVAE-WD images			✓			✓		✓	✓
CVAE-OOD images				✓		✓	✓	✓
Accuracy	58.96%	71.67%	70.26%	69.42%	72.60%	73.25%	70.63%	**74.10%**

The ablation experiments suggest that each type of synthetic images in our method is meaningful, where it greatly improves the student's classification performance compared to the standard KD method. By leveraging all three types of synthetic images, our method improves the generalization and diversity of the training set, which is very effective for the training of the student network.

Hyper-Parameter Analysis Our method **FS-BBT** has one hyper-parameter, that is, the threshold α to determine disqualified mixup images and replace them by CVAE images (see Sect. 3.2). We examine how the different choices of α affect our classification.

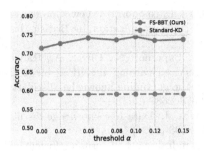

Fig. 4. **FS-BBT**'s accuracy vs. threshold α on CIFAR-10.

As shown in Fig. 4, **FS-BBT** is always better than the standard KD method regardless of α values. More importantly, it is stable with $\alpha \in [0.05, 0.10]$, where its accuracy just slightly changes. When α is too small (i.e. $\alpha < 0.05$), most of mixup images will be considered qualified although many of them are very similar to the original images, leading to few extra meaningful training samples added. The performance of **FS-BBT** is decreased as expected. When α is too large (i.e. $\alpha > 0.10$), **FS-BBT** also slightly reduces its accuracy. This is because many mixup images may become cluttered and semantically meaningless due to a large proportion of two original images blended together, making them difficult for the teacher network to label.

5 Conclusion

Existing standard and few/zero-shot KD methods require lots of original training data or a white-box teacher, which are not realistic in some cases. We present **FS-BBT** – a novel KD method, which is effective even with few training samples and a black-box teacher. **FS-BBT** uses MixUp and CVAE to generate synthetic images to train the student network. Although neither of them is new, combining them is a novel solution to address the problem of black-box KD with few samples. As **FS-BBT** is *unsupervised*, which does not require any ground-truth labels, it can be directly applied to domains where labeled images are difficult to obtain e.g. medical images. We demonstrate the benefits of **FS-BBT** on five benchmark image datasets, where it significantly outperforms SOTA baselines. Our work can cheaply create a white-box proxy of a black-box model, which allows algorithmic assurance [9,14] to verify its behavior along various aspects e.g. robustness, fairness, safety, etc.

Acknowledgment. This research was fully supported by the Australian Government through the Australian Research Council's Discovery Projects funding scheme (project DP210102798). The views expressed herein are those of the authors and are not necessarily those of the Australian Government or Australian Research Council.

References

1. Adriana, R., Nicolas, B., Ebrahimi, S., Antoine, C., Carlo, G., Yoshua, B.: FitNets: hints for thin deep nets. In: ICLR (2015)
2. Ahn, S., Hu, X., Damianou, A., Lawrence, N., Dai, Z.: Variational information distillation for knowledge transfer. In: CVPR, pp. 9163–9171 (2019)

3. Akisato, K., Zoubin, G., Koh, T., Tomoharu, I., Naonori, U.: Few-shot learning of neural networks from scratch by pseudo example optimization. In: British Machine Vision Conference (BMVC), p. 105 (2018)

4. Berthelot, D., Carlini, N., Goodfellow, I., Papernot, N., Oliver, A., Raffel, C.: MixMatch: a holistic approach to semi-supervised learning. In: NIPS, vol. 32 (2019)

5. Bhat, P., Arani, E., Zonooz, B.: Distill on the go: online knowledge distillation in self-supervised learning. In: CVPR, pp. 2678–2687 (2021)

6. Chawla, A., Yin, H., Molchanov, P., Alvarez, J.: Data-free knowledge distillation for object detection. In: CVPR, pp. 3289–3298 (2021)

7. Chen, G., Choi, W., Yu, X., Han, T., Chandraker, M.: Learning efficient object detection models with knowledge distillation. In: NIPS, pp. 742–751 (2017)

8. Chen, H., et al.: Data-free learning of student networks. In: ICCV, pp. 3514–3522 (2019)

9. Gopakumar, S., Gupta, S., Rana, S., Nguyen, V., Venkatesh, S.: Algorithmic assurance: an active approach to algorithmic testing using Bayesian optimisation. In: NIPS, vol. 31 (2018)

10. Gou, J., Yu, B., Maybank, S., Tao, D.: Knowledge distillation: a survey. Int. J. Comput. Vis. **129**(6), 1789–1819 (2021)

11. Guo, G., Zhang, N.: A survey on deep learning based face recognition. Comput. Vis. Image Underst. **189**, 102805 (2019)

12. Guo, H., Mao, Y., Zhang, R.: MixUp as locally linear out-of-manifold regularization. In: AAAI, vol. 33, pp. 3714–3722 (2019)

13. Gyawali, K.: Semi-supervised learning by disentangling and self-ensembling over stochastic latent space. arXiv preprint arXiv:1907.09607 (2019)

14. Ha, H., Gupta, S., Rana, S., Venkatesh, S.: High dimensional level set estimation with Bayesian neural network. In: AAAI, vol. 35, pp. 12095–12103 (2021)

15. He, K., Zhang, X., Ren, S., Sun, J.: Deep residual learning for image recognition. In: CVPR, pp. 770–778 (2016)

16. Higgins, I., et al.: Beta-VAE: learning basic visual concepts with a constrained variational framework. In: ICLR (2017)

17. Hinton, G., Vinyals, O., Dean, J.: Distilling the knowledge in a neural network. arXiv preprint arXiv:1503.02531 (2015)

18. Hongyi, Z., Moustapha, C., Yann, D., David, L.P.: MixUp: beyond empirical risk minimization. In: ICLR (2018)

19. Kim, J., Park, S., Kwak, N.: Paraphrasing complex network: network compression via factor transfer. In: NIPS, pp. 2760–2769 (2018)

20. Kong, S., Guo, T., You, S., Xu, C.: Learning student networks with few data. In: AAAI, vol. 34, pp. 4469–4476 (2020)

21. Krizhevsky, A., Sutskever, I., Hinton, G.: ImageNet classification with deep convolutional neural networks. In: NIPS, vol. 25, pp. 1097–1105 (2012)

22. LeCun, Y., et al.: LeNet-5: convolutional neural networks. **20**(5), 14 (2015). http://yann.lecun.com/exdb/lenet

23. Lee, S., Song, B.C.: Graph-based knowledge distillation by multi-head attention network. arXiv preprint arXiv:1907.02226 (2019)

24. Lopes, R.G., Fenu, S., Starner, T.: Data-free knowledge distillation for deep neural networks. arXiv preprint arXiv:1710.07535 (2017)

25. Ma, H., Chen, T., Hu, T.K., You, C., Xie, X., Wang, Z.: Undistillable: making a nasty teacher that cannot teach students. In: ICLR (2021)

26. Meng, Z., Li, J., Zhao, Y., Gong, Y.: Conditional teacher-student learning. In: ICASSP, pp. 6445–6449. IEEE (2019)

27. Nayak, G.K., Mopuri, K.R., Chakraborty, A.: Effectiveness of arbitrary transfer sets for data-free knowledge distillation. In: CVPR, pp. 1430–1438 (2021)
28. Nayak, K., Mopuri, R., Shaj, V., Radhakrishnan, B., Chakraborty, A.: Zero-shot knowledge distillation in deep networks. In: ICML, pp. 4743–4751 (2019)
29. Nguyen, D., et al.: Knowledge distillation with distribution mismatch. In: Oliver, N., Pérez-Cruz, F., Kramer, S., Read, J., Lozano, J.A. (eds.) ECML PKDD 2021. LNCS (LNAI), vol. 12976, pp. 250–265. Springer, Cham (2021). https://doi.org/10.1007/978-3-030-86520-7_16
30. Passalis, N., Tzelepi, M., Tefas, A.: Heterogeneous knowledge distillation using information flow modeling. In: CVPR, pp. 2339–2348 (2020)
31. Pouyanfar, S., et al.: A survey on deep learning: algorithms, techniques, and applications. ACM Comput. Surv. **51**(5), 1–36 (2018)
32. Santiago, F., Singh, P., Sri, L., et al.: Building Cognitive Applications with IBM Watson Services: Volume 6 Speech to Text and Text to Speech. IBM Redbooks (2017)
33. Sohn, K., Lee, H., Yan, X.: Learning structured output representation using deep conditional generative models. In: NIPS, pp. 3483–3491 (2015)
34. Sreenu, G., Saleem Durai, M.A.: Intelligent video surveillance: a review through deep learning techniques for crowd analysis. J. Big Data **6**(1), 1–27 (2019). https://doi.org/10.1186/s40537-019-0212-5
35. Taigman, Y., Yang, M., Ranzato, M., Wolf, L.: DeepFace: closing the gap to human-level performance in face verification. In: CVPR, pp. 1701–1708 (2014)
36. Tian, Y., Krishnan, D., Isola, P.: Contrastive representation distillation. In: ICLR (2020)
37. Wang, D., Li, Y., Wang, L., Gong, B.: Neural networks are more productive teachers than human raters: active mixup for data-efficient knowledge distillation from a blackbox model. In: CVPR, pp. 1498–1507 (2020)
38. Wang, Z.: Data-free knowledge distillation with soft targeted transfer set synthesis. In: AAAI, vol. 35, pp. 10245–10253 (2021)
39. Wang, Z.: Zero-shot knowledge distillation from a decision-based black-box model. In: ICML (2021)
40. Yim, J., Joo, D., Bae, J., Kim, J.: A gift from knowledge distillation: Fast optimization, network minimization and transfer learning. In: CVPR, pp. 4133–4141 (2017)
41. Yin, H., et al.: Dreaming to distill: data-free knowledge transfer via deepinversion. In: CVPR, pp. 8715–8724 (2020)
42. Yuan, L., Tay, F., Li, G., Wang, T., Feng, J.: Revisiting knowledge distillation via label smoothing regularization. In: CVPR, pp. 3903–3911 (2020)
43. Zhang, S., Yao, L., Sun, A., Tay, Y.: Deep learning based recommender system: a survey and new perspectives. ACM Comput. Surv. **52**(1), 1–38 (2019)

Revisiting Batch Norm Initialization

Jim Davis and Logan Frank[✉]

Department of Computer Science and Engineering,
Ohio State University, Columbus, OH, USA
{davis.1719,frank.580}@osu.edu

Abstract. Batch normalization (BN) is comprised of a normalization component followed by an affine transformation and has become essential for training deep neural networks. Standard initialization of each BN in a network sets the affine transformation scale and shift to 1 and 0, respectively. However, after training we have observed that these parameters do not alter much from their initialization. Furthermore, we have noticed that the normalization process can still yield overly large values, which is undesirable for training. We revisit the BN formulation and present a new initialization method and update approach for BN to address the aforementioned issues. Experiments are designed to emphasize and demonstrate the positive influence of proper BN scale initialization on performance, and use rigorous statistical significance tests for evaluation. The approach can be used with existing implementations at no additional computational cost. Source code is available at https://github.com/osu-cvl/revisiting-bn-init.

1 Introduction

Batch normalization (BN) [15] is a standard component used in deep learning, particularly for convolutional neural networks (CNNs) [7,11,28,30,37] where BN layers typically fall into a convolutional-BN-ReLU sequence [11,13]. BN constrains the intermediate per-channel features in a network by utilizing the statistics among examples in the same batch to normalize (or "whiten") the data, followed by a learnable affine transformation to add further flexibility in training. It has been shown that the aggregation of information in a batch is advantageous as it eases the optimization landscape by creating smoother gradients [29] and enables larger learning rates for faster convergence [4,15]. Additionally, the stochasticity from batch statistics can benefit generalization [15,24].

Typically, the default implementation of BN initializes the affine transformation scale (γ) and shift (β) parameters to 1 and 0, respectively, with the expectation that they can adapt to optimal values during training and can undo the preceding normalization if desired [15]. It is common to take this default initialization "as is", with extensions of BN typically adding additional parameters and computations [9,16,22,23] that increase the model complexity.

By inspection of multiple trained BNs, we have observed that the affine parameters often do not change much from their initial values. So either the

S. Avidan et al. (Eds.): ECCV 2022, LNCS 13681, pp. 212–228, 2022.
https://doi.org/10.1007/978-3-031-19803-8_13

affine transformation is hardly needed (staying close to identity) or perhaps there is a limitation in the learning process keeping these parameters from reaching more optimal values. It is unlikely the affine parameters are optimal near identity settings, therefore we question whether the default affine transformation initialization and update approach are appropriate.

In this work, we present a thorough analysis of BN to address the aforementioned hypothesis and provide a new approach for the initialization and updating of BN to enhance overall performance. We will show that 1) reducing the initialization value of the BN scale parameter and 2) decreasing the learning rate on the BN scale parameter can together lead to significant improvements. These alterations to BN are straightforward adaptions to standard implementations with existing libraries (*e.g.*, PyTorch [25], TensorFlow [1]) and have no impact on model complexity or training time. We additionally present a means to further apply BN to the task of input data normalization.

Experiments are provided to compare our proposed BN method to standard BN across multiple popular benchmark datasets and network architectures, and further compare with alternative and existing methods. Notably, we conduct *multiple* training runs, each using a different random seed, for every experiment to properly show statistically significant differences. Results indicate that the proposed technique can yield significant gains with no additional computational costs. Our contributions are summarized as follows:

1. A new BN initialization and update method for improving performance with no increase in parameters or computations.
2. A method that easily integrates into existing BN implementations.
3. An online BN-based input data normalization process.
4. A statistical schema for reporting/evaluating comparative results that eliminates subjectivity and improvements that could be attributed to randomness.

2 Related Work

BN contains operations for both the normalization and transformation of features. Multiple works have proposed related techniques for inter-network feature normalization and/or transformation to achieve improved performance.

Various types of normalization layers exist and differ on how they select which features to group for normalization. Layer normalization (LN) [3] applies to each instance across all input feature channels and is commonly employed in transformer networks [8,33]. Instance normalization (IN) [32] is computed in a similar manner, except it normalizes each channel individually for each instance (example) and is frequently used in image-to-image translation [41]. Group normalization (GN) [36] falls between LN and IN by normalizing groups of channels in individual instances. When the group size equals the total number of channels, GN becomes LN. Similarly, when each channel is a separate group, GN becomes IN. The aforementioned normalization layers were designed to perform better than BN in situations where the training batch size is limited. However, BN remains dominant in the context of CNNs and image classification due to the ability of having large batch sizes on common datasets [11,28,31,37]. In our work, we focus on improving the affine transformation component in BN, though our work could be applied to any of the normalization layer types.

Related work has appeared to extend the affine transformation component of BN. Rather than using only learnable scale and shift parameters, the approach of [16] predicts scale and shift values using a small autoencoder network and combines them with the standard learnable versions. Similarly, in [22] they combine predicted and learned scale and shift parameters by utilizing a mixture of affine transformations and a feature attention mechanism to obtain the final transformation. A convolutional layer is used to replace the affine transformation in [38]. In [23], an attention-based transformation is introduced to integrate instance-specific information into an extra scale parameter. In [9], two different calibration mechanisms are proposed and integrated into BN to calibrate features and to incorporate instance-specific statistics. These mechanisms consist of an initial centering operation that occurs before normalization and a scaling operation in the affine transformation. Their scaling is similar to [23], differing by using the *normalized* features rather than the *raw* input features for the instance-specific information, as well as employing a different initialization. In [2], it is mentioned that the initial value of the scale parameter could be treated as a hyperparameter, though not experimented or discussed further. Alternative initialization values for the shift parameter and numerical stability constant (ϵ) are explored in [39].

The approaches of [9,16,22,23] all initialize the existing BN affine transformation parameters to the standard values of $\gamma = 1$ and $\beta = 0$, but employ different initializations for their additional parameters. In [16,22], their additional parameters are initialized using samples from a normal distribution, thus their initial scale values are not constant across the network and could have a magnitude >1. In [9], they initialize the additional parameters for their scaling operation such that they "play no role at the beginning of training" [9], however, the resulting initial scale value is actually <1. A grid search is performed in [23] to select the best performing initialization values, which also produces a resulting initial scale value <1, with the "theoretical understanding of the best initialization [left as] future work" [23]. For both [9,23], the resulting scale value is <1, constant across all BNs in the network, and fixed for any scenario. The approaches of [9,23] are most similar to our work, but unlike these methods, our approach does not introduce any additional parameters or computations and instead focuses directly on the initialization and updating of the existing scale parameter γ for each BN.

3   Framework

In this section, we initially review the BN formulation then describe the two main tenets of our approach: BN scale initialization and learning rate reduction. We then derive the influence of BN on the backward gradients and discuss various aspects that are influenced by the inclusion of BN. Lastly, we introduce a new BN for input data normalization.

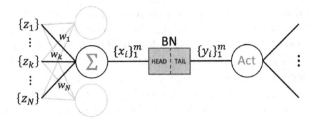

Fig. 1. Flow diagram for a single channel/neuron of BN

3.1 BN Formulation

BN is composed of two sequential channel-wise operations. The first operation, the "head", normalizes the data. The second operation, the "tail", performs an affine transformation on the normalized data. Both operations are applied to each individual channel/neuron across a batch of data.

In the forward pass during training, the head operation first obtains the mean (μ_B) and variance (σ_B^2) of an incoming batch B of data/features containing m examples ($X = \{x_i\}_1^m$) using $\mu_B = \frac{1}{m}\sum_{i=1}^m x_i$ and $\sigma_B^2 = \frac{1}{m}\sum_{i=1}^m (x_i - \mu_B)^2$. With these statistics, the input batch is then normalized to have zero mean and unit standard deviation using

$$\hat{X} = \frac{X - \mu_B}{\sqrt{\sigma_B^2 + \epsilon}} \tag{1}$$

where ϵ is a small value used for numerical stability. Throughout training, μ_B and σ_B^2 are employed to update momentum-based averages of the overall mean and variance, which serve as global statistics at test time. Last, the tail affine transformation $Y = \gamma \cdot \hat{X} + \beta$ is applied to the normalized data ($\hat{X}$) using learnable scale (γ) and shift (β) parameters (again, one for each channel).

The data flow when using BN is shown in Fig. 1, where BN is typically placed between a linear operator and an activation function. The figure depicts a fully-connected layer for ease in explanation and is easily extended to CNNs.

3.2 Proposed Adjustments to γ

The standard procedure for initializing each BN is setting $\gamma = 1$ and $\beta = 0$, with the expectation that the affine transformation can learn optimal values and could undo the preceding normalization if desired [15]. Instead, as we have observed, the learned BN parameters tend to remain close to their initial values which are not likely to be optimal. Furthermore, we have noticed that the BN normalization head (Eq. 1) can often produce overly large values (*e.g.*, $>6\sigma$) as input to the BN affine tail and subsequent convolutional/fully-connected layer (all before another BN), which can be undesirable for learning [15,20,21]. Therefore, there could exist more optimal values of γ not achieved with current learning strategies.

A possible direct solution based on these observations would be to initialize $\gamma < 1$ such that the data is immediately scaled down at the start of training, addressing the presence of overly large values, and furthermore enabling the shift parameter β to have a broader reach on the scaled data before the activation function. Therefore, we propose to treat γ as a hyperparameter (for all BNs in the network) to be initialized in the interval $(0, 1]$ while leaving the default initialization of $\beta = 0$. We will show later that there exists a range of γ initialization values within the interval that can lead to significant increases in test accuracy over the default $\gamma = 1$ initialization.

Since we observed that the learned BN parameters tend to remain somewhat close to their initialization (regardless of the initial value and other hyperparameter settings), it seems necessary to also consider altering the update strategy of these parameters. A seemingly intuitive solution would be to increase the learning rate (α) for the BN parameters only, thus allowing larger updates and the ability to potentially explore more optimal values in the parameter space. However, we have seen this *degrade* performance. Instead, we propose to *reduce* the learning rate for only the scale γ to enable a more fine-grained search, leaving the shift β with larger updates to have a broader and more stable search of the normalized and γ-scaled data. More specifically, we apply a learning rate reduction on γ using $\alpha_\gamma = (\alpha/c)$, where c is a positive constant. Though the value of c could be considered another hyperparameter, we experimented with a wide range of values for c and found that performance gains can be achieved as long as the learning rate for γ is sufficiently and reasonably reduced. Thus, we *fix* this γ learning rate reduction *constant* to $c = 100$ for *all* experiments.

With a proposed smaller initial value for γ, it is important to theoretically understand any effect it will have on the gradients for learning. We next examine the gradients of BN to show the influence of γ and other important relationships.

3.3   BN Gradients

To update a network via gradient descent and backpropagation, loss gradients must be able to propagate through the BN module. For example, parameter w_1 in Fig. 1 is updated using gradient descent by

$$w_1^{new} = w_1^{old} - \alpha \cdot \frac{\partial \mathcal{L}}{\partial w_1} \tag{2}$$

Using the chain rule with a batch of data $\{x_i\}_1^m$, the loss with respect to w_1 is computed as

$$\frac{\partial \mathcal{L}}{\partial w_1} = \frac{1}{m} \sum_{i=1}^{m} \frac{\partial \mathcal{L}}{\partial x_i} \cdot \frac{\partial x_i}{\partial w_1} \tag{3}$$

The BN input x_i is computed from the linear operation $x_i = \sum_{k=1}^{N} w_k \cdot z_{k,i}$, where $z_{k,i}$ is the ith batch value from the kth channel output from the previous layer (see Fig. 1). Therefore $\partial x_i / \partial w_1 = z_{1,i}$ and Eq. 3 becomes

$$\frac{\partial \mathcal{L}}{\partial w_1} = \frac{1}{m} \sum_{i=1}^{m} \frac{\partial \mathcal{L}}{\partial x_i} \cdot z_{1,i} \tag{4}$$

Similarly, the gradient $\partial \mathcal{L} / \partial x_i$ through the BN is computed using the chain rule (described in [15]) as

$$\frac{\partial \mathcal{L}}{\partial x_i} = \frac{\partial \mathcal{L}}{\partial \hat{x}_i} \frac{\partial \hat{x}_i}{\partial x_i} + \frac{\partial \mathcal{L}}{\partial \sigma_B^2} \frac{\partial \sigma_B^2}{\partial x_i} + \frac{\partial \mathcal{L}}{\partial \mu_B} \frac{\partial \mu_B}{\partial x_i} \tag{5}$$

with the x_i dependent gradients

$$\frac{\partial \hat{x}_i}{\partial x_i} = \frac{1}{\sqrt{\sigma_B^2 + \epsilon}} \qquad \frac{\partial \sigma_B^2}{\partial x_i} = \frac{2}{m}(x_i - \mu_B) \qquad \frac{\partial \mu_B}{\partial x_i} = \frac{1}{m} \tag{6}$$

and the remaining gradients

$$\frac{\partial \mathcal{L}}{\partial \hat{x}_i} = \frac{\partial \mathcal{L}}{\partial y_i} \cdot \gamma \tag{7}$$

$$\frac{\partial \mathcal{L}}{\partial \sigma_B^2} = \sum_{i=1}^{m} \frac{\partial \mathcal{L}}{\partial \hat{x}_i}(x_i - \mu_B) \cdot \frac{-1}{2}\left(\sigma_B^2 + \epsilon\right)^{-\frac{3}{2}} \tag{8}$$

$$\frac{\partial \mathcal{L}}{\partial \mu_B} = \left(\sum_{i=1}^{m} \frac{\partial \mathcal{L}}{\partial \hat{x}_i} \cdot \frac{1}{\sqrt{\sigma_B^2 + \epsilon}}\right) + \frac{\partial \mathcal{L}}{\partial \sigma_B^2} \cdot \frac{2}{m} \sum_{i=1}^{m}(x_i - \mu_B) \tag{9}$$

where $\partial \mathcal{L} / \partial y_i$ is the gradient accumulated from all downstream layers. For thoroughness, the gradients for the affine transformation parameters γ and β are

$$\frac{\partial \mathcal{L}}{\partial \gamma} = \sum_{i=1}^{m} \frac{\partial \mathcal{L}}{\partial y_i} \cdot \hat{x}_i \qquad \frac{\partial \mathcal{L}}{\partial \beta} = \sum_{i=1}^{m} \frac{\partial \mathcal{L}}{\partial y_i} \tag{10}$$

Substituting Eqs. 6–9 into Eq. 5, we show that

$$\frac{\partial \mathcal{L}}{\partial x_i} = \left(\frac{\partial \mathcal{L}}{\partial y_i} \cdot \gamma\right)\left(\frac{1}{\sqrt{\sigma_B^2 + \epsilon}}\right) +$$

$$\left(\sum_{i=1}^{m} \frac{\partial \mathcal{L}}{\partial \hat{x}_i}(x_i - \mu_B) \cdot \frac{-1}{2}\left(\sigma_B^2 + \epsilon\right)^{-\frac{3}{2}}\right)\left(\frac{2}{m}(x_i - \mu_B)\right) +$$

$$\left(\left(\sum_{i=1}^{m} \frac{\partial \mathcal{L}}{\partial \hat{x}_i} \cdot \frac{1}{\sqrt{\sigma_B^2 + \epsilon}}\right) + \frac{\partial \mathcal{L}}{\partial \sigma_B^2} \cdot \frac{2}{m} \sum_{i=1}^{m}(x_i - \mu_B)\right)\left(\frac{1}{m}\right) \tag{11}$$

and after multiple reduction steps (novel to our work),

$$\frac{\partial \mathcal{L}}{\partial x_i} = \frac{\gamma}{\sqrt{\sigma_B^2 + \epsilon}} \cdot \left[\frac{\partial \mathcal{L}}{\partial y_i} - \frac{1}{m} \sum_{i=1}^{m} \frac{\partial \mathcal{L}}{\partial y_i}(1 - \hat{x}_i)\right] = \frac{\gamma}{\sqrt{\sigma_B^2 + \epsilon}} \cdot G_i \tag{12}$$

where G_i is a function of the downstream gradients of y_i (*after* the BN layer) and the normalized values $\hat{X}$ (*within* the BN layer). We refer to the leading ratio $\gamma / \sqrt{\sigma_B^2 + \epsilon}$ as the BN 'gradient factor', which is composed of the affine scale parameter γ for this current BN and the variance σ_B^2 of the *incoming* data to that BN. Therefore the update for w_1 (Eq. 2) is computed as

$$w_1^{new} = w_1^{old} - \alpha \cdot \frac{\gamma}{\sqrt{\sigma_B^2 + \epsilon}} \left(\frac{1}{m} \sum_{i=1}^{m} G_i \cdot z_i \right) \tag{13}$$

We will next show how this gradient factor relates to various aspects of learning.

Gradient Influence of γ. Following Fig. 1 at the beginning of training *before any updates*, the incoming data variance σ_B^2 to the BN is

$$\sigma_B^2 = \mathrm{Var}(\{x_i\}_1^m) = \sum_{k=1}^{N} w_k^2 \cdot \mathrm{Var}(\{z_{k,i}\}_1^m) = \sum_{k=1}^{N} w_k^2 \cdot \sigma_k^2 \tag{14}$$

As each of the k input batches $\{z_{k,i}\}_1^m$ come from the output of a *previous* BN (each normalized then scaled with γ_{prev}) that is also passed through an activation function,

$$\sum_{k=1}^{N} w_k^2 \cdot \sigma_k^2 = \sigma^2 \sum_{k=1}^{N} w_k^2 = \sigma_{act}^2 \cdot \gamma_{prev}^2 \sum_{k=1}^{N} w_k^2 = \sigma_{act}^2 \cdot \gamma_{prev}^2 \cdot \omega \tag{15}$$

where σ_{act}^2 is the variance of the normalized (but unscaled) data after being passed through an activation function. For example, a unit Gaussian passed through a ReLU yields a *rectified* normal distribution with an empirical $\sigma_{act}^2 \approx (0.58)^2$. When the normalized data is scaled by γ and passed through an activation, the resulting variance is $\sigma^2 = \sigma_{act}^2 \cdot \gamma^2$.

From Eq. 15, the scale parameter γ_{prev} of the *previous* layer BNs is therefore embedded in the *incoming* data variance (σ_B^2). At the start of training, where $\gamma_{prev} = \gamma_{curr}$, the scales will essentially cancel in the gradient factor of Eq. 12

$$\frac{\gamma_{curr}}{\sqrt{\sigma_B^2 + \epsilon}} = \frac{\gamma_{curr}}{\gamma_{prev} \cdot \sqrt{\sigma_{act}^2 \cdot \omega + \epsilon}} = \frac{1}{\sqrt{\sigma_{act}^2 \cdot \omega + \epsilon}} \tag{16}$$

again assuming a negligible ϵ. Thus for the initial backward pass, the initial BN scale value for γ has *no effect* on the local BN gradients (the first BN layer will be addressed in Sect. 3.4). While γ will not affect the initial backward pass, it will contribute to the forward pass and loss. Though the value of each γ will naturally migrate toward a more optimal value during training, each BN gradient factor should remain non-degenerate. Therefore initializing $\gamma < 1$ will not cause any cascading issues during training.

Network Weight Initialization. Most network weight initialization schemes take into account the number of either incoming or outgoing links in a layer. For example, Kaiming normal initialization [10] initializes the weights in a network following a normal distribution $\mathcal{N}(0, \sigma^2)$ with $\sigma = \mathrm{gain}/\sqrt{\mathrm{fan\_mode}}$, where 'gain' is a constant determined by the activation function used in the network and 'fan_mode' is a value representing either the number of incoming (fan-in) or outgoing (fan-out) links. Thus the number of links affects the standard deviation of the normal distribution, with more links yielding a tighter distribution.

As shown in Eqs. 14 and 15, the variance σ_B^2 of the data going into a BN at the start of training is dependent on the sum of the squared *incoming* weights (ω). Therefore, weight initialization approaches based on *fan-in* will initially balance the gradient factor for each BN across the network. In our experiments we therefore employed fan-in weight initialization in our networks.

3.4 BN-Based Input Normalization

Traditional methods for normalizing the input data typically utilize either "fixed" bounds based on the data type min/max or compute "offline" dataset statistics:

- Fixed: Chooses the mean (μ) as the middle value of the data type and the standard deviation (σ) as the $\pm$ maximum possible value of the mean-subtracted data (*e.g.*, $\mu = \sigma = 128$ for an 8-bit [0–255] image).
- Offline: Preprocess the data to estimate the μ and σ based on the average of averages across batches or individual examples in the dataset.

These methods normalize the data using $(X - \mu) / \sigma$ (as used in Eq. 1 for BN).

The fixed input normalization technique can be problematic for images not spanning the full possible range of values for its data type. For example, with a dataset of low-contrast imagery the true μ and σ would be much smaller. The offline statistics approach obviously requires the extra steps of computing the dataset μ and σ before training.

Consider the BN gradient factor $\gamma/\sqrt{\sigma_B^2 + \epsilon}$ for the weights just before the *first* BN in the network on the *initial* backward pass. Here the variance σ_B^2 is computed from the input data itself (Eq. 14). Examining Eq. 15, we expect this variance to be $\sigma_{act}^2 \cdot \gamma^2 \cdot \omega$ as for all other layers, however neither the scale γ or activation are present. Therefore, a *smaller/larger* σ^2 of the input data, where $\sigma^2 \neq \sigma_{act}^2 \cdot \gamma^2 \cdot \omega$, will result in a *larger/smaller* gradient factor as compared with the other layers in the network.

This bias with traditional input normalization techniques can be removed by conveniently prepending a new BN layer to the network. Since it would not be ideal to immediately threshold the input data with an activation following this new BN layer, we initialize these BNs to have a modified scale value $\hat{\gamma} = \sigma_{act} \cdot \gamma$, where $\hat{\gamma} = 0.58 \cdot \gamma$ for a ReLU-based network, to account for the missing activation function's influence on the variance. For this BN layer, the built-in shift parameter β is unnecessary as no activation function follows and can therefore be removed or fixed to $\beta = 0$. Thus, employing this BN-based input data normalization method will only add a single scale parameter $\hat{\gamma}$ per input channel (*e.g.*, 3 parameters total for an RGB image in a CNN).

4 Experiments

To evaluate our proposed approach, we conducted a series of classification experiments using several datasets and network architectures, examined different possible versions of our approach, and compared to relevant existing methods.

4.1   Datasets and Network Architectures

We employed four established classification datasets for our evaluation. CIFAR-10 [19] contains 10 classes, each with 5K and 1K images for training and testing, respectively. The larger, yet distinct, CIFAR-100 [19] has 100 classes, each with 500 training and 100 testing examples. The fine-grained visual classification (FGVC) dataset CUB-200 [34] contains 200 classes with 5994 training and 5794 testing examples. Finally, Stanford Cars (ST-Cars) [18] is another FGVC dataset that consists of 196 classes with 8144 and 8041 images for training and testing, respectively. In order to have a validation set for each of the datasets, we randomly sampled 10% of the training examples class-wise for validation.

We primarily employed networks from the ResNet [11] architecture family, using ResNet-18 for CIFAR-10, ResNet-34 for CIFAR-100, and ResNet-50 for CUB-200/ST-Cars. Due to the smaller image sizes of CIFAR-10/CIFAR-100, common modifications to its associated model were made which consisted of altering the first convolutional layer to have a 3×3 kernel with stride of 1 and padding of 1 (originally a 7×7 with stride of 2 and padding of 2) and removing the max pooling operation that followed the initial convolutional layer. For initialization, convolutional layer weights used Kaiming normal initialization [10] with 'fan-in' mode for a ReLU nonlinearity, fully connected layer weights were initialized with a uniform distribution (also using 'fan-in'), and all biases (including the BN shift parameter β) were initialized to 0. The BN scale parameter γ will be initialized with various values to demonstrate our approach. We additionally examined RepVGG [7], MobileNetV2 [28], and ResNeXt [37] architectures (with the same initialization strategy).

4.2   Training Details

Training is implemented using a standard regime and in a manner where all hyperparameters are set using typical values. Across all experiments, we used SGD with momentum (0.9) and weight decay (1e−4) on the convolutional and fully connected layer weights. BN parameters and all network biases are properly excluded from weight decay as it is not necessary to impose a constraint to minimize these parameter values. Networks were each trained for 180 epochs with a half-period cosine learning rate scheduler and across multiple initial learning rates (to be presented). We used a batch size of 128 for CIFAR-10/CIFAR-100 and 64 for CUB-200/ST-Cars. Data augmentation schemes for CIFAR-10/CIFAR-100 consisted of random horizontal flipping only and for CUB-200/ST-Cars images were resized to 256×256 then randomly cropped to 224×224, followed by random horizontal flipping. After augmentations, the input data is normalized online using our proposed BN-based input normalization technique with the initialization of $\hat{\gamma} = 0.58 \cdot \gamma$ corresponding to ReLU activations (Sect. 3.4). In our experiments, the epoch yielding the best validation accuracy was used to select the final model. Our approach was implemented using PyTorch [25] and all models were trained and evaluated on a single NVIDIA V100 GPU.

We note that we *purposefully* used minimal regularization techniques in our experiments to show noticeable improvements that can be attributed solely to changes within BN using our approach. Our goal is *not* to provide new SOTA scores on the datasets used for evaluation. However, if more regularization is employed to improve baseline performance, our approach may still provide further gains (as shown in an experiment below).

To demonstrate our proposed BN scale initialization approach, we explored a variety of possible γ values in the half-open unit interval $(0, 1]$ and several learning rates α. Smaller values of γ and larger values of α are typically favored and thus we examined a subset of values for γ and α after the initial CIFAR-10 experiments. As described in Sect. 3.2, we also divided α by $c = 100$ for only γ. For our baseline comparison, referred to as 'BASE', we used the default BN scale initialization ($\gamma = 1$) and no learning rate reduction ($c = 1$), but retained the BN-based input normalization for fair comparison.

4.3   Statistical Significance

As variations in the final score (accuracy) can be caused by different random number generator (RNG) seeds resulting in different network weight initializations and different batching of training data [26,35], we conducted several runs for each experiment and performed a statistically-grounded comparative analysis on our results. For *each* experiment (a specific BN scale value γ and learning rate α), we trained 15 networks (of the same form), each with a different RNG seed, and reported the mean and standard deviation of test accuracy. Our seeds were sequential numbers in the range [1, 15], which were made more complex using MD5 as suggested in [17,27].

A result is judged to be significantly better than BASE according to a one-sided paired t-test [6] with a significance level of $p \le 0.05$ using the scores from the 15 runs. All significant improvements over BASE are emphasized in **bold** in the following tables and the highest mean for each experiment is <u>underlined</u>. We suggest this method as a proper technique to evaluate and compare empirical results to instill confidence for the reader on reported improvements.

4.4   Results

We first conducted experiments on CIFAR-10 using the selected BN scale initialization values, then compared our method with possible alternative BN scale formulations. Next, we evaluated our method on different datasets and network architectures, and then compared with different methods of input normalization. Finally, we compared to relevant established approaches on all of the datasets.

CIFAR-10. For our initial experiments with CIFAR-10, we used $\gamma \in \{1.0, 0.75, 0.5, 0.25, 0.1, 0.05, 0.01\}$ and $\alpha \in \{0.1, 0.01, 0.001\}$. Results on CIFAR-10 are presented in Table 1a. Using the proposed $\gamma < 1$ initialization with the learning rate reduction ($c = 100$), significant improvements are found across all learning rates. These results alone demonstrate that the default settings and learning

Table 1. Accuracy on (a) CIFAR-10 and (b) CIFAR-100, CUB-200, and ST-Cars

(a)

γ	Learning Rate (α)		
	0.1	0.01	0.001
0.01	85.50±0.39	87.11±0.23	80.37±0.58
0.05	90.19±0.32	88.84±0.32	76.98±0.71
0.10	90.80±0.20	87.31±0.37	74.48±0.55
0.25	90.32±0.24	85.33±0.43	73.83±0.64
0.50	90.17±0.19	84.60±0.35	72.80±0.68
0.75	90.19±0.18	84.43±0.30	72.01±0.58
1.00	89.81±0.46	84.48±0.33	71.15±0.56
BASE	89.44±0.45	84.64±0.25	71.32±0.60

(b)

Dataset	γ	Learning Rate (α)	
		0.1	0.01
CIFAR100	0.05	68.18±0.30	64.01±0.54
	0.10	68.80±0.49	62.83±0.48
	0.50	67.74±0.44	59.05±0.41
	BASE	66.01±0.95	58.48±0.53
CUB-200	0.05	58.32±0.54	34.23±0.86
	0.10	58.52±0.69	39.92±0.76
	0.50	50.45±1.22	45.31±0.59
	BASE	46.26±1.59	41.61±1.03
ST-Cars	0.05	78.29±0.44	44.18±1.29
	0.10	78.26±0.61	48.60±1.02
	0.50	70.17±1.45	51.18±2.16
	BASE	64.73±2.87	51.86±1.80

of the BN affine transformation (BASE) are not ideal. For this dataset, there is a noticeable trend that as the learning rate decreases, a smaller initialization value for γ is favored, with smaller values for γ preferred in general. Performance dropped heavily for BASE at lower learning rates, however our approach with smaller γ initializations had much less of a decrease. We also experimented with initially setting the BN scale parameter to $\gamma > 1$, but experiments produced degraded results, as expected.

With only the learning rate reduction method ($c = 100$, $\gamma = 1$), there remained a significant gain over BASE ($c = 1$, $\gamma = 1$) at the highest learning rate ($\alpha = 0.1$). To confirm the importance of learning rate reduction, we ablated it from our method (*i.e.*, $c = 1$, $\gamma < 1$) and results showed *degraded* performance from the scores presented in Table 1a. Thus, combining our proposed BN scale initialization and learning rate reduction *together* is necessary to obtain the best performance.

In additional experiments with a *stronger* BASE model (employing Random-Crop data augmentation [11,12,40]) having 93.79% accuracy, our proposed BN scale initialization at $\gamma = \{1.0, 0.75, 0.5, 0.25, 0.1\}$ and BN scale learning rate reduction at $c = 100$ still provided statistically significant improvements.

Alternative Scale Formulation. Given the standard affine formulation $y = \gamma \cdot \hat{X} + \beta$ of BN (as we employ), two similar scale-based alternatives could be A1: $Y = \gamma(\hat{X} + \beta)$ and A2: $Y = \gamma(\gamma_0 \cdot \hat{X} + \beta)$. In all three formulations, initialization is $0 < \gamma \leq 1$, $\gamma_0 = 1$, and $\beta = 0$. The two alternatives differ from the standard formulation in that they apply scaling to β as well, which we argue could limit the ability to shift the data sufficiently before the ReLU activation. While A1 does not introduce any extra parameters or additional computations (similar to ours), A2 includes the extra γ_0 parameter (and is similar to [14]).

We compared the three formulations on CIFAR-10 using the same γ values and learning rates presented in Table 1a. All approaches gave significant improvements over BASE, further indicating that the default initialization of

BN is not appropriate. At the highest learning rate, there was only a slight difference between the scores (within 0.15% of each other). However, at the lower learning rates the standard formulation (ours) had a clear and significant advantage (up to 7% gain). These results further support our argument that scaling down only the normalized data with γ enables the shift parameter β to act on a broader range for the following activation function.

CIFAR-100, CUB-200, and ST-Cars. We next evaluated our approach on CIFAR-100, CUB-200, and ST-Cars. As mentioned in Sect. 4.1, we employed ResNet-34 for CIFAR-100 and used ResNet-50 for CUB-200/ST-Cars. Networks for CUB-200/ST-Cars typically employ pretrained ImageNet [5] models and finetune, however since pretrained models utilize the default BN initialization (which affects the BN statistics and network weights learned), we therefore train all of our networks from scratch. The results with $\gamma \in \{0.5, 0.1, 0.05\}$ and $\alpha \in \{0.1, 0.01\}$ are reported in Table 1b.

It is clear that our approach with smaller γ initialization and reduced γ updates can still produce significant improvements in test accuracy for these datasets that contain a larger number of classes than CIFAR-10. For the highest learning rate, all examined scale values produced significantly better results, but at the lower learning rate for ST-Cars it was unable to achieve significant gains with any of the initialization values, though one scale value ($\gamma = 0.5$) was not significantly different from BASE. One could argue that this lower learning rate is not adequate for ST-Cars.

Network Depth and Architectures. We further examined how our approach extends to different ResNet depths and other network architectures on CIFAR-10. In particular, we trained and examined the deeper ResNet-50, ResNet-101, and ResNet-152 models, and additionally employed MobileNetV2 [28], RepVGG-A0 [7], and ResNeXt-50 [37]. Again, since CIFAR-10 consists of small input image sizes, modifications were made to the other architectures. For MobileNetV2, the initial convolutional layer and second and third bottleneck blocks were changed to have a stride of 1. Similarly, for RepVGG-A0, stage 0 and stage 1 were adjusted to have a stride of 1. ResNeXt-50 was modified similar to ResNet (Sect. 4.1).

Results are shown in Table 2a for $\gamma \in \{0.5, 0.1, 0.05\}$ and $\alpha \in \{0.1, 0.01\}$. Our performance increase was even greater with the deeper ResNet models (as compared to ResNet-18), which suggests our method may be particularly beneficial for training networks containing more parameters/layers faster than with the default BN initialization. Furthermore, our approach transferred well to the other network architectures, emphasizing the generality of our $\gamma < 1$ initialization and learning rate reduction.

Input Normalization. We next compared our proposed input data normalization BN layer to the standard fixed and offline methods (Sect. 3.4). All experiments were conducted on CIFAR-10 and employed our proposed $\gamma < 1$ initialization and learning rate reduction ($c = 100$). Therefore, any differences reported are solely due to how the input data was normalized. Results showed that all three methods produced similar results. Therefore, our proposed online BN-

Table 2. (a) Accuracy on CIFAR-10 employing various network depths and network architectures. (b) Comparison with RBN and IEBN variations on CIFAR-10, CIFAR-100, CUB-200, and ST-Cars

(a)

Network	γ	Learning Rate (α)	
		0.1	0.01
ResNet-50	0.05	**91.23**±0.20	**89.60**±0.19
	0.10	**91.28**±0.26	87.67±0.20
	0.50	**89.49**±0.27	84.74±0.37
	BASE	86.94±1.23	85.04±0.32
ResNet-101	0.05	**91.58**±0.22	**90.02**±0.22
	0.10	**91.26**±0.18	88.35±0.28
	0.50	**89.89**±0.74	85.23±0.50
	BASE	88.28±1.39	84.74±0.56
ResNet-152	0.05	**91.20**±0.16	**90.00**±0.17
	0.10	**90.89**±0.41	88.31±0.33
	0.50	**90.17**±0.23	85.23±0.62
	BASE	88.73±0.62	84.15±0.79
RepVGG-A0	0.05	89.71±0.30	**88.08**±0.26
	0.10	**90.63**±0.26	86.67±0.28
	0.50	89.96±0.20	84.28±0.47
	BASE	89.59±0.27	83.92±0.38
MobileNetV2	0.05	88.32±0.21	**87.02**±0.38
	0.10	**91.14**±0.17	85.10±0.30
	0.50	91.07±0.21	81.25±0.41
	BASE	90.60±0.19	80.03±0.57
ResNeXt-50	0.05	**92.04**±0.22	**89.06**±0.24
	0.10	**92.02**±0.19	86.10±0.24
	0.50	91.21±0.47	80.31±0.53
	BASE	88.60±1.57	82.60±0.43

(b)

Dataset	Method	Learning Rate (α)	
		0.1	0.01
CIFAR10	RBN	90.17±0.22	84.72±0.29
	RBN⁻	90.11±0.24	84.50±0.36
	IEBN	90.18±0.26	85.34±0.39
	IEBN⁻	90.15±0.24	85.29±0.35
	Ours	**90.80**±0.20	**88.84**±0.32
	BASE	89.44±0.45	84.64±0.25
CIFAR100	RBN	66.95±0.57	58.95±0.42
	RBN⁻	66.82±0.55	58.90±0.61
	IEBN	66.94±0.39	60.61±0.40
	IEBN⁻	66.95±0.32	60.89±0.41
	Ours	**68.80**±0.49	**64.01**±0.54
	BASE	66.01±0.95	58.48±0.53
CUB-200	RBN	48.68±1.56	44.68±0.59
	RBN⁻	47.14±2.72	43.02±1.22
	IEBN	54.12±0.60	44.92±0.74
	IEBN⁻	53.81±0.76	44.09±0.65
	Ours	**58.52**±0.69	**45.31**±0.59
	BASE	46.26±1.59	41.61±1.03
ST-Cars	RBN	68.17±1.84	51.87±1.34
	RBN⁻	67.84±2.96	**52.30**±1.73
	IEBN	73.60±0.92	51.06±0.87
	IEBN⁻	74.04±1.55	51.08±0.78
	Ours	**78.29**±0.44	51.18±2.16
	BASE	64.73±2.87	51.86±1.80

based input normalization method can serve as a replacement for the traditional techniques, where it *automatically* handles input normalization and avoids the previously mentioned issues that may stem from employing the other techniques (Sect. 3.4).

4.5 Related Approaches

Lastly, we examined the existing related methods of Representative BN (RBN) [9] and Instance Enhancement BN (IEBN) [23] that utilize instance-specific statistics to compute an *extra* scaling parameter (as described in Sect. 2). For this work, we focused on the scaling aspect of RBN/IEBN for a more direct comparison of methods. The data normalization component for both approaches is the same as ours (which produces $\hat{X}$), but the affine transformation of RBN/IEBN is $Y = \gamma \cdot \mathcal{S} \cdot \hat{X} + \beta$ with $\mathcal{S} = sigmoid(w_v \cdot \text{GAP}(\mathcal{X}) + w_b)$, where GAP is the global average pooling operation, w_v and w_b are *additional* learnable weights (one of each per channel), and $\mathcal{S}$ is the result of their additional scaling method.

For RBN, $\mathcal{X} = \hat{X}$ (normalized features) and for IEBN $\mathcal{X} = X$ (raw input features). For RBN, the additional parameters w_v and w_b are initialized to 0 and 1, respectively, while IEBN initializes these parameters to $w_v = 0$ and $w_b = -1$. The standard BN parameters are initialized to $\gamma = 1$ and $\beta = 0$ for both approaches. Thus the resulting BN has an initial effective scale of $\gamma \cdot \mathcal{S} \approx 0.731$ for RBN and 0.269 for IEBN. Both approaches have smaller initial scale values (*i.e.*, <1) similar to ours, though these initial values are *fixed* for *all* scenarios. Related to our use of a reduced learning rate for γ, their use of a sigmoid will also force smaller gradient updates on w_v and w_b (that affect the resulting scale) since the derivative of a sigmoid function is $sigmoid(x) \cdot (1 - sigmoid(x))$.

We considered two versions of both approaches, one with the instance-specific statistics (RBN, IEBN) and one that removes the instance-specific statistics and w_v (RBN$^-$, IEBN$^-$). This modifies their scaling method to become $\mathcal{S} = sigmoid(w_b)$ and results in the same initial scale value as previously mentioned. Comparisons of RBN, RBN$^-$, IEBN, IEBN$^-$, and BASE with our approach for all of the datasets are presented in Table 2. We report results for our approach using the best performing γ initialization selected from $\gamma \in \{0.5, 0.1, 0.05\}$.

When evaluated against each other using a one-sided paired t-test (with a significance level of $p \leq 0.05$), our approach significantly outperformed RBN/RBN$^-$ and IEBN/IEBN$^-$ across all datasets and learning rates except for ST-Cars at the lower 0.01 learning rate, where no approach was significantly different from another. As mentioned, this learning rate is arguably insufficient for ST-Cars.

Our work has shown that *flexibility* in the initialization of γ coupled with a reduced learning rate is advantageous to achieve larger performance gains as compared to a *fixed* initial scale value for all situations. Furthermore, the minor differences in results between RBN/IEBN and RBN$^-$/IEBN$^-$ suggest that the contribution of instance-specific information is not as important as the scaling itself. However, it may be possible to incorporate instance-specific statistics with our approach for further gains.

5   Conclusion

We revisited BN to address the observed issues of learned BN parameters remaining close to initialization and passing forward overly large values from the normalization. We derived and empirically demonstrated across multiple datasets and network architectures that initializing the BN scale parameter $\gamma < 1$ and reducing the learning rate on γ can yield statistically improved performance over the default initialization and update strategy, suggesting that current training strategies are preventing BN from achieving the most optimal γ value. The proposed alterations do not structurally change BN (*i.e.*, no additional parameters) and can easily be applied to existing implementations. Additionally, we presented a special prepended BN to automatically handle input data normalization during training.

Acknowledgements. This research was supported by the U.S. Air Force Research Laboratory under Contract #GRT00054740 (Release #AFRL-2021-3711). We also thank the DoD HPCMP for the use of their computational resources.

References

1. Abadi, M., Barham, P., Chen, J., Chen, Z., et al.: TensorFlow: a system for large-scale machine learning. In: 12th USENIX Symposium on Operating Systems Design and Implementation (2016)
2. Arpit, D., Zhou, Y., Kota, B., Govindaraju, V.: Normalization propagation: a parametric technique for removing internal covariate shift in deep networks. In: International Conference on Machine Learning (2016)
3. Ba, J.L., Kiros, J.R., Hinton, G.E.: Layer normalization. arXiv preprint arXiv:1607.06450 (2016)
4. Bjorck, N., Gomes, C.P., Selman, B., Weinberger, K.Q.: Understanding batch normalization. In: Advances in Neural Information Processing Systems (2018)
5. Deng, J., Dong, W., Socher, R., Li, L.J., Li, K., Fei-Fei, L.: ImageNet: a large-scale hierarchical image database. In: IEEE Conference on Computer Vision and Pattern Recognition (2009)
6. Devore, J.L.: Probability & Statistics for Engineering and the Sciences, 8th edn. Brooks/Cole, Cengage Learning (2011)
7. Ding, X., Zhang, X., Ma, N., Han, J., Ding, G., Sun, J.: RepVGG: making VGG-style ConvNets great again. In: IEEE/CVF Conference on Computer Vision and Pattern Recognition (2021)
8. Dosovitskiy, A., et al.: An image is worth 16×16 words: transformers for image recognition at scale. In: International Conference on Learning Representations (2021)
9. Gao, S.H., Han, Q., Li, D., Cheng, M.M., Peng, P.: Representative batch normalization with feature calibration. In: IEEE/CVF Conference on Computer Vision and Pattern Recognition (2021)
10. He, K., Zhang, X., Ren, S., Sun, J.: Delving deep into rectifiers: surpassing human-level performance on ImageNet classification. In: IEEE International Conference on Computer Vision (2015)
11. He, K., Zhang, X., Ren, S., Sun, J.: Deep residual learning for image recognition. In: IEEE Conference on Computer Vision and Pattern Recognition (2016)
12. Hoffer, E., Ben-Nun, T., Hubara, I., Giladi, N., Hoefler, T., Soudry, D.: Augment your batch: improving generalization through instance repetition. In: IEEE/CVF Conference on Computer Vision and Pattern Recognition (2020)
13. Huang, G., Liu, Z., Van Der Maaten, L., Weinberger, K.Q.: Densely connected convolutional networks. In: IEEE Conference on Computer Vision and Pattern Recognition (2017)
14. Huang, L., Qin, J., Liu, L., Zhu, F., Shao, L.: Layer-wise conditioning analysis in exploring the learning dynamics of DNNs. In: Vedaldi, A., Bischof, H., Brox, T., Frahm, J.-M. (eds.) ECCV 2020. LNCS, vol. 12347, pp. 384–401. Springer, Cham (2020). https://doi.org/10.1007/978-3-030-58536-5_23
15. Ioffe, S., Szegedy, C.: Batch normalization: accelerating deep network training by reducing internal covariate shift. In: International Conference on Machine Learning (2015)
16. Jia, S., Chen, D.J., Chen, H.T.: Instance-level meta normalization. In: IEEE/CVF Conference on Computer Vision and Pattern Recognition (2019)
17. Jones, D.: Good practice in (pseudo) random number generation for bioinformatics applications. Technical report, University College London (2010)
18. Krause, J., Stark, M., Deng, J., Fei-Fei, L.: 3D object representations for fine-grained categorization. In: IEEE Workshop on 3D Representation and Recognition (2013)

19. Krizhevsky, A., Hinton, G., et al.: Learning multiple layers of features from tiny images (2009)
20. LeCun, Y., Bottou, L., Bengio, Y., Haffner, P.: Gradient-based learning applied to document recognition. In: Proceedings of the IEEE (1998)
21. LeCun, Y., Bottou, L., Orr, G.B., Müller, K.-R.: Efficient BackProp. In: Orr, G.B., Müller, K.-R. (eds.) Neural Networks: Tricks of the Trade. LNCS, vol. 1524, pp. 9–50. Springer, Heidelberg (1998). https://doi.org/10.1007/3-540-49430-8_2
22. Li, X., Sun, W., Wu, T.: Attentive normalization. In: Vedaldi, A., Bischof, H., Brox, T., Frahm, J.-M. (eds.) ECCV 2020. LNCS, vol. 12362, pp. 70–87. Springer, Cham (2020). https://doi.org/10.1007/978-3-030-58520-4_5
23. Liang, S., Huang, Z., Liang, M., Yang, H.: Instance enhancement batch normalization: an adaptive regulator of batch noise. In: AAAI Conference on Artificial Intelligence (2020)
24. Luo, P., Wang, X., Shao, W., Peng, Z.: Towards understanding regularization in batch normalization. In: International Conference on Learning Representations (2019)
25. Paszke, A., et al.: PyTorch: an imperative style, high-performance deep learning library. In: Advances in Neural Information Processing Systems (2019)
26. Picard, D.: `torch.manual_seed(3407)` is all you need: on the influence of random seeds in deep learning architectures for computer vision. arXiv preprint arXiv:2109.08203 (2021)
27. PyTorch: Torch Generator. https://pytorch.org/docs/stable/generated/torch.Generator.html. Accessed Aug 2021
28. Sandler, M., Howard, A., Zhu, M., Zhmoginov, A., Chen, L.C.: MobileNetV2: inverted residuals and linear bottlenecks. In: IEEE/CVF Conference on Computer Vision and Pattern Recognition (2018)
29. Santurkar, S., Tsipras, D., Ilyas, A., Madry, A.: How does batch normalization help optimization? In: International Conference on Neural Information Processing Systems (2018)
30. Simonyan, K., Zisserman, A.: Very deep convolutional networks for large-scale image recognition. In: International Conference on Learning Representations (2015)
31. Tan, M., Le, Q.: EfficientNet: rethinking model scaling for convolutional neural networks. In: International Conference on Machine Learning (2019)
32. Ulyanov, D., Vedaldi, A., Lempitsky, V.: Instance normalization: the missing ingredient for fast stylization. arXiv preprint arXiv:1607.08022 (2016)
33. Vaswani, A., et al.: Attention is all you need. In: Advances in Neural Information Processing Systems (2017)
34. Wah, C., Branson, S., Welinder, P., Perona, P., Belongie, S.: The caltech-UCSD birds-200-2011 dataset. Technical report, California Institute of Technology (2011)
35. Wightman, R., Touvron, H., Jégou, H.: ResNet strikes back: an improved training procedure in timm. arXiv preprint arXiv:2110.00476 (2021)
36. Wu, Y., He, K.: Group normalization. Int. J. Comput. Vis. **128**(3), 742–755 (2019). https://doi.org/10.1007/s11263-019-01198-w
37. Xie, S., Girshick, R., Dollár, P., Tu, Z., He, K.: Aggregated residual transformations for deep neural networks. In: IEEE Conference on Computer Vision and Pattern Recognition (2017)
38. Xu, Y., et al.: Batch normalization with enhanced linear normalization. arXiv preprint arXiv:2011.14150 (2020)

39. Yang, G., Pennington, J., Rao, V., Sohl-Dickstein, J., Schoenholz, S.S.: A mean field theory of batch normalization. In: International Conference on Learning Representations (2019)
40. Zhang, S., Nezhadarya, E., Fashandi, H., Liu, J., Graham, D., Shah, M.: Stochastic whitening batch normalization. In: Proceedings of the IEEE/CVF Conference on Computer Vision and Pattern Recognition (2021)
41. Zhu, J.Y., Park, T., Isola, P., Efros, A.A.: Unpaired image-to-image translation using cycle-consistent adversarial networks. In: IEEE International Conference on Computer Vision (2017)

SSBNet: Improving Visual Recognition Efficiency by Adaptive Sampling

Ho Man Kwan$^{(\boxtimes)}$ and Shenghui Song

The Hong Kong University of Science and Technology, Kowloon, Hong Kong
hmkwan@connect.ust.hk, eeshsong@ust.hk

Abstract. Downsampling is widely adopted to achieve a good trade-off between accuracy and latency for visual recognition. Unfortunately, the commonly used pooling layers are not learned, and thus cannot preserve important information. As another dimension reduction method, adaptive sampling weights and processes regions that are relevant to the task, and is thus able to better preserve useful information. However, the use of adaptive sampling has been limited to certain layers. In this paper, we show that using adaptive sampling in the building blocks of a deep neural network can improve its efficiency. In particular, we propose SSB-Net which is built by inserting sampling layers repeatedly into existing networks like ResNet. Experiment results show that the proposed SSB-Net can achieve competitive image classification and object detection performance on ImageNet and COCO datasets. For example, the SSB-ResNet-RS-200 achieved 82.6% accuracy on ImageNet dataset, which is 0.6% higher than the baseline ResNet-RS-152 with a similar complexity. Visualization shows the advantage of SSBNet in allowing different layers to focus on different positions, and ablation studies further validate the advantage of adaptive sampling over uniform methods.

Keywords: Convolutional neural networks · Image recognition · Network architecture · Adaptive sampling · Attention mechanism

1 Introduction

Deep learning models such as convolutional neural networks (CNNs) [7,13,22,24] and Transformers [5] have made unprecedented successes in computer vision. However, achieving efficient inference with stringent latency constraints in real-world applications is very challenging. To obtain a good trade-off between accuracy and latency, downsampling is normally used to reduce the number of operations. Most existing CNNs [7,13,22,24] perform downsampling between stages, coupled with the increase in channel dimension to balance the representation power and computational cost. Typical downsampling operations include strided average/max pooling and convolutions [7,13,14,18,22,24], which are uniformly applied in the spatial dimension.

Supplementary Information The online version contains supplementary material available at https://doi.org/10.1007/978-3-031-19803-8_14.

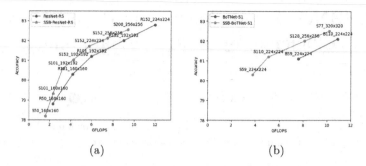

(a)   (b)

Fig. 1. Comparison between the SSB-ResNet-RS and ResNet-RS [2], SSB-BoTNet-S1 and BoTNet-S1 [23] on ImageNet [21] dataset. The proposed SSB-ResNet-RS/SSB-BoTNet-S1 outperforms ResNet-RS and BoTNet-S1 in terms of accuracy to FLOPS ratio. Results of ResNet-RS are from the original paper, where the results of BoTNet-S1 are from reimplementation. See Sect. 4.1.

Besides uniform sampling, there are also non-uniform or adaptive approaches [4,11,12,20,26,32], with which different transformations including zooming, shifting, and deforming can be utilized to selectively focus on the important regions during downsampling. However, the use of adaptive sampling has been limited to certain layers and its application in backbone networks has not been well investigated. Backbone networks are usually pre-trained in some large scale datasets, which are agnostic to the end task like object detection [31]. The challenge for applying adaptive sampling in backbone networks lies in the possible information loss. In particular, later layers cannot access pixels that were skipped by earlier layers, which is quite possible due to the stacking of sampling layers.

Another approach to improve efficiency is to reduce the number of channels. In ResNet [7], the bottleneck layers reduce the channel dimension by using a 1×1 convolution and then perform a costly 3×3 convolution on the low dimensional features to reduce computational complexity. After that, another 1×1 convolution is utilized to restore the dimension and match the shortcut connection. It is noteworthy that residual networks can preserve informative features after the bottleneck operations because the shortcut connection allows signal to bypass the bottleneck.

The bottleneck structure with shortcut connection can be utilized to enable adaptive sampling on backbone networks. In this paper, we propose Saliency Sampling Bottleneck Network (SSBNet), which applies saliency sampler [20,32] in a bottleneck structure to reduce the spatial dimension before costly operations. An inverse operation is then used to restore the feature maps to match the spatial structure of the input that passes through the shortcut connection. Like other bottleneck structures, computationally expensive operations like convolution are applied in a very compact space to save computations. There are two major advantages for applying adaptive sampling over the bottleneck structure. First, by zooming into important regions, SSBNet can better extract features than uniform downsampling. More importantly, with the shortcut connection, each intermediate layer with adaptive sampling can focus on different regions of the feature maps in a very deep network, without loss of information.

In the experiments, we built SSBNets by inserting lightweight convolutional layers and samplers into existing networks to estimate the saliency map and perform down/upsampling. The results in Fig. 1 show that SSBNet can achieve better accuracy/FLOPS ratio than ResNet-RS [2] and BoTNet-S1 [23]. For example, with only 4.4% more FLOPS, the SSB-ResNet-RS-200 with input size of 256×256 achieved 82.6% accuracy on ImageNet dataset [21], which is 0.6% higher than the baseline ResNet-RS-152 with input size of 192×192. The SSB-BoTNet-S1-77 with input size of 320×320 obtained 82.5% accuracy, which is 0.4% higher than BoTNet-S1-110 with input size of 224×224, and required 6% less computation. The contributions of this paper include:

- We investigate the use of adaptive sampling in the building blocks of a deep neural network. By applying adaptive sampling in the bottleneck structure, we propose SSBNet which can be utilized as a backbone network and trained in an end-to-end manner. Note that existing networks only utilized adaptive sampling in specific tasks, where a pre-trained backbone is required for feature extraction.
- We show that the proposed SSBNet can achieve better image classification and object detection performance than the baseline models, and visualize its capability in adaptively sampling different locations at different layers.
- Experiment results and ablation studies validate the advantage of adaptive sampling over uniform sampling. The result in this paper may lead to a new direction of research on network architecture.

2 Related Works

In the following, we explain the connection between the proposed SSBNet and existing works, and highlight the innovation.

Attention Mechanisms. Different types of attention mechanisms have been explored in computer vision tasks. One category of work utilizes attention mechanism to predict a softmask that scales the feature maps. Squeeze-and-Excitation [9] utilizes global context to refine the channel dimension. CBAM [29] uses attention mask to emphasize the important spatial positions.

Besides improving feature maps, another direction of research applies attention as a stand-alone layer that can extract features and act as a replacement for the convolutional layer. Stand-alone self-attention [19] replaces the spatial convolutional layer to efficiently increase the receptive field. Vision Transformer [5] adapts the Transformer [28] structure and takes non-overlapped patches as individual tokens, instead of a map representation that is normally used in vision tasks.

The proposed SSBNet follows the first approach and inserts attention layers to improve efficiency. However, instead of utilizing attention to scale features, SSBNet performs weighted downsampling by the attention map to save computations.

Adaptive Sampling. There are some works [4,11,12,20,26,32] that perform adaptive geometric sampling on the images or feature maps rather than scaling the features, as is done by attention mechanisms. Spatial transformer network [11] uses localization network to predict transformation parameters and performs geometric transformation on the image or feature maps. Saliency sampler [20] applies saliency map estimator to compute the attention map and distorts the input based on this map. Trilinear attention sampling network (TASN) [32] applies trilinear attention to compute the attention map and uses the map to perform sampling in a less distorted way. The sampling mechanism of the proposed SSBNet is inspired by TASN, but with two major differences: 1) SSBNet can be used as a backbone and trained end-to-end, but TASN requires a pretrained backbone; 2) SSBNet performs different sampling at different layers to extract useful features, where TASN only performs sampling once on the image input.

There are only very few works that apply adaptive sampling in the backbone network, which is the core feature extractor for computer vision tasks. One of the exceptions is the Deformable convolutional neural network (DCNN) [4]. DCNN computes the sampling offset to deform the sampling grid of convolutions and RoI poolings, which provides significant performance improvement for object detection and semantic segmentation tasks. Different from DCNN which deforms the convolutions and RoI poolings, SSBNet samples the feature map into a lower dimension to improve efficiency.

In summary, the proposed SSBNet utilizes adaptive sampling in most of its building blocks and allows different sampling at different layers, where most existing works only perform adaptive sampling several times. SSBNet can be used as a backbone network for different tasks like classification and object detection.

Dimension Reduction. Dimension reduction is commonly used in different architectures. Reducing spatial dimensions can save a large amount of computation and increase the effective receptive field of the convolution operations. For example, many CNNs reduce the spatial dimension when they increase the number of channels [7,13,22,24].

There are networks that temporarily reduce the channel dimension. Inception [24] applies 1×1 convolutions to reduce the channel dimension and lower the cost of the following 3×3 and 5×5 convolutions. ResNet [7] has a bottleneck layer design, which reduces the number of channels before the 3×3 convolution and restores the channel dimension afterwards.

There are also applications of the bottleneck structure in the spatial dimension. Spatial bottleneck [18] replaces spatial convolution by a pair of strided convolution and deconvolution to reduce the sampling rate and achieve speedup. HBONet [14] utilizes depthwise convolution and bilinear sampling to perform down/upsampling, where the costly operations are applied in between.

The proposed SSBNet has a similar structure as HBONet, but utilizes adaptive sampling instead of strided convolution or pooling for downsampling. Fur-

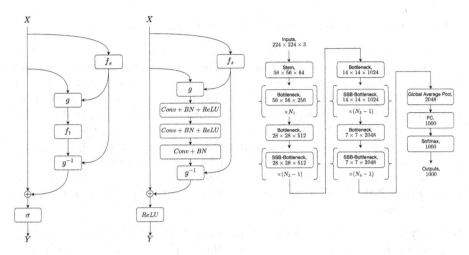

Fig. 2. Left: The structure of SSB layer. Middle: The instantiation of SSB layer built from the bottleneck layer of ResNet [7]. Right: SSB-ResNet, where N_1, N_2, N_3, N_4 follow the configurations of ResNet [7].

thermore, the adaptive sampling can perform spatial transformation like zooming, which could better preserve useful information for feature extraction.

3 Methodology

In this section, we first introduce the SSBNet and then present the details of the building block for SSBNet, i.e. the SSB layer.

3.1 Saliency Sampling Bottleneck Networks

Since the focus of this work is to apply adaptive sampling to improve network efficiency, we modify existing networks to reduce the searching space. To build SSBNet, we insert samplers to the building blocks of the original model such as ResNet [7]. To this end, we only need to determine the sampling size and the position to insert the sampler. In the experiments, we follow the standard approach that shares configuration in a group of building blocks, i.e. same sampling size in one group. Without native implementation of the sampler, some earliest groups that have high spatial dimension will significantly slow down the training. So we skip those earliest groups.

We also skip the first block of each group, i.e. the block that reduces the spatial dimension and increases the number of channels, due to the fact that they usually utilize shortcut connection with strided pooling or/and 1×1 convolution for downsampling [2,7,8], or do not contain shortcut connection [25]. Thus, adding samplers to the first block of each group could lead to loss of information. For example, SSB-ResNet is shown in Fig. 2 (right).

3.2   Saliency Sampling Bottleneck Layer

The SSB layer is the main building block of the SSBNet and is constructed by wrapping a set of layers with the samplers. The SSB layer has a similar structure as the bottleneck layer from ResNet [7], with two branches, i.e., the shortcut branch and the residual branch. The function of the two branches are similar to those in ResNet. Specifically, the shortcut branch passes the signal to the higher level layer and the residual branch performs operations to extract features. The difference is that the residual branch in the SSB layer adaptively samples features in the spatial dimension, but the bottleneck layer of ResNet reduces the channel dimension, and both of them perform the most costly operations in the reduced space. Figure 2 (left) shows the structure of the SSB layer. Next, we introduce the key operations of the SSB layer.

Saliency Map: Given the input feature map $X \in \mathbb{R}^{H_{in} \times W_{in} \times D}$, where H_{in}, W_{in}, D denote the height, the weight and the number of channels, respectively, we first compute the saliency map by $S = f_s(X)$, where S has dimensions of $H_{in} \times W_{in}$. There are many possible choices of f_s. In this paper, we use a 1×1 convolutional layer with one filter, a batch normalization layer [10] and the sigmoid activation, followed by a reshape operation which change the map of $H_{in} \times W_{in} \times 1$ to a 2D matrix of $H_{in} \times W_{in}$. The whole process has negligible overhead in the number of operations and parameters. To stabilize the training, we always initialize the scaling weight γ in the batch normalization layer to zero, such that the network performs uniform sampling at the beginning.

Sampling Output Computation: For a target sampling size of $H_r \times W_r$, we compute the sampling output $X^r = g(X, S)$ with $X^r \in \mathbb{R}^{H_r \times W_r \times D}$. Our approach is close to TASN [32]. Specifically, we apply inverse transform to convert the saliency map into the weights of sampling, where features having higher scores in the saliency map will be sampled with a larger weight into the output feature maps. Unlike TASN, our implementation does not involve bilinear sampling [11]. Instead, we directly compute the sampling weights between the input and output pixels.

To compute X^r with a saliency map $S \in \mathbb{R}^{H_{in} \times W_{in}}$, we first obtain the elements of the saliency vectors $S^y \in \mathbb{R}^{H_{in}}$ and $S^x \in \mathbb{R}^{W_{in}}$ as

$$S_j^y = \frac{\sum_{w=1}^{W_{in}} S_{j,w}}{\sum_{h=1}^{H_{in}} \sum_{w=1}^{W_{in}} S_{h,w}} \quad \forall 1 \leq j \leq H_{in} \tag{1}$$

and

$$S_i^x = \frac{\sum_{h=1}^{H_{in}} S_{h,i}}{\sum_{h=1}^{H_{in}} \sum_{w=1}^{W_{in}} S_{h,w}} \quad \forall 1 \leq i \leq W_{in}. \tag{2}$$

Note that both S^y and S^x are normalized.

We also compute uniform vectors, $U^y \in \mathbb{R}^{H_r}$ and $U^x \in \mathbb{R}^{W_r}$, where

$$U_j^y = \frac{1}{H_r} \quad \forall 1 \leq j \leq H_r \tag{3}$$

$$U_i^x = \frac{1}{W_r} \quad \forall 1 \le i \le W_r. \tag{4}$$

Then, we calculate the cumulative sums C^{S^y}, C^{S^x}, C^{U^y} and C^{U^x}. For example, in the y-axis, we first compute

$$C_j^{S^y} = \sum_{h=1}^{j-1} S_h^y \quad \forall 1 \le j \le H_{in} + 1 \tag{5}$$

$$C_j^{U^y} = \sum_{h=1}^{j-1} U_h^y \quad \forall 1 \le j \le H_r + 1 \tag{6}$$

and then the sampling weights can be determined as

$$G_{i,j}^y = max(min(C_{j+1}^{S^y}, C_{i+1}^{U^y}) - max(C_j^{S^y}, C_i^{U^y}), 0) \tag{7}$$
$$\forall 1 \le j \le H_{in}, 1 \le i \le H_r.$$

The weight matrix in the x-axis, G^x, can be computed similarly. Weight matrices G^y and G^x have dimensions of $H_r \times H_{in}$ and $W_r \times W_{in}$, respectively.

Finally, we can compute the sampling output X^r by

$$X_{i,j,d}^r = \sum_{h=1}^{H_{in}} \sum_{w=1}^{W_{in}} H_r W_r G_{i,h}^y G_{j,w}^x X_{h,w,d} \tag{8}$$
$$\forall 1 \le i \le H_r, 1 \le j \le W_r, 1 \le d \le D.$$

We applied scaling with a factor of $H_r W_r$, such that the average value of the output map is independent of the sampling size.

Feature Extraction: After computing the sampled feature maps X^r, we can extract features by costly operations like convolutions with $Y^r = f_t(X^r)$. When building SSBNet from existing networks with shortcut connections [7], we use the original residual branch as f_t. Figure 2 (middle) shows the SSB layer built from the (channel) bottleneck layer of ResNet.

Inverse Sampling: After the feature extraction stage, an inverse sampling is applied to restore the spatial dimension. For that purpose, we apply the same sampling method, except that the transposed weight matrices, i.e. $(G^y)^T$ and $(G^x)^T$, are utilized. Together with the shortcut connection and the activation function σ, the final output of the SSB layer can be expressed as

$$Y_{i,j,d} = \sigma(X_{i,j,d} + \sum_{h=1}^{H_r} \sum_{w=1}^{W_r} H_{in} W_{in} (G^y)_{i,h}^T (G^x)_{j,w}^T Y_{h,w,d}^r) \tag{9}$$
$$\forall 1 \le i \le H_{in}, 1 \le j \le W_{in}, 1 \le d \le D.$$

Instead of using bilinear sampling [11], we compute the weights between the input and output pixels, and directly use the weighted sum as the output value.

This approach can simplify the calculation, as it does not involve calculation of the coordinates. Furthermore, bilinear sampling may skip some pixels due to the possible non-uniform downsampling, but the proposed method takes all input pixels into account.

Note that the sampling function can be simply implemented by two batch matrix multiplications, which gives a complexity of $O(H_r H_{in} W_{in} D + H_r W_r W_{in} D)$ (when computed in y-axis first). The complexity is higher than bilinear sampling that has a complexity of $O(H_r W_r D)$. However, the weight matrices G^y and G^x contain at most $H_{in} + H_r$ and $W_{in} + W_r$ non-zero elements[1], respectively. If the sampling sizes scaled linearly with the input sizes, the complexity of the sampling function can be reduced to $O(H_r W_r D)$. Thus, an optimized implementation which considers the sparsity of the matrices could significantly reduce the complexity and latency, and allow SSBNet to scale well with high dimension input.

4   Experiments

In this section, we first train SSBNet and the baseline models for image classification tasks on the ImageNet dataset [21], and then fine-tune the models to the object detection and instance segmentation tasks on the COCO dataset [16]. After that, we report the inference performance of SSBNet. All experiments were conducted with TensorFlow 2.6 [1] and Model Garden [30], and ran on TPU v2-8/v3-8 with bfloat16, except for Sect. 4.3. For ease of presentation, we denote the configurations for the last L groups of SSBNets by $(M_1, ..., M_L)$. Here, M_l indicates that the sampling size of the last $(L - l + 1)$-th group is $M_l \times M_l$.

4.1   Image Classification

For image classification, we trained SSBNets and the baseline models on the ImageNet [21] dataset, which contains 1.28M training and 50k validation samples. We built SSBNets based on ResNet-D [8], ResNet-RS [2], EfficientNet [25] and BoTNet-S1 [23], and compare their performance with the original models. Due to limited resources, we only trained some variants of ResNet-RS and found that the results are close to the original work [2]. Thus, we will report other results directly from the original paper. For EfficientNet and BotNet-S1, we were not able to reproduce the same results from the papers [23, 25]. For fair comparison, we trained and reported all variants that have similar complexity as SSB-EfficientNet and SSB-BoTNet-S1.

Note that in this paper, we focus on the theoretical improvement regarding the accuracy-FLOPS trade-off. In Sect. 4.3, we will compare the inference time between SSBNet and the baselines, which shows that real speedup is achievable.

---

[1] Consider a weight matrix G^y with dimensions $H_r \times H_{in}$. If the (i, j)-th element of the weight matrix is non-zero, the next non-zero index will be $(i + \Delta i, j + \Delta j)$, where $\Delta i, \Delta j$ are non-negative integers with either $i + \Delta i > i$ or $j + \Delta j > j$. As a result, there are at most $H_{in} + H_r$ non-zero elements. The same is true for G^x.

Table 1. ImageNet results of (SSB-)ResNet-D and (SSB-)ResNet-RS

Model	Input size	Params	FLOPS	Top-1(%)	Model	Input size	Params	FLOPS	Top-1(%)
R-50	224 × 224	25.6M	4.3G	78.1	R-50	160 × 160	35.7M	2.3G	78.8
S-50	224 × 224	25.6M	3.0G	78.1	S-50	160 × 160	35.7M	1.6G	78.2
R-101	224 × 224	44.6M	8.0G	79.5	R-101	160 × 160	63.6M	4.2G	80.3*
S-101	224 × 224	44.6M	4.3G	78.9	S-101	160 × 160	63.6M	2.3G	79.3
R-152	224 × 224	60.2M	11.8G	80.1	R-101	192 × 192	63.6M	6.0G	81.3
S-152	224 × 224	60.3M	5.6G	79.2	S-101	192 × 192	63.6M	3.2G	80.6
R: ResNet-D [8] S: SSB-ResNet-D					R-152	192 × 192	86.6M	9.0G	82.0*
Model	Input size	Params	FLOPS	Top-1(%)	S-152	192 × 192	86.7M	4.3G	81.0
R-50	224 × 224	25.6M	4.3G	78.2	R-152	224 × 224	86.6M	12.0G	82.5
S-50	224 × 224	25.6M	3.0G	78.2	S-152	224 × 224	86.7M	5.8G	81.7
R-101	224 × 224	44.6M	8.0G	80.0	R-152	256 × 256	86.6M	15.5G	83.0*
S-101	224 × 224	44.6M	4.3G	79.5	S-152	256 × 256	86.7M	7.5G	82.1
R-152	224 × 224	60.2M	11.8G	80.6	R-200	256 × 256	93.2M	20.0G	83.4*
S-152	224 × 224	60.3M	5.6G	80.1	S-200	256 × 256	93.3M	9.4G	82.6
R: ResNet-D [8] + RandAugment [3]					R: ResNet-RS [2] S: SSB-ResNet-RS				
S: SSB-ResNet-D + RandAugment [3]					*: from the original paper				

Comparison with ResNet-D For ResNet-D [8] and SSB-ResNet-D, we trained three scales with the configuration of ResNet50/101/152 [7]. We followed the training and testing settings of [8] with batch size of 1024 and input size of 224×224. The sampling sizes of SSB-ResNet-D are $(16, 8, 4)$. The results are shown in the top-left table of Table 1, which clearly demonstrate the advantage of SSB-ResNet-D. For example, SSB-ResNet-D-50 achieved similar accuracy as ResNet-D-50, where the FLOPS is reduced by 30%. SSB-ResNet-D-101 has the same FLOPS as ResNet-D-50, but achieved 0.8% higher performance. The deepest SSB-ResNet-D-152 also performed only 0.3% worse than ResNet-D-101, with 30% less FLOPS.

In addition, we conducted experiments with RandAugment [3] as data augmentation. The number of transformations and the magnitude were 2 and 5, respectively. It can be observed from the bottom-left table of Table 1 that SSB-ResNet-D-101 outperformed ResNet-D-50 by 1.3% accuracy with the same FLOPS, and SSB-ResNet-D-152 achieved similar accuracy as ResNet-D-101 but saved 30% operations. This indicates that SSBNets can benefit more from stronger regularization.

Comparison with ResNet-RS We also conducted experiments with ResNet-RS [2] by followed the same training settings in the original paper. We trained (SSB-)ResNet-RS-50/101/152/200, with different input sizes of $160 \times 160/192 \times 192/224 \times 224/256 \times 256$, and the sampling sizes are scaled to $(12, 6, 3)/(14, 7, 3)/(16, 8, 4)/(18, 9, 5)$, respectively. The performance comparison between SSB-ResNet-RS and ResNet-RS is shown Table 1(right). The SSB-ResNet-RS

Table 2. ImageNet results of (SSB-)EfficientNet and (SSB-)BoTNet-S1

Model	Input size	Params	FLOPS	Top-1(%)	Model	Input size	Params	FLOPS	Top-1(%)
E-B0	224 × 224	5.3M	0.4G	76.4	B-59	224 × 224	30.5M	7.3G	81.1
S-B0	224 × 224	5.3M	0.3G	75.4	S-59	224 × 224	30.5M	3.8G	80.3
E-B1	240 × 240	7.9M	0.7G	78.5	B-110	224 × 224	51.7M	10.9G	82.1
S-B1	240 × 240	7.9M	0.5G	77.4	S-110	224 × 224	51.8M	5.1G	81.2
E-B2	260 × 260	9.2M	1.0G	79.6	B-128	256 × 256	69.1M	19.3G	82.9
S-B2	260 × 260	9.2M	0.7G	78.6	S-128	256 × 256	69.1M	8.1G	82.0
E-B3	300 × 300	12.3M	1.8G	81.0	B-77	320 × 320	47.9M	23.3G	–
S-B3	300 × 300	12.3M	1.3G	80.1	S-77	320 × 320	47.9M	10.2G	82.5

E: EfficientNet [25]   S: SSB-EfficientNet   B: BoTNet-S1 [23]   S: SSB-BoTNet-S1

achieved competitive results. For example, the SSB-ResNet-RS-200 with input size of 256 × 256 achieved 0.6% higher accuracy than ResNet-RS-152 with input size of 192 × 192, where the FLOPS is only 4.4% higher. Figure 1a compares SSB-ResNet-RS with ResNet-RS with less than 10 GFLOPS and shows that SSB-ResNet-RS achieved better accuracy to FLOPS ratio in different scales.

Comparison with EfficientNet. For EifficientNet [25], we followed the original setting, except that we used a batch size of 1024. Due to the use of 5 × 5 convolutions, we applied larger sampling size for EfficientNet. Specifically, we used (20, 10, 10, 5, 5)/(22, 11, 11, 5, 5)/(24, 12, 12, 6, 6) and (26, 13, 13, 7, 7) for SSB-EfficientNet-B0/1/2/3, respectively.

However, adaptive sampling did not improve EfficientNet in our experiments as shown in Table 2(left). For example, SSB-EfficientNet-B2 has less number of operations than EfficientNet-B2, but nearly the same number of operations and accuracy as EfficientNet-B1. This may be due to the fact that EfficientNet is designed by neural architecture search, thus the network configurations and training parameters do not transfer well to SSB-EfficientNet. We also note that the speed-up in EfficientNet is limited when compared with ResNet. This is because EfficientNet has more groups of layers and we didn't replace the first layer in each group, due to the reason discussed in Sect. 3.1.

Comparison with BoTNet-S1. The recent development of Visual Transformers [5] has gained attention in the research community. However, training Transformers is challenging. For example, larger dataset or additional augmentation is required [5,27]. To evaluate the compatibility of adaptive sampling with self-attention layer, we built SSBNet from BoTNet-S1 [23], which is a hybrid network composed of both convolutional and self-attention layers. It inherited the techniques from modern CNNs, including the choice of normalization layers, optimizers, and training setting.

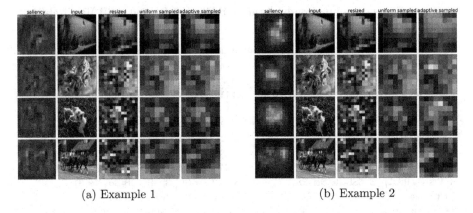

(a) Example 1   (b) Example 2

Fig. 3. Examples of the saliency map and sampling output. (a) and (b) are the samples from different layers of the SSB-ResNet-RS-152.

Table 3. COCO-2017 [16] results of SSB-ResNet-D/ResNet-D [8] with FPN [15] and Mask R-CNN [6]

	Model	AP_{box}	AP_{mask}		Model	AP_{box}	AP_{mask}
12 Epochs	ResNet-D-50	40.14	35.72	36 Epochs	ResNet-D-50	42.50	37.56
	SSB-ResNet-D-50	40.67	35.98		SSB-ResNet-D-50	42.89	37.84
24 Epochs	ResNet-D-50	41.95	37.17				
	SSB-ResNet-D-50	42.36	37.41				

Results in Table 2(right) show that SSB-BoTNet-S1 achieved better accuracy to FLOPS trade-off. For example, SSB-BoTNet-S1-110 performed similar as BoTNet-S1-59, but with 30% less FLOPS; SSB-BoTNet-S1-77 achieved 0.4% higher accuracy than BoTNet-S1-110, but 6% less FLOPS. The results also suggest that adaptive sampling does not only improve CNNs, but also hybrid networks that utilize self-attention. Figure 1b shows the comparison between SSB-BoTNet-S1 and BoTNet-S1 that have less than 11 GFLOPS, where SSB-BoTNet-S1 achieved better accuracy to FLOPS ratio.

Visualization. The outputs of two sampled layers of SSBNet are shown in Fig. 3. While the high dimension features are hard to visualize, we first resized the original images to the same size as the sampler input, and then applied sampling on the resized images for visualization. Figure 3a shows that the first reported layer samples from the whole image, where the background is weighted heavier; Fig. 3b shows that the second reported layer is able to zoom into smaller regions when performing downsampling, which can better preserve the discriminative features in these regions. The results also suggest that different layers of the SSBNet zoom into different regions, which justifies the use of adaptive sampling in multiple layers.

Table 4. Latency comparison between (SSB-)ResNet-RS and (SSB-)BoTNet-S1

Model	Input size	Params	FLOPS	Latency(ms)	Model	Input size	Params	FLOPS	Latency(ms)
R-50	160×160	35.7M	2.3G	130/163	B-59	224×224	30.5M	7.3G	404/469
S-50	160×160	35.7M	1.6G	117/138	S-59	224×224	30.5M	3.8G	291/301
R-101	192×192	63.6M	6.0G	298/381	B-110	224×224	51.7M	10.9G	559/674
S-101	192×192	63.6M	3.2G	235/267	S-110	224×224	51.8M	5.1G	386/406
R-152	224×224	86.6M	12.0G	565/726	B-128	256×256	69.1M	19.3G	925/1127
S-152	224×224	86.7M	5.8G	427/472	S-128	256×256	69.1M	8.1G	612/639
R-200	256×256	93.2M	20.0G	988/1244	B-77	320×320	47.9M	23.3G	1234/1487
S-200	256×256	93.2M	9.4G	744/822	S-77	320×320	47.9M	10.2G	773/784

R: ResNet-RS [2] S: SSB-ResNet-RS	B: BoTNet-S1 [23] S: SSB-BoTNet-S1
First number: Latency on V100 GPU	First number: Latency on V100 GPU
Second number: Latency on 3090 GPU	Second number: Latency on 3090 GPU

4.2 Object Detection and Instance Segmentation

We also evaluated the performance of SSBNet for object detection and instance segmentation tasks on the COCO-2017 dataset [16] which contains 118K images in the training set and 5K images for validation. For that purpose, we used the pre-trained ResNet-D-50 [8] and SSB-ResNet-D-50 with FPN [15] as the backbone, and applied Mask R-CNN [6] for object detection and segmentation. The same was applied to the baseline models for comparison purposes. We used the default setting of Mask R-CNN in Model Garden [30], with input size of 1024×1024, batch size of 64 and a learning rate of 0.01. Horizontal flipping and Scale jitter with a range between 0.8 and 1.25 were applied. For SSB-ResNet-D, we used the sampling sizes of (72, 36, 18) for the last 3 groups. The results of training with 12/24/36 epochs are reported.

The results in Table 3 show that SSBNet is transferable to new tasks with high performance. While the pre-trained ResNet-D-50 and SSB-ResNet-D-50 have similar accuracy on ImageNet [21], the SSB-ResNet-D-50 performs slightly better than ResNet-D-50 on COCO-2017, with less operations. This may be due to two reasons: 1.) there are paddings to the images, but SSBNet can zoom into the non-padding regions such that no computation is wasted, 2.) the images from COCO dataset have higher resolution than those from ImageNet.

4.3 Latency Comparison Between SSBNet and the Original Networks

To explore the actual speed-up by adaptive sampling, we implemented the sampling function in TensorFlow 2.6 [1] and CUDA [17], and performed comparison between ResNet-RS [2], SSB-ResNet-RS, BoTNet-S1 [23], and SSB-BoTNet-S1. Experiments were conducted on V100 and 3090 GPU with float16. We report the results from two GPUs as we noticed the difference in performance. Specifically, V100 is commonly used in the literatures, but our implementation performs bet-

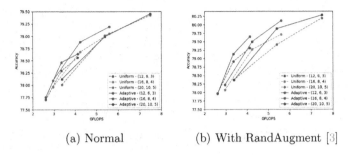

(a) Normal   (b) With RandAugment [3]

Fig. 4. Comparison between uniform and adaptive sampling. In each line, the three points denote SSB-ResNet-D-50/101/152, respectively.

ter in 3090, which is possibly due to the degree of optimization. The results are reported by the batch latency with size of 1024.

The results in Table 4 show that actual speed-up is achievable with adaptive sampling. For example, the latency of SSB-ResNet-RS-200 is reduced by up to 34% when compared with ResNet-RS-200, where ideally the latency can be reduced by 53%. The latency of SSB-BoTNet-S1-77 is 47% lower than BoTNet-S1-77, which is close to the theoretical improvement, i.e. 56%. We would like to highlight that we only did limited implementation optimization over SSBNet. We expect further improvement with better optimization.

5 Ablation Study

In this section, we provide results of additional experiments to justify the use of adaptive sampling in deep neural networks.

5.1 Comparison Between Uniform and Adaptive Sampling

To validate the effectiveness of adaptive sampling utilized in SSBNet, we compared the performance of two SSB-ResNet-D networks, which applied adaptive and uniform sampling, respectively. For a fair comparison, the two networks used the same sampling mechanism (Eq. 8).

The results in Fig. 4a show that, in general, the networks with adaptive sampling outperform the networks that applied uniform sampling. We observed the largest difference from SSB-ResNet101-D, where the adaptive model achieved 0.2% higher accuracy. In Fig. 4b, results with RandAugment [3] are shown, where models with adaptive sampling obtain larger improvement than those with uniform sampling. For example, at sampling sizes (16, 8, 4), the SSB-ResNet152-D with adaptive sampling achieved 0.4% higher accuracy.

The results suggest that adaptive sampling is a better choice for downsampling in SSBNet. In addition, the results show that the SSB-ResNet-D with sampling sizes of (16, 8, 4) achieved a good trade-off between accuracy and FLOPS at different depths. Thus, we used this configuration as default.

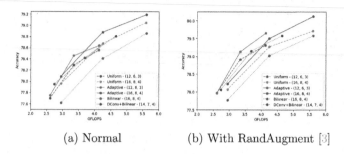

(a) Normal   (b) With RandAugment [3]

Fig. 5. Comparison between adaptive sampling and other sampling methods. In each line, the three points denote SSB-ResNet50/101/152-D, respectively.

5.2 Comparison with Other Sampling Methods

To compare different down/upsampling mechanisms, we conducted experiments with different sampling methods that can be applied in the bottleneck structure: 1) the proposed adaptive sampling; 2) the uniform sampling used in Sect. 5.1; 3) the uniform sampling with bilinear interpolation; and 4) the depthwise convolution for downsampling with bilinear sampling for upsampling [14]. For bilinear sampling, we used sampling sizes of $(16, 8, 4)$ as it is the common choice in our paper. For 4), the kernel size and stride of depthwise convolutions are 5 and 2 respectively, with sampling sizes of $(14, 7, 4)$. For a fair comparison, we included the results of adaptive sampling with sizes $(16, 8, 4)$ and $(12, 6, 3)$, such that the cost of 4) falls between them.

Figure 5a shows the results with basic training setting and Fig. 5b shows the results with RandAugment [3]. In both settings, adaptive sampling outperformed other methods, especially when the model is deeper and additional data augmentation is used. Surprisingly, although method 2) is also a uniform sampling method, it outperformed the widely utilized method 3).

6 Conclusion

In this paper, we proposed a novel architecture to apply adaptive sampling in the main building block of deep neural networks. The proposed SSBNet outperformed other benchmarks in both image classification and object detection tasks. Different from most existing works that applied adaptive sampling for specific tasks [4,11,12,20,26,32] and performed very few sampling operations, the proposed structure can work as a backbone network and be transferred to different tasks. Visualization illustrated SSBNet's capability in sampling different regions at different layers and ablation studies demonstrated that adaptive sampling is more efficient than uniform sampling.

The results in this paper suggest that adaptive sampling is a promising mechanism in deep neural networks. We expect that designing the network with adaptive sampling from scratch and fine-tuning the training process may provide further performance improvement.

Acknowledgment. This work was supported by the Cloud TPUs from Google's TPU Research Cloud (TRC) and the HKUST-WeBank Joint Lab under Grant WEB19EG01-L.

References

1. Abadi, M., et al.: TensorFlow, large-scale machine learning on heterogeneous systems (2015). https://doi.org/10.5281/zenodo.4724125
2. Bello, I., et al.: Revisiting ResNets: improved training and scaling strategies. In: Ranzato, M., Beygelzimer, A., Dauphin, Y., Liang, P., Vaughan, J.W. (eds.) Advances in Neural Information Processing Systems, vol. 34, pp. 22614–22627. Curran Associates, Inc. (2021)
3. Cubuk, E.D., Zoph, B., Shlens, J., Le, Q.: RandAugment: practical automated data augmentation with a reduced search space. In: Larochelle, H., Ranzato, M., Hadsell, R., Balcan, M., Lin, H. (eds.) Advances in Neural Information Processing Systems, vol. 33, pp. 18613–18624. Curran Associates, Inc. (2020)
4. Dai, J., et al.: Deformable convolutional networks. In: Proceedings of the IEEE International Conference on Computer Vision (ICCV) (2017)
5. Dosovitskiy, A., et al.: An image is worth 16×16 words: transformers for image recognition at scale. In: International Conference on Learning Representations (2021)
6. He, K., Gkioxari, G., Dollar, P., Girshick, R.: Mask R-CNN. In: Proceedings of the IEEE International Conference on Computer Vision (ICCV) (2017)
7. He, K., Zhang, X., Ren, S., Sun, J.: Deep residual learning for image recognition. In: Proceedings of the IEEE Conference on Computer Vision and Pattern Recognition (CVPR) (2016)
8. He, T., Zhang, Z., Zhang, H., Zhang, Z., Xie, J., Li, M.: Bag of tricks for image classification with convolutional neural networks. In: Proceedings of the IEEE/CVF Conference on Computer Vision and Pattern Recognition (CVPR) (2019)
9. Hu, J., Shen, L., Sun, G.: Squeeze-and-excitation networks. In: Proceedings of the IEEE Conference on Computer Vision and Pattern Recognition (CVPR) (2018)
10. Ioffe, S., Szegedy, C.: Batch normalization: accelerating deep network training by reducing internal covariate shift. In: International Conference on Machine Learning, pp. 448–456. PMLR (2015)
11. Jaderberg, M., Simonyan, K., Zisserman, A., kavukcuoglu, k.: Spatial transformer networks. In: Cortes, C., Lawrence, N., Lee, D., Sugiyama, M., Garnett, R. (eds.) Advances in Neural Information Processing Systems, vol. 28. Curran Associates, Inc. (2015)
12. Jin, C., Tanno, R., Mertzanidou, T., Panagiotaki, E., Alexander, D.C.: Learning to downsample for segmentation of ultra-high resolution images. In: International Conference on Learning Representations (2022)
13. Krizhevsky, A., Sutskever, I., Hinton, G.E.: ImageNet classification with deep convolutional neural networks. In: Pereira, F., Burges, C., Bottou, L., Weinberger, K. (eds.) Advances in Neural Information Processing Systems, vol. 25. Curran Associates, Inc. (2012)
14. Li, D., Zhou, A., Yao, A.: HBONet: harmonious bottleneck on two orthogonal dimensions. In: Proceedings of the IEEE/CVF International Conference on Computer Vision (ICCV) (2019)
15. Lin, T.Y., Dollar, P., Girshick, R., He, K., Hariharan, B., Belongie, S.: Feature pyramid networks for object detection. In: Proceedings of the IEEE Conference on Computer Vision and Pattern Recognition (CVPR) (2017)

16. Lin, T.-Y., et al.: Microsoft COCO: common objects in context. In: Fleet, D., Pajdla, T., Schiele, B., Tuytelaars, T. (eds.) ECCV 2014. LNCS, vol. 8693, pp. 740–755. Springer, Cham (2014). https://doi.org/10.1007/978-3-319-10602-1_48

17. Nickolls, J., Buck, I., Garland, M., Skadron, K.: Scalable parallel programming with CUDA: is CUDA the parallel programming model that application developers have been waiting for? Queue **6**(2), 40–53 (2008)

18. Peng, J., Xie, L., Zhang, Z., Tan, T., Wang, J.: Accelerating deep neural networks with spatial bottleneck modules. arXiv preprint arXiv:1809.02601 (2018)

19. Ramachandran, P., Parmar, N., Vaswani, A., Bello, I., Levskaya, A., Shlens, J.: Stand-alone self-attention in vision models. In: Wallach, H., Larochelle, H., Beygelzimer, A., d' Alché-Buc, F., Fox, E., Garnett, R. (eds.) Advances in Neural Information Processing Systems, vol. 32. Curran Associates, Inc. (2019)

20. Recasens, A., Kellnhofer, P., Stent, S., Matusik, W., Torralba, A.: Learning to zoom: a saliency-based sampling layer for neural networks. In: Proceedings of the European Conference on Computer Vision (ECCV), pp. 51–66 (2018)

21. Russakovsky, O., et al.: ImageNet large scale visual recognition challenge. Int. J. Comput. Vis. **115**(3), 211–252 (2015). https://doi.org/10.1007/s11263-015-0816-y

22. Simonyan, K., Zisserman, A.: Very deep convolutional networks for large-scale image recognition. In: International Conference on Learning Representations (2015)

23. Srinivas, A., Lin, T.Y., Parmar, N., Shlens, J., Abbeel, P., Vaswani, A.: Bottleneck transformers for visual recognition. In: Proceedings of the IEEE/CVF Conference on Computer Vision and Pattern Recognition (CVPR), pp. 16519–16529 (2021)

24. Szegedy, C., et al.: Going deeper with convolutions. In: Proceedings of the IEEE Conference on Computer Vision and Pattern Recognition (CVPR) (2015)

25. Tan, M., Le, Q.: EfficientNet: rethinking model scaling for convolutional neural networks. In: International Conference on Machine Learning, pp. 6105–6114. PMLR (2019)

26. Thavamani, C., Li, M., Cebron, N., Ramanan, D.: FOVEA: foveated image magnification for autonomous navigation. In: Proceedings of the IEEE/CVF International Conference on Computer Vision (ICCV), pp. 15539–15548 (2021)

27. Touvron, H., Cord, M., Douze, M., Massa, F., Sablayrolles, A., Jégou, H.: Training data-efficient image transformers & distillation through attention. In: International Conference on Machine Learning, pp. 10347–10357. PMLR (2021)

28. Vaswani, A., et al.: Attention is all you need. In: Guyon, I., et al. (eds.) Advances in Neural Information Processing Systems, vol. 30. Curran Associates, Inc. (2017)

29. Woo, S., Park, J., Lee, J.Y., Kweon, I.S.: CBAM: convolutional block attention module. In: Proceedings of the European Conference on Computer Vision (ECCV), pp. 3–19 (2018)

30. Yu, H., et al.: TensorFlow Model Garden (2020). https://github.com/tensorflow/models

31. Zhao, Z.Q., Zheng, P., Xu, S., Wu, X.: Object detection with deep learning: a review. IEEE Trans. Neural Netw. Learn. Syst. **30**(11), 3212–3232 (2019)

32. Zheng, H., Fu, J., Zha, Z.J., Luo, J.: Looking for the devil in the details: learning trilinear attention sampling network for fine-grained image recognition. In: Proceedings of the IEEE/CVF Conference on Computer Vision and Pattern Recognition (CVPR) (2019)

Filter Pruning via Feature Discrimination in Deep Neural Networks

Zhiqiang He[1], Yaguan Qian[1(✉)] (iD), Yuqi Wang[1], Bin Wang[2], Xiaohui Guan[3],
Zhaoquan Gu[4], Xiang Ling[5], Shaoning Zeng[6], Haijiang Wang[1],
and Wujie Zhou[1]

[1] Zhejiang University of Science and Technology, Hangzhou 310023, Zhejiang, China
qianyaguan@zust.edu.cn
[2] Zhejiang Key Laboratory of Multidimensional Perception Technology,
Application and Cybersecurity, Hangzhou 310052, Zhejiang, China
[3] Zhejiang University of Water Resources and Electric Power, Hangzhou 310023,
Zhejiang, China
[4] Cyberspace Institute of Advanced Technology (CIAT), Guang Zhou University,
Guangzhou 510006, Guangdong, China
[5] Institute of Software, Chinese Academy of Sciences, Beijing 100190, China
[6] Yangtze Delta Region Institute, University of Electronic Science and Technology
of China, Huzhou 313000, Zhejiang, China

Abstract. Filter pruning is one of the most effective methods to compress deep convolutional networks (CNNs). In this paper, as a key component in filter pruning, We first propose a feature discrimination based filter importance criterion, namely Receptive Field Criterion (RFC). It turns the maximum activation responses that characterize the receptive field into probabilities, then measure the filter importance by the distribution of these probabilities from a new perspective of feature discrimination. However, directly applying RFC to global threshold pruning may lead to some problems, because global threshold pruning neglects the differences between different layers. Hence, we propose Distinguishing Layer Pruning based on RFC (DLRFC), i.e., discriminately prune the filters in different layers, which avoids measuring filters between different layers directly against filter criteria. Specifically, our method first selects relatively redundant layers by hard and soft changes of the network output, and then prunes only at these layers. The whole process dynamically adjusts redundant layers through iterations. Extensive experiments conducted on CIFAR-10/100 and ImageNet show that our method achieves state-of-the-art performance in several benchmarks.

Keywords: Model compression · Filter pruning · Receptive field criterion · Distinguishing layer pruning

1 Introduction

In the past few years, CNNs have achieved the most excellent performance in various computer vision tasks, such as target classification [9,15], object detec-

S. Avidan et al. (Eds.): ECCV 2022, LNCS 13681, pp. 245–261, 2022.
https://doi.org/10.1007/978-3-031-19803-8_15

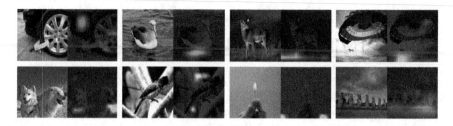

Fig. 1. Feature discrimination. On ImageNet, we randomly select 9 images and visualize the 20th filter in the last convolutional layer of VGG16. If the filter responds more uniformly to each class, then the features learned by the filter will play a small role in discriminating those classes, i.e., contribute less to the classification. We also experimentally demonstrate the effectiveness of this new pruning angle in Subsect. 4.7.

tion [1] and super-resolution [16]. However, over-parameterization is still a severe challenge to the CNNs' deployment in the edge intelligent device. For this reason, many network compression methods have been proposed at present, such as quantification [7], knowledge distillation [12], and network pruning [17,25,28]. Network pruning, as one of the most widely used methods, has attracted extensive attention. According to the pruned objects, network pruning methods are mainly divided into two types: unstructured pruning [8,29] and structured pruning [17,23]. Unstructured pruning removes the specific weights in a filter to obtain a sparse network, which requires special hardware and software for acceleration. Structured pruning directly removes the entire filter without any specially designed acceleration. Therefore, we focus on structured pruning in this paper.

In structured pruning, the filter importance criterion plays a vital role to determine which filters need to be pruned. Previous pruning methods design the filter importance criteria from various perspectives, such as heuristic experience [17], mathematical statistics [28], and network loss [4,26]. In this paper, we create a novel filter importance criterion named Receptive Field Criterion (RFC) from the view of feature discrimination (as illustrated in Fig. 1). Inspired by the receptive field analysis of network interpretability [5,42], we convert the maximum activation responses of a receptive field into probabilities that represent the filter's contribution to each class. Then, from the perspective of feature discrimination, we introduce the information entropy to represent the uniformity of the filter's contribution to all class. Thus, filters with higher information entropy is prone to be pruned. We also compared the RFC with other criterion, and the results show that RFC can better measure filter importance.

Many existing works directly conduct pruning according to a global threshold determined by filtering criteria. However, we find that global threshold pruning ignores the relative importance between layers. To address this problem, we propose a new pruning method: distinguishing layer pruning based on RFC (DLRFC). We select redundant layers by comparing the impact of each layer on network performance. This effect is quantified by both hard and soft labels of the network output vector, and then we prune filters only within redundant layers. The redundant layers are dynamically adjusted in the whole process iteratively. Our contributions are summarized as follows:

- We propose a new filter criterion that utilizes network interpretability to construct a filter maximum response set, and then judges redundancy based on the consistency of filter's response to the class.
- We propose a discriminative layer pruning method that avoids direct global comparison of importance according to filter criteria, which results in better network structures.
- We evaluate the effectiveness of our method on various networks and datasets. Experiment results show that our method achieves state-of-the-art performance.

2 Related Work

Many previous works studied pruning methods and their filter importance criteria. Li [17] used the L1 norm of filters while Liu [23] proposed SD score as the importance score of filters to prune the unimportant filters. Yu [40] applied the feature ranking technique to measure the importance of filters in final response layer. Meng [27] used the stripe of filter as the granularity and took L1 norm of each stripe as the importance criterion to obtain irregular filters. Ding [3] proposed a centripetal SGD to train the network in the hyperspace of parameters and prune the similar filters after training. He [10] proposed a pruning method to prune filters closed to the geometric center of the network. Besides filter importance, Liu [25] considered the scale factor in BN layer as the channel importance to determine which channel to be pruned. Molchanov [28] proposed a new criterion based on the Taylor expansion of network loss change. After scoring all filters using importance criteria, many methods directly perform global pruning. But Wang [39] claimed that pruning in layers with the most structural redundancy outperforms pruning the least important filters across all layers. Therefore, it is better to prune in relatively redundant layers every time. Recently, some researchers have introduced network structure search into pruning. Liu [24,36] applied meta learning to pruning and Lin [21] used artificial bee colony.

Insight into network interpretability can help researchers better understand the network behavior. Zeiler and Fergus [41] use a multi-layer deconvolutional network to project feature activation back to pixel space to learn the representation. Experiments showed that filters of low layers learn low-level features such as color and edge, while filters of high layers learn high-level features such as body parts. Therefore, different layers may not be well pruned according to the filter criterion alone. Zhou [42] visualized the receptive fields by the images with top 5% activation response to filters. Girshick [6] demonstrated that convolutional layers complete most of the learning ability of a CNN and the extracted features are universal.

3   Method

3.1   Receptive Field Criterion (RFC)

Let $N \in \mathbb{R}$ be the number of input images and $C \in \mathbb{R}$ be the number of classes. $M_{ij}(k) \in \mathbb{R}^{h_i \times w_j}$ is the channel generated from the k-th image by the j-th filter in the i-th layer after the activation function. $S_{ij} = \{(M_{ij}(k), v_k), \quad k = 1, 2, \cdots, N\}$ is a set consisting of channel-label pairs, where v_k is the class label of the k-th image. Next, we define the filter's response score to the input image. Define the response score set A_{ij} to represent the activation response of the j-th filter to all images, then the stronger the filter response to the image, the higher the response score is, as shown below:

$$A_{ij} = \{\|M_{ij}(k)\|, \quad k = 1, 2, \cdots, N\} \tag{1}$$

where $\|M_{ij}(k)\| = \sum_{n=1}^{h_i \times w_j} \|m_{ij}^n(k)\|$ and n is the component of the corresponding channel. Zhou et al. [42] used 5% of images with the largest filter response to detect the filter's receptive field, which means that these images reflect the filter's learned features. Therefore, after obtaining all responses in A_{ij}, we construct a maximum response set A_{ij}^* consisting of the top 5% activation responses. With the channel-label pairs corresponding to the responses in A_{ij}^*, we construct the channel-label set:

$$S_{ij}^* = \{(M_{ij}(k), v_k)| \, \|M_{ij}(k)\|_2 \in A_{ij}^*, k = 1, 2, \cdots, N\}. \tag{2}$$

Then we extract the label set V_{ij} from S_{ij}^* as follows:

$$V_{ij} = \{v_k|(M_{ij}(k), v_k) \in S_{ij}^*, \quad k = 1, 2, \cdots, N\} \tag{3}$$

Here, V_{ij} is used to generate the probability distribution of maximum response of the corresponding filter. We convert V_{ij} to the maximum response probability as follows:

$$p_{ij}^n = \frac{e^{|V_{ij}^n|}}{\sum\limits_{n=1}^{C} e^{|V_{ij}^n|}}, n = 1, 2, ..., C \tag{4}$$

where $|V_{ij}|$ is the number of elements in set V_{ij} and $|V_{ij}^n|$ represents the number of elements belong to class n. Note that only when $p_{ij}^n > 0$ will it be added to the next calculation. From the perspective of feature discrimination, we take information entropy as our RFC. With those positive p_{ij}^n, we calculate their information entropy [33]:

$$H_{ij} = \sum_{n=1}^{C} p_{ij}^n \cdot \log \frac{1}{p_{ij}^n} \tag{5}$$

where H_{ij} is the RFC score of the j-th filter in the i-th layer. The greater RFC score indicates the more average contribution to each class, and vice versa. We

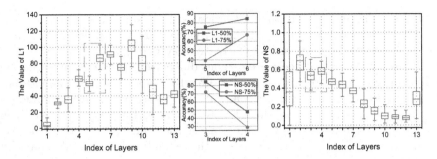

Fig. 2. The upper part is a boxplot of the filter scores (L1 [17], NS [25]) of each layer of VGG16 on CIFAR-10. The middle of the boxplot shows the measured accuracy after only the index layer is selected for trimming. For example, when the index of the middle graph is 5, L1-50% represents the accuracy after pruning only 50% filters of the fifth layer of VGG16 according to the L1 criterion.

demonstrate the effectiveness of RFC in Sect. 4.7, showing that RFC is a good measure of filter importance. Besides, we state in Sect. 4.5 that most of the filters with uniform response are redundant because of their invalid response to the common background of the picture.

For conducting pruning, we define an RFC-score set T_i of all H_{ij} in the i-th layer as follows:

$$T_i = \{H_{ij}, \quad j = 1, 2, ..., O_i\} \tag{6}$$

where O_i is the number of filters in the i-th layer. We denote T_i^* as a set consisting of low RFC values (corresponding to the retained filters). Then the retained filter set K_i^* is defined as follows:

$$K_i^* = \{K_{ij} | H_{ij} \in T_i^*, j = 1, 2, \cdots, O_i\} \tag{7}$$

where K_{ij} is the correspond filter of H_{ij}. In our pruning procedure, we retain the filters in K_i^* to rebuild the network.

3.2   Distinguishing Layer Pruning Based on RFC

Thoughts on Directly Using Criterion Pruning for Global Pruning:
Traditional global threshold pruning methods combine all T_i into a global set $T = \bigcup_{i=1}^{W} T_i$, where W is the total number of convolutional layers in the network. In this case, we cannot simply measure all filters at the same level to construct T^*. As shown in Fig. 2, we observe that the value range of the pruning criterion is usually significantly different between layers. If the global set pruning is simply used, a certain layer may be completely pruned. In addition, we found that criteria for this difference do not compare the importance of filters across layers. As observed in the L1 boxplot of Fig. 2, layer 5 is considered more redundant than layer 6 under global threshold pruning. But from the plot in the middle of the boxplot we know that layer 5 has a bigger impact on network performance,

which is more important. The same situation exists in NS. This means that some filters are considered equally important in global threshold pruning, but their importance to the network varies greatly from layer to layer.

The above shows that there are obvious differences in the pruning situation of different layers. Therefore, we cannot directly compare the filter importance of each layer according to the criteria, but first select the relatively redundant layers, and then prune only in these layers. To this end, we consider each T_i in $T = \bigcup_{i=1}^{W} T_i$ separately during pruning using RFC, first select redundant layers, and then perform pruning. Moreover, the redundant layers are dynamically adjusted in the whole process iteratively.

Distinguishing Layer Pruning Based on RFC: Inspired by the filter redundancy measurement in [4,26,40], we remove each layer in rotation and calculate the network output change to determine the redundant layer.

For a network $\mathcal{F} = (K_1, K_2, \cdots, K_W)$, where K_i represents the filter set of the i-th layer and corresponds to the RFC score set T_i. We remove the same ratio λ of filters in each layer according to T_i to obtain T_i^* as follows:

$$T_i^* = sort_{0.5}(T_i) \tag{8}$$

where $sort_{0.5}$ represents removing 50% of the elements in T_i with the highest H values (50% for a trade-off between effect and efficiency [4]). Thus, T_i^* represents the set of the lowest part of H values in T_i. Corresponding to T_i^*, we construct our network by replacing K_i with K_i^* as presented in Eq. (7):

$$\mathcal{F}_i = (K_1, \cdots, K_i^*, \cdots, K_W) \tag{9}$$

where $\mathcal{F}_i$ represents the network obtained by only pruning the i-th layer of $\mathcal{F}$. Denote $\mathbf{g}_i(\mathbf{g})$ and $y_i(y)$ as the output probability vector and class value of $\mathcal{F}_i(\mathcal{F})$. Since calculating the change of network output on the entire training dataset is time-consuming, we randomly select 5% images from the training set to construct a proxy dataset D_{proxy}. To measure output changes before and after pruning, we measure hard and soft changes. A hard change is a change in the output target class, and a soft change is a change in the output of all classes. We introduce cosine similarity as a soft change, which is widely used to measure similarity [34,37] between vectors. A hard change is combined with the change of target class. We define the layer redundancy R_i as follows:

$$R_i = \gamma E_k \left[sign(|y^k - y_i^k|) \right] + (1 - \gamma)\left(1 - E_k \left[\frac{g^k \cdot g_i^k}{|g^k| \, |g_i^k|} \right] \right), \quad i = 1, 2, \ldots, W \tag{10}$$

where k is the index of the image in D_{proxy} and γ is the balance coefficient between [0,1]. The smaller the value of R_i, the smaller the change of the network performance, the higher the redundancy of the i-th layer. If R_i is large, the corresponding layer will be considered important. We introduce a redundancy threshold ε to control redundant layers in this iteration, so we only prune layers with high redundancy. as follows:

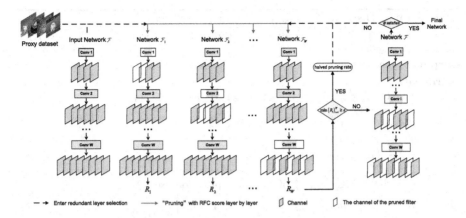

Fig. 3. Distinguishing layer pruning procedure. Conv represents the convolutional layer. Input the proxy dataset to original network $\mathcal{F}$. Then "prune" each layer respectively to obtain each layer's redundancy R_i. If $\min\{R_i\}_{i=1}^{W} \geq \varepsilon$ holds when halved pruning granularity re-enters redundant layer selection. Otherwise, prune the layer of R_i smaller than ε to obtain the network $\mathcal{F}$. Repeat this process until the constraint φ is satisfied.

$$\mathcal{F} \leftarrow \begin{cases} K_i^*, & R_i < \varepsilon \\ K_i, & R_i \geq \varepsilon \end{cases} \tag{11}$$

Here K_i^* represents the layer that has been pruned, and K_i represents the layer that has not been pruned. The network $\mathcal{F}$ is then reconstructed using these layers. The fixed pruning rate in Eq. (8) may result in redundant layers satisfying Eq. (11) not appearing later in the iteration. Therefore, we adjust the ratio by ε, reducing the pruning rate by half to reduce the network output change, and thus perform better pruning. Therefore, when $\min\{R_i\}_{i=1}^{W} \geq \varepsilon$ is satisfied, we permanently halve the pruning rate in Eq. (8) to automatically adjust the pruning granularity. After we prune the redundant layer, we fine-tune the network for one epoch to maintain its stability, which is the same as [13]. The entire procedure (named as DLRFC) is illustrated in Fig. 3 and its pseudocode is shown in Algorithm 1.

4 Experimental Setup

4.1 Experimental Setup

Dataset and Models: As stated in [43], for different size of datasets, a pruning method may lead to different results. We use CIFAR-10/100 [14] and ImageNet [15] for our experiments, which are three popular datasets for pruning evaluation. On CIFAR datasets, we evaluate our method through two classic types of network structures: VGG16 without shortcut connection and ResNet56 with shortcut connection. On ImageNet, we use ResNet50 [9] and MobileNetV2 [31].

Algorithm 1. Distinguishing Layer Pruning based on RFC

Input: Proxy dataset $\mathcal{D}_{proxy}$, redundancy threshold ε, network $\mathcal{F} = (K_1, \cdots, K_W)$, and balance coefficient γ.
Output: Pruned network.

1: **repeat**
2:     Calculate all $\mathbf{g}^k$ and $\mathbf{y}^k$ of $\mathcal{F}$ on the proxy dataset $\mathcal{D}_{proxy}$
3:     **for** $i = 1$ to W **do**
4:         Obtain T_i by RFC
5:         $T_i^* \leftarrow sort_{0.5}(T_i)$
6:         $K_i^* \leftarrow \{K_{ij} | H_{ij} \in T_i^*\}$
7:         $\mathcal{F}_i \leftarrow (K_1, \cdots, K_i^*, \cdots, K_W)$
8:         Calculate all $\mathbf{g}_i^k$ and $\mathbf{y}_i^k$ of $\mathcal{F}_i$ on the proxy dataset $\mathcal{D}_{proxy}$
9:         $R_i = \gamma E_k \left[sign(|y^k - y_i^k|) \right] + (1 - \gamma) \left(1 - E_k \left[\frac{g^k \cdot g_i^k}{|g^k||g_i^k|} \right] \right)$
10:    **end for**
11:    **if** $\min\{R_i\}_{i=1}^W \geq \varepsilon$ **then**
12:       go to 3 **and** halve the pruning granularity in step (5)
13:    **end if**
14:    prune only redundant layers for $\mathcal{F}$
15:    Stablize the network, return to 3.
16: **until** Pruned network satisfies the predefined constraint.

Baseline Setting: Our baseline settings are consistent with those in [21, 25, 27]. On CIFAR-10/100, the model is trained for 160 epochs and the batch size is 64. The initial learning rate is set to 0.1 and divided by 10 at 50% and 75% of the epoch. Simple data augmentation (random cropping and random horizontal flip) is used for training images. On ImageNet, our settings are as same as the popular settings [11, 26].

Pruning Setting: We complete all experiments on NVIDIA RTX 2080 Ti and NVIDIA RTX 3090. We set the balance coefficient $\gamma = 0.8$ and the redundancy threshold $\varepsilon = 0.1$. When pruning ResNet and MobileNetV2, our strategy is similar to [26], i.e. consider all shortcuts at each stage and prune shortcuts and non-shortcuts separately. On CIFAR-10/100, we train the pruned model from scratch using the same FLOPs. On ImageNet, the fine-tuning settings for the pruned model are the same as those in [43].

4.2 Experimental Results on CIFAR-10/100

We prune VGG16 and ResNet56 on CIFAR-10/100 datasets and comprehensively compare our method with other state-of-the-art methods. On CIFAR-10, we obtain two structures (DLRFC-1 and DLRFC-2) from VGG16 and one structure from ResNet56; on CIFAR-100, we obtain one structure for VGG16 and ResNet56, respectively. We record the basline accuracy, pruned model accuracy, accuracy drop, FLOPs and parameters reduction of each model and compare them with other state-of-the-art pruning methods. Comparison results are summarized in Table 1 and Table 2, respectively.

Table 1. Comparison result of VGG16 and ResNet56 on CIFAR-10. Acc↓ is the accuracy drop of pruned model compared to the baseline model. FLOPs↓ and Param↓ represent the reduction of FLOPs and parameters in percentage, respectively.

Model	Method	Baseline Acc.(%)	Pruned Acc.(%)	Acc. ↓ (%)	FLOPs ↓ (%)	Param. ↓ (%)
VGG16	Hinge [18]	93.59	94.02	−0.43	39.07	19.95
	NSPPR [43]	93.88	93.92	−0.04	54.00	-
	AOFP [4]	93.38	93.84	−0.46	60.17	-
	DLRFC-1	**93.25**	**93.93**	**−0.68**	**61.23**	**92.86**
	DPFPS [30]	93.85	93.67	0.18	70.85	93.92
	PFF [27]	93.25	93.65	−0.40	71.16	92.66
	ABC [21]	93.02	93.08	−0.06	73.68	88.68
	HRank [22]	93.96	91.23	2.73	76.50	92.00
	AOFP [4]	93.38	93.28	0.10	75.27	-
	DLRFC-2	**93.25**	**93.64**	**−0.39**	**76.95**	**94.38**
ResNet56	NISP [40]	93.04	93.01	0.03	43.60	42.60
	FPGM [11]	93.59	93.49	0.10	53.00	-
	NSPPR [43]	93.83	93.84	−0.03	47.00	-
	ABC [21]	93.26	93.23	0.03	54.13	54.20
	SRR-GR [39]	93.38	93.75	−0.37	53.80	-
	DPFPS [30]	93.81	93.20	0.61	52.86	46.84
	DLRFC	**93.06**	**93.57**	**−0.51**	**52.58**	**55.63**

Table 2. Comparison result of VGG16 and ResNet56 on CIFAR-100.

Model	Method	Baseline Acc.(%)	Pruned Acc.(%)	Acc. ↓ (%)	FLOPs ↓ (%)	Param. ↓ (%)
VGG16	NS [25]	73.83	74.20	−0.37	38.00	-
	COP [38]	72.59	71.77	0.82	43.10	73.20
	NSPPR [43]	73.83	74.25	−0.42	43.00	-
	DLRFC	**73.54**	**74.09**	**−0.55**	**43.40**	**82.50**
ResNet56	NS [25]	72.49	71.40	1.09	24.00	-
	NSPPR [43]	72.49	72.46	0.03	25.00	-
	DLRFC	**71.14**	**71.41**	**−0.27**	**25.50**	**25.90**

For VGG16, DLRFC-2 reduces 77% FLOPs and 94% parameters; DLRFC-1 reduces 61% FLOPs and 92% parameters on CIFAR-10. Compared with others, DLRFC has the best result, which is higher by 0.49% in accuracy gain than AOFP [4]. On CIFAR-100, DLRFC reduces 43% FLOPs and 82% parameters. In addition, the accuracy gain under the same FLOPs is better than NSPPR.

Table 3. Comparison results of the Top-1 ImageNet accuracy of our method and state-of-the-art pruning methods on ResNet50 and MobileNetV2.

Model	Method	Baseline Acc.(%)	Pruned Acc.(%)	Acc. ↓ (%)	FLOPs ↓ (%)	Param. ↓ (%)
ResNet50	G-SD-B [23]	76.15	75.85	0.30	44	23
	MetaPruning [24]	76.60	75.40	1.20	50	-
	NSPPR [43]	76.15	75.63	0.52	54	-
	DPFPS [30]	76.15	75.55	0.60	46	-
	S-COP [35]	76.15	75.26	0.89	54	52
	LRF-60 [13]	76.15	75.71	0.50	56	53
	DLRFC	**76.13**	**75.84**	**0.29**	**54**	**40**
MobileNetV2	W-Gates [20]	71.80	70.90	0.90	25	-
	DPFPS [30]	72.00	71.10	0.90	25	-
	ManiDP [43]	71.80	71.41	0.39	30	-
	CC [19]	71.88	70.91	0.97	29	-
	DLRFC	**71.80**	**71.88**	**−0.08**	**30**	-

For ResNet56, DLRFC reduces 52% FLOPs and 55% parameters on CIFAR-10. Compared with ABC [21], our model achieves a higher accuracy gain. On CIFAR-100, DLRFC reduces 25% FLOPs and 26% parameters, which outperforms other methods. In brief, DLRFC can produce a more compact model and give better performance.

Compared with ResNet56 on both CIFAR-10/100 datasets, we observe that even at a higher pruning ratio, the pruned VGG16 model can still achieve good performance. A possible explanation is that VGG16 is an extra-large model for CIFAR-10/100, resulting in excessive redundancy. Consequently, pruning can make the model more perfect to fit different datasets.

4.3   Experimental Results on ImageNet

We prune ResNet50 and MobileNetV2 on ImageNet, record the performance of our pruned model and compare it with other methods. As shown in Table 3, our pruned model achieved the best performance. The FLOPs of ResNet50 dropped by 54%, and the accuracy dropped by 0.29%, which was 0.60% lower than S-COP [35] and 0.91% lower than MetaPruning [24]. The FLOPs of MobileNetV2 dropped by 30% and the accuracy increased by 0.08%. This shows that the experimental results still demonstrate the effectiveness of our method on more complex datasets.

Moreover, we demonstrate the effectiveness of our method for wall-clock time speedup on ImageNet. As set by [20], we set the same compression ratio for each layer as a uniform baseline and measure latency using Pytorch on an NVIDIA RTX 2080 Ti GPU. As shown in Table 4, the results show that under the same

Table 4. Comparison results of the Top-1 accuracy and latency of Resnet34 and Resnet50 on ImageNet. Uniform means we set the same pruning ratio for each layer. The network input test batch is set to 100.

Model	DLRFC			Uniform		
	FLOPs(G)	Acc(%)	Latency(ms)	FLOPs(G)	Acc(%)	Latency(ms)
ResNet34	-	-	-	3.7(1X)	73.88	54.04
	2.9	**73.86**	**46.70**	2.9	72.56	49.23
	2.3	**73.28**	**40.65**	2.4	72.05	44.27
	2.0	**72.99**	**37.13**	2.1	71.32	43.47
ResNet50	-	-	-	4.1(1X)	76.15	105.75
	3.0	**76.33**	**95.52**	3.1	75.59	97.87
	2.5	**76.18**	**87.66**	2.6	74.77	91.53
	1.9	**75.81**	**79.83**	2.1	74.42	85.20

Table 5. Results of ablation study. This table shows the results of VGG16 on CIFAR-10 and CIFAR-100 datasets according to different pruning criteria and pruning methods. Different dataset distributions are compared fairly under the same pruning rate.

Criterion	cifar10			cifar100		
	L1(%)	NS(%)	RFC(%)	L1(%)	NS(%)	RFC(%)
GTP	90.56	92.64	92.25	70.90	71.12	71.25
DLP	93.12	93.25	93.38	73.49	73.55	73.82

FLOPs conditions, ResNet50 and ResNet34 pruned by our method can save 17% and 14% of hardware latency without notable accuracy loss. And the model is significantly better than the Uniform baseline in terms of both accuracy and latency.

4.4 Ablation Studies

In this subsection, we investigate the importance of RFC and discriminative layer pruning (called DLP) separately. The results of the ablation studies are summarized in Table 5. For the purpose of ablation experiments, we use the L1 norm [17] (denoted as L1) and the BN scale factor [25] (denoted as NS) to replace the RFC criterion to investigate its importance. We use global threshold pruning (denoted as GTP) to replace DLP to study its importance.

Distinguishing Layer Pruning (DLP): We first study our distinguishing layer pruning algorithm with the fixed criterion RFC. In the RFC column of Table 5, the accuracy of our method is significantly higher than the global threshold pruning of CIFAR-10 and CIFAR-100. This result indicates the effectiveness of our distinguishing layer pruning method. Moreover, we observe that the accuracy of other filter criteria on the DLP method is higher than the global threshold

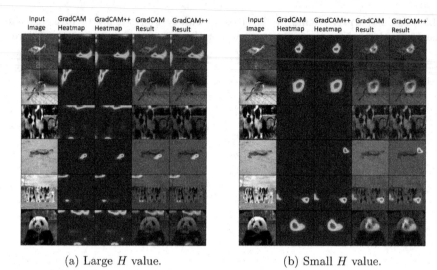

(a) Large H value.   (b) Small H value.

Fig. 4. GradCAM and GradCAM++ visualization for filter selection.

pruning. It shows that the filter criterion alone cannot be used for global comparison, so it is correct that we care about the difference in importance between different layers.

Receptive Field Criterion (RFC): We fixed the pruning method and then replaced RFC with L1 and BN as criteria during pruning. The resulting RFC for the DLP row in Table 5 has better accuracy than L1 and BN, showing that RFC can select filters that should be pruned more to achieve better pruning effect.

4.5 Visualization of Filter Selection

Recall in Sect. 3.1 that H represents the distribution uniformity of the responses. We randomly select 6 animal images in ImageNet. Since the last layer learns the highest-level semantics, we use GradCAM [32] and GradCAM++ [2] to make an visualization analysis of the filter selection in the last layer of the pretrained VGG16, as shown in Fig. 4.

Large H Value: As shown in Fig. 4a, the filters with large H value make high response to most classes, which indicates that the features learned by these filters are not distinguishable and contribute less to classification. Moreover, the response region of these filters with large H values is not on the object. A possible reason is that these filers tend to extract common information of the similar background in the images of different classes.

Small H Value: As shown in Fig. 4b, filters with small H value do not respond to most classes, which shows that these features are distinguishable and contributive to classification. Meanwhile, the response regions generated by the

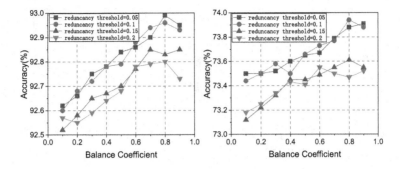

Fig. 5. Hyperparameter analysis of VGG16 on CIFAR10 (left) and CIFAR100 (right).

filters with small H values are roughly located on the object, i.e., these features are relevant to the object. This phenomenon further confirms the reasonability of RFC.

4.6 Hyperparameters

Our DLRFC contains two hyperparameters: (1) balance coefficient γ controlling the relative proportion of soft change and hard change, as shown in Eq. (10); and (2) The redundancy threshold ε controls the network change size and redundancy layer relationship, as shown in Eq. (11).

As shown in Fig. 5, when ε is small, the network selects redundant layers with strict criteria each time. Though this may lead to an increase in accuracy, the entire pruning process will take more time. When ε is too large, the network selects more layers as redundant layers, which will result in the existence of very important layers in the redundant layers and cause accuracy serious decline. So we need to choose ε within a reasonable range to ensure a balance between accuracy and speed. Although different ε may have different fluctuation curves, we found that when $\gamma = 0.8$, there will be better results, that is, we should probably pay more attention to hard changes. But $\gamma = 0.9$ shows that we can't focus too much on hard changes either.

4.7 Other Studies

Feature Discrimination Angle Effectiveness: The level of feature discrimination also represents the uniformity of the filter's response to all class, so we prune filters with high and low uniformity respectively. Figure 6 (left) shows a slight decrease in network performance when pruning the Unif-unimportant filter. However, pruning Unif-important filters wreaks havoc on network performance, suggesting that they are indeed able to measure filter importance. The figure also shows that NS-important has higher accuracy in stage 3 than NS-unimportant, suggesting that NS-important chooses less important filters than NS-unimportant, which is contradictory. It seems that NS cannot distinguish

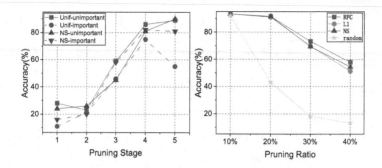

Fig. 6. Left: We divide VGG16 into 5 stages according to the pooling layer, stage x means that the filter of each layer in stage x is only pruned by half, and then the accuracy is obtained. unif-unimportant means to prune all filters that uniformity considers unimportant (that is, filters with high uniformity), unif-important means to prune filters that uniformity considers important, and the same is true for NS. Right: The accuracy of different criteria under the same network pruning structure.

the importance of filters in stage 3 and stage 4, but Unif can distinguish well. The above shows that the idea of class uniformity can be used to judge the redundancy of the filter.

RFC Measuring Redundancy: Recall that the RFC measures redundancy from a new perspective, which is expressed as the H value, as shown in Eq. (5). The higher the H value, the more redundant the filters and the less they contribute to classification. We prune filters with different criteria: RFC, L1 norm, BN, and random selection. After pruning the network by the above criteria, we directly record the accuracy. Figure 6 (right) shows the change in accuracy as the pruning rate increases. When pruning the RFC's filters, the accuracy drop was the smallest among these criteria, i.e. the RFC found the most redundant filters. This result further demonstrates the validity of the RFC guidelines.

5   Conclusion

In this paper, we propose a novel filter importance criterion named as Receptive Field Criterion from the feature discrimination. Our criterion scientifically measures the filter redundancy and effectively guides the pruning procedure. The distinguishing layer pruning based on RFC proposed by us can effectively consider the relative redundancy between the layers of the network. Extensive experiments conducted on CIFAR-10/100 and ImageNet show that our method achieves the state-of-the-art performance in some benchmarks. In the future, we will further explore the more intrinsic relationship between pruning and response class distribution.

Acknowledgement. This work is sponsored by the Zhejiang Provincial Natural Science Foundation of China (LZ22F020007, LGF20F020007), Major Research Plan of the National Natural Science Foundation of China (92167203), National Key R&D Program of China (2018YFB2100400), Natural Science Foundation of China (61902082, 61972357), and the project funded by China Postdoctoral Science Foundation under No.2022M713253.

References

1. Bau, D., Zhou, B., Khosla, A., Oliva, A., Torralba, A.: Network dissection: quantifying interpretability of deep visual representations. In: 2017 IEEE Conference on Computer Vision and Pattern Recognition, pp. 3319–3327 (2017)
2. Chattopadhay, A., Sarkar, A., Howlader, P., Balasubramanian, V.N.: Grad-CAM++: generalized gradient-based visual explanations for deep convolutional networks. In: IEEE Winter Conference on Applications of Computer Vision, pp. 839–847 (2018)
3. Ding, X., Ding, G., Guo, Y., Han, J.: Centripetal SGD for pruning very deep convolutional networks with complicated structure. In: 2019 IEEE Conference on Computer Vision and Pattern Recognition, pp. 4943–4953 (2019)
4. Ding, X., Ding, G., Guo, Y., Han, J., Yan, C.: Approximated oracle filter pruning for destructive CNN width optimization. In: International Conference on Machine Learning, pp. 1607–1616 (2019)
5. Dong, Y., Bao, F., Su, H., Zhu, J.: Towards interpretable deep neural networks by leveraging adversarial examples (2017). arXiv preprint arXiv:1708.05493
6. Girshick, R., Donahue, J., Darrell, T., Malik, J.: Rich feature hierarchies for accurate object detection and semantic segmentation. In: 2014 IEEE Conference on Computer Vision and Pattern Recognition, pp. 580–587 (2014)
7. Han, S., Mao, H., Dally, W.J.: Deep compression: compressing deep neural networks with pruning, trained quantization and Huffman coding. In: International Conference on Learning Representations (2016)
8. Han, S., Pool, J., Tran, J., Dally, W.J.: Learning both weights and connections for efficient neural networks. In: Proceedings of the 28th International Conference on Neural Information Processing Systems, pp. 1135–1143 (2015)
9. He, K., Zhang, X., Ren, S., Sun, J.: Deep residual learning for image recognition. In: IEEE Conference on Computer Vision and Pattern Recognition, pp. 770–778 (2016)
10. He, Y., Ding, Y., Liu, P., Zhu, L., Zhang, H., Yang, Y.: Learning filter pruning criteria for deep convolutional neural networks acceleration. In: Proceedings of the IEEE/CVF Conference on Computer Vision and Pattern Recognition, pp. 2009–2018 (2020)
11. He, Y., Liu, P., Wang, Z., Hu, Z., Yang, Y.: Filter pruning via geometric median for deep convolutional neural networks acceleration. In: Proceedings of the IEEE/CVF Conference on Computer Vision and Pattern Recognition, pp. 4340–4349 (2019)
12. Hinton, G., Vinyals, O., Dean, J.: Distilling the knowledge in a neural network. In: Advances in 28th Neural Information Processing Systems (2015)
13. Joo, D., Yi, E., Baek, S., Kim, J.: Linearly replaceable filters for deep network channel pruning. In: Proceedings of the AAAI Conference on Artificial Intelligence, pp. 8021–8029 (2021)
14. Krizhevsky, A.: Learning multiple layers of features from tiny images. Ph.D. thesis in University of Toronto (2009)

15. Krizhevsky, A., Sutskever, I., Hinton, G.E.: ImageNet classification with deep convolutional neural networks. In: Proceedings of the 25th International Conference on Neural Information Processing Systems, pp. 1097–1105 (2012)

16. Ledig, C., et al.: Photo-realistic single image super-resolution using a generative adversarial network. In: 2017 IEEE Conference on Computer Vision and Pattern Recognition, pp. 4681–4690 (2017)

17. Li, H., Kadav, A., Durdanovic, I., Samet, H., Graf, H.P.: Pruning filters for efficient ConvNets (2016). arXiv preprint arXiv:1608.08710

18. Li, Y., Gu, S., Mayer, C., Gool, L.V., Timofte, R.: Group sparsity: the hinge between filter pruning and decomposition for network compression. In: Proceedings of the IEEE/CVF Conference on Computer Vision and Pattern Recognition, pp. 8018–8027 (2020)

19. Li, Y., et al.: Towards compact CNNs via collaborative compression. In: Proceedings of the IEEE/CVF Conference on Computer Vision and Pattern Recognition, pp. 6438–6447 (2021)

20. Li, Y., et al.: Weight-dependent gates for differentiable neural network pruning. In: Bartoli, A., Fusiello, A. (eds.) ECCV 2020. LNCS, vol. 12539, pp. 23–37. Springer, Cham (2020). https://doi.org/10.1007/978-3-030-68238-5_3

21. Lin, M., Ji, R., Zhang, Y., Zhang, B., Wu, Y., Tian, Y.: Channel pruning via automatic structure search. In: Proceedings of the 29th International Joint Conference on Artificial Intelligence, pp. 673–679 (2020)

22. Lin, M., Ji, R., Zhang, Y., Zhang, B., Wu, Y., Tian, Y.: HRank: filter pruning using high-rank feature map. In: Proceedings of the IEEE/CVF Conference on Computer Vision and Pattern Recognition, pp. 1529–1538 (2020)

23. Liu, Y., Wentzlaff, D., Kung, S.: Rethinking class-discrimination based CNN channel pruning (2020). arXiv preprint arXiv:2004.14492

24. Liu, Z., et al.: MetaPruning: meta learning for automatic neural network channel pruning. In: Proceedings of the IEEE/CVF International Conference on Computer Vision, pp. 3296–3305 (2019)

25. Liu, Z., Li, J., Shen, Z., Huang, G., Yan, S., Zhang, C.: Learning efficient convolutional networks through network slimming. In: Proceedings of the IEEE/CVF International Conference on Computer Vision, pp. 2736–2744 (2017)

26. Luo, J.H., Wu, J.: Neural network pruning with residual-connections and limited-data. In: Proceedings of the IEEE/CVF Conference on Computer Vision and Pattern Recognition, pp. 1458–1467 (2020)

27. Meng, F., et al.: Pruning filter in filter. In: Advances in 33rd Neural Information Processing Systems (2020)

28. Molchanov, P., Tyree, S., Karras, T., Aila, T., Kautz, J.: Pruning convolutional neural networks for resource efficient inference. In: International Conference on Learning Representations (2017)

29. Paszke, A., et al.: Pytorch: an imperative style, high-performance deep learning library. In: Advances in 32nd Neural Information Processing Systems, pp. 8024–8035 (2019)

30. Ruan, X., Liu, Y., Li, B., Yuan, C., Hu, W.: DPFPS: dynamic and progressive filter pruning for compressing convolutional neural networks from scratch. In: Proceedings of the AAAI Conference on Artificial Intelligence, pp. 2495–2503 (2021)

31. Sandler, M., Howard, A., Zhu, M., Zhmoginov, A., Chen, L.C.: MobileNetV2: inverted residuals and linear bottlenecks. In: 2018 IEEE/CVF Conference on Computer Vision and Pattern Recognition, pp. 4510–4520 (2018)

32. Selvaraju, R.R., Cogswell, M., Das, A., Vedantam, R., Parikh, D., Batra, D.: Grad-CAM: visual explanations from deep networks via gradient-based localization. In: Proceedings of the IEEE/CVF International Conference on Computer Vision, pp. 618–626 (2017)
33. Shannon, C.E.: A mathematical theory of communication. Bell Syst. Tech. J. **27**(3), 379–423 (1948)
34. Tang, C., Lv, J., Chen, Y., Guo, J.: An angle-based method for measuring the semantic similarity between visual and textual features. Soft. Comput. **23**(12), 4041–4050 (2018). https://doi.org/10.1007/s00500-018-3051-y
35. Tang, Y., et al.: SCOP: scientific control for reliable neural network pruning (2020). arXiv preprint arXiv:2010.10732
36. Tian, H., Liu, B., Yuan, X.-T., Liu, Q.: Meta-learning with network pruning. In: Vedaldi, A., Bischof, H., Brox, T., Frahm, J.-M. (eds.) ECCV 2020. LNCS, vol. 12364, pp. 675–700. Springer, Cham (2020). https://doi.org/10.1007/978-3-030-58529-7_40
37. Wang, H., et al.: CosFace: large margin cosine loss for deep face recognition. In: 2018 IEEE/CVF Conference on Computer Vision and Pattern Recognition, pp. 5265–5274 (2018)
38. Wang, W., Fu, C., Guo, J., Cai, D., He, X.: COP: customized deep model compression via regularized correlation-based filter-level pruning. In: Proceedings of the 28th International Joint Conference on Artificial Intelligence, pp. 3785–3791 (2019)
39. Wang, Z., Li, C., Wang, X.: Convolutional neural network pruning with structural redundancy reduction. In: 2021 IEEE/CVF Conference on Computer Vision and Pattern Recognition Workshops, pp. 14913–14922 (2021)
40. Yu, R., et al.: NISP: pruning networks using neuron importance score propagation. In: Proceedings of the IEEE Conference on Computer Vision and Pattern Recognition, pp. 9194–9203 (2018)
41. Zeiler, M.D., Fergus, R.: Visualizing and understanding convolutional networks. In: Fleet, D., Pajdla, T., Schiele, B., Tuytelaars, T. (eds.) ECCV 2014. LNCS, vol. 8689, pp. 818–833. Springer, Cham (2014). https://doi.org/10.1007/978-3-319-10590-1_53
42. Zhou, B., Khosla, A., Lapedriza, A., Oliva, A., Torralba, A.: Object detectors emerge in deep scene CNNs. In: International Conference on Learning Representations (2015)
43. Zhuang, T., Zhang, Z., Huang, Y., Zeng, X., Shuang, K., Li, X.: Neuron-level structured pruning using polarization regularizer. In: Advances in 33rd Neural Information Processing Systems (2020)

LA3: Efficient Label-Aware AutoAugment

Mingjun Zhao[1(✉)], Shan Lu[1], Zixuan Wang[2], Xiaoli Wang[2], and Di Niu[1]

[1] University of Alberta, Edmonton, Canada
{zhao2,slu1,dniu}@ualberta.ca
[2] Platform and Content Group, Tencent, Shenzhen, China
{zackiewang,evexlwang}@tencent.com

Abstract. Automated augmentation is an emerging and effective technique to search for data augmentation policies to improve generalizability of deep neural network training. Most existing work focuses on constructing a unified policy applicable to all data samples in a given dataset, without considering sample or class variations. In this paper, we propose a novel two-stage data augmentation algorithm, named *Label-Aware AutoAugment (LA3)*, which takes advantage of the label information, and learns augmentation policies separately for samples of different labels. *LA3* consists of two learning stages, where in the first stage, individual augmentation methods are evaluated and ranked for each label via Bayesian Optimization aided by a neural predictor, which allows us to identify effective augmentation techniques for each label under a low search cost. And in the second stage, a composite augmentation policy is constructed out of a selection of effective as well as complementary augmentations, which produces significant performance boost and can be easily deployed in typical model training. Extensive experiments demonstrate that *LA3* achieves excellent performance matching or surpassing existing methods on CIFAR-10 and CIFAR-100, and achieves a new state-of-the-art ImageNet accuracy of 79.97% on ResNet-50 among auto-augmentation methods, while maintaining a low computational cost.

1 Introduction

Data augmentation has proven to be an effective regularization technique that can improve the generalization of deep neural networks by adding modified copies of existing samples to increase the volume and diversity of data used to train these networks. Traditional ways of applying data augmentation in computer vision include using single augmentation techniques, such as rotation, flipping and cutout [4], adopting randomly selected augmentations [2], and employing a manually crafted augmentation policy consisting of a combination of transformations. However, these methods either do not reach the full potential of data augmentation, or require human expertise in policy design for specific tasks.

Supplementary Information The online version contains supplementary material available at https://doi.org/10.1007/978-3-031-19803-8_16.

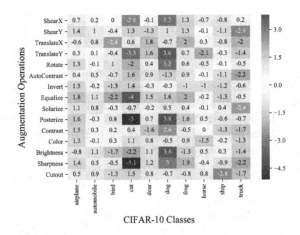

Fig. 1. The effects of different augmentation operations on each class in CIFAR-10, demonstrated by the test accuracy change in each class after each single augmentation is applied to training WRN-40-2.

Recently, automated learning of augmentation policies has become popular to surpass the limitation of manual design, achieving remarkable advances in both the performance and generalization ability on image classification tasks. Different search algorithms such as reinforcement learning [1], population-based training [9], and Bayesian Optimization [16] have been investigated to search effective augmentation policies from data to be used to train target networks. Dynamic augmentation strategies, e.g., PBA [9], AdvAA [25], are also proposed to learn non-stationary policies that vary during model training.

However, most existing methods focus on learning a single policy that is applied to all samples in the dataset equally, without considering variations between samples, classes or labels, which may lead to sub-optimal solutions. Fig. 1 demonstrates the effects of different augmentation operations on different classes of samples in CIFAR-10, from which we can see that the effectiveness of augmentations is different on each class. For example, when the operation "Posterize" is applied in training, the test accuracy of "dog" class increases by 3.8%, whereas the test accuracy of "cat" drops significantly by 5%. It is possible that a certain augmentation used in training has completely different impacts on different labels. This observation implies the limitation of label or sample-invariant dataset-level augmentation policies. MetaAugment [26] proposes to learn a sample-aware augmentation policy by solving a sample re-weighting problem. It uses an augmentation policy network to take an augmentation operation and the corresponding augmented image as inputs, and outputs a weight to adjust the augmented image loss computed by the task network. Despite the benefit of a fine-grained sample-dependent policy, MetaAugment is time-consuming and couples policy network learning with target model training, which may not be convenient in some production scenarios that require functional decomposition.

In this paper, we propose an efficient data augmentation strategy named *Label-Aware AutoAugment (LA3)*, which produces label-aware augmentation policies to overcome the limitation of sample-invariant augmentation while still being computationally efficient as compared to sample-aware or dynamic augmentation strategies. *LA3* achieves competitive performance matching or outperforming a wide range of existing static and dynamic auto-augment methods, and attains the highest ImageNet accuracy on ResNet-50 among all existing augmentation methods including dynamic ones. In the meantime, *LA3* is also a simple scheme which separates augmentation policy search from target network model training, and produces stationary augmentation policies that can easily be applied to enhance deep learning with minimum perturbation to the original target model training routine.

LA3 adopts a two-staged design, which first explores a search space of combinations of operations and evaluates the effectiveness of promising augmentation operations for each class, while in the second stage, forms a composite policy to be used in target model training.

In the first stage of *LA3*, a neural predictor is designed to estimate the effectiveness of operation combinations on each class and is trained online through density matching as the exploration process iterates. We use Bayesian Optimization with a predictor-based sampling strategy to guide search into meaningful regions, which greatly improves the efficiency and reduces search cost.

In the second stage, rather than only selecting top augmentation operations, we introduce a policy construction method based on the minimum-redundancy maximum-reward (mRMR) principle [17] to enhance the performance of the composite augmentation policy when applied to the target model. This is in contrast to most prior methods [1], [16], which simply put together best performing augmentations in evaluation, ignoring their complementary effects.

Extensive experiments show that using the same set of augmentation operations, the proposed *LA3* achieves excellent performance outperforming other low-cost static auto-augmentation strategies, including FastAA and DADA, on CIFAR-10 and CIFAR-100, in terms of the accuracy. On ImageNet, *LA3*, using stationary policies, achieves a new state-of-the-art top-1 accuracy of 79.97% on ResNet-50, which outperforms prior auto-augmentation methods including dynamic strategies such as AdvAA and MetaAug, while being 2× and 3× more computationally efficient, respectively.

2   Related Work

Data augmentation is a popular technique to alleviate overfitting and improve the generalization of neural network models by enlarging the volume and diversity of training data. Various data augmentation methods have been designed, such as Cutout [4], Mixup [24], CutMix [22], etc. Recently, automated augmentation policy search has become popular, replacing human-crafted policies by learning policies directly from data. AutoAugment [1] adopts a reinforcement learning framework that alternatively evaluates a child model and trains an

RNN controller to sample child models to find effective augmentation policies. Although AutoAugment significantly improves the performance, its search process can take thousands of GPU hours which greatly limits its usability.

Multiple strategies are proposed to lower the search cost. Fast AutoAugment [16] proposes a density matching scheme to avoid training and evaluating child models, and uses Bayesian Optimization as the search algorithm. Weight-sharing AutoAugment [18] adopts weight-sharing settings and harvests rewards by fine-tuning child models on a shared pre-trained target network. Faster AutoAugment [7] further reduces the search time by making the search of policies end-to-end differentiable through gradient approximations and targeting to reduce the distance between the original and augmented image distributions. Similarly, DADA [15] relaxes the discrete policy selection to a differentiable optimization problem via Gumbel-Softmax [12] and introduces an unbiased gradient estimator.

Instead of producing stationary augmentation policies that are consistent during the target network training, PBA [9] learns a non-stationary augmentation schedule, inspired by population based training [11], by modeling the augmentation policy search task as a process of hyperparameter schedule learning. AdvAA [25] adopts an adversarial framework that jointly optimizes target network training and augmentation search to find harder augmentation policies that produce the maximum training loss. However, AdvAA must rely on the batch augment trick, where each training batch is enlarged by multiple times with augmented copies, which significantly increases its computational cost. In general, one concern of these dynamic strategies is that they intervene the standard model training procedure, causing extra deployment overhead and may not be applicable in many production environments.

While most previous studies focus on learning augmentation policies for the entire dataset, MetaAugment [26] proposes to learn sample-aware augmentation policies during model training by formulating the policy search as a sample re-weighting problem, and constructing a policy network to learn the weights of specific augmented images by minimizing the validation loss via meta learning. Despite its benefits, MetaAugment is computationally expensive, requiring three forward and backward passes of the target network in each iteration. LB-Aug [19] is a concurrent work that also searches policies dependent on labels, but focuses on a different task under multi-label scenarios, where each sample has multiple labels rather than a single classification label. LB-Aug uses an actor-critic reinforcement learning framework and policy gradient approach for policy learning. Despite the benefits from label-based policies, LB-Aug has potential stability issues due to the use of reinforcement learning, which is generally harder and computational costly to train. In fact, the search cost of LB-Aug is not reported. In contrast, *LA3* targets the classical single-label image classification tasks, e.g., on CIFAR-10/100 and ImageNet benchmarks, on which most other auto-augmentation methods are evaluated. It adopts Bayesian Optimization coupled with a neural predictor to sample and search for label-dependent augmentation policies efficiently. In addition, a policy construction stage is proposed to further form a more effective composite policy for target network training.

3   Methodology

In this section, we first review the task of conventional augmentation search and introduce the formulation of the proposed label-aware augmentation search task. Then we describe the two-stage design of $LA3$, and present the algorithm in detail.

3.1   Conventional Augmentation Search

Given an image recognition task with a training dataset $D^{tr} = \{(x_i, y_i)\}_{i=1}^{|D^{tr}|}$, with x_i and y_i representing the image and label respectively, augmented samples $T(x_i)$ are derived by applying augmentation policy T to sample x_i. Usually, the policy T is composed of multiple sub-policies τ, and each sub-policy is made up by K augmentation operations O, optionally with their corresponding probabilities and magnitudes, which are adopted in the original design of AutoAugment [1], but not included in some of the recent methods such as Weight-sharing AutoAugment [18] and MetaAugment [26].

Conventional augmentation search methods focus on the task whose goal is to construct the optimal policy T^* from given augmentations so that the performance $\mathcal{R}$ of the task network θ_T on the validation dataset D^{val} is maximized:

$$T^* = \arg\max_{T} \mathcal{R}(\theta_T | D^{val}),$$

$$\text{where} \quad \theta_T = \arg\min_{\theta_T} \frac{1}{|D^{tr}|} \sum_{i=1}^{|D^{tr}|} \mathcal{L}_\theta(T(x_i), y_i), \tag{1}$$

and $\mathcal{L}_\theta$ is the loss function of target network θ.

3.2   Label-Aware Augmentation Search

Though learning a dataset-level policy achieves considerable improvements, it is unlikely the optimal solution due to the lack of consideration of sample variations and utilization of label information.

In this paper, we aim to learn a label-aware data augmentation policy $T^* = \{T_{y_0}^*, \cdots, T_{y_n}^*\}$, where for samples of each label y_j, an individual policy T_{y_j} is learned by maximizing the label-specific performance $\mathcal{R}_{y_j}$ of label y_j:

$$T_{y_j}^* = \arg\max_{T_{y_j}} \mathcal{R}_{y_j}(\theta_T | D^{val}),$$

$$\text{where} \quad \theta_T = \arg\min_{\theta_T} \frac{1}{|D^{tr}|} \sum_{i=1}^{|D^{tr}|} \mathcal{L}_\theta(T_{y_i}(x_i), y_i). \tag{2}$$

Similar to conventional augmentation, in our label-aware setting, we define that each policy for a label is composed of multiple augmentation triples, each

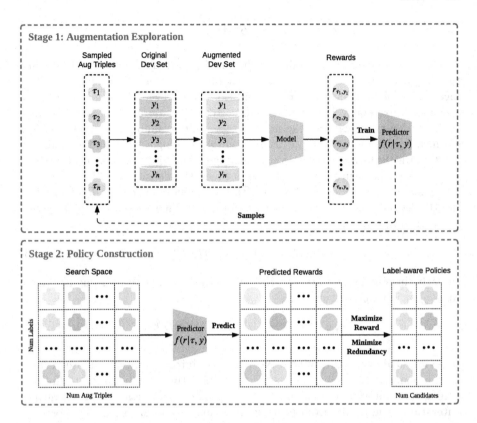

Fig. 2. An overview of the proposed *LA3* method. It contains two stages, where in the first stage, augmentation triples are individually evaluated for each label via Bayesian Optimization with the help of an label-aware neural predictor. In the second stage, the best combination of complementary augmentation triples is selected based on the minimum-redundancy maximum-reward principle.

consisting of three augmentation operations. The magnitude of each augmentation operation is chosen randomly from ranges defined in AutoAugment [1], and is excluded from the search space in order to introduce randomness and diversity into the policy, and allocate more computational resources to assessing the fitness of operations to different classes of samples.

In this paper, we propose a label-aware augmentation policy search algorithm called *LA3*, composed of two stages as presented in Fig. 2. The first augmentation exploration stage aims to search for effective augmentation triples with density matching, and train a neural predictor to provide evaluations on all seen and unseen augmentation triples in the search space. And the goal of the second policy construction stage is to build a composite policy for each label based on the evaluation results from stage 1 by selecting a subset of complementary augmentation triples based on the minimum-redundancy maximum-reward principle.

3.3   Stage 1: Augmentation Exploration

Density Matching is an efficient mechanism originally proposed by Fast AutoAugment [16] to simplify the search process for effective augmentations, since the problem defined by Eq. (1) and Eq. (2) is a bi-level optimization problem, and is extremely hard to solve directly. It calculates the reward of each augmentation triple without the need of repeatedly training the target network. Specifically, given a model θ pre-trained on the training set D^{tr} and a validation set D^{val}, the performance of a certain augmentation triple τ can be evaluated by approximately measuring the distance between the density of D^{tr} and density of augmented validation set $\tau(D^{val})$ with the model performance $\mathcal{R}(\theta|\tau(D^{val}))$. And the reward r is measured by the performance difference caused by applying the augmentation triple τ:

$$r_\tau = \mathcal{R}(\theta|\tau(D^{val})) - \mathcal{R}(\theta|D^{val}). \tag{3}$$

Similarly, in our label-aware setting, the reward r for a certain augmentation triple τ_y at label y is given by

$$r_{\tau,y} = \mathcal{R}_y(\theta|\tau_y(D^{val})) - \mathcal{R}_y(\theta|D^{val}). \tag{4}$$

Bayesian Optimization with a Neural Predictor is a widely adopted framework in many applications such as neural architecture search [20,21] to find the optimal solution within a search space. In standard BO setting, over a sequence of iterations, the results from previous iterations are used to model a posterior distribution to guide the candidate selection of next iteration. And a neural predictor is a neural network that is repeatedly trained on the history evaluated candidates, and provides evaluations on unseen candidates, which increases the utilization efficiency of history evaluations and notably accelerates the search process.

In our *LA3* algorithm, we incorporate a label-aware neural predictor $f(r|\tau, y)$ which takes in an augmentation triple τ and the label y it is evaluated on, and predicts the reward r. In each iteration, the sampled augmentation triples for different labels are evaluated according to Eq. 4, and together with the previous evaluated augmentation triples, are passed to train a new predictor.

Next, we select 100 candidate augmentation triples at the balance of exploration and exploitation, based on the following selection procedure: 1) Generate 10 new candidates by randomly mutating 1 or 2 operations in the chosen augmentation triples of the previous iteration; 2) Randomly sample 50 candidates from all unexplored augmentation triples; 3) Sample 40 candidates from the explored augmentation triples according to their real reward values. Then, for each label y, we choose the augmentation triple τ with the highest predicted reward $\tilde{r}_{\tau,y}$ for evaluation.

Overall workflow of the first stage is summarized in Algorithm 1. To begin with, a warm-up phase of T_0 iterations is incorporated to randomly explore the

---

Algorithm 1: Stage 1: Augmentation Exploration

Input: Pre-trained target network θ, warm up iterations T_0, total iterations T

Output: Well-trained predictor $f^T(r|\tau, y)$

/* warm-up phase   */

1 **for** $t = 0, \cdots, T_0$ **do**

2 $\quad$ randomly generate augmentation triples $\{\tau_{y_0}^t, \cdots, \tau_{y_n}^t\}$ for all labels $\{y_0, \cdots, y_n\}$

3 $\quad$ obtain rewards $\{r_{\tau,y_0}^t, \cdots, r_{\tau,y_n}^t\}$ by Eq. 4

/* search phase   */

4 **for** $t = T_0, \cdots, T$ **do**

5 $\quad$ train $f^t(r|\tau, y)$ with data collected from previous t iterations $\{(\tau, y, r_{\tau,y})\}^t$

6 $\quad$ **for** $y_i = y_0, \cdots, y_n$ **do**

7 $\quad\quad$ generate 100 candidate augmentation triples by exploration and exploitation

8 $\quad\quad$ obtain predicted rewards $\tilde{r}_{\tau,y_i} = f^t(\tau, y_i)$ for 100 candidates

9 $\quad\quad$ $\tau_{y_i}^t = \arg\max_\tau (\tilde{r}_{\tau,y_i})$

10 $\quad$ obtain real rewards $\{r_{\tau,y_0}^t, \cdots, r_{\tau,y_n}^t\}$ for $\{\tau_{y_0}^t, \cdots, \tau_{y_n}^t\}$ by Eq. 4

11 train predictor $f^T(r|\tau, y)$ with all collected data $\{(\tau, y, r_{\tau,y})\}^T$

---

search space, and retrieve the initial training data for learning a label-aware neural predictor $f(r|\tau, y)$. Then, for the following $T - T_0$ iterations, the search phase is adopted. In each iteration, we first train a neural predictor from scratch with data collected from previous iterations. Then, for each label, we apply the forementioned selection procedure to select a set of candidate augmentation triples, and use the trained predictor to choose the augmentation triple for evaluation. After enough training data is collected, a well-trained label-aware neural predictor can be derived to provide accurate evaluations on all augmentation triples for different labels.

3.4 Stage 2: Policy Construction

Policy construction is a process of mapping the evaluation results of stage 1 to the final augmentation policy for training target networks. It is needed because augmentation policies are usually searched on light-weight proxy tasks such as density matching, but are evaluated on the complete tasks of image classification. Even for methods that search on complete tasks such as AutoAugment [1], they still naively concatenate multiple searched policies into a final policy. However, the policies for concatenation usually share a great potion of overlapped transformations, resulting in a high degree of redundancy.

In this paper, we propose an effective policy construction method to iteratively select candidate augmentation triples for the final policy, based on the mutual information criteria of minimum-redundancy maximum-relevance (mRMR) [17]. Specifically, in *LA3*, the relevance metric is defined as the predicted reward $\tilde{r}$ as it provides a direct evaluation on the performance of a certain

---

Algorithm 2: Stage 2: Policy Construction

Input: Well-trained predictor $f^T(r|\tau, y)$, search space A, number of candidates N_{cand}

Output: Label-aware policy $\mathcal{T}^*$

1 **for** $y_i = y_0, \cdots, y_n$ **do**
2   **for** $\tau \in A$ **do**
3   ⌊ predict the reward $\tilde{r}_{\tau, y_i} = f^T(\tau, y_i)$
4   initialize label-specific policy $\mathcal{T}_{y_i} \leftarrow \emptyset$
5   **for** $k = 0, \cdots, N_{cand}$ **do**
6   **for** $\tau \in (A \setminus \mathcal{T}_{y_i})$ **do**
7   ⌊ calculate $v(\tau, y_i)$ using Eq. 5
8   find augmentation triple with highest score $\tau^k = \arg\max_\tau (v(\tau, y_i))$
9   ⌊ $\mathcal{T}_{y_i} \leftarrow \mathcal{T}_{y_i} \cup \tau^k$
10 $\mathcal{T}^* = \{\mathcal{T}_{y_0}, \cdots, \mathcal{T}_{y_n}\}$

---

augmentation triple. And the redundancy of an augmentation triple τ is defined as the average number of intersecting operations between it and the already selected augmentation triples $\mathcal{T}_s$. Formally, in each iteration of policy construction, we define the score $v(\tau, y)$ of each unselected augmentation triple τ at label y as

$$v(\tau, y) = \tilde{r}_{\tau, y} - \alpha \times \overline{r} \times \frac{1}{|\mathcal{T}_s|} \sum_{\tau_s \in \mathcal{T}_s} |\tau \cap \tau_s|, \tag{5}$$

where $|\tau \cap \tau_s|$ refers to the number of overlapped operations between τ and τ_s, $\overline{r}$ is the average predicted reward of all augmentation triples in search space and is used to scale the redundancy, and α is a hyper-parameter adjusting the weight between the reward value and the redundancy value.

Algorithm 2 illustrates the overall process of the policy construction stage where the goal is to find a label-aware policy containing a collection of augmentation triples that maximizes the rewards while keeping a low degree of redundancy. Specifically, for each label y_i, we retrieve the predicted reward $\tilde{r}_{\tau, y_i}$ for each augmentation triple τ in the search space A. Afterwards, a label-specific policy $\mathcal{T}_{y_i}$ is constructed iteratively by calculating the score $v(\tau, y_i)$ of unselected augmentation triples with Eq. 5 and add the augmentation triple with the highest score to the policy until the required number of candidates N_{cand} is met. Eventually, the label-aware policy $\mathcal{T}^*$ is built with each label y_i corresponding to a label-specific policy $\mathcal{T}_{y_i}$.

4 Experiments

In this section, we first describe the details of our experiment settings. Then we evaluate the proposed method, and compare it with previous methods in terms of both performance and search cost. Finally, we perform thorough analysis on the design of different modules in our algorithm. Code and searched policies are released at https://github.com/Simpleple/LA3-Label-Aware-AutoAugment.

4.1   Datasets, Metrics and Baselines

Following previous work, we evaluate our *LA3* method on CIFAR-10/100 [14] and ImageNet [3], across different networks including ResNet [8], WideResnet [23], Shake-Shake [5] and PyramidNet [6]. Test accuracy is reported to assess the effectiveness of the discovered policies, while the cost is assessed by the number of GPU hours measured on Nvidia V100 GPUs. For a fair comparison, we list results of stationary policies produced by static strategies, AutoAugment [1], FastAA [16], and DADA [15]. We also include results from dynamic strategies, PBA [9], AdvAA [25], and MetaAug [26], producing non-stationary policies as target model training progresses.

4.2   Implementation Details

Policy Composition. For a fair comparison, we use the same 15 augmentation operations as PBA and DADA do, which is also the same set used by AA and FastAA with SamplePairing [10] excluded. Additionally, "Identity" operation that returns the original image is introduced in our search space to prevent images from being excessively transformed. Each label-specific policy consists of $N_{cand} = 100$ augmentation triples, while in evaluation, each sample is augmented by an augmentation triple randomly selected from the policy with random magnitudes.

Neural Predictor. The network structure of the neural predictor is composed of two embedding layers of size 100 that map labels and augmentation operations to latent vectors and three fully-connected layers of hidden size 100 with Relu activation function. The representation of an augmentation triple is constructed by combining the three augmentation operation embedding vectors with mean-pooling and concatenating it with the label embedding vector. Then it is passed into the FC layers to derive the predicted reward. The predictor network is trained for 100 epochs with Adam optimizer [13] and a learning rate of 0.01.

Search Details. For CIFAR-10/100, we split the original training set of $50,000$ samples into a training set D^{tr} of size $46,000$ to pre-train the model θ, and a valid set D^{val} of $4,000$ for density matching. We search our policy on WRN-40-2 network and apply the found policy to other networks for evaluation. For ImageNet, we randomly sample 50 examples per class from the original training set, and collect $50,000$ examples in total to form the valid set, where the remaining examples are used as the training set. In the augmentation exploration stage, the total number of iterations is set to $T = 500$, and the warm-up iterations is set to $T_0 = 100$. In the policy construction stage, $\alpha = 2.5$ is used to calculate the reward values of augmentation triples.

Evaluation. The evaluation is performed by training target networks with the searched policies, and the results are reported as the mean test accuracy and standard deviation over three runs with different random seeds. We do not specifically tune the training hyperparameters and use settings consistent with prior work. We include the details in the supplementary materials.

Table 1. Top-1 test accuracy (%) on CIFAR-10 and CIFAR-100. We mainly compare our method *LA3* with methods that also produce stationary augmentation policies, including AA, FastAA and DADA. Results of dynamic policies (PBA, AdvAA and MetaAug) are also provided for reference.

Dataset	Model	Baseline	AA static	FastAA static	DADA static	LA3 static	PBA dynamic	AdvAA dynamic	MetaAug dynamic
CIFAR-10	WRN-40-2	94.7	96.3	96.4	96.4	**97.08 ± 0.08**	–	–	96.79
	WRN-28-10	96.1	97.4	97.3	97.3	**97.80 ± 0.15**	97.42	98.10	97.76
	Shake-Shake (26 2 × 96 d)	97.1	98.0	98.0	98.0	**98.07 ± 0.11**	97.97	98.15	98.29
	Shake-Shake (26 2 × 112 d)	97.2	98.1	98.1	98.0	**98.12 ± 0.08**	97.97	98.22	98.28
	PyramidNet+ShakeDrop	97.3	98.5	98.3	98.3	**98.55 ± 0.02**	98.54	98.64	98.57
CIFAR-100	WRN-40-2	74.0	79.3	79.4	79.1	**81.09 ± 0.28**	–	–	80.60
	WRN-28-10	81.2	82.9	82.8	82.5	**84.54 ± 0.03**	83.27	84.51	83.79
	Shake-Shake (26 2 × 96 d)	82.9	**85.7**	85.4	84.7	85.17 ± 0.13	84.69	85.90	85.97
	PyramidNet+ShakeDrop	86.0	**89.3**	88.3	88.8	89.02 ± 0.03	89.06	89.58	89.46

4.3   Experimental Results

CIFAR-10/100. Table 1 summarizes the CIFAR-10 and CIFAR-100 results of different auto-augmentation methods on a wide range of networks. Among all static methods that produce stationary policies, *LA3* achieves the best performance for all 5 target networks on CIFAR-10 and for 2 out of 4 target networks on CIFAR-100. When extending the comparison to also include dynamic strategies, *LA3* still achieves the best CIFAR-10 and CIFAR-100 accuracies on WRN-40-2, which is the original network on which policy search was performed. When transferring these augmentation policies found on WRN-40-2 to other target network models for evaluation, *LA3* also achieves excellent performance comparable to the current best methods. In particular, *LA3* achieves the highest score for WRN-28-10 on CIFAR-100. These results evidently proves the effectiveness of *LA3* as an augmentation strategy to improve model performance, and demonstrates the strong transferability of our label-aware policies across different neural networks.

ImageNet Performance. In Table 2, we list the top-1 accuracy of different methods evaluated on ResNet-50, as well as their computational cost. For a fair comparison, we also indicate whether the Batch Augment (BA) trick [25], which forms a large batch with multiple copies of transformed samples, is used for each method, with "(BA)" after the method name. We also indicate the number of transformations used in the batch augment. Note that the search cost for dynamic methods is included in the training cost, since they learn a dynamic augmentation policy during the training of the target model. We include the results for *LA3* both with and without batch augment.

From Table 2 we can observe that among all methods without the batch augment trick, *LA3* achieves the best ImageNet top-1 accuracy of 78.71%, while the search only took 29.3 GPU hours, which is 15 times faster than FastAA. Although DADA is faster, *LA3* is substantially better in terms of the ImageNet accuracy achieved.

Meanwhile, *LA3 (BA)* achieves a new state-of-the-art ImageNet accuracy of 79.97% surpassing all existing auto-augmentation strategies including dynamic strategies AdvAA and MetaAug, with a total computational cost 2 times and 3 times lower than theirs, respectively. The high cost of these dynamic policies is due to the fact that augmentation policies may vary for each sample or batch and must be learnt together with model training. By generating static policies, *LA3* is a simpler solution that decouples policy search from model training and evaluation, which is easier to deploy in a production environment, without introducing specialized structures, e.g., the policy networks in AdvAA and MetaAug, into target model training.

Table 2. ResNet-50 top-1 test accuracy (%) and computational cost on ImageNet. Batch Augment (BA) trick is used in the training of *LA3* (BA), AdvAA (BA) and MetaAug (BA). The number of transformations used in batch augment is also given in the table.

	Baseline	AA	FastAA	DADA	LA3	LA3 (BA)	AdvAA (BA)	MetaAug (BA)
		static	static	static	static	static	dynamic	dynamic
Batch augment (BA)	n/a	n/a	n/a	n/a	n/a	×4	×8	×4
ResNet-50 Acc (%)	76.3	77.6	77.6	77.5	**78.71 ± 0.07**	**79.97 ± 0.07**	79.40	79.74
Search cost (h)	–	15,000	450	1.3	29.3	29.3	–	–
Train cost (h)	160	160	160	160	160	640	1,280	1,920
Total cost (h)	160	15,160	610	161.3	189.3	669.3	1,280	1,920

4.4 Ablation Study and Analysis

The reason of the success can be attributed to the following designs in our *LA3* algorithm.

Label-Awareness. One of the main contributions of the paper is to leverage the label information and separately learn policies for samples of different classes, which captures distinct characteristics of data and produces more effective label-aware policies. The results of *LA3* variant without label-awareness (i.e., searching for label-invariant policies) are shown in the first row of Table 3, which are constantly lower than *LA3* in all experimental settings. This confirms that label-aware augmentation policies are effective at improving target network accuracy.

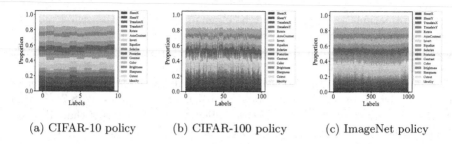

(a) CIFAR-10 policy   (b) CIFAR-100 policy   (c) ImageNet policy

Fig. 3. The proportion of different augmentation operations in policies for different labels in *LA3* searched label-aware policies on CIFAR-10, CIFAR-100 and ImageNet.

Table 3. Ablation analysis results in top-1 test accuracy (%) on CIFAR-10 and CIFAR-100 with different designs removed from the full *LA3* method.

	CIFAR-10		CIFAR-100	
	WRN-40-2	WRN-28-10	WRN-40-2	WRN-28-10
w/o Label-aware	96.70	97.11	80.08	82.76
w/o Stage 2 (top-100)	96.53	97.49	78.57	82.76
w/o Stage 2 (top-500)	96.70	97.26	79.85	84.04
LA3	**97.08**	**97.80**	**81.09**	**84.54**

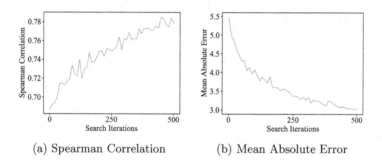

(a) Spearman Correlation   (b) Mean Absolute Error

Fig. 4. The evaluation of the predictor during the policy search on ImageNet given by the Spearman's Rank Correlation and Mean Absolute Error over search iterations.

Figure 3 gives an overview of the searched label-aware policies on CIFAR-10, CIFAR-100 and ImageNet, where we calculate the occurrences of different operations in each label-specific policy and plot their proportions in different colors. We can see that the derived policies possess a high diversity by having all the operations contributing to the final policy, meanwhile making the individual policies notably different among labels. This observation further proves the need for separately treating samples of different labels in augmentation policy search.

Neural Predictor. In addition to using density matching to simplify augmentation assessment during search, we have adopted a label-aware neural predictor to learn the mapping from an augmentation triple to its label-specific reward. We now conduct a thorough evaluation to assess the performance of the neural predictor. For each search iteration, the predictor is trained on 80% of the history data and tested on the remaining 20% data in terms of both the Spearman's Rank Correlation and Mean Abusolute Error (MAE). As shown in Fig. 4, as the policy search on ImageNet progresses and more samples are explored, the predictor can produce more accurate predictions of rewards, obtaining a 0.78 Spearman Correlation and a decreased MAE when the search ends. This allows the predictor to properly guide the search process and find effective policies.

Furthermore, the use of the predictor better utilizes the search history and improves the sample efficiency during searching. As a result, the search cost of our method is significantly reduced and is 15 times lower than FastAA.

Policy Construction. We evaluate the impact of our two-stage design on CIFAR-10 and CIFAR-100 datasets, by showing the performance of model variants with different policy construction methods in row 2 and 3 of Table 3.

We compare our policy construction method based on mRMR to the commonly used Top-k selection method adopted in AA [1], FastAA [16] and DADA [15]. We use two different k value settings of $k = 100$ equaling the number of candidates used in *LA3*, and $k = 500$ following the FastAA setting. We can see that the policy that includes 500 augmentation triples per label with top predicted rewards yields a better performance than the policy with top 100 augmentation triples on both CIFAR-10 and CIFAR-100. This can be attributed to the better diversity as more possibilities of augmentations are contained. However, increasing the k value is not the best solution to improve augmentation diversity as the augmentation triples with high rewards tend to have similar compositions and may result in a high redundancy in the final policy. Our *LA3* incorporates a policy construction method that selects high-reward augmentation triples, and at the same time, keeping the lowest redundancy of the final policy. With the two-stage design, our *LA3* method beats the top-k variants and produces significant improvements in all settings.

Limitation. Unlike dataset-level augmentation policies that can be learned from one dataset and transferred to other datasets [1,9,25], *LA3* learns label-aware policies where labels are specific to a dataset, and hence lacks the transferability across datasets, although *LA3* demonstrates transferability across networks as shown in Table 1. However, when dealing with a large dataset, *LA3* can work on a reduced version of the dataset to search for label-dependent policies efficiently, and requires no tuning on training recipes when applying the found policy to the entire dataset.

5   Conclusion

In this paper, we propose a label-aware data augmentation search algorithm where label-specific policies are learned based on a two-stage algorithm, including an augmentation exploration stage based on Bayesian Optimization and neural predictors as well as a composite policy construction stage. Compared with existing static and dynamic augmentation algorithms, *LA3* is computationally efficient and produces stationary policies that can be easily deployed to improve deep learning performance. *LA3* achieves the state-of-the-art ImageNet accuracy of 79.97% on ResNet-50 among all auto-augmentation methods, at a substantially lower search cost than AdvAA and MetaAugment.

References

1. Cubuk, E.D., Zoph, B., Mané, D., Vasudevan, V., Le, Q.V.: Autoaugment: learning augmentation strategies from data. In: 2019 IEEE/CVF Conference on Computer Vision and Pattern Recognition (CVPR), pp. 113–123. IEEE (2019)
2. Cubuk, E.D., Zoph, B., Shlens, J., Le, Q.V.: Randaugment: practical automated data augmentation with a reduced search space. In: Proceedings of the IEEE/CVF Conference on Computer Vision and Pattern Recognition Workshops, pp. 702–703 (2020)
3. Deng, J., Dong, W., Socher, R., Li, L.J., Li, K., Fei-Fei, L.: Imagenet: a large-scale hierarchical image database. In: 2009 IEEE Conference on Computer Vision and Pattern Recognition, pp. 248–255. IEEE (2009)
4. DeVries, T., Taylor, G.W.: Improved regularization of convolutional neural networks with cutout. arXiv preprint arXiv:1708.04552 (2017)
5. Gastaldi, X.: Shake-shake regularization. arXiv preprint arXiv:1705.07485 (2017)
6. Han, D., Kim, J., Kim, J.: Deep pyramidal residual networks. In: Proceedings of the IEEE Conference on Computer Vision and Pattern Recognition, pp. 5927–5935 (2017)
7. Hataya, R., Zdenek, J., Yoshizoe, K., Nakayama, H.: Faster autoaugment: learning augmentation strategies using backpropagation. In: Vedaldi, A., Bischof, H., Brox, T., Frahm, J.-M. (eds.) ECCV 2020. LNCS, vol. 12370, pp. 1–16. Springer, Cham (2020). https://doi.org/10.1007/978-3-030-58595-2_1
8. He, K., Zhang, X., Ren, S., Sun, J.: Deep residual learning for image recognition. In: Proceedings of the IEEE Conference on Computer Vision and Pattern Recognition, pp. 770–778 (2016)
9. Ho, D., Liang, E., Chen, X., Stoica, I., Abbeel, P.: Population based augmentation: efficient learning of augmentation policy schedules. In: International Conference on Machine Learning, pp. 2731–2741. PMLR (2019)
10. Inoue, H.: Data augmentation by pairing samples for images classification. arXiv preprint arXiv:1801.02929 (2018)
11. Jaderberg, M., et al.: Population based training of neural networks. arXiv preprint arXiv:1711.09846 (2017)
12. Jang, E., Gu, S., Poole, B.: Categorical reparameterization with gumbel-softmax. arXiv preprint arXiv:1611.01144 (2016)
13. Kingma, D.P., Ba, J.: Adam: a method for stochastic optimization. arXiv preprint arXiv:1412.6980 (2014)
14. Krizhevsky, A., Hinton, G., et al.: Learning multiple layers of features from tiny images (2009)
15. Li, Y., Hu, G., Wang, Y., Hospedales, T., Robertson, N.M., Yang, Y.: Differentiable automatic data augmentation. In: Vedaldi, A., Bischof, H., Brox, T., Frahm, J.-M. (eds.) ECCV 2020. LNCS, vol. 12367, pp. 580–595. Springer, Cham (2020). https://doi.org/10.1007/978-3-030-58542-6_35

16. Lim, S., Kim, I., Kim, T., Kim, C., Kim, S.: Fast autoaugment. Adv. Neural. Inf. Process. Syst. **32**, 6665–6675 (2019)
17. Peng, H., Long, F., Ding, C.: Feature selection based on mutual information criteria of max-dependency, max-relevance, and min-redundancy. IEEE Trans. Pattern Anal. Mach. Intell. **27**(8), 1226–1238 (2005)
18. Tian, K., Lin, C., Sun, M., Zhou, L., Yan, J., Ouyang, W.: Improving auto-augment via augmentation-wise weight sharing. Adv. Neural. Inf. Process. Syst. **33**, 19088–19098 (2020)
19. Wang, Y., et al.: Fine-grained autoaugmentation for multi-label classification. arXiv preprint arXiv:2107.05384 (2021)
20. Wen, W., Liu, H., Chen, Y., Li, H., Bender, G., Kindermans, P.-J.: Neural predictor for neural architecture search. In: Vedaldi, A., Bischof, H., Brox, T., Frahm, J.-M. (eds.) ECCV 2020. LNCS, vol. 12374, pp. 660–676. Springer, Cham (2020). https://doi.org/10.1007/978-3-030-58526-6_39
21. White, C., Neiswanger, W., Savani, Y.: Bananas: Bayesian optimization with neural architectures for neural architecture search. In: Proceedings of the AAAI Conference on Artificial Intelligence, vol. 35, pp. 10293–10301 (2021)
22. Yun, S., Han, D., Oh, S.J., Chun, S., Choe, J., Yoo, Y.: Cutmix: regularization strategy to train strong classifiers with localizable features. In: Proceedings of the IEEE/CVF International Conference on Computer Vision, pp. 6023–6032 (2019)
23. Zagoruyko, S., Komodakis, N.: Wide residual networks. In: British Machine Vision Conference 2016. British Machine Vision Association (2016)
24. Zhang, H., Cisse, M., Dauphin, Y.N., Lopez-Paz, D.: mixup: beyond empirical risk minimization. In: International Conference on Learning Representations (2018)
25. Zhang, X., Wang, Q., Zhang, J., Zhong, Z.: Adversarial autoaugment. In: International Conference on Learning Representations (2019)
26. Zhou, F., Li, J., Xie, C., Chen, F., Hong, L., Sun, R., Li, Z.: Metaaugment: sample-aware data augmentation policy learning. In: Proceedings of the AAAI Conference on Artificial Intelligence, vol. 35, pp. 11097–11105 (2021)

Interpretations Steered Network Pruning via Amortized Inferred Saliency Maps

Alireza Ganjdanesh⬤, Shangqian Gao⬤, and Heng Huang(✉)⬤

Department of Electrical and Computer Engineering, University of Pittsburgh,
Pittsburgh, PA 15261, USA
{alireza.ganjdanesh,shg84,heng.huang}@pitt.edu

Abstract. Convolutional Neural Networks (CNNs) compression is crucial to deploying these models in edge devices with limited resources.
Existing channel pruning algorithms for CNNs have achieved plenty of
success on complex models. They approach the pruning problem from
various perspectives and use different metrics to guide the pruning process. However, these metrics mainly focus on the model's 'outputs' or
'weights' and neglect its 'interpretations' information. To fill in this gap,
we propose to address the channel pruning problem from a novel perspective by leveraging the interpretations of a model to steer the pruning
process, thereby utilizing information from both inputs and outputs of
the model. However, existing interpretation methods cannot get deployed
to achieve our goal as either they are inefficient for pruning or may predict non-coherent explanations. We tackle this challenge by introducing a selector model that predicts real-time smooth saliency masks for
pruned models. We parameterize the distribution of explanatory masks
by Radial Basis Function (RBF)-like functions to incorporate geometric
prior of natural images in our selector model's inductive bias. Thus, we
can obtain compact representations of explanations to reduce the computational costs of our pruning method. We leverage our selector model to
steer the network pruning by maximizing the similarity of explanatory
representations for the pruned and original models. Extensive experiments on CIFAR-10 and ImageNet benchmark datasets demonstrate the
efficacy of our proposed method. Our implementations are available at
https://github.com/Alii-Ganjj/InterpretationsSteeredPruning.

Keywords: Convolutional Neural Networks · Model compression ·
Efficient deep learning · Interpretability · Explainable AI

1 Introduction

Convolutional Neural Networks (CNNs) have been continuously achieving state-
of-the-art results on various computer vision tasks [4,10,13,38,44,45,54], but the

---

A. Ganjdanesh and S. Gao—indicates equal contribution.

Supplementary Information The online version contains supplementary material
available at https://doi.org/10.1007/978-3-031-19803-8_17.

required resources of popular deep models [16,23,55] are also exploding. Their substantial computational and storage costs prohibit deploying these models in edge and mobile devices, making the CNN compression problem a crucial task. Many ideas have attempted to address this problem to reduce models' sizes while maintaining their prediction performance. These ideas can usually be classified into one of the model compression methods categories: weight pruning [15], weight quantization [7,43], structural pruning [30], knowledge distillation [21], neural architecture search [20], *etc.*

We focus on pruning channels of CNNs (structural pruning) since it can effectively and practically reduce the computational costs of a deep model without any post-processing steps or specifically designed hardware. Although existing channel pruning methods have achieved excellent results, they do not consider the model's interpretations during the pruning process. They tackle the pruning problem from various perspectives such as reinforcement learning [20], greedy search [62], and evolutionary algorithms [8]. In addition, they have utilized a wide range of metrics like channels' norm [30], loss [11], and accuracy [36] as guidance to prune the model. Thus, they emphasize the model's outputs or weights but ignore its valuable interpretations' information.

We aim to approach the structural model pruning problem from a novel perspective by exploiting the model's interpretations (a subset of input features called saliency maps) to steer the pruning. Our intuition is that the saliency maps of the pruned model should be similar to the ones for the original model. However, the existing interpretation methods are either inefficient or unreliable for pruning. Firstly, locally linear models (*e.g.*, LIME [46] and SHAP [39]) fit a separate linear model to explain the behavior of a nonlinear classifier in the vicinity of each data point. However, they need to fit a new model in each iteration of pruning that the classifier's architecture changes, which makes them inefficient for pruning. Secondly, previous works [1,22] empirically observed that a feature importance assignment of Gradient-based methods (*e.g.*, Grad-CAM [50] and DeepLIFT [52]) might not be more meaningful than random. Moreover, Srinivas and Fleuret [58] theoretically showed that the input gradients used by these methods might seem explanatory as they are related to an implicit generative model hidden in the classifiers [14], not their discriminative function. Thus, their usage for interpreting classifiers should be avoided. Finally, perturbation-based methods [65,71] need multiple forward passes and rely on perturbed samples that are out-of-distribution for the trained model [22] to obtain its explanations. Hence, they are neither efficient nor reliable for pruning. Different from the mentioned methods, **Amortized Explanation Models (AEMs)** [6,26,64] provide a theoretical framework to obtain a model's interpretations. They train a fast saliency prediction model that can be applied in real-time systems as it can provide saliency maps with a single forward pass, making them suitable for pruning. We refer to Sect. 2 for more discussion on interpretation methods.

In this paper, at first, we provide a new AEM method that overcomes the disadvantages of previous AEM models, and then, we employ it to prune convolutional classifiers. Previous AEMs [6,26,64] cannot be applied to guide pruning due to several key drawbacks. REAL-X [26] proved that L2X [6] and INVASE [64] could suffer from degenerate cases where the saliency map selector predicts meaningless explanations. Although REAL-X overcomes this problem, it generates masks independently for each input feature (pixel). Thus, it neglects the geometric prior [5] in natural images that adjacent features (pixels) often correlate to each other. We empirically show in Sect. 3.3 and Fig. 1 that the saliency maps predicted by REAL-X may lack visual interpretability. In addition, the provided explanations have the same size as the input image, which also adds non-trivial computational costs when used for pruning. We propose a novel AEM model to tackle these problems. In contrast with REAL-X, which assumes features' independence, we employ a proper geometric prior in our model. We use a Radial Basis Function (RBF)-like function to parameterize saliency masks' distribution. By doing so, the mask generation is no longer independent for each pixel in our framework. Moreover, it enables us to infer explanations for each image with only three parameters (center coordinates and kernel expansion), saving lots of computations. We utilize such compact saliency representations to steer network pruning by reconstruction in real-time. We also find that merging guidance from the model's interpretations and outputs can further improve the pruning results. Our experimental results on benchmark datasets illustrate that our new interpretation steered pruning method can consistently achieve superior performance compared to baselines. Our contributions are as follows:

- We propose a novel structural pruning method for CNNs designed from a new and different perspective compared to existing methods. We utilize the model's decisions' interpretations to steer the pruning procedure. By doing so, we effectively merge the guidance from the model's interpretations and outputs to discover the high-performance subnetworks.
- We introduce a new Amortized Explanation Model (AEM) such that we embed a proper geometric prior for natural images in the inductive bias of our model and enable it to predict smooth explanations for input images. We parameterize the distribution of saliency masks using RBF-like functions. Thus, our AEM can provide compact explanatory representations and save computational costs. Further, it empowers us to dynamically obtain saliency maps of pruned models and leverage them to steer the pruning procedure.
- Our experimental results on CIFAR-10 and ImageNet datasets clearly demonstrate the added value of using interpretations of CNNs when pruning them.

2   Related Works

Interpretation Methods: Interpretation methods can get classified into four [26] main categories: **1. Gradient-based** methods such as CAM [68], Grad-CAM [50], DeepLIFT [52], and LRP [3] rely on the gradients of outputs of a model $w.r.t$ input features and assume features with larger gradients have more influence on the model's outcome [53,56,57], which is shown is not necessarily a valid assumption [51]. In addition, their feature importance assignment might not be more meaningful than random assignment [1,22,58], which makes them unreliable for pruning. Further, Srinivas and Fleuret [58] theoretically proved that input gradients are equal to the score function for the implicit generative model in classifiers [14] and are not related to the discriminative function of classifiers. Thus, they are not interpretations of the model's predictions. **2. Perturbation-based** models explore the effect of perturbing input features on the model's output or inner layers to conclude their importance [65,69,71]. Yet, they are inefficient for pruning as they need multiple forward passes to obtain importance scores. Also, they may underestimate features' importance [52]. **3. Locally Linear Models** fit a linear model to approximate the behavior of a classifier in the vicinity of each data point [39,46]. However, they require to fit a new model for each sample when the model's architecture changes during pruning, which makes them inefficient for pruning. Also, they rely on the classifier's output for out-of-distribution samples to train the linear model [22], which makes them undependable. **4. Amortized Explanation Models (AEMs)** [6,9,26,64] overcome the inefficiencies of the previous methods by training a *global* model - called *selector* [26] - that *amortizes* the cost of inferring saliency maps for each sample by *selecting* salient input features with a single forward pass. AEMs [6,26,64] provide a theoretical framework to train the selector model. To do so, they use a second *predictor* model that estimates the classifier's output target distribution given an input masked by the selector model's predicted mask. L2X [6] and INVASE [64] jointly train the selector and predictor. However, REAL-X [26] proved that doing so results in degenerate cases. REAL-X overcame this problem by training the predictor model separately with random masks. However, we show in Sect. 3.3 that its predicted masks may not be interpretable for complex image classifiers. Our conjecture for a reason is that it neglects geometric prior [5] of natural images that nearby pixels correlate more to each other.

Network Compression: Weight pruning [15] and quantization [7,43], structural pruning [12,19,30,33,35,41,42,59,60,66,70], knowledge distillation [21], and NAS [20] are popular directions for compressing CNNs. Structural pruning has attracted more attention as it can readily decrease the computational burden of CNN models without any specific hardware changes. Early channel pruning methods [30] propose that the channels with larger norms are more critical and remove weights/filters with small L_1/L_2 norm. L_1 penalty can also be applied to scaling factors of batchnorm [24] to remove redundant channels [37]. Recent channel pruning methods adopt more sophisticated designs. Automatic model compression [20] learns the width of each layer with reinforcement learning. Metapruning [36] generates parameters for subnetworks and uses evolutionary algorithms to find the best subnetwork. Greedy subnetwork selection [62] greedily chooses each channel based on their L_2 norm. Pruning can be also used for fairness [67]. We refer to [32] for a more detailed discussion of pruning techniques.

Network Pruning Using Interpretations: There are a few recent works that attempt to use interpretations of a model to determine importance scores of its weights. Sabih *et al.* [48] leverage DeepLIFT [52]; Yeom *et al.* [63] use LRP [3]; and Yao *et al.* [61] utilize activation maximization [65] to determine weights' importance. However, all these methods use gradient-based methods that, as mentioned above, their predictions are unreliable and should not be used as the model's interpretations. Alqahtani *et al.* [2] visualize feature maps in the input space and use a segmentation model to find the filters that have the highest alignment with visual concepts. Nonetheless, their method needs an accurate segmentation model to find reliable importance scores for filters, which may not be available in some domains. We develop a new AEM model that is theoretically supported and improves REAL-X [26]. Moreover, in contrast with these methods, our pruning method finds the optimal subnetwork end-to-end. We also show in Sect. 4.2 that our model outperforms [2].

3   Methodology

3.1   Overview

We present a novel pruning method in which we steer the pruning process of CNN classifiers using feature-wise interpretations of their decisions. At first, we develop a new intuitive AEM model that overcomes the limitations of REAL-X [26] (state-of-the-art AEM). The reason is that we incorporate the geometric prior of high correlation between adjacent input features (pixels) [5] in the images in the inductive bias of our AEM model. We parameterize the distribution of saliency masks using Radial Basis Function (RBF)-style functions. By doing so, we can represent interpretations (saliency maps) of input images compactly. Then, we elaborate on our pruning method in which we leverage our AEM model to provide interpretations of the original and pruned classifiers. Our intuition is that saliency maps of the original and pruned models should be similar. Thus, we propose a new loss function for pruning that encourages the pruned model to have similar saliency explanations to the original one. In the following subsections, we introduce AEM methods and empirically show the limitations of REAL-X. Then, we elaborate on our method and its intuitions to tackle the drawbacks of previous AEMs. Finally, we present our pruning scheme.

3.2   Notations

We denote our dataset as $\mathcal{D} = \{(x^{(i)}, y^{(i)})\}_{i=1}^{N}$ such that $(x, y) \sim \mathcal{P}(\mathbf{x}, \mathbf{y})$ where $\mathcal{P}$ is the unknown underlying joint distribution over features and targets, and we assume that $x \in \mathbb{R}^D$ and $y \in \{1, 2, \ldots, K\}$. We show the jth feature of sample x by x_j and represent a mask m by the indices of the input features that it preserves, *i.e.*, $m \subseteq \{1, 2, \ldots, D\}$ and a masked input $m(x)$ is defined as follows:

$$m(x) = mask(x, m) = \begin{cases} x_j & j \in m \\ 0 & \text{Otherwise} \end{cases} \qquad (1)$$

We call the model that we aim to prune as the 'classifier' in following sections[1].

---

[1] We use zero values for the masked input features following the literature [6,26,64].

3.3   Amortized Explanation Models (AEMs)

AEMs are a subgroup of Instance-Wise Feature Selection (IWFS) methods that aim to compute a mask with minimum cardinality for each input sample that preserves its outcome-related features. An outcome may be a classifier's predictions (usually calculated as a softmax distribution) for interpretation purposes. It can also be the population distribution of the targets (one-hot representations) when performing dimensionality reduction on the original raw data [6,26,64]. Although previous works [6,26,64] describe their formulation for the latter, we focus on the former in this paper.

Concretely, if $\mathcal{Q}_{class}(\mathbf{y}|\mathbf{x})$ be the classifier's conditional distribution of targets given input features, the objective of AEM models is to find a mask $m(x)$ for each sample x such that

$$\mathcal{Q}_{class}(\mathbf{y}|\mathbf{x} = x) = \mathcal{Q}_{class}(\mathbf{y}|\mathbf{x} = m(x)) \tag{2}$$

AEMs tackle this problem by training a *global* model called *selector* that learns to predict a *local* (sample dependent) mask $m(x)$ for each sample x [26]. They train the selector by encouraging it to follow Eq. 2. To do so, one should quantify the discrepancy between the RHS and LHS of Eq. 2 when the selector model generates the mask m in the RHS. The LHS can be readily calculated by forwarding the sample x into the classifier. However, the classifier should not be used to compute the RHS because the masked sample $m(x)$ is an out-of-distribution input for it [26]. AEMs solve this issue by training a *predictor* model that predicts the conditional distribution of the classifier given a masked input. (RHS of Eq. 2) Then, they train the selector guided by the supervision from the predictor. We present the formulation of REAL-X [26] in supplementary.

Visualization of REAL-X Predictions: We visualize predicted explanations of REAL-X for a ResNet-56 model [16] trained on CIFAR-10 [29] in Fig. 1(a). (we refer to supplementary materials for implementation details) As can be seen, the formulation of REAL-X cannot guide the selector model to learn to select a coherent subset of input pixels of the salient parts of the images. Thus, it may not provide interpretable explanations for the classifier. Our conjecture for the cause is that the formulation of REAL-X does not include a proper inductive bias related to natural images in the selector model. Typically, nearby pixels' values and semantic information are more correlated in natural images, known as their geometric prior [5]. REAL-X does not have such a prior in its formulation because it factorizes the explanatory masks' distribution given an input x as:

$$q_{sel}(m|x; \beta) = \prod_{i=1}^{D} q_i(m_i|x; \beta) \tag{3}$$

where $q_i(m_i|x; \beta) \sim Bernoulli((f_\beta(x))_i)$, *i.e.*, the distribution over the selector's output mask is factorized as a product of marginal Bernoulli distributions over mask's elements, and the parameter for each element gets calculated independently. ($f_\beta(x)$ is the selector model parameterized by β). Hence, the selector

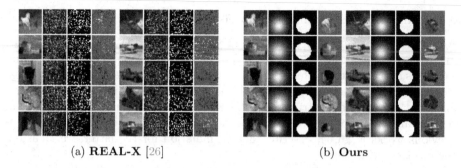

(a) **REAL-X** [26]   (b) **Ours**

Fig. 1. Input features selected by **a) REAL-X** [26] and **b) our model** to explain decisions of a ResNet-56 classifier for samples from CIFAR-10 [29]. In the sub-figures from
left to right: 1st column shows the original image. Both models output an array (2nd
columns) that each value of it is the parameter of the predicted Bernoulli distribution
over the corresponding mask pixel. In the 3rd column, we show the masks generated
such that a pixel's value is one provided that its predicted Bernoulli parameter is bigger
than 0.5 and zero otherwise. The 4th columns show the masked inputs. Our model's
explanations are easier to interpret than the ones by REAL-X that may seem random
for some samples.

model does not have the inductive bias that parameters of nearby Bernoulli
distributions should be close to each other to make the sampled masks coherent. Instead, it should 'discover' such prior during training, which is infeasible
with limited data and training epochs in practice.

3.4   Proposed AEM Model

We introduce a new selector scheme that respects the proximity geometric prior.
To do so, we assume that the parameters of the Bernoulli distributions of mask
pixels should have a Radial Basis Function (RBF) style functional form over
the pixels. The center of the RBF kernel should be on the salient part of the
image most relevant to the classifier's prediction, and the Bernoulli parameters
should decrease as the pixel location gets far from the kernel's center. A parameter σ controls the area of a mask. Our assumption is reasonable for multi-class
classifiers in which, typically, a single object/region in their input image determines the target class. Formally, considering a 2D mask that its coordinates are
parametrized by (z, t) and the parameters of a 2D RBF kernel being (c_z, c_t, σ),
we calculate the Bernoulli parameter (BP) of a pixel at location (z, t) as follows:

$$f_{BP}(z, t; c_z, c_t, \sigma) = \exp\left(\frac{-1}{2\sigma^2}[(z - c_z)^2 + (t - c_t)^2]\right) \tag{4}$$

This formulation has two crucial benefits: 1) It ensures that Bernoulli parameters
of a mask's proximal pixels are close to each other. Thus, the resulting sampled

masks will be much more coherent and smooth than REAL-X. 2) It simplifies the selector model's task significantly. In REAL-X, the selector should learn how to calculate Bernoulli parameters for each pixel that, for instance, will be $224 \times 224 = 50176$ independent functions for the standard ImageNet [10] training. In contrast, in our formulation, the selector should only learn to accurately estimate three values corresponding to the center's coordinates (c_z, c_t) and an expanding parameter σ for the RBF kernel. Given the estimated values, Bernoulli parameters of the output mask's pixels can be readily calculated by Eq. 4. In other words, if the input images have spatial dimensions $M * N$, and we denote the selector function (implemented by a deep neural network) with $f_{sel}(x; \beta)$, our selector's distribution over masks given input images is:

$$
[c_z, c_t, \sigma] = f_{sel}(x; \beta)
$$
$$
q_{i,j}(m_{i,j}|x; \beta) = Bernoulli(f_{BP}(i, j; c_z, c_t, \sigma))
$$
$$
q_{sel}(m|x; \beta) = \prod_{i=1}^{M} \prod_{j=1}^{N} q_{i,j}(m_{i,j}|x; \beta) \tag{5}
$$

In Eq. 5, β denotes the selector's parameters, and we illustrate a predicted RBF kernel by our selector in Fig. 2. In summary, our intuition is that by incorporating the geometric prior in the inductive bias of our framework, the selector will search for proper functional form for Bernoulli parameters over pixels' locations in the RBF family of functions, not all possible ones. As a result, it can find the optimal functional form more readily and robustly. Moreover, our selector model can provide a real-time and compact representation (RBF parameters) for saliency maps, which enables us to efficiently compare the interpretations of the original and pruned models to steer the pruning process. (Sect. 3.6, Fig. 3)

3.5   AEM Training

We train our selector model by encouraging it to generate an explanatory mask m for each sample x such that it follows Eq. 2. To do so, as mentioned in Sect. 3.3, we need to estimate the classifier's conditional distribution of targets given masked inputs (RHS of Eq. 2) to train our selector model. Such an estimate can quantify the quality of a mask generated by the selector model by measuring the discrepancy between the LHS and RHS of Eq. 2.

Predictor Model: We train a predictor model to calculate the classifier's conditional distribution of targets given a masked input. (RHS of Eq. 2) As we designed our selector to predict RBF-style masks (Eq. 5), we train our predictor to predict the classifier's output distribution when the input is masked by a random RBF-style mask. Using random RBF masks allows us to mimic any potential RBF-masked input. Hence, our predictor's training objective is:

$$
\min_{\theta} \mathcal{L}_{pred}(\theta) = \mathbb{E}_{x \sim \mathcal{P}(\mathbf{x})} \mathbb{E}_{c_z', c_t', \sigma'} [\mathbb{E}_{m' \sim \mathcal{B}(m|c_z', c_t', \sigma')} L_\theta(x, m'(x))] \tag{6}
$$

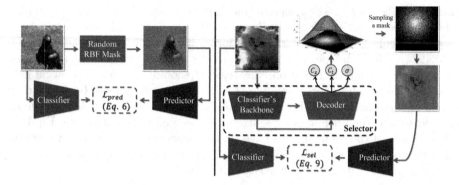

Fig. 2. Our AEM model. The goal is to train the selector model on the right (U-Net model in dashed line) to predict interpretations (saliency maps) of the classifier for each input sample. We train the selector by encouraging it to follow Eq. 2. **(Left):** We train a predictor model that learns to predict the classifier's output distribution given a masked input (RHS of Eq. 2). We do so using inputs masked by random RBF masks as our selector's masks have RBF-style. (Sect. 3.4) **(Right):** Given the trained predictor, we train the selector model using obj. 8 that enforces it to follow Eq. 2. We use the classifier's convolutional backbone as the encoder of the selector and only train its decoder for computational efficiency. Then, we use the trained decoder to prune the encoder. (Fig. 3)

where $L_\theta(\cdot, \ \cdot)$ and $\mathcal{B}(\cdot)$ are defined as:

$$L_\theta(x, m'(x)) = KL(\mathcal{Q}_{class}(\mathbf{y}|\mathbf{x} = x), \ q_{pred}(\mathbf{y}|\mathbf{x} = m'(x); \theta))$$

$$\mathcal{B}(m|c'_z, c'_t, \sigma') = \prod_{i=1}^{M}\prod_{j=1}^{N} Bernoulli(f_{BP}(i, j; c'_z, c'_t, \sigma')) \qquad (7)$$

Equation (6), L_θ form the predictor's objective to learn the conditional distribution of the classifier for targets given masked inputs (RHS of Eq. 2). $\mathcal{B}(\cdot)$ generates random masks with random RBF style (f_{BP}), and KL denotes Kullback-Leibler divergence [27]. Now, we should define the distribution for the parameters c'_z, c'_t, and σ' for a random RBF function. Let us assume that the origin of our 2D coordinate system is the top left of an input image with spatial dimensions M, N. In theory, c'_z and c'_t can have any real values, and the σ' can be any positive real number in Eq. 4. However, considering that the salient part[s] is inside the image region, we are interested that the predictor learns to correctly estimate $\mathcal{Q}_{class}(\mathbf{y}|\mathbf{x} = m(x))$ (RHS of Eq. 2) when the selector predicts that the center of the RBF kernel is inside the image area. Hence, we assume that the distributions of c'_z and c'_t are uniform across image dimensions, i.e., $c'_z \sim U[0, M]$ and $c'_t \sim U[0, N]$. In addition, the parameter σ' determines the degree that an RBF kernel expands on the image, and the values $\sigma' \geq 2 * max\{M, N\}$ practically provide the same Bernoulli parameters for all the mask's pixels when c'_z and c'_t are in the image region. Thus, we can reasonably assume that $\sigma' \sim U[0, \, 2 * max\{M, \, N\}]$ for training the predictor in practice.

Selector Training: Given a predictor model denoted by q_{pred} and trained with random RBF masks, we train our selector model with the following objective:

$$\min_{\beta} \mathcal{L}_{sel}(\beta) = \mathbb{E}_{x \sim \mathcal{P}(\mathbf{x})} \mathbb{E}_{m' \sim q_{sel}(m|x;\beta)} [L(x, m'(x)) + \lambda_1 \mathcal{R}(m') + \lambda_2 \mathcal{S}(m')] \quad (8)$$

such that $L(\cdot, \, \cdot)$, $\mathcal{R}(\cdot)$, and $\mathcal{S}(\cdot)$ are defined as:

$$L(x, m'(x)) = KL(\mathcal{Q}_{class}(\mathbf{y}|\mathbf{x} = x), \, q_{pred}(\mathbf{y}|\mathbf{x} = m'(x))),$$
$$\mathcal{R}(m') = ||m'||_0, \quad \mathcal{S}(m') = \sum_{i=1}^{M} \sum_{j=1}^{N} [(m'_{i,j} - m'_{i+1,j})^2 + (m'_{i,j} - m'_{i,j+1})^2] \quad (9)$$

$L(x, m'(x))$ encourages the selector to follow Eq. 2 as $q_{pred}(\mathbf{y}|\mathbf{x} = m'(x))$ approximates the RHS of Eq. 2 given an input masked by the RBF mask predicted by the selector. $\mathcal{R}(m')$ regularizes the number of selected features. We add the smoothness loss $\mathcal{S}(m')$ to further encourage the selector to output smooth masks. As Eq. 8 requires sampling from predicted distribution by the selector, direct backpropagation of gradients to train its parameters, β, is not possible. Thus, we use the Gumbel-Sigmoid [25,40] trick to train the model. We use a U-Net [47] architecture to implement the selector module of our AEM model, as shown in Fig. 2. We refer to supplementary for more details of our AEM training.

3.6 Pruning

In this section, we introduce our pruning method that leverages interpretations of a classifier to steer its pruning process. Our intuition is that the interpretations (saliency maps) of the original and pruned classifiers should be similar. Thus, we design our pruning method as follows. As discussed in Sect. 3.5 and Fig. 2, we use the convolutional backbone of the classifier as the encoder of the U-Net architecture for the selector model. We keep the encoder weights frozen and only train the decoder when training the selector model for computational efficiency. (Fig. 2) Furthermore, doing so provides us the flexibility to keep the decoder frozen and prune the encoder such that the pruned model should have similar output RBF parameters to the original model. (Fig. 3)

Formally, we employ our trained selector model to predict saliency maps of the original classifier for training samples. For each sample x_k, it provides the parameters of the RBF kernel for its saliency map as $\mathcal{C}_{x_k} = [c_z^k, c_t^k, \sigma^k]$. Then, we insert our pruning gates, parameterized by θ_g, between the layers of the encoder. We represent the architectural vector generated by the gates with $\mathbf{v}$. Finally, we prune the encoder (classifier's backbone) by regularizing the gate parameters to maintain the interpretations and accuracy of the pruned classifier similar to the original one while reducing its computational budget as follows:

$$\min_{\theta_g} L(f(x; \mathcal{W}, \mathbf{v}), y) + \gamma_1 ||\mathcal{C}_x - f_{sel}(x; \beta, \mathbf{v})||_2^2 \, + \gamma_2 \mathcal{R}_{res}(T(\mathbf{v}), pT_{all}) \quad (10)$$

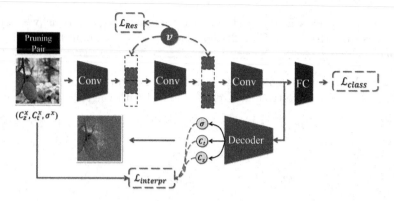

Fig. 3. Our pruning method. The classifier to be pruned is shown on top. (Conv layers and FC). The U-Net (Conv layers and the Decoder) is our trained selector model that can predict RBF parameters of the saliency map of each input for the classifier. The selector model is trained such that the pretrained backbone of the classifier is used as its encoder (Conv layers) and kept frozen during training. (see Fig. 2) Thus, we freeze the selector and classifier's weights and insert our pruning gates between the selector's encoder layers for pruning the classifier. Given a pruning pair (a sample and its RBF saliency map's parameters for the original classifier), we train the gate parameters to prune the classifier such that the pruned model have similar interpretations ($\mathcal{L}_{interpr}$) and accuracy ($\mathcal{L}_{class}$) to the original classifier while requiring lower computational resources ($\mathcal{L}_{Res}$).

where $L(\cdot, \cdot)$ is the classification loss, $f(\cdot; \mathcal{W}, \mathbf{v})$ denotes our classifier (encoder of the U-Net and the FC layer in Fig. 3) parameterized by weights $\mathcal{W}$ and the subnetwork selection vector $\mathbf{v}$. $f_{sel}(x; \beta, \mathbf{v})$ is our trained selector model ($f_{sel}(x; \beta)$ in Eq. 5) augmented by the architecture vector $\mathbf{v}$ after inserting the pruning gates into its encoder. We calculate $\mathbf{v}$ using Gumbel-sigmoid function $g(\cdot)$: $\mathbf{v} = g(\theta_g)$ [25,40], which controls openness or closeness of a channel. The second term in Eq. 10 utilizes the interpretations of the original and pruned classifiers to steer pruning through the selector model $f_{sel}(x; \beta, \mathbf{v})$ by encouraging the similarity of their predicted RBF parameters. $\mathcal{R}_{res}$ is the FLOPs regularization to ensure the pruned model reaches the desired FLOPs rate pT_{all}. T_{all} is the total prunable FLOPs of a model, $T(\mathbf{v})$ is the current FLOPs rate determined by the subnetwork vector $\mathbf{v}$, and p controls the pruning rate. γ_1 and γ_2 are hyperparameters to control the strength of related terms. During pruning, we only optimize θ_g and keep $\mathcal{W}$ and β frozen.

We emphasize that our amortized explanation prediction selector model, $f_{sel}(x; \beta, \mathbf{v})$, enables us to readily perform interpretation-steered pruning because it can dynamically predict each sample's saliency map's RBF parameters ($[c_z, c_t, \sigma]$) given the current subnetwork vector $\mathbf{v}$ with a single forward pass. In contrast, optimization-based explanation methods [39,46] need to fit a new model, and perturbation-based methods [65,69,71] have to make multiple forward passes for the newly selected subnetwork to obtain its explanations. Therefore, they are inefficient to achieve the same goal. We provide the detailed parameterization of channels $(g(\cdot))$ and $\mathcal{R}_{res}$ in supplementary materials.

4 Experiments

We use CIFAR-10 [29] and ImageNet [10] to validate the effectiveness of our proposed model. Due to the space limit, we refer to supplementary for details of our experimental setup. We call our method ISP (**I**nterpretations **S**teered **P**runing) in the experiments.

4.1 Analysis of Different Settings

Before we formally present our experimental results compared to competitive methods, we study the effect of different design choices for our model's components on its performance. We keep the resource regularization ($\mathcal{R}_{res}$) term in obj. 10 and add/drop other ones in all settings.

In our first experiment, we explore the impact of γ_1 by only using interpretations (second term of Obj. 10) to steer the pruning. Figure 5(a,b) and Fig. 4(a) demonstrate the results. We can observe in Fig. 5(a,b) that small γ_1 values (*e.g.*, 0.1) result in a weaker supervision signal from the interpretations and make the exploration of subnetworks unstable (showing high variance), whereas larger ones make the training smooth. Figure 4(a) illustrates the influence of RBF/independent masks' parameterization scheme in

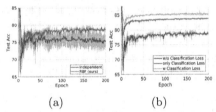

(a)   (b)

Fig. 4. **(a):** Test accuracy of different masks' parameterization schemes. (RBF (ours) *vs.* Independent (REAL-X [26])) **(b):** Test accuracy w/wo using the classification loss. All results are for 3 run times with ResNet-56 on CIFAR-10. Shaded areas represent variance.

Eq. 5 (ours)/Eq. 3 (REAL-X [26]). Our RBF-style model brings better performance than independent parameterization. The latter becomes unstable and less effective when the training proceeds. The instability happens possibly because the pruning gets trapped in some local minima due to noisy and unstructured masks. We can also observe that interpretations on their own provide stable and efficient signals for pruning.

In our second experiment, we examine the impact of γ_2 while utilizing all three terms in objective 10 for pruning. Figure 5(c, d) indicates that small γ_2 (*e.g.*, 1.0) shows higher accuracy but may not be able to push the FLOPs regularization to 0, *i.e.*, reach the predefined pruning rate p. Larger values can satisfy the resource constraint while showing acceptable performance.

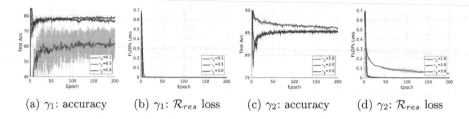

(a) γ_1: accuracy   (b) γ_1: $\mathcal{R}_{res}$ loss   (c) γ_2: accuracy   (d) γ_2: $\mathcal{R}_{res}$ loss

Fig. 5. (a), (b): The model's test accuracy and the FLOPs regularization term when changing γ_1, and **(c), (d):** when varying γ_2. All results are run for 3 times with ResNet-56 on CIFAR-10. Shaded areas represent variance.

Finally, we examine the performance of different combinations of components in objective 10. The results are available in Fig. 4(b). Specifically, 'w/o Classification Loss' represents using the second and third terms, 'only Classification Loss' indicates using the first and third ones, and 'w Classification Loss' means using the full objective function. It is plausible that 'only Classification Loss' performs better than only interpretations ('w/o Classification Loss') since the loss function is a 'less noisy' signal for accuracy compared to the interpretations. Furthermore, incorporating interpretations enhances the supervision signal and yields the best performance. This observation indicates that interpretations contain guidance from different perspectives complementary to the classification loss that only focuses on the model's outputs.

4.2 Comparasion Results

CIFAR-10 Results: Table 1 summarizes the results on CIFAR-10. For **ResNet-56**, ISP outperforms baselines with a similar FLOPs pruning rate. It has a pruning rate on par with EEMC [66], the most recent baseline, while it shows higher Δ-Acc (+0.18% *vs.* +0.06%). For **MobileNet-V2**, ISP simultaneously prunes 18% more FLOPs than DCP and Uniform. It also achieves a better accuracy improvement (+0.10% higher Δ-Acc) than DCP.

ImageNet Results: We present the results on ImageNet in Table 2. For **ResNet-34**, ISP achieves the best trade-off between the performance and FLOPs reduction. It achieves Δ Top-1 close to Taylor [41], but ISP can prune 19.8% more FLOPs. Also, with similar FLOPs pruning rate, ISP outperforms FPGM [19] by 0.84% Δ Top-1. For **ResNet-50**, our model can achieve the largest pruning rate, 56.6%, with the best Δ Top-1/Top-5 being $-0.16\%/-0.12\%$ showing 0.33%/0.23% improvement compared to EEMC [66]. For **ResNet-101**, ISP is the only method that its pruned network has better accuracy than the original one. Also, it accomplishes the highest pruning rate, 56.8%, with a significant 11.7% gap with PFP [33]. For **MobileNetV2**, ISP has a pruning rate competitive (+29.0% *vs.* +30.7%) to MetaPruning [36] and reaches the highest Δ Top-1, with a 0.65% margin with MetaPruning. We also note that ISP significantly outperforms QI [2] (in terms of both accuracy improvement and

Table 1. Comparison of results on CIFAR-10. Δ-Acc represents the performance changes relative to the baseline, and $+/-$ indicates an increase/decrease, respectively.

Model	Method	Baseline Acc	Pruned Acc	Δ-Acc	Pruned FLOPs
ResNet-56	DCP-Adapt [70]	93.80%	93.81%	+0.01%	47.0%
	SCP [28]	93.69%	93.23%	−0.46%	51.5%
	FPGM [19]	93.59%	92.93%	−0.66%	52.6%
	SFP [18]	93.59%	92.26%	−1.33%	52.6%
	FPC [17]	93.59%	93.24%	−0.25%	52.9%
	HRank [34]	93.26%	92.17%	−0.09%	50.0%
	EEMC [66]	93.62%	93.68%	+0.06%	**56.0%**
	ISP (ours)	93.56%	**93.74%**	**+ 0.18%**	54.0%
MobileNetV2	Uniform [70]	94.47%	94.17%	−0.30%	26.0%
	DCP [70]	94.47%	94.69%	+0.22%	26.0%
	ISP (ours)	94.53%	**94.85%**	**+ 0.32%**	**44.0%**

Table 2. Comparison results on ImageNet with ResNet-34/50/101 and MobileNet-V2.

Model	Method	Baseline Top-1 Acc	Baseline Top-5 Acc	Δ-Acc Top-1	Δ-Acc Top-5	Pruned FLOPs
ResNet-34	FPGM [19]	73.92%	91.62%	−1.29%	−0.54%	41.1%
	Taylor [41]	73.31%	–	−0.48%	–	24.2%
	ISP (ours)	73.31%	91.42%	−0.45%	**−0.40%**	**44.0%**
ResNet-50	DCP [70]	76.01%	92.93%	−1.06%	−0.61%	55.6%
	CCP [42]	76.15%	92.87%	−0.94%	−0.45%	54.1%
	FPGM [19]	76.15%	92.87%	−1.32%	−0.55%	53.5%
	ABCP [35]	76.01%	92.96%	−2.15%	−1.27%	54.3%
	QI [2]	74.90%	92.10%	−1.31%	−0.27%	50.0%
	PFP [33]	76.13%	92.86%	−0.92%	−0.45%	44.0%
	EEMC [66]	76.15%	92.87%	−0.49%	−0.35%	56.0%
	ISP (ours)	76.13%	92.86%	**− 0.16%**	**− 0.12%**	**56.6%**
ResNet-101	FPGM [19]	77.37%	93.56%	−0.05%	0.00%	41.1%
	Taylor [41]	77.37%	–	−0.02%	–	39.8%
	QI [2]	76.40%	92.80%	−2.31%	−0.86%	50.0%
	PFP [33]	77.37%	93.56%	−0.94%	−0.44%	45.1%
	ISP (ours)	77.37%	93.56%	**+ 0.40%**	**+ 0.22%**	**56.8%**
MobileNet-V2	Uniform [49]	71.80%	91.00%	−2.00%	1.40%	30.0%
	AMC [20]	71.80%	–	−1.00%	-	30.0%
	CC [31]	71.88%	–	−0.97%	–	28.3%
	MetaPruning [36]	72.00%	–	−0.80%	–	**30.7%**
	ISP (ours)	71.88%	90.29%	**− 0.15%**	**− 0.08%**	29.0%

pruning rate for ResNet-50/101) that aims to perform interpretable pruning by finding filters that are aligned with visual concepts, which illustrates the superiority of our proposed AEM model for pruning compared to other interpretation techniques.

5 Conclusions

We proposed a novel neural network pruning method that utilizes interpretations of the model as guidance for its pruning procedure. We showed that Amortized Explanation Models (AEM) are suitable for our purpose as they can provide real-time explanations of a model. We empirically showed that explanation masks of REAL-X [26], state-of-the-art AEM, might lack a meaningful structure and not be interpretable. Thus, we introduced a new AEM model that overcomes this problem by respecting the geometric prior of natural images and finding the optimal functional form over pixel's Bernoulli parameters of explanatory masks in the RBF functions' family. Finally, we leverage the predictions of our AEM model to steer the pruning process in our formulation. Our experimental results on benchmark data demonstrate that the interpretations of a parameter-heavy classifier provide valuable information to steer its pruning process, complementing the guidance from its outputs, which are the main focus of previous methods.

Acknowledgment. This work was partially supported by NSF IIS 1845666, 1852606, 1838627, 1837956, 1956002, 2217003.

References

1. Adebayo, J., Gilmer, J., Muelly, M., Goodfellow, I., Hardt, M., Kim, B.: Sanity checks for saliency maps. In: Bengio, S., Wallach, H., Larochelle, H., Grauman, K., Cesa-Bianchi, N., Garnett, R. (eds.) Advances in Neural Information Processing Systems, vol. 31. Curran Associates, Inc. (2018)
2. Alqahtani, A., Xie, X., Jones, M.W., Essa, E.: Pruning CNN filters via quantifying the importance of deep visual representations. Comput. Vis. Image Underst. **208**, 103220 (2021)
3. Bach, S., Binder, A., Montavon, G., Klauschen, F., Müller, K.R., Samek, W.: On pixel-wise explanations for non-linear classifier decisions by layer-wise relevance propagation. PLoS One **10**(7), e0130140 (2015)
4. Bojarski, M., et al.: End to end learning for self-driving cars. arXiv preprint arXiv:1604.07316 (2016)
5. Bronstein, M.M., Bruna, J., Cohen, T., Velickovic, P.: Geometric deep learning: grids, groups, graphs, geodesics, and gauges. CoRR abs/2104.13478 (2021). https://arxiv.org/abs/2104.13478
6. Chen, J., Song, L., Wainwright, M., Jordan, M.: Learning to explain: an information-theoretic perspective on model interpretation. In: International Conference on Machine Learning, pp. 883–892. PMLR (2018)
7. Chen, W., Wilson, J., Tyree, S., Weinberger, K., Chen, Y.: Compressing neural networks with the hashing trick. In: International Conference on Machine Learning, pp. 2285–2294 (2015)
8. Chin, T.W., Ding, R., Zhang, C., Marculescu, D.: Towards efficient model compression via learned global ranking. In: Proceedings of the IEEE/CVF Conference on Computer Vision and Pattern Recognition, pp. 1518–1528 (2020)
9. Dabkowski, P., Gal, Y.: Real time image saliency for black box classifiers. In: Guyon, I., von Luxburg, U., Bengio, S., Wallach, H.M., Fergus, R., Vishwanathan, S.V.N., Garnett, R. (eds.) Advances in Neural Information Processing Systems 30:

Annual Conference on Neural Information Processing Systems 2017, 4–9 December 2017, pp. 6967–6976, Long Beach, CA, USA (2017)

10. Deng, J., Dong, W., Socher, R., Li, L.J., Li, K., Fei-Fei, L.: Imagenet: a large-scale hierarchical image database. In: 2009 IEEE Conference on Computer Vision and Pattern Recognition, pp. 248–255. IEEE (2009)

11. Gao, S., Huang, F., Pei, J., Huang, H.: Discrete model compression with resource constraint for deep neural networks. In: Proceedings of the IEEE/CVF Conference on Computer Vision and Pattern Recognition, pp. 1899–1908 (2020)

12. Gao, S., Huang, F., Zhang, Y., Huang, H.: Disentangled differentiable network pruning. In: Proceedings of the European Conference on Computer Vision (ECCV) (2022)

13. Girshick, R.: Fast r-cnn. In: Proceedings of the IEEE International Conference on Computer Vision, pp. 1440–1448 (2015)

14. Grathwohl, W., Wang, K., Jacobsen, J., Duvenaud, D., Norouzi, M., Swersky, K.: Your classifier is secretly an energy based model and you should treat it like one. In: 8th International Conference on Learning Representations, ICLR 2020, Addis Ababa, Ethiopia, 26–30 April 2020. OpenReview.net (2020). https://openreview.net/forum?id=Hkxzx0NtDB

15. Han, S., Pool, J., Tran, J., Dally, W.: Learning both weights and connections for efficient neural network. Adv. Neural Inf. Process. Syst. 1135–1143 (2015)

16. He, K., Zhang, X., Ren, S., Sun, J.: Deep residual learning for image recognition. In: Proceedings of the IEEE Conference on Computer Vision and Pattern Recognition, pp. 770–778 (2016)

17. He, Y., Ding, Y., Liu, P., Zhu, L., Zhang, H., Yang, Y.: Learning filter pruning criteria for deep convolutional neural networks acceleration. In: Proceedings of the IEEE/CVF Conference on Computer Vision and Pattern Recognition, pp. 2009–2018 (2020)

18. He, Y., Kang, G., Dong, X., Fu, Y., Yang, Y.: Soft filter pruning for accelerating deep convolutional neural networks. In: International Joint Conference on Artificial Intelligence (IJCAI), pp. 2234–2240 (2018)

19. He, Y., Liu, P., Wang, Z., Hu, Z., Yang, Y.: Filter pruning via geometric median for deep convolutional neural networks acceleration. In: Proceedings of the IEEE Conference on Computer Vision and Pattern Recognition, pp. 4340–4349 (2019)

20. He, Y., Lin, J., Liu, Z., Wang, H., Li, L.J., Han, S.: Amc: automl for model compression and acceleration on mobile devices. In: Proceedings of the European Conference on Computer Vision (ECCV), pp. 784–800 (2018)

21. Hinton, G., Vinyals, O., Dean, J.: Distilling the knowledge in a neural network. arXiv preprint arXiv:1503.02531 (2015)

22. Hooker, S., Erhan, D., Kindermans, P.J., Kim, B.: A benchmark for interpretability methods in deep neural networks. In: Wallach, H., Larochelle, H., Beygelzimer, A., d'Alché-Buc, F., Fox, E., Garnett, R. (eds.) Advances in Neural Information Processing Systems, vol. 32. Curran Associates, Inc. (2019)

23. Huang, G., Liu, Z., Van Der Maaten, L., Weinberger, K.Q.: Densely connected convolutional networks. In: Proceedings of the IEEE Conference on Computer Vision and Pattern Recognition, pp. 4700–4708 (2017)

24. Ioffe, S., Szegedy, C.: Batch normalization: accelerating deep network training by reducing internal covariate shift. In: Bach, F., Blei, D. (eds.) Proceedings of the 32nd International Conference on Machine Learning. Proceedings of Machine Learning Research, vol. 37, pp. 448–456. PMLR, Lille, France (07–09 Jul 2015). https://proceedings.mlr.press/v37/ioffe15.html

25. Jang, E., Gu, S., Poole, B.: Categorical reparameterization with gumbel-softmax. In: 5th International Conference on Learning Representations, ICLR 2017, Toulon, France, 24–26 April 2017, Conference Track Proceedings. OpenReview.net (2017). https://openreview.net/forum?id=rkE3y85ee

26. Jethani, N., Sudarshan, M., Aphinyanaphongs, Y., Ranganath, R.: Have we learned to explain?: how interpretability methods can learn to encode predictions in their interpretations. In: International Conference on Artificial Intelligence and Statistics, pp. 1459–1467. PMLR (2021)

27. Joyce, J.M.: Kullback-Leibler divergence. Int. Encycl. Stat. Sci. **720**, 722 (2011)

28. Kang, M., Han, B.: Operation-aware soft channel pruning using differentiable masks. In: International Conference on Machine Learning (2020)

29. Krizhevsky, A., Hinton, G., et al.: Learning multiple layers of features from tiny images (2009)

30. Li, H., Kadav, A., Durdanovic, I., Samet, H., Graf, H.P.: Pruning filters for efficient convnets. ICLR (2017)

31. Li, Y., et al.: Towards compact cnns via collaborative compression. In: Proceedings of the IEEE/CVF Conference on Computer Vision and Pattern Recognition, pp. 6438–6447 (2021)

32. Liang, T., Glossner, J., Wang, L., Shi, S., Zhang, X.: Pruning and quantization for deep neural network acceleration: a survey. Neurocomputing **461**, 370–403 (2021)

33. Liebenwein, L., Baykal, C., Lang, H., Feldman, D., Rus, D.: Provable filter pruning for efficient neural networks. In: International Conference on Learning Representations (2020). https://openreview.net/forum?id=BJxkOlSYDH

34. Lin, M., Ji, R., Wang, Y., Zhang, Y., Zhang, B., Tian, Y., Shao, L.: Hrank: filter pruning using high-rank feature map. In: The IEEE Conference on Computer Vision and Pattern Recognition (CVPR) (2020)

35. Lin, M., Ji, R., Zhang, Y., Zhang, B., Wu, Y., Tian, Y.: Channel pruning via automatic structure search. In: Proceedings of the International Joint Conference on Artificial Intelligence (IJCAI), pp. 673–679 (2020)

36. Liu, Z., et al.: Metapruning: meta learning for automatic neural network channel pruning. In: Proceedings of the IEEE International Conference on Computer Vision, pp. 3296–3305 (2019)

37. Liu, Z., Li, J., Shen, Z., Huang, G., Yan, S., Zhang, C.: Learning efficient convolutional networks through network slimming. In: ICCV (2017)

38. Long, J., Shelhamer, E., Darrell, T.: Fully convolutional networks for semantic segmentation. In: Proceedings of the IEEE Conference on Computer Vision and Pattern Recognition, pp. 3431–3440 (2015)

39. Lundberg, S.M., Lee, S.I.: A unified approach to interpreting model predictions. In: Proceedings of the 31st International Conference on Neural Information Processing Systems, pp. 4768–4777 (2017)

40. Maddison, C.J., Mnih, A., Teh, Y.W.: The concrete distribution: a continuous relaxation of discrete random variables. In: 5th International Conference on Learning Representations, ICLR 2017, Toulon, France, 24–26 April 2017, Conference Track Proceedings. OpenReview.net (2017). https://openreview.net/forum?id=S1jE5L5gl

41. Molchanov, P., Mallya, A., Tyree, S., Frosio, I., Kautz, J.: Importance estimation for neural network pruning. In: Proceedings of the IEEE Conference on Computer Vision and Pattern Recognition, pp. 11264–11272 (2019)

42. Peng, H., Wu, J., Chen, S., Huang, J.: Collaborative channel pruning for deep networks. In: International Conference on Machine Learning, pp. 5113–5122 (2019)

43. Rastegari, M., Ordonez, V., Redmon, J., Farhadi, A.: XNOR-Net: ImageNet classification using binary convolutional neural networks. In: Leibe, B., Matas, J., Sebe, N., Welling, M. (eds.) ECCV 2016. LNCS, vol. 9908, pp. 525–542. Springer, Cham (2016). https://doi.org/10.1007/978-3-319-46493-0_32
44. Redmon, J., Divvala, S., Girshick, R., Farhadi, A.: You only look once: unified, real-time object detection. In: Proceedings of the IEEE Conference on Computer Vision and Pattern Recognition, pp. 779–788 (2016)
45. Redmon, J., Farhadi, A.: Yolov3: an incremental improvement. arXiv preprint arXiv:1804.02767 (2018)
46. Ribeiro, M.T., Singh, S., Guestrin, C.: " Why should i trust you?" explaining the predictions of any classifier. In: Proceedings of the 22nd ACM SIGKDD International Conference on Knowledge Discovery and Data Mining, pp. 1135–1144 (2016)
47. Ronneberger, O., Fischer, P., Brox, T.: U-Net: convolutional networks for biomedical image segmentation. In: Navab, N., Hornegger, J., Wells, W.M., Frangi, A.F. (eds.) MICCAI 2015. LNCS, vol. 9351, pp. 234–241. Springer, Cham (2015). https://doi.org/10.1007/978-3-319-24574-4_28
48. Sabih, M., Hannig, F., Teich, J.: Utilizing explainable AI for quantization and pruning of deep neural networks. arXiv preprint arXiv:2008.09072 (2020)
49. Sandler, M., Howard, A., Zhu, M., Zhmoginov, A., Chen, L.C.: Mobilenetv 2: inverted residuals and linear bottlenecks. In: Proceedings of the IEEE Conference on Computer Vision and Pattern Recognition, pp. 4510–4520 (2018)
50. Selvaraju, R.R., Cogswell, M., Das, A., Vedantam, R., Parikh, D., Batra, D.: Gradcam: visual explanations from deep networks via gradient-based localization. In: Proceedings of the IEEE International Conference on Computer Vision, pp. 618–626 (2017)
51. Shah, H., Jain, P., Netrapalli, P.: Do input gradients highlight discriminative features? Adv. Neural Inf. Process. Syst. 34 (2021)
52. Shrikumar, A., Greenside, P., Kundaje, A.: Learning important features through propagating activation differences. In: International Conference on Machine Learning, pp. 3145–3153. PMLR (2017)
53. Simonyan, K., Vedaldi, A., Zisserman, A.: Deep inside convolutional networks: visualising image classification models and saliency maps. In: Workshop at International Conference on Learning Representations. Citeseer (2014)
54. Simonyan, K., Zisserman, A.: Two-stream convolutional networks for action recognition in videos. In: Advances in Neural Information Processing Systems, pp. 568–576 (2014)
55. Simonyan, K., Zisserman, A.: Very deep convolutional networks for large-scale image recognition. In: Bengio, Y., LeCun, Y. (eds.) 3rd International Conference on Learning Representations, ICLR 2015, San Diego, CA, USA, 7–9 May 2015, Conference Track Proceedings (2015). https://arxiv.org/abs/1409.1556
56. Smilkov, D., Thorat, N., Kim, B., Viégas, F., Wattenberg, M.: Smoothgrad: removing noise by adding noise. arXiv preprint arXiv:1706.03825 (2017)
57. Springenberg, J.T., Dosovitskiy, A., Brox, T., Riedmiller, M.A.: Striving for simplicity: the all convolutional net. In: Bengio, Y., LeCun, Y. (eds.) 3rd International Conference on Learning Representations, ICLR 2015, San Diego, CA, USA, 7–9 May 2015, Workshop Track Proceedings (2015). https://arxiv.org/abs/1412.6806
58. Srinivas, S., Fleuret, F.: Rethinking the role of gradient-based attribution methods for model interpretability. In: 9th International Conference on Learning Representations, ICLR 2021, Virtual Event, Austria, 3–7 May 2021. OpenReview.net (2021). https://openreview.net/forum?id=dYeAHXnpWJ4

59. Sui, Y., Yin, M., Xie, Y., Phan, H., Aliari Zonouz, S., Yuan, B.: Chip: channel independence-based pruning for compact neural networks. Adv. Neural Inf. Process. Syst. **34**, 24604–24616 (2021)
60. Wen, W., Wu, C., Wang, Y., Chen, Y., Li, H.: Learning structured sparsity in deep neural networks. In: Advances in Neural Information Processing Systems, pp. 2074–2082 (2016)
61. Yao, K., Cao, F., Leung, Y., Liang, J.: Deep neural network compression through interpretability-based filter pruning. Pattern Recogn. **119**, 108056 (2021)
62. Ye, M., Gong, C., Nie, L., Zhou, D., Klivans, A., Liu, Q.: Good subnetworks provably exist: pruning via greedy forward selection. In: International Conference on Machine Learning (2020)
63. Yeom, S.K., et al.: Pruning by explaining: a novel criterion for deep neural network pruning. Pattern Recogn. **115**, 107899 (2021)
64. Yoon, J., Jordon, J., van der Schaar, M.: Invase: instance-wise variable selection using neural networks. In: International Conference on Learning Representations (2018)
65. Zeiler, M.D., Fergus, R.: Visualizing and understanding convolutional networks. In: Fleet, D., Pajdla, T., Schiele, B., Tuytelaars, T. (eds.) ECCV 2014. LNCS, vol. 8689, pp. 818–833. Springer, Cham (2014). https://doi.org/10.1007/978-3-319-10590-1_53
66. Zhang, Y., Gao, S., Huang, H.: Exploration and estimation for model compression. In: Proceedings of the IEEE/CVF International Conference on Computer Vision, pp. 487–496 (2021)
67. Zhang, Y., Gao, S., Huang, H.: Recover fair deep classification models via altering pre-trained structure. In: Proceedings of the European Conference on Computer Vision (ECCV) (2022)
68. Zhou, B., Khosla, A., Lapedriza, A., Oliva, A., Torralba, A.: Learning deep features for discriminative localization. In: Proceedings of the IEEE Conference on Computer Vision and Pattern Recognition, pp. 2921–2929 (2016)
69. Zhou, J., Troyanskaya, O.G.: Predicting effects of noncoding variants with deep learning-based sequence model. Nat. Methods **12**(10), 931–934 (2015)
70. Zhuang, Z., et al.: Discrimination-aware channel pruning for deep neural networks. In: Advances in Neural Information Processing Systems, pp. 875–886 (2018)
71. Zintgraf, L.M., Cohen, T.S., Adel, T., Welling, M.: Visualizing deep neural network decisions: prediction difference analysis. In: 5th International Conference on Learning Representations, ICLR 2017, Toulon, France, 24–26 April 2017, Conference Track Proceedings. OpenReview.net (2017). https://openreview.net/forum?id=BJ5UeU9xx

BA-Net: Bridge Attention for Deep Convolutional Neural Networks

Yue Zhao[1,2], Junzhou Chen[1,2(✉)], Zirui Zhang[1,2],
and Ronghui Zhang[1,2]

[1] School of Intelligent Systems Engineering, Shenzhen Campus of Sun Yat-sen
University, No. 66, Gongchang Road, Guangming District, Shenzhen 518107,
Guangdong, People's Republic of China
{zhaoy376,zhangzr23}@mail2.sysu.edu.cn
{chenjunzhou,zhangrh25}@mail.sysu.edu.cn
[2] Guangdong Provincial Key Laboratory of Fire Science and Intelligent Emergency
Technology, Sun Yat-sen University, Guangzhou 510006, People's Republic of China

Abstract. In attention mechanism research, most existing methods are
hard to utilize well the information of the neural network with high
computing efficiency due to heavy feature compression in the attention
layer. This paper proposes a simple and general approach named Bridge
Attention to address this issue. As a new idea, BA-Net straightforwardly
integrates features from previous layers and effectively promotes information interchange. Only simple strategies are employed for the model
implementation, similar to the SENet. Moreover, after extensively investigating the effectiveness of different previous features, we discovered
a simple and exciting insight that bridging all the convolution outputs
inside each block with BN can obtain better attention to enhance the
performance of neural networks. BA-Net is effective, stable, and easy to
use. A comprehensive evaluation of computer vision tasks demonstrates
that the proposed approach achieves better performance than the existing channel attention methods regarding accuracy and computing efficiency. The source code is available at https://github.com/zhaoy376/
Bridge-Attention.

Keywords: Channel attention mechanism · Deep neural networks
architecture · Networks optimization

1 Introduction

Deep convolutional neural networks (CNNs) are widely used in the computer
vision community [31], showing excellent performance on various tasks, e.g.,
image classification, object detection, instance segmentation, and semantic segmentation. Since the appearance of AlexNet [14], numerous researches have dedicated to boosting the performance of CNNs [7,12,24,27].

In recent years, the attention mechanism has attracted much attention as a
novel technique to enhance performance. It learns attention weights from the

S. Avidan et al. (Eds.): ECCV 2022, LNCS 13681, pp. 297–312, 2022.
https://doi.org/10.1007/978-3-031-19803-8_18

adjacent convolution layer, thus concentrating on more important features. The channel attention mechanism is one of the attention mechanisms with the most representative method, such as squeeze-and-excitation networks (SENet) [11], which learns the channel attention from an average pooled output on each map, bringing considerable performance gain in various CNNs. Figure 1 shows the block architecture of most attention methods, which consists of stacked convolution layers and one attention layer.

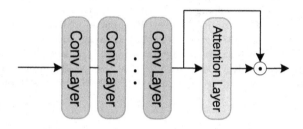

Fig. 1. The block structure of most existing attention methods. The output, coming from stacked convolution layers, passes through the attention layer,thus the attention weights is obtained.

In order to obtain better attention, many methods like [1,4] attempt to use sophisticated strategies on the adjacent convolution output while bringing high model complexity and computation cost. Essentially, attention generation is a process of heavy feature compression, in which the convolution output converts to a vector or a map for channel or spatial attention, respectively. So if we want to get better attention only from a single convolution output, the computational efficiency has to be sacrificed.

To address this issue, we provide new thinking that utilizes previous features. From the view of information transfer, the attention also has an implicit correlation to the previous convolution layers since convolution layers are stacked. Thus bridging previous features can straightforwardly supplement valuable information for the attention. Moreover, the pieces of information from different layers are well interchanged in the attention layer. In this way, we propose the Bridge Attention Net(BA-Net), in which previous features are integrated into the attention layer via simple strategies similar to the SENet. As a result, its model complexity regarding the number of parameters, computation cost, and inference speed is comparable to the SENet. Experimental evaluations on image classification, object detection, and instance segmentation show that BA-Net can perform better than existing channel attention methods.

The major contributions of this article can be summarized as follows:

- We analyze the limitation of traditional channel attention mechanisms and empirically demonstrate that bridging previous features can straightforwardly supplement efficient information from the view of information transfer.

- We propose the Bridge Attention Net (BA-Net) and implement the basic module using only simple strategies. Moreover, we extensively investigate the effectiveness of different previous features and give out the best BA module structure.
- Comprehensive experiments on various computer vision tasks are carried out and show that the proposed BA-Net can achieve higher performance with low model complexity and fast speed compared with existing channel attention methods.

2 Related Work

We mainly revisit attention mechanisms and cross-layer interaction applied in Convolutional Neural Networks(CNNs) in the existing literature.

Attention Mechanisms. The attention mechanism is capable of enhancing the assignment of the most informative feature representations while suppressing the less useful ones, thus allowing the model to focus on the important regions in the context adaptively. The pioneering SENet [11] is the cornerstone of the attention mechanism research field. The method extracted channel-wise features by simple global average pooling and full connection layers, significantly improving the performance of many CNNs with few parameters and computing costs added. The SKNet [16] enhances the expressiveness of the model by passing the feature map through two convolution layers of different kernel sizes, followed by the extraction of channel attention. While extracting channel attention, BAM [19] and CBAM [29] utilize the spatial information and generate spatial attention using convolution. DA-Net Attention [3] concentrates on the relevance of local and global features and combines the two features by summing the attention modules of two branches. ResNeSt [32] adopts a similar split-attention block, which enables the fusion of attention between different groups of the input feature maps. GSoPNet proposes the global second-order pooling to introduce higher-order representation to improve the non-linear capability of CNNs. GSoPNet [4] obtains attention by fully using the second-order statistics of the holistic image. Fca-Net [20] revisits channel attention using frequency analysis and generalizes the pre-processing of channel attention mechanism in the frequency domain. Some methods explore lightweight strategies to reduce the parameters and computing cost of the model with attention. ECA-Net Attention [26] proposes local cross-channel interaction and generates attention by 1D convolution. SA-Net is also a lightweight attention structure inspired by channel shuffling. Half of the features are used to generate spatial attention in SA-Net, and the other half is used to generate channel attention. At the end of the block, features are shuffled along the channel. The above mechanisms provide many novel ways to generate channel or spatial attention. However, one thing in common among them is that they only focus on the features of the layer adjacent to the attention layer. The features in previous layers are ignored. In this paper, we will explore the effect of features in previous layers on the attention mechanism.

Cross-Layer Integration. It is a common strategy to improve network representation by skip connection, which can solve the problem of gradient dispersion and the disappearance of deep networks to some extent. This strategy can train deep networks more adequately, making deeper network structures feasible, and has been widely used in the design of neural network models. The ResNet [7]network first proposed a residual module, which facilitates the fusion of information between different layers. DenseNet [12] also uses a similar structure but differs from ResNet [7]in the form of concatenating for feature stitching. In U-Net [22], which is commonly used in the field of medical segmentation, the decoder-encoder module is connected through a skip connection to make feature extraction achieve higher accuracy.

Actually, cross-layer integration has been used to improve the performance of attention mechanisms. Duo L. et al. [15] propose the DREAL method to optimize parameters of arbitrary attention modules, in which LSTM [9] is used to integrate previous attention weights, and deep reinforce learning is used to update parameters of LSTM and attention layers. DIANet [13] also utilizes LSTM module to integrate previous attention weights and directly outputs attention weights in current block by LSTM. DIANet visualizes the effect of previous features acting on the current attention layer and shows the effect on stabilizing Training. Yu. W. et al. [28] propose the evolving attention to improve the performance of transformers, named EA-AANet. Attention maps in a preceding block are integrated with ones in the current layer by residual connection and 2D convolution. Compared to these works, the proposed BA-Net in this paper has a similar motivation, but this approach integrates the features in previous layers of the current block. The higher performance of our models is displayed in Table 2 demonstrates that feature integration of our method is more effective.

3   Approach

In this section, we first revisit traditional channel attention mechanisms (i.e., SENet [11]) and give out the common form of the mechanisms. Then we demonstrate the limitation of the mechanisms through empirical analysis. It inspires us to come up with the Bridge Attention mechanism, and we will concretely introduce the implementation of the proposed module.

3.1   Traditional Channel Attention Mechanisms

Revisit SENet. Let the output of the SE block be $X \in \mathbb{R}^{C \times H \times W}$, where C, H and W are channel, height and width dimension of the output. Accordingly, the generated attention weights can be computed as:

$$\omega = \sigma(\mathcal{F}_C(gap(X))) \tag{1}$$

where $gap(X) = \frac{1}{HW} \sum_{i=1,j=1}^{H,W} X_{i,j}$ is channel-wise global average pooling, $\sigma(\cdot)$ represents Sigmoid function. $\mathcal{F}_C(\cdot)$ represents two stacked Full Connection(FC) layers, which can be expressed as followed:

$$\mathcal{F}_C(y) = (\boldsymbol{W_2})ReLU(\boldsymbol{W_1}y) \tag{2}$$

In Eq. 2, ReLU [18] represents an activation function. $\boldsymbol{W_1}$ and $\boldsymbol{W_2}$ are matrix used to form the attention weights. The two matrix respectively have size of $C \times (\frac{C}{r})$ and $(\frac{C}{r}) \times C$, in which the reduction factor r is used to avoid heavy computation and high complexity of the attention layer.

We consider that attention mechanism can be divide into two parts, **Integration** and **Generation**. In SENet, the output X is first squeezed by average pooling $gap(\cdot)$ and fully integrated among channels by matrix $\boldsymbol{W_1}$, considered as **Integration** $\mathcal{I}(\cdot)$. And then the features are sequentially fed into $RELU$, matrix $\boldsymbol{W_2}$, $\sigma(\cdot)$, to get the final attention weights, considered as **Generation** $\mathcal{G}(\cdot)$. Thus the common form of attention mechanism can be expressed as :

$$\mathcal{I}(\cdot) = \boldsymbol{W_1}(gap(\cdot)), \ \mathcal{G}(\cdot) = \sigma(\boldsymbol{W_2}(ReLU(\cdot))) \tag{3}$$

$$\omega = \mathcal{G}(\mathcal{I}(X)) \tag{4}$$

In our method, richer features of previous layers are bridged and integrated into $\mathcal{I}(\cdot)$ beside features of the adjacent layer. Thus better attention is generated.

Limitation. Figure 1 shows the block architecture of most existing attention methods, which includes the convolution part and an attention layer. Let $\mathcal{F}(\cdot)$ and $att(\cdot)$ represent the convolution part and the attention layer respectively, thus the whole process can be expressed as:

$$\mathcal{F}_{att}(\cdot) = \mathcal{F}(\cdot) \odot att(\mathcal{F}(\cdot)) \tag{5}$$

$\odot$ represents the element-wise multiplication.

Generally, the convolution part consists of several stacked convolution layers. We assume that the total number of convolution layers is n, thus:

$$\mathcal{F}(\cdot) = F_n(F_{n-1}(\cdots F_2(F_1))) \tag{6}$$

$F_i(\cdot)$ represents the certain convolution layer, where $1 \leq i \leq n$.

Considering the distance, we assume that the outputs of $\mathcal{F}(\cdot)$ are more implicitly correlated with the previous q layers, thus Eq. 6 can be approximately equal to:

$$\mathcal{F}(\cdot) \approx F_n(F_{n-1}(\cdots F_{n-(q-1)}(F_{n-q}))) \Rightarrow \mathcal{F}(F_n, F_{n-1}, \ldots, F_{n-(q-1)}, F_{n-q}) \tag{7}$$

In most existing attention methods, the attention layer only extracts features from the adjacent layer $F_n(\cdot)$. Some methods even have complicated calculations in $att(\cdot)$ for richer information, which weakens the correlation with the previous q convolution layers:

$$att(\cdot) = att(F_n(F_{n-1}(\cdots F_{n-(q-1)}(F_{n-q})))) \approx att(F_n) \tag{8}$$

According to Eq. 8, the generated attention weights lack correlation with previous layers, resulting in insufficient adaptive to outputs of $\mathcal{F}(\cdot)$.

In fact, [13,28] have noticed the above issue, but only the attention weights of previous blocks are fed into the current attention layer. In our method, features of the previous layers inside the block are bridged to the current attention layer.

3.2   Implementation of the BA Module

In this part, we concretely introduce how previous features are integrated into our method and give out the implementation of the Bridge Attention module. Let the output of $F_i(\cdot)$ inside the block be $X_i \in \mathbb{R}^{C_i \times H \times W}$. The outputs are first global average pooled (gap) to the size of $C_i \times 1 \times 1$, and then fed into respective matrices of size $C_i \times (\frac{C_n}{r})$ to get the squeezed features S_i. The size $\frac{C_n}{r} \times 1 \times 1$ is the same as the squeezed feature from the output of $F_n(\cdot)$, which is followed by $att(\cdot)$. Thus the squeezed features from different layers are directly added, and the final integrated feature is obtained.

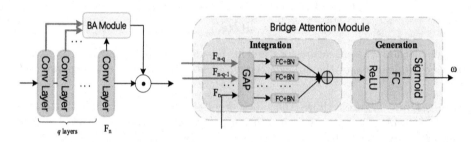

Fig. 2. The overview of Bridge Attention module. Blue arrows indicate that features from previous q layers are bridged to the attention layer. **FC** indicates the matrix to squeeze features and **BN** is BatchNorm Layer. (Color figure online)

We notice that distributions among the squeezed features can be massive differences due to the squeezing process, so we apply Batch Normalization for the features to make them in similar distributions, thus the integration can be more effective. In addition, Batch Normalization improves the nonlinear representation of the features, which also benefits network parameters updating. As a whole, the **Integration** part can be expressed as:

$$S_i = BN_i(\boldsymbol{W}_i(gap(F_i))) \tag{9}$$

$$\mathcal{I}_{BA}(\cdot) = \sum_{n-q}^{n} S_i \tag{10}$$

Then we input the integrated feature into **Generation** part and get the final attention weights. The overview of Bridge Attention module is shown in Fig. 2.

3.3   The Best Structure of the BA Module

Since there are various previous features that can be bridged to the attention layer, we investigate their effectiveness to explore the best structure of the BA module. We evaluate the image classification task based on the backbone of ResNet-50, and the result is shown in Table 1. The row_3 achieves higher accuracy than the row_2, although they are at the same position. Because the attention weights are used to rescale the feature maps, compared with the convolution outputs, they contribute less helpful information to the attention layer. Besides, bridging the proximate features can achieve better performance. Due to the heavy feature compression in the attention layer, more proximate features can straightforwardly supplement more relevant information.

Table 1. The comparison when bridging different features. *att*: the attention weights, *conv*: the convolution outputs, *prev*: the previous block, *curr*: the current block, *conv$_i$*: the i-th convolution layer, *end*: the end of the block.

Backbone	Type	Position	Param.	TOP-1 (%)
SE ResNet-50	*None*	—	28.07M	78.14
BA ResNet-50	*att*	*prev, conv$_3$*	29.16M	78.41
	conv	*prev, conv$_3$*	29.16M	78.49
	conv	*prev, end*	29.16M	78.54
	conv	*curr, conv$_1$*	28.39M	78.78
	conv	*curr, conv$_2$*	28.39M	78.77
	conv	*curr, conv$_{1\&2}$*	28.71M	**78.85**

In conclusion, bridging the closer convolution outputs can achieve better performance. So we merely consider the features within the block, avoiding a significant increase in configuration complexity. Generally, the blocks of existing CNNs contain no more than three convolution layers, such as ResNet [7], ResNext [30], MoblileNetv3 [10], EffcientNet [25], so we bridge all convolution outputs before the attention layer.

For example, the block of the ResNet-50 contains three convolution layers, where the number of channels in each output is C, C, and $4C$. The BA layer follows the last layer. Each output is processed by GAP and converted to a vector of size of $\frac{4C}{r}$ by FC, where r is always set to 16. Then, the vectors will be batch normalized and summed. Another FC converts the sum to $4C$ vector. The total number of neurons in a BA layer is $(C + C + 4C) \times \frac{4C}{r} + 4C \times \frac{4C}{r}$, besides BN.

4 Experiments

In this section, we evaluate our method on three computer vision tasks, including image classification, object detection, and instance segmentation. We first demonstrate the implementation details of the experiments. Then, we give out the performance comparison of our method with other attention methods.

4.1 Implementation Details

For image classification, we evaluate the performance on ImageNet-1K [23] dataset, where we apply our method on various backbone architectures, including

ResNet [7], MobileNet-v3, EfficientNet and ResNeXt. We take the same strategy of the data augmentation and hyperparameter settings in [7] and [8]. The training images are cropped randomly to 224 × 224 with random horizontal flipping, while the testing images are resized to 256 × 256 and cropped from the center to 224 × 224. We use an SGD optimizer with a momentum of 0.9 and a weight decay of 1e-4. In the training phase, the initial learning rate is set to 0.1 for a batch size of 256. All models are trained within 100 epochs with cosine learning rate decay following FcaNet [20].

For object detection and instance segmentation, we evaluate our method on the MS COCO2017 dataset [17]. Faster R-CNN [21] and Mask R-CNN [6] are used as detectors while BA-Net-50 & 101 pretrained on ImageNet-1K are used as backbone. We used MMDetection toolkit [2] to implement all detectors and follow the default settings. The shorter side of input images is resized to 800. All models are optimized using SGD with weight decay of 1e-4, the momentum of 0.9, and batch size set to 8. The total number of training epochs is 12, and the initial learning rate is 0.01, decreased by a factor of 10 at the 8th and 11th epoch, respectively. We construct all models based on the PyTorch framework and experiment on four Nvidia RTX 3090Ti GPUs.

4.2   Image Classification on ImageNet-1K

Performance Comparison with Other Methods. Firstly, we evaluate our method under the backbones of ResNet-50&101, which are the most common backbones used to apply attention mechanisms. Besides traditional channel mechanisms like SENet [11], ECA-Net [26], FcaNet [20], we also compare the performance with the methods using cross-layer integration, like DREAL [15], DIANet [13] and EA-AANet [28]. We give out the metrics from their origin papers. In addition, we noticed that different training settings are used in different mechanisms in their origin papers, so we retrained part of attention models that is reproducible, following the setting of FcaNet [20]. Observed in Table 2, BA-Net has higher performance than other attention mechanisms in *org.* metrics, specifically BA-Net, significantly outperforms SENet by 2.14% and 1.41% in *org.* TOP-1 under the backbones of ResNet-50 and ResNet-101, respectively. Under the same training setting, our method also performs better than SENet, ECA-Net, and FcaNet. Specifically, BA-Net outperforms SENet by 0.71% and 0.62% in *self.* TOP-1 under the two backbones, respectively.

Computing Cost. Observed in Table 2, parameters of BA-Net are slightly larger than parameters of SENet since the features of previous layers are bridged to the attention layer, while FLOPs of them are almost the same. To further illustrate the computation cost of BA-Net, we make additional comparisons on graphics memory usage and speed when training and testing. In Table 3, memory usage when training and testing are slightly increased while training speed and testing speed are slightly decreased. With comparable computing costs, BA-Net outperforms SENet by 0.71% and 0.62% under the two backbones.

Table 2. Performance comparisons of different attention methods on ImageNet-1K in terms of network parameters (Param.), floating point operations per second (FLOPs), and Top-1/Top-5 accuracy. The term *self.* means that the metrics came from the experiments retrained by ourselves while *org.* means that the metrics came from the original paper. Our method and the best records are marked in **bold**.

Attention method	Backbone	Param.	FLOPs	TOP-1 (%)		TOP-5 (%)	
				self. | *org.*		*self.* | *org.*	
SENet	ResNet-50	28.07M	4.13G	78.14 | 76.71		94.05 | 93.38	
ECA-Net		25.56M	4.13G	77.98 | 77.43		93.94 | 93.65	
FcaNet		28.07M	4.13G	78.57 | 78.52		94.16 | 94.14	
SENet+DREAL		28.12M	4.13G	— | 77.85		— | 94.05	
DIANet		28.36M	4.13G	78.31 | 77.24		94.08 | —	
EA-AANet		25.80M	4.35G	— | 78.22		— | 94.21	
BA-Net(ours)		28.71M	4.13G	**78.85**		**94.28**	
SENet	ResNet-101	49.29M	7.86G	79.41 | 77.62		94.62 | 93.93	
ECA-Net		44.55M	7.87G	79.23 | 78.65		94.45 | 94.34	
FcaNet		49.29M	7.86G	79.63 | 79.64		94.66 | 94.63	
SENet+DREAL		49.36M	7.87G	— | 79.27		— | 94.59	
DIANet		47.35M	7.86G	79.47 | —		94.66 | —	
EA-AANet		45.40M	8.60G	— | 79.29		— | 94.81	
BA-Net(ours)		50.49M	7.87G	**80.03**		**94.83**	

Table 3. Computing cost comparisons of BA-Net and SENet in temrs of memory usage and speed (frame per second, FPS) when train and test. M. represents memory usage and S. represents speed.

Method	Backbone	Train M.	Train S.	Test M.	Test S.	TOP-1 (%)
SENet	ResNet-50	34.74G	656 FPS	7.49G	1315 FPS	78.14
BA-Net(Ours)		34.85G	612 FPS	7.67G	1280 FPS	**78.85**
SENet	ResNet-101	46.86G	397 FPS	8.96G	845 FPS	79.41
BA-Net(Ours)		47.54G	362 FPS	9.26G	792 FPS	**80.03**

Table 4. Performance comparisons of BA-Net application on different backbone architectures. The backbones with Bridge Attention and the best records are marked in **bold**.

BackBone	Type	Param.	TOP-1 (%)	TOP-5 (%)
ResNeXt-50	Origin	25.05M	78.77	94.18
	+BA	28.85M	**79.58**	**94.69**
EfficientNet-b0	Origin	5.29M	70.11	89.45
	+BA	8.42M	**71.70**	**90.21**
MobileNetv3-small	Origin	2.54M	**65.87**	86.26
	+BA	2.79M	65.85	**86.48**
MobileNetv3-large	Origin	5.48M	73.29	91.18
	+BA	6.03M	**73.50**	**91.22**

Application on Other Backbones. To further verify the capability of Bridge Attention on other backbone architectures, we apply our method on ResNext, EfficientNet, and MobileNetv3. We retrained all the original backbones while the types with Bridge Attention added, comparisons are shown in Table 4. For ResNeXt-50, BA improves the model by 1.19% on TOP-1 and 0.51% on TOP-5.

EfficientNet-b0 with BA significantly outperforms the origin model by 1.59% and 0.76% on TOP-1 and TOP-5, respectively. However, Bridge Attention seems to have little effect on light-weight backbone like MoblileNetv3, with only a 0.21% improvement on TOP-1 of the large type. So we consider that BA can help improve performance more significantly on heavy backbone architectures.

4.3   Object Detection on COCO2017

In this subsection, we evaluate our BA-Net on object detection tasks using Fast R-CNN and Mask R-CNN. We mainly compare BA-Net with ResNet, SENet, ECA-Net, and FcaNet. We transferred our BA-Net models on the COCO2017 training set and gave out the metrics tested on the validation set. As shown in Table 5, most metrics of BA-Net achieve the highest performance. For Fast R-CNN, our BA-Net outperforms SENet by 1.8% and 2.1% in terms of mAP with the backbones ResNet-50 and ResNet-101, respectively. For Mask R-CNN, our BA-Net outperforms SENet by 2.1% in terms of mAP with ResNet-50.

Table 5. Performance comparisons of different attention methods on obeject detection task. Average Precision (AP) is the main comparison metric.

Backbone	Detector	Param.	FLOPs	mAP	AP_{50}	AP_{75}	AP_S	AP_M	AP_L
ResNet-50	Faster-RCNN	41.53M	215.51G	36.4	58.2	39.2	21.8	40.0	46.2
SENet		44.02M	215.63G	37.7	60.1	40.9	22.9	41.9	48.2
ECA-Net		41.53M	215.63G	38.0	60.6	40.9	23.4	42.1	48.0
FcaNet		44.02M	215.63G	39.0	61.1	42.3	23.7	42.8	49.6
BA-Net		44.66M	215.68G	**39.5**	**61.3**	**43.0**	**24.5**	**43.2**	**50.6**
ResNet-101		60.52M	295.39G	38.7	60.6	41.9	22.7	43.2	50.4
SENet		65.24M	295.58G	39.6	62.0	43.1	23.7	44.0	51.4
ECA-Net		60.52M	295.58G	40.3	62.9	44.0	24.5	44.7	51.3
FcaNet		65.24M	295.58G	41.2	63.3	44.6	23.8	45.2	53.1
BA-Net		66.44M	295.70G	**41.7**	**63.4**	**45.1**	**24.9**	**45.8**	**54.0**
ResNet-50	Mask-RCNN	44.17M	261.81G	37.2	58.9	40.3	22.2	40.7	48.0
SENet		46.66M	261.93G	38.4	60.9	42.1	23.4	42.7	50.0
ECA-Net		44.17M	261.93G	39.0	61.3	42.1	24.2	42.8	49.9
FcaNet		46.66M	261.93G	40.3	**62.0**	44.1	**25.2**	43.9	52.0
BA-Net		47.30M	261.98G	**40.5**	61.7	**44.2**	24.5	**44.3**	**52.1**

4.4   Instance Segmentation on COCO2017

For instance segmentation task, we take Mask R-CNN as the detector for evaluation and the result is shown in Table 6. mAP of BA-Net achieved 36.6% and

38.1% under the two backbones, which performs better than other attention methods. Compared with SENet, our BA-Net notably outperformed by 1.2% and 1.3% in terms of mAP, respectively. Besides image classification, BA-Net also performs well on object detection and instance segmentation tasks, which verifies that our BA-Net has good generalization ability for various tasks.

Table 6. Performance comparisons of different attention methods on instance segmentation task.

Backbone	mAP	AP_{50}	AP_{75}	AP_S	AP_M	AP_L
ResNet-50	34.2	55.9	36.2	16.1	37.5	46.3
SENet	35.4	57.4	37.8	17.1	38.6	51.8
ECA-Net	35.6	58.1	37.7	17.6	39.0	51.8
FcaNet	36.2	58.6	38.1	—	—	—
BA-Net	**36.6**	**58.7**	**38.6**	**18.2**	**39.6**	**52.3**
ResNet-101	35.9	57.7	38.4	16.8	39.7	49.7
SENet	36.8	59.3	39.2	17.2	40.3	53.6
ECA-Net	37.4	59.9	39.8	18.1	41.1	54.1
BA-Net	**38.1**	**60.6**	**40.4**	**18.7**	**41.5**	**54.8**

5 Analysis

5.1 Effectiveness of Bridge Attention

To further analyze how Bridge Attention affects the feature map, we visualize the attention weights distribution of BA-Net and compare it with SENet. Concretely, we randomly sample four classes from ImageNet, which are American chameleon, castle, paintbrush, and a prayer mat, respectively. All images of each class are collected from the validation set of ImageNet, and some example images are shown in Fig. 3.

Fig. 3. Example images of four classes from ImageNet. The images from left to right are American chameleon, castle, paintbrush and prayer mat, respectively.

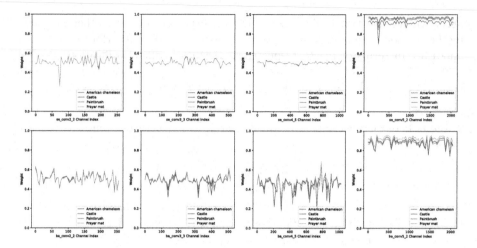

Fig. 4. Visualization of channel attention weights of Block-ij, where i indicate the i-th stage and j is j-th block in i-th stage. The weights learned by SENet50 blocks and BA-Net50 are illustrated in top and bottom row, respectively.

We put the images of the same class into the pretrained BA-Net-50 and SENet-50, then compute the channel attention weights of convolution blocks on average. Figure 4 visualizes the attention weights of four blocks, and each is the last block of four stages. The attention weights of SE blocks are illustrated in the top row, while BA blocks' are illustrated in the bottom row.

In the first stage, the weights distributions of both models are similar, showing that enhancement from Bridge Attention is not significant for coarse feature extraction. Nevertheless, in the later stages for detailed feature extraction, the variance of the weight distribution in BA-Net increases significantly, indicating that the weights become more diverse, especially in the third stage. It demonstrates that BA-Net can effectively capture the more essential features while filtering out the less important ones, thus enhancing the representation of the feature maps. In addition, the SENet's weights curves of different classes in the first three stages almost overlap, while the BA-Net's curves of different classes are clearly distinguishable on some channels. This indicates that BA-Net can distinguish detailed features of different classes sharply. In general, the bridged features of previous convolution layers effectively enhance the representation ability of the output feature maps.

5.2   Importance of the Integrated Features

In our method, the features of different convolution layers in the block are integrated into the attention layer, so we want to explore the relationship between the integrated features and the attention weights and how the features contribute to the attention weights. We consider using the random forest model to reveal the relationship and take the Gini importance [5] from the model as the measurement of feature importance.

The calculating process is referred to as Algorithm 1. There are 16 blocks in the BA-Net-50, where each block contains three convolution layers, and the attention layer follows the third layer. We also use the validation set of ImageNet to inference in the model, and then we get the squeezed features S^i and attention weights ω^i in each block. We fit a random forest model for each block using its S^i and ω^i, and then visualize the feature importance as shown in Fig. 5. We notice that not all S_3 contribute the most to the attention weights, which are adjacent to the attention layer. For example, the contribution of S_2 is comparable to S_3 in B12, or even the integrated features from previous convolution layers are more than important S_3, such as B11, B16. The results demonstrate that the features from previous convolution layers also effectively contribute to the attention weight and even play a dominant role among the integrated features in a particular block.

Algorithm 1: Calculate importance of the squeezed features

Data:
S^i: consisting of S_1^i, S_2^i, S_3^i, indicating all squeezed features in block i;
#The size of S^i is $(b \times c^i \times 3)$, b: training samples, c^i: channels of S^i
ω^i: Channel attention weights in block i;
N: the number of blocks in BA-Net50 backbone;
Result:
The hotmap G about importance of squeezed features in block i;
initialization $G = \emptyset$;
for $i = 1$ *to* N **do**
    $x \longleftarrow [S_1^i, S_2^i, S_3^i]$;
    $x \longleftarrow x.\text{reshape}(b, (c^i \times 3))$;
    $y \longleftarrow \omega^i$;
    Model $\longleftarrow$ RandomForestRegressor();
    Model.fit(x, y)
    Importances $\longleftarrow$ Model.feature_importances_ ;
    # The length of Importances is $(c^i \times 3)$;
    $res = \emptyset; s = 0; cnt = 0$;
    for $k = 0$ *to* $(c^i \times 3)$ **do**
        $s \longleftarrow s + \text{Importances}(k)$;
        $cnt \longleftarrow cnt + 1$;
        if $cnt = c^i - 1$ **then**
            res.add(s);
            $s \longleftarrow 0$;
            $cnt \longleftarrow 0$;
        end
    end
    G.add(res/max(res));
end

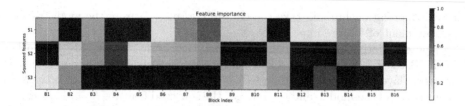

Fig. 5. Visualization of Gini importance of the integrated features. Bi indicates the i-th block in BA-Net50 model and Si is i-th squeezed feature in a certain block. The deeper the color of the square, the more important it is.

6   Conclusion

Traditional channel attention mechanisms heavily rely on the output of the adjacent convolution layer. Faced with this limitation, this paper proposes a novel idea named Bridge Attention to enrich the information for better channel weight estimation. We design the Bridge Attention Module with simple strategies by integrating the features from multiple layers. Experimental evaluation shows that the BA-Net achieves significant performance on various computer vision tasks. Moreover, we verify the features from multiple layers also effectively contribute to the attention weights. In future work, we will consider extending the Bridge Attention by exploring feature integration from the previous block, thus further improving the neural network's performance.

Acknowledgement. This work was partially supported by the Shenzhen Fundamental Research Program (No. JCYJ20200109142217397), Guangdong Natural Science Foundation (No. 2021A1515011794, and 2021B1515120032), Shenzhen Key Science and Technology Program (No. JSGG20210802153412036), and National Natural Science Foundation of China (No.52172350).

References

1. Bello, I., Zoph, B., Vaswani, A., Shlens, J., Le, Q.V.: Attention augmented convolutional networks. In: Proceedings of the IEEE/CVF International Conference on Computer Vision, pp. 3286–3295 (2019)
2. Chen, K., et al.: MMDetection: open mmlab detection toolbox and benchmark. arXiv preprint arXiv:1906.07155 (2019)
3. Fu, J., et al.: Dual attention network for scene segmentation. In: Proceedings of the IEEE/CVF Conference on Computer Vision and Pattern Recognition, pp. 3146–3154 (2019)
4. Gao, Z., Xie, J., Wang, Q., Li, P.: Global second-order pooling convolutional networks. In: Proceedings of the IEEE/CVF Conference on Computer Vision and Pattern Recognition, pp. 3024–3033 (2019)
5. Gregorutti, B., Michel, B., Saint-Pierre, P.: Correlation and variable importance in random forests. Stat. Comput. **27**(3), 659–678 (2016). https://doi.org/10.1007/s11222-016-9646-1

6. He, K., Gkioxari, G., Dollár, P., Girshick, R.: Mask r-cnn. In: Proceedings of the IEEE International Conference on Computer Vision, pp. 2961–2969 (2017)
7. He, K., Zhang, X., Ren, S., Sun, J.: Deep residual learning for image recognition. In: Proceedings of the IEEE Conference on Computer Vision and Pattern Recognition, pp. 770–778 (2016)
8. He, T., Zhang, Z., Zhang, H., Zhang, Z., Xie, J., Li, M.: Bag of tricks for image classification with convolutional neural networks. In: Proceedings of the IEEE/CVF Conference on Computer Vision and Pattern Recognition, pp. 558–567 (2019)
9. Hochreiter, S., Schmidhuber, J.: Long short-term memory. Neural Comput. **9**(8), 1735–1780 (1997)
10. Howard, A., et al.: Searching for mobilenetv3. In: Proceedings of the IEEE/CVF International Conference on Computer Vision, pp. 1314–1324 (2019)
11. Hu, J., Shen, L., Sun, G.: Squeeze-and-excitation networks. In: Proceedings of the IEEE Conference on Computer Vision and Pattern Recognition, pp. 7132–7141 (2018)
12. Huang, G., Liu, Z., van der Maaten, L., Weinberger, K.Q.: Densely connected convolutional networks. In: Proceedings of the IEEE Conference on Computer Vision and Pattern Recognition, pp. 4700–4708 (2017)
13. Huang, Z., Liang, S., Liang, M., Yang, H.: Dianet: dense-and-implicit attention network. In: Proceedings of the AAAI Conference on Artificial Intelligence, vol. 34, pp. 4206–4214 (2020)
14. Krizhevsky, A., Sutskever, I., Hinton, G.E.: Imagenet classification with deep convolutional neural networks. Adv. Neural Inf. Process. Syst. **25**, 1097–1105 (2012)
15. Li, Duo, Chen, Qifeng: Deep reinforced attention learning for quality-aware visual recognition. In: Vedaldi, Andrea, Bischof, Horst, Brox, Thomas, Frahm, Jan-Michael. (eds.) ECCV 2020. LNCS, vol. 12361, pp. 493–509. Springer, Cham (2020). https://doi.org/10.1007/978-3-030-58517-4_29
16. Li, X., Wang, W., Hu, X., Yang, J.: Selective kernel networks. In: Proceedings of the IEEE/CVF Conference on Computer Vision and Pattern Recognition, pp. 510–519 (2019)
17. Lin, Tsung-Yi., et al.: Microsoft COCO: common objects in context. In: Fleet, David, Pajdla, Tomas, Schiele, Bernt, Tuytelaars, Tinne (eds.) ECCV 2014. LNCS, vol. 8693, pp. 740–755. Springer, Cham (2014). https://doi.org/10.1007/978-3-319-10602-1_48
18. Nair, V., Hinton, G.E.: Rectified linear units improve restricted boltzmann machines. In: Icml (2010)
19. Park, J., Woo, S., Lee, J.Y., Kweon, I.S.: Bam: bottleneck attention module. arXiv preprint arXiv:1807.06514 (2018)
20. Qin, Z., Zhang, P., Wu, F., Li, X.: Fcanet: frequency channel attention networks. arXiv preprint arXiv:2012.11879 (2020)
21. Ren, S., He, K., Girshick, R., Sun, J.: Faster r-cnn: towards real-time object detection with region proposal networks. IEEE Trans. Pattern Anal. Mach. Intell. **39**(6), 1137–1149 (2016)
22. Ronneberger, Olaf, Fischer, Philipp, Brox, Thomas: U-Net: convolutional networks for biomedical image segmentation. In: Navab, Nassir, Hornegger, Joachim, Wells, William M.., Frangi, Alejandro F.. (eds.) MICCAI 2015. LNCS, vol. 9351, pp. 234–241. Springer, Cham (2015). https://doi.org/10.1007/978-3-319-24574-4_28
23. Russakovsky, O., et al.: Imagenet large scale visual recognition challenge. Int. J. Comput. Vision **115**(3), 211–252 (2015). https://doi.org/10.1007/s11263-015-0816-y

24. Simonyan, K., Zisserman, A.: Very deep convolutional networks for large-scale image recognition. arXiv preprint arXiv:1409.1556 (2014)
25. Tan, M., Le, Q.: Efficientnet: rethinking model scaling for convolutional neural networks. In: International Conference on Machine Learning, pp. 6105–6114. PMLR (2019)
26. Wang, Q., Wu, B., Zhu, P., Li, P., Zuo, W., Hu, Q.: Eca-net: efficient channel attention for deep convolutional neural networks, 2020 IEEE. In: CVF Conference on Computer Vision and Pattern Recognition (CVPR). IEEE (2020)
27. Wang, X., Girshick, R., Gupta, A., He, K.: Non-local neural networks. In: Proceedings of the IEEE Conference on Computer Vision and Pattern Recognition, pp. 7794–7803 (2018)
28. Wang, Y., et al.: Evolving attention with residual convolutions. arXiv preprint arXiv:2102.12895 (2021)
29. Woo, S., Park, J., Lee, J.Y., Kweon, I.S.: Cbam: convolutional block attention module. In: Proceedings of the European Conference on Computer Vision (ECCV), pp. 3–19 (2018)
30. Xie, S., Girshick, R., Dollár, P., Tu, Z., He, K.: Aggregated residual transformations for deep neural networks. In: Proceedings of the IEEE Conference on Computer Vision and Pattern Recognition, pp. 1492–1500 (2017)
31. Xu, K., et al.: Show, attend and tell: neural image caption generation with visual attention. In: International Conference on Machine Learning, pp. 2048–2057. PMLR (2015)
32. Zhang, H., et al.: Resnest: split-attention networks. arXiv preprint arXiv:2004.08955 (2020)

SAU: Smooth Activation Function Using Convolution with Approximate Identities

Koushik Biswas[1]([⊠]) [iD], Sandeep Kumar[1,3] [iD], Shilpak Banerjee[2] [iD],
and Ashish Kumar Pandey[4] [iD]

[1] Department of Computer Science, IIIT Delhi, New Delhi, India
{koushikb,sandeepk}@iiitd.ac.in
[2] Department of Mathematics and Statistics, IIT Tirupati, Tirupati, India
shilpak@iittp.ac.in
[3] Department of Mathematics, Shaheed Bhagat Singh College, University of Delhi,
New Delhi, India
[4] Department of Mathematics, IIIT Delhi, New Delhi, India
ashish.pandey@iiitd.ac.in

Abstract. Well-known activation functions like ReLU or Leaky ReLU
are non-differentiable at the origin. Over the years, many smooth approximations of ReLU have been proposed using various smoothing techniques. We propose new smooth approximations of a non-differentiable
activation function by convolving it with approximate identities. In particular, we present smooth approximations of Leaky ReLU and show
that they outperform several well-known activation functions in various datasets and models. We call this function Smooth Activation Unit
(SAU). Replacing ReLU by SAU, we get 5.63%, 2.95%, and 2.50%
improvement with ShuffleNet V2 (2.0x), PreActResNet 50 and ResNet 50
models respectively on the CIFAR100 dataset and 2.31% improvement
with ShuffleNet V2 (1.0x) model on ImageNet-1k dataset.

Keywords: Smooth Activation Function · Neural Network

1 Introduction

Deep networks form a crucial component of modern deep learning. Non-linearity
is introduced in such networks by the use of activation functions, and the choice
has a substantial impact on network performance and training dynamics. Designing a new novel activation function is a difficult task. Handcrafted activations
like Rectified Linear Unit (ReLU) [32], Leaky ReLU [29] or its variants are very
common choices for activation functions and exhibits promising performance on
different deep learning tasks. There are many activations that have been proposed so far and some of them are ELU [3], Parametric ReLU (PReLU) [8],

Supplementary Information The online version contains supplementary material
available at https://doi.org/10.1007/978-3-031-19803-8_19.

Swish [36], Padé Activation Unit (PAU) [31], ACON [27], Mish ([30], GELU [10], ReLU6 [20], Softplus [50] etc. Nevertheless, ReLU remains the favourite choice among the deep learning community due to its simplicity and better performance when compared to Tanh or Sigmoid, though it has a drawback known as dying ReLU, in which the network starts to lose the gradient direction due to the negative inputs and produces zero outcome. In 2017, Swish [36] was proposed by the Google brain team. Swish was found by automatic search technique, and it has shown some promising performance across different deep learning tasks.

Activation functions are usually handcrafted. PReLU [8] tries to overcome this problem by introducing a learnable negative component to ReLU [32]. Maxout [6] and Mixout [49] are constructed with piecewise linear components, and theoretically, they are universal function approximators, though they increase the number of parameters in the network. Recently, meta-ACON [27], a smooth activation, has been proposed, which is the generalization of the ReLU and Maxout activations and can smoothly approximate Swish. Meta-ACON has shown some good improvement on both small models and highly optimized large models. PAU [31] is a promising candidate for trainable activations, which have been introduced recently based on rational function approximation.

In this paper, we introduce a smooth approximation of known non-smooth activation functions like ReLU or Leaky ReLU based on the approximation of identity. Our experiments show that the proposed activations improve the performance of different network architectures compared to ReLU on different deep learning problems.

2   Mathematical Formalism

2.1   Convolution

Convolution is a binary operation, which takes two functions f and g as input, and outputs a new function denoted by $f * g$. Mathematically, we define this operation as follows

$$(f * g)(x) = \int_{-\infty}^{\infty} f(y)g(x - y)\, dy. \tag{1}$$

The convolution operation has several properties. Below, we will list two of them which will be used later in this article.

P1. $(f * g)(x) = (g * f)(x)$,

P2. If f is n-times differentiable with compact support over $\mathbb{R}$ and g is locally integrable over $\mathbb{R}$ then $f * g$ is at least n-times differentiable over $\mathbb{R}$.

Property P1 is an easy consequence of definition (1). Property P2 can be easily obtained by moving the derivative operator inside the integral. Note that this exchange of derivative and integral requires f to be of compact support. An immediate consequence of property P2 is that if one of the functions f or g is smooth with compact support, then $f * g$ is also smooth. This observation will be used later in the article to obtain smooth approximations of non-differentiable activation functions.

2.2   Mollifier and Approximate Identities

A smooth function ϕ over $\mathbb{R}$ is called a mollifier if it satisfies the following three properties:

1. It is compactly supported.
2. $\int_{\mathbb{R}} \phi(x)\,dx = 1$.
3. $\lim\limits_{\epsilon \to 0} \phi_\epsilon(x) := \lim\limits_{\epsilon \to 0} \dfrac{1}{\epsilon}\phi(x/\epsilon) = \delta(x)$, where $\delta(x)$ is the Dirac delta function.

We say that a mollifier ϕ is an approximate identity if for any locally integrable function f over $\mathbb{R}$, we have

$$\lim_{\epsilon \to 0}(f * \phi_\epsilon)(x) = f(x) \text{ pointwise for all } x.$$

2.3   Smooth Approximations of Non-differentiable Functions

Let ϕ be an approximate identity. Choosing $\epsilon = 1/n$ for $n \in \mathbb{N}$, one can define

$$\phi_n(x) := n\phi(nx). \tag{2}$$

Using the property of approximate identity, for any locally integrable function f over $\mathbb{R}$, we have

$$\lim_{n \to \infty}(f * \phi_n)(x) = f(x) \text{ pointwise for all } x.$$

That is, for large enough n, $f * \phi_n$ is a good approximation of f. Moreover, since ϕ is smooth, ϕ_n is smooth for each $n \in \mathbb{N}$ and therefore, using property P2, $f * \phi_n$ is a smooth approximation of f for large enough n.

Let $\sigma : \mathbb{R} \to \mathbb{R}$ be any activation function. Then, by definition, σ is a continuous and hence, a locally integrable function. For a given approximate identity ϕ and $n \in \mathbb{N}$, we define a smooth approximation of σ as $\sigma * \phi_n$, where ϕ_n is defined in (2).

3   Smooth Activation Unit (SAU)

Consider the Gaussian function

$$\phi(x) = \frac{1}{\sqrt{2\pi}} e^{-\frac{x^2}{2}}$$

which is a well-known approximate identity. Consider the Leaky Rectified Linear Unit (Leaky ReLU) activation function

$$\text{LeakyReLU}[\alpha](x) = \begin{cases} x & x \geq 0 \\ \alpha x & x < 0 \end{cases}$$

Note that LeakyReLU[α] activation function is hyperparametrized by α and it is non-differentiable at the origin for all values of α except $\alpha = 1$. For $\alpha = 0$, LeakyReLU[α] reduces to well known activation function ReLU [32] while for constant and trainable α, LeakyReLU[α] reduces to Leaky ReLU [29] and Parametric ReLU [8] respectively. For a given $n \in \mathbb{N}$, and $\alpha \neq 1$, a smooth approximation of LeakyReLU[α] is given by

$$G(x, \alpha, n) = (\text{LeakyReLU}[\alpha] * \phi_n)(x) = \frac{1}{2n}\sqrt{\frac{2}{\pi}}e^{\frac{-n^2 x^2}{2}} + \frac{(1+\alpha)}{2}x \qquad (3)$$
$$+ \frac{(1-\alpha)}{2}x \ \text{erf}\left(\frac{nx}{\sqrt{2}}\right)$$

where erf is the Gaussian error function

$$\text{erf}(x) = \frac{2}{\sqrt{\pi}}\int_0^x e^{-t^2}\, dt.$$

For the rest of the paper, we will only consider the approximate identity of Leaky ReLU given in (3) as the activation function. We call this function Smooth Activation Unit (SAU). Approximation of Leaky ReLU ($\alpha = 0.25$) by SAU is given in Fig. 1. It is clear from the Fig. 1 that SAU can smoothly approximate Leaky ReLU (as well as ReLU or its variants) quite well. We note that in GELU [10] paper, the authors use the product of x with the cumulative distribution function of a suitable probability distribution (see [10] for further details).

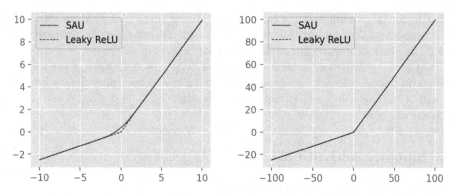

Fig. 1. Approximation of Leaky ReLU ($\alpha = 0.25$) using SAU. The left figure shows that SAU approximates Leaky ReLU smoothly, and in the right figure, we plot the same functions on a larger domain range.

3.1 Learning Activation Parameters via Back-Propagation

Back-propagation algorithm [22] and gradient descent is used in neural networks to update Weights and biases. Parameters in trainable activation functions are updated using the same technique. The forward pass is implemented in both Pytorch [35] & Tensorflow-Keras [1] API and the parameters are updated by automatic differentiation. Alternatively, CUDA [34] can be used to implement (see [29]) the gradients of Eq. 3 for the input x and the parameters α & n and it can be computed as follows:

$$\frac{\partial G}{\partial x} = \frac{-nx}{2}\sqrt{\frac{2}{\pi}}e^{\frac{-n^2x^2}{2}} + \frac{(1+\alpha)}{2} + \frac{(1-\alpha)}{2}\ \mathrm{erf}\left(\frac{nx}{\sqrt{2}}\right) + \frac{n(1-\alpha)}{\sqrt{2\pi}}\ x\ e^{-\frac{n^2x^2}{2}} \tag{4}$$

$$\frac{\partial G}{\partial \alpha} = \frac{x}{2}\left(1 - \mathrm{erf}\left(\frac{nx}{\sqrt{2}}\right)\right). \tag{5}$$

$$\frac{\partial G}{\partial n} = -\frac{1}{2n^2}\sqrt{\frac{2}{\pi}}e^{\frac{-n^2x^2}{2}} - \frac{x^2}{2}\sqrt{\frac{2}{\pi}}e^{\frac{-n^2x^2}{2}} + \frac{x^2(1-\alpha)}{\sqrt{2\pi}}\ e^{-\frac{n^2x^2}{2}}. \tag{6}$$

where

$$\frac{d}{dx}\mathrm{erf}(x) = \frac{2}{\sqrt{\pi}}e^{-x^2}$$

α and n can be either hyperparameters or trainable parameters.

Now, note that the class of neural networks with SAU activation function is dense in $C(K)$, where K is a compact subset of $\mathbb{R}^n$ and $C(K)$ is the space of all continuous functions over K.

The proof follows from the following proposition (see [31]).

Proposition 1. (Theorem 1.1 in Kidger and Lyons, 2020 [16]):- Let $\rho : \mathbb{R} \to \mathbb{R}$ be any continuous function. Let N_n^ρ represent the class of neural networks with activation function ρ, with n neurons in the input layer, one neuron in the output layer, and one hidden layer with an arbitrary number of neurons. Let $K \subseteq \mathbb{R}^n$ be compact. Then N_n^ρ is dense in $C(K)$ if and only if ρ is non-polynomial.

4 Experiments

To explore and compare the performance of SAU, we consider eight popular standard activation functions on different standard datasets and popular network architectures on standard deep learning problems like image classification, object detection, semantic segmentation, and machine translation. We consider the following activations to compare with SAU: ReLU, Leaky ReLU, Parametric ReLU (PReLU), ELU, ReLU6, Softplus, PAU, Swish, and GELU. It is evident from the experimental results in the next sections that SAU outperform in most cases compared to the standard activations. We consider α as a hyperparameter and n as a trainable parameter for the rest of our experiments. The value of n is initialised at 20000 and updated via backpropagation according to Eq. 6. To run the experiments, we use an NVIDIA Tesla V100 GPU with 32 GB RAM.

4.1   Image Classification

MNIST, Fashion MNIST and the Street View House Numbers (SVHN) Database: In this section, we present results on MNIST [24], Fashion MNIST [45], and SVHN [33] datasets. The MNIST and Fashion MNIST databases have a total of 60k training and 10k testing 28 × 28 grey-scale images with ten different classes. SVHN consists of 32 × 32 RGB images with a total of 73257 training images and 26032 testing images with ten different classes. We have applied standard data augmentation methods like rotation, zoom, height shift, and shearing on the three datasets. We report results with LeNet [23], AlexNet [21], and VGG-16 [40] (with batch-normalization [15]) architecture in Table 1, Table 2, and Table 3 respectively. For all the experiments to train a model on these three datasets, we use a batch size of 128, stochastic gradient descent [17,37] optimizer with 0.9 momentum & $5e^{-4}$ weight decay, and trained all networks up-to 100 epochs. We begin with 0.01 learning rate and decay the learning rate with the cosine annealing [26] learning rate scheduler. We report more experiments on these datasets with a custom-designed model in the supplementary material.

Table 1. A detailed comparison between SAU activation function and other baseline activation functions on MNIST, Fashion MNIST, and SVHN datasets for image classification problem with the LeNet architecture. Top-1 test accuracy (in %) is reported in the table for the mean of 10 different runs. We report mean ± std in the table.

Activation function	MNIST	Fashion MNIST	SVHN
ReLU	99.21 ± 0.10	91.51 ± 0.20	92.17 ± 0.19
Leaky ReLU	99.17 ± 0.10	91.61 ± 0.21	92.31 ± 0.18
PReLU	99.27 ± 0.09	91.62 ± 0.18	92.05 ± 0.21
ReLU6	99.29 ± 0.08	91.57 ± 0.17	92.25 ± 0.17
ELU	99.28 ± 0.10	91.48 ± 0.19	92.20 ± 0.18
Softplus	99.06 ± 0.16	91.21 ± 0.23	91.89 ± 0.25
PAU	99.34 ± 0.07	$\mathbf{91.69} \pm 0.12$	92.31 ± 0.22
Swish	99.31 ± 0.07	91.64 ± 0.14	92.39 ± 0.20
GELU	99.29 ± 0.06	91.61 ± 0.14	92.42 ± 0.20
SAU	$\mathbf{99.40} \pm 0.05$	91.47 ± 0.16	$\mathbf{92.61} \pm 0.12$

CIFAR: The CIFAR [19] is one of the most popular databases for image classification problem consists of a total of 60k 32 × 32 RGB images and is divided into 50k training and 10k test images. CIFAR has two different datasets- CIFAR10 and CIFAR100 with a total of 10 and 100 classes, respectively. We report the top-1 accuracy on Table 6 and Table 4 on CIFAR10 and CIFAR100 datasets respectively. We consider MobileNet V1 [11], MobileNet V2 [39], Shufflenet V2 [28],

PreActResNet [9], ResNet [7], Inception V3 [42], squeeze and excitation networks
(SeNet) [12], ResNext [46], LeNet [23], AlexNet [21], DenseNet [13], Xception
[2], Squeezenet [14], WideResNet [47], VGG [40] (with batch-normalization [15]),
and EfficientNet B0 [43]. For all the experiments to train a model on these two
datasets, we use a batch size of 128, stochastic gradient descent [17,37] optimizer
with 0.9 momentum & $5e^{-4}$ weight decay, and trained all networks up-to 200
epochs. We begin with 0.01 learning rate and decay the learning rate by a factor
of 10 after every 60 epochs. Standard data augmentation methods like horizontal
flip and rotation are applied to both datasets. It is noticeable from these two
tables that by replacing ReLU with SAU, there is an increment in top-1 accuracy from 1% to more than 5% in most of the models. More detailed results on
these two datasets with other baseline activations are reported in the supplementary material. Training and test accuracy & loss curves for baseline activation
functions and SAU are given in Figs. 2 and 3 respectively on CIFAR100 dataset
on ShuffleNet V2 (2.0x) network. From these learning curves, it is evident that
after training a few epochs, SAU has stable & smooth learning and higher accuracy and lower loss on the test dataset compared to other baseline activation
functions.

Table 2. A detailed comparison between SAU activation function and other baseline
activation functions on MNIST, Fashion MNIST, and SVHN datasets for image classification problem with the alexnet architecture. Top-1 test accuracy (in %) is reported
in the table for the mean of 10 different runs. We report mean ± std in the table.

Activation function	MNIST	Fashion MNIST	SVHN
ReLU	99.51 ± 0.06	92.77 ± 0.18	95.11 ± 0.14
Leaky ReLU	99.50 ± 0.06	92.79 ± 0.20	95.21 ± 0.17
PReLU	99.48 ± 0.08	92.76 ± 0.18	95.19 ± 0.17
ReLU6	99.55 ± 0.06	93.01 ± 0.16	95.22 ± 0.15
ELU	99.56 ± 0.05	92.89 ± 0.17	95.30 ± 0.18
Softplus	99.22 ± 0.10	92.32 ± 0.25	94.82 ± 0.21
PAU	99.53± 0.08	93.01 ± 0.17	95.22 ± 0.13
Swish	99.58 ± 0.06	92.96 ± 0.16	95.32 ± 0.14
GELU	99.55 ± 0.06	93.05 ± 0.14	95.28 ± 0.14
SAU	**99.64** ± 0.04	**93.17** ± 0.14	**95.45** ± 0.11

Also, We compare the performance of SAU with other baseline activations
with state-of-the-art data augmentation methods like Mixup [48] on CIFAR 100
dataset with ShuffleNet V2 (2.0x), ResNet 18 & ResNet 50 models, and we got
very good improvement over the baseline activations. Results are reported in
Table 5 for the mean of 10 different runs. We use the same experimental setup
as used for the CIFAR100 dataset.

Table 3. A detailed comparison between SAU activation function and other baseline activation functions on MNIST, Fashion MNIST, and SVHN datasets for image classification problem with the VGG16 architecture. Top-1 test accuracy (in %) is reported in the table for the mean of 10 different runs. We report mean ± std in the table.

Activation function	MNIST	Fashion MNIST	SVHN
ReLU	99.55 ± 0.07	93.75 ± 0.14	96.04 ± 0.12
Leaky ReLU	99.59 ± 0.05	93.89 ± 0.14	96.12 ± 0.15
PReLU	99.58 ± 0.07	93.85 ± 0.16	96.12 ± 0.17
ReLU6	99.59 ± 0.05	93.88 ± 0.11	96.18 ± 0.16
ELU	99.51 ± 0.05	93.82 ± 0.16	96.13 ± 0.14
Softplus	99.34 ± 0.12	93.69 ± 0.19	95.88 ± 0.21
PAU	99.58 ± 0.05	94.27 ± 0.12	96.20 ± 0.15
Swish	99.54 ± 0.06	94.10 ± 0.12	96.26 ± 0.13
GELU	99.60 ± 0.04	94.17 ± 0.12	96.23 ± 0.13
SAU	**99.67** ± 0.04	**94.40** ± 0.12	**96.41** ± 0.12

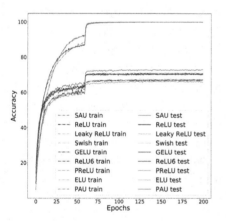

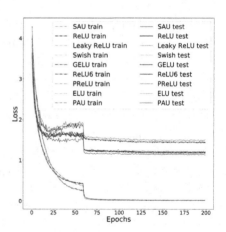

Fig. 2. Top-1 train and test accuracy curves (higher is better) for SAU and baseline activation functions on CIFAR100 dataset with ShuffleNet V2 (2.0x) model.

Fig. 3. Top-1 train and test loss curves (lower is better) for SAU and baseline activation functions on CIFAR100 dataset with ShuffleNet V2 (2.0x) model.

Table 4. A detailed comparison between SAU activation and other baseline activation functions (see supplementary document for more detailed experimental results) on the CIFAR100 dataset for image classification problem with different popular network architectures. Top-1 test accuracy (in %) is reported in the table for the mean of 10 different runs. We report mean ± std in the table.

Model	ReLU	SAU
	Top-1 accuracy (mean ± std)	Top-1 accuracy (mean ± std)
Shufflenet V2 0.5x	61.76 ± 0.27	**64.39** ± 0.23
Shufflenet V2 1.0x	64.12 ± 0.28	**68.41** ± 0.24
Shufflenet V2 1.5x	66.52 ± 0.28	**71.97** ± 0.24
Shufflenet V2 2.0x	66.94 ± 0.24	**72.57** ± 0.21
PreActResNet 18	72.58 ± 0.24	74.01 ± 0.22
PreActResNet 34	72.92 ± 0.24	**75.37** ± 0.24
PreActResNet 50	73.27 ± 0.25	**76.22** ± 0.22
ResNet 18	73.02 ± 0.25	74.27 ± 0.22
ResNet 34	73.12 ± 0.26	**74.64** ± 0.23
ResNet 50	73.89 ± 0.23	**76.39** ± 0.20
MobileNet V1	70.95 ± 0.26	**72.09** ± 0.23
MobileNet V2	73.85 ± 0.24	**75.69** ± 0.19
Inception V3	74.03 ± 0.27	**76.01** ± 0.22
WideResNet 28-10	75.89 ± 0.23	**77.39** ± 0.20
DenseNet 121	75.72 ± 0.27	**77.11** ± 0.23
EffitientNet B0	76.22 ± 0.24	**78.07** ± 0.26
VGG16	71.10 ± 0.30	71.18 ± 0.28

Table 5. Top-1 test accuracy reported with mixup augmentation method on CIFAR100 dataset for the mean of 10 different runs. We report mean ± std in the table.

Activation function	ShuffleNet V2 (2.0x)	ResNet 50	ResNet 18
ReLU	69.10 ± 0.24	75.10 ± 0.23	73.88 ± 0.24
Leaky ReLU	69.04 ± 0.23	75.04 ± 0.23	73.97 ± 0.26
PReLU	69.29 ± 0.25	75.17 ± 0.25	74.12 ± 0.25
ReLU6	69.36 ± 0.23	75.27 ± 0.22	74.17 ± 0.23
ELU	69.34 ± 0.24	75.32 ± 0.24	74.03 ± 0.24
Softplus	68.84 ± 0.28	74.52 ± 0.26	73.69 ± 0.27
Swish	72.78 ± 0.21	76.42 ± 0.22	74.39 ± 0.23
GELU	72.91 ± 0.22	76.54 ± 0.23	74.51 ± 0.23
PAU	73.09 ± 0.22	76.77 ± 0.22	74.62 ± 0.25
SAU	**74.22** ± 0.21	**77.81** ± 0.21	**75.59** ± 0.21

Table 6. A detailed comparison between SAU activation and other baseline activation functions (see supplementary document for more detailed experimental results) on the CIFAR10 dataset for image classification problem with different popular network architectures. Top-1 test accuracy (in %) is reported in the table for the mean of 10 different runs. We report mean ± std in the table.

Model	ReLU	SAU
	Top-1 accuracy (mean ± std)	Top-1 accuracy (mean ± std)
ShuffleNet V2 0.5x	88.01 ± 0.23	**90.50 ± 0.17**
ShuffleNet V2 1.0x	90.74 ± 0.25	**92.78 ± 0.20**
ShuffleNet V2 1.5x	91.07 ± 0.23	**93.20 ± 0.18**
ShuffleNet V2 2.0x	91.32 ± 0.22	**93.52 ± 0.16**
PreActResNet 18	93.36 ± 0.18	94.62 ± 0.15
PreActResNet 34	94.01 ± 0.16	**95.10 ± 0.14**
PreActResNet 50	94.01 ± 0.15	**94.94 ± 0.14**
ResNet 18	93.32 ± 0.20	93.47 ± 0.17
ResNet 34	93.77 ± 0.20	**94.22 ± 0.16**
ResNet 50	93.89 ± 0.19	**94.62 ± 0.16**
MobileNet V1	92.27 ± 0.24	**93.54 ± 0.14**
MobileNet V2	93.89 ± 0.19	**95.37 ± 0.09**
Inception V3	93.89 ± 0.18	**94.51 ± 0.10**
WideResNet 28-10	94.74 ± 0.18	**95.52 ± 0.12**
DenseNet 121	94.41 ± 0.16	**95.31 ± 0.10**
EffitientNet B0	94.64 ± 0.16	**95.52 ± 0.14**
VGG16	93.14 ± 0.23	93.31 ± 0.21

Tiny Imagenet: This section presents results on the Tiny ImageNet dataset, a similar kind of image classification database to the ImageNet Large Scale Visual Recognition Challenge(ILSVRC). Tiny Imagenet dataset contains 64×64 RGB images with total 100,000 training images, 10,000 validation images, and 10,000 test images and have total 200 image classes. We report the mean of 6 different runs for Top-1 accuracy in Table 7 on WideResNet 28-10 (WRN 28-10) [47] and ResNet 18 [7] models. We consider a batch size of 64, 0.2 dropout rate ([41]), SGD optimizer [17,37], He Normal initializer [8], initial learning rate(lr rate) 0.1, and lr rate is reduced by a factor of 10 after every 50 epochs up-to 300 epochs. Standard data augmentation techniques like rotation, width shift, height shift, shearing, zoom, horizontal flip, and fill mode are applied to improve performance. It is evident from the table that the proposed function performs better than the baseline functions, and top-1 accuracy is stable (mean±std) and got a good improvement for SAU over ReLU.

Table 7. A detailed comparison between SAU activation function and other baseline activation functions on tiny ImageNet dataset for image classification problem. Top-1 test accuracy (in %) is reported in the table for the mean of 6 different runs. We report mean $\pm$ std in the table.

Activation function	WideResNet 28-10	ResNet 18
ReLU	62.77 ± 0.46	58.27 ± 0.42
Leaky ReLU	62.72 ± 0.46	58.52 ± 0.44
PReLU	62.70 ± 0.48	58.39 ± 0.44
ReLU6	62.59 ± 0.46	58.67 ± 0.41
ELU	62.58 ± 0.50	58.62 ± 0.43
Softplus	61.77 ± 0.59	58.04 ± 0.47
PAU	63.62 ± 0.44	59.47 ± 0.40
Swish	63.47 ± 0.46	59.02 ± 0.42
GELU	63.26 ± 0.48	59.27 ± 0.39
SAU	**64.07** ± 0.44	**60.12** ± 0.40

ImageNet-1k: ImageNet-1k is a popular image database with more than 1.2 million training images with 1000 classes. We report result on ImageNet-1k with ShuffleNet V2 [28] and ResNet-50 [7] model in Table 8. We use a batch size of 256, SGD optimizer [17,37], 0.9 momentum, and $5e^{-4}$ weight decay. We consider a linear decay learning rate scheduler from 0.1 and trained upto 600k iterations. Experiments on ImageNet-1k are conducted on four NVIDIA V100 GPUs with 32GB RAM each.

Table 8. A detailed comparison between SAU activation function and other baseline activation functions on ImageNet-1k dataset for image classification problem. We report top-1 accuracy in the table.

Activation function	ShuffleNet V2 (1.0x)	ResNet-50
ReLU	69.31	75.50
Leaky ReLU	69.25	75.64
PReLU	69.20	75.48
ReLU6	69.44	75.77
ELU	69.62	75.54
Softplus	69.21	75.37
Swish	70.71	76.39
GELU	70.31	76.30
PAU	70.64	76.42
SAU	**71.62**	**77.47**

4.2   Object Detection

A standard problem in computer vision is object detection, in which the network model tries to locate and identify each object present in the image. Object detection is widely used in face detection, image retrieval, autonomous vehicle etc. In this section, we present our results on challenging Pascal VOC dataset [5] on Single Shot MultiBox Detector(SSD) 300 [25] and we consider VGG-16(with batch-normalization) [40] model as the backbone network. No pre-trained weight is considered for our experiments in the network. The network has been trained with a batch size of 8, SGD optimizer [17,37] with 0.9 momentum, $5e^{-4}$ weight decay, 0.001 learning rate, and trained up to 120000 iterations. We report the mean average precision (mAP) in Table 9 for the mean of 6 different runs.

Table 9. A detailed comparison between SAU activation function and other baseline activation functions on the Pascal VOC dataset for object detection problem with SSD300 network architecture. mAP is reported for the mean of 6 different runs in the table. We report mean ± std in the table.

Activation function	mAP
ReLU	77.2 ± 0.14
Leaky ReLU	77.2 ± 0.19
PReLU	77.2 ± 0.20
ReLU6	77.1 ± 0.15
ELU	75.1 ± 0.22
Softplus	74.2 ± 0.25
PAU	77.4 ± 0.14
Swish	77.3 ± 0.11
GELU	77.3 ± 0.12
SAU	**77.7 ± 0.10**

4.3   Semantic Segmentation

Semantic segmentation is a computer vision problem that narrates the procedure of associating each pixel of an image with a class label. We present our experimental results in this section on the popular Cityscapes dataset [4]. The U-net model [38] is considered as the segmentation framework and is trained up-to 250 epochs, with adam optimizer [18], learning rate $5e^{-3}$, and batch size 32. We report the mean of 6 different runs for pixel accuracy and the mean Intersection-Over-Union (mIOU) on test data in Table 10.

Table 10. A detailed comparison between SAU activation function and other baseline activation functions on the CityScapes dataset for semantic segmentation problem on U-Net model. Pixel accuracy and mIOU is Reported for the mean of 6 different runs in the table. We report mean ± std in the table.

Activation function	Pixel accuracy	mIOU
ReLU	79.45 ± 0.47	69.39 ± 0.28
PReLU	78.88 ± 0.40	68.80 ± 0.40
ReLU6	79.67 ± 0.40	69.79 ± 0.42
Leaky ReLU	79.32 ± 0.40	69.60±0.40
ELU	79.38 ± 0.51	68.10 ± 0.40
Softplus	78.60 ± 0.49	68.20 ± 0.49
PAU	79.52 ± 0.49	69.12 ± 0.31
Swish	79.99 ± 0.47	69.61 ± 0.29
GELU	80.10 ± 0.37	69.39 ± 0.38
SAU	**81.11** ± 0.40	**71.02** ± 0.32

4.4   Machine Translation

Machine Translation is a deep learning technique in which a model translates text or speech from one language to another language. In this section, we report results on WMT 2014, English→German dataset. The database has 4.5 million training sentences. Network performance is evaluated on the newstest2014 dataset using the BLEU score metric. An Attention-based 8-head transformer network [44] in trained with Adam optimizer [18], 0.1 dropout rate [41], and trained up to 100000 steps. Other hyperparameters are kept similar, as mentioned in the original paper [44]. We report the mean of 6 different runs on Table 11 on the test dataset(newstest2014).

5   Baseline Table

In this section, we present a table for SAU and the other baseline functions, which shows that SAU beat or performs equally well compared to baseline activation functions in most cases. We report a detailed comparison with SAU and the baseline activation functions based on all the experiments in earlier sections and supplementary material in Table 12. We notice that SAU performs remarkably well in most of the cases when compared with the baseline activations.

Table 11. A detailed comparison between SAU activation function and other baseline activation functions on the WMT-2014 dataset for machine translation problem on transformer model. BLEU score is reported for the mean of 6 different runs in the table. We report mean ± std in the table.

Activation function	BLEU score on the newstest2014 dataset
ReLU	26.2 ± 0.15
Leaky ReLU	26.3 ± 0.17
PReLU	26.2 ± 0.21
ReLU6	26.1 ± 0.14
ELU	25.1 ± 0.15
Softplus	23.6 ± 0.16
PAU	26.3 ± 0.14
Swish	26.4 ± 0.10
GELU	26.4 ± 0.19
SAU	**26.7±0.12**

Table 12. Baseline table for SAU. In this table, we report the total number of cases in which SAU underperforms, equal, or outperforms when we compare it with the baseline activation functions

Baselines	ReLU	Leaky ReLU	PReLU	ReLU6	ELU	Softplus	PAU	Swish	GELU
SAU > Baseline	71	71	71	71	71	72	67	66	67
SAU = Baseline	0	0	0	0	0	0	0	0	0
SAU < Baseline	1	1	1	1	1	0	5	6	5

6 Conclusion

In this paper, we propose a new novel smooth activation function using approximate identity, and we call it a smooth activation unit (SAU). The proposed function can approximate ReLU or its different variants (like Leaky ReLU etc.) quite well. For our experiments, we consider SAU as a trainable activation function, and we show that in a wide range of experiments on different deep learning problems, the proposed functions outperform the known activations like ReLU, Leaky ReLU or Swish in most cases which shows that replacing the hand-crafted activation functions by SAU can be beneficial in deep networks.

Acknowledgment. The authors are very grateful to Dr. Bapi Chatterjee for lending GPU equipment which helped in carrying out some of the important experiments.

References

1. Chollet, F., et al.: Keras (2015). https://keras.io
2. Chollet, F.: Xception: deep learning with depthwise separable convolutions (2017)

3. Clevert, D.A., Unterthiner, T., Hochreiter, S.: Fast and accurate deep network learning by exponential linear units (elus) (2016)
4. Cordts, M., et al.: The cityscapes dataset for semantic urban scene understanding (2016)
5. Everingham, M., Gool, L., Williams, C.K., Winn, J., Zisserman, A.: The pascal visual object classes (VOC) challenge. Int. J. Comput. Vis. **88**(2), 303–338 (2010)
6. Goodfellow, I.J., Warde-Farley, D., Mirza, M., Courville, A., Bengio, Y.: Maxout networks (2013)
7. He, K., Zhang, X., Ren, S., Sun, J.: Deep residual learning for image recognition (2015)
8. He, K., Zhang, X., Ren, S., Sun, J.: Delving deep into rectifiers: surpassing human-level performance on imagenet classification (2015)
9. He, K., Zhang, X., Ren, S., Sun, J.: Identity mappings in deep residual networks (2016)
10. Hendrycks, D., Gimpel, K.: Gaussian error linear units (gelus) (2020)
11. Howard, A.G., et al.: Mobilenets: efficient convolutional neural networks for mobile vision applications (2017)
12. Hu, J., Shen, L., Sun, G.: Squeeze-and-excitation networks. In: 2018 IEEE/CVF Conference on Computer Vision and Pattern Recognition, pp. 7132–7141 (2018). https://doi.org/10.1109/CVPR.2018.00745
13. Huang, G., Liu, Z., van der Maaten, L., Weinberger, K.Q.: Densely connected convolutional networks (2016)
14. Iandola, F.N., Han, S., Moskewicz, M.W., Ashraf, K., Dally, W.J., Keutzer, K.: Squeezenet: alexnet-level accuracy with 50x fewer parameters and 0.5 mb model size (2016)
15. Ioffe, S., Szegedy, C.: Batch normalization: accelerating deep network training by reducing internal covariate shift (2015)
16. Kidger, P., Lyons, T.: Universal approximation with deep narrow networks (2020)
17. Kiefer, J., Wolfowitz, J.: Stochastic estimation of the maximum of a regression function. Ann. Math. Stat. **23**, 462–466 (1952)
18. Kingma, D.P., Ba, J.: Adam: a method for stochastic optimization. In: Bengio, Y., LeCun, Y. (eds.) 3rd International Conference on Learning Representations, ICLR 2015, San Diego, CA, USA, 7–9 May 2015, Conference Track Proceedings (2015). http://arxiv.org/abs/1412.6980
19. Krizhevsky, A.: Learning multiple layers of features from tiny images. University of Toronto, Technical report (2009)
20. Krizhevsky, A.: Convolutional deep belief networks on cifar-10 (2010)
21. Krizhevsky, A., Sutskever, I., Hinton, G.E.: Imagenet classification with deep convolutional neural networks. In: Proceedings of the 25th International Conference on Neural Information Processing Systems - Volume 1, pp. 1097–1105. NIPS 2012, Curran Associates Inc., Red Hook, NY, USA (2012)
22. LeCun, Y., et al.: Backpropagation applied to handwritten zip code recognition. Neural Comput. **1**(4), 541–551 (1989). https://doi.org/10.1162/neco.1989.1.4.541
23. Lecun, Y., Bottou, L., Bengio, Y., Haffner, P.: Gradient-based learning applied to document recognition. Proc. IEEE **86**(11), 2278–2324 (1998). https://doi.org/10.1109/5.726791
24. LeCun, Y., Cortes, C., Burges, C.: Mnist handwritten digit database. ATT Labs **2** (2010). http://yann.lecun.com/exdb/mnist
25. Liu, W., et al.: SSD: single shot MultiBox detector. In: Leibe, B., Matas, J., Sebe, N., Welling, M. (eds.) ECCV 2016. LNCS, vol. 9905, pp. 21–37. Springer, Cham (2016). https://doi.org/10.1007/978-3-319-46448-0_2

26. Loshchilov, I., Hutter, F.: Sgdr: stochastic gradient descent with warm restarts (2017)
27. Ma, N., Zhang, X., Liu, M., Sun, J.: Activate or not: learning customized activation (2021)
28. Ma, N., Zhang, X., Zheng, H.T., Sun, J.: Shufflenet v2: practical guidelines for efficient cnn architecture design (2018)
29. Maas, A.L., Hannun, A.Y., Ng, A.Y.: Rectifier nonlinearities improve neural network acoustic models. In: in ICML Workshop on Deep Learning for Audio, Speech and Language Processing (2013)
30. Misra, D.: Mish: a self regularized non-monotonic activation function (2020)
31. Molina, A., Schramowski, P., Kersting, K.: Padé activation units: end-to-end learning of flexible activation functions in deep networks (2020)
32. Nair, V., Hinton, G.E.: Rectified linear units improve restricted boltzmann machines. In: Fürnkranz, J., Joachims, T. (eds.) Proceedings of the 27th International Conference on Machine Learning (ICML-10), 21–24 June 2010, Haifa, Israel, pp. 807–814. Omnipress (2010). https://icml.cc/Conferences/2010/papers/432.pdf
33. Netzer, Y., Wang, T., Coates, A., Bissacco, A., Wu, B., Ng, A.Y.: Reading digits in natural images with unsupervised feature learning (2011)
34. Nickolls, J., Buck, I., Garland, M., Skadron, K.: Scalable parallel programming. In: 2008 IEEE Hot Chips 20 Symposium (HCS), pp. 40–53 (2008). https://doi.org/10.1109/HOTCHIPS.2008.7476525
35. Paszke, A., et al.: Pytorch: an imperative style, high-performance deep learning library (2019)
36. Ramachandran, P., Zoph, B., Le, Q.V.: Searching for activation functions (2017)
37. Robbins, H., Monro, S.: A stochastic approximation method. Ann. Math. Stat. **22**, 400–407 (1951)
38. Ronneberger, O., Fischer, P., Brox, T.: U-net: convolutional networks for biomedical image segmentation (2015)
39. Sandler, M., Howard, A., Zhu, M., Zhmoginov, A., Chen, L.C.: Mobilenetv 2: inverted residuals and linear bottlenecks (2019)
40. Simonyan, K., Zisserman, A.: Very deep convolutional networks for large-scale image recognition (2015)
41. Srivastava, N., Hinton, G., Krizhevsky, A., Sutskever, I., Salakhutdinov, R.: Dropout: a simple way to prevent neural networks from overfitting. J. Mach. Learn. Res. **15**(1), 1929–1958 (2014)
42. Szegedy, C., Vanhoucke, V., Ioffe, S., Shlens, J., Wojna, Z.: Rethinking the inception architecture for computer vision (2015)
43. Tan, M., Le, Q.V.: Efficientnet: rethinking model scaling for convolutional neural networks (2020)
44. Vaswani, A., et al.: Attention is all you need (2017)
45. Xiao, H., Rasul, K., Vollgraf, R.: Fashion-mnist: a novel image dataset for benchmarking machine learning algorithms. arXiv preprint arXiv:1708.07747 (2017)
46. Xie, S., Girshick, R., Dollár, P., Tu, Z., He, K.: Aggregated residual transformations for deep neural networks (2017)
47. Zagoruyko, S., Komodakis, N.: Wide residual networks (2016)

48. Zhang, H., Cisse, M., Dauphin, Y.N., Lopez-Paz, D.: mixup: beyond empirical risk minimization. In: International Conference on Learning Representations (2018). https://openreview.net/forum?id=r1Ddp1-Rb
49. Hui-zhen Zhao, Fu-xian Liu, L.y.L.: Improving deep convolutional neural networks with mixed maxout units (2017). https://doi.org/10.1371/journal.pone.0180049
50. Zheng, H., Yang, Z., Liu, W., Liang, J., Li, Y.: Improving deep neural networks using softplus units. In: 2015 International Joint Conference on Neural Networks (IJCNN), pp. 1–4 (2015). https://doi.org/10.1109/IJCNN.2015.7280459

Multi-Exit Semantic Segmentation Networks

Alexandros Kouris[1(✉)], Stylianos I. Venieris[1], Stefanos Laskaridis[1],
and Nicholas Lane[1,2]

[1] Samsung AI Center, Cambridge, UK
{a.kouris,s.venieris,nic.lane}@samsung.com, mail@stefanos.cc
[2] University of Cambridge, Cambridge, UK

Abstract. Semantic segmentation arises as the backbone of many vision systems, spanning from self-driving cars and robot navigation to augmented reality and teleconferencing. Frequently operating under stringent latency constraints within a limited resource envelope, optimising for efficient execution becomes important. At the same time, the heterogeneous capabilities of the target platforms and the diverse constraints of different applications require the design and training of multiple target-specific segmentation models, leading to excessive maintenance costs. To this end, we propose a framework for converting state-of-the-art segmentation CNNs to Multi-Exit Semantic Segmentation (MESS) networks: specially trained models that employ parametrised early exits along their depth to *i)* dynamically save computation during inference on easier samples and *ii)* save training and maintenance cost by offering a post-training customisable speed-accuracy trade-off. Designing and training such networks naively can hurt performance. Thus, we propose a novel two-staged training scheme for multi-exit networks. Furthermore, the parametrisation of MESS enables co-optimising the number, placement and architecture of the attached segmentation heads along with the exit policy, upon deployment via exhaustive search in <1 GPUh. This allows MESS to rapidly adapt to the device capabilities and application requirements for each target use-case, offering a train-once-deploy-everywhere solution. MESS variants achieve latency gains of up to 2.83× with the same accuracy, or 5.33 pp higher accuracy for the same computational budget, compared to the original backbone network. Lastly, MESS delivers orders of magnitude faster architectural customisation, compared to state-of-the-art techniques.

1 Introduction

Semantic segmentation constitutes a core machine vision task that has demonstrated tremendous advancement due to the emergence of deep learning [15]. By predicting dense (every-pixel) semantic labels for an image of arbitrary resolution, semantic segmentation forms one of the finest-grained visual scene understanding tasks, materialised as an enabling technology for myriad applications, including augmented reality [36,63], video conferencing [45,68], navigation [50,61], and semantic mapping [41].

S. I. Venieris and S. Laskaridis—Have contributed equally.

Supplementary Information The online version contains supplementary material available at
https://doi.org/10.1007/978-3-031-19803-8_20.

S. Avidan et al. (Eds.): ECCV 2022, LNCS 13681, pp. 330–349, 2022.
https://doi.org/10.1007/978-3-031-19803-8_20

This wide adoption of segmentation models in consumer applications has pushed their deployment away from the cloud, towards resource-constrained edge devices [22, 63] such as smartphones and home robots. With quality-of-service (QoS) and safety being of utmost importance when deploying such real-time systems, efficient and accurate segmentation becomes a core problem to solve. Additionally, device heterogeneity in the consumer ecosystem (*e.g.* co-existence of top-tier and low-cost smartphones) and the diverse constraints of different applications (*e.g. 30 fps* for AR/VR vs *1 fps* for photo effects), call for segmentation models with variable latency-accuracy characteristics to be designed, trained and distributed to end devices, leading to high maintenance costs.

State-of-the-art segmentation models, however, pose their own challenges to efficient deployment and adaptation, as their impressive accuracy comes at the cost of excessive computational and memory demands. Particularly, the every-pixel nature of the segmentation output calls for high-resolution feature maps to be preserved throughout the network (to avoid eradicating spatial information) [66], while also maintaining a large receptive field on the output (to incorporate context and extract robust semantics) [46], leading to inflated training and inference costs.

Aiming to alleviate this latency burden for on-device inference [1], recent work has focused on the design of lightweight segmentation models either manually [42,72] or through Neural Architecture Search [35,43]. However, such methods typically involve huge search spaces and disallow the re-use of ImageNet [9] pre-trained classification backbones. This leads to long and non-reusable training cycles per model, which often differ for each target device, aggravating prohibitively the training and adaptation time.

Orthogonally, advances in early-exit DNNs offer complementary efficiency gains by adjusting the computation path at run time in an input-dependent manner, while natively providing a tunable speed-accuracy trade-off. However, these solutions [20,24,74] have mainly aimed at image classification so far, leaving challenges in segmentation, such as the design of lightweight exit architectures and exit policies, largely unaddressed. In fact, naively applying early-exiting on segmentation CNNs may not lead to any latency gains due to the inherently heavyweight architecture of segmentation heads, aggravated by the large incoming feature volume. For example, adding a single extra head on DeepLabV3 [6] leads to an overhead of up to 40% of the original model's workload.

In this work, we introduce a novel methodology for deriving and training Multi-Exit Semantic Segmentation (MESS) networks starting from existing CNNs and aiming for efficient and versatile on-device segmentation tailored to the platform and task at hand. MESS brings together architecture customisation and early-exit networks, through a novel training scheme and a compact and highly re-usable search space that allows post-training adaptation through exhaustive search in abridged time frames.

Specifically, MESS uses a given segmentation CNN as a backbone model, pre-trains it in an *early-exit aware* manner (without loss of accuracy) and attaches numerous candidate early-exit architectures (*i.e.* segmentation heads) at different depths, offering predictions with varying workload-accuracy characteristics (Fig. 1). Importantly, through targeted design choices, the *number*, *placement* and *architecture* of exits remain configurable and can be co-optimised upon deployment, to adapt to different-capability devices and diverse application requirements, without the need of retraining, leading to a *train-once, deploy-everywhere* paradigm. The main contributions of this work are:

- The design of MESS networks, combining adaptive inference through early exiting with architecture customisation, to provide a fine-grain speed-accuracy trade-off, tailor-made for semantic segmentation. *This enables efficient and adaptive segmentation based on the use-case requirements and the target device capabilities.*
- A two-stage scheme for training MESS networks, starting with an end-to-end exit-aware pre-training of the backbone that employs a novel exit-dropout loss which pushes the extraction of semantically strong features towards shallow layers of the network without compromising its final accuracy or committing to an exit configuration; followed by a frozen-backbone stage that jointly trains all candidate early-exit architectures through a novel selective distillation scheme. *This mechanism boosts the accuracy of multi-exit networks and decouples training from the deployed MESS configuration, thus enabling rapid post-training adaptation of the architecture.*
- An input-dependent inference pipeline for MESS networks, employing a novel method for estimating the prediction confidence at each exit, used as exit policy, tailored for every-pixel outputs. *This mechanism enables difficulty-based allocation of resources, by early-stopping for "easy" inputs with corresponding performance gains.*

2   Related Work

Efficient Segmentation. Semantic segmentation is rapidly evolving, since the emergence of the first CNN-based approaches [2,38,44,48]. Recent advances have focused on optimising accuracy through stronger backbone CNNs [17,21], dilated convolutions [5,66], multi-scale processing [65,73], multi-path refinement [14,32], knowledge distillation [37] and adversarial training [40]. To reduce the computational cost, the design of lightweight hand-crafted [42,57,64,72] and more recently NAS-crafted [35,43,69] architectures has been explored. MESS is *model-agnostic* and can follow the above advancements by being *applied on top of existent CNN backbones* to achieve complementary gains by exploiting the orthogonal dimension of input-dependent early-exiting.

Adaptive Inference. The key paradigm behind adaptive inference is to save computation on "easy" samples and reduce the overall computation with minimal accuracy degradation [3,12]. Existing methods can be taxonomised into: *1) Dynamic Routing networks* selecting a different sequence of operations to run in an input-dependent manner by skipping layers [53,55,58] or channels [11,13,19,33,56]; and *2) Multi-Exit Networks* forming a class of architectures with intermediate classifiers along their depth [20,27,52,59,60,67]. With earlier exits running faster and deeper ones being more accurate, such networks provide varying accuracy-cost trade-offs. Existing work has mainly focused on image classification, proposing hand-crafted [20,71], model-agnostic [24,52] and deployment-aware architectures [26,27]. Yet, adopting these techniques in segmentation poses additional, still unexplored, challenges.

Multi-Exit Network Training. So far, the training of multi-exit models for classification can be categorised into: *1) End-to-end* schemes jointly training the backbone and early exits [20,24,71], leading to increased accuracy in early exits, at the expense of often downgrading the accuracy deeper on or even causing divergence [20,29] due to early-exit "cross-talk"; and *2) Frozen-backbone* methods which firstly train the backbone until convergence and subsequently attach and train intermediate exits individually [24,27]. This decoupling of the backbone from the exits allows for faster training of the exits, at the expense of an accuracy penalty due to fewer degrees of freedom in parameter tuning. Orthogonally, self-distillation methods have been proposed in the literature [23,28,29,47,70] to further improve the accuracy of early exits by treating them as students of the last exit. In this work, we propose a fused two-stage training scheme, backed by self-distillation with information filtering, that enables exit-aware pre-training and full customisation potential without affecting the final exit's accuracy.

Adaptive Segmentation Networks. Recently, initial efforts on adaptive segmentation have emerged. Li *et al.* [31] combined NAS with a trainable dynamic routing mechanism that generates data-dependent processing paths at run time. NAS approaches, however, compose enormous search spaces with minimum re-use between instances, leading to soaring training times. Furthermore, by incorporating the computation cost to the loss function, this approach is unable to customise the model to meet varying speed-accuracy characteristics without retraining, leading also to inflated adaptation cost. Closer to our work, Layer Cascade (LC) [30] studies *early-stopping* for segmentation. LC treats segmentation as a vast group of independent classification tasks, where *each pixel* propagates to the next exit only if the latest prediction does not surpass a confidence threshold. Nonetheless, due to different *per-pixel* paths, this scheme leads to heavily unstructured computations, for which existing BLAS libraries cannot achieve realistic speedups [62]. LC also constitutes a manually-crafted model, tied to a specific backbone architecture, and non-customisable to the target device's capabilities.

MESS networks bring together benefits of all the above worlds. Our framework supports model customisation within a compact search space of early-exit architectures tailor-made for semantic segmentation, while preserving the ability to re-use pre-trained backbones cutting down training time. Additionally, MESS networks push the limits of efficient inference by incorporating *image-level* confidence-based early exiting, through a novel exit policy that addresses the unique challenges of dense segmentation predictions. Simultaneously, the proposed two-stage training scheme combines end-to-end and frozen-backbone training approaches, boosting the accuracy of shallow exits without compromising deeper ones. Finally, design choices allow us to decouple MESS training from the deployment configuration, enabling exhaustive search to be rapidly performed post-training, in order to customise the architectural configuration for different devices or application-specific requirements, without any parameter fine-tuning.

3 MESS Networks Overview

To enable efficient segmentation, the MESS *framework* employs a target-specific configuration search to obtain a *multi-exit* segmentation network optimised for the platform and task at hand. We call the resulting model a MESS network, with an example depicted in Fig. 1. Constructing a MESS network involves three stages: *i)* starting from a backbone segmentation CNN, we identify several candidate *exit points* along its depth (Sect. 4.1), and *attach* to each of them multiple *early exits* (*i.e.* segmentation heads) of varying architectural configurations (Sect. 4.2), leading to a newly defined *overprovisioned* network; *ii) training* all candidate exits together with the backbone through a novel two-stage scheme (Sect. 4.3); and *iii) tailoring* the overprovisioned network post-training to extract a MESS *instance*, comprising the backbone and a subset of the available exits, considering user-defined constraints and optimisation objectives (Sect. 5.1). Our framework supports various inference settings, ranging from extracting efficient target-specific submodels (meeting accuracy/speed constraints) to progressive refinement of the segmentation prediction and confidence-based exiting (Sect. 5.2). Across all settings, MESS networks save computation by circumventing deeper parts of the network. The next two sections follow the flow of the proposed framework.

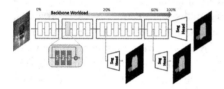

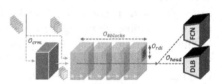

Fig. 1. Multi-exit semantic segmentation network instance.

Fig. 2. Parametrisation of segmentation head architecture.

4   MESS Networks Design and Training

In this section, we go through the design choices that shape MESS networks, their early-exit architectural configuration and training process. This yields an overprovisioned network, ready to be customised for the target application and device at hand.

4.1   Backbone Initialisation and Exit Placement

Initially, a backbone segmentation CNN is provided. Typically, such models aim to preserve large receptive field on the output, while preventing loss of spatial information (*e.g.* by replacing traditional pooling operations with dilated convolutions [66]). As a result, and combined with the increased number of channels integrated, deeper layers demonstrate significantly larger feature volumes, leading to an unbalanced distribution of computational demands across the network (Fig. 1). This motivates the adoption of early-exiting during inference as a means of improving processing speed.

As a first step, the provided backbone is profiled in terms of per-layer workload (FLOPs). Based on the results of this analysis, N *candidate exit points* are identified following an approximately equidistant workload distribution (every $1/N$-th of the total backbone's FLOPs). For simplicity, exit points are restricted to be at the output of individual network blocks[1] b_k. Although some of these exit points may subsequently be dropped during MESS configuration search, this placement currently maximises the distance between subsequent exits, improving the efficiency of our search. An example of the described analysis on a DRN-50 backbone [66] is presented in Fig. 3.

---

[1] *e.g.* Dilated Residual Blocks for ResNet-based [17] backbones, Inverted Residual Blocks for MobileNet-based [49] backbones etc.

4.2 Early-Exit Architecture Search Space Design

Early-exiting in segmentation CNNs faces the challenge of: *i) enlarged feature volumes* of segmentation models, leading to inflated computation cost for the early-exit heads, *ii) limited receptive field* and *iii) weak semantics* in shallow exits. MESS addresses these challenges in a two-fold manner: *i)* by pushing the extraction of semantically strong features to shallower layers of the backbone during training (Sect. 4.3) and *ii)* by introducing a configuration space tailored-made for segmentation head architectures:

1) Channel Reduction Module (CRM): To reduce the computational overhead of each exit without compromising the spatial resolution of the feature volume that is particularly important for accuracy, we optionally include a 1×1 convolutional layer (CRM) that reduces the number of channels fed to the segmentation head by a tunable factor.

2) Extra Trainable Blocks: To address the weak semantics of shallow exits, while avoiding an unnecessary surge in the computational overhead of deeper exits, we allow incorporating a configurable number of additional convolutional blocks in each exit's architecture. These layers are tactically appended *after* the CRM to take advantage of the computational efficiency of its reduced feature-volume width.

3) Rapid Dilation Increase (RDI): To address the limited receptive field of shallow exits, apart from the addition of trainable blocks, we optionally allow the dilation rate employed in the exit layers to be rapidly increased, doubling in each block.

4) Head: MESS currently supports two types of output segmentation blocks from the literature, positioned at the end of each exit: *i)* Fully Convolutional Network-based Head (*FCN-Head*) [38] and *ii)* DeepLabV3-based Head (*DLB-Head*) [6,7].

Overall, the configuration space for each exit architecture (Fig. 2) is shaped as:

1. Channel Reduction Module: $\mathcal{O}_{\mathrm{crm}} = \{/1, /2, /4, /8\} \mapsto \{0, 1, 2, 3\}$
2. Extra Trainable Blocks: $\mathcal{O}_{\#\mathrm{blocks}} = \{0, 1, 2, 3\}$
3. Rapid Dilation Increase: $\mathcal{O}_{\mathrm{rdi}} = \{\mathit{False}, \mathit{True}\} \mapsto \{0, 1\}$
4. Segmentation Head: $\mathcal{O}_{\mathrm{head}} = \{\mathit{FCN\text{-}Head}, \mathit{DLB\text{-}Head}\} \mapsto \{0, 1\}$

Expecting that varying exit-point depths favour different architectural configurations (*e.g.* channel-rich for deeper exits and layer-multitudinous for shallower), MESS allows each early exit to adopt a tailored architecture based on its position in the backbone. Formally, we represent the configuration space for the i-th exit's architecture as:

$$\mathcal{S}_{\mathrm{exit}}^{i} = \mathcal{O}_{\mathrm{crm}} \times \mathcal{O}_{\#\mathrm{blocks}} \times \mathcal{O}_{\mathrm{rdi}} \times \mathcal{O}_{\mathrm{head}} \qquad (1)$$

where $i \in \{1, 2, ..., N\}$ and $\mathcal{O}_{\mathrm{crm}}$, $\mathcal{O}_{\#\mathrm{blocks}}$, $\mathcal{O}_{\mathrm{rdi}}$ and $\mathcal{O}_{\mathrm{head}}$, are the sets of available *options* for the CRM, number of trainable blocks, RDI and exit head, respectively.

4.3 Training Scheme

Two-Stage MESS Training. As aforementioned, early-exit networks are typically either trained *end-to-end* or in a *frozen-backbone* manner [25]. However, both can lead to suboptimal accuracy results in the final or the early exits. For this reason, we combine the best of both worlds by proposing a novel two-stage training scheme.

Stage 1 (end-to-end): In the exit-aware pre-training stage, we aim to fully train the backbone network that will be shared across all candidate exits, specially preparing it for early-exiting by pushing the extraction of semantically strong features at shallow layers, without committing to any particular exit configuration. To achieve this, vanilla FCN-Heads are attached to all candidate exit points, generating an intermediate multi-exit model. This network is trained end-to-end, updating the weights of the backbone and a *single* early exit at each iteration, with the remainder of the exits being dropped-out in a round-robin fashion (Eq. (2), referred to as *exit-dropout loss*). As a result, cross-talk between exits is minimised allowing the final head to reach its full potential, while the backbone remains exposed to gradients from shallower exits. Formally, we denote the segmentation predictions after softmax for each early exit by $y_i \in [0,1]^{R \times C \times M}$ where R and C are the output's number of rows and columns, respectively, and M the number of classes. Given the ground truth labels $\hat{y} \in \{0, 1, ..., M - 1\}^{R \times C}$, the loss function for the proposed exit-aware pre-training stage is formulated as:

$$\mathcal{L}_{\text{pretrain}}^{\text{batch}^{(j)}} = \sum_{i=1}^{N-1} \mathbb{1}(j \bmod i = 0) \cdot \mathcal{L}_{\text{CE}}(y_i, \hat{y}) + \mathcal{L}_{\text{CE}}(y_N, \hat{y}) \qquad (2)$$

where $\mathbb{1}(\cdot)$ is the indicator function and $\mathcal{L}_{\text{CE}}$ the cross entropy. Although after this stage the early exits are not fully trained, their contribution to the loss *guides the backbone towards learning stronger representations throughout, consequently aiding early-exiting.*

Stage 2 (frozen-backbone): At this stage, the backbone and final exit are kept frozen (*i.e.* weights are not updated). The *MESS overprovisioned network* is formed by attaching *all* candidate early-exit architectures of the proposed configuration space $\mathcal{S}_{\text{exit}}^i$ (Sect. 4.2) across *all* candidate exit points $i \in \{1, 2, ..., N\}$ (Sect. 4.1) and training them jointly. Importantly, keeping the backbone unchanged during this stage allows different exit architectures to be: *i)* attached and trained *simultaneously* even to the same candidate exit point *without interfering* with each other, or with the backbone *ii)* trained at significantly reduced cost than the end-to-end approach, while taking advantage of the strong semantics extracted by the backbone due to its early-aware pre-training and *iii)* interchanged at deployment time on top of the shared backbone in a *plug-and-play* manner (without re-training), offering enormous flexibility for customisation (Sect. 5.1).

Positive Filtering Distillation (PFD). In the second stage of our training process, we also exploit the joint potential of knowledge distillation and early-exit networks.

In prior self-distillation works for multi-exit networks, the backbone's final output is used as the teacher for earlier classifiers [70], whose loss function typically combines ground-truth and distillation terms [39,47]. To further exploit what information is back-propagated to the shallow exits, given the pre-trained final exit and taking advantage of the multitude of information available in segmentation predictions due to their dense structure, we propose *Positive Filtering Distillation* (PFD). This technique selectively controls the flow of information of the high-entropy ground-truth reference to earlier exits using only signals from "easier pixels", *i.e.* pixels about which the last exit could yield a correct prediction, while filtering out gradients from more difficult or ambiguous pixels. Our hypothesis is that early-exit heads, having limited learning capacity, can become stronger by only incorporating signals of less ambiguous pixels from the last exit, avoiding noisy gradients and the confusion of trying to mimic contradicting references.

Formally, we express the i-th exit's tensor of predicted classes for each pixel $p = (r, c)$ with $r \in [1, R]$ and $c \in [1, C]$ as $\hat{\boldsymbol{y}}_i \in \{0, 1, ..., M-1\}^{R \times C}$ where $(\hat{\boldsymbol{y}}_i)_p = \arg\max(\boldsymbol{y}_i)_p$ in $\{0, 1, ..., M-1\}$. Given the corresponding output of the final exit $\hat{\boldsymbol{y}}_N$, the ground-truth labels $\hat{\boldsymbol{y}} \in \{0, 1, ..., M-1\}^{R \times C}$ and a hyperparameter α, we employ the following loss during the frozen-backbone stage of our training scheme, where $\mathcal{L}_{\text{KL}}$ is KL-divergence:

$$\mathcal{L}_{\text{PFD}} = \sum_{i=1}^{N} \alpha \cdot \mathbb{1}(\hat{\boldsymbol{y}}_N = \hat{\boldsymbol{y}}) \mathcal{L}_{\text{CE}}(\boldsymbol{y}_i, \hat{\boldsymbol{y}}) + (1 - \alpha) \cdot \mathcal{L}_{\text{KL}}(\boldsymbol{y}_i, \boldsymbol{y}_N) \qquad (3)$$

Fig. 3. Workload breakdown analysis and exit points identification on a DRN-50 [66] backbone ($N = 6$).

Table 1. Cost functions for different inference settings. b_i is the i-th block in the backbone; K_n is the block ordinal of the n-th exit point; $S^{*n}_{\text{exit}} \in S^n_{\text{exit}}$ is the selected architecture for the n-th exit; p_n is the percentage of samples propagated to the n-th exit.

Inference	$cost(s)$
Final-Only	$cost(b_{1:K_N}) + cost(S^{*N}_{\text{exit}})$
Budgeted	$cost(b_{1:K_n}) + cost(S^{*n}_{\text{exit}}), n \leq N$
Anytime	$cost(b_{1:K_N}) + \sum_{n=1}^{N} cost(S^{*n}_{\text{exit}})$
Input-Dep.	$\sum_{n=1}^{N} p_{n-1} \cdot (cost(b_{K_{n-1}:K_n}) + cost(S^{*n}_{\text{exit}})), K_0 = 0, p_0 = 1$

5 MESS Networks Deployment and Inference

Having designed and trained the *overprovisioned* model, here we discuss its customisation to the task- and target-specific deployment for inference. This involves configuring the MESS *instance* architecture via post-training search and crafting the exit policy.

5.1 Deployment-Time Parametrisation

Post-training of the overprovisioned network (comprising *all* candidate exit architectures), MESS instances (comprising a *subset* of the trained exits) can be derived, reflecting on the capabilities of the target device, the required accuracy or latency of the use-case and the intricacy of the inputs.

Inference Settings. To satisfy performance needs under each device and application-specific constraints, MESS networks support different inference settings:

1) Budgeted Inference: in which workload-lighter static submodels, up to a (single) specific exit, are extracted to enable deployment on heterogeneous target platforms.

2) Anytime Inference: in which every sample goes through multiple exits sequentially, initially providing a rapid approximation of the output and progressively refining it through a series of deeper exits until a deadline is met.

3) Input-dependent Inference: where inputs also go through exits sequentially, but each sample dynamically adjusts its path (*i.e.* finalises its output at a different depth) according to its difficulty, as captured by the confidence of each exit's prediction.

Configuration Search. Our framework tailors MESS networks for each of the above settings considering the target use-case, by searching the configuration space post-training. Contrary to most works in multi-exit classification models [20,24,27,71], which employ a uniform architecture across all exits for the sake of simplicity, MESS favours flexibility allowing for per-exit architectural customisation. This is enabled by our overprovisioned training scheme (Sect. 4.3), allowing all trained exits to be interchangeably attached to the same backbone for inference, offering rapid validation of candidate choices that significantly accelerates the search for a tailored design.

The proposed method contemplates all trained exit architectures and exhaustively creates different configurations, trading for example a workload-heavier shallow exit with a more lightweight deeper exit. The search strategy considers the target *inference setting*, along with user-specified requirements in *workload*, *latency* and *accuracy*[2], which can be expressed as a combination of hard constraints and optimisation objectives. As a result, the *number* and *placement* of exits and the *architecture* of each individual exit of the resulting MESS instance are jointly optimised (along with the *exit policy*, discussed in Sect. 5.2, for the input-dependent inference case).

Given the exit-architecture search space $\mathcal{S}^i_{\text{exit}}$ (Eq. 1), we define the overall configuration space of a MESS network as:

$$\mathcal{S} = (\mathcal{S}^1_{\text{exit}} + 1) \times (\mathcal{S}^2_{\text{exit}} + 1) \times ... \times (\mathcal{S}^N_{\text{exit}} + 1) \qquad (4)$$

where the extra term accounts for a *"None"* option for each of the exit positions. Under this formulation, the framework can minimise $workload/latency$, formally expressed as $cost$ for each setting in Table 1, given an $accuracy$ constraint th_{acc}:

$$s^\star = \arg\min_{s \in \mathcal{S}} \{\text{cost}(s) \mid \text{acc}(s) \geq th_{\text{acc}}\} \qquad (5)$$

or optimise for $accuracy$, given a $cost$ constraint th_{cost}:

$$s^\star = \arg\max_{s \in \mathcal{S}} \{\text{acc}(s) \mid \text{cost}(s) \leq th_{\text{cost}}\} \qquad (6)$$

Importantly, a combination of design choices render the *exhaustive exploration* of the search space not only computationally tractable, but extremely efficient. Conversely to heuristic alternatives, this guarantees *optimality* within the examined space. The main enabling factors include: *i)* the informed outlining of the search space (being compact and tailor-made for segmentation), *ii)* the proposed two-stage training scheme (allowing all exits architectures to exploit a shared backbone), *iii)* a vast pruning of configurations at search time (prioritising the less costly constraint verification on latency before

---

[2] Evaluated in a held-out *Calibration Set* during search (equally sized to the target *Test Set*).

evaluating accuracy), and *iv*) prediction memoriisation (eliminating duplicate inference execution by storing and combining per-exit predictions on the calibration set). Finally, in contrast to NAS methods [4], MESS overprovisioned networks are fully trained and can be customised without the need of fine-tuning, offering rapid post-training adaptation.

5.2 Input-Dependent Exit Policy

During input-dependent inference, each input image goes through the selected early exits of the deployed MESS instance sequentially. After a prediction is produced from an exit, a mechanism to calculate its confidence is used to determine whether inference should continue to the next exit or not. In [30], *each pixel* in an image is treated as an independent classification task, exiting early if its prediction confidence in an exit is high, thus yielding irregular computation paths. In contrast, our approach treats the segmentation of *each image* as a single task, aiming to drive each sample through a uniform computation route. To this end, we fill a gap in literature by introducing a novel mechanism to quantify the overall confidence in semantic segmentation predictions.

Confidence Metric. Given the per-pixel confidence map, calculated from the probability distribution across classes of each pixel $c^{\text{map}} = f_c(\boldsymbol{y}) \in [0,1]^{R \times C}$ (where f_c is usually $top1(\cdot)$ [20] or $entropy(\cdot)$ [8]), we introduce a mechanism to reduce these *every-pixel* confidence values to a single *per-image* confidence. The proposed metric considers the *percentage of pixels with high prediction confidence* (i.e. surpassing a tunable threshold th_i^{pix}) in the output of an exit $\boldsymbol{y}_i$:

$$c_i^{\text{img}} = \frac{1}{RC} \sum_{r=1}^{R} \sum_{c=1}^{C} \mathbb{1}(c_{r,c}^{\text{map}}(\boldsymbol{y}_i) \geq th_i^{\text{pix}}) \tag{7}$$

Edge Confidence Enhancement. Moreover, it has been observed that due to the progressive downsampling of the feature volume in CNNs, some spatial information is unavoidably lost. As a result, semantic predictions near object edges are naturally under-confident [54]. Driven by this observation, we enhance our proposed metric to account for these expected low-confidence pixel-predictions, by introducing a preprocessing step for c_i^{img}. Initially, we conduct edge detection on the semantic masks, followed by an erosion filter with kernel equal to the output stride of the respective exit os_i, in order to compute a semantic-edge map (Eq. 8). Thereafter, we apply a median-based smoothing on the confidence values of pixels lying on the semantic edges (Eq. 9).

$$\mathcal{M} = \text{erode}(\text{cannyEdge}(\hat{\boldsymbol{y}}_i), s_i) \tag{8}$$

$$\widehat{c_{r,c}^{\text{map}}}(y_i) = \begin{cases} \text{median}(c_{w_r,w_c}^{\text{map}}(\boldsymbol{y}_i)) & \text{if } \mathcal{M}_{r,c} = 1 \\ c_{r,c}^{\text{map}}(\boldsymbol{y}_i) & \text{otherwise} \end{cases} \tag{9}$$

where $w_l = \{l - 2 \cdot os_i, ..., l + 2 \cdot os_i\}$ is the window size of the filter. *This sets the pixels around semantic edges to inherit the confidence of their neighbouring pixel predictions.*

Exit Policy. At inference time, each sample is sequentially processed by the selected early exits. For each prediction y_i, the proposed metric c_i^{img} is calculated, and a tunable confidence threshold (exposed to the search space) determines whether the sample will exit early ($c_i^{\text{img}} \geq th_i^{\text{img}}$) or be processed further by subsequent backbone layers/exits.

6 Evaluation

6.1 Experimental Setup

Models and Datasets. We apply our methodology on top of DRN-50 [66], DeepLabV3 [6] and SegMBNetV2 [49] segmentation CNNs, using ImageNet [9] pre-trained ResNet50 [17] and MobileNetV2 [49] backbones, representing *high-end* and *edge* use-cases, respectively. We train all backbones on MS COCO [34] and fine-tune early exits on MS COCO and PASCAL VOC [10] (augmented from [16]) independently.

Development and Deployment Setup. MESS networks are implemented on *PyTorch (v1.6.0)*. For inference, we deploy MESS instances on a *high-end* (Nvidia GTX1080Ti; 250W TDP) and an *edge* (Nvidia Jetson AGX Xavier; 30W TDP) compute platform.

Baselines. To compare our work against the following state-of-the-art baselines:

1) **DRN** [66]; *2)* **DLBV3** [7, 66]; *3)* **segMBNetV2** [49]; *4)* **LC** [30]; *5)* **AutoDLB** [35]; *6)* **E2E** [20, 52]; *7)* **Frozen** [24, 27]; *8)* **KD** [18] and *9)* **SelfDistill** [47, 70, 71].

6.2 MESS End-to-End Evaluation

Comparison with Single-Exit Baselines. First, we apply our MESS framework on single-exit segmentation backbones from the literature, namely **DRN**, **DLBV3** and **segMBNetV2**. Table 2 lists the achieved results for MESS instances optimised for varying use-cases (framed as speed/accuracy constraints fed to our configuration search).

Table 2. End-to-end evaluation of MESS network designs

Method		Backbone*	Head	Search targets		Results: MS COCO			Results: PASCAL VOC			
				Error	GFLOPs	mIoU	GFLOPs	Latency†	mIoU	GFLOPs	Latency†
DRN [66]	(i)	ResNet50	FCN	–Baseline–		59.02%	138.63	39.96 ms	72.23%	138.63	39.93 ms
Ours	(ii)	ResNet50	FCN	min	≤1×	64.35%	113.65	37.53 ms	79.09%	113.65	37.59 ms
Ours	(iii)	ResNet50	FCN	≤0.1%	min	58.91%	41.17	17.92 ms	72.16%	44.81	18.63 ms
Ours	(iv)	ResNet50	FCN	≤1%	min	58.12%	34.53	15.11 ms	71.29%	38.51	16.80 ms
DLBV3 [6]	(v)	ResNet50	DLB	–Baseline–		64.94%	163.86	59.05 ms	80.32%	163.86	59.06 ms
Ours	(vi)	ResNet50	DLB	min	≤1×	65.52%	124.10	43.29 ms	82.32%	124.11	43.30 ms
Ours	(vii)	ResNet50	DLB	≤0.1%	min	64.86%	69.84	24.81 ms	80.21%	65.29	24.14 ms
Ours	(viii)	ResNet50	DLB	≤1%	min	64.03%	57.01	20.83 ms	79.30%	50.29	20.11 ms
segMBNetV2 [49]	(ix)	MobileNetV2	FCN	–Baseline–		54.24%	8.78	67.04 ms	69.68%	8.78	67.06 ms
Ours	(x)	MobileNetV2	FCN	min	≤1×	57.49%	8.10	56.05 ms	74.22%	8.10	56.09 ms
Ours	(xi)	MobileNetV2	FCN	≤0.1%	min	54.18%	4.05	40.97 ms	69.61%	3.92	32.79 ms
Ours	(xii)	MobileNetV2	FCN	≤1%	min	53.24%	3.48	38.83 ms	68.80%	3.60	31.40 ms

*Dilated network [66] based on backbone CNN. †Measured on: GTX for ResNet50 and AGX for MobileNetV2 backbone.

Table 3. Comparison with LC (speedup to backbone)

Head	Search target	Exit points	Exit policy	
			LC [30]	Ours
FCN	Error $\leq$ 0.1%	3-exit: $\{\mathcal{E}_1, \mathcal{E}_3, \mathcal{E}_6\}$	1.13×	**3.36×**
FCN	Error $\leq$ 10.0%	2-exit: $\{\mathcal{E}_1, \mathcal{E}_6\}$	0.98×	**6.02×**

Table 4. Comparison with SOTA NAS approach

Method	Approach	ImgNet	Training*	Adaptation*		mIoU	GFLOPs
				Search	Re-training		
DLBV3 [6]	Baseline	✓	192	-Non-adaptive-		80.32%	163.86
AutoDLB [35]	NAS	-	12,248	72	12,176	79.78%	57.61
Ours	MESS	✓	2,580	<1	-	79.94%	51.59

*Initial-training and Adaptation times expressed in GPU-hours.

For a DRN-50 backbone on MS COCO, we observe that a latency-optimised MESS instance achieves a 3.36× workload reduction with no accuracy drop (row (iii)), translating to a latency speedup of 2.23× over the single-exit **DRN** (row (i)). This improvement is amplified to 4.01× in workload (2.65× in latency) for use-cases that can tolerate a controlled accuracy degradation of $\leq$1 pp (row (iv)). Additionally, a MESS instance optimised for accuracy under the same workload budget as **DRN**, can achieve an mIoU gain of 5.33 pp compared to **DRN**, with 1.22× fewer GFLOPs (row (ii)).

Similar results are obtained for **DLBV3**, as well as when targeting PASCAL VOC. Moreover, the gains are consistent on **segMBNetV2**, which forms an inherently efficient segmentation model, with 15.7× smaller workload than DRN-50. This demonstrates the model-agnostic nature of our framework, yielding complementary gains to efficient backbone design, by exploiting the orthogonal dimension of input-dependent inference.

Comparison with Multi-Exit Baselines. Next, we compare MESS networks against *Deep Layer Cascade* (**LC**) [30], the current SOTA in multi-exit segmentation, which proposes *per-pixel* early-exiting through multiple segmentation heads. Due to their unstructured computation, standard BLAS libraries cannot realise true latency benefits from this approach. However, we apply **LC**'s pixel-level exit policy on diverse MESS configurations, and compare with our image-level policy analytically (in GFLOPs), tuning both thresholds so as to meet varying accuracy requirements.

By using SOTA techniques for semantic segmentation, such as larger dilation rates or DeepLab's ASPP, the gains of **LC** rapidly fade away, as for each pixel that propagates deeper on, a substantial feature volume needs to be precomputed. Concretely, when employing **LC** on our designs, up to a substantial 45% of the feature volume at the output of the first exit falls within the receptive field of a *single pixel* in the final output for the case of *FCN-Head*, reaching 100% for *DLB-Head*. As a result, **LC**'s policy presents heavily dissipated to no reduction in workload against the corresponding single-exit baselines, being heavily reliant on the exit placement. In contrast, the respective MESS instances equipped with our proposed exit policy (Sect. 5.2) are able to achieve significant workload reduction, reported in Table 3.

Comparison with NAS Baselines. Finally, we position our work against NAS solutions for deriving efficient segmentation models. We employ Auto-DeepLab (**AutoDLB**) [35] as our strong baseline, due to its SOTA performance both in accuracy and search efficiency, and use our framework to generate a MESS instance matching its accuracy (staring from DeepLabV3 [6] backbone). Table 4 lists our findings on PASCAL VOC.

Remarkably, MESS achieves a better (but comparable) speed-accuracy trade-off than **AutoDLB** ($3.17\times$ vs $2.85\times$ speedup over DeepLabV3), although the latter samples from a larger space during search (10^{19} points vs 10^6) and takes advantage of more degrees of freedom during training. Additionally, being able to exploit ImageNet pre-trained backbones, MESS demonstrates significant training time savings ($4.7\times$ faster) compared to NAS-crafted models like **AutoDLB**, that can only be trained from scratch.

Most importantly, due to our "train-once-deploy-everywhere" design, enabled by the two-stage training approach of MESS, after the initial training of the overprovisioned MESS network *all 10^6 possible MESS instances are ready-to-deploy* without any need for re-training. Alternatively, training end-to-end all 10^6 MESS instances would require >200 million GPU-hours. As a result, different MESS instances can be obtained with a minimal search cost (<1 GPU-hour). Overall, MESS offers up to five orders of magnitude faster adaptation time compared to NAS-based methodologies.

6.3 MESS Training Evaluation

Having shown the benefits of MESS networks against different state-of-the-art methods, we now move to the evaluation of specific components of our framework.

Exit-Aware Pre-training. Initially, we demonstrate the effectiveness of the proposed training scheme. We compare the accuracy of models with uniform exit configuration across all candidate exits points, trained using different strategies. Table 5 summarises the results of this comparison on a DRN-50 backbone with $N = 6$, on MS COCO.

When multiple exits are attached to the backbone and jointly trained end-to-end, as in [20,52], the accuracy of the final exit can notably degrade (row (ii)) compared to a vanilla training of the backbone with solely the final exit attached (row(i)). This is attributed to contradicting gradient signals between the early and the late classifiers and to the larger losses of the early results, which dominate the loss function [3]. On the other hand, freezing the weights of the vanilla backbone of row (i) and independently training the same early exits, as in [24,27], leads to degraded accuracy in shallow exits (row (iv)). This is due to the limited degrees of freedom of this second training stage and the weaker semantics extracted by shallow layers of the frozen backbone.

Our (1st-stage) exit-aware pre-training pushes the extraction of semantically strong features towards shallow parts of the network, while yielding the highest accuracy on the final exit (row (iii)). Similar to observations from [51], we fathom that the extra signal midway through the model acts both as a regulariser and as an extra backpropagation source, reducing the effect of vanishing gradients.

Capitalising on this exit-aware pre-trained backbone, and without any harm of the final exit's accuracy, our subsequent frozen backbone training achieves consistently higher accuracy (up to 12.57 pp) across all exits (row (v)) compared to a traditionally pre-trained segmentation network (**Frozen**), and up to 3.38 pp compared to an end-to-end trained model (**E2E**), which also suffers a 1.57 pp accuracy drop in the final exit.

Table 5. Evaluation of two-stage training scheme on DRN-50 (mIoU).

Method	Init.	Loss	$\mathcal{E}_1$	$\mathcal{E}_2$	$\mathcal{E}_3$	$\mathcal{E}_4$	$\mathcal{E}_5$	$\mathcal{E}_6$
(i) Baseline Init	ImageNet	$\mathcal{L}_{CE}(\mathcal{E}_6)$	-	-	-	-	-	59.02%
(ii) E2E [20,52]	ImageNet	$\mathcal{L}_{CE}(\mathcal{E}_1)+...+\mathcal{L}_{CE}(\mathcal{E}_6)$	29.02%	40.67%	48.64%	51.69%	55.34%	58.33%
(iii) Exit-aware Init	ImageNet	Eq. (2) (Ours)	28.21%	39.61%	47.13%	50.81%	56.11%	59.90%
(iv) Frozen [24,27]	(i)	$\mathcal{L}_{CE}(\mathcal{E}_1), ..., \mathcal{L}_{CE}(\mathcal{E}_5)$	23.94%	31.50%	38.24%	44.73%	54.32%	59.02%
(v) Ours (Sect. 4.3)	(iii)	$\mathcal{L}_{CE}(\mathcal{E}_1), ..., \mathcal{L}_{CE}(\mathcal{E}_5)$	**32.40%**	**43.34%**	**50.81%**	**53.73%**	**57.9%**	**59.90%**

* Experiments repeated 3 times. The sample stdev in mean IoU is at most ± 0.09 in all cases.

Table 6. Evaluation of Positive Filtering Distillation (mIoU)

Method	Loss	DRN-50			MobileNetV2		
		$\mathcal{E}_1$	$\mathcal{E}_2$	$\mathcal{E}_3$	$\mathcal{E}_1$	$\mathcal{E}_2$	$\mathcal{E}_3$
E2E [20,52]	CE	49.96%	55.40%	58.96%	31.56%	41.57%	51.59%
KD [18]	KD	50.33%	55.67%	59.08%	31.04%	41.93%	51.66%
SelfDistill [47,70,71]	CE+KD	50.66%	55.91%	58.84%	32.08%	41.96%	51.58%
Ours (Sect. 4.3)	PFD	**51.02%**	**56.21%**	**59.36%**	**33.36%**	**42.95%**	**52.20%**

CE = Cross-entropy, KD = Knowledge Distillation, PFD = Positive Filtering Distillation

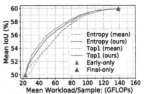

Fig. 4. Comparison of different early-exit policies on a DRN-50-based MESS instance with two exits.

Positive Filtering Distillation. Here, we quantify the benefits of Positive Filtering Distillation (PFD) for the second stage (frozen-backbone) of our training methodology. To this end, we compare against **E2E** utilising cross-entropy loss (**CE**), traditional knowledge distillation (**KD**), and **SelfDistill** approach commonly used in multi-exit classification. Table 6 summarises our results on a representative exit-architecture, on both DRN-50 and MobileNetV2, across MS COCO validation set.

Our proposed loss consistently yields higher accuracy across all cases, achieving up to 1.8, 2.32 and 1.28 pp accuracy gains over **E2E**, **KD** and **SelfDistill**, respectively. This accuracy boost is more salient on shallow exits, whereas a narrower improvement is obtained in deeper exits where the accuracy gap to the final exit is natively bridged.

6.4 MESS Deployment Under Different Settings

In this section, we showcase the effectiveness and flexibility of the proposed *train-once, deploy-everywhere* approach for semantic segmentation. There are three inference settings in MESS networks: *i)* budgeted, *ii)* anytime and *iii)* input-dependent, for which we optimise separately *post-training* (Sect. 5.1). Here, we employ our search to find the best single early-exit architecture for each case, using a 50% mIoU requirement. The results are summarised in Table 7. Figure 5 also depicts the underlying workload-accuracy relationship across the architectural configuration space for DRN-50 backbone. Different points represent different architectures, colour-coded by their placement in the network.

Budgeted Inference. In this setting, we search for a *single-exit submodel* that can execute within a given latency/memory/accuracy target. Our method is able to provide the most efficient MESS instance, tailored to the requirements of the underlying application and target device (Table 7; row (ii)). This optimality gets translated in Fig. 5a, showcasing the cost-accuracy trade-off from the input until the respective early exit of the network, in the presence of candidate design points along the Pareto front of the search space. In this setting, our search tends to favour designs with powerful exit architectures, consisting of multiple trainable layers, mounted earlier in the network (Fig. 6a).

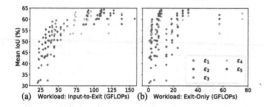

(a) Workload: Input-to-Exit (GFLOPs)   (b) Workload: Exit-Only (GFLOPs)

Fig. 5. Workload-accuracy trade-off between design points. Capturing: (a) input-to-exit workload, (b) the overhead of each exit.

Table 7. DRN-50 with one early exit optimised for different inference schemes (Requirement of 50% mIoU)

	Inference	Workload (GFLOPs)		mIoU	
		Overhead	$\mathcal{E}_{early}$	$\mathcal{E}_{final}$	$\mathcal{E}_{early}$	$\mathcal{E}_{final}$
(i)	Final-Only	-	-	138.63	-	59.90%
(ii)	Budgeted	8.01	28.34	-	51.76%	-
(iii)	Anytime	0.69	39.32	139.33	50.37%	59.90%
(iv)	Input-Dep	2.54	($\mathcal{E}_{sel}$: 23.02)	($\mathcal{E}_{sel}$: 50.03%)		

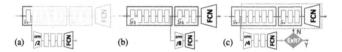

(a)   (b)   (c)

Fig. 6. Selected design points for: (a) budgeted, (b) anytime and (c) input-dependent inference, with the same accuracy target.

Anytime Inference. In this setting, each sample is sequentially processed by multiple exits, progressively refining its prediction. When a deadline is met or a result is needed, the last available output of the multi-exit network is asynchronously returned. This paradigm creates an inherent trade-off: denser exits provide more frequent "checkpoints", whereas each added head adds computational overhead when not explicitly used. To control this trade-off, our method considers the additional computational cost of each exit, when populating the MESS network architecture (Fig. 5b). Contrary to budgeted inference, in this setting our search produces heads with extremely lightweight architecture, sacrificing flexibility for reduced computational overhead, mounted deeper in the network (Fig. 6b). Table 7 showcases that, for anytime inference (row (iii)), our search yields an exit architecture with 11.6× less computational requirements compared to budgeted inference (row (ii)), under the same accuracy constraint.

Input-Dependent Inference. In this setting, each input sample propagates through the selected MESS instance until the model yields a confident-enough prediction ($\mathcal{E}_{sel}$). By selecting different threshold values for the confidence-based exit policy (Sect. 5.2), even the simplest (2-exit) configuration of input-dependent MESS network (Fig. 6c) provides a fine-grained trade-off between workload and accuracy. Exploiting this trade-off, we observe that input-dependent inference (Table 7; row (iv)) offers the highest computational efficiency under the same (50% mIoU) constraint.

Confidence Metric: To evaluate MESS exit-policy, we apply the proposed *image-level* confidence metric for segmentation, on top of both *top1* [20] and *entropy* [52]-based *pixel-level* confidence estimators, commonly used in multi-exit classification. Our experiments with various architectural configurations indicate that the proposed exit-policy offers a consistently better speed-accuracy trade-off compared to corresponding averaging counterparts (directly generalising from classification-based metrics by averaging per-pixel confidences for each image), with accuracy gains of up to 6.34 pp (1.17 pp on average). An example of this trade-off is illustrated in Fig. 4.

7   Conclusion

In this paper, we have presented the concept and realisation of multi-exit semantic segmentation. Applicable to state-of-the-art CNN approaches, MESS models perform efficient semantic segmentation, without sacrificing accuracy. This is achieved by introducing novel training and early-exiting techniques, tailored for MESS networks. Post-training, our framework can customise the MESS network by searching for the optimal multi-exit configuration (number, placement and architecture of exits) according to the target platform, pushing the limits of efficient deployment.

References

1. Almeida, M., Laskaridis, S., Leontiadis, I., Venieris, S.I., Lane, N.D.: EmBench: quantifying performance variations of deep neural networks across modern commodity devices. In: The 3rd International Workshop on Deep Learning for Mobile Systems and Applications (EMDL) (2019)
2. Badrinarayanan, V., Kendall, A., Cipolla, R.: SegNet: a deep convolutional encoder-decoder architecture for image segmentation. IEEE Trans. Pattern Anal. Mach. Intell. (TPAMI) **39**(12), 2481–2495 (2017)
3. Bolukbasi, T., Wang, J., Dekel, O., Saligrama, V.: Adaptive neural networks for efficient inference. In: International Conference on Machine Learning (ICML), pp. 527–536 (2017)
4. Chen, L.-C., et al.: Searching for efficient multi-scale architectures for dense image prediction. In: Advances in Neural Information Processing Systems (NeurIPS), pp. 8699–8710 (2018)
5. Chen, L.-C., Papandreou, G., Kokkinos, I., Murphy, K., Yuille, A.L.: DeepLab: semantic image segmentation with deep convolutional nets, atrous convolution, and fully connected CRFs. IEEE Trans. Pattern Anal. Mach. Intell. (TPAMI) **40**(4), 834–848 (2017)
6. Chen, L.-C., Papandreou, G., Schroff, F., Adam, H.: Rethinking atrous convolution for semantic image segmentation. arXiv preprint arXiv:1706.05587 (2017)
7. Chen, L.-C., Zhu, Y., Papandreou, G., Schroff, F., Adam, H.: Encoder-decoder with atrous separable convolution for semantic image segmentation. In: Ferrari, V., Hebert, M., Sminchisescu, C., Weiss, Y. (eds.) ECCV 2018. LNCS, vol. 11211, pp. 833–851. Springer, Cham (2018). https://doi.org/10.1007/978-3-030-01234-2_49
8. Cheng, F., Zhang, H., Yuan, D., Sun, M.: Leveraging semantic segmentation with learning-based confidence measure. Neurocomputing **329**, 21–31 (2019)
9. Deng, J., Dong, W., Socher, R., Li, L.-J., Li, K., Fei-Fei, L.: ImageNet: a large-scale hierarchical image database. In: IEEE Conference on Computer Vision and Pattern Recognition (CVPR), pp. 248–255 (2009)
10. Everingham, M., Van Gool, L., Williams, C.K.I., Winn, J., Zisserman, A.: The Pascal visual object classes (VOC) challenge. Int. J. Comput. Vis. (IJCV) **88**(2), 303–338 (2010)
11. Fang, B., Zeng, X., Zhang, M.: NestDNN: resource-aware multi-tenant on-device deep learning for continuous mobile vision. In: Annual International Conference on Mobile Computing and Networking (MobiCom), pp. 115–127 (2018)
12. Figurnov, M.: Spatially adaptive computation time for residual networks. In: IEEE Conference on Computer Vision and Pattern Recognition (CVPR), pp. 1039–1048 (2017)

13. Gao, X., Zhao, Y., Dudziak, Ł., Mullins, R., Xu, C.Z.: Dynamic channel pruning: feature boosting and suppression. In: International Conference on Learning Representations (ICLR) (2019)
14. Ghiasi, G., Fowlkes, C.C.: Laplacian pyramid reconstruction and refinement for semantic segmentation. In: Leibe, B., Matas, J., Sebe, N., Welling, M. (eds.) ECCV 2016. LNCS, vol. 9907, pp. 519–534. Springer, Cham (2016). https://doi.org/10.1007/978-3-319-46487-9_32
15. Ghosh, S., Das, N., Das, I., Maulik, U.: Understanding deep learning techniques for image segmentation. ACM Comput. Surv. (CSUR) 52(4), 1–35 (2019)
16. Hariharan, B., Arbeláez, P., Bourdev, L., Maji, S., Malik, J.: Semantic contours from inverse detectors. In: International Conference on Computer Vision (ICCV), pp. 991–998 (2011)
17. He, K., Zhang, X., Ren, S., Sun, J.: Deep residual learning for image recognition. In: IEEE Conference on Computer Vision and Pattern Recognition (CVPR), pp. 770–778 (2016)
18. Hinton, G., Vinyals, O., Dean, J.: Distilling the knowledge in a neural network. In: NeurIPS 2014 Deep Learning Workshop (2014)
19. Hua, W., Zhou, Y., De Sa, C.M., Zhang, Z., Edward Suh, G.: Channel gating neural networks. In: Advances in Neural Information Processing Systems (NeurIPS), pp. 1886–1896 (2019)
20. Huang, G., Chen, D., Li, T., Wu, F., van der Maaten, L., Weinberger, K.: Multi-scale dense networks for resource efficient image classification. In: International Conference on Learning Representations (ICLR) (2018)
21. Huang, G., Liu, Z., Van Der Maaten, L., Weinberger, K.Q.: Densely connected convolutional networks. In: IEEE Conference on Computer Vision and Pattern Recognition (CVPR), pp. 4700–4708 (2017)
22. Ignatov, A., et al.: AI benchmark: all about deep learning on smartphones in 2019. In: International Conference on Computer Vision (ICCV) Workshops (2019)
23. Jiang, J., Wang, X., Long, M., Wang, J.: Resource efficient domain adaptation. In: ACM International Conference on Multimedia (MM) (2020)
24. Kaya, Y., Hong, S., Dumitras, T.: Shallow-deep networks: understanding and mitigating network overthinking. In: International Conference on Machine Learning (ICML) (2019)
25. Laskaridis, S., Kouris, A., Lane, N.D.: Adaptive inference through early-exit networks: design, challenges and directions. In: Proceedings of the 5th International Workshop on Embedded and Mobile Deep Learning (EMDL), pp. 1–6 (2021)
26. Laskaridis, S., Venieris, S.I., Almeida, M., Leontiadis, I., Lane, N.D.: SPINN: synergistic progressive inference of neural networks over device and cloud. In: Annual International Conference on Mobile Computing and Networking (MobiCom). ACM (2020)
27. Laskaridis, S., Venieris, S.I., Kim, H., Lane, N.D.: HAPI: hardware-aware progressive inference. In: International Conference on Computer-Aided Design (ICCAD) (2020)
28. Leontiadis, I., Laskaridis, S., Venieris, S.I., Lane, N.D.: It's always personal: using early exits for efficient on-device CNN personalisation. In: Proceedings of the 22nd International Workshop on Mobile Computing Systems and Applications (HotMobile) (2021)
29. Li, H., Zhang, H., Qi, X., Yang, R., Huang, G.: Improved techniques for training adaptive deep networks. In: IEEE International Conference on Computer Vision (ICCV) (2019)
30. Li, X., Liu, Z., Luo, P., Loy, C.C., Tang, X.: Not all pixels are equal: difficulty-aware semantic segmentation via deep layer cascade. In: IEEE Conference on Computer Vision and Pattern Recognition (CVPR), pp. 3193–3202 (2017)
31. Li, Y., et al.: Learning dynamic routing for semantic segmentation. In: IEEE/CVF Conference on Computer Vision and Pattern Recognition (CVPR), pp. 8553–8562 (2020)
32. Lin, G., Milan, A., Shen, C., Reid, I.: RefineNet: multi-path refinement networks for high-resolution semantic segmentation. In: IEEE Conference on Computer Vision and Pattern Recognition (CVPR), pp. 1925–1934 (2017)
33. Lin, J., Rao, Y., Lu, J., Zhou, J.: Runtime neural pruning. In: Advances in Neural Information Processing Systems (NeurIPS), pp. 2181–2191 (2017)

34. Lin, T.-Y., et al.: Microsoft COCO: common objects in context. In: Fleet, D., Pajdla, T., Schiele, B., Tuytelaars, T. (eds.) ECCV 2014. LNCS, vol. 8693, pp. 740–755. Springer, Cham (2014). https://doi.org/10.1007/978-3-319-10602-1_48

35. Liu, C., et al.: Auto-DeepLab: hierarchical neural architecture search for semantic image segmentation. In: IEEE Conference on Computer Vision and Pattern Recognition (CVPR), pp. 82–92 (2019)

36. Liu, L., Li, H., Gruteser, M.: Edge assisted real-time object detection for mobile augmented reality. In: Annual International Conference on Mobile Computing and Networking (Mobi-Com) (2019)

37. Liu, Y., Chen, K., Liu, C., Qin, Z., Luo, Z., Wang, J.: Structured knowledge distillation for semantic segmentation. In: IEEE Conference on Computer Vision and Pattern Recognition (CVPR) (2019)

38. Long, J., Shelhamer, E., Darrell, T.: Fully convolutional networks for semantic segmentation. In: IEEE Conference on Computer Vision and Pattern Recognition (CVPR), pp. 3431–3440 (2015)

39. Luan, Y., Zhao, H., Yang, Z., Dai, Y.: MSD: multi-self-distillation learning via multi-classifiers within deep neural networks. arXiv:1911.09418 (2019)

40. Luc, P., Couprie, C., Chintala, S., Verbeek, J.: Semantic segmentation using adversarial networks. In: NIPSW on Adversarial Training (2016)

41. McCormac, J., Handa, A., Davison, A., Leutenegger, S.: SemanticFusion: dense 3D semantic mapping with convolutional neural networks. In: 2017 IEEE International Conference on Robotics and Automation (ICRA), pp. 4628–4635. IEEE (2017)

42. Mehta, S., Rastegari, M., Caspi, A., Shapiro, L., Hajishirzi, H.: ESPNet: efficient spatial pyramid of dilated convolutions for semantic segmentation. In: Ferrari, V., Hebert, M., Sminchisescu, C., Weiss, Y. (eds.) ECCV 2018. LNCS, vol. 11214, pp. 561–580. Springer, Cham (2018). https://doi.org/10.1007/978-3-030-01249-6_34

43. Nekrasov, V., Chen, H., Shen, C., Reid, I.: Fast neural architecture search of compact semantic segmentation models via auxiliary cells. In: IEEE Conference on Computer Vision and Pattern Recognition (CVPR), pp. 9126–9135 (2019)

44. Noh, H., Hong, S., Han, B.: Learning deconvolution network for semantic segmentation. In: IEEE International Conference on Computer Vision (ICCV), pp. 1520–1528 (2015)

45. NVIDIA. NVIDIA Maxine - Cloud-AI Video-Streaming Platform (2020). https://developer.nvidia.com/maxine. Accessed 10 Jan 2022

46. Peng, C., Zhang, X., Yu, G., Luo, G., Sun, J.: Large kernel matters-improve semantic segmentation by global convolutional network. In: IEEE Conference on Computer Vision and Pattern Recognition (CVPR), pp. 4353–4361 (2017)

47. Phuong, M., Lampert, C.H.: Distillation-based training for multi-exit architectures. In: IEEE International Conference on Computer Vision (ICCV), pp. 1355–1364 (2019)

48. Ronneberger, O., Fischer, P., Brox, T.: U-Net: convolutional networks for biomedical image segmentation. In: Navab, N., Hornegger, J., Wells, W.M., Frangi, A.F. (eds.) MICCAI 2015. LNCS, vol. 9351, pp. 234–241. Springer, Cham (2015). https://doi.org/10.1007/978-3-319-24574-4_28

49. Sandler, M., Howard, A., Zhu, M., Zhmoginov, A., Chen, L.-C.: MobileNetV2: inverted residuals and linear bottlenecks. In: IEEE Conference on Computer Vision and Pattern Recognition (CVPR), pp. 4510–4520 (2018)

50. Siam, M., Gamal, M., Abdel-Razek, M., Yogamani, S., Jagersand, M., Zhang, H.: A comparative study of real-time semantic segmentation for autonomous driving. In: Conference on Computer Vision and Pattern Recognition (CVPR) Workshops (2018)

51. Szegedy, C., et al.: Going deeper with convolutions. In: IEEE Conference on Computer Vision and Pattern Recognition (CVPR) (2015)

52. Teerapittayanon, S., McDanel, B., Kung, H.-T.: BranchyNet: fast inference via early exiting from deep neural networks. In: 2016 23rd International Conference on Pattern Recognition (ICPR), pp. 2464–2469. IEEE (2016)

53. Veit, A., Belongie, S.: Convolutional networks with adaptive inference graphs. In: Ferrari, V., Hebert, M., Sminchisescu, C., Weiss, Y. (eds.) ECCV 2018. LNCS, vol. 11205, pp. 3–18. Springer, Cham (2018). https://doi.org/10.1007/978-3-030-01246-5_1

54. Vu, T.-H., Jain, H., Bucher, M., Cord, M., Pérez, P.: ADVENT: adversarial entropy minimization for domain adaptation in semantic segmentation. In: IEEE Conference on Computer Vision and Pattern Recognition (CVPR), pp. 2517–2526 (2019)

55. Wang, X., Yu, F., Dou, Z.-Y., Darrell, T., Gonzalez, J.E.: SkipNet: learning dynamic routing in convolutional networks. In: Ferrari, V., Hebert, M., Sminchisescu, C., Weiss, Y. (eds.) ECCV 2018. LNCS, vol. 11217, pp. 420–436. Springer, Cham (2018). https://doi.org/10.1007/978-3-030-01261-8_25

56. Wang, Y., Zhang, X., Hu, X., Zhang, B., Su, H.: Dynamic network pruning with interpretable layerwise channel selection. In: AAAI Conference on Artificial Intelligence (AAAI), pp. 6299–6306 (2020)

57. Wu, H., Zhang, J., Huang, K., Liang, K., Yizhou, Y.: FastFCN: rethinking dilated convolution in the backbone for semantic segmentation. arXiv preprint arXiv:1903.11816 (2019)

58. Wu, Z., et al.: BlockDrop: dynamic inference paths in residual networks. In: IEEE Conference on Computer Vision and Pattern Recognition (CVPR), pp. 8817–8826 (2018)

59. Xin, J., Tang, R., Lee, J., Yu, Y., Lin, J.: DeeBERT: dynamic early exiting for accelerating BERT inference. In: 58th Annual Meeting of the Association for Computational Linguistics (ACL), pp. 2246–2251 (2020)

60. Xing, Q., Xu, M., Li, T., Guan, Z.: Early exit or not: resource-efficient blind quality enhancement for compressed images. In: Vedaldi, A., Bischof, H., Brox, T., Frahm, J.-M. (eds.) ECCV 2020. LNCS, vol. 12361, pp. 275–292. Springer, Cham (2020). https://doi.org/10.1007/978-3-030-58517-4_17

61. Xu, H., Gao, Y., Yu, F., Darrell, T.: End-to-end learning of driving models from large-scale video datasets. In: IEEE Conference on Computer Vision and Pattern Recognition (CVPR), pp. 2174–2182 (2017)

62. Yao, Z., Cao, S., Xiao, W., Zhang, C., Nie, L.: Balanced sparsity for efficient DNN inference on GPU. In: AAAI Conference on Artificial Intelligence (AAAI) 33, pp. 5676–5683 (2019)

63. Yi, J., Lee, Y.: Heimdall: mobile GPU coordination platform for augmented reality applications. In: Annual International Conference on Mobile Computing and Networking (MobiCom) (2020)

64. Yu, C., Wang, J., Peng, C., Gao, C., Yu, G., Sang, N.: BiSeNet: bilateral segmentation network for real-time semantic segmentation. In: Ferrari, V., Hebert, M., Sminchisescu, C., Weiss, Y. (eds.) ECCV 2018. LNCS, vol. 11217, pp. 334–349. Springer, Cham (2018). https://doi.org/10.1007/978-3-030-01261-8_20

65. Yu, F., Koltun, V.: Multi-scale context aggregation by dilated convolutions. In: International Conference on Learning Representations (ICLR) (2016)

66. Yu, F., Koltun, V., Funkhouser, T.: Dilated residual networks. In: IEEE Conference on Computer Vision and Pattern Recognition (CVPR), pp. 472–480 (2017)

67. Yuan, Z., Wu, B., Sun, G., Liang, Z., Zhao, S., Bi, W.: S2DNAS: transforming static CNN model for dynamic inference via neural architecture search. In: Vedaldi, A., Bischof, H., Brox, T., Frahm, J.-M. (eds.) ECCV 2020. LNCS, vol. 12347, pp. 175–192. Springer, Cham (2020). https://doi.org/10.1007/978-3-030-58536-5_11

68. Zakharov, E., Ivakhnenko, A., Shysheya, A., Lempitsky, V.: Fast bi-layer neural synthesis of one-shot realistic head avatars. In: Vedaldi, A., Bischof, H., Brox, T., Frahm, J.-M. (eds.) ECCV 2020. LNCS, vol. 12357, pp. 524–540. Springer, Cham (2020). https://doi.org/10.1007/978-3-030-58610-2_31

69. Zeng, D., et al.: Towards cardiac intervention assistance: hardware-aware neural architecture exploration for real-time 3D cardiac cine MRI segmentation. In: ACM/IEEE International Conference on Computer-Aided Design (ICCAD) (2020)

70. Zhang, L., Song, J., Gao, A., Chen, J., Bao, C., Ma, K.: Be your own teacher: improve the performance of convolutional neural networks via self distillation. In: IEEE International Conference on Computer Vision (ICCV) (2019)

71. Zhang, L., Tan, Z., Song, J., Chen, J., Bao, C., Ma, K.: SCAN: a scalable neural networks framework towards compact and efficient models. In: Advances in Neural Information Processing Systems (NeurIPS) (2019)

72. Zhao, H., Qi, X., Shen, X., Shi, J., Jia, J.: ICNet for real-time semantic segmentation on high-resolution images. In: Ferrari, V., Hebert, M., Sminchisescu, C., Weiss, Y. (eds.) ECCV 2018. LNCS, vol. 11207, pp. 418–434. Springer, Cham (2018). https://doi.org/10.1007/978-3-030-01219-9_25

73. Zhao, H., Shi, J., Qi, X., Wang, X., Jia, J.: Pyramid scene parsing network. In: IEEE Conference on Computer Vision and Pattern Recognition (CVPR), pp. 2881–2890 (2017)

74. Zhou, Z., Chen, X., Li, E., Zeng, L., Luo, K., Zhang, J.: Edge intelligence: paving the last mile of artificial intelligence with edge computing. Proc. IEEE **107**(8), 1738–1762 (2019)

Almost-Orthogonal Layers for Efficient General-Purpose Lipschitz Networks

Bernd Prach[(✉)] and Christoph H. Lampert

Institute of Science and Technology Austria (ISTA), Klosterneuburg, Austria
{bprach,chl}@ist.ac.at

Abstract. It is a highly desirable property for deep networks to be robust against small input changes. One popular way to achieve this property is by designing networks with a small Lipschitz constant. In this work, we propose a new technique for constructing such *Lipschitz networks* that has a number of desirable properties: it can be applied to any linear network layer (fully-connected or convolutional), it provides formal guarantees on the Lipschitz constant, it is easy to implement and efficient to run, and it can be combined with any training objective and optimization method. In fact, our technique is the first one in the literature that achieves all of these properties simultaneously.

Our main contribution is a rescaling-based weight matrix parametrization that guarantees each network layer to have a Lipschitz constant of at most 1 and results in the learned weight matrices to be close to orthogonal. Hence we call such layers *almost-orthogonal Lipschitz (AOL)*. Experiments and ablation studies in the context of image classification with certified robust accuracy confirm that AOL layers achieve results that are on par with most existing methods. Yet, they are simpler to implement and more broadly applicable, because they do not require computationally expensive matrix orthogonalization or inversion steps as part of the network architecture.

We provide code at https://github.com/berndprach/AOL.

Keywords: Lipschitz networks · Orthogonality · Robustness

1 Introduction

Deep networks are often the undisputed state of the art when it comes to solving computer vision tasks with high accuracy. However, the resulting systems tend to be not very *robust*, e.g., against small changes in the input data. This makes them untrustworthy for safety-critical high-stakes tasks, such as autonomous driving or medical diagnosis.

A typical example of this phenomenon are *adversarial examples* [20]: imperceptibly small changes to an image can drastically change the outputs of a

Supplementary Information The online version contains supplementary material available at https://doi.org/10.1007/978-3-031-19803-8_21.

deep learning classifier when chosen in an adversarial way. Since their discovery, numerous methods were developed to make networks more robust against adversarial examples. However, in response a comparable number of new attack forms were found, leading to an ongoing cat-and-mouse game. For surveys on the state of research, see, e.g., [6,17,26].

A more principled alternative is to create deep networks that are robust by design, for example, by restricting the class of functions they can represent. Specifically, if one can ensure that a network has a small *Lipschitz constant*, then one knows that small changes to the input data will not result in large changes to the output, even if the changes are chosen adversarially.

A number of methods for designing such *Lipschitz networks* have been proposed in the literature, which we discuss in Sect. 3. However, all of them have individual limitations. In this work, we introduce the AOL (for *almost-orthogonal Lipschitz*) method. It is the first method for constructing Lipschitz networks that simultaneously meets all of the following desirable criteria:

Generality. AOL is applicable to a wide range of network architectures, in particular most kinds of fully-connected and convolutional layers. In contrast, many recent methods work only for a restricted set of layer types, such as only fully-connected layers or only convolutional layers with non-overlapping receptive fields.

Formal Guarantees. AOL provably guarantees a Lipschitz constant 1. This is in contrast to methods that only encourage small Lipschitz constants, e.g., by regularization.

Efficiency. AOL causes only a small computational overhead at training time and none at all at prediction time. This is in contrast to methods that embed expensive iterative operations such as matrix orthogonalization or inversion steps into the network layers.

Modularity. AOL can be treated as a black-box module and combined with arbitrary training objective functions and optimizers. This is in contrast to methods that achieve the Lipschitz property only when combined with, e.g., specific loss-rescaling or projection steps during training.

AOL's name stems from the fact that the weight matrices it learns are approximately orthogonal. In contrast to prior work, this property is not enforced explicitly, which would incur a computational cost. Instead, almost-orthogonal weight matrices emerge organically during network training. The reason is that AOL's rescaling step relies on an upper bound to the Lipschitz constant that is tight for parameter matrices with orthogonal columns. During training, matrices without that property are put at the disadvantage of resulting in outputs of smaller dynamic range. As a consequence, orthogonal matrices are able to achieve smaller values of the loss and are therefore preferred by the optimizer.

2   Notation and Background

A function $f : \mathbb{R}^n \to \mathbb{R}^m$ is called *L-Lipschitz continuous* with respect to norms $\|.\|_{\mathbb{R}^n}$ and $\|.\|_{\mathbb{R}^m}$, if it fulfills

$$\|f(x) - f(y)\|_{\mathbb{R}^m} \leq L\|x - y\|_{\mathbb{R}^n}, \tag{1}$$

for all x and y, where L is called the *Lipschitz constant*. In this work we only consider Lipschitz-continuity with respect to the Euclidean norm, $\|.\|_2$, and mainly for $L = 1$. For conciseness of notation, we refer to such 1-Lipschitz continuous functions simply as *Lipschitz functions*.

For any linear (actually affine) function f, the Lipschitz property can be verified by checking if the function's Jacobian matrix, J_f, has *spectral norm* $\|J_f\|_{\text{spec}}$ less or equal to 1, where

$$[J_f]_{ij} = \frac{\partial f_i}{\partial x_j} \qquad \text{and} \qquad \|M\|_{\text{spec}} = \max_{\|v\|_2 = 1} \|Mv\|_2. \tag{2}$$

The spectral norm of a matrix M can in fact be computed numerically as it is identical to the largest singular value of the matrix. This, however, typically requires iterative algorithms that are computationally expensive in high-dimensional settings. An exception is if M is an orthogonal matrix, i.e. $M^\top M = I$, for I the identity matrix. In that case we know that all its singular values are 1 and $\|Mv\|_2 = \|v\|_2$ for all v, so the corresponding linear transformation is Lipschitz.

Throughout this work we consider a deep neural network as a concatenation of linear layers (fully-connected or convolutional) alternating with non-linear activation functions. We then study the problem how to ensure that the resulting network function is Lipschitz.

It is known that computing the exact Lipschitz constant of a neural network is an NP-hard problem [24]. However, upper bounds can be computed more efficiently, e.g., by multiplying the individual Lipschitz constants of all layers.

3   Related Work

The first attempts to train deep networks with small Lipschitz constant used ad-hoc techniques, such as weight clipping [2] or regularizing either the network gradients [10] or the individual layers' spectral norms [14]. However, these techniques do not formally guarantee bounds on the Lipschitz constant of the trained network. Formal guarantees are provided by constructions that ensure that each individual network layer is Lipschitz. Combined with Lipschitz activation functions, such as ReLU, MaxMin or tanh, this ensures that the overall network function is Lipschitz.

In the following, we discuss a number of prior methods for obtaining Lipschitz networks. A structured overview of their properties can be found in Table 1.

Table 1. Overview of the properties of different methods for learning Lipschitz networks. Columns indicate: *E (efficiency)*: no internal iterative procedure required, scales well with the input size. *F (formal guarantees)*: provides a guarantee abound the Lipschitz constant of the trained network. *G (generality)*: can be applied to fully-connected as well as convolutional layers. *M (modularity)*: can be used with any training objective and optimization method. $\sim$ symbols indicate that a property is partially fulfilled. Superscripts provide further explanations: [1] requires a regularization loss. [2] internal methods would have to be run to convergence. [3] iterative procedure that can be split between training steps. [4] requires matrix orthogonalization. [5] requires inversion of an input-sized matrix. [6] requires circular padding and full-image kernel size. [7] requires large kernel sizes to ensure orthogonality

Method	E	F	G	M	Methodology
WGAN [2]	✓	✓	✓	✗	Weight clipping
WGAN-GP [10]	✓	✗	✓	$\sim$[1]	Regularization
Parseval Networks [7]	✓	✗	✓	$\sim$[1]	Regularization
OCNN [25]	✓	✗	✓	$\sim$[1]	Regularization
SN [14]	✗	$\sim$[2]	✓	✓	parameter rescaling
LCC [9]	✗	$\sim$[2]	✓	✗	Parameter rescaling
LMT [23]	$\sim$[3]	✗	✓	✗	Loss rescaling
GloRo [12]	$\sim$[3]	$\sim$[2]	✓	✗	Loss rescaling
BCOP [13]	✗[4]	✓	✓	✓	Explicit orthogonalization
GroupSort[1]	✗[4]	$\sim$[2]	✗	✓	Explicit orthogonalization
ONI [11]	✗	$\sim$[2]	✓	✓	Explicit orthogonalization
Cayley Convs [21]	$\sim$[5]	✓	$\sim$[6]	✓	Explicit orthogonalization
SOP [18]	✗	$\sim$[2]	$\sim$[7]	✓	Explicit orthogonalization
ECO [27]	✗[4]	✓	$\sim$[6]	✓	Explicit orthogonalization
AOL (proposed)	✓	✓	✓	✓	Parameter rescaling

Bound-Based Methods. The Lipschitz property of a network layer could be achieved trivially: one simply computes the layer's Lipschitz constant, or an upper bound, and divides the layer weights by that value. Applying such a step after training, however, does not lead to satisfactory results in practice, because the dynamic range of the network outputs is reduced by the product of the scale factors. This can be seen as a reduction of network capacity that prevents the network from fitting the training data well. Instead, it makes sense to incorporate the Lipschitz condition already at training time, such that the optimization can attempt to find weight matrices that lead to a network that is not only Lipschitz but also able to fit the data well.

The *Lipschitz Constant Constraint (LCC)* method [9] identifies all weight matrices with spectral norm above a threshold λ after each weight update and rescales those matrices to have a spectral norm exactly λ. *Lipschitz Margin Training (LMT)* [23] and *Globally-Robust Neural Networks (GloRo)* [12] approximate the overall Lipschitz constant from numeric estimates of the largest singular values of the layers' weight matrices. They integrate this value as a scale factor into their respective loss functions.

In the context of deep learning, controlling only the Lipschitz constant of each layer separately has some drawbacks. In particular, the product of the individual Lipschitz constants might grossly overestimate the network's actual Lipschitz constant. The reason is that the Lipschitz constant of a layer is determined by a single vector direction of maximal expansion. When concatenating multiple layers, their directions of maximal expansion will typically not be aligned, especially with in between nonlinear activations. As a consequence, the actual maximal amount of expansion will be smaller than the product of the per-layer maximal expansions. This causes the variance of the activations to shrink during the forward pass through the network, even though in principle a sequence of 1-Lipschitz operations could perfectly preserve it. Analogously, the magnitude of the gradient signal shrinks with each layer during the backwards pass of backpropagation training, which can lead to vanishing gradient problems.

Orthogonality-Based Method. A way to address the problems of variance-loss and vanishing gradients is to exploit *orthogonality*, which has been found useful in computer vision and machine learning [3,8,15]. Specifically one uses network layers that encode *orthogonal* linear operations. These are 1-Lipschitz, so the overall network will also have that property. However, they are also *isotropic*, in the sense that they preserve data variance and gradient magnitude in all directions, not just a single one.

For fully-connected layers, it suffices to ensure that the weight matrices themselves are orthogonal. The *GroupSort* [1] architecture achieves this using classic results from numeric analysis [4]. The authors parameterize an orthogonal weight matrix as a specific matrix power series, which they embed in truncated form into the network architecture. *Orthogonalization by Newton's Iterations (ONI)* [11] parameterizes orthogonal weight matrices as $(VV^\top)^{-1/2} V$ for a general parameter matrix V. As an approximate representation of the inverse operation the authors embed a number of steps of Newton's method into the network. Both methods, GroupSort and ONI, have the shortcoming that their orthogonalization schemes require the application of iterative computation schemes which incur a trade-off between the approximation quality and the computational cost.

For convolutional layers, more involved constructions are required to ensure that the resulting linear transformations are orthogonal. In particular, enforcing orthogonal kernel matrices is not sufficient in general to ensure a Lipschitz constant of 1 when the convolutions have overlapping receptive fields.

Skew Orthogonal Convolutions (SOC) [18] parameterize orthogonal matrices as the matrix exponentials of skew-symmetric matrices. They embed a truncation of the exponential's power series into the network and bound the resulting error. However, SOC requires a rather large number of iterations to yield good approximation quality, which leads to high computational cost.

Block Convolutional Orthogonal Parameterization (BCOP) [13] relies on a matrix decomposition approach to address the problem of orthogonalizing convolutional layers. The authors parameterize each convolution kernel of size $k \times k$ by a set of $2k-1$ convolutional matrices of size 1×2 or 2×1. These are combined with a final pointwise convolution with orthogonal kernel. However, BCOP also incurs high computation cost, because each of the smaller transforms requires orthogonalizing a corresponding parameter matrix.

Cayley Layers parameterize orthogonal matrices using the Cayley transform [5]. Naively, this requires the inversion of a matrix of size quadratic in the input dimensions. However, in [21] the author demonstrate that in certain situations, namely for full image size convolutions with circular padding, the computations can be performed more efficiently.

Explicitly Constructed Orthogonal Convolutions (ECO) [27] rely on a theorem that relates the singular values of the Jacobian of a circular convolution to the singular values of a set of much smaller matrices [16]. The authors derive a rather efficient parameterization that, however, is restricted to full-size dilated convolutions with non-overlapping receptive fields.

The main shortcomings of Cayley layers and ECO are their restriction to certain full-size convolutions. Those are incompatible with most well-performing network architectures for high-dimensional data, which use local kernel convolutions, such as 3×3, and overlapping receptive fields.

Relation to AOL. The AOL method that we detail in Sect. 4 can be seen as a hybrid of bound-based and orthogonality-based approaches. It mathematically guarantees the Lipschitz property of each network layer by rescaling the corresponding parameter matrix (column-wise for fully-connected layers, channel-wise for convolutions). In contrast to other bound-based approaches it does not use a computationally expensive iterative approach to estimate the Lipschitz constant as precisely as possible, but it relies on a closed-form upper bound. The bound is tight for matrices with orthogonal columns. During training this has the effect that orthogonal parameter matrices are implicitly preferred by the optimizer, because they allow fitting the data, and therefore minimizing the loss, the best. Consequently, AOL benefits from the advantages of orthogonality-based approaches, such as preserving the variance of the activations and the gradient magnitude, without the other methods' shortcomings of requiring difficult parameterizations and being restricted to specific layer types.

4   Almost-Orthogonal Lipschitz (AOL) Layers

In this section, we introduce our main contribution, almost-orthogonal Lipschitz (AOL) layers, which combine the advantages of rescaling and orthogonalization approaches. Specifically, we introduce a weight-dependent rescaling technique for the weights of a linear neural network layer that guarantees them to be 1-Lipschitz. It can be easily computed in closed form and is applicable to fully-connected as well as convolutional layers.

The main ingredient is the following theorem, which provides an elementary formula for controlling the spectral norm of a matrix by rescaling its columns.

Theorem 1. *For any matrix $P \in \mathbb{R}^{n \times m}$, define $D \in \mathbb{R}^{m \times m}$ as the diagonal matrix with $D_{ii} = \left(\sum_j |P^\top P|_{ij} \right)^{-1/2}$ if the expression in the brackets is non-zero, or $D_{ii} = 0$ otherwise. Then the spectral norm of PD is bounded by 1.*

Proof. The upper bound the spectral norm of PD follows from an elementary computation. By definition of the spectral norm, we have

$$\|PD\|_{\text{spec}}^2 = \max_{\|\vec{v}\|_2 = 1} \|PD\vec{v}\|_2^2 = \max_{\|\vec{v}\|_2 = 1} \vec{v}^\top D^\top P^\top PD\vec{v}. \tag{3}$$

We observe that for any symmetric matrix $M \in \mathbb{R}^{n \times n}$ and any $w \in \mathbb{R}^n$:

$$\boldsymbol{w}^T M \boldsymbol{w} \leq \sum_{i,j=1}^n |M_{ij}||w_i||w_j| \leq \sum_{i,j=1}^n \frac{1}{2}|M_{ij}|(w_i^2 + w_j^2) = \sum_{i=1}^n \left(\sum_{j=1}^n |M_{ij}| \right) w_i^2 \tag{4}$$

where the second inequality follows from the general relation $2ab \leq a^2 + b^2$. Evaluating (4) for $M = P^\top P$ and $\boldsymbol{w} = D\vec{v}$, we obtain for all $\vec{v}$ with $\|\vec{v}\|_2 = 1$

$$\vec{v}^\top D^\top P^\top PD \, \vec{v} \leq \sum_{i=1}^n \left(\sum_{j=1}^n |P^\top P|_{ij} \right) (D_{ii} v_i)^2 \leq \sum_{i=1}^n v_i^2 = 1 \tag{5}$$

which proves the bound.

Note that when P has orthogonal columns of full rank, we have that $P^\top P$ is diagonal and $D = (P^\top P)^{-1/2}$, so $D^\top P^\top PD = I$, for I the identity matrix. Consequently, (5) holds with equality and the bound in Theorem 1 is tight.

In the rest of this section, we demonstrate how Theorem 1 allows us to control the Lipschitz constant of any linear layer in a neural network.

4.1   Fully-Connected Lipschitz Layers

We first discuss the case of fully-connected layers.

Lemma 1 (Fully-Connected AOL Layers). *Let $P \in \mathbb{R}^{n \times m}$ be an arbitrary parameter matrix. Then, the fully-connected network layer*

$$f(x) = Wx + b \tag{6}$$

is guaranteed to be 1-Lipschitz, when $W = PD$ for D defined as in Theorem 1.

Proof. The Lemma follows from Theorem 1, because the Lipschitz constant of f is bounded by the spectral norm of its Jacobian matrix, which is simply W.

Discussion. Despite its simplicity, there are a number aspects of Lemma 1 that are worth a closer look. First, we observe that a layer of the form $f(x) = PDx + b$

can be interpreted in two ways, depending on how we (mentally) put brackets into the linear term. In the form $f(x) = P(Dx) + b$, we apply an arbitrary weight matrix to a suitably rescaled input vector. In the form $f(x) = (PD)x + b$, we apply a column-rescaling operation to the weight matrix before applying it to the unchanged input. The two views highlight different aspects of AOL. The first view reflects the flexibility and high capacity of learning with an arbitrary parameter matrix, with only an intermediate rescaling operation to prevent the growth of the Lipschitz constant. The second view shows that AOL layers can be implemented without any overhead at prediction time, because the rescaling factors can be absorbed in the parameter matrix itself, even preserving potential structural properties such as sparsity patterns.

As a second insight from Lemma 1 we obtain how AOL relates to prior methods that rely on orthogonal weight matrices. As derived after Theorem 1, if the parameter matrix, P, has orthogonal columns of full rank, then $W = PD$ is an orthogonal weight matrix. In particular, when P is already an orthonormal matrix, then D will be the identity matrix, and W will be equal to P. Therefore, our method can express any linear map based on an orthonormal matrix, but it can also express other linear maps. If the columns of P are approximately orthogonal, in the sense that $P^\top P$ is approximately diagonal, then the entries of D are dominated by the diagonal entries of the product. The multiplication by D acts mostly as a normalization of the length of the columns of P, and the resulting W is an almost-orthogonal matrix.

Finally, observe that Lemma 1 does not put any specific numeric or structural constraints on the parameter matrix. Consequently, there are no restrictions on the optimizer or objective function when training AOL-networks.

4.2   Convolutional Lipschitz Layers

An analog of Lemma 1 for convolutional layers can, in principle, be obtained by applying the same construction as above: convolutions are linear operations, so we could compute their Jacobian matrix and determine an appropriate rescaling matrix from it. However, this naive approach would be inefficient, because it would require working with matrices that are of a size quadratic in the number of input dimensions and channels. Instead, by a more refined analysis, we obtain the following result.

Lemma 2 (Convolutional AOL Layers). *Let $P \in \mathbb{R}^{k \times k \times c_I \times c_O}$, be a convolution kernel matrix, where $k \times k$ is the kernel size and c_I and c_O are the number of input and output channels, respectively. Then, the convolutional layer*

$$f(x) = P * R(x) + b \tag{7}$$

is guaranteed to be 1-Lipschitz, where $R(x)$ is a channel-wise rescaling that multiplies each channel $c \in \{1, \ldots, c_I\}$ of the input by

$$d_c = \left(\sum_{i,j} \sum_{a=1}^{c_I} \left| \sum_{b=1}^{c_O} P^{(a,b)} * P^{(c,b)} \right|_{i,j} \right)^{-1/2}. \tag{8}$$

We can equivalently write f as $f(x) = W * x + b$, where $W = P * D$ with $D \in \mathbb{R}^{1 \times 1 \times c_I \times c_I}$ given by $D_{1,1}^{(c,c)} = d_c$, and $D_{1,1}^{(c_1,c_2)} = 0$ for $c_1 \neq c_2$.

The proof consists of an explicit derivation of the Jacobian of the convolution operation as a linear map, followed by an application of Theorem 1. The main step is the explicit demonstration that the diagonal rescaling matrix can in fact be bounded by a per-channel multiplication with the result of a self-convolution of the convolution kernel. The details can be found in the supplemental material.

Discussion. We now discuss some favorable properties of Lemma 2. First, as in the fully-connected case, the rescaling operation again can be viewed either as acting on the inputs, or as acting on the parameter matrix. Therefore, the convolutional layer also combines the properties of high capacity and no overhead at prediction time. In fact, for 1×1 convolutions, the construction of Lemma 2 reduces to the fully-connected situation of Lemma 1.

Second, computing the scaling factors is efficient, because the necessary operations scale only with the size of the convolution kernel regardless of the image size. The rescaling preserves the structure of the convolution kernel, e.g. sparsity patterns. In particular, this means that constructs such as dilated convolutions are automatically covered by Lemma 2 as well, as these can be expressed as ordinary convolutions with specific zero entries.

Furthermore, Lemma 2 requires no strong assumption on the padding type, and works as long as the padding itself is 1-Lipschitz. Also, the computation of the scale factors is easy to implement in all common deep learning frameworks using batch-convolution operations with the input channel dimension taking the role of the batch dimension.

5 Experiments

We compare our method to related work in the context of *certified robust accuracy*, where the goal is to solve an image classification task in a way that provably prevents *adversarial examples* [20]. Specifically, we consider an input x as *certifiably robustly classified* by a model under input perturbations up to size ϵ, if $x + \delta$ is correctly classified for all δ with $\|\delta\| \leq \epsilon$. Then the *certified robust accuracy* of a classifier is the proportion of the test set that is certifiably robustly classified.

Consider a function f that generates a score for each class. Define the *margin* of f at input x with correct label y as

$$M_f(x) = \left[f(x)_y - \max_{i \neq y} f(x)_i \right]_+ \qquad \text{with} \qquad [\cdot]_+ = \max\{\cdot, 0\}. \qquad (9)$$

Then the induced classifier, $C_f(x) = \text{argmax}_i f(x)_i$, certifiably robustly classifies an input x if $M_f(x) > \sqrt{2}L\epsilon$, where L is the Lipschitz constant L of f. This relation can be used to efficiently determine (a lower bound to) the certified robust accuracy of Lipschitz networks [23].

Following prior work in the field, we conduct experiments that evaluate the certified robust accuracy for different thresholds, ϵ, on the CIFAR-10 as well

Table 2. Patchwise architecture. For all layers we use zero padding to keep the size the same. For AOL-Small we set w to 16, and we choose $w = 32$ and $w = 48$ for AOL-Medium and AOL-Large. Furthermore, l is the number of classes, and $l = 10$ for CIFAR-10 and $l = 100$ for CIFAR-100. *Concatenation Pooling* stacks all the inputs into a single vector, and *First channels* just selects the first channels and ignores the rest

Layer name	Kernel size	Stride	Activation	Output size	Amount
Concatenation Pooling	4×4	4×4	-	$8 \times 8 \times 48$	1
AOL Conv	1×1	1×1	MaxMin	$8 \times 8 \times 192$	1
AOL Conv	3×3	1×1	MaxMin	$8 \times 8 \times 192$	12
AOL Conv	1×1	1×1	None	$8 \times 8 \times 192$	1
First Channels	–	–	–	$8 \times 8 \times w$	1
Flatten	–	–	–	$64w$	1
AOL FC	–	–	MaxMin	$64w$	13
AOL FC	–	–	None	$64w$	1
First Channels	–	–	–	l	1

as the CIFAR-100 dataset. We also provide ablation studies that illustrate that AOL can be used in a variety of network architectures, and that it indeed learns matrices that are approximately orthogonal. In the following we describe our experimental setup. Further details can be found in the supplemental material. All hyperparameters were determined on validation sets.

Architecture: Our main model architecture is loosely inspired by the *ConvMixer* architecture [22]: we first subdivide the input image into 4×4 patches, which are processed by 14 convolutional layers, most of kernel size 3×3. This is followed by 14 fully connected layers. We report results for three different model sizes, we will refer to the models as AOL-Small, AOL-Medium and AOL-Large. The full architectural details can be found in Table 2.

Other network architectures are discussed in an ablation study in Sect. 6.1.

Initialization: In order to ensure stable training we initialize the parameter matrices so that our bound is tight. In particular, for layers preserving the size between input and output (e.g. the 3×3 convolutions) we initialize the parameter matrix so that the Jacobian is the identity matrix. For any other layers we initialize the parameter matrix so that it has random orthogonal columns.

Loss Function: In order to train the network to achieve good certified robust accuracy we want the score of the correct class to be bigger than any other score by a margin. We use a loss function similar to the one proposed for *Lipschitz-margin training* [23] with a temperature parameter that helps encouraging a margin during training. Our loss function takes as input the model's logit vector,

Table 3. Experimental results: robust image classification on CIFAR-10 for AOL and methods from the literature.Results for concurrent unpublished works (ECO and SOC with Householder activations) are printed in italics. *Standard CNN* refers to our implementation of a simple convolutional network trained without enforcing any robustness, for details see the supplemental material.

Method	Standard Accuracy	Certified Robust Accuracy			
		$\epsilon = \frac{36}{255}$	$\epsilon = \frac{72}{255}$	$\epsilon = \frac{108}{255}$	$\epsilon = 1$
Standard CNN	83.4%	0%	0%	0%	0%
BCOP Large [13]	72.2%	58.3%	–	–	–
GloRo 6C2F [12]	77.0%	58.4%	–	–	–
Cayley Large [21]	75.3%	59.2%	–	–	–
SOC-20 [18]	76.4%	61.9%	–	–	–
SOC-25 (from [27])	–	60.2%	43.7%	28.6%	–
ECO-25 [27]	*75.7 %*	*66.1 %*	*55.6 %*	*45.3 %*	–
SOC-15 (from [19])	*76.4 %*	*63.0 %*	*48.5%*	*35.5 %*	–
AOL-Small	69.8%	62.0%	54.4%	47.1%	21.8%
AOL-Medium	71.1%	63.8%	56.1%	48.6%	23.2%
AOL-Large	71.6%	64.0%	56.4%	49.0%	23.7%

s, as well as a one-hot encoding y of the true label as input, and is given by

$$\mathcal{L}(s,y) = \text{crossentropy}\left(y, \text{softmax}\left(\frac{s-uy}{t}\right)t\right), \qquad (10)$$

for some offset u and some temperature t. For our experiments, we use $u = \sqrt{2}$, which encourages the model to learn to classify the training data certifiably robustly to perturbations of norm 1. Furthermore we use temperature $t = 1/4$, which causes the gradient magnitude to stay close to 1 as long as a training example is classified with margin less than $1/2$.

Optimization: We minimize the loss function (10) using SGD with Nesterov momentum of 0.9 for 1000 epochs. The batch size is 250. The learning rate starts at 10^{-3} and is reduced by a factor of 10 at epochs $900, 990$ and 999. As data augmentation we use spatial transformations (rotations and flipping) as well as some color transformation. The details are provided in the supplemental material. For all AOL layers we also use weight decay with coefficient 5×10^{-4}.

6   Results

The main results can be found in Tables 3 and 4, where we compare the certified robust accuracy of our method to those reported in previous works on orthogonal networks and other networks with bounded Lipschitz constant. For methods that

Table 4. Experimental results: robust image classification on CIFAR-100 for AOL and methods from the literature.We report the standard accuracy on the test set as well as the certified robust accuracy under input perturbations up to size ϵ for different values of ϵ.Results for concurrent unpublished works (ECO and SOC with Householder activations) are printed in italics.

Method	Standard Accuracy	Certified Robust Accuracy			
		$\epsilon = \frac{36}{255}$	$\epsilon = \frac{72}{255}$	$\epsilon = \frac{108}{255}$	$\epsilon = 1$
SOC-30 [18]	43.1%	29.2%	–	–	–
SOC (from [27])	–	28.6%	18.2%	10.9%	–
ECO-25 [27]	*41.7 %*	*32.6 %*	*25.1 %*	*19.2%*	–
SOC (from [19])	*47.8 %*	*34.8 %*	*23.7 %*	*15.8 %*	–
AOL-Small	42.4%	32.5%	24.8%	19.2%	6.7%
AOL-Medium	43.2%	33.7%	26.0%	20.2%	7.2%
AOL-Large	43.7%	33.7%	26.3%	20.7%	7.8%

are presented in multiple variants, such as different networks depths, we include the variant for which the authors list results for large values of ϵ.

The table shows that our proposed methods achieves results comparable with the current state-of-the-art. For small robustness thresholds, it achieves certified robust accuracy on par with published earlier methods, though slightly below that reported in two concurrent preprints [19,27]. Focusing on (more realistic) medium or higher robustness thresholds, AOL achieves certified robust accuracy comparable to or even higher than all other methods. As a reference for future work, we also report values for an even higher robustness threshold than what appeared in the literature so far, $\epsilon = 1$.

Another observation is that on the CIFAR-10 dataset the clean accuracy of AOL is somewhat below other methods. We attribute this to the fact that we mainly focused our training towards high robustness. The accuracy-robustness trade-off can in fact be influenced by the choice of margin at training time, see our ablation study in Sect. 6.1.

6.1 Ablation Studies

In this section we report on a number of ablation studies that shed light on specific aspect of AOL.

Generality: One of the main advantages of AOL is that it is not restricted to a specific architecture or a specific layer type. To demonstrate this, we present additional experiments for a broad range of other architectures. AOL-FC consists simply of 9 fully connected layers. AOL-STD resembles a standard convolutional architecture, where the number of channels doubles whenever the resolution is reduced. AOL-ALT is another convolutional architecture that keeps the number of activations constant wherever possible in the network. AOL-DIL resembles

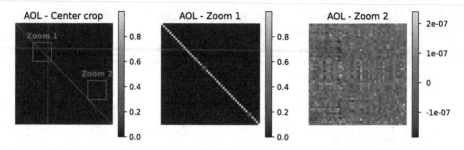

Fig. 1. Evaluation of the orthogonality of the trained model. We consider the third layer of the AOL-Small model. It is a 3×3 convolutions with input size $8 \times 8 \times 192$. We show a center crop of $J^\top J$, for J the Jacobian, as well as two further crops. Note that most diagonal elements are close to 1, and most off-diagonal elements are very close to 0 (note the different color scale in the third subplot). This confirms that AOL did indeed learn an almost-orthogonal weight matrix. Best viewed in color and zoomed in

the architectures used in [27] in that it uses large dilated convolutions instead of small local ones. It also uses circular padding. The details of the architectures are provided in the supplemental.

The results (shown in the supplemental material) confirm that for any of these architectures, we can train AOL-based Lipschitz networks and achieve certified robust accuracy comparable to the results of earlier specialized methods.

Approximate Orthogonality: As a second ablation study, we demonstrate that AOL indeed learns almost-orthogonal weight matrices, thereby justifying its name. In order to do that, we evaluate $J^\top J$ for J the Jacobian of an AOL convolution, and visualize it in Fig. 1. More detailed results including a comparison to standard training are provided in the supplemental material.

Table 5. Experimental results for AOL-Small for different value of u and t in the loss function in Equation (10).We report the standard accuracy on the test seWe report the standard accuracy on the test set as well as the certified robust accuracy under input perturbations up to size ϵ for different values of ϵ.t as well as the certified robust accuracy under input perturbations up to size ϵ for different values of ϵ.

u	t	Standard Accuracy	Certified Robust Accuracy			
			$\epsilon = \frac{36}{255}$	$\epsilon = \frac{72}{255}$	$\epsilon = \frac{108}{255}$	$\epsilon = 1$
$\sqrt{2}/16$	$1/64$	79.8%	45.3%	16.7%	3.3%	0.0%
$\sqrt{2}/4$	$1/16$	77.4%	63.0%	47.6%	33.0%	2.5%
$\sqrt{2}$	$1/4$	70.4%	62.6%	55.0%	47.9%	22.2%
$4\sqrt{2}$	1	59.8%	55.5%	50.9%	46.5%	30.8%
$16\sqrt{2}$	4	48.2%	45.2%	42.2%	39.4%	28.6%

Accuracy-Robustness Tradeoff: The loss function in Eq. (10) allows trading off between clean accuracy and certified robust accuracy by changing the size of the enforced margin. We demonstrate this by an ablation study that varies the offset parameter u in the loss function, and also scales t proportional to u.

The results can be found in Table 5. One can see that using a small margin allows us to train an AOL Network with high clean accuracy, but decreases the certified robust accuracy for larger input perturbations, whereas choosing a higher offset allows us to reach state-of-the-art accuracy for larger input perturbations. Therefore, varying this offset gives us an easy way to prioritize the measure that is important for a specific problem.

7 Limitations

Despite its flexibility, AOL also has limitations. Some of those need to be overcome in order to enable training on high-resolution datasets in the future.

Firstly, while AOL in principle can handle skip connections, as they are used e.g. in ResNets, the bound will (generally) not be tight, and the network will lose dynamic range. We only recommend using skip connections for problems where that is acceptable.

Secondly, optimization seems to be harder for AOL layers. They take longer to converge than unconstrained layers, which manifests itself in more training epochs needed. We believe the reason for this is that the optimizer needs to keep the matrices approximately orthogonal in addition to fitting the training data, and that doing both takes more iterations. Also, local minima emerge, avoiding which needs a careful choice of initialization and learning rate.

Thirdly, AOL is designed for L^2-Lipschitzness. Consequenty, the robustness certificates also hold only for L^2-perturbations, and we can only give very weak guarantees for example for perturbations with bounded L^1 norm.

Finally, the rescaling factors are simple to compute using a matrix multiplication or a convolution. However, the complexity of this calculation grows with the number of channels of the input. A more detailed analysis of the computational complexity can be found in the supplemental material.

8 Conclusion

In this work, we proposed AOL, a method for constructing deep networks that have Lipschitz constant of at most 1 and therefore are robust against small changes in the input data. Our main contribution is a rescaling technique for network layers that ensures them to be 1-Lipschitz. It can be computed and trained efficiently, and is applicable to fully-connected and various types of convolutional layers. Training with the rescaled layers leads to weight matrices that are almost orthogonal without the need for a special parametrization and computationally costly orthogonalization schemes. We present experiments and ablation studies in the context of image classification with certified robustness. They show that AOL-networks achieve results comparable with methods that explicitly enforce orthogonalization, while offering the simplicity and flexibility of earlier bound-based approaches.

References

1. Anil, C., Lucas, J., Grosse, R.B.: Sorting out Lipschitz function approximation. In: International Conference on Machine Learning (ICML) (2019)
2. Arjovsky, M., Chintala, S., Bottou, L.: Wasserstein generative adversarial networks. In: International Conference on Machine Learning (ICML) (2017)
3. Bank, D., Giryes, R.: An ETF view of dropout regularization. In: British Machine Vision Conference (BMVC) (2020)
4. Björck, Å., Bowie, C.: An iterative algorithm for computing the best estimate of an orthogonal matrix. SIAM J. Numer. Anal. **8**(2) (1971)
5. Cayley, A.: About the algebraic structure of the orthogonal group and the other classical groups in a field of characteristic zero or a prime characteristic. J. für die reine und angewandte Mathematik **30** (1846)
6. Chakraborty, A., Alam, M., Dey, V., Chattopadhyay, A., Mukhopadhyay, D.: Adversarial attacks and defences: a survey. arXiv preprint arXiv:1810.00069 (2018)
7. Cissé, M., Bojanowski, P., Grave, E., Dauphin, Y.N., Usunier, N.: Parseval networks: improving robustness to adversarial examples. In: International Conference on Machine Learning (ICML) (2017)
8. Cogswell, M., Ahmed, F., Girshick, R.B., Zitnick, L., Batra, D.: Reducing overfitting in deep networks by decorrelating representations. In: International Conference on Learning Representations (ICLR) (2016)
9. Gouk, H., Frank, E., Pfahringer, B., Cree, M.J.: Regularisation of neural networks by enforcing Lipschitz continuity. Mach. Learn. **110**(2), 393–416 (2020). https://doi.org/10.1007/s10994-020-05929-w
10. Gulrajani, I., Ahmed, F., Arjovsky, M., Dumoulin, V., Courville, A.C.: Improved training of Wasserstein GANs. In: Conference on Neural Information Processing Systems (NeurIPS) (2017)
11. Huang, L., et al.: Controllable orthogonalization in training DNNs. In: Conference on Computer Vision and Pattern Recognition (CVPR) (2020)
12. Leino, K., Wang, Z., Fredrikson, M.: Globally-robust neural networks. In: International Conference on Machine Learning (ICML) (2021)
13. Li, B., Chen, C., Wang, W., Carin, L.: Certified adversarial robustness with additive noise. In: Conference on Neural Information Processing Systems (NeurIPS) (2019)
14. Miyato, T., Kataoka, T., Koyama, M., Yoshida, Y.: Spectral normalization for generative adversarial networks. In: International Conference on Learning Representations (ICLR) (2018)
15. Saxe, A.M., McClelland, J.L., Ganguli, S.: Exact solutions to the nonlinear dynamics of learning in deep linear neural networks. In: International Conference on Learning Representations (ICLR) (2014)
16. Sedghi, H., Gupta, V., Long, P.M.: The singular values of convolutional layers. In: International Conference on Learning Representations (ICLR) (2019)
17. Serban, A., Poll, E., Visser, J.: Adversarial examples on object recognition: a comprehensive survey. ACM Comput. Surv. (CSUR) **53**(3), 1–38 (2020)
18. Singla, S., Feizi, S.: Skew orthogonal convolutions. In: International Conference on Machine Learning (ICML) (2021)

19. Singla, S., Feizi, S.: Improved deterministic l_2 robustness on CIFAR-10 and CIFAR-100. In: International Conference on Learning Representations (ICLR) (2022). https://openreview.net/forum?id=tD7eCtaSkR

20. Szegedy, C., et al.: Intriguing properties of neural networks. In: International Conference on Learning Representations (ICLR) (2014)

21. Trockman, A., Kolter, J.Z.: Orthogonalizing convolutional layers with the Cayley transform. In: International Conference on Learning Representations (ICLR) (2021)

22. Trockman, A., Kolter, J.Z.: Patches are all you need? arXiv preprint arXiv:2201.09792 (2022)

23. Tsuzuku, Y., Sato, I., Sugiyama, M.: Lipschitz-margin training: scalable certification of perturbation invariance for deep neural networks. In: Conference on Neural Information Processing Systems (NeurIPS) (2018)

24. Virmaux, A., Scaman, K.: Lipschitz regularity of deep neural networks: analysis and efficient estimation. In: Conference on Neural Information Processing Systems (NeurIPS) (2018)

25. Wang, J., Chen, Y., Chakraborty, R., Yu, S.X.: Orthogonal convolutional neural networks. In: Conference on Computer Vision and Pattern Recognition (CVPR) (2020)

26. Xu, H., et al.: Adversarial attacks and defenses in images, graphs and text: a review. Int. J. Autom. Comput. **17**(2), 151–178 (2020)

27. Yu, T., Li, J., CAI, Y., Li, P.: Constructing orthogonal convolutions in an explicit manner. In: International Conference on Learning Representations (ICLR) (2022). https://openreview.net/forum?id=Zr5W2LSRhD

PointScatter: Point Set Representation
for Tubular Structure Extraction

Dong Wang[1], Zhao Zhang[2], Ziwei Zhao[2,4,5], Yuhang Liu[3], Yihong Chen[2],
and Liwei Wang[1,2(✉)]

[1] Key Laboratory of Machine Perception, MOE, School of Artificial Intelligence,
Peking University, Beijing, China
wangdongcis@pku.edu.cn, wanglw@cis.pku.edu.cn
[2] Center for Data Science, Peking University, Beijing, China
2201213301@stu.pku.edu.cn, zhaozw@stu.pku.edu.cn, chenyihong@pku.edu.cn
[3] Yizhun Medical AI Co., Ltd, Beijing, China
yuhang.liu@yizhun-ai.com
[4] Peng Cheng Laboratory, Shenzhen, China
[5] Pazhou Laboratory (Huangpu), Guangzhou, China

Abstract. This paper explores the point set representation for tubular
structure extraction tasks. Compared with the traditional mask representation, the point set representation enjoys its flexibility and representation ability, which would not be restricted by the fixed grid as the mask.
Inspired by this, we propose PointScatter, an alternative to the segmentation models for the tubular structure extraction task. PointScatter
splits the image into scatter regions and parallelly predicts points for each
scatter region. We further propose the greedy-based region-wise bipartite
matching algorithm to train the network end-to-end and efficiently. We
benchmark the PointScatter on four public tubular datasets, and the
extensive experiments on tubular structure segmentation and centerline
extraction task demonstrate the effectiveness of our approach. *Code is
available at* https://github.com/zhangzhao2022/pointscatter.

Keywords: Tubular structure · Medical image segmentation ·
Centerline extraction · Point set representation

1 Introduction

Tubular structures broadly exist in computer vision tasks, especially medical
image tasks, such as blood vessels [26,51], ribs [22,52], and nerves [15]. Accurate extraction of these tubular structures performs a decisive role in the downstream tasks. For instance, the diagnosis of eye-related diseases such as hyper-
tension, diabetic retinopathy highly relies on the extraction of retinal vessels.

D. Wang and Z. Zhang—Equal contribution.

Supplementary Information The online version contains supplementary material
available at https://doi.org/10.1007/978-3-031-19803-8_22.

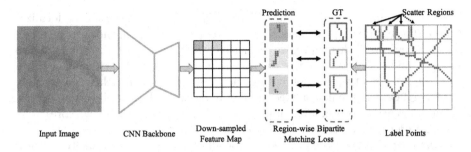

Fig. 1. PointScatter adopts point set representation to perform tubular structure extraction. We exhibit a small input image with size 48×48 to show the details clearly. PointScatter learns to predict points for each scatter region separately. Region-wise bipartite matching is employed in PointScatter to train the network end to end.

Deep learning-based methods usually model the extraction of tubular structures as a regular semantic segmentation task, which predicts segmentation masks as the representation of the structures. Therefore, previous works mostly adopt the following two routines: designing novel network components to incorporate vascular or tubular priors [37], or proposing loss functions that promote topology preservation [38].

Semantic segmentation methods apply successively upsampling on the high-level feature maps to get the predicted segmentation masks. The wide receptive field makes it more suitable to recognize large connected areas in the image. However, the paradigm of semantic segmentation has its inherent defect, which is further amplified in the task of tubular structure extraction. It is widely known that the segmentation models struggle in extracting high-frequency information accurately, such as image contours [8,9,18,19]. In tubular structures, the natural thinness makes almost all foreground regions contact with the structure boundaries. The special characteristics of the tubular structure increase the difficulty of capturing the fine-scale tubular details, which leads to false negatives of the small branches in the tubular structures.

We argue that the limitation lies in the representation of the prediction results. The semantic segmentation methods predict one score map to represent a segmentation result. The score map is arranged on a regular grid where each bin corresponds to a pixel in the input image. The fixed grid limits the flexibility of the representation and therefore restricts the ability of the network to learn fine-scale structures. Compared with the regular grids, point set representation is a more reasonable way for tubular structure extraction. Since the points can be placed at arbitrary real coordinates in the image, the point set representation enjoys more flexibility and expression ability to learn the detailed structures and is not restricted to a fixed grid.

Therefore, in this paper, we propose PointScatter to explore the feasibility of point set representation in tubular structure extraction. PointScatter (Fig. 1) is an alternative of the mask segmentation method and can apply to regular segmentation backbones (*e.g.* U-Net [35]) with minor modifications. Given a downsampled feature map output by the CNN backbone network, each localization of this feature map is responsible for predicting points in the corresponding **scatter region**. In this paper, we regard each patch as a scatter region as shown in Fig. 1, and each localization of the feature map corresponds to the image patch with the same relative position within the whole image. For each scatter region, our `PointScatter` predicts a fixed number of points with their objectness scores. When inference, a threshold is applied to filter out points with low scores. The aggregation of all scatter regions forms the final results.

Our `PointScatter` predicts points for all scatter regions parallelly at once, and the training process is also in an end-to-end and efficient manner. We apply the set matching approach separately for each scatter region to perform label assignment for training our `PointScatter`. Previous works in the object detection area (*e.g.* DETR [5]) adopt Hungarian algorithm [20] to perform one-to-one label assignment. Following this way, a straightforward way is using the Hungarian algorithm iteratively for each scatter region. However, the iteration process is inefficient for large images with thousands of scatter regions. Consequently, we propose the region-wise bipartite matching method which is based on the greedy approach. Our method reduces the computation complexity from $O(N^3)$ to $O(N^2)$ for each scatter region and is easier to be implemented on GPU using the vectorized programming by the deep learning framework (*e.g.* PyTorch [32]).

The advantages of our `PointScatter` and point sets lie in their flexibility and adaptability. 1) For the segmentation methods, each pixel of the output score maps corresponds to the pixel of the input image with the same spatial location, and has to predict the objectness score for this pixel. While in our `PointScatter`, the model can adaptively decide the assignments between the predicted and GT points within each scatter region. Since there are fewer restrictions on the assignments, the model is much easier to fit the complicated fine-scale structures in the training process. 2) During the `PointScatter` training, since we use points as GT rather than the mask, the predicted points can approach the GT points along the continuous spatial dimension. The extra dimension rather than the classification score dimension will reduce the optimization difficulty and provide more paths for the optimization algorithm to find the optimal solution during model training.

Experimentally, we evaluate `PointScatter` on four typical tubular datasets. For each dataset, we compare our methods with their segmentation counterparts on three strong backbone networks. We consider two tasks for tubular structure extraction: tubular structure segmentation and centerline extraction. Extensive experimental results reveal:

1. On the tubular structure segmentation task, according to the volumetric scores, our `PointScatter` achieves superior performance on most of the 12 combinations of the datasets and the backbone networks.
2. On the tubular structure segmentation task, using `PointScatter` as an auxiliary task to learn the centerline, the performance of both volumetric scores and topology-based metrics of the segmentation methods will be boosted.

3. On the centerline extraction task, our `PointScatter` significantly outperforms the segmentation counterparts by a large margin.
4. The qualitative analysis shows that our `PointScatter` is better than the segmentation methods on the small branches or bifurcation points, which verifies the expression ability of our method.

2 Related Work

2.1 Tubular Structure Segmentation

Tubular structure segmentation is a classical task due to the broad existence of tubular structures in medical images. Traditional methods [1–3,6,40] seek to exploit special geometric priors to improve the performance. Fethallah *et al.* [3] proposes an interactive method for tubular structure extraction. Once the physicians click on a small number of points, a set of minimal paths could be obtained through the marching algorithm. Amos *et al.* [40] considers centerline detection as a regression task and estimates the distance in scale space.

As for deep learning-based models, U-Net [35] and FCN [25] are the classical methods for semantic segmentation, which are also appropriate for tubular structures. To further improve the performance, approaches specially designed for tubular structures have been proposed recently. These methods can be coarsely classified into two categories: incorporating tubular priors into the network architecture [37,43,49] and designing topology-preserving loss functions [17,29,30,38]. Wang *et al.* [49] attempt to predict a segmentation mask and a distance map simultaneously for tubular structures. Then the mask could be refined through the shape prior reconstructed from the distance map. Shit *et al.* [38] introduces a new similarity measure called clDice to represent the topology architecture of tubular structures. Moreover, the differentiable version soft-clDice is proposed to train arbitrary segmentation networks. Oner *et al.* [30] proposes a connectivity-oriented loss function for training deep convolutional networks to reconstruct network-like structures. Besides these two ways, some researchers propose special approaches for their specific tasks. For instance, Li *et al.* [23] leverages a deep reinforced tree-traversal agent for efficient coronary artery centerline extraction. Different from the above methods, our `PointScatter` is the first to utilize points as a new representation for tubular structures, which significantly improves the segmentation performance.

2.2 Point Set Representation

Recently, points have become a popular choice to represent objects. Contributing to its flexibility and great expression capability, point representation is applied in various fields, such as image object detection [14,21,53], instance segmentation [54], pose estimation [4,31,48,58], 3D object classification and segmentation [33,34,56], *etc.* Benefiting from the advantage of points for both localization and recognition, RepPoints [53] utilizes point set as a new finer representation of objects instead of the rectangular bounding boxes. For the task of human pose estimation, detecting key points of humans is regarded as the prerequisite. Then, based on the prior knowledge of the human body, the skeletons can be obtained via the spatial connections among the detected key points. In the area of 3D object recognition, the point cloud is an important data structure. Thousands of points represented by the three coordinates (x, y, z) make up the scenes and objects. Qi *et al.* [33] provides a unified architecture for point cloud to achieve object classification and semantic segmentation. In this paper, we introduce the point set representation for tubular structures due to the expression ability of points to capture complex and fine-grained geometric structures.

2.3   Set Prediction by Deep Learning

The paradigm of set prediction has been introduced into the computer vision tasks (*e.g.* Object Detection [5,46,60]) firstly by DETR [5]. In DETR, a bipartite matching between ground truth and prediction is constructed based on the Hungarian algorithm [20], which guarantees that each target corresponds to a unique prediction. Following DETR, Wang *et al.* [50] and Sun *et al.* [42] perform one-to-one label assignment for classification to enable end-to-end object detection. More recently, researchers attempt to utilize the pattern of set prediction to improve the performance of other high-level tasks [10,11,45,50,61]. Cheng *et al.* [11] reformulates semantic segmentation as a mask set prediction problem and shows excellent empirical results. Wang *et al.* [50] predicts instance sequences directly via instance sequence set matching for video instance segmentation. In [10,61], the HOI instances can make up the triplet instance sets for both ground truth and prediction, which provides a simple and effective manner for Human Object Interaction (HOI) detection. Moreover, in the task of instance-aware human part parsing, [58] designs a specific differentiable matching method to generate the matching results for predicted limbs with different categories. In this paper, to train our `PointScatter`, we divide the image by predefined scatter regions and perform set predictions between predicted points and GT points on each of the regions in parallel.

3   Methodology

The `PointScatter` receives 2D images and produces point sets to represent the tubular structure. The training process of the set prediction task is end-to-end and efficient contributed by the region-wise bipartite matching method. We will first introduce the architecture of `PointScatter` in Sect. 3.1. Then Sect. 3.2 elaborates on the training process. An overview of our proposed `PointScatter` is shown in Fig. 2.

3.1   PointScatter Architecture

Our `PointScatter` formulates the tubular structure extraction task as a point set prediction task. The pipeline of the inference process of `PointScatter` is

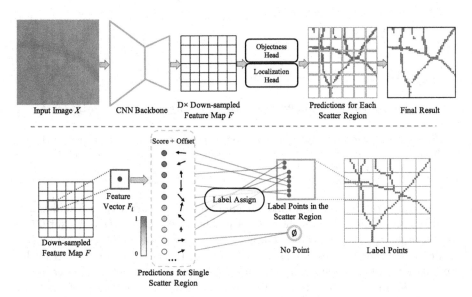

Fig. 2. The pipeline of PointScatter. The top part illustrates the pipeline of point set prediction of PointScatter. It predicts points for each scatter region separately and gathers them to form the final result. The bottom part exhibits the approach of label assignment for each scatter region. We obtain point-to-point assignments to supervise the network training precisely. The predicted points without match will be allocated a "no point" class.

illustrated in the top part of Fig. 2. Given an input image X with shape $\mathbb{H} \times \mathbb{W}$, it is firstly fed into the CNN backbone network, and we obtain the corresponding down-sampled feature map $F \in \mathbb{R}^{C \times H \times W}$, where C is the channel size, H and W indicate the shape of the feature map. Let D denote the downsampling rate of the CNN backbone, we have

$$H = \mathbb{H}/D, \quad W = \mathbb{W}/D. \tag{1}$$

Note that we assume that $\mathbb{H}$ and $\mathbb{W}$ are divisible by D, which is the same situation as semantic segmentation.

Next, we introduce the concept of **scatter region**. In PointScatter, each spatial localization F_i in F is responsible for predicting the corresponding points that situate in a predefined region of the input image. i denotes the spatial index in $H \times W$. We call this predefined specific area **scatter region**. Note that the scatter region could be of arbitrary shape. In this paper, considering the natural grid shape of the feature map F, we define the scatter region as the $D \times D$ patch which has the same relative position in the input image as F_i in F. The top part of Fig. 2 provides an intuitive illustration.

We employ two head networks to perform point prediction for each scatter region. The objectness head and the localization head are responsible for producing point scores and offsets, respectively. The points of all scatter regions jointly constitute the final output.

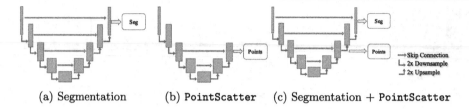

(a) Segmentation   (b) `PointScatter`   (c) Segmentation + `PointScatter`

Fig. 3. Illustrations of applying segmentation method or our `PointScatter` on the U-Net backbone. We show an abstractive version of U-Net for ease of presentation. We set the downsample scale $D = 4$.

The points prediction mechanism from a high-level feature map F makes our `PointScatter` different from the mask segmentation methods (*e.g.* U-Net [35]). Instead of generating a grid of mask with the same shape as the original image, our `PointScatter` utilizes flexible points to describe the tubular structures. The ampliative representation ability enhances the power of the network to learn the complicated fine-scale structures. We will then introduce the details of the head and backbone networks in the following.

Head Networks. The head networks are responsible for predicting points for each image scatter region. They are composed of the Objectness Head (ObjHead) and the Localization Head (LocHead). For each scatter region, `PointScatter` generates N point candidates with their objectness scores and their localization, where N should be set greater than the maximum number of label points within a scatter region.

Formally, given F_i from the downsampled feature map F, where i indicates the spatial localization in $H \times W$, we denote the center localization of the corresponding image scatter region in the input image as $c_i = (X_i^c, Y_i^c)$. Then we predict the objectness score for N points and regress their coordination offsets relative to c_i by ObjHead and LocHead, respectively:

$$\text{score}_i = \text{Sigmoid}(\text{ObjHead}(F_i)) \in \mathbb{R}^N, \quad \text{offset}_i = \text{LocHead}(F_i) \in \mathbb{R}^{N \times 2}. \quad (2)$$

Note that we apply Sigmoid operation after ObjHead to normalize the objectness score to the scale of $[0, 1]$. To acquire the coordinate of the points, we can simply apply the regressed offsets to the center point c_i, *i.e.* $p_i^j = (X_i^c + \text{offset}_i^{j,1}, Y_i^c + \text{offset}_i^{j,2})$, where p_i^j is the j_{th} point generated from F_i. During inference, the points with scores lower than a threshold T will be eliminated. Sliding these two heads on the whole feature map F and merging all predicted points, we can obtain the final results.

In practice, we instantiate ObjHead and LocHead both as a single linear layer, which can be implemented by the convolutional layer with kernel size 1×1. Although the transformer-like architecture [44] is proven to promote the interaction between object items in prior works [5,60], to maintain simplicity and focus on the point representation itself, we adopt the fully convolutional architecture in our `PointScatter`.

Backbone Networks. As introduced above, in `PointScatter`, the only requirement on the backbone network is that it should produce a $D\times$ downsampled feature map relative to the input image. The universality of `PointScatter` makes it compatible with almost all common backbone networks in semantic segmentation [25,35]. In this section, we take as an example the most famous model for medical image segmentation U-Net [35] to show how we apply `PointScatter` to a regular segmentation network.

We illustrate the utilization of the backbone network (*i.e.* U-Net) in Fig. 3. Traditional segmentation methods use the feature map with the same shape as the input image to generate the corresponding segmentation mask (Fig. 3a). Our `PointScatter` (Fig. 3b) passes the $D\times$ downsampled feature map to the head networks, while the successive upsampled feature maps are removed from the computational graph. In Fig. 3c, we show that we can simultaneously apply segmentation and `PointScatter` to the backbone network, which can be regarded as the multitask learning manner. We find that multitask learning will boost the performance of mask segmentation in the following experiments section.

3.2 Training `PointScatter`

The training of `PointScatter` also complies with the paradigm of scatter regions. Therefore, for each scatter region, we should assign the class label and the offset label for each predicted point. To achieve this goal, following prior works [5,60], we first define the cost function between predicted and ground-truth points, and then perform bipartite matching to produce one-to-one label assignment with a low global cost (bottom part of Fig. 2).

We first discuss the cost function. The matching cost should take into account both the objectness scores and the distance of the predicted and ground-truth points. Specifically, for each scatter region, we have a set of K ground-truth points $G = \{g_i\}_{i=1}^K$ and N predicted points $P = \{p_i\}_{i=1}^N$. Note that we omit the index of scatter region in this subsection for simplicity. For each predicted point p_i, its objectness score is denoted as s_i. Since the common assumption is $K \leq N$, we consider G also a set of size N, where the rest part is complemented by $\varnothing$ (no point). Therefore, for a permutation of N elements $\sigma \in \mathfrak{S}_N$, we define the cost for each point assignment as

$$\mathcal{L}_{\text{match}}(g_i, p_{\sigma(i)}) = [L_1(g_i, p_{\sigma(i)})]^\eta \cdot |s_{\sigma(i)} - \mathbb{1}(i \leq K)|^{1-\eta}, \quad (3)$$

where the first term in the equation describes the matching quality of point localization, and the last item indicates the classification error. L_1 is the manhattan distance in this equation, and η is a hyper-parameter determined by cross-validation. Note that we use multiplication instead of addition across the two cost terms, since the effectiveness of multiplication has been proven in [47].

Label Assignment with Region-wise Bipartite Matching. The second step is to get the optimal permutation σ. Previous works such as DETR [5] adopt the Hungarian algorithm [20] to perform set matching. Following this way, a direct generalization to our problem is to compute the bipartite matching iteratively for each scatter region. However, due to the large number of scatter regions in the images, it is inefficient to execute the iteration.

To tackle this problem, we propose a greedy-based bipartite matching method. We present the matching for each image scatter region in Algorithm 1. The greedy bipartite matching iterates the ground-truth points and finds the predicted point with the minimum cost from the left predicted points. The greedy method reduces the computational complexity of the Hungarian algorithm from $O(N^3)$ to $O(N^2)$, and is easy to be implemented on GPU using the deep learning framework (*i.e.* PyTorch) for batched computation. We provide an efficient implementation of the greedy bipartite matching in the supplementary materials.

The greedy method could not generate the optimal matching results. However, the network predictions become gradually closer to the ground-truth points during training. The optimization of the network improves the quality of predicted points, which makes the matching problem easier, hence the weak greedy method is capable of allocating the point targets.

Algorithm 1 Greedy Bipartite Matching

1: **Input:** $G = \{g_1, g_2, ..., g_K\}$, $P = \{p_1, p_2, ..., p_N\}$, $C \in \mathbb{R}^{K \times N}$
2: G is the list of ground truth points, P is the list of predicted points, C is the cost matrix, $C_{i\cdot}$ is the i-th row of C, $C_{\cdot j}$ is the j-th column of C
3: **Output:** $S = \{\sigma(1), \sigma(2), ..., \sigma(K)\}$, $\sigma(i)$ represents that the predicted point $p_{\sigma(i)}$ is assigned to the ground truth point g_i; the rest of predicted points $\{p_{\sigma(K+1)}, ..., p_{\sigma(N)}\}$ are assigned to "no point"
4: **begin**
5:    **for** $i = 1$ **to** K
6:        $n \leftarrow \text{argmin } C_{i\cdot}$
7:        $\sigma(i) \leftarrow n$
8:        $C_{\cdot n} \leftarrow \text{inf}$
9:    **end**
10:    **return** S
11: **end**

Loss Functions. To train PointScatter, the loss function is composed of objectness loss and regression loss:

$$\mathcal{L}_{\text{total}} = \mathcal{L}_{\text{obj}} + \lambda \mathcal{L}_{\text{reg}}, \tag{4}$$

where $\mathcal{L}_{\text{obj}}$ is instantiated as Focal Loss [24] to deal with the unbalanced distribution of objectness targets and we use L_1 loss for $\mathcal{L}_{\text{reg}}$. Note that the regression loss is only applied to the positive points and the points matched "no point" will be eliminated. Practically, we normalize the total loss by dividing the number of ground-truth points to keep the optimization process stable.

It is worth mentioning that almost all current datasets for tubular structure extraction provide mask annotation, therefore we should convert the mask annotation to points to supervise the training of `PointScatter`. We accomplish this goal by replacing each pixel with one point located in the center of this pixel. Concretely, a mask is represented as a matrix with binary values $\mathbf{Y}^{\mathbb{H} \times \mathbb{W}} \in \{0, 1\}$, and we convert it to the point sets $\{(i, j) | Y_{i,j} = 1, i \in [1, \mathbb{H}], j \in [1, \mathbb{W}]\}$.

4   Experiments

4.1   Experimental Setup

Datasets. We evaluate our `PointScatter` on four public tubular datasets, including two medical datasets and two satellite datasets. DRIVE [41] and STARE [16] are two retinal datasets that are commonly adopted in the medical image segmentation problem to evaluate the performance of vessel segmentation. The Massachusetts Roads (MassRoad) dataset [28] and DeepGlobe [13] are labeled with the pixel-level annotation for road segmentation. We use the official data split for DRIVE and STARE in MMSegmentation [12] and follow the data split method in previous works [38,39] for the other two datasets. We report the performance on the test set.

Tasks and Metrics. In this paper, we focus on two different tasks relevant to the understanding of tubular structures: tubular structure segmentation and centerline extraction. The above four datasets are used for the image segmentation task in previous works, and the most popular dataset for centerline extraction is the MICCAI 2008 Coronary Artery Tracking (CAT08) dataset [36]. But unfortunately, the CAT08 dataset and the evaluation server are not publicly available now. Therefore, we generate the centerline labels using the skeleton extraction method in [38] to fulfill the evaluation of centerline extraction. The labelled centerline is a set of connected pixels with a line-like structure where the width is 1 pixel. It is a more challenging task to extract the centerlines accurately by deep models. We then introduce the metrics we utilize for these two tasks.

For the tubular structure segmentation task, we consider two types of metrics: volumetric and topology-based. The volumetric scores include Dice coefficient, Accuracy, AUC, and the recently proposed clDice [38]. We also calculate the topology-based scores including the mean of absolute Betti Errors for the Betti Numbers β_0 and β_1 and the mean absolute error of Euler characteristic. We follow [38] to compute the topology-based scores.

For the centerline extraction task, we report the Dice coefficient, Accuracy, AUC, Precision, and Recall as the volumetric scores. To increase the robustness of the evaluation, we apply a three-pixel tolerance region around the centerline annotation following [15]. We adopt the same topology-based metrics as the tubular structure segmentation task.

The above metrics are designed for mask prediction, while our `PointScatter` generates points to describe the foreground structures. Therefore, we should convert the points to the segmentation mask in order to accommodate the evaluation

Table 1. Main results on tubular structure segmentation task. The gray lines use our `PointScatter`. We mark the best performance by bold numbers.

Dataset	Backbone	Method	Volumetric Scores (%) ↑				Topological Error ↓		
			AUC	Dice	clDice	ACC	β_0	β_1	χ_{error}
DRIVE	UNet	softDice	97.05	81.09	80.69	95.28	1.504	1.129	1.806
		clDice	96.84	81.15	81.55	95.21	1.072	0.993	1.354
		PointScatter	**97.69**	**81.63**	**82.89**	95.23	1.317	1.250	1.628
		softDice+PSAUX	97.27	81.59	81.43	**95.37**	1.004	0.980	1.269
		clDice+PSAUX	96.97	81.51	82.54	95.24	**0.873**	**0.944**	**1.131**
	UNet++	softDice	96.42	80.96	80.55	95.24	1.698	1.106	1.978
		clDice	96.77	81.10	81.48	95.17	1.105	0.965	1.359
		PointScatter	**97.45**	**81.38**	**82.34**	95.17	1.290	1.225	1.600
		softDice+PSAUX	96.45	81.31	81.03	**95.29**	**0.936**	0.956	1.184
		clDice+PSAUX	96.51	81.28	81.62	95.22	0.924	**0.937**	1.189
	ResUNet	softDice	97.78	82.11	82.28	95.49	1.284	1.067	1.562
		clDice	97.09	81.43	82.48	95.21	1.005	1.006	1.272
		PointScatter	97.87	81.85	82.75	95.34	1.547	1.273	1.834
		softDice+PSAUX	**97.97**	**82.45**	82.64	**95.59**	1.372	1.023	1.628
		clDice+PSAUX	97.36	82.02	**84.62**	95.31	**0.883**	**1.019**	**1.142**
STARE	UNet	softDice	94.86	82.27	84.87	97.45	1.093	0.667	1.260
		clDice	96.82	82.29	85.22	97.44	0.790	0.665	0.943
		PointScatter	**97.86**	82.73	85.83	97.45	0.818	0.774	0.978
		softDice+PSAUX	96.42	82.78	85.44	97.51	0.727	0.625	0.887
		clDice+PSAUX	97.32	**83.11**	**86.45**	**97.54**	**0.631**	**0.614**	**0.778**
	UNet++	softDice	95.05	82.22	84.60	97.45	1.005	0.667	1.163
		clDice	96.48	82.62	85.72	97.49	0.801	0.648	0.968
		PointScatter	**97.85**	82.80	85.98	97.43	0.844	0.745	0.997
		softDice+PSAUX	95.59	82.85	85.54	**97.53**	0.658	0.649	0.801
		clDice+PSAUX	96.36	**82.96**	**86.11**	97.53	**0.650**	**0.617**	**0.800**
	ResUNet	softDice	96.27	81.65	84.11	97.38	0.913	0.695	1.051
		clDice	96.65	82.51	85.33	97.47	0.731	0.650	0.884
		PointScatter	**97.77**	82.40	85.00	97.38	0.949	0.730	1.093
		softDice+PSAUX	96.59	81.80	83.55	97.41	0.796	0.670	0.944
		clDice+PSAUX	96.04	**82.68**	**85.60**	**97.48**	**0.601**	**0.636**	**0.748**

Dataset	Backbone	Method	Volumetric Scores (%) ↑				Topological Error ↓		
			AUC	Dice	clDice	ACC	β_0	β_1	χ_{error}
MassRoads	UNet	softDice	97.02	76.96	86.33	96.86	0.686	1.361	1.356
		clDice	95.76	76.11	85.68	96.68	0.679	1.380	1.334
		PointScatter	**97.65**	77.57	86.42	96.87	0.944	1.353	1.616
		softDice+PSAUX	97.59	**78.14**	**87.38**	96.98	0.526	**1.257**	1.190
		clDice+PSAUX	96.60	77.68	87.34	96.88	**0.498**	1.316	**1.187**
	UNet++	softDice	97.10	76.88	86.08	96.82	0.690	1.373	1.351
		clDice	95.80	76.39	86.15	96.72	0.685	1.455	1.373
		PointScatter	**97.62**	77.65	86.40	96.90	0.836	1.315	1.503
		softDice+PSAUX	97.60	**78.10**	87.24	96.99	0.559	1.306	1.252
		clDice+PSAUX	96.41	77.81	**87.34**	96.91	**0.498**	1.316	**1.181**
	ResUNet	softDice	96.93	76.04	85.57	96.73	0.992	1.478	1.658
		clDice	96.12	75.97	85.69	96.68	0.887	1.521	1.571
		PointScatter	**97.40**	76.34	85.07	96.74	1.448	1.423	2.039
		softDice+PSAUX	97.40	**77.08**	86.31	96.85	0.745	**1.416**	1.435
		clDice+PSAUX	96.69	76.67	**86.36**	96.76	0.803	1.456	1.472
DeepGlobe	UNet	softDice	97.65	74.71	80.08	97.89	1.154	0.605	1.166
		clDice	96.03	74.96	81.16	97.90	0.691	0.556	0.751
		PointScatter	**98.64**	78.07	82.38	98.12	0.855	0.541	0.907
		softDice+PSAUX	98.27	**78.00**	83.96	98.15	0.492	0.449	0.530
		clDice+PSAUX	96.87	77.20	83.31	98.07	**0.435**	**0.472**	**0.485**
	LinkNet34	softDice	97.51	75.64	81.58	97.95	0.704	0.549	0.763
		clDice	97.03	75.63	82.03	97.94	0.590	0.646	0.706
		PointScatter	**98.59**	79.21	84.04	98.20	0.710	0.543	0.802
		softDice+PSAUX	98.00	78.88	**85.43**	**98.23**	0.491	0.446	0.549
		clDice+PSAUX	97.55	78.58	85.08	98.18	**0.451**	**0.448**	**0.516**
	DinkNet34	softDice	97.45	75.60	81.59	97.95	0.604	0.524	0.655
		clDice	97.07	75.23	82.18	97.92	0.938	0.562	1.009
		PointScatter	**98.66**	79.39	84.36	98.20	0.749	0.558	0.833
		softDice+PSAUX	98.30	78.95	**85.33**	98.21	0.513	**0.440**	0.571
		clDice+PSAUX	97.78	78.29	85.01	98.16	**0.511**	0.549	0.613

protocol. Specifically, an image can be regarded as a grid with the size of each bin 1×1, and each point is expected to be located in one bin. We first initialize an empty score map with the same size as the input image. For each bin in the output score map, we directly set the objectness score of the point located in this bin as its score. The bins without any point will be endowed with zero scores. To get the segmentation mask, we can threshold the score map by 0.5.

Implementation Details. As discussed in Sect. 3.1, our `PointScatter` is compatible with various segmentation backbones with an encoder-decoder shape, the adjustable parameters are the downsample rate D and the number of points in each scatter region N. Experimentally, we set $D = 4$ and $N = 16$ by default. The threshold of objectness score during inference is $T = 0.1$. During training, we set $\eta = 0.8$ in Eq. 3 to balance the localization cost and classification cost. Additional implementation details are depicted in the supplementary materials. We implement our model based on PyTorch and MMSegmentation [12].

4.2   Main Results

Our `PointScatter` can be regarded as an alternative for the segmentation approach. We compare our `PointScatter` with two very competitive segmentation methods (*i.e.* softDice [27] and clDice [38]) on various mainstream backbone networks [7, 35, 55, 57, 59]. We use the same training settings for the segmentation methods with our `PointScatter`, including the optimizer, training schedule, *etc.*

Table 2. Main results on centerline extraction task.

Dataset	Backbone	Method	Volumetric Scores (%) ↑					Topological Error ↓		
			AUC	Dice	Prec	Recall	ACC	β_0	β_1	χ_{error}
DRIVE	UNet	softDice	89.53	73.41	90.97	61.52	97.63	3.177	1.843	3.555
		PointScatter	94.46	81.92	92.52	73.51	98.05	5.203	2.612	5.509
		softDice+PS	93.13	75.92	91.08	65.08	97.76	2.677	1.753	3.051
	UNet++	softDice	83.83	72.06	90.48	59.87	97.54	5.651	2.371	6.006
		PointScatter	93.29	82.23	91.14	74.91	98.04	1.959	1.657	2.282
		softDice+PS	87.88	72.93	91.29	60.72	97.61	6.360	2.600	6.671
	ResUNet	softDice	90.83	74.86	91.36	63.40	97.70	2.774	1.723	3.147
		PointScatter	94.79	83.91	91.73	77.31	98.18	3.169	1.983	3.495
		softDice+PS	95.40	81.52	92.95	72.60	98.12	2.479	1.673	2.853
STARE	UNet	softDice	86.99	72.14	93.01	58.91	98.91	3.053	1.562	3.253
		PointScatter	94.52	81.77	92.09	73.52	99.10	2.158	1.424	2.303
		softDice+PS	88.34	75.10	92.51	63.20	98.98	1.870	1.219	2.061
	UNet++	softDice	84.94	73.08	92.87	60.24	98.93	3.388	1.556	3.588
		PointScatter	93.07	80.03	92.74	70.38	99.07	2.582	1.613	2.743
		softDice+PS	84.91	74.20	93.20	61.64	98.96	2.300	1.368	2.487
	ResUNet	softDice	86.56	73.93	92.66	61.49	98.95	2.568	1.341	2.760
		PointScatter	95.93	82.44	92.15	74.58	99.12	2.495	1.451	2.641
		softDice+PS	93.08	77.55	93.24	66.39	99.04	1.964	1.199	2.152

Dataset	Backbone	Method	Volumetric Scores (%) ↑					Topological Error ↓		
			AUC	Dice	Prec	Recall	ACC	β_0	β_1	χ_{error}
MassRoads	UNet	softDice	95.09	66.24	72.36	61.08	99.06	2.225	2.589	2.919
		PointScatter	93.59	69.63	70.28	68.99	99.01	5.955	2.244	6.135
		softDice+PS	96.23	67.60	73.74	62.40	99.09	1.990	2.438	2.683
	UNet++	softDice	95.07	66.01	71.94	60.99	99.05	2.315	2.699	3.011
		PointScatter	96.54	69.93	71.18	68.73	99.03	2.353	2.407	3.033
		softDice+PS	96.05	67.76	73.06	63.17	99.08	2.329	2.582	3.030
	ResUNet	softDice	94.84	65.84	71.52	61.01	99.04	2.816	2.784	3.512
		PointScatter	95.42	67.45	70.83	64.88	99.02	5.666	2.651	5.409
		softDice+PS	96.43	67.52	73.00	62.82	99.08	2.295	2.628	2.996
DeepGlobe	LinkNet34	softDice	96.59	56.58	62.56	51.64	99.60	1.823	1.157	1.845
		PointScatter	97.84	62.78	66.38	59.55	99.62	2.127	1.059	2.145
		softDice+PS	97.59	61.17	67.08	56.21	99.63	1.358	1.001	1.380
		softDice	96.62	57.42	62.82	52.87	99.60	1.481	1.108	1.503
	DinkNet34	PointScatter	95.04	59.36	63.85	55.46	99.60	9.880	1.933	8.516
		softDice+PS	97.44	61.55	66.97	56.95	99.63	1.395	1.022	1.417
		softDice	96.08	56.42	62.37	51.51	99.60	1.528	1.121	1.549
	DinkNet34	PointScatter	95.54	60.89	64.20	57.91	99.60	7.341	1.375	6.520
		softDice+PS	97.71	61.71	66.89	57.77	99.63	1.436	0.997	1.458

These methods are also implemented by MMSegmentation for a fair comparison. Except for using PointScatter directly, we also study the effect of using our PointScatter as an auxiliary task for the segmentation method. We combine these two methods as shown in Fig. 3c and use the sum of the loss function of these two methods as the objective to train the network. We denote this method as PSAUX (abbreviation for PointScatter AUXiliary). We use the centerline labels to train the PointScatter branch in PSAUX.

Tubular Structure Segmentation. We exhibit the results in Table 1. According to the volumetric metrics, we can conclude that our PointScatter achieves superior performance compared to the segmentation methods on most of the combinations of the datasets and the backbone networks, which confirms the effectiveness of our PointScatter. When applying PSAUX to the segmentation method, we also observe improvements for most of the cases. The performance of PSAUX certifies that the point set representation leads to better feature learning for the backbone network. Our PointScatter obtains inferior performance than clDice according to the topology-based scores. We argue that it is because our PointScatter can capture more fine-scale structures which cannot be discovered by the segmentation models. These detailed predictions are beneficial to the volumetric scores but harmful to the topology. We will qualitatively analyze this phenomenon later. In addition, it is worth mentioning that PSAUX can improve the topology scores as shown in Table 1.

Centerline Extraction. We also conduct extensive experiments to validate the advantage of PointScatter for the centerline extraction task. As shown in Table 2, our PointScatter consistently surpasses the performance of the segmentation methods by a large margin according to the volumetric scores. Our PointScatter achieves similar precision to softDice, while complies with significantly higher recall values. It confirms again that our PointScatter can capture fine-scale details which cannot be detected by the segmentation model. The effect of PSAUX is similar to the tubular structure segmentation task.

Table 3. Ablation on N. ($D = 4$)

Dataset	N	Segmentation Dice (%)	clDice (%)	ACC (%)	Centerline Dice (%)	ACC (%)
DRIVE	8	64.80	66.71	92.27	78.31	97.79
	16	**81.63**	**82.89**	**95.23**	**81.92**	**98.05**
	32	78.73	80.73	94.60	79.07	97.85
	64	78.33	80.57	94.54	80.08	97.91
MassRoads	8	57.61	58.23	95.20	64.73	98.94
	16	**77.57**	86.42	96.87	69.63	99.01
	32	77.52	**86.55**	96.87	70.05	99.03
	64	77.54	86.40	**96.89**	**70.38**	**99.04**

Table 4. Ablation on D.

Dataset	D	Segmentation Dice (%)	clDice (%)	ACC (%)	Centerline Dice (%)	ACC (%)
DRIVE	2	81.26	82.16	95.20	**82.70**	**98.07**
	4	**81.63**	**82.89**	**95.23**	81.92	98.05
	8	79.80	80.48	94.77	78.59	97.81
MassRoads	2	**77.90**	**86.92**	**96.93**	**69.87**	99.02
	4	77.57	86.42	96.87	69.63	99.01
	8	77.54	86.31	96.86	68.79	**99.03**

4.3   Ablation Study

Number of Points (N). We ablate the number of predicted points (N) within each scatter region in Table 3. With $D = 4$, the maximum number of ground-truth points in each scatter region is 16. Therefore, the performance is not satisfactory when $N = 8$. Increasing N has marginal improvement on the performance when $N \geq 16$.

Downsample Rate (D). We compare the effect of different downsample rates D in Table 4. For the DRIVE dataset, $D = 4$ shows the best performance on the segmentation task while $D = 2$ is slightly better on the centerline extraction task. For the MassRoads dataset, different D yield similar performances on both tasks.

Greedy Bipartite Matching. Our greedy bipartite matching is theoretically faster than the Hungarian method and can be easily implemented on GPU. We compare the running time in each training iteration of these two methods in Table 5. We execute the greedy method on GPU TITAN RTX and the Hungarian algorithm on Intel(R) Xeon(R) CPU E5-2680 v4. The results show that our greedy method is at least three orders of magnitude faster than the Hungarian algorithm. The latency of our greedy method is negligible compared to the computation time of neural networks, whereas the latency of the Hungarian algorithm is unaffordable for large images.

Table 5. Running time (seconds) of Greedy and Hungarian bipartite matching. We set $D = 4$ and batchsize $= 4$.

Method	Complexity	Image size	Running time (seconds)
Greedy	$O(M^2)$	384×384	0.0076
		768×768	0.0100
		1024×1024	0.0123
Hungarian	$O(M^3)$	384×384	3.0043
		768×768	12.7027
		1024×1024	20.9922

4.4   Qualitative Analysis

We qualitatively compare our method and the mask segmentation methods in Fig. 4. Our `PointScatter` performs better on small branches or bifurcation points. It shows a better ability for our `PointScatter` to learn the complicated fine-scale information, which is contributed by the flexibility of the point set representation. Note that sometimes the small branches detected by `PointScatter` are not densely connected (*e.g.* the top left image), which decreases the performance on the topology-based metrics. However, it is better to extract tubular segments than miss the whole branch. We will leave future work to improve the topology performance of our `PointScatter`.

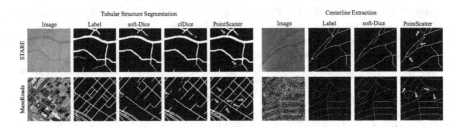

Fig. 4. Visual comparison for our `PointScatter` with other methods (zoom for details). The areas pointed by the arrows are missed by other models, while extracted by our `PointScatter`. More qualitative results can be found in the supplementary materials.

5   Conclusion

This paper proposes `PointScatter`, a novel architecture that introduces the point set representation for tubular structure extraction. This network can be trained end-to-end and efficiently with our proposed greedy bipartite matching algorithm. The extensive experiments reveal that our `PointScatter` achieves superior performance to the segmentation counterparts on the tubular structure segmentation task in most of the experiments, and significantly surpasses other methods on the centerline extraction task.

This novel design presents the potential of point set representation for tubular structures, and future work may include:

- Exploring the performance of `PointScatter` on the more challenging 3D tubular extraction tasks such as coronary vessel extraction.
- Improving the topology of predicted points of `PointScatter` to enhance the performance of the topology-based metrics.
- Promoting the point set representation for the general segmentation task.

Acknowledgement. This work is supported by Exploratory Research Project of Zhejiang Lab (No. 2022RC0AN02), Project 2020BD006 supported by PKUBaidu Fund.

References

1. Alvarez, L., et al.: Tracking the aortic lumen geometry by optimizing the 3D orientation of its cross-sections. In: Descoteaux, M., Maier-Hein, L., Franz, A., Jannin, P., Collins, D.L., Duchesne, S. (eds.) MICCAI 2017. LNCS, vol. 10434, pp. 174–181. Springer, Cham (2017). https://doi.org/10.1007/978-3-319-66185-8_20
2. Bauer, C., Pock, T., Sorantin, E., Bischof, H., Beichel, R.: Segmentation of interwoven 3d tubular tree structures utilizing shape priors and graph cuts. Med. Image Anal. **14**(2), 172–184 (2010)
3. Benmansour, F., Cohen, L.D.: Tubular structure segmentation based on minimal path method and anisotropic enhancement. Int. J. Comput. Vision **92**(2), 192–210 (2011)
4. Cao, Z., Simon, T., Wei, S.E., Sheikh, Y.: Realtime multi-person 2d pose estimation using part affinity fields. In: Proceedings of the IEEE Conference on Computer Vision and Pattern Recognition, pp. 7291–7299 (2017)
5. Carion, N., Massa, F., Synnaeve, G., Usunier, N., Kirillov, A., Zagoruyko, S.: End-to-end object detection with transformers. In: Vedaldi, A., Bischof, H., Brox, T., Frahm, J.-M. (eds.) ECCV 2020. LNCS, vol. 12346, pp. 213–229. Springer, Cham (2020). https://doi.org/10.1007/978-3-030-58452-8_13
6. Caselles, V., Kimmel, R., Sapiro, G.: Geodesic active contours. Int. J. Comput. Vision **22**(1), 61–79 (1997)
7. Chaurasia, A., Culurciello, E.: LinkNet: exploiting encoder representations for efficient semantic segmentation. In: 2017 IEEE Visual Communications and Image Processing (VCIP), pp. 1–4. IEEE (2017)
8. Chen, L.C., Papandreou, G., Kokkinos, I., Murphy, K., Yuille, A.L.: DeepLab: semantic image segmentation with deep convolutional nets, Atrous convolution, and fully connected CRFs. IEEE Trans. Pattern Anal. Mach. Intell. **40**(4), 834–848 (2017)
9. Chen, L.-C., Zhu, Y., Papandreou, G., Schroff, F., Adam, H.: Encoder-decoder with Atrous separable convolution for semantic image segmentation. In: Ferrari, V., Hebert, M., Sminchisescu, C., Weiss, Y. (eds.) ECCV 2018. LNCS, vol. 11211, pp. 833–851. Springer, Cham (2018). https://doi.org/10.1007/978-3-030-01234-2_49
10. Chen, M., Liao, Y., Liu, S., Chen, Z., Wang, F., Qian, C.: Reformulating HOI detection as adaptive set prediction. In: Proceedings of the IEEE/CVF Conference on Computer Vision and Pattern Recognition, pp. 9004–9013 (2021)
11. Cheng, B., Schwing, A., Kirillov, A.: Per-pixel classification is not all you need for semantic segmentation. Advances in Neural Information Processing Systems 34 (2021)
12. MMS Contributors: MMSegmentation: OpenMMLab semantic segmentation toolbox and benchmark (2020). www.github.com/open-mmlab/mmsegmentation
13. Demir, I., et al.: DeepGlobe 2018: a challenge to parse the earth through satellite images. In: Proceedings of the IEEE Conference on Computer Vision and Pattern Recognition Workshops, pp. 172–181 (2018)
14. Duan, K., Bai, S., Xie, L., Qi, H., Huang, Q., Tian, Q.: CenterNet: keypoint triplets for object detection. In: Proceedings of the IEEE/CVF International Conference on Computer Vision, pp. 6569–6578 (2019)
15. Guimaraes, P., Wigdahl, J., Ruggeri, A.: A fast and efficient technique for the automatic tracing of corneal nerves in confocal microscopy. Transl. Vision Sci. Technol. **5**(5), 7 (2016)

16. Hoover, A., Kouznetsova, V., Goldbaum, M.: Locating blood vessels in retinal images by piecewise threshold probing of a matched filter response. IEEE Trans. Med. Imaging **19**(3), 203–210 (2000)
17. Hu, X., Li, F., Samaras, D., Chen, C.: Topology-preserving deep image segmentation. In: Advances in Neural Information Processing Systems 32 (2019)
18. Kirillov, A., Levinkov, E., Andres, B., Savchynskyy, B., Rother, C.: InstanceCut: from edges to instances with MultiCut. In: Proceedings of the IEEE Conference on Computer Vision and Pattern Recognition, pp. 5008–5017 (2017)
19. Kirillov, A., Wu, Y., He, K., Girshick, R.: PointRend: image segmentation as rendering. In: Proceedings of the IEEE/CVF Conference on Computer Vision and Pattern Recognition, pp. 9799–9808 (2020)
20. Kuhn, H.W.: The Hungarian method for the assignment problem. Nav. Res. Logist. Q. **2**(1–2), 83–97 (1955)
21. Law, H., Deng, J.: CornerNet: detecting objects as paired keypoints. In: Ferrari, V., Hebert, M., Sminchisescu, C., Weiss, Y. (eds.) Computer Vision – ECCV 2018. LNCS, vol. 11218, pp. 765–781. Springer, Cham (2018). https://doi.org/10.1007/978-3-030-01264-9_45
22. Lenga, M., Klinder, T., Bürger, C., von Berg, J., Franz, A., Lorenz, C.: Deep learning based rib centerline extraction and labeling. In: Vrtovec, T., Yao, J., Zheng, G., Pozo, J.M. (eds.) MSKI 2018. LNCS, vol. 11404, pp. 99–113. Springer, Cham (2019). https://doi.org/10.1007/978-3-030-11166-3_9
23. Li, Z., Xia, Q., Hu, Z., Wang, W., Xu, L., Zhang, S.: A deep reinforced tree-traversal agent for coronary artery centerline extraction. In: de Bruijne, M., et al. (eds.) MICCAI 2021. LNCS, vol. 12905, pp. 418–428. Springer, Cham (2021). https://doi.org/10.1007/978-3-030-87240-3_40
24. Lin, T.Y., Goyal, P., Girshick, R., He, K., Dollár, P.: Focal loss for dense object detection. In: Proceedings of the IEEE International Conference on Computer Vision, pp. 2980–2988 (2017)
25. Long, J., Shelhamer, E., Darrell, T.: Fully convolutional networks for semantic segmentation. In: Proceedings of the IEEE Conference on Computer Vision and Pattern Recognition, pp. 3431–3440 (2015)
26. Ma, Y., et al.: ROSE: a retinal OCT-angiography vessel segmentation dataset and new model. IEEE Trans. Med. Imaging **40**(3), 928–939 (2020)
27. Milletari, F., Navab, N., Ahmadi, S.A.: V-Net: fully convolutional neural networks for volumetric medical image segmentation. In: 2016 Fourth International Conference on 3D Vision (3DV), pp. 565–571. IEEE (2016)
28. Mnih, V.: Machine learning for aerial image labeling. University of Toronto (Canada) (2013)
29. Mosinska, A., Marquez-Neila, P., Koziński, M., Fua, P.: Beyond the pixel-wise loss for topology-aware delineation. In: Proceedings of the IEEE Conference on Computer Vision and Pattern Recognition, pp. 3136–3145 (2018)
30. Oner, D., Koziński, M., Citraro, L., Dadap, N.C., Konings, A.G., Fua, P.: Promoting connectivity of network-like structures by enforcing region separation. arXiv preprint arXiv:2009.07011 (2020)
31. Papandreou, G., Zhu, T., Chen, L.-C., Gidaris, S., Tompson, J., Murphy, K.: PersonLab: person pose estimation and instance segmentation with a bottom-up, part-based, geometric embedding model. In: Ferrari, V., Hebert, M., Sminchisescu, C., Weiss, Y. (eds.) Computer Vision – ECCV 2018. LNCS, vol. 11218, pp. 282–299. Springer, Cham (2018). https://doi.org/10.1007/978-3-030-01264-9_17

32. Paszke, A., et al.: PyTorch: an imperative style, high-performance deep learning library. In: Wallach, H.M., Larochelle, H., Beygelzimer, A., d'Alché-Buc, F., Fox, E.B., Garnett, R. (eds.) NeurIPS (2019)

33. Qi, C.R., Su, H., Mo, K., Guibas, L.J.: PointNet: deep learning on point sets for 3d classification and segmentation. In: Proceedings of the IEEE Conference on Computer Vision and Pattern Recognition, pp. 652–660 (2017)

34. Qi, C.R., Yi, L., Su, H., Guibas, L.J.: Pointnet++: deep hierarchical feature learning on point sets in a metric space. In: Advances in Neural Information Processing Systems 30 (2017)

35. Ronneberger, O., Fischer, P., Brox, T.: U-Net: convolutional networks for biomedical image segmentation. In: Navab, N., Hornegger, J., Wells, W.M., Frangi, A.F. (eds.) MICCAI 2015. LNCS, vol. 9351, pp. 234–241. Springer, Cham (2015). https://doi.org/10.1007/978-3-319-24574-4_28

36. Schaap, M., et al.: Standardized evaluation methodology and reference database for evaluating coronary artery centerline extraction algorithms. Med. Image Anal. **13**(5), 701–714 (2009)

37. Shin, S.Y., Lee, S., Yun, I.D., Lee, K.M.: Deep vessel segmentation by learning graphical connectivity. Med. Image Anal. **58**, 101556 (2019)

38. Shit, S., et al.: clDice-a novel topology-preserving loss function for tubular structure segmentation. In: Proceedings of the IEEE/CVF Conference on Computer Vision and Pattern Recognition, pp. 16560–16569 (2021)

39. Singh, S., et al.: Self-supervised feature learning for semantic segmentation of overhead imagery. In: BMVC, vol. 1, p. 4 (2018)

40. Sironi, A., Lepetit, V., Fua, P.: Multiscale centerline detection by learning a scale-space distance transform. In: Proceedings of the IEEE Conference on Computer Vision and Pattern Recognition, pp. 2697–2704 (2014)

41. Staal, J., Abràmoff, M.D., Niemeijer, M., Viergever, M.A., Van Ginneken, B.: Ridge-based vessel segmentation in color images of the retina. IEEE Trans. Med. Imaging **23**(4), 501–509 (2004)

42. Sun, P., et al.: What makes for end-to-end object detection? In: International Conference on Machine Learning, pp. 9934–9944. PMLR (2021)

43. Tetteh, G., et al.: DeepVesselNet: vessel segmentation, centerline prediction, and bifurcation detection in 3-d angiographic volumes. Front. Neurosci., 1285 (2020)

44. Vaswani, A., et al.: Attention is all you need. In: Advances in Neural Information Processing Systems 30 (2017)

45. Wang, H., Zhu, Y., Adam, H., Yuille, A., Chen, L.C.: MaX-DeepLab: end-to-end panoptic segmentation with mask transformers. In: Proceedings of the IEEE/CVF Conference on Computer Vision and Pattern Recognition, pp. 5463–5474 (2021)

46. Wang, J., Song, L., Li, Z., Sun, H., Sun, J., Zheng, N.: End-to-end object detection with fully convolutional network. In: Proceedings of the IEEE/CVF Conference on Computer Vision and Pattern Recognition, pp. 15849–15858 (2021)

47. Wang, J., Song, L., Li, Z., Sun, H., Sun, J., Zheng, N.: End-to-end object detection with fully convolutional network. In: Proceedings of the IEEE/CVF Conference on Computer Vision and Pattern Recognition (CVPR), pp. 15849–15858, June 2021

48. Wang, J., et al.: Deep high-resolution representation learning for visual recognition. IEEE Trans. Pattern Anal. Mach. Intell. **43**(10), 3349–3364 (2020)

49. Wang, Y., et al.: Deep distance transform for tubular structure segmentation in CT scans. In: Proceedings of the IEEE/CVF Conference on Computer Vision and Pattern Recognition, pp. 3833–3842 (2020)

50. Wang, Y., et al.: End-to-end video instance segmentation with transformers. In: Proceedings of the IEEE/CVF Conference on Computer Vision and Pattern Recognition, pp. 8741–8750 (2021)
51. Wu, H., Wang, W., Zhong, J., Lei, B., Wen, Z., Qin, J.: SCS-Net: a scale and context sensitive network for retinal vessel segmentation. Med. Image Anal. **70**, 102025 (2021)
52. Yang, J., Gu, S., Wei, D., Pfister, H., Ni, B.: RibSeg dataset and strong point cloud baselines for rib segmentation from CT scans. In: de Bruijne, M., et al. (eds.) MICCAI 2021. LNCS, vol. 12901, pp. 611–621. Springer, Cham (2021). https://doi.org/10.1007/978-3-030-87193-2_58
53. Yang, Z., Liu, S., Hu, H., Wang, L., Lin, S.: RepPoints: point set representation for object detection. In: Proceedings of the IEEE/CVF International Conference on Computer Vision, pp. 9657–9666 (2019)
54. Yang, Z., et al.: Dense RepPoints: representing visual objects with dense point sets. In: Vedaldi, A., Bischof, H., Brox, T., Frahm, J.-M. (eds.) ECCV 2020. LNCS, vol. 12366, pp. 227–244. Springer, Cham (2020). https://doi.org/10.1007/978-3-030-58589-1_14
55. Zhang, Z., Liu, Q., Wang, Y.: Road extraction by deep residual U-Net. IEEE Geosci. Remote Sens. Lett. **15**(5), 749–753 (2018)
56. Zhao, H., Jiang, L., Jia, J., Torr, P.H., Koltun, V.: Point transformer. In: Proceedings of the IEEE/CVF International Conference on Computer Vision, pp. 16259–16268 (2021)
57. Zhou, L., Zhang, C., Wu, M.: D-LinkNet: LinkNet with pretrained encoder and dilated convolution for high resolution satellite imagery road extraction. In: Proceedings of the IEEE Conference on Computer Vision and Pattern Recognition Workshops, pp. 182–186 (2018)
58. Zhou, T., Wang, W., Liu, S., Yang, Y., Van Gool, L.: Differentiable multi-granularity human representation learning for instance-aware human semantic parsing. In: Proceedings of the IEEE/CVF Conference on Computer Vision and Pattern Recognition, pp. 1622–1631 (2021)
59. Zhou, Z., Rahman Siddiquee, M.M., Tajbakhsh, N., Liang, J.: UNet++: a nested U-Net architecture for medical image segmentation. In: Stoyanov, D., et al. (eds.) DLMIA/ML-CDS -2018. LNCS, vol. 11045, pp. 3–11. Springer, Cham (2018). https://doi.org/10.1007/978-3-030-00889-5_1
60. Zhu, X., Su, W., Lu, L., Li, B., Wang, X., Dai, J.: Deformable DETR: deformable transformers for end-to-end object detection. arXiv preprint arXiv:2010.04159 (2020)
61. Zou, C., et al.: End-to-end human object interaction detection with HOI transformer. In: Proceedings of the IEEE/CVF Conference on Computer Vision and Pattern Recognition, pp. 11825–11834 (2021)

Check and Link: Pairwise Lesion Correspondence Guides Mammogram Mass Detection

Ziwei Zhao[1,4,5], Dong Wang[2], Yihong Chen[1], Ziteng Wang[3], and Liwei Wang[1,2(✉)]

[1] Center for Data Science, Peking University, Beijing, China
zhaozw@stu.pku.edu.cn, chenyihong@pku.edu.cn
[2] Key Laboratory of Machine Perception, MOE, School of Artificial Intelligence, Peking University, Beijing, China
wangdongcis@pku.edu.cn, wanglw@cis.pku.edu.cn
[3] Yizhun Medical AI Co., Ltd., Beijing, China
ziteng.wang@yizhun-ai.com
[4] Pazhou Laboratory (Huangpu), Guangzhou, China
[5] Peng Cheng Laboratory, Shenzhen, China

Abstract. Detecting mass in mammogram is significant due to the high occurrence and mortality of breast cancer. In mammogram mass detection, modeling pairwise lesion correspondence explicitly is particularly important. However, most of the existing methods build relatively coarse correspondence and have not utilized correspondence supervision. In this paper, we propose a new transformer-based framework CL-Net to learn lesion detection and pairwise correspondence in an end-to-end manner. In CL-Net, View-Interactive Lesion Detector is proposed to achieve dynamic interaction across candidates of cross views, while Lesion Linker employs the correspondence supervision to guide the interaction process more accurately. The combination of these two designs accomplishes precise understanding of pairwise lesion correspondence for mammograms. Experiments show that CL-Net yields state-of-the-art performance on the public DDSM dataset and our in-house dataset. Moreover, it outperforms previous methods by a large margin in low FPI regime.

Keywords: Pairwise lesion correspondence · Mammogram mass · Object detection

1 Introduction

With the highest incidence of cancers in women, breast cancer has become a serious threat to human health worldwide. In recent years, mammography screening

---

Z. Zhao and D. Wang—Equal contribution.

Supplementary Information The online version contains supplementary material available at https://doi.org/10.1007/978-3-031-19803-8_23.

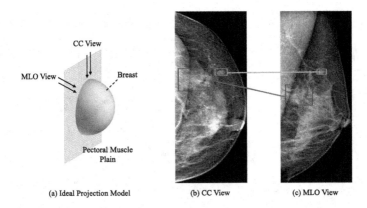

(a) Ideal Projection Model   (b) CC View   (c) MLO View

Fig. 1. (a) In mammograms, the CC view is a top-down view, while the MLO view is taken at a certain angle from the side. (b–c) show an example. Lesions connected by a line from different views are the projections of the same mass instance

has been used by most hospitals as a common examination for its effectiveness and non-invasiveness. Detecting mass is one of the core objectives for mammography screening since mass behaved spiculated and irregular is a typical sign of breast cancer. However, gland overlap and occlusion are great obstacles for distinguishing mass from the gland, accordingly identifying suspicious lesions on mammogram is difficult for both radiologists and deep learning models.

In clinical practice, as shown in Fig. 1, each breast is taken from two different angles, which are cranio-caudal (CC) view and mediolateral oblique (MLO) view, respectively. The complementary information of the ipsilateral view (CC view and MLO view of the same breast) will help radiologists to make better decisions for lesion detection. They usually cross-check the possible lesion locations in CC view and MLO view repeatedly. Once the relevant evidences are found in both views, the existence of the lesion can be confirmed. We call the co-existence of the same mass manifestations in both of the two views **pairwise lesion correspondence**. An example breast mammogram with two lesion pairs is shown in Fig. 1 (b–c).

As for deep models, it is also particularly important to model the pairwise lesion correspondence explicitly for lesion detectors. Firstly, once the model is empowered with the ability to model pairwise lesion correspondences, the complementary information from the auxiliary view will help to distinguish the suspicious regions of the examined view, which is in line with the analysis logic of radiologists. Besides, the correspondences are also important supervision signals to train the network. The supervision of pairwise correspondences can guide the network to establish more accurate relations across the two views, which can further improve the detection performance.

Previous works have attempted to model lesion correspondences [17, 18, 20, 35], however, the correspondence captured by these works is not accurate enough to represent pairwise lesion correspondence. For example, previous SOTA

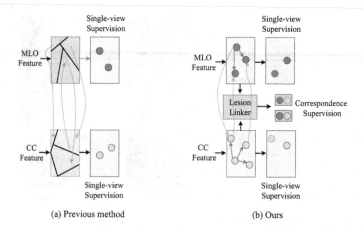

(a) Previous method   (b) Ours

Fig. 2. (a) Previous methods [17] split mammograms into several parts and model part-level relationships without correspondence supervision. (b) We establish lesion-level interaction across views, and leverage correspondence supervision to guide the network training procedure explicitly

method BG-RCNN [17] divides the image into multiple parts and builds part-wise correspondence using a graph neural network (Fig. 2(a)), which leads to relatively coarse correspondence. Meanwhile, the utilization of correspondence supervision is not considered by previous works.

In this paper, we propose **CL-Net** to model more precise pairwise lesion correspondence. We design a transformer-based network structure to learn the lesion detection and pairwise correspondence in an end-to-end manner. As shown in Fig. 2(b), our CL-Net can not only build pairwise lesion correspondence for lesion candidates detected by single-view lesion detectors, but also leverage correspondence supervision to guide the network training procedure for discovering accurate and sensible pairwise lesion correspondence.

Specifically, we first propose **View-Interactive Lesion Detector** (VILD) to achieve dynamic interaction across lesion candidates of MLO and CC views. We build our model upon modern transformer-based object detectors (*e.g.* DETR [5]). These detectors often adopt the query mechanism, where each object query can be regarded as an abstract representation of a lesion candidate, and the information flow across queries is suitable for capturing the correspondences for lesion pairs. Therefore, we apply the inter-attention layer between the object queries' outputs of MLO and CC views to build relationships for the two views, which captures pairwise lesion correspondences in an elegant and efficient way.

Furthermore, we propose **Lesion Linker** to learn the precise pairwise lesion correspondence during network training. Lesion linker summarizes all lesion information from MLO and CC views by taking all lesion candidates generated by object queries as inputs, and then employs the **link query** and a decoder-like net structure to produce paired lesion outputs. Like DETR, we use a set prediction approach to output lesion pairs, where each pair is a point in the set. Hence, the lesion linker can also be trained with a set matching loss. Under the guidance of pair supervision, the inter-attention layer in VILD can obtain more direct and precise correspondence, which will benefit the training of the detector.

Experimentally, the results show that the proposed approach outperforms the previous SOTA methods by a large margin on both the public dataset DDSM [13] and an in-house dataset. The ablation study validates the effectiveness of each part in our design.

In a nutshell, our contributions are three-folds:

- To the best of our knowledge, our work is the first to model and learn pairwise lesion correspondence explicitly for mammogram mass detection, which is essential for cross-view reasoning.
- VILD and lesion linker are proposed to achieve precise lesion correspondence.
- We propose a novel framework, which achieves a new SOTA performance for mammogram mass detection with ipsilateral views and surpasses all previous methods by a large margin.

2 Related Work

2.1 Mammogram Mass Detection

Traditional approaches [3,11,21,31] usually use complex preprocessing and design hand-crafted features for mammogram mass detection. However, due to the low representation ability, the performance of these methods is not satisfactory. In the past few years, deep learning has been introduced to this area. Most of works [1,4,26,34] only use a single view for detection, while recently several studies [17,18,20,35] attempt to establish cross-view reasoning mechanism for mammogram mass detection. Ma *et al.* [20] and Yang *et al.* [35] use relation module [14] to model the relationships of lesion proposals across views. Liu *et al.* [17] seeks to leverage bipartite graph convolutional network to achieve part-level correspondence. C2-Net [18] preprocesses the mammograms for column-wise alignment and performs column-wise correspondence between cross-views, since they assume that the perpendicular distance to the chest of the same lesion in CC view and MLO view is roughly the same. Although these methods model the correspondence of the two views to a certain extent, however, the correspondence is generated freely without any pairwise supervision. Perek *et al.* [24] proposes a Siamese approach to achieve cross-view mass matching, while the performance of mass detection is not considered. Different from above approaches, our CL-Net can model and learn the pairwise lesion correspondence explicitly, which significantly improves the detection performance.

2.2 Object Detection and HOI Detection with Transformer

Transformer [32] has drawn great attention in computer vision recently [5,9,33, 38]. In the area of object detection, the first representative of the transformer-based detector is DETR [5]. DETR employs a transformer encoder-decoder architecture with object queries to hit the instances in the images. It regards object detection as a set prediction task, and uses a set matching method [5] to train the network. Afterwards, Deformable DETR [38] is proposed as a variant of DETR. Deformable DETR uses the local receptive fields for attention layers, which reduces computational complexity significantly and speeds up convergence. Moreover, DETR has also been applied to the task of Human-Object Interaction detection [6,15,37,39]. Chen *et al.* [6] and Zou *et al.* [39] reformulate HOI detection as a set prediction task and predict humans, objects and their interactions directly. HOTR [15] utilizes HO Pointers to associate the outputs of two parallel decoders, which leverages the self-attention mechanisms to exploit the contextual relationships between humans and objects. It is worth mentioning that HOI detection focuses on predicting the associations of humans and objects, while in this paper mammogram mass detection is evaluated by the detection results of each single image view. Different from HOI detection, the correspondence of MLO and CC views is regarded as the auxiliary supervision to promote the detection model. Our proposed lesion linker takes the advantage of this supervision to guide the training of VILD.

2.3   Learnable Image Matching

The well-known image matching in computer vision aims to establish dense correspondences across images for camera pose recovery and scene structure estimation in geometric vision tasks, such as Structure-from-Motion (SfM) and Simultaneous Localization and Mapping (SLAM) [2,8,10,22,25,28,30,36]. These methods rely on dense interest points as local descriptors to build pixel-to-pixel dense correspondences for multiple views. However, in mammograms, the two views are two different projections of 3D breast, which means there is no precise pixel-to-pixel correspondence. Therefore, we can only model the sparse lesion-to-lesion correspondence for accurate lesion detection. Compared with pixel-level matching, extracting the pairwise lesion correspondence is a high-level vision task that requires the network to understand lesion instances in advance. Therefore, we design the lesion linker and use link queries after the detector to learn lesion matching.

3   Methodology

In this section, we will elaborate on the design of the proposed CL-Net. The name CL stands that our method can Cross-Check the two views and Link the corresponding lesions across views. An overview of the whole pipeline is illustrated in Fig. 3. To be specific, we first explain how the proposed View-Interactive Lesion Detector (VILD) along with the Lesion Linker establishes pairwise lesion correspondence. Then we discuss how to effectively train the network by presenting the training details including label assignment rules for lesion correspondence and the final loss function.

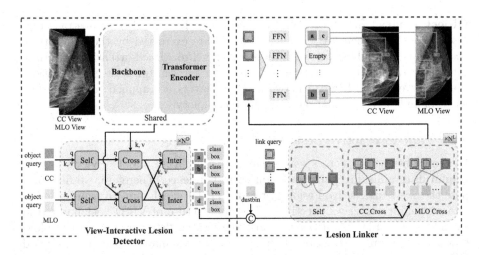

Fig. 3. Overview of our proposed CL-Net. A pair of mammograms are firstly processed by View-Interactive Lesion Detector (VILD) to achieve dynamic interaction across lesion candidates of MLO and CC views. Then, the embeddings outputted by the last decoder layer in VILD are provided for Lesion Linker to learn the precise pairwise lesion correspondence by learnable link queries

3.1 Reviewing DETR

Recently, DETR [5] has drawn great attention since it proposes a novel paradigm for object detection through transformer encoder-decoder architecture. It reformulates object detection as a set prediction task and adopts one-to-one label assignment between ground truth and predicted objects, which achieves an end-to-end object detector.

Multi-head Attention. Attention is the core component in Transformer architecture. The standard version of attention can be written as follows:

$$\text{Attention}(Q, K, V) = \text{softmax}(\frac{QK^T}{\sqrt{d_k}})V, \tag{1}$$

where Q, K, V stand for query vector, key vector and value vector, respectively. d_k is the vector dimension.

Multi-head attention is the extension of the standard version:

$$\text{MultiHeadAttn}(Q, K, V) = \text{Concat}(H_1, H_2, ..., H_m), \tag{2}$$

$$H_i = \text{Attention}(QW_i^Q, KW_i^K, VW_i^V), \tag{3}$$

where m is the number of heads, W_i^Q, W_i^K, W_i^V are projection matrices in the i-th head to map the original vector into a vector with lower dimension. For convenience, we use $\mathcal{M}$ to denote MultiHeadAttn in the following.

Object Query. In DETR, object queries can be regarded as abstract representations of objects. After image features are extracted by the transformer encoder, queries will interact with these features through self-attention and cross-attention layers in the transformer decoder to aggregate instance information. Finally, several feed-forward network (FFN) layers are applied to decode box location and class information for each object query.

3.2   View-Interactive Lesion Detector

Dynamic interaction across lesion candidates of MLO and CC views is very helpful in establishing pairwise lesion correspondence. Therefore, we first propose the View-Interactive Lesion Detector (VILD) which aims to transfer lesion information across views effectively. The architecture of VILD is elaborated in the left part of Fig. 3. VILD is a transformer-based detector that also employs object query as an abstraction of object. VILD takes mammogram of MLO and CC views as input and passes them through the shared backbone and feature encoder to encode the image content. Afterwards, two sets of object queries (one for MLO and one for CC) are fed into a specially designed decoder to predict lesions' position and class for each view while taking the lesion information from the ipsilateral view into consideration.

To be specific, we append an additional inter-attention layer at the end of each transformer decoder block to achieve dynamic interaction across views. Object queries can be regarded as abstract representations of objects, thus directly applying cross-view inter-attention can be realized as an elegant and efficient way to capture pairwise lesion correspondence. The cross-view inter-attention is also instantiated as a multi-head attention block which takes intermediate embedding of one view as queries and intermediate embedding of the other view as keys and values. Formally, suppose the number of object queries of each view is N and denote the embeddings output by cross-attention layer in the i-th decoder layer as E_i^c, $E_i^m \in \mathbb{R}^{N \times D}$ for CC view and MLO view respectively, then the enhanced embeddings are obtained through attention mechanism which could be expressed as (take CC view for example),

$$E_i^{c*} = E_i^c + \mathcal{M}(E_i^c + P^c, E_i^m + P^m, E_i^m), \qquad (4)$$

where P^m and P^c denote the positional encodings for MLO and CC view's embedding, respectively. The positional encodings are learnable vectors, which are the same as Deformable DETR. $\mathcal{M}$ is MultiHeadAttn as defined in Sect. 3.1. The enhanced embedding for MLO view is obtained vice versa:

$$E_i^{m*} = E_i^m + \mathcal{M}(E_i^m + P^m, E_i^c + P^c, E_i^c). \qquad (5)$$

By passing through the decoder layer for several times, cross-view lesion correspondence is gradually transferred and formed bidirectionally with the help of inter-attention block. This aligns with how radiologists identify lesions. They usually search for potential lesions in both views back and forth. Once a suspicious region is discovered in one view, they will check all possible positions in the other view in order to find the corresponding lesion with similar spatial and visual information.

Denote the embeddings for CC view and MLO view outputted by the last decoder layer as E^c, $E^m \in \mathbb{R}^{N \times D}$, the detection results are then predicted by FFN layers with E^c and E^m as input.

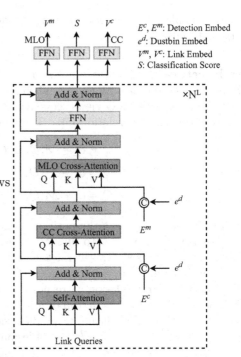

Fig. 4. Architecture of Lesion Linker

3.3 Lesion Linker

In VILD, the establishment of cross-view dynamic interaction endows lesions from one view with the ability to form correspondence with lesions from the other view. We argue that by explicitly utilizing the guidance of the pair supervision, a more accurate pairwise lesion correspondence could be achieved and the detection ability of the network could be further boosted. We propose Lesion Linker, a transformer decoder-like structure to take full advantage of the pair supervision. The architecture of lesion linker is illustrated in the right part of Fig. 3. Lesion linker adopts link query, which is initialized as a set of learnable vectors, as abstract representations of possible pairwise relationships. Given output embeddings E^c and E^m from VILD as input, link queries will interact with them to extract lesion information and gradually focus on specific lesion pairs. Each link query will finally predict a triplet including link embeddings for CC and MLO views and lesion pair score through FFN layers. Given these embeddings, corresponding detection results in MLO view and CC view could be linked together to form pairwise lesion detection results. In the following, we will elaborate on the key designs of our lesion linker.

Dustbin Embedding. In clinical practice, mammogram is a projection along the X-ray direction in which lots of information is lost, thus some mass instances can only be seen in one view. To cope with this special situation for lesion linker, we set a learnable vector $e^d \in \mathbb{R}^D$, named dustbin embedding. Detection embeddings that have no correspondence should be linked to it.

We concatenate detection embeddings from CC view and MLO view with dustbin embedding to obtain the complete version $\tilde{E}^c, \tilde{E}^m \in \mathbb{R}^{(N+1) \times D}$:

$$\tilde{E}^c = \text{Concat}(E^c, e^d), \tag{6}$$

$$\tilde{E}^m = \text{Concat}(E^m, e^d). \tag{7}$$

More explanations about dustbin embedding can be found in the supplementary materials.

Architecture. As illustrated in Fig. 4, at first link queries Q are passed through the multi-head self-attention layer. Then they will interact with detection embeddings from CC and MLO views sequentially to extract view-dependent information to form pairwise relationships. The process could be written as

$$\dot{Q} = Q + \mathcal{M}(Q, Q, Q), \tag{8}$$

$$\ddot{Q} = \dot{Q} + \mathcal{M}(\dot{Q}, \tilde{E}^c + P^c, \tilde{E}^c), \tag{9}$$

$$\hat{Q} = \ddot{Q} + \mathcal{M}(\ddot{Q}, \tilde{E}^m + P^m, \tilde{E}^m), \tag{10}$$

where P^c and P^m denote the positional encoding for $\tilde{E}^c$ and $\tilde{E}^m$. Finally, $\hat{Q}$ is processed by a FFN layer to further enhance the representative ability. Above layers can be stacked for several times. Link queries transformed by stacked attention have fully explored lesion-level relationships from MLO view and CC view and the pairwise lesion correspondence is gradually formed.

Motivated by [15], at the top of lesion linker, we decode the correspondence by applying three FFN layers to predict the link embedding for CC and MLO views $V^c \in \mathbb{R}^{M \times D}$, $V^m \in \mathbb{R}^{M \times D}$ and lesion pair classification score $S \in \mathbb{R}^{M \times 1}$, respectively. M is the number of the link queries and D is the feature dimension. The predicted link embeddings V^c and V^m are used for indexing the detection results, which will be introduced later. The classification score S denotes the confidence that whether the pair of detection results captured by the link query is true positive.

Lesion Correspondence Extracting. The output of lesion linker can be reformulated as a set of M triplets, $\{\langle v_i^c, v_i^m, s_i \rangle\}_{i=1}^M$, where $v_i^c, v_i^m \in \mathbb{R}^D$ and $s_i \in \mathbb{R}^1$ are the i-th row of V^c, V^m and S. The pairwise lesion correspondence could be explicitly established by first calculating the feature similarity between detection embeddings $\tilde{e}_j^t \in \mathbb{R}^D$ and link embeddings v_i^t for each view and then taking the index of the detection embedding with the highest similarity as result. Here $t \in \{c, m\}$ denotes CC view or MLO view, and $\tilde{e}_j^t$ is the j-th row of $\tilde{E}^t$. Formally, this process could be expressed as

$$c_i = \arg\max_j(\text{sim}(v_i^c, \tilde{e}_j^c)), \quad m_i = \arg\max_j(\text{sim}(v_i^m, \tilde{e}_j^m)), \tag{11}$$

where we use cosine similarity to measure the feature similarity:

$$\text{sim}(x, y) = \frac{x^T y}{||x||_2 ||y||_2}. \tag{12}$$

Finally, for each link query q_i, we could obtain its extracted lesion correspondence pair $\langle c_i, m_i \rangle$ as result. Next we will discuss how to effectively train our network.

3.4 Training Details

We will elaborate on training details of our proposed CL-Net in this section. To be specific, we first explain the label assignment rule for pairwise lesion correspondence. Then we introduce the loss function of our CL-Net.

Label Assignment for Lesion Correspondence. In original DETR, a one-to-one label assignment based on bipartite matching is used to assign training targets for the predicted bounding boxes. In our CL-Net, we also aim to establish a similar rule to assign the pairwise ground truth lesion boxes to the set of link triplets predicted by lesion linker.

Our VILD shares a similar structure and training strategy with DETR, therefore through the label assignment rule for detection, we can obtain the assignment relationships between ground truth boxes and detection embeddings. Thus the pairwise ground truth boxes can be naturally converted to pairwise detection embeddings. We denote the conversion results as $y = \langle e^c, e^m, a = 1 \rangle$. e^c and e^m denote the detection embedding converted from ground truth boxes for CC view and MLO view. For a lesion that can only be viewed in CC view, the converted result is $y = \langle e^c, e^d, a = 1 \rangle$, in which e^d denotes the dustbin embedding defined in Sect. 3.3. The same is for the lesion that can only be viewed in MLO view.

Suppose the number of unique ground truth lesions is K. Then the set of converted lesion triplets from the ground truth lesions could be denoted as $Y = \{y_i\}_{i=1}^{K}$. The set of M predictions from lesion linker could be similarly denoted as $\hat{Y} = \{\hat{y}_j = \langle v_j^c, v_j^m, s_j \rangle\}_{j=1}^{M}$. Since K is less than M in mammogram, we pad the ground truth set Y with $\langle \varnothing, \varnothing, a = 0 \rangle$ (no lesion pair) to the size of M, similar to DETR. We aim to find an optimal bipartite matching between these two sets by searching for a permutation of M elements $\pi \in \Pi_M$ with the lowest cost:

$$\hat{\pi} = \arg\min_{\pi \in \Pi} \sum_{i=1}^{M} \mathcal{L}_{\text{match}}(y_i, \hat{y}_{\pi(i)}), \tag{13}$$

where $\mathcal{L}_{\text{match}}$ is a matching cost between ground truth y_i and prediction $\hat{y}_{\pi(i)}$. We consider two aspects when calculating the matching cost, which are the prediction scores and the similarity of ground truth embeddings and predicted link embeddings:

$$\mathcal{L}_{\text{match}}(y_i, \hat{y}_{\pi(i)}) = -\mathbb{1}_{\{a_i \neq 0\}} \cdot [\mathcal{L}_{\text{emd}}(i, \pi(i))]^\alpha \cdot [\mathcal{L}_{\text{score}}(i, \pi(i))]^{1-\alpha}, \tag{14}$$

where $\mathcal{L}_{\text{emd}}$ and $\mathcal{L}_{\text{score}}$ denote cost of feature similarity and classification score. The operation of $+1$ in Eq. 15 aims to guarantee that $\mathcal{L}_{\text{emd}}$ is positive.

$$\mathcal{L}_{\text{emd}}(i, j) = \beta \text{sim}(e_i^c, v_j^c) + (1 - \beta)\text{sim}(e_i^m, v_j^m) + 1, \tag{15}$$

$$\mathcal{L}_{\text{score}}(i, j) = s_j. \tag{16}$$

We adopt the weighted geometric mean of the feature similarity $\mathcal{L}_{\text{emd}}$ and classification score $\mathcal{L}_{\text{score}}$, in which $\alpha \in [0, 1]$ is the balance hyper-parameter.

The ablation study of the cost function and analysis can be found in Table 5. β is set to 0.5 by default to adjust the ratio of feature similarity in CC view and MLO view. The optimal bipartite assignment can be obtained through the Hungarian algorithm efficiently as in [29].

Training Loss. The final loss function can be written as follows:

$$\mathcal{L} = \mathcal{L}_\mathrm{D} + \mathcal{L}_\mathrm{Link}, \tag{17}$$

where $\mathcal{L}_\mathrm{D}$ is the loss function in DETR, $\mathcal{L}_\mathrm{Link}$ is defined as

$$\mathcal{L}_\mathrm{Link} = \sum_{i=1}^{M}[\mathbf{1}_{\{a_i \neq 0\}}\lambda_\mathrm{sim}\mathcal{L}_\mathrm{sim}(i, \pi(i)) + \lambda_\mathrm{cls}\mathcal{L}_\mathrm{cls}(a_i, s_{\pi(i)})], \tag{18}$$

where λ_sim and λ_cls are weight hyper-parameters. We adopt focal loss [16] as the loss function $\mathcal{L}_\mathrm{cls}$ for lesion pair classification.

Following [15], we first calculate the similarity scores $S^t \in \mathbb{R}^{N+1}$, where $t \in \{c, m\}$ denotes the CC view and MLO view, and the j-th item of S^t is $\mathrm{sim}(v^t_{\pi(i)}, \tilde{e}^t_j)$. Then, we use Cross-Entropy Loss to localize the ground truth embeddings:

$$\mathcal{L}_\mathrm{sim}(i, \pi(i)) = \mathrm{CrossEntropyLoss}(S^c, i) + \mathrm{CrossEntropyLoss}(S^m, i). \tag{19}$$

3.5   Discussion of Match Learning Strategy

Our lesion linker learns the paired relationships of lesions by learning to predict MLO and CC embeddings which are close to the corresponding lesion pairs. Our match learning strategy is a soft way, which gradually pushes the link embeddings to get closer to the ground-truth embeddings during training. Although there are also other alternative approaches for this task, learning lesion matching is not trivial. In this subsection, we compare our method with two other seemingly reasonable solutions, to strengthen the advantages of our method.

Pair Verification. A straightforward solution to predict match pairs is to verify whether every two lesions from ipsilateral views are truly paired lesions. Following this design, we need to output a 2D matrix that represents the match probabilities of all possible pairs. The shape of the matrix should be $N \times N$, where N is number of lesion candidates per view. However, since the number of possible lesion pairs is much larger than the number of truly paired lesions, it is difficult to extract useful training signals from such a small amount of pairwise annotation information.

Compared to the verification approach, the introduction of link queries decouples the pairwise training from the number of object queries N. The number of link queries M could be in the same order of magnitude as N, thus the pair supervision signal could be fully utilized, leading to an easier optimization process.

Table 1. Comparison with baselines and previous SOTA on DDSM dataset (%)

Method	R@0.25	R@0.5	R@1.0	R@2.0	R@4.0
Mask RCNN [17]	-	76.0	82.5	88.7	91.4
Mask RCNN, DCN [17]	-	76.7	83.9	89.4	91.8
Deformable DETR [38]	73.8	78.4	83.7	88.7	93.7
BG-RCNN [17]	-	79.5	86.6	91.8	94.5
CL-Net	**78.1**	**83.1**	**88.0**	**92.4**	**95.0**

Table 2. Comparison with previous works on DDSM dataset (%)

Method	R@t
Campanini et al. [3]	80@1.1
Eltonsy et al. [11]	92@5.4, 88@2.4, 81@0.6
Sampat et al. [27]	88@2.7, 85@1.5, 80@1.0
CVR-RCNN [20]	92@4.4, 88@1.9, 85@1.2
CL-Net	**96@4.4, 92@1.9, 89@1.2**

Paired Lesion Query. Another seemingly straightforward way is to predict pairwise lesions with query mechanism directly. With this paired lesion query, the network can output a pair of detected boxes in the two views for each query. Then, the form of outputted lesion pairs is similar to the extracted lesion pairs of lesion linker. Therefore, we can also adopt a similar set matching loss to train the network. With the paired lesion query, the object query for each view is not required anymore.

However, the optimization of paired lesion query is much harder than our lesion linker. Our CL-Net first detects lesion candidates from each view (in VILD), therefore the lesion linker only focus on extracting the pairwise correspondence. While using the paired lesion query, the detection of objects and pairing are performed in the same step, which increases the difficulty of network training and results in inferior performance.

We elaborate on the implementation details of above two methods in the supplementary materials. The experimental results are presented in Sect. 4.4.

4 Experiments

4.1 Implementation Details

Our model is based on Deformable DETR [38] for its flexibility and fast convergence. We adopt ResNet-50 [12] pre-trained from ImageNet [7] as backbone. The number of object queries N and link queries M are set to 125 and 16, respectively. The loss weights λ_{sim} and λ_{cls} are 0.125 and 1.0 by default. We set $\alpha = 0.5$ and $\gamma = 2.0$ for the focal loss $\mathcal{L}_{cls}$. It is worth mentioning that since

Table 3. Ablation study on different components of CL-Net on DDSM dataset (%). VILD: View-Interactive Lesion Detector. LL: Lesion Linker. "not using VILD" means we use Deformable DETR directly

VILD	LL	R@0.25	R@0.5	R@1.0	R@2.0	R@4.0
		73.8	78.4	83.7	88.7	93.7
✓		76.1	81.7	86.4	91.7	94.4
	✓	74.1	80.1	86.0	88.7	93.4
✓	✓	**78.1**	**83.1**	**88.0**	**92.4**	**95.0**

we mainly focus on the task of lesion detection, the final predictions come from VILD in the inference process.

We implement our network with PyTorch [23]. We train the network in an end-to-end manner on 8 GPUs for 25k iterations. For each GPU, we use 4 images containing two mammogram pairs. Following Deformable DETR [38], we train our model using AdamW Optimizer [19] with base learning rate of 2×10^{-4}. We use the same multiplied factors for learning rates as [38], while the learning rates of lesion linker parameters are multiplied by 0.25. In addition, we adopt cosine learning rate schedule with warm-up. To avoid overfitting, we use several data augmentation methods (random flip, random crop, random normalization) in training.

4.2 Datasets

We conduct experiments on the public DDSM dataset and our in-house dataset.

DDSM Dataset. DDSM [13] is a widely used public dataset. It contains 2620 patient cases, and each case has four images, including MLO view and CC view for both breasts. We use the same data split method with previous studies [3,17, 20,27]. The original dataset does not provide lesion correspondence annotations, hence we fulfill the annotations with experienced radiologists.

In-House Dataset. We collect an in-house mammography dataset with 3,160 cases. Each case is annotated by at least two experts. We randomly split the dataset into train, validation, and test set with the ratio of 8:1:1.

Evaluation Metric. We report recall (R) at t false positives per image (FPI) to evaluate the performance following [17,20]. The metric can be simplified as $R@t$.

4.3 Compare with State-of-the-Art Methods

We compare our methods with previous works on DDSM dataset in Table 1 and Table 2. In Table 1, the results of Mask RCNN, Mask RCNN DCN, and BG-RCNN are from [17], and Deformable DETR is implemented by ourselves. In

Table 2, we use the same FPIs as in CVR-RCNN [20] and compare our method with previous works. From these two tables, we can draw a conclusion that our CL-Net outperforms all baselines by a large margin and surpasses previous SOTA [17,20]. The performance of our method is more significant in low FPIs, outperforming BG-RCNN [17] by 3.6 at $R@0.5$, which could benefit clinical practice a lot. The results on the in-house dataset are reported in the supplementary materials. Similar improvement over baselines on in-house dataset also demonstrates the superiority of our approach.

4.4   Ablation Study

In this section, we elaborate on ablation studies for CL-Net. Other ablation experiments are presented in the supplementary materials.

Different Components of CL-Net. We ablate the impact of different components of CL-Net on detection performance in Table 3. There are mainly two important modules in CL-Net, VILD and lesion linker. As shown in the table, using VILD can significantly improve the detection performance, while the improvement of employing lesion linker alone is marginal. Considering that learning accurate correspondences relies on the expression ability of VILD, it is explainable that the contribution of lesion linker is limited without VILD. The effect of lesion linker in CL-Net is guiding the interaction process more precisely in the inter-attention layer of VILD. The experimental results also verifies our conjecture. The joint contributions of VILD and lesion linker improve the detection performance of VILD significantly ($+2.0$ at $R@0.25$).

Table 4. Different strategies for match learning on DDSM dataset (%). PV: Pair Verification. PL Query: Paired Lesion Query

Method	R@0.25	R@0.5	R@1.0	R@2.0
VILD	76.1	81.7	86.4	91.7
PV	75.7	82.1	86.4	90.7
PL Query	68.8	75.1	81.7	87.0
CL-Net	**78.1**	**83.1**	**88.0**	**92.4**

Table 5. Ablation study on cost function of label assignment. Default parameter is marked by *

Method	α	R@0.25	R@0.5	R@1.0	R@2.0
Add	0.25	77.7	82.7	87.7	90.4
	0.5	73.8	81.1	86.4	90.0
	0.75	75.1	80.1	86.7	91.7
Mul	0.25	76.1	**83.7**	**89.7**	91.7
	0.5*	**78.1**	83.1	88.0	**92.4**
	0.75	74.8	80.4	85.4	90.0

Different Strategies for Match Learning. We present the results of different strategies for match learning in Table 4. The methods described in Sect. 3.5 are adopted. Pair verification method yields similar performance as VILD solely, which indicates that it is hard for the model to mine useful correspondences from plenty of feasibilities. In addition, paired lesion query performs much worse than VILD (-7.3 at $R@0.25$) due to the difficulty of optimization. Our CL-Net achieves the best performance attributing the success to the design of link query.

Cost Function of Label Assignment. We investigate the effect of different forms of cost function for label assignment on our model in Table 5. Method 'Mul' denotes the cost function in Eq. 14, while 'Add' refers to the weighted sum of $\mathcal{L}_{emd}$ and $\mathcal{L}_{score}$, where α is also the weighting factor. The experimental results show that method 'Mul' achieves better performance than 'Add', which could be mainly attributed to the sensitivity to both $\mathcal{L}_{emd}$ and $\mathcal{L}_{score}$ in the form of multiplication.

The visualization and error analysis can be found in the supplementary materials.

5   Conclusion

In this work, we present CL-Net, a novel mammogram mass detector based on transformer architecture. Our CL-Net can not only model precise pairwise lesion correspondence, but also leverage correspondence supervision to guide the network training. The experimental results conducted on the public DDSM dataset and an in-house dataset show that CL-Net surpasses the state-of-the-art methods by a large margin.

Acknowledgement. This work is supported by Exploratory Research Project of Zhejiang Lab (No. 2022RC0AN02), Project 2020BD006 supported by PKUBaidu Fund.

References

1. Agarwal, R., Diaz, O., Lladó, X., Yap, M.H., Martí, R.: Automatic mass detection in mammograms using deep convolutional neural networks. J. Med. Imaging **6**(3), 031409 (2019)
2. Brachmann, E., Rother, C.: Neural-guided RanSAC: learning where to sample model hypotheses. In: ICCV (2019)
3. Campanini, R., et al.: A novel featureless approach to mass detection in digital mammograms based on support vector machines. Phys. Med. Biol. **49**(6), 961 (2004)
4. Cao, Z., et al.: DeepLima: deep learning based lesion identification in mammograms. In: ICCV Workshops (2019)
5. Carion, N., Massa, F., Synnaeve, G., Usunier, N., Kirillov, A., Zagoruyko, S.: End-to-end object detection with transformers. In: Vedaldi, A., Bischof, H., Brox, T., Frahm, J.-M. (eds.) ECCV 2020. LNCS, vol. 12346, pp. 213–229. Springer, Cham (2020). https://doi.org/10.1007/978-3-030-58452-8_13
6. Chen, M., Liao, Y., Liu, S., Chen, Z., Wang, F., Qian, C.: Reformulating hoi detection as adaptive set prediction. In: CVPR (2021)
7. Deng, J., Dong, W., Socher, R., Li, L.J., Li, K., Fei-Fei, L.: Imagenet: a large-scale hierarchical image database. In: CVPR (2009)
8. DeTone, D., Malisiewicz, T., Rabinovich, A.: Superpoint: self-supervised interest point detection and description. In: CVPR Workshops (2018)
9. Dosovitskiy, A., et al.: An image is worth 16x16 words: transformers for image recognition at scale. arXiv preprint arXiv:2010.11929 (2020)

10. Dusmanu, M., Rocco, I., Pajdla, T., Pollefeys, M., Sivic, J., Torii, A., Sattler, T.: D2-net: a trainable CNN for joint detection and description of local features. arXiv preprint arXiv:1905.03561 (2019)
11. Eltonsy, N.H., Tourassi, G.D., Elmaghraby, A.S.: A concentric morphology model for the detection of masses in mammography. IEEE Trans. Med. Imaging **26**(6), 880–889 (2007)
12. He, K., Zhang, X., Ren, S., Sun, J.: Deep residual learning for image recognition. In: CVPR (2016)
13. Heath, M., Bowyer, K., Kopans, D., Moore, R., Kegelmeyer, W.P.: The digital database for screening mammography. In: Proceedings of the 5th International Workshop on Digital Mammography, pp. 212–218. Medical Physics Publishing (2000)
14. Hu, H., Gu, J., Zhang, Z., Dai, J., Wei, Y.: Relation networks for object detection. In: CVPR (2018)
15. Kim, B., Lee, J., Kang, J., Kim, E.S., Kim, H.J.: HOTR: end-to-end human-object interaction detection with transformers. In: CVPR (2021)
16. Lin, T.Y., Goyal, P., Girshick, R., He, K., Dollár, P.: Focal loss for dense object detection. In: ICCV (2017)
17. Liu, Y., Zhang, F., Zhang, Q., Wang, S., Wang, Y., Yu, Y.: Cross-view correspondence reasoning based on bipartite graph convolutional network for mammogram mass detection. In: CVPR (2020)
18. Liu, Y., et al.: Compare and contrast: detecting mammographic soft-tissue lesions with c2-net. Med. Image Anal. **71**, 101999 (2021)
19. Loshchilov, I., Hutter, F.: Decoupled weight decay regularization. arXiv preprint arXiv:1711.05101 (2017)
20. Ma, J., et al.: Cross-view relation networks for mammogram mass detection. In: ICPR (2020)
21. Mudigonda, N.R., Rangayyan, R.M., Desautels, J.L.: Detection of breast masses in mammograms by density slicing and texture flow-field analysis. IEEE Trans. Med. Imaging **20**(12), 1215–1227 (2001)
22. Ono, Y., Trulls, E., Fua, P., Yi, K.M.: LF-net: learning local features from images. arXiv preprint arXiv:1805.09662 (2018)
23. Paszke, A., et al.: PyTorch: an imperative style, high-performance deep learning library. In: Wallach, H.M., Larochelle, H., Beygelzimer, A., d'Alché-Buc, F., Fox, E.B., Garnett, R. (eds.) NeurIPS (2019)
24. Perek, S., Hazan, A., Barkan, E., Akselrod-Ballin, A.: Siamese network for dual-view mammography mass matching. In: Stoyanov, D., et al. (eds.) RAMBO/BIA/TIA -2018. LNCS, vol. 11040, pp. 55–63. Springer, Cham (2018). https://doi.org/10.1007/978-3-030-00946-5_6
25. Ranftl, R., Koltun, V.: Deep fundamental matrix estimation. In: Ferrari, V., Hebert, M., Sminchisescu, C., Weiss, Y. (eds.) ECCV 2018. LNCS, vol. 11205, pp. 292–309. Springer, Cham (2018). https://doi.org/10.1007/978-3-030-01246-5_18
26. Ribli, D., Horváth, A., Unger, Z., Pollner, P., Csabai, I.: Detecting and classifying lesions in mammograms with deep learning. Sci. Rep. **8**(1), 1–7 (2018)
27. Sampat, M.P., Bovik, A.C., Whitman, G.J., Markey, M.K.: A model-based framework for the detection of spiculated masses on mammography a. Med. Phys. **35**(5), 2110–2123 (2008)
28. Sarlin, P.E., DeTone, D., Malisiewicz, T., Rabinovich, A.: Superglue: learning feature matching with graph neural networks. In: CVPR (2020)
29. Stewart, R., Andriluka, M., Ng, A.Y.: End-to-end people detection in crowded scenes. In: CVPR (2016)

30. Sun, J., Shen, Z., Wang, Y., Bao, H., Zhou, X.: LoFTR: detector-free local feature matching with transformers. In: CVPR (2021)
31. Tai, S.C., Chen, Z.S., Tsai, W.T.: An automatic mass detection system in mammograms based on complex texture features. IEEE J. Biomed. Health Inform. **18**(2), 618–627 (2013)
32. Vaswani, A., et al.: Attention is all you need. In: NIPS (2017)
33. Wang, Y., et al.: End-to-end video instance segmentation with transformers. In: CVPR (2021)
34. Xi, P., Shu, C., Goubran, R.: Abnormality detection in mammography using deep convolutional neural networks. In: 2018 IEEE International Symposium on Medical Measurements and Applications (MeMeA), pp. 1–6. IEEE (2018)
35. Yang, Z., et al.: Momminet-v2: mammographic multi-view mass identification networks. Med. Image Anal. **73**, 102204 (2021)
36. Yi, K.M., Trulls, E., Ono, Y., Lepetit, V., Salzmann, M., Fua, P.: Learning to find good correspondences. In: CVPR (2018)
37. Zhang, A., et al.: Mining the benefits of two-stage and one-stage hoi detection. arXiv preprint arXiv:2108.05077 (2021)
38. Zhu, X., Su, W., Lu, L., Li, B., Wang, X., Dai, J.: Deformable DETR: deformable transformers for end-to-end object detection. arXiv preprint arXiv:2010.04159 (2020)
39. Zou, C., et al.: End-to-end human object interaction detection with hoi transformer. In: CVPR (2021)

Graph-Constrained Contrastive Regularization for Semi-weakly Volumetric Segmentation

Simon Reiß[1(✉)] [iD], Constantin Seibold[1] [iD], Alexander Freytag[2] [iD],
Erik Rodner[3] [iD], and Rainer Stiefelhagen[1] [iD]

[1] Karlsruhe Institute of Technology, 76131 Karlsruhe, Germany
{simon.reiss,constantin.seibold,rainer.stiefelhagen}@kit.edu
[2] Carl Zeiss AG, 07745 Jena, Germany
alexander.freytag@zeiss.com
[3] University of Applied Sciences Berlin, 12459 Berlin, Germany
erik.rodner@htw-berlin.de

Abstract. Semantic volume segmentation suffers from the requirement of having voxel-wise annotated ground-truth data, which requires immense effort to obtain. In this work, we investigate how models can be trained from *sparsely annotated volumes*, *i.e.* volumes with only individual slices annotated. By formulating the scenario as a semi-weakly supervised problem where only some regions in the volume are annotated, we obtain surprising results: expensive dense volumetric annotations can be replaced by cheap, partially labeled volumes with limited impact on accuracy *if* the hypothesis space of valid models gets properly constrained during training. With our *Contrastive Constrained Regularization (Con2R)*, we demonstrate that 3D convolutional models can be trained with less than 4% of only two dimensional ground-truth labels and still reach up to 88% accuracy of fully supervised baseline models with dense volumetric annotations. To get insights into *Con2R*s success, we study how strong semi-supervised algorithms transfer to our new volumetric semi-weakly supervised setting. In this manner, we explore retinal fluid and brain tumor segmentation and give a detailed look into accuracy progression for scenarios with extremely scarce labels.

Keywords: Volumetric semantic segmentation · Semi-weakly supervised learning · Regularization · Contrastive learning

1 Introduction

Over the last decades, healthcare and natural sciences underwent a drastic increase in efficiency in analyzing data by exploiting semantic segmentation algorithms. Not surprisingly, current products and solutions in these domains

---

Supplementary Information The online version contains supplementary material available at https://doi.org/10.1007/978-3-031-19803-8_24.

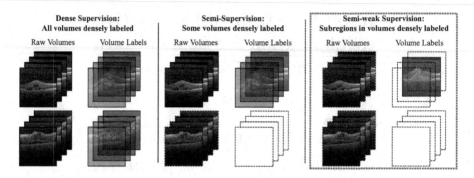

Fig. 1. In which setting can 3D segmentation become relevant in practise? *Left*: densely supervised volume segmentation requires fully annotated volumes – hardly possible in practise. *Center*: semi-supervision allows some volumes to be unlabeled – better, but still with fully annotated volumes. *Right*: we propose semi-weakly volume segmentation as the missing step for bringing 3D segmentation to practise at affordable costs

are built with neural networks, as their performance has proven superior in most use cases [1,7,16]. And still, one major challenge often limits scaling applications further: the need for precisely annotated data. This especially holds for segmentation networks to generalize well to new examples – which in these applications is not only of academic interest, but of utmost importance. However, *e.g.* in healthcare, only trained experts are able to provide correct annotations. These experts are hard to get for annotation tasks, as their main job is often not less but to save lives. Constructing large labeled datasets therefore becomes expensive and difficult. Even worse, the wide-spread use of volumetric image data with all of its benefits, *e.g.* as prevalent in computed tomography [25], optical coherence tomography [7], or magnetic resonance imaging [1,54], amplifies this annotation problem by going from 2D pixel- to even more laborious 3D voxel annotations (if you do not agree with this sentence, you should spend at least one hour on annotating volume data yourself).

These observations clearly show the urgent need for training schemes for 3D segmentation networks to become more economic and more annotation-efficient. We will therefore investigate how these models can be trained with partially labeled as well as entirely unlabeled volumes. We aim at answering the question *Can we circumvent the additional effort to annotate entire volumes?* Partially labeled volumes, *e.g.* volumes that have at most few individual image-slices annotated, can be considered weak labels for the 3D volumetric segmentation task (Fig. 1). As we train with weak annotations and cheaper unlabeled volumes, we refer to it as semi-weakly supervised volumetric segmentation (as in weakly- and semi-supervised [13,50]). Our contributions can be summarized as follows:

- We establish the task of semi-weakly supervised volumetric segmentation and set up thorough training and evaluation protocols for it.
- We analyze and transfer established semi-supervised methods from 2D and 3D to the semi-weakly supervised volume segmentation setting, which gives strong baselines and insights into performance implications.

- We propose the *Con2R* objective for training volumetric models on sparsely labeled data, integrating *smoothness-* and *semantic coherence constraints.*
- By considering the mismatch in training and testing targets, we achieve performances of up to 88% as compared to densely supervised models on the RETOUCH dataset with merely two dozen labels (a fraction of 3.5% labels) and outperform all semi-supervised models on BraTS.

2 Related Work

Semantic Segmentation In semantic segmentation literature steep progress on commonly known natural image benchmarks [17,20,41,71] has been made. Impressive performance is achieved using convolutional [11,27] or transformer-based architectures [56,67] and novel training strategies [4,74]. These models are often trained or pre-trained on gigantic datasets [14,26,74], to itch out every performance improvement, which for domains that are more distant from natural imagery and do not encompass this data-richness, often lies beyond reach. This might be one reason that arguably one of the most successful architectures for segmentation in domains distant from ImageNet [53] is the UNet architecture [51] and its 3D counterpart [15] for volumetric data. In our work, we are interested in domains distant from natural imagery and mainly explore medical data [1,7] where limited amounts of semantic labels are available.

Volumetric Semantic Segmentation. We are further interested in processing volumetric data, which started in the neural network era with video processing [32,34,58] and was shortly after adapted to voxel-wise prediction tasks [35,59]. With their introduction of the 3D UNet Çiçek *et al.* [15] set of a string of works that culminate in the state-of-the-art volumetric segmentation architectures as indicated by 3D approaches [30,31,43,45,46,69] dominating leaderboards of common benchmarks [3,25]. A lot of flavors of the 3D UNet have been proposed: adding multiple pathways [33], deep supervision [63], self-supervised training objectives [46] as well as specifically considering boundaries [24,33,63] . We lay emphasis on exploring how 3D models can cope with weaker training signals than dense volume annotations. Closest to our work are [18], a 3D segmentation model trained on retinal OCT scans, which is done partly on sparse labels as in [15] and [50] which shares the very low-data regimen for retinal fluid segmentation.

Semi- and Weak Volume Supervision. Coping with fewer labels for volumetric segmentation has seen a lot of interest recently and was most commonly posed as semi-supervised task, *i.e.* labeled and unlabeled volumes are used for training. For this, a variety of approaches were tested, *e.g.* based on adversarial learning [47], integrating the 3D shape of the input data by training distinctly on multiple views and fuse model predictions on unlabeled volumes [72]. Mean-Teachers [57] were also successfully applied in volumetric segmentation [61,62,66] often in combination with uncertainty modeling. Uncertainty is also integrated in [42], yet rather than previous approaches which leverage classical Monte Carlo

Dropout [22] they base the uncertainty measure on predictions from multiple UNet decoding scales and directly minimize it. Aside from designing new training strategies by splitting the training data into different sets [28], contrastive learning has seen some application in semi-supervised volume segmentation recently [64,65,68]. In these works, contrastive learning is used on a voxel-level [64] and slice-level [65,68], which is coarsely related to our work through the idea of enforcing similarities. Yet, we don't set up positives and negatives, we deliberately design target voxel-similarities based on positional- and semantic proximity.

A lot of semi-supervised algorithms consider graphs [48,73], while many graphs are built between labeled and unlabeled samples [29,38], we bring this view to the voxel level within individual volumes. Comatch [38] considers semi-supervised contrastive learning as graph-regularization for 2D and builds embedding graphs across different images, rather than different voxel-embeddings. Our method also coarsely relates to segmentation post-processing methods such as CRFs [8,10,36,70], which view individual images as graphs and pixels as vertices.

We restrict our supervision types to unlabeled- alongside sparsely annotated volumes, which is related to weakly supervised literature [5,40]. In the medical domain, scribbles which are also partial labels, were used in [60] to learn 2D segmentation via an adversarial objective and access to unpaired dense labels. Singular points as partial annotations were explored in [49], where a segmentation model is bootstrapped by iteratively pseudo-labeling unlabeled regions of histopathology images. For volumetric segmentation, labeling only extreme points on the three dimensional entity to segment built the foundation of [52], which, like our method, views input volumes as graphs.

3   Proposed Approach

In this chapter, we introduce our notation, define the task of semi-weakly supervised volumetric segmentation, and discuss relevant network related architectural choices. Then, we outline our *Contrastive Constrained Regularization (Con2R)* method that can be understood as graph constraints on the learned feature space. Via its design as contrastive loss, it encompasses a *receptive field smoothness constraint* and a *semantic coherence constraint*.

3.1   Preliminaries

Supervision Modality and Notation. We leverage a volume dataset of size N for semantic segmentation, with the specification of:

$$\mathcal{D} = \{v_1, ..., v_N | v_i \in \mathbb{R}^{c_{dim} \times D \times H \times W}\}, \tag{1}$$

where c_{dim} is the number of volume input channels, its depth D, height H, and width W. In the general setting of volumetric segmentation, an input volume v_i

is accompanied by a ground-truth $m_i \in \mathbb{R}^{C \times D \times H \times W}$, with C classes to segment. Our setting reduces the requirement for densely labeled ground-truths as follows:

$$\mathcal{M} = \{(m_1, a_1), ..., (m_N, a_N) | (m_i, a_i) \in (\mathbb{R}^{C \times D \times H \times W}, \{0,1\}^D)\}. \quad (2)$$

In addition to ground-truth annotations m_i, we use binary variables $a_i^d \in \{0,1\}$ to indicate the availability of annotation information at each slice location $1 \leq d \leq D$ in a volume v_i. An indicator a_i that only contains zeros corresponds to m_i not containing any annotation information, whereas an indicator a_i containing e.g. two ones indicates the locations of two annotated slices within m_i.

Generally, we care about the setting where indicators satisfy $\sum_{d=1}^{D} a_i^d \ll D$, i.e. v_i are very sparsely annotated. We further speak of semi-weakly supervised volume segmentation if these sparse annotations are distributed among all volumes in the dataset: $\sum_{i,d=1}^{N,D} a_i^d \ll N \cdot D$. The goal for a learning algorithm stays consistent with traditional volumetric segmentation, given any unseen v, predict the full corresponding semantic m.

We found that this scenario is important in practice when experts are asked to add pixel-wise semantic labels to slices within volumetric data. The question this formulation poses is: Can three dimensional segmentation also be performed well when only weak two dimensional annotations are available?

Volume Indexing and -Processing. Given an input volume v, we refer to v^x as the input-values at voxel location x. Throughout our experiments, we leverage 3D segmentation architectures that produce voxel-wise features $f \in \mathbb{R}^{f_{dim} \times D \times H \times W}$ and voxel-wise semantic predictions $p \in \mathbb{R}^{C \times D \times H \times W}$ (for instance 3D Encoder-Decoder models [15]). Here, the predictions $p = \kappa(f)$ are the result of the output-head $\kappa(\cdot)$, which is parameterized by C $1 \times 1 \times 1$ convolution kernels. Similarly, our method processes the voxel-wise features and transforms them via $\tau(f)$ into embeddings $e \in \mathbb{R}^{e_{dim} \times D \times H \times W}$. The transformation function $\tau(\cdot)$ is parameterized by a sequence of: normalization layer, $1 \times 1 \times 1$ convolution, non-linearity (i.e. LeakyReLU) and a final $1 \times 1 \times 1$ convolution layer. With this dual-head 3D segmentation architecture, each voxel v^x from the input volume can be described by a semantic prediction p^x as well as a high dimensional voxel-embedding e^x.

3.2 Graph Constraints as Regularization

In the absence of densely labeled data, we fall back to designing data-driven constraints on the hypothesis space to address the train-test target mismatch to be suitable. In particular, we take the commonly chosen view on the input data as a graph as also done in the excellent papers [10,36,38,70].

Our method considers a complete bi-partite weighted graph $\mathcal{G} = (\mathcal{Q}, \mathcal{N}, \mathcal{E}, \sigma)$. In this graph, we have two sets of vertices, the Query-set $\mathcal{Q}$ and Neighborhood-set $\mathcal{N}$ which both contain voxel-embeddings e^x sampled from all voxel-embeddings e in the current volume (w.l.o.g. we choose $|\mathcal{Q}| = |\mathcal{N}|$). Important note: we do not restrict these sets to local neighbors in the volume, but instead sample globally from all possible pairs of voxels during training. The vertices, i.e. embeddings $e^x \in \mathcal{Q}$, are connected to embeddings in $e^y \in \mathcal{N}$ by edges $(x, y) \in \mathcal{E}$

and weighted by $\sigma(x,y) = e^{x^T} e^y/(||e^x||||e^y||)$. Thus, our graph $\mathcal{G}$ describes the similarity between voxel-embeddings of a volume.

We can now exploit this graph to regularize model training by preferring solutions where the weights in the differentiable graph $\mathcal{G}$ take specific target values. The question remains: what are sensible choices for a function $\mathcal{T}(\cdot)$ to define target values for each edge? In the standard case of full supervision, $\mathcal{T}(\cdot)$ can simply set the weights in $\mathcal{E}$ to class-agreement between the vertices based on their labels. As we lack this option, we need to design these targets on the basis of practical assumptions that integrate knowledge about the relationship between unlabeled and labeled data [6].

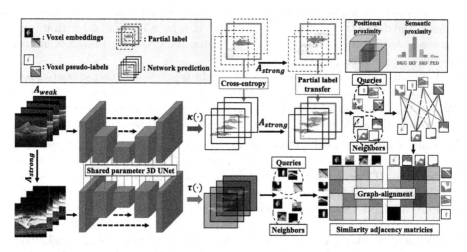

Fig. 2. Our method *Con2R* processes weakly- and strongly augmented volumes to generate voxel-wise embeddings and form a similarity graph. We align this graph to a target similarity graph that we compute via positional- and semantic proximity constraints using network predictions and partial labels if available. This alignment process enables us to learn consistent 3D predictions, merely using unlabeled or partially labeled data.

Receptive Smoothness Constraint. The well-known smoothness assumption [9], which states that *samples close to each other likely share a class label*, is the basis of much recent work [21,57], which enforce consistent predictions between differently perturbed versions of the same input. Similar but differently, we further condition the smoothness assumption on the magnitude of such perturbations: *samples closer to each other are more likely to share a class label*. With the similarity graph-based design introduced above, we are now able to integrate this assumption easily. By considering translations as a form of perturbation, we can enforce the similarity between voxel-embeddings to be proportional to their relative position in the volume. Thus, we condition the smoothness assumption on the magnitude of the translation, *i.e.* on the relative position.

To integrate this assumption into our target similarity weights, let us consider two embeddings $e^x \in \mathcal{Q}$ and $e^y \in \mathcal{N}$. We propose to compute *positional proximity* of the two voxel-embeddings in the volume by using the relative intersection of sub-volumes centered at x and y (smoothed by a small ε if the intersection approaches 0):

$$\rho(x, y, \mathcal{R}(\cdot)) = \max(\frac{|\mathcal{R}(x) \cap \mathcal{R}(y)|}{|\mathcal{R}(x)|}, \varepsilon), \tag{3}$$

where the receptive field function $\mathcal{R}(\cdot)$ returns for a voxel x all spatially related voxels that fall into the sub-volume centered at x. For a simplified depiction (2D case), see Fig. 3, where in (2) voxel B shares a larger receptive portion with A than with C or D, therefore B's voxel-embedding should be _closest_ to A's. This positional similarity is marginalized over neighborhood embeddings $e^z \in \mathcal{N}$:

$$\mathcal{P}(x, y, \mathcal{R}(\cdot)) = \frac{\rho(x, y, \mathcal{R}(\cdot))}{\sum_{e^z \in \mathcal{N}} \rho(x, z, \mathcal{R}(\cdot))}. \tag{4}$$

When no semantic information on class membership is present, constraining a model to be coherent with respect to $\mathcal{P}(\cdot)$ results in models that draw conclusions concerning embedding-similarity exclusively on the basis of relative positioning. In this case, the resulting models will lead to embeddings which consider the full extent of three dimensional receptive volumes. As it will turn out, this is useful in our setting with extremely few annotated volume slices.

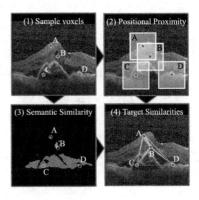

Fig. 3. Graph constraints (simplified 2D): Pairs of voxels are related by positional proximity measured in overlap of receptive field/volume and similarity in class-predictions.

Semantic Coherence Constraint. Besides positional proximity, we also enforce coherence of the embeddings for voxels with similar semantics. This is important to offset the position constraint for voxel-embeddings that share semantics but lie far apart, _e.g._ voxel C and D in (3) of Fig. 3 share the class prediction, hence C's voxel-embedding should be _more similar_ to D than to A or B. For two embeddings $e^x \in \mathcal{Q}$ and $e^y \in \mathcal{N}$, we take into account the semantic predictions p^x and p^y produced by the segmentation output-head $\kappa(\cdot)$, which is trained with the few given labels. To measure _semantic proximity_, different functions $\mathcal{S}(\cdot)$ have been proposed [36]. We base our measure on the symmetrized negative Kullback-Leibler divergence:

$$\text{SN-KL}(p^x, p^y) = -\frac{1}{2} \cdot \left(p^y \cdot \log\left(\frac{p^y}{p^x}\right) + p^x \cdot \log\left(\frac{p^x}{p^y}\right) \right), \tag{5}$$

which we marginalize over the predictions at the locations of the neighborhood voxels:

$$\mathcal{S}(x, y, p) = \frac{\exp(\text{SN-KL}(p^x, p^y))}{\sum_{e^z \in \mathcal{N}} \exp(\text{SN-KL}(p^x, p^z))}. \tag{6}$$

With the semantic proximity $\mathcal{S}(\cdot)$ and the positional proximity $\mathcal{P}(\cdot)$, we are now able to set up the function $\mathcal{T}(\cdot)$, which produces target similarity-weights for $\mathcal{G}$.

Graph-Based Contrastive Constraints. To restrict the similarity weights of our embedding graph $\mathcal{G}$, we first define a function $\mathcal{T}$ to obtain the target similarities between pairs of voxel-embeddings. For a given edge (x, y) between voxel-embeddings, the model should produce a similarity $\sigma(x,y)$ that matches:

$$\mathcal{T}(x, y, \mathcal{R}(\cdot), p) = \alpha \cdot \mathcal{P}(x, y, \mathcal{R}(\cdot)) + (1 - \alpha) \cdot \mathcal{S}(x, y, p). \tag{7}$$

The weight $\alpha \in [0, 1]$ allows to trade-off the contribution of the *receptive smoothness-* and *semantic coherence constraints*. With $\mathcal{T}$, we can align the voxel-embeddings for a given volume to these similarity targets. For this alignment process, we leverage the common contrastive similarity formulation:

$$\mathcal{O}(e^x, e^y) = \frac{\exp(\sigma(x,y))}{\sum_{e^z \in \mathcal{N}} \exp(\sigma(x,z))}, \tag{8}$$

which encodes the current voxel-embedding similarities in the graph $\mathcal{G}$. The final loss is formed by minimizing the cross-entropy between similarities and targets:

$$L(\mathcal{Q}, \mathcal{N}) = - \sum_{e^x \in \mathcal{Q}, e^y \in \mathcal{N}} \log(\mathcal{O}(e^x, e^y)) \cdot \mathcal{T}(x, y, \mathcal{R}(\cdot), p). \tag{9}$$

Finally, we symmetrize this loss and follow the example of [12] by only backpropagating through either $\mathcal{Q}$ or $\mathcal{N}$. Therefore, our proposed L_{Con2R} loss function resolves to:

$$L_{Con2R}(\mathcal{Q}, \mathcal{N}) = \frac{1}{2} \cdot (L(\mathcal{Q}, \bar{\mathcal{N}}) + L(\mathcal{N}, \bar{\mathcal{Q}})). \tag{10}$$

Here, $\bar{\mathcal{Q}}$ and $\bar{\mathcal{N}}$ indicate the respective voxel-embedding sets being detached from the computation graph, *i.e.* we treat them as constants in backpropagation.

3.3   Graph-Constrained Semi-weak Learning

To put L_{Con2R} to work, we propose the following training scheme which is also visualized in Fig. 2. First, we take an input volume v_i and augment it weak and strong, yielding $\mathcal{A}_{weak}(v_i)$ and $\mathcal{A}_{strong}(v_i)$. We train the output-head $\kappa(\cdot)$ with only the weakly augmented volumes by minimizing standard categorical cross-entropy $L_{Entropy}$ using the few partially labeled annotations. We use the predictions p from the weakly augmented volumes as input to generate our target similarities $\mathcal{T}(\cdot)$. When sparse annotations for v_i are present, we adapt p_i to p_i^*:

$$p_i^* = p_i \cdot (1 - a_i) + m_i \cdot a_i, \tag{11}$$

substituting ground-truth annotations in regions of the volume, where we are supplied with them. The embeddings we use for setting up the similarity graph $\mathcal{G}$ are taken from the strongly augmented input, *i.e.* embeddings produced by forwarding $\mathcal{A}_{strong}(v_i)$ through the network as well as the embedding output-head $\tau(\cdot)$. Put together, we optimize our semi-weakly supervised 3D segmentation model by minimizing $L_{total} = L_{Entropy} + L_{Con2R}$.

4   Evaluation

4.1   Protocol

Datasets. We evaluate our approach on two well-known volumetric datasets. The RETOUCH OCT dataset [7] for retinal fluid segmentation contains classes: Intraretinal fluid (IRF), Subretinal fluid (SRF), and Pigment Epithelium Detachment (PED). While different vendors of OCT devices are covered, we focus on Spectralis, for which the volumes have a depth of 49 B-scans. Further, we evaluate our approach on brain tumor sub-region segmentation in magnetic resonance images. We use the data as supplied in [1] which contains multiple BraTS challenges [2,3,44]. We segment tumor sub-regions edema (EDM), enhancing tumor (EN), non-enhancing tumor (NEN) within volumes of depth 155.

Experimental Setup. We intend to analyze extremely scarce annotation scenarios. Thus, we need to carefully design a suitable evaluation protocol. Therefore, we split the labeled data five times into train and test splits, where the train portion is further divided into train and validation volumes (train/val/test: RETOUCH: 14/10/10, BraTs: 242/121/121). This five-fold cross-validation enables us to report mean and standard deviation for the performance of all models which is crucially important when working with few labels [50]. In each train-val fold, we randomly select B-scans to be annotated, thereby marginalizing effects of individual annotated slices. We make sure that the set of annotated scans covers all classes. As such, in each fold a sequence of scenarios where only $3, 6, 12,$ or 24 label-masks are available gives detailed insight into effects of adding annotations. With *e.g.* $\mathcal{M}(12)$ we refer to a scenario that from all training volumes only has access to 12 annotated slices, distributed among all volumes ($\sum_{i,d=1}^{N,D} a_i^d = 12$). In a fold, higher supervision scenarios extend labels of lower supervision scenarios.

Evaluation Metric. For evaluating the performance of our methods, we use the mean Intersection over Union (mIoU), which is defined as the average classwise Intersection of segmentation and ground-truth over their Union. We report mIoU averaged over five cross-validation folds and the standard deviation.

4.2   Implementation Details

Data Augmentation. For RETOUCH, we resize the input volumes to $49 \times 160 \times 160$ and crop out 16 slices for training, while for BraTS, we resize to $155 \times 110 \times 110$ and crop out $32 \times 110 \times 110$-sized volumes. As described in Sect. 3.3, we require weak and strong augmentations for computing pseudo-labels and voxel-embeddings. Weak augmentations are in our setting flipping the input volume in the longitudinal- and the vertical direction with a probability of 50%. To compute embeddings, the input is flipped in all three directions with a probability of 50% and always altered via photometric perturbations with sampled magnitudes. Here, we find adjusting the brightness and sharpness to be most effective. Furthermore, we extend CutOut [19] for volumetric inputs, where we always set a randomly placed cube of size $16 \times 16 \times 16$ in the volume to zero.

Network Configuration. For all experiments and baselines, we leverage 3D UNets [15] with $64, 128, 256, 256$ channels in each encoder and decoder layer. We train the networks using a batchsize of two, where we oversample the partially labeled volumes and ensure that in each iteration, one of the volumes is partially labeled. We apply Xavier initialization [23], use a learning rate of 0.01, and use SGD with momentum of 0.9 and a weight decay of 0.00001. As lower bound on performance, we train models that merely employ cross-entropy on partially labeled volumes and do not consider unlabeled volumes or unlabeled regions. These naive 3D UNet baselines serve as initialization to the semi-supervised models. Training is conducted in 100 epochs and validated every 10 epochs, where the best epoch is then evaluated once on the testing set. All experiments were carried out on 11GB NVIDIA RTX 2080 Ti GPUs. The code is made publicly available at https://github.com/Simael/Con2R.

4.3   Baselines and Setup for Semi-weak Volumetric Segmentation

We implement common methods from semi-supervised literature and tune them for semi-weakly volumetric segmentation. Thus, we select the most common [37] and successful 2D methods [55] and methods that have seen success on volumetric medical use-cases [39,66] and also a naive **3D UNet** as a lower bound. With this we explore how they compare and transfer to partially labeled scenarios.

Pseudo-label (PL) [37,74]. We implement a pseudo-labeling baseline which is a common, classical semi-supervised approach. As we have access to partially labeled volumes, in pseudo-labeling we use the network predictions and augment them via Eq. (11). This simple transfer of the method did not perform well in our setting; we tune it by using the self-training normalization scheme of [74].

Mean-Teacher (MT) [57]. A commonly used semi-supervised framework is the Mean-Teacher, which we transfer to volumetric inputs and dense predictions. The adaptation of this approach to segmentation has been modeled multiple times [39,50]. We train by aligning the student predictions to the teacher predictions as obtained by forward passing differently augmented volumes. Then, we reverse geometric augmentations on the teacher predictions to maintain pixel-alignment between student- and teacher outputs for the consistency loss. We find an exponential-moving average decay factor 0.5 to perform well.

FixMatch [55]. FixMatch is a successful method originally designed for 2D classification. It mixes pseudo-labeling and consistency regularization by using weak and strong augmentations (we use augmentations from Sec. 4.2). As we adapt this approach to segmentation, we consider the alignment of predictions from the strongly augmented branch to the weakly augmented branch, which we do similarly as in the Mean-Teacher. A confidence threshold of 0.5 was suitable.

Uncertainty-Aware Mean-Teacher (UA MT) [66]. This Mean-Teacher flavor adds uncertainty estimation using Monte-Carlo dropout [22]. By estimating and thresholding voxel-wise uncertainty, the consistency loss is applied selectively in unlabeled regions. We find a threshold of 0.5 and 8 forward passes to work well.

Contrastive Constrained Regularization (Con2R). We train our *Con2R* method on RETOUCH by sampling $|\mathcal{Q}| + |\mathcal{N}| = 3456$ voxels from the volume-graph (BraTS: 6750) each iteration and optimize the alignment to our computed target graph. The composition of positional- and semantic constraints for the target graph is moderated by $\alpha = 0.2$. The receptive volume size $\mathcal{R}$ is $16 \times 16 \times 16$ and $32 \times 32 \times 32$ for RETOUCH and BraTS, we set $e_{dim} = 64$ and $\varepsilon = 10^{-7}$.

4.4 Quantitative Results

RETOUCH. When looking at Table 1, the first observation is that the lower accuracy bound for scenarios with $3, 6, 12, 24$ annotations is set by the 3D UNet. In the lowest supervision scenario $\mathcal{M}(3)$, results are as expected very poor and most semi-supervised models can not meaningfully exceed the plain 3D UNet. With additional supervision, semi-supervised methods start to show improvements due to modeling concistency in unlabeled data. Interestingly, FixMatch gives smallest gains in $\mathcal{M}(6)$ while in later scenarios, it is comparable to competing approaches. *Con2R* is able to outperform all methods with clear margins, especially Uncertainty-aware Mean-Teacher and FixMatch, which are the strongest competitors in $\mathcal{M}(12)$ and $\mathcal{M}(24)$. With full annotations, the baselines and *Con2R* achieve, within a small margin, comparable results, as no additional unlabeled data is leveraged. UA MT further improves $\mathcal{M}(\textbf{full})$ slightly, which might be due to the integrated dropout layers. The results show that semi-supervised methods generally work for the proposed semi-weakly supervised learning with partially labeled volumes. Yet, by explicitly modeling the properties of partially labeled data with our constraints in *Con2R*, we see consistent gains of $+1.8\%$, $+1.9\%$, $+2.1\%$, $+2.0\%$, as compared to the best competing methods.

Table 1. RETOUCH results in mIoU for semi-weakly supervised learning, number of annotated B-scans successively increased from 3 to 24 and **full** access as upper limit

Method	$\mathcal{M}(3)$	$\mathcal{M}(6)$	$\mathcal{M}(12)$	$\mathcal{M}(24)$	$\mathcal{M}(\textbf{full})$
3D UNet [15]	12.0 ± 5.6	18.1 ± 11.5	31.1 ± 12.4	43.8 ± 2.5	54.9 ± 0.9
PL [37,74]	13.0 ± 6.3	20.6 ± 13.4	30.9 ± 11.5	45.7 ± 2.2	55.4 ± 1.5
MT [39,57]	12.0 ± 6.6	20.2 ± 12.4	34.4 ± 11.4	45.3 ± 3.1	53.4 ± 1.9
FixMatch [55]	10.4 ± 5.7	18.7 ± 10.6	34.7 ± 6.8	46.2 ± 3.8	54.4 ± 3.3
UA MT [66]	13.0 ± 6.7	20.0 ± 11.9	36.5 ± 9.2	45.7 ± 1.9	$\mathbf{56.3 \pm 1.7}$
Con2R (Ours)	$\mathbf{14.8 \pm 8.7}$	$\mathbf{22.5 \pm 10.0}$	$\mathbf{38.6 \pm 7.5}$	$\mathbf{48.2 \pm 3.1}$	54.6 ± 1.2

We can get more nuanced insights by comparing class-wise segmentation performance in Table 2. It is evident that even with few annotations, *Con2R* is able to segment Subretinal Fluid (SRF) and Pigment Epithelium Detachments (PED) better than alternative approaches which holds true for all scenarios. In $\mathcal{M}(24)$, our method segments Subretinal Fluid with an IoU of 79.1% which is close to the best fully supervised result of 84.4% reached by Uncertainty-aware Mean-Teacher with access to a total of 686 annotated OCT B-scans.

Table 2. RETOUCH class-wise results in mIoU for semi-weakly supervised learning, number of annotated B-scans successively increased from 3 to 24

Method	$\mathcal{M}(3)$			$\mathcal{M}(6)$			$\mathcal{M}(12)$			$\mathcal{M}(24)$		
	IRF	SRF	PED	IRF	SRF	PED	IRF	SRF	PED	IRF	SRF	PED
3D UNet [15]	21.1	11.5	3.3	21.0	24.6	8.6	23.4	49.9	20.0	30.5	73.0	27.8
PL [37,74]	**22.4**	13.0	3.7	**23.5**	27.3	11.0	24.2	52.9	15.6	32.3	73.9	30.8
MT [39,57]	18.4	12.9	4.8	20.7	29.4	10.5	24.5	59.7	19.0	30.9	76.6	28.3
FixMatch [55]	16.5	13.1	1.4	21.4	27.7	7.0	20.0	64.9	19.2	**33.4**	76.8	28.3
UA MT [66]	22.3	12.9	3.7	21.1	29.6	9.4	27.2	61.1	21.2	31.9	75.9	29.3
Con2R (Ours)	20.2	**16.4**	**7.8**	22.1	**31.8**	**13.6**	**27.3**	**65.2**	**23.3**	31.6	**79.1**	**34.0**

Table 3. BraTS class-wise results in mIoU for semi-weakly supervised learning, number of annotated B-scans is set at 24 and **full** access is shown as upper limit

Method	$\mathcal{M}(24)$				$\mathcal{M}(\textbf{full})$
	EDM	EN	NEN	AVG	AVG
3D UNet [15]	48.7	19.6	48.1	38.8 ± 3.4	51.7 ± 7.0
PL [37,74]	49.1	21.3	50.5	40.3 ± 2.5	52.2 ± 8.4
MT [39,57]	49.1	21.7	45.0	38.6 ± 4.5	53.7 ± 5.7
FixMatch [55]	50.1	**24.2**	53.1	42.4 ± 4.9	51.0 ± 6.5
UA MT [66]	49.2	22.6	51.3	41.1 ± 3.5	52.6 ± 6.0
Con2R (Ours)	**51.8**	23.9	**53.9**	$\mathbf{43.2 \pm 3.5}$	$\mathbf{54.6 \pm 7.7}$

BraTS. In Table 3, we see the same methods evaluated for brain tumor segmentation. Due to generally long training times for 3D segmentation models, we report only one semi-weakly supervised setting, namely $\mathcal{M}(24)$. Here, we see that especially edema (EDM) and non-enhancing tumor (NEN) sub-regions benefit from our modeling, which leads to superior results. It is noteworthy that in this scenario, 37, 486 slices are not annotated while only 24 have associated labels. Hence, even in this highly unbalanced setting between unlabeled and labeled scans, our method is well suited and exceeds all semi-supervised baselines.

4.5 Ablation and Hyperparameter Sensitivity Studies

We carry out all experiments in this section on the RETOUCH dataset with the 24 annotation scenario. First, we study the effect of the weight α, which interpolates between the *positional* and *semantic constraints* (Table 6). We see that semantic constraints in isolation ($\alpha = 0.0$) produce solid results, only positional constraints surprisingly too ($\alpha = 1.0$), but best results are found with $\alpha = 0.2$. Next, we report in Table 4 how chosing the receptive field function $\mathcal{R}$ impacts accuracy. The best results are achieved with $16 \times 16 \times 16$, which is the maximum depth of the input volume crops (therefore, we adjust $\mathcal{R}$ to $32 \times 32 \times 32$ for the BraTS task). Larger receptive volume sizes degrade the performance, and we expect that the shape and size of objects to segment in a given dataset also plays an important role regarding this choice.

Finally, the number of sampled edges from the volume-graph to tune is varied in Table 5. We see that increasing this number also steadily increases the benefit of *Con2R*. We set this hyperparameter to $1,728$ for RETOUCH and to $3,375$ for BraTS, which relates to the maximum GPU capacity available to us.

4.6 Qualitative Results

RETOUCH. An example of the qualitative segmentation improvement between different methods while adding annotations are shown in Fig. 4. With 3 annotated slices in training, none of the methods achieve satisfying results, merely a small fluid portion of **Subretinal Fluid (SRF)** is in some cases segmented coarsely. Adding three annotations more, most approaches over-confidently identify **Pigment Epithelium Detachments (PED)** as **Intraretinal Fluid (IRF)**, merely

Table 4. Effect of receptive volume size $\mathcal{R}$ on the mean IoU

$\mathcal{R}$	validation mIoU
$16 \times 16 \times 16$	$49.1 \pm 4.7\%$
$32 \times 32 \times 32$	$47.1 \pm 2.7\%$
$64 \times 64 \times 64$	$46.3 \pm 2.3\%$
$160 \times 160 \times 160$	$46.5 \pm 6.1\%$

Table 5. Effect number of vertices in graph $\mathcal{G}$ on the mean IoU

$|\mathcal{Q}|, |\mathcal{N}|$	validation mIoU
216	$46.9 \pm 4.5\%$
512	$46.9 \pm 3.4\%$
1000	$47.8 \pm 5.0\%$
1728	$49.1 \pm 4.7\%$

Table 6. Validation performance of *Con2R* when tuning α, IoU reported along five validation splits with mean and standard deviation displayed

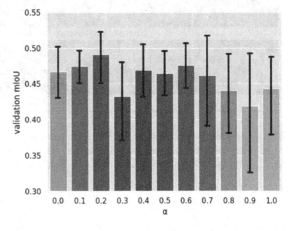

our method starts to segment this area correctly. FixMatch and Uncertainty-aware Mean-Teacher are the only other methods that correctly pick up the spatial relations between PED and SRF with 12 annotated slices. For this supervision scenario, our method is able to already pick up the correct location of IRF pockets in the retina. Using 24 annotations, our method further is the only one to correctly delineate the SRF and PED and making consistent spatial segmentations without class confusion that we see in the remaining methods. We attribute this to our smoothness priors regarding both semantics <u>and</u> locality.

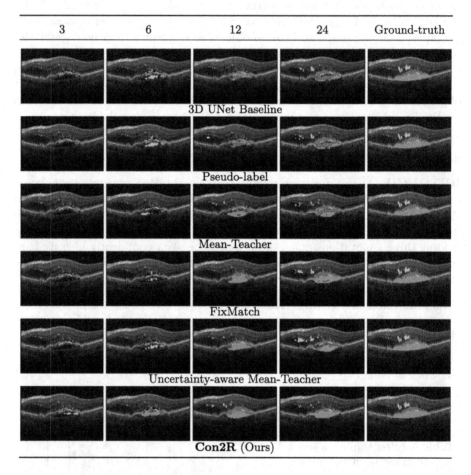

Fig. 4. Segmentation progression when increasing the number of annotations from 3 to 24 in semi-weak retinal fluid segmentation, results for IRF, SRF and PED overlayed with input OCT scan. Method names are below rows, right column: ground-truth.

5   Discussion

We believe that our proposed concept of semi-weakly supervised volumetric segmentation as formulated in Sect. 3.1 is worth exploring further since it gives detailed insights into how labeling can be optimized. Especially in application fields where labeling budget is tight or where time of expert annotators is limited, flexible learning algorithms such as *Con2R* can become enabling technologies to build useful solutions. To reduce the expert label costs further, we see potential in using annotations that only consider sub-regions within a slice in a volume. This variation from our setting would further put emphasis on intuitive expert-selected region annotation, which is one additional step towards an expert-centric process. By design, our *Con2R* method is applicable to such scenarios and we are curious to see them being analyzed in future investigations.

6   Conclusion

We introduced and explored semi-weakly volumetric segmentation to reduce the need for dense expert-labels on volumetric data. Motivated by designing flexible learning algorithms which can use partial labels, we transferred a variety of semi-supervised algorithms. It became evident that these methods indeed add performance but leave behind uncollected rewards. Our method *Con2R* recovers those by explicitly modelling the semi-weak scenario. We carefully constructed positional smoothness- and semantic coherence constraints in embedding space, and we were able to consistently raise segmentation accuracy on two medical datasets. We expect that flexible algorithms like *Con2R* which exploit unlabeled and partially labeled volume data can enable applications where annotations at scale are otherwise too costly or even impossible to obtain.

References

1. Antonelli, M., et al.: The medical segmentation decathlon. arXiv preprint arXiv:2106.05735 (2021)
2. Bakas, S., et al.: Advancing the cancer genome atlas glioma MRI collections with expert segmentation labels and radiomic features. Sci. Data 4(1), 1–13 (2017)
3. Bakas, S., et al.: Identifying the best machine learning algorithms for brain tumor segmentation, progression assessment, and overall survival prediction in the brats challenge. arXiv preprint arXiv:1811.02629 (2018)
4. Bao, H., Dong, L., Wei, F.: Beit: Bert pre-training of image transformers. arXiv preprint arXiv:2106.08254 (2021)
5. Bearman, A., Russakovsky, O., Ferrari, V., Fei-Fei, L.: What's the point: semantic segmentation with point supervision. In: Leibe, B., Matas, J., Sebe, N., Welling, M. (eds.) ECCV 2016. LNCS, vol. 9911, pp. 549–565. Springer, Cham (2016). https://doi.org/10.1007/978-3-319-46478-7_34
6. Ben-David, S., Lu, T., Pál, D.: Does unlabeled data provably help? worst-case analysis of the sample complexity of semi-supervised learning. In: COLT, pp. 33–44 (2008)

7. Bogunović, H., et al.: Retouch: the retinal oct fluid detection and segmentation benchmark and challenge. IEEE Trans. Med. Imaging **38**(8), 1858–1874 (2019)

8. Chandra, S., Kokkinos, I.: Fast, exact and multi-scale inference for semantic image segmentation with deep gaussian CRFs. In: Leibe, B., Matas, J., Sebe, N., Welling, M. (eds.) ECCV 2016. LNCS, vol. 9911, pp. 402–418. Springer, Cham (2016). https://doi.org/10.1007/978-3-319-46478-7_25

9. Chapelle, O., Zien, A.: Semi-supervised classification by low density separation. In: International Workshop on Artificial Intelligence and Statistics, pp. 57–64. PMLR (2005)

10. Chen, L.C., Papandreou, G., Kokkinos, I., Murphy, K., Yuille, A.L.: Semantic image segmentation with deep convolutional nets and fully connected crfs. arXiv preprint arXiv:1412.7062 (2014)

11. Chen, L.C., Zhu, Y., Papandreou, G., Schroff, F., Adam, H.: Encoder-decoder with atrous separable convolution for semantic image segmentation. In: Proceedings of the European Conference on Computer Vision (ECCV), pp. 801–818 (2018)

12. Chen, X., He, K.: Exploring simple siamese representation learning. In: Proceedings of the IEEE/CVF Conference on Computer Vision and Pattern Recognition, pp. 15750–15758 (2021)

13. Choe, J., Oh, S.J., Lee, S., Chun, S., Akata, Z., Shim, H.: Evaluating weakly supervised object localization methods right. In: Proceedings of the IEEE/CVF Conference on Computer Vision and Pattern Recognition, pp. 3133–3142 (2020)

14. Chollet, F.: Xception: Deep learning with depthwise separable convolutions. In: Proceedings of the IEEE Conference on Computer Vision and Pattern Recognition, pp. 1251–1258 (2017)

15. Çiçek, Ö., Abdulkadir, A., Lienkamp, S.S., Brox, T., Ronneberger, O.: 3D U-Net: learning dense volumetric segmentation from sparse annotation. In: Ourselin, S., Joskowicz, L., Sabuncu, M.R., Unal, G., Wells, W. (eds.) MICCAI 2016. LNCS, vol. 9901, pp. 424–432. Springer, Cham (2016). https://doi.org/10.1007/978-3-319-46723-8_49

16. Cityscapes-team: semantic understanding of urban street scenes: pixel-level semantic labeling task. www.cityscapes-dataset.com/benchmarks/. Accessed 03 Mar 2022

17. Cordts, M., et al.: The cityscapes dataset for semantic urban scene understanding. In: Proceedings of the IEEE Conference on Computer Vision and Pattern Recognition, pp. 3213–3223 (2016)

18. De Fauw, J., et al.: Clinically applicable deep learning for diagnosis and referral in retinal disease. Nat. Med. **24**(9), 1342–1350 (2018)

19. DeVries, T., Taylor, G.W.: Improved regularization of convolutional neural networks with cutout. arXiv preprint arXiv:1708.04552 (2017)

20. Everingham, M., Van Gool, L., Williams, C.K., Winn, J., Zisserman, A.: The pascal visual object classes (VOC) challenge. Int. J. Comput. Vision **88**(2), 303–338 (2010)

21. French, G., Laine, S., Aila, T., Mackiewicz, M., Finlayson, G.: Semi-supervised semantic segmentation needs strong, varied perturbations. arXiv preprint arXiv:1906.01916 (2019)

22. Gal, Y., Ghahramani, Z.: Dropout as a Bayesian approximation: representing model uncertainty in deep learning. In: International Conference on Machine Learning, pp. 1050–1059. PMLR (2016)

23. Glorot, X., Bengio, Y.: Understanding the difficulty of training deep feedforward neural networks. In: Proceedings of the Thirteenth International Conference on Artificial Intelligence and Statistics, pp. 249–256. JMLR Workshop and Conference Proceedings (2010)

24. Hatamizadeh, A., Terzopoulos, D., Myronenko, A.: Edge-gated cnns for volumetric semantic segmentation of medical images. arXiv preprint arXiv:2002.04207 (2020)
25. Heller, N., et al.: The state of the art in kidney and kidney tumor segmentation in contrast-enhanced CT imaging: results of the kits19 challenge. Med. Image Anal. **67**, 101821 (2021)
26. Hinton, G., Vinyals, O., Dean, J.: Distilling the knowledge in a neural network. arXiv preprint arXiv:1503.02531 (2015)
27. Huang, S., Lu, Z., Cheng, R., He, C.: Fapn: feature-aligned pyramid network for dense image prediction. In: Proceedings of the IEEE/CVF International Conference on Computer Vision, pp. 864–873 (2021)
28. Huo, X., et al.: Atso: asynchronous teacher-student optimization for semi-supervised image segmentation. In: Proceedings of the IEEE/CVF Conference on Computer Vision and Pattern Recognition, pp. 1235–1244 (2021)
29. Iscen, A., Tolias, G., Avrithis, Y., Chum, O.: Label propagation for deep semi-supervised learning. In: Proceedings of the IEEE/CVF Conference on Computer Vision and Pattern Recognition, pp. 5070–5079 (2019)
30. Isensee, F., Kickingereder, P., Wick, W., Bendszus, M., Maier-Hein, K.H.: No new-net. In: Crimi, A., Bakas, S., Kuijf, H., Keyvan, F., Reyes, M., van Walsum, T. (eds.) BrainLes 2018. LNCS, vol. 11384, pp. 234–244. Springer, Cham (2019). https://doi.org/10.1007/978-3-030-11726-9_21
31. Isensee, F., Maier-Hein, K.H.: An attempt at beating the 3D U-Net. arXiv preprint arXiv:1908.02182 (2019)
32. Ji, S., Xu, W., Yang, M., Yu, K.: 3D convolutional neural networks for human action recognition. IEEE Trans. Pattern Anal. Mach. Intell. **35**(1), 221–231 (2012)
33. Kamnitsas, K., et al.: Efficient multi-scale 3D CNN with fully connected CRF for accurate brain lesion segmentation. Med. Image Anal. **36**, 61–78 (2017)
34. Karpathy, A., Toderici, G., Shetty, S., Leung, T., Sukthankar, R., Fei-Fei, L.: Large-scale video classification with convolutional neural networks. In: Proceedings of the IEEE conference on Computer Vision and Pattern Recognition, pp. 1725–1732 (2014)
35. Kleesiek, J., et al.: Deep MRI brain extraction: a 3D convolutional neural network for skull stripping. Neuroimage **129**, 460–469 (2016)
36. Krähenbühl, P., Koltun, V.: Parameter learning and convergent inference for dense random fields. In: International Conference on Machine Learning, pp. 513–521. PMLR (2013)
37. Lee, D.H., et al.: Pseudo-label: the simple and efficient semi-supervised learning method for deep neural networks. In: Workshop on Challenges in Representation Learning, ICML, vol. 3, p. 896 (2013)
38. Li, J., Xiong, C., Hoi, S.C.: Comatch: semi-supervised learning with contrastive graph regularization. In: Proceedings of the IEEE/CVF International Conference on Computer Vision, pp. 9475–9484 (2021)
39. Li, X., Yu, L., Chen, H., Fu, C.W., Xing, L., Heng, P.A.: Transformation-consistent self-ensembling model for semisupervised medical image segmentation. IEEE Trans. Neural Netw. Learn. Syst. **32**(2), 523–534 (2020)
40. Lin, D., Dai, J., Jia, J., He, K., Sun, J.: Scribblesup: scribble-supervised convolutional networks for semantic segmentation. In: Proceedings of the IEEE Conference on Computer Vision and Pattern Recognition, pp. 3159–3167 (2016)
41. Lin, T.Y., et al.: Microsoft COCO: common objects in context. In: Fleet, D., Pajdla, T., Schiele, B., Tuytelaars, T. (eds.) ECCV 2014. LNCS, vol. 8693, pp. 740–755. Springer, Cham (2014). https://doi.org/10.1007/978-3-319-10602-1_48

42. Luo, X., et al.: Efficient semi-supervised gross target volume of nasopharyngeal carcinoma segmentation via uncertainty rectified pyramid consistency. In: de Bruijne, M., et al. (eds.) MICCAI 2021. LNCS, vol. 12902, pp. 318–329. Springer, Cham (2021). https://doi.org/10.1007/978-3-030-87196-3_30

43. McKinley, R., Meier, R., Wiest, R.: Ensembles of densely-connected CNNs with label-uncertainty for brain tumor segmentation. In: Crimi, A., Bakas, S., Kuijf, H., Keyvan, F., Reyes, M., van Walsum, T. (eds.) BrainLes 2018. LNCS, vol. 11384, pp. 456–465. Springer, Cham (2019). https://doi.org/10.1007/978-3-030-11726-9_40

44. Menze, B.H., et al.: The multimodal brain tumor image segmentation benchmark (brats). IEEE Trans. Med. Imaging **34**(10), 1993–2024 (2014)

45. Mu, G., Lin, Z., Han, M., Yao, G., Gao, Y.: Segmentation of kidney tumor by multi-resolution VB-nets (2019)

46. Myronenko, A.: 3D MRI brain tumor segmentation using autoencoder regularization. In: Crimi, A., Bakas, S., Kuijf, H., Keyvan, F., Reyes, M., van Walsum, T. (eds.) BrainLes 2018. LNCS, vol. 11384, pp. 311–320. Springer, Cham (2019). https://doi.org/10.1007/978-3-030-11726-9_28

47. Nie, D., Gao, Y., Wang, L., Shen, D.: ASDNet: attention based semi-supervised deep networks for medical image segmentation. In: Frangi, A.F., Schnabel, J.A., Davatzikos, C., Alberola-López, C., Fichtinger, G. (eds.) MICCAI 2018. LNCS, vol. 11073, pp. 370–378. Springer, Cham (2018). https://doi.org/10.1007/978-3-030-00937-3_43

48. Ouali, Y., Hudelot, C., Tami, M.: An overview of deep semi-supervised learning. arXiv preprint arXiv:2006.05278 (2020)

49. Qu, H., et al.: Weakly supervised deep nuclei segmentation using partial points annotation in histopathology images. IEEE Trans. Med. Imaging **39**(11), 3655–3666 (2020)

50. Reiß, S., Seibold, C., Freytag, A., Rodner, E., Stiefelhagen, R.: Every annotation counts: multi-label deep supervision for medical image segmentation. In: Proceedings of the IEEE/CVF Conference on Computer Vision and Pattern Recognition, pp. 9532–9542 (2021)

51. Ronneberger, O., Fischer, P., Brox, T.: U-Net: convolutional networks for biomedical image segmentation. In: Navab, N., Hornegger, J., Wells, W.M., Frangi, A.F. (eds.) MICCAI 2015. LNCS, vol. 9351, pp. 234–241. Springer, Cham (2015). https://doi.org/10.1007/978-3-319-24574-4_28

52. Roth, H., et al.: Weakly supervised segmentation from extreme points. In: Zhou, L., et al. (eds.) LABELS/HAL-MICCAI/CuRIOUS -2019. LNCS, vol. 11851, pp. 42–50. Springer, Cham (2019). https://doi.org/10.1007/978-3-030-33642-4_5

53. Russakovsky, O., et al.: Imagenet large scale visual recognition challenge. Int. J. Comput. Vision **115**(3), 211–252 (2015)

54. Simpson, A.L., et al.: A large annotated medical image dataset for the development and evaluation of segmentation algorithms. arXiv preprint arXiv:1902.09063 (2019)

55. Sohn, K., et al.: Fixmatch: simplifying semi-supervised learning with consistency and confidence. arXiv preprint arXiv:2001.07685 (2020)

56. Tao, A., Sapra, K., Catanzaro, B.: Hierarchical multi-scale attention for semantic segmentation. arXiv preprint arXiv:2005.10821 (2020)

57. Tarvainen, A., Valpola, H.: Mean teachers are better role models: weight-averaged consistency targets improve semi-supervised deep learning results. arXiv preprint arXiv:1703.01780 (2017)

58. Tran, D., Bourdev, L., Fergus, R., Torresani, L., Paluri, M.: Learning spatiotemporal features with 3D convolutional networks. In: Proceedings of the IEEE International Conference on Computer Vision, pp. 4489–4497 (2015)

59. Tran, D., Bourdev, L., Fergus, R., Torresani, L., Paluri, M.: Deep end2end voxel2voxel prediction. In: Proceedings of the IEEE Conference on Computer Vision and Pattern Recognition Workshops, pp. 17–24 (2016)
60. Valvano, G., Leo, A., Tsaftaris, S.A.: Learning to segment from scribbles using multi-scale adversarial attention gates. IEEE Trans. Med. Imaging **40**(8), 1990–2001 (2021)
61. Xia, Y., et al.: 3D semi-supervised learning with uncertainty-aware multi-view co-training. In: Proceedings of the IEEE/CVF Winter Conference on Applications of Computer Vision, pp. 3646–3655 (2020)
62. Xia, Y., et al.: Uncertainty-aware multi-view co-training for semi-supervised medical image segmentation and domain adaptation. Med. Image Anal. **65**, 101766 (2020)
63. Yang, X., et al.: Towards automatic semantic segmentation in volumetric ultrasound. In: Descoteaux, M., et al. (eds.) MICCAI 2017. LNCS, vol. 10433, pp. 711–719. Springer, Cham (2017). https://doi.org/10.1007/978-3-319-66182-7_81
64. You, C., Zhao, R., Staib, L., Duncan, J.S.: Momentum contrastive voxel-wise representation learning for semi-supervised volumetric medical image segmentation. arXiv preprint arXiv:2105.07059 (2021)
65. You, C., Zhou, Y., Zhao, R., Staib, L., Duncan, J.S.: Simcvd: simple contrastive voxel-wise representation distillation for semi-supervised medical image segmentation. arXiv preprint arXiv:2108.06227 (2021)
66. Yu, L., Wang, S., Li, X., Fu, C.-W., Heng, P.-A.: Uncertainty-aware self-ensembling model for semi-supervised 3D left atrium segmentation. In: Shen, D., et al. (eds.) MICCAI 2019. LNCS, vol. 11765, pp. 605–613. Springer, Cham (2019). https://doi.org/10.1007/978-3-030-32245-8_67
67. Yuan, Y., Chen, X., Chen, X., Wang, J.: Segmentation transformer: object-contextual representations for semantic segmentation. In: European Conference on Computer Vision (ECCV), vol. 1 (2021)
68. Zeng, D., et al.: Positional contrastive learning for volumetric medical image segmentation. In: de Bruijne, M., et al. (eds.) MICCAI 2021. LNCS, vol. 12902, pp. 221–230. Springer, Cham (2021). https://doi.org/10.1007/978-3-030-87196-3_21
69. Zhang, Y., et al.: Cascaded volumetric convolutional network for kidney tumor segmentation from CT volumes. arXiv preprint arXiv:1910.02235 (2019)
70. Zheng, Set al.: Conditional random fields as recurrent neural networks. In: Proceedings of the IEEE International Conference on Computer Vision, pp. 1529–1537 (2015)
71. Zhou, B., Zhao, H., Puig, X., Fidler, S., Barriuso, A., Torralba, A.: Scene parsing through ade20k dataset. In: Proceedings of the IEEE Conference on Computer Vision and Pattern Recognition, pp. 633–641 (2017)
72. Zhou, Y., Wang, Y., Tang, P., Bai, S., Shen, W., Fishman, E., Yuille, A.: Semi-supervised 3D abdominal multi-organ segmentation via deep multi-planar co-training. In: 2019 IEEE Winter Conference on Applications of Computer Vision (WACV), pp. 121–140. IEEE (2019)
73. Zhu, X., Ghahramani, Z., Lafferty, J.D.: Semi-supervised learning using gaussian fields and harmonic functions. In: Proceedings of the 20th International Conference on Machine learning (ICML-2003), pp. 912–919 (2003)
74. Zoph, B., et al.: Rethinking pre-training and self-training. arXiv preprint arXiv:2006.06882 (2020)

Generalizable Medical Image Segmentation via Random Amplitude Mixup and Domain-Specific Image Restoration

Ziqi Zhou[1,2], Lei Qi[3(✉)], and Yinghuan Shi[1,2(✉)]

[1] State Key Laboratory for Novel Software Technology, Nanjing University,
Nanjing, China
zhouzq@smail.nju.edu.cn
[2] National Institute of Healthcare Data Science, Nanjing University, Nanjing, China
syh@nju.edu.cn
[3] School of Computer Science and Engineering, Southeast University,
Dhaka, Bangladesh
qilei@seu.edu.cn

Abstract. For medical image analysis, segmentation models trained on one or several domains lack generalization ability to unseen domains due to discrepancies between different data acquisition policies. We argue that the degeneration in segmentation performance is mainly attributed to overfitting to source domains and domain shift. To this end, we present a novel generalizable medical image segmentation method. To be specific, we design our approach as a multi-task paradigm by combining the segmentation model with a self-supervision *domain-specific image restoration* (DSIR) module for model regularization. We also design a *random amplitude mixup* (RAM) module, which incorporates low-level frequency information of different domain images to synthesize new images. To guide our model be resistant to domain shift, we introduce a semantic consistency loss. We demonstrate the performance of our method on two public generalizable segmentation benchmarks in medical images, which validates our method could achieve the state-of-the-art performance. (Code is available at https://github.com/zzzqzhou/RAM-DSIR).

Keywords: Medical image segmentation · Domain generalization · Self-supervision

1 Introduction

Recently, deep convolution neural networks (DCNNs) have progressed remarkably in computer vision tasks (*e.g.*, image classification, semantic segmentation,

---

Supplementary Information The online version contains supplementary material available at https://doi.org/10.1007/978-3-031-19803-8_25.

S. Avidan et al. (Eds.): ECCV 2022, LNCS 13681, pp. 420–436, 2022.
https://doi.org/10.1007/978-3-031-19803-8_25

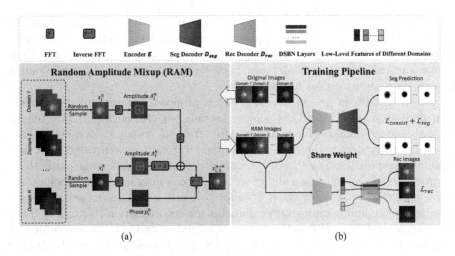

(a)   (b)

Fig. 1. The overall architecture of our method. (a) Random Amplitude Mixup (RAM): We extract the amplitude maps from two random sampled images of different domains and incorporate the amplitude maps of them. Then we can synthesize new images that have different domain styles and preserve original semantic information. (b) The synthesized images from RAM module are utilized to train the segmentation model and DSIR decoder. Basic segmentation loss combined with semantic consistency loss and image recovering loss are employed to train our network.

object detection, *etc.*). Especially in medical image segmentation tasks, deep learning based methods have taken over the dominant position [29,33]. Usually, DCNNs require large numbers of annotated training images to alleviate the risk of overfitting. However, datasets in medical image segmentation tasks are often relatively small in amount than those in natural image segmentation tasks. Moreover, it is notoriously time-consuming to acquire segmentation annotations of medical images. Accurate annotations also requires specific expertise in radiodiagnosis. Except for the data amounts and annotations problem, basic deep learning methods assume that training data and test data share same distribution information. This assumption requires that training and test data are collected from the same distribution, which is a strong assumption. Due to data distribution shifts, this assumption usually becomes invalid in the real clinical setting. It is known that the quality of medical images varies greatly due to many factors, such as different scanners, imaging protocols, and operators. As a result, the segmentation model directly trained on a set of training images may lack generalization ability on test images drawn from another hospital or medical center, which follows a different distribution.

To fight against distribution shift, tremendous researchers have investigated several practical settings, such as unsupervised domain adaptation (UDA), domain generalization (DG), *etc.* UDA-based segmentation methods have gained much popularity in medical image segmentation [9,18,44]. To be specific, UDA attempts to learn a segmentation network on single or multiple source domain images including the annotations along with unlabeled target domain images.

UDA-based methods intend to narrow the domain gap between source and target domains. However, this prerequisite is sometimes impractical or infeasible in real-world application. Since data privacy protection is rigorous in medical image scenarios, we may sometimes have no chance to access target domain images from some medical centers.

Recently, domain generalization (DG) is proposed to alleviate the application limitation in UDA. DG is a more feasible yet challenging setting requiring only source domains for training. After training on source domain images, we can directly deploy the segmentation model to new unseen target domains. Recently, several literature have developed domain generalization methods to improve model generalization ability with multiple source domains. Among these previous methods, most of them attempt to learn a domain-irrelevant feature representation among multi-source domains for generalization [11,22–24]. Some data augmentation based methods have emerged to tackle the problem of lack of prior information from target domains [40,43] by synthesizing newly stylized images to expand diversities of source domain images. Some pioneers have proposed self-supervised tasks (*i.e.*, solving a Jigsaw Puzzles) to help regularize the model [3,37]. These methods indicate that an auxiliary self-supervised task can better help the model learn domain-invariant knowledge, thus improving model regularization. However, solving a Jigsaw Puzzles may not be a sufficient self-supervision for DG segmentation tasks. To this end, we aim to design a more complex self-supervision to better learn domain-invariant semantic representation for medical image segmentation.

In our work, we present a new framework based on vanilla generalizable medical image segmentation model. To be specific, we first introduce a *random amplitude mixup* (RAM) module by utilizing the Fourier transform to capture frequency space signals from different source domain images and incorporating low-level frequency information of different source domain images to generate new images with different styles. We then use these synthetic images as data augmentation to train the segmentation model and improve robustness. To further regularize our model and combat domain shifts, we employ a semantic consistency training loss to minimize the discrepancy between predictions of real source domain images and synthetic images. To learn more robust feature representation, we introduce a *domain-specific image restoration* (DSIR) decoder to recover low-level features from synthetic images to original source domain images. We demonstrate the effectiveness of our approach on two DG medical image segmentation benchmarks. Our method achieves the state-of-the-art performance compared with competitive methods. We display the overall architecture of our method in Fig. 1.

2   Related Work

Unsupervised Domain Adaptation. Unsupervised Domain Adaptation (UDA) is a particular branch of Domain Adaptation (DA) that leverages labeled data from one or multiple source domains along with unlabeled data from the target domain to learn a classifier for the target domain [4,5,9,18,27,36,44].

Under such a problem setting, data from the target domain can be utilized to guide the optimization procedure. The general motivation of UDA is to align the source domain and target domain distributions. Some methods adopted a generative model to narrow the pixel-level distribution gap between source and target domains [7,9,18,44]. Dou *et al*. [12] aligned the feature distribution between source and target domains by adversarial training to keep semantic features consistent in different domains. Differently, some methods attempted to narrow the distribution gap between source and target domains in output space level [8,34–36]. However, due to data privacy protection, some unlabeled target domain data can not be accessed in some cases. The target domain is not available in the training process, making UDA methods impractical in some real-world applications.

Domain Generalization. In contrast to UDA, Domain Generalization (DG) purely trains a model on one or more related source domains and directly generalizes to target domains. A large amount of DG methods have been proposed recently [6,13,14,17,32,40,41]. Some methods tried to minimize the domain discrepancy across multiple source domains to learn domain-invariant representations [15,19,24]. With the recent advance of the episodic training strategy for domain generalization [1,11,22,23], some meta-learning-based methods have been developed to generalize models to unseen domains. Li *et al*. [23] proposed an episodic training procedure to simulate domain shift at runtime to improve the robustness of the network. Unlike previous meta-learning-based methods, our method is based on vanilla training policy by aggregating different source domain images. We apply a self-supervised image-level-recovering task and semantic consistency training policy to improve the generalization performance on unseen target domains. In medical image segmentation, several prior literature have studied DG segmentation. For instance, Zhang *et al*. [43] proposed a deep-stacked transformation approach that utilized a stack of image transformations to simulate domain shift in medical imaging. Liu *et al*. [26] introduced a shape-aware supervision combined with meta-learning to help generalizable prostate image segmentation. Wang *et al*. [38] stored domain-specific prior knowledge in a pool as domain attributes for domain aggregation. Liu *et al*. [25] proposed a continuous frequency space augmentation with episodic training policy to improve the generalization ability across different domains. Similar to Liu *et al*. [25], we apply frequency space information for image augmentation in our method. However, we utilize augmented images for image segmentation and the auxiliary image-level-recovering task. This will help our model be more robust to domain shifts and alleviate overfitting.

Self-supervisied Regularization. Self-supervised learning have gained much attention in computer vision, natural language processing *etc*. [2,10,16], recently. It utilizes annotation-free tasks to learn feature representations of data for the downstream tasks. In DG scenario, some methods have also introduced self-supervision tasks to regularize the semantic feature learning [3,37]. We also develop an image-level-recovering self-supervision task to help regularize the model. Different from [3,37] solving a Jigsaw Puzzles, our image-level-recovering task is more complicated, which can better regularize the model.

3   Our Method

3.1   Definition and Overview

We denote a set of K source domains as $D_s = \{(x_i^k, y_i^k)_{i=1}^{N_k}\}_{k=1}^{K}$, where x_i^k is the i-th image from k-th source domain; y_i^k is the segmentation label of x_i^k; N_k is the number of samples in k-th source domain. We aim to learn a generalizable medical image segmentation model F_θ on D_s. The model F_θ is expected to show a satisfactory generalization performance on unseen target domain $D_t = \{x_i\}_{i=1}^{N_t}$, where x_i represent the i-th image in target domain, and N_t is the number of image samples in target domain.

Our proposed method contains an encoder-decoder segmentation model with an auxiliary *domain-specific image restoration* (DSIR) decoder. In front of our training pipeline, we introduce a data augmentation and corruption module named as *random amplitude mixup* (RAM). The workflow of our method contains three steps. First, in the RAM module, we apply the Fourier transform on two source domain images that share different domain labels to obtain their frequency space signals; then, we incorporate their low-frequency signals and utilize inverse Fourier transform to generate new images. Secondly, in our DSIR module, the encoder of the segmentation model obtains low-level features of images generated by RAM. A decoder with domain-specific batch normalization is trained to recover original images in a specific source domain from the low-level features. Finally, the encoder-decoder segmentation model is trained by the segmentation loss of source domain images and augmented images; also we adopt a consistency loss between the outputs of source domain images and augmented images to help the segmentation model better resist domain shifts. We discuss all of these components next in detail.

3.2   Random Amplitude Mixup

To address the restriction of domain discrepancy between source and target domains, a reasonable idea is to apply data augmentation on source domains to diversify source domain data. In this case, we can regularize the model and alleviate overfitting to source domains. Among plenty of data augmentation methods, Mixup [42] has been widely used in image recognition tasks. Image-level-Mixup (IM) incorporates two different images from the training dataset. However, IM will also disturb the semantic information of images, which may negatively influence semantic segmentation tasks. Inspired by prior literature [25,39], we propose to exploit the inherent information of source domains in the frequency space and incorporate distribution information (*i.e.*, style) in the amplitude spectrum of different images. We name our module as *random amplitude mixup* (RAM).

To be specific, we randomly take a sample image $x_i^k \in \mathbb{R}^{H \times W \times C}$ (C represents the number of image channels; H and W are height and width of the image) from source domain k. Then, we perform the Fourier transform [31] $\mathcal{F}$ to obtain the frequency space signal of image x_i^k, which can be written as:

$$\mathcal{F}(x_i^k)(u, v, c) = \sum_{h=0}^{H-1} \sum_{w=0}^{W-1} x_i^k(h, w, c) e^{-j2\pi(\frac{h}{H}u + \frac{w}{W}v)}, j^2 = -1. \tag{1}$$

After the Fourier transform, we can decompose the frequency signal $\mathcal{F}(x_i^k)$ into an amplitude spectrum $\mathcal{A}_i^k \in \mathbb{R}^{H \times W \times C}$ and a phase image $\mathcal{P}_i^k \in \mathbb{R}^{H \times W \times C}$, where the amplitude spectrum contains low-level statistics (*e.g.*, style) while the phase image includes high-level (*e.g.*, object) semantics of the original image. We incorporate the amplitude spectrum of different images from multiple source domains. To this end, we randomly select another sample image $x_j^n(n \neq k)$ from source domain n and perform the Fourier transform on it as well. So that, we obtain another amplitude $\mathcal{A}_j^n$ of image x_j^n. To incorporate the low-frequency component within amplitude $\mathcal{A}_i^k$ and $\mathcal{A}_j^n$, we introduce a binary mask $\mathcal{M}$ which can control the scale of low-frequency component in amplitude spectrum to be incorporated. After that, we incorporate the amplitude information of image x_i^k and image x_j^n by:

$$\mathcal{A}_{i,\lambda}^{n \to k} = \mathcal{A}_i^k * (1 - \mathcal{M}) + ((1 - \lambda)\mathcal{A}_i^k + \lambda \mathcal{A}_j^n) * \mathcal{M}, \tag{2}$$

where $\mathcal{A}_{i,\lambda}^{n \to k}$ is the newly interpolated amplitude spectrum; λ is a parameter that used to adjust the ratio between $\mathcal{A}_i^k$ and $\mathcal{A}_j^n$. Finally, we can transform the merged amplitude $\mathcal{A}_{i,\lambda}^{n \to k}$ into a newly stylized image through inverse Fourier transform $\mathcal{F}^{-1}$ as follows:

$$x_{i,\lambda}^{n \to k} = \mathcal{F}^{-1}(\mathcal{A}_{i,\lambda}^{n \to k}, \mathcal{P}_i^k), \tag{3}$$

where the generated image $x_{i,\lambda}^{n \to k}$ contains the semantic information of x_i^k and its low-level information (*e.g.*, style) is a mixture of low-level information of x_i^k and x_j^n. In our implementation, we follow [25] to dynamically sample λ from $[0.0, 1.0]$ to generate images. Figure 1(a) illustrates the overall architecture of RAM.

To further indicates that RAM can increase the diversity of source domain and narrow the domain discrepancy. We show the t-SNE [28] visualization of image features in **Fundus** dataset in Fig. 2. Figure 2(a) shows the original distribution information of different domains in the **Fundus** dataset. From the visualization, we can observe that the image features from different domains are clearly separated. This leads to the problem that training the model on original source domains make the model easily overfit to specific source domains, which

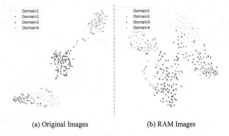

(a) Original Images   (b) RAM Images

Fig. 2. t-SNE visualization of features of original images and RAM augmented images from **Fundus** dataset. We use different colors and markers to denote different domains.

might degrade generalization performance on target domains. However, in Fig. 2(b), we discover that, by applying RAM on original source domains, we can narrow domain gaps significantly, showing domain invariant representation. The distribution of different domains is more compacted and diversified.

3.3   Semantic Consistency Training

To segment images from the target domain, one straightforward method is to train a vanilla segmentation model in a unified fashion by directly feeding multi-source domain images into the model. We name training such a vanilla segmentation model as "DeepAll". Although the "DeepAll" method might have good generalization performance on multi-source domains, it may not preserve satisfactory segmentation performance on target domain images. Training a vanilla segmentation model on multi-source domains does not introduce supervision to combat domain shifts. Also, we have mentioned that original multi-source domain images lack sufficient diversity in feature distribution, which may lead to overfitting to a specific source domain.

We design a semantic consistency training strategy to tackle problems of the "DeepAll" method. To be specific, we introduce an encoder-decoder structure [33] as our segmentation model. The encoder E will extract low-level semantic features from images while the segmentation decoder D_{seg} is used to predict segmentation masks. We formulate the forward propagation of the segmentation model on source domain image x_i^k as:

$$\hat{y}_i^k = D_{seg}(E(x_i^k)), \tag{4}$$

where $\hat{y}_i^k$ is the predicting segmentation mask. Since we utilize RAM to generate newly stylized images from original source domains, we can use these augmented images to help train the segmentation model. This can also regularize the segmentation model and improve its generalization performance on target domains. Similar to Eq. (4), the forward propagation on $x_{i,\lambda}^{n \to k}$ can be written as:

$$\hat{y}_{i,\lambda}^{n \to k} = D_{seg}(E(x_{i,\lambda}^{n \to k})), \tag{5}$$

where $\hat{y}_{i,\lambda}^{n \to k}$ represents the prediction. Then, we utilize the unified cross-entropy (CE) loss [30] and Dice loss [29] as our segmentation loss to optimize the model. The CE and dice loss on original source domain k are formulated as:

$$\mathcal{L}_{ce}^k = -\frac{1}{N} \sum_{i=0}^{N-1} \left(y_i^k \log \hat{y}_i^k + (1 - y_i^k) \log(1 - \hat{y}_i^k) \right), \tag{6}$$

$$\mathcal{L}_{dice}^k = 1 - \frac{2 \sum_{i=0}^{N-1} \hat{y}_i^k y_i^k}{\sum_{i=0}^{N-1} (\hat{y}_i^k + y_i^k + \epsilon)}, \tag{7}$$

where y_i^k is the shared ground truth of x_i^k and $x_{i,\lambda}^{n \to k}$; N represents the number of samples from domain k; ϵ is a smooth factor to avoid dividing by 0. The CE loss $\mathcal{L}_{ce}^{n \to k}$ and dice loss $\mathcal{L}_{dice}^{n \to k}$ on the generated images are similar as above. So, segmentation losses on x_i^k and $x_{i,\lambda}^{n \to k}$ can be written as:

$$\mathcal{L}_{seg}^k = \mathcal{L}_{dice}^k + \mathcal{L}_{ce}^k, \quad \mathcal{L}_{seg}^{n \to k} = \mathcal{L}_{dice}^{n \to k} + \mathcal{L}_{ce}^{n \to k}. \tag{8}$$

To combat domain shifts, we propose a novel semantic consistency loss in our method. Specifically, we regard the generated image $x_{i,\lambda}^{n \to k}$ as a style augmentation of x_i^k. We intend to force the segmentation model to predict consistent segmentation results from x_i^k and $x_{i,\lambda}^{n \to k}$. So that the segmentation model can be less sensitive to domain shift. We design a loss term to minimize the Kullback-Leibler (KL) divergence [21] between soft predictions $\hat{y}_i^k$ and $\hat{y}_{i,\lambda}^{n \to k}$. Our semantic consistency loss is as follows:

$$\mathcal{L}_{consist}^k = \frac{1}{N} \sum_{i=0}^{N-1} \left(\text{KL}(\hat{y}_i^k \| \hat{y}_{i,\lambda}^{n \to k}) + \text{KL}(\hat{y}_{i,\lambda}^{n \to k} \| \hat{y}_i^k) \right), \tag{9}$$

where KL represents the KL-divergence [21]. We compute a symmetric version of KL-divergence between $\hat{y}_i^k$ and $\hat{y}_{i,\lambda}^{n \to k}$. By explicitly enhancing the consistency of results, the segmentation model can extract semantic features more robust to domain shift, thus improving performance on unseen target domains.

3.4   Domain-Specific Image Restoration

To further regularize the segmentation model and reduce overfitting on source domains, we propose a self-supervised auxiliary task to help train a more robust segmentation model. To be specific, we introduce an image restoration decoder with domain-specific batch normalization (DSBN) layers [5]. The image restoration decoder is utilized to recover image from the low-level features extracted by the segmentation encoder E from the RAM image $x_{i,\lambda}^{n \to k}$.

To better recover images of different source domains, we add DSBN in our image restoration decoder. Let our image restoration decoder denote as $D_{rec} = \{D_{rec}^1, D_{rec}^2, \cdots, D_{rec}^K\}$, where K represents the number of source domain, D_{rec}^k is used to recover images from low-level features of RAM images generated by k-th source domain images. All of the decoders in D_{rec} share the same model parameters but have different batch normalization layers [20]. Since distribution information of multi-source domains is quite different, using different batch normalization layers in different domains can better preserve domain intrinsic features for image restoration. The forward propagation of the image restoration module on source domain k are as follows:

$$\hat{x}_i^k = D_{rec}^k(E(x_{i,\lambda}^{n \to k})), \tag{10}$$

where E is the encoder in our segmentation model; $\hat{x}_i^k$ is the recovering image from $x_{i,\lambda}^{n \to k}$. We utilize this image restoration decoder as a regularization of the segmentation encoder E. We show detailed information of our image restoration module in Fig. 1(b).

To train the image restoration module, we employ L2 distance as recovering loss to optimize D_{rec} and E. The recovering loss on k-th source domain are:

$$\mathcal{L}_{rec}^k = \frac{1}{NHWC} \sum_{i=0}^{N-1} \sum_{h=0}^{H-1} \sum_{w=0}^{W-1} \sum_{c=0}^{C-1} \left(x_i^k(h,w,c) - \hat{x}_i^k(h,w,c) \right)^2, \tag{11}$$

where N represents the number of samples from domain K; H, W, C are width, height and channel of the image.

Overall, we can formulate our whole framework as a multi-task learning paradigm. The total training loss are as follows:

$$\mathcal{L}_{total} = \frac{1}{K} \sum_{k=1}^{K} \left(\lambda_1 \mathcal{L}_{seg}^{k} + \lambda_2 \mathcal{L}_{seg}^{n \to k} + \lambda_3 \mathcal{L}_{rec}^{k} + \lambda_4 \mathcal{L}_{consist}^{k} \right), \tag{12}$$

where K represents the number of source domains; λ_1, λ_2, λ_3, and λ_4 are hyperparameters to balance the weights of basic segmentation loss, consistency loss, and image restoration loss respectively.

4   Experiments

4.1   Datasets

We evaluate our method on two public DG medical image segmentation datasets as popular used in [25,26,38]: **Fundus** [38] and **Prostate** [26]. The **Fundus** dataset contains retinal fundus images from 4 different medical centers for optic cup and disc segmentation. Each domain has been split into training and testing sets. For pre-processing, we follow the prior literature [38] and center-crop disc regions with a 800×800 bounding-box for all of images in **Fundus** dataset. After that, we randomly resize and crop a 256×256 region on each cropped images as network input. The **Prostate** dataset collected T2-weighted MRI prostate images from 6 different data sources for prostate segmentation. All of the images have been cropped to 3D prostate region and 2D slices in axial plane have been resized to 384×384. For model training, we feed 2D slices of prostate images into our model. We normalize the data individually to $[-1, 1]$ in intensity values on both datasets.

4.2   Implementation Details

We employ a UNet-based [33] encoder-decoder structure as our segmentation model. The DISR decoder is similar to our segmentation decoder by replacing batch normalization layers with DSBN layers. We implement our experiment with the PyTorch framework on 1 Nvidia RTX 2080Ti GPU with 11 GB memory. We train our model for 400 epochs on **Fundus** dataset and 200 epochs on **Prostate** dataset. For each dataset, we set 8 as training batch size. We also employ the Adam optimizer with an initial learning rate of 0.001 to optimize our model. To stabilize the training process, the learning rate is decayed by the polynomial rule. Last but not least, we set λ_1, λ_2, λ_3, and λ_4 as 1, 1, 0.1 and 0.5 empirically in Eq. (12).

Since the **Fundus** dataset has already split each domain into training and testing sets, we train our model on training sets of source domains and evaluate on testing sets of target domains. During testing, we first resize 800×800 test images to size of 256×256 and get 256×256 segmentation masks. We then resize segmentation masks to 800×800 and compute evaluation metrics on them. For **Prostate** dataset, we directly train segmentation model on source domains and test on target domains. Since original images of **Prostate** dataset are all 3D volumes, we first get 2D predictions and concatenate all 2D predictions of each 3D sample, then compute evaluation metrics on 3D predictions. When testing on **Prostate** dataset, we also skip those 2D slices that not contain any prostate region. All of implementations on datasets follow previous methods [26, 38]. For evaluation, we adopt commonly-used metric of Dice coefficient (Dice) and Average Surface Distance (ASD) to quantitatively evaluate the segmentation results of whole region and the surface shape respectively. Higher Dice coefficient represents better performance and ASD is the opposite. To avoid randomness, we repeat our experiments for 3 times and report the average performance.

4.3   Comparison with Other DG Methods

Experiment Setting. In our experiments, we follow the practice in prior literature of domain generalization and employ the leave-one-domain-out strategy, *i.e.*, training on K source domains and test on the left one target domain (total $K + 1$ domains). So that, for **Fundus** and **Prostate** datasets, we have four and six distinguished tasks, respectively.

We choose five recent state-of-the-art domain generalization methods to compare with ours and reproduce their results. First of all, the JiGen [3] is an effective self-supervised based DG methods for model regularization by solving jigsaw puzzles. The BigAug [43] is an augmentateion based DG method. SAML [26] and FedDG [25] are two meta-learning based generalizable medical image segmentation methods. Finally, the DoFE [38] is a domain-invariant feature representation learning approach. We further train a vanilla segmentation model by simply aggregating all source domain images as our baseline model.

In Tables 1 and 2, we show Dice coefficient and ASD results of different domains in **Fundus** dataset. All of the methods successfully outperform our baseline method except BigAug [43] (Dice coefficient 85.49% *vs.* 85.63%; ASD 14.18 voxel *vs.* 13.98 voxel). We assume that this is because BigAug [43] was first designed to augment grey-scale medical images (*e.g.*, CT, MRI, *etc.*) for domain generalization segmentation tasks. Images in **Fundus** dataset are all RGB images which have quite different image properties compared with other medical images. So that the generalization performance of BigAug [43] could be degraded. Other methods gain improvements above baseline more or less and prove that different regularization and generalization strategies can help the model to learn more robust feature representation. Compared with these methods, we achieve higher average Dice coefficient and better average ASD on **Fundus** dataset. This thanks to our RAM and DSIR module. The RAM helps to diversify our source domain images to alleviate overfitting. Also, the image restoration tasks can regularize our model to learn more robust feature representation. Last but not least, we adopt a semantic consistency training policy to resist to domain shift. All of these key components contribute to success

Table 1. Dice coefficient of different methods on **Fundus** segmentation task (%). We mark the top results in **bold**.

Task	Optic cup/disc segmentation				Avg.
Unseen site	Domain 1	Domain 2	Domain 3	Domain 4	
JiGen [3]	82.45/95.03	77.05/87.25	87.01/**94.94**	80.88/91.34	86.99
BigAug [43]	77.68/93.32	75.56/87.54	83.33/92.68	81.63/92.20	85.49
SAML [26]	83.72/95.03	77.68/87.57	84.20/94.49	82.08/92.78	87.19
FedDG [25]	81.72/95.62	77.87/88.71	83.96/94.83	81.90/93.37	87.25
DoFE [38]	84.17/94.96	**81.03**/89.29	86.54/91.67	**87.28**/93.04	88.50
Baseline	81.44/95.52	77.20/87.96	85.11/94.56	72.30/90.97	85.63
Ours	**85.48/95.75**	78.82/**89.43**	**87.44**/94.67	85.84/**94.10**	**88.94**

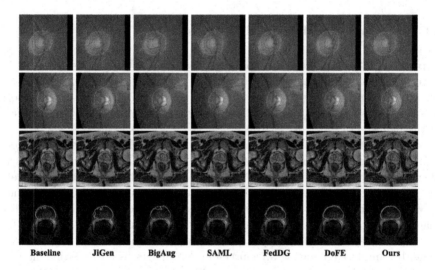

Fig. 3. Visualization on segmentation results of different methods on **Fundus** (top two rows) and **Prostate** datasets (bottom two rows). The red contours indicate the boundaries of ground truths while the green and blue contours are predictions. (Color figure online)

of our method on **Fundus** dataset. Compared with baseline, our method achieves consistent improvements over baseline across all unseen domain settings, with the average performance increase of 3.31% in Dice coefficient and 3.66 voxel average improvement in ASD.

To further indicate effectiveness of our method, we provide experiment results on **Prostate** dataset in Tables 3 and 4. For prostate segmentation task, all of the comparison DG method outperform baseline. Our method also obtains the highest Dice coefficient and ASD across most unseen domains. The average Dice coefficient 88.08% and ASD 1.37 voxel are the best compared with other DG methods. Specially, compared with baseline, the increase in overall Dice coefficient of our method is 4.04% and ASD decreases 1.55 voxel. In Fig. 3, we show

Table 2. Average Surface Distance (ASD) of different methods on **Fundus** segmentation task (voxel). We mark the top results in **bold**.

Task	Optic cup/disc segmentation				Avg.
Unseen site	Domain 1	Domain 2	Domain 3	Domain 4	
JiGen [3]	18.57/9.43	17.29/19.53	9.15/**6.99**	15.84/12.14	13.62
BigAug [43]	22.61/12.53	17.95/17.64	11.48/10.33	11.57/9.36	14.18
SAML [26]	17.08/9.01	16.72/18.63	10.87/7.87	16.28/8.64	13.14
FedDG [25]	18.57/7.69	15.87/16.93	11.09/7.28	10.23/7.51	11.90
DoFE [38]	16.07/7.18	**13.44**/17.06	10.12/10.75	**8.14**/7.29	11.26
Baseline	18.16/8.99	15.67/17.95	11.96/9.42	20.03/9.64	13.98
Ours	**16.05/7.12**	14.01/**13.86**	**9.02**/7.11	8.29/**7.06**	**10.32**

Table 3. Dice coefficient of different methods on **Prostate** segmentation task (%). We mark the top results in **bold**.

Task	Prostate segmentation						Avg.
Unseen site	Domain 1	Domain 2	Domain 3	Domain 4	Domain 5	Domain 6	
JiGen [3]	85.45	89.26	85.92	87.45	86.18	83.08	86.22
BigAug [43]	85.73	89.34	84.49	88.02	81.95	87.63	86.19
SAML [26]	86.35	90.18	85.03	88.20	86.97	87.69	87.40
FedDG [25]	86.43	89.59	85.30	88.95	85.93	87.39	87.27
DoFE [38]	**89.64**	87.56	85.08	**89.06**	86.15	87.03	87.42
Baseline	85.30	87.56	82.33	87.37	80.49	81.40	84.04
Ours	87.56	**90.20**	**86.92**	88.72	**87.17**	**87.93**	**88.08**

the visualization results of two sample images from target domains of **Fundus** and **Prostate** datasets. It is explicit that our method can accurately segment the objective structure of unseen domain images and the boundary of the structure is smoother while other methods may fail to do so.

4.4   Analysis of Our Method

We conduct extensive ablation studies on our method. Firstly, we investigate the effectiveness of our random amplitude mixup for data augmentation and DSIR module on **Fundus** and **Prostate** dataset. We need to note that, without RAM, our DISR module cannot be implemented. Since our RAM module is utilized to conduct style augmentation and image corruption at the same time, here we discuss the style augmentation and image corruption separately. The experimental results are illustrated in Tables 5 and 6. The RAM_{Aug} indicates that the RAM style augmentation is employed in our method and DSIR represents the domain-specific image restoration module with image corruption. The method without these two components (*i.e.*, the first row in Tables 5 and 6) is the baseline method, which is the same with the baseline results in Tables 1 and 3. From Tables 5 and 6, we observe that each component plays a significant role in our

Table 4. Average Surface Distance (ASD) of different methods on **Prostate** segmentation task (voxel). We mark the top results in **bold**.

Task	Prostate segmentation						Avg.
Unseen site	Domain 1	Domain 2	Domain 3	Domain 4	Domain 5	Domain 6	
JiGen [3]	1.11	1.81	2.61	1.66	**1.71**	2.43	1.89
BigAug [43]	1.13	1.78	4.01	1.25	1.92	1.89	2.00
SAML [26]	1.09	1.54	2.52	1.41	2.01	1.77	1.72
FedDG [25]	1.30	1.67	2.36	1.37	2.19	1.94	1.81
DoFE [38]	**0.92**	1.49	2.74	1.46	1.89	1.53	1.68
Baseline	1.22	1.95	4.68	1.51	3.95	4.23	2.92
Ours	1.04	**0.81**	**2.23**	**1.16**	1.81	**1.15**	**1.37**

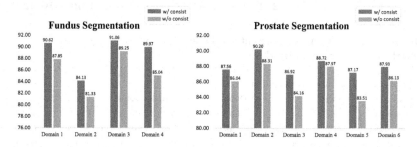

Fig. 4. Ablation study of our semantic consistency training policy. Green and blue bars represent average Dice coefficient of our complete method and the method without consistency loss respectively. We show results on different domains from **Fundus** and **Prostate** datasets. (Color figure online)

method. By adding RAM style augmentation in our method, the overall segmentation performance on fundus segmentation task can increase 2.12% in Dice coefficient and on prostate segmentation tasks the improvements of Dice coefficient is 3.23%. Besides, when equipping with domain-specific image restoration module, our model can gain 1.58% and 1.03% overall improvements in Dice coefficient on **Fundus** and **Prostate** datasets respectively. Based on these results, we justify that, our RAM and DSIR module can help regularize our segmentation model and improve the generalization ability. Last rows in Tables 5 and 6 display the results by adding all of the components in our method, which are the same as results of our method in Tables 1 and 3.

As aforementioned, during the training process, we employed a semantic consistency loss as a supervision signal to make the model resistant to domain shift. In Fig. 4, we investigate the effectiveness of our semantic consistency loss on **Fundus** and **Prostate** datasets. We observe that without the semantic consistency loss, all of the results degenerate on both datasets. This indicates that the semantic consistency loss do help improve the generalization performance of our model which means our model can be more robust to domain shift.

Table 5. Ablation Study of key components in our method on **Fundus** Segmentation Task (%). We mark the top results in **bold**.

Task		Optic cup/disc segmentation				Avg.
RAM$_{Aug}$	DSIR	Domain 1	Domain 2	Domain 3	Domain 4	
–	–	81.44/95.52	77.20/87.96	85.11/94.56	72.30/90.97	85.63
✓	–	83.06/94.86	78.09/89.04	86.73/**95.01**	82.28/92.89	87.75
–	✓	83.76/95.31	77.43/88.07	85.84/94.19	81.58/91.48	87.21
✓	✓	**85.48/95.75**	**78.82/89.43**	**87.44**/94.67	**85.84/94.10**	88.94

Table 6. Ablation Study of key components in our method on **Prostate** Segmentation Task (%). We mark the top results in **bold**.

Task		Prostate segmentation						Avg.
RAM$_{Aug}$	DSIR	Domain 1	Domain 2	Domain 3	Domain 4	Domain 5	Domain 6	
–	–	85.30	87.56	82.33	87.37	80.49	81.40	84.04
✓	–	87.28	89.94	85.45	87.86	86.17	86.94	87.27
–	✓	86.57	88.04	83.19	87.42	82.08	83.14	85.07
✓	✓	**87.56**	**90.20**	**86.92**	**88.72**	**87.17**	**87.93**	**88.08**

Table 7. Dice coefficient of different consistency loss on **Fundus** segmentation task (%). We mark the top results in **bold**.

Task	Optic cup/disc segmentation				Avg.
Unseen site	Domain 1	Domain 2	Domain 3	Domain 4	
MSE	85.45/95.13	77.96/89.14	86.73/**94.76**	**85.93/94.16**	88.65
JS-Div	85.04/94.91	78.02/88.27	86.32/93.91	85.14/93.87	88.19
KL-Div	**85.48/95.75**	**78.82/89.43**	**87.44**/94.67	85.84/94.10	**88.94**

Moreover, we experiment different types of consistency loss on **Fundus** dataset. In Table 7, we show the results of different kinds of consistency loss. Except for KL-divergence (KL-Div), we also employ mean squared error (MSE) and Jensen-Shannon divergence (JS-Div). We observe that using different consistency loss will not affect the overall results of our method much, which means our method is robust to different types of consistency loss.

5   Conclusion

We present a novel generalizable medical image segmentation method for fundus and prostate image segmentation. To combat with overfitting in DG segmentation, we introduce random amplitude mixup (RAM) module to synthesize images with different domain style. We utilize the synthetic images as data augmentation to train the segmentation model and propose a self-supervised domain-specific image restoration (DSIR) module to recover the original images from synthetic images. Moreover, to further make the model resistant to domain shift and learn more domain invariant feature representation, we employ a semantic consistency loss in our training process. Our experimental results and ablation analysis indicate that all of the proposed components can help regularize the model and improve generalization performance on unseen target domains.

Acknowledgements. This work was supported by NSFC Major Program (62192783), CAAI-Huawei MindSpore Project (CAAIXSJLJJ-2021-042A), China Postdoctoral Science Foundation Project (2021M690609), Jiangsu Natural Science Foundation Project (BK20210224), and CCF-Lenovo Bule Ocean Research Fund.

References

1. Balaji, Y., Sankaranarayanan, S., Chellappa, R.: Metareg: towards domain generalization using meta-regularization (2018)
2. Bao, H., Dong, L., Piao, S., Wei, F.: BEit: BERT pre-training of image transformers. In: ICLR (2022)
3. Carlucci, F.M., D'Innocente, A., Bucci, S., Caputo, B., Tommasi, T.: Domain generalization by solving jigsaw puzzles. In: CVPR (2019)
4. Chang, W.L., Wang, H.P., Peng, W.H., Chiu, W.C.: All about structure: adapting structural information across domains for boosting semantic segmentation. In: CVPR (2019)
5. Chang, W.G., You, T., Seo, S., Kwak, S., Han, B.: Domain-specific batch normalization for unsupervised domain adaptation. In: CVPR (2019)
6. Chattopadhyay, P., Balaji, Y., Hoffman, J.: Learning to balance specificity and invariance for in and out of domain generalization. In: Vedaldi, A., Bischof, H., Brox, T., Frahm, J.-M. (eds.) ECCV 2020. LNCS, vol. 12354, pp. 301–318. Springer, Cham (2020). https://doi.org/10.1007/978-3-030-58545-7_18
7. Chen, C., Dou, Q., Chen, H., Qin, J., Heng, P.A.: Synergistic image and feature adaptation: towards cross-modality domain adaptation for medical image segmentation. In: AAAI (2019)
8. Chen, Y., Li, W., Van Gool, L.: Road: Reality oriented adaptation for semantic segmentation of urban scenes. In: CVPR (2018)
9. Chen, Y.C., Lin, Y.Y., Yang, M.H., Huang, J.B.: CrDoCo: pixel-level domain transfer with cross-domain consistency. In: CVPR (2019)
10. Devlin, J., Chang, M.W., Lee, K., Toutanova, K.: Bert: pre-training of deep bidirectional transformers for language understanding. In: NAACL (2019)
11. Dou, Q., Coelho de Castro, D., Kamnitsas, K., Glocker, B.: Domain generalization via model-agnostic learning of semantic features. In: NeurIPS (2019)
12. Dou, Q., Ouyang, C., Chen, C., Chen, H., Heng, P.A.: Unsupervised cross-modality domain adaptation of convnets for biomedical image segmentations with adversarial loss. In: IJCAI (2018)
13. Du, Y., et al.: Learning to learn with variational information bottleneck for domain generalization. In: Vedaldi, A., Bischof, H., Brox, T., Frahm, J.-M. (eds.) ECCV 2020. LNCS, vol. 12355, pp. 200–216. Springer, Cham (2020). https://doi.org/10.1007/978-3-030-58607-2_12
14. Gong, R., Li, W., Chen, Y., Gool, L.V.: DLOW: domain flow for adaptation and generalization. In: CVPR (2019)

15. Gong, Y., Lin, X., Yao, Y., Dietterich, T.G., Divakaran, A., Gervasio, M.: Confidence calibration for domain generalization under covariate shift. In: ICCV (2021)
16. He, K., Fan, H., Wu, Y., Xie, S., Girshick, R.: Momentum contrast for unsupervised visual representation learning. In: CVPR (2020)
17. Hoffer, E., Ben-Nun, T., Hubara, I., Giladi, N., Hoefler, T., Soudry, D.: Augment your batch: improving generalization through instance repetition. In: CVPR (2020)
18. Hoffman, J., et al.: CyCADA: cycle-consistent adversarial domain adaptation. In: ICML (2018)
19. Hsu, Y.C., Lv, Z., Kira, Z.: Learning to cluster in order to transfer across domains and tasks. In: ICLR (2018)
20. Ioffe, S., Szegedy, C.: Batch normalization: accelerating deep network training by reducing internal covariate shift. In: ICML (2015)
21. Kullback, S., Leibler, R.A.: On information and sufficiency. Ann. Math. Stat. $22(1)$, 79–86 (1951)
22. Li, D., Yang, Y., Song, Y.Z., Hospedales, T.M.: Learning to generalize: meta-learning for domain generalization. In: AAAI (2018)
23. Li, D., Zhang, J., Yang, Y., Liu, C., Song, Y.Z., Hospedales, T.M.: Episodic training for domain generalization. In: ICCV (2019)
24. Li, H., Pan, S.J., Wang, S., Kot, A.C.: Domain generalization with adversarial feature learning. In: CVPR (2018)
25. Liu, Q., Chen, C., Qin, J., Dou, Q., Heng, P.A.: FedDG: federated domain generalization on medical image segmentation via episodic learning in continuous frequency space. In: CVPR (2021)
26. Liu, Q., Dou, Q., Heng, P.-A.: Shape-aware meta-learning for generalizing prostate MRI segmentation to unseen domains. In: Martel, A.L., et al. (eds.) MICCAI 2020. LNCS, vol. 12262, pp. 475–485. Springer, Cham (2020). https://doi.org/10.1007/978-3-030-59713-9_46
27. Liu, Z., et al.: Open compound domain adaptation. In: CVPR (2020)
28. Van der Maaten, L., Hinton, G.: Visualizing data using t-SNE. JMLR (2008)
29. Milletari, F., Navab, N., Ahmadi, S.A.: V-net: fully convolutional neural networks for volumetric medical image segmentation. In: 3DV (2016)
30. Murphy, K.P.: Machine Learning: A Probabilistic Perspective. MIT Press, Cambridge (2012)
31. Nussbaumer, H.J.: The fast Fourier transform. In: Nussbaumer, H.J. (ed.) Fast Fourier Transform and Convolution Algorithms. Springer Series in Information Sciences, vol. 2, pp. 80–111. Springer, Heidelberg (1981). https://doi.org/10.1007/978-3-662-00551-4_4
32. Qiao, F., Zhao, L., Peng, X.: Learning to learn single domain generalization. In: CVPR (2020)
33. Ronneberger, O., Fischer, P., Brox, T.: U-net: convolutional networks for biomedical image segmentation. In: Navab, N., Hornegger, J., Wells, W.M., Frangi, A.F. (eds.) MICCAI 2015. LNCS, vol. 9351, pp. 234–241. Springer, Cham (2015). https://doi.org/10.1007/978-3-319-24574-4_28
34. Tsai, Y.H., Hung, W.C., Schulter, S., Sohn, K., Yang, M.H., Chandraker, M.: Learning to adapt structured output space for semantic segmentation. In: CVPR (2018)
35. Tsai, Y.H., Sohn, K., Schulter, S., Chandraker, M.: Domain adaptation for structured output via discriminative patch representations. In: ICCV (2019)
36. Vu, T.H., Jain, H., Bucher, M., Cord, M., Pérez, P.: ADVENT: adversarial entropy minimization for domain adaptation in semantic segmentation. In: CVPR (2019)

37. Wang, S., Yu, L., Li, C., Fu, C.-W., Heng, P.-A.: Learning from extrinsic and intrinsic supervisions for domain generalization. In: Vedaldi, A., Bischof, H., Brox, T., Frahm, J.-M. (eds.) ECCV 2020. LNCS, vol. 12354, pp. 159–176. Springer, Cham (2020). https://doi.org/10.1007/978-3-030-58545-7_10
38. Wang, S., Yu, L., Li, K., Yang, X., Fu, C.W., Heng, P.A.: DoFE: domain-oriented feature embedding for generalizable fundus image segmentation on unseen datasets. IEEE TMI **39**, 4237–4248 (2020)
39. Yang, Y., Soatto, S.: FDA: Fourier domain adaptation for semantic segmentation. In: CVPR (2020)
40. Yue, X., Zhang, Y., Zhao, S., Sangiovanni-Vincentelli, A., Keutzer, K., Gong, B.: Domain randomization and pyramid consistency: simulation-to-real generalization without accessing target domain data. In: ICCV (2019)
41. Zakharov, S., Kehl, W., Ilic, S.: DeceptionNet: network-driven domain randomization. In: ICCV (2019)
42. Zhang, H., Cisse, M., Dauphin, Y.N., Lopez-Paz, D.: Mixup: beyond empirical risk minimization. In: ICLR (2018)
43. Zhang, L., et al.: Generalizing deep learning for medical image segmentation to unseen domains via deep stacked transformation. IEEE TMI **39**, 2531–2540 (2020)
44. Zhang, Y., Qiu, Z., Yao, T., Liu, D., Mei, T.: Fully convolutional adaptation networks for semantic segmentation. In: CVPR (2018)

Auto-FedRL: Federated Hyperparameter Optimization for Multi-institutional Medical Image Segmentation

Pengfei Guo[1]([⊠]), Dong Yang[2], Ali Hatamizadeh[2], An Xu[3], Ziyue Xu[2], Wenqi Li[2], Can Zhao[2], Daguang Xu[2], Stephanie Harmon[4], Evrim Turkbey[5], Baris Turkbey[4], Bradford Wood[5], Francesca Patella[6], Elvira Stellato[7], Gianpaolo Carrafiello[7], Vishal M. Patel[1], and Holger R. Roth[2]

[1] Johns Hopkins University, Baltimore, USA
pguo4@jhu.edu
[2] NVIDIA, Santa Clara, USA
[3] University of Pittsburgh, Pittsburgh, USA
[4] National Cancer Institute, Bethesda, USA
[5] National Institutes of Health, Bethesda, USA
[6] ASST Santi Paolo e Carlo, Milan, Italy
[7] University of Milan, Milan, Italy

Abstract. Federated learning (FL) is a distributed machine learning technique that enables collaborative model training while avoiding explicit data sharing. The inherent privacy-preserving property of FL algorithms makes them especially attractive to the medical field. However, in case of heterogeneous client data distributions, standard FL methods are unstable and require intensive hyperparameter tuning to achieve optimal performance. Conventional hyperparameter optimization algorithms are impractical in real-world FL applications as they involve numerous training trials, which are often not affordable with limited compute budgets. In this work, we propose an efficient reinforcement learning (RL)-based federated hyperparameter optimization algorithm, termed Auto-FedRL, in which an online RL agent can dynamically adjust hyperparameters of each client based on the current training progress. Extensive experiments are conducted to investigate different search strategies and RL agents. The effectiveness of the proposed method is validated on a heterogeneous data split of the CIFAR-10 dataset as well as two real-world medical image segmentation datasets for COVID-19 lesion segmentation in chest CT and pancreas segmentation in abdominal CT.

Keywords: FL · Reinforcement learning · Hyperparameter optimization

P. Guo—Work done during an internship at NVIDIA. NVFlare [39] implementation of this work is available at https://nvidia.github.io/NVFlare/research/auto-fed-rl.

Supplementary Information The online version contains supplementary material available at https://doi.org/10.1007/978-3-031-19803-8_26.

S. Avidan et al. (Eds.): ECCV 2022, LNCS 13681, pp. 437–455, 2022.
https://doi.org/10.1007/978-3-031-19803-8_26

1   Introduction

A large amount of data is needed to train robust and generalizable machine learning models. A single institution often does not have enough data to train such models effectively. Meanwhile, there are emerging regulatory and privacy concerns about the data sharing and management [13,21]. Federated Learning (FL) [34] mitigates such concerns as it leverages data from different clients or institutions to collaboratively train a global model while allowing the data owners to control their private datasets. Unlike the conventional centralized training, FL algorithms open the potential for multi-institutional collaborations in a privacy-preserving manner [63]. This multi-institutional collaboration scenario often refers to *cross-silo* FL [20] and is the main focus of this paper. In this FL setting, clients are autonomous data owners, such as medical institutions storing patients' data, and collaboratively train a general model to overcome the data scarcity issue and privacy concerns [63]. This makes *cross-silo* FL applications especially attractive to the healthcare sector [14,43]. Several methods have already been proposed to leverage FL for multi-institutional collaborations in digital healthcare [15,44,50,59].

The most recently introduced FL frameworks [15,27,38,59] are variations of the Federated Averaging (FedAvg) [34] algorithm. The training process of FedAvg consists of the following steps: (i) clients perform local training and upload model parameters to the server. (ii) The server carries out the averaging aggregation over the received parameters from clients and broadcasts aggregated parameters to clients. (iii) Clients update local models and evaluate its performance. After sufficient communication rounds between clients and the server, a global model can be obtained. The design of FedAvg is based on standard Stochastic Gradient Descent (SGD) learning with the assumption that data is uniformly distributed across clients [34]. However, in real-world applications, one has to deal with underlying unknown data distributions that are likely not independent and identically distributed (non-iid). The heterogeneity of data distributions has been identified as a critical problem that causes the local models to diverge during training and consequently sub-optimal performance of the trained global model [27,31,38].

To achieve the required performance, the proper tuning of hyperparameters (*e.g.*, the learning rate, the number of local iterations, aggregation weights, *etc.*) plays a critical role for the success of FL [38,59]. [29] shows that the learning rate decay is a necessary condition of the convergence for FL on non-iid data. While the general hyperparameter optimization has been intensively studied [6,53,58], the unique setting of FL makes federated hyperparameters optimization especially difficult [24]. Reinforcement learning (RL) provides a promising solution to approach this complex optimization problem. Compared to other methods for finding the optimal hyperparameters, RL-based methods do not require the prior knowledge of the complicated underlying system dynamics [47]. Thus, federated hyperparameter optimization can be reduced to defining appropriate reward metrics, search space, and RL agents.

In this paper, we aim to make the automated hyperparameter optimization applicable in realistic FL applications. An online RL algorithm is proposed to dynamically tune hyperparameters during a single trial. Specifically, the proposed Auto-FedRL formulates hyperparameter optimization as a task of discovering optimal policies for the RL agent. Auto-FedRL can dynamically adjust hyperparameters at each communication round based on relative loss reduction. Without the need for multiple training trails, an online RL agent is introduced to maximize the rewards in small intervals, rather than the sum of all rewards.

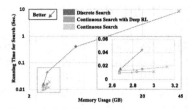

Fig. 1. The computational details of different search strategies under the same setting on CIFAR-10 when the number of clients equals to 2 ($\triangle$), 4 (+), 6 ($\Diamond$), and 8 ($\times$). The green box shows the zoomed-in region.

While RL-based hyperparameter optimization method has been explored in [38], our experiments show that the prior work has several deficiencies impeding its practical use in real-world applications. (i) The discrete action space (*i.e.*, hyperparameter search space) not only leads to limited available actions but also suffers from scalability issues. At each optimization step, the gradient of all possible hyperparameter combinations is retained, which causes high memory consumption and computational inefficiency. Therefore, as shown in Fig. 1, the hardware limitation can be reached quickly, when one needs to collaborate with multiple institutions using a large search space. To circumvent this challenge, Auto-FedRL can leverage continuous search space. Its memory usage is practically constant as the memory consumption per hyperparameter is negligible and does not explode with increased search space and the number of involved clients. Meanwhile, its computational efficiency is significantly improved compared to discrete search space. (ii) The flexibility of hyperparameter search space is limited. [38] focuses on a small number of hyperparameters (*e.g.*, one or two hyperparameters) in less general settings. In contrast, our method is able to tune a wide range of hyperparameters (*e.g.*, client/server learning rates, the number of local iterations, and the aggregation weight of each client) in a realistic FL setting. It is worth noting that the averaging model aggregation is replaced by a pseudo-gradient optimization [42] in Auto-FedRL. Thus, we are able to search server-side hyperparameters. To this end, we propose a more practical federated hyperparameter optimization framework with notable computational efficiency and flexible search space.

Our main contributions in this work are summarized as follows:

- A novel federated hyperparameter optimization framework Auto-FedRL is proposed, which enables the dynamic tuning of hyperparameters via a single trial.
- Auto-FedRL makes federated hyperparameter optimization more practical in real-world applications by efficiently incorporating continuous search space and the deep RL agent to tune a wide range of hyperparameters.
- Extensive experiments on multiple datasets show the superior performance and notable computational efficiency of our methods over existing FL baselines.

2   Related Works

Federated Learning on Heterogeneous Data. The heterogeneous data distribution across clients impedes the real-world deployment of FL applications and draws emerging attentions. Several methods [7,23,29,35,48,61,65] have been proposed to address this issue. FedOpt [42] introduced the adaptive federated optimization, which formulated a more flexible FL optimization framework but also introduced more hyperparameters, such as the server learning rate and server-side optimizers. FedProx [27] and Agnostic Federated Learning (AFL) [37] are variants of FedAvg [34] which attempted to address the learning bias issue of the global models for local clients by imposing additional regularization terms. FedDyn [2] was proposed to address the problem that the minima of the local-device level loss are inconsistent with those of the global loss by introducing a dynamic regularizer for each device. Those works demonstrated good theoretical analysis but are evaluated only on manually created toy datasets. Recently, FL-MRCM [15] was proposed to address the domain shift issue among different clients by aligning the distribution of latent features between the source domain and the target domain. Although those methods [15,30] achieved promising results in overcoming domain shift in the multi-institutional collaboration, directly sharing latent features between clients increased privacy concerns.

Conventional Hyperparameter Optimization. Grid and random search [6] can perform automated hyperparameter tuning but require long running time due to often exploring unpromising regions of the search space. While advanced random search [5] and Bayesian optimization-based search methods [53,58] require fewer iterations, several training trails are required to evaluate the fitness of hyperparameter configurations. Repeating the training process multiple times is impractical in the FL setting, especially for deep learning models, due to the limited communication and compute resources in real-world FL setups.

Federated Hyperparameter Optimization. Auto-FedAvg [59] is a recent automated search method, which only is compatible with differentiable hyperparameters and focuses on searching client aggregation weights. The method proposed in [38] is the most relevant to our work. However, as discussed in the previous section, it suffers from limited practicability and flexibility of search space in real-world applications. Inspired by the recent hyperparameter search [3,11,12] and differentiable [8,32], evolutionary [41,60] and RL-based automated machine learning methods [4,66], we propose an efficient automated approach with flexible search space to discover a wide range of hyperparameters.

3   Methodology

In this section, we first introduce the general notations of FL and the adaptive federated optimization that provides the theoretical foundation of tuning FL server-side hyperparameters (Sect. 3.1). Then, we describe our method in detail (Sect. 3.2), including online RL-based hyperparameter optimization, the discrete/continuous search space, and the deep RL agent. In addition, we provide theoretical analysis to guarantee the convergence of Auto-FedRL in the supplementary material.

3.1 Federated Learning

In a FL system, suppose K clients collaboratively train a global model. The goal is to solve the optimization problem as follows:

$$\min_{x \in \mathbb{R}^d} \frac{1}{K} \sum_{k=1}^{K} \mathcal{L}_k(x), \tag{1}$$

where $\mathcal{L}_k(x) = \mathbb{E}_{z \sim \mathcal{D}_k}[\mathcal{L}_k(x, z)]$ is the loss function of the kth client. $z \in \mathcal{Z}$, and $\mathcal{D}_k$ represents the data distribution of the kth client. Commonly, for two different clients i and j, $\mathcal{D}_i$ and $\mathcal{D}_j$ can be dissimilar, so that Eq. 1 can become nonconvex. A widely used method for solving this optimization problem is FedAvg [34]. At each round, the server broadcasts the global model to each client. Then, all clients conduct local training on their own data and send back the updated model to the server. Finally, the server updates the global model by a weighted average of these local model updates. FedAvg's server update at round q can be formulated as follows:

$$\Theta^{q+1} = \sum_{k=1}^{K} \alpha_k \Theta_k^q, \tag{2}$$

where Θ_k^q denotes the local model of kth client and α_k is the corresponding aggregation weight. The update of global model Θ^{q+1} in Eq. 2 can be further rewritten as follows:

$$\begin{aligned}
\Theta^{q+1} &= \Theta^q - \sum_{k=1}^{K} \alpha_k(\Theta^q - \Theta_k^q) \\
&= \Theta^q - \sum_{k=1}^{K} \alpha_k \Delta_k^q \\
&= \Theta^q - \Delta^q,
\end{aligned} \tag{3}$$

where $\Delta_k^q := \Theta^q - \Theta_k^q$ and $\Delta^q := \sum_{k=1}^{K} \alpha_k \Delta_k^q$. Therefore, the server update in FedAvg is equivalent to applying optimization to the *pseudo-gradient* $-\Delta^q$ with a learning rate $\gamma = 1$. This general FL optimization formulation refers to adaptive federated optimization [42]. Auto-FedRL utilizes this *pseudo-gradient* update formulation to enable the server-side hyperparameter optimization, such as the server learning rate γ.

3.2 Auto-FedRL

Online RL Hyperparameter Optimization. The online setting in the targeted task is very challenging since the same actions at different training stages may receive various responses. Several methods [1,19,40] have been proposed in the literature to deal with such non-stationary problems. However, these methods require multiple training runs, which is usually not affordable in FL settings where clients often have limited computation resources. Typically, a client can run only one training procedure at the same time and the resources for parallelization as would be done in a cluster environment is not available. To circumvent the limitations of conventional hyperparameter optimization methods and inspired by previous works [4,38,66], we introduce an online RL-based approach to directly learn the proper hyperparameters from data at the clients' side during a single training trial. At round q, a set of hyperparameters h^q can be sampled from the distribution $P(\mathcal{H}|\psi^q)$. We denote the validation loss of client k at round q as $\mathcal{L}^q_{\mathrm{val}_k}$ and the hyperparameter loss at round q as

$$\mathcal{L}^q_h = \frac{1}{K} \sum_{k=1}^{K} \mathcal{L}^q_{\mathrm{val}_k}. \tag{4}$$

The relative loss reduction reward function of the RL agent is defined as follows:

$$r^q = \frac{\mathcal{L}^q_h - \mathcal{L}^{q+1}_h}{\mathcal{L}^q_h}. \tag{5}$$

The goal of the RL agent at round q is to maximize the objective as follows:

$$J^q = \mathbb{E}_{P(h^q|\psi^q)}[r^q]. \tag{6}$$

By leveraging the one-sample Monte Carlo estimation technique [57], we can approximate the derivative of J^q as follows:

$$\nabla_{\psi^q} J^q = r^q \nabla_{\psi^q} \log(P(h^q|\psi^q)). \tag{7}$$

To this end, we can evaluate Eq. 6 and use it to update the condition of hyperparameter distribution ψ^q. To formulate an online algorithm, we utilize the averaged rewards in a small interval ("window") rather than counting the sum of all rewards to update ψ^q as follows:

$$\psi^{q+1} \leftarrow \psi^q - \gamma_h \sum_{\tau=q-Z}^{\tau=q} (r^\tau - \hat{\tau}^q) \nabla_{\psi^\tau} \log(P(h^\tau|\psi^\tau)), \tag{8}$$

where Z is the size of the update window and γ_h is the RL agent learning rate. The averaged rewards $\hat{\tau}^q$ in the interval $[q - Z, q]$ are defined as follows:

$$\hat{\tau}^q = \frac{1}{Z+1} \sum_{\tau=q-Z}^{\tau=q} r^\tau. \tag{9}$$

Discrete Search. Selecting the form of hyperparameter distribution $P(\mathcal{H}|\psi)$ is non-trivial, since it determines the available actions in the search space.

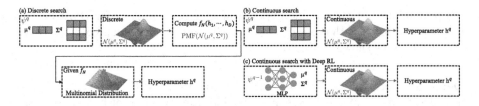

Fig. 2. The sampling workflow comparison of different search strategies in the proposed Auto-FedRL. PMF denotes the probability mass function.

We denote the proposed method using discrete search (DS) space as Auto-FedRL(DS). Here, $P(\mathcal{H}|\psi)$ is defined by a D-dimensional discrete Gaussian distribution, where D denotes the number of searchable hyperparameters. For each hyperparameter, there is a finite set of available selections. Therefore, $\mathcal{H}$ is a grid that consists of all possible combinations of available hyperparameters. A hyperparameter combination h^q at round q is a point on $\mathcal{H}$ as follows:

$$P(h^q|\psi^q) = \mathcal{N}(h^q|\mu^q, \Sigma^q), \tag{10}$$

where $h^q = \{h_1^q, \ldots, h_D^q\}$. ψ^q is defined by the mean vector μ^q and the covariance matrix Σ^q, which are learnable parameters that the RL agent targets to optimize. To increase the stability of RL training and encourage learning in all directions, different types of predefined hyperparameter selections are normalized to the same scale with zero-mean when constructing the search space. This hyperparameter sampling procedure is presented in Fig. 2(a).

Continuous Search. While defining a discrete action space can be more controllable for hyperparameter optimization, as discussed in Sect. 1, it limits the scalability of the search space. The gradients of all possible hyperparameter combinations are retained in the discrete search during the windowed update as in Eq. 8, which requires a large amount of memory. To overcome this issue, we extend Auto-FedRL(DS) to Auto-FedRL(CS), that can utilize a continuous search (CS) space for the RL agent. Instead of constructing a gigantic grid that stores all possible hyperparameter combinations, one can directly sample a choice from a continuous multivariate Gaussian distribution $\mathcal{N}(\mu^q, \Sigma^q)$. It is worth noting that with the expansion of search space, the increase of memory usage of Auto-FedRL(CS) is negligible. A comparison between the hyperparameter sampling workflows in discrete and continuous search are presented in Fig. 2. The main difference between DS and CS lies in the sampling process. In practice, one can adopt the Box-Muller transform [55] for sampling the continuous Gaussian distribution. However, as shown in Fig. 2(a), the sampling for multivariate discrete Gaussian distributions typically involves the following steps: **(i)** We compute the probabilities of all possible combinations. **(ii)** Given the probabilities, we draw a choice from the multinomial distribution or alternatively can use the "inverse CDF" method [49]. In either way, we need to compute the probabilities of all possible hyperparameter combinations for DS, which is not required for CS. Hence, our CS is much more efficient for hyperparameter optimization, as shown in Fig. 1.

Deep RL Agent. An intuitive extension of Auto-FedRL(CS) is to leverage neural networks (NN) as the agent to update the condition of hyperparameter distribution ψ^q rather than the direct optimization. A more complicated RL agent design could deal with potentially more complex search spaces [17]. To investigate the potential of NN-based agent in our setting, we further propose the Auto-FedRL(MLP), which leverages a multilayer perceptron (MLP) as the agent to update the ψ. The sampling workflow of Auto-FedRL(MLP) is presented in Fig. 2(c). The proposed MLP takes the condition of previous hyperparameter distribution ψ^{q-1} as the network's input and predicts the updated ψ^q. Meanwhile, due to our online setting (*i.e.* limited optimization steps), we have to keep the learnable parameters in MLP small but effective. The detailed network configuration can be found in the supplementary material.

Full Algorithm. The overview of Auto-FedRL framework is presented in Algorithm 1 and Fig. 3. At each training round q, the training of Auto-FedRL consists of following steps: (i) As shown in Fig. 3(a), clients receive the global model Θ^q and hyperparameters h^q. Clients perform LocalTrain based on the received hyperparameters. (ii) The updated local models are then uploaded to the server as shown in Fig. 3(b). Instead of performing the average aggregation, we use *pseudo-gradient* $-\Delta^q$ in Eq. 3 to carry out the server update with a searchable server learning rate. (iii) Clients evaluate the received the updated global model Θ^{q+1} and upload the validation loss $\mathcal{L}_{\text{val}_k}^{q+1}$ to the server. The server performs the RL update as shown in RLUpdate of Algorithm 1. Here, we consider the applicability in a real-world scenario, in which each client maintains its own validation data rather than relying on validation data being available on the server. Then, the server computes the reward r^{q+1} as in Eq. 5 and updates the RL agent (RLOpt) as in Eq. 8. Finally, hyperparameters for the next training round h^{q+1} can be sampled from the updated hyperparameter distribution $P(\mathcal{H}|\psi^{q+1})$. As shown in Fig. 3(c), the proposed method requires one extra round of communication between clients and the server for $\mathcal{L}_{\text{val}_k}$. It is worth noting that the message size of $\mathcal{L}_{\text{val}_k}$ is negligible. Thus, this extra communication can still be considered practical under our targeted scenario in which all clients have a reliable connection (*i.e.*, multi-institutional collaborations in cross-silo FL).

3.3   Datasets and Implementation Details

CIFAR-10. We simulate an environment in which the number of data points and label proportions are imbalanced across clients. Specifically, we partition the standard CIFAR-10 training set [25] into 8 clients by sampling from a Dirichlet distribution ($\alpha = 0.5$) as in [56]. The original test set in CIFAR-10 is considered as the global test set used to measure performance. VGG-9 [51] is used as the

---

Algorithm 1: Auto-FedRL

Input: initial global model Θ^1; initial
hyperparameter combination h^1; server optimizer
`ServerOpt`; client optimizer `ClientOpt`; RL
optimizer `RLOpt`; RL learning rate γ_h .

for q = 1 to Q **do**
  for k = 1 to K **in parallel do**
    ▷ deploy h^q to clients
    if q = 1 **then**
      ▷ deploy Θ^q to clients
    ▷ unpack P^q and γ_k^q, from h^q
    $\Theta_k^q \leftarrow$ `LocalTrain` $(\Theta^q, P^q, \gamma_k^q)$
    ▷ $\Delta_k^q = \Theta^q - \Theta_k^q$
    ▷ upload Δ_k^q to the server
  ▷ unpack α_k^q and γ^q, from h^q
  ▷ $\Delta^q = \sum_{k=1}^{K} \alpha_k^q \Delta_k^q$
  $\Theta^{q+1} \leftarrow$ `ServerOpt`$(\Theta^q, -\Delta^q, \gamma^q)$
  $h^{q+1} \leftarrow$ `RLUpdate`(Θ^{q+1}, γ_h)
return Θ^Q

`LocalTrain`$(\Theta^q, P^q, \gamma_k^q)$:
  $\Theta_k^{q,1} \leftarrow \Theta^q$
  for p = 1 to P **do**
    ▷ compute the gradients $g_k^{q,p}$
    ▷ $\Theta_k^{q,p+1} =$ `ClientOpt`$(\Theta_k^{q,p}, g_k^{q,p}, \gamma_k)$
  return Θ_k^q
`RLUpdate`(Θ^{q+1}, γ_h):
  ▷ deploy Θ^{q+1} to clients
  for k = 1 to K **in parallel do**
    ▷ compute and upload $\mathcal{L}_{\mathrm{val}_k}^{q+1}$ to the server
  $\mathcal{L}_h^{q+1} = \frac{1}{K} \sum_{k=1}^{K} \mathcal{L}_{\mathrm{val}_k}^{q+1}$
  ▷ Compute r^q with Eq. 5
  $\psi^{q+1} \leftarrow$ `RLOpt`(r^{q+1}, γ_h) with Eq. 8
  $h^{q+1} \sim P(\mathcal{H}|\psi^{q+1})$
  return h^{q+1}

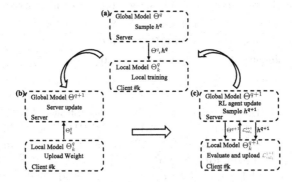

Fig. 3. The schematics of Auto-FedRL at round q.

classification network. All models are trained using the following settings: Adam
optimizer for RL; SGD optimizer for clients and the server; γ_h of 1×10^{-2};
initial learning rate of 1×10^{-2}; maximum rounds of 100; initial local epochs of
20; batch size of 64.

Multi-national COVID-19 Lesion Segmentation. This dataset contains
3D computed tomography (CT) scans of COVID-19 infected patients collected
from three medical centers[1] [16,46,59,62]. We partition this dataset into three
clients based on collection locations as following: 671 scans from China (Client
I), 88 scans from Japan (Client II), and 186 scans from Italy (Client III). Each
voxel containing a COVID-19 lesion was annotated by two expert radiologists.

---

[1] https://wiki.cancerimagingarchive.net/display/Public/CT+Images+in+COVID-
19.

Table 1. CIFAR-10 classification results. **Bold** and <u>Underline</u> indicate the best and the second best performance, respectively.

Method	Accuracy (%)
FedAvg [34]	88.43
FedProx [27]	89.45
Mostafa *et al.* [38]	89.86
Auto-FedAvg [59]	89.16
Auto-FedRL(DS)	90.70
Auto-FedRL(CS)	<u>90.85</u>
Auto-FedRL(MLP)	**91.27**
Centralized	92.56

Table 2. The computational details of different search strategies under the same setting on CIFAR-10.

Search Space type	Memory usage	Running time for search
Discrete	42.8 GB	8.246 s
Continuous	**3.00 GB**	**0.012 s**
Continuous MLP	3.13 GB	<u>0.019 s</u>

The training/validation/testing data splits are as follows: 447/112/112 (Client I), 30/29/29 (Client II), and 124/31/31 (Client III). The architecture of the segmentation network is 3D U-Net [10]. All models are trained using the following settings: Adam optimizer for RL and clients; γ_h of 1×10^{-2}; SGD optimizer for the server; initial learning rate of 1×10^{-3}; initial local iterations of 300; maximum rounds of 300; batch size of 16.

Multi-institutional Pancreas Segmentation. Here, we utilize 3D CT scans from three public datasets, including 281 scans from the pancreas segmentation subset of the Medical Segmentation Decathlon [52] as Client I, 82 scans from the Cancer Image Archive (TCIA) Pancreas-CT dataset [45] as Client II, and 30 scans from Beyond the Cranial Vault (BTCV) Abdomen dataset [22] as Client III. The training/validation/testing data splits are as follows: 95/93/93 (Client I), 28/27/27 (Client II), and 10/10/10 (Client III). All models are trained using the same network architecture and settings as COVID-19 lesion segmentation except that the maximum rounds are 50.

4 Experiments and Results

In this section, the effectiveness of our approach is first validated on a heterogeneous data split of the CIFAR-10 dataset (Sect. 4.1). Then, experiments are conducted on two multi-institutional medical image segmentation datasets (*i.e.*, COVID-19 lesion segmentation and pancreas segmentation) to investigate the real-world potential of the proposed Auto-FedRL (Sect. 4.2). Finally, detailed comparisons between discrete and continuous search space, and the exploration of deep RL agents are provided (Sect. 4.3). We evaluate the performance of our method against the following popular FL methods: FedAvg [34] and FedProx [27] as well as FL-based hyperparameter optimization methods: Auto-FedAvg [59], and Mostafa *et al.* [38].

4.1 CIFAR-10

Table 1 shows the quantitative performance of different methods in terms of the average accuracy across 8 clients. We denote the model that is directly trained with all available data as *Centralized* in Table 1. We treat it as an upper bound when data can be shared. As can be seen from this table, the proposed Auto-FedRL methods clearly outperform the other competing FL alternatives. Auto-FedRL(MLP) gains the best performance improvement by taking the advantage of a more complex RL agent design. To investigate the underlying hyperparameter change, we plot the evolution of aggregation weights in Fig. 4. We found that the proposed RL agent is able to reveal more informative clients (i.e., clients containing more unique labels) and assign larger aggregation weights to those client's model updates. In particular, in Fig. 4(a), C4 (red), C5 (purple), and C8 (gray) are gradually assigned three of the largest aggregation weights. As shown in Fig. 4(b), although those three clients do not contain the largest number of images, all have the most number of unique labels (*i.e.* 10 in CIFAR-10). This behavior further demonstrates the effectiveness of Auto-FedRL. Moreover, we provide the computational details of different search strategies to investigate their practicability under a same setting in Table 2. Without losing performance, the proposed continuous search requires only 7% memory usage but is 690× faster compared to the discrete search. While Auto-FedRL(MLP) introduces the deep RL agent, it is still 430× faster compared to the discrete version. Additional multi-dimensional comparisons [9] are provided in the supplementary material. The notable computational efficiency and low memory usage of Auto-FedRL validate our motivation of making federated hyperparameter optimization more practical in real-world applications.

4.2 Real-World FL Medical Image Segmentation

Multi-national COVID-19 Lesion Segmentation: The quantitative results are presented in Table 3. We show the segmentation results of different methods for qualitative analysis in Fig. 5(a). Dice score is used to evaluate the quality of segmentation. We repeatedly run all FL algorithms 3 times and report the mean and standard deviation. The main metric of evaluating the generalizability of the global model is *Global Test Avg.*, which is computed by the average performance of the global model across all clients. In the first three rows of Table 3, we evaluate three locally trained models as the baseline. Due to the domain shift, all locally

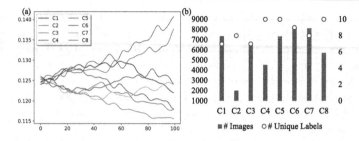

Fig. 4. Analysis of the learning process of Auto-FedRL(MLP) in CIFAR-10. (a) the evolution of aggregation weights during the training. (b) the data statistics of different clients.

Table 3. Multi-national COVID-19 lesion segmentation. † indicates significant improvement (p ≪ 0.05 in the Wilcoxon signed rank test) of the global model over the best counterpart.

Method	Client I	Client II	Client III	Global Test Avg.
Local only - I	59.8	61.8	51.8	57.8
Local only - II	41.9	59.9	50.2	50.7
Local only - III	34.5	52.5	65.9	51.0
FedAvg [34]	59.9	63.8	60.5	61.4 ± 0.2
FedProx [27]	60.3	64.9	60.5	61.9 ± 0.5
Mostafa *et al.* [38]	60.9	64.6	65.6	63.7 ± 0.3
Auto-FedAvg [59]	60.3	65.3	64.8	63.5 ± 0.2
Auto-FedRL(DS)	59.3	65.6	$68.9^\dagger$	$\underline{64.6 \pm 0.2}$
Auto-FedRL(CS)	59.9	$66.1^\dagger$	$68.2^\dagger$	$\mathbf{64.7 \pm 0.1}$
Auto-FedRL(MLP)	57.8	65.6	$68.5^\dagger$	64.0 ± 0.4
Centralized	61.1	65.9	69.3	65.4

trained models exhibit low generalizability on the other clients. By leveraging the additional regularization on weight changes, FedProx (with the empirically best $\mu = 0.001$) can slightly outperform the FedAvg baseline. Mostafa *et al.* that uses the RL agent to perform discrete search can achieve slightly better performance than Auto-FedAvg. We find that with the nearly constant memory usage and notable computational efficiency, the proposed Auto-FedRL(CS) achieves the best performance, outperforming the most competitive method [38] by 1.0% in terms of the global model performance, by 1.5% and 2.6% on clients II and III, respectively. The performance gap between the FL algorithm and centralized training is shrunk to only 0.7%. Figure 6 presents the analysis of learning process in our best performing model. As shown in Fig. 6(a), we can observe that the RL agent is able to naturally form the training scheduler for each hyperparameter (*e.g.*, the learning rate decay for the client/server), which is aligned with the theoretical analysis about the convergence on non-iid data of FL algorithms [29].

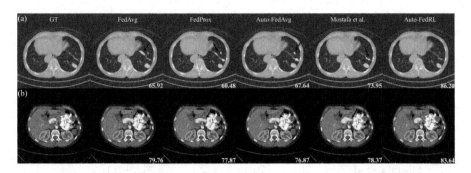

Fig. 5. Qualitative results of different methods that correspond to (a) COVID-19 lesion segmentation of Client III and (b) Pancreas segmentation of Client II. GT shows human annotations in green and others show the segmentation results from different methods. Red arrows point to erroneous segmentation. The dice score is presented in the lower-right corner of each subplot. (Color figure online)

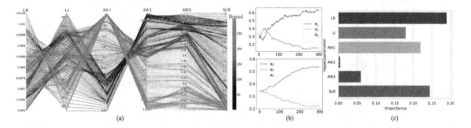

Fig. 6. Analysis of the learning process of Auto-FedRL(CS) in COVID-19 lesion segmentation. (a) The parallel plot of the hyperparameter change during the training. LR, LI, AW, and SLR denote the learning rate, local iterations, the aggregation weight of each client, and the server learning rate, respectively. (b) The aggregation weights evolution of Auto-FedAvg in the *top row* and Auto-FedRL(CS) in the *bottom row*. (c) The importance analysis of different hyperparameters.

Since Auto-FedAvg specially aims to learn the optimal aggregation weights, we compare the aggregation weights learning process between our approach and Auto-FedAvg in Fig. 6(b). It can be observed that the two methods exhibit a similar trend of learning aggregation weights, which further demonstrates the effectiveness of Auto-FedRL in aggregation weights searching. Finally, we use FANOVA [18] to assess the hyperparameter importance. As shown in Fig. 6(c), LR, SLR, and AW1 rank as the top-3 most important hyperparameters, which implies the necessity of tuning server-side hyperparameters in FL setting.

Multi-institutional Pancreas Segmentation. Table 4 and Fig. 5(b) present the quantitative and qualitative results on this dataset, respectively. Similar to the results on COVID-19 segmentation, our Auto-FedRL algorithms achieves the significantly better overall performance. In particular, Auto-FedRL(MLP) outperforms the best counterpart by 1.3%. We aslo observe that our methods

Table 4. Multi-institutional pancreas segmentation. † indicates significant improvement of the global model over the best counterpart.

Method	Clinet I	Clinet II	Clinet III	Global Test Avg.
Local only - I	69.4	71.4	63.8	68.2
Local only - II	49.7	75.5	53.0	59.3
Local only - III	42.4	61.2	51.1	51.3
FedAvg [34]	71.9	78.4	69.1	73.1 ± 0.3
FedProx [27]	72.0	78.4	69.6	73.3 ± 0.3
Mostafa *et al.* [38]	74.4	79.4	72.1	75.3 ± 0.1
Auto-FedAvg [59]	71.3	79.9	71.5	74.2 ± 0.3
Auto-FedRL(DS)	72.8	80.8†	74.7†	76.1 ± 0.4
Auto-FedRL(CS)	73.0	82.2†	74.5†	<u>76.5 ± 0.3</u>
Auto-FedRL(MLP)	73.2	81.2†	75.3†	**76.6 ± 0.3**
Centralized	74.5	82.6	72.0	76.3

Table 5. The search space ablation study on CIFAR-10.

Search space				Search strategy		
LR	LE	AW	SLR	Discrete	Continuous	Continuous MLP
✓				89.83	<u>90.02</u>	**90.12**
✓	✓			89.86	<u>90.10</u>	**90.49**
✓	✓	✓		90.43	<u>90.52</u>	**90.87**
✓	✓	✓	✓	90.70	<u>90.85</u>	**91.27**

exhibits better generalizability on the relatively smaller clients. Specifically, on Client III, Auto-FedRL(MLP) improves the Dice score from 51.1% to 75.3%, which is even 3.28% higher than the centralized training. These results implies that by leveraging the dynamic hyperparameter tuning during the training, Auto-FedRL algorithms can achieve better generalization and are more robust towards the heterogeneous data distribution. As shown in Fig. 5(b), the proposed methods have a better capacity of handling the challenging cases, which is consistent with the quantitative results. The detailed hyperparameter evolution analysis on pancreas segmentation is provided in the supplementary material.

4.3 Ablation Study

The effectiveness of the proposed continuous search and NN-based RL agent is demonstrated by the previous sets of experiments in three datasets. Here, we conduct a detailed ablation study to analyze the benefit of individually adding each hyperparameter into the search space. As shown in Table 5, the performance of trained global model can be further improved with the expansion of the search space, which also validates our motivation that the proper hyperparameter tuning is crucial for the success of FL algorithms. More visualizations, experimental results, and the theoretical analysis to guarantee the convergence of Auto-FedRL are provided in the supplementary material.

5   Conclusion and Discussion

In this work, we proposed an online RL-based federated hyperparameter optimization framework for realistic FL applications, which can dynamically tune the hyperparameters during a single trial, resulting in improved performance compared to several existing baselines. To make federated hyperparameter optimization more practical in real-world applications, we proposed Auto-FedRL(CS) and Auto-FedRL(MLP), which can operate on continuous search space, demand nearly constant memory and are computationally efficient. By integrating the adaptive federated optimization, Auto-FedRL supports a more flexible search space to tune a wide range of hyperparameters. The empirical results on three datasets with diverse characteristics reveal that the proposed method can train global models with better performance and generalization capabilities under heterogeneous data distributions.

While our proposed method yielded a competitive performance, there are potential areas for improvement. First, we are aware that the performance improvement brought by the proposed method is not uniform across participating clients. Since the proposed RL agent jointly optimizes the whole system, minimizing an aggregate loss can lead to potentially advantage or disadvantage a particular client's performance. We can also observe that all FL methods exhibit a relatively small improvement on the client with the largest amount of data. This is a common phenomenon of FL methods since the client itself already provides diverse and rich training and testing data. Future research could include additional fairness constraints [26,28,33,36,64] to achieve a more uniform performance distribution across clients and reduce potential biases. Second, the NN-based RL agent could be benefiting from transfer learning. The effectiveness of RL transfer learning has been demonstrated in the literature for related tasks [54]. Pre-training the NN-based agent on large-scale FL datasets and then finetuning on target tasks may further boost the performance of our approach.

References

1. Abdallah, S., Kaisers, M.: Addressing environment non-stationarity by repeating q-learning updates. J. Mach. Learn. Res. **17**(1), 1582–1612 (2016)
2. Acar, D.A.E., Zhao, Y., Matas, R., Mattina, M., Whatmough, P., Saligrama, V.: Federated learning based on dynamic regularization. In: International Conference on Learning Representations (2020)
3. Andrychowicz, M., et al.: Learning to learn by gradient descent by gradient descent. In: Advances in Neural Information Processing Systems, pp. 3981–3989 (2016)
4. Baker, B., Gupta, O., Naik, N., Raskar, R.: Designing neural network architectures using reinforcement learning. arXiv preprint arXiv:1611.02167 (2016)

5. Bergstra, J., Bardenet, R., Bengio, Y., Kégl, B.: Algorithms for hyper-parameter optimization. Adv. Neural Inf. Process. Syst. **24**, 1–9 (2011)
6. Bergstra, J., Bengio, Y.: Random search for hyper-parameter optimization. J. Mach. Learn. Res. **13**(2) (2012)
7. Chen, X., Chen, T., Sun, H., Wu, Z.S., Hong, M.: Distributed training with heterogeneous data: Bridging median-and mean-based algorithms. arXiv preprint arXiv:1906.01736 (2019)
8. Chen, X., Xie, L., Wu, J., Tian, Q.: Progressive differentiable architecture search: Bridging the depth gap between search and evaluation. In: Proceedings of the IEEE/CVF International Conference on Computer Vision, pp. 1294–1303 (2019)
9. Chopra, A., et al.: Adasplit: adaptive trade-offs for resource-constrained distributed deep learning. arXiv preprint arXiv:2112.01637 (2021)
10. Çiçek, Ö., Abdulkadir, A., Lienkamp, S.S., Brox, T., Ronneberger, O.: 3D U-Net: learning dense volumetric segmentation from sparse annotation. In: Ourselin, S., Joskowicz, L., Sabuncu, M.R., Unal, G., Wells, W. (eds.) MICCAI 2016. LNCS, vol. 9901, pp. 424–432. Springer, Cham (2016). https://doi.org/10.1007/978-3-319-46723-8_49
11. Cubuk, E.D., Zoph, B., Mane, D., Vasudevan, V., Le, Q.V.: Autoaugment: learning augmentation policies from data. arXiv preprint arXiv:1805.09501 (2018)
12. Cubuk, E.D., Zoph, B., Shlens, J., Le, Q.V.: Randaugment: practical automated data augmentation with a reduced search space. In: Proceedings of the IEEE/CVF Conference on Computer Vision and Pattern Recognition Workshops, pp. 702–703 (2020)
13. Geiping, J., Bauermeister, H., Dröge, H., Moeller, M.: Inverting gradients-how easy is it to break privacy in federated learning? arXiv preprint arXiv:2003.14053 (2020)
14. Guo, P., et al.: Learning-based analysis of amide proton transfer-weighted MRI to identify tumor progression in patients with post-treatment malignant gliomas. Available at SSRN 4049653
15. Guo, P., Wang, P., Zhou, J., Jiang, S., Patel, V.M.: Multi-institutional collaborations for improving deep learning-based magnetic resonance image reconstruction using federated learning. In: Proceedings of the IEEE/CVF Conference on Computer Vision and Pattern Recognition, pp. 2423–2432 (2021)
16. Harmon, S.A., Sanford, T.H., Xu, S., Turkbey, E.B., Roth, H., Xu, Z., Yang, D., Myronenko, A., Anderson, V., Amalou, A., et al.: Artificial intelligence for the detection of covid-19 pneumonia on chest ct using multinational datasets. Nat. Commun. **11**(1), 1–7 (2020)
17. Henderson, P., Islam, R., Bachman, P., Pineau, J., Precup, D., Meger, D.: Deep reinforcement learning that matters. In: Proceedings of the AAAI Conference on Artificial Intelligence, vol. 32 (2018)
18. Hutter, F., Hoos, H., Leyton-Brown, K.: An efficient approach for assessing hyper-parameter importance. In: Proceedings of the 31st International Conference on Machine Learning. Proceedings of Machine Learning Research, vol. 32, pp. 754–762. PMLR (2014)
19. Jaakkola, T., Singh, S.P., Jordan, M.I.: Reinforcement learning algorithm for partially observable markov decision problems. Adv. Neural Inf. Process. Syst. **7**, 345–352 (1995)
20. Kairouz, P., et al.: Advances and open problems in federated learning. arXiv preprint arXiv:1912.04977 (2019)
21. Kaissis, G., et al.: End-to-end privacy preserving deep learning on multi-institutional medical imaging. Nat. Mach. Intell. **3**(6), 473–484 (2021)

22. Kaissis, G.A., Makowski, M.R., Rückert, D., Braren, R.F.: Secure, privacy-preserving and federated machine learning in medical imaging. Nat. Mach. Intell. **2**(6), 305–311 (2020)

23. Karimireddy, S.P., Kale, S., Mohri, M., Reddi, S., Stich, S., Suresh, A.T.: Scaffold: stochastic controlled averaging for federated learning. In: International Conference on Machine Learning, pp. 5132–5143. PMLR (2020)

24. Khodak, M., et al.: Federated hyperparameter tuning: challenges, baselines, and connections to weight-sharing. Adv. Neural Inf. Process. Syst. **34**, 19184–19197 (2021)

25. Krizhevsky, A., Hinton, G., et al.: Learning multiple layers of features from tiny images (2009)

26. Li, T., Hu, S., Beirami, A., Smith, V.: Ditto: fair and robust federated learning through personalization. In: International Conference on Machine Learning, pp. 6357–6368. PMLR (2021)

27. Li, T., Sahu, A.K., Zaheer, M., Sanjabi, M., Talwalkar, A., Smith, V.: Federated optimization in heterogeneous networks. arXiv preprint arXiv:1812.06127 (2018)

28. Li, T., Sanjabi, M., Beirami, A., Smith, V.: Fair resource allocation in federated learning. arXiv preprint arXiv:1905.10497 (2019)

29. Li, X., Huang, K., Yang, W., Wang, S., Zhang, Z.: On the convergence of fedavg on non-iid data. In: International Conference on Learning Representations (2020). https://openreview.net/forum?id=HJxNAnVtDS

30. Li, X., Gu, Y., Dvornek, N., Staib, L.H., Ventola, P., Duncan, J.S.: Multi-site fmri analysis using privacy-preserving federated learning and domain adaptation: Abide results. Med. Image Anal. **65**, 101765 (2020)

31. Li, X., Jiang, M., Zhang, X., Kamp, M., Dou, Q.: Fedbn: Federated learning on non-iid features via local batch normalization. arXiv preprint arXiv:2102.07623 (2021)

32. Liu, H., Simonyan, K., Yang, Y.: Darts: differentiable architecture search. arXiv preprint arXiv:1806.09055 (2018)

33. Lyu, L., Xu, X., Wang, Q., Yu, H.: Collaborative fairness in federated learning. In: Yang, Q., Fan, L., Yu, H. (eds.) Federated Learning. LNCS (LNAI), vol. 12500, pp. 189–204. Springer, Cham (2020). https://doi.org/10.1007/978-3-030-63076-8_14

34. McMahan, B., Moore, E., Ramage, D., Hampson, S., y Arcas, B.A.: Communication-efficient learning of deep networks from decentralized data. In: Artificial Intelligence and Statistics, pp. 1273–1282. PMLR (2017)

35. Mei, Y., Guo, P., Patel, V.M.: Escaping data scarcity for high-resolution heterogeneous face hallucination. In: Proceedings of the IEEE/CVF Conference on Computer Vision and Pattern Recognition, pp. 18676–18686 (2022)

36. Michieli, U., Ozay, M.: Are all users treated fairly in federated learning systems? In: Proceedings of the IEEE/CVF Conference on Computer Vision and Pattern Recognition, pp. 2318–2322 (2021)

37. Mohri, M., Sivek, G., Suresh, A.T.: Agnostic federated learning. In: International Conference on Machine Learning, pp. 4615–4625. PMLR (2019)

38. Mostafa, H.: Robust federated learning through representation matching and adaptive hyper-parameters. arXiv preprint arXiv:1912.13075 (2019)

39. Nvidia Corporation: Nvidia FLARE (2022). https://doi.org/10.5281/zenodo.6780567, https://github.com/NVIDIA/nvflare

40. Padakandla, S., K. J., P., Bhatnagar, S.: Reinforcement learning algorithm for non-stationary environments. Appl. Intell. **50**(11), 3590–3606 (2020). https://doi.org/10.1007/s10489-020-01758-5

41. Real, E., Aggarwal, A., Huang, Y., Le, Q.V.: Regularized evolution for image classifier architecture search. In: Proceedings of the AAAI Conference on Artificial Intelligence, vol. 33, pp. 4780–4789 (2019)
42. Reddi, S., et al.: Adaptive federated optimization. arXiv preprint arXiv:2003.00295 (2020)
43. Rieke, N., et al.: The future of digital health with federated learning. NPJ Dig. Med. **3**(1), 1–7 (2020)
44. Roth, H.R., et al.: Federated learning for breast density classification: a real-world implementation. In: Albarqouni, S., et al. (eds.) DART/DCL -2020. LNCS, vol. 12444, pp. 181–191. Springer, Cham (2020). https://doi.org/10.1007/978-3-030-60548-3_18
45. Roth, H.R., et al.: DeepOrgan: multi-level deep convolutional networks for automated pancreas segmentation. In: Navab, N., Hornegger, J., Wells, W.M., Frangi, A.F. (eds.) MICCAI 2015. LNCS, vol. 9349, pp. 556–564. Springer, Cham (2015). https://doi.org/10.1007/978-3-319-24553-9_68
46. Roth, H.R., et al.: Rapid artificial intelligence solutions in a pandemic-the covid-19-20 lung ct lesion segmentation challenge. Research Square (2021)
47. Ruvolo, P., Fasel, I., Movellan, J.: Optimization on a budget: a reinforcement learning approach. Adv. Neural Inf. Process. Syst. **21**, 1–8 (2008)
48. Sattler, F., Wiedemann, S., Müller, K.R., Samek, W.: Robust and communication-efficient federated learning from non-iid data. IEEE Trans. Neural Netw. Learn. Syst. **31**(9), 3400–3413 (2019)
49. Shaw, W.T.: Sampling student's t distribution-use of the inverse cumulative distribution function. J. Comput. Finan. **9**(4), 37 (2006)
50. Sheller, M.J., et al.: Federated learning in medicine: facilitating multi-institutional collaborations without sharing patient data. Sci. Rep. **10**(1), 1–12 (2020)
51. Simonyan, K., Zisserman, A.: Very deep convolutional networks for large-scale image recognition. arXiv preprint arXiv:1409.1556 (2014)
52. Simpson, A.L., et al.: A large annotated medical image dataset for the development and evaluation of segmentation algorithms. arXiv preprint arXiv:1902.09063 (2019)
53. Snoek, J., Larochelle, H., Adams, R.P.: Practical bayesian optimization of machine learning algorithms. Adv. Neural Inf. Process. Syst. **25**, 1–9 (2012)
54. Taylor, M.E., Stone, P.: Transfer learning for reinforcement learning domains: a survey. J. Mach. Learn. Res. **10**(7) (2009)
55. Thistleton, W.J., Marsh, J.A., Nelson, K., Tsallis, C.: Generalized box-müller method for generating q-gaussian random deviates. IEEE Trans. Inf. Theory **53**(12), 4805–4810 (2007)
56. Wang, H., Yurochkin, M., Sun, Y., Papailiopoulos, D., Khazaeni, Y.: Federated learning with matched averaging. arXiv preprint arXiv:2002.06440 (2020)
57. Williams, R.J.: Simple statistical gradient-following algorithms for connectionist reinforcement learning. Mach. Learn. **8**(3), 229–256 (1992)
58. Wu, J., Chen, X.Y., Zhang, H., Xiong, L.D., Lei, H., Deng, S.H.: Hyperparameter optimization for machine learning models based on bayesian optimization. J. Electron. Sci. Technol. **17**(1), 26–40 (2019)
59. Xia, Y., et al.: Auto-fedavg: learnable federated averaging for multi-institutional medical image segmentation. arXiv preprint arXiv:2104.10195 (2021)
60. Xie, L., Yuille, A.: Genetic cnn. In: Proceedings of the IEEE International Conference on Computer Vision, pp. 1379–1388 (2017)
61. Xu, A., et al.: Closing the generalization gap of cross-silo federated medical image segmentation. In: Proceedings of the IEEE/CVF Conference on Computer Vision and Pattern Recognition, pp. 20866–20875 (2022)

62. Yang, D.: Federated semi-supervised learning for covid region segmentation in chest ct using multi-national data from china, italy, japan. Med. Image Anal. **70**, 101992 (2021)
63. Yang, Q., Liu, Y., Chen, T., Tong, Y.: Federated machine learning: concept and applications. ACM Trans. Intell. Syst. Technol. (TIST) **10**(2), 1–19 (2019)
64. Yu, H., et al.: A fairness-aware incentive scheme for federated learning. In: Proceedings of the AAAI/ACM Conference on AI, Ethics, and Society, pp. 393–399 (2020)
65. Zhao, Y., Li, M., Lai, L., Suda, N., Civin, D., Chandra, V.: Federated learning with non-iid data. arXiv preprint arXiv:1806.00582 (2018)
66. Zoph, B., Le, Q.V.: Neural architecture search with reinforcement learning. arXiv preprint arXiv:1611.01578 (2016)

Personalizing Federated Medical Image Segmentation via Local Calibration

Jiacheng Wang[1], Yueming Jin[2], and Liansheng Wang[1](✉)

[1] Department of Computer Science at School of Informatics, Xiamen University, Xiamen, China
jiachengw@stu.xmu.edu.cn, lswang@xmu.edu.cn
[2] Wellcome/EPSRC Centre for Interventional and Surgical Sciences (WEISS) and Department of Computer Science, University College London, London, UK
yueming.jin@ucl.ac.uk

Abstract. Medical image segmentation under federated learning (FL) is a promising direction by allowing multiple clinical sites to collaboratively learn a global model without centralizing datasets. However, using a single model to adapt to various data distributions from different sites is extremely challenging. Personalized FL tackles this issue by only utilizing partial model parameters shared from global server, while keeping the rest to adapt to its own data distribution in the local training of each site. However, most existing methods concentrate on the partial parameter splitting, while do not consider the *inter-site in-consistencies* during the local training, which in fact can facilitate the knowledge communication over sites to benefit the model learning for improving the local accuracy. In this paper, we propose a personalized federated framework with **Local Calibration** (LC-Fed), to leverage the inter-site in-consistencies in both *feature- and prediction- levels* to boost the segmentation. Concretely, as each local site has its alternative attention on the various features, we first design the contrastive site embedding coupled with channel selection operation to calibrate the encoded features. Moreover, we propose to exploit the knowledge of prediction-level in-consistency to guide the personalized modeling on the ambiguous regions, e.g., anatomical boundaries. It is achieved by computing a disagreement-aware map to calibrate the prediction. Effectiveness of our method has been verified on three medical image segmentation tasks with different modalities, where our method consistently shows superior performance to the state-of-the-art personalized FL methods. Code is available at https://github.com/jcwang123/FedLC.

1 Introduction

As a data-driven approach, deep learning model heavily relies on the data quantities to prompt its efficacy. Collaborative training using the data across mul-

---

J. Wang and Y. Jin—Contributed equally.

Supplementary Information The online version contains supplementary material available at https://doi.org/10.1007/978-3-031-19803-8_27.

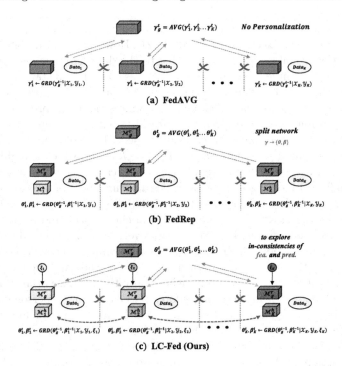

Fig. 1. Federated frameworks. Dash lines with arrow denote the parameter communication. (a) FedAVG, the classical federated framework that designs the global model averaging all parameters from local sites. (b) FedRep, the latest personalized framework under federation, which splits the model into representation part and head part. The former is updated through global averaging while the latter is trained only using local data. (c) Our method LC-Fed, that explores inter-site in-consistencies to calibrate the local learning from both feature- and prediction-levels.

tiple medical sites is increasingly essential for yielding the maximal potential of deep models for medical image segmentation [9,28,38]. However, it is generally infeasible to accomplish the data communication over multiple sites owing to the privacy protection for patients [15]. Federated Learning (FL) [16] has recently received significant research interests from the community [15,24,27], as it enables the different sites to jointly train a global model with no need to share and centralize the data. Instead, each local client (e.g., medical site) trains the model from their own data, and the coordinating is achieved by aggregating the model parameters from the local clients to a global server and broadcasting the updated parameters to them. See a typical and standard federate paradigm in Fig. 1(a), a single global model is generated in the server by averaging the model parameters from the local clients.

Although FL has recently achieved the promising progress in medical image segmentation [18,19,21,29], most existing works fall into the standard federate learning paradigm, i.e., concentrating on learning *a single global model* with more robustness and generalization on clients via balanced average weight [19], image simulation [18], image style transformation [21]. However, the single global model can not perform well on all local sites due to the data heterogeneity, where the underlying data sample distribution of local sites could be substantially different from each other [10,33]. The potential model degradation is more severe in the medical scenario, where the difference of scanners, imaging protocols, patient populations bring the high diversity of data distribution. In this work, we focus on improving the performance of each local client, by exploiting the data of all clients but learning *a personalized model for each client*, which is highly desired for practical usage yet still underexplored in medical image segmentation tasks.

Personalized FL emerges and establishes a promising approach for improving the quality of each local client model [1,6,7,20,36,37]. Among them, the vanilla solution is delivering the global model to local clients back and using their own data to do the model finetuning [36,37]. However, these methods adjust the full-dimensional parameters, which may destroy the common representation gained by FL and negatively affect the performance. Recent advances reduce the communication part of local parameters, where only the partial parameters will be sent to the global server for updating (global part) and others (personalized part) are maintained in the local site. The personalized part can be concluded into two streams. One is at feature-level such as the high-frequency components of convolutional parameters [6] or Batch Normalization layers [1,20]. The other one is at the prediction level, i.e., the prediction head layers [7] (as shown in Fig. 1(b)). However, the two streams still only consider the intra-site information during local training, while they have ignored to exploit the *inter-site inconsistency*. The valuable knowledge from other sites shall be inevitably lost. Additionally, most existing literature on personalized FL tackles the classification problem, in which the classification models contain much fewer and simpler layers than the segmentation models so that whether they are useful and how to effectively form the personalization for segmentation tasks are still under-explored so far.

In this paper, we propose a personalized federated segmentation framework that is able to unify the personalized feature representation and target prediction through **Local Calibration**, so-called **LC-Fed** as shown in Fig. 1(c). The feature- and prediction-level personalization is respectively achieved by the Personalized Channel Selection (PCS) module and the Head Calibration (HC) module.

- **PCS** can calibrate the encoded features after standard encoding layers depending on our proposed *contrastive site embedding*, which is unique for each site and inter-site contrastive. Specifically, given a site embedding and the encoded features, as each site pays its personalized attention to the various channels, the PCS module augments the site embedding and yields an attention channel factor to calibrate the features.
- **HC** is designed with the insight that, the inter-site in-consistency at prediction-level always implies the most ambiguous areas which demand more concentration in model training. In order to take advantage of this prior knowledge, HC gathers prediction heads from other sites and calculates a *disagreement-aware map* to calibrate its own prediction.

We conduct comparison experiments with several personalized FL methods on three typical medical image segmentation tasks, which are prostate segmentation on T2-weighted MR images (PMR), polyp segmentation of endoscopic images (EndoPolyp), and optic disc/cup segmentation of retinal fundus images (RIF). We evaluate the local accuracy of all federated sites and calculate the averaged score to assess the performance. Experimental results demonstrate the effectiveness of the proposed method, consistently achieving better segmentation results than the state-of-the-arts.

2 Related Work

2.1 Medical Image Segmentation

Medical image segmentation aims to predict a certain region from an input image, such as organ at risk from MR image [35,38], optic disc and cup from retinal fundus image [28,34], and polyp from endoscopic image [9,11,40]. It contributes a lot to the improvement of clinical efficiency, treatment effect, and quality control. A large proportion of current research focuses on architecture adjustment to improve representation ability, by attention-like mechanism [9], multi-scale feature fusion [11], hyper-architecture [28] and so on. However, learning powerful representation requires a large amount of data in general, or the performance will meet a serious drop. To increase the data amount, collecting data over different sites is mostly necessary as each institution has limited patients especially for some rare diseases, while the data communication is sometimes hard to come true due to privacy protection of patients' information. Hence, instead of improving the architectures, we pay attention to building a federated segmentation framework with no need to centralize data from different sites. Also, we make efforts to personalize the federation so that local accuracy can be extensively improved that benefits the local application.

2.2 Federated Learning

With the consideration of increasing attention on privacy legislation, federated learning is catching more and more eyes in recent years, particularly in the medical area, which requires no need to centralize data over different sites [15,19,27,31]. The federated learning paradigm is meant to protect patients' privacy and can even achieve competitive performance compared to that of models trained on centralized data [15]. Its workflow can be realised with several different topologies, i.e. centralized server and decentralized sever, but the goal remains the same that is to aggregate knowledge from different sites without data communication [27]. For example, the most classical one, FedAVG [24], proposes to average parameters from all local sites at the centralized server. In the medical area, Sheller et al. [29] firstly conducts a pilot study to investigate the usefulness of FL in multi-site brain tumor segmentation and recent studies aim to tackle the quantity imbalance over sites [18,39] or enhance the generalization ability during federated setting [21] In other areas, numerous methods have been introduced to solve the various FL challenges [14], such as reducing communication cost [24,26], privacy protection [41]. However, in whatever areas, when applied for practice, the goal of each participated host is to obtain an accurate model for its local data, while using a single global model to adapt to different data distribution is extremely hard. With the motivation to boost the local accuracy as much as possible and ignore the probable performance drop on the unseen domain, we propose to personalize the federated medical image segmentation, in which each site has its own parameters and simultaneously catch knowledge from other sites.

2.3   Personalized Federated Learning

The data heterogeneity, differences in data distribution, makes it hard to learn a single global model that can be applied to all sites. To cope with this issue, personalized federated learning is introduced to personalize the global model uniquely for each participating client in the setup [17]. Some work treats personalized federated learning as a multi-task learning problem where each site's learning process is a unique task [8,23]. Other approaches divide the network architecture into shared and personalized layers, where the shared layers are aggregated by FedAVG at the centralized server and the personalized layers are not. The shared layers could be batch normalization layers [20], high-frequency convolution layers [6] or prediction head layers [7]. However, these setups are all designed and evaluated for classification tasks while the segmentation models have more complex architecture so the effectiveness has not been verified. Additionally, these methods have not adequately investigated the inter-site disagreement at both feature- and prediction-level, which is beneficial to concurrently learn the personalization and communication. To fill this gap, our work introduces a novel personalized FL paradigm considering the inter-site information in the local training and demonstrates the promising performance on medical image segmentation task.

3   Method

An overall of our personalized federated segmentation framework of LC-Fed is visualized in Fig. 2. It takes the first attempt to enhance the inter-site communication by exploring inconsistencies between sites in the local training. We start with introducing the overview of our personalized federation paradigm with local calibration, then describe the two modules in detail at the rest parts.

3.1   Locally Calibrated Federation Paradigm

Denote $(\mathcal{X}, \mathcal{Y})$ as the joint image and label space with K sites. For the k-th site, the data samples establish its own data distribution $(x_k, y_k) \sim D_k$, where $x_k \in \mathcal{X}_k$ and $y_k \in \mathcal{Y}_k$. Instead learning a single shared model, our LC-Fed aims at

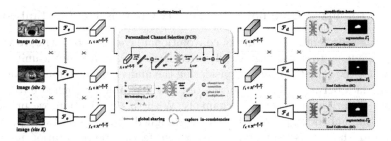

Fig. 2. Overview of our personalized federated learning framework with local calibration, LC-Fed. It locally calibrates the features and predictions using the personalized channel selection (PCS) module and head calibration (HC) module. In PCS, we propose an unique and contrastive site embedding for each site, through which we calculate a channel selection map to calibrate the feature representation. In HC, we gather all sites' prediction heads and measure their in-consistency as the prediction-level disagreement to calibrate segmentation map.

learning K unique models stylized for K local sites $\{\mathcal{M}_i\}_{i=1}^K : \mathcal{X} \to \mathcal{Y}$ using the whole data space. The models hold the same network architecture, containing two components: a base body for representation learning $\mathcal{M}^r$ with parameter θ, a prediction head to map the representation to produce predicted values for each class $\mathcal{M}^h$ with parameter β. Specifically, an U-shape network is exploited as the base body $\mathcal{M}^r$, consisting of five encoding-decoding stages. Our feature-level calibration is achieved by injecting the contrastive site embedding ξ_k into the final encoding stage in the local training, to incorporate the stylized information of each local site into the representations from coarse to fine. Our prediction-level calibration is established within the prediction head $\mathcal{M}^h$, which contains two cascaded fully-connected layers, to produce a coarse map and a calibrated segmentation map, respectively.

To learn K unique local models, our LC-Fed alternates between the local site update and global server update on each communication round. At each federated round t, all local sites receive the same parameters θ_g^{t-1} for the base body part from the global server at the last round, while the parameters of the prediction head are initialized from the local training itself, i.e., β_k^{t-1} in k-th local site. Each site will update the model for its optimal solution using its local data $(\mathcal{X}_k, \mathcal{Y}_k)$ and the stylized site embedding ξ_k as

$$\theta_k^t, \beta_k^t \leftarrow \text{GRD}(\theta_g^{t-1}, \beta_k^{t-1} | \mathcal{X}_k, \mathcal{Y}_k, \xi_k), \tag{1}$$

where GRD(.) represents the local gradient-based update. After the update finished in all local sites, the global server then collects the parameters for the representation portion θ^t to update the global model. We employ the most popular federated averaging algorithm (FedAvg) [24], which performs an average operation on the local parameters for global model updating, i.e., $\theta_g^t = \frac{1}{K}\sum_{i=1}^K \theta_i^t$. Till now, the current federated round finishes and the global server shall deliver the updated representation θ_g^t to local sites to turn to the next round.

3.2 Personalized Channel Selection via Contrastive Site Embedding

The strong representation ability of convolutional layers can be owing to various feature channels to some degree, where each channel represents a unique perspective for the target learning. Considering the underlying distribution variance of image data between different local sites, it is desirable for each site to pay its personal attention to alternative channels. With this motivation, we propose a stylized site embedding, coupled with the designed channel selection operation, to calibrate the local sites to pursue their own feature representation modeling with different directions. Moreover, the simple site embedding design invokes the inter-site communication during the local feature learning, which prompts the inter-site inconsistency in the feature level. It is achieved by incorporating the contrastive objective on the site embeddings to incite them to be dissimilar.

Concretely, in the k-th local site, the encoded feature of a image data at the l-th encoding stage is denoted as $f_k^l \in \mathbb{R}^{C \times \frac{H}{2^l} \times \frac{W}{2^l}}$, where C is the channel number and (H, W) are the image size and $l = 5$ in this work. To simplify the communication cost, we initialize the site embedding as a one-hot vector, with the length set as the site number K: $\xi_k \in \mathbb{R}^K$. The k-th value is 1 and others are 0. We further integrate the textural semantics from the feature in the current stage f_k^l to enhance the site embedding. To achieve this, we first extend the length of site embedding to keep balance with the textural semantics for better training stability, i.e., the updated one $\xi_k^* \in \mathbb{R}^C$. We employ two fully-connected layers, with instance normalization and Relu activation in between, to accomplish the extension. We then perform the global averaging on each channel of the feature f_k^l, to generate a channel descriptor that can represent the abundant textural information and save the computational cost. The feature concatenation on channel descriptor and ξ_k^*, followed by a full-connection and a gating sigmoid activation is used for augmenting site embedding by the textural knowledge. The augmented site embedding $\hat{\xi}_k$ can serve as the attentive factor for selecting feature channels. We use the residual design for reducing the negative effects caused by wrong selection: $f_k' = f_k + f_k \otimes \hat{\xi}_k$, where $\otimes$ denotes the pixel-wise multiplication. f_k' is then fed into the decoder followed by the prediction head to generate the segmentation map. As the initially injected site embeddings ξ_k are mutually independent and different among local clients, they can generate different augmented versions to calibrate the feature representation learning to adapt to their own data distributions and not affect others.

Site-Contrast Regularization. To prompt the inter-site inconsistency in the current feature-level calibration, we present the site-contrast regularization to encourage a larger distance between different site embeddings. Taking the k-th site's regularization as an example, we sequentially couple f_k with each site embedding in $\{\xi_i\}_{i=1}^K$, and feed them into the generator $\mathcal{F}_{cs}$ one by one to obtain a set of augmented version $\{\hat{\xi}_i\}_{i=1}^K$, which are used for channel selection. It is noteworthy that the site embeddings from other sites are one-hot vectors so that the calculation requires no extra transmissions and the privacy protection

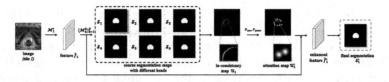

Fig. 3. Illustration of head calibration. It starts with calculating an in-consistency map, then encourages the map to concentrate on ambiguous boundaries, and finally utilizes a spatial attending mechanism to empower representations.

is guaranteed. We **maximize** distance between k-th augmented site embedding $\hat{\xi}_k$ and others as:

$$\mathcal{L}_{con} = -\frac{1}{K-1} \sum\nolimits_{i=1}^{K} |\hat{\xi}_k - StopGradient(\hat{\xi}_i)|, \text{ s.t. } i \neq k. \tag{2}$$

Note that we stop the gradient when augmenting the site embeddings designed for other sites. To this end, the inter-site feature learning can be facilitated towards different directions by pushing apart the site embeddings.

3.3   Disagreement-Aware Head Calibration

Previous studies share the base body with the global server while storing the prediction head locally. The personalized head is verified to be beneficial for the performance improvement of each site. In fact, they can be wisely utilized to estimate the inconsistency in prediction level across different sites, and these disagreement regions generally imply the most ambiguous areas that demand more concentration in model training. For example, the ambiguous boundary of anatomy in Fig. 3. In this regard, we propose to impose disagreement-aware calibration to incorporate the knowledge of prediction-level inter-site inconsistency, which can guide the model optimization focusing on these challenging regions.

We first extract the inter-site prediction inconsistencies. Considering that the prediction head part $\mathcal{M}^h$ is a simple full-connection layer with few parameters, we collect all sites' heads in each local site, that are $\{\mathcal{M}_i^h\}_{i=1}^{K}$. For the k-th site, we input the feature $\hat{f}_k$ extracted from its base body, into these prediction heads, and result in a set of segmentation maps $\{\mathcal{S}_i\}_{i=1}^{K}$, where each $\mathcal{S}_k \in \mathbb{R}^{N \times H \times W}$ and N is the number of classes (i.e., one for prostate segmentation and two for optic disc/cup segmentation). Then we construct the disagreement-aware calibration map $\mathcal{U}_k$ by calculating the standard deviation along each class channel:

$$\mathcal{U}_k^c = \sqrt{\frac{1}{N-1} \sum\nolimits_{i=1}^{K} (\mathcal{S}_k^c - \mathcal{S}_i^c)^2}, \tag{3}$$

where c denotes the class channel. The calibration map keeps the same size as the segmentation map and the pixel value can indicate the disagreement between the other sites and the current local site. The larger value suggests more difference that desires more attention in model optimization.

We do not utilize the map directly, instead, we further emphasize the most disagreement regions which can better benefit the model training (see experiments in Sect. 4.4). To do this, we first utilize the Non-Maximum Suppression (NMS) operator $\mathcal{F}_{\mathrm{nms}}$ to identify such regions. Given each element u_i in $\mathcal{U}_i$, it is only kept when its value is the largest in the surrounding $\delta \times \delta$ values, otherwise, the value is set as 0, where δ is set as 11 by default, We then employ a Gaussian filter $\mathcal{F}_{\mathrm{Gauss}}$ to enlarge the attention area, which is also beneficial for stabilizing the training process [13]. The updated calibration map with the same size as the original one is obtained. We finally perform a pixel-wise multiplication between the updated calibration map and the representation feature $\hat{f}_k$, enhanced by a residual design, to incorporate the prediction-level inter-site inconsistency knowledge into the model training: $\hat{f}_i^* = \mathcal{F}_{\mathrm{Gauss}}(\mathcal{F}_{\mathrm{nms}}(\mathcal{U}_i)) * \hat{f}_i + \hat{f}_i$. The refined feature is fed into another full-connection layer with Sigmoid activation to predict the segmentation map $\mathcal{S}_k^*$.

3.4   Overall Objective in Local Training

Our model predicts two segmentation maps, i.e., the coarse map $\mathcal{S}_k$ and calibrated map $\mathcal{S}_k^*$ in each local site k. We utilize Dice loss to minimize their difference between the ground-truth segmentation map $\tilde{\mathcal{S}}_k$, as $\mathcal{L}_{coarse} = 1 - 2 * \frac{|\mathcal{S}_k * \tilde{\mathcal{S}}_k|}{|\mathcal{S}_k| + |\tilde{\mathcal{S}}_k|}$ and $\mathcal{L}_{calib} = 1 - 2 * \frac{|\mathcal{S}_k^* * \tilde{\mathcal{S}}_k|}{|\mathcal{S}_k^*| + |\tilde{\mathcal{S}}_k|}$. Apart from the segmentation loss, the site-contrast regularization enforces our model to yield different site embeddings. To this end, the overall joint loss for each local site is defined as: $\mathcal{L}_{joint} = \mathcal{L}_{coarse} + \mathcal{L}_{calib} + \lambda \mathcal{L}_{con}$, where λ is used to balance the regularization and segmentation. As too large regularization leads to meaningless selection maps, we set it to 0.1 empirically.

4   Experiments

4.1   Datasets and Evaluation Metrics

Datasets: Extensive experiments are conducted to verify the effectiveness of our proposed framework on various medical modalities, including the prostate segmentation from T2-weighted MR images, the polyp segmentation from endoscopic images, and the optic disc/cup segmentation from retinal fundus images.

- Prostate MR (**PMR**) images are collected and labeled from six different public data sources for prostate segmentation [22]. All of them have been resampled to the same spacing and center-cropped with the size of 384×384. We follow the site division [21] to divide them into six sites, each of which contains $\{261, 384, 158, 468, 421, 175\}$ slices as well as the labels.
- Endoscopic polyp (**EndoPolyp**) images are collected and labeled from four different centers [3,4,12,30] for polyp segmentation. All the images and annotations are resized to 384×384 following the general setting. We follow the latest work [5] to divide the sites into four parts, each of which contains $\{1000, 380, 196, 612\}$ images and labels.

- Retinal fundus (**RIF**) images are collected and labeled from four different clinical centers for optic disc and cup segmentation [2, 25, 32]. We pre-process the data following general setting [21], where a 800×800 disc region in each image is center-cropped uniformly and then resized to 384×384. We follow the site division [21] to split them into four sites, each of which contains $\{101, 159, 400, 400\}$ images as well as the labels.

We employ the standard $80\% - 20\%$ train-test split widely used in medical vision field for PMR and RIF. The train-test split protocol is slightly different in EndoPolyp where we follow the standard split in the latest work for polyp segmentation [5].

Metrics: We quantitatively evaluate each local site's optimized model on its test data by two commonly-used metrics, including a region-based metric, IoU, and a boundary-based metric, ASSD. The larger IoU and smaller ASSD represent the better segmentation results. The averaged scores of all local sites are used for the eventual assessment.

4.2 Implementation Details

In the federated learning process, all sites adopt the same hyper-parameters. δ in the NMS operator and Gauss filter size are set to 11, and λ is set to 0.1, empirically. The Adam optimizer with an initial learning rate of 0.0001 is used to optimize the parameters and the batch size is set as six in all experiments. Totally, we train the network with 200 rounds as the global model has converged stably and in each federated round, each local site's network is trained with one epoch. The whole training process is achieved on the PyTorch platform using one NVIDIA Titan X GPU.

4.3 Comparison with State-of-the-Arts

Experimental Setting. We compare our methods to several federated frameworks including the conventional federation, FedAVG [24], and recent state-of-the-art personalized federation methods, i.e., FedAVG with fine-tuning (FT) [36], PRR-FL [6], FedBN [20], and FedRep [7]. For implementation, as these methods are originally designed for the image classification task, we try our best to keep their design principle and adapt them to our image segmentation task. Specifically, we personalize all model parameters in FT; the high-frequency components of convolutional layer parameters in PRR-FL; all the BN layers in FedBN; and the final full-connection layer in FedRep. We also compare with the baseline setting (Local Train) where each local model is trained using its own data.

Quantitative Comparison. Table 1 presents the quantitative results of the PMR dataset. It could be seen that with participating in the federated learning paradigm, the IoU score of Site F largely increases. The underlying reason is due to the patient distribution variance, some institutions like Site F have little data to train a powerful deep model if only using their own data. Thanks to

Table 1. Quantitative results on PMR dataset. "FT" means the FedAVG with fine-tuning and * denotes the personalized federation.

Sites	IoU ↑							ASSD ↓						
	A	B	C	D	E	F	Avg.	A	B	C	D	E	F	Avg.
Local Train	77.01	74.15	77.80	76.73	79.67	45.39	71.79	0.60	0.93	0.53	0.84	0.86	12.40	2.69
FedAVG [24]	79.74	80.89	84.91	82.59	83.69	73.27	80.85	0.47	0.52	0.32	0.59	0.36	2.02	0.71
FT* [36]	81.66	81.51	83.04	80.93	82.09	72.76	80.33	0.41	0.59	0.36	0.68	0.39	1.00	0.57
PRR-FL* [6]	75.10	68.67	79.67	79.71	69.99	51.05	70.70	0.79	1.60	0.46	0.79	1.34	12.69	2.95
FedBN* [20]	78.91	52.30	77.15	61.75	77.58	64.14	68.64	0.54	19.95	0.49	13.80	0.60	1.67	6.17
FedRep* [7]	81.09	81.41	84.70	83.46	82.31	73.81	81.13	0.41	0.49	0.32	0.58	0.39	**0.64**	0.47
LC-Fed (Ours)	**85.91**	**82.27**	**86.28**	**85.31**	**86.08**	**79.47**	**84.22**	**0.35**	**0.48**	**0.25**	**0.49**	**0.32**	0.75	**0.44**

Table 2. Quantitative results on EndoPolyp dataset. "FT" means the FedAVG with fine-tuning and * denotes the personalized federation.

Sites	IoU ↑					ASSD ↓				
	A	B	C	D	Avg.	A	B	C	D	Avg.
Local Train	48.27	55.26	38.37	62.74	51.16	27.89	21.14	36.66	22.62	27.08
FedAVG [24]	64.56	86.76	61.28	65.93	69.63	18.12	2.85	15.33	17.69	13.50
FT* [36]	65.95	87.45	60.63	69.04	70.77	17.43	2.62	16.42	13.65	12.53
PRR-FL* [6]	15.29	71.69	43.37	73.39	50.93	116.87	13.18	31.14	13.15	43.58
FedBN* [20]	51.76	78.23	31.21	60.55	55.44	30.59	15.16	105.40	28.41	44.89
FedRep* [7]	67.23	**88.94**	61.17	69.56	71.73	16.36	**2.11**	18.69	16.77	13.48
LC-Fed (Ours)	**69.21**	88.51	**68.10**	**76.68**	**75.63**	**15.59**	2.64	**11.60**	**12.00**	**10.46**

the federation, these institutions obtain a great opportunity to train an employable model by multi-site data collaboration under privacy protection. We can also see that PRR-FL and FedBN have the interior performance to the basic version (FedAVG), behind which the possible reason is the training collapse. Straightforward modifying the parameters of convolution or normalization in the personalized part will cause mis-matching of the current feature distribution and desired distribution of convolutional layers. In comparison, exploring shared representation and personalizing the prediction layers (FedRep) are slightly useful for the local accuracy improvement. By investigating the in-consistencies at feature- and prediction levels, our method consistently achieves superior performance over FedRep on all metrics, especially 3.1% increase on averaged IoU.

Results on EndoPolyp further support the advancement of our method. Segmentation on this dataset is more challenging because images in each local site only cover a few patients and present limited variance. Federated learning brings great benefits on this dataset, by leveraging the diverse data from other sites to enhance model learning. Excitingly, our personalized LC-Fed further attains large result improvement, surpassing FedRep over around 4% averaged IoU.

As for the RIF dataset, FedAVG shows a close performance compared with "Local Train". The reason is that in the RIF dataset, each local site's data is enough to train a satisfactory model. Vanilla federated learning provides limited

Table 3. Quantitative results on RIF dataset. "FT" means the FedAVG with fine-tuning and * denotes the personalized federation.

Sites	IoU ↑					ASSD ↓				
	A	B	C	D	Avg.	A	B	C	D	Avg.
Local Train	82.80	78.55	84.80	85.58	82.93	5.88	5.12	3.72	2.76	4.37
FedAVG [24]	84.81	77.88	83.91	84.51	82.77	5.19	5.68	3.99	3.00	4.46
FT* [36]	85.84	80.21	84.58	85.20	83.96	4.62	4.56	3.82	2.85	3.96
PRR-FL* [6]	81.24	78.49	83.75	83.19	81.67	7.57	5.09	4.10	3.34	5.02
FedBN* [20]	84.70	78.01	85.01	85.13	83.21	5.05	5.32	3.65	2.84	4.22
FedRep* [7]	85.33	79.81	83.95	83.53	83.15	4.84	4.93	3.95	3.14	4.21
LC-Fed (Ours)	**86.33**	**81.91**	**85.15**	**86.81**	**85.05**	**4.54**	**4.29**	**3.62**	**2.51**	**3.74**

Table 4. Ablation study about two components, PCS and HC. We report the averaged IoU and ASSD of three public datasets in this table. The first row without any components denotes the result of FedRep.

PCS	HC	PMR		EndoPolyp		RIF	
		IoU ↑	ASSD ↓	IoU ↑	ASSD ↓	IoU ↑	ASSD ↓
		81.13	0.47	72.56	11.40	83.15	3.88
✓		82.97	0.44	73.57	11.23	83.47	4.23
	✓	81.65	0.46	72.21	13.10	84.10	3.94
✓	✓	**84.22**	**0.44**	**75.63**	**10.46**	**85.05**	**3.74**

assistance. Notably, our method still consistently outperforms FedRep across all the metrics on this dataset. It demonstrates that, even in the situation that most local sites can provide enough data to train their employable models ($IoU \geq 80\%$), our LC-Fed can still yield great efficacy on personalized federation by considering the inter-site in-consistency.

Visual Comparison. Figure 4 visually compares the segmentation results on three datasets produced by our method and other personalized methods. Apparently, without any federated learning process (LT), the target is hard to be determined in challenging cases (EndoPolyp). Using federation (FT) can boost the segmentation in most cases while it fails on some samples. The results of PRR-FL and FedBN show huge fluctuation, demonstrating that personalization on the normalization layers and high-frequency convolutional parameters is not stable. FedRep yields stable and better performance while it sometimes includes the negatives and the determination of boundaries is not precise. In contrast, our method consistently produces the best segmentation masks.

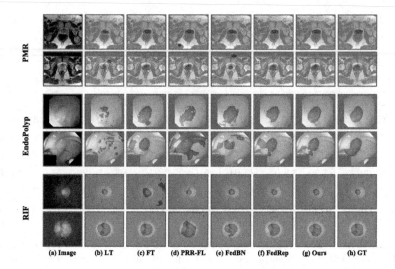

Fig. 4. Visualized comparison of the personalized methods on three datasets. From each dataset, we randomly select two samples from different sites to form the visualization. (a) Input images from two sites on each dataset; (b–g) Segmentation results by model trained with "Local Train" (LT), FedAVG with fine-tuning (FT) [24], PRR-FL [6], FedBN [20], FedRep [7], and our method LC-Fed; (h) Ground truths (denoted as 'GT');

4.4 Analytical Ablation Studies

Contribution of Key Components. To prove that the feature- and prediction-level personalization are both useful to improve the local accuracy, we perform an ablation study on all datasets and present the results in Table 4. The first row denotes our baseline, FedRep [7]. Comparing it to the second row, we can see that when personalizing the feature representation with our PCS module, the IoU score gains improvement of $1.84\%, 1.01\%, 0.32\%$ on the three datasets. Shown in the third row, only using the HC module can achieve better results on PMR and RIF datasets. It is noteworthy that the improvement of using the HC module is smaller than that of PCS, since the segmentation maps are relatively similar without feature calibration, lacking the ability to measure prediction-level in-consistency. Furthermore, results in the last row from LC-Fed, largely outperform others, demonstrating the complementary advantage of both modules. Thanks to the feature-level calibration, each site's prediction head adapts to its own feature space so that the HC module can measure prediction-level in-consistency better and the disagreement map contributes to the performance increase.

Contrastive Site Embedding. Previous experiments have verified that the contrastive site embedding is able to strengthen the local accuracy. To further prove that the performance improvements come from the contrastive comparison instead of extra computation, we conduct the experiment where site embeddings of all local clients are initialized as the same ($\{\xi_i = [1, 1, 1...1]\}_{i=1}^{K}$) and the site-

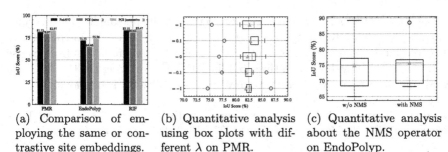

(a) Comparison of employing the same or contrastive site embeddings.

(b) Quantitative analysis using box plots with different λ on PMR.

(c) Quantitative analysis about the NMS operator on EndoPolyp.

Fig. 5. Detailed analysis about the PCS module (a–b) and the HC module (c). The triangles denote the average scores.

contrast regularization is removed. As shown in Fig. 5a, the performance unexpectedly drops significantly on all datasets compared with the baseline. While using contrastive ξ for each site and adding the site-contrast regularization, our method outperforms the baseline obviously. It indicates that our PCS module improves the local accuracy by exploring inter-site contrastive features, rather than the extra computation.

Site-Contrast Regularization Factor. We further investigate the influence of the hyper-parameter λ, which is a key factor in the PCS module by controlling the regularization weight in the overall loss. We vary different $\lambda \in \{-1, -0.1, 0, 0.1, 1\}$ and present results on the PMR dataset in Fig. 5b. It shows that the site-contrast regularization can help the module produce more accurate segmentation when comparing $\lambda = \{0\}$ and $\lambda = \{0.1\}$. In addition, when using opposite regularization ($\lambda = \{-1, -0.1\}$) to pull site embeddings over different sites to be more similar, performances slightly drop as our expectation. These results demonstrate that repelling site embeddings by our site-contrast regularization is desired and can benefit the feature-level calibration.

NMS Operator. In the HC module, the NMS operator is utilized to identify the most disagreement regions. Figure 5c shows the evaluation results of (not) using the NMS operator on the EndoPolyp dataset. It is seen that the NMS boosts the IoU score from 74.92% into 75.63%, indicating that using the NMS operator to filter regions can benefit the model learning.

5 Conclusion

In this paper, we propose to personalize the federated medical image segmentation via unifying the feature- and prediction-level personalization by local calibration. The learning paradigm, LC-Fed, is able to calibrate the feature representation and prediction during local training through the Personalized Channel Selection (PCS) module and the Head Calibration (HC) module. The PCS module aims to calculate contrastive site embedding for each unique local site and couple it with channel selection operation to pursue the personalized representation modeling. The HC module is designed to explore the inter-site in-consistency at prediction-level as a disagreement map to calibrate the prediction from coarse to fine. LC-Fed is evaluated on three public datasets, achieving the best IoU and ASSD on all test sets, compared to previous personalized FL methods.

Acknowledgement. This work was supported by the Ministry of Science and Technology of the People's Republic of China (2021ZD0201900)(2021ZD0201903).

References

1. Andreux, M., du Terrail, J.O., Beguier, C., Tramel, E.W.: Siloed federated learning for multi-centric histopathology datasets. In: Albarqouni, S., et al. (eds.) DART/DCL -2020. LNCS, vol. 12444, pp. 129–139. Springer, Cham (2020). https://doi.org/10.1007/978-3-030-60548-3_13
2. Batista, F.J.F., Diaz-Aleman, T., Sigut, J., Alayon, S., Arnay, R., Angel-Pereira, D.: Rim-one dl: A unified retinal image database for assessing glaucoma using deep learning. Image Anal. Stereology **39**(3), 161–167 (2020). https://doi.org/10.5566/ias.2346, https://www.ias-iss.org/ojs/IAS/article/view/2346
3. Bernal, J., Sánchez, F.J., Fernández-Esparrach, G., Gil, D., Rodríguez, C., Vilariño, F.: WM-DOVA maps for accurate polyp highlighting in colonoscopy: validation vs. saliency maps from physicians. Comput. Med. Imaging Graph. **43**, 99–111 (2015)
4. Bernal, J., Sánchez, J., Vilarino, F.: Towards automatic polyp detection with a polyp appearance model. Pattern Recogn. **45**(9), 3166–3182 (2012)
5. Bo, D., Wenhai, W., Deng-Ping, F., Jinpeng, L., Huazhu, F., Ling, S.: Polyp-pvt: polyp segmentation with pyramidvision transformers (2021)
6. Chen, Z., Zhu, M., Yang, C., Yuan, Y.: Personalized retrogress-resilient framework for real-world medical federated learning. In: de Bruijne, M., et al. (eds.) MICCAI 2021. LNCS, vol. 12903, pp. 347–356. Springer, Cham (2021). https://doi.org/10.1007/978-3-030-87199-4_33
7. Collins, L., Hassani, H., Mokhtari, A., Shakkottai, S.: Exploiting shared representations for personalized federated learning. arXiv preprint. arXiv:2102.07078 (2021)
8. Dinh, C.T., Vu, T.T., Tran, N.H., Dao, M.N., Zhang, H.: Fedu: a unified framework for federated multi-task learning with laplacian regularization. arXiv preprint. arXiv:2102.07148 (2021)
9. Dong, B., Wang, W., Fan, D.P., Li, J., Fu, H., Shao, L.: Polyp-pvt: polyp segmentation with pyramid vision transformers. arXiv preprint. arXiv:2108.06932 (2021)
10. Fallah, A., Mokhtari, A., Ozdaglar, A.: Personalized federated learning with theoretical guarantees: a model-agnostic meta-learning approach. In: Advances in Neural Information Processing Systems vol. 33, pp. 3557–3568 (2020)
11. Fan, D.P., Ji, G.P., Zhou, T., Chen, G., Fu, H., Shen, J., Shao, L.: Pranet: Parallel reverse attention network for polyp segmentation. In: International conference on medical image computing and computer-assisted intervention. pp. 263–273. Springer (2020)
12. Jha, D., Smedsrud, P.H., Riegler, M.A., Halvorsen, P., de Lange, T., Johansen, D., Johansen, H.D.: Kvasir-seg: A segmented polyp dataset. In: International Conference on Multimedia Modeling. pp. 451–462. Springer (2020)

13. Ji, W., Yu, S., Wu, J., Ma, K., Bian, C., Bi, Q., Li, J., Liu, H., Cheng, L., Zheng, Y.: Learning calibrated medical image segmentation via multi-rater agreement modeling. In: Proceedings of the IEEE/CVF Conference on Computer Vision and Pattern Recognition (CVPR). pp. 12341–12351 (June 2021)
14. Kairouz, P., McMahan, H.B., Avent, B., Bellet, A., Bennis, M., Bhagoji, A.N., Bonawitz, K., Charles, Z., Cormode, G., Cummings, R., et al.: Advances and open problems in federated learning. arXiv preprint arXiv:1912.04977 (2019)
15. Kaissis, G.A., Makowski, M.R., Rückert, D., Braren, R.F.: Secure, privacy-preserving and federated machine learning in medical imaging. Nature Machine Intelligence 2(6), 305–311 (2020)
16. Konečnỳ, J., McMahan, H.B., Yu, F.X., Richtárik, P., Suresh, A.T., Bacon, D.: Federated learning: Strategies for improving communication efficiency. arXiv preprint arXiv:1610.05492 (2016)
17. Kulkarni, V., Kulkarni, M., Pant, A.: Survey of personalization techniques for federated learning. In: 2020 Fourth World Conference on Smart Trends in Systems, Security and Sustainability (WorldS4). pp. 794–797. IEEE (2020)
18. Li, D., Kar, A., Ravikumar, N., Frangi, A.F., Fidler, S.: Federated simulation for medical imaging. In: International Conference on Medical Image Computing and Computer-Assisted Intervention. pp. 159–168. Springer (2020)
19. Li, W., Milletarì, F., Xu, D., Rieke, N., Hancox, J., Zhu, W., Baust, M., Cheng, Y., Ourselin, S., Cardoso, M.J., et al.: Privacy-preserving federated brain tumour segmentation. In: International workshop on machine learning in medical imaging. pp. 133–141. Springer (2019)
20. Li, X., Jiang, M., Zhang, X., Kamp, M., Dou, Q.: Fedbn: Federated learning on non-iid features via local batch normalization. In: International Conference on Learning Representations (2021), https://openreview.net/pdf?id=6YEQUn0QICG
21. Liu, Q., Chen, C., Qin, J., Dou, Q., Heng, P.A.: Feddg: federated domain generalization on medical image segmentation via episodic learning in continuous frequency space. In: Proceedings of the IEEE/CVF Conference on Computer Vision and Pattern Recognition, pp. 1013–1023 (2021)
22. Liu, Q., Dou, Q., Yu, L., Heng, P.A.: MS-Net: Multi-site network for improving prostate segmentation with heterogeneous MRI data. IEEE Trans. Med. Imaging 39(9), 2713–2724 (2020)
23. Marfoq, O., Neglia, G., Bellet, A., Kameni, L., Vidal, R.: Federated multi-task learning under a mixture of distributions. In: Advances in Neural Information Processing Systems, vol. 34 (2021)
24. McMahan, B., Moore, E., Ramage, D., Hampson, S., y Arcas, B.A.: Communication-efficient learning of deep networks from decentralized data. In: Artificial Intelligence and Statistics, pp. 1273–1282. PMLR (2017)
25. Orlando, J.I., et al.: Refuge challenge: a unified framework for evaluating automated methods for glaucoma assessment from fundus photographs. Med. Image Anal. 59, 101570 (2020)
26. Reisizadeh, A., Mokhtari, A., Hassani, H., Jadbabaie, A., Pedarsani, R.: Fedpaq: a communication-efficient federated learning method with periodic averaging and quantization. In: International Conference on Artificial Intelligence and Statistics, pp. 2021–2031. PMLR (2020)
27. Rieke, N., et al.: The future of digital health with federated learning. NPJ Digit. Med. 3(1), 1–7 (2020)
28. Sarhan, A., et al.: Utilizing transfer learning and a customized loss function for optic disc segmentation from retinal images. In: Proceedings of the Asian Conference on Computer Vision (2020)

29. Sheller, M.J., Reina, G.A., Edwards, B., Martin, J., Bakas, S.: Multi-institutional deep learning modeling without sharing patient data: a feasibility study on brain tumor segmentation. In: Crimi, A., Bakas, S., Kuijf, H., Keyvan, F., Reyes, M., van Walsum, T. (eds.) BrainLes 2018. LNCS, vol. 11383, pp. 92–104. Springer, Cham (2019). https://doi.org/10.1007/978-3-030-11723-8_9

30. Silva, J., Histace, A., Romain, O., Dray, X., Granado, B.: Toward embedded detection of polyps in WCE images for early diagnosis of colorectal cancer. Int. J. Comput. Assist. Radiol. Surg. **9**(2), 283–293 (2013). https://doi.org/10.1007/s11548-013-0926-3

31. Silva, S., Gutman, B.A., Romero, E., Thompson, P.M., Altmann, A., Lorenzi, M.: Federated learning in distributed medical databases: meta-analysis of large-scale subcortical brain data. In: 2019 IEEE 16th International Symposium on Biomedical Imaging (ISBI 2019), pp. 270–274. IEEE (2019)

32. Sivaswamy, J., Krishnadas, S., Chakravarty, A., Joshi, G., Tabish, A.S., et al.: A comprehensive retinal image dataset for the assessment of glaucoma from the optic nerve head analysis. JSM Biomed. Imaging Data Pap. **2**(1), 1004 (2015)

33. Tan, A.Z., Yu, H., Cui, L., Yang, Q.: Towards personalized federated learning. IEEE Trans. Neural Networks Learn. Syst. (2022)

34. Thakur, N., Juneja, M.: Optic disc and optic cup segmentation from retinal images using hybrid approach. Expert Syst. Appl. **127**, 308–322 (2019)

35. Tian, Z., Liu, L., Zhang, Z., Fei, B.: Psnet: prostate segmentation on MRI based on a convolutional neural network. J. Med. Imaging **5**(2), 021208 (2018)

36. Wang, K., Mathews, R., Kiddon, C., Eichner, H., Beaufays, F., Ramage, D.: Federated evaluation of on-device personalization. arXiv preprint. arXiv:1910.10252 (2019)

37. Yu, T., Bagdasaryan, E., Shmatikov, V.: Salvaging federated learning by local adaptation. arXiv preprint. arXiv:2002.04758 (2020)

38. Zavala-Romero, O., et al.: Segmentation of prostate and prostate zones using deep learning. Strahlenther. Onkol. **196**(10), 932–942 (2020). https://doi.org/10.1007/s00066-020-01607-x

39. Zhang, L., Lei, X., Shi, Y., Huang, H., Chen, C.: Federated learning with domain generalization. arXiv preprint. arXiv:2111.10487 (2021)

40. Zhang, Q.L., Yang, Y.B.: Sa-net: shuffle attention for deep convolutional neural networks. In: ICASSP 2021–2021 IEEE International Conference on Acoustics, Speech and Signal Processing (ICASSP), pp. 2235–2239. IEEE (2021)

41. Zhu, W., Kairouz, P., McMahan, B., Sun, H., Li, W.: Federated heavy hitters discovery with differential privacy. In: International Conference on Artificial Intelligence and Statistics, pp. 3837–3847. PMLR (2020)

One-Shot Medical Landmark Localization by Edge-Guided Transform and Noisy Landmark Refinement

Zihao Yin[1], Ping Gong[2], Chunyu Wang[3], Yizhou Yu[4], and Yizhou Wang[5,6](✉)

[1] Center for Data Science, Peking University, Beijing, China
silvermouse@pku.edu.cn
[2] Deepwise AI Lab, Beijing, China
gongping@deepwise.com
[3] Microsoft Research Asia, Beijing, China
chnuwa@microsoft.com
[4] The University of Hong Kong, Pok Fu Lam, Hong Kong
yizhouy@acm.org
[5] Center on Frontiers of Computing Studies, School of Computer Science,
Peking University, Beijing, China
yizhou.wang@pku.edu.cn
[6] Institute for Artificial Intelligence, Peking University, Beijing, China

Abstract. As an important upstream task for many medical applications, supervised landmark localization still requires non-negligible annotation costs to achieve desirable performance. Besides, due to cumbersome collection procedures, the limited size of medical landmark datasets impacts the effectiveness of large-scale self-supervised pre-training methods. To address these challenges, we propose a two-stage framework for one-shot medical landmark localization, which first infers landmarks by unsupervised registration from the labeled exemplar to unlabeled targets, and then utilizes these noisy pseudo labels to train robust detectors. To handle the significant structure variations, we learn an end-to-end cascade of global alignment and local deformations, under the guidance of novel loss functions which incorporate edge information. In stage II, we explore self-consistency for selecting reliable pseudo labels and cross-consistency for semi-supervised learning. Our method achieves state-of-the-art performances on public datasets of different body parts, which demonstrates its general applicability. Code is available at https://github.com/GoldExcalibur/EdgeTrans4Mark.

Keywords: Medical landmark localization · One-shot learning

1 Introduction

Landmark localization is an essential step for many medical image applications, such as dental radiography [1,2], bone age assessment [3,4], vertebra labeling [5] and per-operative measurements [6]. Although fully supervised methods [7–9]

Supplementary Information The online version contains supplementary material available at https://doi.org/10.1007/978-3-031-19803-8_28.

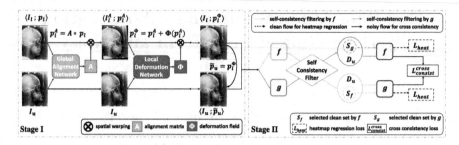

Fig. 1. Overview of the proposed framework. In stage I, unsupervised registration is learned through an end-to-end cascade of global alignment and subsequent local deformations, which aims to predict pseudo landmarks $\tilde{p}_u$ by registering the labeled exemplar I_l to unlabeled targets I_u. Inferred noisy landmarks are further refined in stage II, where two robust landmark detectors f, g are co-trained, by utilizing both self-consistency for sample selection and cross-consistency for semi-supervised learning

achieve the state-of-the-art results, the required manual annotations take considerable cost and time. In contrast, given few exemplars and proper instructions, experts are ready to generalize these landmark concepts to unseen targets and annotate them accurately. This motivates us to explore the challenging task of one-shot medical landmark localization.

Besides the scarce supervision, significant differences in spatial structures between images for landmark datasets also increase the difficulty of this task. While they can be quite different in scale, orientation, or intensity due to patient positioning or imaging quality as in hand radiography [3], there are also substantial variations in local structures, such as the front teeth in dental radiography [1]. Furthermore, because of cumbersome acquisition procedures, medical landmark datasets are too expensive to collect in large numbers. Thus, the amount of unlabeled data available is often limited.

Considering these challenges, landmark localization in the low data regime is in urgent need and explored by [10–12]. 3FabRec [10] is a method for few-shot face alignment. They first train an autoencoder for face reconstruction and then retask the decoder to heatmap prediction through fine-tuning on labeled sets. However, when having access to only one exemplar and hundreds of data as in our work, qualities of reconstructed images are too poor to perform landmark localization. Motivated by the recent success of contrastive learning, CC2D [11] proposes to detect target landmarks by first solving a self-supervised patch matching task and uses these pseudo labels to retrain new detectors. However, their method overlooks the global spatial relationships of landmarks and is prone to yield inaccurate predictions once over fitting to the local appearance of specific instances. Conversely, DAG [8] employs graph convolution network (GCN) to capture topological constraints of landmarks. Few-shot DAG [12] extends DAG to the few-shot (e.g., five-shot) setting. They report impressive results on several datasets but fail to converge under the extreme one-shot setting.

In order to fully exploit the exemplar and available data, we propose to propagate the landmarks from exemplar to unlabeled images through registration, which not only considers global anatomical constraints, but also performs precise matching of local structures. In fact, the dense correspondence between instances learned by registration can be directly leveraged by landmark localization. Besides, registration can be learned efficiently without the need of a large amount of data to produce reasonable results. As shown in Fig. 1, our novel two-stage framework first learns unsupervised registration from the labeled exemplar to unlabeled targets for inferring pseudo landmarks, and then trains robust landmark detectors by exploiting consistency between clean annotations and noisy pseudo labels. For better adaptation to landmark localization, we make several non-trivial contributions to solve the following challenges.

First, there might be a chicken-and-egg issue if you want to infer landmarks for unseen targets through registration, since registration itself usually requires detected landmarks, either for alignment in pre-processing steps [13], or to guide the learning process as extra structural information [14]. To avoid this dilemma, we decompose the total spatial transform into an end-to-end cascade of global alignment and local deformations. To facilitate the registration learning, powerful attention blocks [15] are employed, including self-attention for capturing long-range dependencies and cross-attention for fusing multi-resolution features.

Second, classical reconstruction terms for registration, which mainly consider image similarity based on the distribution of pixel values, are insufficient to constrain the structural consistency of landmarks. Hence we propose novel loss functions that incorporate edge information and landmark locations. Specifically, our reconstruction term further involves the masked similarities of edge structures around interested landmarks. Besides, since different anatomical parts tend to have different displacements, it is beneficial to relax the smoothness constraints of deformation field around boundaries.

Last, under the interference of certain nuisances (e.g., background, abnormal appearance), deformation learned by the low-level registration task can not perfectly capture the high-level semantic correspondence of landmarks. Thus, an essential second stage is introduced to refine noisy predictions with large biases. We train robust landmark detectors, utilizing self-consistency between different views of the same model for sample selection and cross-consistency between different views of different models for semi-supervised learning.

We conduct experiments on public medical landmark datasets of different body parts, including head, hand and chest. Our method consistently outperforms other baselines with notable margins and further narrows the gap with the supervised upper bound. To summarize, our contributions are three-fold:

1. We propose an unsupervised training strategy for inferring pseudo landmarks through registration, which learns an end-to-end cascade of global alignment and local deformations, with the guidance of novel loss functions incorporating edge information.
2. We introduce an effective scheme for training robust landmark detectors with noisy labels, which utilizes self-consistency for selecting reliable pseudo labels and cross-consistency for semi-supervised learning.
3. We conduct experiments on public medical landmark datasets of different body parts. Results show our method stably advances the state-of-the-art for all three applications.

2   Related Work

We briefly review most related works, including one-shot, few-shot and semi-supervised methods for landmark localization, and medical image registration.

2.1   One-Shot and Few-Shot Landmark Localization

As mentioned, CC2D [11] is motivated by contrastive learning: features for the original patch and its randomly augmented counterparts at the same location are matched using cosine similarity. With the learned matching network and template patches, pseudo-labels are inferred for retraining a multi-task UNet [16] from scratch. Despite their promising results on the cephalometric dataset [1], CC2D overlooks valuable global structure constraints [8], making it difficult to handle multiple similar local structures, such as fingertips. Another interesting work, 3FabRec [10] achieves impressive performance for few-shot face alignment. They first train an adversarial autoencoder for unsupervised face reconstruction, then fine-tune with interleaved layers to the landmark detection task with few labels. 3FabRec demonstrates great benefits of dense pixel-level pre-training for landmark localization. However, for medical applications where the amount of data is orders of magnitude less, it is rather difficult to achieve satisfactory results through pre-training of image reconstruction.

2.2   Semi-supervised Landmark Localization

Recent advances can be divided into two streams: consistency-based approaches [17,18] and synthetic image based approaches [19,20]. The equivariant landmark transformation (ELT) constraint [17] is built on the intuition that, given a transformed image, the model should produce similarly transformed landmarks. Semantic Consistency [18] encourages learning similar features for landmarks with the same semantics across images. Synthetic image approaches focus on generating desired training data. StyleAlign [19] first disentangles face images to style and structure space, then transfers randomly sampled styles to images with known structures, greatly enriching training space.

2.3   Learning-Based Deformable Image Registration

Our work is closely related to learning-based image registration [13,14,21,22]. [14] proposes to utilize detected landmarks as extra structural information to guide the training of registration. VoxelMorph [13] proposes to use a convolutional neural network (CNN) g to learn the registration field Φ unsupervisedly, by optimizing the image similarity between the fixed and moving images, and the smoothness of Φ. [13] requires image pairs to be affinely aligned in the pre-processing step and then focus on the nonlinear correspondence. [13] can further be extended as in DataAug [23] for one-shot medical segmentation, by learning independent spatial and appearance transform for data augmentation.

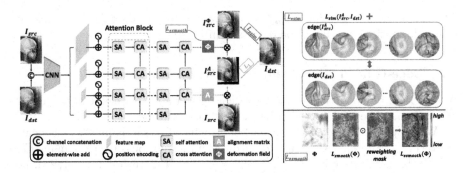

Fig. 2. The architecture of registration model consists of a CNN backbone and cascades of attention blocks. Red lines denote the flow for global alignment, while blue lines denote the flow for local deformation. Besides the image similarity, $\mathcal{L}_{esim}$ is introduced to further penalize local similarities of edge structures around inferred pseudo landmarks, masked by their gaussian heatmaps. $\mathcal{L}_{esmooth}$ relaxes the smoothness constraint around boundaries, to avoid mutual interference between different regions (e.g., anatomical parts, background & foreground) (Color figure online)

3 Method

Let I_l, I_u be two images defined over a 2-D spatial domain Ω. $I_l \in \mathbb{R}^{H \times W}$ is the labeled exemplar with N annotated landmarks $p_l = \{(x_l^j, y_l^j) | j = 1, \cdots, N\}$, and I_u is the unlabeled target. I_l and I_u share similar appearance distribution, and landmarks p_l are defined at locations with particular anatomical structures. Our goal is to learn a spatial transformation from I_l to I_u through registration, so that we can infer reliable landmarks for I_u based on p_l, according to the equivariant property of landmarks.

3.1 Reformulation of Classical Registration Framework

First, in order to adapt to the downstream landmark localization, we reformulate the classical framework for unsupervised registration as follows:

$$\hat{A}, \hat{\Phi} = \arg\min_{A,\phi} \mathcal{L}_{total}(I_{src}, I_{dst} \mid \tilde{p}_{src}), A = g_\theta(I_{src}, I_{dst}), \Phi = g_\theta(I_{src}^A, I_{dst}) \quad (1)$$

$$\mathcal{L}_{total} = \mathcal{L}_{global}(I_{src}^A, I_{dst}) + \mathcal{L}_{local}(I_{src}^\Phi, I_{dst} \mid \tilde{p}_{src}^\Phi) + \mathcal{L}_{esmooth}(\Phi \mid I_{src}^A) \quad (2)$$

$$I_{src}^A = A \otimes I_{src}, \ I_{src}^\Phi = \Phi \otimes I_{src}^A, \ \tilde{p}_{src}^A = A \circ \tilde{p}_{src}, \ \tilde{p}_{src}^\Phi = \tilde{p}_{src}^A + \Phi(\tilde{p}_{src}^A) \quad (3)$$

where we learn an end-to-end cascade of global affine alignment $A \in \mathbb{R}^{2 \times 3}$ and local deformation $\Phi \in \mathbb{R}^{H \times W \times 2}$. During training, $\langle I_{src}, I_{dst} \rangle$ is a pair of images randomly sampled from the mini-batch. For inference, I_{src} is fixed as the exemplar I_l and we set I_{dst} as the unlabeled target I_u to predict pseudo landmarks $\tilde{p}_u$. The local similarity $\mathcal{L}_{local}$ is conditioned on $\tilde{p}_{src}^\Phi$ (Eq. 3), where $\tilde{p}_{src}$ is an exponential moving average of e-th epoch prediction $\tilde{p}_{src}^e$ after certain epoch M:

$$\tilde{p}_{src} = \tau\tilde{p}_{src} + (1 - \tau)\tilde{p}_{src}^e, \ e \geq M \quad (4)$$

The smoothness constraint $\mathcal{L}_{esmooth}$ is extraly conditioned on I_{src}^{Φ}, to utilize its edge information, which will be discussed in Eq. 16.

3.2 Edge-Guided Global and Local Transform

As in Fig. 2, our registration model g_θ consists of a CNN backbone for feature extraction and several attention blocks for feature fusion.

We adopt the HRNet18 [24] as backbone, which takes a channel-wise concatenation of I_{src} and I_{dst} as input, and outputs four resolutions of feature maps $F_i \in \mathbb{R}^{C \times H_i \times W_i}$ with stride S_i ($H_i = \frac{H}{S_i}, W_i = \frac{W}{S_i}, S_i \in \{32, 16, 8, 4\}, i \in \{1, 2, 3, 4\}$). For each F_i, we use a 1×1 convolution to change its channel dimension into a unified value d_{model} and then reshape it to $\mathbb{R}^{d_{model} \times H_i W_i}$, since the attention blocks expect a sequence as input. Following [25,26], we adopt a concatenation of two 1D learned positional encodings as the recovered order information.

Because of the significant structural differences between I_{src} and I_{dst}, distance between their corresponding pixels could be large. To capture these long-range dependencies, we furnish our model with powerful transformer layers [15]:

$$\text{Attention}(Q, K, V) = \text{softmax}(\frac{QK^T}{\sqrt{d_k}})V \tag{5}$$

$$\text{MultiHead}(Q, K, V) = \text{Concat}(\text{H}_1, \cdots, \text{H}_h)W^O \tag{6}$$

$$\text{H}_i = \text{Attention}(QW_i^Q, KW_i^K, VW_i^V) \tag{7}$$

where Q, K, V are embeddings of the same feature map, projected into different spaces for the self-attention module (SA). It is also crucial to fully exploit features from multiple resolutions for registration learning. Thus, we further utilize the cross-attention module (CA) for cross-resolution feature fusion, where K, V are embeddings of the feature map from branch of lower-resolution than Q. For each layer of attention blocks, we stack both one SA module and one CA module following feature maps from each resolution, which progressively incorporates the information from lower resolutions to higher resolutions, and enables the model to gradually figure out the optimal transformation from I_{src} to I_{dst}.

Global Transform. Since high-level features are sufficient to capture global relationships, features of lower resolutions (i.e., F_1, F_2) are passed into transformer layers and we use the aggregated representation of the last output state for affine estimation. It is then passed to a two-layer MLP and tanh function to obtain $o \in \mathbb{R}^6$, each element of which denotes the relative changes in translation (t_x, t_y), scale (s_x, s_y), rotation α, and shear β:

$$o = \tanh(\text{MLP}(H)) \tag{8}$$

$$t_x = o_1, \quad s_x = 1 + o_3 * sf_x, \quad \alpha = o_5 * rot \tag{9}$$

$$t_y = o_2, \quad s_y = 1 + o_4 * sf_y, \quad \beta = o_6 * sh \tag{10}$$

where sf_x, sf_y, rot, sh are four hyper parameters controlling transformation intensities. Then the affine matrix $A \in \mathbb{R}^{2 \times 3}$ can be computed as follows:

$$\begin{pmatrix} s_x \cos \alpha & s_x(\cos \alpha \tan \beta + \sin \alpha) & t_x \\ -s_y \sin \alpha & s_y(-\sin \alpha \tan \beta + \cos \alpha) & t_y \end{pmatrix}$$

which is a composite of several basic transforms. Then I_{src}^A is obtained through differentiable bilinear interpolation based on the spatial transformer module [27].

Local Deformation Field. Based on the global transform A, features are again extracted for $\langle I_{src}^A, I_{dst} \rangle$. For a more precise pixel-level correspondence, we mainly utilize high-resolution features to predict a deformation field $\Phi \in \mathbb{R}^{H \times W \times 2}$. Since global transform already roughly aligns two images, the target pixel for a certain location of I_{src}^A is more likely to be within a local neighborhood in I_{dst}. Thus, for high-resolution features (i.e., F_3, F_4), we can reduce their spatial scale through reshaping them from $C \times H_i W_i$ to R^2 sequences (e.g., $R = 4$) with size $C \times \frac{H_i W_i}{R^2}$ and perform attention mechanism on each sequence.

The final hidden state from the highest-resolution branch is fed into a linear layer for regressing displacements $(\Delta x, \Delta y)$, which implies that $I_{src}^G(x +\Delta x, y + \Delta y)$ corresponds to $I_{dst}(x, y)$ $(x \in \{1, \cdots, h\}; y \in \{1, \cdots, w\})$. With the deformation field Φ, we further improve I_{src}^A to I_{src}^Φ through bilinear interpolation.

Loss and Training Strategy. For learning of the challenging unsupervised deformation, we apply the local deformation cascade iteratively for N_Φ times. Thus, the total loss is a weighted combination of one global similarity $\mathcal{L}_{global}$, local similarity $\mathcal{L}_{local}$ and regularization $\mathcal{L}_{reg}$ of Φ_i for each step.

$$\mathcal{L}_{stage_I} = \mathcal{L}_{global}(I_{src}^A, I_{dst}) + \lambda_1 \sum_{i=1}^{N_\Phi} [\mathcal{L}_{local}(I_{src}^{\Phi_i}, I_{dst}) + \mathcal{L}_{reg}(\Phi_i)] \tag{11}$$

$$\mathcal{L}_{reg}(\Phi_i) = \mathcal{L}_{smooth}(\Phi_i) + \lambda_2 \mathcal{L}_{inv}(\Phi_i) + \lambda_3 \mathcal{L}_{syn} \tag{12}$$

Our ultimate goal is to find the discrete semantic correspondence between landmarks, instead of image registration. Similarity terms during the deformation process should gradually weaken impacts of appearance and focus more on structural information. We simply use $\mathcal{L}_1$ for $\mathcal{L}_{global}$. While for $\mathcal{L}_{local}$, we propose to enhance the original image similarity with an additional masked similarity term between their edge maps as follows:

$$\mathcal{L}_{esim} = \mathcal{L}_{sim}(I_{src}^\Phi, I_{dst}) + \mathcal{L}_{sim}(\text{edge}(I_{src}^\Phi), \text{edge}(I_{dst})) \odot \text{Mask}(p_{src}^\Phi) \tag{13}$$

$$\text{Mask}(p) = \frac{1}{N} \sum_{i=1}^{N} \exp(-\frac{1}{2\sigma^2}||u - p_i||^2), \ p \in \mathbb{R}^{N \times 2}, \ \forall u \in \Omega \tag{14}$$

where edge$(\cdot)$ denotes the operator for edge detection (e.g., sobel) and Mask$(\cdot)$ generates the averaged gaussian heatmaps with fixed deviation σ, centered on landmarks p_{src}^Φ. $\mathcal{L}_{esim}$ considers the similarity between not only image pairs, but also their local edge maps around landmarks, which is beneficial to enforce the structural consistency of landmarks across images. We adopt the robust structural similarity (SSIM) [28] as $\mathcal{L}_{sim}$ in Eq. 13.

Besides, we observe that different anatomical parts tend to exhibit different displacements. Thus, the original smoothness constraint $\mathcal{L}_{smooth}$ (Eq. 15), which penalizes the approximated spatial gradients of Φ for all pixels, should be relaxed around the boundaries of these parts. We propose to re-weight $\mathcal{L}_{smooth}$ based on the magnitudes of detected edge vectors as in Eq. 16:

$$\mathcal{L}_{smooth}(\Phi) = ||\nabla\Phi(u)||^2, \ \forall u \in \Omega \tag{15}$$

$$\mathcal{L}_{esmooth}(\Phi|I_{src}^{\Phi}) = \mathcal{L}_{smooth}(\Phi) \odot \exp(-||\text{edge}(I_{src}^{\Phi})||^2/T) \tag{16}$$

where T is a hyper parameter to control the sharpness of distribution. In this way, weights for boundaries is lowered by their large magnitudes in edge maps and attenuates the mutual interference between different parts. As in [13], we also adopt $\mathcal{L}_{inv}$ to enforce the invertibility of Φ. For ease of early optimization, we introduce $\mathcal{L}_{syn}$, where we apply random perspective transform to I_{src} and use synthetic pairs with known correspondence to supervise the learning of Φ.

3.3   Stage II: Noisy Landmark Refinement

With the learned spatial correspondence from the exemplar (I_l, p_l) to I_u, we can infer pseudo landmarks $\tilde{p}_u$ for I_u. $h(\cdot)$ computes gaussian heatmaps with fixed standard deviation σ centered on landmark locations. Instead of simply train a new landmark detector with these pseudo-labels, as [11] did, we propose a robust learning scheme for noisy landmarks, coined as *Consistency Co-Teaching* (C2T).

As shown in Algorithm 1, C2T builds on the seminal co-teaching framework [29]. Two networks f and g are co-trained to select relatively clean samples S_f and S_g (line 5–6) for the other network (line 7–9), leveraging the small-loss assumption [29–31]. C2T's main novelties are two ingredients: self-consistency filtering $\mathcal{L}_{filter}$ (Eq. 17–19) and cross-consistency loss $\mathcal{L}_{con}^{cross}$ (Eq. 20), which not only stabilize training, but also boost performance.

$$\mathcal{L}_{heat}(f, x, h(\tilde{p}_x)) = ||f(x) - h(\tilde{p}_x)||_2 \tag{17}$$

$$\mathcal{L}_{con}^{self}(f, x) = ||f(T_h(x)) - T_{e \to h}(f(T_e(x)))||_2 \tag{18}$$

$$\mathcal{L}_{filter}(f, x, h) = \mathcal{L}_{heat}(f, x, h) + w\mathcal{L}_{con}^{self}(f, x) \tag{19}$$

As pointed out in [32], in later training epochs, two networks trained by co-teaching could harmfully converge to a consensus. To keep f and g healthily diverged, we introduce $\mathcal{L}_{con}^{self}$ (Eq. 18) into $\mathcal{L}_{filter}$. (T_e, T_h) is a pair of easy (weak augmentations) and hard (strong augmentations) views of the original images. Intuitively, if heatmaps predicted by f (g) for x are equivariant to different transformations [17], its pseudo label is more likely to be clean.

Algorithm 1. C2T: Consistency Co-Teaching

Input: $L : \{(I_l, H_l)\}, U : \{(I_u, \hat{H}_u)\}_{u=1}^{N_u}$
Parameter: f, g: landmark detectors; ϵ: filter rate
Output: f, g: landmark detectors

1: **Shuffle** L and U.
2: **for** $T = 1, \cdots, T_{max}$ **do**
3:     **Fetch** mini-batch D_l, D_u from L, U respectively.
4:     **Sample** random augmentations T_e, T_h and compute transform $T_{e \to h}$.
5:     $S_g = \underset{D' \geq \epsilon |D_u|}{\arg\min} \sum_{(x,h) \in D'} L_{filter}(g, x, h), D' \subset D_u$.
6:     $S_f = \underset{D' \geq \epsilon |D_u|}{\arg\min} \sum_{(x,h) \in D'} L_{filter}(f, x, h), D' \subset D_u$.
7:     $\mathcal{L}_f^{update} = \sum_{(x,h) \in D_l \cup S_g} \mathcal{L}_{heat}(f, x, h) + \sum_{(x,h) \in D_l \cup D_u} \mathcal{L}_{con}^{cross}(f, g, x)$.
8:     $\mathcal{L}_g^{update} = \sum_{(x,h) \in D_l \cup S_f} \mathcal{L}_{heat}(g, x, h) + \sum_{(x,h) \in D_l \cup D_u} \mathcal{L}_{con}^{cross}(g, f, x)$.
9:     **Update** f by $\nabla_f \mathcal{L}_f^{update}$ and g by $\nabla_g \mathcal{L}_g^{update}$.
10: **end for**
11: **Return** f, g

Instead of simply discarding filtered samples as in [29], we involve them along with selected samples, in $\mathcal{L}_{con}^{cross}$ (Eq. 20) to explore the consistency between

$$\mathcal{L}_{con}^{cross}(f, g, x) = ||f(T_h(x)) - T_{e \to h}(g(T_e(x)))||_2 \tag{20}$$

predictions of different models on different views. Motivated by semi-supervised methods [33], we utilize the confident predictions of each detector on easy views, to enforce consistency of the other detector on hard views. The overall loss function consists of the heatmap regression loss $\mathcal{L}_{heat}$ on the exemplar and selected samples, and the cross-consistency loss $\mathcal{L}_{con}^{cross}$ between the easy-hard pairs.

4 Experiments

We evaluate our method and state-of-the-art methods on multiple public X-ray datasets of different body parts. Furthermore, we conduct ablation studies to demonstrate how different components contribute to our final performance.

4.1 Dataset

Head: This dataset is a widely-used open-source dataset collected for IEEE ISBI 2015 challenge [1,34], which consists of 400 cephalometric radiographs. Two medical experts annotate 19 landmarks manually and we compute their average as the ground truth like [5,11]. The entire dataset is officially split into three parts: the first 150 images are training set, the next 250 images are test set. The original resolution is 2400×1935 and the pixel spacing is 0.1 mm.

Hand: This dataset is a public dataset of hand radiographs collected by [35]. [5] further annotate 37 landmarks on fingertips and bone joints. They assume the length between two endpoints of the wrist is 50 mm. The whole dataset is split into a training set of 609 images and a test set of 300 images as in [36].

Chest: This dataset is from a Kaggle challenge. [36] select a subset of 279 images by excluding abnormal cases and annotate six landmarks at the boundaries of the lung. Following [36], we use pixel distance at fixed resolution (512×512) for evaluation, since no pixel spacing information is provided.

4.2 Implementation

For both stages, the input resolution for head and hand datasets is 320×256, while chest images are resized into 256×256 to keep the aspect ratio. Data augmentations used in both stages include random rotation and random scaling. Random horizontal flipping is only applied in stage II. β_1, β_2 for Adam optimizer is set to $0.99, 0.0$ respectively and weight decay is 1e−4.

For stage I, we adopt pretrained HRNet18 [7] as backbone. The channel dimension of extracted feature maps are adjusted to $d_{model} = 64$ through 1×1 convolution, as the input dimension for attention blocks. Self (cross) attention modules are implemented as the encoder (decoder) block designed in [15], with multi-head attention ($N_h = 2$) and dropout $p = 0.1$. For each step of deformation, we stack $N_l = 2$ attention blocks for feature fusion. For alignment estimation, we set sf_x, sf_y, rot, sh to $1, 1, \frac{\pi}{2}, \frac{\pi}{2}$ respectively. We set $\sigma = 3$ for heatmap generation in Eq. 13 and $T = 0.1$ in Eq. 16.

We train the model for 750 epochs. For the first 250 epochs, learning rate lr is fixed as 1e−4 and ramps the weight for local deformation λ_1 (Eq. 11) from 0 to 1. For the remaining epochs, lr is decayed to 5e−5 with the cosine annealing strategy. In Eq. 12, λ_2 is set as 0.25 and λ_3 cosinely ramps down from 5.0 to 0.0. For each mini-batch, half of them are synthesized source-target pairs with known pixel correspondence, while the others are obtained by shuffling images within the current batch. In consideration of computation overhead and memory, all models are trained with one global step and two subsequent local steps ($N_\Phi = 2$). We start to infer pseudo labels for the training set after 200 epochs and compute its exponential moving average with a τ of 0.9 in Eq. 4.

For stage II, we retrain two HRNet18 [7] detectors, both initialized from pre-trained weights. We set $\sigma = 3$ for the standard deviation of the gaussian heatmap. Initial lr is 1e−3 and decays by 0.1 at 60 epochs and 80 epochs, until a total of 100 epochs. In the first 30 epochs, filter rate ϵ ramps from 0.0 to 0.8.

4.3 Evaluation

Metrics. Mean radial error (MRE) and successful detection rate (SDR) are adopted as evaluation metrics. MRE computes the average Euclidean distances between predicted landmarks and ground truth landmarks. Given several thresholds, SDR calculates the proportion of predictions with an error below these thresholds respectively. The unit of MRE is mm if pixel spacing is provided. Otherwise, it is reported as raw pixel distance. We use the same thresholds for

Table 1. Evaluation on the head, hand and chest dataset. * denotes original reported results in paper. # denotes reproduced performances under the one-shot landmark setting. Supervised method YOLO [36] serves as an universal upper bound. The best results are in **bold** and the second best results are underlined. Strictly using the same exemplar, our result outperforms all other one-shot methods. Performance of stage I is reported for fair comparison with CC2D-SSL

Method	Head					Hand				Chest			
	MRE↓	SDR↑(%)				MRE↓	SDR↑(%)			MRE↓	SDR↑(%)		
	(mm)	2mm	2.5mm	3mm	4mm	(mm)	2mm	4mm	10mm	(px)	3px	6px	9px
YOLO*	1.54	77.79	84.65	89.41	94.93	0.84	95.4	99.35	99.75	5.57	57.33	82.67	89.33
3FabRec#	20.12	2.42	3.86	4.98	7.23	9.81	3.98	15.24	60.92	48.67	0.67	2.33	4.67
DataAug#	3.18	32.81	44.42	55.12	73.16	2.51	48.87	85.67	98.91	10.15	15.67	40.67	61.67
CC2D-SSL#	3.41	40.63	49.58	60.31	72.14	2.93	51.59	81.29	95.59	17.37	9.87	27.99	42.11
CC2D-TPL#	2.72	42.59	53.18	66.48	83.22	2.47	54.95	87.16	97.84	12.91	12.67	38.67	57.67
Ours-stage I	2.70	42.78	54.88	65.03	81.01	2.13	60.93	89.43	99.21	10.16	12.33	39.00	60.33
Ours-stage II	**2.13**	**54.69**	**67.47**	**77.85**	**90.02**	**1.82**	**66.39**	**92.93**	**99.97**	**6.89**	**17.33**	**50.33**	**75.33**

SDR as [36], where they developed a fully-supervised universal landmark detector trained on the mix of all three datasets aforementioned. We list their results in Table 1 as the supervised upper bound.

4.4 Comparison with Baseline Methods

As shown in Table 1, we compare with 3FabRec, DataAug and CC2D on all three datasets. Our results outperform other one-shot methods by notable margins, which demonstrates both effectiveness and general applicability of our method.

As the weak baseline, with only access to hundreds of images, 3FabRec can hardly reconstruct the fine-grained details in X-ray images and thus yield relatively poor results. Our method also shows consistent improvements against the strong baseline DataAug, which relies on the affine alignment in the preprocessing step. While for some cases with drastic changes in spatial structure as in Fig. 3, our end-to-end learned alignment is more beneficial for the subsequent local deformations, since the total transformation learning is extraly guided by our carefully-designed constraints for landmarks.

Compared to the state-of-the-art method CC2D, we achieve superior performance by decreasing the MRE of stage I and stage II by 20.8% (3.41 mm → 2.70 mm) and 21.7% (2.72 mm → 2.13 mm) respectively. Improvements over CC2D might be attributed to the following two aspects. First, the pretext task of image-patch matching used in [11], is prone to overfitting when having difficulties discriminating local regions centered on those densely-labeled landmarks. Besides, they do not consider the global spatial relationships among these patches. In contrast, our way of inferring landmarks by registration, implicitly takes such constraints into consideration, and thus naturally avoid abnormal predictions, which can be justified by the obvious increase of SDR@4 mm in stage I (72.14% → 81.01%). Second, compared to simply retraining with synthesized samples as in DataAug, or performing majority-voting as in CC2D, our

I_l	I_l^A	I_l^{Φ}	I_u (Stage I)	I_u (Stage II)	DataAug	CC2D

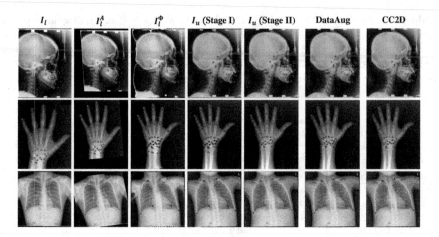

Fig. 3. Visualization of learned transformations and comparison with baseline methods. From left to right, we display the exemplar (I_{src}), intermediate warped results (I_l^A, I_l^{Φ}) and the unlabeled target image I_u. **Green dots** denote locations of the transformed exemplar landmarks. **Red dots** denote the ground truth landmark locations of I_u. Most of the stage I predictions with large biases could be corrected in stage II (Color figure online)

C2T makes better use of the common landmark knowledge contained in pseudo labels. Specifically, reliable labels can be effectively selected to provide more supervision for heatmap regression. On the other hand, remaining instances are not wasted by contributing to the consistency learning. It is especially crucial to handle challenging cases, such as the second row in Fig. 3, which successfully correct the large biases introduced in stage I, for landmarks around wrists.

Table 2. Ablation of spatial transform. "L" denotes the alignment is learned

Global Alignment Type	Local Step N_{Φ}	Head				
		MRE↓ (mm)	SDR↑(%) 2mm	2.5mm	3mm	4mm
✗	2	3.42	30.78	41.96	52.02	69.36
sift	2	3.10	35.31	47.58	58.23	74.02
affine (L)	1	2.73	39.64	52.19	63.45	80.50
affine (L)	2	2.70	42.78	54.88	65.03	81.01
perspective (L)	2	2.80	40.17	52.48	63.41	79.35

Table 3. Configurations of stage I network

backbone	N_l	N_h	Head				
			MRE↓ (mm)	SDR↑(%) 2mm	2.5mm	3mm	4mm
hrnet	0	0	2.93	36.76	48.36	59.58	76.11
	1	1	2.85	37.37	50.08	60.67	78.36
	2	1	2.82	39.87	52.61	63.47	78.25
	2	2	2.70	42.78	54.88	65.03	81.01
unet	2	2	2.95	34.86	47.81	58.63	76.42

4.5   Ablation Study

Here we conduct experiments on the head dataset, to analyze the contributions of different components from multiple aspects including spatial transformation, network architecture, loss function and robustness to exemplar selection.

Spatial Transformation. We remove the global alignment in the first row of Table 2 and witness a great drop in our performance. Besides, compared to alignment computed by traditional methods (e.g., sift detector), learned alignment is more desirable to reduce the complexity for subsequent local deformations. Compared to single step of local deformation, one more step benefits our performance, decreasing MRE from 2.73 mm to 2.70 mm. This observation is well-aligned with [37]. We also try to learn perspective transform with more degrees of freedom, but do not observe further improvements as expected. We argue that this might be restricted by the complexity of the head dataset.

Stage I Network Configurations. We remove all attention blocks in the first row of Table 3 and achieve a MRE of 2.93 mm. Furnishing backbone with more layers of attention blocks ($N_l = 0 \rightarrow 2$) and multi-head attention ($N_h = 1 \rightarrow 2$) contributes positively to our final performance. Our method still achieves competitive performance if we switch our backbone to the commonly-used UNet [38].

Table 4. Ablation of loss function for stage I

Loss	Head				
	MRE↓	SDR↑(%)			
	(mm)	2mm	2.5mm	3mm	4mm
w/o $\mathcal{L}_{inv}$	3.24	32.67	44.95	55.52	71.81
w/o $\mathcal{L}_{smooth}$	2.97	39.01	50.23	60.46	75.85
w/o $\mathcal{L}_{syn}$	2.86	39.54	51.43	61.68	77.14
$\mathcal{L}_{esim} \rightarrow \mathcal{L}_{sim}$	3.17	33.31	45.64	57.31	73.01
$\mathcal{L}_{esmooth} \rightarrow \mathcal{L}_{smooth}$	2.75	40.27	52.95	64.65	81.12
ours	2.70	42.78	54.88	65.03	81.01

Table 5. Ablation for stage II

$\mathcal{L}_{filter}$	$\mathcal{L}_{con}^{cross}$	Head				
		MRE↓	SDR↑(%)			
		(mm)	2mm	2.5mm	3mm	4mm
✗	✗	2.53	44.38	57.37	67.52	83.43
w $\mathcal{L}_{con}^{self}$	✗	2.29	50.80	63.64	74.36	87.53
w/o $\mathcal{L}_{con}^{self}$	✓	2.17	53.81	67.18	77.43	89.70
w $\mathcal{L}_{con}^{self}$	✓	2.13	54.69	67.47	77.85	90.02

Loss Function for StageI. In the first three rows of Table 4, we remove one regularization term of Φ at a time and find they all contribute to our results. They require the deformation field to be smooth, reversible, and applicable to real images respectively, thus avoiding intermediate abnormal warping results.

To study the contributions of $\mathcal{L}_{esim}$, we replace it with $\mathcal{L}_{sim}$ and find that MRE increases greatly by 17.4%. $\mathcal{L}_{sim}$ only considers image similarity based on pixel values, while our $\mathcal{L}_{esim}$ further incorporates the local structural similarity around landmarks based on edge maps, which is crucial to enforce the consistency across instances and thus adapts better to landmark localization task. Compared to $\mathcal{L}_{esmooth}$, $\mathcal{L}_{smooth}$ also leads to slight degradation in performance. Taking landmarks annotated near boundaries between foreground and background for example, they might be biased towards background due to the strict

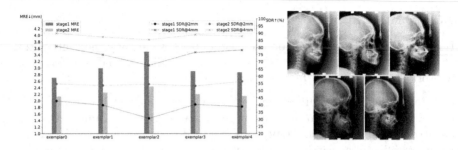

Fig. 4. Experiments for five candidate exemplars on the head dataset

smoothness enforced by $\mathcal{L}_{smooth}$. $\mathcal{L}_{esmooth}$ is tolerant to discontinuity between different regions and thus mitigates such phenomenon.

Ablation for Stage II. As in Table 5, we achieve a MRE of 2.53 mm by simply retraining with pseudo labels in stage I. Filtering out noisy pseudo labels by heatmap loss $\mathcal{L}_{heat}$ can improve MRE to 2.29 mm. And $\mathcal{L}_{con}^{cross}$ involves these filtered samples for semi-supervised learning, which further decreases MRE to 2.17 mm. If $\mathcal{L}_{con}^{self}$ is also taken into consideration for filtering, selected pseudo labels can provide more reliable supervision since they are also robust against spatial transformations, which enables us to achieve the final MRE of 2.13 mm.

Exemplar Selection. In Fig. 4, we show five different candidate exemplars and their corresponding results on the head dataset. Although there might be certain variations in the performances of stage II, our retraining scheme introduced in stage II effectively stabilizes the final performance, with a mean MRE of 2.25 mm.

5   Conclusion

We propose a novel two-stage framework for one-shot medical landmark localization. In stage I, an image transform model is learned through unsupervised registration. The total transform is decomposed to an end-to-end cascade of global alignment and local deformations, with the guidance of novel loss functions incorporating edge information. Pseudo landmarks are inferred on unlabeled targets with the exemplar and learned transform model. In stage II, we use these noisy labels to train robust landmark detectors by exploring self-consistency for selecting reliable samples and cross-consistency for semi-supervised learning. Extensive experiments on multiple datasets demonstrate our method surpasses other one-shot methods and further narrows the gap with supervised methods.

Acknowledgements. This work is supported in part by MOST-2018AAA0102004 and NSFC-62061136001.

References

1. Wang, C.-W., et al.: A benchmark for comparison of dental radiography analysis algorithms. Med. Image Anal. **31**, 63–76 (2016)
2. Chen, R., Ma, Y., Chen, N., Lee, D., Wang, W.: Cephalometric landmark detection by attentive feature pyramid fusion and regression-voting. In: Shen, D., et al. (eds.) MICCAI 2019. LNCS, vol. 11766, pp. 873–881. Springer, Cham (2019). https://doi.org/10.1007/978-3-030-32248-9_97
3. Escobar, M., González, C., Torres, F., Daza, L., Triana, G., Arbeláez, P.: Hand pose estimation for pediatric bone age assessment. In: Shen, D., et al. (eds.) MICCAI 2019. LNCS, vol. 11769, pp. 531–539. Springer, Cham (2019). https://doi.org/10.1007/978-3-030-32226-7_59
4. Gong, P., Yin, Z., Wang, Y., Yu, Y.: Towards robust bone age assessment: rethinking label noise and ambiguity. In: Martel, A.L., et al. (eds.) MICCAI 2020. LNCS, vol. 12266, pp. 621–630. Springer, Cham (2020). https://doi.org/10.1007/978-3-030-59725-2_60
5. Payer, C., Štern, D., Bischof, H., Urschler, M.: Integrating spatial configuration into heatmap regression based CNNs for landmark localization. Med. Image Anal. **54**, 207–219 (2019)
6. Liu, W., Wang, Yu., Jiang, T., Chi, Y., Zhang, L., Hua, X.-S.: Landmarks detection with anatomical constraints for total hip arthroplasty preoperative measurements. In: Martel, A.L., et al. (eds.) MICCAI 2020. LNCS, vol. 12264, pp. 670–679. Springer, Cham (2020). https://doi.org/10.1007/978-3-030-59719-1_65
7. Wang, J., et al.: Deep high-resolution representation learning for visual recognition. IEEE trans. Pattern Anal. Mach. Intell. **43**, 3349–3364 (2020)
8. Li, W., et al.: Structured landmark detection via topology-adapting deep graph learning. In: Vedaldi, A., Bischof, H., Brox, T., Frahm, J.-M. (eds.) ECCV 2020. LNCS, vol. 12354, pp. 266–283. Springer, Cham (2020). https://doi.org/10.1007/978-3-030-58545-7_16
9. Liu, H., Liu, F., Fan, X., Huang, D.: Polarized self-attention: towards High-quality Pixel-wise Regression. arXiv preprint arXiv:2107.00782 (2021)
10. Browatzki, B., Wallraven, C.: 3FabRec: fast few-shot face alignment by reconstruction. In: Proceedings of the IEEE/CVF Conference on Computer Vision and Pattern Recognition, pp. 6110–6120 (2020)
11. Yao, Q., Quan, Q., Xiao, L., Zhou, S.K.: One-shot medical landmark detection. arXiv preprint arXiv:2103.04527 (2021)
12. Zhou, X-Y., et al.: Scalable semi-supervised landmark localization for X-ray images using few-shot deep adaptive graph. arXiv preprint arXiv:2104.14629 (2021)
13. Balakrishnan, G., Zhao, A., Sabuncu, M.R., Guttag, J., Dalca, A.V.: An unsupervised learning model for deformable medical image registration. In: Proceedings of the IEEE Conference on Computer Vision and Pattern Recognition, pp. 9252–9260 (2018)
14. Lee, M.C.H., Oktay, O., Schuh, A., Schaap, M., Glocker, B.: Image-and-spatial transformer networks for structure-guided image registration. In: Shen, D., et al. (eds.) MICCAI 2019. LNCS, vol. 11765, pp. 337–345. Springer, Cham (2019). https://doi.org/10.1007/978-3-030-32245-8_38
15. Vaswani, A., et al.: Attention is all you need. In: Advances in Neural Information Processing Systems, pp. 5998–6008 (2017)
16. Yao, Q., He, Z., Han, H., Zhou, S.K.: Miss the point: targeted adversarial attack on multiple landmark detection. In: Martel, A.L., et al. (eds.) MICCAI 2020. LNCS,

vol. 12264, pp. 692–702. Springer, Cham (2020). https://doi.org/10.1007/978-3-030-59719-1_67

17. Honari, S., Molchanov, P., Tyree, S., Vincent, P., Pal, C., Kautz, J.: Improving landmark localization with semi-supervised learning. In: Proceedings of the IEEE Conference on Computer Vision and Pattern Recognition, pp. 1546–1555 (2018)

18. Moskvyak, O., Maire, F., Dayoub, F., Baktashmotlagh, M.: Semi-supervised keypoint localization. arXiv preprint arXiv:2101.07988 (2021)

19. Qian, S., Sun, K., Wu, W., Qian, C., Jia, J.: Aggregation via separation: boosting facial landmark detector with semi-supervised style translation. In: Proceedings of the IEEE/CVF International Conference on Computer Vision, pp. 10153–10163 (2019)

20. Kumar, A., Chellappa, R.: S2LD: Semi-supervised landmark detection in low-resolution images and impact on face verification. In: Proceedings of the IEEE/CVF Conference on Computer Vision and Pattern Recognition Workshops, pp. 758–759 (2020)

21. Uzunova, H., Wilms, M., Handels, H., Ehrhardt, J.: Training CNNs for image registration from few samples with model-based data augmentation. In: Descoteaux, M., Maier-Hein, L., Franz, A., Jannin, P., Collins, D.L., Duchesne, S. (eds.) MIC-CAI 2017. LNCS, vol. 10433, pp. 223–231. Springer, Cham (2017). https://doi.org/10.1007/978-3-319-66182-7_26

22. Li, H., Fan, Y.: Non-rigid image registration using self-supervised fully convolutional networks without training data. In: 2018 IEEE 15th International Symposium on Biomedical Imaging (ISBI 2018), pp. 1075–1078. IEEE (2018)

23. Zhao, A., Balakrishnan, G., Durand, F., Guttag, J.V., Dalca, A.V.: Data augmentation using learned transformations for one-shot medical image segmentation. In: Proceedings of the IEEE/CVF Conference on Computer Vision and Pattern Recognition, pp. 8543–8553 (2019)

24. Sun, K., Xiao, B., Liu, D., Wang, J.: Deep high-resolution representation learning for human pose estimation. In: Proceedings of the IEEE/CVF Conference on Computer Vision and Pattern Recognition, pp. 5693–5703 (2019)

25. Parmar, N., et al.: Image transformer. In: International Conference on Machine Learning, pp. 4055–4064. PMLR (2018)

26. Carion, N., Massa, F., Synnaeve, G., Usunier, N., Kirillov, A., Zagoruyko, S.: End-to-end object detection with transformers. In: Vedaldi, A., Bischof, H., Brox, T., Frahm, J.-M. (eds.) ECCV 2020. LNCS, vol. 12346, pp. 213–229. Springer, Cham (2020). https://doi.org/10.1007/978-3-030-58452-8_13

27. Jaderberg, M., Simonyan, K., Zisserman, A., et al.: Spatial transformer networks. Adv. Neural. Inf. Process. Syst. **28**, 2017–2025 (2015)

28. Wang, Z., Simoncelli, E.P., Bovik, A.C.: Multiscale structural similarity for image quality assessment. In: 2003 the Thrity-Seventh Asilomar Conference on Signals, Systems and Computers, vol. 2, pp. 1398–1402. IEEE (2003)

29. Han, B., et al.: Co-teaching: robust training of deep neural networks with extremely noisy labels. arXiv preprint arXiv:1804.06872 (2018)

30. Zhang, C., Bengio, S., Hardt, M., Recht, B., Vinyals, O.: Understanding deep learning requires rethinking generalization. arXiv:abs/1611.03530 (2017)

31. Arpit, D., et al.: A closer look at memorization in deep networks. In: International Conference on Machine Learning, pp. 233–242. PMLR (2017)

32. Yu, X., Han, B., Yao, J., Niu, G., Tsang, I., Sugiyama, M.: How does disagreement help generalization against label corruption? In: International Conference on Machine Learning pp. 7164–7173 (2019)

33. Sohn, K., et al.: FixMatch: simplifying semi-supervised learning with consistency and confidence. arXiv preprint arXiv:2001.07685 (2020)

34. Wang, C.-W., et al.: Evaluation and comparison of anatomical landmark detection methods for cephalometric X-ray images: a grand challenge. IEEE Trans. Med. Imaging **34**(9), 1890–1900 (2015)

35. Gertych, A., Zhang, A., Sayre, J., Pospiech-Kurkowska, S., Huang, HK.: Bone age assessment of children using a digital hand atlas. Comput. Med. Imaging Graph. **31**(4–5), 322–331 (2007)

36. Zhu, H., Yao, Q., Xiao, L., Zhou, S.K.: You only learn once: universal anatomical landmark detection. arXiv preprint arXiv:2103.04657 (2021)

37. Zhao, S., et al.: Recursive cascaded networks for unsupervised medical image registration. In: Proceedings of the IEEE/CVF International Conference on Computer Vision, pp. 10600–10610 (2019)

38. Ronneberger, O., Fischer, P., Brox, T.: U-Net: convolutional networks for biomedical image segmentation. In: Navab, N., Hornegger, J., Wells, W.M., Frangi, A.F. (eds.) MICCAI 2015. LNCS, vol. 9351, pp. 234–241. Springer, Cham (2015). https://doi.org/10.1007/978-3-319-24574-4_28

Ultra-High-Resolution Unpaired Stain Transformation via Kernelized Instance Normalization

Ming-Yang Ho$^{(\boxtimes)}$ ⓘ, Min-Sheng Wu ⓘ, and Che-Ming Wu ⓘ

aetherAI, Taipei, Taiwan
{kaminyouho,vincentwu,uno}@aetherai.com
https://www.aetherai.com/

Abstract. While hematoxylin and eosin (H&E) is a standard staining procedure, immunohistochemistry (IHC) staining further serves as a diagnostic and prognostic method. However, acquiring special staining results requires substantial costs. Hence, we proposed a strategy for ultra-high-resolution unpaired image-to-image translation: Kernelized Instance Normalization (KIN), which preserves local information and successfully achieves seamless stain transformation with constant GPU memory usage. Given a patch, corresponding position, and a kernel, KIN computes local statistics using convolution operation. In addition, KIN can be easily plugged into most currently developed frameworks without re-training. We demonstrate that KIN achieves state-of-the-art stain transformation by replacing instance normalization (IN) layers with KIN layers in three popular frameworks and testing on two histopathological datasets. Furthermore, we manifest the generalizability of KIN with high-resolution natural images. Finally, human evaluation and several objective metrics are used to compare the performance of different approaches. Overall, this is the first successful study for the ultra-high-resolution unpaired image-to-image translation with constant space complexity. Code is available at: https://github.com/Kaminyou/URUST.

Keywords: Unpaired image-to-image translation ·
Ultra-high-resolution · Stain transformation · Whole slide image

1 Introduction

Histological staining, highlighting cellular components with dyes, is crucial in clinical diagnosis [1], which enables visualization of cells and extracellular matrix and abnormal identification. Since specific cellular components or biomarkers can be distinguished when particular dyes attach specific molecules in tissues,

Supplementary Information The online version contains supplementary material available at https://doi.org/10.1007/978-3-031-19803-8_29.

© The Author(s), under exclusive license to Springer Nature Switzerland AG 2022
S. Avidan et al. (Eds.): ECCV 2022, LNCS 13681, pp. 490–505, 2022.
https://doi.org/10.1007/978-3-031-19803-8_29

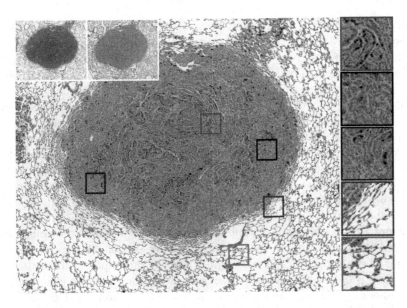

Fig. 1. An ultra-high-resolution translated result ($7,328 \times 8,899$ pixels) from our Kernelized Instance Normalization (KIN). The whole slide image (WSI) was translated from source stain to target stain (on the upper left) with constant space complexity (GPU memory) via KIN, and local appearance was preserved. On the right side, five close-ups demonstrate the detail.

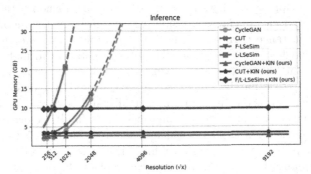

Fig. 2. Comparison of GPU memory usage among different unpaired image-to-image translation approaches. Compared with the models using Instance Normalization (IN), which has limitation (marked by the dashed line) on a 32G GPU (NVIDIA V-100), our Kernelized Instance Normalization (KIN) approach can translate an ultra-high-resolution image with constant GPU memory usage (less than 5GB).

different staining methods are applied to diagnose various diseases and their subtypes [4,11,15]. The standard stain (or routine stain) is hematoxylin and eosin (H&E). While hematoxylin stains nuclei, eosin can stain cytoplasm. Immuno-histochemistry (IHC) protocol is further developed to detect the presence of specific protein markers. For example, Ki-67 and ER staining can quantify the presence of Ki-67 and ER biomarkers, respectively. In clinical practice, high Ki-67 expression is considered a poor prognostic factor [23], while the presence of ER indicates the suitability of choosing specific target therapies that benefit related disease subtypes [26].

However, compared with H&E staining, the IHC staining process is much more expensive and requires extra biopsies, which are limited materials. With the development of deep learning-based image-to-image translation, virtually translating H&E into different IHC staining can be achieved. For example, de Haan et al. proposed a supervised deep learning approach via CycleGAN [33] to transform stained images from H&E to Masson's Trichrome (MT) staining [13]. While supervised pair-wise training is desirable, this approach requires perfectly paired staining images, necessitating de-staining and re-staining processes, and is not practically efficient in a clinical scenario. Most datasets are composed of unpaired H&E and IHC images from consecutive sections. Several methodologies have been proposed and successfully tackled the unpaired image-to-image translation problem [27]. Regardless of the astonishing performance, the existing methods are limited to low-resolution images and rarely explore the images with ultra-high-resolution. In histopathology, whole slide images (WSIs) are usually larger than $10,000 \times 10,000$ pixels. The main challenge of transforming a WSI is the limitation of GPU memory capacity. Patch-wise inference with an assembly process can tackle ultra-high-resolution image-to-image translation, but tiling artifacts between adjacent patches would be a critical problem. Traditionally, overlapping windows have been leveraged to smooth the transitions but have limited effectiveness. Considering the mean and standard deviation calculated in instance normalization (IN) layers might influence hue and contrast, recently, Chen et al. developed Thumbnail Instance Normalization (TIN) for both ultra-high-resolution style transfer as well as image-to-image translation tasks [8]. Unfortunately, while their approach could overcome the resolution limitation, their erroneous assumption that all patches share global mean and standard deviation would lead to dramatically over/under-colorizing according to our comprehensive experiment, which is confirmed in Sect. 5.3.

To compensate for all the above limitations, we proposed a Kernelized Instance Normalization (KIN) layer that can replace the original IN layer during the inference process without re-training the models. With the help of KIN, images with arbitrary resolution can be translated with constant GPU memory space (as demonstrated in Fig. 1 and 2). Moreover, utilizing the statistics of neighboring patches instead of global ones like TIN, our approach can further preserve the hue and contrast locally, which is especially paramount in stain transformation tasks. Besides the translation of H&E to four IHC staining, we additionally demonstrated the generalizability of KIN with natural images by translating summer to autumn style. Our novel contribution can be summarized as follows:

- To the best of our knowledge, this is the first successful study for the ultra-high-resolution unpaired image-to-image translation with constant space complexity (GPU memory), which manifests state-of-the-art outcomes in stain transformation and can also be generalized to natural images.

- Without re-training the models, our KIN module can be seamlessly inserted into most currently developed frameworks that have IN layers, such as Cycle-GAN [33], CUT [28], and LSeSim [32].
- With the KIN module, local contrast and hue information in translated images can be well preserved. Besides, different kernels can be further applied to subtly adjust the translated images.

2 Related Works

2.1 Unpaired Image-to-Image Translation

Several frameworks have been proposed for unpaired image-to-image translation. CycleGAN [33], DiscoGAN [19], and DualGAN [31] were first presented to overcome the supervised pairing constraint via cycle consistency. However, subtle information was forced to be retained in the translated image to achieve better reconstruction, causing detrimental effects when two domains are substantially different such as dog-to-cat translation. Besides, a reverse mapping function might not always exist, which inevitably leads to artifacts in translated images. Recently, strategies beyond cyclic loss have been developed to reach one-sided unpaired image-to-image translation. While DistanceGAN [3] enforced distance consistency between different parts of the same sample in each domain, CUT [28] leveraged contrastive loss to maximize the patch-wise similarity between domains and achieved remarkable results. LSeSim [32] further utilized spatially correlation to maximize structural similarity and eliminate the domain-specific features.

2.2 Image-to-Image Translation for Stain Transformation

Transforming one stained tissue into another specific stain will dramatically save laboratory resources and money. Hence, growing research has leveraged unsupervised image-to-image translation to conduct stain transformation in several medical scenarios. Levy *et al.* translated H&E to trichrome staining via Cycle-GAN for liver fibrosis staging [22]. Kapil *et al.* translated Cytokeratin to PD-L1 staining to bypass re-staining for segmentation [18]. de Haan *et al.* translated H&E to Masson's Trichrome, periodic acid-Schiff, and Jones silver stain for improving preliminary diagnosis for kidney diseases via CycleGAN with perfectly paired images [13]. Lahiani *et al.* further broke the limitation of 256×256-pixel image patches by applying perceptual embedding consistency for H&E to FAP-CK transformation [21]. However, the lack of detailed description hampers the implementation of their methodology.

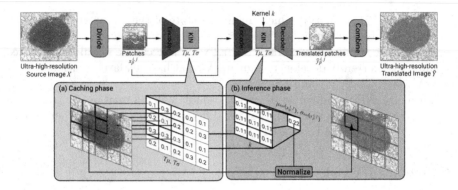

Fig. 3. Overall framework of proposed method. An ultra-high-resolution H&E image is passed through the caching phase and inference phase to be translated into an ultra-high-resolution IHC image. (a) In the caching phase, all mean μ and standard deviation σ values of patches will be cached in caching tables T_μ and T_σ by the Kernelized Instance Normalization (KIN) layer. (b) In the inference phase, a kernel k will convolute the caching table to compute μ_{KIN} and σ_{KIN} for instance normalization. Taking the neighboring statistics into account, our method can preserve local appearance.

2.3 Ultra-High Resolution Image-to-Image Translation

Ultra-high-resolution images are ubiquitous in photography, artwork, posters, ultra-high (*e.g.*, 8K) videos, and especially, WSIs in digital pathology (usually, larger than $10,000 \times 10,000$). Due to the massive computational costs, transforming these images into different styles will be difficult. Traditionally, strategies have been proposed to address the problem of tiling artifacts created by patchwise-based methods, including utilizing a larger overlapping window [20] or freezing IN layers during testing time [2]. By providing a patch-wise style transfer network with Thumbnail Instance Normalization (TIN), Chen *et al.* performed ultra-high-resolution style transformation with constant GPU memory usage [8]. Also, they applied their framework to an image-to-image translation task. However, according to our experiment, TIN may result in over/under-colorizing for their fallacious assumption that all patches can be normalized with the same global mean and standard deviation.

3   Proposed Method

3.1   Overall Framework

Our framework targets one-sidedly translating an ultra-high-resolution image X in domain $\mathcal{X}$ (*e.g.*, H&E stain domain) into image $\hat{Y}$ in domain $\mathcal{Y}$ (*e.g.*, IHC domain), in which $X, \hat{Y} \in R^{H \times W \times C}$, H and W are the height and width of X, via a mapping function, generator $\mathcal{G}$.

$$\hat{Y} = \mathcal{G}(X), \mathcal{G} : \mathcal{X} \to \mathcal{Y} \tag{1}$$

Collections of unpaired $\mathbf{X}$ in $\mathcal{X}$ and $\mathbf{Y}$ in $\mathcal{Y}$ would be first cropped into patches with the size of 512×512 pixels to train a generator $\mathcal{G}$.

As our KIN module is only applied during the testing time and can be inserted into any framework with IN layers, we followed the original training process and hyperparameters proposed in the paper of CycleGAN [33], CUT [28], and LSeSim [32] to train the corresponding generators with their specific designed losses without any modification.

During the testing process, all the IN layers in $\mathcal{G}$ are replaced with KIN layers. Given an image X, non-overlapped patches $x_p^{i,j}$ are cropped with the size of 512×512. The coordinates i, j of each patch $x_p^{i,j}$ corresponding to the original X would be recorded simultaneously. For example, an $M \times N$ image would be cropped into $\lfloor M/512 \rfloor \times \lfloor N/512 \rfloor$ patches with coordinates of $\{0, 1, ..., \lfloor M/512 \rfloor\}$ $\times \{0, 1, ..., \lfloor N/512 \rfloor\}$. Two caching tables of size $\lfloor M/512 \rfloor \times \lfloor N/512 \rfloor \times C$, in which C denotes the number of channels, would be initialized in each KIN for caching mean and standard deviation calculated.

As illustrated in Fig. 3, we divide the testing process into two phases: caching and inference. During caching phase, each patch $x_p^{i,j}$ with its corresponding coordinates i, j are the input of the generator $\mathcal{G}$, and the calculated mean $\mu(x_p^{i,j})$ and standard deviation $\sigma(x_p^{i,j})$ after passing the KIN will be cached. During the inference phase, $x_p^{i,j}$, its corresponding coordinates i, j and a kernel k are the input of the generator $\mathcal{G}$. The kernel $k \in R^{h \times w}$, where h and w are the height and width of k, is adjustable. When passing through the KIN layer, a region with the same size of kernel k extended from i, j will be extracted from the caching table and convolute with kernel k to compute mean $\mu_{KIN}(x_p^{i,j})$ and standard deviation $\sigma_{KIN}(x_p^{i,j})$ which are used to normalize the feature maps. All the cropped patches will be passed to the $\mathcal{G}$ in the aforementioned manner to yield translated patches $\hat{y}_p^{i,j}$. Eventually, all $\hat{y}_p^{i,j}$ are assembled into an ultra-high-resolution translated image $\hat{Y}$.

3.2 Kernelized Instance Normalization (KIN)

IN [29] has been widely used in GAN-based models for image generation and dramatically improved image quality [27]. Besides, multiple styles can be obtained by conditionally replacing the μ and σ in the IN layer [9]. IN can be formulated by:

$$IN(X) = \gamma(\frac{X - \mu(X)}{\sigma(X)}) + \beta \tag{2}$$

For each instance in a batch, $\mu(X)$ and $\sigma(X)$ are calculated in a channel-wise manner, in which $\mu(X), \sigma(X) \in R^{B \times C}$, B denotes the batch size and γ and β are trainable parameters.

We hypothesize that adjacent patches share similar statistics including the μ and σ computed in IN, and thus proposed KIN that could further alleviate the subtle incongruity that induces the tiling artifacts when adjacent patches are assembled. KIN is the extension of the original IN layer with extra two caching tables T_μ and T_σ to spatially store $\mu(X)$ and $\sigma(X)$ values and additionally supports convolution operation on the caching tables with a given kernel k. During the caching phase, KIN input a cropped patch $x_p^{i,j}$ with its spatial information, i, j. $\mu(x_p^{i,j})$ and $\sigma(x_p^{i,j})$ are computed as the original IN and cached.

$$T_\mu[i,j] := \mu(x_p^{i,j}), x_p^{i,j} \text{ is cropped from } X_{i,j} \tag{3}$$

$$T_\sigma[i,j] := \sigma(x_p^{i,j}), x_p^{i,j} \text{ is cropped from } X_{i,j} \tag{4}$$

During the inference phase, given a kernel k with the size of $2q+1$, $\mu_{KIN}(x_p^{i,j})$ and $\sigma_{KIN}(x_p^{i,j})$ are computed by convoluting k on cache tables to generate translated images. To address the boundary cases, the cache tables would be padded initially with edge values.

$$\mu_{KIN}(x_p^{i,j}) = \sum_{u=-q}^{q} \sum_{v=-q}^{q} T_\mu[i+u, j+v] \cdot K[q+u, q+v], \forall i, j \tag{5}$$

$$\sigma_{KIN}(x_p^{i,j}) = \sum_{u=-q}^{q} \sum_{v=-q}^{q} T_\sigma[i+u, j+v] \cdot K[q+u, q+v], \forall i, j \tag{6}$$

$$KIN(x_p^{i,j}, i, j) = \gamma(\frac{x_p^{i,j} - \mu_{KIN}(x_p^{i,j})}{\sigma_{KIN}(x_p^{i,j})}) + \beta \tag{7}$$

4   Datasets

4.1   Automatic Non-rigid Histological Image Registration (ANHIR)

Automatic Non-rigid Histological Image Registration (ANHIR) dataset [5–7, 10,12,24] consists of high-resolution WSIs from different tissue samples (lesions, lung lobes, breast tissue, kidney tissue, gastric tissue, colon adenocarcinoma, and mammary gland). The acquired images are organized in sets of consecutive tissue slices stained by various dyes, including H&E, Ki-67, ER/PR, CD4/CD8/CD68, etc., with sizes vary from $15,000 \times 15,000$ to $50,000 \times 50,000$ pixels. We randomly sampled three types of tissues to conduct our experiments. Each experiment comprises H&E stain and one target IHC stain: breast tissue (from H&E to PR), colon adenocarcinoma (COAD) (from H&E to CD4&CD68), and lung lesion (from H&E to Ki-67).

4.2   Glioma

The private glioma dataset was collected from H&E ($98,304 \times 93,184$ pixels) and epidermal growth factor receptor (EGFR) IHC ($102,400 \times 93,184$ pixels) stained tissue microarrays, and each comprised 105 tissue samples corresponding to 105 different patients. Totally 105 H&E stained tissue images with their consecutive EGFR counterparts were cropped from the microarrays and the image sizes vary from $7,000 \times 7,000$ to $10,000 \times 10,000$ pixels. We randomly selected 55 samples as the training set while the other 50 pairs as the testing set.

4.3 Kyoto Summer2autumn

An extra natural image dataset was used to validate the generalizability of our methodology. We collected 17 and 20 high-resolution (3456 × 5184 pixels) unpaired images taken in Tokyo during summer and autumn, respectively, as the training set and additional four summer images were used as a testing set. This Kyoto summer2autumn dataset[1] was released to facilitate solving ultra-high-resolution-related problems that most computer vision studies might encounter.

5 Experiments

5.1 Experimental Settings

Three popular unpaired image-to-image translation frameworks: CycleGAN [33], CUT [28], and L-LSeSim [32], were utilized to verify our approach. We followed the hyperparameter settings described in the original papers during the training process except for the model output size, which was changed from 256 × 256 to 512 × 512. We trained the CycleGAN, CUT, and L-LSeSim for 50, 100, and 100 epochs. Models were trained and tested on three datasets: ANHIR, glioma, and Kyoto summer2autumn. Due to the insufficiency of WHIs in ANHIR dataset, we could only inference on the training set (note that training was in an unsupervised manner) while glioma and Kyoto summer2autumn datasets can be further split into training and testing sets. We replaced all IN layers with KIN layers in the generators during the inference process. One ultra-high-resolution image would be cropped into non-overlapped patches and pass through the KIN module. Translated patches were assembled to the final translated output. Constant and Gaussian kernels with sizes of 3, 7, and 11 were used to generate the best results. Translated images generated with KIN were compared with those from IN and TIN. Due to the GPU memory limitation, translated images generated with IN were also in a patch-wise (512 × 512) manner, which is the same as the patch-wise IN in Chen *et al.*'s work [8].

5.2 Metrics

In addition to the visualization of the translated images, we calculated Fréchet inception distance (FID) [14], histogram correlation, Sobel gradients [16] in YCbCr color domain, perception image quality evaluator (PIQE) [30], and natural image quality evaluator (NIQE) [25] to comprehensively evaluate the quality of translated ultra-high-resolution images.

However, due to the limitations of the available metrics that the tiling artifacts are difficult to be fairly graded and the unavailability of the perfectly

---

[1] Kyoto summer2autumn dataset is available at: https://github.com/Kaminyou/Kyoto-summer2autumn.

matched counterpart, we conducted two human evaluation studies with five specialists: (a) quality challenge: given one source, one reference, and three translated images generated by patch-wise IN, TIN, and our KIN methods, respectively, specialists were asked to select the best among three translated images in 30 s. Since the images generated by CycleGAN and L-LSeSim were atrocious, we only chose images generated by CUT; (b) fidelity challenge: given one real image and one translated image, specialists were asked to select the one which is personally considered realistic in 10 s. We followed the protocol of the AMT perceptual studies from Isola *et al.* [17] but adjusted the time limitation as our images are extremely large. Since the data in ANHIR breast, COAD, and lung lesion subdatasets are insufficient, we combined these subdatasets as single ANHIR dataset and randomly selected pairs of real and translated WSIs from it.

5.3   Results

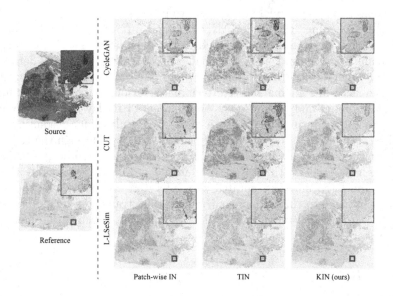

Fig. 4. H&E-to-PR stain transformation results on ANHIR breast dataset $(10, 205 \times 10, 933$ **pixels)** generated by different frameworks with IN, TIN, and KIN layers. Red arrows indicate tiling artifacts; green arrows indicate over/under-colorizing. CUT+KIN achieved the best performance. Zoom in for better view.

Stain Transformation. Figures 4, 5, 6 and S5 and S6 show the translated images for three ANHIR subdatasets (breast tissue, COAD, and lung lesion) and glioma dataset, respectively. With only IN layers, CUT yields the images with best quality with some tiling artifacts, while CycleGAN led to checkerboard artifacts. L-LSeSim powerfully preserves spatial information but compromises

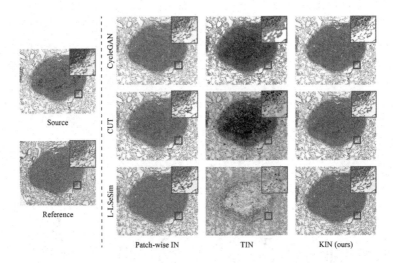

Fig. 5. H&E-to-Ki-67 stain transformation results on ANHIR lung lesion dataset (7,336 × 8,915 pixels) generated by different frameworks with IN, TIN, and KIN layers. Red arrows indicate tiling artifacts; green arrows indicate over/under-colorizing. CUT+KIN achieved the best performance. Zoom in for better view.

Table 1. Quantitative results for ANHIR dataset. For each experiment, the bold shows the best performance; the underline indicates that KIN surpasses IN and TIN.

		Breast					COAD					Lung lesion				
		FID↓	Corr.↑	Grad.↓	PIQE↓	NIQE↓	FID↓	Corr.↑	Grad.↓	PIQE↓	NIQE↓	FID↓	Corr.↑	Grad.↓	PIQE↓	NIQE↓
CycleGAN	IN*	98.60	−0.07	13.62	**4.95**	9.39	103.25	75.25	15.08	5.26	**9.08**	76.15	−4.49	9.92	**62.69**	13.14
	TIN	179.14	−28.91	14.37	6.16	9.56	**100.78**	**79.53**	16.68	15.79	9.55	239.19	**17.46**	**9.53**	67.79	11.96
	KIN	**96.09**	**11.53**	**12.93**	5.29	**7.36**	108.32	43.60	**14.95**	**5.15**	9.69	103.48	−2.16	9.94	63.81	12.16
CUT	IN*	**71.00**	**35.56**	14.55	**3.00**	12.15	95.87	74.64	14.76	4.50	8.96	**54.86**	−5.79	**10.41**	58.32	12.20
	TIN	125.18	39.50	17.04	3.42	10.98	**91.81**	33.29	15.49	11.96	9.02	251.48	**80.14**	11.80	**32.08**	12.20
	KIN	72.59	36.32	**14.05**	3.27	**10.66**	93.68	**76.45**	**14.60**	**4.49**	**8.94**	56.38	−9.63	10.58	60.13	**12.08**
L-LSeSim	IN*	**65.82**	31.57	15.04	**3.03**	13.36	100.42	48.15	13.64	**4.23**	8.45	**56.30**	−3.82	**9.71**	46.40	13.88
	TIN	89.94	22.16	**12.75**	3.29	13.18	100.50	41.37	15.67	9.56	**8.14**	231.13	**59.71**	12.68	**44.29**	**11.13**
	KIN	67.46	**31.58**	14.31	3.19	**12.35**	**100.04**	**51.62**	**13.34**	4.44	8.22	62.74	−4.77	9.91	47.99	13.48

IN*: Patch-wise IN; Corr.: Histogram correlation; Grad.: Sobel gradients; ↓: the lower the better; ↑: the higher the better

color information. With TIN, all the translated images showed dramatically over/under-colorizing. With our KIN, translated images can have minor tiling artifacts and preserve their local features. However, if the original framework generated severe tiling artifacts, our KIN could alleviate but be hard to eliminate. Considering the similarity (FID and histogram correlation) and quality metrics (Sobel gradient, PIQE and NIQE), our KIN is superior to patch-wise IN and TIN in most cases (see Tables 1 and 2). Although KIN does not always obtain the best scores, a possible reason is that no appropriate metrics can reflect the performance of such unpaired WSIs stain transformation task. Thus, we established two human evaluation studies to pertinently evaluate the image

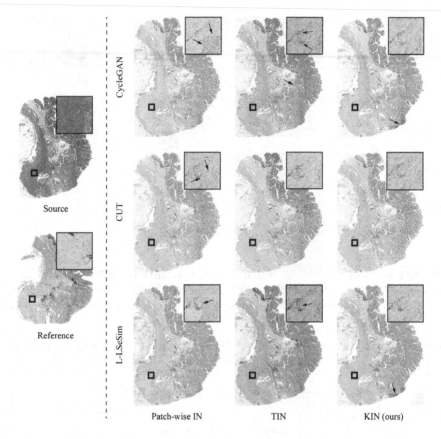

Fig. 6. H&E-to-CD4&CD8 stain transformation results on ANHIR COAD dataset (9,816 × 8,433 pixels) generated by different frameworks with IN, TIN, and KIN layers. Red arrows indicate tiling artifacts; green arrows indicate over/under-colorizing. CUT+KIN achieved the best performance. Zoom in for better view.

quality and fidelity. As shown in Fig. 8, our KIN achieved the best performance in both.

Translation for Natural Images. Our KIN module also performed well on natural images (as shown in Fig. 7 and S7). As described above, KIN can alleviate the tiling artifacts generated by patch-wise IN while TIN would lead to over/under-colorizing. However, when it comes to natural images, over/under-colorizing would not be as obtrusive as in stain transformation cases, since people sometimes prefer over-stylized images. For example, High-Dynamic Range (HDR) or contrast adjustment techniques are popular to beautify photographs and render the photos more attractive. Table 3 and Fig. 8 provided the metrics evaluation results, and our KIN obtained the best performance among all methodologies in human evaluation. Considering the FID, CUT with our KIN is

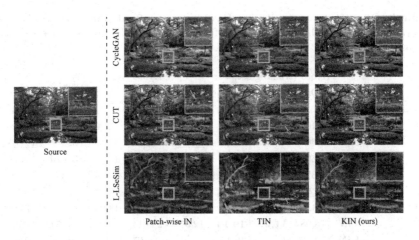

Fig. 7. Image-to-image translation results on Kyoto summer2autumn testing set $(3,456 \times 5,184$ **pixels)** generated by different frameworks with IN, TIN, and KIN layers. Red arrows indicate tiling artifacts; green arrows indicate over/under-colorizing. CUT+KIN achieved the best performance. Zoom in for better view.

Table 2. Quantitative results for Glioma dataset. For each experiment, the bold shows the best performance; the underline indicates that KIN surpasses IN and TIN.

		Glioma (training set)					Glioma (testing set)				
		FID↓	Corr.↑	Grad.↓	PIQE↓	NIQE↓	FID↓	Corr.↑	Grad.↓	PIQE↓	NIQE↓
CycleGAN	IN*	**136.32**	0.26	11.91	**21.83**	13.64	**142.28**	0.28	10.57	**23.73**	13.76
	TIN	220.00	**0.28**	**5.42**	39.05	12.01	207.03	**0.38**	**4.65**	41.16	11.99
	KIN	157.26	0.14	7.22	27.89	<u>**11.27**</u>	150.93	0.19	6.31	29.87	<u>**11.54**</u>
CUT	IN*	105.22	**0.85**	14.81	**23.76**	13.99	105.66	**0.85**	13.48	**24.02**	14.05
	TIN	214.22	0.54	**10.02**	34.52	**13.37**	200.56	0.64	**8.64**	35.01	**13.37**
	KIN	108.20	0.81	12.84	31.26	13.70	<u>**100.90**</u>	0.80	11.58	31.94	13.86
L-LSeSim	IN*	**107.74**	0.41	11.83	**21.09**	10.70	**105.59**	0.48	10.67	**21.25**	10.62
	TIN	203.70	0.10	**8.22**	24.87	10.94	191.44	0.19	**7.58**	23.34	10.75
	KIN	113.92	<u>0.41</u>	8.64	26.00	<u>**10.63**</u>	106.90	0.46	7.69	26.85	<u>**10.40**</u>

IN*: Patch-wise IN; Corr.: Histogram correlation; Grad.: Sobel gradients; ↓: the lower the better; ↑: the higher the better

superior or competitive to other methods. Although Sobel gradients are higher in some cases, the high contrast level of one image might also contribute to higher gradients. On the other hand, there are only minor differences in PIQE and NIQE between methods. However, none of the metrics can effectively evaluate ultra-high-resolution images with tiling artifacts.

5.4 Ablation Study

Kernel and Kernel Size. To elucidate the effect of different kernels and kernel size on the translated images, we applied constant and Gaussian kernels with the size of 1, 3, 7, 11, and ∞ in the KIN module (see Fig. S8 and S9). It is noteworthy that when kernel size is set to 1, the KIN module will operate in a

Table 3. Quantitative results for Kyoto summer2autumn dataset. For each experiment, the bold shows the best performance; the underline indicates that KIN surpasses IN and TIN.

		Kyoto (training set)				Kyoto (testing set)			
		FID↓	Grad.↓	PIQE↓	NIQE↓	FID↓	Grad.↓	PIQE↓	NIQE↓
CycleGAN	IN*	**79.11**	18.40	**43.62**	12.20	**171.88**	16.52	**37.00**	11.26
	TIN	87.10	**12.39**	54.29	12.24	180.50	**10.49**	52.56	11.92
	KIN	93.60	17.08	44.65	<u>12.11</u>	192.25	15.12	39.53	<u>11.10</u>
CUT	IN*	77.59	17.87	43.81	13.40	**157.04**	18.29	**37.74**	**11.41**
	TIN	98.37	**17.44**	43.30	**12.11**	181.13	**15.33**	40.97	11.89
	KIN	<u>75.27</u>	18.53	<u>40.21</u>	12.98	167.15	17.24	38.30	12.31
L-LSeSim	IN*	**178.19**	14.86	19.35	**11.89**	**248.81**	13.05	14.14	11.42
	TIN	178.98	**11.27**	**19.13**	12.07	253.14	**9.74**	**12.21**	11.18
	KIN	192.42	16.41	19.19	12.01	265.07	16.12	13.00	<u>10.54</u>

IN*: Patch-wise IN; Grad.: Sobel gradients; ↓: the lower the better

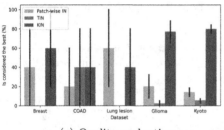
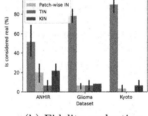

(a) Quality evaluation   (b) Fidelity evaluation

Fig. 8. Human evaluation results. In quality evaluation, KIN achieved the best or competitive performance among all datasets while images generated via TIN obtained the worst quality. For the fidelity evaluation, although real consecutive section of tissue is easily to be distinguished from the fake ones, KIN is still the most deceptive among all methods. It can be noticed that translated natural images are hardly to deceive human since their complicated content are difficult to be fabricated.

manner of patch-wise IN, whereas it would be like TIN when kernel size is set to ∞ (bounded by the input image size). KIN is an eclectic approach that combines the advantages of patch-wise IN and TIN and avoids extremes of single and global features calculated in patch-wise IN and TIN. When kernel size increases from one to ∞, the translated results gradually change from patch-wise IN to TIN. On the other hand, the constant kernel can help generate smoother results, while the Gaussian kernel will emphasize local features more.

6   Discussions

Our experiments showed that KIN performed well on multiple datasets, and unseen testing data can even be successfully inferred when sufficient training data are available. The over/under-colorizing problem caused by TIN is also revealed, which might be innocuous when natural images are used but would be detrimental when targeting stain transformation. Pathological features, which are essential for clinical judgment, would be compromised when global mean and standard deviation are applied in the TIN.

Although KIN can be inserted into any IN-based framework, the performance would be compromised if the original framework has amateurish performance, such as CycleGAN, which generates results diversely among adjacent patches. KIN can hardly eliminate all the tiling artifacts undertaking such cases. Interestingly, we found that CUT can yield more consistent results among adjacent patches, especially for the hue. On the other hand, LSeSim meticulously preserves all the structure but ignores the consistency of the hue, which is reasonable as CUT captures domain-specific features, but LSeSim focuses on spatial features according to their loss functions. Despite KIN achieving the best performance surpassing all previous approaches in human evaluation studies, its strength cannot be manifested due to the inadequacy of appropriate metrics for evaluating the quality and fidelity of unpaired ultra-high-resolution WSIs. Finally, ultra-high-resolution images are commonly used in daily life but there is no public dataset available for a fair comparison. To facilitate related researches, we released the Kyoto summer2autumn dataset.

7   Conclusion

This study presents Kernelized Instance Normalization (KIN) for ultra-high-resolution stain transformation with constant space complexity. KIN can be easily inserted into popular unpaired image-to-image translation frameworks without re-training the model. Comprehensive experiments with two WSI datasets were conducted and evaluated by human evaluation studies and appropriate metrics. An extra ultra-high-resolution natural image dataset was also utilized and demonstrated the generalizability of KIN. Overall, KIN surpassed all the previous approaches and generated state-of-the-art outcomes. Henceforth, ultra-high-resolution stain transformation or image-to-image translation, can be easily accomplished and applied in clinical practice.

Acknowledgements. We thank Chao-Yuan Yeh, the CEO of aetherAI, for providing computing resources, which enabled this study to be performed, and Cheng-Kun Yang for his revision suggestions.

References

1. Alturkistani, H.A., Tashkandi, F.M., Mohammedsaleh, Z.M.: Histological stains: a literature review and case study. Global J. Health Sci. **8**(3), 72 (2016)
2. de Bel, T., Hermsen, M., Kers, J., van der Laak, J., Litjens, G.: Stain-transforming cycle-consistent generative adversarial networks for improved segmentation of renal histopathology. In: International Conference on Medical Imaging with Deep Learning-Full Paper Track (2018)

3. Benaim, S., Wolf, L.: One-sided unsupervised domain mapping. In: NIPS (2017)
4. Birkman, E.M., et al.: Gastric cancer: immunohistochemical classification of molecular subtypes and their association with clinicopathological characteristics. Virchows Arch. **472**(3), 369–382 (2018)
5. Borovec, J., et al.: Anhir: automatic non-rigid histological image registration challenge. IEEE Trans. Med. Imaging **39**(10), 3042–3052 (2020)
6. Borovec, J., Munoz-Barrutia, A., Kybic, J.: Benchmarking of image registration methods for differently stained histological slides. In: 2018 25th IEEE International Conference on Image Processing (ICIP), pp. 3368–3372. IEEE (2018)
7. Bueno, G., Deniz, O.: Aidpath: academia and industry collaboration for digital pathology (2019)
8. Chen, Z., Wang, W., Xie, E., Lu, T., Luo, P.: Towards ultra-resolution neural style transfer via thumbnail instance normalization. In: Proceedings of the AAAI Conference on Artificial Intelligence (2022)
9. Dumoulin, V., Shlens, J., Kudlur, M.: A learned representation for artistic style (2017)
10. Fernandez-Gonzalez, R., et al.: System for combined three-dimensional morphological and molecular analysis of thick tissue specimens. Microsc. Res. Tech. **59**(6), 522–530 (2002)
11. Fragomeni, S.M., Sciallis, A., Jeruss, J.S.: Molecular subtypes and local-regional control of breast cancer. Surg. Oncol. Clin. **27**(1), 95–120 (2018)
12. Gupta, L., Klinkhammer, B.M., Boor, P., Merhof, D., Gadermayr, M.: Stain independent segmentation of whole slide images: a case study in renal histology. In: 2018 IEEE 15th International Symposium on Biomedical Imaging (ISBI 2018), pp. 1360–1364. IEEE (2018)
13. de Haan, K., et al.: Deep learning-based transformation of H&E stained tissues into special stains. Nat. Commun. **12**(1), 1–13 (2021)
14. Heusel, M., Ramsauer, H., Unterthiner, T., Nessler, B., Hochreiter, S.: GANs trained by a two time-scale update rule converge to a local nash equilibrium. In: Advances in Neural Information Processing Systems, vol. 30 (2017)
15. Inamura, K.: Update on immunohistochemistry for the diagnosis of lung cancer. Cancers **10**(3), 72 (2018)
16. Irwin, F., et al.: An isotropic 3x3 image gradient operator. Presentation Stanford AI Project **2014**(02) (1968)
17. Isola, P., Zhu, J.Y., Zhou, T., Efros, A.A.: Image-to-image translation with conditional adversarial networks. In: Proceedings of the IEEE Conference on Computer Vision and Pattern Recognition, pp. 1125–1134 (2017)
18. Kapil, A., et al.: DASGAN-joint domain adaptation and segmentation for the analysis of epithelial regions in histopathology PD-L1 images. arXiv preprint arXiv:1906.11118 (2019)
19. Kim, T., Cha, M., Kim, H., Lee, J.K., Kim, J.: Learning to discover cross-domain relations with generative adversarial networks. In: International Conference on Machine Learning, pp. 1857–1865. PMLR (2017)
20. Lahiani, A., Gildenblat, J., Klaman, I., Albarqouni, S., Navab, N., Klaiman, E.: Virtualization of tissue staining in digital pathology using an unsupervised deep learning approach. In: Reyes-Aldasoro, C.C., Janowczyk, A., Veta, M., Bankhead, P., Sirinukunwattana, K. (eds.) ECDP 2019. LNCS, vol. 11435, pp. 47–55. Springer, Cham (2019). https://doi.org/10.1007/978-3-030-23937-4_6
21. Lahiani, A., Klaman, I., Navab, N., Albarqouni, S., Klaiman, E.: Seamless virtual whole slide image synthesis and validation using perceptual embedding consistency. IEEE J. Biomed. Health Inform. **25**(2), 403–411 (2020)

22. Levy, J.J., Jackson, C.R., Sriharan, A., Christensen, B.C., Vaickus, L.J.: Preliminary evaluation of the utility of deep generative histopathology image translation at a mid-sized NCI cancer center. bioRxiv (2020)
23. Luo, Z.W., Zhu, M.G., Zhang, Z.Q., Ye, F.J., Huang, W.H., Luo, X.Z.: Increased expression of KI-67 is a poor prognostic marker for colorectal cancer patients: a meta analysis. BMC Cancer **19**(1), 1–13 (2019)
24. Mikhailov, I., Danilova, N., Malkov, P.: The immune microenvironment of various histological types of EBV-associated gastric cancer. Virchows Arch. **473**, S168–S168 (2018)
25. Mittal, A., Soundararajan, R., Bovik, A.C.: Making a "completely blind" image quality analyzer. IEEE Signal Process. Lett. **20**(3), 209–212 (2012)
26. Oshi, M., et al.: Degree of early estrogen response predict survival after endocrine therapy in primary and metastatic ER-positive breast cancer. Cancers **12**(12), 3557 (2020)
27. Pang, Y., Lin, J., Qin, T., Chen, Z.: Image-to-image translation: methods and applications. IEEE Trans. Multimedia (2021)
28. Park, T., Efros, A.A., Zhang, R., Zhu, J.-Y.: Contrastive learning for unpaired image-to-image translation. In: Vedaldi, A., Bischof, H., Brox, T., Frahm, J.-M. (eds.) ECCV 2020. LNCS, vol. 12354, pp. 319–345. Springer, Cham (2020). https://doi.org/10.1007/978-3-030-58545-7_19
29. Ulyanov, D., Vedaldi, A., Lempitsky, V.: Instance normalization: the missing ingredient for fast stylization. arXiv preprint arXiv:1607.08022 (2016)
30. Venkatanath, N., Praneeth, D., Bh, M.C., Channappayya, S.S., Medasani, S.S.: Blind image quality evaluation using perception based features. In: 2015 Twenty First National Conference on Communications (NCC), pp. 1–6. IEEE (2015)
31. Yi, Z., Zhang, H., Tan, P., Gong, M.: Dualgan: unsupervised dual learning for image-to-image translation. In: Proceedings of the IEEE International Conference on Computer Vision, pp. 2849–2857 (2017)
32. Zheng, C., Cham, T.J., Cai, J.: The spatially-correlative loss for various image translation tasks. In: Proceedings of the IEEE Conference on Computer Vision and Pattern Recognition (2021)
33. Zhu, J.Y., Park, T., Isola, P., Efros, A.A.: Unpaired image-to-image translation using cycle-consistent adversarial networks. In: 2017 IEEE International Conference on Computer Vision (ICCV) (2017)

Med-DANet: Dynamic Architecture Network for Efficient Medical Volumetric Segmentation

Wenxuan Wang[1] , Chen Chen[2] , Jing Wang[1] , Sen Zha[1] , Yan Zhang[1] , and Jiangyun Li[1(✉)]

[1] School of Automation and Electrical Engineering, University of Science and Technology Beijing, Beijing, China
{s20200579,m202120718,g20198675,m202110578}@xs.ustb.edu.cn,
leejy@ustb.edu.cn
[2] Center for Research in Computer Vision, University of Central Florida, Orlando, USA
chen.chen@crcv.ucf.edu

Abstract. For 3D medical image (e.g. CT and MRI) segmentation, the difficulty of segmenting each slice in a clinical case varies greatly. Previous research on volumetric medical image segmentation in a slice-by-slice manner conventionally use the identical 2D deep neural network to segment all the slices of the same case, ignoring the data heterogeneity among image slices. In this paper, we focus on multi-modal 3D MRI brain tumor segmentation and propose a dynamic architecture network named Med-DANet based on adaptive model selection to achieve effective accuracy and efficiency trade-off. For each slice of the input 3D MRI volume, our proposed method learns a *slice-specific decision* by the Decision Network to dynamically select a suitable model from the predefined Model Bank for the subsequent 2D segmentation task. Extensive experimental results on both BraTS 2019 and 2020 datasets show that our proposed method achieves comparable or better results than previous state-of-the-art methods for 3D MRI brain tumor segmentation with much less model complexity. Compared with the state-of-the-art 3D method TransBTS, the proposed framework improves the model efficiency by up to 3.5× without sacrificing the accuracy. Our code will be publicly available at https://github.com/Wenxuan-1119/Med-DANet.

Keywords: Segmentation · Brain tumor · MRI · Dynamic network · Adaptive inference

1 Introduction

Gliomas are the most common malignant brain tumors with different levels of aggressiveness. The precise measurements of gliomas can assist doctors in mak-

Supplementary Information The online version contains supplementary material available at https://doi.org/10.1007/978-3-031-19803-8_30.

ing accurate diagnosis and further treatment planning. Traditionally, the lesion regions are delineated by clinicians heavily relying on clinical experiences, which is time-consuming and prone to mistakes. Therefore, to improve the accuracy and efficiency of clinical diagnosis, automated and accurate segmentation of these malignancies on Magnetic Resonance Imaging (MRI) [12] is of vital importance.

In the past few years, deep neural networks, convolutional neural networks (CNNs) in particular, have achieved great success in medical image segmentation task. The mainstream methods can be divided into two categories: (1) applying 2D networks for slice-wise (i.e. slice-by-slice) predictions and (2) utilizing 3D models (e.g. 3D CNNs) to process image volumes with multiple slices. 3D CNNs such as 3D U-Net [8] and V-Net [22] employing 3D convolutions to capture the correlation between adjacent slices, have achieved impressive segmentation results. However, these 3D CNN architectures come with high computational overheads due to multiple layers of 3D convolutions, making them prohibitive for practical large-scale applications. Similarly, the 2D U-Net [27] and its variants such as [24,36,37] are also confronted with the same problem because of the unique architecture. Specifically, to obtain the multi-scale feature representation and fine-grained local details, multiple skip connections and stacked stacked convolutional layers are employed to improve model performance, but leading to unbearable computational overheads simultaneously.

Since the efficiency of a network determines the practical application value of the model deployment, model efficiency is as important as segmentation accuracy. In order to cope with the high computational costs brought by 3D medical image itself and the segmentation networks mentioned above, many lightweight networks [4,7,16,18,23,26] have been developed to realize efficient medical image segmentation. However, these proposed lightweight networks are designed from the perspective of efficient architecture without the consideration of data itself, treating all different inputs equally. Although these models effectively make the structural improvements to achieve lightweight architectures, they suffer from segmentation accuracy degradation due to reduced modeling capacity. Moreover, they can not **adaptively** make appropriate adjustments to different input data due to fixed network structure. Therefore, a natural question arises:

For volumetric medical image segmentation task, is it possible to achieve dynamic inference with adjustable network structures for better accuracy and efficiency trade-offs by considering the characteristics of the input data (e.g. the level of segmentation difficulty of each image slice)?

To answer this question, we take a brain tumor segmentation dataset BraTS 2019 [1,2,21] as an example to seek some insights. Figure 1(a) shows the distribution of a 3D multi-modal brain tumor image along the slice dimension for one case. Due to several factors, such as the MRI process, shape of the organ (e.g. brain), and the location of the disease (e.g. glioma), the image content varies significantly across different MRI slices. For example, the 1st row of Fig. 1(a) shows the first 5 slices that barely capture any tissue content of the brain. These slices can be simply predicted as containing all "background" pixels (i.e. no lesion pixel) without model inference (i.e. "skip" mode), saving the computational cost.

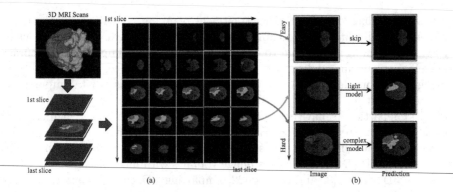

Fig. 1. (a) The illustration of image content distribution along slice dimension of an MRI case (Axial View) from the BraTS 2019 dataset. The blue regions denote the enhancing tumors, the red regions denote the non-enhancing tumors, and the green ones denote the peritumoral edema. (b) The main idea of our proposed framework for dynamic inference. For image slices with diverse segmentation difficulty, our framework realizes efficient and accurate segmentation by adaptively adjusting the architecture, selecting the optimal network in the Model Bank which consists of several networks with different model complexities. In this way, our framework can dynamically decide to "slack off" or "work hard" according to different samples. (Color figure online)

For MRI slices contain lesions, the level of difficulty for segmentation also varies a lot. Some slices contain only certain categories of the foreground or tumor morphology is easy to segment (as highlighted with blue boxes in Fig. 1(b)), and some difficult-to-segment slices contain multiple types of tumors that are extremely irregular in shape and difficult to recognize (as highlighted with red boxes in Fig. 1(b)). From the analysis of the MRI data, the answer to the above question is Yes. It is possible to adjust the model complexity according to the input (e.g. image slice) for effective accuracy and efficiency trade-offs.

Our Solution. In this paper we tackle the aforementioned high computational overload problem of medical volumetric segmentation from a different perspective. Rather than designing more lightweight networks with static structure, we propose a highly efficient framework with **d**ynamic **a**rchitecture for **med**ical volumetric segmentation (Med-DANet). As illustrated in Fig. 1(b), taking a 2D image slice as input data, the Decision Network firstly generates a slice-dependent choice which represents the level of segmentation difficulty for the current slice. Then, according to the optimal choice made by the Decision Network, our method can adaptively determine to skip the current slice (i.e. directly output the segmentation map with only zero – background class) as highlighted with green boxes in Fig. 1(b) or utilize the corresponding candidate segmentation network in the pre-defined Model Bank to accurately segment the current slice. The Model Bank consists of several networks with different model complexities. In this way, a reasonable allocation of computing resources for each slice is achieved by our adaptive segmentation framework. The main contributions of this work can be summarized as follows:

- This work presents the *first attempt* to explore the potential of dynamic inference in medical volumetric segmentation task. We focus on the 3D MRI brain tumor segmentation and propose a new framework with dynamic architectures to achieve a good balance between segmentation accuracy and efficiency. The proposed Med-DANet is generic and can be applied to any volumetric segmentation tasks (see Supplementary for the experiments of our Med-DANet on liver tumor segmentation with CT images).
- By exploiting the special characteristics of multi-modal MRI brain tumor segmentation data that different slices have diverse degree of difficulty for segmentation, a comprehensive choice metric is designed to acquire the supervision signal for Decision Network, achieving the trade-off between accuracy and computational complexity of the model.
- Our proposed Med-DANet has strong scalability and flexibility. Any 2D networks can be incorporated into the Model Bank to meet various accuracy and efficiency requirements.
- Extensive experiments on two benchmark datasets (BraTS 2019 and BraTS 2020) for multi-modal 3D MRI brain tumor segmentation demonstrate that our method reaches competitive or better performance than previous state-of-the-art methods with much less model complexity.

2   Related Work

2.1   Static and Lightweight CNNs for Medical Image Segmentation

For medical image segmentation task, U-Net [27] and its variants [8,24,37] have achieved great success recently. However, the expensive computational costs impede the timely segmentation for assisting clinical diagnosis. To this end, great efforts have been made to design lightweight networks with improved model efficiency. For example, 3D-ESPNet [23] generalizes the efficient ESPNet [20] for 2D semantic segmentation to 3D medical volumetric segmentation, achieving satisfactory results on medical images. S3D-UNet [7] takes advantages of the separable 3D convolution to improve model efficiency. DMFNet [4] develops a novel 3D dilated multi-fiber network to bridge the gap between model efficiency and accuracy for 3D MRI brain tumor segmentation. HDCNet [18] replaces 3D convolutions with a novel hierarchical decoupled convolution (HDC) module to achieve a light-weight but efficient pseudo-3D model. [16] introduces a lightweight 3D U-Net with depth-wise separable convolution (DSC), which can not only avoid over fitting but also improve the generalization ability. In addition, knowledge distillation is also a popular method to achieve lightweight networks (i.e. student network). For example, [26] proposes an efficient architecture by distilling knowledge from well-trained medical image segmentation networks to train another lightweight network for efficient medical image segmentation.

2.2   Dynamic Networks for Efficient Inference

Lightweight models operates on the input data with the same static architecture, which cannot adaptively achieve the trade-off between accuracy and computational cost. To cope with this problem, dynamic networks are developed for efficient and adaptive inference [31–35,38]. From the perspective of model architecture, the dynamic structure of network includes dynamic depth and dynamic width. For instance, slimmable networks [35] dynamically adjust the network width to achieve accuracy and efficient trade-offs at inference time. Moreover, adjusting input resolution is also an effective way to balance between accuracy and efficiency. DRNet [38] presents a novel dynamic-resolution network in which the resolution is determined dynamically based on each input sample.

Apart from the research on dynamic inference mostly for the classification task, a few works aim to achieve dynamic inference in pixel labeling tasks. Kong et al. [13] propose Pixel-wise Attention Gating to selectively process each pixel, allocating more computing power to pixels of fuzzy targets under specific resource constraints. Dynamic Multi-scale Network (DMN) [11] adaptively learns weights of convolution kernels according to different input instances, arranging multiple DMN branches to learn multi-scale semantic information in parallel. Li et al. [15] introduce the concept of dynamic routing to generate data-dependent routes. Based on the scale distribution of objects in an image, the proposed soft condition gates can adaptively select scale transformation routes in an end-to-end manner.

3   Methodology

3.1   Overview

An overview of our Med-DANet is shown in Fig. 2. In general, our framework consists of an extremely lightweight Decision Network ($\mathcal{D}$) and a Model Bank ($\mathcal{B}$) which contains n different medical image segmentation networks ($M_1, M_2..., M_n$). Models in the bank should be diverse in terms of the number of parameters and computational cost. To deal with the medical image datasets where segmentation targets are sparsely distributed among slices, we learn a *slice-specific* decision by the Decision Network to dynamically select a suitable model from the Model Bank for the subsequent segmentation task, as formulated by Eq. 1.

$$y = \mathcal{D}(x) \circ \mathcal{B}(x), \tag{1}$$

where x denotes the input image and y is the corresponding prediction. $\mathcal{D} \circ \mathcal{B}$ indicates to take the matched element with index $\mathcal{D}$ in the collection $\mathcal{B}$, and the calculation details will be explained in the next subsection.

Roughly speaking, the Decision Network will comprehensively considers the segmentation accuracy and efficiency of each model, making the most appropriate choice. As for the Model Bank, any 2D networks can be included to meet various accuracy and efficiency requirements. More discussions on the model choices and ablation study are presented in Sect. 4.1 and Sect. 4.3.

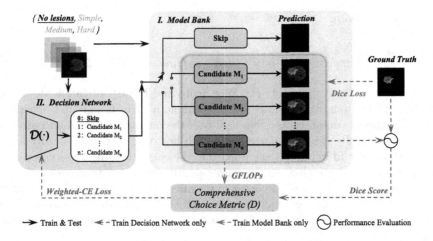

Fig. 2. The illustration of the overall architecture of our proposed Med-DANet. Taking a 2D image slice as input data, the Decision Network generates a slice-dependent choice which represents the level of segmentation difficulties for the current slice. Then, according to the optimal choice made by the Decision Network, our method can adaptively determine to skip the current slice (i.e. directly output a segmentation map with only zero – "background" class) or utilize the corresponding candidate network in the pre-defined Model Bank (containing several networks with different model complexities) to accurately segment the current slice.

3.2 Dynamic Selection Policy

We reduce the channel size of ShuffleNetV2 [19] to get an extremely lightweight classification network as our Decision Network so that its computational overhead is negligible in the entire framework. The Decision Network undertakes a $n + 1$-class classification task, and the $n + 1$ categories refer to the n candidate networks and a skip procedure. Therefore, the Decision Network and Model Bank can be respectively formulated as

$$\mathcal{D}(x) = \{\hat{D}|x; \theta\}, \tag{2}$$

$$\mathcal{B}(x) = [\varnothing, M_1(x), M_2(x), ..., M_n(x)]. \tag{3}$$

θ represents all the parameters of the Decision Network and $\hat{D}$ is the prediction of $\mathcal{D}(x)$. $M_1 \sim M_n$ denote the model candidates and $\varnothing$ indicates the skip procedure.

To be specific, when encountering a slice with only background (background slice, lesions are considered as foreground), the Decision Network will choose to directly skip the subsequent segmentation process. Otherwise, the Decision Network dynamically selects an appropriate segmentation model considering the recognition difficulty of foreground objects. During training process, the supervision of the Decision Network comes from the trade-off between model performance and efficiency. The calculation of the supervision signal of the decision process is as follows

$$D = \begin{cases} 0, & P_f < 1 \\ argmax((1 - \alpha) * S_i + \alpha * softmax(\frac{1}{F_i})) + 1, & P_f \geqslant 1 \end{cases}, \qquad (4)$$

where S_i and F_i is respectively the Dice Score and FLOPs of candidate model M_i during the model training. P_f denotes the number of foreground pixels (all pixels of segmentation targets). Specifically, if the number of foreground pixels is less than 1 (i.e. $P_f < 1$), the current slice will be considered without any lesion areas, which should be directly skipped (i.e. the corresponding supervision is 0) during inference. Note that we normalize $\frac{1}{F_i}$ through the softmax operation to avoid the negative effects of the order of magnitude difference between accuracy and computations, in case that the acquired D is dominated by either model performance or complexity. In addition, α is a coefficient to moderate the impact of Dice Score and FLOPs.

Given the choice $\hat{D}$ predicted by $\mathcal{D}(x)$ and the ground-truth D calculated with Eq. 4, we apply the weighted cross-entropy loss to supervise our Decision Network. This allows the network to learn to skip (assigning all pixels directly to the background class without going through the segmentation models) the pure background slices in the dataset and comprehensively measure the accuracy (S_i) as well as efficiency ($\frac{1}{F_i}$) of different models for the segmentation targets from individual slice. In practice, the skip procedure is essential and can be widely applied because some background slices barely capturing any image content are very common in medical volumes, it is pointless to invest too much computation on these background slices. Moreover, the recognition difficulty of segmentation targets varies from slice to slice, it is more efficient to dynamically select segmentation models of different complexities.

3.3   Training and Inference Strategy

Training. The training process of the entire framework consists of two steps. First, the ensemble training of segmentation models. To save the training time cost, the n segmentation models are jointly trained, minimizing the mean average of the dice-losses of all models and performing gradient back-propagation synchronously.

$$diceloss_j = \sum_{i=1}^{C}(1 - \frac{2|pred_i \cap truth_i|}{|pred_i| + |truth_i|}), \qquad (5)$$

$$Loss_B = \frac{1}{n}\sum_{j=1}^{n} diceloss_j. \qquad (6)$$

Here C denotes the number of segmentation classes of the dataset, $diceloss_j$ is the dice-loss of candidate segmentation model $M_j(j \in \{1, 2, ..., n\})$ and $Loss_B$ is the overall loss when training the Model Bank.

After that, we train the Decision Network with a weighted cross-entropy loss:

$$Loss_{\mathcal{D}} = WCE(D, \hat{D}) = -\sum_{i=0}^{n} w_i * d_i * log(\hat{d}_i), \tag{7}$$

where WCE is short for weighted cross-entropy, d_i and $\hat{d}_i$ are respectively the ground-truth and logits predicted by the Decision Network for model candidate i, w_i represents the corresponding loss weight.

To cope with the problem of class imbalance (background slices make up a considerable portion of the dataset) and further pursue a better trade-off between segmentation accuracy and model complexity, we slightly enlarge the loss weights of candidate models with better performance (i.e. relatively lower the loss weight of the skip procedure).

Inference. After the two-step training phase mentioned above, the well-trained decision network and predefined Model Bank are cascaded sequentially to achieve the final model structure at inference stage. Given a 2D slice as input image, our extremely lightweight Decision Network will decide to skip the current slice or choose the most appropriate segmentation network in the Model Bank based on the segmentation difficulty of the current slice. Following the specific selective choice made by Decision Network, the current slice will be directly skipped (i.e. output the corresponding segmentation maps with all zeros) or segmented by the single activated segmentation network included in the Model Bank. In this way, a dynamic slice-dependent framework with greatly improved efficiency is realized by our method. On one hand, compared with the previously proposed lightweight networks with static structure, our Med-DANet makes dynamic structure adjustments for different inputs instead of treating all inputs equally. On the other hand, compared with the previously proposed dynamic methods that utilize prediction confidence to determine whether the cascaded architecture need to early exit or not, our highly efficient Med-DANet can achieve the accurate segmentation in a one-pass manner.

4   Experiments

4.1   Experimental Setup

Data and Evaluation Metric. The first 3D MRI dataset used in the experiments is provided by the Brain Tumor Segmentation (BraTS) 2019 challenge [1,2,21]. It comprises 335 patient cases for training and 125 cases for validation. Each sample is composed of 3D brain MRI scans with four modalities. Each modality has a volume of $240 \times 240 \times 155$ that has already been aligned into the same space. The ground truth include 4 classes: background (label 0), necrotic and non-enhancing tumor (label 1), peritumoral edema (label 2) and GD-enhancing tumor (label 4). The segmentation accuracy is measured by the Dice score and the Hausdorff distance (95%) metrics for enhancing tumor region (ET, label 4), regions of the tumor core (TC, labels 1 and 4), and the whole tumor region (WT, labels 1, 2 and 4), while the computational complexity is evaluated by the FLOPs metric. The second 3D MRI dataset is provided by the Brain Tumor Segmentation Challenge (BraTS) 2020 [1,2,21]. It is comprised of 369 cases for training, 125 cases for validation. Except for the number of samples in the dataset, the other information about these two MRI datasets are identical.

Implementation Details. The proposed Med-DANet is implemented on Pytorch [25] and trained with 2 NVIDIA Geforce RTX 3090 GPUs (each has 24 GB memory). For the **training** aspect, we first jointly train the Model Bank for 400 epochs from scratch with a batch size of 64. To prevent the small-scale candidates in the Model Bank from overfitting and make sure the large models can be fully optimized, we let small-scale candidates detach the training process at the epoch of 300 and make large-scale candidates continue to back propagate in the remaining epochs. After acquiring the training labels for Decision Network using our proposed comprehensive choice metric, the Decision Network is trained for 50 epochs from scratch with a batch size of 64. The Adam optimizer and the poly learning rate strategy with warm-up are utilized to train both two parts of our method. The initial learning rate for training the Decision Network and Model Bank are 0.01 and 0.0001, respectively. Random cropping, random mirror flipping and random intensity shift are applied as the data augmentation techniques for training both the Decision Network and the segmentation candidates. The softmax Dice loss and weighted cross-entropy loss are employed to train the Model Bank and the Decision Network respectively. Besides, $L2$ Norm is applied for model regularization with a weight decay rate of 10^{-5}.

As for the aspect of **model candidate selection** in the Model Bank, we choose the modified 2D UNet with various channel sizes (i.e. model width) and the 2D version of TransBTS [30] with different scales (i.e. model depth) in this paper. The reason of choosing these two baselines is that both of them are state-of-the-art methods for brain tumor segmentation with excellent performance and they also represent two popular network architectures (i.e. CNN and vision transformer) that can extract complementary information from the data. Compared with the original UNet [27], the modified version make improvements on both segmentation accuracy and efficiency. Taking consideration of both model depth and width, modified 2D UNet with a base channel of 12 (i.e. M1), modified 2D UNet with a base channel of 16 (i.e. M2), the light version of 2D TransBTS with 1-layer Transformer (i.e. M3), and 2D TransBTS with the original 4-layer Transformer (i.e. M4) are selected as the 4 model candidates in the Model Bank. According to the policy made by the Decision Network, the modified 2D UNet can segment the easy slice with greatly reduced computations, while the 2D version of TransBTS achieves precise segmentation of the difficult slices by modeling explicit long-range dependency. In this way, with the well-trained Decision Network and the splendid segmentation candidates in Model Bank, our framework can achieve great trade-off between segmentation accuracy and efficiency.

4.2   Results and Analysis

BraTS 2019. We conduct experiments on the BraTS 2019 validation set and compare our Med-DANet with previous state-of-the-art (SOTA) approaches.

Table 1. Performance comparison on BraTS 2019 validation set. Per case and per slice denote the computational costs of segmenting a 3D case and a 2D slice separately.

Method	Dice score (%) ↑			Hausdorff dist. (mm) ↓			FLOPs (G) ↓	
	ET	WT	TC	ET	WT	TC	Per case	Per slice
3D U-Net [8]	70.86	87.38	72.48	5.062	9.432	8.719	1,669.53	13.04
V-Net [22]	73.89	88.73	76.56	6.131	6.256	8.705	749.29	5.85
Attention U-Net [24]	75.96	88.81	77.20	5.202	7.756	8.258	132.67	1.04
Wang et al. [29]	73.70	89.40	80.70	5.994	5.677	7.357	-	-
Chen et al. [6]	74.16	**90.26**	79.25	4.575	**4.378**	7.954	-	-
Li et al. [14]	77.10	88.60	81.30	6.033	6.232	7.409	-	-
Frey et al. [9]	78.70	89.60	80.00	6.005	8.171	8.241	-	-
TransUNet [5]	78.17	89.48	78.91	4.832	6.667	7.365	1205.76	9.42
Swin-UNet [3]	78.49	89.38	78.75	6.925	7.505	9.260	250.88	1.96
TransBTS [30]	78.36	88.89	**81.41**	5.908	7.599	7.584	333.09	2.60
Ours	**79.99**	90.13	80.83	**4.086**	5.826	**6.886**	**77.78**	**0.61**

The **quantitative results** are presented in Table 1. Our method achieves the Dice scores of 79.99%, 90.13%, 80.83% on ET, WT, TC, respectively, which are comparable or higher results than previous SOTA methods presented in Table 1. Besides, a considerable improvement has also been achieved for segmentation in terms of Hausdorff distance metric. It is worth noting that the model complexity of our Med-DANet is significantly less than other SOTA methods, while the segmentation performance of ours is extraordinary. For example, the computational complexity of TransBTS [30] is **3.5** times that of the proposed Med-DANet, and the model computational complexity of TransUNet [5] is surprisingly **15.4** times that of our method, which fully validates the effectiveness of adaptive architecture for dynamic inference.

For **qualitative analysis**, the brain tumor segmentation results of various methods are shown in Fig. 3 for a visual comparison (more visual comparison on BraTS 2019 dataset can be seen in Supplementary), including 3D U-Net [8], V-Net [22], Attention U-Net [24], and our Med-DANet. Since the labels for the validation set are not available, the five-fold cross-validation evaluation is conducted on the training set for all methods. It is obvious from Fig. 3 that our framework can delineate the brain tumors more accurately and generate much better segmentation masks with the powerful candidates as our dynamic options. Since we successfully take advantage of both CNNs and Transformer for different inputs, both local details and global context can be captured by our method to achieve accurate segmentation of tumors.

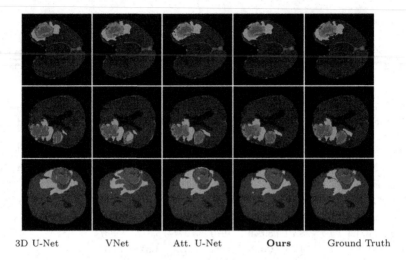

| 3D U-Net | VNet | Att. U-Net | **Ours** | Ground Truth |

Fig. 3. The visual comparison of MRI brain tumor segmentation results. The blue regions denote the enhancing tumors, the red regions denote the non-enhancing tumors, and the green ones denote the peritumoral edema. (Color figure online)

BraTS 2020. We also evaluate our Med-DANet on BraTS 2020 validation set and the segmentation results are reported in Table 2. With the hyper-parameters on BraTS 2019 directly adopted for model training, our method achieves Dice scores of 80.57%, 90.28%, 81.34% and HD of 6.474 mm, 6.718 mm, 7.416 mm on ET, WT, TC. Considerable gain has been made by our method in terms of ET. Besides, compared with 3D U-Net [8], V-Net [22] and Residual 3D U-Net, our method makes great improvements in both metrics. It is clear that our method not only shows significant superiority in model performance but also has the great advantage of computational efficiency, which reveals the benefit of leveraging dynamic inference for medical volumetric segmentation task.

4.3   Ablation Studies

We conduct extensive ablation experiments to verify the effectiveness of our framework and justify the rationale of its design choices based on five-fold cross-validation evaluations on the BraTS 2019 training set. (1) We make a fair comparison with each single candidate in the predefined Model Bank in terms of segmentation performance and computational cost. (2) We investigate the effect of different designs for the final choice metric, which stands for the acquired supervision signal for Decision Network to help the proposed framework achieve optimal trade-off between accuracy and efficiency. (3) We explore the effect of different lightweight networks for our Decision Network. (4) We also analyze the effect of different numbers of candidate networks in the Model Bank. Besides, please check Supplementary for more ablation study on BraTS 2019 training set.

Table 2. Performance comparison on BraTS 2020 validation set. Per case and per slice denote the computational costs of segmenting a 3D case and a 2D slice separately.

Method	Dice score (%) ↑			Hausdorff Dist. (mm) ↓			FLOPs (G) ↓	
	ET	WT	TC	ET	WT	TC	Per case	Per slice
3D U-Net [8]	68.76	84.11	79.06	50.983	13.366	13.607	1,669.53	13.04
V-Net [22]	61.79	84.63	75.26	47.702	20.407	12.175	749.29	5.85
Deeper V-Net [22]	68.97	86.11	77.90	43.518	14.499	16.153	-	-
3D Residual U-Net [36]	71.63	82.46	76.47	37.422	12.337	13.105	407.37	3.18
Liu et al. [17]	76.37	88.23	80.12	21.390	6.680	**6.490**	-	-
Vu et al. [28]	77.17	**90.55**	**82.67**	27.040	**4.990**	8.630	-	-
Ghaffari et al. [10]	78.00	90.00	82.00	-	-	-	-	-
TransUNet [5]	78.42	89.46	78.37	12.851	5.968	12.840	1205.76	9.42
Swin-UNet [3]	78.95	89.34	77.60	**11.005**	7.855	14.594	250.88	1.96
TransBTS [30]	78.50	89.00	81.36	16.716	6.469	10.468	333.09	2.60
Ours	**80.57**	90.28	81.34	**6.474**	6.718	7.416	**77.71**	**0.61**

Comparison with Each Single Candidate in Model Bank. We first compare our Med-DANet with all the candidates in Model Bank to demonstrate the powerful potential of dynamic architecture for medical volumetric segmentation. It is worth noting that the comparison is made under two different common settings to comprehensively evaluate the proposed framework. The first setting is to utilize the cropped image with a spatial resolution of 128×128 for training process and use slide-window technique to inference on original input with the spatial resolution of 240×240 (i.e. full resolution), while the second setting is to utilize the full resolution for both training and inference. As presented in Table 3, considerable improvements are achieved by our method in terms of both segmentation accuracy and model efficiency. Compared with the candidate M4 which has the largest model complexity under setting 1, our method achieves comparable performance with up to **8x** less computational costs. The same situation can be clearly seen under setting 2 in Table 3. With much less model complexity and great segmentation performance, our proposed Med-DANet pursues the best trade-off between accuracy and efficiency, demonstrating the significance of adaptive architecture for dynamic inference.

Effect of Different Designs for the Comprehensive Choice Metric. To seek the optimal trade-off between model complexity and performance, we further investigate the effect of different designs for our proposed comprehensive choice metric (as illustrated in Eq. 4). As described in Sect. 3, we introduce α and softmax operation to moderate the impact of Dice Score and FLOPs, in case that the acquired ground truth for Decision Network is dominated by either accuracy or complexity. The ablation results are listed in Table 4. It shows that $\alpha = 0.001$ is the sweet spot for the whole framework to achieve the optimal balance between accuracy and efficiency. Specifically, increasing α will make our method focus more on model efficiency, while the decreasing of α will push our

Table 3. Comparison with each single candidate in the predefined Model Bank.

Under setting 1 (w/ slide window)

Method	Dice score (%) ↑			FLOPs (G) ↓			
	ET	WT	TC	All cases	Per case	Per slice	Per inference
M1(Modified 2D UNet-12)	75.49	90.21	81.58	**99,026.40**	**1,500.40**	**9.68**	**0.61**
M2(Modified 2D UNet-16)	78.31	90.61	82.59	174,646.57	2,646.16	17.07	1.07
M3(2D TransBTS-light)	78.72	90.30	82.99	385,957.45	5,847.84	37.73	2.36
M4(2D TransBTS)	77.21	**91.08**	**83.27**	814,962.73	12,347.92	79.66	4.98
Ours	**78.75**	90.40	83.13	102,398.01	1,551.485	10.01	0.63

Under setting 2 (w/o slide window)

Method	Dice score (%) ↑			FLOPs (G) ↓			
	ET	WT	TC	All cases	Per case	Per slice	Per inference
M1(Modified 2D UNet-12)	76.86	90.16	80.43	**21,748.98**	**329.53**	**2.13**	**2.13**
M2(Modified 2D UNet-16)	77.22	89.99	81.61	38,362.50	581.25	3.75	3.75
M3(2D TransBTS-light)	76.64	90.16	82.21	90,862.86	1,376.71	8.88	8.88
M4(2D TransBTS)	76.48	90.57	**83.21**	203,351.94	3,081.09	19.88	19.88
Ours	**77.73**	**90.65**	82.72	38,211.12	578.96	3.74	3.74

method to pursue model accuracy without the consideration of computational cost. Similarly, the drop of softmax operation on either Dice Scores or FLOPs will cause our framework to extremely pursue either the model performance or efficiency. By adopting the optimal configuration ($\alpha = 0.001$, with softmax on FLOPs), our Med-DANet achieves greatly reduced computational complexity and competitive model accuracy.

Effect of Different Lightweight Networks for Decision Network. After investigating of the best design for the choice metric, we verify the effectiveness of our method with different Decision Networks. To achieve the highly efficient overall framework, the computational cost brought by the Decision Network should be controlled within acceptable limits. Therefore, four lightweight CNNs (MobileNetV2, GhostNet, ShuffleNetV2, and our modified ShuffleNetV2) are selected to study the influence of the Decision Network. To be noticed, the modified ShuffleNetV2 is acquired by greatly cutting down the channel size (i.e. model width). As shown in Table 5, with our modified ShuffleNetV2 as the Decision Network, our Med-DANet yields the best trade-off between accuracy and computational cost. Although our method achieves the best Dice Scores with MobileNetV2 as the Decision Network, the model complexity of MobileNetV2 and the overall FLOPs resulted by the guidance of MobileNetV2 are not acceptable. Specifically, the model complexity of the modified ShuffleNetV2 is approximately **1/3** of GhostNet or ShuffleNetV2 and nearly **1/23** of MobileNetV2, which shows the effectiveness and efficiency of our optimal Decision Network. It is clear that employing modified ShuffleNetV2 enables our framework to show great superiority in terms of computation with competitive model performance.

Table 4. Ablation study on effect of different design for the proposed comprehensive choice metric. "*S*", "*F*" denote the Dice Scores and FLOPs respectively, w/o and w/ denote with or without softmax on corresponding metrics (i.e. Dice Scores and FLOPs).

Comprehensive choice metric design	Dice score (%) ↑			FLOPs (G) ↓			
	ET	WT	TC	All cases	Per case	Per slice	Per inference
$\alpha = 0.0001$	**78.84**	**90.48**	**83.28**	129,768.88	1,966.20	12.69	0.79
$\alpha = 0.001$	77.00	90.17	82.34	51,994.98	787.80	5.08	0.32
$\alpha = 0.01$	77.21	90.19	81.80	49,951.03	756.83	4.88	0.31
$\alpha = 0.001$, w/ S & F	77.00	90.17	82.34	51,994.98	787.80	5.08	0.32
$\alpha = 0.001$, w/o F	75.57	90.10	81.85	**48,255.83**	**731.15**	**4.72**	**0.29**
$\alpha = \mathbf{0.001}$, **w/o S**	78.75	90.40	83.13	102,398.01	1,551.485	10.01	0.63
$\alpha = 0.001$, w/o S & F	77.12	90.31	82.66	69,618.70	1,054.83	6.81	0.43

Table 5. Ablation study on effect of different choices for Decision Network. DN denotes the Decision Network, while ShuffleNetV2-M denotes our modified ShuffleNetV2.

Decision network	DN's FLOPs (G)	Dice score (%) ↑			Overall FLOPs (G) ↓			
		ET	WT	TC	All cases	Per case	Per slice	Per inference
MobileNetV2	1.758	**78.54**	**90.22**	**82.44**	334,046.58	5,061.31	32.65	2.04
GhostNet	0.278	75.57	90.19	81.48	82,536.60	1,250.56	8.07	0.50
ShuffleNetV2	0.247	77.20	90.19	81.48	96,606.43	1,463.73	9.44	0.59
ShuffleNetV2-M	0.078	77.00	90.17	82.34	**51,994.98**	**787.80**	**5.08**	**0.32**

Effect of Different numbers of Candidate Networks in Model Bank.
Finally, we conduct experiments to investigate the influence of the number of candidates in Model Bank on segmentation performance and efficiency. The quantitative results are illustrated in Table 6. First of all, with no candidates (only skip procedure), the framework will naturally not work at all. Then we add the lightest CNN and Transformer as candidates ($n = 2$), a good result has been achieved already. After that, the largest CNN and Transformer are also incorporated to Model Bank ($n = 4$), making the segmentation performance and efficiency of the network both improve. Compared to 2 candidates, 4 candidates give the network more options for pursuing either performance or efficiency. However, when we further add 2 medium-sized CNN and Transformer to the Model Bank ($n = 6$), although the network performance (i.e. segmentation accuracy) is further improved because of more optional network candidates, the computational cost is also increased. Moreover, more candidate networks in the model bank would also increase the training cost. If higher precision requirements is necessary for the segmentation tasks, more candidates can be plugged into the Model bank to further boost the final performance. In conclusion, 4 candidates in Model Bank achieve the best balance between the accuracy and efficiency.

Table 6. Ablation study on effect of different numbers of candidate networks (n).

Number of candidate networks	Dice score (%) ↑			FLOPs (G) ↓			
	ET	WT	TC	All cases	Per case	Per slice	Per inference
0 (only skip)	9.09	0.00	0.00	0.00	0.00	0.00	0.00
2 (1 CNN + 1 TR)	75.60	90.15	82.11	54,247.84	821.94	5.30	0.33
4 (2 CNN + 2 TR)	77.00	90.17	82.34	**51,994.98**	**787.80**	**5.08**	**0.32**
6 (3 CNN + 3 TR)	**78.71**	**90.76**	**82.92**	84,130.02	1,274.70	8.22	0.51

5 Conclusion

We present the *first attempt* to explore the potential of dynamic inference in medical volumetric segmentation task. We focus on the 3D MRI brain tumor segmentation and propose a new framework named Med-DANet with dynamic architectures to achieve the trade-off between segmentation accuracy and efficiency. The proposed Med-DANet is generic and not limited to MRI brain tumor segmentation, which can be applied to any volumetric segmentation tasks. It is also worth noting that our proposed Med-DANet has strong scalability and flexibility. Any 2D state-of-the-art methods can be incorporated into our framework to satisfy different accuracy and efficiency requirements. Extensive experiments on two benchmark datasets (BraTS 2019 and BraTS 2020) for multi-modal 3D MRI brain tumor segmentation demonstrate that our Med-DANet reaches competitive or better performance than previous state-of-the-art methods with greatly improved model complexity.

Acknowledgement. This work was supported by the Fundamental Research Funds for the China Central Universities of USTB (FRF-DF-19-002), Scientific and Technological Innovation Foundation of Shunde Graduate School, USTB (BK20BE014).

References

1. Bakas, S., et al.: Advancing the cancer genome atlas glioma MRI collections with expert segmentation labels and radiomic features. Sci. Data **4**, 170117 (2017)
2. Bakas, S., et al.: Identifying the best machine learning algorithms for brain tumor segmentation, progression assessment, and overall survival prediction in the brats challenge. arXiv preprint arXiv:1811.02629 (2018)
3. Cao, H., et al.: Swin-Unet: Unet-like pure transformer for medical image segmentation. arXiv preprint arXiv:2105.05537 (2021)
4. Chen, C., Liu, X., Ding, M., Zheng, J., Li, J.: 3D dilated multi-fiber network for real-time brain tumor segmentation in MRI. In: Shen, D., et al. (eds.) MICCAI 2019. LNCS, vol. 11766, pp. 184–192. Springer, Cham (2019). https://doi.org/10.1007/978-3-030-32248-9_21
5. Chen, J., et al.: TransUNet: transformers make strong encoders for medical image segmentation. arXiv preprint arXiv:2102.04306 (2021)
6. Chen, M., Wu, Y., Wu, J.: Aggregating multi-scale prediction based on 3D U-Net in brain tumor segmentation. In: Crimi, A., Bakas, S. (eds.) BrainLes 2019. LNCS,

vol. 11992, pp. 142–152. Springer, Cham (2020). https://doi.org/10.1007/978-3-030-46640-4_14

7. Chen, W., Liu, B., Peng, S., Sun, J., Qiao, X.: S3D-UNet: separable 3D U-Net for brain tumor segmentation. In: Crimi, A., Bakas, S., Kuijf, H., Keyvan, F., Reyes, M., van Walsum, T. (eds.) BrainLes 2018. LNCS, vol. 11384, pp. 358–368. Springer, Cham (2019). https://doi.org/10.1007/978-3-030-11726-9_32

8. Çiçek, Ö., Abdulkadir, A., Lienkamp, S.S., Brox, T., Ronneberger, O.: 3D U-Net: learning dense volumetric segmentation from sparse annotation. In: Ourselin, S., Joskowicz, L., Sabuncu, M.R., Unal, G., Wells, W. (eds.) MICCAI 2016. LNCS, vol. 9901, pp. 424–432. Springer, Cham (2016). https://doi.org/10.1007/978-3-319-46723-8_49

9. Frey, M., Nau, M.: Memory efficient brain tumor segmentation using an autoencoder-regularized U-Net. In: Crimi, A., Bakas, S. (eds.) BrainLes 2019. LNCS, vol. 11992, pp. 388–396. Springer, Cham (2020). https://doi.org/10.1007/978-3-030-46640-4_37

10. Ghaffari, M., Sowmya, A., Oliver, R.: Brain tumour segmentation using cascaded 3D densely-connected u-net. arXiv preprint arXiv:2009.07563 (2020)

11. He, J., Deng, Z., Qiao, Y.: Dynamic multi-scale filters for semantic segmentation. In: Proceedings of the IEEE/CVF International Conference on Computer Vision, pp. 3562–3572 (2019)

12. Huo, Y., et al.: Robust multicontrast MRI spleen segmentation for splenomegaly using multi-atlas segmentation. IEEE Trans. Biomed. Eng. **65**(2), 336–343 (2017)

13. Kong, S., Fowlkes, C.: Pixel-wise attentional gating for scene parsing. In: 2019 IEEE Winter Conference on Applications of Computer Vision (WACV), pp. 1024–1033. IEEE (2019)

14. Li, X., Luo, G., Wang, K.: Multi-step cascaded networks for brain tumor segmentation. In: Crimi, A., Bakas, S. (eds.) BrainLes 2019. LNCS, vol. 11992, pp. 163–173. Springer, Cham (2020). https://doi.org/10.1007/978-3-030-46640-4_16

15. Li, Y., et al.: Learning dynamic routing for semantic segmentation. In: Proceedings of the IEEE/CVF Conference on Computer Vision and Pattern Recognition, pp. 8553–8562 (2020)

16. Li, Z., Pan, J., Wu, H., Wen, Z., Qin, J.: Memory-efficient automatic kidney and tumor segmentation based on non-local context guided 3D U-Net. In: Martel, A.L., et al. (eds.) MICCAI 2020. LNCS, vol. 12264, pp. 197–206. Springer, Cham (2020). https://doi.org/10.1007/978-3-030-59719-1_20

17. Liu, C., et al.: Brain tumor segmentation network using attention-based fusion and spatial relationship constraint. In: Crimi, A., Bakas, S. (eds.) BrainLes 2020. LNCS, vol. 12658, pp. 219–229. Springer, Cham (2021). https://doi.org/10.1007/978-3-030-72084-1_20

18. Luo, Z., Jia, Z., Yuan, Z., Peng, J.: HDC-Net: hierarchical decoupled convolution network for brain tumor segmentation. IEEE J. Biomed. Health Inform. **25**(3), 737–745 (2020)

19. Ma, N., Zhang, X., Zheng, H.T., Sun, J.: Shufflenet v2: practical guidelines for efficient CNN architecture design. In: Proceedings of the European Conference on Computer Vision (ECCV), pp. 116–131 (2018)

20. Mehta, S., Rastegari, M., Caspi, A., Shapiro, L., Hajishirzi, H.: ESPNet: efficient spatial pyramid of dilated convolutions for semantic segmentation. In: Proceedings of the European Conference on Computer Vision (ECCV), pp. 552–568 (2018)

21. Menze, B.H., et al.: The multimodal brain tumor image segmentation benchmark (brats). IEEE Trans. Med. Imaging **34**(10), 1993–2024 (2014)

22. Milletari, F., Navab, N., Ahmadi, S.A.: V-net: fully convolutional neural networks for volumetric medical image segmentation. In: 2016 Fourth International Conference on 3D Vision (3DV), pp. 565–571. IEEE (2016)

23. Nuechterlein, N., Mehta, S.: 3D-ESPNet with pyramidal refinement for volumetric brain tumor image segmentation. In: Crimi, A., Bakas, S., Kuijf, H., Keyvan, F., Reyes, M., van Walsum, T. (eds.) BrainLes 2018. LNCS, vol. 11384, pp. 245–253. Springer, Cham (2019). https://doi.org/10.1007/978-3-030-11726-9_22

24. Oktay, O., et al.: Attention U-Net: learning where to look for the pancreas. arXiv preprint arXiv:1804.03999 (2018)

25. Paszke, A., et al.: Pytorch: an imperative style, high-performance deep learning library. In: Advances in Neural Information Processing Systems, vol. 32 (2019)

26. Qin, D., et al.: Efficient medical image segmentation based on knowledge distillation. IEEE Trans. Med. Imaging 40(12), 3820–3831 (2021)

27. Ronneberger, O., Fischer, P., Brox, T.: U-Net: convolutional networks for biomedical image segmentation. In: Navab, N., Hornegger, J., Wells, W.M., Frangi, A.F. (eds.) MICCAI 2015. LNCS, vol. 9351, pp. 234–241. Springer, Cham (2015). https://doi.org/10.1007/978-3-319-24574-4_28

28. Vu, M.H., Nyholm, T., Löfstedt, T.: Multi-decoder networks with multi-denoising inputs for tumor segmentation. In: Crimi, A., Bakas, S. (eds.) BrainLes 2020. LNCS, vol. 12658, pp. 412–423. Springer, Cham (2021). https://doi.org/10.1007/978-3-030-72084-1_37

29. Wang, F., Jiang, R., Zheng, L., Meng, C., Biswal, B.: 3D U-Net based brain tumor segmentation and survival days prediction. In: Crimi, A., Bakas, S. (eds.) BrainLes 2019. LNCS, vol. 11992, pp. 131–141. Springer, Cham (2020). https://doi.org/10.1007/978-3-030-46640-4_13

30. Wang, W., Chen, C., Ding, M., Yu, H., Zha, S., Li, J.: TransBTS: multimodal brain tumor segmentation using transformer. In: de Bruijne, M., et al. (eds.) MICCAI 2021. LNCS, vol. 12901, pp. 109–119. Springer, Cham (2021). https://doi.org/10.1007/978-3-030-87193-2_11

31. Wang, Y., Huang, R., Song, S., Huang, Z., Huang, G.: Not all images are worth 16x16 words: dynamic vision transformers with adaptive sequence length. arXiv e-prints pp. arXiv-2105 (2021)

32. Yang, L., Han, Y., Chen, X., Song, S., Dai, J., Huang, G.: Resolution adaptive networks for efficient inference. In: Proceedings of the IEEE/CVF Conference on Computer Vision and Pattern Recognition, pp. 2369–2378 (2020)

33. Yang, T., Zhu, S., Chen, C., Yan, S., Zhang, M., Willis, A.: MutualNet: adaptive ConvNet via mutual learning from network width and resolution. In: Vedaldi, A., Bischof, H., Brox, T., Frahm, J.-M. (eds.) ECCV 2020. LNCS, vol. 12346, pp. 299–315. Springer, Cham (2020). https://doi.org/10.1007/978-3-030-58452-8_18

34. Yang, T., et al.: Mutualnet: adaptive convnet via mutual learning from different model configurations. IEEE Trans. Pattern Anal. Mach. Intell. (2021)

35. Yu, J., Yang, L., Xu, N., Yang, J., Huang, T.: Slimmable neural networks. arXiv preprint arXiv:1812.08928 (2018)

36. Zhang, Z., Liu, Q., Wang, Y.: Road extraction by deep residual U-Net. IEEE Geosci. Remote Sens. Lett. 15(5), 749–753 (2018)

37. Zhou, Z., Rahman Siddiquee, M.M., Tajbakhsh, N., Liang, J.: UNet++: a nested U-Net architecture for medical image segmentation. In: Stoyanov, D., et al. (eds.) DLMIA/ML-CDS -2018. LNCS, vol. 11045, pp. 3–11. Springer, Cham (2018). https://doi.org/10.1007/978-3-030-00889-5_1

38. Zhu, M., et al.: Dynamic resolution network. In: Advances in Neural Information Processing Systems, vol. 34 (2021)

ConCL: Concept Contrastive Learning for Dense Prediction Pre-training in Pathology Images

Jiawei Yang[1,2], Hanbo Chen[1(✉)], Yuan Liang[2], Junzhou Huang[3], Lei He[2], and Jianhua Yao[1(✉)]

[1] Tencent AI Lab, Bellevue, USA
jiawei118@ucla.edu, hanbochen@tencent.com, jianhua.yao@gmail.com
[2] University of California, Los Angeles, Los Angeles, USA
[3] University of Texas at Arlington, Arlington, USA

Abstract. Detecting and segmenting objects within whole slide images is essential in computational pathology workflow. Self-supervised learning (SSL) is appealing to such annotation-heavy tasks. Despite the extensive benchmarks in natural images for *dense* tasks, such studies are, unfortunately, absent in current works for pathology. Our paper intends to narrow this gap. We first benchmark representative SSL methods for dense prediction tasks in pathology images. Then, we propose **con**cept **c**ontrastive **l**earning (ConCL), an SSL framework for dense pre-training. We explore how ConCL performs with concepts provided by different sources and end up with proposing a simple dependency-free concept generating method that does not rely on external segmentation algorithms or saliency detection models. Extensive experiments demonstrate the superiority of ConCL over previous state-of-the-art SSL methods across different settings. Along our exploration, we distill several important and intriguing components contributing to the success of dense pre-training for pathology images. We hope this work could provide useful data points and encourage the community to conduct ConCL pre-training for problems of interest. Code is available at https://github.com/TencentAILabHealthcare/ConCL.

Keywords: Pathology image analysis · Whole slide image · Self-supervised learning · Object detection · Instance segmentation · Pre-training

1 Introduction

Computational pathology is an emerging area in modern healthcare. More whole slide images (WSIs) are now analyzed by deep learning (DL) models [29]. To alleviate the heavy annotation burden required by DL models, reusing weights from

---

J. Yang—Work done during an internship at Tencent AI Lab.

Supplementary Information The online version contains supplementary material available at https://doi.org/10.1007/978-3-031-19803-8_31.

S. Avidan et al. (Eds.): ECCV 2022, LNCS 13681, pp. 523–539, 2022.
https://doi.org/10.1007/978-3-031-19803-8_31

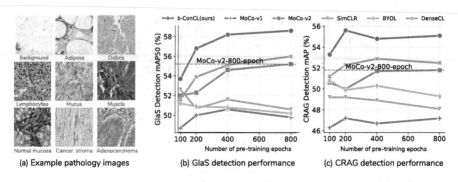

Fig. 1. (a) Example pathology images with tissue class names. (b, c) Comparisons of pre-trained models by fine-tuning on the GlaS [28] and CRAG [9] datasets. The detector is Mask-RCNN [14] with a ResNet-18 backbone [15], and an FPN head [20]. Results are averaged over 5 independent runs.

pre-trained models has become a common practice. Besides transferring from fully-supervised models, recent attention has been attracted to self-supervised learning (SSL) methods [3,10,12]. They are annotation-free but can achieve comparable or even better performance when transferring.

The breakthrough of SSL methods starts with contrastive learning [3,4,11, 12,34], where the most popular task is instance discrimination [34]. It requires a model to discriminate among individual instances. To achieve that, it first defines some positive pairs and negative pairs. It then optimizes a model to maximize the representation similarity between positive pairs and minimize it between negative pairs. Later, more SSL methods based on cross-view prediction are proposed, e.g., [2,3,10,38]. However, these methods are optimized for image-level representations and might be sub-optimal for dense prediction tasks such as object detection and instance segmentation. This motivates works for detection-friendly pre-training methods, e.g., DenseCL [33], InsLoc [37], *Self-EMD* [22], SCRL [27], and more [16,30,35,36]. Despite many interests raised in the natural image domain for dense prediction problems, such studies, which are of important clinical and practical values, are *absent* in the pathology image domain. Our research is intended to bridge the gap between SSL in natural images and pathology images for dense prediction tasks, as well as to distill the key components to the success of dense pre-training in the pathology data.

To that end, we start by presenting a general **Con**cept **C**ontrastive **L**earning (ConCL) framework. Rather than contrasting image-level representations [3,12, 34], it contrasts "concepts" that mark different local (semantic) regions. ConCL is an abstraction of dense contrasting frameworks that can resemble most concurrent related works. We first benchmark current leading image-level SSL methods and a grid-level dense SSL method (*i.e.*, DenseCL [33]) in two public datasets. We observe a considerable performance gap between DenseCL [33] and the others. These gaps indicate the importance of contrasting densely (grid-level) than roughly (image-level). Then, directed by the performance differences and the characteristics of pathology images, we gradually develop and improve ConCL via a series of explorations. Specifically, we explore: 1) *what makes the success of dense prediction pre-training?* 2) *what kind of concepts are good for pathology images?* The nature of having rich low-level patterns in pathology images (see Fig. 1-(a)) gives some surprising and intriguing results, *e.g.*, a randomly initialized model can group meaningful concepts and help dense pre-training. Along the exploration, we distill several key components contributing to the transferring performance for dense tasks. At the end of exploration, the presented ConCL can surpass various state-of-the-art SSL methods by solid and consistent margins across different downstream datasets, detector architectures, fine-tuning schedules, and pre-training epochs. For example, as shown in Fig. 1-(b), the 200-epoch pre-trained ConCL wins all the other methods but with 4× to 8× fewer epochs. To summarize, this paper makes the following contributions:

- It makes one of the earliest attempts to systematically study and benchmark self-supervised learning methods for dense prediction problems in pathology images, which are of high practical and clinical interest but, unfortunately, *absent* in existing works. We hope this work could narrow the gap between studies in natural images and pathology images.
- It presents ConCL, an SSL framework for dense pre-training. We show how ConCL performs with concepts provided by different sources and find that a randomly initialized model could learn semantic concepts and improve itself without expert-annotation or external algorithms while achieving competitive, if not the best, results.
- It shows how important the *dense* pre-training is in pathology images for dense tasks and provides some intriguing observations that could contribute to other applications such as few-shot and semi-supervised segmentation and detection, or more, in pathology image analysis or beyond.

We hope this work could provide useful data points and encourage the community to conduct ConCL pre-training for problems of interest.

2 Related Work

Contrastive Learning. The success of deep learning is mainly attributed to mining a large amount of data. When limited data is provided for specific tasks, an alternative is to transfer knowledge by re-using pre-trained models [8,13]. SSL methods learn good pre-trained models from label-free pretext tasks, *e.g.*, colorization [39,40], denoising [31], and thus attract much attention. Recently, contrastive learning [2–4,12,24,34], a typical branch of SSL, has made significant progress in many fields, where instance discrimination [3,4,11,12,34] serves as a pretext task. It requires a model to discriminate among individual instances, *i.e.*, image-level representations [34]. MoCo [4,12] and SimCLR [3] are two representatives. Specifically, they generate two views of the same image via random data augmentations (*e.g.*, color jittering, random cropping) and mark them as a positive pair. Then, views from other different images are marked as negative instances or pairs. After that, they learn embeddings by maximizing the similarity between the representations of positive pairs while minimizing it between the representations of negative pairs. Later methods combine contrasting with clustering, *e.g.*, SwAV [2] proposes to contrast views' cluster assignments, and PCL [19] contrasts instances with cluster prototypes.

Dense Prediction Pre-training. Despite their success in transferring to classification tasks, good image-level representations do not necessarily result in better performance in dense prediction tasks. Therefore, recent efforts have been made for dense prediction pre-training. Related works are mostly concurrent [16,22,27,30,33,35–37]. Among them, DenseCL [33] learns the correspondence among pixels of a positive pair and optimizes a pairwise contrastive loss at a pixel level, yielding a dense contrasting behavior. *Self*-EMD [22] does dense predicting in a non-contrastive manner as in BYOL [10], *i.e.*, predicting a grid-level feature vector from one view when given its counterpart from another (positive) view. SCRL [27] argues the importance of spatially consistent representations, so it maximizes the similarity of box region features in the intersected area. The most relevant works concurrent to ours are [16,30]. They also optimize contrastive loss over mask-averaged representations. Those masks are generated by external algorithms that are successful for natural images, *e.g.*, Felzenszwalb-Huttenlocher algorithm [7], or models, *e.g.*, MCG [1], BASNet [25], and DeepUSPS [23]. However, the success of such mask generators is unfortunately unverified in pathology images. In this paper, we provide some of their empirical results. Their different performances yield the disparity between natural and pathology images, from which we are motivated to propose a dependency-free concept mask generator. It directly bootstraps the structural concepts inherent in pathology images, learns from *scratch*, and has better potential.

SSL in Pathology Images. Studying SSL methods in pathology images is still at an early stage. In addition to studies on natural images, SimCLR [3] is also studied and benchmarked for classification, regression, and segmentation tasks in pathology images [6]. Some domain-specific self-supervised pretext tasks, *e.g.*, magnification prediction, JigMag prediction, and hematoxylin channel prediction, are proposed and studied [18]. However, despite interest raised in natural images for dense problems, existing works have not studied, to our knowledge, detection/segmentation-friendly SSL methods in pathology images. Our work aims to bridge this gap and provide our exploration roadmap toward better dense prediction performance for pathology images.

3   Method

3.1   Preliminary: Instance Contrastive Learning

MoCo [12] abstracts the instance discrimination task as a dictionary look-up problem. Specifically, for each encoded query q, there is a set of encoded keys $\{k_0, k_1, k_2, ...\}$ in a dictionary. The instance discrimination task is to pull closer q and its matched positive key k_+ in the dictionary while spreading q away from all

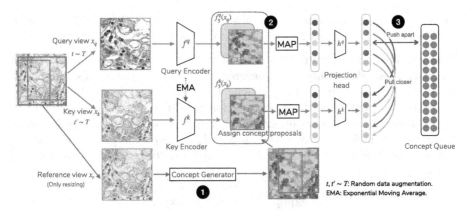

Fig. 2. ConCL overview. ConCL has three steps: (1) Given a query view x_q and a key view x_k, their union region is cropped as a reference view x_r. ConCL obtains concept proposals by processing x_r with a "concept generator." (2) For the shared concepts, ConCL computes their representations via masked average pooling (MAP). (3) ConCL optimizes concept contrastive loss (Eq. (2)), and enqueues the concept prototypes from the key encoder to the concept queue.

other negative keys k_-. When using the dot-product as similarity measurement, a form of contrastive loss function based on InfoNCE [24] becomes:

$$L_q = -\log \frac{\exp(q \cdot k_+/\tau)}{\exp(q \cdot k_+/\tau) + \sum_{k_-} \exp(q \cdot k_-/\tau)} \quad (1)$$

where τ is a temperature hyper-parameter [34]. Queries q and keys k are computed by a query encoder and a key encoder, respectively [4,12]. Formally, $q = h(\text{GAP}(f_5(x_q)))$, where h is a MLP projection head as per [3]; $\text{GAP}(\cdot)$ denotes global-average-pooling, and $f_5(x)$ represents the outputs from the stage-5 of a ResNet [15]. Keys k are computed similarly using the key encoder. In MoCo [12], the negative keys are stored in a queue to avoid using large batches [3].

3.2   Concept Contrastive Learning

Instance contrastive methods [3,12,34] do well in discriminating among image-level instances, but dense prediction tasks usually require discriminating among local details, e.g., object instances or object parts. We abstract such local details, or say, fine-grained semantics as "concepts." A concept does not necessarily represent an object. Instead, any sub-region in an image could be a concept since it contains certain different semantics. From the perspective of dense prediction, it is desirable to build concept-sensitive representations. For example, one WSI patch usually contains multiple small objects, e.g., nucleus, glands, and multiple texture-like tissues, e.g., mucus [17,29]. To successfully detect and segment objects in such images, models need to learn more information from local details.

To this end, we propose a simple but effective framework—***Con**cept **C**ontrastive Learning* (ConCL). Figure 2 shows its overview, which we elaborate on below.

Concept Discrimination. We first define a pretext task named concept discrimination. Similar to instance discrimination [11,34], concept discrimination requires a model to discriminate among the representations of the same but augmented concepts and the representations of different concepts. We formulate concept discrimination by extending the instance-level queries and keys to concept-level. Specifically, given an encoded query concept q^c and a set of encoded key concepts $\{k_0^c, k_1^c, k_2^c, ...\}$, we derive concept contrastive loss as:

$$L_c = -\log \frac{\exp(q^c \cdot k_+^c/\tau)}{\exp(q^c \cdot k_+^c/\tau) + \sum_{k_-^c} \exp(q^c \cdot k_-^c/\tau)} \tag{2}$$

where τ is the same temperature parameter and k_-^c are keys in the concept queue—the queue to store concept representations. This objective brings representations of different views of the same concept closer and spreads representations of views from different concepts apart.

Concept Mask Proposal. We use masks to annotate fine-grained concepts explicitly. Assume a mask generator is given, as diagramed at the bottom of Fig. 2; we first pass a reference view x_r, defined as the circumscribed rectangle crop of the union of two views, into the mask generator to obtain a set of concept masks—$\mathcal{M}_r = \{m_i\}_{i=1}^K$, where K is the number of concepts. Since the reference view contains both the query view and the key view, their concept masks $\mathcal{M}_q$ and $\mathcal{M}_k$ are immediately obtained if we restore them in the reference view. Then, we derive concept representations in both views by masked average pooling (MAP) with resized concept masks. Specifically, we compute $q^c = h\left(\mathtt{MAP}\left(f_5(x_q), m_c\right)\right)$ and k^c similarly, where $\mathtt{MAP}(z, m) = \sum_{ij} m_{ij} \cdot z_{ij}/\sum_{ij} m_{ij}$, and $z \in \mathbb{R}^{CHW}$ denotes feature maps, $m \in \{0, 1\}^{HW}$ is a binary indicator for each concept. Here, only the shared concepts in both views are considered, *i.e.*, $m_c \in \mathcal{M}_q \cap \mathcal{M}_k$.

Our analysis hereafter focuses on 1) What makes the success of dense prediction pre-training? 2) What kind of concepts are good *for pathology images*? Different answers to these two questions reveal the characteristics of pathology images and the disparity between natural and pathology images, as we explore in Sect. 4. Below, we first introduce the benchmark pipeline and setups.

3.3 Benchmark Pipeline

Despite the extensive benchmarks in natural images for dense tasks, to our knowledge, such studies are unfortunately *absent* in current works for pathology. Note that studying SSL methods in pathology images is still at an early stage. Most current works focus on employing image-level SSL methods for classification tasks. Orthogonal to theirs, we investigate a wider range of SSL methods for object detection and instance segmentation tasks, which are of high clinical value. We hope our work could provide useful data points for future work.

Implementations. For implementation details, please refer to Appendix B. We briefly introduce the datasets here and elaborate on them in Appendix C:

- *Pre-training dataset.* We use NCT-CRC-HE-100K [17] dataset, referred to as NCT, for pre-training. It contains 100,000 non-overlapping patches extracted from hematoxylin and eosin (H&E) stained colorectal cancer and normal tissues. All images are of size 224 × 224 at 0.5 MPP (20× magnification). We randomly choose 80% of NCT to be the pre-training dataset.
- *Transferring dataset.* We use two public datasets, the gland segmentation in pathology images challenge (GlaS) dataset [28] and the colorectal adenocarcinoma gland (CRAG) dataset [9], and follow their official train/test splits for evaluation. GlaS [28] collects images of 775 × 522 from H&E stained slides with object-instance-level annotation; the images include both malignant and benign glands. CRAG [9] collects 213 H&E stained images taken from 38 WSIs with a pixel resolution of 0.55 μm/pixel at 20× magnification. Images are mostly of size 1512 × 1516 with object-instance-level annotation. We study the performance of object detection and instance segmentation.

Experimental Setup. We pre-train all the methods on the NCT training set for 200 epochs. For ConCL pre-training, we warm up the model by optimizing instance contrastive loss (Eq. (1)) for the first 20 epochs and switch to concept contrastive loss (Eq. (2)). Then, we use the pre-trained backbones to initialize the detectors, fine-tune them on the training sets of transferring datasets, and test them in the corresponding test sets. Unless otherwise specified, we run all the transferring experiments 5 times and report the averaged performance.

4   Towards Better Concepts: A Roadmap

In this section, we first benchmark some popular state-of-the-art SSL methods for dense pathology tasks. Then, we start with DenseCL [33] and derive better concepts along the way, directed by the questions raised in the previous section.

4.1   Benchmarking SSL Methods for Dense Pathology Tasks

Benchmark Results. Table 1 (baselines and prior SSL arts) shows the transferring performance for GlaS dataset (left columns) and CRAG dataset (right columns), respectively. We report results using 200-epoch pre-trained models and a 1× fine-tuning schedule. On the GlaS dataset [28], we observe that the gap between training from randomly initialized models and training from supervised pre-trained models is relatively smaller compared to those in the natural image domain [3–5,10]. Nonetheless, state-of-the-art SSL methods all exceed supervised pre-training, meeting the same expectation as in natural images. Yet, on the CRAG dataset [9], most of the pre-trained models, including both the self-supervised ones and the supervised one, fail to achieve competitive performance compared to training from randomly initialized weights. The only exception is DenseCL [33], a dense contrasting method.

Table 1. Main results of object detection and instance segmentation. AP^{bb}: bounding box mAP, AP^{mk}: mask mAP.

Category	Methods	GlaS				CRAG			
		Detect		Segment		Detect		Segment	
		AP^{bb}	AP^{bb}_{75}	AP^{mk}	AP^{mk}_{75}	AP^{bb}	AP^{bb}_{75}	AP^{mk}	AP^{mk}_{75}
Baselines	Rand. Init.	49.8	57.3	52.1	60.7	51.1	57.0	50.6	57.3
	Supervised	50.2	56.9	53.2	62.1	49.2	55.2	49.4	55.0
Sect. 4.1 Prior SSL arts	SimCLR [3]	50.7	56.9	53.6	62.7	49.2	54.8	49.1	54.7
	BYOL [10]	50.9	57.7	53.9	62.6	49.9	55.8	49.3	55.3
	PCL-v2† [19]	49.4	55.9	51.9	61.0	51.0	56.6	50.5	56.7
	MoCo-v1 [12]	50.0	56.2	52.1	59.9	47.2	51.1	47.5	52.0
	MoCo-v2 [4]	52.3	60.0	55.3	65.0	50.0	55.7	50.3	56.8
	DenseCL [33]	53.9	62.0	56.5	66.2	52.3	58.2	52.2	59.8
Our differently instantiated ConCLs:									
Sect. 4.2 Grid concepts	(1) g-ConCL(s = 3)	54.9	64.1	57.1	66.3	55.4	62.3	54.4	62.0
	(2) g-ConCL(s = 5)	55.4	65.2	57.4	67.2	55.5	62.7	54.6	62.2
	(3) g-ConCL(s = 7)	54.9	63.8	57.0	66.5	55.3	62.5	54.7	62.6
Sect. 4.3 Natural-image priors concepts	(4) fh-ConCL(s = 50)	55.8	65.6	58.3	68.8	54.8	60.7	54.1	60.7
	(5) fh-ConCL(s = 500)	56.2	65.9	57.7	67.9	54.7	61.9	53.8	60.5
	(6) bas-ConCL	56.1	66.1	58.1	68.1	54.2	61.1	53.4	60.8
Sect. 4.4 Bootstrapped concepts									
	(7) b-ConCL(f_4)	**56.8**	**66.2**	**58.7**	**68.9**	55.1	62.2	54.1	61.4
	(8) b-ConCL(f_5)	56.1	65.6	57.8	67.7	**56.5**	**63.3**	**55.3**	**62.9**

Among the image-level SSL methods, MoCo-v2 [4] performs the best in GlaS and the second-best in CRAG. Enhanced by dense contrasting, DenseCL [33] achieves the best results in both datasets. It should be emphasized that DenseCL [33] gets $+ 1.6$ AP^{bb} for GlaS by using grid-level contrasting. This demonstrates the importance of designing dense pre-training frameworks when transferring to dense tasks since all the stragglers are only optimized for image-level representations. Thus, we here conclude *dense contrasting matters*.

4.2 Correspondence Matters

From the previous section, we find dense contrasting is favored in both natural and pathology images, where DenseCL [33] all achieves top performance. The next question is: *can we improve the dense contrasting framework?* To answer it, we first summarize the overall pipeline of DenseCL [33]. DenseCL

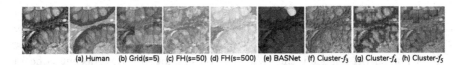

(a) Human   (b) Grid(s=5)   (c) FH(s=50)   (d) FH(s=500)   (e) BASNet   (f) Cluster-f_3 (g) Cluster-f_4 (h) Cluster-f_5

Fig. 3. Concept descriptors. (a) Tissue concept illustration. (b) Grid concepts (s: grid number). (c–d) FH concepts (s: scale). (e) Binary saliency concepts, obtained from BASNet [25]. (f–h) Clustering concepts (f_i: ResNet output stage). The image is resized to 448×448 for better visualization.

computes the dense representations of two views without global average pooling, *i.e.*, $f_5(x_q), f_5(x_k)$, and passes them to a dense projection head to obtain final grid features of size $\mathbb{R}^{128 \times 7 \times 7}$. Then it sets the most similar (measured by cosine similarity) grids in two views as positive pairs. As such, the correspondence of positive pairs is learned. However, the reliability of learned correspondence remains questionable and would affect the quality of learned representations.

To address that, we instantiate DenseCL [33] in ConCL by regarding the grid-prior as a form of concept, as shown in Fig. 3-(b). We denote this ConCL instance as g-ConCL. Compared with DenseCL [33] (learned matching), ConCL naturally restores the positive correspondence from a reference view (precise matching Fig. 2-x_r). Table 1-(1–3) compares the original DenseCL [33] and ConCL-instantiated g-ConCL. The results indicate that g-ConCL with precise correspondence can boost DenseCL [33] by a large margin. Even with the simplest form of concepts, g-ConCL already has topped entries above it in Table 1. We believe other dense pre-training methods that learn the matching between grids, *e.g.*, *Self*-EMD [22], should perform similarly to DenseCL [33], and g-ConCL could outperform them. Thus, we conclude that *correspondence matters.*

4.3 Natural Image Priors in Pathology Images

ConCL is a general framework for using masks as supervision to discriminate concepts. Some previous works in natural image [16,30,32,41,42] also combines masks with contrastive learning, where the masks are provided by ground truth annotation [16,32,42], or supervised/unsupervised pseudo-mask generation [16,30,41]. The mask generators can be graph-based (*e.g.*, Felzenszwalb-Huttenlocher algorithm [7]), MCG [1], or other saliency detection models [23,25] trained on designated natural image datasets. However, those methods werer originally proposed for nature images, and their success for pathology images remains unknown.

Here we instantiate ConCL by using Felzenszwalb-Huttenlocher (FH) algorithm [7] and BASNet [25] as concept generators, dubbed as fh-ConCL and bas-ConCL, respectively. FH [7] is a conventional graph-based segmentation algorithm that relies on local neighborhoods, while BASNet [25] is a deep neural network pre-trained on a curated saliency detection dataset, which only contains daily natural objects. We use these two as representatives to study if these natural image priors win twice in both natural and pathology images.

532   J. Yang et al.

Specifically, we use the FH algorithm in the scikit-image package and set both "scale" and "size" hyper-parameters to s. We use the pre-trained BASNet provided by [25]. Figure 3-(c–e) shows some examples. Table 1 reports the results.

It is not surprising that the BASNet [25] cannot generate decent concept masks (Fig. 3-(e)) for pathology images since it is pre-trained on curated saliency detection datasets. What is surprising is that bas-ConCL does yield satisfactory results (Table 1-(6)). Similar observations are also found in fh-ConCLs (Table 1-(4,5)) that though the generated concept masks are coarse-grained, the resulted transferring performances are unexpectedly good. After inspecting more examples, we find that the generated masks maintain high coherence and integrity despite their coarse-grained nature. That said, each concept contains semantic-consistent objects or textures. For example, Fig. 3-(d, e) can be seen as special cases of Fig. 3-(a) that merge fine-grained semantics with coarse-grained ones. This property makes the major difference between fh-/bas-ConCLs and g-ConCLs, where the grid-concepts are less likely to have coherent semantics.

Thus, we here conclude that *coherence matters* and natural image priors also work in pathology images, though they mostly provide coarse-grained concepts.

4.4 Pathology Image Priors in Pathology Images

Can we obtain concept masks away with natural image priors? External dependency is not always wanted and sometimes may fail to provide the desired masks (*e.g.*, Fig. 3-(e)). We thus task ourselves to find a dependency-free concept proposal method. One of the key characteristics in pathology images is that they have rich low-level patterns and tissue structures. Can we use that prior instead?

Figure 3-(f–h) shows the clustering visualization from intermediate feature maps generated by a 10-epoch warmed-up MoCo-v2 [4]. Thanks to the rich structural patterns in pathology images, we find that simply clustering over the feature maps provided by a barely trained model can already generate meaningful structural concept proposals. We thus build upon this "free lunch" and use a "bootstrap your own *perception*" mechanism that is similar to the "bootstrap your own latent" mechanism in BYOL [10]. ConCL generates concept proposals from the momentum key encoder's perception while simultaneously improving and refining it via the online query encoder, leading to a "bootstrapping" behavior. Thus, we denote such ConCL as bootstrapped-ConCL (b-ConCL). We provide an additional introduction to BYOL and "bootstrapping" in Appendix A.

b-ConCL. The concept generator is now instantiated as a KMeans grouper. We first pass the reference view x_r to the key encoder to obtain a reference feature map from ResNet stage-i: $f_i(x_r) \in \mathbb{R}^{CHW}$. Then, we apply K-Means to group K underlying concepts. b-ConCL relies on neither external segmentation algorithms nor designated saliency detection models for natural images.

Our default setting is $K = 8$, and clustering from f_4 or f_5. We postpone the study of hyper-parameters, *i.e.*, the number of clusters in KMeans, and the clustering stage f_i to Sect. 5.2 and report the main results in Table 1-(7, 8). We find b-ConCL tops other entries. Compared to MoCo-v2 [4], our direct baseline, b-ConCL outperforms it by $+4.5$ AP^{bb} and $+3.1$ AP^{mk}. Moreover, b-ConCL obtains more gains in terms of AP_{75} ($+6.2$ AP_{75}^{bb}, $+3.7$ AP_{75}^{mk}) compared to MoCo-v2 [4], which means it improves MoCo-v2 [4] by more accurate bounding box regression and instance mask prediction. This aligns with our motivation for ConCL since discriminating local concepts helps shape object borders.

Table 2. Detection performance using different detectors. Results are averaged over 5 trials.

Detector	Pretrain	GlaS detection		CRAG detection	
		AP^{bb}	AP_{75}^{bb}	AP^{bb}	AP_{75}^{bb}
MaskRCNN-C4	Rand. Init.	52.9	59.9	49.4	54.2
	Supervised	49.1(-3.8)	55.1(-4.8)	46.1(-3.3)	50.6(-2.3)
	MoCo-v2 [4]	53.6($+0.7$)	61.8($+1.9$)	48.3(-1.1)	52.6(-1.6)
	b-ConCL	55.8($+2.9$)	63.6($+3.7$)	49.8($+0.4$)	54.3($+0.1$)
MaskRCNN-FPN	Rand. Init.	49.8	57.3	51.1	57.0
	Supervised	50.2($+0.4$)	56.9(-0.4)	49.2(-1.9)	55.2(-1.8)
	MoCo-v2 [4]	52.3($+2.5$)	60.0($+2.7$)	50.0(-1.1)	55.7(-1.3)
	b-ConCL	56.8($+7.0$)	66.2($+8.9$)	55.1($+4.0$)	62.2($+5.2$)
RetinaNet	Rand. Init.	46.4	51.0	45.2	47.6
	Supervised	44.7(-1.7)	48.4(-2.6)	43.1(-2.1)	44.8(-2.8)
	MoCo-v2 [4]	47.2($+0.8$)	50.9(-0.1)	43.1(-2.1)	43.8(-3.8)
	b-ConCL	52.6($+6.2$)	58.6($+7.6$)	48.4($+3.2$)	51.9($+4.3$)

Closing Remarks. So far, we have included: i) dense contrasting matters; ii) correspondence matters; iii) coherence matters; iv) natural image priors, though they might only provide coarse-grained concepts, work in pathology images as well; and find v) a randomly initialized or barely trained convolutional neural network, thanks to the rich low-level patterns in pathology images and good network initialization, can generate good proposals that are *dense, fine-grained* and *coherent*, as shown in Fig. 3. Though the coarse-grained concepts generated from natural image priors could also help tasks in our studied benchmarks, they might underperform when a fine-grained dense prediction task is given. We hope our closing remarks could be intriguing and guide future works in designing dense pre-training methods for pathology images and beyond.

5 More Experiments

In the previous section, we have explored how we can obtain concepts, what concepts are good, and find b-ConCL to be the best. We here conduct more experiments to study b-ConCL. Some visual comparisons are in Appendix D.

5.1   Robustness to Transferring Settings

Transferring with Different Detectors. Here we investigate the transferring performance with other detectors, *i.e.*, Mask-RCNN-C4 (C4) [26] and RetinaNet [21]. RetinaNet is a single-stage detector. It uses ResNet-FPN backbone features as Mask-RCNN-FPN but directly generates predictions without region proposal [26]. C4 detector adopts a similar two-stage fashion as Mask-RCNN but uses the outputs of the 4-th residual block as backbone features and re-targets the 5-th block to be the detection head instead of building a new one. These three representative detectors evaluate pre-trained models under different detector architectures. Results together with Mask-RCNN-FPN's are shown in Table 2. b-ConCL performs the best with all three detectors in both datasets. Notably, training from scratch (Rand. Init.) is one of the top competitors when the C4 detector is used. We conjecture that the pre-trained models are possibly overfitted to their pretext tasks in their 5-th blocks and thus are harder to be tuned than a randomly initialized 5-th block. In CRAG detection, only b-ConCL pre-trained models consistently outperform randomly initialized models. In addition, the most significant gap between MoCo-v2 [4] and b-ConCL is found in the RetinaNet detector [21]. As also noted by [22], RetinaNet [21] is a single-stage detector, where the local representations from the backbone become more important than other two-stage detectors since results are directly predicted from them. b-ConCL is tasked to discriminate local concepts, and subsequently, the learned representations could be better than other pre-training methods here.

Transferring with Different Schedules. To investigate if b-ConCL's lead could persist with longer fine-tuning, we fine-tune Mask-RCNN-FPN with $0.5\times$, $1\times$, $2\times$, $3\times$, and $5\times$ schedules. Table 3 shows the results. b-ConCL maintains its noticeable gains in longer schedules in both datasets, *e.g.*, b-ConCL achieves 56.2 mAP with a $0.5\times$ schedule, which is better than MoCo-v2 [4] with a $5\times$ schedule but costs $10\times$ less fine-tuning time. Similar observations are also found in CRAG, where the gap between b-ConCL and MoCo-v2 [4] becomes larger (see Δ row). Together, these results confirm b-ConCL's superiority across different fine-tuning schedules.

5.2   Ablation Study

In this section, we ablate the key factors in b-ConCL. Our default setting clusters $K = 8$ concepts from ResNet stage-4 ($f_4(\cdot)$). Since b-ConCL is built on MoCo-v2 [4], we use it as our direct baseline for comparisons.

Concept Loss Weight λ. We here study the generalized concept contrastive loss: $L = (1 - \lambda)L_q + \lambda L_c$, where $\lambda \in [0, 1]$ is a concept loss weight parameter. It shows a natural way to combine concept contrastive loss with instance contrastive loss. We start by asking whether instance contrastive loss is indispensable during the training process of b-ConCL. We alter the concept loss weight λ, and Table 4a reports the results. We see a monotonically increasing performance as λ increases in both datasets, which emphasizes the importance of concept

Table 3. Detection performance under different fine-tuning schedules. Results other than 1× schedule are averaged over 3 runs. Δ row shows b-ConCL's improvement over MoCo-v2. We report AP^{bb} here.

Method	GlaS dataset					CRAG dataset				
	Fine-tuning schedule					Fine-tuning schedule				
	0.5×	1×	2×	3×	5×	0.5×	1×	2×	3×	5×
Rand. Init.	49.1	49.8	51.4	51.8	52.7	50.2	51.1	51.9	52.4	52.8
Supervised	48.6	50.2	51.4	52.7	54.0	50.0	49.2	50.5	50.1	50.3
MoCo-v2 [4]	51.4	52.3	53.7	54.2	55.7	50.2	50.0	50.2	50.8	51.8
b-ConCL	**56.2**	**56.8**	**57.7**	**58.3**	**59.0**	**54.8**	**55.1**	**55.4**	**55.6**	**56.0**
Δ	+4.8	+4.5	+4.0	+4.1	+3.3	+4.6	+5.1	+5.2	+4.8	+4.2

loss. When no warm-up is used (last row in Table 4a), only a slight performance drop is observed, meaning that warm-up is not the key component of b-ConCL. Warming-up with instance loss (Eq. (2)) is a special case of b-ConCL, where at the early training stage, each instance is regarded as a concept, and we then gradually increase the number of concepts as training goes on. Thus, the overall findings in this ablation support b-ConCL's advance over MoCo-v2 [4].

Number of Concepts K. Here, we investigate how the number of concepts clustered during pre-training affects performance in downstream tasks. We report the results of different K in Table 4b. b-ConCL performs reasonably well when $K >= 4$, with most of performance peaking at $K = 8$. This demonstrates the robustness of b-ConCL to the choice of K. Note that the best performance for the GlaS dataset is higher than our default setting and outperforms all entries in Table 1, showing the potential room for b-ConCL.

Where to Group $f_i(\cdot)$. b-ConCL groups concepts from a model's intermediate feature maps. Our default setting uses feature maps from stage-4 of a ResNet [15], denoted as $f_4(\cdot)$. We now ablate this choice in Table 4c. Clustering concepts from $f_4(\cdot)$ and $f_5(\cdot)$ works similarly well across two datasets. We choose $f_4(\cdot)$ as the default since it achieves top two performance in both datasets under both metrics. Besides, b-ConCL exceeds MoCo-v2 [4], whichever stage it groups concepts from. This again confirms the effectiveness and robustness of b-ConCL.

Longer Pre-training. We compare the pre-training efficiency of different SSL methods w.r.t. training epochs in Fig. 1-(b, c) with the numerical results in Appendix D. Interestingly, we find SimCLR [3] and BYOL [10] fail to benefit from longer pre-training. This shows the disparity between pathology image data and natural image data. In the latter field, a monotonically increasing performance in downstream tasks is usually observed [2, 3, 10, 12, 16]. For MoCo-v1/v2 [4, 12], DenseCL [33] and our b-ConCL, we observe the performance consistently improves as the pre-training epoch increases in GlaS dataset [28]. Note that the 200-epoch b-ConCL surpasses the 800-epoch MoCo-v2 [4] and DenseCL [33] by a large margin (Fig. 1-(b)). In the CRAG dataset, we observe all pre-training methods saturate and achieve the best performance in around 200-epoch and 400-epoch. Among them, b-ConCL is still the best (Fig. 1-(c)).

Table 4. Ablation Study. We study the effect of different hyper-parameters to b-ConCL. Default settings are marked in gray and MoCo-v2 baselines are marked by gray. In (a), "\ w." means no warm-up.

λ	GlaS		CRAG	
	AP^{bb}	AP^{bb}_{75}	AP^{bb}	AP^{bb}_{75}
0.0	52.3	60.0	50.0	55.7
0.1	53.6	61.1	50.5	55.9
0.3	53.6	61.8	51.7	57.1
0.5	53.6	61.8	51.3	57.0
0.7	55.2	64.1	53.1	59.9
0.9	56.0	65.1	53.6	59.6
1.0	**56.8**	**66.2**	**55.1**	**62.2**
1.0\w.	56.1	**66.2**	54.0	60.6

(a) **Concept loss weight.**

K	GlaS		CRAG	
	AP^{bb}	AP^{bb}_{75}	AP^{bb}	AP^{bb}_{75}
1	52.3	60.0	50.0	55.7
2	54.5	64.1	52.9	60.1
4	55.6	64.7	53.4	59.7
6	56.3	65.1	53.7	60.2
8	56.8	**66.2**	**55.1**	**62.2**
10	57.0	66.0	**55.1**	61.0
12	**57.4**	**66.2**	54.2	60.1
16	55.7	65.3	54.5	61.3

(b) **Number of concepts.**

K	GlaS		CRAG	
	AP^{bb}	AP^{bb}_{75}	AP^{bb}	AP^{bb}_{75}
None	52.3	60.0	50.0	55.7
$f_1(\cdot)$	55.0	65.1	53.3	60.0
$f_2(\cdot)$	55.0	64.7	53.7	60.4
$f_3(\cdot)$	<u>56.2</u>	**66.4**	53.0	59.6
$f_4(\cdot)$	**56.8**	<u>66.2</u>	<u>55.1</u>	<u>62.2</u>
$f_5(\cdot)$	56.1	65.6	**56.5**	**63.3**

(c) **Clustering stage.**

	GlaS Detection			
Pretrain	ResNet-18		ResNet-50	
	AP^{bb}	AP^{bb}_{75}	AP^{bb}	AP^{bb}_{75}
Rand.	49.8	57.3	49.9	56.1
Sup.	50.2	56.9	47.9	54.2
MoCo.v2	52.3	60.0	53.1	60.5
b-ConCL	**56.8**	**66.2**	**57.0**	**65.9**

(d) **Backbone capacities.**

Larger Model Capacity. Table 4d shows the results of using a larger backbone, ResNet-50. b-ConCL maintains its leading position. For consistency to the previous ablation, a $1\times$ schedule is also used here, which could put ResNet-50 at a disadvantage since it has more parameters to tune in a relatively short schedule.

6   Conclusion and Broader Impact

In this work, we have benchmarked some of the current SSL methods for dense tasks in pathology images and presented the ConCL framework. Along our exploration, we have distilled several key components to the success of transferring to dense tasks: i) dense contrasting matters, ii) correspondence matters, iii) coherence matters, and more. Finally, we ended up with a dependency-free concept generator that directly bootstraps the underlying concepts inherent in the data and learns from *scratch*. It was shown to be robust and competitive.

While our initial results are presented only for pre-training and fine-tuning, many applications could embrace ConCL. One example is to combine it with few-shot detection or segmentation, where clustering from feature arrays can be an approach for mining latent objects. Another example can be semi-supervised learning, where ConCL can be used as an additional branch for unlabeled data. *Beyond* pathology image analysis, we also hope ConCL would help in speech or tabular data, where little priors can be used. Unsupervised clustering in representation space is likely to be modality-agnostic. Learned by using contrastive learning and clustering, fine-grained "concepts" could also be mined from those data modalities.

References

1. Arbeláez, P., Pont-Tuset, J., Barron, J.T., Marques, F., Malik, J.: Multiscale combinatorial grouping. In: Proceedings of the IEEE Conference on Computer Vision and Pattern Recognition, pp. 328–335 (2014)
2. Caron, M., Misra, I., Mairal, J., Goyal, P., Bojanowski, P., Joulin, A.: Unsupervised learning of visual features by contrasting cluster assignments. arXiv preprint arXiv:2006.09882 (2020)
3. Chen, T., Kornblith, S., Norouzi, M., Hinton, G.: A simple framework for contrastive learning of visual representations. In: International Conference on Machine Learning, pp. 1597–1607. PMLR (2020)
4. Chen, X., Fan, H., Girshick, R., He, K.: Improved baselines with momentum contrastive learning. arXiv preprint arXiv:2003.04297 (2020)
5. Chen, X., He, K.: Exploring simple siamese representation learning. In: Proceedings of the IEEE/CVF Conference on Computer Vision and Pattern Recognition, pp. 15750–15758 (2021)
6. Ciga, O., Xu, T., Martel, A.L.: Self supervised contrastive learning for digital histopathology. arXiv preprint arXiv:2011.13971 (2020)
7. Felzenszwalb, P.F., Huttenlocher, D.P.: Efficient graph-based image segmentation. Int. J. Comput. Vision **59**(2), 167–181 (2004)
8. Girshick, R., Donahue, J., Darrell, T., Malik, J.: Rich feature hierarchies for accurate object detection and semantic segmentation. In: Proceedings of the IEEE Conference on Computer Vision and Pattern Recognition, pp. 580–587 (2014)
9. Graham, S., et al.: MILD-Net: minimal information loss dilated network for gland instance segmentation in colon histology images. Med. Image Anal. **52**, 199–211 (2019)
10. Grill, J.B., et al.: Bootstrap your own latent: a new approach to self-supervised learning. arXiv preprint arXiv:2006.07733 (2020)
11. Hadsell, R., Chopra, S., LeCun, Y.: Dimensionality reduction by learning an invariant mapping. In: 2006 IEEE Computer Society Conference on Computer Vision and Pattern Recognition (CVPR 2006), vol. 2, pp. 1735–1742. IEEE (2006)
12. He, K., Fan, H., Wu, Y., Xie, S., Girshick, R.: Momentum contrast for unsupervised visual representation learning. In: Proceedings of the IEEE/CVF Conference on Computer Vision and Pattern Recognition, pp. 9729–9738 (2020)
13. He, K., Girshick, R., Dollár, P.: Rethinking imagenet pre-training. In: Proceedings of the IEEE/CVF International Conference on Computer Vision, pp. 4918–4927 (2019)
14. He, K., Gkioxari, G., Dollár, P., Girshick, R.: Mask R-CNN. In: Proceedings of the IEEE International Conference on Computer Vision, pp. 2961–2969 (2017)

15. He, K., Zhang, X., Ren, S., Sun, J.: Deep residual learning for image recognition. In: Proceedings of the IEEE Conference on Computer Vision and Pattern Recognition, pp. 770–778 (2016)

16. Hénaff, O.J., Koppula, S., Alayrac, J.B., Oord, A.V.D., Vinyals, O., Carreira, J.: Efficient visual pretraining with contrastive detection. arXiv preprint arXiv:2103.10957 (2021)

17. Kather, J.N., Halama, N., Marx, A.: 100,000 histological images of human colorectal cancer and healthy tissue, April 2018. https://doi.org/10.5281/zenodo.1214456

18. Koohbanani, N.A., Unnikrishnan, B., Khurram, S.A., Krishnaswamy, P., Rajpoot, N.: Self-path: self-supervision for classification of pathology images with limited annotations. IEEE Trans. Med. Imaging **40**(10), 2845–2856 (2021)

19. Li, J., Zhou, P., Xiong, C., Hoi, S.C.: Prototypical contrastive learning of unsupervised representations. arXiv preprint arXiv:2005.04966 (2020)

20. Lin, T.Y., Dollár, P., Girshick, R., He, K., Hariharan, B., Belongie, S.: Feature pyramid networks for object detection. In: Proceedings of the IEEE Conference on Computer Vision and Pattern Recognition, pp. 2117–2125 (2017)

21. Lin, T.Y., Goyal, P., Girshick, R., He, K., Dollár, P.: Focal loss for dense object detection. In: Proceedings of the IEEE International Conference on Computer Vision, pp. 2980–2988 (2017)

22. Liu, S., Li, Z., Sun, J.: Self-EMD: self-supervised object detection without ImageNet. arXiv preprint arXiv:2011.13677 (2020)

23. Nguyen, D.T., et al.: Deepusps: deep robust unsupervised saliency prediction with self-supervision. arXiv preprint arXiv:1909.13055 (2019)

24. Oord, A.V.D., Li, Y., Vinyals, O.: Representation learning with contrastive predictive coding. arXiv preprint arXiv:1807.03748 (2018)

25. Qin, X., Zhang, Z., Huang, C., Gao, C., Dehghan, M., Jagersand, M.: Basnet: boundary-aware salient object detection. In: Proceedings of the IEEE/CVF Conference on Computer Vision and Pattern Recognition, pp. 7479–7489 (2019)

26. Ren, S., He, K., Girshick, R., Sun, J.: Faster R-CNN: towards real-time object detection with region proposal networks. Adv. Neural. Inf. Process. Syst. **28**, 91–99 (2015)

27. Roh, B., Shin, W., Kim, I., Kim, S.: Spatially consistent representation learning. In: Proceedings of the IEEE/CVF Conference on Computer Vision and Pattern Recognition, pp. 1144–1153 (2021)

28. Sirinukunwattana, K., et al.: Gland segmentation in colon histology images: the GlaS challenge contest. Med. Image Anal. **35**, 489–502 (2017)

29. Srinidhi, C.L., Ciga, O., Martel, A.L.: Deep neural network models for computational histopathology: a survey. Med. Image Anal. **67**, 101813 (2021)

30. Van Gansbeke, W., Vandenhende, S., Georgoulis, S., Van Gool, L.: Unsupervised semantic segmentation by contrasting object mask proposals. arXiv preprint arXiv:2102.06191 (2021)

31. Vincent, P., Larochelle, H., Bengio, Y., Manzagol, P.A.: Extracting and composing robust features with denoising autoencoders. In: Proceedings of the 25th International Conference on Machine Learning, pp. 1096–1103 (2008)

32. Wang, W., Zhou, T., Yu, F., Dai, J., Konukoglu, E., Van Gool, L.: Exploring cross-image pixel contrast for semantic segmentation. arXiv preprint arXiv:2101.11939 (2021)

33. Wang, X., Zhang, R., Shen, C., Kong, T., Li, L.: Dense contrastive learning for self-supervised visual pre-training. In: Proceedings of the IEEE/CVF Conference on Computer Vision and Pattern Recognition, pp. 3024–3033 (2021)

34. Wu, Z., Xiong, Y., Yu, S.X., Lin, D.: Unsupervised feature learning via non-parametric instance discrimination. In: Proceedings of the IEEE Conference on Computer Vision and Pattern Recognition, pp. 3733–3742 (2018)

35. Xie, E., et al.: DetCo: unsupervised contrastive learning for object detection. In: Proceedings of the IEEE/CVF International Conference on Computer Vision, pp. 8392–8401 (2021)

36. Xie, Z., Lin, Y., Zhang, Z., Cao, Y., Lin, S., Hu, H.: Propagate yourself: exploring pixel-level consistency for unsupervised visual representation learning. In: Proceedings of the IEEE/CVF Conference on Computer Vision and Pattern Recognition, pp. 16684–16693 (2021)

37. Yang, C., Wu, Z., Zhou, B., Lin, S.: Instance localization for self-supervised detection pretraining. In: Proceedings of the IEEE/CVF Conference on Computer Vision and Pattern Recognition, pp. 3987–3996 (2021)

38. Zbontar, J., Jing, L., Misra, I., LeCun, Y., Deny, S.: Barlow twins: self-supervised learning via redundancy reduction. arXiv preprint arXiv:2103.03230 (2021)

39. Zhang, R., Isola, P., Efros, A.A.: Colorful image colorization. In: Leibe, B., Matas, J., Sebe, N., Welling, M. (eds.) ECCV 2016. LNCS, vol. 9907, pp. 649–666. Springer, Cham (2016). https://doi.org/10.1007/978-3-319-46487-9_40

40. Zhang, R., Isola, P., Efros, A.A.: Split-brain autoencoders: unsupervised learning by cross-channel prediction. In: Proceedings of the IEEE Conference on Computer Vision and Pattern Recognition, pp. 1058–1067 (2017)

41. Zhao, N., Wu, Z., Lau, R.W., Lin, S.: Distilling localization for self-supervised representation learning. arXiv preprint arXiv:2004.06638 (2020)

42. Zhao, X., et al.: Contrastive learning for label efficient semantic segmentation. In: Proceedings of the IEEE/CVF International Conference on Computer Vision, pp. 10623–10633 (2021)

CryoAI: Amortized Inference of Poses for Ab Initio Reconstruction of 3D Molecular Volumes from Real Cryo-EM Images

Axel Levy[1,2]([✉]) [iD], Frédéric Poitevin[1] [iD], Julien Martel[2] [iD], Youssef Nashed[3] [iD],
Ariana Peck[1] [iD], Nina Miolane[4] [iD], Daniel Ratner[3] [iD], Mike Dunne[1],
and Gordon Wetzstein[2] [iD]

[1] LCLS, SLAC National Accelerator Laboratory, Menlo Park, CA, USA
[2] Department of Electrical Engineering, Stanford University, Stanford, CA, USA
axlevy@stanford.edu
[3] ML Initiative, SLAC National Accelerator Laboratory, Menlo Park, CA, USA
[4] Department of Electrical and Computer Engineering, University of California
Santa Barbara, Santa Barbara, CA, USA

Abstract. Cryo-electron microscopy (cryo-EM) has become a tool of fundamental importance in structural biology, helping us understand the basic building blocks of life. The algorithmic challenge of cryo-EM is to jointly estimate the unknown 3D poses and the 3D electron scattering potential of a biomolecule from millions of extremely noisy 2D images. Existing reconstruction algorithms, however, cannot easily keep pace with the rapidly growing size of cryo-EM datasets due to their high computational and memory cost. We introduce cryoAI, an *ab initio* reconstruction algorithm for homogeneous conformations that uses direct gradient-based optimization of particle poses and the electron scattering potential from single-particle cryo-EM data. CryoAI combines a learned encoder that predicts the poses of each particle image with a physics-based decoder to aggregate each particle image into an implicit representation of the scattering potential volume. This volume is stored in the Fourier domain for computational efficiency and leverages a modern coordinate network architecture for memory efficiency. Combined with a symmetric loss function, this framework achieves results of a quality on par with state-of-the-art cryo-EM solvers for both simulated and experimental data, one order of magnitude faster for large datasets and with significantly lower memory requirements than existing methods.

Keywords: Cryo-electron microscopy · Neural scene representation

1 Introduction

Understanding the 3D structure of proteins and their associated complexes is crucial for drug discovery, studying viruses, and understanding the function of the

---

Supplementary Information The online version contains supplementary material available at https://doi.org/10.1007/978-3-031-19803-8_32.

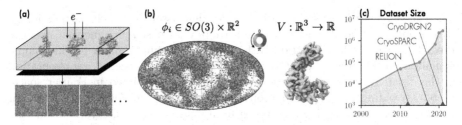

Fig. 1. (a) (Top) Illustration of a cryo-EM experiment. Molecules are frozen in a random orientation and their electron scattering potential (i.e., volume) V interacts with an electron beam imaged on a detector. (Bottom) Noisy projections (i.e., particles) of V selected from the full micrograph measured by the detector. (b) Output of a reconstruction algorithm: poses ϕ_i and volume V. Each pose is characterized by a rotation in $SO(3)$ (hue represents in-plane rotation) and a translation in $\mathbb{R}^2$ (not shown). An equipotential surface of V is shown on the right. (c) Evolution of the maximum number of images collected in one day [29] and established and emerging state-of-the-art reconstruction methods.

fundamental building blocks of life. Towards this goal, cryo-electron microscopy (cryo-EM) of isolated particles has been developed as the go-to method for imaging and studying molecular assemblies at near-atomic resolution [21,31,39]. In a cryo-EM experiment, a purified solution of the molecule of interest is frozen in a thin layer of vitreous ice, exposed to an electron beam, and randomly oriented projections of the electron scattering potential (i.e., the volume) are imaged on a detector (Fig. 1(a)). These raw *micrographs* are then processed by an algorithm that reconstructs the volume and estimates the unknown pose, including orientation and centering shift, of each particle extracted from the micrographs (Fig. 1(b)).

Recent advances in sample preparation, instrumentation, and data collection capabilities have resulted in very large amounts of data being recorded for each cryo-EM experiment [4,29] (Fig. 1(c)). Millions of noisy (images of) particles, each with an image size on the order of 100^2–400^2 pixels, need to be processed by the reconstruction algorithm to jointly estimate the pose of each particle and the unknown volume. Most existing algorithms that have been successful with experimental cryo-EM data address this problem using a probabilistic approach that iteratively alternates between updating the volume and the estimated poses [37,44,59,61]. The latter "orientation matching" step, however, is computationally expensive, requiring an exhaustive search in a 5-dimensional space ($\phi_i \in SO(3) \times \mathbb{R}^2$) for each particle. In spite of using smart pose search strategies and optimization schedules, the orientation matching step is the primary bottleneck of existing cryo-EM reconstruction algorithms, requiring hours to estimate a single volume and scaling poorly with increasing dataset sizes.

We introduce cryoAI, a technique that uses direct gradient-based optimization to jointly estimate the poses and the electron scattering potential of a non-deformable molecule (*homogeneous* reconstruction). Our method operates in an unsupervised manner over a set of images with an encoder–decoder pipeline.

The encoder learns a discriminative model that associates each particle image with a pose and the decoder is a generative physics-based pipeline that uses the predicted pose and a description of the volume to predict an image. The volume is maintained by an implicit, i.e., neural network–parameterized, representation in the decoder, and the image formation model is simulated in Fourier space, thereby avoiding the approximation of integrals via the Fourier-slice theorem (see Sect. 3.1). By learning a mapping from images to poses, cryoAI avoids the computationally expensive step of orientation matching that limits existing cryo-EM reconstruction methods. Our approach thus amortizes over the size of the dataset and provides a scalable approach to working with modern, large-scale cryo-EM datasets. We demonstrate that cryoAI performs homogeneous reconstructions of a comparable resolution but with nearly one order of magnitude faster runtime than state-of-the-art methods using datasets containing millions of particles.

Specifically, our contributions include

- a framework that learns to map images to particle poses while reconstructing an electron scattering potential for homogeneous single-particle cryo-EM;
- demonstration of reconstruction times and memory consumption that amortize over the size of the dataset, with nearly an order of magnitude improvement over existing algorithms on large datasets;
- formulations of a symmetric loss function and an implicit Fourier-domain volume representation that enable the high-quality reconstructions we show.

Source code is available at https://github.com/compSPI/cryoAI.

2   Related Work

Estimating the 3D structure of an object from its 2D projections with known orientations is a classical problem in tomography and has been solved using backprojection-based methods [18,43] or compressive sensing–style solvers [8,12]. In cryo-EM, the reconstruction problem is complicated by several facts: (1) the poses of the unknown object are also unknown for all projections; (2) the signal-to-noise ratio (SNR) is extremely low (around −20 dB for experimental datasets [5,6]); (3) the molecules in a sample can deform and be frozen in various (unknown) conformations. Unlike homogeneous reconstruction methods, heterogeneous methods take into account the deformations of the molecule and reconstruct a discrete set or a low-dimensional manifold of conformations. Although they give more structural information, most recent heterogeneous methods [9,36,59,62] assume the poses to be known. For each particle i, a pose ϕ_i is defined by a rotation $R_i \in SO(3)$ and a translation $\mathbf{t}_i \in \mathbb{R}^2$. In this work, we do not assume the poses to be known and aim to estimate the electron scattering function V of a unique underlying molecule in a homogeneous setting. We classify previous work on pose estimation into two inference categories [11]: non-amortized and amortized.

Non-amortized Inference refers to a class of methods where the posterior distribution of the poses $p(\phi_i|Y_i, V)$ is computed independently for each image Y_i. Common-line approaches [16,35,47,51,55,57], projection-matching strategies [3,33] and Bayesian formulations [10,24,37,45] belong to this category. The software package RELION [44] widely popularized the Bayesian approach by performing Maximum-A-Posteriori (MAP) optimization through Expectation–Maximization (EM). Posterior distributions over the poses (and the optional *conformational* states) are computed for each image in the expectation step and all frequency components of the volume are updated in the maximization step, which makes the approach computationally costly. The competing software cryoSPARC [37] proposed to perform MAP optimization jointly using stochastic gradient descent (SGD) to optimize the volume V and branch-and-bound algorithms [22] to estimate the poses ϕ_i. While a gradient-based optimization scheme for V circumvents the costly updates in the maximization step of RELION, a pose must be estimated for each image by aligning each 2D projection Y_i with the estimated 3D volume V. Although branch-and-bound algorithms can accelerate the pose search, this step remains computationally expensive and is one of the bottlenecks of the method in terms of runtime. Ullrich *et al.* [50] proposed a variational and differentiable formulation of the optimization problem in the Fourier domain. Although they demonstrated that their method can estimate the volume when poses are known, they also showed that jointly optimizing the pose posterior distributions by SGD fails due to the high non-convexity of the problem. Instead of parameterizing the volume with a 3D voxel array, Zhong *et al.* proposed in cryoDRGN [59–61] to use a coordinate-based representation (details in Sect. 3.4) to directly approximate the electron scattering function in Fourier space. Their neural representation takes 3D Fourier coordinates and a latent vector encoding the conformational state as input, therefore accounting for continuous deformations of the molecule. The latest published version of cryoDRGN [59] reports excellent results on the reconstruction of conformation heterogeneities but assumes the poses to be determined by a consensus reconstruction. Poses are jointly estimated with V in cryoDRGN-BNB [60] and cryoDRGN2 [61], but in spite of a frequency-marching strategy, the use of a branch-and-bound algorithm and a later introduced multi-resolution approach the global 5D pose search remains the most computationally expensive step in their pipeline.

Amortized Inference techniques, on the other hand, learn a parameterized function $q_\xi(Y_i)$ that approximates the posterior distribution of the poses $p(\phi_i|Y_i, V)$ [14]. At the expense of optimizing the parameter ξ, these techniques avoid the orientation matching step which is the main computational bottleneck in non-amortized methods. Lian *et al.* [23] demonstrated the possibility of using a convolutional neural network to approximate the mapping between cryo-EM images and orientations, but their method cannot perform end-to-end volume reconstruction. In cryoVAEGAN [27], Miolane *et al.* showed that the in-plane rotation could be disentangled from the contrast transfer function (CTF) parameters in the latent space of an encoder. Rosenbaum *et al.* [41] were the first to demonstrate volume reconstruction from unknown poses in a framework of amortized inference. In their work, distributions of poses and conformational states are predicted by the encoder of a Variational Autoencoder (VAE) [20]. In their model-based decoder, the predicted conformation is used to deform a base backbone frame of Gaussian blobs and the predicted pose is used to make a projection of these blobs. The reconstructed image is compared to the measurement in order to optimize the parameters of both the encoder and the decoder. While this method is able to account for conformational heterogeneity in a dataset, it requires *a priori* information about the backbone frame. CryoPoseNet [30] proposed a non-variational autoencoder framework that can perform homogeneous reconstruction with a random initialization of the volume, avoiding the need for prior information about the molecule. Although it demonstrated the possibility of using a non-variational encoder to predict the orientations R_i, cryoPoseNet assumes the translations $\mathbf{t}_i$ to be given and the volume is stored in real space in the decoder (while the image formation model is in Fourier space, see Sect. 3.1), thereby requiring a 3D Fourier transform at each forward pass and making the overall decoding step slow. The volume reconstructed by cryoPoseNet often gets stuck in local minima, which is a problem we also address in this paper (see Sect. 3.5). Finally, the two last methods only proved they could be used with simulated datasets and, to the best of our knowledge, no amortized inference technique for volume estimation from unknown poses have been proven to work with experimental datasets in cryo-EM.

Previous methods differ in the way poses are inferred in the generative model. Yet, the only variable of interest is the description of the conformational state (for heterogeneous methods) and associated molecular volumes, while poses can be considered "nuisance" variables. As a result, recent works have explored methods that avoid the inference of poses altogether, such as GAN-based approaches [1]. CryoGAN [17], for example, used a cryo-EM simulator and a discriminator neural network to optimize a 3D volume. Although preliminary results are shown on experimental datasets, the reconstruction cannot be further refined with other methods due to the absence of predicted poses.

Our approach performs an amortized inference of poses and therefore circumvents the need for expensive searches over $SO(3) \times \mathbb{R}^2$, as in non-amortized techniques. In the implementation, no parameter needs to be statically associated with each image. Consequently, the memory footprint and the runtime of our algorithm does not scale with the number of images in the dataset. We introduce a loss function called "symmetric loss" that prevents the model from getting stuck in local minima with spurious planar symmetries. Finally, in contrast to previous amortized inference techniques, our method can perform volume reconstruction on experimental datasets.

3 Methods

3.1 Image Formation Model and Fourier-Slice Theorem

In a cryo-EM sample, the charges carried by each molecule and their surrounding environment create an electrostatic potential that scatters probing electrons, which we refer to as the electron scattering "volume," and consider as a mapping

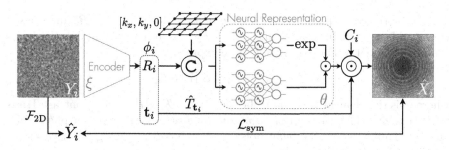

Fig. 2. Overview of our pipeline. The encoder, parameterized by ξ learns to map images Y_i to their associated pose $\phi_i = (R_i, \mathbf{t}_i)$. The matrix R_i rotates a slice of 3D coordinates in Fourier space. The coordinates are fed into a neural representation of $\hat{V}$, parameterized by θ. The output is multiplied by the CTF C_i and the translation operator $\hat{T}_{\mathbf{t}_i}$ to build $\hat{X}_i$, a noise-free estimation of $\mathcal{F}_{2D}[Y_i] = \hat{Y}_i$. $\hat{X}_i$ and $\hat{Y}_i$ are compared *via* the symmetric loss $\mathcal{L}_{\text{sym}}$. Differentiable parameters are represented in blue. (Color figure online)

$$V : \mathbb{R}^3 \to \mathbb{R}. \tag{1}$$

In the sample, each molecule i is in an unknown orientation $R_i \in SO(3) \subset \mathbb{R}^{3 \times 3}$. The probing electron beam interacts with the electrostatic potential and its projections

$$Q_i : (x, y) \mapsto \int_z V\left(R_i \cdot [x, y, z]^T\right) dz \tag{2}$$

are considered mappings from $\mathbb{R}^2$ to $\mathbb{R}$. The beam then interacts with the lens system characterized by the Point Spread Function (PSF) P_i and individual particles are cropped from the full micrograph. The obtained images may not be perfectly centered on the molecule and small translations are modeled by $\mathbf{t}_i \in \mathbb{R}^2$. Finally, taking into account signal arising from the vitreous ice into which the molecules are embedded as well as the non-idealities of the lens and the detector, each image Y_i is generally modeled as

$$Y_i = T_{\mathbf{t}_i} * P_i * Q_i + \eta_i \tag{3}$$

where $*$ is the convolution operator, $T_{\mathbf{t}}$ the $\mathbf{t}$-translation kernel and η_i white Gaussian noise on $\mathbb{R}^2$ [44,53].

With a formulation in real space, both the integral over z in Eq. (2) and the convolution in Eq. (3) make the simulation of the image formation model computationally expensive. A way to avoid these operations is to use the Fourier-slice Theorem [7], which states that for any volume V and any orientation R_i,

$$\mathcal{F}_{2D}[Q_i] = \mathcal{S}_i[\mathcal{F}_{3D}[V]], \tag{4}$$

where $\mathcal{F}_{2D}$ and $\mathcal{F}_{3D}$ are the 2D and 3D Fourier transform operators and $\mathcal{S}_i$ the "slice" operator defined such that for any $\hat{V} : \mathbb{R}^3 \to \mathbb{C}$,

$$\mathcal{S}_i[\hat{V}] : (k_x, k_y) \mapsto \hat{V}\left(R_i \cdot [k_x, k_y, 0]^T\right). \tag{5}$$

That is, $\mathcal{S}_i[\hat{V}]$ corresponds to a 2D slice of $\hat{V}$ with orientation R_i and passing through the origin. In a nutshell, if $\hat{Y}_i = \mathcal{F}_{2D}[Y_i]$ and $\hat{V} = \mathcal{F}_{3D}[V]$, the image formation model in Fourier space can be expressed as

$$\hat{Y}_i = \hat{T}_{\mathbf{t}_i} \odot C_i \odot \mathcal{S}_i[\hat{V}] + \hat{\eta}_i, \tag{6}$$

where $\odot$ is the element-wise multiplication, $C_i = \mathcal{F}_{2D}[P_i]$ is the Contrast Transfer Function (CTF), $\hat{T}_{\mathbf{t}}$ the $\mathbf{t}$-translation operator in Fourier space (phase shift) and $\hat{\eta}_i$ complex white Gaussian noise on $\mathbb{R}^2$. Based on this generative model, cryoAI solves the inverse problem of inferring $\hat{V}$, R_i and $\mathbf{t}_i$ from $\hat{Y}_i$ assuming C_i is known.

3.2 Overview of CryoAI

CryoAI is built with an autoencoder architecture (see Fig. 2). The encoder takes an image Y_i as input and outputs a predicted orientation R_i along with a predicted translation $\mathbf{t}_i$ (Sect. 3.3). R_i is used to rotate a 2-dimensional grid of L^2 3D-coordinates $[k_x, k_y, 0] \in \mathbb{R}^3$ which are then fed into the neural network $\hat{V}_\theta$. This neural network is an implicit representation of the current estimate of the volume $\hat{V}$ (in Fourier space), and this query operation corresponds to the "slicing" defined by Eq. (5) (Sect. 3.4). Based on the estimated translation $\mathbf{t}_i$ and given CTF parameters C_i, the rest of the image formation model described in Eq. (6) is simulated to obtain $\hat{X}_i$, a noise-free estimation of $\hat{Y}_i$. These images are compared using a loss described in Sect. 3.5 and gradients are backpropagated throughout the differentiable model in order to optimize both the encoder and the neural representation.

3.3 Pose Estimation

CryoAI uses a Convolutional Neural Network (CNN) to predict the parameters R_i and $\mathbf{t}_i$ from a given image, thereby avoiding expensive orientation matching computations performed by other methods [37,44,61]. The architecture of this encoder has three layers.

1. *Low-pass filtering*: $Y_i \in \mathbb{R}^{L \times L}$ is fed into a bank of Gaussian low-pass filters.
2. *Feature extraction*: the filtered images are stacked channel-wise and fed into a CNN whose architecture is inspired by the first layers of VGG16 [46], which is known to perform well on image classification tasks.
3. *Pose estimation*: this feature vector finally becomes the input of two separate fully-connected neural networks. The first one outputs a vector of dimension 6 of $S^2 \times S^2$ [63] (two vectors on the unitary sphere in $\mathbb{R}^3$) and converted into a matrix $R_i \in \mathbb{R}^{3 \times 3}$ using the PyTorch3D library [38]. The second one outputs a vector of dimension 2, directly interpreted as a translation vector $\mathbf{t}_i \in \mathbb{R}^2$.

We call ξ the set of differentiable parameters in the encoder described above. We point the reader to Supp. B for more details about the architecture of the encoder.

3.4 Neural Representation in Fourier Space (FourierNet)

Instead of using a voxel-based representation, we maintain the current estimate of the volume using a neural representation. This representation is parameterized by θ and can be see seen as a mapping $\hat{V}_\theta : \mathbb{R}^3 \to \mathbb{C}$.

In imaging and volume rendering, neural representations have been used to approximate signals defined in real space [2,13,25,32,49]. Neural Radiance Field (NeRF) [26] is a successful technique to maintain a volumetric representation of a real scene. A view-independent NeRF model, for example, maps real 3D-coordinates $[x, y, z]$ to a color vector and a density scalar using positional encoding [52] and a set of fully-connected layers with ReLU activation functions. Sinusoidal Representation Networks (SIRENs) [48] can also successfully approximate 3D signed distance functions with a shallow fully-connected neural network using sinusoidal activation functions. However, these representations are tailored to approximate signals defined in real space. Here, we want to directly represent the Fourier transform of the electrostatic potential of a molecule. Since this potential is a smooth function of the spatial coordinates, the amplitude of its Fourier coefficients $\hat{V}(\mathbf{k})$ is expected to decrease with $|\mathbf{k}|$, following a power law (see Supp. C for more details). In practice, this implies that $|\hat{V}|$ can vary over several orders of magnitude and SIRENs, for example, are known to poorly approximate these types of functions [48]. The first method to use neural representations for volume reconstruction in cryo-EM, cryoDRGN [60,61], proposed to use a Multi-Layer Perceptron (MLP) with positional encoding in Hartley space (where the FST still applies).

With our work, we introduce a new kind of neural representation (FourierNet), tailored to represent signals defined in the Fourier domain, inspired by the success of SIRENs for signals defined in real space. Our idea is to allow a SIREN to represent a signal with a high dynamic range by raising its output in an exponential function. Said differently, the SIREN only represents a signal that scales logarithmically with the approximated function. Since Fourier coefficients are defined on the complex plane, we use a second network in our implicit representation to account for the phase variations. This architecture is summarized in Fig. 2 and details on memory requirements are given in Supp. C. Input coordinates $[k_x, k_y, k_z]$ are fed into two separate SIRENs outputting 2-dimensional vectors. For one of them, the exponential function is applied element-wise and the two obtained vectors are finally element-wise mutliplied to produce a vector in $\mathbb{R}^2$, mapped to $\mathbb{C}$ with the Cartesian coordinate system. Since $\hat{V}_\theta$ must represent the Fourier transform of real signals, we know that it should verify $\hat{V}_\theta(-\mathbf{k}) = \hat{V}_\theta(\mathbf{k})^*$. We enforce this property by defining

$$\hat{V}_\theta(\mathbf{k}) = \hat{V}_\theta(-\mathbf{k})^* \quad \text{if } k_x < 0. \tag{7}$$

Benefits of this neural representation are shown on 2-dimensional signals in the Supp. C.

The neural representation is queried for a set of L^2 3D-coordinates $[k_x, k_y, k_z]$, thereby producing a discretized slice $\mathcal{S}_i[\hat{V}_\theta] \in \mathbb{C}^{L \times L}$. The rest of the image formation model (6) is simulated by element-wise multiplying $\mathcal{S}_i[\hat{V}_\theta]$ by the CTF C_i and a translation matrix,

$$\hat{X}_i = \hat{T}_{\mathbf{t}_i} \odot C_i \odot \mathcal{S}_i[\hat{V}_\theta], \tag{8}$$

where $\hat{T}_{\mathbf{t}_i}$ is defined by

$$\hat{T}_{\mathbf{t}_i}(\mathbf{k}) = \exp\left(-2j\pi\mathbf{k} \cdot \mathbf{t}_i\right). \tag{9}$$

The parameters of the CTF are provided by external CTF estimation softwares such as CTFFIND [40]. The whole encoder–decoder pipeline can be seen as a function that we call $\Gamma_{\xi,\theta}$, such that $\hat{X}_i = \Gamma_{\xi,\theta}(Y_i)$.

3.5 Symmetric Loss

In the image formation model of Eq. (3), the additive noise η_i is assumed to be Gaussian and uncorrelated (white Gaussian noise) [44,53], which means that its Fourier transform $\hat{\eta}_i$ follows the same kind of distribution. Therefore, maximum likelihood estimation on a batch $\mathcal{B}$ amounts to the minimization of the L2-loss.

Nonetheless, we empirically observed that using this loss often led the model to get stuck in local minima where the estimated volume showed spurious planar symmetries (see Sect. 4.3). We hypothesize that this behaviour is linked to the fundamental ambiguity contained in the image formation model in which, given unknown poses, one cannot distinguish two "mirrored" versions of the same volume [42]. We discuss this hypothesis in more detail in Supp. D. To solve this problem, we designed a loss that we call "symmetric loss" defined as

$$\mathcal{L}_{\text{sym}} = \sum_{i \in \mathcal{B}} \min\left\{\|\hat{Y}_i - \Gamma_{\xi,\theta}(Y_i)\|^2, \|\mathcal{R}_\pi[\hat{Y}_i] - \Gamma_{\xi,\theta}\left(\mathcal{R}_\pi[Y_i]\right)\|^2\right\} \tag{10}$$

where $\mathcal{R}_\pi$ applies an in-plane rotation of π on $L \times L$ images. Using the symmetric loss, the model can be supervised on a set of images Y_i in which the predicted in-plane rotation (embedded in the predicted matrix R_i) can always fall in $[-\pi/2, \pi/2]$ instead of $[-\pi, \pi]$. As shown in Sect. 4.3 and explained in Supp. D, this prevents cryoAI from getting stuck in spuriously symmetrical states.

4 Results

We qualitatively and quantitatively evaluate cryoAI for *ab initio* reconstruction of both simulated and experimental datasets. We first compare cryoAI to the state-of-the-art method cryoSPARC [37] in terms of runtime on a simulated dataset of the *80S* ribosome with low levels of noise. We then compare our method with baseline methods in terms of resolution and pose accuracy on simulated datasets with and without noise (*spike, spliceosome*). Next, we show that cryoAI can perform *ab initio* reconstruction on an experimental cryo-EM dataset (*80S*), which is the first time for a method estimating poses in an amortized fashion. Finally, we highlight the importance of a tailored neural representation in the decoder and the role of the symmetric loss in an ablation study.

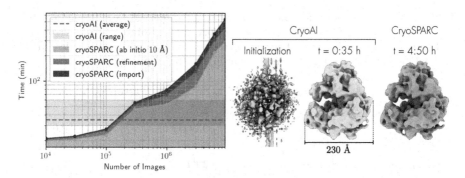

Fig. 3. (Left) Time to reach 10 Å of resolution with cryoAI (range and average over 5 runs per datapoint) and cryoSPARC vs. number of images in the simulated 80S dataset. (Right) Estimated volume at initialization and after 35 min of running cryoAI vs. cryoSPARC after convergence, with 9M images.

4.1   Reconstruction on Simulated Datasets

Experimental Setup. We synthesize three datasets from deposited Protein Data Bank (PDB) structures of the Plasmodium falciparum 80S ribosome (PDB: 3J79 and 3J7A) [56], the SARS-CoV-2 spike protein (PDB: 6VYB) [54] and the pre-catalytic spliceosome (PDB: 5NRL) [34]. First, a 3D grid map, the *ground-truth volume*, is generated in ChimeraX [15] from each atomic model using the steps described in Supp. A. Then a dataset is generated from the ground-truth volume using the image formation model described in Sect. 3.1. Images are sampled at $L = 128$. Rotations R_i are randomly generated following a uniform distribution over $SO(3)$ and random translations $\mathbf{t}_i$ are generated following a zero-mean Gaussian distribution ($\sigma = 20$ Å). The defocus parameters of the CTFs are generated with a log-normal distribution. We build noise-free (ideal) and noisy versions of each dataset (SNR = 0 dB for 80S, SNR = −10 dB for the others, see Supp. E for details). We compare cryoAI with three baselines: the state-of-the-art software cryoSPARC v3.2.0 [37] with default settings, the neural network–based method cryoDRGN2 [61] and the autoencoder-based method cryoPoseNet [30] (with the image formation model in real space in the decoder, see Supp. A). We quantify the accuracy of the reconstructed volume by computing the Fourier Shell Correlations (FSC) between the reconstruction and the ground truth and reporting the resolution at the 0.5 cutoff. All experiments are run on a single Tesla V100 GPU with 8 CPUs.

Convergence Time. We compare cryoAI with cryoSPARC in terms of runtime for datasets of increasing size in Fig. 3. We use the simulated 80S dataset and define the running time as the time needed to reach a resolution of 10 Å (2.65 pixels), which is a sufficiently accurate resolution to perform refinement with cryoSPARC (see workflow in Supp. A). With default parameters, cryoSPARC's ab initio reconstruction must process all images in the dataset.

Table 1. Accuracy of pose and volume estimation for simulated data. Resolution (Res.) is reported using the FSC = 0.5 criterion, in pixels ($\downarrow$). Rotation (Rot.) error is the median square Frobenius norm between predicted and ground truth matrices R_i ($\downarrow$). Translation (Trans.) error is the mean square L2-norm, in pixels ($\downarrow$).

Dataset		cryoPoseNet	cryoSPARC	cryoDRGN2	cryoAI
Spliceosome (ideal)	Res.	2.78	**2.13**	–	**2.13**
	Rot.	0.004	**0.0002**	–	0.0004
	Trans.	–	0.006	–	**0.001**
Spliceosome (noisy)	Res.	3.15	**2.61**	–	**2.61**
	Rot.	0.01	**0.002**	–	0.007
	Trans.	–	**0.007**	–	0.01
Spike (ideal)	Res.	16.0	2.33	–	**2.29**
	Rot.	5	0.0003	**0.0001**	0.0003
	Trans.	–	0.007	–	**0.001**
Spike (noisy)	Res.	16.0	3.56	**2.03**	2.91
	Rot.	6	0.02	**0.01**	**0.01**
	Trans.	–	0.008	–	**0.003**

We show the time required by cryoSPARC for importing data and for the refinement step. CryoAI processes images batch-wise and does not statically associates variables to each image, making the convergence time (for reaching the specified resolution) independent from the size of the dataset. By contrast, the computation time of cryoSPARC increases with the number of images and can reach 5 hours with a dataset of 9M particles. We additionally show in Supp F the time required to estimate all the poses of the dataset with cryoAI's encoder.

Accuracy. We compare cryoAI with baseline methods on the *spike* and *spliceosome* datasets in Table 1. We compare the reconstructed variables (volume and poses) with their ground truth values (from simulation). Results of cryoDRGN2 are reported from available data in [59]. Images were centered for cryoPoseNet since the method does not predict $\mathbf{t}_i$. A "tight" adaptive mask was used with cryoSPARC. The performance of cryoAI is comparable with the baselines. The splicesome and the noise-free spike protein are reconstructed with state-of-the-art accuracy. In the noisy spike dataset, the accuracy of cryoAI and cryoSPARC decreases, which may be due to the pseudo-symmetries shown by the molecule (visual reconstruction in Supp. F). CryoPoseNet gets stuck for at least 24 h in a state where the the resolution is very poor on both spike datasets.

4.2 Reconstruction on Experimental Datasets

Experimental Setup. We use the publicly available 80S experimental dataset EMPIAR-10028 [19,56,58] containing 105,247 images of length $L = 360$ (1.34 Å

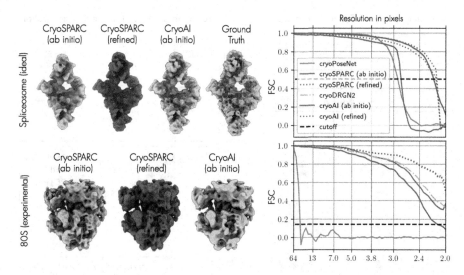

Fig. 4. (Top left) Volume reconstruction on a noise-free simulated dataset of the spliceosome ($L = 128$, pixel size = 4.25 Å). (Bottom left) Volume reconstruction for the experimental 80S dataset ($L = 128$, pixel size = 3.77 Å). (Right) Fourier Shell Correlations, reconstruction-to-ground-truth (top) or reconstruction-to-reconstruction (bottom). A resolution of 2.0 pixels corresponds to the Nyquist frequency. CryoAI can be refined using the software cryoSPARC.

per pixel), downsampled to $L = 256$. The dataset is evenly split in two, each method runs independent reconstructions on each half and the FSC are measured between the two reconstructions. We compare cryoAI with cryoPoseNet and cryoSPARC. The dataset fed to cryoAI and cryoPoseNet is masked with a circular mask of radius 84 pixels, while cryoSPARC adaptively updates a "tight" mask. CryoAI and cryoPoseNet reconstruct a volume of size 128^3. For cryoSPARC, both the *ab initio* volume and the volume subsequently homogeneously refined from it were downsampled to the same size 128^3. We also demonstrate the possibility of refining cryoAI's output with the software cryoSPARC. Finally, we report the results published for cryoDRGN2 [61] that were obtained on a filtered version of the same dataset [58] downsampled to $L = 128$ prior reconstruction.

Results. We report quantitative and qualitative results in Fig. 4. CryoAI is the first amortized method to demonstrate proper volume reconstruction on an experimental dataset, although techniques predicting poses with an orientation-matching step (like cryoDRGN2) or followed by an EM-based refinement step (like cryoSPARC) can reach slightly higher resolutions. State-of-the-art results can be obtained with cryoSPARC's refinement, initialized from either cryoSPARC's or cryoAI's *ab initio*. Since simulated datasets were built using the same image formation model as the one cryoAI uses in its decoder, the gap in performance between the experimental and simulated datasets suggests that improvements could potentially be achieved with a more accurate physics model.

Ablation Study on Symmetrized Loss

Method/Loss		Time	Rot. Error
cryoPoseNet	L2	4:35 h	0.01
	Sym.	0:30 h	0.01
cryoAI	L2	1:35 h	0.005
	Sym.	**0:09 h**	**0.004**

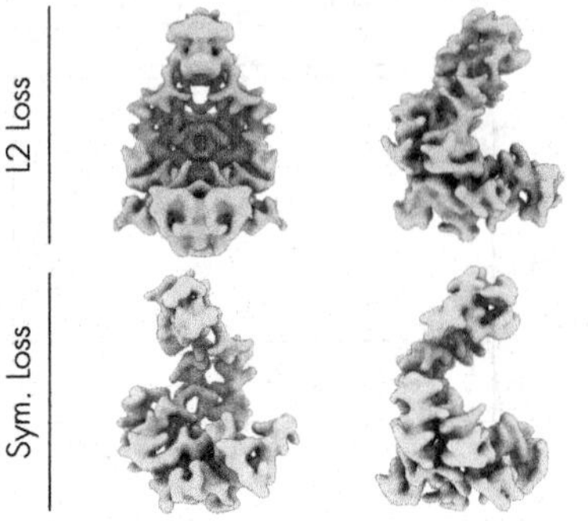

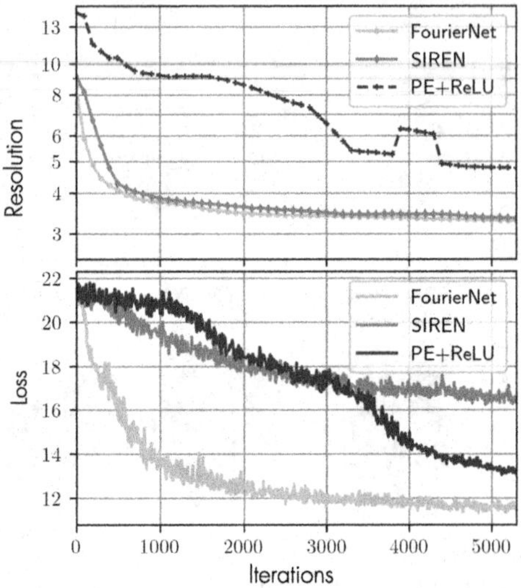

Ablation Study on Neural Representation

Fig. 5. (Top left) Ablation study on the symmetric loss with cryoAI and cryoPoseNet with simulated noise-free adenylate kinase ($L = 64$). We report the minimal convergence time out of 5 runs. CryoPoseNet is always slower and achieves worse results. The symmetric loss always accelerates convergence. (Bottom left) Volume reconstruction when using a L2 loss vs. the symmetric loss. The latter prevents the model from getting stuck in a symmetrical local minimum. (Right) Loss and resolution (in pixels, FSC = 0.143 cutoff) vs. number of iterations with a FourierNet, a SIREN [48] and an MLP with ReLU activation functions and positional encoding (32 images per batch).

4.3 Ablation Study

Importance of Symmetric Loss. The purpose of the symmetric loss is to prevent the model from getting stuck in local minima where the volume shows incorrect planar symmetries. Ullrich *et al.* showed in [50] that optimizing the poses using a gradient-based method often leads the model to fall in sub-optimal minima, due to the high non-convexity of the optimization problem. In [61], Zhong *et al.* implemented an autoencoder-based method (dubbed PoseVAE), and compared it to cryoDRGN2. The method is unable to properly reconstruct a synthetic hand, and a spurious planar symmetry appears in their reconstruction. We use a noisy dataset ($L = 128$) generated from a structure of Adenylate kinase (PDB 4AKE) [28]. We show in Fig. 5 that our method presents the same kind of artifact when using a L2 loss and validate that the symmetric loss prevents these artifacts. In Fig. 5, we compare our method to cryoPoseNet with and without the symmetric loss on a simulated ideal dataset of the same molecule ($L = 64$). Both methods use an autoencoder-based architecture and both converge significantly faster with the symmetric loss. With the same loss, cryoAI is always faster than cryoPoseNet since our method operates in Fourier space and avoids the approximation of integrals using the FST.

Comparison of Neural Representations. We replaced FourierNet with other neural representations in the decoder and compared the convergence rate of these models on the noisy Adenylate kinase dataset (L=128). In Fig. 5, we compare our architecture with a multi-layer perceptron (MLP) with sinusoidal activation functions (i.e., a SIREN [48]) and an MLP with ReLU activation function and positional encoding, as used by cryoDRGN2 [61]. We keep approximately 300k differentiable parameters in all representations. FourierNet significantly outperforms the two other architectures in terms of convergence speed.

5 Discussion

The amount of collected cryo-EM data is rapidly growing [29], which increases the need for efficient *ab initio* reconstruction methods. CryoAI proposes a framework of amortized inference to meet this need by having a complexity that does not grow with the size of the dataset. Since CryoAI jointly estimates volume and poses, it can be followed by reconstruction methods that address conformational heterogeneities, such as the ones available in cryoSPARC [37], RELION [44], or cryoDRGN [59]. The ever increasing size of cryo-EM datasets is necessary to provide sufficient sampling of conformational heterogeneities with increasing accuracy, in particular when imaging molecules that display complex dynamics. However, existing methods that tackle the more complex inference task of heterogeneous reconstruction also see their runtime suffer as datasets grow bigger, again showing the need for new developments that leverage amortized inference.

Future work on cryoAI includes adding features to the image formation model implemented in the decoder. CTFs, for example, are currently only characterized by three parameters (two defoci parameters and an astigmatism angle) but could be readily enhanced to account for higher-order effects (see e.g. [64]). A richer noise model, currently assumed to be Gaussian and white, could also improve the performance of the algorithm. In order to tackle the case of very noisy experimental datasets, adaptive masking techniques, such as those used by cryoSPARC, could be beneficial. In terms of hardware development, cryoAI would benefit from being able to run on more than a single GPU using data parallelism and/or model parallelism, thereby improving both runtime and efficiency. CryoAI, as described here, belongs to the class of homogeneous reconstruction methods; future developments should explore its performance in an heterogenous reconstruction setting, where conformational heterogeneity is baked in the generative model and the encoder is enhanced to predict descriptions of conformational states in low-dimensional latent space along with the poses.

Acknowledgment. We thank Wah Chiu for numerous discussions that helped shape this project. This work was supported by the U.S. Department of Energy, under DOE Contract No. DE-AC02-76SF00515. N.M. acknowledges support from the National Institutes of Health (NIH), grant No. 1R01GM144965-01. We acknowledge the use of the computational resources at the SLAC Shared Scientific Data Facility (SDF).

References

1. Akçakaya, M., Yaman, B., Chung, H., Ye, J.C.: Unsupervised deep learning methods for biological image reconstruction and enhancement: an overview from a signal processing perspective. IEEE Signal Process. Mag. **39**, 28–44 (2022)
2. Atzmon, M., Lipman, Y.: SAL: sign agnostic learning of shapes from raw data. In: Proceedings of the IEEE/CVF Conference on Computer Vision and Pattern Recognition, pp. 2565–2574 (2020)
3. Baker, T.S., Cheng, R.H.: A model-based approach for determining orientations of biological macromolecules imaged by cryoelectron microscopy. J. Struct. Biol. **116**, 120–130 (1996)
4. Baldwin, P.R., et al.: Big data in cryoEM: automated collection, processing and accessibility of EM data. Curr. Opin. Microbiol. **43**, 1–8 (2018)
5. Bendory, T., Bartesaghi, A., Singer, A.: Single-particle cryo-electron microscopy: mathematical theory, computational challenges, and opportunities. IEEE Signal Process. Mag. **37**, 58–76 (2020)
6. Bepler, T., Kelley, K., Noble, A.J., Berger, B.: Topaz-denoise: general deep denoising models for cryoEM and cryoET. Nat. Commun. **11**, 1–12 (2020)
7. Bracewell, R.N.: Strip integration in radio astronomy. Aust. J. Phys. **9**, 198–217 (1956)
8. Candes, E., Romberg, J., Tao, T.: Robust uncertainty principles: exact signal reconstruction from highly incomplete frequency information. IEEE Trans. Inf. Theory **52**, 489–509 (2006)
9. Chen, M., Ludtke, S.J.: Deep learning-based mixed-dimensional Gaussian mixture model for characterizing variability in cryo-EM. Nat. Methods **18**, 930–936 (2021)
10. Dempster, A.P., Laird, N.M., Rubin, D.B.: Maximum likelihood from incomplete data via the EM algorithm. J. Roy. Stat. Soc.: Ser. B (Methodol.) **39**, 1–22 (1977)
11. Donnat, C., Levy, A., Poitevin, F., Miolane, N.: Deep generative modeling for volume reconstruction in cryo-electron microscopy. arXiv: 2201.02867 (2022)
12. Donoho, D.: Compressed sensing. IEEE Trans. Inf. Theory **52**, 1289–1306 (2006)
13. Genova, K., Cole, F., Vlasic, D., Sarna, A., Freeman, W.T., Funkhouser, T.: Learning shape templates with structured implicit functions. In: Proceedings of the IEEE/CVF International Conference on Computer Vision, pp. 7154–7164 (2019)
14. Gershman, S., Goodman, N.: Amortized inference in probabilistic reasoning. In: Proceedings of the Annual Meeting of the Cognitive Science Society, vol. 36 (2014)
15. Goddard, T.D., et al.: UCSF chimeraX: meeting modern challenges in visualization and analysis. Protein Sci. **27**, 14–25 (2018)
16. Greenberg, I., Shkolnisky, Y.: Common lines modeling for reference free ab-initio reconstruction in cryo-EM. J. Struct. Biol. **200**, 106–117 (2017)
17. Gupta, H., McCann, M.T., Donati, L., Unser, M.: CryoGAN: a new reconstruction paradigm for single-particle cryo-EM via deep adversarial learning. IEEE Transactions on Computational Imaging **7**, 759–774 (2021)
18. Hertle, A.: On the problem of well-posedness for the radon transform. In: Herman, G.T., Natterer, F. (eds.) Mathematical Aspects of Computerized Tomography. Lecture Notes in Medical Informatics, vol. 8, pp. 36–44. Springer, Heidelberg (1981). https://doi.org/10.1007/978-3-642-93157-4_5
19. Iudin, A., Korir, P., Salavert-Torres, J., Kleywegt, G., Patwardhan, A.: EMPIAR: a public archive for raw electron microscopy image data. Nat. Methods **13**, 387–388 (2016)

20. Kingma, D.P., Welling, M.: An introduction to variational autoencoders. arXiv preprint arXiv:1906.02691 (2019)
21. Kühlbrandt, W.: The resolution revolution. Science **343**, 1443–1444 (2014)
22. Lawler, E.L., Wood, D.E.: Branch-and-bound methods: a survey. Oper. Res. **14**, 699–719 (1966)
23. Lian, R., Huang, B., Wang, L., Liu, Q., Lin, Y., Ling, H.: End-to-end orientation estimation from 2D cryo-EM images. Acta Crystallogr. Sect. D: Struct. Biol. **78**, 174–186 (2022)
24. Mallick, S., Agarwal, S., Kriegman, D., Belongie, S., Carragher, B., Potter, C.: Structure and view estimation for tomographic reconstruction: a Bayesian approach. In: 2006 IEEE Computer Society Conference on Computer Vision and Pattern Recognition (CVPR 2006), vol. 2, pp. 2253–2260 (2006)
25. Michalkiewicz, M., Pontes, J.K., Jack, D., Baktashmotlagh, M., Eriksson, A.: Implicit surface representations as layers in neural networks. In: Proceedings of the IEEE/CVF International Conference on Computer Vision, pp. 4743–4752 (2019)
26. Mildenhall, B., Srinivasan, P.P., Tancik, M., Barron, J.T., Ramamoorthi, R., Ng, R.: NeRF: representing scenes as neural radiance fields for view synthesis. In: Vedaldi, A., Bischof, H., Brox, T., Frahm, J.-M. (eds.) ECCV 2020. LNCS, vol. 12346, pp. 405–421. Springer, Cham (2020). https://doi.org/10.1007/978-3-030-58452-8_24
27. Miolane, N., Poitevin, F., Li, Y.T., Holmes, S.: Estimation of orientation and camera parameters from cryo-electron microscopy images with variational autoencoders and generative adversarial networks. In: 2020 IEEE/CVF Conference on Computer Vision and Pattern Recognition Workshops (CVPRW), pp. 4174–4183. IEEE (2020)
28. Müller, C., Schlauderer, G., Reinstein, J., Schulz, G.E.: Adenylate kinase motions during catalysis: an energetic counterweight balancing substrate binding. Structure **4**, 147–156 (1996)
29. Namba, K., Makino, F.: Recent progress and future perspective of electron cryomicroscopy for structural life sciences. Microscopy **71**, i3–i14 (2022)
30. Nashed, Y.S.G., et al.: CryoPoseNet: end-to-end simultaneous learning of single-particle orientation and 3D map reconstruction from cryo-electron microscopy data. In: Proceedings of the IEEE/CVF International Conference on Computer Vision (ICCV) Workshops, pp. 4066–4076 (2021)
31. Nogales, E.: The development of cryo-EM into a mainstream structural biology technique. Nat. Methods **13**, 24–27 (2016)
32. Park, J.J., Florence, P., Straub, J., Newcombe, R., Lovegrove, S.: DeepSDF: learning continuous signed distance functions for shape representation. In: Proceedings of the IEEE/CVF Conference on Computer Vision and Pattern Recognition, pp. 165–174 (2019)
33. Penczek, P.A., Grassucci, R.A., Frank, J.: The ribosome at improved resolution: new techniques for merging and orientation refinement in 3D cryo-electron microscopy of biological particles. Ultramicroscopy **53**, 251–270 (1994)
34. Plaschka, C., Lin, P.C., Nagai, K.: Structure of a pre-catalytic spliceosome. Nature **546**, 617–621 (2017)
35. Pragier, G., Shkolnisky, Y.: A common lines approach for ab-initio modeling of cyclically-symmetric molecules. Inverse Prob. **35**, 124005 (2019)
36. Punjani, A., Fleet, D.J.: 3D flexible refinement: structure and motion of flexible proteins from cryo-EM. BioRxiv (2021)

37. Punjani, A., Rubinstein, J.L., Fleet, D.J., Brubaker, M.A.: cryoSPARC: algorithms for rapid unsupervised cryo-EM structure determination. Nat. Methods **14**, 290–296 (2017)
38. Ravi, N., et al.: Accelerating 3D deep learning with PyTorch3D. arXiv: 2007.08501 (2020)
39. Renaud, J.P., et al.: Cryo-EM in drug discovery: achievements, limitations and prospects. Nat. Rev. Drug Discov. **17**, 471–492 (2018)
40. Rohou, A., Grigorieff, N.: CTFFIND4: fast and accurate defocus estimation from electron micrographs. J. Struct. Biol. **192**, 216–221 (2015)
41. Rosenbaum, D., et al.: Inferring a continuous distribution of atom coordinates from cryo-EM images using VAEs. arXiv:2106.14108 (2021)
42. Rosenthal, P.B., Henderson, R.: Optimal determination of particle orientation, absolute hand, and contrast loss in single-particle electron cryomicroscopy. J. Mol. Biol. **333**, 721–745 (2003)
43. Rudin, L.I., Osher, S., Fatemi, E.: Nonlinear total variation based noise removal algorithms. Phys. D **60**, 259–268 (1992)
44. Scheres, S.H.: RELION: implementation of a Bayesian approach to cryo-EM structure determination. J. Struct. Biol. **180**, 519–530 (2012)
45. Sigworth, F.J.: A maximum-likelihood approach to single-particle image refinement. J. Struct. Biol. **122**, 328–339 (1998)
46. Simonyan, K., Zisserman, A.: Very deep convolutional networks for large-scale image recognition. arXiv preprint arXiv:1409.1556 (2014)
47. Singer, A., Coifman, R.R., Sigworth, F.J., Chester, D.W., Shkolnisky, Y.: Detecting consistent common lines in cryo-EM by voting. J. Struct. Biol. **169**, 312–322 (2010)
48. Sitzmann, V., Martel, J., Bergman, A., Lindell, D., Wetzstein, G.: Implicit neural representations with periodic activation functions. Adv. Neural. Inf. Process. Syst. **33**, 7462–7473 (2020)
49. Sitzmann, V., Zollhöfer, M., Wetzstein, G.: Scene representation networks: continuous 3D-structure-aware neural scene representations. Adv. Neural. Inf. Process. Syst. **32** (2019)
50. Ullrich, K., Berg, R.V.D., Brubaker, M., Fleet, D., Welling, M.: Differentiable probabilistic models of scientific imaging with the Fourier slice theorem. arXiv preprint arXiv:1906.07582 (2019)
51. Vainshtein, B., Goncharov, A.: Determination of the spatial orientation of arbitrarily arranged identical particles of unknown structure from their projections. In: Soviet Physics Doklady, vol. 31, p. 278 (1986)
52. Vaswani, A., et al.: Attention is all you need. Adv. Neural. Inf. Process. Syst. **30** (2017)
53. Vulović, M., et al.: Image formation modeling in cryo-electron microscopy. J. Struct. Biol. **183**, 19–32 (2013)
54. Walls, A.C., Park, Y.J., Tortorici, M.A., Wall, A., McGuire, A.T., Veesler, D.: Structure, function, and antigenicity of the SARS-CoV-2 spike glycoprotein. Cell **181**, 281–292 (2020)
55. Wang, L., Singer, A., Wen, Z.: Orientation determination of cryo-EM images using least unsquared deviations. SIAM J. Imag. Sci. **6**, 2450–2483 (2013)
56. Wong, W., et al.: Cryo-EM structure of the plasmodium falciparum 80s ribosome bound to the anti-protozoan drug emetine. Elife **3**, e03080 (2014)
57. Zehni, M., Donati, L., Soubies, E., Zhao, Z.J., Unser, M.: Joint angular refinement and reconstruction for single-particle cryo-EM. IEEE Trans. Image Process. **29**, 6151–6163 (2020)

58. Zhong, E.: cryoDRGN-empiar (2022). https://github.com/zhonge/cryodrgn_empiar

59. Zhong, E.D., Bepler, T., Berger, B., Davis, J.H.: CryoDRGN: reconstruction of heterogeneous cryo-EM structures using neural networks. Nat. Methods **18**, 176–185 (2021)

60. Zhong, E.D., Bepler, T., Davis, J.H., Berger, B.: Reconstructing continuous distributions of 3D protein structure from cryo-EM images. arXiv:1909.05215 (2019)

61. Zhong, E.D., Lerer, A., Davis, J.H., Berger, B.: CryoDRGN2: ab initio neural reconstruction of 3D protein structures from real cryo-EM images. In: Proceedings of the IEEE/CVF International Conference on Computer Vision, pp. 4066–4075 (2021)

62. Zhong, E.D., Lerer, A., Davis, J.H., Berger, B.: Exploring generative atomic models in cryo-EM reconstruction. arXiv:2107.01331 (2021)

63. Zhou, Y., Barnes, C., Lu, J., Yang, J., Li, H.: On the continuity of rotation representations in neural networks. arXiv: 1812.07035 (2020)

64. Zivanov, J., et al.: New tools for automated high-resolution cryo-EM structure determination in RELION-3. Elife **7**, e42166 (2018)

UniMiSS: Universal Medical Self-supervised Learning via Breaking Dimensionality Barrier

Yutong Xie[1], Jianpeng Zhang[2], Yong Xia[2], and Qi Wu[1](✉)

[1] The University of Adelaide, Adelaide, Australia
qi.wu01@adelaide.edu.au

[2] School of Computer Science and Engineering, Northwestern Polytechnical University, Xi'an, China

Abstract. Self-supervised learning (SSL) opens up huge opportunities for medical image analysis that is well known for its lack of annotations. However, aggregating massive (unlabeled) 3D medical images like computerized tomography (CT) remains challenging due to its high imaging cost and privacy restrictions. In this paper, we advocate bringing a wealth of 2D images like chest X-rays as compensation for the lack of 3D data, aiming to build a universal medical self-supervised representation learning framework, called UniMiSS. The following problem is how to break the dimensionality barrier, *i.e.*, making it possible to perform SSL with both 2D and 3D images? To achieve this, we design a pyramid U-like medical Transformer (MiT). It is composed of the switchable patch embedding (SPE) module and Transformers. The SPE module adaptively switches to either 2D or 3D patch embedding, depending on the input dimension. The embedded patches are converted into a sequence regardless of their original dimensions. The Transformers model the long-term dependencies in a sequence-to-sequence manner, thus enabling UniMiSS to learn representations from both 2D and 3D images. With the MiT as the backbone, we perform the UniMiSS in a self-distillation manner. We conduct expensive experiments on six 3D/2D medical image analysis tasks, including segmentation and classification. The results show that the proposed UniMiSS achieves promising performance on various downstream tasks, outperforming the ImageNet pre-training and other advanced SSL counterparts substantially. Code is available at `https://github.com/YtongXie/UniMiSS-code`.

Keywords: Self-supervised learning · Cross-dimension · Medical image analysis · Transformer

1 Introduction

Medical image analysis, a key process in computer-aided diagnosis, is well known by its lack of labels for training, especially for the 3D task. Recent research

Supplementary Information The online version contains supplementary material available at https://doi.org/10.1007/978-3-031-19803-8_33.

S. Avidan et al. (Eds.): ECCV 2022, LNCS 13681, pp. 558–575, 2022.
https://doi.org/10.1007/978-3-031-19803-8_33

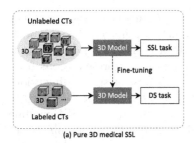
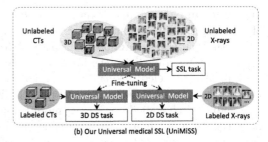

Fig. 1. (a) Pure 3D medical SSL learns representations with only 3D CT scans; (b) our proposed UniMiSS brings a wealth of 2D X-rays to offset the lack of 3D data, thus enables the large-scale SSL for better pre-training performance. Besides, the pre-trained model is generic to various downstream (DS) applications, without the restriction on the dimensionality barrier.

work suggests that the self-supervised learning (SSL) is promising to ease the annotation cost by making the best of unlabeled data [8,9,40,41,47,54,56,57]. Although setting label free, SSL still heavily relies on the large-scale unlabeled data to explore the feature representations. Unfortunately, publicly available 3D medical data is relatively limited due to the high imaging cost and data privacy. Most of 3D medical datasets just contain a few thousands of cases. For example, Zhou *et al.* [54] utilized the LUNA dataset [38], containing about 1000 CT cases, for self-supervised pre-training. Such a small data scale may limit the potential of SSL in 3D medical image analysis.

In comparison to 3D data, it is easy to collect hundreds of thousands of 2D medical images such as X-rays due to its fast imaging speed, low radiation and low cost. Accordingly, we advocate to bring a wealth of 2D medical images to the 3D SSL process, aiming at learning strong representations with large-scale images, as shown in Fig. 1. Comparing to the pure 3D medical SSL, this practice benefits the medical SSL in terms of three significant merits. First, 2D data serves as a compensation for the lack of 3D data, enabling the large-scale SSL pre-training. Second, there is the anatomy correlation between 2D and 3D images, like chest X-ray and CT. Such an intrinsic relevance may contribute for strong associated representations. Third, the pre-trained model is generic enough to be applied to both 3D and 2D downstream tasks. To achieve the universal SSL purpose, on the technical side, we need to build a versatile model that is able to process both 2D and 3D images. The common practice in medical image analysis is to design 2D convolutional neural networks (CNNs) for 2D images [49,50,54] and 3D CNNs for 3D images [47,48,51,54,56], respectively. Restricted to the dimensionality barrier, it is almost impossible to design a dimension-free CNN network for this purpose.

Recent months have witnessed the success of Transformer in computer vision [15]. A vision Transformer usually takes a sequence of image patches, represented by the learned linear embedding, as the input to model the long-term dependencies among the sequence elements. Owing to the sequence modeling, Transformer can accept the data of any dimensions, including but not limited to

2D images and 3D volumetric data. Therefore, Transformer offers the possibility of breaking the dimensionality barrier and constructing a universal SSL model.

In this paper, we propose a **Universal Medical Self-Supervised** representation learning framework (UniMiSS) that learns general representations from 2D and 3D unlabeled medical images. To achieve this, we design a dimension-free pyramid U-like **Medical Transformer** (MiT), which is mainly composed of switchable patch embedding (SPE) module and Transformers. The SPE module converts the input images to a sequence by using 2D or 3D patch embedding, depending on the input dimension. The Transformer layer processes the embedded tokens in a sequence-to-sequence manner, regardless of their original dimension. We perform the self-supervised learning by the self-distillation of student and teacher networks, both of which take the MiT as the backbone. The student network learns to predict the output distribution obtained with the momentum teacher network, following the view consistency. Moreover, the 3D volumetric image should be identical with their slices due to the same imaging content. The volume-slice consistency is adopted as a cross-dimension regularization to boost the representations. We conduct the SSL experiments based on 5,022 3D CT volumes, which are augmented by 108,948 2D X-ray images. Benefit from the huge augmented 2D data, the proposed UniMiSS achieves the obvious performance improvement on the downstream 3D classification/segmentation tasks. Besides, the UniMiSS pre-trained model can be freely applied to 2D downstream tasks, which beats strong competitors like ImageNet pre-training on the downstream 2D medical tasks.

To summarise, our contributions are three-fold: (1) we are the first to augment 3D medical images with the easily accessible unpaired 2D ones for the SSL purpose, aiming at addressing the limitation of 3D data amounts during the SSL process; (2) the proposed MiT breaks the dimensionality barrier and enables the joint SSL training with both 2D and 3D images; and (3) our UniMiSS pre-training achieves the advanced performance on six downstream tasks, covering the 3D/2D medical image classification/segmentation.

2   Related Work

2.1   Self-supervised Learning

SSL has been extensively studied in the literature. According to the pretext tasks, these studies can be broadly categorized into the discriminative methods [6,11,17,19,21,28,33–35,42] and generative methods [26,27,36,37,52]. The contrastive learning [11,17,19,21,33,35,42] has drawn significant research attention and achieved advanced performance on many vision tasks. Most of the previous work were built on the CNN-based network. More recently, Transformer has become an increasingly popular alternative architecture in computer vision. There has been a trend towards combining the merits of Transformer and SSL, advancing the self-supervised vision Transformers. The seminal work is iGPT [10], which follows the masked auto-regressive language modelling to pretrain the self-supervised vision Transformer. Besides, some attempts have also been made to pre-train vision Transformers using the contrastive learning [7] or Siamese distillation [13], which outperform the CNN-based SSL approaches, setting a new record on ImageNet.

The success of SSL in computer vision also benefits to the medical community [8,9,40,41,47,54,56,57]. Typical attempts include pre-training a CNN by restoring the content of raw images [9,41,54,56,57] and tailoring contrastive SSL to medical images [8,40,41,47]. These efforts constitute an important and timely step forward towards better SSL approaches to medical image analysis. However, they suffer two limitations. First, the CNN architecture enables the pre-training on either 2D or 3D medical images, failing to process both of them simultaneously. The resulting representations would be trapped especially for the limited 3D data. Consequently, the pre-trained CNN can only be transferred to the dimension-specific downstream task. Second, the above SSL approaches capture the spatial context of 3D medical images from either slices [8] or volume [41,56,57]. Few of them consider the inherent consistency relation between volume and its slices.

2.2 Cross-Domain Training for Medical Imaging

In the medical context, the cross-domain training usually jointly utilizes two or more datasets acquired at different sites [24,30] or using different imaging modalities [16,29,53] to train a single model that could perform well on diverse datasets. Karani et al. [24] and Liu et al. [30] trained a single CNN with shared convolutional layers and specific batch normalization layers using the MRI data acquired at each site individually, aiming to tackle the statistical divergence explicitly. Zhang et al. [53] simultaneously learned a volume-to-volume translation using the unpaired CT and MRI data and strong segmentors using synthetic data, which were translated from another modality. Dou et al. [16] derived a variant of knowledge distillation (KD) to leverage the shared across-modality information between CT and MRI for accurate segmentation of anatomical structures. Li et al. [29] also introduced KD to the cross-modality analysis of CT and MRI data, but they simultaneously exploited abundant unlabeled data. These studies are dedicated to analyzing multi-modal/site but fixed dimension (3D) medical images, failing to address the dimensionality barrier in our scenario.

3   Methods

3.1   Overview

UniMiSS is a universal medical SSL framework that is superior to learn general image representations with large scale mixed 2D and 3D unlabeled medical images. Figure 2 illustrates the pipeline of UniMiSS. Let us denote the mixed 2D and 3D data pool by $\{\mathbb{D}^{2D}, \mathbb{D}^{3D}\}$. To enable UniMiSS to process both 2D and 3D medical images, we build the MiT as its backbone, which is mainly constituted by the dimension-adaptive SPE module and Transformer layers. We perform the SSL process in the self-distillation manner, and utilize a standard cross-entropy loss to maximize the consistency between the student and teacher outputs. Besides, to get the utmost out of 3D volumetric information, we introduce

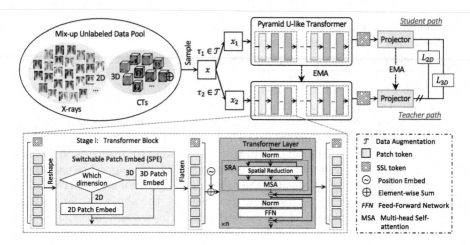

Fig. 2. Illustration of the proposed UniMiSS framework. It has a dual path architecture, *i.e.*, a student and a teacher. Taking both 2D X-rays and 3D CTs as input, UniMiSS is trained by the self-distillation strategy, *i.e.*, maximizing the agreement of both paths. To break the dimensionality barrier between X-rays and CTs, the MiT network, composed of the switchable patch embedding (SPE) module and Transformers, processes the 3D/2D data in a sequence-to-sequence manner.

the volume-slice consistency constraint, which encourages UniMiSS to model the consistency cross dimensions. It is intuitively conducive to learning strong feature representations from the volumetric images. We now delve into the details of this framework.

3.2 MiT: A Dimension-Free Architecture

Although achieving great success in computer vision, vision Transformer [15] still remains challenging to process high resolution 3D images, due to the high computation cost and memory requirement. Inspired by [45], we design the MiT with a pyramid architecture to process both 2D and 3D images efficiently. To break the dimensionality barrier, we propose a simple yet efficient SPE module to adaptively choose the 2D or 3D patch embedding according to the input type. MiT has an encoder-decoder architecture that facilitates the various applications, including segmentation and classification. We now describe each part of MiT, and more details can be found in Appendix.

SPE. As shown in Fig. 2, the SPE module plays an important role to obtain the dimension-specific embedding, *i.e.*, using 2D patch embedding operation for 2D inputs and using 3D patch embedding operation for 3D inputs. Notice that the implementations of SPE in the encoder and decoder are different. The SPE in the encoder refers to a switchable 2D and 3D convolution block with the stride of 2, which reduces the feature resolution. In contrast, the SPE in the decoder is a switchable 2D and 3D transpose convolution block, which increases the feature resolution.

Encoder-Decoder. The MiT encoder follows a progressive shrinking pyramid Transformer, as done in [45]. It consists explicitly of four stages, each of which is composed of a SPE module and several stacked Transformers. In each stage, the SPE module down-samples the input features and generates the dimension-specific embedded sequence. Notably, we append an extra learnable SSL token [7, 13] to the patch embedded sequence. The SSL token is similar to the [CLS] token in ViT, which is able to aggregate information from the whole patch embedding tokens via the self-attention. The resultant sequences, combined with the learnable positional embedding, are inputted into the following Transformers for the long-term dependency modeling. Each Transformer layer includes a self-attention module and a feed-forward network (FFN) with two hidden layers. To enable MiT to process high-resolution images, we follow the spatial-reduction attention (SRA) layer [45]. Given a query q, a key k, and a value v as the input, SRA first reduces the spatial resolution of k and v, and then feeds q, reduced k, and reduced v to a multi-head self-attention (MSA) layer to produce refined features. This process can be formally expressed as follows

$$SRA(q, k, v) = MSA(q, F(\sigma(R(k))), F(\sigma(R(v)))), \qquad (1)$$

where $\sigma(\cdot)$ represents a linear projection, *i.e.*, strided 2D or 3D convolution operation, that reduces the feature map resolution, $R(\cdot)$ reshapes the input sequence to a feature map of the original spatial size, and $F(\cdot)$ flattens the input into a 1D sequence. MiT has a symmetric decoder structure that consists of three stages. In each stage, the input feature map is first up-sampled by the SPE module, and then refined by the stacked Transformer layers. Besides, we also add skip connections between the encoder and decoder to keep more low-level but high-resolution information.

3.3 Objective of UniMiSS

The proposed UniMiSS framework is based on the student-teacher paradigm. Each path comprises a MiT network $\mathcal{F}_\theta(\cdot)$ and a projector $\mathcal{P}_\theta(\cdot)$. $\mathcal{P}_\theta(\cdot)$ is a n-layer multi-layer perceptron (MLP) head, θ represents the parameter set of this path. The SPE layers switch to perform the 2D patch embedding or 3D patch embedding during the feed-forward computing that is denoted as $\mathcal{F}_\theta(\cdot; 2D)$ and $\mathcal{F}_\theta(\cdot; 3D)$, respectively. During the SSL process, we only extract the SSL token from the output of $\mathcal{F}_\theta(\cdot; 2D/3D)$ as the input of the projector. Since the Transformer sets the dimension free, our UniMiSS is able to learn image representations from both 2D and 3D unlabeled medical images.

Both of paths share an identical architecture. However, they differ in the following two items. First, the teacher network is formulated as a momentum version of the student network, which updated by an exponential moving average strategy, defined as

$$\mu \leftarrow \lambda\mu + (1 - \lambda)\theta, \qquad (2)$$

where λ increases from 0.996 to 1 using a cosine schedule during training [7]. Second, a stop-gradient operator is performed to the teacher network to avoid model collapse.

Objective for 2D Domain Data. Taking a mini-batch of 2D data x for example, we first create two augmented views x_1 and x_2 by using the data augmentation module $\mathcal{T}$, and then feed them into the student and teacher networks. The obtained SSL token is inputted into the projector to produce the output vector, denoted as $f_1 = \mathcal{P}_\theta(\mathcal{F}_\theta(x_1; 2D))$, $f_2 = \mathcal{P}_\mu(\mathcal{F}_\mu(x_2; 2D))$. The objective of UniMiSS is to maximize the consistency between the output vectors obtained with student and teacher networks, formulated by

$$\mathcal{H}(f_1, f_2) = -\text{softmax}(\frac{f_2 - \mathcal{C}}{\tau_t}) * \log(\text{softmax}(\frac{f_1}{\tau_s})), \tag{3}$$

where $\mathcal{C}$ is the centering of teacher outputs, τ_t and τ_s are sharpening temperature parameters for student and teacher network. The centering operation heartens the model to the uniform distribution while the sharpening has the opposite effect, $i.e.$, encouraging one dimension to dominate. Both of them are jointly used together to avoid model collapse [7]. Specifically, the temperature τ_t is set to a small value in the teacher path for the sharpening purpose. The center $\mathcal{C}$ is first computed via averaging the teacher's outputs of the min-batch data and then updated with an exponential moving average strategy to aggregate the center across the whole batches, shown as follows

$$\mathcal{C} \leftarrow \omega * \mathcal{C} + (1 - \omega) * \widehat{f_2} \tag{4}$$

where ω is a rate parameter, and $\widehat{f_2}$ refers to the mean of teacher output in a mini-batch. We define a symmetrized loss for 2D images as:

$$\mathcal{L}^{2D} = \mathbb{E}_{x \sim \mathbb{D}^{2D}}[\mathcal{H}(f_1, f_2) + \mathcal{H}(f_2, f_1)] \tag{5}$$

Objective for 3D Domain Data. In medical domain, 3D volumes can be viewed as the stacking of 2D images along with the inter-slice dimension. The volume data has the inherent consistency to their slices, which inspires us to model the volume-slice consistency for SSL. Given a 3D data x sampled from the 3D medical dataset, we denote its two augmented views as x_1 and x_2, each containing m 2D slices. We compute the global volumetric representations by the student and teacher networks in a 3D mode, $i.e.$, $f_1 = \mathcal{P}_\theta(\mathcal{F}_\theta(x_1; 3D))$, and $f_2 = \mathcal{P}_\mu(\mathcal{F}_\mu(x_2; 3D))$. Meanwhile, we stack m slices of each augmented view in a batch, and use them as 2D inputs to calculate the slice-wise representations in a 2D mode, and then treat the average outputs of all slices as the holistic slice representations, $i.e.$, $f_1' = \frac{1}{m}\sum_{i=1}^{m} \mathcal{P}_\theta(\mathcal{F}_\theta([x_1]^i; 2D))$, and $f_2' = \frac{1}{m}\sum_{i=1}^{m} \mathcal{P}_\mu(\mathcal{F}_\mu([x_2]^i; 2D))$, where $[x]^i$ represents the i-th slice extracted from the 3D data x. After that, we build the following objective function

$$\begin{aligned}\mathcal{L}^{3D} = \mathbb{E}_{x \sim \mathbb{D}^{3D}}[&\mathcal{H}(f_1, f_2) + \mathcal{H}(f_1, f_2') + \mathcal{H}(f_1', f_2) + \mathcal{H}(f_1', f_2') \\ &+ \mathcal{H}(f_2, f_1) + \mathcal{H}(f_2, f_1') + \mathcal{H}(f_2', f_1) + \mathcal{H}(f_2', f_1')]\end{aligned} \tag{6}$$

The above objective function encourages to learn the refined consistency with 3D medical data in terms of three aspects, $i.e.$, volume to volume, slice to slice, and volume to slice.

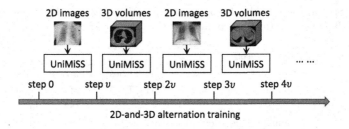

Fig. 3. Illustration of 2D-and-3D alternation training.

We introduce an alternative training scheme to solve this multi-objective optimization problem. As shown in Fig. 3, we first sample 2D images to train the UniMiSS from step 0 to step v, and then take turn to sample 3D volumes in the next v steps. The following training process will continue in a circular manner until the model converges. The proposed iterative training scheme has two merits: (1) it bypasses the difficulty of using both 2D and 3D images in the same batch; and (2) it can reduce the instability caused by the distribution discrepancy between 2D and 3D data.

4   Experiments

4.1   Datasets

Pre-Training Datasets. We collected 5,022 3D CT scans from five datasets (*i.e.*MOTS dataset [51], LIDC-IDRI dataset [5], Tianchi dataset [2], RibFrac dataset [23], TCIACT dataset [4]), and collected 108,948 2D images from NIH ChestX-ray8 dataset [46] to train UniMiSS in a self-supervised manner.

Downstream Datasets. Table 1 gives the details of six downstream tasks, which can be grouped into (1) 3D downstream: CT-based segmentation (BCV) and classification (RICORD), MRI-based segmentation (CHAOS); (2) 2D downstream: multi-organ segmentation (JSRT) and pneumonia classification (ChestXR), and skin lesion segmentation (ISIC). Note that the CHAOS and ISIC datasets are different from the pre-training data in terms of modalities (*i.e.*, 3D CT vs. MRI, 2D X-ray vs. dermoscopy). They are used to evaluate the unseen-modality transferability.

4.2   Experimental Details

Pre-Training Setup. We set the size of input 2D patches to 224×224 and 3D patches to $16 \times 96 \times 96$, aiming to weigh the balance between reserving enough information for SSL and reducing computational and spatial complexity to an affordable level. We applied a rich set of data augmentations to create positive views, including colour jittering, Gaussian blur/noise, random crop, zooming, and flip to the inputs for producing two views. Following [7], we adopted the AdamW optimizer [32] with a cosine decaying learning rate [31], a warm-up

Table 1. Six datasets for the downstream evaluation. Noticed that we used two test sets, *i.e.* offline test set (off) and online test set (on), for the BCV dataset.

Downstream evaluation datasets				
Name	Tasks	Modalities	#Train	#Test
BCV [1]	Multi-organ segmentation	3D CT	24	6 (off) + 20 (on)
RICORD [43]	COVID-19 screening		182	45
CHAOS [25]	Abdominal organ segmentation	3D MRI	48	12
JSRT [39,44]	Multi-organ segmentation	2D X-ray	124	123
ChestXR [3]	Pneumonia classification		17,955	3,430
ISIC [14]	Skin lesion segmentation	2D dermoscopy	2000	600

period of 10 epochs, to train our UniMiSS. We empirically set the initial learning rate to 0.0008, batch size to 192, maximum epochs to 200, rate parameter ω to 0.9, and temperature parameter τ_t and τ_s to 0.04 and 0.1, respectively. It took about 2.5 days to pre-train the UniMiSS using 8 NVIDIA V100 GPUs. We understand this is a big GPU consumption but it saves large amount of time and money to collect 3D medical image data, as we use easily-collected 2D data as the fuel.

Downstream Training Setup. For the classification, we extracted the pre-trained MiT encoder and appended a FC layer with the output channel as the number of classes for prediction. For the segmentation, we took the pre-trained MiT encoder and decoder while removing the SSL token, and appended a segmentation head for prediction. This head includes a transposed convolutional layer, a Conv-IN-LeakyReLU, and a convolutional layer with the kernel size of 1 and the output channel as the number of classes. The segmentation performance is measured by the Dice coefficient scores. The classification performance is measured by the area under the receiver operator curve (AUC). Note that we randomly split 25% training samples as a validation set to select the hyperparameters of UniMiSS in the ablation study. The detailed training setups for each downstream task are shown in Appendix.

4.3   Results on 3D Downstream Tasks

Dimension-Specific SSL *vs.* Cross-dimension SSL. In this section, we evaluate the SSL performance on two downstream 3D taks, *i.e.*, multi-organ segmentation (BCV) and COVID-19 screening (RICORD). The UniMiSS pre-training is compared with the random initialization (Rand. init.) and five advanced SSL methods, including MoCo v2/v3 [12,13], PGL [47], PCRL [54], and DINO [7]. Note that MoCo v2, PGL, and PCRL take the CNN as their encoder backbone, *i.e.*, a 3D ResNet with 50 learnable layers. During the SSL process, MoCo v2 and PGL only pre-train the encoder part, while PCRL additionally pre-trains a decoder by using the reconstruction task. Besides, MoCo v3, DINO, and our UniMiSS use the Transformer model as the backbone, which contains

Table 2. Segmentation and classification performance of using different pre-training strategies on the BCV offline test set and RICORD test set.

Methods	Backbone	BCV (CT, seg)			RICORD (CT, cls)		
		20%	40%	100%	20%	40%	100%
Rand. init.	CNN	68.44	73.14	79.93	69.72	74.66	83.36
MoCo v2 [12]		71.22	75.09	82.05	73.46	77.81	85.46
PGL [47]		72.05	75.86	82.57	73.76	77.96	85.61
PCRL [54]		72.80	76.05	82.73	75.11	79.01	86.21
Rand. init.	Transformer	70.09	74.60	79.97	71.36	76.06	83.21
MoCo v3 [13]		74.54	78.16	82.02	75.56	79.66	85.16
DINO [7]		75.33	78.88	82.61	76.31	80.11	85.91
UniMiSS (Ours)		**77.96**	**80.97**	**84.99**	**78.71**	**82.96**	**89.06**

both encoder and decoder. We employ the U-like PVT as the backbone for MoCo v3 and DINO, which has a similar architecture of MiT but the different patch embedding module. The lack of SPE make them fail to process both 2D and 3D images simultaneously, resulting in the dimension-specific SSL with only 3D data. For a fair comparison, all of these SSL methods are pre-trained on the 5,022 unlabeled 3D CT scans. Somewhat differently, the proposed UniMiSS introduces the additional 2D X-rays to the 3D SSL training, benefiting from the universality. We make more detailed comparisons between the proposed UniMiSS and other dimension-specific CNN/Transformer SSL methods. Table 2 shows the results of three label settings (20%,40%, and 100% label available). We summarize this table in the following points: (1) The Transformer-based models outperform obviously the CNN-based methods, mainly owing to the SSL pre-training. It reflects that the Transformer is a competitive architecture and the SSL pre-training is essential for the Transformer to achieve good performance. (2) The proposed UniMiSS is superior to MoCo v3 and DINO. The performance gains over DINO are +2.38% for segmentation and +3.15% for classification when 100% labels are available. It proves the effectiveness of using a wealth of 2D medical images to assist the 3D SSL process. (3) Besides, it is really encouraging to see that the proposed UniMiSS is able to achieve the comparable or even superior performance while less annotations, even a half. Taking BCV for example, UniMiSS with 40% label achieves 80.97% segmentation Dice, which is better than the 79.97% of the random initialized method with 100% labels.

Comparisons on the BCV Online Test Set. To be more persuasive, we also compared the proposed UniMiSS with other state-of-the-art segmentation methods on the BCV online test set. As listed in Table 3, these compared methods include PaNN [55], UNETR [18], nnUnet [22] and DoDnet [51]. Note that the performance records of these competitors come from their original paper. It reveals that our UniMiSS, without using any ensemble strategy, still achieves the competitive performance, the best Hausdorff distance (HD) and average mean

Table 3. Comparisons on the BCV online test set.

Metrics	PaNN [55]	UNETR [18]	nnUnet [22]	DoDnet [51]	UniMiSS	UniMiSS
Ensemble	5	5	10	5	1	10
Dice	85.00	85.55	87.62	86.44	87.05	**88.11**
HD	18.47	\	\	15.62	13.92	**13.17**
SD	1.45	\	\	1.17	1.02	**0.90**

Table 4. Segmentation and classification performance of using different pre-training strategies on two 2D test sets.

Methods	Backbone	JSRT (X-ray, seg)			ChestXR (X-ray, cls)		
		20%	40%	100%	20%	40%	100%
Rand. init.	CNN	84.05	87.63	90.96	92.05	94.83	97.54
INpre [20]		87.90	90.01	91.73	94.78	96.26	98.13
MoCo v2 [12]		88.65	91.03	92.32	95.22	96.61	98.67
PGL [47]		89.01	91.39	92.76	95.56	96.96	98.87
PCRL [54]		89.55	91.53	93.07	95.88	97.43	98.99
Rand. init.	Transformer	85.55	88.83	91.22	92.80	95.20	97.04
MoCo v3 [13]		90.07	91.75	92.68	95.99	97.33	98.59
DINO [7]		90.40	92.16	93.03	96.44	97.69	98.70
UniMiSS		**91.88**	**93.15**	**94.08**	**97.09**	**98.14**	**99.07**

surface distance (SD), and second highest Dice on the online test set, outperforming the DoDNet with supervised pre-training. When using the coarse-to-fine ensemble strategy like [22], our UniMiSS can obtain the best performance in terms of all metrics.

Results on 2D Downstream Tasks. Since pre-training on both 2D and 3D medical images, our UniMiSS can be freely applied to 2D downstream tasks. Table 4 makes the comparisons on the 2D medical image segmentation and classification tasks. The compared methods include the Rand. init., ImageNet pre-training (INpre), CNN-based SSL methods (*i.e.*MoCo v2, PGL and PCRL), and Transformer-based SSL methods (*i.e.*MoCo v3 and DINO). Different from the 3D scenarios, a 2D ResNet-50 is used as the backbone in MoCo v2, PGL, and PCRL. MoCo v3, and DINO still take the U-like PVT as the backbone, but modify the patch embedding to adapt for the 2D inputs. Here, all compared SSL methods are pre-trained on the same 2D unlabeled medical images. As for UniMiSS, we directly apply the previous pre-trained model to the 2D tasks, without any modification or further re-training. From the results, we can find that (1) the SSL methods have surpassed INpre in both tasks, revealing that pre-training on a large-scale medical image dataset is more friendly to medical domain downstream tasks than pre-training on natural images; (2) although the number of 3D data is much smaller than 2D, *i.e.*, about one in twenty,

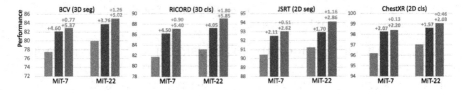

Fig. 4. Results of MiT with fewer Transformer layers. Here, MiT-7 and MiT-22 denote MiT with 7 and 22 Transformer layers, respectively. ■ Rand. init., ■ Dimension-specific pre-training, ■ UniMiSS. Note that the performance gain with yellow and orange color is computed by comparing to the Rand. init., and dimension-specific pre-training baseline, respectively. (Color figure online)

Table 5. Segmentation and classification performance on two 3D validation sets with or without using volume-slice consistency.

Objective for 3D		BCV (seg)			RICORD (cls)		
Volume	Slices	20%	40%	100%	20%	40%	100%
✓		72.08	76.04	80.94	69.87	74.61	80.96
✓	✓	**74.56**	**77.97**	**82.36**	**72.46**	**76.89**	**82.43**

the UniMiSS pre-training still achieves the performance gain over the pure 2D SSL method, like DINO. This may account in part for the inherent correlation between X-rays and CTs. Such a correlation information can be captured by the UniMiSS, thus contributed for the performance gain.

4.4 Discussions

Effectiveness of Volume-Slice Consistency. We design the volume-slice consistency mechanism for learning rich representations with 3D medical images. To evaluate the effectiveness of this mechanism, we pre-trained UniMiSS on 3D medical images with or without using the volume-slice consistency. Table 5 gives the downstream performance on the validation of two 3D datasets. The proposed volume-slice consistency can substantially improve the 3D segmentation/classification accuracy under different label ratios. The performance gain is at least by 1.42% on segmentation and by 1.47% on classification.

Number of Iteration Interval. The UniMiSS is optimized in a 2D-3D alternation training way, where the iteration interval v is a critical parameter. A smaller v may lead to insufficient training for each domain. A larger v may make the network forget the information learned from another domain. To set a suitable v, we pre-trained UniMiSS with various of v, varying from 1 to 3, and fine-tuned them on four downstream tasks. Table 6 shows that the pre-trained UniMiSS can achieve the best performance on four downstream tasks when v equals 2, and below or above 2 gives rise to the performance loss. Hence, we suggest setting the iteration interval to 2 during the cross-domain pre-training.

Table 6. Segmentation and classification performance of our UniMiSS with different iteration intervals on the validation sets.

Iteration interval	BCV (3D seg)	RICORD (3D cls)	JSRT (2D seg)	ChestXR (2D cls)
1	82.70	82.95	92.33	96.65
2	**83.56**	**84.26**	**93.48**	**97.57**
3	83.28	83.65	93.12	97.16

Table 7. Segmentation performance of using the random initialization and three pre-training strategies on CHAOS dataset (unseen MRI scans) and ISIC dataset (unseen dermoscopic images).

Methods	Downstream data					
	2D dermoscopic			3D MRI		
	20%	40%	100%	20%	40%	100%
Rand. init.	76.31	79.92	85.07	73.28	83.64	88.38
MoCo v3	78.66	81.46	86.04	78.42	87.22	89.83
DINO	79.11	81.89	86.21	79.16	87.79	90.52
UniMiSS	**79.78**	**82.33**	**86.67**	**80.50**	**88.58**	**91.36**

MiT with Different Transformer Scales. Transformer is the dominant component in the MiT backbone. We investigate the effect of Transformer scales in MiT. Specifically, we compare a MiT with 22 Transformer layers (MiT-22) and another with seven layers (MiT-7). The segmentation and classification performance is given in Fig. 4, from which three conclusions can be drawn: (1) increasing the Transformer layers boosts the performance of MiT in all downstream tasks; (2) as MiT goes deeper, the performance gain of the dimension-specific pre-training over the random initialization becomes smaller, while the performance gain of our UniMiSS with cross-dimension pre-training is basically impregnable; and (3) the superiority of our UniMiSS pre-training over the dimension-specific pre-training is more evident with the increase of Transformer layers.

Transferability on Unseen Modality Data. In the above experiments, the pre-training and downstream tasks are all based on CT and X-ray images. To evaluate the transferability of UniMiSS on unseen modalities, we further tested the MoCo v3, DINO and our UniMiSS on the CHAOS dataset (MRI scans) and ISIC dataset (dermoscopic images). The results in Table 7 show that UniMiSS can consistently improve at least 2.98% on the CHAOS dataset, and 1.60% on the ISIC dataset, compared to the random initialization. It demonstrates that UniMiSS has a great potential in transferring learned knowledge to the unseen modality. Besides, our UniMiSS also outperforms two popular Transformer-based SSL methods on both CHAOS and ISIC datasets.

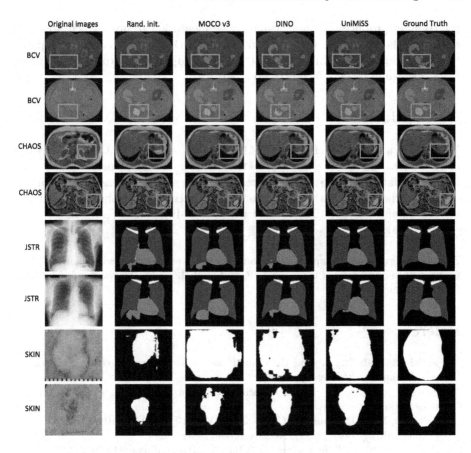

Fig. 5. Visualization of segmentation results of 8 cases selected from four datasets. The regions in red rectangles indicate our superiority. Our UniMiSS pre-training results in more accurate results than random initialization and other two pre-training strategies. Each type of organs and tumors in single dataset is denoted by a unique color. (Color figure online)

Necessity of SPE. Without the SPE module, a straightforward solution is to flatten the pixels or patches and then use a linear layer for the embedding. Such a crude flattening operation suffers the high computation complexity and memory requirements, especially for 3D images. Accordingly, SPE is an indispensable part of UniMiSS, which enables to (1) adaptively choose the patch embedding according to the input type; and (2) lessen the length of the sequence to reduce computation cost when the network goes deep.

Visualization of Segmentation Results. In Fig. 5, we visualize the segmentation results obtained by the segmentation network, which is initialized (1) randomly, (2) by using the pre-trained MoCo v3 [13], (3) by using the pre-trained DINO [7], or (4) by using our pre-trained UniMiSS. It shows that our UniMiSS pre-training produces the higher-quality segmentation results, which are more similar to the ground truth, than MoCo v3 and DINO pre-training. Compared to other competitors, UniMiSS pre-training is superior to process challenging cases, like small objects or blurry boundaries.

5   Conclusion

We propose a simple yet effective UniMiSS framework, which introduces a wealth of 2D medical images (*i.e.* X-rays) to the 3D SSL, aiming at making up for the lack of 3D data (*i.e.* CT scans). To break the difficulty of dimensionality barrier, we design the MiT as a bridge to connect different dimensions. In the future, we will extend our UniMiSS to deal with more dimensions (*e.g.* clinic text or genetic data).

Acknowledgement. Jianpeng Zhang and Yong Xia were supported by National Natural Science Foundation of China under Grants 62171377. Qi Wu was funded by ARC DE190100539.

References

1. Multi-atlas labeling beyond the cranial vault - workshop and challenge. https://www.synapse.org/#!Synapse:syn3193805/wiki/217789
2. Tianchi dataset. https://tianchi.aliyun.com/competition/entrance/231601/information?from=oldUrl
3. Akhloufi, M.A., Chetoui, M.: Chest XR COVID-19 detection. https://cxr-covid19.grand-challenge.org/ (2021). Accessed September 2021
4. An, P., et al.: CT images in COVID-19. https://doi.org/10.7937/TCIA.2020.GQRY-NC81. The Cancer Imaging Archive (2020)
5. Armato, S.G., III.: The lung image database consortium (LIDC) and image database resource initiative (IDRI): a completed reference database of lung nodules on CT scans. Med. Phys. **38**(2), 915–931 (2011)
6. Caron, M., Bojanowski, P., Joulin, A., Douze, M.: Deep clustering for unsupervised learning of visual features. In: ECCV, pp. 132–149 (2018)
7. Caron, M., et al.: Emerging properties in self-supervised vision transformers. In: ICCV (2021)
8. Chaitanya, K., Erdil, E., Karani, N., Konukoglu, E.: Contrastive learning of global and local features for medical image segmentation with limited annotations. In: NeurIPS, vol. 33 (2020)
9. Chen, L., Bentley, P., Mori, K., Misawa, K., Fujiwara, M., Rueckert, D.: Self-supervised learning for medical image analysis using image context restoration. Med. Image Anal. **58**, 101539 (2019)
10. Chen, M., et al.: Generative pretraining from pixels. In: ICML, pp. 1691–1703 (2020)
11. Chen, T., Kornblith, S., Norouzi, M., Hinton, G.: A simple framework for contrastive learning of visual representations. In: ICML (2020)
12. Chen, X., Fan, H., Girshick, R., He, K.: Improved baselines with momentum contrastive learning. arXiv preprint arXiv:2003.04297 (2020)

13. Chen*, X., Xie*, S., He, K.: An empirical study of training self-supervised vision transformers. In: ICCV (2021)
14. Codella, N.C., et al.: Skin lesion analysis toward melanoma detection: a challenge at the 2017 international symposium on biomedical imaging (ISBI), hosted by the international skin imaging collaboration (ISIC). In: ISBI, pp. 168–172. IEEE (2018)
15. Dosovitskiy, A., et al.: An image is worth 16x16 words: transformers for image recognition at scale. In: ICLR (2021)
16. Dou, Q., Liu, Q., Heng, P.A., Glocker, B.: Unpaired multi-modal segmentation via knowledge distillation. IEEE Trans. Med. Imaging **39**(7), 2415–2425 (2020)
17. Grill, J.B., et al.: Bootstrap your own latent-a new approach to self-supervised learning. In: NeurIPS (2020)
18. Hatamizadeh, A., et al.: UNETR: transformers for 3D medical image segmentation. In: Proceedings of the IEEE/CVF Winter Conference on Applications of Computer Vision, pp. 574–584 (2022)
19. He, K., Fan, H., Wu, Y., Xie, S., Girshick, R.: Momentum contrast for unsupervised visual representation learning. In: CVPR, pp. 9729–9738 (2020)
20. He, K., Zhang, X., Ren, S., Sun, J.: Deep residual learning for image recognition. In: Proceedings of the IEEE Conference on Computer Vision and Pattern Recognition, pp. 770–778 (2016)
21. Hjelm, R.D., et al.: Learning deep representations by mutual information estimation and maximization. In: ICLR (2019)
22. Isensee, F., Jaeger, P.F., Kohl, S.A., Petersen, J., Maier-Hein, K.H.: NNU-net: a self-configuring method for deep learning-based biomedical image segmentation. Nat. Methods **18**(2), 203–211 (2021)
23. Jin, L., et al.: Deep-learning-assisted detection and segmentation of rib fractures from CT scans: development and validation of FracNet. EBioMedicine (2020)
24. Karani, N., Chaitanya, K., Baumgartner, C., Konukoglu, E.: A lifelong learning approach to brain MR segmentation across scanners and protocols. In: Frangi, A.F., Schnabel, J.A., Davatzikos, C., Alberola-López, C., Fichtinger, G. (eds.) MICCAI 2018. LNCS, vol. 11070, pp. 476–484. Springer, Cham (2018). https://doi.org/10.1007/978-3-030-00928-1_54
25. Kavur, A.E., Selver, M.A., Dicle, O., Barış, M., Gezer, N.S.: CHAOS - combined (CT-MR) healthy abdominal organ segmentation challenge data (2019). https://doi.org/10.5281/zenodo.3362844
26. Larsson, G., Maire, M., Shakhnarovich, G.: Colorization as a proxy task for visual understanding. In: CVPR, pp. 6874–6883 (2017)
27. Ledig, C., et al.: Photo-realistic single image super-resolution using a generative adversarial network. In: CVPR, pp. 4681–4690 (2017)
28. Lee, H., Hwang, S.J., Shin, J.: Self-supervised label augmentation via input transformations. In: ICML (2020)
29. Li, K., Wang, S., Yu, L., Heng, P.A.: Dual-teacher++: exploiting intra-domain and inter-domain knowledge with reliable transfer for cardiac segmentation. IEEE Trans. Med. Imaging **40**, 2771–2782 (2020)
30. Liu, Q., Dou, Q., Yu, L., Heng, P.A.: MS-NET: multi-site network for improving prostate segmentation with heterogeneous MRI data. IEEE Trans. Medical Imaging **39**(9), 2713–2724 (2020)
31. Loshchilov, I., Hutter, F.: Sgdr: Stochastic gradient descent with warm restarts. In: ICLR (2017)
32. Loshchilov, I., Hutter, F.: Fixing weight decay regularization in Adam (2018)
33. Misra, I., Maaten, L.v.d.: Self-supervised learning of pretext-invariant representations. In: CVPR, pp. 6707–6717 (2020)

34. Noroozi, M., Favaro, P.: Unsupervised learning of visual representations by solving jigsaw puzzles. In: Leibe, B., Matas, J., Sebe, N., Welling, M. (eds.) ECCV 2016. LNCS, vol. 9910, pp. 69–84. Springer, Cham (2016). https://doi.org/10.1007/978-3-319-46466-4_5

35. Oord, A.v.d., Li, Y., Vinyals, O.: Representation learning with contrastive predictive coding. arXiv preprint arXiv:1807.03748 (2018)

36. Pathak, D., Krahenbuhl, P., Donahue, J., Darrell, T., Efros, A.A.: Context encoders: feature learning by inpainting. In: CVPR, pp. 2536–2544 (2016)

37. Radford, A., Metz, L., Chintala, S.: Unsupervised representation learning with deep convolutional generative adversarial networks. arXiv preprint arXiv:1511.06434 (2015)

38. Setio, A.A.A., et al.: Validation, comparison, and combination of algorithms for automatic detection of pulmonary nodules in computed tomography images: the luna16 challenge. Med. Image Anal. 42, 1–13 (2017)

39. Shiraishi, J., et al.: Development of a digital image database for chest radiographs with and without a lung nodule: receiver operating characteristic analysis of radiologists' detection of pulmonary nodules Am. J. Roentgenol. 174(1), 71–74 (2000). https://db.jsrt.or.jp/eng.php

40. Sowrirajan, H., Yang, J., Ng, A.Y., Rajpurkar, P.: MoCo pretraining improves representation and transferability of chest x-ray models. In: MIDL, pp. 728–744. PMLR (2021)

41. Taleb, A., et al.: 3D self-supervised methods for medical imaging. In: NeurIPS, vol. 33, pp. 18158–18172 (2020)

42. Tian, Y., Krishnan, D., Isola, P.: Contrastive multiview coding. In: Vedaldi, A., Bischof, H., Brox, T., Frahm, J.-M. (eds.) ECCV 2020. LNCS, vol. 12356, pp. 776–794. Springer, Cham (2020). https://doi.org/10.1007/978-3-030-58621-8_45

43. Tsai, E.B., et al.: The RSNA international COVID-19 open radiology database (RICORD). Radiology 299(1), E204–E213 (2021)

44. Van Ginneken, B., Stegmann, M.B., Loog, M.: Segmentation of anatomical structures in chest radiographs using supervised methods: a comparative study on a public database. Med. Image Anal. 10(1), 19–40 (2006). https://www.isi.uu.nl/Research/Databases/SCR/index.php

45. Wang, W., et al.: Pyramid vision transformer: a versatile backbone for dense prediction without convolutions. In: ICCV (2021)

46. Wang, X., Peng, Y., Lu, L., Lu, Z., Bagheri, M., Summers, R.M.: ChestX-ray8: hospital-scale chest x-ray database and benchmarks on weakly-supervised classification and localization of common thorax diseases. In: CVPR, pp. 2097–2106 (2017)

47. Xie, Y., Zhang, J., Liao, Z., Xia, Y., Shen, C.: PGL: prior-guided local self-supervised learning for 3D medical image segmentation. arXiv preprint arXiv:2011.12640 (2020)

48. Xie, Y., Zhang, J., Shen, C., Xia, Y.: CoTr: efficiently bridging CNN and transformer for 3D medical image segmentation. In: de Bruijne, M., et al. (eds.) MICCAI 2021. LNCS, vol. 12903, pp. 171–180. Springer, Cham (2021). https://doi.org/10.1007/978-3-030-87199-4_16

49. Xie, Y., Zhang, J., Xia, Y., Shen, C.: A mutual bootstrapping model for automated skin lesion segmentation and classification. IEEE Trans. Med. Imaging 39(7), 2482–2493 (2020)

50. Zhang, J., et al.: Viral pneumonia screening on chest x-rays using confidence-aware anomaly detection. IEEE Trans. Med. Imaging 40(3), 879–890 (2020)

51. Zhang, J., Xie, Y., Xia, Y., Shen, C.: DoDNet: learning to segment multi-organ and tumors from multiple partially labeled datasets. In: CVPR, pp. 1195–1204 (2021)
52. Zhang, R., Isola, P., Efros, A.A.: Split-brain autoencoders: unsupervised learning by cross-channel prediction. In: CVPR, pp. 1058–1067 (2017)
53. Zhang, Z., Yang, L., Zheng, Y.: Translating and segmenting multimodal medical volumes with cycle-and shape-consistency generative adversarial network. In: CVPR, pp. 9242–9251 (2018)
54. Zhou, H.Y., Lu, C., Yang, S., Han, X., Yu, Y.: Preservational learning improves self-supervised medical image models by reconstructing diverse contexts. In: ICCV, pp. 3499–3509 (2021)
55. Zhou, Y., et al.: Prior-aware neural network for partially-supervised multi-organ segmentation. In: ICCV, pp. 10672–10681 (2019)
56. Zhou, Z., Sodha, V., Pang, J., Gotway, M.B., Liang, J.: Models genesis. Med. Image Anal. **67**, 101840 (2021)
57. Zhu, J., Li, Y., Hu, Y., Ma, K., Zhou, S.K., Zheng, Y.: Rubik's cube+: a self-supervised feature learning framework for 3D medical image analysis. Med. Image Anal. **64**, 101746 (2020)

DLME: Deep Local-Flatness Manifold Embedding

Zelin Zang[1,2], Siyuan Li[1,2], Di Wu[1,2], Ge Wang[1,2], Kai Wang[3], Lei Shang[3], Baigui Sun[3], Hao Li[3], and Stan Z. Li[1,2(✉)]

[1] Zhejiang University, Hangzhou 310000, China
{zangzelin,stan.zq.li}@westlake.edu.cn
[2] AI Lab, School of Engineering, Westlake University, Hangzhou 310000, China
[3] Alibaba Group, Hangzhou, China

Abstract. Manifold learning (ML) aims to seek low-dimensional embedding from high-dimensional data. The problem is challenging on real-world datasets, especially with under-sampling data, and we find that previous methods perform poorly in this case. Generally, ML methods first transform input data into a low-dimensional embedding space to maintain the data's geometric structure and subsequently perform downstream tasks therein. The poor local connectivity of under-sampling data in the former step and inappropriate optimization objectives in the latter step leads to two problems: *structural distortion* and *underconstrained embedding*. This paper proposes a novel ML framework named Deep Local-flatness Manifold Embedding (DLME) to solve these problems. The proposed DLME constructs semantic manifolds by data augmentation and overcomes the structural distortion problem using a smoothness constrained based on a *local flatness* assumption about the manifold. To overcome the underconstrained embedding problem, we design a loss and theoretically demonstrate that it leads to a more suitable embedding based on the local flatness. Experiments on three types of datasets (toy, biological, and image) for various downstream tasks (classification, clustering, and visualization) show that our proposed DLME outperforms state-of-the-art ML and contrastive learning methods.

1 Introduction

The intrinsic dimension of high-dimensional data is usually much lower and how to effectively learn a low-dimensional representation is a fundamental problem in traditional machine learning [31], data mining [1], and pattern recognition [6]. Manifold learning (ML), based on solid theoretical foundations and assumptions, discusses manifold representation problems under unsupervised conditions and

---

Z. Zang and S. Li—Equal contribution.

Supplementary Information The online version contains supplementary material available at https://doi.org/10.1007/978-3-031-19803-8_34.

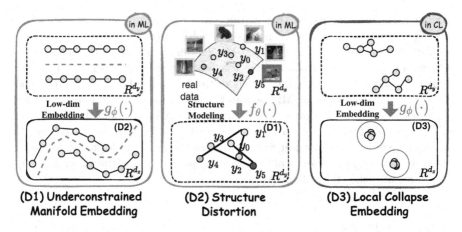

(D1) Underconstrained Manifold Embedding   **(D2) Structure Distortion**   **(D3) Local Collapse Embedding**

Fig. 1. Problems in ML and CL. **(D1)** Local field of view & first-order (similarity/dissimilarity) constraints → underconstrained manifold embedding. **(D2)** complexity of real-world data (ultra-high dimensionality or non well-sampling) → broke the local connectivity of manifold → structure distortions. **(D3)** unsmoothed losses function → local collapse embedding.

has a far-reaching impact. However, practical applications of the manifold learning method are limited in real-world scenarios, and we attribute the reasons to the following two reasons. **(D1) Underconstrained manifold embedding.** ML methods focus on local relationships, while it is prone to distorted embeddings that affect the performance of downstream tasks (in Fig. 1 (D2) and Fig. 6). Paper [18,19] suggests even the most advanced ML methods lose performance on downstream tasks due to inadequate constraints on the latent space. The reason is attributed to the limitations of traditional ML methods based on similarity/dissimilarity loss function design. **(D2) Structural distortion.** ML methods focus on handcraft or easy datasets and are not satisfactory in handling real-world datasets. Most of these approaches use the locally connected graphs constructed in the input space to define structure-preserving unsupervised learning loss functions [27,28]. These methods introduce a stringent assumption (local connectivity assumption (LCA)) which suggests the metric of input data well describes the data's neighbor relationship. However, LCA requires the data to be densely sampled and too ideal in the real world, e.g., pictures of two dogs are not necessarily similar in terms of pixel metric (in Fig. 1 (D2)).

Meanwhile, Contrastive Learning (CL) is enthusiastically discussed in the image and NLP fields [3,11,14]. These methods have shown excellent performance by introducing prior knowledge of the data with the help of data augmentation. However, we have encountered significant difficulties applying such techniques to the ML domain. The above methods require a large amount of data for pre-training [37,40], so it is not easy to achieve good results in areas where data is expensive (e.g., biology, medicine, etc.). We consider that the core issues can be summarized as **(D3) Local collapse embedding.** The unsmoothed loss of the CL leads to the model that is prone to local collapse and requires a large diversity of data to learn valid knowledge (in Fig. 2 (D3)).

We want to propose a novel deep ML model to constrain the latent space better and solve the structural distortion problem with the help of CL. At the same time, we hope the proposed method avoids the local collapse phenomenon in the CL. The process of ML perspective includes *structural modeling sub-processes* and *low-dimensional embedding sub-processes*. The structural modeling sub-process obtains the graph structures of data manifolds by measuring the relationship of each sample pair which serves as the guidance for low-dimensional embedding. The low-dimensional embedding process maps the provided graph structures into the embedding space.

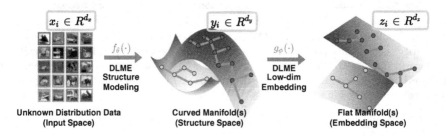

Fig. 2. DLME includes the structure modeling network $f_\theta(\cdot)$ and low-dim embedding network $g_\phi(\cdot)$. The $f_\theta(\cdot)$ maps the input data into structure space to describe the data relationship. The $g_\phi(\cdot)$ maps the curled manifold into the flat embedding space to improve the discriminative performance and friendliness to downstream tasks. $f_\theta(\cdot)$ and $g_\phi(\cdot)$ are compatible with any neural network.

We propose a novel deep ML framework named deep local-flatness manifold embedding (DLME) to solve both problems by merging the advantages of ML and CL. Firstly, a novel local flatness assumption (LFA) is proposed to obtain a reasonable latent space by adding a second-order manifold curvature constraint (for **D1**), thus improving the performance on downstream tasks. Secondly, a new neural network framework is designed to accommodate data augmentation and enhance the net work training (for **D2**). DLME framework accomplishes the two sub-processes with two networks ($f_\theta(\cdot)$ and $g_\phi(\cdot)$) optimized by the proposed DLME loss between the latent space of $f_\theta(\cdot)$ and $g_\phi(\cdot)$ in an end-to-end manner (framework is in Fig. 2). Furthermore, an LFA-based smoother loss function is designed to accommodate data augmentation. It is based on a long-tailed t-distribution and guides the network learning through the two latent spaces (for **D3**). Finally, we further illustrate mathematically: (1) the differences between DLME loss and conventional CL loss and (2) why DLME loss can obtain a locally flat embedding.

In short, DLME makes the following contributions: (1) DLME provides a novel deep ML framework that utilizes neural networks instead of distance metrics in data space to better model structural relationships, thus overcoming structural distortions. (2) DLME put forward the concept of local flatness and theoretically discusses that the DLME loss can enhance the flatness of manifolds and obtain transfer abilities to downstream tasks. (3) The effectiveness of DLME is demonstrated on three downstream tasks with three types of datasets (toy, biological, and image). Experiment results show that DLME outperforms current state-of-the-art ML and CL methods.

2   Related Works

In **manifold learning**, MDS [20], ISOMAP [36], and LLE [32] model the structure of data manifolds based on local or global distances (dissimilarity) and linearly project to the low-dimensional space. SNE [16], t-SNE [27] and UMAP [28] use normal distribution to define local similarities and apply the Gaussian or t-distribution kernel to transform the distance into the pair-wise similarity for *structural modeling*. They perform the manifold embedding by preserving the local geometric structures explored from the input data.

In **deep manifold learning**, Parametric t-SNE (P-TSNE) [26] and Parametric UMAP [33] learn more complex manifolds by non-linear neural networks and can transfer to unseen data. However, they inherit the original *structural modeling* strategies in t-SNE and UMAP. Topological autoencoder (TAE), Geometry Regularized AutoEncoders (GRAE) [7], and ivis [35] abandon the accurate modeling of input data and directly achieve *low-dimensional embedding* using distances or contrast training.

In **self-supervised contrastive learning**, contrastive-based methods [3,11, 14,39] which learns instance-level discriminative representations by contrasting positive and negative views have largely reduced the performance gap between supervised models on various downstream tasks. Deep clustering methods is another popular form of self-supervised pertraining.

3   Methods

3.1   Problem Description and Local Flatness Assumptions

According to Nash embedding theorems [30], we mainly discuss manifolds represented in Euclidean coordinates and provide the definitions of manifold learning (ML) and deep manifold learning (DML) in practical scenarios.

Definition 1 (Manifold Learning, ML). Let $\mathcal{M}$ be a d-dimensional embedding in Euclidean space $\mathbb{R}^d$ and $f : \mathcal{M} \to \mathbb{R}^D$ be a diffeomorphic embedding map, for $D > d$, the purpose of manifold learning is to find $\{z_i\}_{i=1}^N, z_i \in \mathcal{M}$ from the sufficient sampled(observed) data $X = \{x_i\}_{i=1}^N, x_i \in \mathbb{R}^D$.

Based on Definition 1, the DML aims finding the embedding $\{z_i\}_{i=1}^N, z_i \in \mathcal{M}$ by mapping $g_\theta : \mathbb{R}^D \to \mathbb{R}^d$ with the neural network parameters θ. Each ML method designs a loss function based on the specific manifold assumption to map the observed data $\{x_i\}$ back to the intrinsic manifold $\{z_i\}$. For example, LLE [32] assumes that the local manifold is linear, and UMAP [28] assumes that the local manifold is uniform. We propose a novel assumption, considering the nature of the manifold is local flatness.

Assumptions 1 (Local Flatness Assumption, LFA). Let $\mathcal{M}$ be a manifold, and $\{x_i\}$ be a set of observations in the manifold. We expect each data point and its neighbors to lie on or close to a local flatness patch. The mean curvature $\overline{K}_{\mathcal{M}}$ is introduced to quantify the flatness of high-dimensional manifolds according to the Gauss-Bonnet theorem [34],

$$
\begin{aligned}
\overline{K}_{\mathcal{M}} &= \sum_{x_i \in X} k(x_i) \\
k(x_i) &= 2\pi\chi(\mathcal{M}) - \theta(x_{|\mathrm{H}_1(x_i)|}, x_i, x_0) - \sum_{j \in \{0,1,\cdots,|\mathrm{H}_1(x_i)|-1\}} \theta(x_j, x_i, x_{j+1}),
\end{aligned}
\tag{1}
$$

where $\chi(\mathcal{M})$ is Euler Characteristic [13]. The $\mathrm{H}_1(x_i)$ is the hop-1 neighbor of x_i, and $\theta(x_i, x_j, x_k)$ is the angle of three point x_i x_j, x_k.

From First-Order Constraint to Second-Order Curvature Constraint. ML methods (e.g., LLE and UMAP) design distance-preserving or similarity-preserving objective functions, hoping to guarantee the first-order relationship of the data. However, first-order relation preservation is not a tight enough constraint if the local structure of the manifold is simple, thus leading to underconstrained manifold embedding in ML. We introduce a second-order (curvature) constraint to solve the distortion problem. Due to the expensive complexity of second-order losses, we directly minimize the manifold's curvature by a mundane flatness assumption.

The Empirical Benefits of LFA. Similar to most ML and CL methods, LFA is an assumption of latent space, which is beneficial for downstream tasks. In the case of the single-manifold, the assumption of 'Local Flatness' reduces curling in the unsuitable embedding space (see Fig. 6), thus avoiding distortion during embedding. In the case of the multi-manifolds, assuming 'Local Flatness' can simplify the discriminative relations of multi-manifolds. Therefore, the proposed assumption can avoid representation collapse. Meanwhile, it also reduces the possibility of different manifolds overlapping so that the downstream can be accomplished by a simple linear model easily.

3.2   DLME Framework

As shown in Fig. 3, the DLME framework contains two neural networks (f_θ and g_ϕ) and a DLME loss function L_D. The network f_θ achieves *structural modeling* in its structure space $\mathbb{R}^{d_y}$, and the network g_ϕ learns *low-dimensional embedding* in the embedding space $\mathbb{R}^{d_z}$. The DLME loss is calculated based on the A_{ij} and the pairwise similarity in spaces $\mathbb{R}^{d_y}$ and $\mathbb{R}^{d_z}$ used to train two neural networks

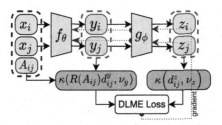

Fig. 3. The framework of DLME. (x_i, x_j) is a pair of input sample, and the neighbor relationship A_{ij} indicates whether x_i and x_j are homologous pairs. The red dashed line marks the direction of the gradient back-propagation. (Color figure online)

from scratch. The A_{ij} indicate the homologous relationships, if x_i and x_j are augmentations of the same original data, then $A_{ij} = 1$ else $A_{ij} = 0$.

Data Augmentation for Solving Structural Distortion. ML methods have difficulty efficiently identifying neighboring nodes, causing structural distortions, when dealing with complex and not well-sampled data. DLME solves this problem with a priori knowledge provided by data augmentation. Data augmentation schemes have been widely used in self-supervised contrastive learning (CL) to solve problems in CV and NLP. From the ML perspective, data augmentation is a technique to make new observations in the intrinsic manifold based on prior knowledge. Since data augmentation changes the semantics of the original data as little as possible, it generates specific neighborhood data for each isolated data when the local connectivity of ML data is broken. DLME trains a neural network $f_\theta(\cdot)$. The $f_\theta(\cdot)$ is guided by data augmentation and loss functions to map the data into a latent space that better guarantees local connectivity.

Data augmentation is designed based on domain knowledge. For example, in CV datasets, operations such as color jittering [41], random cropping [4], applying Gaussian blur [9], Mixup [21,24,25] are proven useful. In biology and some easy datasets, linear combinations $\tau_{lc}(\cdot)$ in k-nearest neighbor data is a simple and effective way. The linear combinations is

$$\tau_{lc}(x) = rx + (1 - r)x^n, x^n \sim \text{KNN}(x), \tag{2}$$

where x^n is sampled from the neighborhood set of data x, and $r \in [0, 1]$ is a combination parameter. For special domain data, the prior knowledge in the domain can be used to establish data augmentation.

The forward propagation of DLME is,

$$
\begin{aligned}
y_i &= f_\theta(x_i), y_i \in \mathbb{R}^{d_y}, x_i \sim \tau(x), x_j \sim \tau(x), \\
z_i &= g_\phi(y_i), z_i \in \mathbb{R}^{d_z}, d_z < d_y,
\end{aligned}
\tag{3}
$$

where x_i and x_j sampled form different random augmentation of raw data x, the d_y and d_z are the dimension number of $\mathbb{R}^{d_y}$ and $\mathbb{R}^{d_z}$.

The loss function of DLME is,

$$L_{\mathrm{D}} = E_{x_i, x_j}\left[\mathcal{D}\left(\kappa\left(R(A_{ij})d_{ij}^y, \nu_y\right), \kappa\left(d_{ij}^z, \nu_z\right)\right)\right], \tag{4}$$

where $d_{ij}^y = d(y_i, y_j)$, $d_{ij}^z = d(z_i, z_j)$ and d_{ij}^y, d_{ij}^z are the distance metrics of data node i and j in spaces $\mathbb{R}^{d_v}$ and $\mathbb{R}^{d_z}$. The two-way divergence [22] $\mathcal{D}(p, q)$ is introduced to measure the dis-similarity between two latent spaces,

$$\mathcal{D}(p, q) = p \log q + (1 - p) \log(1 - q), \tag{5}$$

where $p \in [0, 1]$. Notice that $\mathcal{D}(p, q)$ is a continuous version of the cross-entropy loss. The two-way divergence is used to guide the pairwise similarity of two latent spaces to fit each other. The effect of the loss function on the two networks will be discussed in Sect. 3.3 and Sect. 3.4.

The structure space requires a larger dimensionality to accurately measure data relationships, while the embedding space requires sufficient compression of the output dimension. Thus the t-distribution kernel function is used to calculate the pairwise similarity. The different degrees of freedom ν_y and ν_z in different spaces are essential to enhance the flatness of embedding space (in Sect. 3.4).

$$\kappa(d, \nu) = \frac{\mathrm{Gam}\left(\frac{\nu+1}{2}\right)}{\sqrt{\nu\pi}\,\mathrm{Gam}\left(\frac{\nu}{2}\right)} \left(1 + \frac{d^2}{\nu}\right)^{-\frac{\nu+1}{2}}, \tag{6}$$

where $\mathrm{Gam}(\cdot)$ is the Gamma function, and the degrees of freedom ν controls the shape of the kernel function.

DLME design $R(A_{ij})$ to integrate the neighborhood information in A_{ij}.

$$R(A_{ij}) = 1 + (\alpha - 1)A_{ij} = \begin{cases} \alpha & \text{if } A_{ij} = 1 \\ 1 & \text{otherwise} \end{cases}, \tag{7}$$

where $\alpha \in [0, 1]$ is a hyperparameters. If x_i is the neighbor of x_j, the distance in *structure space* will be reduced by α, and the similarity of x_i and x_j will increase.

3.3   Against Local Collapse by a Smoother CL Framework

The CL loss in self-supervised contrastive learning (CL) frameworks is

$$L_C = -\mathbb{E}_{x_i, x_j}\left[A_{ij} \log \kappa(d_{ij}^z) + (1 - A_{ij}) \log(1 - \kappa(d_{ij}^z))\right], \tag{8}$$

where similarity kernel function $\kappa(d_{ij}^z)$ is defined in Eq. (6). The CL is not smooth and can be analogous to bang-bang control [8] in control systems. Because the learning target of the point pair will switch between $\log \kappa(d_{ij}^z)$ and $\log(1 - \kappa(d_{ij}^z))$ with the change of A_{ij}.

The proposed framework is a smoother CL framework because DLME compromises the learning process and avoids sharp conflicts in gradients. To compare the difference between the DLME loss and the CL loss, we assume that $g_\phi(\cdot)$ satisfies K-Lipschitz continuity [10], then

$$d_{ij}^z = k^* d_{ij}^y, k^* \in [1/K, K], \tag{9}$$

where k^* is a Lipschitz constant. The difference of CL loss and DLME loss is

$$|L_{\mathrm{D}} - L_{\mathrm{c}}| = \mathbb{E}_{x_j, x_j} \left[A_{ij} - \kappa \left((1 + (\alpha - 1)A_{ij})k^* d_{ij}^z \right) \log\left(\frac{1}{\kappa(d_{ij}^z)} - 1\right) \right],$$ (10)

The detailed derivation is provided in Appendix B. If i and j are neighbors, $A_{ij} = 1$, when $\alpha \to 0$, then $\alpha k^* d_{ij}^z \to 0$ and then $1 - \kappa(\alpha k^* d_{ij}^z) \to 0$, finally we have the $|L_{\mathrm{D}} - L_{\mathrm{c}}| \to 0$. When $\alpha \to 0$, the two losses have the same effect on the samples within each neighbor system. When $\alpha > 0$, the optimal solution of L_{D} retain a remainder about the embedding structure d_{ij}^z (in Appendix) which indicates that the DLME loss does not maximize the similarity of the neighborhood as the CL loss, but depends on the current embedding structure. Equation (10) indicates that the DLME loss is smoother and can preserve the data structure in the embedding space. When $\alpha > 0$, the DLME loss is a smooth version of the CL loss, which causes a minor collapse of local structures.

Generally, $f_\theta(\cdot)$ explores the structure of the prior manifolds defined by the given data augmentations smoothly, which can model the manifold structure more accurately than previous ML and DML methods.

3.4 Why DLME Leads to Local Flatness

This section discusses why the DLME loss optimizes the local curvature to be flatter. Network $f_\theta(\cdot)$ maps the data in the input space to the structure space for accurate structural modeling, although it is not guaranteed to obtain locally flat manifolds. Curling can cause overlap and deformation of the manifold, which can cause degradation of downstream task performance. To improve the performance in downstream tasks, we need to obtain an embedding space as flat as possible. The simplest linear methods can perform the discriminative tasks (classification, clustering, visualization).

DLME loss can enforce the flatness of the manifold in the embedded space. Similar to t-SNE, we use the kernel function of the long-tailed t-distribution to transform the distance metric into similarity. Further, we apply different 'degrees of freedom' parameters ν in the two latent spaces. The differences in the degree of freedom ν form two different kernel functions $\kappa(d, \nu_y)$ and $\kappa(d, \nu_z)$, and the difference of kernel functions will make the manifold in the embedding space flatter during the training process.

As described by Eq. (1), we use the local curvature description of the discrete surface to represent the flatness of the manifold. Next, we theoretically discuss why DLME's loss can minimize the local curvature. We use the Push-pull property to describe the action of DLME loss on the embedding space.

Lemma 1 (Push-pull property). let $\nu^y > \nu^z$ and let $d^{z+} = \kappa^{-1}(\kappa(d, \nu^y), \nu^z)$ be the solution of minimizing L_{D}. Then exists d_p so that $(d^y - d_p)(d^{z+} - d^y) > 0$.

The proof of Lemma 1 is detailed in Appendix. Lemma 1 describes the push-pull property of the DLME loss between sample pairs in the embedding space. L_D decreases the distance between sample pairs within the threshold d_p (as similar pairs) and increases the distance between sample pairs beyond d_p (as dis-similar pairs), which shows pushing and pulling effects between two kinds of sample pairs. Next, we prove that the DLME loss minimizes the average local curvature of the embedding based on the push-pull property (Fig. 4).

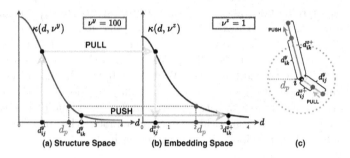

Fig. 4. Push-pull property: if $d^y < d_p$ then $d^{z+} < d^y$ (in yellow), if $d^y > d_p$ then $d^{z+} > d^y$ (in pink). (Color figure online)

Lemma 2. Assume $f_\theta(\cdot)$ satisfies HOP1-2 order preserving: $\max(\{d_{ij}^y\}_{j\in H_1(x_i)}) < \min(\{d_{ij}^z\}_{j\in H_2(x_i)})$ Then $\overline{K}_{\mathcal{M}}^{z+} < \overline{K}_{\mathcal{M}}^y$ where $\overline{K}_{\mathcal{M}}^y$ is the mean curvature in the structure space, and $\overline{K}_{\mathcal{M}}^{z+}$ is the mean curvature optimization results of L_D in the embedding space.

Lemma 2 indicates that the DLME loss encourages the flatness of the embedding space by decreasing the local average curvature. As Fig. 6, Lemma 2 describes that the optimization result of DLME loss is to flatten the manifold of the embedded space, which means that we can represent the data in a latent space as linear as possible. **DLME's pseudo-code** is shown in Algorithm 1.

4   Experiments

In this section, we evaluate the effectiveness of the proposed DLME on four downstream tasks (classification/linear test, clustering, visualization) and analyze each proposed component with the following questions.
(**Q1**) How to intuitively understand structural distortions? (**Q2**) Does DLME overcome structural distortions? (**Q3**) How to intuitively understand underconstrained manifold embedding? (**Q4**) Does DLME overcome underconstrained

---

Algorithm 1. The DLME algorithm

Input: Data: $\mathcal{X} = \{x_i\}_{i=1}^{|\mathcal{X}|}$, Learning rate: η, Epochs: E, Batch size: B, α, ν^y, ν^z, Network: f_θ, g_ϕ, **Output**: Graph Embedding: $\{e_i\}_{i=1}^{|\mathcal{X}|}$.

1: **while** $i = 0$; $i < E$; $i{+}{+}$ **do**
2:     $X^+ \leftarrow X \cup \tau(X)$. # Data augmentation
3:     **while** $b = 0$; $b < [|\mathcal{X}|/B]$; $b{+}{+}$ **do**
4:         $\{x_{a,1}, x_{a,2} \sim X^+\}_{a \in \mathcal{B}}$, $\mathcal{B} = \{1, \cdots, B\}$; # Sampling
5:         $\{y_{a,0}, y_{a,1} \leftarrow f_\theta(x_{a,0}), f_\theta(x_{a,1})\}_{a \in \mathcal{B}}$; # Map to $\mathbb{R}^{d_y}$
6:         $\{z_{a,0}, z_{a,1} \leftarrow g_\phi(y_{a,0}), g_\phi(y_{a,1})\}_{a \in \mathcal{B}}$; # Map to $\mathbb{R}^{d_z}$
7:         $\{d_{a,ij}^y \leftarrow d(y_{a,0}, y_{a,1})\}_{a \in \mathcal{B}}$; $\{d_{a,ij}^z \leftarrow d(z_{a,0}, z_{a,1})\}_{a \in \mathcal{B}}$; #Cal. dist in $\mathbb{R}^{d_y}$ & $\mathbb{R}^{d_z}$
8:         $\{S_a^y \leftarrow \kappa(R(B_{a,ij})d_{a,ij}^y, \nu_y)\}_{a \in \mathcal{B}}$; $\{S_a^z \leftarrow \kappa(d_{a,ij}^z, \nu_z)\}_{a \in \mathcal{B}}$; #Cal. sim in $\mathbb{R}^{d_y}$ & $\mathbb{R}^{d_z}$
9:         $\mathcal{L}_{\mathrm{D}} \leftarrow E(\{D(S_a^y, S_a^z)\}_{a \in \mathcal{B}})$ by Eq. (4); # Cal. loss function
10:        $\theta \leftarrow \theta - \eta \frac{\partial \mathcal{L}_{\mathrm{D}}}{\partial \theta}$, $\phi \leftarrow \phi - \eta \frac{\partial \mathcal{L}_{\mathrm{D}}}{\partial \phi}$; # Update parameters
11:    **end while**
12: **end while**
13: $\{z_i \leftarrow f_\theta(g_\phi(x_i))\}_{i \in \{1,2,\cdots,\mathcal{X}\}}$; # Cal. the embedding result

---

manifold embedding and obtain locally flat embeddings? (**Q5**) How much does DLME improve the performance of downstream tasks on ML and CL datasets? (**Q6**) Can smoother losses bring better performance to CL?

4.1 Visualization of Structural Distortions (Q1, Q2)

Experimental Setups. This section illustrates structural distortions on image datasets and experimentally demonstrates that DLME can overcome structural distortions by introducing prior knowledge of data augmentation. In this experiment, all the data are mapped to a 2-D latent space to facilitate the visualization. All compared ML methods (t-SNE, PUMAP, ivis, and PHA) will fail in the CIFAR dataset; we only show the results of UMAP.

Structural Distortions. The ML approach uses distance metrics from observations to model the structure. The complexity of the data (data with dimensionality and not-well sampling) leads to a failure of the distance metric, confusing the semantic nearest neighbors and subsequently destroying local connectivity, ultimately creating structural distortions in the ML process. DLME constructs a smoother CL framework with the help of data augmentation. The proposed framework obtains richer prior knowledge with data augmentation. It maps the data into the latent space for structural modeling with neural networks, which can achieve more accurate modeling and thus overcome structural distortion.

4.2 Visualization of Underconstrained Manifold Embedding (Q3, Q4)

This section illustrates underconstrained manifold embedding with toy datasets and experimentally demonstrates the DLME potential to solve this problem by constraining the local curvature.

Experimental Setups. The experiments include two 3D toy datasets, Twain-SwissRoll and StarFruit. The TwainSwissRoll dataset has two tangled but disjoint SwissRolls. The StarFruit dataset has a locally curved surface. The input data and outputs of compared methods are shown in Fig. 6. The details of the datasets and outputs are shown in Appendix.

Underconstrained Manifold Embedding. Figure 6 shows that the compared ML methods produce bends that should not exist. We attribute these bends to inadequate constraints on the loss function. These bends affect downstream tasks such as classification and clustering. In addition, these bends may cause more significant damage when the data situation is more complex (Fig. 5).

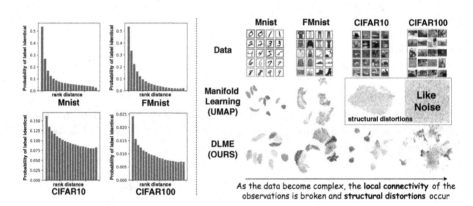

Fig. 5. (left) The Bar plot of probabilities of identical label v.s. rank distance. A higher left end of the bar plot indicates a higher probability of the same label for the nearest neighbor sample, implying that local connectivity is guaranteed. (right) The results of ML methods (UMAP) for four image datasets. For complex data, local connectivity cannot be guaranteed, leading to the embedding failure of the ML method. The proposed DLME method has better embedding results on the more complex CIFAR dataset.

Benefits of Local Flat Embedding. Since a flat localization is assumed, DLME tries to obtain a locally flat embedding. The statistics of the mean curvature show that DLME can receive a flatter local manifold. We consider that a flat embedding possesses practical benefits. A flatter local manifold can achieve better performance in downstream tasks and is more suitable for interpretable analysis of deep models. For example, it is easy to distinguish two sub-manifolds of TwainSwissRoll using a linear classifier, and it is easy to perform regression tasks on StarFruit.

4.3   Comparison on Traditional ML Datasets (Q5, Q6)

Experimental Setups: The compared methods include two ML methods (UMAP [28], t-SNE (tSNE) [15]) and three deep ML methods (PHATE (PHA)

[29], ivis [35] and parametric UMAP (PUM) [33].) The experiments are on six image datasets (Digits, Coil20, Coil100, Mnist, EMnist, and KMnist) and six biological datasets (Colon, Activity (Acti), MCA, Gast, SAMUSIK (SAMU), and HCL). For a fair comparison, all the compared methods map the input data into a 2D space and then evaluated by 10-fold cross-validation. The MLP architecture of f_θ is $[-1, 500, 300, 80]$, where -1 is the dimension of input data. The MLP architecture of g_ϕ is $[80, 500, 80, 2]$. The comparison results of linear SVM and k-means are shown in Table 1. Details of datasets, baseline methods, and evaluation metrics are in Appendix.

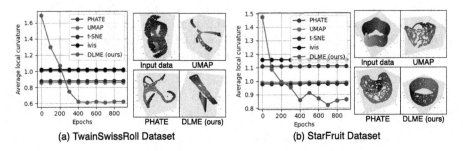

(a) TwainSwissRoll Dataset   (b) StarFruit Dataset

Fig. 6. Average local curvature and scatter plot on TwainSwissRoll and StarFruit dataset. The two examples indicate that traditional ML produces distorted embeddings, which affect the performance of downstream tasks. In contrast, DLME can get as flat embeddings as possible by optimizing the local curvature.

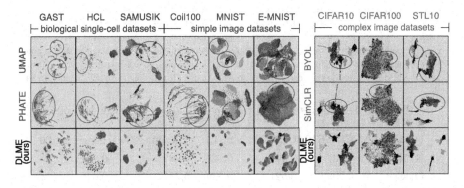

Fig. 7. Visualization results of biological datasets, simple image datasets and complex image datasets. The red circle indicates the clusters confused by the baseline method. (Color figure online)

Analyse: DLME has advantages over all 12 datasets, and DLME is 5% higher than other methods in 14 items (24 items in total). We observe that the proposed DLME has advantages in classification and clustering metrics. We summarize the reasons why DLME has performance advantages as follows. (1) Compared with ML methods, DLME overcomes structural distortions to a certain extent to model the structure more accurately. (2) DLME reduces the overlap of different clusters, improving the performance of classification and clustering. (3) The locally flat embeddings learned by DLME are linearly characterized and more suitable for the linear model.

4.4   Comparison on CL Datasets (Q5, Q6)

Experimental Setups: Due to structural distortions, ML methods fail in CV Datasets, and our comparison is limited to the CL and deep clustering (DC) domain. The compared methods include CL methods (NPID [39], ODC [41], Sim-CLR [3], MOCO.v2 [14] and BYOL [11]) and deep clustering methods (DAC [12], DDC [2], DCCM [38], PICA [17], CC [23], and CRLC [5]). The datasets include six image datasets: CIFAR10, CIFAR100, STL10, TinyImageNet, ImageNet-Dog

Table 1. Performance comparison on 12 datasets. **Bold** denotes the best result and **Underline** denotes 5% higher than others.

	Classification accuracy (linear SVM)						Clustering accuracy (K-means)					
	tSNE	UMAP	PUM	ivis	PHA	DLME	tSNE	UMAP	PUM	ivis	PHA	DLME
Digits	0.949	0.960	0.837	0.767	0.928	**0.973**	0.938	0.875	0.763	0.726	0.794	**0.956**
Coil20	0.799	0.834	0.774	0.672	0.828	<u>**0.909**</u>	0.763	0.821	0.722	0.612	0.655	<u>**0.899**</u>
Coil100	0.760	0.756	N/A	0.542	0.653	<u>**0.952**</u>	0.763	0.785	N/A	0.492	0.515	<u>**0.944**</u>
Mnist	0.963	0.966	0.941	0.671	0.796	**0.976**	0.904	0.801	0.772	0.466	0.614	<u>**0.977**</u>
EMnist	0.420	0.588	0.384	0.190	0.416	<u>**0.657**</u>	0.478	0.537	0.363	0.178	0.352	<u>**0.641**</u>
KMnist	0.738	0.656	0.674	0.547	0.607	<u>**0.782**</u>	0.586	0.668	0.706	0.522	0.594	**0.712**
Colon	0.932	0.893	0.918	0.942	0.930	**0.947**	0.862	0.847	0.861	0.922	0.855	**0.924**
Acti	0.861	0.844	0.849	0.831	0.798	<u>**0.921**</u>	0.784	0.639	0.783	0.681	0.679	<u>**0.898**</u>
MCA	0.719	0.675	0.667	0.634	0.552	<u>**0.774**</u>	0.475	0.532	0.464	0.443	0.414	**0.563**
Gast	0.821	0.846	0.706	0.687	0.676	<u>**0.918**</u>	0.534	0.546	0.512	0.427	0.523	<u>**0.598**</u>
SAMU	0.556	0.678	0.599	0.625	0.675	**0.700**	0.335	0.387	0.345	0.328	0.511	<u>**0.572**</u>
HCL	**0.874**	0.863	0.767	0.454	0.393	**0.874**	0.689	0.743	0.619	0.308	0.263	**0.753**

Table 2. The linear-test Performance comparison on image datasets.

Dataset	CIFAR10	CIFAR100	STL10	TinyImageNet	ImageNet100
NPID	0.827	0.571	0.825	0.382	0.721
ODC	0.799	0.521	0.734	0.287	0.645
SimCLR	0.882	0.574	0.869	0.384	0.756
MoCo.v2	0.886	0.614	0.856	0.374	0.780
BYOL	0.881	0.644	0.887	0.388	0.785
DLME	<u>0.913</u>	0.661	0.901	<u>0.449</u>	0.793
DLME-A1	0.910	0.653	0.881	0.428	0.785
DLME-A2	0.902	0.626	0.879	0.432	0.791
DLME-A3	0.888	0.624	0.873	0.401	0.783

Table 3. The clustering Performance comparison on image datasets.

Dataset	CIFAR10	CIFAR100	STL10	TinyImageNet	ImageNet-Dog
DAC	0.522	0.238	0.470	0.066	0.219
DCCM	0.623	0.327	0.482	0.108	0.321
PICA	0.696	0.337	0.713	0.098	0.352
CC	0.747	0.429	0.850	0.140	0.445
CRLC	0.799	0.425	0.818	0.153	0.461
DLME	**0.822**	**0.441**	**0.883**	**0.182**	**0.483**
DLME-A1	0.792	0.417	0.872	0.145	0.479
DLME-A2	0.783	0.421	0.859	0.133	0.480
DLME-A3	0.779	0.417	0.852	0.134	0.477

and ImageNet100. The f_θ is ResNet50, and g_ϕ is MLP with architecture of [2048, 256]. We use the same settings as SimCLR for the linear test and use the same settings as CC [23] for deep clustering. The results are shown in Table 2 and Table 3 and the detailed setup is in Appendix.

Analyse: In all datasets, DLME outperformed the SOTA method by a large margin. And it beat the other techniques by 2% in 6 items (out of 10 items). The reason is the smoother DLME framework avoids problems such as falling into local collapse. Another reason is locally flat embeddings learned by DLME are linearly characterized and more suitable for a linear model.

Ablation Study. We designed ablation experiments to demonstrate the effectiveness of DLME. **Ablation 1 (DLME-A1)**, we detach the L_D's gradient on the model $f_\theta(\cdot)$ and replace it with the CL loss (in Eq. (8)). The model is divided into two separate parts. One obtains embedding with CL, and the other emphasizes the flatness of manifold with similarity loss. **Ablation 2 (DLME-A2)**, based on DLME-A1, We ablate the t-distribution kernel and use a standard distribution kernel in both spaces. **Ablation 3 (DLME-A3)**, finally, we further ablate the structure of the two networks and transform the model into a CL method. The results of ablation experiments are in Table 2 and Table 3. The experimental results show that the three critical operations of DLME can improve the performance in complex manifold embedding tasks.

4.5 Visualization of ML and CV Datasets (Q5, Q6)

DLME is an appropriate method for visualizing high-dimensional data. A typical setup for data visualization using DLME is to embed the data directly into 2D space. As the selected visualization results are shown in Fig. 7, DLME significantly outperforms other methods in terms of visualization results. Because the distortion problem is overcome, the DLME embedding results in a minimum mixture of different clusters with clear boundaries. The detailed results are shown in Appendix.

5   Conclusion

We propose Deep Local-flatness Manifold Embedding (DLME), a novel ML framework to obtain reliable manifold embedding by reducing distortion. In the experiments, by demonstrating the effectiveness of DLME on downstream classification, clustering, and visualization tasks with three types of datasets (toy, biological, and image), our experimental results show that DLME outperforms SOTA ML & CL methods.

Acknowledgement. This work is supported by National Natural Science Foundation of China, named Geometric Deep Learning and Applications in Proteomics-Based Cancer Diagnosis (No. U21A20427). This work is supported by Alibaba Innovative Research (AIR) Programme.

References

1. Agrawal, R., Gehrke, J., Gunopulos, D., Raghavan, P.: Automatic subspace clustering of high dimensional data for data mining applications. In: Proceedings of the 1998 ACM SIGMOD International Conference on Management of Data, pp. 94–105 (1998)
2. Chang, J., Guo, Y., Wang, L., Meng, G., Xiang, S., Pan, C.: Deep discriminative clustering analysis. arXiv:1905.01681 [cs, stat] (2019)
3. Chen, T., Kornblith, S., Norouzi, M., Hinton, G.: A simple framework for contrastive learning of visual representations. arXiv:2002.05709 [cs, stat] (2020)
4. Cheng, B., Wu, W., Tao, D., Mei, S., Mao, T., Cheng, J.: Random cropping ensemble neural network for image classification in a robotic arm grasping system. IEEE Trans. Instrum. Meas. **69**(9), 6795–6806 (2020)
5. Do, K., Tran, T., Venkatesh, S.: Clustering by maximizing mutual information across views (2021)
6. Donoho, D.L., et al.: High-dimensional data analysis: the curses and blessings of dimensionality. AMS Math Challenges Lecture **1**(2000), 32 (2000)
7. Duque, A.F., Morin, S., Wolf, G., Moon, K.: Extendable and invertible manifold learning with geometry regularized autoencoders. In: 2020 IEEE International Conference on Big Data (Big Data) (2020). https://doi.org/10.1109/bigdata50022.2020.9378049
8. Flugge-Lotz, I.: Discontinuous Automatic Control. Princeton University Press (2015)
9. Flusser, J., Farokhi, S., Höschl, C., Suk, T., Zitova, B., Pedone, M.: Recognition of images degraded by Gaussian blur. IEEE Trans. Image Process. **25**(2), 790–806 (2015)
10. Gouk, H., Frank, E., Pfahringer, B., Cree, M.: Regularisation of neural networks by enforcing lipschitz continuity. arXiv:1804.04368 [cs, stat] (2018)
11. Grill, J.B., et al.: Bootstrap your own latent: a new approach to self-supervised learning. arXiv:2006.07733 [cs, stat] (2020)
12. Haeusser, P., Plapp, J., Golkov, V., Aljalbout, E., Cremers, D.: Associative deep clustering: training a classification network with no labels. In: Brox, T., Bruhn, A., Fritz, M. (eds.) GCPR 2018. LNCS, vol. 11269, pp. 18–32. Springer, Cham (2019). https://doi.org/10.1007/978-3-030-12939-2_2

13. Harer, J., Zagier, D.: The Euler characteristic of the moduli space of curves. Invent. Math. **85**(3), 457–485 (1986)
14. He, K., Fan, H., Wu, Y., Xie, S., Girshick, R.: Momentum contrast for unsupervised visual representation learning. arXiv:1911.05722 [cs] (2020)
15. Hinton, G.E., Salakhutdinov, R.R.: Reducing the dimensionality of data with neural networks. Science **313**(5786), 504–507 (2006). https://doi.org/10.1126/science.1127647
16. Hinton, G.E., Roweis, S.T.: Stochastic neighbor embedding. In: Advances in Neural Information Processing Systems, pp. 857–864 (2003)
17. Huang, J., Gong, S., Zhu, X.: Deep semantic clustering by partition confidence maximisation, pp. 8849–8858 (2020)
18. Kobak, D., Linderman, G.C.: UMAP does not preserve global structure any better than t-SNE when using the same initialization. BioRxiv (2019)
19. Kobak, D., Linderman, G.C.: Initialization is critical for preserving global data structure in both t-SNE and UMAP. Nat. Biotechnol. **39**(2), 156–157 (2021)
20. Kruskal, J.B.: Nonmetric multidimensional scaling: a numerical method. Psychometrika **29**(2), 115–129 (1964)
21. Li, S., Liu, Z., Wu, D., Liu, Z., Li, S.Z.: Boosting discriminative visual representation learning with scenario-agnostic mixup. arXiv preprint arXiv:2111.15454 (2021)
22. Li, S.Z., Zang, Z., Wu, L.: Deep manifold transformation for dimension reduction. arXiv preprint arXiv:2010.14831 (2020)
23. Li, Y., Hu, P., Liu, Z., Peng, D., Zhou, J.T., Peng, X.: Contrastive clustering. AAAI2021 (2021). https://arxiv.org/abs/2009.09687
24. Liu, Z., Li, S., Di Wu, Z.C., Wu, L., Guo, J., Li, S.Z.: AutoMix: unveiling the power of mixup (2021)
25. Liu, Z., Li, S., Wang, G., Tan, C., Wu, L., Li, S.Z.: Decoupled mixup for data-efficient learning. arXiv preprint arXiv:2203.10761 (2022)
26. van der Maaten, L.: Learning a parametric embedding by preserving local structure. In: Artificial Intelligence and Statistics, pp. 384–391. PMLR (2009). https://proceedings.mlr.press/v5/maaten09a.html. ISSN 1938-7228
27. van der Maaten, L., Hinton, G.: Visualizing data using t-SNE. J. Mach. Learn. Res. **9**(Nov), 2579–2605 (2008)
28. McInnes, L., Healy, J., Melville, J.: UMAP: uniform manifold approximation and projection for dimension reduction. arXiv:1802.03426 [cs, stat] (2018). Version: 1
29. Moon, K.R., van Dijk, D.: Visualizing structure and transitions in high dimensional biological data. Nat. Biotechnol. **37**(12), 1482–1492 (2019)
30. Nash, J.: The imbedding problem for Riemannian manifolds. Ann. Math. 20–63 (1956)
31. Pers, T.H., Albrechtsen, A., Holst, C., Sørensen, T.I., Gerds, T.A.: The validation and assessment of machine learning: a game of prediction from high-dimensional data. PLoS One **4**(8), e6287 (2009)
32. Roweis, S.T., Saul, L.K.: Nonlinear dimensionality reduction by locally linear embedding. Science **290**(5500), 2323–2326 (2000)
33. Sainburg, T., McInnes, L., Gentner, T.Q.: Parametric UMAP embeddings for representation and semi-supervised learning. arXiv:2009.12981 [cs, q-bio, stat] (2021)
34. Satake, I.: The Gauss-Bonnet theorem for V-manifolds. J. Math. Soc. Jpn. **9**(4), 464–492 (1957)
35. Szubert, B., Cole, J.E., Monaco, C., Drozdov, I.: Structure-preserving visualisation of high dimensional single-cell datasets. Sci. Rep. **9**(1), 8914 (2019)

36. Tenenbaum, J.B.: A global geometric framework for nonlinear dimensionality reduction. Science **290**(5500), 2319–2323 (2000). https://doi.org/10.1126/science.290.5500.2319. https://www.sciencemag.org/lookup/doi/10.1126/science.290.5500.2319

37. Weng, L.: Contrastive representation learning. lilianweng.github.io (2021). https://lilianweng.github.io/posts/2021-05-31-contrastive/

38. Wu, J., et al.: Deep comprehensive correlation mining for image clustering, pp. 8150–8159 (2019)

39. Wu, Z., Xiong, Y., Yu, S., Lin, D.: Unsupervised feature learning via non-parametric instance-level discrimination. arXiv:1805.01978 [cs] (2018)

40. Zbontar, J., Jing, L., Misra, I., LeCun, Y., Deny, S.: Barlow twins: self-supervised learning via redundancy reduction. In: International Conference on Machine Learning, pp. 12310–12320. PMLR (2021)

41. Zhan, X., Xie, J., Liu, Z., Ong, Y.S., Loy, C.C.: Online deep clustering for unsupervised representation learning. In: Proceedings of the IEEE/CVF Conference on Computer Vision and Pattern Recognition, pp. 6688–6697 (2020)

Semi-supervised Keypoint Detector and Descriptor for Retinal Image Matching

Jiazhen Liu[1,2] , Xirong Li[1,2(✉)] , Qijie Wei[2,3], Jie Xu[4], and Dayong Ding[3]

[1] MoE Key Lab of DEKE, Renmin University of China, Beijing, China
xirong@ruc.edu.cn
[2] AIMC Lab, School of Information, Renmin University of China, Beijing, China
[3] Vistel AI Lab, Visionary Intelligence Ltd, Beijing, China
[4] Institute of Ophthalmology, Tongren Hospital, Beijing, China

Abstract. For retinal image matching (RIM), we propose *SuperRetina*, the first end-to-end method with jointly trainable keypoint detector and descriptor. SuperRetina is trained in a novel semi-supervised manner. A small set of (nearly 100) images are incompletely labeled and used to supervise the network to detect keypoints on the vascular tree. To attack the incompleteness of manual labeling, we propose Progressive Keypoint Expansion to enrich the keypoint labels at each training epoch. By utilizing a keypoint-based improved triplet loss as its description loss, Super-Retina produces highly discriminative descriptors at full input image size. Extensive experiments on multiple real-world datasets justify the viability of SuperRetina. Even with manual labeling replaced by auto labeling and thus making the training process fully manual-annotation free, SuperRetina compares favorably against a number of strong baselines for two RIM tasks, *i.e.* image registration and identity verification.

Keywords: Retinal image matching · Trainable detector and descriptor · Progressive keypoint expansion

1 Introduction

This paper is targeted at retinal image matching (RIM), which is to match color fundus photographs based on their visual content. Matching criteria are task-dependent. As the retinal vasculature is known to be unique, stable across ages and naturally anti-counterfeiting [28], retinal images are used for high-security *identity verification* [19]. In this context, two retinal images are considered matched if they were taken from the same eye. RIM is also crucial for *retinal image registration*, which is to geometrically align two or more images

---

Supplementary Information The online version contains supplementary material available at https://doi.org/10.1007/978-3-031-19803-8_35.

S. Avidan et al. (Eds.): ECCV 2022, LNCS 13681, pp. 593–609, 2022.
https://doi.org/10.1007/978-3-031-19803-8_35

taken from different regions of the same retina (at different periods). Aligned images can be used for wide-field imaging [4], precise cross-session assessment of retinal condition progress [8], and accurate laser treatment on the retina [31]. RIM is thus a valuable topic in computer vision.

Developing a generic method for RIM is nontrivial. Due to varied factors in fundus photography such as illumination conditions, abnormal retinal changes and natural motions of the fixating eye, retinal images of the same eye may vary significantly in terms of their visual appearance. Common lesions in diabetic retinopathy such as microaneurysm and intraretinal hemorrhage appear as dark dots, while cotton-wool spots look like white blobs [34]. The classical SIFT detector [17], which finds corners and blobs in a scale-invariant manner, tends to respond around the lesions and the boundary between the circular foreground and the dark background, see Fig. 1. SIFT keypoints detected at these areas lack both repeatability and reliability.

Recently, GLAMpoints [31] is proposed as a trainable detector for RIM. GLAMpoints learns to detect keypoints in a self-supervised manner, exploiting known spatial correspondence between a specific image and its geometric transformation produced by a controlled homography[1]. Such full self-supervision has a downside of having many detections on non-vascular areas that are adverse to high-resolution image registration, see Fig. 1. The non-vascular areas are also unreliable for identity verification. As GLAMPoints is a detector, an external descriptor, *e.g.* rootSIFT [3], is needed. To the best of our knowledge, RIM with jointly trainable keypoint detector and descriptor is non-existing.

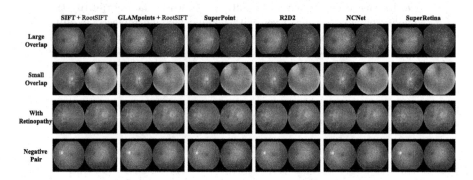

Fig. 1. Retinal image matching by different methods. Keypoints corresponding to geometrically valid/invalid matches are shown in green/red dots. The first three rows are positive pairs, i.e. retinal images taken from the eye. More green dots and fewer red dots on the positive pairs indicate better matching. For the negative pair, fewer green is better. Best viewed on screen (Color figure online)

We depart from SuperPoint [7], a pivotal work on natural image matching with end-to-end keypoint detection and description. SuperPoint is a deep net-

---

[1] As fundus images depict small area of retina, it is justified to apply the planar assumption in generating homographies [4,31].

work with one encoder followed by two independent decoders. Given a $h \times w$ gray-image input, SuperPoint first uses the encoder to generate a down-sized feature map of $\frac{h}{8} \times \frac{w}{8} \times 128$. With the feature map as a common input, one decoder produces a full-sized keypoint detection map, while the other decoder produces 256-dimensional descriptor per pixel on a $\frac{h}{8} \times \frac{w}{8}$ image. Despite its encouraging performance on natural image matching, directly applying SuperPoint for RIM is problematic due to the following issues. First, in order to optimize its descriptor, SuperPoint has to compute hinge losses between all pixels, resulting in a complexity of $O((w \times h)^2)$ for both computation and memory footprint. Such a high complexity significantly limits the input image size, in particular for training, making SuperPoint suboptimal for high-resolution retinal image registration. Second, the description loss is computed without taking the detected keypoints into account, making the learned descriptors less discriminative for disentangling genuine pairs from impostors for identity verification. Lastly, while the loss is computed on the $\frac{h}{8} \times \frac{w}{8} \times 256$ descriptor tensor, the tensor has to be upsampled to $h \times w \times 256$ to provide descriptors for keypoints detected at the original size. Such an inherent discrepancy between descriptors used in the training and the inference stages affects the performance, see our ablation study. More recent advances such as R2D2 [21] and NCNet [23] have similar or other issues, as we will discuss in Sect. 2, motivating us to develop a novel method for RIM.

We propose *SuperRetina*, a semi-**Super**vised deep learning method for joint detection and description of keypoints for **Retina**l image matching. In contrast to [7,21,31] which limit themselves to fully self-supervised (without using any manual annotation), we opt to initialize the training procedure with a relatively small set of (nearly 100) images, sparsely labeled to make the labeling cost well affordable. Such small-scale, incomplete yet precise supervision lets SuperRetina quickly focus on specific vascular points such as crossover and bifurcation that are more stable and repeatable. To overcome the incompleteness of manual labeling, we propose *Progressive Keypoint Expansion* (PKE) to enrich the labeled set at each training epoch. This allows SuperRetina to detect keypoints at previously untouched areas of the vascular tree. Moreover, we modify the network architecture of SuperPoint to directly produce a full-sized descriptor tensor of $h \times w \times 256$, see Fig. 2b. Consequently, our description loss is a keypoint-based improved triplet loss, which not only leads to highly discriminative descriptors but also has a quadratic complexity w.r.t. the number of detected keypoints. As this number is much smaller than $h \times w$, SuperRetina allows a larger input for training. Hence, SuperRetina detects keypoints that are spread over the image plane and at the same time on the vascular tree, making it versatile for multiple RIM tasks. In sum, our contributions are as follows:

• We propose SuperRetina, the first end-to-end method for RIM with jointly trainable keypoint detector and descriptor.
• We propose PKE to address the incompleteness of manual labeling in semi-supervised learning. To enlarge the input size for both training and inference and for highly discriminative descriptors, we re-purpose and adapt a triplet loss

as our keypoint-based description loss.

• Extensive experiments on two RIM tasks, *i.e.* retinal image registration and retina-based identity verification, show the superior performance of SuperRetina against the previous methods including three dedicated to RIM, *i.e.* PBO [19], REMEP [8] and GLAMpoints [31], and four generics, *i.e.* SuperPoint [7], R2D2 [21], SuperGlue [25] and NCNet [23]. Code is available at GitHub[2].

2   Related Work

Progress on Retinal Image Matching. Previous works on RIM are tailored to a specific task, let it be single-modal [8,31] or multi-modal [1,15,33] image registration, or identity verification [2,14,19]. For retinal image registration, LoSPA [1] and DeepSPA as its deep learning variant [15] focus on describing image patches by step pattern analysis (SPA), with keypoints found by detecting intersection points. Designed for feature matching between multi-modal retinal images of the same eye, the SPA descriptor lacks discrimination in revealing eye identity. GLAMpoints [31] is trained in a labeling-free manner by exploiting spatial correspondences between a given image and its geometric transformations. However, such full self-supervision tends to detect many keypoints on non-vascular areas. REMPE [8] first finds many candidate points by vessel bifurcation detection and the SIFT detector [17], and then performs point pattern matching (PPM) based on eye modeling and camera pose estimation to identify geometrically valid matches. The PPM algorithm involves expensive online optimization, requiring over three minutes to complete a registration, and thus putting its practical use into question.

For identity verification, existing works focus on detecting a few landmarks on the vascular tree, mainly crossover and bifurcation points known to be unique and stable across persons and ages [2,14,19]. With the detected landmarks as input, PPM is then performed. PBO [19] improves PPM by considering principal bifurcation orientations. BGM [14] formulates the retinal vasculature as a spatial graph and consequently implements PPM by graph matching. Aleem *et al.*[2] enhance point patterns of a given image based on spatial relationships between the landmarks, and then vectorize the patterns to a matching template. The number of keypoints required for identity verification is much less than that for image registration. Probably due to this reason, we see no attempt to re-purpose an identity verification method for image registration. In short, while there are few separated efforts on trainable detector (GLAMpoints) and descriptor (DeepSPA) for RIM, a joint effort remains missing.

Progress on Natural Image Matching. In contrast to RIM, a number of end-to-end methods exist for natural image matching, including SuperPoint [7], R2D2 [21], SuperGlue [25], NCNet [23], LoFTR [29], COTR [10], PDC-Net [32], *etc.*. As the newly developed methods focus on natural scenes where detecting repeatable keypoints is difficult due to the lack of repetitive texture patterns, we notice a

---

[2] https://github.com/ruc-aimc-lab/SuperRetina.

new trend of keypoint-free image matching. R2D2 softens the notion of keypoint detection by producing two probabilistic maps to measure the reliability and the repeatability per pixel. In NCNet, all pairwise feature matches are computed, resulting in a quadratic complexity w.r.t. the number of pixels. As a consequence, the feature map used for matching has to be substantially downsized to make the computation affordable. LoFTR improves over SuperGlue with transformers to exploit self-/inter- correlations among the dense-positioned local features. These dense features are powerful for finding correspondences in low-texture areas, desirable for scene image matching. However, this will produce many unwanted matches in non-vascular areas when matching retinal images.

3   Proposed Method

SuperRetina is a deep neural network that takes as input a (gray-scale) $h \times w$ retinal image I, detects and describes keypoints in the given image with high repeatability and reliability in a single forward pass. We describe the network architecture in Sect. 3.1, followed by the proposed training algorithms in Sect. 3.2. The use of SuperRetina for RIM is given in Sect. 3.3.

3.1   Network Architecture

We adapt the SuperPoint network. Conceptually, our network consists of an encoder to extract down-sized feature maps F from the given image I. The feature map is then fed in parallel into two decoders, one for keypoint detection and the other for keypoint description, which we term Det-Decoder and Des-Decoder, respectively. The Det-Decoder generates a full-sized probabilistic map P, where $P_{i,j}$ indicates the probability of a specific pixel being a keypoint, $i = 1, \ldots, h$ and $j = 1, \ldots, w$. The Des-Decoder produces a $h \times w \times d$ tensor D, where $D_{i,j}$ denotes a d-dimensional descriptor. Note that in the inference stage, Non-Maximum Suppression (NMS) is applied on P to obtain a binary mask $\widehat{P}$ as the final detection result. We formalize the above process as follows:

$$\begin{cases} F \leftarrow \text{Encoder}(I), \\ P \leftarrow \text{Det-Decoder}(F), \\ D \leftarrow \text{Des-Decoder}(F), \\ \widehat{P} \leftarrow \text{NMS}(P). \end{cases} \tag{1}$$

As illustrated in Fig. 2b, we modify both Det-Decoder and Des-Decoder for RIM.

U-Net as Det-Decoder. Effectively capturing low-level patterns such as crossover and bifurcation on the vascular tree is crucial for detecting retinal keypoints in a reliable and repeatable manner. We therefore opt to use U-Net [24], originally developed for biomedical image segmentation with its novel design of re-using varied levels of features from the encoder in the decoder by skip connections. In order to support high-resolution input, our encoder is relatively shallow, with a conv layer to generate low-level full-sized feature maps, followed by three conv blocks, each consisting of two conv layers, 2×2 max pooling and ReLU. Consequently, the high-level feature maps F have a size of $\frac{h}{8} \times \frac{w}{8} \times 128$. In order to recover full-sized feature maps, our Det-Decoder uses three conv blocks, each having two conv layers, followed by bilinear upsampling[3], ReLU and concatenation to merge the corresponding feature maps from the encoder. Lastly, a conv. block consisting of three conv. layers and one sigmoid activation is applied on the full-sized feature maps to produce the detection map P.

Full-Sized Des-Decoder. Different from SuperPoint which computes its description loss on a down-sized tensor of $\frac{h}{8} \times \frac{w}{8} \times d$, we target optimizing the descriptors on the full size of $h \times w$, where each pixel is associated with a d-dimensional descriptor. Naturally, such dense results are obtained by interpolation, meaning gradient correlation between each keypoint and its neighborhood during backpropagation. Enlarging the neighborhood enhances the correlation, and is thus helpful for training with a larger receptive field [5]. In that regard, our Des-Decoder first downsizes F to more compact feature maps of $\frac{h}{16} \times \frac{w}{16} \times d$, and then uses an upsampling block (using transposed conv) to generate the full-sized descriptor tensor D of $h \times w \times d$. All the descriptors are l_2-normalized.

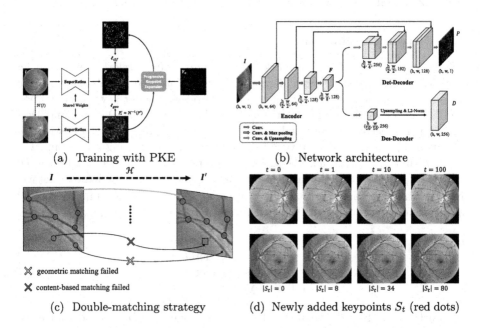

(a) Training with PKE

(b) Network architecture

(c) Double-matching strategy

✗ geometric matching failed
✗ content-based matching failed

(d) Newly added keypoints S_t (red dots)

Fig. 2. Proposed **SuperRetina**. Green/orange markers in (c) indicate genuine/ fake keypoints. Blue/red dots in (d) indicate the initial keypoints (autodetected by PBO [19])/iteratively detected keypoints for training. (Color figure online)

---

[3] We use bilinear upsampling, as transposed convolutions originally used by U-Net are computationally more expensive, and introduce unwanted checkerboard artifact[13].

Our network adaption may seem to be conceptually trivial. Note that producing a full-sized descriptor tensor is computationally prohibitive for a pixel-based description loss as used in SuperPoint and NCNet. A keypoint-based description loss is needed. Nonetheless, keypoint-based training is nontrivial, as inadequate annotations will make the network quickly converge to a local, suboptimal solution. However, having many training images adequately labeled is known to be expensive. To tackle the practical challenge, we develop a semi-supervised training algorithm that works with a small amount of incompletely labeled images.

3.2 Training Algorithm

Semi-supervised Training of Det-Decoder. We formulate keypoint detection as a pixel-level binary classification task [7,31]. Due to the sparseness and incompleteness of manually labeled keypoints, training Det-Decoder using a common binary cross-entropy (CE) loss is difficult. To attack the sparseness (and the resultant class imbalance) issue, we leverage two tactics. The first tactic, borrowed from Pose Estimation [35], is to convert the binary labels Y to soft labels $\tilde{Y}$ by 2D Gaussian blur, where each keypoint is a peak surrounded by neighbors with their values decaying exponentially. The second tactic is to use the Dice loss [18], found to be more effective than the weighted CE loss and the Focal loss to handle extreme class imbalance [34]. The Dice-based classification loss ℓ_{clf} per image is computed as

$$\ell_{clf}(I;Y) = 1 - \frac{2 \cdot \sum_{i,j} (P \circ \tilde{Y})_{i,j}}{\sum_{i,j} (P \circ P)_{i,j} + \sum_{i,j} (\tilde{Y} \circ \tilde{Y})_{i,j}}, \tag{2}$$

where $\circ$ denotes element-wise multiplication.

To attack the incompleteness issue, we propose **Progressive Keypoint Expansion** (PKE). The basic idea is to progressively expand the labeled keypoint set Y by adding novel and reliable keypoints found by Det-Detector, which itself is continuously improving after each epoch. To distinguish from such a dynamic Y, for each training image we now use Y_0 to indicate its initial keypoints, and S_t to denote keypoints detected at the t-th epoch, $t = 1, 2, \ldots$. We obtain the expanded keypoint set Y_t as $Y_0 \cup S_t$, which is used for training at the t-th epoch.

As S_t is auto-constructed, improper keypoints are inevitable, in particular at the early stage when the Det-Decoder is relatively weak. Given that a good detector shall detect the same keypoint under different viewpoints and scales, GLAMpoints performs a geometric matching to identify keypoints that can be repeatedly detected from a given image and its projective transformations. We improve over GLAMpoints by adding a content-based matching, making it a *double*-matching strategy. As Fig. 2c shows, suppose a keypoint detected in a non-vascular area in I (orange circle) has a geometrically matched keypoint (orange square) in $I' = \mathcal{H}(I)$, with $\mathcal{H}$ as a specific homography. Non-vascular areas lack specificity in visual appearance, meaning descriptors extracted from such areas relatively close. Hence, even if the square is the best match to the circle in the descriptor space, it is not sufficiently different from the second-best match to pass Lowe's ratio test [17]. Double matching is thus crucial.

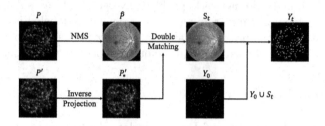

Fig. 3. Key dataflow within the PKE module

As illustrated in Fig. 3, the PKE module works as follows:

1) Construct I', a geometric mapping of I, using $I' = \mathcal{H}(I)$.

2) Feed I' to SuperRetina to obtain its probabilistic detection map P'. The inverse projection of the map w.r.t. I is obtained as $P'_* = \mathcal{H}^{-1}(P')$.

3) Geometric matching: For each point (i, j) in $\widehat{P}$, add it to S_t if $(P'_*)_{i,j} > 0.5$.

4) Content-based matching: For each point (i, j) in S_t, we obtain its descriptor by directly sampling the output of the Des-Decoder, resulting in a descriptor set D_t. Similarly, we extract D'_t from I' based on $\mathcal{H}(S_t)$. Each descriptor in D_t is used as a query to perform the nearest neighbor search on D'_t. A point (i, j) will be preserved in S_t, only if its spatial correspondence (i', j') passes the ratio test.

The above procedure allows us to progressively find new and reliable keypoints, see Fig. 2d. Moreover, in order to improve the holistic consistency between the detection maps of I and its geometric transformation I', we additionally compute the Dice loss between P and P'_*, termed as $\ell_{geo}(I, \mathcal{H})$. Our detection loss ℓ_{det} conditioned on Y_t and $\mathcal{H}$ is computed as

$$\ell_{det}(I; Y_t, \mathcal{H}) = \ell_{clf}(I; Y_t) + \ell_{geo}(I, \mathcal{H}). \tag{3}$$

Self-Supervised Training of Des-Decoder. Ideally, the output of the Des-Decoder shall be invariant to homography. That is, for each keypoint (i, j) detected in I, its descriptor shall be identical to the descriptor extracted at the corresponding location (i', j') in I'. To avoid a trivial solution of yielding a constant descriptor, we choose to optimize a triplet loss [27] such that the distance between paired keypoints shall be smaller than the distance between unpaired keypoints. Recall that keypoints are automatically provided by the Det-Decoder, our Des-Decoder is trained in a fully self-supervised manner. Such a property lets the Des-Decoder learn from unlabeled data with ease.

Feeding I and I' separately into SuperRetina allows us to access their full-sized descriptor tensors D and D'. For each element (i, j) in the non-maximum suppressed keypoint set $\widehat{P}$, let $D_{i,j}$ be its descriptor. As (i, j) and (i', j') shall be paired, the distance of their descriptors, denoted as $\phi_{i,j}$, has to be reduced. With (i', j') excluded, we use $\phi_{i,j}^{rand}$ to indicate the descriptor distance between (i, j) and a point chosen randomly from $\mathcal{H}(\widehat{P})$. Let $\phi_{i,j}^{hard}$ be the minimal distance. We argue that using $\phi_{i,j}^{rand}$ or $\phi_{i,j}^{hard}$ alone as the negative term in the triplet loss is problematic. As the requirement of $\phi_{i,j} < \phi_{i,j}^{rand}$ is relatively easy to fulfill, using $\phi_{i,j}^{rand}$ alone is inadequate to obtain descriptors of good discrimination. Meanwhile, as the network at its early training stage lacks ability to produce good descriptors, using $\phi_{i,j}^{hard}$ exclusively will make the network hard to train. To resolve the issue, we propose a simple trick by using the mean of $\phi_{i,j}^{rand}$ and $\phi_{i,j}^{hard}$ as the negative term. Our description loss ℓ_{des} is thus defined as

$$\ell_{des}(I; \mathcal{H}) = \sum_{(i,j) \in \widehat{P}} \max(0, m + \phi_{i,j} - \frac{1}{2}(\phi_{i,j}^{rand} + \phi_{i,j}^{hard})), \tag{4}$$

where $m > 0$ is a hyper-parameter controlling the margin. Note that ℓ_{des} has a quadratic time complexity w.r.t. the size of $\widehat{P}$, which is much smaller than $h \times w$. Hence, our description loss is much more efficient than its counterpart in SuperPoint, which is quadratic w.r.t. $h \times w$. As such, given the same amount of GPU resources, SuperRetina can be trained on higher-resolution images.

While we describe the training algorithms of Det-Decoder and Des-Decoder separately, they are jointly trained by minimizing the following combined loss:

$$\ell(I; Y_t, \mathcal{H}) = \ell_{det}(I; Y_t, \mathcal{H}) + \ell_{des}(I; \mathcal{H}), \tag{5}$$

where the homography $\mathcal{H}$ varies per mini-batch.

3.3   Keypoint-Based Retinal Image Matching

Once trained, the use of SuperRetina for RIM is simple. Given a query image I_q and a reference image I_r, we feed them separately into SuperRetina to obtain their keypoint probabilistic maps P_q and P_r and associated descriptor tensors D_q and D_r. NMS is performed on P_q and P_r to obtain keypoints as Kp_q and Kp_r. Recall that D_q and D_r are full-sized, so the corresponding descriptors $desc_q$ and $desc_r$ are fetched directly from the two tensors. Initial matches between Kp_q and Kp_r are obtained by an OpenCV brute-force matcher. The homography matrix $\mathcal{H}$ are then computed using the matched pairs to register q w.r.t. r. As for identity verification, $\mathcal{H}$ is reused to remove outliers. The two images are accepted as *genuine*, *i.e.* from the same eye, if the number of matched points exceeds a predetermined threshold, and *impostor* otherwise. The above process can be written in just a few lines of Python-style code, see the supplement.

4   Evaluation

To evaluate SuperRetina in a real scenario, we train it on fixed data. The model is then applied directly (w/o re-training) for different RIM tasks on multiple testsets independent of the training data (Table 1).

4.1   Common Setup

Training data. We built a small labeled set as follows. We invited 10 members (staffs and students) from our lab. With ages ranging from 22 to 42, the subjects are with normal retinal condition. Multiple color fundus images of the posterior pole (FoV of 45°) were taken per eye, using a SYSEYE Reticam 3100 fundus camera. We collected 97 images in total. The number of keypoints manually labeled[4] per image is between 46 and 147 with a mean value of 93.3. We term the labeled dataset *Lab*. In addition, to support training of our Des-Decoder, we collected an auxiliary dataset of 844 retinal images from 120 subjects having varied retinal diseases. Recall that Des-Decoder is trained in a fully self-supervised manner, so the auxiliary dataset requires no extra annotation.

Implementation. We implement SuperRetina using PyTorch. Subject to our GPU resource (an NVIDIA GeForce RTX 2080 Ti), we choose a training input size of 768×768. The network is trained end-to-end by SGD with mini-batch size of 1. The optimizer is Adam [12], with $\beta = (0.9, 0.999)$ and an initial learning rate of 0.001. Standard data augmentation methods are used: gaussian blur, changes of contrast, and illumination. The number of maximum training epochs is 150. The descriptor length d is 256. For inference, the NMS size is 10×10 pixels. For homography fitting, we use `cv2.findHomography` with LMEDS.

Table 1. Our experimental data. Large cross-dataset divergence w.r.t. subjects, retinal conditions, imaging FoV *etc.*. allows us to evaluate the effectiveness and generalization ability of SuperRetina. All test images are resized to 768×768, except for images from VAIRA which use 512×512 due to their smaller FoV

Dataset	Subjects	Eyes	Images	Image pairs		
				Total	Genuine	Impostor
Training sets:						
Lab (labeled)	10	20	97	–	–	–
Auxiliary (unlabeled)	120	215	844	–	–	–
Test set for retinal image registration						
FIRE[9]	–	–	129	134	134	–
Test sets for retina based identity verification						
VARIA [20]	–	139	233	27,028	155	26,873
CLINICAL	100	180	691	16,203	1,473	14,730
BES [11,36]	2,066	4,132	24,880	99,846	49,923	49,923

---

[4] Keypoint labeling requires little medical knowledge. The first author performed the labeling task in 4 working hours, which we believe was affordable.

4.2   Task 1. Retinal Image Registration

Test set. We adopt FIRE [9], a benchmark set consisting of 129 images of size $2,912 \times 2,912$ acquired with a Nidek AFC-210 fundus camera (FOV of 45°) and 134 registered image pairs. The pairs have been divided into three groups according to their registration difficulty: *Easy* (71 pairs with high overlap and no anatomical change), *Moderate* (14 pairs with high overlap and large anatomical changes), and *Hard* (49 pairs with small overlap and no anatomical changes).

Performance Metrics. Following [31], we report three sorts of rates, *i.e.* failed, inaccurate and acceptable. Given a query image I_q and its reference I_r, a registration is considered failed if the number of matches is less than 4, the minimum required to estimate a homography $\mathcal{H}$. Otherwise, for each query point p_q in I_q, we compute the l_2 distance between $\mathcal{H}(p_q)$ and its reference p_r in I_r. Per query image, the median distance is defined as the median error (MEE), with the maximum distance as the maximum error (MAE). A registration is considered acceptable if MEE < 20 and MAE < 50, and inaccurate otherwise. Besides, we report Area Under Curve (AUC) proposed by [9], which estimates the expectation of the acceptance rates w.r.t. the decision threshold, and thus reflects the overall performance of a specific method. Following [9], we compute AUC per category, *i.e.* Easy, Mod and Hard, and take their mean (mAUC) as an overall measure. Higher acceptance rate/AUC and lower inaccurate/failed rates are better. All the metrics are computed on the original size of 2912×2912.

Baselines. For a reproducible comparison, we choose competitor methods that have either source code or pre-trained models released by paper authors. Accordingly, we have eight baselines as follows:

- SIFT detector [17] plus RootSIFT descriptor [3], using OpenCV APIs.
- PBO [19], a traditional keypoint extraction and matching method with author-provided Matlab implementation.
- REMPE [8], performing retinal image registration through eye modelling and pose estimation[5].
- SuperPoint[6] [7] trained on MS-COCO [16].
- GLAMpoints[7] [31] (+ RootSIFT descriptor) trained on private fundus images.
- R2D2[8] [21], trained on the Aachen dataset [26].
- SuperGlue[9] [25], trained on ScanNet [6].
- NCNet[10] [23], pretrained on the Indoor Venues Dataset [22].

Due to the natural domain gap between retinal images and natural images, the baseline models pretrained on natural images might not be in their optimal condition for RIM. We take this into account by finetuning SuperPoint, GLAMpoints, R2D2 and NCNet on our training data.

---

[5] https://projects.ics.forth.gr/cvrl/rempe/.

[6] https://github.com/rpautrat/SuperPoint.

[7] https://github.com/PruneTruong/GLAMpoints_pytorch.

[8] https://github.com/naver/r2d2.

[9] https://github.com/magicleap/SuperGluePretrainedNetwork.

[10] https://github.com/ignacio-rocco/ncnet.

Comparison with the Existing Methods. As shown in Table 2, SuperRetina, with zero failure, an inaccurate rate of 1.49% and an acceptance rate of 98.51% is the best. Interestingly, we find that REMPE, which relies on traditional image processing enhanced by geometric modeling of the retina, performs better than the deep learning based alternatives including GLAMpoints, R2D2, SuperPoint, SuperGlue and NCNet. SuperRetina beats this strong baseline.

Table 2. Performance of the state-of-the-art for two RIM tasks, *i.e.* **retinal image registration and retina based identity verification.** Methods postfixed with *finetune* have been finetuned on our training data. The proposed SuperRetina compares favorably against the existing methods, even with the initial keypoint set Y_0 automatically detected by the PBO method

Methods	Image Registration (FIRE as the test set)							Identity Verification (EER [%])		
	Failed [%]	Inaccurate [%]	Acceptable [%]	AUC-Easy	AUC-Mod	AUC-Hard	mAUC	VARIA	CLINICAL	BES
Traditional:										
SIFT, IJCV04 [17]	0	20.15	79.85	0.903	0.474	0.341	0.573	0.65	3.64	4.67
PBO, ICIP10 [19]	0.75	28.36	70.89	0.844	0.691	0.122	0.552	0.65	4.96	4.33
REMPE, JBHI20[8]	0	2.99	97.01	**0.958**	0.660	**0.542**	0.720	–	–	–
Deep learning based:										
SuperPoint, CVPRW18 [7]	0	5.22	94.78	0.882	0.649	0.490	0.674	0.01	1.06	2.00
SuperPoint-*finetune*	0	6.72	93.28	0.909	0.609	0.465	0.661	0.01	2.89	3.91
GLAMpoints, ICCV19 [31]	0	7.46	92.54	0.850	0.543	0.474	0.622	0.02	4.32	2.95
GLAMpoints-*finetune*	0	7.46	92.54	0.825	0.517	0.490	0.611	0.03	6.74	4.83
R2D2, NIPS19 [21]	0	12.69	87.31	0.900	0.517	0.386	0.601	0.05	6.23	7.16
R2D2-*finetune*	0	4.48	95.52	0.928	0.666	0.540	0.711	0.05	1.83	7.76
SuperGlue, CVPR20 [25]	0.75	3.73	95.52	0.885	0.689	0.488	0.687	0	2.38	2.35
NCNet, TPAMI22 [23]	0	37.31	62.69	0.588	0.386	0.077	0.350	14.19	22.13	30.67
NCNet-*finetune*	0	14.18	85.82	0.817	0.609	0.410	0.612	7.97	3.05	19.87
SuperRetina										
Y_0: Pretraining	0	2.99	97.01	0.922	0.720	0.502	0.715	0	1.04	1.93
Y_0: PBO	0	3.73	96.27	0.944	**0.789**	0.516	0.750	0	1.02	**1.10**
Y_0: Manual labeling	0	**1.49**	**98.51**	0.940	0.783	**0.542**	**0.755**	0	**0.83**	1.18

Similar results are observed in terms of AUC scores. The only exception is on the Easy group, where REMPE obtains a higher AUC (0.958 versus 0.940). Recall that images in this group have large overlap and no anatomic change, so the heavy modeling of the retinal structure in REMPE is advantageous. The benefit of end-to-end learning becomes more evident when dealing with the Moderate and Hard groups. SuperRetina scores a substantially higher AUC-Mod than REMPE (0.783 versus 0.660). Moreover, while REMPE takes 198 s to perform one registration, SuperRetina is far more efficient, requiring 1 s, most of which is spent on data IO and preprocessing. As only the query image has to be computed on the fly, while images in the database can be precomputed, the entire image matching process can be much accelerated. In short, the advantage of SuperRetina over REMPE is three-fold: (i) The end-to-end learned detector is more reliable than REMPE's vessel bifurcation detector for handling images with large anatomical changes, (ii) SuperRetina works for both image registration and identity verification, and (iii) SuperRetina is nearly 200x faster.

Manual Labeling versus Auto-Labeling for Y_0. The last three rows of Table 2 are SuperRetina with distinct choices of the initial keypoint set Y_0. Pre-training means we tried to first train SuperRetina on the synthetic corner dataset as used by SuperPoint, and then use this pre-trained SuperRetina to produce Y_0. The second-last row means using PBO-detected keypoints as Y_0. Their results show that even with the auto-produced Y_0, SuperRetina compares favorably against the current methods. In particular, using PBO-based Y_0 obtains mAUC of 0.750. The number, although lower than using the manual Y_0 (mAUC 0.755), clearly outperforms the best baseline, *i.e.* REMPE (mAUC 0.720). At the cost of merely 0.66% relative loss in performance, SuperRetina can indeed be trained in a manual-annotation free manner.

Evaluating the Influence of PKE. As Table 3 shows, SuperRetina w/o PKE suffers from a clear performance drop. Without PKE, the average number of keypoints detected by SuperRetina is substantially reduced, from 530 to 109 per image. We also tried PKE without content-based matching, making it effectively the keypoint selection strategy used by GLAMpoints. Its lower performance (row#3 in Table 3) verifies the necessity of the proposed double-matching strategy. The above results justify the effectiveness of PKE for expanding the annotation data for semi-supervised learning.

For the description loss, we simultaneously leverage the hard negative instance and a random negative for computing the negative term in Eq. (4). We tried an alternative strategy of semi-hard negative sampling, where the negative ranked at the middle among all candidate negatives in a given mini-batch is chosen for computing the negative term. This alternative strategy (row#4 in Table 3) is ineffective.

In addition, we re-run the same training pipeline, but *w/o* descriptor upsampling, *w/o* 2D Gaussain blur and using the (weighted) CE loss instead of Dice, respectively. Their consistent lower performance supports the necessity of the proposed changes regarding the network and its training strategy.

4.3   Task 2. Retina-Based Identity Verification

Test Sets. We use three test sets: VARIA [20], Beijing Eye Study (BES) [11,36], and a private set. VARIA has 233 gray-scale retinal images from 139 eyes, acquired with a Topcon NW-100 camera. The images are optic disc centered, with a small FoV of around 20°. BES, acquired for a population-based study conducted in Beijing between 2001 and 2011, has 24,880 color fundus photos taken from 4,132 eyes at different periods. As images taken at earlier periods were digital scans of printed photos, the image quality of BES varies. Our private set, termed CLINICAL, consists of 691 images from 100 patients, acquired with a Topcon Trc-Nw6 fundus camera at an outpatient clinic of ophthalmology with due ethics approval. CLINICAL exhibits more diverse abnormal conditions such as old macula lesion, retinitis pigmentosa and macular edema. The joint use of the testsets leads to a systematic evaluation covering retinas in normal (VARIA)/abnormal (CLINICAL) conditions and across ages (BES).

Table 3. Ablation study. Larger mAUC on FIRE and lower EER on VARIA, CLINICAL and BES are better

Setup	FIRE($\uparrow$)	VARIA($\downarrow$)	CLINICAL($\downarrow$)	BES($\downarrow$)
Full-setup	0.755	0	0.83	1.18
w/o PKE	0.685	0.01	5.14	3.11
PKE *w/o* content-based mathcing	0.670	0	1.48	1.19
Semi-hard negative sampling	0.407	2.75	10.18	7.83
w/o upsampling	0.697	0.03	3.46	4.15
w/o Gaussian blur	0.574	8.38	7.44	10.82
Dice $\rightarrow$ CE	0.653	0.65	4.20	2.48
Dice $\rightarrow$ weighted CE	0.704	0.02	1.79	1.32
Compare with other detectors:				
Det: SIFT, Des: SuperRetina	0.585	0	4.40	4.23
Det: GLAMpoints, Des: SuperRetina	0.605	0	2.84	1.51
Det: SuperPoint, Des: SuperRetina	0.673	0	1.60	1.68
Compare with other descriptors:				
Det: SuperRetina, Des: RootSIFT	0.705	0	2.81	2.10
Det: SuperRetina, Des: SOSNet	0.712	0	0.88	1.78

Performance Metric. We report Equal Error Rate (EER). As a common metric for evaluating a biometric system, EER is the value when the system's False Accept Rate and False Reject Rate are equal. Lower is better.

Baselines. We re-use the baselines from Sect. 4.2 except for REMPE [8], which is inapplicable for identity verification.

Comparison with State-of-the-Art. As Table 2 shows, SuperRetina, with EER of 0% on VARIA, 0.83% on CLINICAL and 1.18% on BES, compares favorably against the baselines. All the deep learning based methods perform well on VARIA, which has a small FoV with clearly visible vessels. However, their performance decreases noticeably on CLINICAL and BES, especially for GLAMpoints and R2D2, both using self-supervised training. As shown in Fig. 1, GLAMpoints and R2D2 tend to detect keypoints on non-vascular areas. By contrast, SuperRetina keypoints are mostly distributed along the vascular tree, thus more suited for identity verification.

Ablation Study. Table 3 shows that PKE also matters for identity verification. As for the choice of Y_0, using the PBO-produced labels achieves comparable results for two out of the three test sets, *i.e.* VARIA and BES. Note that its higher EER of 1.02% on CLINICAL remains better than the best baseline, *i.e.* SuperPoint with EER of 1.06%. We compare the SuperRetina detector with three existing detectors, *i.e.* SIFT, SuperPoint and GLAMpoints, all using the SuperRetina descriptor. We also compare the SuperRetina descriptor with two existing descriptors, *i.e.* RootSIFT previously used by GLAMPoints for RIM and SOSNet, a widely used deep descriptor [30]. Table 3 shows that our detector and descriptor remain competitive even used separately.

5   Conclusions

Real-world experiments allow us to conclude as follows. The proposed PKE strategy is effective for resolving the incompleteness of manual labeling for semi-supervised training, improving mAUC from 0.685 to 0.755 for retinal image registration on the FIRE dataset and reducing EER from 5.14% to 0.83% for retina-based identity verification on the most challenging CLINICAL dataset. Super-Retina beats the best baselines, *i.e.* REMPE for image registration (mAUC: 0.755 versus 0.720), and SuperPoint for identity verification (EER: 0.83% versus 1.06% on CLINICAL, 1.18% versus 2.00% on BES). Even with the manually labeled training data fully replaced by auto-labeling, and thus making the training process fully manual annotation free, SuperRetina preserves mostly its performance and compares favorably against the previous methods for RIM.

Acknowledgments. This work was supported by NSFC (No. 62172420, No. 62072463), BJNSF (No. 4202033), and Public Computing Cloud, Renmin University of China.

References

1. Addison Lee, J., et al.: A low-dimensional step pattern analysis algorithm with application to multimodal retinal image registration. In: CVPR (2015)
2. Aleem, S., Sheng, B., Li, P., Yang, P., Feng, D.D.: Fast and accurate retinal identification system: using retinal blood vasculature landmarks. IEEE Trans. Industr. Inf. **15**(7), 4099–4110 (2018)
3. Arandjelović, R., Zisserman, A.: Three things everyone should know to improve object retrieval. In: CVPR (2012)
4. Cattin, P.C., Bay, H., van Gool, L., Székely, G.: Retina mosaicing using local features. In: MICCAI (2006)
5. Chen, L.C., Papandreou, G., Kokkinos, I., Murphy, K., Yuille, A.L.: Deeplab: semantic image segmentation with deep convolutional nets, atrous convolution, and fully connected crfs. IEEE Trans. Pattern Anal. Mach. Intell. **40**(4), 834–848 (2017)
6. Dai, A., Chang, A.X., Savva, M., Halber, M., Funkhouser, T., Nießner, M.: Scan-Net: richly-annotated 3D reconstructions of indoor scenes. In: CVPR (2017)
7. DeTone, D., Malisiewicz, T., Rabinovich, A.: SuperPoint: self-supervised interest point detection and description. In: CVPR Workshops (2018)
8. Hernandez-Matas, C., Zabulis, X., Argyros, A.A.: REMPE: registration of retinal images through eye modelling and pose estimation. IEEE J. Biomed. Health Inform. **24**(12), 3362–3373 (2020)

9. Hernandez-Matas, C., Zabulis, X., Triantafyllou, A., Anyfanti, P., Douma, S., Argyros, A.A.: FIRE: fundus image registration dataset. Model. Artif. Intell. Ophthalmol. **1**(4), 16–28 (2017)

10. Jiang, W., Trulls, E., Hosang, J., Tagliasacchi, A., Yi, K.M.: COTR: correspondence transformer for matching across images. In: ICCV (2021)

11. Jonas, J.B., Xu, L., Wang, Y.: The Beijing eye study. Acta Ophthalmol. **87**(3), 247–261 (2009)

12. Kingma, D.P., Ba, J.: Adam: a method for stochastic optimization. In: ICLR (2015)

13. Laibacher, T., Weyde, T., Jalali, S.: M2U-Net: effective and efficient retinal vessel segmentation for real-world applications. In: CVPRW (2019)

14. Lajevardi, S.M., Arakala, A., Davis, S.A., Horadam, K.J.: Retina verification system based on biometric graph matching. IEEE Trans. Image Process. **22**(9), 3625–3635 (2013)

15. Lee, J.A., Liu, P., Cheng, J., Fu, H.: A deep step pattern representation for multimodal retinal image registration. In: ICCV (2019)

16. Lin, T.Y., et al.: Microsoft COCO: common objects in context. In: ECCV (2014)

17. Lowe, D.G.: Distinctive image features from scale-invariant keypoints. Int. J. Comput. Vis. **60**(2), 91–110 (2004)

18. Milletari, F., Navab, N., Ahmadi, S.A.: V-Net: fully convolutional neural networks for volumetric medical image segmentation. In: 3DV (2016)

19. Oinonen, H., Forsvik, H., Ruusuvuori, P., Yli-Harja, O., Voipio, V., Huttunen, H.: Identity verification based on vessel matching from fundus images. In: ICIP (2010)

20. Ortega, M., Penedo, M.G., Rouco, J., Barreira, N., Carreira, M.J.: Retinal verification using a feature points-based biometric pattern. EURASIP J. Adv. Signal Process. **2009**(1), 1–13 (2009). https://doi.org/10.1155/2009/235746

21. Revaud, J., Weinzaepfel, P., de Souza, C.R., Humenberger, M.: R2D2: repeatable and reliable detector and descriptor. In: NeurIPS (2019)

22. Rocco, I., Cimpoi, M., Arandjelović, R., Torii, A., Pajdla, T., Sivic, J.: Neighbourhood consensus networks. In: NeurIPS (2018)

23. Rocco, I., Cimpoi, M., Arandjelović, R., Torii, A., Pajdla, T., Sivic, J.: NCNet: neighbourhood consensus networks for estimating image correspondences. IEEE Trans. Pattern Anal. Mach. Intell. **44**(2), 1020–1034 (2022)

24. Ronneberger, O., Fischer, P., Brox, T.: U-Net: convolutional networks for biomedical image segmentation. In: MICCAI (2015)

25. Sarlin, P.E., DeTone, D., Malisiewicz, T., Rabinovich, A.: SuperGlue: learning feature matching with graph neural networks. In: CVPR (2020)

26. Sattler, T., et al.: Benchmarking 6DOF outdoor visual localization in changing conditions. In: CVPR (2018)

27. Schroff, F., Kalenichenko, D., Philbin, J.: FaceNet: a unified embedding for face recognition and clustering. In: CVPR (2015)

28. Simon, C.: A new scientific method of identification. N. Y. State J. Med. **35**(18), 901–906 (1935)

29. Sun, J., Shen, Z., Wang, Y., Bao, H., Zhou, X.: LoFTR: detector-free local feature matching with transformers. In: CVPR (2021)

30. Tian, Y., Yu, X., Fan, B., Wu, F., Heijnen, H., Balntas, V.: SOSNet: second order similarity regularization for local descriptor learning. In: CVPR (2019)

31. Truong, P., Apostolopoulos, S., Mosinska, A., Stucky, S., Ciller, C., Zanet, S.D.: GLAMpoints: greedily learned accurate match points. In: ICCV (2019)

32. Truong, P., Danelljan, M., Van Gool, L., Timofte, R.: Learning accurate dense correspondences and when to trust them. In: CVPR (2021)

33. Wang, Y., et al.: A segmentation based robust deep learning framework for multi-modal retinal image registration. In: ICASSP (2020)

34. Wei, Q., et al.: Learn to segment retinal lesions and beyond. In: ICPR (2020)

35. Wei, S.E., Ramakrishna, V., Kanade, T., Sheikh, Y.: Convolutional pose machines. In: CVPR (2016)

36. Wei, W., et al.: Subfoveal choroidal thickness: the Beijing eye study. Ophthalmology **120**(1), 175–180 (2013)

Graph Neural Network for Cell Tracking in Microscopy Videos

Tal Ben-Haim[✉] and Tammy Riklin Raviv

Ben-Gurion University of the Negev,
Be'er Sheva, Israel
benhait@post.bgu.ac.il, rrtammy@ee.bgu.ac.il

Abstract. We present a novel graph neural network (GNN) approach for cell tracking in high-throughput microscopy videos. By modeling the entire time-lapse sequence as a direct graph where cell instances are represented by its nodes and their associations by its edges, we extract the entire set of cell trajectories by looking for the maximal paths in the graph. This is accomplished by several key contributions incorporated into an end-to-end deep learning framework. We exploit a deep metric learning algorithm to extract cell feature vectors that distinguish between instances of different biological cells and assemble same cell instances. We introduce a new GNN block type which enables a mutual update of node and edge feature vectors, thus facilitating the underlying message passing process. The message passing concept, whose extent is determined by the number of GNN blocks, is of fundamental importance as it enables the 'flow' of information between nodes and edges much behind their neighbors in consecutive frames. Finally, we solve an edge classification problem and use the identified active edges to construct the cells' tracks and lineage trees.

We demonstrate the strengths of the proposed cell tracking approach by applying it to 2D and 3D datasets of different cell types, imaging setups, and experimental conditions. We show that our framework outperforms current state-of-the-art methods on most of the evaluated datasets. The code is available at https://github.com/talbenha/cell-tracker-gnn.

Keywords: Cell tracking · Graph Neural Network · Microscopy videos

1 Introduction

Time-lapse microscopy imaging is a common tool for the study of biological systems and processes. However, probing complex and dynamic cellular events requires quantitative analysis at the single cell level of a huge amount of data,

Supplementary Information The online version contains supplementary material available at https://doi.org/10.1007/978-3-031-19803-8_36.

S. Avidan et al. (Eds.): ECCV 2022, LNCS 13681, pp. 610–626, 2022.
https://doi.org/10.1007/978-3-031-19803-8_36

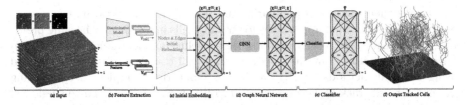

Fig. 1. An outline of the proposed cell tracking framework. (a) The input is composed of a live cell microscopy sequence of length T and the corresponding sequence of label maps. (b) Each cell instance in the sequence is represented by a feature vector which includes DML and spatio-temporal features. (c) The entire microscopy sequence is encoded as a direct graph where the cell instances are represented by its nodes and their associations are represented by the graph edges. Each node and edge in the graph has its own embedded feature vector. (d) These feature vectors are encoded and updated using Graph Neural Network (GNN). The GNN (which is illustrated in Fig. 2a) is composed of L message passing blocks which enable an update of edge and node features by their L-th order neighbors (i.e., cell instances which are up to L frames apart). (e) The GNN's edge feature output is the input for an edge classifier network which classifies the edges into active (solid lines) and non-active (dashed lines). During training, the predicted classification $\hat{\mathbf{Y}}$ is compared to the GT classification $\mathbf{Y}$ for the loss computation. Since all the framework components are connected in an end-to-end manner the loss backpropogates throughout the entire network. (f) At inference time, cell tracks are constructed by concatenating sequences of active edges that connect cells in consecutive frames.

which far surpasses human annotators' abilities. Therefore, automatic cell tracking which aims to identify and associate instances of the same biological cells and their offspring along microscopy sequences is an active field of study.

The automatic construction of cell trajectories is a challenging problem since same-sequence cells often have similar visual traits yet individual cells may change their appearance or even divide over the course of time. In addition, a cell may temporarily occlude another, exit and reenter the frame field of view. On top of these, frequent mitotic events, the high cell density, high cell migration rate and low frame rate render cell tracking even more difficult.

Classical cell tracking methods include cell association algorithms which solve the tracking problem in a temporarily local manner, and global frameworks which aim to solve cell tracking for an entire time-lapse microscopy sequence by simultaneous extraction of entire tracks. Frame-to-frame association algorithms connect cell instances in consecutive frames based on their visual traits and pose similarity [4, 21] as well as cell motion prediction [1, 2]. Methods that look for globally optimal cell tracking solutions usually represent a microscopy sequence by a graph, encoding detected cell instances and their potential links to neighboring frames by the graph nodes and edges, respectively. In most cases, linear programming and combinatorial algorithms were used to extract, multiple, non-overlapping cell trajectories [5, 17, 18, 20, 27, 30, 31, 35, 36].

Despite their increasing popularity and state-of-the-art performance in various fields, deep learning approaches for tracing cells in a sequence became prevalent only lately. Many recent methods use convolutional neural networks (CNNs) for cell segmentation, but the construction of cell trajectories is still performed using classical methods e.g., [15,34,37]. A pioneering complete deep learning method for cell tracking was proposed in [14] however it is limited to single cell tracking. In [11] two separate U-nets [32] were proposed for cell likelihood detection and movement estimation. In a later work by that group, a single U-Net was exploited to perform both tasks at once [12]. A further elaboration was proposed in [26] using both backward and forward propagation between nearby frames. Both [29] and [38] presented recurrent neural network (RNN) approaches for the time-series analysis of microscopy videos. Other recent cell tracking approaches include a deep reinforcement learning method [41] and a pipeline of Siamese networks [8,28]. All of these deep learning approaches predict frame-to-frame cell associations rather than providing a global tracking solution. In contrast, for the first time (to the best of our knowledge), we present a graph neural network (GNN) framework for the tracking of multiple cell instances (represented by the graph nodes and associated by its edges) in high-throughput microscopy sequences. This approach allows us to simultaneously extract entire cell tracks for the construction of complete lineage trees.

A GNN is a neural network that operates on data structured as a graph. It is designed to capture graph dependencies via message passing between its nodes. Specifically, node feature vectors are computed by recursively aggregating and transforming feature vectors of their neighbors [10]. The number of message passing neural network (MPNN) blocks determines the extent of the long range interactions of nodes and edges in detached frames. Many GNN variants with different neighborhood aggregation schemes have been proposed and applied to node classification, including Graph Convolutional Network (GCN) [19] and Graph Attention Network (GAT) [40]. The latter is an extension of the GCN in which the weighting of neighboring nodes is inferred by an attention mechanism. In a very recent framework called Pathfinder Discovery Network Convolution (PDN-Conv), it has been proposed to use incoming edge features to weight their influence on the nodes they connect [33].

We extend the PDN-Conv block and design a unique MPNN paradigm based on an edge encoding network and a mutual update mechanism of node and edge features that facilitate the message passing process. Moreover, since we formulate the construction of cell trajectories by a problem of finding paths in a graph, we can address it by solving a binary edge classification problem, where 'active' edges are those which connect cell instances in consecutive frames that are associated with the same biological cell. The update of the edge features is therefore an important aspect of our method. In [7,43] GNNs have been used with different message passing schemes for vehicle and pedestrian tracking. Yet, cell tracking poses different challenges than tracking cars or people. Cell dynamics appear completely random, as there are no paths or roads neither common motion directions or speed. Moreover, cells within the same sequence may look very similar, yet they change their appearance along the sequence and even divide. Furthermore, in many cases, due to frequent mitotic events (cell divisions), cell population increases very rapidly such that frames, mainly toward the end of the sequence, become extremely dense and cluttered. There might be hundreds of cell instances in a frame, and therefore, frequent cell overlap and occlusions [9,25].

Cell overlap, visual similarity, and gradual change in appearance often render manually selected features such as position, intensity, and shape insufficient for accurate tracking. To address some of these difficulties, Arbelle et al. exploited the Kalman filter to predict changes in cell shapes in addition to their estimated pose and motion [2]. Some CNN-based methods learn cell features implicitly but mainly for the purpose of cell segmentation and separation of nearby cell instances. In this work, we use a deep metric learning (DML) technique to learn discriminative cell instance features. Specifically, we utilize the multi-similarity loss as proposed by [42] to differentiate between instances of different cells and to associate instances of the same biological cells. The DML features of each cell instance are the input to the proposed GNN.

Figure 1 presents the outline of our end-to-end cell tracking framework. The input to our framework is composed of a time-lapse microscopy sequence of living cells and their annotations. The outputs are the cell trajectories and lineage trees. The feature embedding networks, the GNN, and the edge classifier are connected such that the classifier loss backpropagates throughout the entire network compound. Our method is based on several key steps and contributions: **1)** We address cell tracking by the simultaneous construction of all cell trajectories in the entire sequence. **2)** We are the first to use deep metric learning to learn features that distinguish between instances of different biological cells and to assemble same cell instances. **3)** We represent cell instances and their features as nodes in a direct graph and connect them by edges which represent their potential associations in consecutive frames. **4)** We are the first to apply a GNN and a message passing mechanism as a solution to the cell tracking task. Specifically, we look for paths in a graph that models the studied microscopy sequence, where each path represents a cell trajectory. **5)** We address cell tracking as an edge classification problem for identifying active and non-active edges. We, therefore, focus on edge features and introduce a new GNN block that enables mutual node and edge feature update.

We demonstrate our cell tracking framework by applying it to a variety of datasets, both 2D and 3D of different cell types, imaging conditions, and experimental setups. We show that our framework outperforms current state-of-the-art methods on most of the evaluated datasets. Specifically, we perform cell tracking on the challenging C2C12 dataset [9] and show that our method outperforms five other competing methods and achieves state-of-the-art results. We also competed in the Cell Tracking Challenge (CTC) [23,39] as BGU-IL (5). The table published on the CTC website shows that our method was ranked first for three different datasets and second for another one.

2   Method

Addressing the problem of cell tracking via GNN enables a simultaneous construction of all tracks in a sequence. Here, we present the method's building blocks and our contributions. The reader is also referred to Fig. 1 for a visualization of the method outline. We consider cell tracking as a global problem applied to the entire sequence at once. This tracking model is formulated in Sect. 2.1. The representation of the entire microscopy sequence as a graph, where cell's instances are encoded by its nodes and their associations by its edges, is introduced in Sect. 2.2. This representation allows us to address cell tracking as an edge classification problem. In Sect. 2.3 we discuss cell instance feature extraction using deep metric learning. In Sect. 2.4 we present the proposed GNN blocks which are designed to facilitate a message passing strategy and introduce our innovative mechanism for mutual node and edge feature update. The edge classifier and the corresponding loss function are presented in Sect. 2.5. Finally, in Sects. 2.6 and 2.7 we discuss our approach which utilizes the proposed representation for inference and mitosis detection, respectively.

2.1   Cell Tracking Problem Formulation

The input to our framework is a sequence of frames $\{I_t\}_{t=1}^T$ and its corresponding sequence of label maps $\{\mathcal{L}_t\}_{t=1}^T$, where T is the length of the sequence. Each frame in the sequence $I_t \colon \Omega \to \mathbb{R}+$ is a gray-scale image presenting K_t cell instances, where Ω denotes a 2D or 3D image domain. The associated label map $\mathcal{L}_t \colon \Omega \to \{l^0, l^1, \ldots, l^{K_t}\}$ partitions Ω into K_t connected components, each corresponds to an individual cell, and a background which is labeled by $l^0 = 0$ regardless of the frame number. We note that the cell labeling in each frame is arbitrary and the number of cell instances K_t may vary from frame to frame due to entrance/exit of cells to/from the field of view and mitotic events. We further define by $s_t^k = \{\forall \rho \in \Omega | \mathcal{L}_t(\rho) = l^k\}$ the set of pixels/voxels ρ that are associated with the k–th cell in frame I_t. Note that s_t^k can either include all the pixels/voxels that belong to a particular cell or a representative subset, depending whether $\mathcal{L}_t$ is the segmentation map of the cells in the frame or represents a set of K_t markers at approximately the cell centers.

Let N denote the total number of biological cells that were depicted in the entire sequence, and let $c_t^n = \{s_t^n, t\}$ denote a cell object which represents an instance of the n–th cell in frame t. We further denote by t_{init}^n and t_{fin}^n the first and the last time points (respectively) in which a cell is depicted in a sequence n. Note that $1 \le t_{\text{init}} \le t_{\text{fin}} \le T$. To avoid confusion between the indices of the actual cells and their instances in the frame sequence, we define a cell function ψ which, given a cell instance, returns the index of its corresponding biological cell. Note that if $\psi(c_t^k) = \psi(c_{t+1}^l)$ than c_t^k and c_{t+1}^l are instances of the same cell. We aim to compose a set of N trajectories $\{\mathcal{T}_n\}_{n=1}^N$, where $\mathcal{T}_n = \{c_{t_{\text{init}}}^n, \ldots, c_{t_{\text{fin}}}^n\}$ is the maximal-length sequence of associated cell instances in consecutive frames that correspond to the same biological cell. Here, we set $c_t^n \equiv c_t^k$ for different values of k along the sequence if $\psi(c_t^k) = n$.

We assume that cells are depicted continuously; i.e., $t_{i+1} = t_i + 1$. Therefore, if a particular cell disappears due to an occlusion or a temporary exit from the field of view, its reappearance initiates a new track and it gets a new cell index. To identify mitosis we define a parent function $P: \{1, \ldots, N\} \rightarrow \{1, \ldots, N\}$ such that $P(n) = n'$ when n' is the parent of cell n and $P(n) = 0$ if the cell's appearance is not a result of a mitotic event. For convenience we set $n' < n$. Note that a cell cannot be a parent of itself, therefore $n' \neq n$. A complete trajectory object of the n−th biological cell is defined as follows, where $\mathcal{T}_n = \{\mathcal{T}_n, P(n), t_{\text{init}}^n, t_{\text{fin}}^n\}$. The cell tracking task goal is to find the set $\{\mathcal{T}_1, \ldots, \mathcal{T}_N\}$ that best explains the observations.

2.2 Graph Formulation

We use a direct, acyclic graph to model cell-to-cell associations in microscopy sequences. Let $\mathcal{G} = (\mathcal{V}, \mathcal{E})$ define a graph represented by its vertices (nodes) $\mathcal{V}$ and edges (links) $\mathcal{E}$. Let $M = \sum_{t=1}^{T} K_t$ represent all cell instances in the entire frame sequence. A graph representation of cells and their associations is composed of $|\mathcal{V}| = M$ vertices, where each node $\nu_i \in \mathcal{V}$, $i = 1, \ldots, M$ represents a single cell instance $c_{t=\tau}^k$. For convenience, we can set $i = \sum_{t=1}^{\tau-1} K_t + k$.

An edge $e_{i,j} \in \mathcal{E}$ represents a potential association between a pair of vertices ν_i, ν_j, representing cell instances in consecutive frames. To reduce the number of edges, we connect a pair of cells only if their spatial Euclidean distance is within a neighborhood region, which is calculated based on the training set as detailed in Section A.1 in the Appendix.

We address cell tracking as an edge classification problem. The desired output are labeled sets of edges defined by an edge function $Y: \mathcal{E} \rightarrow \{0, 1\}$. Let ν_i, ν_j represent cell instances denoted by c_t^k and c_{t+1}^l, respectively.

$$Y(e_{i,j}) = y_{i,j} = \begin{cases} 1, & \text{if } \psi(c_t^k) = \psi(c_{t+1}^l) \\ 0, & \text{otherwise} \end{cases} \tag{1}$$

Accurate prediction of $Y(e_{i,j})$ for the complete set of graph edges provides the entire cell lineage associated with the observed microscopy sequence. A cell trajectory $\mathcal{T}_n$ can be either defined by a sequence of cell instances represented by the graph's vertices $\{\nu_{i_1}, \nu_{i_2}, \ldots \nu_{i_n}\}$, or by a sequence of edges $\mathbf{e}_n = \{e_{i_1 i_2}, \ldots, e_{i_{n-1} i_n}\}$, that connect cell instances in consecutive frames, where $\{e_{ij} \in \mathbf{e}_n \mid Y(e_{ij}) = 1\}$.

We assume that a non-dividing cell instance has at most a single successor while a cell that undergoes mitosis may have two successors and even more (in rare occurrences). Ideally, if two (or more) different nodes in a frame $\nu_j \neq \nu_{j'}$ are connected to the same node ν_i in a previous frame, i.e.; $Y(e_{i,j}) = Y(e_{i,j'}) = 1$, then we can assume that $P(\psi(c_{t+1}^l)) = P(\psi(c_{t+1}^{l'})) = \psi(c_t^k)$ and detect a mitosis event. In practice, often the visual features of daughter cells differ from those of their parent and an additional process is required to identify and validate parent-daughter relations. The complete representation of the proposed graph is defined by the following attribute matrices: i) A node feature matrix $\mathbf{X} \in \mathbb{R}^{|\mathcal{V}| \times d_{\mathcal{V}}}$ with $d_{\mathcal{V}}$ features per node. ii) A graph connectivity matrix $\mathbf{E} \in \mathbb{N}^{2 \times |\mathcal{E}|}$ which represents all possible linked cell indices from source to target. iii) An edge feature matrix $\mathbf{Z} \in \mathbb{R}^{|\mathcal{E}| \times d_{\mathcal{E}}}$, where each row in $\mathbf{Z}$ consists of $d_{\mathcal{E}}$ features of an edge e_{ij} in the graph. We aim to predict $\hat{\mathbf{Y}} \in \mathbb{R}_{[0,1]}^{|\mathcal{E}| \times 1}$ that represents the probability to represent an actual cell association. Next, we present the initial graph embedding.

2.3   Feature Extraction

The success of cell tracking algorithms depends on correct associations of instances of the same biological cells. We consider instances of the same cell as members of the same class. Altogether, we have N mutually exclusive classes.

Deep Metric Learning (DML) Features. We use *deep metric learning* to learn cell feature embeddings that allow us to assemble instances of the same biological cells and distinguish between different ones. For this purpose, we use the cell segmentation maps or marker annotations to crop each frame into sub-images of all cell instances. Following [42] we use a *hard mining* strategy and a *multi-similarity loss* function to train a ResNet network [13] to predict such embeddings. Specifically, we generate batches of cell sub-images, where each is composed of m same-class instances from κ classes. Since the cell's appearance gradually changes during the sequence we perform the *m-per-class* sampling [24] using temporally adjacent frames. To calculate the loss, we consider pairs of within-class and between-class cell instances which form the positive and negative examples, respectively. To conduct the hard mining, an affinity matrix $\mathbb{A} \in \mathbb{R}^{m\kappa \times m\kappa}$ is constructed based on the cosine similarity function applied to the 'learned' feature vectors of each of the pairs. A column i in $\mathbb{A}$ presents the proximity of all the batch instances to the i–th instance. An instance j forms a *hard negative* example with i if i and j are not within the same class and j is more similar to i than another instance k that form a positive example with it. In the same manner, an instance l forms a *hard positive* example with i if i and l are within the same class and l is less similar to i than another instance r that form a negative example with it. The multi-similarity loss is a measure of the *hard positive* and *hard negative* examples. When there are no such examples the embedded feature vectors are adequately clustered. The node feature vectors extracted using DML approach are denoted in a matrix form as follows: $\mathbf{V}_{\text{DML}} \in \mathbb{R}^{|\mathcal{V}| \times d_{\text{DML}}}$, where d_{DML} denotes the number of DML features.

Spatio-Temporal Features. We also consider temporal and global spatial cells' features which include the coordinates of the cell center, its frame number, and intensity statistics (minimum, maximum, and average). In the case where we have an instance segmentation mask, the cell's area, the minor and major axes of a bounding ellipse, and bounding-box coordinates are also considered. We denote by $\mathbf{V}_{\text{ST}} \in \mathbb{R}^{|\mathcal{V}| \times d_{\text{ST}}}$ the spatio-temporal (ST) feature matrix, which is composed of the d_{ST}-dimensional feature vectors of all nodes.

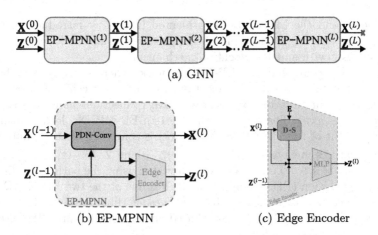

(a) GNN

(b) EP-MPNN   (c) Edge Encoder

Fig. 2. (a) A Graph Neural Network (GNN). The GNN is composed of L EP-MPNN blocks where L determines the message passing extent. The l-th EP-MPNN block updates the nodes and edge features, i.e., $\mathbf{X}^{(l-1)} \to \mathbf{X}^{(l)}$ and $\mathbf{Z}^{(l-1)} \to \mathbf{Z}^{(l)}$. **(b) Edge-oriented Pathfinder - Message Passing Network (EP-MPNN) Layer.** The basic layer in the graph neural network step comprises a PDN-Conv and an edge encoder. The PDN-Conv updates the node feature vectors based on their current values and an edge attention model. **(c) Edge encoder.** Updates the edge feature vectors. Its $\boldsymbol{D}\text{-}\boldsymbol{S}$ block calculates the distance and similarity between the feature vectors of each pair of nodes by an edge. The output of the $\boldsymbol{D}\text{-}\boldsymbol{S}$ block along with the nodes and the current edge features compose the input of an MLP which outputs the new feature vectors of the edges. The concatenation (denoted by '$\otimes$') of the $\boldsymbol{D}\text{-}\boldsymbol{S}$ block's output along with the current node and edge features formulated in Eq. 4, is the input for an MLP which is trained to learn a new edges representation

Initial Edge and Node Features. The complete feature matrix of all nodes in the graph includes both the learned and the spatio-temporal features and is denoted by $\mathbf{V}_{\mathcal{V}} \in \mathbb{R}^{|\mathcal{V}| \times d_{\mathcal{V}}}$, where, $d_{\mathcal{V}} = d_{\text{ST}} + d_{\text{DML}}$. It is generated by a concatenation of $\mathbf{V}_{\text{DML}}$ and $\mathbf{V}_{\text{ST}}$. Having $\mathbf{V}_{\mathcal{V}}$ we construct the initial edge feature matrix $\mathbf{V}_{\mathcal{E}}$ using the *distance & similarity* operation defined in Eq. 3. Since $\mathbf{V}_{\text{DML}}$ and $\mathbf{V}_{\text{ST}}$ are from different sources and are in different scales, we homogenize them and reduce the complete feature vector dimension via mapping by multi-layer perceptron (MLP) networks. These MLPs are connected to the proposed GNN (see Sect. 2.4) in an end-to-end manner. We denote the initial node feature vector of a vertex ν_i by $\mathbf{x}_i^{(0)}$, where $\mathbf{x}_i^{(0)}$ is the i-th row in $\mathbf{X}^{(0)}$.

2.4 Graph Neural Network

The core of the proposed cell tracking framework is the graph neural network (GNN) illustrated in Fig. 2a. Exploiting the GNN model and the message passing paradigm allows us to simultaneously trace entire cells tracks rather than locally associate cell instances in a frame-by-frame manner. One of our main contributions is the graph message passing block presented in Fig. 2b called the Edge-oriented Pathfinder Message Passing Neural Network (EP-MPNN). Specifically, we extend the MPNN block presented in [33] by introducing an edge encoder, thus enabling an interplay between the edge and node feature update simultaneously with an edge-attention mechanism.

The GNN is composed of L EP-MPNN blocks where L determines the message passing extent. In other words, the associations of cell instances in consecutive frames are affected by the respective connections along the sequence up to L frames away. The input to the $l + 1$-th EP-MPNN block (which is, in fact, the output of the l-th EP-MPNN block) is composed of the updated node and edge features, denoted by $\mathbf{X}^{(l)} = \{x_i^{(l)}\}_{\nu_i \in \mathcal{V}}$ and $\mathbf{Z}^{(l)} = \{z_{ij}^{(l)}\}_{e_{ij} \in \mathcal{E}}$, respectively, where $l = 0, \ldots, L$. The nodes are updated using the pathfinder discovery network convolution (PDN-Conv) [33] which is one of the two EP-MPNN components. The other component is the *edge encoder* (illustrated in Fig. 2c) which is trained to embed the edge features based on the node features. We introduce the edge encoder in the following.

Node Feature Update. The features of each node ν_i are updated based on the weights of the incoming edges. These weights are learned using an attention mechanism. Let $f_{\text{edge}}^{\text{PDN}} \colon \mathbb{R}^{d_\mathcal{E}} \to \mathbb{R}$ define a function implemented by an MLP that is trained to output scalars which represent the weights of the edges, given their current features. Let $f_{\text{node}}^{\text{PDN}} \colon \mathbb{R}^{d_\mathcal{V}} \to \mathbb{R}^{d_\mathcal{V}}$ define a vector function implemented by an MLP that is trained to output updated feature vectors given the current ones. The updated feature vector of a node ν_i is obtained by a weighted sum of its own and its neighboring nodes, as follows:

$$\mathbf{x}_i^{(l)} = \sum_{j \in \mathcal{N}(i) \cup \{i\}} \overbrace{f_{\text{edge},l}^{\text{PDN}}(\mathbf{z}_{j,i}^{(l)})}^{\omega_{ji}^l} \overbrace{f_{\text{node},l}^{\text{PDN}}(\mathbf{x}_j^{(l-1)})}^{\tilde{x}_j^{(l-1)}}, \tag{2}$$

where $\mathcal{N}(i)$ denotes the neighbors of ν_i; i.e., all the nodes ν_j for which there exist $e_{j,i} \in \mathcal{E}$. Note that $f_{\text{edge},l}^{\text{PDN}}$ and $f_{\text{node},l}^{\text{PDN}}$ are trained separately for each block. Equation 2 can be interpreted as attention through edges, where, $\omega_{ji}^l = f_{edge,l}^{\text{PDN}}(\mathbf{z}_{j,i}^{(l)})$ is the predicted attention parameter of an edge $e_{j,i}$ ($\omega_{ii}^l = 1$) and $\tilde{\mathbf{x}}_j^{(l-1)} = f_{\text{node},l}^{\text{PDN}}(\mathbf{x}_j^{(l-1)})$ is the *mapped* feature vector of a node ν_j in the l-th EP-MPNN.

Edge Feature Update. The main contribution of the proposed GNN framework is a mechanism for edge feature update that enhances the message passing process. Unlike the GNN presented in [33] here, the edge and node features are alternately updated. We denote by $\boldsymbol{D\text{-}S}$ a function that returns the distance & similarity vector of two feature vectors of connected nodes as follows:

$$\boldsymbol{D\text{-}S}(\mathbf{v}_i, \mathbf{v}_j) = [|v_i^1 - v_j^1|, \ldots, |v_i^{d_\nu} - v_j^{d_\nu}|, \frac{\mathbf{v}_i \cdot \mathbf{v}_j}{\|\mathbf{v}_i\| \|\mathbf{v}_j\|}] \tag{3}$$

which is a concatenation of the absolute values of the differences between corresponding elements in $\mathbf{v}_i$ and $\mathbf{v}_j$ and their cosine similarity $\frac{\mathbf{v}_i \cdot \mathbf{v}_j}{\|\mathbf{v}_i\| \|\mathbf{v}_j\|}$. In the

l-th block $\mathbf{v}_i = \mathbf{x}_i^{(l)}$ and $\mathbf{v}_j = \mathbf{x}_j^{(l)}$. In the initial phase, when the input to the first GNN block is formed, $\mathbf{v}_i$ and $\mathbf{v}_j$ are the i-th and the j-th rows in $\mathbf{V}_\mathcal{V}$, respectively. The construction of the initial feature matrix $\mathbf{V}_\mathcal{V}$ is described in Sect. 2.3.

The edge update function $f_{\text{edge},l}^{\text{EE}}$ (implemented as an MLP) returns the updated features of each edge $e_{i,j}$ given the concatenation of the current edge features, the updated feature vectors of the nodes it connects, and the output of the $\boldsymbol{D}$-$\boldsymbol{S}$ block applied to these nodes. Formally,

$$\mathbf{z}_{ij}^{(l)} = f_{\text{edge},l}^{\text{EE}}([\mathbf{z}_{ij}^{(l-1)}, \mathbf{x}_i^{(l)}, \mathbf{x}_j^{(l)}, \boldsymbol{D}\text{-}\boldsymbol{S}(\mathbf{x}_i^{(l)}, \mathbf{x}_j^{(l)})]) \tag{4}$$

The simultaneous edge and node feature update facilitates the message passing mechanism. Let ν_i be a node in frame t and let $\mathcal{N}(i)$ define the set of nodes connected to it in frame $t-1$. Consider a node $\nu_j \in \mathcal{N}(i)$. In the first GNN block ($l = 1$) the features of an edge $e_{j,i}$ are updated based on the features of ν_i and ν_j. In the same block ν_j is updated based on the features of its neighbors $\mathcal{N}(j)$ that are nodes representing cell instances in frame $t-2$. The update is determined by the weights of the edges connecting them. In the next GNN block ($l = 2$) the features of an edge $e_{j,i}$ are again updated based on the features of ν_i and ν_j. However, this time the features of a node ν_j are already influenced by its neighbors. Therefore, when the features of ν_i are updated they are already affected by the neighbors of its neighbors which are cell instances that are two frames away. In the same manner, in the L-th block, cell instances and their first-order connections are influenced by cell-to-cell associations and higher-order connections along L frames.

2.5 Classifier and Training

The output edge feature vectors are the inputs to the edge classifier network. The classifier is an MLP with three linear layers each is followed by a ReLU activation, when a Sigmoid function is applied to the output layer. The output is a vector $\hat{\mathbf{Y}} \in \mathbb{R}_{[0,1]}^{|\mathcal{E}| \times 1}$ that represents the probability for each edge to be active ($= 1$) or not ($= 0$). We use the ground-truth (GT) edge activation vector $\mathbf{Y}$ to train the model. Since most of the edges in the graph dataset are not active (i.e., do not link nodes), our data are highly imbalanced. Therefore, we use a weighted cross-entropy loss function with adaptive weights which are determined by the average number of neighbors in a batch, i.e., $\left(\frac{1}{|\mathcal{N}|}, \frac{|\mathcal{N}|-1}{|\mathcal{N}|}\right)$. Note that since the size of the neighborhood region remains fixed throughout the sequence, the number of neighbors increases as the frames become denser.

2.6 Cell Tracking Inference

The output of the proposed deep learning framework is a probability matrix which identifies active edges. It is used together with the connection matrix $\mathbf{E}$ to construct candidates for cell trajectories as described in Sect. 2.2. Specifically, predictions of cell tracks are obtained at the inference phase in the form

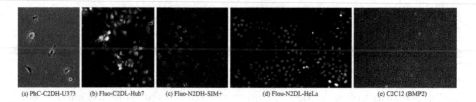

(a) PhC-C2DH-U373   (b) Fluo-C2DL-Huh7   (c) Fluo-N2DH-SIM+   (d) Flou-N2DL-HeLa   (e) C2C12 (BMP2)

Fig. 3. Example frames from five evaluated 2D datasets. Note the different appearance of the cells and the entire frames.

of a directed graph with soft edge weights (the output of a sigmoid). The edges in the graph represent only outgoing, potential associations between consecutive frames. The soft weights (association probabilities) allow us to partition the graph edges into active and non-active. Considering the outgoing/incoming edges of a specific node, there could be one of the following outcomes: 1) All outgoing/incoming edges are non-active - which may indicate end/beginning of a track. 2) Only one outgoing edge is active. 3) Two or more outgoing edges are active which may indicate mitosis (cell division). 4) More than a single incoming edge is active - i.e., when different cell instances are associated to the same cell instance. Above 99% of incoming/outgoing edges conflicts are avoided thanks to the proposed training scheme. We note that the network is implicitly trained to prefer bijection cell associations thanks to the attention-based mechanism of the GNN blocks and the weighted loss function (see Sect. 2.5). Nevertheless, to ensure one-to-two mapping at most (case 3), in case that the association probabilities of more than two outgoing edges are higher than 0.5 (extremely rare events) only the top-2 are considered as active. In addition, to ensure injective mapping (case 4), only the incoming edge with the highest association probability (as long as it is higher than 0.5) is considered active. This obviously feasible ad-hoc strategy ensures a single path to each cell.

2.7   Mitosis Detection

Since daughter cells usually have different visual features than their parent, it is not very frequent for a node to have two active outgoing edges. In most mitotic events the parent track terminates whereas two new tracks initiate. To associate pairs of daughter cells to their parents we consider the detected tracks of all cells. We then look for triplets of trajectories $(\mathcal{T}_k, \mathcal{T}_l, \mathcal{T}_m)$ where $k, l, m \in \{1, \ldots, N\}$ such that $t_{\text{init}}^k = t_{\text{init}}^l = t_{\text{fin}}^m + 1$. If the spatial coordinates of $c_{t_{\text{init}}}^k, c_{t_{\text{init}}}^l$ and $c_{t_{\text{fin}}}^m$ are within the same neighborhood region, then we set $P(k) = P(l) = m$.

3   Experiments

We evaluated our model on six datasets from two different sources: an open dataset [9] we call C2C12 and five (2D and 3D) datasets from the Cell Tracking Challenge (CTC) [23,39]. The C2C12 dataset is composed of 16 sequences

Table 1. C2C12 cell tracking results [9]. A comparison of our association accuracy (left) and target effectiveness (right) scores to the scores obtained by five other methods. The top five rows present results for the original frame rate (best appears in **bold**) and the bottom two rows refer to the lower ($\times$5) frame rate setup (best is <u>underlined</u>)

Method	Association Accuracy					Target Effectiveness				
	control	FGF2	BMP2	FGF2+ BMP2	Avg.	control	FGF2	BMP2	FGF2+ BMP2	Avg.
AGC [4]	0.604	0.499	0.801	0.689	0.648	0.543	0.448	0.621	0.465	0.519
ST-GDA [5]	0.826	0.775	0.855	0.942	0.843	0.733	0.710	0.788	0.633	0.716
BFP [26]	0.955	0.926	0.982	0.976	0.960	0.869	0.806	0.970	0.911	0.881
MPM [12]	0.947	0.952	**0.991**	**0.987**	0.969	0.803	0.829	0.958	0.911	0.875
Ours	**0.981**	**0.973**	**0.991**	0.986	**0.983**	**0.894**	**0.843**	**0.976**	**0.914**	**0.907**
CDM($\times$5) [11]	0.883	0.894	0.971	0.951	0.927	0.832	0.813	0.958	0.895	0.875
Ours ($\times$5)	<u>0.958</u>	<u>0.942</u>	<u>0.988</u>	<u>0.970</u>	<u>0.964</u>	<u>0.905</u>	<u>0.852</u>	<u>0.981</u>	<u>0.919</u>	<u>0.914</u>

acquired with four different cell growth factors. Representative frames are presented in Fig. 3 for each of the 2D data sequences. Implementation details and further experiments including qualitative results (figures and videos) and ablation studies are provided in Sections A and B (respectively) of the appendix.

3.1 C2C12 Myoblast Datasets

In the following experiments, we focus on C2C12 [9], which is considered a challenging cell tracking dataset (see trajectories in Fig. 1). It is composed of high-throughput time-lapse sequences of C2C12 mouse myoblast cells acquired by phase-contrast microscopy under four growth factor conditions, including with fibroblast growth factor 2 (FGF2), bone morphogenetic protein 2 (BMP2), FGF2 + BMP2, and control (no growth factor). For each condition, four image sequences were captured, each consists of 780 frames (12 frames-per-hour, 1392×1040 pixels). The GT annotation includes a list of coordinates of the cell instances' centers along with the corresponding indices of the depicted biological cells. There is a complete cell annotation for only one sequence, where three cells and their lineage trees were marked in the others.

Experimental Setting and Evaluated Metrics. To quantify the tracking performance for the C2C12 dataset, we used the association accuracy (AA) and the target effectiveness (TE) measures as suggested by [12,26]. All comparisons were made with respect to human-annotated target cells and their frame-to-frame associations, which are considered the GT. The AA measure is defined by the ratio between the number of true positive associations and the total number of GT associations. The TE measure [6] considers the number of cell instances correctly associated within a track with respect to the total number of GT cell instances associated within that track. Training-test split was as in [12] where the test sequences of the C2C12 were annotated by the nnU-Net network [16].

Table 2. Cell Tracking Challenge (CTC) results. Our tracking scores (TRA measure [22]) for the test sequences of five different datasets as published by the CTC organizers. The table presents the top three scores (our scores appear in bold) and our ranks with respect to the number of competing methods. The difference between our score and the best one appears in parentheses

Dataset	Our-Rank(diff)	1st	2nd	3rd
PhC-C2DH-U373	1/25	**0.985**	0.982	0.981
Fluo-N2DH-SIM+	1/35	**0.978**	0.975	0.973
Fluo-N3DH-SIM+	1/11	**0.974**	0.972	0.967
Fluo-C2DL-Huh7	2/6(0.026)	0.960	**0.934**	0.865
Fluo-N2DL-HeLa	4/34(0.004)	0.993	0.991	0.991

C2C12 Tracking Results. The AA and the TE scores are reported in Table 1 for the four different types of C2C12 growth factor conditions. The top part of the table compares the performances of our framework with respect to the reported scores of four other methods: AGC [4], ST-GDA [5], BFP [26], MPM [12], where the latter two were considered the best performing methods for this dataset [12, 26]. The bottom part of the table presents tracking scores for subsampled C2C12 sequences, simulating ×5 lower frame rate. Our scores are compared with those obtained by the CDM method [11] which was reported to have the best performance for this setup. Our tracking framework is shown to outperform all other methods, for almost all cell growth factor conditions in both setups. The advantage of our method over the classical global cell tracking approaches which are based on combinatorial algorithms such as AGC [4] and ST-GDA [5] can be explained by the fact that the optimization process is performed via training through the loss functions. Moreover, the uniquely designed message passing scheme which considers long term cell associations is preferable over the local, greedy and therefore sub-optimal frame-by-frame association paradigms such as MPM [12], BFP [26], and CDM [11].

3.2   Cell Tracking Challenge (CTC)

We competed in the CTC for five datasets [23, 39] to further assess our method. Figure 3 presents representative examples for each of the datasets, demonstrating their variability. The CTC is an excellent platform for objective and unbiased comparisons of the performances of different cell tracking methods when applied to a variety of 2D and 3D microscopy sequences of different acquisition methods (e.g., fluorescence or phase-contrast microscopy) and different cell types. Each CTC dataset is split into training and test sequences where the annotations of the test sets are deliberately unavailable to the competitors. The scores and ranks for all competing methods are calculated and published by the challenge organizers[1].

---

[1] The Cell Tracking Benchmark web page is available at http://celltrackingchallenge. net/latest-ctb-results/.

Table 3. Quantitative ablation study. ST and DML stand for spatio-temporal and deep-metric-learning feature extraction, respectively. EE stands for the proposed edge encoder (Fig. 2c). MPNN is the chosen message passing scheme. The symbols ✓ and ✗ indicate included or excluded, respectively. AA and TE stand for association accuracy and target effectiveness scores

Components				Results	
ST	DML	EE	MPNN	AA	TE
✓	✓	✓	GAT	0.805	0.353
✓	✓	✗	GCN	0.775	0.271
✓	✓	✓	GCN	0.871	0.359
✓	✓	✗	PDN	0.205	0.109
✗	✓	✓	EP-MPNN	0.989	0.960
✓	✗	✓	EP-MPNN	0.987	0.978
✓	✓	✓	EP-MPNN	**0.994**	**0.989**

To quantify the tracking results the CTC organizers use the TRA measure [22]. The TRA measure is based on a comparison of the nodes and edges of acyclic oriented graphs representing cells and their associations in both the GT and the evaluated method. It computes the weighted sum of the required operations to transform the predicted cell lineage tree into the GT cell lineage tree and captures all the required information for tracking assessment, including mitotic events. For the CTC experiments, we used a publicly available segmentation method [3] to predict segmentation maps for the test datasets.

Results. Table 2 presents the TRA scores for five CTC datasets: PhC-C2DH-U373, Fluo-N2DH-SIM+, Fluo-N3DH-SIM+, Fluo-C2DL-Huh7 and Fluo-N2DL-HeLa. Our scores are compared to the scores of the three-best performing methods. Our ranks are presented with respect to the number of competing methods that took part in the CTC for each dataset. Our method was ranked **first** for three out of five datasets and achieved the second- and the fourth-best ranks for the two other datasets. Our tracking results appear under BGU-IL (5).

3.3   Ablation Studies

We conduct ablation studies using the C2C12 dataset [9] to demonstrate the contribution of each component of our framework to the overall cell tracking performance. The first three rows in Table 3 present a comparison of the proposed EP-MPNN to two other commonly used message passing schemes, namely, GCN [19] and GAT [40]. The PDN method is similar to ours but does not have the edge encoder in the GNN block. The comparisons to the PDN and to the GCN without edge encoder assessed its importance. To demonstrate the significance of both the DML and the ST features we conducted two more experiments that are presented in the fifth and the sixth rows in the table. The DML and ST features both contribute to our tracking results. Further ablation study experiments are presented in Section B.4 of the Appendix.

4 Conclusions

We introduced an end-to-end deep learning framework for the simultaneous detection of complete cell trajectories in high-throughput microscopy sequences. This was accomplished by representing cell instances and their potential associations by nodes and edges (respectively) in a direct, acyclic graph; using deep metric learning for the extraction of distinguishing node features; and by using GNN and a uniquely designed message passing scheme to apply long range interactions between nodes and edges. The GNN's edge feature outputs were exploited to detect active edges that form paths in the graph, where each such path represents a cell trajectory.

Ablation study experiments presented in Sect. 3.3 assess the contribution of each of the proposed method components to the tracking accuracy. State-of-the-art tracking results are shown for a variety of 2D and 3D publicly available microscopy sequences. The code is released for comparisons and future study.

Acknowledgments. This study was partially supported by The Israel Ministry of Science, Technology and Space (MOST 3-14344 T.R.R.) and The United States - Israel Binational Science Foundation (BSF 2019135 T.R.R.).

References

1. Amat, F., et al.: Fast, accurate reconstruction of cell lineages from large-scale fluorescence microscopy data. Nat. Methods **11**(9), 951–958 (2014)
2. Arbelle, A., Reyes, J., Chen, J.Y., Lahav, G., Riklin Raviv, T.: A probabilistic approach to joint cell tracking and segmentation in high-throughput microscopy videos. Med. Image Anal. **47**, 140–152 (2018)
3. Arbelle, A., Riklin Raviv, T.: Microscopy cell segmentation via convolutional LSTM networks. In: IEEE International Symposium on Biomedical Imaging (ISBI), pp. 1008–1012. IEEE (2019)
4. Bensch, R., Ronneberger, O.: Cell segmentation and tracking in phase contrast images using graph cut with asymmetric boundary costs. In: IEEE International Symposium on Biomedical Imaging (ISBI), pp. 1220–1223. IEEE (2015)
5. Bise, R., Yin, Z., Kanade, T.: Reliable cell tracking by global data association. In: IEEE International Symposium on Biomedical Imaging (ISBI), pp. 1004–1010. IEEE (2011)
6. Blackman, S.S.: Multiple-target Tracking with Radar Applications. Artech House Inc., Dedham (1986)
7. Brasó, G., Leal-Taixé, L.: Learning a neural solver for multiple object tracking. In: IEEE Conference on Computer Vision and Pattern Recognition (CVPR), pp. 6247–6257 (2020)
8. Chen, Y., et al.: Cell track R-CNN: a novel end-to-end deep neural network for cell segmentation and tracking in microscopy images. In: IEEE International Symposium on Biomedical Imaging (ISBI), pp. 779–782. IEEE (2021)
9. Eom, S., et al.: Phase contrast time-lapse microscopy datasets with automated and manual cell tracking annotations. Sci. Data **5**(1), 1–12 (2018)
10. Gilmer, J., Schoenholz, S.S., Riley, P.F., Vinyals, O., Dahl, G.E.: Neural message passing for quantum chemistry. In: International Conference on Machine Learning (ICML), pp. 1263–1272. PMLR (2017)

11. Hayashida, J., Bise, R.: Cell tracking with deep learning for cell detection and motion estimation in low-frame-rate. In: Shen, D., et al. (eds.) MICCAI 2019. LNCS, vol. 11764, pp. 397–405. Springer, Cham (2019). https://doi.org/10.1007/978-3-030-32239-7_44

12. Hayashida, J., Nishimura, K., Bise, R.: MPM: joint representation of motion and position map for cell tracking. In: IEEE Conference on Computer Vision and Pattern Recognition (CVPR). (2020)

13. He, K., Zhang, X., Ren, S., Sun, J.: Deep residual learning for image recognition. In: IEEE Conference on Computer Vision and Pattern Recognition (CVPR), pp. 770–778 (2016)

14. He, T., Mao, H., Guo, J., Yi, Z.: Cell tracking using deep neural networks with multi-task learning. Image Vis. Comput. **60**, 142–153 (2017)

15. Hernandez, D.E., Chen, S.W., Hunter, E.E., Steager, E.B., Kumar, V.: Cell tracking with deep learning and the viterbi algorithm. In: International Conference on Manipulation, Automation and Robotics at Small Scales (MARSS), pp. 1–6. IEEE (2018)

16. Isensee, F., Jaeger, P.F., Kohl, S.A., Petersen, J., Maier-Hein, K.H.: nnU-Net: a self-configuring method for deep learning-based biomedical image segmentation. Nat. Methods **18**(2), 203–211 (2021)

17. Jug, F., Levinkov, E., Blasse, C., Myers, E.W., Andres, B.: Moral lineage tracing. In: IEEE Conference on Computer Vision and Pattern Recognition (CVPR), pp. 5926–5935 (2016)

18. Kausler, B.X., et al.: A discrete chain graph model for 3d+t cell tracking with high misdetection robustness. In: Fitzgibbon, A., Lazebnik, S., Perona, P., Sato, Y., Schmid, C. (eds.) ECCV 2012. LNCS, vol. 7574, pp. 144–157. Springer, Heidelberg (2012). https://doi.org/10.1007/978-3-642-33712-3_11

19. Kipf, T.N., Welling, M.: Semi-supervised classification with graph convolutional networks. In: International Conference on Learning Representations (ICLR) (2017)

20. Magnusson, K.E., Jaldén, J., Gilbert, P.M., Blau, H.M.: Global linking of cell tracks using the viterbi algorithm. IEEE Trans. Med. Imaging **34**(4), 911–929 (2014)

21. Maška, M., Daněk, O., Garasa, S., Rouzaut, A., Munoz-Barrutia, A., Ortiz-de Solorzano, C.: Segmentation and shape tracking of whole fluorescent cells based on the Chan-Vese model. IEEE Trans. Med. Imaging **32**(6), 995–1006 (2013)

22. Matula, P., Maška, M., Sorokin, D.V., Matula, P., Ortiz-de Solórzano, C., Kozubek, M.: Cell tracking accuracy measurement based on comparison of acyclic oriented graphs. PLoS ONE **10**(12), e0144959 (2015)

23. Maška, M., et al.: A benchmark for comparison of cell tracking algorithms. Bioinformatics **30**(11), 1609–1617 (2014)

24. Musgrave, K., Belongie, S., Lim, S.-N.: A metric learning reality check. In: Vedaldi, A., Bischof, H., Brox, T., Frahm, J.-M. (eds.) ECCV 2020. LNCS, vol. 12370, pp. 681–699. Springer, Cham (2020). https://doi.org/10.1007/978-3-030-58595-2_41

25. Neumann, B., et al.: Phenotypic profiling of the human genome by time-lapse microscopy reveals cell division genes. Nature **464**(7289), 721–727 (2010)

26. Nishimura, K., Hayashida, J., Wang, C., Ker, D.F.E., Bise, R.: Weakly-supervised cell tracking via backward-and-forward propagation. In: Vedaldi, A., Bischof, H., Brox, T., Frahm, J.-M. (eds.) ECCV 2020. LNCS, vol. 12357, pp. 104–121. Springer, Cham (2020). https://doi.org/10.1007/978-3-030-58610-2_7

27. Padfield, D., Rittscher, J., Roysam, B.: Coupled minimum-cost flow cell tracking for high-throughput quantitative analysis. Med. Image Anal. **15**(4), 650–668 (2011)

28. Panteli, A., Gupta, D.K., Bruijn, N., Gavves, E.: Siamese tracking of cell behaviour patterns. In: Medical Imaging with Deep Learning, pp. 570–587. PMLR (2020)

29. Payer, C., Štern, D., Feiner, M., Bischof, H., Urschler, M.: Segmenting and tracking cell instances with cosine embeddings and recurrent hourglass networks. Med. Image Anal. **57**, 106–119 (2019)
30. Rempfler, M., et al.: Efficient algorithms for moral lineage tracing. In: IEEE International Conference on Computer Vision (ICCV), pp. 4695–4704 (2017)
31. Rempfler, M., et al.: Tracing cell lineages in videos of lens-free microscopy. Med. Image Anal. **48**, 147–161 (2018)
32. Ronneberger, O., Fischer, P., Brox, T.: U-Net: convolutional networks for biomedical image segmentation. In: Navab, N., Hornegger, J., Wells, W.M., Frangi, A.F. (eds.) MICCAI 2015. LNCS, vol. 9351, pp. 234–241. Springer, Cham (2015). https://doi.org/10.1007/978-3-319-24574-4_28
33. Rozemberczki, B., Englert, P., Kapoor, A., Blais, M., Perozzi, B.: Pathfinder discovery networks for neural message passing. In: Proceedings of the Web Conference, pp. 2547–2558 (2021)
34. Scherr, T., Löffler, K., Böhland, M., Mikut, R.: Cell segmentation and tracking using CNN-based distance predictions and a graph-based matching strategy. PLoS ONE **15**(12), e0243219 (2020)
35. Schiegg, M., Hanslovsky, P., Haubold, C., Koethe, U., Hufnagel, L., Hamprecht, F.A.: Graphical model for joint segmentation and tracking of multiple dividing cells. Bioinformatics **31**(6), 948–956 (2015)
36. Schiegg, M., Hanslovsky, P., Kausler, B.X., Hufnagel, L., Hamprecht, F.A.: Conservation tracking. In: IEEE International Conference on Computer Vision (ICCV), pp. 2928–2935 (2013)
37. Sixta, T., Cao, J., Seebach, J., Schnittler, H., Flach, B.: Coupling cell detection and tracking by temporal feedback. Mach. Vis. Appl. **31**(4), 1–18 (2020). https://doi.org/10.1007/s00138-020-01072-7
38. Spilger, R., Imle, A., Lee, J.Y., Mueller, B., Fackler, O.T., Bartenschlager, R., Rohr, K.: A recurrent neural network for particle tracking in microscopy images using future information, track hypotheses, and multiple detections. IEEE Trans. Image Process. **29**, 3681–3694 (2020)
39. Ulman, V., et al.: An objective comparison of cell-tracking algorithms. Nat. Methods **14**(12), 1141–1152 (2017)
40. Veličković, P., Cucurull, G., Casanova, A., Romero, A., Liò, P., Bengio, Y.: Graph attention networks. In: International Conference on Learning Representations (ICLR) (2018)
41. Wang, J., Su, X., Zhao, L., Zhang, J.: Deep reinforcement learning for data association in cell tracking. Front. Bioeng. Biotechnol. **8**, 298 (2020)
42. Wang, X., Han, X., Huang, W., Dong, D., Scott, M.R.: Multi-similarity loss with general pair weighting for deep metric learning. In: IEEE Conference on Computer Vision and Pattern Recognition (CVPR), pp. 5022–5030 (2019)
43. Weng, X., Wang, Y., Man, Y., Kitani, K.M.: Gnn3dmot: graph neural network for 3d multi-object tracking with 2d–3d multi-feature learning. In: IEEE Conference on Computer Vision and Pattern Recognition (CVPR), pp. 6499–6508 (2020)

CXR Segmentation by AdaIN-Based Domain Adaptation and Knowledge Distillation

Yujin Oh[ID] and Jong Chul Ye[(✉)][ID]

Kim Jaechul Graduate School of AI, Korea Advanced Institute of Science and Technology (KAIST), Daejeon, South Korea
jong.ye@kaist.ac.kr

Abstract. As segmentation labels are scarce, extensive researches have been conducted to train segmentation networks with domain adaptation, semi-supervised or self-supervised learning techniques to utilize abundant unlabeled dataset. However, these approaches appear different from each other, so it is not clear how these approaches can be combined for better performance. Inspired by recent multi-domain image translation approaches, here we propose a novel segmentation framework using adaptive instance normalization (AdaIN), so that a single generator is trained to perform both domain adaptation and semi-supervised segmentation tasks via knowledge distillation by simply changing task-specific AdaIN codes. Specifically, our framework is designed to deal with difficult situations in chest X-ray radiograph (CXR) segmentation, where labels are only available for normal data, but the trained model should be applied to both normal and abnormal data. The proposed network demonstrates great generalizability under domain shift and achieves the state-of-the-art performance for abnormal CXR segmentation.

Keywords: Chest X-ray · Segmentation · Domain adaptation · Knowledge distillation · Self-supervised learning

1 Introduction

High-accuracy image segmentation often serves as the first step in various medical image analysis tasks [6,16]. Recently, deep learning (DL) approaches have become the state-of-the-art (SOTA) techniques for medical image segmentation tasks thanks to their superior performance compared to the classical methods [6].

The performance of DL-based segmentation algorithm usually depends on large amount of labels, but segmentation masks are scarce due to expensive and

---

Supplementary Information The online version contains supplementary material available at https://doi.org/10.1007/978-3-031-19803-8_37.

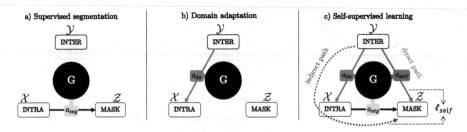

Fig. 1. Overview of the proposed unified framework. A single generator G transfers domains by simply changing task-specific AdaIN codes a_{seg}, a_{da} and a_{self} for each supervised segmentation, domain adaptation and self-supervised learning task, respectively

time-consuming annotation procedures. Another difficulty in DL-based segmentation is the so-called domain shift, i.e., a segmentation network trained with data in a specific domain often undergoes drastic performance degradation when applied to unseen test domains.

For example, in the field of chest X-ray radiograph (CXR) analysis [2], segmentation networks trained with normal CXR data often produce under-segmentation when applied to abnormal CXRs with severe infectious diseases such as viral or bacterial pneumonia [14,21]. The missed regions from under-segmentation mostly contain crucial features, such as pulmonary consolidations or ground-glass opacity, for classifying the infectious diseases. Thus, highly-accurate lung segmentation results without under-segmentation are required to guarantee that DL-based classification algorithms fully learn crucial lung features, while alleviating irrelevant factors outside the lung to prevent shortcut learning [7].

To solve the label scarcity and domain shift problems, there have been extensive researches to train segmentation networks in a semi-supervised manner using limited training labels, or in a self-supervised or unsupervised manner even without labeled dataset [1,3,13,15,17,22,23,25]. However, these approaches appear different from each other, and there exist no consensus in regard to how these different approaches can be synergistically combined. Inspired by success of Star-GANv2 for transferring style between various domains [4], here we propose a style transfer-based knowledge distillation framework that can synergistically combine supervised segmentation, domain adaptation and self-supervised knowledge distillation tasks to improve unsupervised segmentation performance. Specifically, our framework is designed to deal with difficult but often encountered situations where segmentation masks are only available for normal data, but the trained method should be applied to both normal and abnormal images.

The key idea is that a single generator trained along with the adaptive instance normalization (AdaIN) [9] can perform supervised segmentation as well as domain adaptation between normal and abnormal domains by simply changing the AdaIN codes, as shown in Fig. 1a and b, respectively. The network is also trained in a self-supervised manner using another AdaIN code in order to force direct segmentation results (illustrated as a red arrow in Fig. 1c) to be matched to indirect segmentation results through domain adaptation and subsequent segmentation (illustrated as a blue arrow in Fig. 1c). Since a single generator is used for all these tasks, the network can synergistically learn common features from different dataset through knowledge distillation.

To validate the concept of the proposed framework, we train our network using labeled normal CXR dataset and unlabeled pneumonia CXR dataset, and test the model performance on unseen dataset composed of COVID-19 pneumonia CXRs [11,21]. We further evaluate the network performance on domain-shifted CXR datasets for both normal and abnormal cases, and compared the results with other SOTA techniques. Experimental results confirm that our method has great promise in providing robust segmentation results for both in-domain and out-of-domain dataset. We release our source code[1] for being utilized in various CXR analysis tasks presented in Supplementary Section S1.

2   Related Works

To make this paper self-contained, here we review several existing works that are necessary to understand our method.

Image Style Transfer. The aim of the image style transfer is to convert a content image into a certain stylized image. Currently, two types of approaches are often used for image style transfer.

First, when a pair of content image and a reference style image is given, the goal is to convert the content image to imitate the reference style. For example, the adaptive instance normalization (AdaIN) has been proposed as a simple but powerful method [9] for image style transfer. Specifically, AdaIN layers of a network estimate means and variance of the given reference style features and use the learned parameters to adjust those of the content image.

On the other hand, unsupervised style transfer approaches such as Cycle-GAN [26] learn target reference style distribution rather than individual style given a single image. Unfortunately, the CycleGAN approach requires $N(N-1)$ generators to translate between N domains. To deal with this, multi-domain image translation approaches have been proposed. In particular, StarGANv2 [4] introduces an advanced single generator-based framework, which transfers styles over multiple domains by training domain-specific style codes of AdaIN.

Semi and Self-supervised Learning. For medical image segmentation, a DL-based model trained with labeled dataset in a specific domain (e.g. normal CXR)

---

[1] https://github.com/yjoh12/CXR-Segmentation-by-AdaIN-based-Domain-Adaptation-and-Knowledge-Distillation.git.

is often needed to be refined for different domain dataset in semi-supervised, self-supervised or unsupervised manners [3,13,15,17,22,23,25]. These approaches try to take advantage of learned features from a specific domain to generate pseudo-labels or distillate the learned knowledge to another domain.

Specifically, Tang et al. [22] applies a semi-supervised learning approach by generating pseudo CXRs via an image-to-image style transfer framework, and achieves improved segmentation performance by training a segmentation network with both labeled and pseudo-labeled dataset.

Self-supervised learning approaches can also bring large improvements in image segmentation tasks, by promoting consistency between model outputs given a same input with different perturbations or by training auxiliary proxy tasks [13,15,25]. In general, DL models trained with auxiliary self-consistency losses are proven to achieve better generalization capability as well as better primary task performance, especially when training with abundant unlabeled dataset.

Teacher-Student Approaches. Teacher-student approaches can be utilized for semi or self-supervised learning framework. These methods consist of two individual networks, i.e., a student and a teacher model. The student model is trained in a supervised manner, as well as in a self-supervised manner which enforces the student model outputs to be consistent with outputs from the teacher model [13,17,23].

Specifically, Li et al. [13] introduce a dual-teacher framework on segmentation task, which consists of two teacher models: a traditional teacher model for transferring intra-domain knowledge and an additional teacher model for transferring inter-domain knowledge. To leverage inter-domain dataset, images from different domain are firstly style-transferred as pseudo-images using CycleGAN [26]. Then the student network is trained to predict consistent outputs with those of the inter-domain teacher given the style-transferred images, so that the acquired inter-doamin knowledge can be integrated into the student network.

3   Methods

3.1   Key Idea

One of the unique features of StarGANv2 [4] is that it can synergistically learn common features across multiple image domains via shared layers to fully utilize all different datasets, but still allow domain-specific style transfer using different style codes. Inspired by this idea, our framework adapts AdaIN layers to perform style transfer between normal and abnormal domains and further utilizes an additional style code for self-supervised learning.

Specifically, our framework categorizes the training data into three distinct groups: the segmentation mask [MASK], their matched input image domain [INTRA], and domain-shifted input images with no segmentation labels [INTER]. Due to the domain shift between [INTRA] and [INTER] domains, a network trained in a supervised manner using only [INTRA] dataset does not generalize well for [INTER] domain. To mitigate this problem, we propose a single generator to perform supervised segmentation (see Fig. 1a) as well as domain adaptation between [INTRA] and [INTER] domains using different AdaIN codes (see Fig. 1b).

Similar to the existing teacher-student approaches, we then introduce a self-consistency loss between different model outputs given learned task-specific AdaIN codes. The teacher network considers the indirect segmentation through domain adaptation followed by segmentation (indicated as the blue arrow in Fig. 1c), and the student network considers the direct segmentation (indicated as the red arrow in Fig. 1c). The network is trained in a self-supervised manner that enforces the direct segmentation results to be consistent with the indirect segmentation results, so that unlabeled domain images can be directly segmented. This enables knowledge distillation from learned segmentation and domain adaptation tasks to the self-supervised segmentation task.

Once the network is trained, only a single generator and pre-built AdaIN codes can be simply utilized at the inference phase, which makes the proposed method more practical.

3.2 Overall Framework

Overall architecture of our network is shown in Fig. 2, which is composed of a single generator G, AdaIN code generators for the encoder and decoder, F_e and F_d, respectively, a style encoder S, and a multi-head discriminator D.

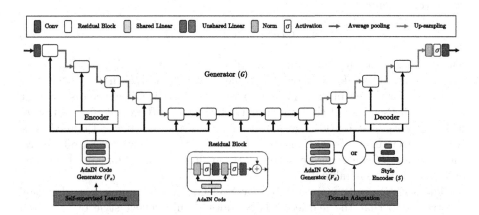

Fig. 2. The architecture of generator connected to two AdaIN code generators and a style encoder. The codes generated from either AdaIN code generators or the style encoder are connected to AdaIN layers of each residual block

The generator G is composed of encoder and decoder modules. Specifically, the encoder part is composed of four downsampling residual blocks and two

intermediate residual blocks. The decoder part is composed of two intermediate
residual blocks and four up-sampling residual blocks. Each residual block is composed of AdaIN layers, activation layers, and convolution layers. All the AdaIN
layers are connected to the code generators F_e and F_d, and the style encoder S is
also connected to the decoder module. Detailed network specification is provided
in Supplementary Section S2.

One of key ideas of our framework is introducing independent code generators
F_e and F_d to each encoder and decoder module. Thanks to the two separate code
generators, the generator G can perform segmentation, domain adaptation and
self-supervised learning tasks, by simply changing combinations of the AdaIN
codes, as shown in Table 1.

Table 1. AdaIN codes combination for three different tasks

AdaIN codes.	Task	F_e (mean, var)	F_d (mean, var)	Training type
a_{seg}	[INTRA] → [MASK]	(0, 1)	(0, 1)	Segmentation
a'_{seg}	[INTRA] → [MASK]	(0, 1)	Learnable	Dummy segmentation code
a_{da}^X	[INTER] → [INTRA]	(0, 1)	Learnable	Domain adaptation
a_{da}^Y	[INTRA] → [INTER]	(0, 1)	Learnable	Domain adaptation
a_{self}	[INTER] → [MASK]	Learnable	(0, 1)	Self-supervised

Specifically, let $\mathcal{X}, \mathcal{Y}$ and $\mathcal{Z}$ refer to the [INTRA], [INTER] and [MASK]
domains associated with the probability distribution P_X, P_Y and P_Z. Then, our
generator is defined by

$$v = G(u, a), \quad a := (F_e, F_d) \tag{1}$$

where u is the input image either in $\mathcal{X}$ or $\mathcal{Y}$, $a \in \{a_{seg}, a'_{seg}, a_{da}^X, a_{da}^Y, a_{self}\}$
refers the AdaIN code, as shown in Table 1, and F_e and F_d indicate the code
generators for the encoder and the decoder, respectively. Given the task-specific
code a, AdaIN layers of the generator G efficiently shift weight distribution to
desirable style distribution, by adjusting means and variances. Detailed style
transfer mechanism of AdaIN is provided in Supplementary Section S3. Hence,
the generator G can generate output v either in $\mathcal{X}, \mathcal{Y}$, or $\mathcal{Z}$ domain, depending
on different codes combination.

The style encoder is introduced by StyleGANv2 to impose an additional
constraint, so that the learned AdaIN codes should reflect style of the given
reference images [4]. In our framework, the style encoder S encodes the generated
output into a code for imposing code-level cycle-consistency. Another role of the
style encoder S is to generate reference-guided codes given reference images.
By alternatively generating codes using the style encoder S or the AdaIN code
generator F_d, as illustrated as the *or* module in Fig. 2, the learned codes can be
regularized to reflect the reference styles.

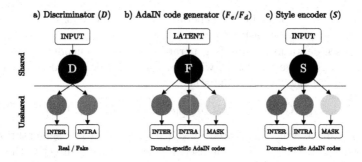

Fig. 3. Multi-head structure of a) Discriminator, b) AdaIN code generator, and c) Style encoder. Each module is composed of shared layers and domain-specific layers

The discriminator D is composed of shared convolution layers followed by multi-headed unshared convolution layers for each image domain, as shown in Fig. 3a. In the discriminator, the input image can be classified as 1 or 0 for each domain separately, where 1 indicates real and 0 indicates fake. The AdaIN code generator and the style encoder are also composed of shared layers followed by domain-specific unshared layers, as shown in Fig. 3b and c. Thanks to the existence of the shared layers, learned features from a specific domain can be shared with other domains, improving overall performance of each module.

In the following, we provide more detailed description how this network can be trained.

3.3   Neural Network Training

Our training losses are extended from traditional style transfer framework, with specific modification to include the segmentation and the self-supervised learning tasks. The details are as follows.

Supervised Segmentation. This part is a unique contribution of our work compared to traditional style transfer methods. Figure 1a shows the supervised segmentation, which can be considered as conversion from $\mathcal{X}$ to $\mathcal{Z}$. In this case, the generator is trained by the following:

$$\min_{G,F_d,S} \lambda_{seg}\ell_{seg}(G) + \lambda_{style}\ell_{style}(G, F_d, S), \qquad (2)$$

where λ_{seg} and λ_{style} are hyper-parameters, and the segmentation loss ℓ_{seg} is defined by the cross-entropy loss between generated output and its matched label:

$$\ell_{seg}(G) = -\mathbb{E}_{x\sim P_X}\left[z_i \log p_i(G(x, a_{seg}))\right], \qquad (3)$$

where z_i denotes the i-th pixel of the ground truth segmentation mask $z \in \mathcal{Z}$ with respect to the input image $x \in \mathcal{X}$, $p_i(G)$ denotes the softmax probability function of the i-th pixel in the generated image, and $G(x, a_{seg})$ denotes the supervised segmentation task output.

Once a segmentation result is generated, the style encoder S encodes the generated image to be consistent with the dummy AdaIN code a'_{seg}. This can be achieved by using the following style loss:

$$\ell_{style}(G, F_d, S) = \mathbb{E}_{x \sim P_X} \left[\|a'_{seg} - S(G(x, a_{seg}))\|_1 \right], \tag{4}$$

where a'_{seg} can be either generated by $F_d(z)$ or $S(z)$, given segmentation mask $z \in \mathcal{Z}$. Although this code is not used for segmentation directly, the generation of this dummy AdaIN code turns out to be important to train the shared layers in the AdaIN code generator and the style encoder. We analyzed contribution of different losses for the supervised segmentation task, as analyzed in Supplementary Section S4.

Domain Adaptation. Figure 1b shows the training scheme for the domain adaptation between $\mathcal{X}$ and $\mathcal{Y}$. The training of domain adaptation solves the following optimization problem:

$$\min_{G, F_e, F_d, S} \max_D \ell_{da}(G, F_e, F_d, S, D). \tag{5}$$

The role of Eq. 5 is to train the generator G to synthesize style-transfered images given domain-specific AdaIN codes a_{da}, while fooling the discriminator D. As this step basically follows traditional style transfer methods, the detailed domain adaptation loss is deferred to Supplementary Section S5.

Self-supervised Learning. This part is another unique contribution of our work. The goal of the self-supervised learning is to directly transfer an unlabeled image in $\mathcal{Y}$ to segmentation mask $\mathcal{Z}$, illustrated as the red arrow in Fig. 1c.

Specifically, since [INTER] domain $\mathcal{Y}$ lacks segmentation mask, knowledge learned from both the supervised learning and domain adaptation need to be distilled. Thus, our contribution comes from introducing novel constraints: (1) the direct segmentation outputs trained in a self-supervised manner, illustrated as the red arrow in Fig. 1c should be consistent with indirect segmentation outputs, illustrated as the blue arrow in Fig. 1c. (2) At the inference phase, it is often difficult to know which domain the input comes from. Therefore, a single AdaIN code should deal with both [INTRA] and [INTER] domain image segmentation. This leads to the following self-consistency loss:

$$\ell_{self}(G, F_e) \tag{6}$$

$$= \lambda_{inter} \ell_{inter}(G, F_e) + \lambda_{intra} \ell_{intra}(G, F_e) \tag{7}$$

$$= \mathbb{E}_{y \sim P_Y} \left[\|G(G(y, a_{da}^T), a_{seg}) - G(y, a_{self})\|_1 \right] \tag{8}$$

$$+ \mathbb{E}_{x \sim P_X} \left[\|G(x, a_{self}) - G(x, a_{seg})\|_1 \right], \tag{9}$$

where ℓ_{inter} and ℓ_{intra} denote inter-domain and intra-domain self-consistency loss, respectively, and λ_{inter} and λ_{intra} are hyper-parameters for each. The role of Eq. (8) is for emposing the constraint (1), and Eq. (9) is for emposing the constraint (2).

In fact, this procedure can be regarded as a teacher-student approach. The indirect path is a teacher network that guides the training procedure of the direct path, which regards the student network. In contrast to the existing teacher-student approaches [13,17,23], our approach does not need two separate networks: instead, the single generator with different AdaIN codes combinations can be served as the teacher or the student network, which is another big advantage of our method.

4 Experiments

4.1 Experimental Settings

Dataset. For training the supervised segmentation task, normal CXRs were acquired from JSRT dataset [20] with their paired lung segmentation labels from SCR dataset [24]. For training domain adaptation task, we collected pneumonia CXRs from RSNA [8] and Cohen dataset [5]. Detailed dataset information is described in Table 2.

Table 2. Chest X-ray dataset resources

Domain	Dataset	Label	Disease class	Bit	View	Total	Train	Val	Test	DS level	
										Weak	Harsh
Labeled train set	JSRT	O	Normal, Nodule	12	PA	247	178	20	49	–	
Unlabeled train set	RSNA	–	PN (COVID-19)	10	AP	218	218	–	–	–	
	Cohen et al.	–	PN (COVID-19, Viral, Bacterial, TB)	8	PA, AP	680	640	–	40	–	
External testset	NLM	O	Normal	8	PA	80	–	–	80	80	80
	BIMCV-13	O	PN (COVID-19)	16	PA, AP	13	–	–	13	13	13
	BIMCV	–	PN (COVID-19)	16	AP	374	–	–	374	–	–
	BRIXIA	–	PN (COVID-19)	16	AP	2384	–	–	2384	–	–

Note: PN, pneumonia; TB, tuberculosis; DS level, distribution shift level.

To test the proposed network performance on external datasets, we utilized three external resources. For normal CXR segmentation evaluation, NLM dataset with paired lung labels were utilized [12]. For abnormal CXR segmentation evaluation, BIMCV dataset [11] and BRIXIA dataset [21] were utilized. Besides, additional 13 CXRs from the BIMCV dataset (indicated as BIMCV-13), with labeled consolidation or ground glass opacities features by radiologists, were utilized for quantitative evaluation of abnormal CXRs segmentation.

For further analyzing the model performance on domain-shifted conditions, external labeled dataset were prepared with three different levels of modulation, defined as distribution shift level. *None*-level indicates original inputs. *Weak*-and *Harsh*-level indicate intensity and contrast modulated inputs with random scaling factors within ±30% and ±60% range, followed by addition of Gaussian noise with standard deviation of 0.5 and 1, respectively.

All the input CXRs and labels are resized to 256 × 256. We did not perform any pre-processing or data augmentation except for normalization of pixel intensity range to [−1,0, 1.0].

Implementation Details. The proposed network was trained by feeding input images from a pair of two randomly chosen domains: one for the source domain and the other for the target domain. For example, if a domain pair composed of [INTER] and [INTRA] domains fed into the network, the network was trained for the domain adaptation task. When a domain pair, composed of [INTRA] as source and [MASK] as target domain, fed into the network, the network was trained for the supervised segmentation task. For self-supervised learning, an image from [INTER] domain, as well as from [INTRA], was fed as the source domain to output the segmentation mask. Implementation details for training the proposed network are provided in Supplementary Section S6.

For the domain adaptation task, we utilized CycleGAN [26], MUNIT [10] and StarGANv2 [4] as baseline models for comparative studies. For the segmentation task, we utilized U-Net [18] as a baseline model. All the baseline models were trained with identical conditions to that of the proposed model. To evaluate unified performance of the domain adaptation task and the segmentation task, we utilized available models for performing abnormal CXR segmentation, i.e., XLSor [22] and lungVAE [19]. Implementation details for all the comparative models are provided in Supplementary Section S7.

Evaluation Metric. For normal CXRs, quantitative segmentation performance of both lungs was evaluated using dice similarity score (Dice) index. The abnormal CXR segmentation performance was evaluated quantitatively using true positive ratio (TPR) of the annotated abnormalities labels. Moreover, for unlabeled abnormal dataset, domain adaptation and segmentation performance were qualitatively evaluated based on generation of expected lung structure covered with highly-consolidated regions.

4.2   Results

Unified Domain Adaptation and Segmentation. The unified performance was evaluated on the internal test set. We defined our model trained with segmentation loss (Eq. (2)) and domain adaptation loss (Eq. (5)) as *Proposed*, and the model trained with additional self-consistency loss (Eq. (6)) as *Proposed+ℓ_{self}*. As shown in Fig. 4a, compared to CycleGAN and MUNIT, *Proposed* model utilizing StarGANv2 framework successfully transferred highly consolidated regions in abnormal CXRs into normal lungs.

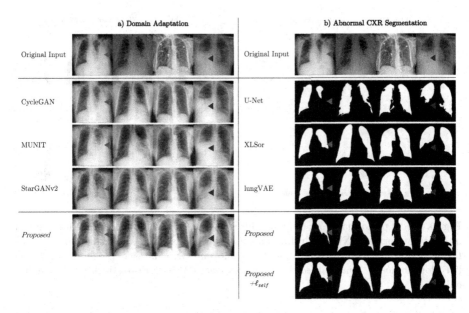

Fig. 4. The network performance on the internal test set. a) Domain adaptation performance comparison with traditional style transfer methods. b) Segmentation performance comparison. Red and blue triangles indicate highly consolidated lung regions in CXRs (Color figure online)

Abnormal CXR segmentation results are presented in Fig. 4b. All the comparative models failed to segment highly consolidated lung regions, indicated as red and blue triangles. Note that *Proposed* and *Proposed+ℓ_{self}* models were the only methods that successfully segmented abnormal lungs as like normal lungs.

Quantitative Evaluation on Domain-Shifted External Dataset. For quantitative evaluation, we utilized labeled dataset for both normal and abnormal CXRs (NLM and BIMCV-13, respectively). To verify that the proposed methods could still retain segmentation performance on domain-shifted dataset, we further tested the model performance on distribution modulated inputs (*Weak-* and *Harsh*-level) for both normal and abnormal dataset.

As illustrated in Fig. 5a, *Proposed* model successfully adapted shifted distribution of lung area intensity to be similar to the train set distribution. Thanks to the successful domain adaptation performance, both *Proposed* and *Proposed+ℓ_{self}* models maintained robust segmentation performance compared to other models, as distribution gap increases (see blue bar plots of Fig. 5b and c).

Specifically, as reported in Table 3, for the abnormal CXR segmentation task, all the models showed promising performance by achieving TPR of around 0.90 for the original (*None*-level) inputs, illustrated as black bar plots in Fig. 5c. However, XLSor and lungVAE performance drastically dropped to around 0.60

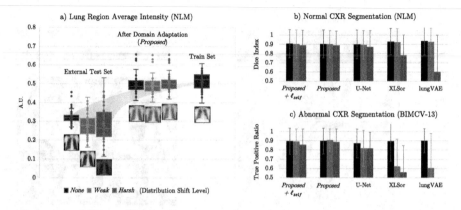

Fig. 5. Model performance on domain-shifted inputs. a) Box plot of average lung region intensity of normal CXRs with different distribution shift levels. Bar plots of segmentation performance on b) Normal, and c) Abnormal CXR dataset. Black, red and blue bal plots indicate *None*-, *Weak*- and *Harsh*-level dataset, respectively (Color figure online)

for *Weak*-level inputs, while *Proposed* model performance rather improved, as illustrated in red bar plots. For *Harsh*-level inputs, lung structures were only correctly segmented by *Proposed* and *Proposed+ℓ_{self}* models with above 0.85 of TPR, as illustrated in blue bar plots.

Corresponding segmentation contours are also presented in Fig. 6. The qualitative segmentation performance was surprising since artificial perturbation, which seemed tolerable for human eye, brought strong performance degradation to the existing DL-based algorithms. Specifically, for abnormal CXR segmentation, all the comparative UDS/Self methods (XLSor and lungVAE) failed to be generalized to several out-of-distribution cases from *Harsh*-level inputs (see Fig. 6b). The UDS/Self methods have no additional domain adaptation process, but the networks themselves are trained with augmented data distribution, e.g., images added with random noise or pseudo-pneumonia images. The degraded performance indicates that the above data augmentation techniques are still limited to be generalized to way-shifted data distribution. U-Net with or without style-transfer based pre-processing (CycleGAN or StarGANv2), rather endured harsh-distribution shift, however, lung contours showed irregular shapes with rough boundary. On the other hand, *Proposed* and *Proposed+ℓ_{self}* models showed stable segmentation performance on majority of domain-shifted cases. In particular, *Proposed+ℓ_{self}* model showed most promising performance, with the least over-segmentation artifact for both normal and abnormal datasets.

Qualitative Evaluation on COVID-19 Dataset. For evaluating the model performance on real-world dataset, we utilized COVID-19 pneumonia dataset (BIMCV and BRIXIA), which are obtained from more than 12 hospitals. Figure 7 presents qualitative results of abnormal CXR segmentation on COVID-

Table 3. Segmentation performance on external test set

Method	Normal CXR (Dice Index)			Abnormal CXR (True Positive Ratio)		
	Distribution Shift Level			Distribution Shift Level		
	None	*Weak*	*Harsh*	*None*	*Weak*	*Harsh*
SS						
U-Net [18]	0.90 ± 0.15	0.89 ± 0.16	0.87 ± 0.18	0.87 ± 0.16	0.82 ± 0.20	0.82 ± 0.18
DA+SS						
CycleGAN [26]+U-Net	0.89 ± 0.17	0.89 ± 0.17	0.86 ± 0.18	0.88 ± 0.17	0.84 ± 0.22	0.85 ± 0.17
StarGANv2 [4]+U-Net	**0.90 ± 0.15**	**0.90 ± 0.15**	0.88 ± 0.15	**0.90 ± 0.13**	0.90 ± 0.12	0.88 ± 0.16
Proposed	**0.90 ± 0.01**	**0.90 ± 0.14**	**0.89 ± 0.15**	**0.90 ± 0.14**	**0.91 ± 0.12**	**0.89 ± 0.14**
UDS/Self						
XLSor [22]	0.93 ± 0.14	0.92 ± 0.15	0.78 ± 0.22	**0.90 ± 0.22**	0.62 ± 0.30	0.56 ± 0.29
lungVAE [19]	**0.94 ± 0.15**	**0.93 ± 0.15**	0.60 ± 0.40	**0.90 ± 0.13**	0.61 ± 0.38	0.10 ± 0.26
Proposed+ℓ_{self}	0.91 ± 0.15	0.90 ± 0.15	**0.89 ± 0.16**	**0.90 ± 0.14**	**0.89 ± 0.14**	**0.86 ± 0.17**

Note: SS, supervised segmentation; DA, domain adaptation; UDS, unified DA+SS; Self, self-supervised segmentation.

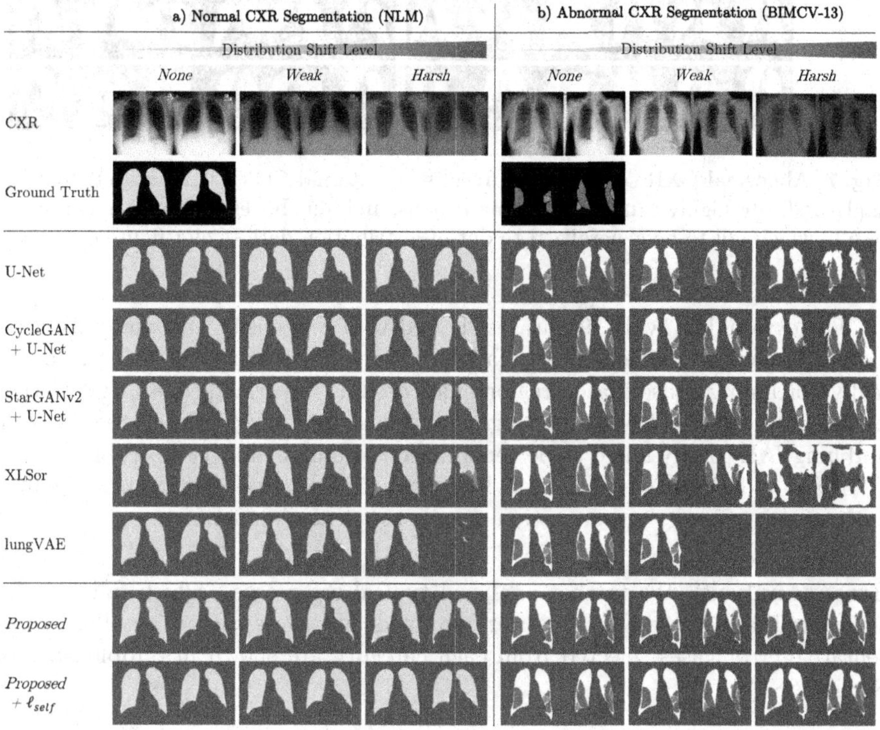

Fig. 6. Qualitative segmentation performance for a) Normal CXRs, and b) Abnormal CXRs. Green ground truth masks indicates lung labels, red and blue masks indicate consolidation and ground-glass opacity labels, respectively (Color figure online)

19 pneumonia dataset. Representative cases were randomly selected from each dataset.

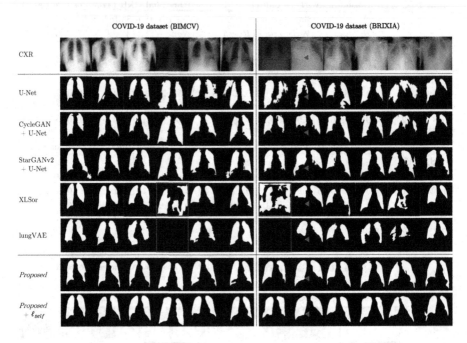

Fig. 7. Abnormal CXR segmentation results on external COVID-19 dataset. Red triangles indicate highly consolidated lung regions, and blue boxes indicate segmentation results which fail to be generalized to out-of-distribution data (Color figure online)

The external COVID-19 dataset showed varied intensity and noise distribution. Comparative models mostly failed to segment regular lung shapes. Specifically, for highly consolidated regions indicated as red triangles, all the existing models were suffered from under-segmentation artifacts. For several cases, XLSor and lungVAE totally failed to be generalized to domain-shift issues (blue boxes). *Proposed* and *Proposed+ℓ_{self}* models showed reliable segmentation performance without severe under-segmentation or over-segmentation artifacts.

Error Analysis. We further analyzed typical error cases, which failed to be segmented, and the error cases were grouped into three categories. The representative error cases selected from each category are shown in Supplementary Section S8.

5   Conclusions

We present a novel framework, which can perform segmentation, domain adaptation and self-supervised learning tasks within a single generator in a cost-effective manner (see Supplementary Section S9). The proposed network can fully leverage knowledge learned from each task by utilizing shared network parameters, thus the model performance can be synergistically improved via knowledge distillation between multiple tasks, so that achieves SOTA performance on the unsupervised abnormal CXR segmentation task. The experimental results demonstrate that the proposed unified framework can solve domain shift issues with great generalizability, even on dataset with way-shifted distribution. Last but not the least, the proposed model does not need any pre-processing techniques but shows superior domain adaptation performance, which presents a promising direction to solve the generalization problem of DL-based segmentation methods.

Acknowledgement. This research was supported by the Korea Medical Device Development Fund grant funded by the Korea government (the Ministry of Science and ICT, the Ministry of Trade, Industry and Energy, the Ministry of Health & Welfare, the Ministry of Food and Drug Safety) (Project Number: 1711137899, KMDF_PR_20 200901_0015), the MSIT (Ministry of Science and ICT), Korea, under the ITRC (Information Technology Research Center) support program(IITP-2022-2020-0-01461) supervised by the IITP (Institute for Information & communications Technology Planning & Evaluation), the National Research Foundation of Korea under Grant NRF-2020R1A2B5B03001980, and the Field-oriented Technology Development Project for Customs Administration through National Research Foundation of Korea (NRF) funded by the Ministry of Science & ICT and Korea Customs Service (NRF-2021M3I1A1097938).

References

1. Bai, W., et al.: Semi-supervised learning for network-based cardiac MR image segmentation. In: Descoteaux, M., Maier-Hein, L., Franz, A., Jannin, P., Collins, D.L., Duchesne, S. (eds.) MICCAI 2017. LNCS, vol. 10434, pp. 253–260. Springer, Cham (2017). https://doi.org/10.1007/978-3-319-66185-8_29
2. Çallı, E., Sogancioglu, E., van Ginneken, B., van Leeuwen, K.G., Murphy, K.: Deep learning for chest x-ray analysis: a survey. Med. Image Anal. **72**, 102125 (2021)
3. Chen, C., Dou, Q., Chen, H., Qin, J., Heng, P.A.: Unsupervised bidirectional cross-modality adaptation via deeply synergistic image and feature alignment for medical image segmentation. IEEE Trans. Med. Imaging **39**(7), 2494–2505 (2020)
4. Choi, Y., Uh, Y., Yoo, J., Ha, J.W.: Stargan v2: diverse image synthesis for multiple domains. In: Proceedings of the IEEE/CVF Conference on Computer Vision and Pattern Recognition, pp. 8188–8197 (2020)
5. Cohen, J.P., Morrison, P., Dao, L.: COVID-19 image data collection. arXiv preprint arXiv:2003.11597 (2020). https://github.com/ieee8023/covid-chestxray-dataset
6. de Fauw, J., et al.: Clinically applicable deep learning for diagnosis and referral in retinal disease. Nat. Med. **24**(9), 1342–1350 (2018)
7. DeGrave, A.J., Janizek, J.D., Lee, S.I.: AI for radiographic COVID-19 detection selects shortcuts over signal. Nature Machine Intelligence **3**(7), 610–619 (2021)
8. Desai, S., et al.: Chest imaging representing a COVID-19 positive rural us population. Scientific data **7**(1), 1–6 (2020)

9. Huang, X., Belongie, S.: Arbitrary style transfer in real-time with adaptive instance normalization. In: Proceedings of the IEEE International Conference on Computer Vision, pp. 1501–1510 (2017)

10. Huang, X., Liu, M.-Y., Belongie, S., Kautz, J.: Multimodal unsupervised image-to-image translation. In: Ferrari, V., Hebert, M., Sminchisescu, C., Weiss, Y. (eds.) ECCV 2018. LNCS, vol. 11207, pp. 179–196. Springer, Cham (2018). https://doi.org/10.1007/978-3-030-01219-9_11

11. de la Iglesia Vayá, M., et al.: Bimcv covid-19+: a large annotated dataset of RX and CT images from COVID-19 patients (2020)

12. Jaeger, S., Candemir, S., Antani, S., Wáng, Y.X.J., Lu, P.X., Thoma, G.: Two public chest X-ray datasets for computer-aided screening of pulmonary diseases. Quant. Imaging Med. Surg. **4**(6), 475 (2014)

13. Li, X., Yu, L., Chen, H., Fu, C.W., Xing, L., Heng, P.A.: Transformation-consistent self-ensembling model for semisupervised medical image segmentation. In: IEEE Transactions on Neural Networks and Learning Systems (2020)

14. Oh, Y., Park, S., Ye, J.C.: Deep learning COVID-19 features on CXR using limited training data sets. IEEE Trans. Med. Imaging **39**(8), 2688–2700 (2020). https://doi.org/10.1109/TMI.2020.2993291

15. Orbes-Arteaga, M., et al.: Multi-domain adaptation in brain MRI through paired consistency and adversarial learning. In: Wang, Q., et al. (eds.) DART/MIL3ID -2019. LNCS, vol. 11795, pp. 54–62. Springer, Cham (2019). https://doi.org/10.1007/978-3-030-33391-1_7

16. Ouyang, X., et al.: Dual-sampling attention network for diagnosis of COVID-19 from community acquired pneumonia. IEEE Trans. Med. Imaging **39**(8), 2595–2605 (2020)

17. Perone, C.S., Ballester, P., Barros, R.C., Cohen-Adad, J.: Unsupervised domain adaptation for medical imaging segmentation with self-ensembling. Neuroimage **194**, 1–11 (2019)

18. Ronneberger, O., Fischer, P., Brox, T.: U-Net: convolutional networks for biomedical image segmentation. In: Navab, N., Hornegger, J., Wells, W.M., Frangi, A.F. (eds.) MICCAI 2015. LNCS, vol. 9351, pp. 234–241. Springer, Cham (2015). https://doi.org/10.1007/978-3-319-24574-4_28

19. Selvan, R., et al.: Lung segmentation from chest X-rays using variational data imputation (2020)

20. Shiraishi, J., et al.: Development of a digital image database for chest radiographs with and without a lung nodule. Am. J. Roentgenol. **174**(1), 71–74 (2000). https://doi.org/10.2214/ajr.174.1.1740071

21. Signoroni, A., et al.: BS-Net: learning COVID-19 pneumonia severity on a large chest X-ray dataset. Med. Image Anal. **71**, 102046 (2021)

22. Tang, Y.B., Tang, Y.X., Xiao, J., Summers, R.M.: XLsor: a robust and accurate lung segmentor on chest x-rays using criss-cross attention and customized radorealistic abnormalities generation. In: International Conference on Medical Imaging with Deep Learning, pp. 457–467. PMLR (2019)

23. Tarvainen, A., Valpola, H.: Mean teachers are better role models: weight-averaged consistency targets improve semi-supervised deep learning results. arXiv preprint arXiv:1703.01780 (2017)

24. Van Ginneken, B., Stegmann, M.B., Loog, M.: Segmentation of anatomical structures in chest radiographs using supervised methods: a comparative study on a public database. Med. Image Anal. **10**(1), 19–40 (2006)

25. Xue, Y., Feng, S., Zhang, Y., Zhang, X., Wang, Y.: Dual-task self-supervision for cross-modality domain adaptation. In: Martel, A.L., et al. (eds.) MICCAI 2020. LNCS, vol. 12261, pp. 408–417. Springer, Cham (2020). https://doi.org/10.1007/978-3-030-59710-8_40
26. Zhu, J.Y., Park, T., Isola, P., Efros, A.A.: Unpaired image-to-image translation using cycle-consistent adversarial networks. In: Proceedings of the IEEE International Conference on Computer Vision (ICCV) (2017)

Accurate Detection of Proteins in Cryo-Electron Tomograms from Sparse Labels

Qinwen Huang[iD], Ye Zhou[iD], Hsuan-Fu Liu[iD], and Alberto Bartesaghi[(✉)][iD]

Duke University, Durham, NC 27708, USA
{qinwen.huang,ye.zhou867,hl325,alberto.bartesaghi}@duke.edu

Abstract. Cryo-electron tomography (CET) combined with sub-volume averaging (SVA), is currently the only imaging technique capable of de-termining the structure of proteins imaged inside cells at molecular reso-lution. To obtain high-resolution reconstructions, sub-volumes containing randomly distributed copies of the protein of interest need be identified, extracted and subjected to SVA, making accurate particle detection a critical step in the CET processing pipeline. Classical template-based methods have high false-positive rates due to the very low signal-to-noise ratios (SNR) typical of CET volumes, while more recent neural-network based detection algorithms require extensive labeling, are very slow to train and can take days to run. To address these issues, we propose a novel particle detection framework that uses positive-unlabeled learning and exploits the unique properties of 3D tomograms to improve detec-tion performance. Our end-to-end framework is able to identify particles within minutes when trained using a single partially labeled tomogram. We conducted extensive validation experiments on two challenging CET datasets representing different experimental conditions, and observed more than 10% improvement in mAP and F1 scores compared to existing particle picking methods used in CET. Ultimately, the proposed framework will facilitate the structural analysis of challenging biomedical targets imaged within the native environment of cells.

Keywords: Cryo-Electron Microscopy · Cryo-electron tomography · 3D detection · Positive-unlabeled training · Contrastive learning

1 Introduction

Cryo-electron tomography (CET) combined with sub-volume averaging (SVA) is currently the only imaging technique capable of determining the structure

Supplementary Information The online version contains supplementary material available at https://doi.org/10.1007/978-3-031-19803-8_38.

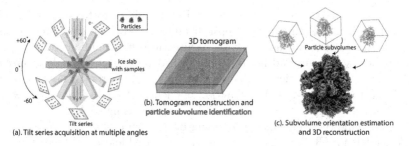

Fig. 1. Overall processing pipeline for CET. (a) Projections of the protein sample are acquired at different angles by rotating the microscope stage using small tilt increments. (b) The acquired tilt-series are aligned and used to reconstruct 3D tomograms containing a few hundred sub-volumes which are identified and extracted. (c) Orientations of each extracted sub-volume are estimated followed by averaging to obtain the final high-resolution 3D reconstruction.

of proteins imaged inside cells at molecular resolution [8]. Bypassing the need for protein purification, CET allows determination of protein structures within their native context while also providing information on their distribution and partner interactions. Unlike cryo-EM single particle analysis (SPA) that requires sample purification and collects 2D projections of particles [2], CET can recover 3D information from proteins by recording a series of 2D images as the biological sample is rotated around a tilt axis (Fig. 1). The sequence of 2D images, termed a *tilt-series*, is then aligned and used to calculate a 3D tomographic reconstruction or *tomogram* of the sample. A typical CET dataset usually contains between tens to a few hundred tomograms and each tomogram contains a few hundred copies of the same protein of interest. To obtain a single high-resolution structure, tens of thousands of sub-volumes containing randomly oriented and distributed copies of the protein of interest first need to be detected within tomograms in a process commonly referred to as *particle picking*. Sub-volumes are then extracted, aligned and combined in 3D using SVA, making the detection task critical for the downstream data processing. The low signal-to-noise ratios (SNR) characteristic of CET images, caused in part by the limited electron doses used during acquisition to prevent radiation damage of the biological samples, makes particle localization very challenging. High false-positive rates can prevent successful 3D reconstruction altogether due to the presence of confounding sub-volumes corresponding to noise, while high true-positive rates are desirable as they can lead to better denoising performance and increased resolution of the final reconstruction. For 2D SPA data, fully-supervised and semi-supervised learning-based particle picking methods can achieve good results due to the higher SNRs and availability of large annotated datasets [14]. In contrast, training of deep learning-based 3D CET particle picking algorithms remains impractical due to: (1) the lack of enough annotated CET datasets caused by the time consuming nature of doing manual labeling of 3D tomograms, and (2) the challenges imposed by the intrinsically lower SNR of tomographic projections and the effects caused by molecular

crowding in native cellular environments. Recent efforts to tackle particle picking from CET tomograms using deep-learning only work on simulated datasets
with full annotation, and use network architectures with millions of parameters
that take days to train and hours to perform detection on a single tomogram,
making their use impractical in real applications [11]. Currently, particle picking
from CET tomograms remains a major bottleneck that has slowed down the
reconstruction of high-resolution protein structures using SVA.

To overcome the challenges in training deep learning-based particle identification models for CET, we propose a semi-supervised learning-based framework
that only requires a few annotations on a single tomogram. The proposed method
can be trained within minutes, which makes it suitable for a data-specific model.
Specifically, our approach uses a positive unlabeled learning-based center localization module, allowing us to leverage information from both annotated and
unlabeled data, effectively removing the burden of doing full data annotation.
To enable better feature representation learning, we adopt a voxel-level contrastive learning module. The proposed module exploits both supervised and
self-supervised contrastive learning and improves learned features. To validate
our approach, we carried out extensive experiments on two challenging CET
datasets acquired under different SNR conditions. We show that our method is
able to outperform existing methods, while requiring smaller amounts of training
data (less than 0.5% of the total data) and being time-efficient (under 10 min).

To summarize, the main contributions of this paper are:

1. We propose a 3D particle detection framework that achieves high localization
   accuracy with only a few annotations. The framework consists of two modules:
   (1) a positive unlabeled learning-based particle center localization module,
   and (2) a debiased voxel-level contrastive learning module. Both modules
   leverage information from annotated and unannotated data.
2. To the best of our knowledge, our work is the first to enable protein identification of hundreds of tomograms within minutes (training time included).
3. Through extensive experiments, we demonstrate that our framework is robust
   and performs well, even under the challenging SNR conditions of CET.

2   Related Work

Object Detection and Applications in Cryo-Electron Microscopy (EM). Neural
network based object detection algorithms have been applied and shown promising results in various fields ranging from photography to medical imaging. Existing object detection approaches can be broadly divided into two categories:
anchor-based and anchor-free. Representative examples of anchor-based methods
include faster R-CNN [26], a region-based two-stage object detector, and YOLO
[25] and SSD [21], which are one-stage object detectors. To address problems
with class imbalance, the use of a focal loss term was proposed in [20]. Building on top of anchor-based methods, anchor-free methods were later introduced.

This category includes FCOS [31], which performs per-pixel bounding box prediction, and CenterNet [36], which predicts bounding box location by estimating its center coordinates. Following the success of object detection algorithms based on neural networks, there have been multiple CNN-based particle picking algorithms for 2D cryo-EM SPA [1,13,23], including Topaz [3], a positive-unlabeled learning-based algorithm that learns to identify particles by minimizing both the supervised classification loss and the divergence between estimated empirical distribution and prior distribution; and crYOLO [32], a YOLO-based fully supervised particle detector. In contrast, there is very limited work on particle identification from 3D CET tomograms, where the most commonly used particle detection method is template matching [28]. Examples include recently proposed 3D-CNN based methods [11,22,34], and concurrent work, DeepPict [30], that uses a 2D-CNN for segmentation and a 3D-CNN for particle localization. These methods all require a large amount of annotated data and long training time.

Positive Unlabeled Learning. PU learning can be broadly generalized into two categories: (1) two-step techniques that first identify reliable negative examples and learn based on labeled positives and reliable negatives; (2) class prior incorporation. The two-step techniques are similar to the teacher-student model that have been widely adopted in semi-supervised learning [16,27,33]. Class prior information can be incorporated in two ways: (1) the expected distribution of the classified unlabeled data should match the known prior distribution (this is a form of posterior regularization called GE criteria [9] and this approach is adopted by [3]), and (2) unbiased PU learning, where the unlabeled data is used as negatives while being properly down-weighted [18,24]. Based on unbiased PU learning, debiased instance level contrastive learning that takes sampling bias into account was also proposed [7].

Contrastive Representation Learning. The goal of contrastive learning is to learn an embedding space in which similar sample pairs are close to each other while dissimilar pairs are far apart. Our proposed contrastive learning utilizes the InfoNCE loss, which has been adopted by many self-supervised contrastive learning frameworks such as simCLR [5] and MoCo [12]. In most self-supervised contrastive learning frameworks, heavy data augmentation, large batch size and hard negative sampling are crucial components. More recently, supervised contrastive learning [17] using InfoNCE was proposed and shown to be a generalization of triplet loss and N-pair loss. In addition to image-wise contrastive learning, there are pixel-wise contrastive learning frameworks used for image segmentation [4,35]. In our case, instead of using contrastive learning as a pre-training framework, we use it as a regularization component to the detection task.

3 Methodology

We first introduce the problem formulation of semi-supervised protein localization in crowded CET volumes and some special characteristics of CET data. We then give an overview of our proposed framework, which consists of two modules: positive unlabeled learning-based protein center localization, and voxel-level

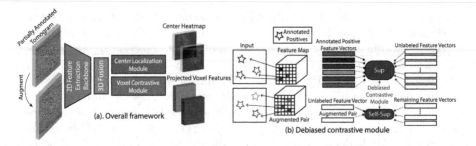

Fig. 2. (Left) Proposed framework for 3D protein detection. We use a combination of 2D and 3D convolutional layers. The 2D CNN-based feature extractor follows a encoder-decoder architecture. The feature extractor is applied to each slice of the tomogram. The extracted features are then fused together through 3D convolutional layers. The fused 3D features are used for: (1) center coordinate heatmap prediction, and (2) voxel-level contrastive learning. During inference, only the heatmap is used for particle identification. **(Right) Voxel-level debiased contrastive learning module.** For illustration purposes, we use a 2D image with stars in different orientations. These stars represent naturally augmented positive pairs. Feature vectors at the star locations encode information about the location of the objects and the feature vectors serve as input to our contrastive learning module.

debiased contrastive feature learning. A detailed description of each module is then given. Finally, we present the overall training objective.

3.1   Characteristics of CET Volumes

There are two important properties of CET tomograms, apart from their low SNR nature (Fig. 3). First, due to the use of limited tilt angle ranges, the reconstructed tomograms contain a "missing-wedge" of information that distorts particle images due to lack of full orientation information. This distortion is especially obvious from the $Y - Z$ view of the data which is perpendicular to the specimen plane. Second, there is data recurrence within each tomogram since a single tomogram usually contains up to a few hundred sub-volumes of the protein-of-interest. These copies are all present in different relative orientations (with respect to the missing wedge) and are distorted in different ways. Our particle detection technique leverages these unique properties of CET datasets.

3.2   Problem Formulation

The aim of semi-supervised protein localization in CET volumes is to obtain a model that is able to detect locations of proteins-of-interest in 3D tomograms, by learning from just a few annotated examples. A typical CET dataset $\mathcal{D}$ contains j tomograms $\{T_i \in R^{W \times H \times D}, i = 1, ..., j\}$, with j ranging from tens to a few hundreds. A single tomogram T_i is scattered with a few hundreds to thousands of proteins. In

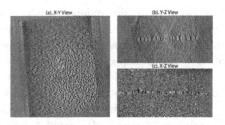

Fig. 3. An example CET slice from all three views. X-Y view provides most amount of useful information for particle identification.

the semi-supervised protein identification setting, in order to reduce the labor of manual labeling, the training set $\mathcal{D}_{tr}$ includes one tomogram T_{tr} with a few proteins annotated. The remaining tomograms are used as testing set $\mathcal{D}_{te}$. Unlike standard object detection algorithms which aim to produce bounding box locations of objects-of-interest, in most cryo-EM applications, center coordinates of proteins are the desired outputs for the particle detection task. Therefore, instead of outputting bounding box locations and sizes, inspired by [36], we aim to train the particle detector using $\mathcal{D}_{tr}$ to produce a center point heatmap $\hat{Y} \in [0,1]^{C \times \frac{W}{R_1} \times \frac{H}{R_1} \times \frac{D}{R_2}}$ where R_i is the output stride and C is the number of protein species. The output stride downsamples the prediction by a factor R_i on each dimension. We set $C = 1$ as we only consider monodisperse samples and omit the dimension in the following sections. We extend the method used by [19] to generate the ground truth heatmap $Y \in [-1,1]^{\frac{W}{R_1} \times \frac{H}{R_1} \times \frac{D}{R_2}}$ using the partially annotated tomogram. For each annotated center coordinate position $p = (x, y, z)$, its downsampled equivalent is computed as $\tilde{p} = (\lfloor \frac{x}{R_1} \rfloor, \lfloor \frac{y}{R_1} \rfloor, \lfloor \frac{z}{R_2} \rfloor)$. For each $\tilde{p}$ on Y, we apply a Gaussian kernel $K_{xyz} = \exp\left(-\frac{(x-\tilde{p}_x)^2 + (y-\tilde{p}_y)^2 + (z-\tilde{p}_z)^2}{2\sigma_k^2}\right)$ where σ_k is determined by the particle size [19]. The remaining unlabeled coordinates on Y have a value of -1.

3.3   Proposed Approach

Overview. As shown in Fig. 2, our framework is composed of: (a) an encoder-decoder feature extraction backbone, (b) a protein center localization module, and (c) a voxel-level contrastive feature learning module. We used a fully convolutional architecture for the backbone and since the input training tomogram is only partially labeled, we incorporated a positive unlabeled learning-based strategy for both the localization and contrastive learning modules.

Feature Extraction Backbone. Even though the input is a 3D tomogram, our network is composed of mostly 2D convolutional layers. 3D convolutional layers are only applied in the last two layers. Essentially, the network first extracts features of each slice independently and then merges the extracted 2D features into 3D at the final layers. The combination of 2D and 3D layers is inspired by the actual manual particle picking process: to identify a particle, the $X - Y$ view of each slice is inspected most carefully (as it contains no distortions), while the $X - Z$ and $Y - Z$ views only provide very limited information (due to the heavy missing-wedge distortions, Fig. 3). This architecture design has two advantages: first, since 3D information is only considered during the final layers, it can reduce the missing-wedge effect; second, the resulting architecture has fewer parameters than a pure 3D CNN, greatly reducing memory requirements and running time. We provide more details in the supplementary material.

Protein Center Localization Module. For the input tomogram T and its output heatmap $\hat{Y}$, protein localization can be viewed as a per-voxel classification problem such that each voxel $v_{i,j,k}$ at position (i, j, k) is the input and the corresponding $\hat{y}_{i,j,k} \in [0, 1]$ is the classification output.

Positive Negative (PN) Learning: Denote $p(v)$ as the underlying data distribution from which $v_{i,j,k}$ is sampled, $p(v)$ can be decomposed as follows:

$$p(v) = \pi_p p_p(v|y = 1) + \pi_n p_n(v|y = 0) \tag{1}$$

where $p_p(v|y = 1)$ is the positive class conditional probability of protein voxels, $p_n(v|y = 0)$ is the negative class conditional probability of background voxels, and π_p and π_n are the class prior probabilities. Underscripts n, p, u denote negative, positive and unlabeled, respectively. Denote $g : \mathbb{R}^d \to \mathbb{R}$, an arbitrary classifier that can be parameterized by a neural network, $l(g(v) = \hat{y}, y)$ being the loss between model outputs $\hat{y}$ and ground truth y. When all the voxels are labeled, this is essentially a binary classification problem that can be optimized using a standard PN learning approach with the following risk minimization:

$$\tilde{R}_{pn} = \pi_p \tilde{R}_p^+(g) + \pi_n \tilde{R}_n^-(g) \tag{2}$$

where $\tilde{R}_p^+(g)$ is the mean positive loss $\mathbb{E}_{v \sim p_p(v)}[l(g(v^p), y = 1)]$ and can be estimated as $1/n_p \sum_{i=1}^{n_p} l(\hat{y}_p^i, 1)$, $\tilde{R}_n^-(g)$ is the mean negative loss $\mathbb{E}_{v \sim p_n(v)}[l(g(v^n), y = 0)]$ and can be estimated as $1/n_n \sum_{i=1}^{n_n} l(\hat{y}_n^i, 0)$, n_p and n_n are the number of positive and negative voxels.

Positive Unlabeled (PU) Learning: When only a few positive voxels are labeled and the remainder of the data is unlabeled, we re-formulate the problem into the PU setting: the positive labeled voxels are sampled from $p_p(v|y = 1)$ and the remaining unlabeled voxels are sampled from $p(v)$. As shown in [24], by rearranging Eq. 1 and 2, we obtain $\pi_n p_n(v) = p(v) - \pi_p p_p(v)$ and $\pi_n \tilde{R}_n^-(g) = \tilde{R}_u^-(g) - \pi_p \tilde{R}_p^-(g)$. We therefore rewrite the risk minimization as:

$$R_{pu} = \pi_p \tilde{R}_p^+(g) - \pi_p \tilde{R}_p^-(g) + \tilde{R}_u^-(g) \tag{3}$$

with $\tilde{R}_u^-(g) = \mathbb{E}_{v \sim p(v)}[l(g(v), y = 0)]$ and $\tilde{R}_p^-(g) = \mathbb{E}_{v \sim p_p(v)}[l(g(v), y = 0)]$. In order to prevent overfitting in Eq. 3, we adopted the non-negative risk estimation as in [18]:

$$\tilde{R}_{pu} = \pi_p \tilde{R}_p^+(g) + \max\{0, \tilde{R}_u^-(g) - \pi_p \tilde{R}_p^-(g)\} \tag{4}$$

Soft Positives and True Positives: Since the ground-truth heatmap is splatted with Gaussian kernels, the labels are not strictly binary. Positive labels are split into two groups: true positives (tp) where $y_{i,j,k} = 1$, which is the center of each Gaussian kernel (protein center), and soft positives (sp) where $0 < y_{i,j,k} < 1$ (voxels that are close to the center). Unlabeled voxels are labeled as -1. With this, the positive distribution $p_p(v)$ and positive associated losses $\tilde{R}_p^+(g)$, $\tilde{R}_p^-(g)$ are decomposed into:

$$p_p(v) = \pi_{tp} p_{tp}(v|y = 1) + \pi_{sp} p_{sp}(v|0 < y < 1)$$
$$\tilde{R}_p^+(g) = \pi_{tp} \tilde{R}_{tp}^+(g) + \pi_{sp} \tilde{R}_{sp}^+(g), \ \tilde{R}_p^-(g) = \pi_{tp} \tilde{R}_{tp}^-(g) + \pi_{sp} \tilde{R}_{sp}^-(g) \tag{5}$$

We adopt voxel-wise logistic regression with focal loss for $l(g(v), y)$. Specifically, we have:

$$\tilde{R}_{tp}^+(g) = (1 - \hat{y}_{ijk})^\alpha \log(\hat{y}_{ijk}), \ \tilde{R}_{sp}^+(g) = (1 - y_{ijk})^\beta (\hat{y}_{ijk})^\alpha \log(1 - \hat{y}_{ijk})$$
$$\tilde{R}_{tp}^-(g) = \hat{y}_{ijk}^\alpha \log(1 - \hat{y}_{ijk}), \ \tilde{R}_{sp}^-(g) = (y_{ijk})^\beta (1 - \hat{y}_{ijk})^\alpha \log(\hat{y}_{ijk}) \tag{6}$$
$$\tilde{R}_u^-(g) = (\hat{y}_{ijk})^\alpha \log(1 - \hat{y}_{ijk})$$

where α, β are the focal loss parameters and we use $\alpha = 2, \beta = 4$. By combining Eq. 4, 5 and 6, we obtain the final minimization:

$$\tilde{R}_{pu} = \pi_p(\pi_{tp} \tilde{R}_{tp}^+(g) + \pi_{sp} \tilde{R}_{sp}^+(g)) + \max\{0, \tilde{R}_u^-(g) - \pi_p(\pi_{tp} \tilde{R}_{tp}^-(g) + \pi_{sp} \tilde{R}_{sp}^-(g))\} \tag{7}$$

Voxel Level Debiased Contrastive Learning Module. For the input tomogram $T \in \mathbb{R}^{W \times H \times D}$ and its augmented pair $\tilde{T}$, denote the output from the feature extraction backbone as $M \in \mathbb{R}^{Ch \times \frac{W}{R} \times \frac{H}{R} \times \frac{D}{R}}$ and the augmented pair $\tilde{M}$. M and $\tilde{M}$ are used to generate: (1) the output heatmap $\hat{Y}$ and its augmented pair $\tilde{Y}$, and (2) the projected feature map F and $\tilde{F}$. As suggested in [5], instead of using M, it is beneficial to map the representations to a new space through a projection head composed of $1 \times 1 \times 1$ convolutional layer where a contrastive loss is applied. Denote $m_{i,j,k} \in \mathbb{R}^{Ch}$ and $\tilde{m}_{i,j,k}$ as the feature vector at the (i, j, k) position of the feature map M and its augmented counterpart. There exists a total of $\frac{W}{R} \times \frac{H}{R} \times \frac{D}{R} = N$ such vectors. Each of these feature vectors is responsible for predicting $\hat{y}_{i,j,k}$. If $y_{i,j,k} = 1$, $m_{i,j,k}$ and its projection $f_{i,j,k}$ should encode particle-related features. For a partially annotated T, the voxel-level feature vectors f can be separated into positive and unlabeled classes. Therefore, the voxel-level contrastive loss is composed of: (1) positive supervised debiased contrastive, and (2) unlabeled self-supervised debiased contrastive terms.

Positive Supervised Debiased Contrastive Loss: Denote $\mathcal{F}^p = \{f_{i,j,k}^p : y_{i,j,k} = 1\}$ as the set of positive feature vectors obtained from n_p annotated proteins and its augmented counterpart $\tilde{\mathcal{F}}^p = \{\tilde{f}_{i,j,k}^p : \tilde{y}_{i,j,k} = 1\}$, $\mathcal{F}^u = \{f_{i,j,k}^u : y_{i,j,k} < 1\}$ as the set of unlabeled (including the soft positives) feature vectors with a total of n_n.

Since each tomogram contains up to a few hundred sub-volumes of the protein of interest, and each of these sub-volumes are the same protein with different relative orientations and are distorted in different ways, for a feature vector $f_i^p \in \mathcal{F}^p$, the remaining $2n_p - 1$ feature vectors $f_j^p, j = 1, ..., 2n_p - 1$ in $\mathcal{F}^p$ and $\tilde{\mathcal{F}}^p$ can be treated as its naturally augmented pair. Unlabeled feature vectors $f_k^u \in \mathcal{F}^u, k = 1, ..., 2n_n$ which includes the augmented unlabeled features are treated as negatives. However, since the unlabeled set $\mathcal{F}^u$ can contain positive feature vectors, the naive supervised contrastive loss as proposed in [17] will be biased. We therefore adopt a modified debiased supervised contrastive loss based on [7]:

$$\mathcal{L}_{sup}^{db} = \mathbb{E}\left[-\log \left[\frac{1/(2n_p - 1) \sum_{j=1}^{2n_p-1} e^{f_i^{pT} f_j^p}}{1/(2n_p - 1) \sum_{j=1}^{2n_p-1} e^{f_i^{pT} f_j^p} + g_{sup}(f_i^p, \{f_j^p\}_{j=1}^{2n_p-1}, \{f_k^u\}_{k=1}^{2n_n})} \right] \right] \tag{8}$$

where the second term in the denominator is:

$$g_{sup}(\cdot) = \max \left\{ \frac{1}{\pi_n} \left(\frac{1}{2n_n} \sum_{k=1}^{2n_n} e^{f_i^{pT} f_k^u} - \pi_p \frac{1}{2n_p - 1} \sum_{j=1}^{2n_p-1} e^{f_i^{pT} f_j^p} \right), e^{-1/t} \right\} \tag{9}$$

with π_n and π_p being the class prior probabilities and t the temperature.

Unlabeled Self-supervised Debiased Contrastive loss: For the unlabeled feature vector f_k^u, the only known positive is its augmented pair $\tilde{f}_k^u$ and the remaining vectors are treated as negatives. Denote $\{f_l^r\}_{l=1}^{2N-2}$ as the set of remaining vectors. The resulting contrastive loss for an unlabeled feature vector is:

$$\mathcal{L}_{unsup} = \mathbb{E}\left[-\log \left[\frac{e^{f_k^{uT} \tilde{f}_k^u}}{e^{f_k^{uT} \tilde{f}_k^u} + g_{unsup}(f_k^u, \tilde{f}_k^u, \{f_l^r\}_{l=1}^{2N-2})} \right] \right] \tag{10}$$

It should be noted that $g(\cdot)$ involves class prior probabilities, however, the actual class of the unlabeled feature vectors is unknown. Therefore, we used the output probabilities from $\hat{Y}$ and the final unlabeled contrastive loss is calculated as the weighted average based on the probabilities of the feature vector belonging to the positive class:

$$\mathcal{L}_{unsup}^{db} = \hat{Y}\mathcal{L}_{unsup}^p + (1 - \hat{Y})\mathcal{L}_{unsup}^n \tag{11}$$

where for $\mathcal{L}_{unsup}^p$, the denominator $g_{unsup}^p(\cdot)$ is:

$$g_{unsup}^p(\cdot) = \max \left\{ \frac{1}{\pi_n} \left(\frac{1}{2N - 2} \sum_{l=1}^{2N-2} e^{f_k^{uT} f_l^r} - \pi_n e^{f_k^{uT} \tilde{f}_k^u} \right), e^{-1/t} \right\} \tag{12}$$

and for $\mathcal{L}_{unsup}^n$, the denominator $g_{unsup}^n(\cdot)$ is:

$$g_{unsup}^n(\cdot) = \max \left\{ \frac{1}{\pi_p} \left(\frac{1}{2N - 2} \sum_{l=1}^{2N-2} e^{f_k^{uT} f_l^r} - \pi_p e^{f_k^{uT} \tilde{f}_k^u} \right), e^{-1/t} \right\} \tag{13}$$

Overall Training Objective. In addition, we added a consistency regularization loss for the output heatmap $\hat{Y}$ and its augmented version $\tilde{Y}$ such that the probability of a voxel containing a protein should be invariant to augmentations:

$$\mathcal{L}_{cons} = MSE(\hat{Y}, \tilde{Y}) \tag{14}$$

The final training objective is:

$$\mathcal{L} = \tilde{R}_{pu} + \lambda_1(\mathcal{L}_{sup}^{db} + \lambda_2\mathcal{L}_{unsup}^{db}) + \lambda_3\mathcal{L}_{cons} \tag{15}$$

where λ_1 is the weight of the total contrastive module, λ_2 is the weight of the unsupervised contrastive loss, and λ_3 is the weight of consistency regularization. The resulting loss serves two purposes: 1) the contrastive term maximizes similarities for encoded features belonging to the same group (particle and background) and minimizes such similarities if features are from different groups, and 2) the heatmap loss term forces predicted particle probabilities to be higher when they are closer to the true center location. To remove duplicate predictions, non-max suppression is applied to the predicted heatmap using 3D max-pooling.

4   Validation Experiments

We evaluate the performance of our algorithm on two real CET datasets. For each dataset, we evaluated the performance when 5%, 10%, 30%, 50% and 70% of the data from a single tomogram is annotated. We perform ablation studies over the contrastive and positive unlabeled learning components. Performance is measured using mean average precision (mAP) scores calculated against manually labeled particle locations.

4.1   Datasets

We evaluate our method on two publicly available CET datasets from the electron microscopy public image archive (EMPIAR) [14]: EMPIAR-10304 [10] and EMPIAR-10499 [29]. These datasets represent the two most common types of CET biological samples, more details are included in supplementary material.

4.2   Experimental Setup

Implementation Details. We initialize the network using weights obtained from a trained network that identifies whether a slice contains particles. However, random initialization of the network is able to achieve similar performance. During training, instead of using the whole tomogram, we cropped sub-tomograms of size $64 \times 64 \times 5$ as input to the network in batches of 2. Training time is thus independent of input size. Inference is performed on the entire tomogram. The network is implemented with PyTorch and trained/tested on an NVIDIA

Tesla V100 GPU. The proposed framework is trained in an end-to-end manner using Adam optimizer with default parameter values and an initial learning rate of 0.001. We decrease the learning rate by a factor of 10 every 200 iterations. Training takes around 3 to 5 min for 600 iterations and inference on each full tomogram takes less than a second. In all our experiments, we trained the network for 600 iterations. We used experimentally determined values: $\lambda_1 = 0.1$, $\lambda_2 = 0.5$ and $\lambda_1 = 0.1$. For EMPIAR-10304, we used $\pi_p = 0.6$, and $t = 0.07$. For EMPIAR-10499, we used $\pi_p = 0.1$, and $t = 0.02$.

Evaluation Metrics. We use mean average precision (mAP) scores calculated against manually labeled particle locations for evaluation. To account for small variations in the detected particle centers, instead of looking at a single pixel, we also look at pixels located within a certain radius from the center. If the detected particle position is within a certain radius of a ground truth particle position, it is considered as a true positive match. Similarly, if there is no ground truth particle within a certain radius of a detected particle position, it is considered as a false positive. We use radius values of 2 and 5 and denote the corresponding mAP values as mAP_{r2} and mAP_{r5}.

Baseline Methods. We compare our method with one conventional CET particle detection method, template matching, and one recently developed deep learning-based method, crYOLO-3D [32]. Even though there are many available deep-learning based particle picking methods for 2D SPA cryo-EM, there are only a few methods for 3D CET. crYOLO-3D is the only deep learning-based algorithm that is available to use. Template matching is implemented using the EMAN2 package [28]. We use a low-pass filtered ribosome reconstruction as template. Even though crYOLO-3D is termed as "3D" picking, it is really a 2D picking method. For each 3D tomogram input, crYOLO-3D performs per-slice particle detection using a pretrained 2D model. The detected 2D coordinates on each slice are combined into 3D coordinates through a tracking algorithm. The pretrained model is trained using 43 fully labeled datasets with more than 44,000 labeled particles. We use their official software available online[1] and fine tune the pretrained weights with images and labels from our training samples (Note: we had to convert 3D labels to 2D (slice-level) for crYOLO training, and therefore we used 360 annotations for EMPIAR-10304 and 1100 annotations for EMPIAR-10499). For the baseline methods, we are only able to obtain precision and recall values, as their implementation does not output detection scores and we can only select a cut-off threshold. Therefore, for comparing with our framework, we also calculated the corresponding precision-recall score using the same threshold (0.25).

---

[1] https://cryolo.readthedocs.io/en/stable/.

4.3 Results

In Table 2, we show mAP_{r2} and mAP_{r5} scores for both datasets obtained using our approach. We show qualitative visualization of detection results on selected slices of tomograms from each dataset in Fig. 4. To improve particle visibility, we use averages of multiple slices

Table 1. Precision, Recall and F1 scores for our proposed method and baseline methods

Method	EMPIAR 10304			EMPIAR 10499		
	Precision	Recall	F1	Precision	Recall	F1
5%	80.4	59.2	68.2	49.6	58.1	53.5
10%	81.8	53.6	64.7	50.1	58.2	53.8
30%	79.5	76.5	78.0	55.9	60.3	58.0
50%	83.8	72.1	77.5	53.0	65.1	58.4
70%	82.3	77.6	80.0	54.9	66.7	60.2
crYOLO	47.6	14.6	22.4	47.8	56.8	52.0
EMAN2	58.9	65.5	62.0	26.1	55.3	35.5

instead of a single slice. Our method is able to outperform the two baseline methods by a significant margin, as shown in Table 1. We also show that when trained only using a very small amount of annotated data (5% and 10%), our approach is still able to obtain satisfactory results. When more annotations are available for training, performance improves (especially from 5% to 30%). Template matching from EMAN2 tends to pick up more false positives and is less accurate in identifying the true center of the particle. It tends to miss more particles when SNR is lower. While crYOLO-3D is more robust to noise compared to template matching, it still results in many missed particles. In addition, it performs poorly on the extremely crowded dataset (EMPIAR-10304) even though the SNR is much higher. This is because crYOLO-3D is actually a 2D particle detector. Instead of processing the entire tomogram as one 3D volume, the inputs are individual 2D slices: it performs particle detection on each slice first. The 2D coordinate outputs on each slice are then merged in the post-processing step (multi-slice tracing) into 3D coordinates. During the merging step, the actual 3D tomogram is not used, only the 2D coordinates are used as inputs to the post-processing step. When particles are crowded, tracing fails and the subsequent detection also fails. Since our algorithm uses the whole 3D tomogram as input, we are able to avoid these problems. Our method is also able to avoid contamination areas, as features corresponding to these areas are learned to be distinct from features characteristic of true particles.

In terms of running time and level of annotation, template matching takes 2–5 min and a template is required. When a template is not available, a Gaussian blob is used, which results in even higher false positive rates. crYOLO-3D takes a total of 30–40 min to run including model fine-tuning. Our proposed method takes 5–10 min to run and requires a minimum of 20–50 labeled particles.

Ablation Studies. To evaluate the effectiveness of our proposed method we perform ablations studies on: (1) voxel-level contrastive learning module, and (2) positive unlabeled learning in two modules. For (1), we remove the proposed voxel-level contrastive module and the corresponding term in the loss function.

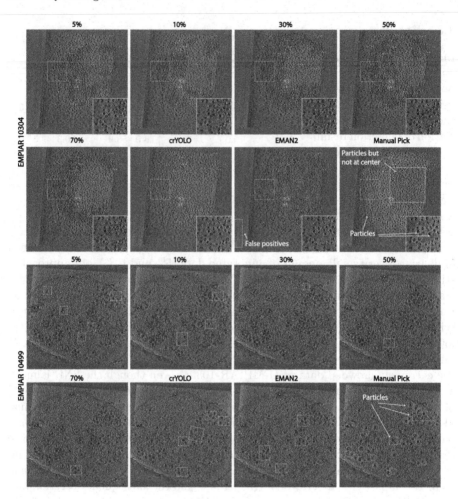

Fig. 4. Detection results on selected tomograhic slices from EMPIAR-10304 and EMPIAR-10499. Top two rows: Slice averages from tomograms of EMPIAR-10304. Zoomed-in views are provided at the bottom right. Bottom two rows: Slices averages from tomograms of EMPIAR-10499. We show detected particles trained using 5%, 10%, 30%, 50% and 70% of particles annotated on a single tomogram. We also show particle detection results using crYOLO-3D and EMAN2. Our method is able to detect more particles with highere precision. As more data annotation is available, detection performance increases (especially from 5% to 50%). EMAN2 tends to pick up more false positives. Note that manual picked results are not necessarily ground truth, as it is possible to miss several particles during manual picking (as shown). We highlighted several missed particles regions in light yellow.

As shown in Table 2, without this module, the performance degrades, especially under lower SNR scenarios. This shows that our proposed module improves the feature learning of input tomograms and in turn facilitates the detection

Table 2. Particle detection results obtained using different levels of annotations available for training. *First row*: mAP scores for our proposed method with both positive unlabeled center localization module and debiased voxel-level contrastive learning module. *Second row*: mAP scores for our proposed method without the contrastive learning module. *Third row*: Our proposed method without positive unlabeled learning and debiased contrastive learning.

mAP	EMPIAR-10304									
	5%		10%		30%		50%		70%	
	r5	r2	r5	r2	r5	r2	r5	r2	r5	r2
Ours	**54.5**	**44.0**	**57.0**	**45.2**	**67.9**	**56.8**	**71.5**	**62.0**	**72.1**	**62.5**
Ours no CR	53.0	42.1	54.1	43.2	65.1	55.7	67.5	58.1	65.8	57.4
Ours no PU	32.2	14.1	38.3	22.9	41.5	15.4	40.2	20.0	41.1	23.1
mAP	EMPIAR-10499									
	5%		10%		30%		50%		70%	
	r5	r2	r5	r2	r5	r2	r5	r2	r5	r2
Ours	**31.1**	**22.0**	**33.2**	**22.4**	**40.1**	**29.8**	**41.3**	**30.2**	**42.5**	**31.3**
Ours no CR	24.2	14.1	24.3	14.2	33.9	24.0	31.8	19.1	34.5	24.1
Ours no PU	11.4	2.1	9.4	1.7	16.2	4.1	14.8	3.5	20.0	9.2

of particles when only limited amount of training samples are provided. In (2), for the center localization module, we treat all unlabeled regions as negatives and adopted a standard focal loss as in [36]; for the contrastive module, we adopted a combination of supervised contrastive loss as in [17] for labeled regions and self-supervised InfoNCE for unlabeled regions. As shown in Table 2, the detection outcome decreases significantly without positive unlabeled learning, which implies the importance of debiasing when there is lack of annotated data. We also evaluated the effect of feature extraction backbone choices on detection outcomes. For this, we looked at: (1) 2D convolution vs. 3D convolution, and (2) depth of the network. For (1), even though for volumetric data 3D convolution-based architectures are more commonly used [6,15], due to the unique properties of CET data and the lack of training data, we experimentally found out that full 3D convolution-based architectures (3D ResNet and UNet) failed to learn any useful information, which is why we did not include their corresponding results in this section. For (2), as objects-of-interest in CET are small, increasing the depth of networks (which increases the receptive field size) can actually worsen performance. We include more details in the supplementary material.

Limitations. The main limitation of our proposed method is the necessary knowledge of the class prior probabilities π. For crowded samples like EMPIAR-10304, if we use a very small positive prior such as 0.1, the trained model tends to produce more false negatives. On the contrary, for less crowded samples like EMPIAR-10499, if we use a large positive prior, more false positives get identified. Therefore, a reliable estimation of π is required. Such estimation can be obtained by visually inspecting the tomogram when doing annotations. In addition, the performance of our method is limited under very low SNR levels.

5   Conclusion

We propose a novel 3D particle detection framework that enables accurate localization of proteins from CET datasets within minutes when trained using a small amount of labeled data. By leveraging the internal data statistics of CET tomograms, we design a novel architecture for 3D particle identification that incorporates positive unlabeled and contrastive learning. Extensive experiments demonstrate that our proposed framework achieves superior performance on real cryo-ET datasets compared to previous methods. The proposed framework will expedite the current cryo-ET data processing pipeline and facilitate the structural analysis of challenging biomedical targets imaged within cells.

Acknowledgments. This study utilized the computational resources offered by Duke Research Computing (https://rc.duke.edu/). We thank C. Kneifel, K. Kilroy, M. Newton, V. Orlikowski, T. Milledge and D. Lane from the Duke Office of Information Technology and Research Computing for providing assistance with the computing environment. This work was supported by a Visual Proteomics Imaging grant from the Chan Zuckerberg Initiative (CZI) to AB.

References

1. Al-Azzawi, A., Ouadou, A., Tanner, J.J., Cheng, J.: Autocryopicker: an unsupervised learning approach for fully automated single particle picking in cryo-EM images. BMC Bioinformatics **20**(1), 1–26 (2019)
2. Bendory, T., Bartesaghi, A., Singer, A.: Single-particle cryo-electron microscopy: mathematical theory, computational challenges, and opportunities. IEEE Sig. Process. Mag. **37**(2), 58–76 (2020). https://doi.org/10.1109/MSP.2019.2957822
3. Bepler, T., Morin, A., Noble, A.J., Brasch, J., Shapiro, L., Berger, B.: Positive-unlabeled convolutional neural networks for particle picking in cryo-electron micrographs. Nat. Methods **16**, 1–8 (2019)
4. Chaitanya, K., Erdil, E., Karani, N., Konukoglu, E.: Contrastive learning of global and local features for medical image segmentation with limited annotations. arXiv abs/2006.10511 (2020)
5. Chen, T., Kornblith, S., Norouzi, M., Hinton, G.E.: A simple framework for contrastive learning of visual representations. arXiv abs/2002.05709 (2020)
6. Chen, W., Liu, B., Peng, S., Sun, J., Qiao, X.: S3D-UNet: separable 3D U-net for brain tumor segmentation. In: Crimi, A., Bakas, S., Kuijf, H., Keyvan, F., Reyes, M., van Walsum, T. (eds.) BrainLes 2018. LNCS, vol. 11384, pp. 358–368. Springer, Cham (2019). https://doi.org/10.1007/978-3-030-11726-9_32
7. Chuang, C.Y., Robinson, J., Lin, Y.C., Torralba, A., Jegelka, S.: Debiased contrastive learning. arXiv (2020)
8. Doerr, A.: Cryo-electron tomography. Nat. Methods **14**(1), 34–34 (2017). https://doi.org/10.1038/nmeth.4115

9. Druck, G., Mann, G.S., McCallum, A.: Learning from labeled features using generalized expectation criteria. In: SIGIR'08 (2008)
10. Eisenstein, F., Danev, R., Pilhofer, M.: Improved applicability and robustness of fast cryo-electron tomography data acquisition. J. Struct. Biol. **208**(2), 107–114 (2019). https://doi.org/10.1016/j.jsb.2019.08.006
11. Gubins, I., et al.: SHREC 2021: Classification in cryo-electron tomograms (2021)
12. He, K., Fan, H., Wu, Y., Xie, S., Girshick, R.B.: Momentum contrast for unsupervised visual representation learning. In: 2020 IEEE/CVF Conference on Computer Vision and Pattern Recognition (CVPR), pp. 9726–9735 (2020)
13. Huang, Q., Zhou, Y., Liu, H.F., Bartesaghi, A.: Weakly supervised learning for joint image denoising and protein localization in cryo-electron microscopy. In: 2022 IEEE/CVF Winter Conference on Applications of Computer Vision (WACV), pp. 3260–3269 (2022)
14. Iudin, A., Korir, P.K., Salavert-Torres, J., Kleywegt, G.J., Patwardhan, A.: EMPIAR: a public archive for raw electron microscopy image data. Nat. Methods **13**, 387–388 (2016)
15. Jin, Q., Meng, Z.P., Sun, C., Wei, L., Su, R.: RA-UNeT: A hybrid deep attention-aware network to extract liver and tumor in CT scans. Front. Bioeng. Biotechnol. **8**, 1471 (2020)
16. Ke, Z., Wang, D., Yan, Q., Ren, J.S.J., Lau, R.W.H.: Dual student: Breaking the limits of the teacher in semi-supervised learning. In: 2019 IEEE/CVF International Conference on Computer Vision (ICCV), pp. 6727–6735 (2019)
17. Khosla, P., et al.: Supervised contrastive learning. arXiv abs/2004.11362 (2020)
18. Kiryo, R., Niu, G., du Plessis, M.C., Sugiyama, M.: Positive-unlabeled learning with non-negative risk estimator. arXiv (2017)
19. Law, H., Deng, J.: Cornernet: Detecting objects as paired keypoints. arXiv abs/1808.01244 (2018)
20. Lin, T.Y., Goyal, P., Girshick, R.B., He, K., Dollár, P.: Focal loss for dense object detection. IEEE Trans. Pattern Anal. Mach. Intell. **42**, 318–327 (2020)
21. Liu, W., et al.: SSD: single shot multibox detector. In: Leibe, B., Matas, J., Sebe, N., Welling, M. (eds.) ECCV 2016. LNCS, vol. 9905, pp. 21–37. Springer, Cham (2016). https://doi.org/10.1007/978-3-319-46448-0_2
22. Moebel, E., et al.: Deep learning improves macromolecule identification in 3D cellular cryo-electron tomograms. Nat. Methods (2021)
23. Nguyen, N.P., Ersoy, I., Gotberg, J., et al.: DRPnet: automated particle picking in cryo-electron micrographs using deep regression. BMC Bioinf. **22**, 55 (2021). https://doi.org/10.1186/s12859-020-03948-x
24. du Plessis, M.C., Niu, G., Sugiyama, M.: Analysis of learning from positive and unlabeled data. In: NIPS (2014)
25. Redmon, J., Divvala, S.K., Girshick, R.B., Farhadi, A.: You only look once: unified, real-time object detection. In: 2016 IEEE Conference on Computer Vision and Pattern Recognition (CVPR), pp. 779–788 (2016)
26. Ren, S., He, K., Girshick, R.B., Sun, J.: Faster r-cnn: Towards real-time object detection with region proposal networks. IEEE Trans. Pattern Anal. Mach. Intell. **39**, 1137–1149 (2015)
27. Sohn, K., Zhang, Z., Li, C.L., Zhang, H., Lee, C.Y., Pfister, T.: A simple semi-supervised learning framework for object detection. arXiv (2020)
28. Tang, G., et al.: Eman2: an extensible image processing suite for electron microscopy. J. Struct. Biol. **157**(1), 38–46 (2007)

29. Tegunov, D., Xue, L., Dienemann, C., Cramer, P., Mahamid, J.: Multi-particle cryo-em refinement with m visualizes ribosome-antibiotic complex at 3.5 å in cells. Nat. Methods **18**, 186–193 (2021)
30. de Teresa, I., et al.: Convolutional networks for supervised mining of molecular patterns within cellular context. bioRxiv (2022)
31. Tian, Z., Shen, C., Chen, H., He, T.: Fcos: fully convolutional one-stage object detection. In: 2019 IEEE/CVF International Conference on Computer Vision (ICCV), pp. 9626–9635 (2019)
32. Wagner, T., et al.: SPHIRE-crYOLO is a fast and accurate fully automated particle picker for cryo-EM. Commun. Biol. **2**(1), 218 (2019)
33. Xu, M., et al.: End-to-end semi-supervised object detection with soft teacher. In: 2021 IEEE/CVF International Conference on Computer Vision (ICCV), pp. 3040–3049 (2021)
34. Zeng, X., Kahng, A., Xue, L., Mahamid, J., Chang, Y.W., Xu, M.: Disca: high-throughput cryo-et structural pattern mining by deep unsupervised clustering. bioRxiv (2021)
35. Zhao, X., et al.: Contrastive learning for label-efficient semantic segmentation. arXiv abs/2012.06985 (2020)
36. Zhou, X., Wang, D., Krähenbühl, P.: Objects as points. arXiv abs/1904.07850 (2019)

k-SALSA: k-Anonymous Synthetic Averaging of Retinal Images via Local Style Alignment

Minkyu Jeon[1,2] , Hyeonjin Park[5], Hyunwoo J. Kim[2(✉)] ,
Michael Morley[3,4(✉)] , and Hyunghoon Cho[1(✉)]

[1] Broad Institute of MIT and Harvard, Cambridge, MA, USA
{mjeon,hhcho}@broadinstitute.org
[2] Korea University, Seoul, Republic of Korea
hyunwoojkim@korea.ac.kr
[3] Harvard Medical School, Boston, MA, USA
[4] Ophthalmic Consultants of Boston, Boston, MA, USA
mgmorley@eyeboston.com
[5] NAVER CLOVA, Seoul, Republic of Korea
hyeonjin.park.ml@navercorp.com

Abstract. The application of modern machine learning to retinal image analyses offers valuable insights into a broad range of human health conditions beyond ophthalmic diseases. Additionally, data sharing is key to fully realizing the potential of machine learning models by providing a rich and diverse collection of training data. However, the personally-identifying nature of retinal images, encompassing the unique vascular structure of each individual, often prevents this data from being shared openly. While prior works have explored image de-identification strategies based on synthetic averaging of images in other domains (e.g. facial images), existing techniques face difficulty in preserving both privacy and clinical utility in retinal images, as we demonstrate in our work. We therefore introduce k-SALSA, a generative adversarial network (GAN)-based framework for synthesizing retinal fundus images that summarize a given private dataset while satisfying the privacy notion of k-anonymity. k-SALSA brings together state-of-the-art techniques for training and inverting GANs to achieve practical performance on retinal images. Furthermore, k-SALSA leverages a new technique, called local style alignment, to generate a synthetic average that maximizes the retention of fine-grain visual patterns in the source images, thus improving the clinical utility of the generated images. On two benchmark datasets of diabetic retinopathy (EyePACS and APTOS), we demonstrate our improvement upon existing methods with respect to image fidelity, classification performance, and mitigation of membership inference attacks. Our work represents a step toward broader sharing of retinal images for scientific collaboration. Code is available at https://github.com/hcholab/k-salsa.

H. Park—This work was performed while the author was at Korea University.

Supplementary Information The online version contains supplementary material available at https://doi.org/10.1007/978-3-031-19803-8_39.

Keywords: Medical image privacy · k-anonymity · Generative
adversarial networks · Fundus imaging · Synthetic data generation ·
Style transfer

1   Introduction

Retinal imaging is a fast, non-invasive, and cost-effective platform to study a
range of systemic diseases, e.g. cardiovascular and neurological disorders [46].
Recent advances in machine learning (ML) are accelerating this transformation, equipping researchers with tools to recognize clinically relevant biomarkers
across diverse imaging modalities, such as fundus imaging and optical coherence
tomography (OCT). Studies have demonstrated the effectiveness of deep learning
models in predicting clinical traits such as cardiovascular risk factors as well as
other health-related information such as age, sex, and smoking status [26,36,49].

However, privacy concerns prevent the sharing of retinal images, presenting a
hurdle for ML in ophthalmology [43,44]. Despite not being legally recognized as
a biometric identifier in certain cases (e.g. HIPAA [45]), retinal images are widely
regarded as sensitive because they include individual-specific patterns like blood
vessel structure [28]. Reflecting these concerns, medical institutions have begun
to refrain from using retinal images in grand rounds, lectures, and publications,
leading to difficulties in research and education. We aim to tackle these challenges
by transforming retinal images to protect privacy while preserving clinical utility.

To this end, a seminal work by Newton et al. [33] on face de-identification
introduced a class of techniques known as the "k-Same" algorithms, wherein
mutually disjoint clusters of k images in the dataset are individually replaced
with a single representative synthetic image that summarizes the visual characteristics of the images in each cluster. This naturally leads to a synthetic dataset
satisfying the classical privacy notion of k-anonymity [41], which requires that
each data instance in the released dataset cannot be distinguished among at least
k underlying individuals. k-anonymity has been widely considered in the medical
literature as a meaningful privacy notion and has been used as a core principle
in real-world systems and polices [10,12,19]. Furthermore, recent successes of
generative adversarial networks (GANs) [13,15] in synthesizing realistic images
in diverse domains suggest a promising approach for generating high-quality representatives of individual clusters by taking an average of images in the latent
embedding space of a GAN, also known as the k-Same-Net algorithm [30].

Despite the promise of these approaches, several key challenges remain
in applying these methods to retinal images. First, while several works have
explored the use of GANs to generate synthetic retinal images [4–7,34], none
to our knowledge have addressed the problem of effectively summarizing these
images in the latent space, making the feasibility of this approach for retinal
images an unknown. Next, the difficulty of capturing fine-grain visual patterns of
retinal images (e.g. hemorrhages or lipid deposits) poses an additional challenge
in preserving the clinical utility of these images. Finally, because k-anonymity
does not directly imply privacy (individual images could potentially be inferred

from the average), a direct evaluation of privacy offered by k-anonymity in the context of retinal images is needed before these tools may be used in practice [35].

To address these challenges, we developed k-SALSA, an end-to-end pipeline for synthesizing a k-anonymous dataset given a private dataset of retinal images. We modernize the approach of k-Same-Net to use state-of-the-art techniques for training and inverting GANs. This allows us to map the source images to an embedding space, "average" them, and generate a representative synthetic image. We improve upon the existing methodology of taking the Euclidean average of embedding vectors by introducing a new technique called *local style alignment*, which aims to maximize the retention of local texture information from the source images. This ensures that the output keeps clinically relevant features.

We evaluate our pipeline on two benchmark datasets (APTOS and EyePACS) and demonstrate the enhanced visual fidelity of the synthetic images generated by our approach with respect to the Fréchet inception distance [18], a standard quality metric for synthetic images. We also show that the synthetic dataset generated by our approach enables accurate training of downstream classifiers for predicting varying degrees of diabetic retinopathy. Lastly, we evaluate the privacy of our approach with respect to membership inference attacks (MIA), where an adversary tries to predict whether a given retinal image was part of the cluster represented by a specific synthetic image. Our results show that synthetic images generated by k-SALSA provide strong mitigation of MIA, while prior k-Same approaches using pixel-wise or eigenvector-based averaging fail to do so, despite the fact that all of these approaches ostensibly satisfy k-anonymity.

Summary of Our Contributions. (1) We demonstrate the feasibility of GAN-based k-anonymization of retinal images. (2) We present a modernized k-Same algorithm using state-of-the-art GAN techniques, which are crucial for practical performance. (3) We introduce a novel technique—local style alignment—for generating a synthetic average with enhanced fidelity and downstream utility. (4) We perform comprehensive experiments on two datasets, evaluating the fidelity, utility, and privacy of our method compared to existing techniques.

2   Related Work

Traditional approaches for removing identifying features from private images (e.g., faces and medical images) involve direct manipulation of pixels, including masking, blurring, and pixelation [3,31,38,39]. However, these heuristics have been found to provide insufficient privacy protection [1,37]. In response, a *learning*-based approach to de-identification has been increasingly studied [14]. This is enabled by recent advances in GANs, which intuitively provide a more powerful approach to manipulate images according to their intrinsic manifold [15].

The existing literature on GAN-based transformation of images for privacy protection largely focuses on face de-identification. A common approach for formalizing privacy protection in this problem is to combine multiple images to obtain k-anonymity through the k-Same framework [21,30,33]. A key difficulty in these works has been generating high-quality images that capture useful information in the original image. To this end, recent works have focused on developing techniques to disentangle and preserve non-identity attributes of the image, such as pose and facial expression [20,21,29,50]. However, these methods are not directly applicable to our setting given the unclear distinction between identity vs. non-identity features in retinal images beyond the blood vessel structure. GAN-based approaches to generate images with differential privacy [8] have also been proposed [27,52], but current techniques lead to significant degradation of image quality (see supplement for an example application to retinal images).

Several recent works have successfully explored the use of GANs for generating realistic retinal images. Niu et al. [34] proposed a method to generate an image consistent with the given pathological descriptors. Both Zhou et al. [54] and Chen et al. [6] developed GAN models to synthesize retinal images conditioned on a semantic segmentation to improve disease classification performance. Yu et al. [53] introduced multi-channel GANs that improve the quality of generated retinal images by separately considering different elements of the image, including the blood vessels and the optic disc.

3   Method

3.1   Overview of k-SALSA

We consider a dataset D of retinal fundus images that the user wishes to release in a privatized form. We assume that the user has access to an auxiliary dataset D_0 that can be used to pre-train the GAN components of k-SALSA. Note that D_0 could simply be a publicly available dataset like the ones we used in our work or a subset of D. This choice does not affect the k-anonymity property of k-SALSA. Given these datasets, k-SALSA proceeds in four steps:

1. **Pre-training.** We first train a GAN on D_0. Let $G(\cdot)$ be the trained generator, which maps a latent code $w \in \mathcal{W}$ to a synthetic image $G(w)$. This step intuitively constructs the latent embedding space $\mathcal{W}$, which we will later rely on for the averaging operation. Next, k-SALSA trains a GAN inversion model $E(\cdot)$ (can be viewed as an encoder), which maps an image $x \in \mathcal{X}$ to a particular latent code $E(x) \in \mathcal{W}$. Note that this inversion process is lossy in that the synthetic image $G(E(x))$ will only be approximately similar to the original image x, constrained by the limitations of encoder E and generator G. Together, these two functions approximate a bijection between the space of retinal images $\mathcal{X}$ and the latent embedding space $\mathcal{W}$.
2. **Clustering.** Next, k-SALSA performs *same-size clustering* of the target input dataset D based on the inverted codes $E(x)$ for each $x \in D$, partitioning D into groups of exactly k similar images. Here k is the user parameter determining the k-anonymity of the final output. If the size of D is not divisible by k, one can disregard a small number of samples to resolve the issue, given that k is typically small (e.g. 10).

3. **Averaging.** For each cluster, *k*-SALSA summarizes the *k* source images as a single representative image via local style alignment—our new approach. This leads to *k*-anonymity, since each average image represents *k* individuals as a whole and does not distinguish among them.

4. **Release.** Finally, *k*-SALSA constructs a *k*-anonymous synthetic dataset $\tilde{D}$ to release by associating each average image (one per cluster) with the aggregated labels of the *k* images in the corresponding cluster (if labels were provided in the input dataset). This synthetic dataset can then be used for downstream analysis, such as training a classifier to predict the labels.

A graphical illustration of our workflow is provided in Fig. 1.

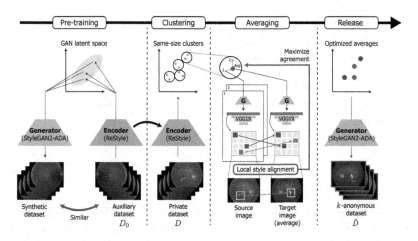

Fig. 1. Workflow of *k*-SALSA. GAN generator and inversion encoder are first trained to be used in subsequent steps. Same-size clustering groups images into groups of *k*, then the representative of each cluster is optimized via our local style alignment approach to preserve salient visual patterns. Images are synthesized from the optimized averages and released. Avg: average, G: generator

3.2   Local Style Alignment: Our New Approach to Image Averaging

While prior *k*-Same approaches developed for facial images have considered the Euclidean average of latent codes within each cluster as the representative, we found that this straightforward approach leads to significant loss of detail in synthetic retinal images, where clinically relevant patterns such as hemorrhages and exudates are often omitted (see Fig. 2).

We make the following two observations toward addressing this key limitation. First, unlike facial images where the salient structural features (e.g. eyes and nose) generally appear in consistent regions within the image, which facilitates the disentanglement of latent features, important patterns in retinal images

---

Algorithm 1. k-SALSA

Input: Private dataset $X = (x_1, \ldots, x_n)$, auxiliary dataset X_0 for GAN model training, integer $k > 1$ (assume $n = mk$ for integer m without loss of generality), number of iterations T, loss ratio parameter $\tilde{\lambda}$

Output: Synthetic dataset $\tilde{X}$ of size m with k-anonymity

1: Train a GAN generator G and a GAN inversion encoder E on X_0
2: Obtain latent code $w_i = E(x_i)$ for each $i \in [n]$ and let $W = \{w_i\}_{i=1}^n$
3: $(C_1, \ldots, C_m) = \mathsf{SameSizeClustering}(W, k) \triangleright C_j \subset W, |C_j| = k, |C_j \cap C_{j' \neq j}| = 0, \forall j$
4: Initialize $\tilde{X} = \emptyset$
5: **for** each cluster $j \in [m]$ **do**
6:      Let $C_j = (w'_1, \ldots, w'_k)$, and x'_i the original image of w'_i for each i
7:      Compute $w_0 = \frac{1}{k} \sum_{i=1}^k w'_i$ and generate $x_0 = G(w_0)$
8:      Initialize $w_{\text{avg}}^{(0)} = w_0$
9:      **for** each iteration $t \in [T]$ **do**
10:          Generate $x_{\text{avg}}^{(t-1)} = G(w_{\text{avg}}^{(t-1)})$
11:          Compute content loss $\mathcal{L}_{\text{content}}(x_0, x_{\text{avg}}^{(t-1)})$ using Eq. 6
12:          Compute local style alignment loss $\mathcal{L}_{\text{style}}((x'_1, \ldots, x'_k), x_{\text{avg}}^{(t-1)})$ using Eq. 7
13:          Compute total loss $\mathcal{L}_{\text{total}} = \lambda \mathcal{L}_{\text{content}} + (1 - \lambda) \mathcal{L}_{\text{style}}$
14:          Update $w_{\text{avg}}^{(t)}$ using $w_{\text{avg}}^{(t-1)}$ and the gradient $\nabla_{w_{\text{avg}}^{(t-1)}} \mathcal{L}_{\text{total}}$
15:      **end for**
16:      Add $G(w_{\text{avg}}^{(T)})$ to $\tilde{X}$
17: **end for**
18: **return** $\tilde{X}$

---

can appear in different areas and thus are more easily diluted when averaging the features in the latent space. Second, in contrast to the importance of shape information in facial images, the patterns of interest in retinal images that are not directly linked to personal identity tend to be associated with *texture-level* information (e.g. colored dots of varying granularity and frequency). In fact, the geometric structure of the blood vessels is a prominent identifying feature of concern that we are interested in obfuscating in the image via averaging.

Our local style alignment technique takes advantage of these observations to obtain higher quality representative images of each cluster. We first draw the connection between texture patterns of interest and the "style" of the image from the style transfer literature [11]. Since we are interested in local texture patterns in the image, we capture the *local style features* by constructing the feature covariance matrix in a sliding window of image patches, rather than over the whole image. We then consider the correspondence of the local style features between the source images in the cluster and the target representative image, allowing for source texture patterns to appear in different locations in the target and simultaneously enforcing that these patterns are recapitulated somewhere in the target image. Optimizing the latent code for the representative image with respect to the augmented loss function considering both the local style features and general content similarity, we obtain an enhanced representative image for each cluster. We provide the details of each step below and in Algorithm 1.

Construction of Local Style Features. Following the approach of style transfer, we view style and texture information as being captured by the cross-channel feature correlations in the intermediate layers of a pre-trained convolutional neural network (CNN), such as VGG19 [40].

Formally, let $F_{\text{source}}^{(i)}$ and F_{target} be n-by-n-by-c tensors for the i-th source image and the target representative, respectively, representing the activation output of an n-by-n intermediate CNN layer across c channels. Note that we use the second layer of VGG19 in all our experiments. We spatially partition the activation output into a grid of p submatrices, $\{F_{\text{source},j}^{(i)}\}_{j=1}^{p}$ and $\{F_{\text{target},j}\}_{j=1}^{p}$, each corresponding to a local patch in the image. For each patch j, we define the local style features $S_{\text{source},j}^{(i)}$ and $S_{\text{target},j}$ as c-by-c matrices, where

$$(S_{\text{source},j}^{(i)})_{u,v} := \langle \mathsf{Vec}((F_{\text{source},j}^{(i)})_{:,:,u}), \mathsf{Vec}((F_{\text{source},j}^{(i)})_{:,:,v}) \rangle \tag{1}$$

$$(S_{\text{target},j})_{u,v} := \langle \mathsf{Vec}((F_{\text{target},j})_{:,:,u}), \mathsf{Vec}((F_{\text{target},j})_{:,:,v}) \rangle \tag{2}$$

and $\mathsf{Vec}(\cdot)$ denotes vectorization, $\langle \cdot, \cdot \rangle$ denotes dot product, and $M_{:,:,u}$ for a tensor M denotes a slice corresponding to channel u. The sets $\{S_{\text{source},j}^{(i)}\}_{j=1}^{p}$ for each source image i in the cluster and $\{S_{\text{target},j}\}_{j=1}^{p}$ for the target fully characterize the local texture information we aim to capture in our model.

Alignment of Local Style Features. To introduce flexibility in determining where a visual pattern from the source image appears in the target image, we quantify the agreement in local style features via a correspondence. Inspired by the recent work of Wang et al. on dense contrastive learning [47], we compute the cosine similarity of style features between every pair of patches between the source and the target and take the optimal match for each patch in the source image to be included in the loss function. This induces positional flexibility while penalizing complete omission of texture patterns from the source. Note that the prior work [47] did not consider style information in their approach.

We define correspondence index $a(i,j)$ for patch j in the source image i as:

$$a(i,j) := \arg\max_{j' \in \{1,\dots,p\}} \mathsf{CosineSimilarity}(\mathsf{Vec}(S_{\text{source},j}^{(i)}), \mathsf{Vec}(S_{\text{target},j'})). \tag{3}$$

It is worth noting that, while a naïve implementation of all pairwise comparison of patches leads to significant runtime overhead, our implementation efficiently utilizes matrix operations to maintain computational efficiency.

Optimization of Representative Images. To synthesize an informative representative image for each cluster, leveraging the correspondence of local style features, we frame the process as an optimization problem as follows.

Let $E(\cdot)$ and $G(\cdot)$ be the encoder of the pre-trained GAN inversion model and the pre-trained GAN generator, respectively. We directly optimize the target latent code w_{avg} whose corresponding image $G(w_{\text{avg}})$ is the desired representative of the cluster. We initialize w_{avg} to the baseline Euclidean average w_0 of the source image embeddings given by

$$w_0 := \frac{1}{k} \sum_{i=1}^{k} E(x^{(i)}), \tag{4}$$

where $x^{(i)}$ denotes the i-th image in the cluster. We then iteratively optimize the solution using gradient descent with the loss function

$$\mathcal{L}_{\mathrm{total}} = \lambda \mathcal{L}_{\mathrm{content}} + (1 - \lambda) \mathcal{L}_{\mathrm{style}}, \tag{5}$$

where λ determines the ratio between the two terms given by

$$\mathcal{L}_{\mathrm{content}} = 1 - \langle F(G(w_0)), F(G(w_{\mathrm{avg}})) \rangle, \tag{6}$$

$$\mathcal{L}_{\mathrm{style}} = \sum_{i=1}^{k} \sum_{j=1}^{p} \|S_{\mathrm{source},j}^{(i)} - S_{\mathrm{target},a(i,j)}(w_{\mathrm{avg}})\|_{\mathcal{F}}^2. \tag{7}$$

Note that $\|\cdot\|_{\mathcal{F}}$ denotes the Frobenius norm, and $F(\cdot)$ represents a pre-trained encoder network, which we use to induce high-level similarity between the optimized representative and the Euclidean average to avoid degenerate cases and to prioritize refining of the baseline solution. In our experiments, we set F to the pre-trained MoCo network [16], which was trained on the ImageNet dataset [9] via unsupervised contrastive learning. MoCo is recognized for its effectiveness in capturing semantic information of natural images beyond the available labels in the original dataset. We also note that, although style transfer approaches typically take many iterations to converge, our initialization scheme using the Euclidean average greatly simplifies this process, requiring fewer iterations to obtain the final solutions in our experiments.

3.3   GAN-based Image Generation and Encoding

We train a GAN model, StyleGAN2-ADA [22], on retinal images to learn to generate realistic fundus images from a latent vector space. The StyleGAN family of methods [22–24] generate high-resolution images using a progressive architecture, where increasingly fine-grain details are added to the image as we get deeper into the network. We consider the latent space associated with this network to be extended multi-scale $\mathcal{W}$, which modulates the activation of units in all layers of the generator hierarchy. StyleGAN2-ADA is one of the latest in this class, which stabilizes training on limited data using the *adaptive discriminator augmentation* (ADA) mechanism. Likely because the size of the public retinal image datasets is small compared to other types of image datasets, we observed that the use of ADA leads to a considerable improvement in image quality. We also note that the existing work on GANs for retinal images (e.g. [6,34,53,54]) leverages additional labeled information such as vessel segmentation, and thus are not directly applicable to our setting where we use the raw fundus images.

To manipulate and summarize real retinal images in the latent space equipped with a generator to synthesize new images, we need an encoder to map a given image to the GAN latent space, a task known as GAN inversion [51]. In our framework, we use this encoder to invert every image in the input dataset, then use the latent codes both to define the clusters of size k to be averaged and to find the Euclidean centroid for the cluster to use as an initialization point, as described in the previous sections. To this end, we use ReStyle [2], a recently developed approach to GAN inversion which achieved a significant scalability improvement over the previous methods by adopting an iterative refinement approach. The ReStyle model takes the target image and the current synthetic image (the result of inversion) as input, and learns to generate an update to the latent code that improves consistency between the two images. For k-SALSA, adopting this approach was key to building a practical pipeline—it reduced the inversion time by an order of magnitude (from 80 to 3 s per image).

While the generator and the encoder individually draws from prior work, we note that the combination of these state-of-the-art techniques have not been previously studied in the context of privatizing retinal images and were in fact key enabling factors of the practical performance of k-SALSA in our experiments.

3.4 Same-Size Clustering

To partition the input dataset into groups of exactly k images to average, we employ a greedy nearest neighbor clustering to the inverted latent codes of the input images. At each iteration, a point with the maximum average distance to the rest of the dataset is chosen, with the goal of prioritizing outliers. Then $k - 1$ nearest neighbors of the chosen point are identified to form a new cluster of size k. The points in the new cluster are removed from the dataset and the above process is repeated. In our experiments, we downsample the dataset to a multiple of k to avoid a leftover cluster smaller than k. Our experiments show the effectiveness of this efficient clustering approach in downstream tasks.

4 Experiments

4.1 Benchmark Datasets and Evaluation Setting

Our experiments are conducted on public fundus image datasets APTOS[1] and EyePACS[2], widely used for diabetic retinopathy (DR) classification. The images in both datasets are labeled by ophthalmologists with five grades of DR based on severity: 0 (normal), 1 (mild DR), 2 (moderate DR), 3 (severe DR), and 4 (proliferative DR). EyePACS images were acquired from different imaging devices, leading to variations in image resolution, aspect ratio, intensity, and quality. Hence, EyePACS represents a more challenging evaluation setting.

---

[1] https://www.kaggle.com/c/aptos2019-blindness-detection.
[2] https://www.kaggle.com/c/diabetic-retinopathy-detection.

For both datasets, we train the GAN generator and the GAN inversion model on the training set (see supplement for details). We then apply k-SALSA to the training set with the pre-trained GAN models to generate a k-anonymous dataset of synthetic images with aggregated labels. To evaluate the downstream utility of the synthetic dataset, we trained DR classifiers based on the synthetic images and evaluated the classifiers on the test set using real images and labels.

4.2   Baseline Approaches

We compare k-SALSA with the following baseline methods. To demonstrate the advantage of our novel local style alignment-based averaging scheme, we consider the same method as k-SALSA, except using the Euclidean average (centroid) of each cluster in our GAN latent space to generate the representative image (k-**Centroid**). To illustrate the importance of GANs in synthetic averaging of retinal images, we also evaluate less sophisticated schemes based on pixel-wise averaging (k-**Same-Pixel**) and averaging in the low-dimensional latent space obtained by principal components analysis (k-**Same-PCA**). Note that k-Same-PCA is equivalent to the method proposed in the original work on k-Same algorithms [33], and k-Centroid represents the best achievable performance following the general framework of k-Same-Net [30] leveraging our GAN approaches. We applied all averaging methods to the same set of clusters we constructed using

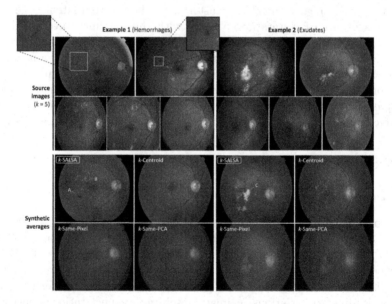

Fig. 2. Examples of synthetic average of retinal images. Two example clusters ($k = 5$) of real retinal images (*top*) along with synthetic averages generated by different methods (*bottom*). k-SALSA better captures clinically relevant features such as hemorrhages (A) and exudates (B and C)

the latent space of k-SALSA. For some comparisons, we also consider the performance based on the non-averaged synthetic images generated from the inversion of each original image, i.e. $G(E(x))$ given an image x (**GAN-Inverted**).

4.3 Fidelity of Synthetic Images

To evaluate the visual quality of synthetic retinal images, we first compare the Fréchet inception distance (FID) [18], a standard performance metric for images generated using GANs, across the methods we considered. Note that, unlike pixel-wise metrics such as PSNR and SSIM [48] (see supplement for additional discussion), FID measures the divergence between the multivariate Gaussian distributions induced by the real vs. synthetic images in the activation of the Inception V3 model [42] trained on ImageNet [9]. Intuitively, FID quantifies how different the synthetic images are from a reference set of real images in a manner that reflects human visual perception. We use the original retinal images from each dataset as the reference to calculate FID on the corresponding synthetic images. As shown in Table 1, k-SALSA consistently obtains the best (the lowest) FID among all averaging methods for different values of k (2, 5, and 10) on both datasets. For all methods, averaging leads to worse FID relative to GAN-Inverted images, with the gap increasing as k becomes larger. This suggests that generating a realistic image becomes more difficult as we average more images. Nevertheless, k-SALSA's FID remains closest to GAN-Inverted even for $k = 10$.

Table 1. Comparison of fidelity of synthetic images

Method	Metric	APTOS			EyePACS		
		$k = 2$	$k = 5$	$k = 10$	$k = 2$	$k = 5$	$k = 10$
GAN-Inverted	FID	11.47	18.12	25.45	9.65	14.65	19.77
k-Same-Pixel	FID	128.23	131.69	138.89	65.21	113.45	144.13
k-Same-PCA	FID	131.691	128.225	138.891	159.57	164.69	173.15
k-Centroid	FID	12.7	22.71	31.09	11.24	20.58	28.49
k-SALSA	FID	**11.84**	**20.09**	**28.4**	**9.95**	**15.07**	**21.28**

In Fig. 2, we provide examples of synthetic averages generated by different methods for $k = 5$ for visual comparison. k-SALSA images more clearly capture the fine-grain, clinically-relevant patterns in the source images, including exudates (appearing as grainy yellow patches) and hemorrhages (appearing as dark spots), both of which are well-established biomarkers of diabetes [32]. k-Centroid generates realistic images, but tend to omit important fine-grain patterns, which initially motivated this work. k-Same-Pixel and k-Same-PCA lead to low-fidelity images that even fail to align the boundaries of the photographs due to their linearity. Examples for other values of k are provided in the supplement.

4.4   Downstream Classification Performance

In addition to generating more realistic and informative summaries of each cluster of retinal images, we are interested in enabling downstream analysis with our synthetic data. We tested whether k-SALSA's synthetic dataset can lead to accurate classifiers of clinical labels, in our case the grading of diabetic retinopathy (DR). In EyePACS, we evaluated normal vs. DR binary classification due to the highly imbalanced number of labels (in contrast to the five-class setting in Kaggle). We tested multi-class prediction with all five labels in APTOS.

The number of images in the training set was 3,000 for APTOS and 10,000 for EyePACS, where the latter was subsampled for efficiency. For each set, we used our clustering approach to obtain same-size clusters for each of $k \in \{2, 5, 10\}$, which were then individually averaged to obtain training images for a classifier. We also evaluated the classifiers trained on original or GAN-Inverted images, which were subsampled to the same number of training examples as the synthetic datasets for each k for comparison. We provide experimental details and a comparison without subsampling in the supplement.

Table 2. Comparison of diabetic retinopathy classification performance

Method	Metric	APTOS			EyePACS		
		$k = 2$	$k = 5$	$k = 10$	$k = 2$	$k = 5$	$k = 10$
Original	Accuracy	0.771	0.752	0.700	0.794	0.767	0.725
	Cohen's κ	0.903	0.888	0.856	0.414	0.327	0.297
GAN-Inverted	Accuracy	0.744	0.702	0.651	0.731	0.730	0.708
	Cohen's κ	0.865	0.828	0.814	0.140	0.140	0.058
k-Same-Pixel	Accuracy	0.502	0.318	0.366	0.361	0.296	0.434
	Cohen's κ	0.663	0.273	0.140	0.029	0.000	0.043
k-Same-PCA	Accuracy	0.572	0.394	0.293	0.3360	0.361	0.657
	Cohen's κ	0.651	0.559	0.253	0.010	0.029	0.096
k-Centroid	Accuracy	**0.688**	0.688	0.646	0.680	0.664	0.611
	Cohen's κ	**0.786**	0.745	0.647	**0.268**	0.185	0.160
k-**SALSA**	Accuracy	0.687	**0.712**	**0.673**	**0.704**	**0.688**	**0.705**
	Cohen's κ	0.773	**0.769**	**0.710**	0.254	**0.222**	**0.225**

The results in Table 2 show that the k-SALSA synthetic datasets generally outperform the alternative approaches with respect to both accuracy and Cohen's κ statistic (with quadratic weighting) on the test set. k-Centroid achieves slightly better performance for $k = 2$, but remains comparable to our approach. Since Euclidean averaging may introduce greater distortions for larger values of k, we expect the advantage of k-SALSA to be more pronounced for moderate to large k, which is consistent with our results. As expected, performance based on original images is higher than the synthetic dataset, but part of this gap is ascribed to the limitations of the current GAN models as suggested by the lower performance of the non-averaged, GAN-inverted images compared to the original. Interestingly, for EyePACS $k = 10$, k-SALSA outperforms GAN-Inverted, suggesting that summarizing salient features may even be beneficial for classification when the data is limited. We include in the supplement additional results illustrating the impact of k and a promising extension of k-SALSA which uses data augmentation to mitigate dataset reduction due to averaging.

4.5 Mitigation of Membership Inference Attacks

To compare the privacy properties of the methods, we implemented a membership inference attack (MIA), where an adversary holding a synthetic dataset attempts to infer whether a target person was part of a specific cluster. We trained ResNet18 [17] on the training set to classify cluster membership using the synthetic averages generated by each method. We then evenly divided the test set into two parts, generated cluster averages on the first, then evaluated the performance of the classifier in ranking the images in *both* test sets for membership in each cluster, based only on its synthetic average. For each cluster size k, we calculated the top-K accuracy (i.e., mean fraction of top K samples in the ranking that correspond to correct guesses) with $K = k$.

Table 3. Membership inference attack top-K accuracy (%) with $K = k$.

Method	APTOS			EyePACS		
	$k = 2$	$k = 5$	$k = 10$	$k = 2$	$k = 5$	$k = 10$
k-Same-Pixel	100.0	91.76	84.21	97.96	94.28	86.67
k-Same-PCA	98.98	84.29	2.5	98.98	86.21	2.63
k-Centroid	78.57	41.42	2.1	88.63	45.92	2.63
k-SALSA	**77.55**	**40.0**	**1.0**	**71.42**	**35.17**	**0.52**

The results are summarized in Table 3. Note that an adversary with access to the encoder would achieve an expected accuracy of 50% for all values of k, since in any neighborhood a random half of the samples correspond to negative matches that were not included in the private dataset. This represents a realistic scenario where the attacker does not have *a priori* knowledge of individuals in the private dataset. For a worst-case evaluation, we assume that the target's image is identical to the one in the dataset; any protection offered by noisy re-acquisition of images is likely to be bypassed with more sophisticated MIA (e.g., using vessel structures). We observed that pixel-averaging provides little to no privacy. k-Same-PCA and k-Centroid lower the risks, the latter to a greater extent. k-SALSA results in the strongest mitigation with MIA accuracy of 1% and 0.52% for APTOS and EyePACS, respectively, for $k = 10$. Our improvement over k-Centroid is likely due to the fact that the addition of our local style loss prioritizes similarity in high-level visual patterns over low-level content, potentially reducing the amount of identity-related information that can be exploited by the attack. None of the methods provide strong privacy at $k = 2$, which reflects an insufficient amount of variability between the two source images that could be leveraged for privacy; however, we expect our approach to provide meaningful privacy protection for larger values of k as our results show.

4.6   Ablation Study

We conducted an ablation study to evaluate the importance of individual components of our methodology. Recall that the loss function of k-SALSA includes the content loss and the local style loss (see Eq. 5). We considered four alternative models with: only style loss, only content loss, both but using global style features computed over the whole image, and both without the flexible alignment (i.e., each local style is directly compared to that of the corresponding patch in the other image at the same location). All of these alternatives performed considerably worse than k-SALSA in downstream classification performance (Table 4). The especially poor performance without alignment suggests that enforcing style preservation without spatial flexibility can in fact be harmful for the method.

Table 4. Ablation study (APTOS, $k = 5$)

Method	Accuracy	Cohen's κ
Style loss only (local, with alignment)	0.685	0.735
Content loss only	0.673	0.712
Content loss, Global style loss	0.687	0.761
Content loss, Local style loss, No alignment	0.57	0.417
k-SALSA	**0.712**	**0.769**

5   Discussion and Conclusions

We presented k-SALSA, an end-to-end pipeline for synthesizing a k-anonymous retinal image dataset given a private input dataset. We leverage local style alignment, our new approach for summarizing source images in a cluster while preserving local texture information. Our results demonstrate that k-anonymization of retinal images, preserving both privacy and clinical utility, is feasible.

We would like to address several limitations of the current method in future work. First, k-SALSA's performance is dependent on the quality of the underlying GAN and GAN inversion models. We plan to devise strategies tailored to retinal images (e.g., separately modelling different parts of the image) to further improve GAN models. Next, we plan to explore more rigorous frameworks for privacy such as differential privacy (DP) [8]. While it is generally difficult to apply DP to high-dimensional data such as images, certain relaxations of DP [25] may lead to a practical solution. Lastly, we plan to explore the application of our methodology to other imaging modalities for the retina, including the OCT.

Our work demonstrates that domain-inspired techniques can be combined with the state-of-the-art GAN techniques to design effective approaches to privatizing sensitive data. The methodological insights introduced by our work is of general interest to other domains (e.g. genomics), where privacy-aware aggregation of sensitive data may overcome challenges in data sharing.

Acknowledgement. M.J. is supported by the Ministry of Trade, Industry, and Energy in Korea, under Human Resource Development Program for Industrial Innovation (Global) (P0017311) supervised by the Korea Institute for Advancement of Technology. H.C. is supported by NIH DP5 OD029574-01 and by the Schmidt Fellows Program at Broad Institute.

References

1. Abramian, D., Eklund, A.: Refacing: reconstructing anonymized facial features using GANS. In: 2019 IEEE 16th International Symposium on Biomedical Imaging (ISBI 2019) (2019)
2. Alaluf, Y., Patashnik, O., Cohen-Or, D.: Restyle: A residual-based stylegan encoder via iterative refinement. In: Proceedings of the IEEE/CVF International Conference on Computer Vision (2021)
3. Bischoff-Grethe, A., et al.: A technique for the deidentification of structural brain MR images. Hum. Brain Mapp. **28**(9), 892–903 (2007)
4. Burlina, P., Paul, W., Liu, T.Y.A., Bressler, N.M.: Detecting anomalies in retinal diseases using generative, discriminative, and self-supervised deep learning. JAMA Ophthalmol. **140**(2), 185–189 (2022)
5. Burlina, P.M., Joshi, N., Pacheco, K.D., Liu, T.Y.A., Bressler, N.M.: Assessment of deep generative models for high-resolution synthetic retinal image generation of age-related macular degeneration. JAMA Ophthalmol. **137**(3), 258–264 (2019)
6. Chen, Y., Long, J., Guo, J.: RF-GANs: a method to synthesize retinal fundus images based on generative adversarial network. Comput. Intell. Neurosci. (2021)
7. Coyner, A.S., et al.: Diagnosability of synthetic retinal fundus images for plus disease detection in retinopathy of prematurity. In: AMIA Symposium (2020)
8. Dwork, C., Roth, A., et al.: The algorithmic foundations of differential privacy. Found. Trends Theor. Comput. Sci. **9**(3–4), 211–407 (2014)
9. Fei-Fei, L., Deng, J., Li, K.: ImageNet: constructing a large-scale image database. J. Vis. **9**(8), 1037–1037 (2009)
10. Garfinkel, S., et al.: De-identification of Personal Information: US Department of Commerce. National Institute of Standards and Technology (2015)
11. Gatys, L.A., Ecker, A.S., Bethge, M.: Image style transfer using convolutional neural networks. In: Proceedings of the IEEE Conference on Computer Vision and Pattern Recognition (2016)
12. Gkoulalas-Divanis, A., Loukides, G., Sun, J.: Publishing data from electronic health records while preserving privacy: a survey of algorithms. J. Biomed. Inf. **50**, 4–19 (2014)

13. Goodfellow, I.: Nips 2016 tutorial: generative adversarial networks. arXiv preprint. arXiv:1701.00160 (2016)
14. der Goten, V., Alexander, L., Hepp, T., Akata, Z., Smith, K.: Conditional de-identification of 3d magnetic resonance images. arXiv preprint. arXiv:2110.09927 (2021)
15. Gui, J., Sun, Z., Wen, Y., Tao, D., Ye, J.: A review on generative adversarial networks: Algorithms, theory, and applications. IEEE Trans. Knowl. Data Eng. (2021)
16. He, K., Fan, H., Wu, Y., Xie, S., Girshick, R.: Momentum contrast for unsupervised visual representation learning. In: Proceedings of the IEEE/CVF Conference on Computer Vision and Pattern Recognition (2020)
17. He, K., Zhang, X., Ren, S., Sun, J.: Deep residual learning for image recognition. In: Proceedings of the IEEE Conference on Computer Vision and Pattern Recognition (2016)
18. Heusel, M., Ramsauer, H., Unterthiner, T., Nessler, B., Hochreiter, S.: Gans trained by a two time-scale update rule converge to a local nash equilibrium. In: Advances in Neural Information Processing Systems (2017)
19. Jakob, C.E., Kohlmayer, F., Meurers, T., Vehreschild, J.J., Prasser, F.: Design and evaluation of a data anonymization pipeline to promote open science on COVID-19. Sci. Data $7(1)$, 1–10 (2020)
20. Jeong, Y., et al.: FICGAN: facial identity controllable GAN for de-identification. arXiv preprint. arXiv:2110.00740 (2021)
21. Jourabloo, A., Yin, X., Liu, X.: Attribute preserved face de-identification. In: 2015 International Conference on Biometrics (ICB) (2015)
22. Karras, T., Aittala, M., Hellsten, J., Laine, S., Lehtinen, J., Aila, T.: Training generative adversarial networks with limited data. In: Advances in Neural Information Processing Systems (2020)
23. Karras, T., Laine, S., Aila, T.: A style-based generator architecture for generative adversarial networks. In: Proceedings of the IEEE/CVF Conference on Computer Vision and Pattern Recognition (2019)
24. Karras, T., Laine, S., Aittala, M., Hellsten, J., Lehtinen, J., Aila, T.: Analyzing and improving the image quality of stylegan. In: Proceedings of the IEEE/CVF Conference on Computer Vision and Pattern Recognition (2020)
25. Kifer, D., Machanavajjhala, A.: Pufferfish: a framework for mathematical privacy definitions. ACM Trans. Database Syst. (TODS) $39(1)$, 1–36 (2014)
26. Korot, E., et al.: Predicting sex from retinal fundus photographs using automated deep learning. Sci. Rep. $11(1)$, 1–8 (2021)
27. Long, Y., et al.: G-PATE: scalable differentially private data generator via private aggregation of teacher discriminators. In: Advances in Neural Information Processing Systems (2021)
28. Mariño, C., Penedo, M.G., Penas, M., Carreira, M.J., Gonzalez, F.: Personal authentication using digital retinal images. Pattern Anal. Appl. **9**, 21 (2006)
29. Maximov, M., Elezi, I., Leal-Taixé, L.: Ciagan: conditional identity anonymization generative adversarial networks. In: Proceedings of the IEEE/CVF Conference on Computer Vision and Pattern Recognition (2020)
30. Meden, B., Emeršič, Ž, Štruc, V., Peer, P.: k-same-Net: k-anonymity with generative deep neural networks for face deidentification. Entropy $20(1)$, 60 (2018)
31. Milchenko, M., Marcus, D.: Obscuring surface anatomy in volumetric imaging data. Neuroinformatics **11**, 65–75 (2013). https://doi.org/10.1007/s12021-012-9160-3
32. Mohamed, Q., Gillies, M.C., Wong, T.Y.: Management of diabetic retinopathy: a systematic review. Jama **298**(8), 902–916 (2007)

33. Newton, E.M., Sweeney, L., Malin, B.: Preserving privacy by de-identifying face images. IEEE Trans. Knowl. Data Eng. **17**(2), 232–243 (2005)
34. Niu, Y., Gu, et al.: Pathological evidence exploration in deep retinal image diagnosis. In: Proceedings of the AAAI Conference on Artificial Intelligence (2019)
35. Paul, W., Cao, Y., Zhang, M., Burlina, P.: Defending medical image diagnostics against privacy attacks using generative methods. arXiv preprint. arXiv:2103.03078 (2021)
36. Poplin, R., et al.: Prediction of cardiovascular risk factors from retinal fundus photographs via deep learning. Nat. Biomed. Eng. **2**(3), 158–164 (2018)
37. Ravindra, V., Grama, A.: De-anonymization attacks on neuroimaging datasets. In: Proceedings of the 2021 International Conference on Management of Data (2021)
38. Ribaric, S., Pavesic, N.: An overview of face de-identification in still images and videos. In: 2015 11th IEEE International Conference and Workshops on Automatic Face and Gesture Recognition (FG) (2015)
39. Schimke, N., Kuehler, M., Hale, J.: Preserving privacy in structural neuroimages. In: Li, Y. (ed.) DBSec 2011. LNCS, vol. 6818, pp. 301–308. Springer, Heidelberg (2011). https://doi.org/10.1007/978-3-642-22348-8_26
40. Simonyan, K., Zisserman, A.: Very deep convolutional networks for large-scale image recognition. In: International Conference on Learning Representations (2015)
41. Sweeney, L.: k-anonymity: a model for protecting privacy. Int. J. Uncertainty Fuzziness Knowl.-Based Syst. **10**(05), 557–570 (2002)
42. Szegedy, C., Vanhoucke, V., Ioffe, S., Shlens, J., Wojna, Z.: Rethinking the inception architecture for computer vision. In: Proceedings of the IEEE Conference on Computer Vision and Pattern Recognition (2016)
43. Taylor, R.: AI and the retina: finding Patterns of Systemic Disease. EyeNet Magazine (2021)
44. Tom, E., et al.: Protecting data privacy in the age of AI-enabled ophthalmology. Transl. Vis. Sci. Technol. **9**(2), 36–36 (2020)
45. Dept, U.S.: of Health and Human Services: Standards for privacy of individually identifiable health information. Final Rule, Federal Registrar (2002)
46. Wagner, S.K., et al.: Insights into systemic disease through retinal imaging-based oculomics. Trans. Vis. Sci. Technol. **9**(2), 6 (2020)
47. Wang, X., Zhang, R., Shen, C., Kong, T., Li, L.: Dense contrastive learning for self-supervised visual pre-training. In: Proceedings of the IEEE/CVF Conference on Computer Vision and Pattern Recognition (2021)
48. Wang, Z., Bovik, A.C., Sheikh, H.R., Simoncelli, E.P.: Image quality assessment: from error visibility to structural similarity. IEEE Trans. Image Process. **13**(4), 600–612 (2004)
49. Wisely, C.E., et al.: Convolutional neural network to identify symptomatic alzheimer's disease using multimodal retinal imaging. Br. J. Ophthalmol. **106**(3), 388–395 (2022)
50. Wu, Y., Yang, F., Xu, Y., Ling, H.: Privacy-protective-GAN for privacy preserving face De-identification. J. Comput. Sci. Technol. **34**(1), 47–60 (2019). https://doi.org/10.1007/s11390-019-1898-8
51. Xia, W., Zhang, Y., Yang, Y., Xue, J.H., Zhou, B., Yang, M.H.: Gan inversion: a survey. arXiv preprint. arXiv:2101.05278 (2021)
52. Xu, C., Ren, J., Zhang, D., Zhang, Y., Qin, Z., Ren, K.: GANobfuscator: mitigating information leakage under GAN via differential privacy. IEEE Trans. Inf. Forensics Secur. **14**(9), 2358–2371 (2019)

53. Yu, Z., Xiang, Q., Meng, J., Kou, C., Ren, Q., Lu, Y.: Retinal image synthesis from multiple-landmarks input with generative adversarial networks. Biomed. Eng. Online **18**(1), 1–15 (2019)
54. Zhou, Y., Wang, B., He, X., Cui, S., Shao, L.: DR-GAN: conditional generative adversarial network for fine-grained lesion synthesis on diabetic retinopathy images. IEEE J. Biomed. Health Inform. (2020)

RadioTransformer: A Cascaded Global-Focal Transformer for Visual Attention–Guided Disease Classification

Moinak Bhattacharya$^{(\boxtimes)}$ ⓘ, Shubham Jain ⓘ, and Prateek Prasanna ⓘ

Stony Brook University, Stony Brook, New York, USA
{moinak.bhattacharya,prateek.prasanna}@stonybrook.edu

Abstract. In this work, we present *RadioTransformer*, a novel student-teacher transformer framework, that leverages radiologists' gaze patterns and models their visuo-cognitive behavior for disease diagnosis on chest radiographs. Domain experts, such as radiologists, rely on visual information for medical image interpretation. On the other hand, deep neural networks have demonstrated significant promise in similar tasks even where visual interpretation is challenging. Eye-gaze tracking has been used to capture the viewing behavior of domain experts, lending insights into the complexity of visual search. However, deep learning frameworks, even those that rely on attention mechanisms, do not leverage this rich domain information for diagnostic purposes. *RadioTransformer* fills this critical gap by learning from radiologists' visual search patterns, encoded as 'human visual attention regions' in a cascaded global-focal transformer framework. The overall 'global' image characteristics and the more detailed 'local' features are captured by the proposed global and focal modules, respectively. We experimentally validate the efficacy of *RadioTransformer* on 8 datasets involving different disease classification tasks where eye-gaze data is not available during the inference phase. Code: https://github.com/bmi-imaginelab/radiotransformer

Keywords: Eye-gaze · Visual attention · Chest radiographs · Disease classification

1 Introduction

Medical image interpretation and associated diagnosis relies largely on how domain experts study images. Radiologists hone their image search skills during years of training on medical images from different domains. In fact, studies have shown that systematic visual search patterns can lead to improved diagnostic performance [15,43]. Current diagnostic and prognostic models, however, are limited to image content semantics such as disease location, annotation, and

---

Supplementary Information The online version contains supplementary material available at https://doi.org/10.1007/978-3-031-19803-8_40.

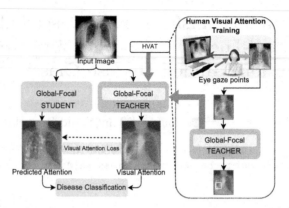

Fig. 1. Overview of proposed work. Visual search patterns of radiologists on chest radiographs are used to first train a global-focal teacher network, referred to as *Human Visual Attention Training* (Sect. 3.3). This pre-trained teacher network teaches the global-focal student network to learn visual attention using a novel *Visual Attention Loss* (Sect. 3.2). The student-teacher network is implemented to explicitly integrate radiologist visual attention for improving disease classification on chest radiographs.

severity level, and do not take this rich auxiliary domain knowledge into account. They primarily implement hand-crafted descriptors or deep architectures that learn textural and spatial features of diseases [5,62]. The spatial dependencies of intra-image disease patterns, often implicitly interpreted by expert readers, may not be adequately captured via image feature representation learning alone.

Recent works have utilized transformer-based architectures that leverage attention from radiological scans to provide better diagnosis [54,59]. This is a significant advancement, as the models learn self-attention across image patches to determine diagnostically relevant regions-of-interest. Although these approaches integrate long-range feature dependencies and learn high-level representations, they lack apriori domain knowledge, fundamentally rooted in disease pathophysiology and its manifestation on images. Recently, it has been demonstrated that deep-learning networks can be trained to learn radiologists' attention level and decisions [48]. However, it is still unclear how effectively and efficiently such search patterns can be used to improve a model's decision-making ability. To address this gap, we propose to leverage domain experts' systematic viewing patterns, as the basis of underlying attention and intention, to guide a deep learning network towards improved disease diagnosis.

Motivation. The motivation for our approach stems from a) understanding the importance of human visual attention in medical image interpretation, and b) understanding the medical experts' search heuristics in decision-making. Medical image interpretation is a complex process that broadly comprises a global-focal approach involving a) identifying suspicious regions from a global perspective, and b) identifying specific abnormalities with a focal perspective. During the global screening process, a radiologist scans for coarse low-contrast features in which certain textural attributes are analyzed and prospective abnormal regions of interest are identified. In the focal process, the regions of abnormalities are re-examined to determine the severity, type of disease, or reject the assumption of abnormality. For example, while analyzing a chest radiograph for COVID-19, a radiologist skims through the thoracic region at a glance to identify suspicious regions based on intensity variations. This helps in selective identification by eliminating 'obviously healthy' regions. The focal feature learning process involves a more critical analysis of the suspicious regions to understand the structural and morphological characteristics of specific regions and their surroundings. This typically involves domain-specific features such as distribution of infiltrates and accumulation of fluid. We use this as a motivation to design *Radio Transformer*, a global-focal transformer that integrates a radiologist's visual cognition with the self-attention-based learning of transformers. This improves their class activation regions, leading to a probabilistic score from attention features that correlates highly with human visual attention based diagnosis.

The objective of our work is *to augment the learning capabilities of deep networks in a disease diagnosis setting with domain-specific expert viewing patterns in a cognitive-aware manner.*

Contributions. The primary contributions of this work can be summarized as follows:

1. A novel *student-teacher based global-focal* **Radio Transformer** *architecture,* constituting transformer blocks with shifting windows, is proposed to leverage the radiologists' visual attention in order to improve the diagnostic accuracy. The global module learns high-level coarse representations and the focal module learns low-level granular representations with two-way lateral connections to address the semantic attention gap with smoothed moving average training.
2. A novel *visual attention loss* (VAL) is proposed to train the student network with the visual attention regions from the teacher network. This loss teaches the student network to focus on regions from teacher-generated visual attention using a weighted combination of attention region overlap and regression of center and boundary points.

Figure 1 shows an overview of the proposed *Radio Transformer* architecture consisting of the global-focal student-teacher network with a novel Visual Attention Loss. While the underlying concepts of the proposed framework are domain-agnostic, in this work we have validated it on pulmonary and thoracic disease classification on chest radiographs.

2   Related Work

Eye-Gaze Tracking in Radiology. Eye-tracking studies have been conducted in radiology to draw insights into the visual diagnosis process [15,40]. Experts' visual search patterns have been studied in various diseases [33,39,50,55,89,92] to understand their relationship with the diagnostic performance of radiologists [2,14,82]. Clinical error in diagnostic interpretation has often been

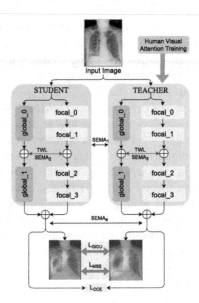

Fig. 2. Global-Focal Student-Teacher network implemented using shifting window blocks cascaded in series with TWL connections and layered SEMA.

attributed to reader fatigue and strain, which has been extensively validated via eye-tracking studies [17,73,80,83]. Variations in cognition and perceptual patterns while viewing images can cause the same image being interpreted differently by different experts. This has led to a few studies displaying eye-positions from experts as a visual aid to improve diagnostic performance of novice readers [37,43]. The dependence of diagnostic decisions on visual search patterns presents a unique opportunity to integrate this rich auxiliary domain information in computer-aided diagnosis systems.

Visual Attention–Driven Learning. In the context of image interpretation, visual attention refers to the cognitive operations that direct an observer's attention to specific regions in an image. We represent visual attention as saliency maps constructed by tracking users' eye movements. Eye-gaze [35] has been used in several computer vision [30,53] studies for head-pose estimation, human-computer interaction, driver vigilance monitoring, etc. Human eyes tend to focus on visual features, such as corners [46], luminance [72], visual onsets [75,76], dynamic events [24,25], color, intensity, and orientation [26,27,60]. Image perception, in general, is hence tightly coupled with visual attention of the observer. Several methods, involving gaze analysis, have been proposed for tasks such as object detection [58,90,91], image segmentation [52,66], object referring [79], action recognition [22,41,49,81], and action localization [69]. Other specialized methods use visual attention for goal-oriented localization [44] and egocentric activity recognition [51]. A recent work incorporated sonographer knowledge in the form of gaze tracking data on ultrasounds to enhance anatomy classification tasks [61]. In another study [71], Convolutional Neural Networks (CNN) trained on eye tracking data were shown to be equivalent to the ones trained on manually annotated masks for the task of tumor segmentation.

Despite evidence of the importance of expert gaze patterns in improving image interpretation, their role in machine-learning driven disease classification in radiology, is still under explored. The interpretation of radiology images is a complex task, requiring specialized viewing patterns unlike the more general visual attention in other tasks. For example, determining whether a lesion is cancerous or not involves the following hierarchical steps: a) detecting the presence of a lesion, b) recognizing whether it is pathologic, c) determining the type, and finally, d) providing a diagnosis. These sequential analysis patterns, to some extent, are captured by the visual search patterns which are not leveraged by machine learning models. To bridge this gap, our proposed work uses the visual attention knowledge from radiologists to train a transformer-based model for improving disease classification on chest radiographs.

Disease Classification on Chest Radiographs. Reliable classification of cardiothoracic and pulmonary diseases on chest radiographs is a crucial task in Radiology, owing to the high morbidity and mortality resulting from such abnormalities. Several methods have been proposed to address this, of which the most prominent baselines, ChexNet [65], and CheXNext [64], use a Densenet-121 [21] backbone. Attention-based models such as A^3Net [84], and DuaLAnet [74], have also been proposed for this diagnostic task. CheXGCN [6] and SSGE [7] are Graph Convolutional Network (GCN)–based methods; the latter proposes a student-teacher based SSL method. More recently, attempts have been made to develop methods for diagnosis and prognosis of COVID-19 from chest radiographs. Most of these methods [3,23,47,85,87] use backbones of deep convolution neural network for COVID-19 prediction. Although, CNN-based methods have achieved tremendous success through generic feature extraction strategies, these architectures often fail to comprehensively encode spatial features from a biological viewpoint [36].

To address this limitation, transformer-based approaches, such as vision transformers [12], have been proposed. The self-attention mechanism in transformers integrates global information by encoding the relative locations of the patches. Few recent works have proposed vision transformers for COVID-19 prediction task [54,59]. However, the efficacy of shifting window based [45] transformer architectures has not been evaluated in this domain. These recent methods compute self-attention among patches within local windows. As an example, Swin-UNet [4] implements swin transformer blocks for medical image segmentation. These blocks are well suited to characterize intra-image disease heterogeneity, a very crucial factor affecting diagnosis and patient prognosis. This motivates our choice of using shifting window blocks in the proposed global-focal network.

3   Proposed Methodology

Figure 2 presents an overview of the end-to-end framework of the proposed *RadioTransformer* global-focal student-teacher network. This comprises two par-

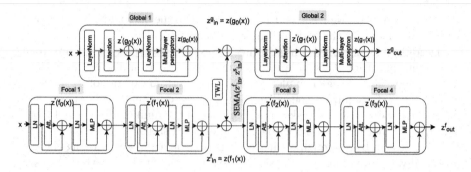

Fig. 3. Overall global-focal network. There are two global networks, and four focal networks connected in parallel inside a Student or Teacher network. The components of the global and focal network are similar, where LN: Layer Normalization, Att.: Attention, MLP: Multi-layer Perceptron. The output of Focal 2 is connected with Global 1 with a TWL connection with SEMA applied to it.

allel architectures, a student and a teacher model. Both student and teacher networks have global and focal network components. Four focal blocks in each model are cascaded with two global blocks in parallel. The global and focal blocks are connected via a two-way lateral (TWL) connection [10,13,42] with smoothed exponential moving average (SEMA). SEMA regulates the attention features shared between the global and focal blocks to bridge the attention gap caused by different learning scales across these networks.

The teacher model is trained with human visual attention obtained from visual search patterns of radiologists. The student model learns from the teacher network using VAL and a classification loss. There are two TWL connections between the teacher and student models coupled with layered SEMA. The proposed architecture is explained in the following subsections.

3.1   Global-Focal Architecture

Global-focal networks can be described as a single-stream architecture where the two components operate in parallel. The global network consists of two and the focal network consists of four shifting-window transformer blocks (Fig. 3). This draws its analogy from the pathways that involve the Parvo, Magno, and Konio ganglion cells [56,88]. The focal network is inspired by the functioning of slow responding Parvo cells (in the 'what' pathway), and the global network is inspired by the fast Magno cells (in the 'where' pathway).

Global-focal network. The teacher and student networks are variants of global-focal architecture. The primary idea of the global-focal architecture is to pseudo-replicate learning of attention in a detailed shifting window fashion as shown in Supplementary Fig. 1. The focal and global layers are represented as f_i and g_j, respectively, where $i \in \{0, 1, 2, 3\}$ and $j \in \{0, 1\}$.

Focal network. The focal network is implemented to learn high contrast and focal information from shifting the windows incrementally on four blocks that are cascaded in a series. The first block of the focal network has multi-layer perceptron head, $h_{f_0}^{mlp} = 64$, attention head, $h_{f_0}^{att} = 2$, and shift size, $s_{f_0} = 0$. The second, third and fourth blocks operate with incremental shifting window size $s_{f_i} = \{1, 2, 3\}$, $h_{f_i}^{att} = \{4, 4, 8\}$ and $h_{f_i}^{mlp} = \{128, 128, 256\}$, where $i \in \{1, 2, 3\}$.

Global Network. The global network consists of two shifting-window blocks cascaded in series. The motivation for implementing global network is to learn low contrast global information from two incremental shift sizes. The first block in the global network has a shift size $s_{g_0} = 0$ and the second block has a shift size $s_{g_1} = 1$. The multi-layer perceptron head of the global network is incremental and can be represented as $h_{g_j}^{mlp} = \{128, 256\}$. The attention head of the global network is incremental and can be represented as $h_{g_j}^{att} = \{4, 8\}$, where $j \in \{0, 1\}$.

TWL Connections. TWL connections between global and focal architectures are introduced to address the inherent semantic attention averaging between the two. The TWL connections are established between layers $\{f_1, g_0\}$ and $\{f_3, g_1\}$. These constitute weighted addition of the outputs from the aforementioned layers coupled with SEMA on the weighted addition outputs. This can be represented as,

$$z_p^{gf} = \lambda_{p_1}^{gf} . g_p(x) + \lambda_{p_2}^{gf} . f_p(x) \tag{1}$$

where, $\lambda_{p_1}^{gf}$ and $\lambda_{p_2}^{gf}$ are the hyper-parameters for weighted addition of the outputs from the global-focal networks represented as gf. $z(g_p(.))$ is the output from the global network and $z(f_p(.))$ is the output from the focal network, $p \in \{in, out\}$ where in is the intermediate, and out is the final output. $\{z_{in}^f, z_{in}^g\} : \{z(f_{in}(.)), z(g_{in}(.))\}$ are the outputs from the intermediate layers of the focal and global networks, respectively. $\{z_{out}^f, z_{out}^g\} : \{z(f_{out}(.)), z(g_{out}(.))\}$ are the final outputs from the focal and global networks, respectively. This is shown in Fig. 3. The smoothed moving average s_v is given by,

$$s_{v_p}(z_p^{gf}) = \hat{\delta}_p^{gf} . s_{v'_p}(z_p^{gf}) + (1 - \hat{\delta}_p^{gf}) . v_p(z_p^{gf}) \tag{2}$$

where s_{v_p} is the smoothed-value of the current variable v in the current iteration for different p, and $s_{v'}$ is the smoothed-value of the variable from the previous iteration for a different p. $\hat{\delta}_p^{gf}$ is the smoothing decay hyperparameter of the global-focal TWL connection. This is represented as $\hat{\delta}_p^{gf} = 1 - \frac{1}{N}$, where N is the number of samples in the current iteration.

Student-Teacher Network. A student-teacher network is proposed in this work. The teacher network learns visual attention patterns only from radiologist's eye gaze maps, while the student learns more specific disease attributes directly from the medical images by leveraging attention information provided by the teacher. Generally, the visual attention maps from radiologists can be noisy and may exhibit variability. Incorporating this variability in addition to distinct disease patterns is not feasible in single-stream architectures. Hence, we need a student-teacher learning framework so that the student can learn this soft information from the teacher. Also, the student-teacher network reduces the complexity of training a single network with the visual attention maps and further fine-tuning for downstream tasks. Here, the model is compressed with just the teacher trained with the visual attention maps.

Teacher Network. The teacher network is a cascaded global-focal learning network with two global and four local blocks connected in parallel, represented as:

$$z_{in}^t = \lambda_{t_1}^{l_0}.g_0^t(x^t) + \lambda_{t_2}^{l_0}.f_1^t(f_0^t(x^t)) \tag{3}$$

$$z_{out}^t = \lambda_{t_1}^{l_1}.g_1^t(z_{in}^t) + \lambda_{t_2}^{l_1}.f_3^t(f_2^t(z_{in}^t)) \tag{4}$$

where x^t is the input to the teacher network, which is subject to hard augmentation techniques with stateless high-value intervals of brightness, contrast, hue, and saturation. z_{in}^t is the intermediate output of the teacher network with $\{\lambda_{t_1}^{l_0}, \lambda_{t_2}^{l_0}\}$, and $\{\lambda_{t_1}^{l_1}, \lambda_{t_2}^{l_1}\}$ as the hyperparameters for weighted addition of the intermediate and final outputs from global and focal blocks, respectively.

Student Network. The input to the student network is softly augmented with stateless relatively low-value intervals of brightness, contrast, hue, and saturation as compared to the teacher network. The student predicts probability values of the disease classes along with an attention region. This attention region is subjected to VAL, described in Sect. 3.2, with the output of the attention region from the teacher network. The student network can be represented as

$$z_{in}^s = \lambda_{s_1}^{l_0}.g_0^s(x^s) + \lambda_{s_2}^{l_0}.f_1^s(f_0^s(x^s)) \tag{5}$$

$$z_{out}^s = \lambda_{s_1}^{l_1}.g_1^s(z_{in}^s) + \lambda_{s_2}^{l_1}.f_3^s(f_2^s(z_{in}^s)) \tag{6}$$

where x^s is the input to the student network. z_{in}^s is the intermediate output of the student network with $\{\lambda_{s_1}^{l_0}, \lambda_{s_2}^{l_0}\}$, and $\{\lambda_{s_1}^{l_1}, \lambda_{s_2}^{l_1}\}$ as the hyperparameters for weighted addition of the intermediate and final outputs from the global and focal blocks of the student network, respectively.

TWL Connections. TWL connections between student and teacher architectures are introduced between layers $\{f_{in}, g_{in}\}$ and $\{f_{out}, g_{out}\}$. The weighted addition of the outputs from the aforementioned layers are coupled with SEMA. This is represented as:

$$z_{in}^{st} = \lambda_{in_1}^s.z_{in}^s + \lambda_{in_2}^t.z_{in}^t \tag{7}$$

$$s_v(z_{in}^{st}) = \hat{\delta}_{in}^{st}.s_{v'}(z_{in}^{st}) + (1 - \hat{\delta}_{in}^{st}).v(z_{in}^{st}) \tag{8}$$

where z_{in}^{st} is the output from the intermediate TWL connection of student-teacher network and s_v is the SEMA from this layer.

$$z_{out}^{st} = \lambda_{out_1}^s.z_{out}^s + \lambda_{out_2}^t.z_{out}^t \tag{9}$$

$$s_v(z_{out}^{st}) = \hat{\delta}_{out}^{st}.s_{v'}(z_{out}^{st}) + (1 - \hat{\delta}_{out}^{st}).v(z_{out}^{st}) \tag{10}$$

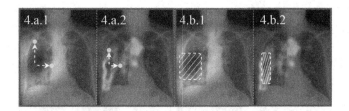

Fig. 4. Visual Attention Loss, $\mathcal{L}_{VAL}$. 4.a.* illustrates the computation of $\mathcal{L}_{MSE}$, where the red dot is the center point of the attention region, and the yellow dots are the height, and width. 4.b.* shows $\mathcal{L}_{GIoU}$, where the attention region overlap is shown with dashed boxes. {4.a.1, 4.b.1} are the predicted attention regions, and {4.a.2, 4.b.2} are the human visual attention regions.

where z_{out}^{st} is the output from the final layer of student-teacher network and $\{s_v(z_{in}^{st}), s_v(z_{out}^{st})\}$ are the $\{SEMA_1, SEMA_4\}$, as shown in Fig. 2. Also, $\{SEMA_2, SEMA_3\}$ are the SEMAs for the intermediate layers of the student global-focal, and teacher global-focal network. The augmentation strategies are explained in the Supplementary section.

3.2 Visual Attention Loss

The visual attention regions are obtained from the teacher network and the predicted attention regions are obtained from the student network. We propose a novel visual attention loss (VAL) function to train the student network. VAL includes a GIoU and a MSE loss, as shown in Fig. 4. We use a hyperparameter $\lambda_{l_i} \in \mathbb{R}^+$ to induce weights in the losses with $i \in \{1, 2\}$.

$$\mathcal{L}_{GIoU} = 1 - \left\{ \frac{|(\mathcal{A}_{pred} \cap \mathcal{A}_{hva})|}{|(\mathcal{A}_{pred} \cup \mathcal{A}_{hva})|} - \frac{|C \setminus (\mathcal{A}_{pred} \cup \mathcal{A}_{hva})|}{|C|} \right\} \quad (11)$$

where $\mathcal{A}_{hva}$ is the visual attention region predicted from the teacher network and $\mathcal{A}_{pred}$ is the attention region predicted from the student network. C is the smallest convex hull of $\mathcal{A}_{hva}$ and $\mathcal{A}_{pred}$. The regression loss between the predicted keypoints and keypoints from visual attention is represented as

$$\mathcal{L}_{MSE} = \frac{1}{n} \sum_{k=1}^{n} \|(\mathcal{K}_{c_x, c_y, h, w})k - (\hat{\mathcal{K}}_{c_x, c_y, h, w})k\|_2^2 \quad (12)$$

where $\{c_x, c_y\}$ are the center points and $\{h, w\}$ are height, and width of the attention region. $\mathcal{K}_{(.)}$ is the keypoint of $\mathcal{A}_{pred}$. $\hat{\mathcal{K}}_{(.)}$ is the keypoint of $\mathcal{A}_{hva}$. n is the number of samples in a particular batch. The final loss is calculated as:

$$\mathcal{L}_{VAL} = \lambda_{l_1}.\mathcal{L}_{GIoU} + \lambda_{l_2}.\mathcal{L}_{MSE} \quad (13)$$

where $\mathcal{L}_{VAL}$ is the proposed VAL and $\{\lambda_{l_1}, \lambda_{l_2}\}$ are the hyperparameters used for weighted addition of the two losses.

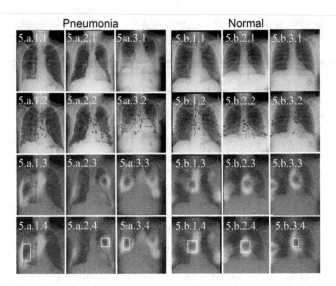

Fig. 5. Human Visual Attention. 5.a.*.* series represents Pneumonia and 5.b.*.* series represents normal examples from [32]. Chest X-Rays from patient are shown in the first row as 5.*.*.1, the raw eye-gaze points from radiologists is shown in the second row as 5.*.*.2, human visual attention maps are shown in the third row as 5.*.*.3, and the corresponding bounding boxes are shown in the fourth row as 5.*.*.4.

3.3 Human Visual Attention

Pre-processing. In this subsection, we discuss the methodology for extracting visual search patterns from eye-tracking data and generating visual attention maps of radiologists. The eye-tracking data [32] consists primarily of a) raw eye-gaze information (as shown in Fig. 5.*.*.2), and b) fixations information, captured from radiologists while they are analyzing chest radiographs in a single-screen setting. The eye-gaze points are reflective of the diagnostic search patterns. The cumulative attention regions, represented as heatmaps (Fig. 5.*.*.3), are human attention regions reflective of diagnostically important areas. A multi-dimensional Gaussian filter with standard deviation, $\sigma = 64$, is used to generate these attention heatmaps. Contours from these attention heatmaps are selected with a thresholding value of $\lambda = 140$ and, subsequently, bounding boxes are generated from the contour with the largest area, as shown in Fig. 5.*.*.4.

Human Visual Attention Training (HVAT). Next, the teacher network is trained with the eye-tracking data from [32]. The teacher network has a classification head to provide an output probability value and a detection head to output key points. The probability value is a $1 \times n$ vector, where n represents the number of different types of disease labels. The key-points output is $\{x_c, y_c, h, w\}$, where (x_c, y_c) are the x and y coordinates of the center, and (h, w) are the height and width respectively. Also, Categorical Crossentropy loss is used for classification,

Table 1. Train-Validation-Test splits used across all experiments

Name	Cell	RSNA	SIIM	Rad	NIH	VBD	MIDRC	SBU
Train	4200	21158	4433	14815	77871	47539	-	-
Valid	1032	3022	633	2116	17304	6791	-	-
Test	624	6045	1266	4233	25596	13582	1241	14220

and weighted addition of Generalized Intersection-with-Union (GIoU) loss [67] and Mean Squared Error (MSE) loss for detection.

4 Datasets and Environment

Datasets. The proposed architecture is evaluated on eight different datasets consisting of two pneumonia classification, four COVID-19 classification (TCIA-SBU [11,68], and MIDRC [11,77,78] only for testing), and two thoracic disease classification cohorts. Further dataset details are provided in the Supplementary section. The datasets along with the train-validation-test splits are shown in Table 1.

Environment. All experiments were performed on the Google Cloud Platform in a compute node with 2 vCPUs, 16 GB RAM, and 20 GB disk memory. The baselines and proposed architectures were trained on a cloud TPU of either type v2-8 or v3-8 with version 2.8.0. All implementations are in TensorFlow [1] and Keras [8] v2.8.0.

5 Experiments and Results

Implementation. During HVAT, the teacher network is trained on eye-gaze data from [16,31] which contains radiologist eye-gaze points on 1083 chest x-rays from the MIMIC-CXR dataset [16,28,29] (details in Subsect. 3.3). All the images are resized to 256×256 pixels. The output of the teacher network is a 1×3 vector of probability values and a 1×4 vector of keypoints. All the baseline models are trained with images uniformly resized to 256×256 pixels. They are trained with Adam optimizer with a batch size of 64 for 50 epochs. The initial learning rate (LR) is set to 1×10^{-2}. The LR is scheduled with an exponential LR scheduler with decay steps $= 10^5$ and decay rate $= 0.2$. There is an early stopping criteria with patience $= 20$ with the task to minimize the validation loss. The proposed *RadioTransformer* architecture follows the same training standards.

5.1 Quantitative Results

We report the F1 Score and Area-Under-Curve (AUC) for all experiments. Detailed results are shown in the Supplementary section. We compare our method with architectures such as different variations of ResNet [19],

Table 2. Quantitative Comparison. F1(↑) and AUC(↑) are reported for the baselines and *RadioTransformer*(RadT)

Classification→	Pneumonia				COVID-19				14-Thoracic				COVID-19 (Test)			
Dataset→	Cell [34]		RSNA [70]		SIIM [38]		Rad [9,63]		NIH [86]		VBD [57]		MIDRC [77,78]		SBU [11,68]	
Architectures↓	F1	AUC	F1	AUC	F1	AUC	F1	AUC	F1	AUC	F1	AUC	F1	AUC	F1	AUC
R50 [19]	59.78	81.70	93.75	98.91	43.01	98.85	94.03	99.27	11.91	74.04	21.76	95.86	23.04	96.32	15.11	65.16
R101 [19]	71.93	83.64	94.84	99.21	39.22	96.98	85.36	97.62	11.20	73.30	32.77	96.24	22.31	93.87	24.22	99.20
R152 [19]	74.30	87.49	91.97	98.57	43.04	98.18	70.21	87.90	10.67	71.37	32.42	96.58	19.22	83.09	24.58	99.61
R50v2 [20]	78.96	87.32	96.60	99.44	47.99	99.79	92.82	99.06	11.42	73.11	34.11	96.32	23.93	98.72	18.71	78.27
R101v2 [20]	52.11	71.23	96.39	99.33	45.83	99.26	97.46	99.82	11.99	73.46	32.18	96.55	04.86	42.13	19.43	82.47
R152v2 [20]	53.44	71.97	95.30	99.01	47.10	99.71	97.76	99.82	11.93	73.23	32.69	96.54	23.07	95.89	23.03	86.25
D121 [21]	70.05	81.97	96.25	99.34	47.59	99.82	95.72	99.51	13.81	78.83	28.71	96.01	24.88	99.82	20.67	88.35
D169 [21]	59.18	76.56	88.86	95.60	46.40	99.68	94.33	99.52	15.21	79.90	32.90	96.46	24.97	99.84	20.13	85.95
D201 [21]	71.93	82.98	95.43	99.04	48.17	99.83	97.81	99.85	14.84	81.38	34.66	96.41	24.99	99.99	21.08	89.53
ViT-B16 [12]	33.85	83.40	76.35	86.06	36.22	95.74	88.25	98.42	05.50	82.06	34.80	95.69	08.47	42.15	11.49	50.22
ViT-B32 [12]	70.02	76.41	79.11	90.74	30.42	92.12	86.73	98.09	06.51	83.77	30.57	94.58	17.50	76.52	18.26	77.75
ViT-L16 [12]	69.59	83.31	85.41	94.53	34.16	95.75	90.11	98.70	08.16	81.60	33.99	95.40	11.17	47.79	15.54	62.72
ViT-L32 [12]	76.38	87.07	69.32	88.86	28.45	92.54	88.40	98.35	06.35	84.96	33.24	95.36	10.21	47.35	03.92	30.82
CCT [18]	62.10	71.18	80.60	92.04	32.63	95.33	92.52	99.11	08.05	85.37	30.25	95.12	23.98	98.53	19.43	83.21
Swin0 [45]	66.04	83.74	96.27	99.57	47.63	99.66	97.53	99.92	07.90	74.62	34.30	95.08	13.74	63.07	17.77	75.47
Swin1 [45]	73.74	86.91	96.65	99.58	47.30	99.56	94.94	99.64	08.30	74.18	34.27	95.13	15.47	69.00	17.64	73.68
RadT	**77.40**	**88.80**	**98.75**	**99.85**	**48.74**	99.65	**99.39**	**99.98**	04.21	**85.43**	**37.32**	**96.84**	18.17	79.60	22.18	94.76

ResNetv2 [20], DenseNet [21], Vision Transformer [12], Compact Convolution Transformers [18], and two variations of Swin Transformers [45]. Note that we show our comparison results primarily on the most prominent backbones (DenseNet-121 [21], vision transformer [12], etc.) used by the baselines [54,64,65] and not on individual implementations. As shown in Table 2, our proposed architecture, mentioned as *RadT*, outperforms other methods on all six datasets. Note that the F1 scores are computed without any standard averaging such as macro, micro or weighted. This is why, F1 scores on 14-class classification datasets, such as, NIH, and VinBigData are comparatively lower than the reported scores on RSNA, Radiography, etc. However, in these datasets where lower F1 scores are reported, the AUC of the proposed framework still outperforms the baselines.

Table 3. Ablation Study. Accuracy(↑), AUC(↑), F1(↑), Precision(↑), and Recall(↑) are shown for different ablations on three datasets

Dataset→	RSNA [70]					Radiography [9,63]					VinBigData [57]				
Ablations↓	Ac	AUC	F1	Pr	Re	Ac	AUC	F1	Pr	Re	Ac	AUC	F1	Pr	Re
Focal	85.01	92.69	80.96	85.01	85.01	91.05	98.92	90.82	91.38	90.60	63.18	95.62	28.34	94.84	48.19
Global	86.45	93.99	83.26	86.45	86.45	89.91	98.65	88.90	90.38	89.44	62.46	95.46	25.79	**95.53**	47.54
Focal+HVAT	87.00	94.12	84.15	87.00	87.00	92.33	99.08	91.46	92.82	91.55	65.43	96.35	33.18	90.24	51.81
Global+HVAT	90.46	96.29	88.60	90.46	90.46	91.26	98.76	90.41	91.52	91.00	65.02	96.32	32.56	92.27	50.17
Focal+HVAT+VAL	89.68	95.88	87.62	89.68	89.68	93.04	99.22	92.66	93.35	92.66	65.32	96.31	33.49	92.30	50.44
Global+HVAT+VAL	89.76	96.00	87.51	89.76	89.76	91.05	98.76	90.32	91.47	90.60	64.97	96.16	31.85	91.73	50.41
GF+HVAT+VAL(**RadT**)	98.94	99.85	98.75	98.94	98.94	99.43	99.98	99.39	99.48	99.41	66.54	96.84	37.32	82.35	57.90

Ablation Experiments. Here, we discuss the categorical inference on all the individual components of our proposed network. In Table 3, the ablation experiment results for different components are summarized for three different datasets. The global network outperforms the focal network for the binary classification

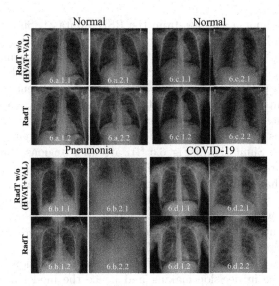

Fig. 6. Qualitative Comparison. Comparison of the class activation maps from *RadioTransformer* are shown on two datasets. {6.a.*.* , 6.b.*.*} are from {normal, pneumonia} classes of the RSNA dataset, and {6.c.*.*, 6.d.*.*} are from {normal, COVID-19} of the Radiography dataset. {6.*.*.1, 6.*.*.2} are the class activation maps generated from {RadT w/o (HVAT+HVAL), RadT}.

task in the RSNA dataset. This signifies that for simple binary classification, where global feature representations generally lead to a clear distinction between labels, the global network performs better. This is, in fact, true for radiologists' decision making as well; the results provide a justification for the designed global-focal approach. For the Radiography and VinBigData datasets, which are multi-class classification tasks, focal network performs better than the global network owing to diagnostic relevance of the more granular details in the images. It is also evident from the results that when HVAT is used along with global-focal networks, the scores improve. Interestingly, when VAL is added, scores are not significantly higher than the previous ablations. There are primarily two reasons: a) VAL lacks in distilling the visual attention from the teacher to the student when using only individual global and focal blocks; the performance improves when VAL distills the visual attention from combined global-focal blocks of the teacher, and b) attention loss between the two visual attention regions may not converge well with regression of key-points and minimizing of GIoU.

5.2   Qualitative Results

Figure 6 illustrates the qualitative differences between *RadT w/o (HVAT+VAL)*, and *RadT*. *RadT w/o (HVAT+VAL)* is the basic backbone of our proposed *RadioTransformer* architecture, i.e., the global-focal student-teacher network without HVAT and VAL. The first column, Fig. 6.a.*.*, and Fig. 6.b.*.*, are normal and pneumonia samples from the RSNA dataset. Similarly, Fig. 6.c.*.* are normal, and Fig. 6.d.*.* are COVID-19, from the Radiography dataset. The images in Fig. 6.*.*.1 and Fig. 6.*.*.2 are the class activation maps from RadT w/o (HVAT+VAL) and RadT, respectively. We can observe clear differences in attention region patterns between these two rows. The attention regions in the first row are relatively discretized and the inconsistency in overlap with the white regions (infiltrates/fluids) is quite prominent. However, in the second row, relatively continuous attention regions are observed with consistent overlap with the disease patterns. Similarly, in Fig. 6.c.*.1, attention regions observed are more discrete in nature, unlike Fig. 6.c.*.2. For normal chest radiographs, this potentially signifies that RadT focuses intrinsically on regions that may be significant for a radiologist to diagnose and reject the presence of infiltrates/fluids. On the contrary, RadT w/o (HVAT+VAL) attempts to identify non-overlapping regions with visual attention to reject the presence of infiltrates/fluids. Also, we observe that the attention regions from RadT w/o (HVAT+VAL) cover a larger area than those from RadT, implying that lack of visual attention knowledge leads to low confidence in decision-making and hence the model needs to search a comparatively larger space to conclusively accept or reject a claim. In 6.b.2.*, it is observed that for a lung densely filled with fluid, RadT w/o (HVAT+VAL) focuses on a comparatively sparse and large region. However, RadT focuses on regions with dense fluid accumulation. These qualitative findings suggest that *Radio Transformer* inherently analyzes the regions with a visuo-cognitive approach similar to that of a radiologist.

6   Conclusion

This paper presents *Radio Transformer*, a novel visual attention–driven transformer framework, motivated by radiologists' visuo-cognitive approaches. Unlike existing techniques that rely only on visual information for diagnostic tasks, *Radio Transformer* leverages eye-gaze patterns from experts to train a global-focal student-teacher network. Our framework learns and implements hierarchical search patterns to improve the diagnostic performance of transformer architectures. When evaluated on eight datasets, comprising over 260,000 images, the proposed architecture outperforms SOTA approaches. Our qualitative analysis shows that by integrating visual attention into the network, *Radio Transformer* focuses on diagnostically relevant regions of interest leading to higher confidence in decision making. To the best of our knowledge, no method has been proposed that integrates gaze data from expert radiologists to improve the diagnostic performance of deep learning architectures. This work paves the way for radiologist-in-the-loop computer-aided diagnosis tools.

Acknowledgement. The reported research was partly supported by NIH 1R21CA258493-01A1, NIH 75N92020D00021 (subcontract), and the OVPR and IEDM seed grants at Stony Brook University. The content is solely the responsibility of the authors and does not necessarily represent the official views of the National Institutes of Health.

References

1. Abadi, M., et al.: TensorFlow: large-scale machine learning on heterogeneous distributed systems. arXiv preprint arXiv:1603.04467 (2016)
2. Bertram, R., et al.: Eye movements of radiologists reflect expertise in CT study interpretation: a potential tool to measure resident development. Radiology 281(3), 805–815 (2016)
3. Canayaz, M.: MH-COVIDNet: diagnosis of COVID-19 using deep neural networks and meta-heuristic-based feature selection on X-ray images. Biomed. Signal Process. Control 64, 102257 (2021)
4. Cao, H., et al.: Swin-Unet: Unet-like pure transformer for medical image segmentation. arXiv preprint arXiv:2105.05537 (2021)
5. Cheerla, A., Gevaert, O.: Deep learning with multimodal representation for pancancer prognosis prediction. Bioinformatics 35(14), i446–i454 (2019)
6. Chen, B., Li, J., Lu, G., Yu, H., Zhang, D.: Label co-occurrence learning with graph convolutional networks for multi-label chest x-ray image classification. IEEE J. Biomed. Health Inform. 24(8), 2292–2302 (2020)
7. Chen, B., Zhang, Z., Li, Y., Lu, G., Zhang, D.: Multi-label chest x-ray image classification via semantic similarity graph embedding. IEEE Trans. Circuits Syst. Video Technol. 32(4), 2455–2468 (2021)
8. Chollet, F., et al.: Keras: deep learning library for Theano and TensorFlow. https://keras.io/k 7(8), T1 (2015)
9. Chowdhury, M.E.H., et al.: Can AI help in screening viral and COVID-19 pneumonia? IEEE Access 8, 132665–132676 (2020). https://doi.org/10.1109/ACCESS.2020.3010287
10. Christoph, R., Pinz, F.A.: Spatiotemporal residual networks for video action recognition. In: Advances in Neural Information Processing Systems, pp. 3468–3476 (2016)
11. Clark, K., et al.: The cancer imaging archive (TCIA): maintaining and operating a public information repository. J. Digit. Imaging 26(6), 1045–1057 (2013)
12. Dosovitskiy, A., et al.: An image is worth 16×16 words: transformers for image recognition at scale. arXiv preprint arXiv:2010.11929 (2020)
13. Feichtenhofer, C., Fan, H., Malik, J., He, K.: SlowFast networks for video recognition. In: Proceedings of the IEEE/CVF International Conference on Computer Vision, pp. 6202–6211 (2019)
14. Fox, S.E., Faulkner-Jones, B.E.: Eye-tracking in the study of visual expertise: methodology and approaches in medicine. Frontline Learn. Res. 5(3), 29–40 (2017)
15. van der Gijp, A., et al.: How visual search relates to visual diagnostic performance: a narrative systematic review of eye-tracking research in radiology. Adv. Health Sci. Educ. 22(3), 765–787 (2016). https://doi.org/10.1007/s10459-016-9698-1
16. Goldberger, A.L., et al.: PhysioBank, PhysioToolkit, and PhysioNet: components of a new research resource for complex physiologic signals. Circulation 101(23), e215–e220 (2000)
17. Hanna, T.N., et al.: The effects of fatigue from overnight shifts on radiology search patterns and diagnostic performance. J. Am. Coll. Radiol. 15(12), 1709–1716 (2018)
18. Hassani, A., Walton, S., Shah, N., Abuduweili, A., Li, J., Shi, H.: Escaping the big data paradigm with compact transformers. arXiv preprint arXiv:2104.05704 (2021)

19. He, K., Zhang, X., Ren, S., Sun, J.: Deep residual learning for image recognition. In: Proceedings of the IEEE Conference on Computer Vision and Pattern Recognition, pp. 770–778 (2016)
20. He, K., Zhang, X., Ren, S., Sun, J.: Identity mappings in deep residual networks. In: Leibe, B., Matas, J., Sebe, N., Welling, M. (eds.) ECCV 2016. LNCS, vol. 9908, pp. 630–645. Springer, Cham (2016). https://doi.org/10.1007/978-3-319-46493-0_38
21. Huang, G., Liu, Z., Van Der Maaten, L., Weinberger, K.Q.: Densely connected convolutional networks. In: Proceedings of the IEEE Conference on Computer Vision and Pattern Recognition, pp. 4700–4708 (2017)
22. Huang, Y., Cai, M., Li, Z., Lu, F., Sato, Y.: Mutual context network for jointly estimating egocentric gaze and action. IEEE Trans. Image Process. **29**, 7795–7806 (2020)
23. Hussain, E., Hasan, M., Rahman, M.A., Lee, I., Tamanna, T., Parvez, M.Z.: CoroDet: a deep learning based classification for COVID-19 detection using chest X-ray images. Chaos, Solitons Fractals **142**, 110495 (2021)
24. Itti, L.: Quantifying the contribution of low-level saliency to human eye movements in dynamic scenes. Vis. Cogn. **12**(6), 1093–1123 (2005)
25. Itti, L., Baldi, P.: Bayesian surprise attracts human attention. Vision. Res. **49**(10), 1295–1306 (2009)
26. Itti, L., Koch, C.: A saliency-based search mechanism for overt and covert shifts of visual attention. Vision. Res. **40**(10–12), 1489–1506 (2000)
27. Itti, L., Koch, C.: Computational modelling of visual attention. Nat. Rev. Neurosci. **2**(3), 194–203 (2001)
28. Johnson, A., Bulgarelli, L., Pollard, T., Horng, S., Celi, L.A., Mark IV, R.: MIMIC-IV (version 0.4). PhysioNet (2020)
29. Johnson, A., Pollard, T., Mark, R., Berkowitz, S., Horng, S.: MIMIC-CXR database. PhysioNet (2019). https://doi.org/10.13026/C2JT1Q
30. Kar, A., Corcoran, P.: A review and analysis of eye-gaze estimation systems, algorithms and performance evaluation methods in consumer platforms. IEEE Access **5**, 16495–16519 (2017)
31. Karargyris, A., et al.: Eye gaze data for chest x-rays
32. Karargyris, A., et al.: Creation and validation of a chest x-ray dataset with eye-tracking and report dictation for AI development. Sci. Data **8**(1), 1–18 (2021)
33. Kelly, B.S., Rainford, L.A., Darcy, S.P., Kavanagh, E.C., Toomey, R.J.: The development of expertise in radiology: in chest radiograph interpretation, "expert" search pattern may predate "expert" levels of diagnostic accuracy for pneumothorax identification. Radiology **280**(1), 252–260 (2016)
34. Kermany, D.S., et al.: Identifying medical diagnoses and treatable diseases by image-based deep learning. Cell **172**(5), 1122–1131 (2018)
35. Kleinke, C.L.: Gaze and eye contact: a research review. Psychol. Bull. **100**(1), 78 (1986)
36. Konwer, A., et al.: Attention-based multi-scale gated recurrent encoder with novel correlation loss for COVID-19 progression prediction. In: de Bruijne, M., et al. (eds.) MICCAI 2021. LNCS, vol. 12905, pp. 824–833. Springer, Cham (2021). https://doi.org/10.1007/978-3-030-87240-3_79
37. Kundel, H.L., Nodine, C.F., Krupinski, E.A.: Computer-displayed eye position as a visual aid to pulmonary nodule interpretation. Invest. Radiol. **25**(8), 890–896 (1990)
38. Lakhani, P., et al.: The 2021 SIIM-FISABIO-RSNA machine learning COVID-19 challenge: annotation and standard exam classification of COVID-19 chest radiographs (2021)

39. Lee, A., et al.: Identification of gaze pattern and blind spots by upper gastrointestinal endoscopy using an eye-tracking technique. Surg. Endosc. **36**, 2574–2581 (2021). https://doi.org/10.1007/s00464-021-08546-3

40. Lévêque, L., Bosmans, H., Cockmartin, L., Liu, H.: State of the art: eye-tracking studies in medical imaging. IEEE Access **6**, 37023–37034 (2018)

41. Li, Y., Liu, M., Rehg, J.: In the eye of the beholder: gaze and actions in first person video. IEEE Trans. Pattern Anal. Mach. Intell. (2021)

42. Lin, T.Y., Dollár, P., Girshick, R., He, K., Hariharan, B., Belongie, S.: Feature pyramid networks for object detection. In: Proceedings of the IEEE Conference on Computer Vision and Pattern Recognition, pp. 2117–2125 (2017)

43. Litchfield, D., Ball, L.J., Donovan, T., Manning, D.J., Crawford, T.: Viewing another person's eye movements improves identification of pulmonary nodules in chest x-ray inspection. J. Exp. Psychol. Appl. **16**(3), 251 (2010)

44. Liu, Y., et al.: Goal-oriented gaze estimation for zero-shot learning. In: Proceedings of the IEEE/CVF Conference on Computer Vision and Pattern Recognition, pp. 3794–3803 (2021)

45. Liu, Z., et al.: Swin transformer: hierarchical vision transformer using shifted windows. arXiv preprint arXiv:2103.14030 (2021)

46. Mackworth, N.H., Morandi, A.J.: The gaze selects informative details within pictures. Percept. Psychophys. **2**(11), 547–552 (1967)

47. Mahmud, T., Rahman, M.A., Fattah, S.A.: CovXNet: a multi-dilation convolutional neural network for automatic COVID-19 and other pneumonia detection from chest X-ray images with transferable multi-receptive feature optimization. Comput. Biol. Med. **122**, 103869 (2020)

48. Mall, S., Brennan, P.C., Mello-Thoms, C.: Can a machine learn from radiologists' visual search behaviour and their interpretation of mammograms–a deep-learning study. J. Digit. Imaging **32**(5), 746–760 (2019)

49. Mathe, S., Sminchisescu, C.: Dynamic eye movement datasets and learnt saliency models for visual action recognition. In: Fitzgibbon, A., Lazebnik, S., Perona, P., Sato, Y., Schmid, C. (eds.) ECCV 2012. LNCS, vol. 7573, pp. 842–856. Springer, Heidelberg (2012). https://doi.org/10.1007/978-3-642-33709-3_60

50. McLaughlin, L., Hughes, C., Bond, R., McConnell, J., Cairns, A., McFadden, S.: The effect of a digital training tool to aid chest image interpretation: hybridising eye tracking technology and a decision support tool. Radiography **27**(2), 505–511 (2021)

51. Min, K., Corso, J.J.: Integrating human gaze into attention for egocentric activity recognition. In: Proceedings of the IEEE/CVF Winter Conference on Applications of Computer Vision, pp. 1069–1078 (2021)

52. Mishra, A., Aloimonos, Y., Fah, C.L.: Active segmentation with fixation. In: 2009 IEEE 12th International Conference on Computer Vision, pp. 468–475. IEEE (2009)

53. Modi, N., Singh, J.: A review of various state of art eye gaze estimation techniques. In: Advances in Computational Intelligence and Communication Technology, pp. 501–510 (2021)

54. Mondal, A.K., Bhattacharjee, A., Singla, P., Prathosh, A.P.: xViTCOS: explainable vision transformer based COVID-19 screening using radiography. IEEE J. Transl. Eng. Health Med. **10**, 1–10 (2021)

55. Moser, T., Lohmeyer, Q., Meboldt, M., Distler, O., Becker, M.O.: Visual assessment of digital ulcers in systemic sclerosis analysed by eye tracking: implications for wound assessment. Clin. Exp. Rheumatol. **38**(3), 137–139 (2020)

56. Murray, I., Plainis, S.: Contrast coding and magno/parvo segregation revealed in reaction time studies. Vision. Res. **43**(25), 2707–2719 (2003)
57. Nguyen, H.Q., et al.: VinDr-CXR: an open dataset of chest X-rays with radiologist's annotations. Sci. Data **9**, 429 (2022). https://doi.org/10.1038/s41597-022-01498-w
58. Papadopoulos, D.P., Clarke, A.D.F., Keller, F., Ferrari, V.: Training object class detectors from eye tracking data. In: Fleet, D., Pajdla, T., Schiele, B., Tuytelaars, T. (eds.) ECCV 2014. LNCS, vol. 8693, pp. 361–376. Springer, Cham (2014). https://doi.org/10.1007/978-3-319-10602-1_24
59. Park, S., et al.: Vision transformer for COVID-19 CXR diagnosis using chest x-ray feature corpus. arXiv preprint arXiv:2103.07055 (2021)
60. Parkhurst, D., Law, K., Niebur, E.: Modeling the role of salience in the allocation of overt visual attention. Vision. Res. **42**(1), 107–123 (2002)
61. Patra, A., et al.: Efficient ultrasound image analysis models with sonographer gaze assisted distillation. In: Shen, D., et al. (eds.) MICCAI 2019. LNCS, vol. 11767, pp. 394–402. Springer, Cham (2019). https://doi.org/10.1007/978-3-030-32251-9_43
62. Prasanna, P., et al.: Radiographic-deformation and textural heterogeneity (r-DepTH): an integrated descriptor for brain tumor prognosis. In: Descoteaux, M., Maier-Hein, L., Franz, A., Jannin, P., Collins, D.L., Duchesne, S. (eds.) MICCAI 2017. LNCS, vol. 10434, pp. 459–467. Springer, Cham (2017). https://doi.org/10.1007/978-3-319-66185-8_52
63. Rahman, T., et al.: Exploring the effect of image enhancement techniques on COVID-19 detection using chest x-ray images. Comput. Biol. Med. **132**, 104319 (2021)
64. Rajpurkar, P., et al.: Deep learning for chest radiograph diagnosis: a retrospective comparison of the CheXNeXt algorithm to practicing radiologists. PLoS Med. **15**(11), e1002686 (2018)
65. Rajpurkar, P., et al.: CheXnet: radiologist-level pneumonia detection on chest x-rays with deep learning. arXiv preprint arXiv:1711.05225 (2017)
66. Ramanathan, S., Katti, H., Sebe, N., Kankanhalli, M., Chua, T.-S.: An eye fixation database for saliency detection in images. In: Daniilidis, K., Maragos, P., Paragios, N. (eds.) ECCV 2010. LNCS, vol. 6314, pp. 30–43. Springer, Heidelberg (2010). https://doi.org/10.1007/978-3-642-15561-1_3
67. Rezatofighi, H., Tsoi, N., Gwak, J., Sadeghian, A., Reid, I., Savarese, S.: Generalized intersection over union: a metric and a loss for bounding box regression. In: Proceedings of the IEEE/CVF Conference on Computer Vision and Pattern Recognition, pp. 658–666 (2019)
68. Saltz, J., et al.: Stony brook university COVID-19 positive cases [data set] (2021)
69. Shapovalova, N., Raptis, M., Sigal, L., Mori, G.: Action is in the eye of the beholder: eye-gaze driven model for spatio-temporal action localization. In: Advances in Neural Information Processing Systems, pp. 2409–2417. Citeseer (2013)
70. Shih, G., et al.: Augmenting the national institutes of health chest radiograph dataset with expert annotations of possible pneumonia. Radiol. Artif. Intell. **1**(1), e180041 (2019)
71. Stember, J.N., et al.: Eye tracking for deep learning segmentation using convolutional neural networks. J. Digit. Imaging **32**(4), 597–604 (2019)
72. Tatler, B.W., Baddeley, R.J., Vincent, B.T.: The long and the short of it: spatial statistics at fixation vary with saccade amplitude and task. Vision. Res. **46**(12), 1857–1862 (2006)
73. Taylor-Phillips, S., Stinton, C.: Fatigue in radiology: a fertile area for future research. Br. J. Radiol. **92**(1099), 20190043 (2019)

74. Teixeira, V., Braz, L., Pedrini, H., Dias, Z.: DuaLAnet: dual lesion attention network for thoracic disease classification in chest X-rays. In: 2020 International Conference on Systems, Signals and Image Processing (IWSSIP), pp. 69–74. IEEE (2020)

75. Theeuwes, J.: Stimulus-driven capture and attentional set: selective search for color and visual abrupt onsets. J. Exp. Psychol. Hum. Percept. Perform. **20**(4), 799 (1994)

76. Theeuwes, J., Kramer, A.F., Hahn, S., Irwin, D.E., Zelinsky, G.J.: Influence of attentional capture on oculomotor control. J. Exp. Psychol. Hum. Percept. Perform. **25**(6), 1595 (1999)

77. Tsai, E.B., et al.: Data from medical imaging data resource center (MIDRC) - RSNA international COVID radiology database (RICORD) release 1C - chest X-ray, COVID+ (MIDRC-RICORD-1C). Cancer Imaging Archive **6**(7), 13 (2021)

78. Tsai, E.B., et al.: The RSNA international COVID-19 open radiology database (RICORD). Radiology **299**(1), E204–E213 (2021)

79. Vasudevan, A.B., Dai, D., Van Gool, L.: Object referring in videos with language and human gaze. In: Proceedings of the IEEE Conference on Computer Vision and Pattern Recognition, pp. 4129–4138 (2018)

80. Vertinsky, T., Forster, B.: Prevalence of eye strain among radiologists: influence of viewing variables on symptoms. Am. J. Roentgenol. **184**(2), 681–686 (2005)

81. Vig, E., Dorr, M., Cox, D.: Space-variant descriptor sampling for action recognition based on saliency and eye movements. In: Fitzgibbon, A., Lazebnik, S., Perona, P., Sato, Y., Schmid, C. (eds.) ECCV 2012. LNCS, vol. 7578, pp. 84–97. Springer, Heidelberg (2012). https://doi.org/10.1007/978-3-642-33786-4_7

82. Waite, S., et al.: Analysis of perceptual expertise in radiology-current knowledge and a new perspective. Front. Hum. Neurosci. **13**, 213 (2019)

83. Waite, S., et al.: Tired in the reading room: the influence of fatigue in radiology. J. Am. Coll. Radiol. **14**(2), 191–197 (2017)

84. Wang, H., Wang, S., Qin, Z., Zhang, Y., Li, R., Xia, Y.: Triple attention learning for classification of 14 thoracic diseases using chest radiography. Med. Image Anal. **67**, 101846 (2021)

85. Wang, L., Lin, Z.Q., Wong, A.: COVID-Net: a tailored deep convolutional neural network design for detection of COVID-19 cases from chest X-ray images. Sci. Rep. **10**(1), 1–12 (2020). https://doi.org/10.1038/s41598-020-76550-z

86. Wang, X., Peng, Y., Lu, L., Lu, Z., Bagheri, M., Summers, R.M.: ChestX-ray8: hospital-scale chest x-ray database and benchmarks on weakly-supervised classification and localization of common thorax diseases. In: Proceedings of the IEEE Conference on Computer Vision and Pattern Recognition, pp. 2097–2106 (2017)

87. Wong, A., et al.: COVID-Net S: towards computer-aided severity assessment via training and validation of deep neural networks for geographic extent and opacity extent scoring of chest X-rays for SARS-CoV-2 lung disease severity. arXiv preprint arXiv:2005.12855 (2020)

88. Yoonessi, A., Yoonessi, A.: Functional assessment of magno, parvo and koniocellular pathways; current state and future clinical applications. J. Ophthalmic Vis. Res. **6**(2), 119 (2011)

89. Yoshie, T., et al.: The influence of experience on gazing patterns during endovascular treatment: eye-tracking study. J. Neuroendovascular Ther. oa–2021 (2021)

90. Yun, K., Peng, Y., Samaras, D., Zelinsky, G.J., Berg, T.L.: Exploring the role of gaze behavior and object detection in scene understanding. Front. Psychol. **4**, 917 (2013)

91. Yun, K., Peng, Y., Samaras, D., Zelinsky, G.J., Berg, T.L.: Studying relationships between human gaze, description, and computer vision. In: Proceedings of the IEEE Conference on Computer Vision and Pattern Recognition, pp. 739–746 (2013)
92. Zimmermann, J.M., et al.: Quantification of avoidable radiation exposure in interventional fluoroscopy with eye tracking technology. Invest. Radiol. **55**(7), 457–462 (2020)

Differentiable Zooming for Multiple Instance Learning on Whole-Slide Images

Kevin Thandiackal[1,2]([✉])[ID], Boqi Chen[1,2][ID], Pushpak Pati[1][ID],
Guillaume Jaume[3][ID], Drew F. K. Williamson[3][ID], Maria Gabrani[1][ID],
and Orcun Goksel[2,4][ID]

[1] IBM Research Europe, Zurich, Switzerland
{kth,che,pus,mga}@zurich.ibm.com
[2] ETH Zurich, Zurich, Switzerland
[3] Brigham and Women's Hospital, Harvard Medical School, Boston, USA
{gjaume,dwilliamson}@bwh.harvard.edu
[4] Uppsala University, Uppsala, Sweden
orcun.goksel@it.uu.se

Abstract. Multiple Instance Learning (MIL) methods have become increasingly popular for classifying gigapixel-sized Whole-Slide Images (WSIs) in digital pathology. Most MIL methods operate at a *single* WSI magnification, by processing *all* the tissue patches. Such a formulation induces high computational requirements and constrains the contextualization of the WSI-level representation to a single scale. Certain MIL methods extend to multiple scales, but they are computationally more demanding. In this paper, inspired by the pathological diagnostic process, we propose ZOOMMIL, a method that *learns* to perform multi-level zooming in an end-to-end manner. ZOOMMIL builds WSI representations by aggregating tissue-context information from multiple magnifications. The proposed method outperforms the state-of-the-art MIL methods in WSI classification on two large datasets, while significantly reducing computational demands with regard to Floating-Point Operations (FLOPs) and processing time by 40–50×. Our code is available at: https://github.com/histocartography/zoommil.

Keywords: Whole-slide image classification · Multiple instance learning · Multi-scale zooming · Efficient computational pathology

1 Introduction

Histopathological diagnosis consists of examining tissue samples to characterize their phenotype, morphology, and the topological distribution of their constituents. With advancements in slide-scanning technologies, tissue specimens

---

K. Thandiackal and B. Chen—Contributed equally.
G. Jaume—Work done while at IBM Research Europe.

Supplementary Information The online version contains supplementary material available at https://doi.org/10.1007/978-3-031-19803-8_41.

can now be digitized into Whole-Slide Images (WSIs) with high resolution, enabling the pathological assessment to be conducted on a computer rather than under a microscope. A WSI contains rich tissue information and can be up to $100\,000\times100\,000$ pixels in size at $40\times$ magnification ($0.25\mu m$/pixel). Due to the image size, complexity, and multi-scale nature of biological systems, a pathologist generally examines a WSI in a hierarchical manner, *i.e.*, detecting informative regions at a *low* magnification, and evaluating selected areas at a *high* magnification, as shown in Fig. 1(a). However, such manual examination of a gigapixel-sized WSI can be cumbersome, time-consuming, and prone to inter- and intra-observer variability [14,16].

To alleviate the aforementioned challenges, Deep Learning (DL)-based diagnosis tools are being developed in digital pathology. However, these tools encounter additional challenges pertaining to the size of WSIs, and the difficulty of acquiring fine-grained annotations. To this end, DL methods have been proposed, in particular, using Multiple Instance Learning (MIL). Here, a WSI is decomposed into a bag of patches, which are individually encoded by a Convolutional Neural Network (CNN) backbone. A pooling operation then combines the patch embeddings into a slide-level representation that is finally mapped to the slide label. Although MIL methods have achieved remarkable performance on several pathology tasks, *e.g.*, tumor classification [10,32,39,42], tumor segmentation [22,30], and survival prediction [44], they pose the following drawbacks.

First, the performance of MIL methods relies on a carefully tuned context-resolution trade-off [6,36,41], *i.e.*, an optimal operating resolution that includes adequate context in a patch. As the dimensions of diagnostically relevant tissue vary significantly in histopathology, patches of different sizes across magnifications convey different context information about the tissue microenvironment. Thus, identifying an optimal resolution and patch size involves several tailored and tedious steps. Typical MIL methods use patches at a *single* magnification (Fig. 1(b)) and disregard the spatial distribution of patches, causing the above problem. Although [33,40] address this via visual self-attention, they are constrained by expensive computations of attention scores on a large number of patches in a WSI. Differently, [26] addresses the issue via random patch sampling and sparse convolutions, consequently preventing deterministic inference. In the literature, other methods [17,19,41] are extracting concentric patches across multiple magnifications (Fig. 1(c)) to acquire richer context per patch. However, they are computationally more expensive as they need to encode all patches at high magnification and the corresponding patches across lower magnifications.

Second, most MIL methods process *all* tissue patches at high magnification, thus processing a large number of uninformative patches, which increases computational cost, inference time, and memory requirements. For instance, inference on a WSI of $50\,000 \times 50\,000$ pixels using CLAM [32], an MIL method, requires $\approx$150 Tera Floating-Point Operations (FLOPs), which is $37\,500\times$ the processing of an ImageNet [12] sample by ResNet34 [18]. Further, the high memory footprint of MIL methods inhibits their scalability to large histopathology images, *e.g.*, prostatectomy slides which can be $300\,000\times400\,000$ pixels at $40\times$ magnification. Such computational requirements can in turn hinder the clinical deployment of

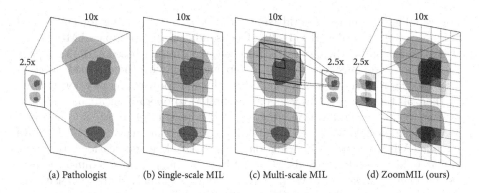

Fig. 1. Comparison of different methods for the diagnosis of WSIs

these methods. Their adoption becomes even prohibitive when computational resources are scarce due to limited access to GPUs or cloud services. In view of the above challenges, a multi-scale context-aware MIL method with high computational efficiency is desired.

In this paper, we propose ZOOMMIL, a novel method inspired by the hierarchical diagnostic process of pathologists. We first select Regions-of-Interest (ROIs) at low magnification, and zoom in on them at high magnification for finer analysis, as in Fig. 1(d). The RoI selection is performed through a gated-attention and a differentiable top-K (DIFF-TOPK) module, which learns where to zoom, in an end-to-end manner, while moderating computational requirements at high magnifications. The process can be repeated across an arbitrary number of magnifications, *e.g.*, $5\times \to 10\times \to 20\times$, as per the task at hand. Finally, we aggregate the information acquired across multiple scales to obtain a context-aware WSI representation for downstream pathology tasks, as shown in Fig. 2. In summary, our contributions are:

1. A novel multi-scale context-aware MIL method that learns to perform multi-level zooming in an end-to-end manner for WSI classification.
2. A computationally more efficient method compared to the state of the art in MIL, *e.g.*, $40\times$ faster inference on a WSI of size $26\,009\times18\,234$ pixels at $10\times$ magnification, while achieving better (2/3 datasets) or comparable (1/3 datasets) WSI classification performance.
3. Comprehensive benchmarking of the method with regard to WSI classification performance and computational requirements (on GPU and CPU) on multiple datasets across multiple organs and pathology tasks, *i.e.*, tumor subtyping, grading, and metastasis detection.

2 Related Work

2.1 Multiple Instance Learning in Histopathology

MIL in histopathology was introduced in [20] to classify breast and colon RoIs. The experiments established the superiority of *attention*-based pooling over *max* and *mean* pooling. Concurrently, [10] scaled MIL to WSIs for grading prostate biopsies. They proposed Neural Network (RNN)-based pooling for end-to-end training. Later, several works [31,32,44] consolidated attention-based MIL across several organs and pathology tasks. Recently, transformer-based MIL [33,40] has been proposed to consider inter-patch dependencies, with the downside of computing a quadratic number of interactions, which introduces memory constraints. Further, all the above MIL methods are limited to operate on *all* patches in a WSI at a single magnification. In view of the benefits of multi-scale information in histopathology [4,15,19,28,36,43], a few recent methods [17,27] have extended MIL to combine information across multiple magnifications. However, similar to single-scale methods, these multi-scale versions also require the processing of *all* patches in a WSI, which is computationally more expensive. In contrast, our proposed ZooMMIL*learns* to identify informative regions at low magnification and subsequently zooms in on these regions at high magnification for efficient and comprehensive analysis. Differently, several other approaches aim to learn the inter-instance relations in histopathology via Graph Neural Networks (GNNs) [1–3,29,36,38,45] or CNNs [26,39,42].

2.2   Instance Selection Strategies in Histopathology

Most MIL methods encode all patches in a WSI irrespective of their functional types. This compels MIL to be computationally expensive for large WSIs. To reduce the computational memory requirements, [26] randomly sampled a subset of instances, with the consequence of potentially missing vital information, especially when the informative set is small, *e.g.*, in metastasis detection. Differently, reinforcement learning-based methods [13,37] have also been developed to this end. [37] proposed to sequentially identify some of the diagnostically relevant RoIs in a WSI by following a parameterized policy. However, the method leverages a very coarse context for the RoI identification and is limited to utilizing only single-scale information for the diagnosis. Additionally, the reinforcement learning method [13] and the recurrent visual attention-based model [7] aim to select patches, which mimics pathological diagnosis. However, these methods require pixel-level annotations to learn discriminative regions, which is expensive to acquire on large WSIs. In contrast to the above methods, ZooMMILrequires only WSI-level supervision. Our method is flexible to attend to several magnifications, while efficiently classifying WSIs with high performance.

The attention-score-based iterative sampling strategy proposed in [23,25] closely relates to our work. For the final classification, the selected patch embeddings are simply concatenated, analogous to average pooling. Instead, ZooMMILincorporates a dual gated-attention module between two consecutive magnifications to simultaneously learn to select the relevant instances to be zoomed in on, and learn an improved WSI-level representation for the lower magnification.

The patch selection module employed in our work is inspired by the perturbed optimizer-based [8] differentiable Top-K algorithm proposed in [11]. ZooMMILadvances upon [11] by extending to several magnifications, *i.e.*, multi-level zooming, and scaling the applications to gigapixel-sized WSIs.

3   MIL with Differentiable Zooming

In this section, we present ZOOMMIL, which identifies informative patches at low magnification and zooms in on them for fine-grained analysis. In Sect. 3.1, we introduce the gated-attention mechanism determining the informative patches at a given magnification. In Sect. 3.2, we describe how to enable the attention-based patch selection to be differentiable while employing multiple magnifications. Finally, we present in Sect. 3.3 our overall architecture, in particular our proposed Dual Gated Attention and multi-scale information aggregation.

3.1   Attention-Based MIL

In MIL, an input X is considered as a bag of instances $X = \{\mathbf{x}_1, ..., \mathbf{x}_N\}$. Given a classification task with C labels, there exists an *unknown* label $\mathbf{y}_i \in C$ for each instance and a *known* label $\mathbf{y} \in C$ for the bag. In our context, the input is a WSI and the instances denote the extracted patches. We follow the embedding-based MIL approaches [20,32,40], where a patch-level feature extractor h maps each patch $\mathbf{x}_i$ to a feature vector $\mathbf{h}_i = h(\mathbf{x}_i) \in \mathbb{R}^D$. Afterwards, a pooling operator $g(\cdot)$ aggregates the feature vectors $\mathbf{h}_{i=1:N}$ to a single WSI-level feature representation. Finally, a classifier $f(\cdot)$ uses the WSI representation to predict the WSI-level label $\hat{\mathbf{y}} \in C$. The end-to-end process can be summarized as:

$$\hat{\mathbf{y}} = f\Big(g\big(\{h(\mathbf{x}_1), \ldots, h(\mathbf{x}_N)\}\big)\Big). \tag{1}$$

To aggregate the patch features, we use attention-pooling, specifically, Gated Attention (GA) from [20]. Let $\mathbf{H} = [\mathbf{h}_1, \ldots, \mathbf{h}_N]^\top \in \mathbb{R}^{N \times D}$ be the patch-level feature matrix, then the WSI-level representation $\mathbf{g}$ is computed as:

$$\mathbf{g} = \sum_{i=1}^{N} a_i \mathbf{h}_i, \qquad a_i = \frac{\exp\{\mathbf{w}^\top(\tanh(\mathbf{V}\mathbf{h}_i) \odot \eta(\mathbf{U}\mathbf{h}_i))\}}{\sum_{j=1}^{N} \exp\{\mathbf{w}^\top(\tanh(\mathbf{V}\mathbf{h}_j) \odot \eta(\mathbf{U}\mathbf{h}_j))\}}, \tag{2}$$

where $\mathbf{w} \in \mathbb{R}^{L \times 1}$, $\mathbf{V} \in \mathbb{R}^{L \times D}$, $\mathbf{U} \in \mathbb{R}^{L \times D}$ are learnable parameters with hidden dimension L, $\odot$ is element-wise multiplication, and $\eta(\cdot)$ is the sigmoid function. While previous attention-based MIL methods [20,32] were designed to operate at a *single* magnification, we propose an efficient and flexible framework that can be extended to arbitrarily many magnifications while being fully differentiable.

3.2   Attending to Multiple Magnifications

We assume the WSI is accessible at magnifications indexed by $m \in \{1, \ldots, M\}$, where the highest magnification is at M and the magnification at $m + 1$ is twice that at m, consistent with the pyramidal format of WSIs. To efficiently extend MIL to multiple magnifications, we hierarchically identify informative patches from low-to-high magnifications and aggregate their features to get the WSI representation. To identify the patches at m, we first compute $\mathbf{a}_m \in \mathbb{R}^N$,

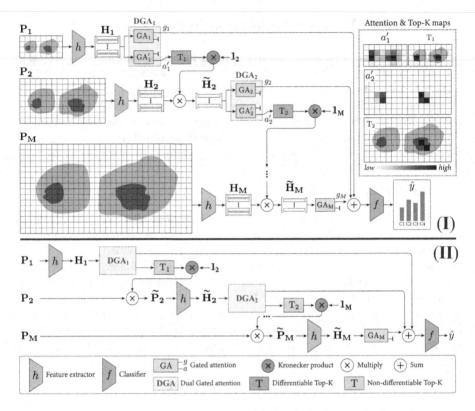

Fig. 2. Overview of the proposed ZOOMMIL. **(I)** and **(II)** present the distinct training and inference modes, generically exemplified for M magnifications.

which includes an attention score per patch. Then, the top K patches with the highest scores are selected for further processing at a higher magnification. The corresponding selected patch feature matrix is denoted by

$$\widetilde{\mathbf{H}}_m = \mathbf{T}_m^\top \mathbf{H}_m \,, \tag{3}$$

where $\mathbf{T}_m \in \{0,1\}^{N \times K}$ is an indicator matrix and $\mathbf{H}_m \in \mathbb{R}^{N \times D}$ is the patch feature matrix at m.

Instead of a handcrafted approach, we propose to drive the patch selection at m directly by the prediction output of $f(\cdot)$. This could be achieved via a backpropagation path from the output of $f(\cdot)$ to the attention module at m, without introducing any additional loss or associated hyperparameters. However, this naive formulation is non-differentiable as it involves a Top-K operation. To address this problem, we build on the perturbed maximum method [8] to make the Top-K selection differentiable, inspired by [11], and apply it to the attention weights $\mathbf{a}_m$ at magnification m. Specifically, $\mathbf{a}_m$ is first perturbed by adding uniform Gaussian noise $\mathbf{Z} \in \mathbb{R}^N$. Then, a linear program is solved for each of the perturbed attention weights, and their results are averaged. The forward pass of the differentiable Top-K module can thus be written as:

$$\mathbf{T} = \mathop{\mathbb{E}}_{\mathbf{Z} \sim \mathcal{N}(\mathbf{0}, \mathbb{K})} \left[\arg\max_{\hat{\mathbf{T}}} \langle \hat{\mathbf{T}}, (\mathbf{a}_m + \sigma \mathbf{Z}) \mathbf{1}^\top \rangle \right], \tag{4}$$

where $\mathbf{1}^\top = [1 \cdots 1] \in \mathbb{R}^{1 \times K}$ and $(\mathbf{a}_m + \sigma \mathbf{Z})\mathbf{1}^\top \in \mathbb{R}^{N \times K}$ denotes the perturbed attention weights repeated K times, and $\langle \cdot \rangle$ is a scalar product preceded by a vectorization of the matrices. The corresponding Jacobian is defined as:

$$J_{\mathbf{a}_m}\mathbf{T} = \mathop{\mathbb{E}}_{\mathbf{Z} \sim \mathcal{N}(\mathbf{0}, \mathbb{K})} \left[\arg\max_{\hat{\mathbf{T}}} \langle \hat{\mathbf{T}}, (\mathbf{a}_m + \sigma \mathbf{Z}) \mathbf{1}^\top \rangle \mathbf{Z}^\top / \sigma \right]. \tag{5}$$

More details on the derivation are provided in the supplemental material. The differentiable Top-K operator enables to *learn* the parameters of the attention module that weighs the patches at specific magnifications. Unlike [11], where patch sizes are scaled proportionally to the magnifications, we maintain a constant patch size across magnifications. This renders the number of patches proportional to the magnifications. It also provides different fields-of-view of the tissue microenvironment and enables us to capture a variety of contexts. This is crucial for analyzing WSIs as they contain diagnostically relevant constituents of various sizes. To achieve the zooming objective, we expand the indicator matrix $\mathbf{T}_m$ to select from the patch features $\mathbf{H}_{m'} \in \mathbb{R}^{N \cdot 4^{(m'-m)} \times D}$, where $m' > m$. Specifically, we compute the Kronecker product between $\mathbf{T}_m$ and the identity matrix $\mathbb{K}_{m'} = \text{diag}(1, \cdots, 1) \in \mathbb{R}^{4^{(m'-m)} \times 4^{(m'-m)}}$ to obtain the expanded indicator matrix $\mathbf{T}_{m'} \in \{0,1\}^{N \cdot 4^{(m'-m)} \times K \cdot 4^{(m'-m)}}$. Analogously to Eq. (3), patch selection at m' using the attention weights from m can be performed using

$$\widetilde{\mathbf{H}}_{m'} = \left(\mathbf{T}_m \otimes \mathbb{K}_{m'}\right)^\top \mathbf{H}_{m'}, \tag{6}$$

where $\mathbf{H}_{m'}$ is the feature matrix at m' and $\widetilde{\mathbf{H}}_{m'}$ is the selected feature matrix.

3.3 Dual Gated Attention and Multi-scale Aggregation

Figure 2 shows ZOOMMIL in its training (**I**) and inference (**II**) mode.

Training Mode: The feature matrix $\mathbf{H}_1$ at $m{=}1$ passes through a Dual Gated Attention (DGA) block. DGA consists of two gated-attention modules GA_1 and GA_1'. GA_1 is trained to obtain an optimal attention-pooled WSI-level representation $\mathbf{g}_1$ at low magnification. GA_1' calculates attention weights $\mathbf{a}_1'$ that are used to identify important patches to zoom in. Alternatively, a single attention module could be used for both tasks. However, this would prevent optimal zooming, as the selected low-magnification patches would aim to optimize the classification performance only with information from the low magnification. Employing separate attention modules decouples the optimization tasks, and in turn, enables to obtain *complementary* information from both magnifications. Subsequently, the differentiable Top-K selection module, $\mathbf{T}_1$, is employed to learn to select the most informative patches. The following selected higher-magnification patch feature matrix $\widetilde{\mathbf{H}}_2$ is obtained via Eq. (6).

706 K. Thandiackal et al.

The process of selecting patch features for every subsequent higher magnification is repeated until the highest magnification M. The selected patch features $\widetilde{\mathbf{H}}_M$ at M go through a last gated-attention block GA_M to produce $\mathbf{g}_M$. Finally, the attention-pooled features from all magnifications, $\mathbf{g}_1, \mathbf{g}_2, \ldots, \mathbf{g}_M$, are aggregated via sum-pooling to get a multi-scale, context-aware representation for the WSI. Inspired by residual learning [18], sum-pooling is used, as the features across different magnifications are closely related and the summation leverages their complementarity. The final classifier $f(\cdot)$ maps the WSI representation to the label $y \in C$ by producing the model prediction $\hat{\mathbf{y}}$. The training phase can be regarded as extending Eq. (1) with sum-pooling over multiple magnifications:

$$\hat{\mathbf{y}} = f\Big(\mathbf{g}_1(\mathbf{H}_1) + \mathbf{g}_2(\widetilde{\mathbf{H}}_2), \cdots + \mathbf{g}_M(\widetilde{\mathbf{H}}_M)\Big) . \tag{7}$$

Inference Mode: The differentiable Top-K operator in our model learns to identify informative patches during training. However, this operator includes random perturbations to the attention weights, and thus makes the forward pass of the model non-deterministic. Therefore, we replace differentiable Top-K with conventional non-differentiable Top-K during inference, which is also faster as no perturbations have to be computed. As shown in Fig. 2, another crucial difference to the training mode is that the patch selection directly operates on the WSI patches, $\mathbf{P}_{m'} \in \mathbb{R}^{N \cdot 4^{(m'-1)} \times p_h \times p_w \times p_c}$, instead of the pre-extracted patch features $\mathbf{H}_{m'}$. This avoids the extraction of features for uninformative patches during inference, unlike other MIL methods. It significantly reduces the computational requirements and speeds up model inference.

4 Experiments

4.1 Datasets

We benchmark ZooMMILon three H&E stained, public WSI datasets.

CRC [34] contains 1133 colorectal biopsy and polypectomy slides from *non-neoplastic, low-grade,* and *high-grade* lesions, accounting for 26.5%, 48.7%, 24.8% of the data. The slides were acquired at the IMP Diagnostics laboratory, Portugal, and were digitized by a Leica GT450 scanner at 40×. We split the data into 70%/10%/20% stratified sets for training, validation, and testing.

BRIGHT [9] consists of breast WSIs from *non-cancerous, precancerous,* and *cancerous* subtypes. The slides were acquired at the Fondazione G. Pascale, Italy, and scanned by an Aperio AT2 scanner at 40×. We used the BRIGHT challenge splits[1] containing 423, 80, and 200 WSIs for training, validation, and testing.

CAMELYON16 [5] includes 270 WSIs, 160 normal and 110 with metastases, for training, and 129 slides for testing. The slides were scanned by 3DHIS-TECH and Hamamatsu scanners at 40× at the Radboud University Medical Center and the University Medical Center Utrecht, Netherlands. We split the 270 slides into 90%/10% stratified sets for training and validation.

---

[1] www.research.ibm.com/haifa/Workshops/BRIGHT.

The average number of (pixels, patches), within the tissue area, at 20× magnification for CRC, BRIGHT, and CAMELYON16 datasets are (227.28 Mpx, 3468), (1.04 Gpx, 15872), and (648.28 Mpx, 9892), respectively.

4.2   Implementation Details

Preprocessing: For each WSI, we detect the tissue area using a Gaussian tissue detector [21] and divide the tissue into 256×256 patches at all considered magnifications. We ensure that each high-magnification patch is associated with the corresponding lower-magnification patch. We encode the patches with ResNet-50 [18] pre-trained on ImageNet [12] and apply adaptive average pooling after the third residual block to obtain 1024-dimensional embeddings.

ZoomMIL: The gated-attention module comprises three 2-layer Multi-Layer Perceptrons (MLPs), where the first two are followed by Hyperbolic Tangent and Sigmoid activations, respectively. The classifier is a 2-layer MLP with ReLU activation. We use a dropout probability of 0.25 in all fully-connected layers.

Implementation: All methods are implemented in PyTorch [35] and run on a single NVIDIA A100 GPU. ZoomMILuses $K = \{16, 12, 300\}$ on CRC, BRIGHT, and CAMELYON16, respectively, and our more efficient variant ZoomMIL-Eff uses $K = \{12, 8\}$ on CRC and BRIGHT, respectively. We use the Adam optimizer [24] with 0.0001 learning rate and plateau scheduler (patience=5 epochs, decay rate=0.8). The experiments are run for 100 epochs with a batch size of one. For CRC & CAMELYON16, the models with the best validation loss are saved for testing. On BRIGHT, we observed that the baselines perform poorly compared to ZoomMILwhen using validation loss as the model selection criterion. We therefore employ best validation weighted-F1 for model selection on BRIGHT since it improves the baselines, giving them a better competitive chance against ZoomMIL.

4.3   Results and Discussion

Baselines: We compare ZoomMILwith state-of-the-art MIL methods. Specifically, we compare with ABMIL [20], which uses a gated-attention pooling, and its variant CLAM [32], which also includes an instance-level clustering loss. We further compare with two spatially-aware methods, namely, TransMIL [40] which models instance-level dependencies using transformer-based pooling, and SparseConvMIL [26] which selects random subsets of patches and employs sparse convolutions for pooling. In addition, we compare with multi-scale methods MSMIL [17] and DSMIL [27], which are computationally less efficient than ZoomMILas they encode all patches in a WSI across all considered magnifications. For completeness, we also include vanilla MIL methods based on max-pooling (MaxMIL) [26] and mean-pooling (MeanMIL) [26], following SparseConvMIL's strategy of random patch selection. Additional implementation details and hyper-parameters are provided in the supplemental material. For a fair comparison, preprocessing including the extraction of patch embeddings is done consistently in the same manner, as described in Sect. 4.2.

Table 1. Performance and efficiency measurement on CRC [34]. The best and second-best classification results are in **bold** and <u>underlined</u>, respectively.

Methods	Classification		Computation	
	Weighted-F1(%)	Accuracy(%)	TFLOPs	Time(s)
MaxMIL [26] (20×)	82.2±0.9	82.2±1.2	0.96	0.13
MeanMIL [26] (20×)	84.3±0.8	84.1±1.2	0.96	0.12
SparseConvMIL [26] (20×)	89.6±1.3	89.6±0.9	0.96	0.13
ABMIL [20] (20×)	90.1±0.6	90.2±0.5	13.63	4.85
CLAM-SB [32] (20×)	90.9±0.6	90.9±0.5	13.63	4.85
TransMIL [40] (20×)	89.8±1.1	90.2±0.9	13.63	4.85
MSMIL [17] (5× + 10× + 20×)	84.6±0.1	84.9±0.2	17.88	6.37
DSMIL [27] (5× + 10× + 20×)	<u>91.1 ± 1.1</u>	<u>91.2 ± 1.1</u>	17.94	6.37
ZoomMIL-Eff (5× → 10×)	90.3±1.3	90.3±1.3	1.06	0.38
ZoomMIL(5× → 10× → 20×)	**92.0 ± 0.6**	**92.1 ± 0.7**	1.40	0.50

Table 2. Performance and efficiency measurement on BRIGHT [9]. The best and second-best classification results are in **bold** and <u>underlined</u>, respectively.

Methods	Classification		Computation	
	Weighted-F1	Accuracy	TFLOPs	Time(s)
MaxMIL [26] (10×)	46.8±3.7	51.3±1.7	0.96	0.13
MeanMIL [26] (10×)	44.9±2.8	47.1±0.1	0.96	0.12
SparseConvMIL [26] (10×)	53.2±3.6	55.3±3.7	0.96	0.13
ABMIL [20] (10×)	63.5±2.7	65.5±1.9	16.45	5.86
CLAM-SB [32] (10×)	63.1±1.7	64.3±1.7	16.45	5.86
TransMIL [40] (10×)	65.5±2.8	66.0±2.7	16.46	5.86
MSMIL [17] (1.25× + 2.5× + 10×)	61.7±0.6	62.5±1.1	21.59	7.69
DSMIL [27] (1.25× + 2.5× + 10×)	63.1±1.6	64.0±1.1	21.66	7.69
ZoomMIL-Eff (1.25× → 2.5×)	<u>66.0 ± 1.9</u>	<u>66.5 ± 1.5</u>	0.40	0.14
ZoomMIL(1.25× → 2.5× → 10×)	**68.3 ± 1.1**	**69.3 ± 1.0**	1.29	0.46

WSI Classification Performance: We present the classification results in terms of weighted F1-score and accuracy in Table 1, 2, and 3. Mean±standard deviation of the metrics is computed over three runs with different weight initializations. Corresponding magnifications of operation are shown alongside each method for each dataset. We include two versions of ZoomMILusing either 2 or 3 magnifications, denoted as ZoomMIL-Eff (efficient) and ZoomMIL.

On CRC, ZoomMILoutperforms CLAM-SB and TransMILby 1.1% and 2.2% weighted F1-score, and ZoomMIL-Eff achieves comparable performance. Furthermore, ZoomMILshows superior performance compared to the multi-scale methods MSMILand DSMIL. For the individual classes, Zoom-MILachieves 94.3%, 93.6%, and 86.4% average F1-scores in the one-vs-rest setting.

Table 3. Performance and efficiency measurement on CAMELYON16 [5]. The best and second-best classification results are in **bold** and underlined, respectively.

Methods	Classification		Computation	
	Weighted-F1(%)	Accuracy(%)	TFLOPs	Time(s)
MAXMIL[26] (20×)	64.0±3.0	67.1±0.9	0.96	0.13
MEANMIL [26] (20×)	63.5±1.1	65.9±1.6	0.96	0.12
SPARSECONVMIL [26] (20×)	67.7±0.6	68.7±0.1	0.96	0.13
ABMIL [20] (20×)	83.2±1.7	84.0±1.3	39.12	13.92
CLAM-SB [32] (20×)	83.3±1.5	84.0±1.3	39.12	13.92
TRANSMIL [40] (20×)	**83.6 ± 2.6**	**85.3 ± 1.9**	39.12	13.92
MSMIL [17] (10× + 20×)	81.4±1.1	82.4±1.0	48.87	17.41
DSMIL [27] (10× + 20×)	78.5±0.42	79.6±0.3	48.95	17.41
ZOOMMIL(10× → 20×)	<u>83.3 ± 0.3</u>	<u>84.2 ± 0.4</u>	14.94	5.32

WSIs in BRIGHT are 4.5× larger than in CRC and thus provide a better evaluation ground for efficient scaling. ZOOMMILachieves the best performance, outperforming MSMILby 6.6%, CLAM-SB and DSMILby 5.2%, and TRANS-MILby 2.8% in weighted F1-score. Notably, ZOOMMIL-EFF achieves the second-best results. For the individual classes, ZOOMMILreaches average F1-scores of 70.4%, 56.5%, and 77.8%. The performance is lowest for the challenging pre-cancerous class, which often resembles the other two classes.

For CAMELYON16, we set the lowest magnification to 10× as the metastatic regions can be extremely small (see Fig. 4). Nevertheless, it still adversely impacts the performance, resulting in 1.1% lower average accuracy than TRANS-MIL. However, this translates to misclassifying only 1–2 test WSIs.

Overall, ZOOMMILperforms better on CRC and BRIGHT, while being comparable to the state of the art on CAMELYON16. It also consistently outperforms ZOOMMIL-EFF, highlighting the apparent performance-efficiency trade-off, *i.e.*, performance reduction in exchange for gains in computational efficiency.

Efficiency Measurements: We analyze the efficiency in terms of FLOPs and average processing time for inference (see Table 1, 2, and 3). Note that the computational cost in the MIL modules is negligible compared to patch feature extraction, which is computationally the most expensive. The FLOPs and processing time for different methods can therefore appear to be equal as their difference only becomes visible several digits after the decimal point. On CRC, ZOOMMILuses ≈10× less FLOPs and time than CLAM-SB and TRANSMIL. Compared to MSMILand DSMIL, this factor increases to >12×. On BRIGHT, our efficient variant reduces computational requirements by >50× compared to MSMILand DSMIL, and >40× compared to CLAM-SB and TRANSMILwhile providing comparable performance. On CAMELYON16, ZOOMMILuses ≈ 1/3 FLOPs compared to MSMIL, DSMIL, CLAM-SB, and TRANSMIL. The rela-

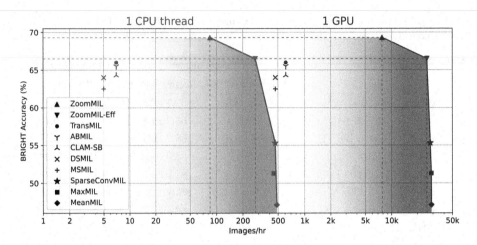

Fig. 3. Throughput vs classification accuracy for different MIL methods on BRIGHT, (left) on 1 single-core CPU, (right) on 1 NVIDIA A-100 GPU. Efficiency frontier curves are drawn in red and blue for CPU and GPU, respectively. (Color figure online)

tively lower efficiency gain is due to the fact that metastatic regions occupy only a small fraction of a WSI, and thus need to be analyzed at a finer magnification. Across all datasets, the methods adopting random patch selection (MAXMIL, MEANMIL, and SPARSECONVMIL) have similar computational requirements as ZOOMMILbut perform significantly worse.

To further highlight our efficiency gain, we show in Fig. 3 the model throughput (images/hour) against the performance (accuracy) for all methods on BRIGHT. The marked efficiency frontier curves signify the best possible accuracies for different minimal throughput requirements. Noticeably, ZOOMMIL-EFF running on a single-core CPU processor ($\approx$300 images/h) provides similar throughput to MSMIL, DSMIL, CLAM-SB, and TRANSMILrunning on a cutting-edge NVIDIA A100 GPU ($\approx$500–600 images/h). ZOOMMIL's low computational requirements make it more practical and suitable for clinical deployment, where IT infrastructures are often under-developed and need large investments to establish and maintain a digital workflow.

Interpretability. We interpret ZOOMMILby qualitatively analyzing its patch-level attention maps. Figure 4(a,b) show the maps for two cancerous WSIs in BRIGHT at 1.25$\times$, and Fig. 4(c-f) show the maps for four metastatic WSIs in CAMELYON16 at 10$\times$. We further include corresponding tumor regions annotated by an expert pathologist for comparison. Brighter regions in the maps mark higher attention scores, $i.e.$, more influential for model prediction.

For the BRIGHT WSIs, ZOOMMILcorrectly attends to cancerous areas in (a,b), pays lower attention to the pre-cancerous area in (b), and least attention to the remaining non-cancerous areas that include non-cancerous epithelium, stroma, and adipose tissue. For the CAMELYON16 WSIs, (c,d) are correctly

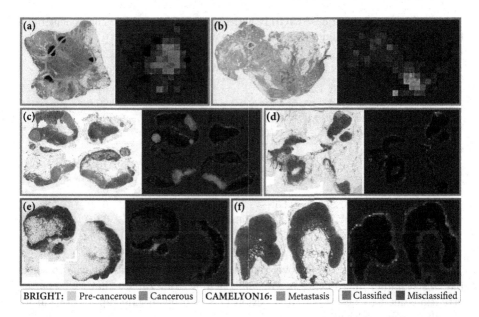

BRIGHT: ▨ Pre-cancerous ▨ Cancerous | CAMELYON16: ▨ Metastasis | ▨ Classified ▨ Misclassified

Fig. 4. Annotated tumor regions and attention maps from the lowest magnification of ZOOMMILare presented for (a,b) BRIGHT and (c-f) CAMELYON16 WSIs.

classified as ZOOMMILgives high attention to the metastatic regions of different sizes. However, the extremely small metastases in (e,f) get low attention and are disregarded by the Top-K module leading to misclassifying the WSIs. Notably, for cases with tiny metastases, relatively higher attention is imparted to the periphery of the tissues. This is consistent with the fact that metastases generally appear in the subcapsular zone of lymph nodes, as can be observed in (c-f). The presented visualizations are obtained from low magnifications, which signifies ZOOMMIL's ability to learn to zoom in. More interpretability maps for other classes and fine-grained attention maps from higher attention modules in ZOOMMILare provided in the supplemental material.

Ablation Study: We ablated different modules in ZOOMMIL-EFF, due to its simple 2-magnification model. The results on BRIGHT are given in Table 4.

Differentiable Patch Selection: We compared our attention-based differentiable patch selection (DIFF-TOPK) against three alternatives: random selection at the lowest magnification (RANDOMK @ 1.25×), random selection at the highest magnification (RANDOM4K @ 2.5×), and the non-differentiable Top-K selection (NONDIFF-TOPK) at the lowest magnification. The top rows in Table 4 show the superiority of DIFF-TOPK. Due to its differentiability, it learns to select patches via the gradient optimization of the model's prediction.

Dual Gated Attention: We examined DGA consisting of two separate gated attention modules GA_1 and GA_1' at low magnification, as discussed in Sect. 3.3.

Table 4. Ablation study on BRIGHT, with the varied algorithmic component tabulated in the left-most column. All experiments use $K = 8$.

	Methods	Weighted F1(%)	Accuracy(%)
Patch sel.	RANDOM K @ 1.25×	61.0	61.0
	RANDOM 4K @ 2.5×	59.6	60.0
	NONDIFF-TOPK K @ 1.25×	59.9	60.0
	DIFF-TOPK K @ 1.25× (Ours)	**68.1**	**68.0**
Attn.	Single GA @ 1.25×	59.6	61.0
	DGA @ 1.25× (Ours)	**68.1**	**68.0**
Feat.	Features @2.5×	62.7	63.5
	Features @1.25× || @2.5×	64.9	65.0
	Features @1.25× + @2.5× (Ours)	**68.1**	**68.0**

The former computes a slide-level representation and the latter learns to select patches at higher magnification. We can conclude from Table 4 that two separate attentions lead to better patch selection and improved slide representation for overall improved classification.

Feature Aggregation: We aggregate slide-level representations across magnifications through sum-pooling, as shown in Eq. (7). Among several alternatives, we compared with: using the highest-magnification features (Features@2.5×) and fusing representations via concatenation (represented as @1.25× \|\| @2.5×). Table 4 shows that concatenation improves performance, indicating the value of multi-scale information. However, our sum-pooling, which is inspired by residual learning [18], significantly outperforms concatenation as it leverages the complementarity of the two magnifications more effectively.

5   Conclusion

In this work, we introduced ZOOMMIL, a novel framework for WSI classification. The method is more than an order of magnitude faster than previous state-of-the-art methods during inference while achieving comparable or better accuracy. Essential for our method is the concept of differentiable zooming that allows the model to learn which patches are informative and thus worth zooming in on. We conduct extensive quantitative and qualitative evaluations on three different datasets and demonstrate the importance of each component in our model with a detailed ablation study. Finally, we show that ZOOMMILis a modular architecture that can easily be deployed in different flavors, depending on the performance-efficiency requirements in a given application. In future work, it would be interesting to further study the attention maps of ZoomMIL and compare them with the visual attention of pathologists.

Author contributions. K. Thandiackal and B. Chen—Contributed equally.

References

1. Adnan, M., Kalra, S., Tizhoosh, H.: Representation learning of histopathology images using graph neural networks. In: IEEE/CVF Conference on Computer Vision and Pattern Recognition (CVPR) Workshops, pp. 988–989 (2020)
2. Anklin, V., et al.: Learning whole-slide segmentation from inexact and incomplete labels using tissue graphs. In: de Bruijne, M., et al. (eds.) MICCAI 2021. LNCS, vol. 12902, pp. 636–646. Springer, Cham (2021). https://doi.org/10.1007/978-3-030-87196-3_59
3. Aygüneş, B., Aksoy, S., Cinbiş, R., Kösemehmetoğlu, K., Önder, S., Üner, A.: Graph convolutional networks for region of interest classification in breast histopathology. In: SPIE Medical Imaging 2020: Digital Pathology, vol. 11320, pp. 134–141. SPIE (2020)
4. Bejnordi, B., Litjens, G., Hermsen, M., Karssemeijer, N., van der Laak, J.: A multi-scale superpixel classification approach to the detection of regions of interest in whole slide histopathology images. In: SPIE Medical Imaging 2015: Digital Pathology, vol. 9420, pp. 99–104. SPIE (2015)
5. Bejnordi, B., et al.: Diagnostic assessment of deep learning algorithms for detection of lymph node metastases in women with breast cancer. JAMA **318**, 2199–2210 (2017)
6. Bejnordi, B., et al.: Context-aware stacked convolutional neural networks for classification of breast carcinomas in whole-slide histopathology images. J. Med. Imaging **4**(4), 044504 (2017)
7. BenTaieb, A., Hamarneh, G.: Predicting cancer with a recurrent visual attention model for histopathology images. In: Frangi, A.F., Schnabel, J.A., Davatzikos, C., Alberola-López, C., Fichtinger, G. (eds.) MICCAI 2018. LNCS, vol. 11071, pp. 129–137. Springer, Cham (2018). https://doi.org/10.1007/978-3-030-00934-2_15
8. Berthet, Q., Blondel, M., Teboul, O., Cuturi, M., Vert, J., Bach, F.: Learning with differentiable pertubed optimizers. Adv. Neural. Inf. Process. Syst. **34**, 9508–9519 (2020)
9. Brancati, N., et al.: BRACS: a dataset for BReAst carcinoma subtyping in H&E histology images. arXiv:2111.04740 (2021)
10. Campanella, G., et al.: Clinical-grade computational pathology using weakly supervised deep learning on whole slide images. Nat. Med. **25**, 1301–1309 (2019)
11. Cordonnier, J., Mahendran, A., Dosovitskiy, A.: Differentiable patch selection for image recognition. In: IEEE/CVF Conference on Computer Vision and Pattern Recognition (CVPR), pp. 2351–2360 (2021)
12. Deng, J., Dong, W., Socher, R., Li, L., Li, K., Fei-Fei, L.: Imagenet: a large-scale hierarchical image database. In: IEEE/CVF Conference on Computer Vision and Pattern Recognition (CVPR), pp. 248–255 (2009)
13. Dong, N., Kampffmeyer, M., Liang, X., Wang, Z., Dai, W., Xing, E.: Reinforced auto-zoom net: towards accurate and fast breast cancer segmentation in whole-slide images. In: International Conference on Medical Image Computing and Computer Assisted Intervention (MICCAI) Workshop, pp. 317–325 (2018)
14. Elmore, J., et al.: Diagnostic concordance among pathologists interpreting breast biopsy specimens. JAMA **313**, 1122–1132 (2015)
15. Gao, Y., et al.: Multi-scale learning based segmentation of glands in digital colorectal pathology images. In: SPIE Medical Imaging 2016: Digital Pathology, vol. 9791, pp. 175–180. SPIE (2016)

16. Gomes, D., Porto, S., Balabram, D., Gobbi, H.: Inter-observer variability between general pathologists and a specialist in breast pathology in the diagnosis of lobular neoplasia, columnar cell lesions, atypical ductal hyperplasia and ductal carcinoma in situ of the breast. Diagn. Pathol. **9**, 1–9 (2014)

17. Hashimoto, N., et al.: Multi-scale domain-adversarial multiple-instance CNN for cancer subtype classification with unannotated histopathological images. In: IEEE/CVF Conference on Computer Vision and Pattern Recognition (CVPR), pp. 3852–3861 (2020)

18. He, K., Zhang, X., Ren, S., Sun, J.: Deep residual learning for image recognition. In: IEEE/CVF Conference on Computer Vision and Pattern Recognition (CVPR), pp. 770–778 (2016)

19. Ho, D., et al.: Deep multi-magnification networks for multi-class breast cancer image segmentation. Comput. Med. Imaging Graph. **88**, 101866 (2021)

20. Isle, M., Tomczak, J., Welling, M.: Attention-based deep multiple instance learning. In: International Conference on Machine Learning (ICML), vol. 35, pp. 2127–2136 (2018)

21. Jaume, G., Pati, P., Anklin, V., Foncubierta-Rodríguez, A., Gabrani, M.: Histocartography: a toolkit for graph analytics in digital pathology. In: MICCAI Workshop on Computational Pathology, pp. 117–128. PMLR (2021)

22. Jia, Z., Huang, X., Eric, I., Chang, C., Xu, Y.: Constrained deep weak supervision for histopathology image segmentation. IEEE Trans. Med. Imaging **36**, 2376–2388 (2017)

23. Katharopoulos, A., Fleuret, F.: Processing megapixel images with deep attention-sampling models. In: International Conference on Machine Learning (ICML), vol. 36, pp. 3282–3291. PMLR (2019)

24. Kingma, D., Ba, J.: Adam: a method for stochastic optimization. In: International Conference on Learning Representations (ICLR) arXiv preprint arXiv:1412.6980 (2014)

25. Kong, S., Henao, R.: Efficient classification of very large images with tiny objects. arXiv:2106.02694 (2021)

26. Lerousseau, M., Vakalopoulou, M., Deutsch, E., Paragios, N.: SparseConvMIL: sparse convolutional context-aware multiple instance learning for whole slide image classification. In: MICCAI Workshop on Computational Pathology, pp. 129–139. PMLR (2021)

27. Li, B., Li, Y., Eliceiri, K.: Dual-stream multiple instance learning network for whole slide image classification with self-supervised contrastive learning. In: IEEE/CVF Conference on Computer Vision and Pattern Recognition (CVPR), pp. 14318–14328 (2021)

28. Li, J., et al.: A multi-resolution model for histopathology image classification and localization with multiple instance learning. Comput. Biol. Med. **131**, 104253 (2021)

29. Li, R., Yao, J., Zhu, X., Li, Y., Huang, J.: Graph CNN for survival analysis on whole slide pathological images. In: Frangi, A.F., Schnabel, J.A., Davatzikos, C., Alberola-López, C., Fichtinger, G. (eds.) MICCAI 2018. LNCS, vol. 11071, pp. 174–182. Springer, Cham (2018). https://doi.org/10.1007/978-3-030-00934-2_20

30. Liang, Q., et al.: Weakly supervised biomedical image segmentation by reiterative learning. IEEE J. Biomed. Health Inform. **23**, 1205–1214 (2018)

31. Lu, M., et al.: AI-based pathology predicts origins for cancers of unknown primary. Nature **594**, 106–110 (2021)

32. Lu, M., Williamson, D., Chen, T., Chen, R., Barbieri, M., Mahmood, F.: Data efficient and weakly supervised computational pathology on whole slide images. Nat. Biomed. Eng. **5**, 555–570 (2021)
33. Myronenko, A., Xu, Z., Yang, D., Roth, H.R., Xu, D.: Accounting for dependencies in deep learning based multiple instance learning for whole slide imaging. In: de Bruijne, M., et al. (eds.) MICCAI 2021. LNCS, vol. 12908, pp. 329–338. Springer, Cham (2021). https://doi.org/10.1007/978-3-030-87237-3_32
34. Oliveira, S., et al.: CAD systems for colorectal cancer from WSI are still not ready for clinical acceptance. Sci. Rep. **11**(1), 1–15 (2021)
35. Paszke, A., et al.: PyTorch: an imperative style, high-performance deep learning library. In: Advances in Neural Information Processing Systems (NeurIPS), vol. 33, pp. 8024–8035 (2019)
36. Pati, P., et al.: Hierarchical graph representations in digital pathology. Med. Image Anal. **75**, 102264 (2021)
37. Qaiser, T., Rajpoot, N.: Learning where to see: a novel attention model for automated immunohistochemical scoring. IEEE Trans. Med. Imaging **38**, 2620–2631 (2019)
38. Raju, A., Yao, J., Haq, M.M.H., Jonnagaddala, J., Huang, J.: Graph attention multi-instance learning for accurate colorectal cancer staging. In: Martel, A.L., et al. (eds.) MICCAI 2020. LNCS, vol. 12265, pp. 529–539. Springer, Cham (2020). https://doi.org/10.1007/978-3-030-59722-1_51
39. Shaban, M., et al.: Context-aware convolutional neural network for grading of colorectal cancer histology images. IEEE Trans. Med. Imaging **39**, 2395–2405 (2020)
40. Shao, Z., et al.: TransMIL: transformer based correlated multiple instance learning for whole slide image classification. Adv. Neural. Inf. Process. Syst. **35**, 2136–2147 (2021)
41. Sirinukunwattana, K., Alham, N.K., Verrill, C., Rittscher, J.: Improving whole slide segmentation through visual context - a systematic study. In: Frangi, A.F., Schnabel, J.A., Davatzikos, C., Alberola-López, C., Fichtinger, G. (eds.) MICCAI 2018. LNCS, vol. 11071, pp. 192–200. Springer, Cham (2018). https://doi.org/10.1007/978-3-030-00934-2_22
42. Tellez, D., Litjens, G., van der Laak, J., Ciompi, F.: Neural image compression for gigapixel histopathology image analysis. IEEE Trans. Pattern Anal. Mach. Intell. **43**, 567–578 (2019)
43. Tokunaga, H., Teramoto, Y., Yoshizawa, A., Bise, R.: Adaptive weighting multi-field-of-view CNN for semantic segmentation in pathology. In: IEEE/CVF Conference on Computer Vision and Pattern Recognition (CVPR), pp. 12597–12606 (2019)
44. Yao, J., Zhu, X., Jonnagaddala, J., Hawkins, N., Huang, J.: Whole slide images based cancer survival prediction using attention guided deep multiple instance learning networks. Med. Image Anal. **65**, 101789 (2020)
45. Zhao, Y., et al.: Predicting lymph node metastasis using histopathological images based on multiple instance learning with deep graph convolution. In: IEEE/CVF Conference on Computer Vision and Pattern Recognition (CVPR), pp. 4837–4846 (2020)

Learning Uncoupled-Modulation CVAE for 3D Action-Conditioned Human Motion Synthesis

Chongyang Zhong[1,2], Lei Hu[1,2], Zihao Zhang[1,2], and Shihong Xia[1,2]

[1] Institute of Computing Technology, Chinese Academy of Sciences, Beijing, China
{zhongchongyang,hulei19z,zhangzihao,xsh}@ict.ac.cn
[2] University of Chinese Academy of Sciences, Beijing, China

Abstract. Motion capture data has been largely needed in the movie and game industry in recent years. Since the motion capture system is expensive and requires manual post-processing, motion synthesis is a plausible solution to acquire more motion data. However, generating the action-conditioned, realistic, and diverse 3D human motions given the semantic action labels is still challenging because the mapping from semantic labels to real motion sequences is hard to depict. Previous work made some positive attempts like appending label tokens to pose encoding and performing action bias on latent space. However, how to synthesize diverse motions that accurately match the given label is still not fully explored. In this paper, we propose the Uncoupled-Modulation Conditional Variational AutoEncoder (UM-CVAE) to generate action-conditioned motions from scratch in an uncoupled manner. The main idea is twofold: (i) training an action-agnostic encoder to weaken the action-related information to learn the easy-modulated latent representation; (ii) strengthening the action-conditioned process with FiLM-based action-aware modulation. We conduct extensive experiments on the HumanAct12, UESTC, and BABEL datasets, demonstrating that our method achieves state-of-the-art performance both qualitatively and quantitatively with potential applications.

Keywords: Human motion synthesis · Action-conditioned synthesis · CVAE · Uncoupled modulation

1 Introduction

With the development of the movie and game industry, a growing amount of motion data is required to achieve more life-like animation. To acquire the motion data, one straightforward method is to use motion capture technology. However, it is not feasible to capture all kinds of motion data because, on some occasions, rather than pre-record the motion data, the motion data is required to follow the users' intention. To solve this problem, motion synthesis is a plausible way.

Supplementary Information The online version contains supplementary material available at https://doi.org/10.1007/978-3-031-19803-8_42.

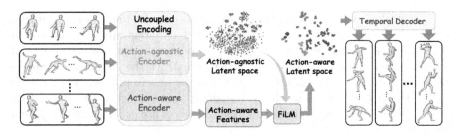

Fig. 1. Overview. We assume that a piece of white and blank paper can be drawn well, which means that it is easier to learn something as an "unskilled kid" than as an adult. Thus we perform uncoupled encoding to learn the action-agnostic latent space as the "unskilled kid" and the action-aware features as the "action skills". In the condition process, we compute FiLM parameters from the action-aware features to "teach" the action-agnostic latent representation how to perform action skills.

Especially, we focus on generating motion sequences based on the user-specific semantic action labels in this problem.

Though motion synthesis has emerged as a powerful solution for acquiring motion data, the problem of generating motion sequences based on given semantic action labels is still challenging. The reasons are mainly three-fold: (i) Firstly, it is hard to learn an appropriate correspondence between motion sequences and semantic action labels, which can ensure the generated motions meet the label constraints. For example, previous work [10] tries to build the correspondence on the single frame, but the generated results may suffer from discontinuity. Petrovich et al. [30] embed labels into transformer token and train a transformer-VAE to encode the entire motion sequence and label token coupledly, then add action bias in latent representation to strengthen the action constraint. However, we argue that this coupled manner will make the learned latent representation contain more or less label-related information, which may lead to conflict with that contained in the condition labels (discussed in "Qualitative comparison" of Sect. 4.2). Imagine when you teach a person who has already learned boxing to play golf, the subconscious boxing skills in his mind may distract him from learning golf. (ii) Secondly, the spatio-temporal properties in human motion are difficult to learn, especially when dealing with complex motions within diverse action categories. While the prior works [10,30] consider temporal modeling of motion dynamics, they directly input the original motion representation into the network without considering the spatial relationship between body joints. (iii) Lastly, the generated motion requires diversity, realism, and continuity.

To solve the above problems, we introduce the UM-CVAE to learn the correspondence between action labels and motion sequences in an uncoupled manner. The main idea is twofold: (i) *reducing* the action-related information in latent representation; (ii) *extracting* spatio-temporal action-aware features and *strengthening* the action-conditioned process via FiLM.

Specifically, as shown in Fig. 1, we first encode the motion sequence into *action-agnostic*(which means easy-modulated) latent space via an action-agnostic encoder. For the *action-aware* features extraction, we perform label-motion fusion and train an extra encoder to extract the action-aware spatio-temporal features. Unlike direct concatenation or bias in previous work [10,30], we use FiLM [29] instead to obtain an action-aware latent space. Finally, the variable-length action-conditioned motion sequences are generated through temporal decoder.

Extensive experiments are conducted on HumanAct12, UESTC, and BABEL datasets. We demonstrate that our method achieves significant improvement over the state-of-the-art works both qualitatively and quantitatively. The main contributions of our work can be summarized as follow:

1. We introduce UM-CVAE, a novel sequence-level CVAE to learn the latent representation in an uncoupled manner, which makes the generated motions conform better to the given action labels;
2. We learn the action-aware features through spatio-temporal extraction and utilize FiLM as the modulation method in action-conditioned motion generation, making the condition process more reasonable and powerful;
3. We carry out extensive experiments on HumanAct12, UESTC and BABEL to demonstrate that our method outperforms state-of-the-art works and has potential applications.

2   Related Works

In this section, we briefly review related works, including research on diverse motion prediction, constrained motion synthesis, and sequence-level VAE.

2.1   Diverse Motion Prediction

Human motion prediction aims to predict the human motion in the future period from a given historical motion sequence, which we refer to here as motion synthesis conditioned on the historical sequence. From traditional statistical methods [4,39] to deep neural networks based works like RNN [14,27,44], GCN [8,26,34,45], VAE [38,42] and GAN [3,17], exciting progress has been made in motion prediction. Among these works, diverse human motion prediction based on generative models is more relevant to our work. Using past sequences as conditions, CVAE-based works [38,42] build a probability model on the existing motion data to predict a variety of results through sampling and prediction. Moreover, GAN-based works [3,17] are conditioned on the latent space modeled by standard normal distribution to generate various motions and use GAN to optimize the quality of the prediction. In addition, some other condition ways include conditioned on contextual cues and interaction with objects [7], conditioned on music [20], etc. Unlike these works, the problem we want to solve is conditioned on action labels to generate motion sequences without any initial frame or past sequence.

2.2 Constrained Motion Synthesis

Generating human motion that meets user constraints has always been a challenging problem. Depending on the type of the given constraint, we divide the related work into content-constrained and semantic-constrained motion synthesis.

Content-Constrained Motion Synthesis. Content constraints refer to motion content information, such as velocity, direction, joint trajectory, etc. Through training an unconstrained generative model using RNN [40] or TCN [13] and then performing an optimization-based approach to constrain and edit the motion generation, some works use a two-stage method to generate content-constrained motion, which is too time-consuming to realize real-time generation. To solve this problem, researchers directly parameterize the control signal as the input of the generative model [12,35,36,43], which is equivalent to making an unconstrained generative model conditioned on the control parameters. This class of work relies on sufficiently informative motion representations and achieves high-quality locomotion generation. Unlike the generative methods, another kind of work is named "motion matching" [6,11], which generates motion sequences by searching the animation database based on users-input in real-time to find the most appropriate next frame or next clip. These works generate high-quality motions but badly depend on the quantity and quality of the dataset while being computationally intensive.

Semantic-Constrained Motion Synthesis. Rather than specific content constraints, sometimes users prefer to generate motions using semantic constrain like action labels, styles, descriptive sentences, and music, etc., which can help users without professional skills get the data more conveniently. Text2Action [1] and Language2Pose [2] investigate how to generate a motion sequence from a text description, and some other work generates motion conditioned on music [18,19] or styles [28,41]. Some works focus on more detailed aspects, generating motion from semantic action labels. DVGAN [21] uses a language model to encode the action labels and generates motion by RNN and CNN, and GAN is used to improve the realism of the generation. Their work cannot generate high-quality motions due to the difficulty of learning the correspondence between labels and sequences. Recently, A2M [10] and ACTOR [30] propose to use the CVAE-based framework, which not only performs coupled encoding on labels and motion sequences but also treats action labels as conditions to modulate the latent space, resulting in natural and diverse generated motions.

While most previous works learn the label-sequence correspondence in a coupled manner, we observe that the learned label-related features in latent representation and that in the given condition-label may conflict with each other during the condition process. Therefore, we perform uncoupled encoding to learn the action-agnostic latent space and the action-aware features, then adopt FiLM as the condition method instead of concatenation or bias to perform a more powerful action modulation.

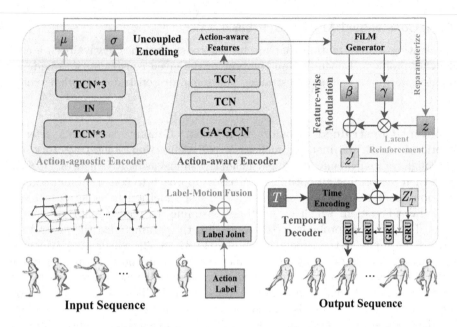

Fig. 2. UM-CVAE architecture. We encode the motion sequence into action-agnostic latent space via TCN and employ instance normalization to weaken action-related information. To strengthen the action-conditioned process, we learn the action-aware spatio-temporal features from action labels and motion sequences through label-motion fusion and spatio-temporal modeling. Then we use FiLM to compute modulation parameters γ and β to perform linear modulation on the learned latent representation. Finally, the GRU decoder is used to generate variable-length motion sequences in conjunction with temporal encoding and latent reinforcement.

2.3   Sequence-Level VAE

Action labels usually correspond to the whole motion sequence rather than a single frame, so to better learn the correspondence between labels and sequences, we use sequence-level VAE. The main problem of sequence-level VAE is how to learn the mappings in the sequence-latent-sequence transformation. To solve this problem, [38] and [42] use GRU to encode and recover sequences, embedding the hidden state of the last frame to the latent space, which may result in temporal information not being fully learned. Some works use a transformer instead to apply attention mechanism on feature extraction [5,9,16,30]. Since transformer cannot get a single latent code directly, [16] learns latent code for each frame, [5] simply averages the hidden states to get a single latent code, and [9] uses attention average at encoding stage and maps the latent code to L vectors at decoding stage. [30] learns the latent space by taking the first two outputs of transformer encoder corresponding to the distribution parameter tokens, then directly using the latent representation as the key and value of transformer decoder and the temporal positional encoding as the query to generate motion sequences. These works mainly focus on temporal modeling of the input but lack spatial terms. Therefore, we use GAGCN [45] to learn the complex spatial properties of human motion and use TCN for smooth temporal modeling, which learns more expressive action-aware features.

3   Methods

Problem Formulation. The problem we aim to solve is to generate a motion sequence $X_{1:T} = \{x_1, x_2, ..., x_T\}$ according to the given action label $a \in A$. Here A is the predefined action categories set, T is the desired length and $x_t \in \mathbb{R}^{24 \times 6 + 3}$ is the SMPL [23] pose of a single frame, including the root joint translation and 24 joint rotations represented by the continuous 6D rotation representation.

Overview. As shown in Fig. 2, we encode the motion sequence into action-agnostic latent space via TCN and employ instance normalization [37] on the intermediate features to weaken the action-related features. For the feature extraction, we embed the action labels into a latent representation as an extra *label joint* of the human body for the purpose of reinforcing the action information, which we call "label-motion fusion". After that, GAGCN [45] and TCN are used to extract the action-aware spatio-temporal features of the fused input, where spatial feature extraction is lacking in previous works. For the action-condition method, we use FiLM instead of direct concatenation or bias in previous work. Specifically, we input the learned spatio-temporal features into a fully connected layer to compute modulation parameters γ and β, and perform linear modulation on the action-agnostic latent representation, so that the action-aware features are better integrated into the latent representation. Finally, the GRU is used to generate variable-length motion sequences in conjunction with temporal encoding and latent reinforcement.

3.1   Uncoupled-Modulation CVAE

Action-Agnostic Latent Representation. Following previous work [10,30], we adopt a CVAE-based framework for action-conditioned motion generation. Previous works encode the labels and sequences coupledly to learn the latent representation, which makes the learned latent representation contain more or less action-related information. When random sampling from the latent space, the latent representation may contain the information of an arbitrary action label a, and if we modulate it with another action label b, the conflict between them will result in the generated motion not matching action label b.

We assume that a piece of white and blank paper can be drawn well, which means that it is easier to learn something as an "unskilled kid" than as an adult. So we need to learn an action-agnostic latent representation, just like an unskilled kid who only knows the basic movement laws. As shown in the upper left corner of Fig. 2, we use 6 TCN layers as an action-agnostic encoder(AAGE) denoted as Ψ_{AAGE} and add an instance normalization layer between the third and fourth layers to weaken the action-related information contained in the input $X_{1:T}$. Finally, the encoder outputs μ and σ to obtain $z \in \mathbb{R}^{256}$ by reparameterization:

$$\mu, \sigma = \Psi_{AAGE}(X_{1:T}), \quad p(z) = N(z|\mu, \sigma) \tag{1}$$

Action-Aware Modulation. Since the learned latent space is action-agnostic, the action condition method is required to be more powerful to make the generated motion match the given label. A professional teacher needs two capabilities: being good at learning action skills from motion sequences; knowing how to teach the skills to others, i.e. feature extraction and action condition.

In order to extract action-aware features, we need to fuse the label and motion and learn the spatio-temporal dynamics of the input motion sufficiently. Intuitively, the action label of a motion sequence is related to whole-body joints, so we encode the action label into an embedding vector by a linear projection, treating it as an *"label   joint"*. Then we concatenate the embedded vector and other joint features to get the labeled poses $X_{1:T}^l$, which we call it as "label-motion fusion" shown in the lower left corner of Fig. 2. GAGCN is a novel variant of GCN proposed by [45] to learn the complex spatial characteristics of human motion. Here we train an action-aware encoder(AAWE) with spatial GAGCN (denoted as Ψ_{AAWE}^s) and TCN (denoted as Ψ_{AAWE}^t) to learn the spatial dependencies between joints and the temporal dynamics to get the action-aware spatio-temporal features f_{st}. The whole encoder can be formulated as follows:

$$f_{st} = \Psi_{AAWE}^t(\Psi_{AAWE}^s(X_{1:T}^l)) \tag{2}$$

In order to make our action-aware feature to know how to "teach" the latent representation, we use FiLM as the modulation method instead of the simple concatenation or bias in previous work(shown in the upper right corner of Fig. 2). We use a fully connected layer(denoted as Φ) as FiLM generator to compute the modulation parameters $\gamma \in \mathbb{R}^{256}$ and $\beta \in \mathbb{R}^{256}$ from action-aware features, and then perform linear modulation on the latent representation z to obtain the action-aware latent representation $z' \in \mathbb{R}^{256}$:

$$\gamma, \beta = \Phi(f_{st}), \quad z' = \gamma * z + \beta \tag{3}$$

Temporal Decoder. To carry out action-conditioned motion generation, we pre-compute FiLM parameters for each action offline and save them with the corresponding labels. At runtime, given a prescribed action label, we randomly select a corresponding FiLM parameter to modulate the randomly sampling z. For more details, please refer to the supplementary material. Once we get the modulated latent representation z', to better recover a temporal sequence from a single latent z', we perform time encoding on the input length T via positional encoding and project $z' \in \mathbb{R}^d$ into $Z'_T \in \mathbb{R}^{d \times T}$ with the help of time encoding and a linear layer to get T vectors $[z'_1, \ldots, z'_T]$. After that, we input Z'_T into 4 GRU layers to generate an action-conditioned motion sequence(shown in the lower right corner of Fig. 2). Our uncoupled modulation is able to further enhance the diversity of the generated motion by operation on the modulation parameter like interpolation(seeing Sect. 4.4). In our experiments, we find that the strong condition may lead to posterior collapse, so we take a "latent reinforcement" approach [22] by adding the unmodulated z to the input of the last three layers of GRU to make the decoder's attention focus more on z. This trick solves the problem to some extent.

3.2   Training

The implementation details of our UM-CVAE are shown in the supplementary material. Here we only formulate our training loss. Following [30], we adopt 3 loss terms to train out model, the total loss is the weighted sum of these loss terms: $L = \lambda_{pr}L_{pr} + \lambda_{vr}L_{vr} + \lambda_{kl}L_{kl}$.

Pose reconstruction loss L_{pr}: We use L2 parametric to calculate the loss between our reconstruction results $\widetilde{X}_{1:T} = \{\widetilde{x}_1, \widetilde{x}_2, ..., \widetilde{x}_T\}$ and Ground Truth $X_{1:T} = \{x_1, x_2, ..., x_T\}$, formulated as: $L_{pr} = \frac{1}{T}\sum_{i=1}^{T} \|\widetilde{x}_i - x_i\|_2$.

Vertex coordinates reconstruction loss L_{vr}: For a more refined reconstruction results, we adopt an extra reconstruction loss on mesh Vertex coordinates. Specifically, we use differentiable SMPL layer to transform poses $X_{1:T} = \{x_1, x_2, ..., x_T\}$ into mesh vertices $V_{1:T} = \{v_1, v_2, ..., v_T\}$, the loss is formulated as: $L_{vr} = \frac{1}{T}\sum_{i=1}^{T} \|\widetilde{v}_i - v_i\|_2$.

KL divergence loss L_{kl}: We adopt the standard KL divergence loss, i.e. minimizing the KL divergence between Θ-parametrized approximate posterior distribution$q_{\Theta}(z|X_{1:T})$ and standard Gaussian distribution $p(z)$, it can be formulated as: $L_{kl} = D_{kl}\{q_{\Theta}(z|X_{1:T})\|p(z)\}$.

Fig. 3. Qualitative results of our method. We illustrate our generations of "Cartwheel" and "Kick" actions from BABEL, and each action consists of 2 sequences. These results demonstrate that our method can generate complex, realistic, diverse, and label-compliant motions. More results are shown in the supplementary material.

4   Experiments

In this section, we evaluate the proposed method. First, we will show the details of the used benchmark dataset and evaluation metrics in Sect. 4.1. The quantitative and qualitative comparison results with the state-of-the-art method will be given in Sect. 4.2. Then, we will analyze the main components of our method in Sect. 4.3. Finally, we will show the applications of our method in Sect. 4.4.

4.1   Datasets and Evaluation Metrics

Datasets. Here we briefly introduce the datasets we used. Please refer to supplementary material for more details about the datasets

HumanAct12 [10] is adopted from an existing dataset PHSPD [46], consisting of 1,191 motion clips and 90,099 frames in total. All motions are organized into 12 action categories.

UESTC [15] consists of 25K sequences across 40 action categories and 118 persons collected using Microsoft Kinect v2 sensors. [30] use VIBE to obtain SMPL sequences, which we use for training and testing. The processed dataset has 10650 sequences for training and 13350 sequences for testing.

BABEL [31] leverages the recently introduced AMASS dataset [25] for mocap sequences. BABEL contains action annotations for about 43.5 h of mocap performed by over 346 subjects from AMASS represented by SMPL-H [32], with 15472 unique language labels.

Evaluation Metrics. Following [10], we measure Frechet Inception Distance(FID), action recognition accuracy(Acc.), overall diversity(Div.), and multimodality(MM.) for quantitative evaluations. For HumanAct12 and UESTC, we use the provided recognition models of [10] and [30] to extract motion features to compute evaluation metrics. For BABEL, since the dataset is complicated and challenging for action recognition, we only use their provided recognition models [33] to compute the recognition accuracy for evaluation, including Top-1, Top-5, and Top-1-norm accuracy.

4.2   Comparisons with the State-of-the-Art Methods

To the best of our knowledge, the prior works focus on action-conditioned motion generation are A2M [10] and ACTOR [30], so we compare with their works qualitatively and quantitatively on HumanAct12, UESTC, and BABEL.

Quantitative Comparison. We used their publicly available code and pre-trained model to obtain results. It is worth noting that A2M does not experiment on UESTC, so we use their code to train on UESTC for 1500 epochs. And it is mentioned in [30] that their model can get better results by training more epochs. To be fair, we use their code to train 1500 epochs on UESTC, so the results we report are slightly different from those in ACTOR (better than the results demonstrated in [30]). We use the evaluation metrics in Sect. 4.1 to perform quantitative comparison on HumanAct12 and UESTC, the results are shown in Table 1. And we evaluate the comparison of recognition accuracy on BABEL. The results are shown in the third to sixth rows of Table 2.

Table 1. Quantitative comparison to the state-of-the-art works on UESTC and HumanAct12. We use the evaluation metrics in Sect. 4.1 and the best results are marked in bold. We can see that our method outperforms the state-of-the-art in both datasets.

Methods	UESTC					HumanAct12			
	FID_{tr} ↓	FID_{te} ↓	Acc.↑	Div.→	MM.→	FID_{tr} ↓	Acc.↑	Div.→	MM.→
Original	2.93 ±0.26	2.79 ±0.29	98.8 ±0.10	33.34 ±0.32	14.16 ±0.06	0.02 ±0.00	99.4 ±0.00	6.86 ±0.03	2.60 ±0.01
A2M [10]	25.78 ±1.31	27.01 ±1.99	88.1 ±0.57	31.78 ±0.41	15.44 ±0.11	2.46 ±0.08	92.3 ±0.20	7.03 ±0.04	2.87 ±0.04
ACTOR [30]	16.81 ±1.70	18.95 ±1.41	91.7 ±0.31	32.70 ±0.59	14.53 ±0.08	0.12 ±0.00	95.5 ±0.80	6.84 ±0.03	2.53 ±0.02
Ours	**9.12** 0.30	**±8.58** 0.23	**±93.0** 0.24	±31.85 ±0.29	15.08 ±0.09	**0.09** 0.00	**±95.8** 0.42	**±6.81** ±0.02	2.93 ±0.01

Table 2. Quantitative results on BABEL. The fourth to sixth rows show the comparison with state-of-the-art, and the best results are underlined. The recognition accuracy of our method is the highest and also the closest to the real data. The comparison between the "Original" row and the "Augmented" row shows that our method can augment the action recognition dataset and improve the action recognition accuracy.

Methods	BABEL-60		
	Top-5	Top-1	Top-1-norm
Original	67.83	33.41	30.42
A2M [10]	52.34	26.17	24.06
ACTOR [30]	48.24	25.37	23.49
Ours	57.14	29.04	27.81
Augmented	**70.01**	**35.14**	**32.18**

Thanks to our uncoupled latent spatial learning strategy and action-aware modulation, our results show a significant improvement over A2M and ACTOR on all datasets, especially on UESTC and BABEL. These two datasets have more motion types and motion sequences compared to HumanAct12, which indicates that our approach can generate realistic, diverse, and label-constrained motion on the more challenging dataset. It is worth noting that because there are more categories and more complex data in BABEL, the evaluation results of all methods are relatively worse than the real data, where our method is still the best. Also, we found that ACTOR performs worse than A2M on BABEL. We guess it is because ACTOR uses a single z as key and value for transformer decoder, which is not enough to learn the multi-head attention, resulting in unsatisfactory results on the complex dataset.

Qualitative Comparison. We visualize the generated results to demonstrate the advantages of our approach. Because of the limitations of previous methods, the motions they generate may have problems such as unnatural, falling into a stationary state, and confusing action types, etc. Our experimental results indicate that we solve these problems well. We demonstrate qualitative comparison results here in Fig. 4 and the motion generation results on BABEL in Fig. 3.

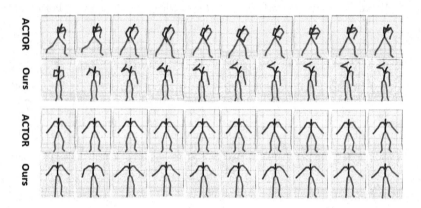

Fig. 4. Qualitative comparison of our method and ACTOR [30]. We illustrate the generations of "Drinking" (Top) on HumanAct12 and "Wrist-circling" (Bottom) on UESTC. In order to make the contrast effect more intuitive, we used the skeleton instead of the shape. While ACTOR have some issues like falling into a stationary state and confusing action types, our method solves these problems well.

The comparison of results generated on "Drinking" is worthy to notice. When given the "drinking" action label as the condition to the latent representation, ACTOR [30] generates a motion sequence in which the lower body is "warming up" and the upper body is lifting just like "drinking", and the generated motion of ours meets the labels well. This means that the action-related features learned in the latent representation indeed conflict with that contained in the user-specified label, which is strong support for our motivation.

The comparison of "Wrist-circling" is also convincing. In the movement of "Wrist-circling", only the wrist is circling with a small amplitude, and other joints are basically static. Generating this kind of motion requires us to learn the spatio-temporal characteristics of the motion well and reconstruct the temporal dynamics of the motion when decoding. We can see that the motion generated by ACTOR is stuck in a stationary state, while the motion generated by our method can normally perform wrist-circling. This is because we take the temporal dynamics into account when performing the reconstruction by mapping z' into Z'_T, while a single z is used as key and value in ACTOR to recover the motion sequence. More qualitative results (figure and video) are shown in the supplementary material.

4.3   Ablation Study

We do ablation studies to evaluate the effect of key components in our method: action-aware modulation, instance normalization, and latent reinforcement.

Effect of action-aware modulation: For better action-conditioned motion generation, we propose action-aware modulation to learn spatio-temporal features and modulate the latent space using FiLM. To demonstrate the advantages of our action-aware modulation, we remove action-aware encoder and directly input the motion sequences and action labels into action-agnostic encoder without IN, and use the action bias method in [30] for modulation. The experimental results are shown in the row starting with "w/o FiLM" in Table 3. It can be seen that the experimental results are significantly worse on FID and Acc. without our action-aware modulation, which means that the generated results have worse conformity to the action types of the original dataset. Moreover, the Div. and MM. increase instead due to the possibility of generating some artificial motions without action-aware modulation. To illustrate the effect of action-aware modu-

Table 3. Ablation study. We perform ablation studies to evaluate the effect of key components in our method on UESTC and HumanAct12, including action-aware modulation (FiLM), instance normalization (IN), and latent reinforcement (LR).

Methods	UESTC					HumanAct12			
	$FID_{tr}\downarrow$	$FID_{te}\downarrow$	Acc.↑	Div.→	MM.→	$FID_{tr}\downarrow$	Acc.↑	Div.→	MM.→
w/o IN	16.89 ±0.74	16.42 ±0.55	91.6 ±0.59	34.51 ±0.53	16.58 ±0.21	0.23 ±0.04	93.9 ±0.57	6.92 ±0.12	3.07 ±0.04
w/o FiLM	23.94 ±1.58	25.17 ±2.14	88.9 ±0.68	32.52 ±0.54	16.21 ±0.13	0.52 ±0.42	92.7 ±0.44	5.97 ±0.06	2.27 ±0.03
w/o LR	11.88 ±0.41	12.71 ±0.38	92.7 ±0.30	26.78 ±0.29	12.07 ±0.07	0.12 ±0.00	95.0 ±0.34	5.18 ±0.02	2.17 ±0.01
Ours	**9.12** 0.30	±**8.58** 0.23	±**93.0** 0.24	±31.85 ±0.29	15.08 ±0.09	**0.09** 0.00	±**95.8** 0.42	±6.81 ±0.02	2.93 ±0.01

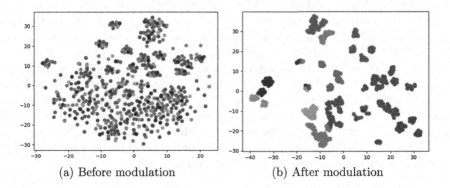

(a) Before modulation   (b) After modulation

Fig. 5. Latent space visualization. We visualize the latent space before and after modulation using T-SNE [24]. The latent space before modulation is randomly distributed (action-agnostic). After modulation, the latent variables are separated from each other according to the action types, making the latent space action-aware.

lation more intuitively, we visualize the latent space before and after modulation with TSNE [24], and the results are shown in Fig. 5. The latent space is clearly clustered according to action types after modulation, which indicates that our method knows how to "teach" the latent space action skills.

Effect of instance normalization: According to the above description, the learned latent space should be action-agnostic as the way to avoid conflicting with modulation. Inspired by [37], we use instance normalization to weaken the action-related information contained in the input sequence. To verify the effectiveness of this component, we directly remove it and the results are shown in the row starting with "w/o IN" in Table 3. When our encoder does not contain instance normalization, FID and Acc. become significantly worse, while Div. and MM. rise instead. The reason may be that the encoder without instance normalization learns more or less information related to the label and conflicts with the given label when modulating. The generated results will be different from the real human motion and increase the "diversity", which is obviously not what we want indeed. The visualized latent space in Fig. 5(a) is scattered, which also proves that the learned latent space is action-agnostic to some extent.

Effect of latent reinforcement: In our experiments, we find that since our action-aware modulation is too strong and weakens the effect of the latent space, which may reduce the diversity of generated motions. It is a problem known as posterior collapse. Inspired by [22], we add the unmodulated z to the input of the last three layers of GRU decoder to emphasize the importance of the latent variable, which is named latent reinforcement. The ablation results are shown in the row starting with "w/o LR" in Table 3, where FID and Acc. change very slightly and Div. and MM. decrease a lot. This indicates that the lack of latent reinforcement does reduce the diversity of the generated motions.

4.4 Applications

Generating Variable-Length Motions. Similar to [30], we add length T as input to the encoder stage to achieve variable-length motion generation through temporal encoding, latent variable expansion, and GRU decoder. We use a model trained on UETSC with fixed length 64 to generate motions of different lengths from 40 to 100 (with 4 frames interval), and then use our evaluation metrics to compute the FID_{te} and Acc. of the generated motions. To show the superiority of our model, we compare it with ACTOR, and the experimental results are plotted in Fig. 6. The results show that our method ensures higher Acc. and lower FID_{te} for different lengths of motion, which is a significant improvement compared to ACTOR. Besides, the standard deviation of our method is smaller, which indicates that our method is more robust.

Augmentation for Action Recognition. Our method generates high-quality action-conditioned motions, thus a very straightforward application is augmenting the action recognition dataset to help improve action recognition accuracy. We report the augmentation of BABEL because the current state-of-the-art

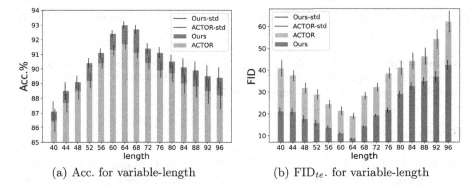

(a) Acc. for variable-length (b) FID$_{te}$. for variable-length

Fig. 6. Generating variable-length motions. We report the Acc. (left) and FID$_t e$ (right) of the motion from 40 to 100 frames at 4 frame intervals generated by a model trained on 64 frames and compare them with ACTOR [30]. The bars indicate the mean and the lines indicate the standard deviation. The results show that our method generates high-quality variable-length motions without training on other lengths and outperforms previous work.

action recognition method gets unsatisfactory accuracy on it. Specifically, we generate 30 motion clips for each motion category in BABEL-60(1800 in total), adding 9.11% data to BABEL-60. The augmented data is then used to train the motion recognition model [33]. The Acc. in the row starting with "Augmented" in Table 2 is higher than the "Original" row, which demonstrates that the data generated by our method can indeed augment the action recognition dataset.

Motion Interpolation. Thanks to our action-aware modulation method, we can interpolate different motions of the same action label to get more diverse results. Specifically, we select several different modulation parameters learned from a given label and interpolate them to generate interpolated motion. In this way, the motions we generate will be more diverse while maintaining the properties of the given label. The results are shown in the supplementary material.

5   Conclusions

We propose a novel action-conditioned motion generation model called UM-CVAE. Specifically, we learn the action-agnostic latent representation and action-aware spatio-temporal feature in an uncoupled manner, then perform action-aware feature-wise linear modulation via FiLM. The generated motions are realistic, diverse, and label-compliant, which show significant improvement over prior works and have some useful applications. However, there are still limitations to our approach. For example, althoug h our decoding approach is carefully designed, how to better recover motion sequence from a single latent variable remains to be explored. Also, our method relies on the quality of the dataset and cannot be conveniently extended to new actions or unseen body size.

Acknowledgement. This work was supported by the National Key R&D Program of Science and Technology for Winter Olympics (No. 2020YFF0304701) and the National Natural Science Foundation of China (No. 61772499).

References

1. Ahn, H., Ha, T., Choi, Y., Yoo, H., Oh, S.: Text2Action: generative adversarial synthesis from language to action. In: 2018 IEEE International Conference on Robotics and Automation (ICRA), pp. 5915–5920. IEEE (2018)
2. Ahuja, C., Morency, L.P.: Language2Pose: natural language grounded pose forecasting. In: 2019 International Conference on 3D Vision (3DV), pp. 719–728. IEEE (2019)
3. Barsoum, E., Kender, J., Liu, Z.: HP-GAN: probabilistic 3D human motion prediction via GAN. In: Proceedings of the IEEE Conference on Computer Vision and Pattern Recognition Workshops, pp. 1418–1427 (2018)
4. Brand, M., Hertzmann, A.: Style machines. In: Proceedings of the 27th Annual Conference on Computer Graphics and Interactive Techniques, pp. 183–192 (2000)
5. Cheng, X., Xu, W., Wang, T., Chu, W.: Variational semi-supervised aspect-term sentiment analysis via transformer. arXiv preprint arXiv:1810.10437 (2018)
6. Clavet, S.: Motion matching and the road to next-gen animation. In: Proceedings of the GDC (2016)
7. Corona, E., Pumarola, A., Alenya, G., Moreno-Noguer, F.: Context-aware human motion prediction. In: Proceedings of the IEEE/CVF Conference on Computer Vision and Pattern Recognition, pp. 6992–7001 (2020)
8. Cui, Q., Sun, H., Yang, F.: Learning dynamic relationships for 3D human motion prediction. In: Proceedings of the IEEE/CVF Conference on Computer Vision and Pattern Recognition, pp. 6519–6527 (2020)
9. Fang, L., Zeng, T., Liu, C., Bo, L., Dong, W., Chen, C.: Transformer-based conditional variational autoencoder for controllable story generation. arXiv preprint arXiv:2101.00828 (2021)
10. Guo, C., et al.: Action2Motion: conditioned generation of 3D human motions. In: Proceedings of the 28th ACM International Conference on Multimedia, pp. 2021–2029 (2020)
11. Holden, D., Kanoun, O., Perepichka, M., Popa, T.: Learned motion matching. ACM Trans. Graph. **39**(4), 53:1–53:12 (2020)
12. Holden, D., Komura, T., Saito, J.: Phase-functioned neural networks for character control. ACM Trans. Graph. **36**(4), 1–13 (2017)
13. Holden, D., Saito, J., Komura, T.: A deep learning framework for character motion synthesis and editing. ACM Trans. Graph. **35**(4), 1–11 (2016)
14. Jain, A., Zamir, A.R., Savarese, S., Saxena, A.: Structural-RNN: deep learning on spatio-temporal graphs. In: Proceedings of the IEEE Conference on Computer Vision and Pattern Recognition, pp. 5308–5317 (2016)
15. Ji, Y., Xu, F., Yang, Y., Shen, F., Shen, H.T., Zheng, W.S.: A large-scale RGB-D database for arbitrary-view human action recognition. In: Proceedings of the 26th ACM International Conference on Multimedia, pp. 1510–1518 (2018)

16. Jiang, J., Xia, G.G., Carlton, D.B., Anderson, C.N., Miyakawa, R.H.: Transformer VAE: a hierarchical model for structure-aware and interpretable music representation learning. In: ICASSP 2020 IEEE International Conference on Acoustics, Speech and Signal Processing (ICASSP), pp. 516–520. IEEE (2020)
17. Kundu, J.N., Gor, M., Babu, R.V.: BiHMP-GAN: bidirectional 3D human motion prediction GAN. In: Proceedings of the AAAI Conference on Artificial Intelligence, vol. 33, pp. 8553–8560 (2019)
18. Lee, H.Y., et al.: Dancing to music. Adv. Neural Inf. Process. Syst. **32** (2019)
19. Li, J., et al.: Learning to generate diverse dance motions with transformer. arXiv preprint arXiv:2008.08171 (2020)
20. Li, R., Yang, S., Ross, D.A., Kanazawa, A.: AI choreographer: music conditioned 3D dance generation with AIST++. In: Proceedings of the IEEE/CVF International Conference on Computer Vision, pp. 13401–13412 (2021)
21. Lin, X., Amer, M.R.: Human motion modeling using DVGANs. arXiv preprint arXiv:1804.10652 (2018)
22. Ling, H.Y., Zinno, F., Cheng, G., Van De Panne, M.: Character controllers using motion VAEs. ACM Trans. Graph. **39**(4), 40:1–40:12 (2020)
23. Loper, M., Mahmood, N., Romero, J., Pons-Moll, G., Black, M.J.: SMPL: a skinned multi-person linear model. ACM Trans. Graph. **34**(6), 1–16 (2015)
24. Van der Maaten, L., Hinton, G.: Visualizing data using t-SNE. J. Mach. Learn. Res. **9**(11) (2008)
25. Mahmood, N., Ghorbani, N., Troje, N.F., Pons-Moll, G., Black, M.J.: AMASS: archive of motion capture as surface shapes. In: Proceedings of the IEEE/CVF International Conference on Computer Vision, pp. 5442–5451 (2019)
26. Mao, W., Liu, M., Salzmann, M.: History repeats itself: human motion prediction via motion attention. In: Vedaldi, A., Bischof, H., Brox, T., Frahm, J.-M. (eds.) ECCV 2020. LNCS, vol. 12359, pp. 474–489. Springer, Cham (2020). https://doi.org/10.1007/978-3-030-58568-6_28
27. Martinez, J., Black, M.J., Romero, J.: On human motion prediction using recurrent neural networks. In: Proceedings of the IEEE Conference on Computer Vision and Pattern Recognition, pp. 2891–2900 (2017)
28. Mason, I., Starke, S., Komura, T.: Real-time style modelling of human locomotion via feature-wise transformations and local motion phases. arXiv preprint arXiv:2201.04439 (2022)
29. Perez, E., Strub, F., De Vries, H., Dumoulin, V., Courville, A.: FiLM: visual reasoning with a general conditioning layer. In: Proceedings of the AAAI Conference on Artificial Intelligence, vol. 32 (2018)
30. Petrovich, M., Black, M.J., Varol, G.: Action-conditioned 3D human motion synthesis with transformer VAE. In: Proceedings of the IEEE/CVF International Conference on Computer Vision, pp. 10985–10995 (2021)
31. Punnakkal, A.R., Chandrasekaran, A., Athanasiou, N., Quiros-Ramirez, A., Black, M.J.: BABEL: bodies, action and behavior with English labels. In: Proceedings of the IEEE/CVF Conference on Computer Vision and Pattern Recognition, pp. 722–731 (2021)
32. Romero, J., Tzionas, D., Black, M.J.: Embodied hands: modeling and capturing hands and bodies together. ACM Trans. Graph. (Proc. SIGGRAPH Asia) **36**(6) (2017)
33. Shi, L., Zhang, Y., Cheng, J., Lu, H.: Two-stream adaptive graph convolutional networks for skeleton-based action recognition. In: Proceedings of the IEEE/CVF Conference on Computer Vision and Pattern Recognition, pp. 12026–12035 (2019)

34. Sofianos, T., Sampieri, A., Franco, L., Galasso, F.: Space-time-separable graph convolutional network for pose forecasting. In: Proceedings of the IEEE/CVF International Conference on Computer Vision, pp. 11209–11218 (2021)
35. Starke, S., Zhang, H., Komura, T., Saito, J.: Neural state machine for character-scene interactions. ACM Trans. Graph. **38**(6), 178:1–178:14 (2019)
36. Starke, S., Zhao, Y., Komura, T., Zaman, K.: Local motion phases for learning multi-contact character movements. ACM Trans. Graph. **39**(4), 54:1–54:13 (2020)
37. Ulyanov, D., Vedaldi, A., Lempitsky, V.: Improved texture networks: maximizing quality and diversity in feed-forward stylization and texture synthesis. In: Proceedings of the IEEE Conference on Computer Vision and Pattern Recognition, pp. 6924–6932 (2017)
38. Walker, J., Marino, K., Gupta, A., Hebert, M.: The pose knows: video forecasting by generating pose futures. In: Proceedings of the IEEE International Conference on Computer Vision, pp. 3332–3341 (2017)
39. Wang, J.M., Fleet, D.J., Hertzmann, A.: Gaussian process dynamical models for human motion. IEEE Trans. Pattern Anal. Mach. Intell. **30**(2), 283–298 (2007)
40. Wang, Z., Chai, J., Xia, S.: Combining recurrent neural networks and adversarial training for human motion synthesis and control. IEEE Trans. Visual Comput. Graphics **27**(1), 14–28 (2019)
41. Xia, S., Wang, C., Chai, J., Hodgins, J.: Realtime style transfer for unlabeled heterogeneous human motion. ACM Trans. Graph. **34**(4), 1–10 (2015)
42. Yuan, Y., Kitani, K.: DLow: diversifying latent flows for diverse human motion prediction. In: Vedaldi, A., Bischof, H., Brox, T., Frahm, J.-M. (eds.) ECCV 2020. LNCS, vol. 12354, pp. 346–364. Springer, Cham (2020). https://doi.org/10.1007/978-3-030-58545-7_20
43. Zhang, H., Starke, S., Komura, T., Saito, J.: Mode-adaptive neural networks for quadruped motion control. ACM Trans. Graph. **37**(4), 1–11 (2018)
44. Zhong, C., Hu, L., Xia, S.: Spatial–temporal modeling for prediction of stylized human motion. Neurocomputing **511**, 34–42 (2022)
45. Zhong, C., Hu, L., Zhang, Z., Ye, Y., Xia, S.: Spatio-temporal gating-adjacency GCN for human motion prediction. In: Proceedings of the IEEE/CVF Conference on Computer Vision and Pattern Recognition, pp. 6447–6456 (2022)
46. Zou, S., et al.: 3D human shape reconstruction from a polarization image. In: Vedaldi, A., Bischof, H., Brox, T., Frahm, J.-M. (eds.) ECCV 2020. LNCS, vol. 12359, pp. 351–368. Springer, Cham (2020). https://doi.org/10.1007/978-3-030-58568-6_21

Towards Grand Unification of Object Tracking

Bin Yan[1], Yi Jiang[2](✉), Peize Sun[3], Dong Wang[1](✉), Zehuan Yuan[2], Ping Luo[3], and Huchuan Lu[1,4]

[1] School of Information and Communication Engineering,
Dalian University of Technology, Dalian, China
wdice@dlut.edu.cn
[2] ByteDance, Beijing, China
jiangyi.enjoy@bytedance.com
[3] The University of Hong Kong, Pok Fu Lam, Hong Kong
[4] Peng Cheng Laboratory, Shenzhen, China

Abstract. We present a unified method, termed Unicorn, that can simultaneously solve four tracking problems (SOT, MOT, VOS, MOTS) with a single network using the same model parameters. Due to the fragmented definitions of the object tracking problem itself, most existing trackers are developed to address a single or part of tasks and over-specialize on the characteristics of specific tasks. By contrast, Unicorn provides a unified solution, adopting the same input, backbone, embedding, and head across all tracking tasks. For the first time, we accomplish the great unification of the tracking network architecture and learning paradigm. Unicorn performs on-par or better than its task-specific counterparts in 8 tracking datasets, including LaSOT, TrackingNet, MOT17, BDD100K, DAVIS16-17, MOTS20, and BDD100K MOTS. We believe that Unicorn will serve as a solid step towards the general vision model. Code is available at https://github.com/MasterBin-IIAU/Unicorn.

Keyword: Object tracking

1 Introduction

Compared with weak AI designed for solving one specific task, artificial general intelligence (AGI) is expected to understand or learn any intellectual task that a human being can. Although there is still a large gap between this ambitious goal and the intellectual algorithms of today, some recent works [19,20,48,76] have begun to explore the possibility of building general vision models to address several vision tasks simultaneously.

Object tracking is one of the fundamental tasks in computer vision, which aims to build pixel-level or instance-level correspondence between frames and

---

B. Yan—This work was performed while Bin Yan worked as an intern at ByteDance.

Supplementary Information The online version contains supplementary material available at https://doi.org/10.1007/978-3-031-19803-8_43.

S. Avidan et al. (Eds.): ECCV 2022, LNCS 13681, pp. 733–751, 2022.
https://doi.org/10.1007/978-3-031-19803-8_43

to output trajectories typically in the forms of boxes or masks. Over the years, according to different application scenarios, the Object tracking problem has been mainly divided into four separate sub-tasks: Single Object Tracking (SOT) [17,39], Multiple Object Tracking (MOT) [37,75], Video Object Segmentation (VOS) [43], and Multi-Object Tracking and Segmentation (MOTS) [57, 75]. As a result, most tracking approaches are developed for only one of or part of the sub-tasks. Despite convenience for specific applications, this fragmented situation brings into the following drawbacks: (1) Trackers may over-specialize on the characteristic of specific sub-tasks, lacking in the generalization ability. (2) Independent model designs cause redundant parameters. For example, recent deep-learning-based trackers usually adopt similar backbones architectures, but the separate design philosophy hinders the potential reuse of parameters. It is natural to ask a question: Can all main-stream tracking tasks be solved by a unified model?

Although some works [33,36,58,60,66] attempt to unify SOT&VOS or MOT&MOTS by adding a mask branch to the existing box-level tracking system, there is still little progress towards the unification of SOT and MOT. There are mainly three obstacles hindering this process. (1) The characteristics of tracked objects vary. MOT usually tracks tens even hundreds of instances of specific categories. In contrast, SOT needs to track one target given in the reference frame no matter what class it belongs to. (2) SOT and MOT require different types of correspondence. SOT requires distinguishing the target from the background. However, MOT needs to match the currently detected objects with previous trajectories. (3) Most SOT methods [3,5,9,15,27,72] only take a small search region as the input to save computation and filter potential distractors. However, MOT algorithms [2,8,36,63,69,79,84] usually take the high-resolution full image as the input for detecting instances as completely as possible.

To conquer these challenges, we propose two core designs: the target prior and the pixel-wise correspondence. To be specific, (1) the target prior is an additional input for the detection head and serves as the switch among four tasks. For SOT&VOS, the target prior is the propagated reference target map, enabling the head to focus on the tracked target. For MOT&MOTS, by setting the target prior as zero, the head degenerates into the usual class-specific detection head smoothly. (2) The pixel-wise correspondence is the similarity between all pairs of points from the reference frame and the current frame. Both the SOT correspondence ($\mathbf{C}^{\mathrm{SOT}} \in \mathbb{R}^{h'w' \times hw}$) and the MOT correspondence ($\mathbf{C}^{\mathrm{MOT}} \in \mathbb{R}^{M \times N}$) are subsets of the pixel-wise correspondence ($\mathbf{C}_{\mathrm{pix}} \in \mathbb{R}^{hw \times hw}$). (3) With the help of the informative target prior and the accurate pixel-wise correspondence, the design of the search region becomes unnecessary for SOT, leading to unified inputs as the full image for SOT and MOT.

Towards the **unification** of **object tracking**, we propose Unicorn, a single network architecture to solve four tracking tasks. It takes the reference frame and the current frame as the inputs and produces their visual features by a weight-shared backbone. Then a feature interaction module is exploited to build pixel-wise correspondence between two frames. Based on the correspondence, a target prior is generated by propagating the reference target to the current frame. Finally, the target prior and the visual features are fused and sent to the detection head to get the tracked objects for all tasks.

With the unified network architecture, Unicorn can learn from various sources of tracking data and address four tracking tasks with the same model parameters. Extensive experiments show that Unicorn performs on-par or better than task-specific counterparts on 8 challenging benchmarks from four tracking tasks.

We summarize that our work has the following contributions:

- For the first time, Unicorn accomplishes the great unification of the network architecture and the learning paradigm for four tracking tasks.
- Unicorn bridges the gap among methods of four tracking tasks by the target prior and the pixel-wise correspondence.
- Unicorn puts forwards new state-of-the-art performance on 8 challenging tracking benchmarks with the same model parameters. This achievement will serve as a solid step towards the general vision model.

2   Related Work

2.1   Task-Specific Trackers

SOT typically specifies one tracked target with a bounding box on the first frame, then requires trackers to predict boxes for the tracked target in the following frames. Considering the uniqueness and the motion continuity of the tracked target, most of the algorithms in SOT [3,5,9,15,27,70,72] track on a small search region rather than the whole image to reduce computation and to filter distractors. Although achieving great success in the SOT field, search-region-based trackers suffer from the following drawbacks: (1) Due to the limited visual field, it is difficult for these methods to recover from temporary tracking failure, especially in the long-term tracking scenarios. (2) The speed of these methods drops drastically as the number of tracked instances increases. The inefficiency problem restricts the application of SOT trackers in scenarios such as MOT, where there are tens or hundreds of targets to track. To overcome the first problem, some works [23,58] propose a global-detection-based tracking paradigm. However, these methods either require large modifications to the original detection architecture to integrate the target information or rely on complicated dynamic programming to pick the best tracklet. Besides, both Global-Track [23] and Siam R-CNN [23] are developed on two-stage Faster R-CNN, whose detection pipeline is tedious and relies on hand-crafted anchors and ROI-Align. By contrast, in this work, we build our method based on a one-stage, anchor-free detector [18]. Furthermore, we demonstrate that only with minimal change to the original detector architecture, we could transform an object detector into a powerful SOT tracker.

Different from SOT, MOT does not have any given prior on the first frame. Trackers of MOT are required to find and associate all instances of specific classes by themselves. The mainstream methods [41,49,63,79,84] follow the tracking-by-detection paradigm. Specifically, an MOT system typically has two main components, an object detector and a certain association strategy. Commonly used detectors include Faster R-CNN [45], the YOLO series [18,44], CenterNet

[85], Sparse R-CNN [50], and Deformable DETR [88], etc. Popular association methods include IoU matching [4,49], Kalman Filter [4,63,79], ReID embedding [41,63,65,79], Transformer [36,49,77], or the combination of them [78]. Although there are some works [12,87] introducing SOT trackers for the association, these SOT trackers [3,14] are completely independent with the MOT networks, without any weight sharing. There is still a large gap between methods of SOT and MOT.

The goal of VOS is to predict masks for the tracked instances based on the high-quality mask annotations of the first frame. This field is now dominated by memory-network-based methods [10,40,74]. Although achieving great performance, these methods suffer from the following disadvantages: (1) The memory network brings huge time and space complexity, especially when dealing with high spatial resolution and the long sequence. While these scenarios are quite common in sequences of SOT and MOT. Specifically, the long-term tracking benchmarks [17,55] in SOT usually have thousands of frames per sequence, being more than 20x longer than DAVIS [43]. Meanwhile, the image size in MOT [75] can reach 720×1280, while the image size of DAVIS is usually only 480×854. (2) SOTA methods assume that there are always high-quality mask annotations on the first frame. However, high-quality masks demand expensive labor costs and are usually unavailable in real-world applications. To overcome this problem, some works [33,58,60] attempt to develop weakly-annotated VOS algorithms, which only require box annotation on the first frame.

MOTS is highly related to MOT by changing the form of boxes to fine-grained representation of masks. MOTS benchmarks [57,75] are typically from the same scenarios as those of MOT [37,75]. Besides, many MOTS methods are developed upon MOT trackers. Representative approaches include 3D-convolution-based Track R-CNN [57] and Stem-Seg [1], Transformer-based TrackFormer [36], tracking-assisting-detection Trades [66] and Prototype-based PCAN [26].

2.2   General Vision Models

Despite the great success of specialized models for diverse tasks, there is still a large gap between the current AI with human-like, omnipotent Artificial General Intelligence (AGI). An important step towards this grand goal is to build a generalist model supporting a broad range of AI tasks. Recent pioneering works [19,20,48,76] attempt to approach this goal from different perspectives. Specifically, MuST [19] introduces a multi-task self-training pipeline, which harnesses the knowledge in independent specialized teacher models to train a single general student model. INTERN [48] proposes a new learning paradigm, which learns with supervisory signals from multiple sources in multiple stages. The developed general vision model generalizes well to different tasks but also has lower requirements on downstream data. Florence [76] is a new computer vision foundation model, which expands the representations to different tasks along space, time, and modality. Florence has great transferability and achieves new SOTA results on a wide range of vision benchmarks. OMNIVORE [20] proposes a modality-agnostic model which can classify images, videos, and single-view 3D data using the same model parameters.

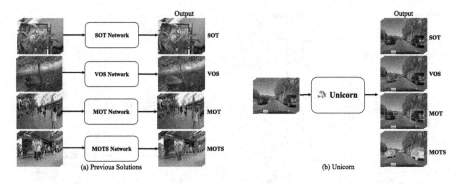

Fig. 1. Comparison between previous solutions and Unicorn.

2.3 Unification in Object Tracking

In the literature, some works [60,62,66] attempted to design a unified framework for supporting multiple tracking tasks. Specifically, SiamMask [60] is the first work to address SOT and VOS simultaneously. Similarly, TraDes [66] can solve both MOT and MOTS by introducing an extra mask head. Besides, UniTrack [62] proposes a high-level tracking framework, which consists of a shared appearance model and a series of unshared tracking heads. It demonstrates that different tracking tasks can share one appearance model for either propagation or association. However, the large discrepancy in tracking heads hinders it from exploiting a large amount of tracking data. Consequently, its performance lags far behind that of SOTA task-specific methods. Moreover, when used for MOT or MOTS, UniTrack requires extra, independent object detectors to provide observation. The extra object detector and the appearance model do not share the same backbone, bringing heavy burdens in parameters. By contrast, Unicorn solves four tracking tasks with one unified network with the same parameters. Besides, Unicorn can learn powerful representation from a large amount of labeled tracking data, achieving superior performance on 8 challenging benchmarks. Figure 1 shows the comparison between task-specific methods and Unicorn.

2.4 Correspondence Learning

Learning accurate correspondence is the key to many vision tasks, such as optical flow [51], video object segmentation [25,80], geometric matching [53,54], etc. The dense correspondence is usually obtained by computing correlation between the embedding maps of two frames. Most existing methods [25,51,80] obtain the embedding maps without considering the information exchange between two images. This could lead to ambiguous or wrong matching when there are many similar patterns or instances on the input images. Although some works [53, 54] attempt to relieve this problem, they usually require complex optimization or uncertainty modeling. Different from the local comparison, Transformer [56]

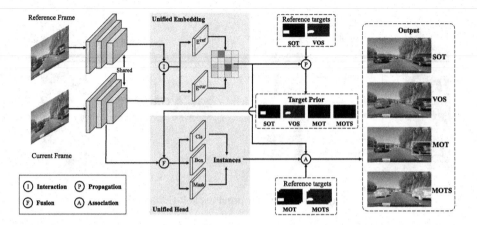

Fig. 2. Unicorn consists of three main components: (1) Unified inputs and backbone (2) Unified embedding (3) Unified head.

and its variants [88] exploit the attention mechanism to capture the long-range dependency within the input sequence. In this work, we demonstrate that these operations can help to learn precise correspondence in object tracking.

3   Approach

We propose a unified solution for Object tracking, called Unicorn, which consists of three main components: unified inputs and backbone; unified embedding and unified head. Three components are responsible for obtaining powerful visual representation, building precise correspondence and detecting diverse tracked targets respectively. The framework of Unicorn is demonstrated in Fig. 2. Given the reference frame $\mathbf{I}_{ref}$, the current frame $\mathbf{I}_{cur}$, and the reference targets, Unicorn aims at predicting the states of the tracked targets on the current frame for four tasks with a unified network.

3.1   Unified Inputs and Backbone

For efficiently localizing multiple potential targets, Unicorn takes the whole image (for both the reference frame and the current frame) instead of local search regions as the inputs. This also endows Unicorn high resistance to tracking failure and the ability to re-detect tracked target after disappearance.

During the feature extraction, the reference frame and the current frame are passed through a weight-sharing backbone to get feature pyramid representations(FPN) [30]. To maintain important details and reduce the computational burden during computing correspondence, we choose the feature map with stride 16 as the input of the following embedding module. The corresponding features from the reference and the current frame are termed $\mathbf{F}_{ref}$ and $\mathbf{F}_{cur}$ respectively.

3.2   Unified Embedding

The core task of Object tracking is to build accurate correspondence between frames in a video. For SOT and VOS, pixel-wise correspondence propagates the user-provided target from the reference frame (usually the 1st frame) to the tth frame, providing strong prior information for the final box or mask prediction. Besides, for MOT and MOTS, instance-level correspondence helps to associate the detected instances on the tth frame to the existing trajectories on the reference frame (usually the $t-1^{th}$ frame).

   In Unicorn, given the spatially flattened reference frame embedding $\mathbf{E}_{ref} \in \mathbb{R}^{hw \times c}$ and the current frame embedding $\mathbf{E}_{cur} \in \mathbb{R}^{hw \times c}$, pixel-wise correspondence $\mathbf{C}_{pix} \in \mathbb{R}^{hw \times hw}$ is computed by the matrix multiplication between them. For SOT&VOS taking the full image as the inputs, the correspondence is the pixel-wise correspondence itself. For MOT&MOTS, assume that there are M trajectories on the reference frame and N detected instances on the current frame respectively, the instance-level correspondence $\mathbf{C}_{inst} \in \mathbb{R}^{N \times M}$ is the matrix multiplication of the reference instance embedding $\mathbf{e}_{ref} \in \mathbb{R}^{M \times c}$ and the current instance embedding $\mathbf{e}_{cur} \in \mathbb{R}^{N \times c}$. The instance embedding $\mathbf{e}$ is extracted from the frame embedding $\mathbf{E}$, where the center of the instance is located.

$$\begin{aligned} \mathbf{C}_{pix} &= \mathrm{softmax}(\mathbf{E}_{cur}\mathbf{E}_{ref}{}^{T}) \\ \mathbf{C}_{inst} &= \mathrm{softmax}(\mathbf{e}_{cur}\mathbf{e}_{ref}{}^{T}) \end{aligned} \qquad (1)$$

It can be seen that the instance-level correspondence $\mathbf{C}_{inst}$ required by MOT and MOTS is the sub-matrix of the pixel-wise correspondence $\mathbf{C}_{pix}$. Besides, learning highly discriminative embedding $\{\mathbf{E}_{ref}, \mathbf{E}_{cur}\}$ is the key to building precise correspondence for all tracking tasks.

Feature Interaction. Due to its advantages of capturing long-range dependency, Transformer [56] is an intuitive choice to enhance the original feature representation $\{\mathbf{F}_{ref}, \mathbf{F}_{cur}\}$. However, this could lead to huge memory cost when dealing with high-resolution feature maps, because the memory consumption increases with the length of the input sequence quadratically. To alleviate this problem, we replace the full attention with more memory-efficient deformable attention [88]. For more accurate correspondence, the enhanced feature maps are upsampled by 2× to obtain high-resolution embeddings on the stride of 8.

$$\{\mathbf{E}_{ref}, \mathbf{E}_{cur}\} = \mathrm{Upsample}(\mathrm{Attention}(\mathbf{F}_{ref}, \mathbf{F}_{cur})) \qquad (2)$$

Loss. Ideal embedding should work well on both propagation (SOT, VOS) and association (MOT, MOTS). For SOT&VOS, although there is no human-annotated label for dense correspondence between frames, the embedding can be supervised by the difference between the propagated result $\widetilde{\mathbf{T}}_{cur}$ and the ground-truth target map $\mathbf{T}_{cur}$. Specifically, the shape of target map $\mathbf{T}$ is $hw \times 1$. The regions where the tracked target exists are equal to one and the other regions are equal to zero. During the propagation, the pixel-wise correspondence $\mathbf{C}_{pix}$

transforms the reference target map $\mathbf{T}_{\mathrm{ref}}$ to the estimation of the current target map $\widetilde{\mathbf{T}}_{\mathrm{cur}}$.

$$\widetilde{\mathbf{T}}_{\mathrm{cur}}(i,j) = \sum_k \mathbf{C}_{\mathrm{pix}}(i,k) \cdot \mathbf{T}_{\mathrm{ref}}(k,j) \tag{3}$$

Besides, for MOT and MOTS, the instance-level correspondence can be learned with standard contrastive learning paradigm. Specifically, assume that the instance i from the current frame is matched with the instance j from the reference frame, then the corresponding ground-truth matrix $\mathbf{G}$ should satisfies that

$$\mathbf{G}_{i,k} = \begin{cases} 0 & k \neq j \\ 1 & k = j \end{cases} \tag{4}$$

Finally, the unified embedding can be optimized end-to-end by Dice Loss [38] for SOT&VOS or Cross-Entropy Loss for MOT&MOTS.

$$\mathbf{L}_{\mathrm{corr}} = \begin{cases} \mathrm{Dice}(\widetilde{\mathbf{T}}_{\mathrm{cur}}, \mathbf{T}_{\mathrm{cur}}) & \text{task in } \{\mathrm{SOT}, \mathrm{VOS}\} \\ \mathrm{CrossEntropy}(\mathbf{C}_{\mathrm{inst}}, \mathbf{G}) & \text{task in } \{\mathrm{MOT}, \mathrm{MOTS}\} \end{cases} \tag{5}$$

3.3   Unified Head

To achieve the grand unification of Object tracking, another important and challenging problem is designing a unified head for four tracking tasks. Specifically, MOT shall detect objects of specific categories. However, SOT needs to detect any target given in the reference frame. To bridge this gap, Unicorn introduces an extra input (called target prior) to the original detector head [18,52]. Without any further modification, Unicorn can easily detect various objects needed for four tasks with this unified head. More details about the head architecture can be found in the supplementary materials.

Target Prior. As mentioned in Sect. 3.2, given the reference target map $\mathbf{T}_{\mathrm{ref}}$, the propagated target map $\widetilde{\mathbf{T}}_{\mathrm{cur}}$ can provide strong prior information about the state of the tracked target. This motivates us to take it as a target prior when detecting targets for SOT&VOS. To be compatible with the original input of the detection head, we first reshape it to $h \times w \times 1$ (i.e. $\widetilde{\mathbf{T}}_{\mathrm{cur}}^{\mathrm{reshape}} \in \mathbb{R}^{h \times w \times 1}$). Meanwhile, when dealing with MOT&MOTS, we can simply set this prior to zero. Formally, the target prior $\mathbf{P}$ satisfies that

$$\mathbf{P} = \begin{cases} \widetilde{\mathbf{T}}_{\mathrm{cur}}^{\mathrm{reshape}} & \text{task in } \{\mathrm{SOT}, \mathrm{VOS}\} \\ 0 & \text{task in } \{\mathrm{MOT}, \mathrm{MOTS}\} \end{cases} \tag{6}$$

Feature Fusion. The unified head takes the original FPN feature $\mathbf{F} \in \mathbb{R}^{h \times w \times c}$ and the target prior $\mathbf{P} \in \mathbb{R}^{h \times w \times 1}$ as the inputs. Unicorn fuses these two inputs with broadcast sum and passes the fused feature $\mathbf{F}' \in \mathbb{R}^{h \times w \times c}$ to the original detection head. This fusion strategy has the following advantages. (1)

The fused features are seamlessly compatible with four tasks. Specifically, for MOT&MOTS, the target prior is equal to zero. Then the fused feature $\mathbf{F}'$ degenerates back to the original FPN feature $\mathbf{F}$ to detect objects of specific classes. For SOT&VOS, the target prior with strong target information can enhance the original FPN feature and makes the network focus on the tracked target.(2) The architecture is simple, without introducing complex changes to the original detection head. Furthermore, the consistent architecture also enables Unicorn to fully exploit the pretrained weights of the original object detector.

3.4 Training and Inference

Training. The whole training process divides into two stages: SOT-MOT joint training and VOS-MOTS joint training. In the first stage, the network is end-to-end optimized with the correspondence loss and the detection loss using data from SOT&MOT. In the second stage, a mask branch is added and optimized with the mask loss using data from VOS&MOTS with other parameters fixed.

Inference. During the test phase, for SOT&VOS, the reference target map is generated once on the first frame and kept fixed in the following frames. Unicorn directly picks the box or mask with the highest confidence score as the final tracking result, without any hyperparameter-sensitive post-processing like cosine window. Besides, Unicorn only needs to run the heavy backbone and the correspondence once, while running the lightweight head rather than the whole network N times, leading to higher efficiency. For MOT&MOTS, Unicorn detects all objects of the given categories and simultaneously outputs corresponding instance embeddings. The later association is performed based on the embeddings and the motion model for BDD100K and MOT17 respectively.

4   Experiments

4.1   Implementation Details

When comparing with state-of-the-art methods, we choose ConvNeXt-Large [31] as the backbone. In ablations, we report the results of our method with ConvNeXt-Tiny [31] and ResNet-50 [21] as the backbone. The input image size is 800×1280 and the shortest side ranges from 736 to 864 during multi-scale training. The model is trained on 16 NVIDIA Tesla A100 GPU with a global batch size of 32. To avoid inaccurate statistics estimation, we replace all Batch Normalization [24] with Group Normalization [67]. Two training stages randomly sample data from SOT&MOT datasets and VOS&MOTS datasets, respectively. Each training stage consists of 15 epochs with 200,000 pairs of frames in every epoch. The optimizer is Adam-W [32] with weight decay of $5e^{-4}$ and momentum of 0.9. The initial learning rate is $2.5e^{-4}$ with 1 epoch warm-up and the cosine annealing schedule. More details can be found in the supplementary materials.

Table 1. State-of-the-art comparison on LaSOT [17] and TrackingNet [39].

Method	Source	LaSOT [17]			TrackingNet [39]		
		Success	P_{norm}	P	Success	P_{norm}	P
SiamFC [3]	ECCVW2016	33.6	42.0	33.9	57.1	66.3	53.3
UniTrack [62]	NeurIPS2021	35.1	–	32.6	–	–	–
ATOM [15]	CVPR2019	51.5	57.6	50.5	70.3	77.1	64.8
SiamPRN++ [27]	CVPR2019	49.6	56.9	49.1	73.3	80.0	69.4
DiMP [5]	ICCV2019	56.9	65.0	56.7	74.0	80.1	68.7
GlobalTrack [23]	AAAI2020	52.1	–	52.7	70.4	75.4	65.6
SiamFC++ [70]	AAAI2020	54.4	62.3	54.7	75.4	80.0	70.5
D3S [33]	CVPR2020	–	–	–	72.8	76.8	66.4
PrDiMP [16]	CVPR2020	59.8	68.8	60.8	75.8	81.6	70.4
Siam R-CNN [58]	CVPR2020	64.8	72.2	–	81.2	85.4	80.0
KYS [6]	ECCV2020	55.4	63.3	–	74.0	80.0	68.8
Ocean [82]	ECCV2020	56.0	65.1	56.6	–	–	–
TrDiMP [59]	CVPR2021	63.9	–	61.4	78.4	83.3	73.1
TransT [9]	CVPR2021	64.9	73.8	69.0	81.4	86.7	80.3
AutoMatch [81]	ICCV2021	58.2	–	59.9	76.0	–	72.6
SAOT [86]	ICCV2021	61.6	70.8	–	–	–	–
KeepTrack [35]	ICCV2021	67.1	77.2	70.2	–	–	–
STARK [72]	ICCV2021	67.1	77.0	–	82.0	86.9	–
Unicorn	Ours	68.5	76.6	74.1	83.0	86.4	82.2

In Sect. 4.2, 4.3, 4.4 and 4.5, we compare Unicorn with task-specific counterparts in 8 tracking datasets. In each benchmark, the red bold font and the blue font indicate the best two results. Unicorn in four tasks uses the same model parameters.

4.2 Evaluations on Single Object Tracking

We compare Unicorn with state-of-the-art SOT trackers on two popular and challenging benchmarks, LaSOT [17] and TrackingNet [39]. Both datasets evaluate the tracking performance with the following measures: Success, precision (P) and normalized precision (P_{norm}). All these measures are the higher the better.

LaSOT. LaSOT [17] is a large-scale long-term tracking benchmark, which contains 280 videos in the test set with an average length of 2448 frames. Table 1 shows that Unicorn achieves new state-of-the-art Success and Precision of 68.5% and 74.1% respectively. It is also worth noting that Unicorn surpasses the previous best global-detection-based tracker Siam R-CNN [58] by a large margin

Table 2. State-of-the-art comparison on MOT17 [37] test set.

Tracker	MOTA↑	IDF1↑	HOTA↑	MT↑	ML↓	FP↓	FN↓	IDs↓
TrackFormer [36]	65.0	63.9	–	–	–	70443	123552	3528
Chained-Tracker [42]	66.6	57.4	49.0	37.8%	18.5%	22284	160491	5529
CenterTrack [84]	67.8	64.7	52.2	34.6%	24.6%	18498	160332	3039
QuasiDense [41]	68.7	66.3	53.9	40.6%	21.9%	26589	146643	3378
TraDes [66]	69.1	63.9	52.7	36.4%	21.5%	20892	150060	3555
SOTMOT [83]	71.0	71.9	–	42.7%	15.3%	39537	118983	5184
TransCenter [68]	73.2	62.2	54.5	40.8%	18.5%	23112	123738	4614
MOTR [77]	73.4	68.6	57.8	42.9%	19.1%	27939	119589	2439
FairMOT [79]	73.7	72.3	59.3	43.2%	17.3%	27507	117477	3303
CSTrack [28]	74.9	72.6	59.3	41.5%	17.5%	23847	114303	3567
TransTrack [49]	75.2	63.5	54.1	55.3%	10.2%	50157	86442	3603
OMC [29]	76.3	72.3	–	44.8%	15.5%	–	–	–
CorrTracker [61]	76.5	73.6	60.7	47.6%	12.7%	29808	99510	3369
TransMOT [13]	76.7	75.1	61.7	51.0%	16.4%	36231	93150	2346
Unicorn	77.2	75.5	61.7	58.7%	11.2%	50087	73349	5379

Table 3. State-of-the-art comparison on BDD100K [75] tracking validation set.

Method	Split	mMOTA↑	mIDF1↑	MOTA↑	IDF1↑	FN↓	FP↓	ID Sw.↓	MT↑	ML↓	mAP↑
Yu et al. [75]	val	25.9	44.5	56.9	66.8	122406	52372	8315	8396	3795	28.1
QDTrack [41]	val	36.6	50.8	63.5	71.5	108614	46621	6262	9481	3034	32.6
Unicorn	val	41.2	54.0	66.6	71.3	95454	41648	10876	10296	2505	41.4

(68.5% vs 64.8%) with a much simpler network architecture and tracking strategy (directly picking the top-1 vs tracklet dynamic programming).

TrackingNet. TrackingNet [39] is a large-scale short-term tracking benchmark containing 511 videos in the test set. As reported in Table 1, Unicorn surpasses all previous methods with a Success of 83.0% and a Precision of 82.2%.

4.3   Evaluations on Multiple Object Tracking

We compare Unicorn with state-of-the-art MOT trackers on two challenging benchmarks: MOT17 [37] and BDD100K [75]. The common metrics include Multiple-Object Tracking Accuracy (MOTA), Identity F1 Score (IDF1), False Positives (FP), False Negatives (FN), the percentage of Mostly Tracked Trajectories (MT) and Mostly Lost Trajectories (ML), Identity Switches (IDS). Among them, MOTA is the primary metric to measure the overall detection and tracking performance, IDF1 is used to measure the trajectory identity accuracy.

MOT17. The MOT17 focuses on pedestrian tracking and includes 7 sequences in the training set and 7 sequences in the test set. We compare Unicorn with previous methods under the private detection protocol on the test set of MOT17. Table 2 demonstrates that Unicorn achieves the best MOTA and IDF1, surpassing the previous SOTA method by 0.5% and 0.4% respectively.

Table 4. State-of-the-art comparison on the validation set of the DAVIS-2016 and the DAVIS-2017. OL: online learning, Memory: using an external memory bank.

Init	Method	OL	Memory	$(\mathcal{J\&F})^{16}$	$\mathcal{J}^{16}$	$\mathcal{F}^{16}$	$(\mathcal{J\&F})^{17}$	$\mathcal{J}^{17}$	$\mathcal{F}^{17}$
mask	FAVOS [11]	✗	✗	81.0	82.4	79.5	58.2	54.6	61.8
	OSMN [34]	✗	✗	73.5	74.0	72.9	54.8	52.5	57.1
	VideoMatch [22]	✗	✗	–	81.0	–	56.5	–	–
	UniTrack [62]	✗	✓	–	–	–	–	58.4	–
	RANet [64]	✗	✗	85.5	85.5	85.4	65.7	63.2	68.2
	FRTM [46]	✓	✓	83.5	83.6	83.4	76.7	73.9	79.6
	TVOS [80]	✗	✓	–	–	–	72.3	69.9	74.7
	LWL [7]	✓	✓	–	–	–	81.6	79.1	84.1
	STM [40]	✗	✓	89.3	88.7	89.9	81.8	79.2	84.3
	CFBI [74]	✗	✓	89.4	88.3	90.5	81.9	79.1	84.6
	HMMN [47]	✗	✓	90.8	89.6	92.0	84.7	81.9	87.5
	STCN [10]	✗	✓	91.6	90.8	92.5	85.4	82.2	88.6
bbox	SiamMask [60]	✗	✗	69.8	71.7	67.8	56.4	54.3	58.5
	D3S [33]	✗	✗	74.0	75.4	72.6	60.8	57.8	63.8
	Siam R-CNN [58]	✗	✗	–	–	–	70.6	66.1	75.0
	Unicorn	✗	✗	87.4	86.5	88.2	69.2	65.2	73.2

BDD100K MOT. BDD100K is a large-scale dataset of visual driving scenes and requires tracking 8 categories of instances. To evaluate the average performance across 8 classes, BDD100K additionally introduces two measures: mMOTA and mIDF1. Different from MOT17, BDD100K is annotated at only 5 FPS. The low frame-rate brings difficulty to motion models commonly used for MOT17. As shown in Table 3, Unicorn achieves the best performance, largely surpassing the previous SOTA method QDTrack [41] on the val set. Specifically, the improvement is up to 4.6% and 3.2% in terms of mMOTA and mIDF1 respectively.

4.4 Evaluations on Video Object Segmentation

We further evaluate the ability of Unicorn to perform VOS on DAVIS [43] 2016 and 2017. Both datasets evaluate methods with the region similarity $\mathcal{J}$, the contour accuracy $\mathcal{F}$, and the average of them $\mathcal{J\&F}$.

DAVIS-16. DAVIS-16 includes 20 single-object videos in the validation set. Table 4 demonstrates that Unicorn achieves the best results among methods with bounding-box initialization, even surpassing RANet [64] and FRTM [46] with mask initialization. Meanwhile, Unicorn outperforms its multi-task counterparts SiamMask [60] by a large margin of 17.6% in terms of $\mathcal{J\&F}$.

DAVIS-17. DAVIS-17 contains 30 videos in the validation set and there could be multiple tracked targets in each sequence. As shown in Table 4, compared with

Table 5. State-of-the-art comparison on the MOTS [57] test set.

Method	sMOTSA↑	IDF1↑	MT↑	ML ↓	FP↓	FN↓	ID Sw.↓
Track R-CNN [57]	40.6	42.4	38.7%	21.6%	1261	12641	567
TraDeS [66]	50.8	58.7	49.4%	18.3%	1474	9169	492
TrackFormer [36]	54.9	63.6	–	–	2233	7195	278
PointTrackV2 [71]	62.3	42.9	56.7%	12.5%	963	5993	541
Unicorn	65.3	65.9	64.9%	10.1%	1364	4452	398

Table 6. State-of-the-art comparison on the BDD100K MOTS validation set.

Method	Online	mMOTSA↑	mMOTSP↑	mIDF1↑	ID Sw.↓	mAP↑
SortIoU	✓	10.3	59.9	21.8	15951	22.2
MaskTrackRCNN [73]	✓	12.3	59.9	26.2	9116	22.0
STEm-Seg [1]	✗	12.2	58.2	25.4	8732	21.8
QDTrack-mots [41]	✓	22.5	59.6	40.8	1340	22.4
QDTrack-mots-fix [41]	✓	23.5	66.3	44.5	973	25.5
PCAN [26]	✓	27.4	66.7	45.1	876	26.6
Unicorn	✓	29.6	67.7	44.2	1731	32.1

the previous best box-initialized method Siam R-CNN [58], Unicorn achieves competitive results with a much simpler architecture. Specifically, Siam R-CNN [58] uses an extra Box2Seg network, which is completely independent from the box-based tracker without any weight sharing. However, Unicorn can predict both boxes and masks with a unified head. Although there is still gap between the performance of Unicorn with that of SOTA VOS methods with mask initialization, Unicorn can address four tracking tasks with the same model parameters, while HMMN [47] and STCN [10] can only be used in the VOS task.

4.5 Evaluations on Multi-object Tracking and Segmentation

Finally, we evaluate the ability of Unicorn for MOTS on MOTS20 [57] and BDD100K MOTS [75]. The main evaluation metrics are sMOTSA and mMOTSA.

MOTS20 Challenge. MOTS20 Challenge has 4 sequences in the test set. As shown in Table 5, Unicorn achieves state-of-the-art performance, surpassing the second-best method PoinTrackV2 [71] by a large margin of 3.3% on sMOTSA.

BDD100K MOTS Challenge. BDD100K MOTS Challenge includes 37 sequences in the validation set. Table 6 demonstrates that Unicorn outperforms the previous best method PCAN [26] by a large margin (i.e. mMOTSA +2.2%, mAP +5.5%). Meanwhile, Unicorn does not use any complex design like space-time memory or prototypical network as in PCAN, bringing into a simpler pipeline.

Table 7. Ablations and comparisons. Our baseline model are underlined.

Experiment	Method	SOT LaSOT (AUC)	MOT BDD (mMOTA)	VOS DAVIS17 ($\mathcal{J}\&\mathcal{F}$)	MOTS BDD (mMOTSA)	FPS
Backbone	ConvNeXt-Tiny	67.7	39.9	68.0	29.7	14
	ResNet-50	65.3	35.1	66.2	30.8	13
Interaction	Deformable Att	67.7	39.9	68.0	29.7	14
	Full Att	67.1	38.5	66.9	26.7	13
	Conv	66.8	37.6	66.6	27.0	15
Fusion	Broad Sum	67.7	39.9	68.0	29.7	14
	Concat	66.8	38.3	66.7	27.2	14
	W/o Prior	50.9	37.6	29.2	27.8	14
Single task	Unification	67.7	39.9	68.0	29.7	14
	SOT only	67.5	–	–	–	14
	MOT only	–	39.6	–	–	14
	VOS only	–	–	68.4	–	14
	MOTS only	–	–	–	28.1	14
Speed	Ours	67.7	39.9	68.0	29.7	14
	Ours-RT	67.1	37.5	66.8	26.2	23

4.6 Ablations and the Other Analysis

For the ablations, we choose Unicorn with ConvNeXt-Tiny [31] backbone as the baseline. The detailed results are demonstrated in Table 7.

Backbone. We implement a variant of Unicorn with ResNet-50 [21] as the backbone. Although the overall performance of this version is lower than the baseline, this variant still achieves superior performance on four tasks.

Interaction. Besides the memory-efficient deformable attention [88], we compare the full attention [56] and the convolution operation, which does not exchange information between frames. Experiments show that deformable attention obtains better performance than the full attention, while consuming much less memory. Moreover, the results of the convolution are lower than the baseline, showing the importance of interaction for accurate correspondence.

Fusion. Apart from broadcast sum, we compare other two methods: concatenation, and without the target prior. The performance of SOT and VOS drops significantly after removing the target prior, demonstrating the importance of this design. Besides, broadcast sum performs better than concatenation.

Single Task. We compare with training four independent models for different tasks. Experiments show that our unified model performs on-par with independently trained counterparts, while being much more parameter-efficient.

Speed. We develop a light-weight variant with a lower input resolution of 640×1024. Experiments show that the real-time version does not only achieves competitive performance but also can run in real-time at more than 20 FPS.

5 Conclusions

We propose Unicorn, a unified approach to address four tracking tasks using a single model with the same model parameters. For the first time, it achieves the unification of network architecture and learning paradigm for Object tracking. Extensive experiments demonstrate that Unicorn performs on-par or better than task-specific counterparts on 8 challenging benchmarks. We hope that Unicorn can serve as a solid step towards the general vision model.

Acknowledgement. Thank the reviewers for their insightful comments. Huchuan Lu and Dong Wang are supported in part by the National Natural Science Foundation of China under Grant nos. 62022021, 61806037, 61725202, U1903215 and 61829102, and in part by the Science and Technology Innovation Foundation of Dalian under Grant no. 2020JJ26GX036 and Dalian Innovation leader's support Plan under Grant no. 2018RD07. Ping Luo is supported by the General Research Fund of HK No. 27208720, No. 17212120, and No. 17200622.

References

1. Athar, A., Mahadevan, S., Ošep, A., Leal-Taixé, L., Leibe, B.: STEm-Seg: spatio-temporal embeddings for instance segmentation in videos. In: Vedaldi, A., Bischof, H., Brox, T., Frahm, J.-M. (eds.) ECCV 2020. LNCS, vol. 12356, pp. 158–177. Springer, Cham (2020). https://doi.org/10.1007/978-3-030-58621-8_10
2. Bergmann, P., Meinhardt, T., Leal-Taixe, L.: Tracking without bells and whistles. In: ICCV (2019)
3. Bertinetto, L., Valmadre, J., Henriques, J.F., Vedaldi, A., Torr, P.H.S.: Fully-convolutional siamese networks for object tracking. In: ECCVW (2016)
4. Bewley, A., Ge, Z., Ott, L., Ramos, F., Upcroft, B.: Simple online and realtime tracking. In: ICIP (2016)
5. Bhat, G., Danelljan, M., Gool, L.V., Timofte, R.: Learning discriminative model prediction for tracking. In: ICCV (2019)
6. Bhat, G., Danelljan, M., Van Gool, L., Timofte, R.: Know your surroundings: exploiting scene information for object tracking. In: Vedaldi, A., Bischof, H., Brox, T., Frahm, J.-M. (eds.) ECCV 2020. LNCS, vol. 12368, pp. 205–221. Springer, Cham (2020). https://doi.org/10.1007/978-3-030-58592-1_13
7. Bhat, G., Lawin, F.J., Danelljan, M., Robinson, A., Felsberg, M., Van Gool, L., Timofte, R.: Learning what to learn for video object segmentation. In: Vedaldi, A., Bischof, H., Brox, T., Frahm, J.-M. (eds.) ECCV 2020. LNCS, vol. 12347, pp. 777–794. Springer, Cham (2020). https://doi.org/10.1007/978-3-030-58536-5_46
8. Brasó, G., Leal-Taixé, L.: Learning a neural solver for multiple object tracking. In: CVPR (2020)
9. Chen, X., Yan, B., Zhu, J., Wang, D., Yang, X., Lu, H.: Transformer tracking. In: CVPR (2021)
10. Cheng, H.K., Tai, Y.W., Tang, C.K.: Rethinking space-time networks with improved memory coverage for efficient video object segmentation. In: NeurIPS (2021)
11. Cheng, J., Tsai, Y.H., Hung, W.C., Wang, S., Yang, M.H.: Fast and accurate online video object segmentation via tracking parts. In: CVPR (2018)

12. Chu, P., Ling, H.: FAMNet: Joint learning of feature, affinity and multi-dimensional assignment for online multiple object tracking. In: ICCV (2019)
13. Chu, P., Wang, J., You, Q., Ling, H., Liu, Z.: TransMOT: spatial-temporal graph transformer for multiple object tracking. arXiv preprint arXiv:2104.00194 (2021)
14. Danelljan, M., Bhat, G., Khan, F.S., Felsberg, M.: ECO: efficient convolution operators for tracking. In: CVPR (2017)
15. Danelljan, M., Bhat, G., Khan, F.S., Felsberg, M.: ATOM: accurate tracking by overlap maximization. In: CVPR (2019)
16. Danelljan, M., Gool, L.V., Timofte, R.: Probabilistic regression for visual tracking. In: CVPR (2020)
17. Fan, H., et al.: LaSOT: a high-quality benchmark for large-scale single object tracking. In: CVPR (2019)
18. Ge, Z., Liu, S., Wang, F., Li, Z., Sun, J.: YOLOX: exceeding yolo series in 2021. arXiv preprint arXiv:2107.08430 (2021)
19. Ghiasi, G., Zoph, B., Cubuk, E.D., Le, Q.V., Lin, T.Y.: Multi-task self-training for learning general representations. In: ICCV (2021)
20. Girdhar, R., Singh, M., Ravi, N., van der Maaten, L., Joulin, A., Misra, I.: Omnivore: a single model for many visual modalities. arXiv preprint arXiv:2201.08377 (2022)
21. He, K., Zhang, X., Ren, S., Sun, J.: Deep residual learning for image recognition. In: CVPR (2016)
22. Hu, Y.-T., Huang, J.-B., Schwing, A.G.: VideoMatch: matching based video object segmentation. In: Ferrari, V., Hebert, M., Sminchisescu, C., Weiss, Y. (eds.) ECCV 2018. LNCS, vol. 11212, pp. 56–73. Springer, Cham (2018). https://doi.org/10.1007/978-3-030-01237-3_4
23. Huang, L., Zhao, X., Huang, K.: GlobalTrack: a simple and strong baseline for long-term tracking. In: AAAI (2020)
24. Ioffe, S., Szegedy, C.: Batch normalization: accelerating deep network training by reducing internal covariate shift. In: ICML (2015)
25. Jabri, A., Owens, A., Efros, A.: Space-time correspondence as a contrastive random walk. In: NeurIPS (2020)
26. Ke, L., Li, X., Danelljan, M., Tai, Y.W., Tang, C.K., Yu, F.: Prototypical cross-attention networks for multiple object tracking and segmentation. In: NeurIPS (2021)
27. Li, B., Wu, W., Wang, Q., Zhang, F., Xing, J., Yan, J.: SiamRPN++: evolution of siamese visual tracking with very deep networks. In: CVPR (2019)
28. Liang, C., et al.: Rethinking the competition between detection and ReID in multi-object tracking. arXiv preprint arXiv:2010.12138 (2020)
29. Liang, C., Zhang, Z., Zhou, X., Li, B., Lu, Y., Hu, W.: One more check: making "fake background" be tracked again. arXiv preprint arXiv:2104.09441 (2021)
30. Lin, T.Y., Dollár, P., Girshick, R., He, K., Hariharan, B., Belongie, S.: Feature pyramid networks for object detection. In: CVPR (2017)
31. Liu, Z., Mao, H., Wu, C.Y., Feichtenhofer, C., Darrell, T., Xie, S.: A convnet for the 2020s. arXiv preprint arXiv:2201.03545 (2022)
32. Loshchilov, I., Hutter, F.: Decoupled weight decay regularization. arXiv preprint arXiv:1711.05101 (2017)
33. Lukezic, A., Matas, J., Kristan, M.: D3S-a discriminative single shot segmentation tracker. In: CVPR (2020)
34. Maninis, K.K., et al.: Video object segmentation without temporal information. TPAMI (2018)

35. Mayer, C., Danelljan, M., Paudel, D.P., Van Gool, L.: Learning target candidate association to keep track of what not to track. In: ICCV (2021)
36. Meinhardt, T., Kirillov, A., Leal-Taixe, L., Feichtenhofer, C.: TrackFormer: multi-object tracking with transformers. arXiv preprint arXiv:2101.02702 (2021)
37. Milan, A., Leal-Taixé, L., Reid, I., Roth, S., Schindler, K.: MOT16: a benchmark for multi-object tracking. arXiv preprint arXiv:1603.00831 (2016)
38. Milletari, F., Navab, N., Ahmadi, S.A.: V-Net: fully convolutional neural networks for volumetric medical image segmentation. In: 3DV (2016)
39. Müller, M., Bibi, A., Giancola, S., Alsubaihi, S., Ghanem, B.: TrackingNet: a large-scale dataset and benchmark for object tracking in the wild. In: Ferrari, V., Hebert, M., Sminchisescu, C., Weiss, Y. (eds.) ECCV 2018. LNCS, vol. 11205, pp. 310–327. Springer, Cham (2018). https://doi.org/10.1007/978-3-030-01246-5_19
40. Oh, S.W., Lee, J.Y., Xu, N., Kim, S.J.: Video object segmentation using space-time memory networks. In: ICCV (2019)
41. Pang, J., et al.: Quasi-dense similarity learning for multiple object tracking. In: CVPR (2021)
42. Peng, J., Wang, C., Wan, F., Wu, Y., Wang, Y., Tai, Y., Wang, C., Li, J., Huang, F., Fu, Y.: Chained-Tracker: Chaining Paired Attentive Regression Results for End-to-End Joint Multiple-Object Detection and Tracking. In: Vedaldi, A., Bischof, H., Brox, T., Frahm, J.-M. (eds.) ECCV 2020. LNCS, vol. 12349, pp. 145–161. Springer, Cham (2020). https://doi.org/10.1007/978-3-030-58548-8_9
43. Pont-Tuset, J., Perazzi, F., Caelles, S., Arbeláez, P., Sorkine-Hornung, A., Van Gool, L.: The 2017 DAVIS challenge on video object segmentation. arXiv preprint arXiv:1704.00675 (2017)
44. Redmon, J., Farhadi, A.: YOLOv3: an incremental improvement. arXiv preprint arXiv:1804.02767 (2018)
45. Ren, S., He, K., Girshick, R., Sun, J.: Faster R-CNN: towards real-time object detection with region proposal networks. In: NeurIPS (2015)
46. Robinson, A., Lawin, F.J., Danelljan, M., Khan, F.S., Felsberg, M.: Learning fast and robust target models for video object segmentation. In: CVPR (2020)
47. Seong, H., Oh, S.W., Lee, J.Y., Lee, S., Lee, S., Kim, E.: Hierarchical memory matching network for video object segmentation. In: ICCV (2021)
48. Shao, J., et al.: INTERN: a new learning paradigm towards general vision. arXiv preprint arXiv:2111.08687 (2021)
49. Sun, P., et al.: TransTrack: multiple-object tracking with transformer. arXiv preprint arXiv:2012.15460 (2020)
50. Sun, P., et al.: Sparse R-CNN: end-to-end object detection with learnable proposals. In: Proceedings of the IEEE/CVF Conference on Computer Vision and Pattern Recognition, pp. 14454–14463 (2021)
51. Teed, Z., Deng, J.: RAFT: recurrent all-pairs field transforms for optical flow. In: Vedaldi, A., Bischof, H., Brox, T., Frahm, J.-M. (eds.) ECCV 2020. LNCS, vol. 12347, pp. 402–419. Springer, Cham (2020). https://doi.org/10.1007/978-3-030-58536-5_24
52. Tian, Z., Shen, C., Chen, H.: Conditional convolutions for instance segmentation. In: Vedaldi, A., Bischof, H., Brox, T., Frahm, J.-M. (eds.) ECCV 2020. LNCS, vol. 12346, pp. 282–298. Springer, Cham (2020). https://doi.org/10.1007/978-3-030-58452-8_17
53. Truong, P., Danelljan, M., Gool, L.V., Timofte, R.: GoCor: bringing globally optimized correspondence volumes into your neural network. In: NeurIPS (2020)
54. Truong, P., Danelljan, M., Van Gool, L., Timofte, R.: Learning accurate dense correspondences and when to trust them. In: CVPR (2021)

55. Valmadre, J., Bertinetto, L., Henriques, J.F., Tao, R., Vedaldi, A., Smeulders, A.W.M., Torr, P.H.S., Gavves, E.: Long-term tracking in the wild: a benchmark. In: Ferrari, V., Hebert, M., Sminchisescu, C., Weiss, Y. (eds.) ECCV 2018. LNCS, vol. 11207, pp. 692–707. Springer, Cham (2018). https://doi.org/10.1007/978-3-030-01219-9_41

56. Vaswani, A., et al.: Attention is all you need. In: NeurIPS (2017)

57. Voigtlaender, P., et al.: MOTS: multi-object tracking and segmentation. In: CVPR (2019)

58. Voigtlaender, P., Luiten, J., Torr, P.H., Leibe, B.: Siam R-CNN: visual tracking by re-detection. In: CVPR (2020)

59. Wang, N., Zhou, W., Wang, J., Li, H.: Transformer meets tracker: exploiting temporal context for robust visual tracking. In: CVPR (2021)

60. Wang, Q., Zhang, L., Bertinetto, L., Hu, W., Torr, P.H.S.: Fast online object tracking and segmentation: a unifying approach. In: CVPR (2019)

61. Wang, Q., Zheng, Y., Pan, P., Xu, Y.: Multiple object tracking with correlation learning. In: CVPR (2021)

62. Wang, Z., Zhao, H., Li, Y.L., Wang, S., Torr, P., Bertinetto, L.: Do different tracking tasks require different appearance models? In: NeurIPS (2021)

63. Wang, Z., Zheng, L., Liu, Y., Li, Y., Wang, S.: Towards real-time multi-object tracking. In: Vedaldi, A., Bischof, H., Brox, T., Frahm, J.-M. (eds.) ECCV 2020. LNCS, vol. 12356, pp. 107–122. Springer, Cham (2020). https://doi.org/10.1007/978-3-030-58621-8_7

64. Wang, Z., Xu, J., Liu, L., Zhu, F., Shao, L.: RANet: ranking attention network for fast video object segmentation. In: ICCV (2019)

65. Wojke, N., Bewley, A., Paulus, D.: Simple online and realtime tracking with a deep association metric. In: ICIP (2017)

66. Wu, J., Cao, J., Song, L., Wang, Y., Yang, M., Yuan, J.: Track to detect and segment: an online multi-object tracker. In: CVPR (2021)

67. Wu, Y., He, K.: Group Normalization. Int. J. Comput. Vision **128**(3), 742–755 (2019). https://doi.org/10.1007/s11263-019-01198-w

68. Xu, Y., Ban, Y., Delorme, G., Gan, C., Rus, D., Alameda-Pineda, X.: Transcenter: transformers with dense queries for multiple-object tracking. arXiv preprint arXiv:2103.15145 (2021)

69. Xu, Y., Osep, A., Ban, Y., Horaud, R., Leal-Taixé, L., Alameda-Pineda, X.: How to train your deep multi-object tracker. In: CVPR (2020)

70. Xu, Y., Wang, Z., Li, Z., Yuan, Y., Yu, G.: SiamFC++: towards robust and accurate visual tracking with target estimation guidelines. In: AAAI (2020)

71. Xu, Z., Yang, W., Zhang, W., Tan, X., Huang, H., Huang, L.: Segment as points for efficient and effective online multi-object tracking and segmentation. TPAMI (2021)

72. Yan, B., Peng, H., Fu, J., Wang, D., Lu, H.: Learning spatio-temporal transformer for visual tracking. In: ICCV (2021)

73. Yang, L., Fan, Y., Xu, N.: Video instance segmentation. In: ICCV (2019)

74. Yang, Z., Wei, Y., Yang, Y.: Collaborative video object segmentation by foreground-background integration. In: Vedaldi, A., Bischof, H., Brox, T., Frahm, J.-M. (eds.) ECCV 2020. LNCS, vol. 12350, pp. 332–348. Springer, Cham (2020). https://doi.org/10.1007/978-3-030-58558-7_20

75. Yu, F., et al.: BDD100K: a diverse driving dataset for heterogeneous multitask learning. In: CVPR (2020)

76. Yuan, L., et al.: Florence: a new foundation model for computer vision. arXiv preprint arXiv:2111.11432 (2021)

77. Zeng, F., Dong, B., Wang, T., Zhang, X., Wei, Y.: MOTR: end-to-end multiple-object tracking with transformer. arXiv preprint arXiv:2105.03247 (2021)
78. Zhang, Y., et al.: ByteTrack: multi-object tracking by associating every detection box. arXiv preprint arXiv:2110.06864 (2021)
79. Zhang, Y., Wang, C., Wang, X., Zeng, W., Liu, W.: FairMOT: on the fairness of detection and re-identification in multiple object tracking. IJCV (2021)
80. Zhang, Y., Wu, Z., Peng, H., Lin, S.: A transductive approach for video object segmentation. In: CVPR (2020)
81. Zhang, Z., Liu, Y., Wang, X., Li, B., Hu, W.: Learn to match: automatic matching network design for visual tracking. In: ICCV (2021)
82. Zhang, Z., Peng, H., Fu, J., Li, B., Hu, W.: Ocean: object-aware anchor-free tracking. In: Vedaldi, A., Bischof, H., Brox, T., Frahm, J.-M. (eds.) ECCV 2020. LNCS, vol. 12366, pp. 771–787. Springer, Cham (2020). https://doi.org/10.1007/978-3-030-58589-1_46
83. Zheng, L., Tang, M., Chen, Y., Zhu, G., Wang, J., Lu, H.: Improving multiple object tracking with single object tracking. In: CVPR (2021)
84. Zhou, X., Koltun, V., Krähenbühl, P.: Tracking objects as points. In: Vedaldi, A., Bischof, H., Brox, T., Frahm, J.-M. (eds.) ECCV 2020. LNCS, vol. 12349, pp. 474–490. Springer, Cham (2020). https://doi.org/10.1007/978-3-030-58548-8_28
85. Zhou, X., Wang, D., Krähenbühl, P.: Objects as points. arXiv preprint arXiv:1904.07850 (2019)
86. Zhou, Z., Pei, W., Li, X., Wang, H., Zheng, F., He, Z.: Saliency-associated object tracking. In: ICCV (2021)
87. Zhu, J., Yang, H., Liu, N., Kim, M., Zhang, W., Yang, M.-H.: Online multi-object tracking with dual matching attention networks. In: Ferrari, V., Hebert, M., Sminchisescu, C., Weiss, Y. (eds.) ECCV 2018. LNCS, vol. 11209, pp. 379–396. Springer, Cham (2018). https://doi.org/10.1007/978-3-030-01228-1_23
88. Zhu, X., Su, W., Lu, L., Li, B., Wang, X., Dai, J.: Deformable DETR: deformable transformers for end-to-end object detection. In: ICLR (2020)

Author Index

Printed in the United States
by Baker & Taylor Publisher Services